Fifth Edition

P9-CEH-463

501
SPANISH VERBS

Fifth Edition

501

SPANISH VERBS

fully conjugated in all the tenses
and moods in a new easy-to-learn
format, alphabetically arranged

by

Christopher Kendris

B.S., M.S., Columbia University
M.A., Ph.D., Northwestern University
Diplômé, Faculté des Lettres, Sorbonne
Former Chairman
Department of Foreign Languages
Farmingdale High School
Farmingdale, New York

and

Theodore Kendris

B.A., Union College
M.A., Northwestern University
Ph.D., Université Laval, Quebec, Canada
University of St. Francis, Joliet, Illinois

BARRON'S EDUCATIONAL SERIES, INC.

© Copyright 2003 by Barron's Educational Series, Inc.

Prior editions © 1996, 1990, 1982, 1971, 1963 by
Barron's Educational Series, Inc.

All rights reserved.
No part of this book may be reproduced in any
form, by photostat, microfilm, xerography, or any
other means, or incorporated into any information
retrieval system, electronic or mechanical, without
the written permission of the copyright owner.

All inquiries should be addressed to:
Barron's Educational Series, Inc.
250 Wireless Boulevard
Hauppauge, New York 11788
http://www.barronseduc.com

Library of Congress Catalog Card No. 2002038363
International Standard Book No. 0-7641-2428-5

Library of Congress Cataloging-in-Publication Data

Kendris, Christopher.
  501 Spanish verbs / by Christopher Kendris & Theodore Kendris.—5th ed.
  p.   cm.
  Includes indexes.
  ISBN 0-7641-2428-5
  1. Spanish language—Verb—Tables. I. Title: Five hundred and one
Spanish verbs. II. Title: Five hundred one Spanish verbs. III. Kendris,
Theodore. IV. Title.

PC4271 .K38 2003
468.2'421—dc21   2002038363

PRINTED IN THE UNITED STATES OF AMERICA
9 8 7 6 5 4 3 2

*To St. Sophia Greek Orthodox Church
of Albany, New York*

and

*Yolanda, Alex, Tina, Fran, Bryan, Daniel, Matthew, Andrew,
Athena, Tom, Donna, Amanda, Laura, Thomas,
Mary Ann, Hilda, Arthur, Karen, George, Christopher, Matthew,
Delores, Faith, Demetra, and Stephanie*

With love

About the Authors

Dr. Christopher Kendris has worked as interpreter and translator of French for the U.S. State Department at the American Embassy in Paris. He earned his B.S. and M.S. degrees at Columbia University in the City of New York, where he held a New York State Scholarship, and his M.A. and Ph.D. degrees at Northwestern University in Evanston, Illinois, where he held a Teaching Assistantship and Tutorial Fellowship for four years. He also earned two diplomas with *Mention très Honorable* at the Université de Paris (en Sorbonne), Faculté des Lettres, École Supérieure de Préparation et de Perfectionnement des Professeurs de Français à l'Étranger, and at the Institut de Phonétique, Paris. In 1986 he was one of 95 teachers in the United States who was awarded a Rockefeller Foundation Fellowship for Teachers of Foreign Languages in American High Schools. He has taught French at the College of The University of Chicago as visiting summer lecturer, at Colby College, Duke University, Rutgers—The State University of New Jersey, and the State University of New York at Albany. He was Chairman of the Department of Foreign Languages and Supervisor of 16 foreign language teachers on the secondary level at Farmingdale High School, Farmingdale, New York, where he was also a teacher of all levels of French and Spanish, and prepared students for the New York State French and Spanish Regents, SAT exams, and AP tests. Dr. Kendris is the author of 22 school and college books, workbooks, and other language guides of French and Spanish. He is listed in *Contemporary Authors* and *Directory of American Scholars.*

Dr. Theodore Kendris earned his B.A. degree in Modern Languages at Union College, Schenectady, New York, where he received the Thomas J. Judson Memorial Book Prize for modern language study. He went on to earn his M.A. degree in French Language and Literature at Northwestern University, Evanston, Illinois, where he held a Teaching Assistantship. He earned his Ph.D. degree in French Literature at Université Laval in Quebec City, where he studied the Middle Ages and Renaissance. While at Université Laval he taught French writing skills as a *chargé de cours* in the French as a Second Language program and, in 1997, he was awarded a doctoral scholarship by the *Fondation de l'Université Laval.* Dr. Kendris is coauthor of *Spanish Fundamentals,* published by Barron's in 1992. He is currently teaching in the Department of English and Foreign Languages at the University of St. Francis in Joliet, Illinois.

Contents

Preface to the Fifth Edition

This anniversary edition has been updated to take into account the many technological advances that have taken place over the past several years. Increased globalization and social changes have also made it necessary to ensure that *501 Spanish Verbs* will continue to provide the guidance that students and travelers like you have come to expect.

We have, therefore, added a number of related words and idiomatic expressions, along with English meanings, at the bottom of every page from 1 to 501. We also hope that you will take advantage of the section on verb drills and tests with answers explained, beginning on page 619. There, you will find a lot of practice in Spanish verb forms and tenses in a variety of tests and word games to determine your strengths and weaknesses yourself and to make some things clearer in your mind. Also, it would be a good idea to get acquainted with the section on definitions of basic grammatical terms, with examples that begins on page 666. Many students who study a foreign language do not understand certain grammatical terms. If you know what they are, what they are called, and how they are used in the grammatical structure of a sentence, you will improve your skill in speaking and writing Spanish.

In your spare time, especially if you are planning a trip abroad, it would be a good idea to consult the two sections on travel vocabulary, especially commonly used verbs, in the back pages. One section, which begins on page 564, contains thirty practical situations you may find yourself in while visiting a Spanish-speaking country or region of the world. Notice the variety of topical situations and don't miss new Spanish verbs listed in the English to Spanish index, which begins on page 505. That is a handy index to consult if you can't remember the Spanish verb you need to use.

Have you wondered about what preposition goes with what verb? Many people do. Check out page 541 where they begin.

Beginning on page 595, there is a section that gives you many popular phrases, words and expressions (including verbs, of course!), abbreviations, signs, and notices in Spanish and English in one alphabetical listing. This allows you to look in one place instead of two for an entry, whether in Spanish or English. Also, cognates and near-cognates in both languages are given in a single entry.

On page 563 there is a simple system of sound transcriptions to help you pronounce Spanish words effectively. From time to time, refer to page 564, which explains the reasons for the use of hyphens in the transcriptions of sounds.

We hope that you will make full of all the features of this anniversary edition and that you will enjoy your exploration of Spanish language and culture.

Christopher Kendris and Theodore Kendris

Introduction

This self-teaching book of 501 commonly used Spanish verbs for students and travelers provides fingertip access to correct verb forms.

Verb conjugations are usually found scattered in Spanish grammar books and they are difficult to find quickly when needed. Verbs have always been a major problem for students no matter what system or approach the teacher uses. You will master Spanish verb forms if you study this book for a few minutes every day, especially the pages before and after the alphabetical listing of the 501 verbs.

This book will help make your work easier and at the same time will teach you Spanish verb forms systematically. It is a useful book because it provides a quick and easy way to find the full conjugation of many Spanish verbs.

The 501 verbs included here are arranged alphabetically by infinitive at the top of each page. The book contains many common verbs of high frequency, both reflexive and nonreflexive, which you need to know. It also contains many other frequently used verbs which are irregular in some way. Beginning on page 550 there are over 1,100 Spanish verbs that can be conjugated in the same way as model verbs among the 501. If the verb you have in mind is not given among the 501, consult this list.

The subject pronouns have been omitted from the conjugations in order to emphasize the verb forms. The subject pronouns are given on page xlii. Turn to that page now and become acquainted with them.

The first thing to do when you use this book is to become familiar with it from cover to cover—in particular, the front and back pages where you will find valuable and useful information to make your work easier and more enjoyable. Take a minute right now and turn to the table of contents at the beginning of this book as we guide you in the following way:

(a)   Beginning on page xi you can learn how to form a present participle regularly in Spanish with examples. There, you will find the common irregular present participles and the many uses of the present participle.

(b)   Beginning on page xii you can learn how to form a past participle regularly in Spanish with examples. There, you will find the common irregular past participles and the many uses of the past participle.

(c)   On page xiv the Passive and Active voices are explained with numerous examples.

(d)   Beginning on page xvi you will find the principal parts of some important Spanish verbs. This is useful because, if you know these, you are well on your way to mastering Spanish verb forms.

(e)   Beginning on page xviii we give you a sample English verb conjugation so that you can get an idea of the way a verb is expressed in the English tenses. Many people do not know one tense from another because they have never learned the use of verb tenses in a systematic and organized way—not even in English! How can you, for example, know that you need the conditional form of a verb in Spanish when you want to say *"I would go* to the movies if . . ."* or the pluperfect tense in Spanish if you want to say *"I had gone . . ."*? The sample English verb conjugation with the names of the tenses and their numerical ranking will help you to distinguish one tense from another so that you will know what tense you need in order to express a verb in Spanish.

(f)   On page xx you will find a summary of meanings and uses of Spanish verb tenses and moods as related to English verb tenses and moods. That section is very important and useful because the seven simple tenses are separated from the seven compound tenses. You are given the name of each tense in Spanish and English starting with the present indicative, which we call tense number one because it is the tense most frequently used. We assign a number to each tense name so that you can fix each one in your mind and associate the tense names and numbers in their logical order. We explain briefly what each tense is, when you use it, and we give examples using verbs in sentences in Spanish and English. At the end of each tense you are shown how to form that tense for regular verbs.

(g)   Beginning on page xxxiv we explain the Imperative, which is a mood, not a tense, and give numerous examples using it.

(h)   Beginning on page xxxvi the progressive forms of tenses are explained with examples. Also note the future subjunctive and the future perfect subjunctive. We explain how these two rarely used tenses are formed, and we give examples of what tenses are used in place of them in informal writing and in conversation.

(i)   Beginning on page xxxviii we give you a summary of all the fourteen tenses in Spanish with English equivalents, which we have divided into the seven simple tenses and the seven compound tenses. After referring to that summary frequently, you will soon know that tense number 1 is the present indicative, tense number 2 is the imperfect indicative, and so on. We also explain how each compound tense is based on each simple tense. Try to see these two divisions as two frames, two pictures, with the seven simple tenses in one frame and the seven compound tenses in another frame. Place them side by side in your mind, and you will see how tense number 8 is related to tense number 1, tense number 9 to tense number 2, and so on. If you study the numerical arrangement of each of the seven simple tenses and associate the tense number with the tense name, you will find it very easy to learn the names of the seven compound tenses, how they rank numerically according to use, how they are formed, and when they are used. Spend at least ten minutes every day studying these preliminary pages to help you understand better the fourteen tenses in Spanish.

Finally, in the back pages of this book there are useful indexes: an index of English-Spanish verbs, an index of common irregular Spanish verb forms identified by infinitive, and a list of over 1,100 Spanish verbs that are conjugated like model verbs among the 501. We also give many examples of Spanish verbs used in idiomatic expressions and simple sentences, verbs that require certain prepositions, and Spanish proverbs and weather expressions using verbs—all of which are special features. If you refer to these back pages each time you look up verb tense forms for a particular verb, you will increase your knowledge of Spanish vocabulary and Spanish idioms by leaps and bounds.

We sincerely hope that this book will be of some help to you in learning and using Spanish verbs.

Christopher Kendris and Theodore Kendris

Formation of the Present and Past Participles in Spanish

Formation of the present participle in Spanish

A present participle is a verb form which, in English, ends in *-ing*; for example, *singing, eating, receiving.* In Spanish, a present participle is regularly formed as follows:

drop the **ar** of an **-ar** ending verb, like **cantar,** and add **ando: cantando**/singing

drop the **er** of an **-er** ending verb, like **comer,** and add **iendo: comiendo**/eating

drop the **ir** of an **-ir** ending verb, like **recibir,** and add **iendo: recibiendo**/receiving

In English, a gerund also ends in **-ing,** but there is a distinct difference in use between a gerund and a present participle in English. In brief, it is this: in English, when a present participle is used as a noun it is called a gerund; for example, *Reading is good.* As a present participle in English, it would be used as follows: *While reading,* the boy fell asleep.

In the first example (*Reading is good*), *reading* is a gerund because it is the subject of the verb *is.* In Spanish, however, we do not use the present participle form as a noun to serve as a subject; we use the infinitive form of the verb: *Leer es bueno.*

Common irregular present participles

INFINITIVE		PRESENT PARTICIPLE	
caer	to fall	**cayendo**	falling
conseguir	to attain, to achieve	**consiguiendo**	attaining, achieving
construir	to construct	**construyendo**	constructing
corregir	to correct	**corrigiendo**	correcting
creer	to believe	**creyendo**	believing
decir	to say, to tell	**diciendo**	saying, telling
despedirse	to say good-bye	**despidiéndose**	saying good-bye
destruir	to destroy	**destruyendo**	destroying
divertirse	to enjoy oneself	**divirtiéndose**	enjoying oneself
dormir	to sleep	**durmiendo**	sleeping
huir	to flee	**huyendo**	fleeing
ir	to go	**yendo**	going
leer	to read	**leyendo**	reading
mentir	to lie (tell a falsehood)	**mintiendo**	lying
morir	to die	**muriendo**	dying
oír	to hear	**oyendo**	hearing
pedir	to ask (for), to request	**pidiendo**	asking (for), requesting
poder	to be able	**pudiendo**	being able
reír	to laugh	**riendo**	laughing
repetir	to repeat	**repitiendo**	repeating
seguir	to follow	**siguiendo**	following
sentir	to feel	**sintiendo**	feeling
servir	to serve	**sirviendo**	serving
traer	to bring	**trayendo**	bringing
venir	to come	**viniendo**	coming
vestir	to dress	**vistiendo**	dressing
vestirse	to dress oneself	**vistiéndose**	dressing oneself

Uses of the present participle

1. To form the progressive tenses: **The Progressive Present** is formed by using **estar** in the present tense plus the present participle of the main verb you are using. **The Progressive Past** is formed by using **estar** in the imperfect indicative plus the present participle of the main verb you are using. (See pages xxxvi–xxxvii for a complete description of the uses and formation of the progressive tenses.)

2. To express vividly an action that occurred (preterit + present participle): *El niño entró llorando en la casa/*The little boy came into the house crying.

3. To express the English use of *by* + present participle in Spanish, we use the gerund form, which has the same ending as a present participle explained above: *Trabajando, se gana dinero/*By working, one earns (a person earns) money; *Estudiando mucho, Pepe recibió buenas notas/*By studying hard, Joe received good grades.

   Note that no preposition is used in front of the present participle (the Spanish gerund) even though it is expressed in English as *by* + present participle.

   Note, too, that in Spanish we use **al** + inf. (not + present part.) to express *on* or *upon* + present part. in English: *Al entrar en la casa, el niño comenzó a llorar/*Upon entering the house, the little boy began to cry.

4. To form the Perfect Participle: **habiendo hablado/**having talked.

Formation of the past participle in Spanish

A past participle is a verb form which, in English, usually ends in *-ed*: for example, *worked, talked, arrived,* as in *I have worked, I have talked, I have arrived.* There are many irregular past participles in English; for example, *gone, sung,* as in *She has gone, We have sung.* In Spanish, a past participle is regularly formed as follows:

drop the **ar** of an **-ar** ending verb, like **cantar,** and add **ado: cantado/**sung

drop the **er** of an **-er** ending verb, like **comer,** and add **ido: comido/**eaten

drop the **ir** of an **-ir** ending verb, like **recibir,** and add **ido: recibido/**received

Common irregular past participles

INFINITIVE	PAST PARTICIPLE
abrir to open	**abierto** opened
caer to fall	**caído** fallen
creer to believe	**creído** believed
cubrir to cover	**cubierto** covered
decir to say, to tell	**dicho** said, told
descubrir to discover	**descubierto** discovered
deshacer to undo	**deshecho** undone
devolver to return (something)	**devuelto** returned (something)
escribir to write	**escrito** written
hacer to do, to make	**hecho** done, made
imponer to impose	**impuesto** imposed
imprimir to print	**impreso** printed
ir to go	**ido** gone
leer to read	**leído** read
morir to die	**muerto** died
oír to hear	**oído** heard
poner to put	**puesto** put
poseer to possess	**poseído** possessed
rehacer to redo, to remake	**rehecho** redone, remade
reír to laugh	**reído** laughed
resolver to resolve, to solve	**resuelto** resolved, solved
romper to break	**roto** broken
sonreír to smile	**sonreído** smiled
traer to bring	**traído** brought
ver to see	**visto** seen
volver to return	**vuelto** returned

Uses of the past participle

1. To form the seven compound tenses

2. To form the Perfect Infinitive: *haber hablado*/to have spoken

3. To form the Perfect Participle: *habiendo hablado*/having spoken

4. To serve as an adjective, which must agree in gender and number with the noun it modifies: *El señor Molina es muy respetado por todos los alumnos*/ Mr. Molina is very respected by all the students; *La señora González es muy conocida*/Mrs. González is very well known.

5. To express the result of an action with **estar** and sometimes with **quedar** or **quedarse**: *La puerta está abierta*/The door is open; *Las cartas están escritas*/The letters are written; *Los niños se quedaron asustados*/The children remained frightened.

6. To express the passive voice with **ser**: *La ventana fue abierta por el ladrón*/ The window was opened by the robber.

Passive voice means that the action of the verb falls on the subject; in other words, the subject receives the action: *La ventana fue abierta por el ladrón*/The window was opened by the robber. Note that *abierta* (really a form of the past part. *abrir/abierto*) is used as an adjective and it must agree in gender and number with the subject that it describes.

Active voice means that the subject performs the action and the subject is always stated: *El ladrón abrió la ventana*/The robber opened the window.

To form the true passive, use **ser** + the past part. of the verb you have in mind; the past part. then serves as an adjective and it must agree in gender and number with the subject that it describes. In the true passive, the agent (the doer) is always expressed with the prep. **por** in front of it. The formula for the true passive construction is: subject + tense of **ser** + past part. + **por** + the agent (the doer): *Estas composiciones fueron escritas por Juan*/These compositions were written by John.

The reflexive pronoun **se** may be used to substitute for the true passive voice construction. When you use the **se** construction, the subject is a thing (not a person) and the doer (agent) is not stated: *Aquí se habla español*/Spanish is spoken here; *Aquí se hablan español e inglés*/Spanish and English are spoken here; *Se venden libros en esta tienda*/Books are sold in this store.

There are a few standard idiomatic expressions that are commonly used with the pronoun **se**. These expressions are not truly passive, the pronoun **se** is not truly a reflexive pronoun, and the verb form is in the 3rd pers. sing. only. In this construction, there is no subject expressed; the subject is contained in the use of **se** + the 3rd pers. sing. of the verb at all times and the common translations into English are: it is . . . , people . . . , they . . . , one . . .

Se cree que . . . It is believed that . . . , people believe that . . . , they believe that . . . , one believes that . . .

Se cree que este criminal es culpable. It is believed that this criminal is guilty.

Se dice que . . . It is said that . . . , people say that . . . , they say that . . . , one says that . . . , you say . . .

Se dice que va a nevar esta noche. They say that it's going to snow tonight.
¿Cómo se dice en español "ice cream"? How do you say *ice cream* in Spanish?

Se sabe que . . . It is known that . . . , people know that . . . , they know that . . . , one knows that . . .

Se sabe que María va a casarse con Juan./People know that Mary is going to marry John.

The **se** reflexive pronoun construction is avoided if the subject is a person because there can be ambiguity in meaning. For example, how would you translate into English the following? **Se da un regalo.** Which of the following two meanings is intended? She (he) is being given a present, *or* She (he) is giving a present to himself (to herself). In correct Spanish you would have to say: **Le da (a María, a Juan, etc.) un regalo**/He (she) is giving a present to Mary (to John, etc.). Avoid using the **se** construction in the passive when the subject is a person; change your sentence around and state it in the active voice to make the meaning clear. Otherwise, the pronoun **se** seems to go with the verb, as if the verb is reflexive, which gives an entirely different meaning. Another example: **Se miró** would mean *He (she) looked at himself (herself)*, not *He (she) was looked at!* If you mean to say *He (she) looked at her,* say: **La miró** or, if in the plural, say: **La miraron**/They looked at her.

Abbreviations

adj.   adjetivo (adjective)
ant.   anterior
comp.   compuesto (compound, perfect)
e.g.   for example
fut.   futuro (future)
i.e.   that is, that is to say
imp.   imperfecto (imperfect)
ind.   indicativo (indicative)
inf.   infinitivo (infinitive)
p.   página (page)
part.   participio (participle)
part. pas.   participio de pasado, participio pasivo (past participle)
part. pr.   participio de presente, participio activo, gerundio (present participle)
pas.   pasado, pasivo (past, passive)
perf.   perfecto (perfect)
perf. ind.   perfecto de indicativo (present perfect indicative)
perf. subj.   perfecto de subjuntivo (present perfect or past subjunctive)
plpf.   pluscuamperfecto (pluperfect)
pot.   potencial (conditional)
pot. comp.   potencial compuesto (conditional perfect)

pr. or *pres.*   presente (present)
prep.   preposición (preposition)
pres. or *pr.*   presente (present)
pret.   pretérito (preterit)
subj.   subjuntivo (subjunctive)

Principal Parts of Some Important Spanish Verbs

INFINITIVE	(GERUNDIO) PRESENT PARTICIPLE	PAST PARTICIPLE	PRESENT INDICATIVE	PRETERIT
abrir	abriendo	abierto	abro	abrí
andar	andando	andado	ando	anduve
caber	cabiendo	cabido	quepo	cupe
caer	cayendo	caído	caigo	caí
conseguir	consiguiendo	conseguido	consigo	conseguí
construir	construyendo	construido	construyo	construí
corregir	corrigiendo	corregido	corrijo	corregí
creer	creyendo	creído	creo	creí
cubrir	cubriendo	cubierto	cubro	cubrí
dar	dando	dado	doy	di
decir	diciendo	dicho	digo	dije
descubrir	descubriendo	descubierto	descubro	descubrí
deshacer	deshaciendo	deshecho	deshago	deshice
despedirse	despidiéndose	despedido	me despido	me despedí
destruir	destruyendo	destruido	destruyo	destruí
devolver	devolviendo	devuelto	devuelvo	devolví
divertirse	divirtiéndose	divertido	me divierto	me divertí
dormir	durmiendo	dormido	duermo	dormí
escribir	escribiendo	escrito	escribo	escribí
estar	estando	estado	estoy	estuve
haber	habiendo	habido	he	hube
hacer	haciendo	hecho	hago	hice
huir	huyendo	huido	huyo	huí
ir	yendo	ido	voy	fui
irse	yéndose	ido	me voy	me fui
leer	leyendo	leído	leo	leí
mentir	mintiendo	mentido	miento	mentí
morir	muriendo	muerto	muero	morí
oír	oyendo	oído	oigo	oí
oler	oliendo	olido	huelo	olí
pedir	pidiendo	pedido	pido	pedí
poder	pudiendo	podido	puedo	pude
poner	poniendo	puesto	pongo	puse
querer	queriendo	querido	quiero	quise
reír	riendo	reído	río	reí
repetir	repitiendo	repetido	repito	repetí
resolver	resolviendo	resuelto	resuelvo	resolví
romper	rompiendo	roto	rompo	rompí
saber	sabiendo	sabido	sé	supe
salir	saliendo	salido	salgo	salí

INFINITIVE	(GERUNDIO) PRESENT PARTICIPLE	PAST PARTICIPLE	PRESENT INDICATIVE	PRETERIT
seguir	siguiendo	seguido	sigo	seguí
sentir	sintiendo	sentido	siento	sentí
ser	siendo	sido	soy	fui
servir	sirviendo	servido	sirvo	serví
tener	teniendo	tenido	tengo	tuve
traer	trayendo	traído	traigo	traje
venir	viniendo	venido	vengo	vine
ver	viendo	visto	veo	vi
vestir	vistiendo	vestido	visto	vestí
volver	volviendo	vuelto	vuelvo	volví

Tip

In the present indicative and the preterit columns above only the 1st person singular (**yo**) forms are given to get you started. If you cannot recall the remaining verb forms in the present indicative and the preterit tenses of the verbs listed above in the first column under **infinitive,** please practice them by looking them up in this book where the infinitive form of the verb is listed alphabetically at the top of each page from page 1 to 501. When you find them, say them aloud at the same time you practice writing them in Spanish. This is a very useful exercise to do.

Sample English Verb Conjugation

INFINITIVE **to eat**
PRESENT PARTICIPLE **eating**   *PAST PARTICIPLE* **eaten**

Tense no.	The seven simple tenses
1 *Present* *Indicative*	I eat, you eat, he (she, it) eats; we eat, you eat, they eat
	or: I do eat, you do eat, he (she, it) does eat; we do eat, you do eat, they do eat
	or: I am eating, you are eating, he (she, it) is eating; we are eating, you are eating, they are eating
2 *Imperfect* *Indicative*	I was eating, you were eating, he (she, it) was eating; we were eating, you were eating, they were eating
	or: I ate, you ate, he (she, it) ate; we ate, you ate, they ate
	or: I used to eat, you used to eat, he (she, it) used to eat: we used to eat, you used to eat, they used to eat
3 *Preterit*	I ate, you ate, he (she, it) ate; we ate, you ate, they ate
	or: I did eat, you did eat, he (she, it) did eat; we did eat, you did eat, they did eat
4 *Future*	I shall eat, you will eat, he (she, it) will eat; we shall eat, you will eat, they will eat
5 *Conditional*	I would eat, you would eat, he (she, it) would eat; we would eat, you would eat, they would eat
6 *Present* *Subjunctive*	that I may eat, that you may eat, that he (she, it) may eat; that we may eat, that you may eat, that they may eat
7 *Imperfect or* *Past Subjunctive*	that I might eat, that you might eat, that he (she, it) might eat; that we might eat, that you might eat, that they might eat

Tense no.	The seven compound tenses
8 *Past Perfect or Past Indefinite*	I have eaten, you have eaten, he (she, it) has eaten; we have eaten, you have eaten, they have eaten
9 *Pluperfect Indic. or Past Perfect*	I had eaten, you had eaten, he (she, it) had eaten; we had eaten, you had eaten, they had eaten
10 *Past Anterior or Preterit Perfect*	I had eaten, you had eaten, he (she, it) had eaten; we had eaten, you had eaten, they had eaten
11 *Future Perfect or Future Anterior*	I shall have eaten, you will have eaten, he (she, it) will have eaten; we shall have eaten, you will have eaten, they will have eaten
12 *Conditional Perfect*	I would have eaten, you would have eaten, he (she, it) would have eaten; we would have eaten, you would have eaten, they would have eaten
13 *Present Perfect or Past Subjunctive*	that I may have eaten, that you may have eaten, that he (she, it) may have eaten; that we may have eaten, that you may have eaten that they may have eaten
14 *Pluperfect or Past Perfect Subjunctive*	that I might have eaten, that you might have eaten, that he (she, it) might have eaten; that we might have eaten, that you might have eaten, that they might have eaten
Imperative or Command	—— eat, let him (her) eat; let us eat, eat, let them eat

A Summary of Meanings and Uses of Spanish Verb Tenses and Moods as Related to English Verb Tenses and Moods

A verb is where the action is! A verb is a word that expresses an action (like *go, eat, write*) or a state of being (like *think, believe, be*). Tense means time. Spanish and English verb tenses are divided into three main groups of time: past, present, and future. A verb tense shows if an action or state of being took place, is taking place, or will take place.

Spanish and English verbs are also used in moods, or modes. Mood has to do with the *way* a person regards an action or a state that he expresses. For example, a person may merely make a statement or ask a question—this is the Indicative Mood, which we use most of the time in Spanish and English. A person may say that he *would do* something if something else were possible or that he *would have* done something if something else had been possible—this is the Conditional. A person may use a verb *in such a way* that he indicates a wish, a fear, a regret, a joy, a request, a supposition, or something of this sort—this is the Subjunctive Mood. The Subjunctive Mood is used in Spanish much more than in English. Finally, a person may command someone to do something or demand that something be done—this is the Imperative Mood. English Conditional is not a mood. (There is also the Infinitive Mood, but we are not concerned with that here.)

There are six tenses in English: Present, Past, Future, Present Perfect, Past Perfect, and Future Perfect. The first three are simple tenses. The other three are compound tenses and are based on the simple tenses. In Spanish, however, there are fourteen tenses, seven of which are simple and seven of which are compound. The seven compound tenses are based on the seven simple tenses. In Spanish and English a verb tense is simple if it consists of one verb form, e.g., *estudio.* A verb tense is compound if it consists of two parts—the auxiliary (or helping) verb plus the past participle, e.g., *he estudiado.* See the Summary of verb tenses and moods in Spanish with English equivalents on page xxxviii. We have numbered each tense name for easy reference and recognition.

In Spanish there is also another tense which is used to express an action in the present. It is called the Progressive Present. It is used only if an action is actually in progress at the time; for example, *Estoy leyendo*/I am reading (right now). It is formed by using the Present Indicative of *estar* plus the present participle of the verb. There is still another tense in Spanish which is used to express an action that was taking place in the past. It is called the Progressive Past. It is used if an action was actually in progress at a certain moment in the past; for example, *Estaba leyendo cuando mi hermano entró*/I was reading when my brother came in. The Progressive Past is formed by using the Imperfect Indicative of *estar* plus the present participle of the verb.

In the pages that follow, the tenses and moods are given in Spanish and the equivalent name or names in English are given in parentheses. Although some of the names given in English are not considered to be tenses (there are only six), they are given for the purpose of identification as they are related to the Spanish names. The comparison includes only the essential points you need to know about the meanings and uses of Spanish verb tenses and moods as related to English usage. We shall use examples to illustrate their meanings and uses. This is not intended to be a detailed treatise. It is merely a summary. We hope you find it helpful.

Tense No. 1   Presente de Indicativo
                        (Present Indicative)

This tense is used most of the time in Spanish and English. It indicates:

(a) An action or a state of being at the present time.
   EXAMPLES:
   1. **Hablo** español. *I speak* Spanish.
                        I am speaking Spanish.
                        I do speak Spanish.
   2. **Creo en** Dios. *I believe* in God.

(b) Habitual action.
   EXAMPLE:
   Voy a la biblioteca todos los días.
   I go to the library every day.
   I do go to the library every day.

(c) A general truth, something which is permanently true.
   EXAMPLES:
   1. Seis menos dos **son** cuatro.
      Six minus two *are* four.
   2. El ejercicio **hace** maestro al novicio.
      Practice *makes* perfect.

(d) Vividness when talking or writing about past events.
   EXAMPLE:
   El asesino **se pone** pálido. **Tiene** miedo. **Sale** de la casa y **corre** a lo largo del río.
   The murderer *turns* pale. *He is* afraid. *He goes out* of the house and *runs* along the river.

(e) A near future.
   EXAMPLES:
   1. Mi hermano **llega** mañana.
      My brother *arrives* tomorrow.
   2. ¿**Escuchamos** un disco ahora?
      Shall we *listen* to a record now?

(f) An action or state of being that occurred in the past and *continues up to the present.*
   In Spanish this is an idiomatic use of the present tense of a verb with **hace,** which is also in the present.
   EXAMPLE:
   Hace tres horas que **miro** la televisión.
   I have been watching television for three hours.

(g) The meaning of *almost* or *nearly* when used with **por poco.**
   EXAMPLE:
   Por poco me **matan.**
   They almost *killed* me.

This tense is regularly formed as follows:

Drop the -ar ending of an infinitive, like **hablar,** and add the following endings: **o, as, a; amos, áis, an**

You then get: **hablo, hablas, habla;**
                  hablamos, habláis, hablan

Drop the -er ending of an infinitive, like **beber,** and add the following endings: **o, es, e; emos, éis, en**

You then get: **bebo, bebes, bebe;**
                  bebemos, bebéis, beben

Drop the -ir ending of an infinitive, like **recibir,** and add the following endings: **o, es, e; imos, ís, en**

You then get: **recibo, recibes, recibe;**
                  recibimos, recibís, reciben

Tense No. 2   Imperfecto de Indicativo
(Imperfect Indicative)

This is a past tense. Imperfect suggests incomplete. The imperfect tense expresses an action or a state of being that was continuous in the past and its completion is not indicated. This tense is used, therefore, to express:

(a) An action that was going on in the past at the same time as another action.
     EXAMPLE:
     Mi hermano **leía** y mi padre **hablaba.**
     My brother *was reading* and my father *was talking.*

(b) An action that was going on in the past when another action occurred.
     EXAMPLE:
     Mi hermana **cantaba** cuando yo entré.
     My sister *was singing* when I came in.

(c) An action that a person did habitually in the past.
     EXAMPLE:
     1. Cuando **estábamos** en Nueva York, **íbamos** al cine todos los sábados.
        When *we were* in New York, *we went* to the movies every Saturday.
        When *we were* in New York, *we used to go* to the movies every Saturday.
     2. Cuando **vivíamos** en California, **íbamos** a la playa todos los días.
        When *we used to live* in California, *we would go* to the beach every day.
     NOTE: In this last example, *we would go* looks like the conditional, but it is not. It is the imperfect tense in this sentence because habitual action in the past is expressed.

(d) A description of a mental, emotional, or physical condition in the past.
     EXAMPLES:
     1. (mental condition)   **Quería** ir al cine.
                             I *wanted* to go to the movies.
        Common verbs in this use are **creer, desear, pensar, poder, preferir, querer, saber, sentir.**
     2. (emotional condition)   **Estaba** contento de verlo.
                               I *was* happy to see him.
     3. (physical condition)   Mi madre **era** hermosa cuando **era** pequeña.
                              My mother *was* beautiful when she *was* young.

(e) The time of day in the past.
EXAMPLES:
1. ¿Qué hora **era**?
What time *was* it?
2. **Eran** las tres.
It was three o'clock.

(f) An action or state of being that occurred in the past and *lasted for a certain length of time* prior to another past action. In English it is usually translated as a pluperfect tense and is formed with *had been* plus the present participle of the verb you are using. It is like the special use of the presente de indicativo explained in the above section in paragraph (f), except that the action or state of being no longer exists at present. This is an idiomatic use of the imperfect tense of a verb with **hacía,** which is also in the imperfect.
EXAMPLE:
Hacía tres horas que **miraba** la televisión cuando mi hermano entró.
I had been watching television for three hours when my brother came in.

(g) An indirect quotation in the past.
EXAMPLE:
Present: Dice que **quiere** venir a mi casa.
               He says *he wants* to come to my house.
Past: Dijo que **quería** venir a mi casa.
               He said *he wanted* to come to my house.

This tense is regularly formed as follows:

Drop the **-ar** ending of an infinitive, like **hablar,** and add the following endings: **aba, abas, aba; ábamos, abais, aban**
You then get: **hablaba, hablabas, hablaba;**
                  hablábamos, hablabais, hablaban

The usual equivalent in English is: I was talking OR I used to talk OR I talked; you were talking OR you used to talk OR you talked, etc.

Drop the **-er** ending of an infinitive, like **beber,** or the **-ir** ending of an infinitive, like **recibir,** and add the following endings: **ía, ías, ía; íamos, íais, ían**
You then get: **bebía, bebías, bebía;**
                  bebíamos, bebíais, bebían

                  recibía, recibías, recibía;
                  recibíamos, recibíais, recibían

The usual equivalent in English is: I was drinking OR I used to drink OR I drank; you were drinking OR you used to drink OR you drank, etc.; I was receiving OR I used to receive OR I received; you were receiving OR you used to receive OR you received, etc.

Verbs irregular in the imperfect indicative:

ir/to go	**iba, ibas, iba;** (I was going, I used to go, etc.)
	íbamos, ibais, iban
ser/to be	**era, eras, era;** (I was, I used to be, etc.)
	éramos, erais, eran
ver/to see	**veía, veías, veía;** (I was seeing, I used to see, etc.)
	veíamos, veíais, veían

Tense No. 3   Pretérito
(Preterit)

This tense expresses an action that was completed at some time in the past.

EXAMPLES:
1. Mi padre **llegó** ayer.
   My father *arrived* yesterday.
   My father *did arrive* yesterday.
2. María **fue** a la iglesia esta mañana.
   Mary *went* to church this morning.
   Mary *did go* to church this morning.
3. ¿Qué **pasó?**
   What *happened*?
   What *did happen*?
4. **Tomé** el desayuno a las siete.
   I *had* breakfast at seven o'clock.
   I *did have* breakfast at seven o'clock.
5. **Salí** de casa, **tomé** el autobús y **llegué** a la escuela a las ocho.
   I left the house, *I took* the bus and *I arrived* at school at eight o'clock.

In Spanish, some verbs that express a mental state have a different meaning when used in the preterit.

EXAMPLES:
1. La **conocí** la semana pasada en el baile.
   I *met* her last week at the dance.
   (**Conocer,** which means *to know* or *be acquainted with,* means *met,* that is, introduced to for the first time, in the preterit.)
2. **Pude** hacerlo.
   I *succeeded* in doing it.
   (**Poder,** which means *to be able,* means *succeeded* in the preterit.)
3. **No pude** hacerlo.
   I *failed* to do it.
   (**Poder,** when used in the negative in the preterit, means *failed* or *did not succeed.*)
4. **Quise** llamarle.
   I *tried* to call you.
   (**Querer,** which means *to wish* or *want,* means *tried* in the preterit.)
5. **No quise** hacerlo.
   I *refused* to do it.
   (**Querer,** when used in the negative in the preterit, means *refused.*)
6. **Supe** la verdad.
   I *found out* the truth.
   (**Saber,** which means *to know,* means *found out* in the preterit.)
7. **Tuve** una carta de mi amigo Roberto.
   I *received* a letter from my friend Robert.
   (**Tener,** which means *to have,* means *received* in the preterit.)

This tense is regularly formed as follows:

Drop the **-ar** ending of an infinitive, like **hablar,** and add the following endings: **é, aste, ó; amos, asteis, aron**
You then get: **hablé, hablaste, habló;**
                    hablamos, hablasteis, hablaron

The usual equivalent in English is: I talked OR I did talk; you talked OR you did talk, etc. OR I spoke OR I did speak; you spoke OR you did speak, etc.

Drop the **-er** ending of an infinitive, like **beber,** or the **-ir** ending of an infinitive, like **recibir,** and add the following endings: **í, iste, ió; imos, isteis, ieron**

You then get: **bebí, bebiste, bebió;**
                 bebimos, bebisteis, bebieron
                 recibí, recibiste, recibió;
                 recibimos, recibisteis, recibieron

The usual equivalent in English is: I drank OR I did drink; you drank OR you did drink, etc.; I received OR I did receive, etc.

Tense No. 4   Futuro
(Future)

In Spanish and English, the future tense is used to express an action or a state of being that will take place at some time in the future.

> EXAMPLES:
> 1. Lo **haré.**
>   *I shall do* it.
>   *I will do* it.
> 2. **Iremos** al campo la semana que viene.
>   *We shall go* to the country next week.
>   *We will go* to the country next week.

Also, in Spanish the future tense is used to indicate:

(a) Conjecture regarding the present.
> EXAMPLES:
> 1. ¿Qué hora **será**?
>   *I wonder* what time *it is.*
> 2. ¿Quién **será** a la puerta?
>   Who *can that be* at the door?
>   *I wonder who is* at the door.

(b) Probability regarding the present.
> EXAMPLES:
> 1. **Serán** las cinco.
>   *It is probably* five o'clock.
>   *It must be* five o'clock.
> 2. **Tendrá** muchos amigos.
>   *He probably has* many friends.
>   *He must have* many friends.
> 3. María **estará** enferma.
>   Mary *is probably* sick.
>   Mary *must be* sick.

(c) An indirect quotation.
> EXAMPLE:
> María dice que **vendrá** mañana.
> Mary says that she *will come* tomorrow.

Finally, remember that the future is never used in Spanish after *si* when *si* means *if.*

This tense is regularly formed as follows:

Add the following endings to the whole infinitive: **é, ás, á; emos, éis, án**

Note that these Future endings happen to be the endings of **haber** in the present indicative: **he, has, ha; hemos, habéis, han.** Also note the accent marks on the Future endings, except for **emos.**

You then get: **hablaré, hablarás, hablará;**
                 hablaremos, hablaréis, hablarán

                 beberé, beberás, beberá;
                 beberemos, beberéis, beberán

                 recibiré, recibirás, recibirá;
                 recibiremos, recibiréis, recibirán

Tense No. 5   Potencial Simple
                          (Conditional)

The conditional is used in Spanish and in English to express:

(a) An action that you *would do* if something else were possible.
    EXAMPLE:
    Iría a España si tuviera dinero.
    I would go to Spain if I had money.

(b) A conditional desire. This is a conditional of courtesy.
    EXAMPLE:
    Me **gustaría** tomar una limonada.
    I would like (I should like) to have a lemonade . . . (if you are willing to let me have it).

(c) An indirect quotation.
    EXAMPLES:
    1. María **dijo** que **vendría** mañana.
       Mary *said* that she *would come* tomorrow.
    2. María **decía** que **vendría** mañana.
       Mary *was saying* that she *would come* tomorrow.
    3. María **había dicho** que **vendría** mañana.
       Mary *had said* that she *would come* tomorrow.

(d) Conjecture regarding the past.
    EXAMPLE:
    ¿Quién **sería?**
    I wonder who that was.

(e) Probability regarding the past.
    EXAMPLE:
    Serían las cinco cuando salieron.
    It was probably five o'clock when they went out.

This tense is regularly formed as follows:

Add the following endings to the whole infinitive:

    ía, ías, ía; íamos, íais, ían

Note that these conditional endings are the same endings of the imperfect indicative for **-er** and **-ir** verbs.

You then get: **hablaría, hablarías, hablaría;**
hablaríamos, hablaríais, hablarían

bebería, beberías, bebería;
beberíamos, beberíais, beberían

recibiría, recibirías, recibiría;
recibiríamos, recibiríais, recibirían

The usual translation in English is: I would talk, you would talk, etc.; I would drink, you would drink, etc.; I would receive, you would receive, etc.

Tense No. 6   Presente de Subjuntivo
(Present Subjunctive)

The subjunctive mood is used in Spanish much more than in English. In Spanish the present subjunctive is used:

(a)   To express a command in the **usted** or **ustedes** form, either in the affirmative or negative.
EXAMPLES:
1. **Siéntese Ud.** *Sit down.*
2. **No se siente Ud.** *Don't sit down.*
3. **Cierren Uds. la puerta.** *Close the door.*
4. **No cierren Uds. la puerta.** *Don't close the door.*
5. **Dígame Ud. la verdad.** *Tell me the truth.*

(b)   To express a negative command in the familiar form (**tú**).
EXAMPLES:
1. **No te sientes.** *Don't sit down.*   3. **No duermas.** *Don't sleep.*
2. **No entres.** *Don't come in.*   4. **No lo hagas.** *Don't do it.*

(c)   To express a negative command in the second person plural (**vosotros**).
EXAMPLES:
1. **No os sentéis.** *Don't sit down.*   3. **No durmáis.** *Don't sleep.*
2. **No entréis.** *Don't come in.*   4. **No lo hagáis.** *Don't do it.*

(d)   To express a command in the first person plural, either in the affirmative or negative (**nosotros**).
EXAMPLES:
1. **Sentémonos.** *Let's sit down.*
2. **No entremos.** *Let's not go in.*

See also **Imperativo** (Imperative) farther on.

(e)   After a verb that expresses some kind of wish, insistence, preference, suggestion, or request.
EXAMPLES:
1. *Quiero* que María lo **haga.**
I want Mary to do it.
NOTE: In this example, English uses the infinitive form, *to do.* In Spanish, however, a new clause is needed introduced by *que* because there is a new subject, María. The present subjunctive of *hacer* is used (haga) because the main verb is *Quiero,* which indicates a wish. If there were no change in subject, Spanish would use the infinitive form, as we do in English, for example, *Quiero hacerlo*/I want to do it.

2. *Insisto* en que María lo **haga.**
   I insist that Mary *do* it.
3. *Prefiero* que María lo **haga.**
   I prefer that Mary *do* it.
4. *Pido* que María lo **haga.**
   I ask that Mary *do* it.
NOTE: In examples 2, 3, and 4 here, English also uses the subjunctive form *do*. Not so in example no. 1, however.

(f) After a verb that expresses doubt, fear, joy, hope, sorrow, or some other emotion. Notice in the following examples, however, that the subjunctive is not used in English.
EXAMPLES:
1. *Dudo* que María lo **haga.**
   I doubt that Mary *is doing* it.
   I doubt that Mary *will do* it.
2. *No creo* que María **venga.**
   I don't believe (I doubt) that Mary *is coming.*
   I don't believe (I doubt) that Mary *will come.*
3. *Temo* que María **esté** enferma.
   I fear that Mary *is* ill.
4. *Me alegro* de que **venga** María.
   I'm glad that Mary *is coming.*
   I'm glad that Mary *will come.*
5. *Espero* que María no **esté** enferma.
   I hope that Mary *is* not ill.

(g) After certain impersonal expressions that show necessity, doubt, regret, importance, urgency, or possibility. Notice, however, that the subjunctive is not used in English in some of the following examples.
EXAMPLES:
1. *Es necesario que* María lo **haga.**
   It is necessary for Mary to do it.
   It is necessary that Mary *do* it.
2. *No es cierto que* María **venga.**
   It is doubtful (not certain) that Mary *is coming.*
   It is doubtful (not certain) that Mary *will come.*
3. *Es lástima que* María no **venga.**
   It's too bad (a pity) that Mary *isn't coming.*
4. *Es importante que* María **venga.**
   It is important for Mary to come.
   It is important that Mary *come.*
5. *Es preciso que* María **venga.**
   It is necessary for Mary to come.
   It is necessary that Mary *come.*
6. *Es urgente que* María **venga.**
   It is urgent for Mary to come.
   It is urgent that Mary *come.*

(h) After certain conjunctions of time, such as, **antes (de) que, cuando, en cuanto, después (de) que, hasta que, mientras,** and the like. The subjunctive form of the verb is used when introduced by any of these time conjunctions if the time referred to is either indefinite or is expected to take place in the future. However, if the action was completed in the past, the indicative mood is used.

EXAMPLES:

1. Le hablaré a María cuando **venga.**
   I shall talk to Mary when she *comes.*
2. Vámonos antes (de) que **llueva.**
   Let's go before *it rains.*
3. En cuanto la **vea** yo, le hablaré.
   As soon as *I see her,* I shall talk to her.
4. Me quedo aquí hasta que **vuelva.**
   I'm staying here until *he returns.*

NOTE: In the above examples, the subjunctive is not used in English.

(i)   After certain conjunctions that express a condition, negation, purpose, such as, **a menos que, con tal que, para que, a fin de que, sin que, en caso (de) que,** and the like. Notice, however, that the subjunctive is not used in English in the following examples.

EXAMPLES:

1. Démelo con tal que **sea** bueno.
   Give it to me provided that *it is* good.
2. Me voy a menos que **venga.**
   I'm leaving unless *he comes.*

(j)   After certain adverbs, such as, **acaso, quizá,** and **tal vez.**

EXAMPLE:

Acaso **venga** mañana.
Perhaps *he will come* tomorrow.
Perhaps *he is coming* tomorrow.

(k)   After **aunque** if the action has not yet occurred.

EXAMPLE:

Aunque María **venga** esta noche, no me quedo.
Although Mary *may come* tonight, I'm not staying.
Although Mary *is coming* tonight, I'm not staying.

(l)   In an adjectival clause if the antecedent is something or someone that is indefinite, negative, vague, or nonexistent.

EXAMPLES:

1. Busco un libro que **sea** interesante.
   I'm looking for a book that *is* interesting.
   NOTE: In this example, *que* (which is the relative pronoun) refers to *un libro* (which is the antecedent). Since *un libro* is indefinite, the verb in the following clause must be in the subjunctive *(sea)*. Notice, however, that the subjunctive is not used in English.
2. ¿Hay alguien aquí que **hable** francés?
   Is there anyone here who *speaks* French?
   NOTE: In this example, *que* (which is the relative pronoun) refers to *alguien* (which is the antecedent). Since *alguien* is indefinite and somewhat vague—we do not know who this anyone might be—the verb in the following clause must be in the subjunctive *(hable)*. Notice, however, that the subjunctive is not used in English.
3. No hay nadie que **pueda** hacerlo.
   There is no one who *can* do it.
   NOTE: In this example, *que* (which is the relative pronoun) refers to *nadie* (which is the antecedent). Since *nadie* is nonexistent, the verb in the following clause must be in the subjunctive *(pueda)*. Notice, however, that the subjunctive is not used in English.

(m) After **por más que** or **por mucho que.**
EXAMPLES:
1. **Por más que hable usted,** no quiero escuchar.
   No matter how much you talk, I don't want to listen.
2. **Por mucho que se alegre,** no me importa.
   No matter how glad he is, I don't care.

(n) After the expression **ojalá (que),** which expresses a great desire. This interjection means *would to God!* or *may God grant!* . . . It is derived from the Arabic, *ya Allah!* (Oh, God!)
EXAMPLE:
¡Ojalá que vengan mañana!
Would to God that they come tomorrow!
May God grant that they come tomorrow!
How I wish that they would come tomorrow!
If only they would come tomorrow!

Finally, remember that the present subjunctive is never used in Spanish after *si* when *si* means *if.*

The present subjunctive of regular verbs and many irregular verbs is normally formed as follows:

Go to the present indicative, 1st pers. sing., of the verb you have in mind, drop the ending **o,** and

for an **-ar** ending type, add: **e, es, e; emos, éis, en**
for an **-er** or **-ir** ending type, add: **a, as, a; amos, áis, an**

As you can see, the characteristic vowel in the present subjunctive endings for an **-ar** type verb is **e** in the six persons.

As you can see, the characteristic vowel in the present subjunctive endings for an **-er** or **-ir** type verb is **a** in the six persons.

Since the present subjunctive of some irregular verbs is not normally formed as stated above (*e.g.,* **dar, dormir, haber, ir, secar, sentir, ser, tocar**), you must look up the verb you have in mind in the alphabetical listing in this book.

Tense No. 7   Imperfecto de Subjuntivo
(Imperfect Subjunctive)

This past tense is used for the same reasons as the presente de subjuntivo—that is, after certain verbs, conjunctions, impersonal expressions, etc., which were explained and illustrated above in tense no. 6. The main difference between these two tenses is the time of the action.

If the verb in the main clause is in the present indicative or future or present perfect indicative or imperative, the *present subjunctive* or the *present perfect subjunctive* is used in the dependent clause—provided, of course, that there is some element which requires the use of the subjunctive.

However, if the verb in the main clause is in the imperfect indicative, preterit, conditional, or pluperfect indicative, the *imperfect subjunctive* (this tense) or *pluperfect subjunctive* is ordinarily used in the dependent clause—provided, of course, that there is some element which requires the use of the subjunctive.

EXAMPLES:
1. *Insistí* en que María lo **hiciera.**
   I insisted that Mary *do* it.
2. Se lo *explicaba* a María **para que lo comprendiera.**
   I was explaining it to Mary *so that she might understand it.*

Note that the imperfect subjunctive is used after **como si** to express a condition contrary to fact.

EXAMPLE:

Me habla como si **fuera** un niño.

He speaks to me as if *I were* a child.

NOTE: In this last example, the subjunctive is used in English also for the same reason.

Finally, note that **quisiera** (the imperfect subjunctive of **querer**) can be used to express politely a wish or desire, as in *I should like:* **Quisiera hablar ahora/**I should like to speak now.

The imperfect subjunctive is regularly formed as follows:

For all verbs, drop the **ron** ending of the 3rd pers. pl. of the preterit and add the following endings:

> **ra, ras, ra;** OR **se, ses, se;**
> **ramos, rais, ran** **semos, seis, sen**

The only accent mark on the forms of the imperfect subjunctive is on the 1st pers. pl. form (**nosotros**) and it is placed on the vowel which is right in front of the ending **ramos** or **semos**.

THE SEVEN COMPOUND TENSES

Tense No. 8 Perfecto de Indicativo
(Present Perfect Indicative)

This is the first of the seven compound tenses that follow here. This tense expresses an action that took place at no definite time in the past. It is also called the past indefinite. It is a compound tense because it is formed with the present indicative of **haber** (the auxiliary or helping verb) plus the past participle of your main verb. Note the translation into English in the examples that follow. Then compare this tense with the **perfecto de subjuntivo,** which is tense no. 13. For the seven simple tenses of **haber** (which you need to know to form these seven compound tenses), see **haber** listed alphabetically among the 501 verbs in this book.

EXAMPLES:

1. (Yo) **he hablado.**
   I have spoken.
2. (Tú) no **has venido** a verme.
   You have not come to see me.
3. Elena **ha ganado** el premio.
   Helen *has won* the prize.

Tense No. 9 Pluscuamperfecto de Indicativo
(Pluperfect *or* Past Perfect Indicative)

This is the second of the compound tenses. In Spanish and English, this past tense is used to express an action which happened in the past *before* another past action. Since it is used in relation to another past action, the other past action is ordinarily expressed in the preterit. However, it is not always necessary to have the other past action expressed, as in example 2 on the following page.

In English, this tense is formed with the past tense of *to have* (had) plus the past participle of your main verb. In Spanish, this tense is formed with the imperfect indicative of **haber** plus the past participle of the verb you have in mind. Note the translation into English in the examples that follow. Then compare this tense with the **pluscuamperfecto de subjuntivo,** which is tense no. 14. For the seven simples tenses of **haber** (which you need to know to form these seven compound tenses), see **haber** listed alphabetically among the 501 verbs in this book.

EXAMPLES:

1. Cuando **llegué a casa, mi hermano había salido.**
   When I *arrived* home, my brother *had gone out.*
   NOTE: *First,* my brother went out; *then,* I arrived home. Both actions happened in the past. The action that occurred in the past *before* the other past action is in the pluperfect, and in this example, it is *my brother had gone out* (**mi hermano había salido).**
   NOTE also that **llegué** *(I arrived)* is in the preterit because it is an action that happened in the past and it was completed.

2. Juan lo **había perdido** en la calle.
   John *had lost* it in the street.
   NOTE: In this example, the pluperfect indicative is used even though no other past action is expressed. It is assumed that John *had lost* something *before* some other past action.

Tense No. 10 Pretérito Anterior or Pretérito Perfecto
(Past Anterior *or* Preterit Perfect)

This is the third of the compound tenses. This past tense is compound because it is formed with the preterit of **haber** plus the past participle of the verb you are using. It is translated into English like the pluperfect indicative, which is tense no. 9. This tense is not used much in spoken Spanish. Ordinarily, the pluperfect indicative is used in spoken Spanish (and sometimes even the simple preterit) in place of the past anterior.

This tense is ordinarily used in formal writing, such as history and literature. It is normally used after certain conjunctions of time, e.g., **después que, cuando, apenas, luego que, en cuanto.**

EXAMPLE:

Después que **hubo hablado,** salió.
After *he had spoken,* he left.

Tense No. 11 Futuro Perfecto
(Future Perfect *or* Future Anterior)

This is the fourth of the compound tenses. This compound tense is formed with the future of **haber** plus the past participle of the verb you have in mind. In Spanish and in English, this tense is used to express an action that will happen in the future *before* another future action. In English, this tense is formed by using *shall have* or *will have* plus the past participle of the verb you have in mind.

EXAMPLE:

María llegará mañana y **habré terminado** mi trabajo.
Mary will arrive tomorrow and *I shall have finished* my work.

NOTE: *First,* I shall finish my work; *then,* Mary will arrive. The action that will occur in the future *before* the other future action is in the **Futuro perfecto,** and in this example it is (yo) **habré terminado mi trabajo.**

Also, in Spanish the future perfect is used to indicate conjecture or probability regarding recent past time.

EXAMPLES:

1. María **se habrá acostado.**
   Mary *has probably gone to bed*
   Mary *must have gone to bed.*
2. José **habrá llegado.**
   Joseph *has probably arrived.*
   Joseph *must have arrived.*

Tense No. 12   Potencial Compuesto
(Conditional Perfect)

This is the fifth of the compound tenses. It is formed with the conditional of **haber** plus the past participle of your main verb. It is used in Spanish and English to express an action that you *would have done* if something else had been possible; that is, you would have done something *on condition* that something else had been possible.

In English it is formed by using *would have* plus the past participle of the verb you have in mind. Observe the difference between the following example and the one given for the use of the potencial simple.

EXAMPLE:

Habría ido a España si hubiera tenido dinero.
I would have gone to Spain if I had had money.

Also, in Spanish the conditional perfect is used to indicate probability or conjecture in the past.

EXAMPLES:

1. **Habrían sido** las cinco cuando salieron.
   It must have been five o'clock when they went out.
   (Compare this with the example given for the simple conditional.)
2. ¿Quién **habría sido**?
   Who *could that have been*? (*or* I wonder *who that could have been*.)
   (Compare this with the example given for the simple conditional.)

Tense No. 13   Perfecto de Subjuntivo
(Present Perfect *or* Past Subjunctive)

This is the sixth of the compound tenses. It is formed by using the present subjunctive of **haber** as the helping verb plus the past participle of the verb you have in mind.

If the verb in the main clause is in the present indicative, future, or present perfect tense, the present subjunctive is used *or* this tense is used in the dependent clause—provided, of course, that there is some element which requires the use of the subjunctive.

The present subjective is used if the action is not past. However, if the action is past, this tense (present perfect subjunctive) is used, as in the examples given below.

EXAMPLES:
1. María duda que yo le **haya hablado** al profesor.
   Mary doubts that *I have spoken* to the professor.
2. Siento que tú no **hayas venido** a verme.
   I am sorry that you *have not come* to see me.
3. Me alegro de que Elena **haya ganado** el premio.
   I am glad that Helen *has won* the prize.

In these three examples, the auxiliary verb **haber** is used in the present subjunctive because the main verb in the clause that precedes is one that requires the subjunctive mood of the verb in the dependent clause.

Tense No. 14   Pluscuamperfecto de Subjuntivo
(Pluperfect *or* Past Perfect Subjunctive)

This is the seventh of the compound tenses. It is formed by using the imperfect subjunctive of **haber** as the helping verb plus the past participle of your main verb.

The translation of this tense into English is often like the pluperfect indicative.

If the verb in the main clause is in a past tense, this tense is used in the dependent clause—provided, of course, that there is some element which requires the use of the subjunctive.

EXAMPLES:
1. Sentí mucho que **no hubiera venido** María.
   I was very sorry that Mary *had not come.*
2. Me alegraba de que **hubiera venido** María.
   I was glad that Mary *had come.*
3. No creía que María **hubiera llegado.**
   I did not believe that Mary *had arrived.*

So much for the seven simple tenses and the seven compound tenses. Now, let's look at the Imperative Mood.

Imperativo
(Imperative *or* Command)

The imperative mood is used in Spanish and in English to express a command. We saw earlier that the subjunctive mood is used to express commands in the **Ud.** and **Uds.** forms, in addition to other uses of the subjunctive mood.

Here are other points you ought to know about the imperative.

(a) An indirect command or deep desire expressed in the third pers. sing. or pl. is in the subjunctive. Notice the use of *Let* or *May* in the English translations. **Que** introduces this kind of command.

EXAMPLES:
1. ¡Que lo **haga** Jorge!
   Let George do it!
2. ¡Que Dios se lo **pague!**
   May God reward you!
3. ¡Que **vengan** pronto!
   Let them come quickly!
4. ¡Que **entre** Roberto!
   Let Robert enter!
5. ¡Que **salgan!**
   Let them leave!
6. ¡Que **entren** las muchachas!
   Let the girls come in!

(b) In some indirect commands, **que** is omitted. Here, too, the subjunctive is used.
EXAMPLE:
¡**Viva** el presidente!
Long live the president!

(c) The verb form of the affirmative sing. familiar (**tú**) is the same as the 3rd pers. sing. of the present indicative when expressing a command.
EXAMPLE:
1. ¡**Entra** pronto!
   Come in quickly!
2. ¡**Sigue** leyendo!
   Keep on reading!
   Continue reading!

(d) There are some exceptions, however, to (c) above. The following verb forms are irregular in the affirmative sing. imperative (**tú** form only).

di (decir)	**sal** (salir)	**val** (valer)
haz (hacer)	**sé** (ser)	**ve** (ir)
hé (haber)	**ten** (tener)	**ven** (venir)
pon (poner)		

(e) In the affirmative command, 1st pers. pl., instead of using the present subjunctive hortatory command, **vamos a** (*Let's* or *Let us*) + **inf.** may be used.
EXAMPLES:
1. **Vamos a** comer/Let's eat.
   or: **Comamos** (1st pers. pl., present subj., hortatory command)
2. **Vamos a** cantar/Let's sing.
   or: **Cantemos** (1st pers. pl., present subj., hortatory command)

(f) In the affirmative command, 1st pers. pl., **vamos** may be used to mean *Let's go:*
Vamos al cine/Let's go to the movies.

(g) However, if in the negative *(Let's not go),* the present subjunctive of **ir** must be used: **No vayamos** al cine/Let's not go to the movies.

(h) Note that **vámonos** (1st pers. pl. of **irse,** imperative) means *Let's go,* or *Let's go away,* or *Let's leave.* See (m) below.

(i) Also note that **no nos vayamos** (1st pers. pl. of **irse,** present subjunctive) means *Let's not go,* or *Let's not go away,* or *Let's not leave.*

(j) The imperative in the affirmative familiar plural (**vosotros, vosotras**) is formed by dropping the final **r** of the inf. and adding **d.**
EXAMPLES:
1. ¡**Hablad!**/Speak!   3. ¡**Id!**/Go!
2. ¡**Comed!**/Eat!   4. ¡**Venid!**/Come!

(k) When forming the affirmative familiar plural (**vosotros, vosotras**) imperative of a reflexive verb, the final **d** on the inf. must be dropped before the reflexive pronoun **os** is added, and both elements are joined to make one word.
EXAMPLES:
1. ¡**Levantaos!**/Get up!   2. ¡**Sentaos!**/Sit down!

(l) Referring to (k) above, when the final **d** is dropped in a reflexive verb ending in **-ir,** an accent mark must be written on the **i.**
EXAMPLES:
1. ¡**Vestíos!**/Get dressed!   2. ¡**Divertíos!**/Have a good time!

(m) When forming the 1st pers. pl. affirmative imperative of a reflexive verb, final s must drop before the reflexive pronoun **os** is added, and both elements are joined to make one word. This requires an accent mark on the vowel of the syllable that was stressed before **os** was added.

EXAMPLE:

Vamos + nos changes to: **¡Vámonos!**/*Let's go!* or *Let's go away!* or *Let's leave!* See (h) above.

(n) All negative imperatives in the familiar 2nd pers. sing. (**tú**) and plural (**vosotros, vosotras**) are expressed in the present subjunctive.

EXAMPLES:

1. **¡No corras (tú)!**/Don't run!
2. **¡No corráis (vosotros or vosotras)!**/Don't run!
3. **¡No vengas (tú)!**/Don't come!
4. **¡No vengáis (vosotros or vosotras)!**/Don't come!

(o) Object pronouns (direct, indirect, or reflexive) with an imperative verb form in the **affirmative** are attached to the verb form.

EXAMPLES:

1. **¡Hágalo (Ud.)!**/Do it!
2. **¡Díganoslo (Ud.)!**/Tell it to us!
3. **¡Dímelo (tú)!**/Tell it to me!
4. **¡Levántate (tú)!**/Get up!
5. **¡Siéntese (Ud.)!**/Sit down!
6. **¡Hacedlo (vosotros, vosotras)!**/Do it!
7. **¡Démelo (Ud.)!**/Give it to me!

(p) Object pronouns (direct, indirect, or reflexive) with an imperative verb form in the **negative** are placed in front of the verb form. Compare the following examples with those given in (o) above:

EXAMPLES:

1. **¡No lo haga (Ud.)!**/Don't do it!
2. **¡No nos lo diga (Ud.)!**/Don't tell it to us!
3. **¡No me lo digas (tú)!**/Don't tell it to me!
4. **¡No te levantes (tú)!**/Don't get up!
5. **¡No se siente (Ud.)!**/Don't sit down!
6. **¡No lo hagáis (vosotros, vosotras)!**/Don't do it!
7. **¡No me lo dé (Ud.)!**/Don't give it to me!

(q) Note that in some Latin American countries the 2nd pers. pl. familiar (**vosotros, vosotras**) forms are avoided. In place of them, the 3rd pers. pl. **Uds.** forms are customarily used.

The Progressive forms of tenses: a note

(1) In Spanish, there are also progressive forms of tenses. They are the Progressive Present and the Progressive Past.

(2) The **Progressive Present** is formed by using *estar* in the present tense plus the present participle of your main verb; e.g., *Estoy hablando*/I am talking, i.e., I am (in the act of) talking (right now).

(3) The **Progressive Past** is formed by using *estar* in the imperfect indicative plus the present participle of your main verb; e.g., *Estaba hablando*/I was talking, i.e., I was (in the act of) talking (right then).

(4) The progressive forms are generally used when you want to emphasize or intensify an action; if you don't want to do that, then just use the simple present or simple imperfect; e.g., say *Hablo,* not *Estoy hablando;* or *Hablaba,* not *Estaba hablando.*

(5) Sometimes *ir* is used instead of *estar* to form the progressive tenses; e.g., *Va hablando*/He (she) keeps right on talking, *Iba hablando*/He (she) kept right on talking. Note that they do not have the exact same meaning as *Está hablando* and *Estaba hablando.* See (2) and (3) above.

(6) Also, at times *andar, continuar, seguir,* and *venir* are used as helping verbs in the present or imperfect indicative tenses plus the present participle to express the progressive forms: *Los muchachos andaban cantando*/The boys were walking along singing; *La maestra seguía leyendo a la clase*/The teacher kept right on reading to the class.

The Future Subjunctive and the Future Perfect Subjunctive: a note

The future subjunctive and the future perfect subjunctive exist in Spanish, but they are rarely used. Nowadays, instead of using the future subjunctive, one uses the present subjunctive of the present indicative. Instead of using the future perfect subjunctive, one uses the future perfect indicative or the present perfect subjunctive. However, if you are curious to know how to form the future subjunctive and the future perfect subjunctive in Spanish, the following is offered:

(1) To form the future subjunctive, take the third person plural of the preterit of any Spanish verb and change the ending -ron to re, res, re; remos, reis, ren. An accent mark is needed as shown below on the first person plural form to preserve the stress.
EXAMPLES:

amar	**amare, amares, amare;** **amáremos, amareis, amaren**
comer	**comiere, comieres, comiere;** **comiéremos, comiereis, comieren**
dar	**diere, dieres, diere;** **diéremos, diereis, dieren**
haber	**hubiere, hubieres, hubiere;** **hubiéremos, hubiereis, hubieren**
hablar	**hablare, hablares, hablare;** **habláremos, hablareis, hablaren**
ir *or* **ser**	**fuere, fueres, fuere;** **fuéremos, fuereis, fueren**

(2) Let's look at the forms of **amar** above to see what the English translation is of this tense:

(que) yo amare, (that) I love . . .
(que) tú amares, (that) you love . . .
(que) Ud. (él, ella) amare, (that) you (he, she) love . . .
(que) nosotros (-tras) amáremos, (that) we love . . .
(que) vosotros (-tras) amareis, (that) you love . . .
(que) Uds. (ellos, ellas) amaren, (that) you (they) love . . .

(3) To form the future perfect subjunctive, use the future subjunctive form of **haber** (shown above) as your auxiliary plus the past participle of the verb you have in mind.

EXAMPLES:

(que) hubiere amado, hubieres amado, hubiere amado;
(que) hubiéremos amado, hubiereis amado, hubieren amado

English translation:
(that) I have *or* I shall have loved, (that) you have *or* will have loved, etc.

Summary of verb tenses and moods in Spanish with English equivalents

Los siete tiempos simples *The seven simple tenses*		Los siete tiempos compuestos *The seven compound tenses*	
Tense No.	Tense Name	Tense No.	Tense Name
1	**Presente de indicativo** *Present indicative*	**8**	**Perfecto de indicativo** *Present perfect indicative*
2	**Imperfecto de indicativo** *Imperfect indicative*	**9**	**Pluscuamperfecto de indicativo** *Pluperfect or Past perfect indicative*
3	**Pretérito** *Preterit*	**10**	**Pretérito anterior (Pret. perfecto)** *Past anterior or Preterit perfect*
4	**Futuro** *Future*	**11**	**Futuro perfecto** *Future perfect or Future anterior*
5	**Potencial simple** *Conditional*	**12**	**Potencial compuesto** *Conditional perfect*
6	**Presente de subjuntivo** *Present subjunctive*	**13**	**Perfecto de subjuntivo** *Present perfect or Past subjunctive*
7	**Imperfecto de subjuntivo** *Imperfect subjunctive*	**14**	**Pluscuamperfecto de subjuntivo** *Pluperfect or Past perfect subjunctive*

The imperative is not a tense; it is a mood.

In Spanish, there are 7 simple tenses and 7 compound tenses. A simple tense means that the verb form consists of one word. A compound tense means that the verb form consists of two words (the auxiliary verb and the past participle). The auxiliary verb is also called a helping verb and in Spanish, as you know, it is any of the 7 simple tenses of **haber** *(to have).*

TIP

Each compound tense is based on each simple tense. The 14 tenses given on the previous page are arranged in the following logical order:

Tense number 8 is based on Tense number 1 of **haber;** in other words, you form the **Perfecto de indicativo** by using the auxiliary **haber** in the **Presente de indicativo** plus the past participle of the verb you are dealing with.

Tense number 9 is based on Tense number 2 of **haber;** in other words, you form the **Pluscuamperfecto de indicativo** by using the auxiliary **haber** in the **Imperfecto de indicativo** plus the past participle of the verb you are dealing with.

Tense number 10 is based on Tense number 3 of **haber;** in other words, you form the **Pretérito anterior** by using the auxiliary **haber** in the **Pretérito** plus the past participle of the verb you are dealing with.

Tense number 11 is based on Tense number 4 of **haber;** in other words, you form the **Futuro perfecto** by using the auxiliary **haber** in the **Futuro** plus the past participle of the verb you are dealing with.

Tense number 12 is based on Tense number 5 of **haber;** in other words, you form the **Potencial compuesto** by using the auxiliary **haber** in the **Potencial simple** plus the past participle of the verb you are dealing with.

Tense number 13 is based on Tense number 6 of **haber;** in other words, you form the **Perfecto de subjuntivo** by using the auxiliary **haber** in the **Presente de subjuntivo** plus the past participle of the verb you are dealing with.

Tense number 14 is based on Tense number 7 of **haber;** in other words, you form the **Pluscuamperfecto de subjuntivo** by using the auxiliary **haber** in the **Imperfecto de subjuntivo** plus the past participle of the verb you are dealing with.

What does all the above mean? This: If you ever expect to know or even recognize the meaning of any of the 7 compound tenses, you certainly have to know **haber** in the 7 simple tenses. If you do not, you cannot form the 7 compound tenses. This is one perfect example to illustrate that learning Spanish verb forms is a cumulative experience. Look up **haber** where it is listed alphabetically among the 501 verbs in this book and study the 7 simple tenses.

An Easy Way to Form the Seven Compound Tenses in Spanish

haber in the following simple tenses + PLUS the past participle of the verb you have in mind* = EQUALS the following compound tenses

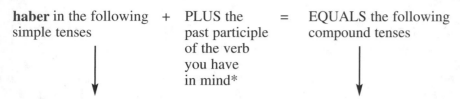

1. **Presente de indicativo**	8. **Perfecto de indicativo**
2. **Imperfecto de indicativo**	9. **Pluscuamperfecto de indicativo**
3. **Pretérito**	10. **Pretérito anterior (Pret. perfecto)**
4. **Futuro**	11. **Futuro perfecto**
5. **Potencial simple**	12. **Potencial compuesto**
6. **Presente de subjuntivo**	13. **Perfecto de subjuntivo**
7. **Imperfecto de subjuntivo**	14. **Pluscuamperfecto de subjuntivo**

*To know how to form a past participle, see page xii.

Subject Pronouns

(a) The subject pronouns for all verb forms on the following pages have been omitted in order to emphasize the verb forms, which is what this book is all about.

(b) The subject pronouns that have been omitted are, as you know, as follows:

singular	*plural*
yo	**nosotros (nosotras)**
tú	**vosotros (vosotras)**
Ud. (él, ella)	**Uds. (ellos, ellas)**

The Spanish Alphabet and the New System of Alphabetizing

The Association of Spanish Language Academies met in Madrid for its 10th Annual Congress on April 27, 1994 and voted to eliminate **CH** and **LL** as separate letters of the Spanish alphabet.

Words beginning with **CH** will be listed alphabetically under the letter **C.** Words beginning with **LL** will be listed alphabetically under the letter **L.** The two separate letters historically have had separate headings in dictionaries and alphabetized word lists. Spanish words that contain the letter **ñ** are now alphabetized accordingly with words that do not contain the tilde over the **n.** For example, the Spanish system of alphabetizing used to place the word **andar** before **añadir** because the **ñ** would fall in after all words containing **n.** According to the new system, **añadir** is placed before **andar** because alphabetizing is now done letter by letter. The same applies to words containing **rr.**

The move was taken to simplify dictionaries, to make Spanish more compatible with English, and to aid translation and computer standardization. The vote was 17 in favor, 1 opposed, and 3 abstentions. Ecuador voted "no" and Panama, Nicaragua, and Uruguay abstained. (*The New York Times,* International Section, May 1, 1994, p. 16).

Alphabetical Listing of
501 Spanish Verbs
Fully Conjugated in
All the Tenses and Moods

Subject Pronouns

singular	plural
yo	nosotros (nosotras)
tú	vosotros (vosotras)
Ud. (él, ella)	Uds. (ellos, ellas)

to knock down, to overthrow, to throw down

The Seven Simple Tenses		The Seven Compound Tenses	
Singular	Plural	Singular	Plural
1 presente de indicativo		8 perfecto de indicativo	
abato	**abatimos**	he abatido	hemos abatido
abates	**abatís**	has abatido	habéis abatido
abate	**abaten**	ha abatido	han abatido
2 imperfecto de indicativo		9 pluscuamperfecto de indicativo	
abatía	**abatíamos**	había abatido	habíamos abatido
abatías	**abatíais**	habías abatido	habíais abatido
abatía	**abatían**	había abatido	habían abatido
3 pretérito		10 pretérito anterior	
abatí	**abatimos**	hube abatido	hubimos abatido
abatiste	**abatisteis**	hubiste abatido	hubisteis abatido
abatió	**abatieron**	hubo abatido	hubieron abatido
4 futuro		11 futuro perfecto	
abatiré	**abatiremos**	habré abatido	habremos abatido
abatirás	**abatiréis**	habrás abatido	habréis abatido
abatirá	**abatirán**	habrá abatido	habrán abatido
5 potencial simple		12 potencial compuesto	
abatiría	**abatiríamos**	habría abatido	habríamos abatido
abatirías	**abatiríais**	habrías abatido	habríais abatido
abatiría	**abatirían**	habría abatido	habrían abatido
6 presente de subjuntivo		13 perfecto de subjuntivo	
abata	**abatamos**	haya abatido	hayamos abatido
abatas	**abatáis**	hayas abatido	hayáis abatido
abata	**abatan**	haya abatido	hayan abatido
7 imperfecto de subjuntivo		14 pluscuamperfecto de subjuntivo	
abatiera	**abatiéramos**	hubiera abatido	hubiéramos abatido
abatieras	**abatierais**	hubieras abatido	hubierais abatido
abatiera	**abatieran**	hubiera abatido	hubieran abatido
OR		OR	
abatiese	**abatiésemos**	hubiese abatido	hubiésemos abatido
abatieses	**abatieseis**	hubieses abatido	hubieseis abatido
abatiese	**abatiesen**	hubiese abatido	hubiesen abatido

imperativo

—	**abatamos**
abate; no abatas	**abatid; no abatáis**
abata	**abatan**

Words and expressions related to this verb
abatidamente dejectedly
el abatimiento abasement, depression, discouragement
abatir el ánimo to feel discouraged, low in spirit

batir to beat, strike
batir palmas to applaud, clap
abatido, abatida dejected

Consult the sections on verbs used in idiomatic expressions, verbs with prepositions,
and the list of over 1,100 verbs conjugated like model verbs in the back pages.

to burn, to set on fire

The Seven Simple Tenses		The Seven Compound Tenses	
Singular	Plural	Singular	Plural
1 presente de indicativo		8 perfecto de indicativo	
abraso	abrasamos	he abrasado	hemos abrasado
abrasas	abrasáis	has abrasado	habéis abrasado
abrasa	abrasan	ha abrasado	han abrasado
2 imperfecto de indicativo		9 pluscuamperfecto de indicativo	
abrasaba	abrasábamos	había abrasado	habíamos abrasado
abrasabas	abrasabais	habías abrasado	habíais abrasado
abrasaba	abrasaban	había abrasado	habían abrasado
3 pretérito		10 pretérito anterior	
abrasé	abrasamos	hube abrasado	hubimos abrasado
abrasaste	abrasasteis	hubiste abrasado	hubisteis abrasado
abrasó	abrasaron	hubo abrasado	hubieron abrasado
4 futuro		11 futuro perfecto	
abrasaré	abrasaremos	habré abrasado	habremos abrasado
abrasarás	abrasaréis	habrás abrasado	habréis abrasado
abrasará	abrasarán	habrá abrasado	habrán abrasado
5 potencial simple		12 potencial compuesto	
abrasaría	abrasaríamos	habría abrasado	habríamos abrasado
abrasarías	abrasaríais	habrías abrasado	habríais abrasado
abrasaría	abrasarían	habría abrasado	habrían abrasado
6 presente de subjuntivo		13 perfecto de subjuntivo	
abrase	abrasemos	haya abrasado	hayamos abrasado
abrases	abraséis	hayas abrasado	hayáis abrasado
abrase	abrasen	haya abrasado	hayan abrasado
7 imperfecto de subjuntivo		14 pluscuamperfecto de subjuntivo	
abrasara	abrasáramos	hubiera abrasado	hubiéramos abrasado
abrasaras	abrasarais	hubieras abrasado	hubierais abrasado
abrasara	abrasaran	hubiera abrasado	hubieran abrasado
OR		OR	
abrasase	abrasásemos	hubiese abrasado	hubiésemos abrasado
abrasases	abrasaseis	hubieses abrasado	hubieseis abrasado
abrasase	abrasasen	hubiese abrasado	hubiesen abrasado

	imperativo	
—		abrasemos
abrasa; no abrases		abrasad; no abraséis
abrase		abrasen

Words and expressions related to this verb

abrasadamente   ardently, fervently
abrasado, abrasada   burning; flushed with anger
el abrasamiento   burning, excessive passion

abrasarse vivo   to burn with passion
abrasarse de amor   to be passionately in love
abrasarse en deseos   to become full of desire

Get acquainted with what preposition goes with what verb on pages 541–549.

to embrace, to hug; to clamp

The Seven Simple Tenses		The Seven Compound Tenses	
Singular	Plural	Singular	Plural
1 presente de indicativo		**8 perfecto de indicativo**	
abrazo	**abrazamos**	**he abrazado**	**hemos abrazado**
abrazas	**abrazáis**	**has abrazado**	**habéis abrazado**
abraza	**abrazan**	**ha abrazado**	**han abrazado**
2 imperfecto de indicativo		**9 pluscuamperfecto de indicativo**	
abrazaba	**abrazábamos**	**había abrazado**	**habíamos abrazado**
abrazabas	**abrazabais**	**habías abrazado**	**habíais abrazado**
abrazaba	**abrazaban**	**había abrazado**	**habían abrazado**
3 pretérito		**10 pretérito anterior**	
abracé	**abrazamos**	**hube abrazado**	**hubimos abrazado**
abrazaste	**abrazasteis**	**hubiste abrazado**	**hubisteis abrazado**
abrazó	**abrazaron**	**hubo abrazado**	**hubieron abrazado**
4 futuro		**11 futuro perfecto**	
abrazaré	**abrazaremos**	**habré abrazado**	**habremos abrazado**
abrazarás	**abrazaréis**	**habrás abrazado**	**habréis abrazado**
abrazará	**abrazarán**	**habrá abrazado**	**habrán abrazado**
5 potencial simple		**12 potencial compuesto**	
abrazaría	**abrazaríamos**	**habría abrazado**	**habríamos abrazado**
abrazarías	**abrazaríais**	**habrías abrazado**	**habríais abrazado**
abrazaría	**abrazarían**	**habría abrazado**	**habrían abrazado**
6 presente de subjuntivo		**13 perfecto de subjuntivo**	
abrace	**abracemos**	**haya abrazado**	**hayamos abrazado**
abraces	**abracéis**	**hayas abrazado**	**hayáis abrazado**
abrace	**abracen**	**haya abrazado**	**hayan abrazado**
7 imperfecto de subjuntivo		**14 pluscuamperfecto de subjuntivo**	
abrazara	**abrazáramos**	**hubiera abrazado**	**hubiéramos abrazado**
abrazaras	**abrazarais**	**hubieras abrazado**	**hubierais abrazado**
abrazara	**abrazaran**	**hubiera abrazado**	**hubieran abrazado**
OR		OR	
abrazase	**abrazásemos**	**hubiese abrazado**	**hubiésemos abrazado**
abrazases	**abrazaseis**	**hubieses abrazado**	**hubieseis abrazado**
abrazase	**abrazasen**	**hubiese abrazado**	**hubiesen abrazado**

imperativo	
—	**abracemos**
abraza; no abraces	**abrazad; no abracéis**
abrace	**abracen**

Words related to this verb
un abrazo embrace, hug
el abrazamiento embracing
un abrazo de Juanita Love, Juanita

una abrazada embrace
una abrazadera clamp, clasp

Be sure to consult the sections on verbs used in idiomatic expressions, verbs with prepositions, and the list of over 1,100 verbs conjugated like model verbs in the back pages.

abrir

Gerundio **abriendo** Part. pas. **abierto**

to open

The Seven Simple Tenses		The Seven Compound Tenses	
Singular	Plural	Singular	Plural
1 presente de indicativo		**8 perfecto de indicativo**	
abro	abrimos	he abierto	hemos abierto
abres	abrís	has abierto	habéis abierto
abre	abren	ha abierto	han abierto
2 imperfecto de indicativo		**9 pluscuamperfecto de indicativo**	
abría	abríamos	había abierto	habíamos abierto
abrías	abríais	habías abierto	habíais abierto
abría	abrían	había abierto	habían abierto
3 pretérito		**10 pretérito anterior**	
abrí	abrimos	hube abierto	hubimos abierto
abriste	abristeis	hubiste abierto	hubisteis abierto
abrió	abrieron	hubo abierto	hubieron abierto
4 futuro		**11 futuro perfecto**	
abriré	abriremos	habré abierto	habremos abierto
abrirás	abriréis	habrás abierto	habréis abierto
abrirá	abrirán	habrá abierto	habrán abierto
5 potencial simple		**12 potencial compuesto**	
abriría	abriríamos	habría abierto	habríamos abierto
abrirías	abriríais	habrías abierto	habríais abierto
abriría	abrirían	habría abierto	habrían abierto
6 presente de subjuntivo		**13 perfecto de subjuntivo**	
abra	abramos	haya abierto	hayamos abierto
abras	abráis	hayas abierto	hayáis abierto
abra	abran	haya abierto	hayan abierto
7 imperfecto de subjuntivo		**14 pluscuamperfecto de subjuntivo**	
abriera	abriéramos	hubiera abierto	hubiéramos abierto
abrieras	abrierais	hubieras abierto	hubierais abierto
abriera	abrieran	hubiera abierto	hubieran abierto
OR		OR	
abriese	abriésemos	hubiese abierto	hubiésemos abierto
abrieses	abrieseis	hubieses abierto	hubieseis abierto
abriese	abriesen	hubiese abierto	hubiesen abierto

	imperativo
—	abramos
abre; no abras	abrid; no abráis
abra	abran

Sentences using this verb and words related to it
La maestra dijo a los alumnos: — Abrid los libros en la página diez, por favor.
Todos los alumnos abrieron los libros en la página diez y Pablo comenzó a leer la lectura.

un abrimiento opening
abrir paso to make way

La puerta está abierta. The door is open.
Los libros están abiertos. The books are open.
en un abrir y cerrar de ojos in a wink

The Seven Simple Tenses		The Seven Compound Tenses	
Singular	Plural	Singular	Plural

1   presente de indicativo

		8 perfecto de indicativo	
absuelvo	absolvemos	he absuelto	hemos absuelto
absuelves	absolvéis	has absuelto	habéis absuelto
absuelve	absuelven	ha absuelto	han absuelto

2   imperfecto de indicativo

		9 pluscuamperfecto de indicativo	
absolvía	absolvíamos	había absuelto	habíamos absuelto
absolvías	absolvíais	habías absuelto	habíais absuelto
absolvía	absolvían	había absuelto	habían absuelto

3   pretérito

		10 pretérito anterior	
absolví	absolvimos	hube absuelto	hubimos absuelto
absolviste	absolvisteis	hubiste absuelto	hubisteis absuelto
absolvió	absolvieron	hubo absuelto	hubieron absuelto

4   futuro

		11 futuro perfecto	
absolveré	absolveremos	habré absuelto	habremos absuelto
absolverás	absolveréis	habrás absuelto	habréis absuelto
absolverá	absolverán	habrá absuelto	habrán absuelto

5   potencial simple

		12 potencial compuesto	
absolvería	absolveríamos	habría absuelto	habríamos absuelto
absolverías	absolveríais	habrías absuelto	habríais absuelto
absolvería	absolverían	habría absuelto	habrían absuelto

6   presente de subjuntivo

		13 perfecto de subjuntivo	
absuelva	absolvamos	haya absuelto	hayamos absuelto
absuelvas	absolváis	hayas absuelto	hayáis absuelto
absuelva	absuelvan	haya absuelto	hayan absuelto

7   imperfecto de subjuntivo

		14 pluscuamperfecto de subjuntivo	
absolviera	absolviéramos	hubiera absuelto	hubiéramos absuelto
absolvieras	absolvierais	hubieras absuelto	hubierais absuelto
absolviera	absolvieran	hubiera absuelto	hubieran absuelto
OR		OR	
absolviese	absolviésemos	hubiese absuelto	hubiésemos absuelto
absolvieses	absolvieseis	hubieses absuelto	hubieseis absuelto
absolviese	absolviesen	hubiese absuelto	hubiesen absuelto

imperativo

—	absolvamos
absuelve; no absuelvas	absolved; no absolváis
absuelva	absuelvan

Words and expressions related to this verb

la absolución   absolution, acquittal, pardon
absolutamente   absolutely
absoluto, absoluta   absolute, unconditional
en absoluto   absolutely
nada en absoluto   nothing at all

el absolutismo   absolutism, despotism
la absolución libre   not guilty verdict
salir absuelto   to come out clear of any charges

The subject pronouns are found on the page facing page 1.

abstenerse

Gerundio **absteniéndose**

Part. pas. **abstenido**

to abstain

The Seven Simple Tenses		The Seven Compound Tenses	
Singular	Plural	Singular	Plural
1 presente de indicativo		**8 perfecto de indicativo**	
me abstengo	nos abstenemos	me he abstenido	nos hemos abstenido
te abstienes	os abstenéis	te has abstenido	os habéis abstenido
se abstiene	se abstienen	se ha abstenido	se han abstenido
2 imperfecto de indicativo		**9 pluscuamperfecto de indicativo**	
me abstenía	nos absteníamos	me había abstenido	nos habíamos abstenido
te abstenías	os absteníais	te habías abstenido	os habíais abstenido
se abstenía	se abstenían	se había abstenido	se habían abstenido
3 pretérito		**10 pretérito anterior**	
me abstuve	nos abstuvimos	me hube abstenido	nos hubimos abstenido
te abstuviste	os abstuvisteis	te hubiste abstenido	os hubisteis abstenido
se abstuvo	se abstuvieron	se hubo abstenido	se hubieron abstenido
4 futuro		**11 futuro perfecto**	
me abstendré	nos abstendremos	me habré abstenido	nos habremos abstenido
te abstendrás	os abstendréis	te habrás abstenido	os habréis abstenido
se abstendrá	se abstendrán	se habrá abstenido	se habrán abstenido
5 potencial simple		**12 potencial compuesto**	
me abstendría	nos abstendríamos	me habría abstenido	nos habríamos abstenido
te abstendrías	os abstendríais	te habrías abstenido	os habríais abstenido
se abstendría	se abstendrían	se habría abstenido	se habrían abstenido
6 presente de subjuntivo		**13 perfecto de subjuntivo**	
me abstenga	nos abstengamos	me haya abstenido	nos hayamos abstenido
te abstengas	os abstengáis	te hayas abstenido	os hayáis abstenido
se abstenga	se abstengan	se haya abstenido	se hayan abstenido
7 imperfecto de subjuntivo		**14 pluscuamperfecto de subjuntivo**	
me abstuviera	nos abstuviéramos	me hubiera abstenido	nos hubiéramos abstenido
te abstuvieras	os abstuvierais	te hubieras abstenido	os hubierais abstenido
se abstuviera	se abstuvieran	se hubiera abstenido	se hubieran abstenido
OR		OR	
me abstuviese	nos abstuviésemos	me hubiese abstenido	nos hubiésemos abstenido
te abstuvieses	os abstuvieseis	te hubieses abstenido	os hubieseis abstenido
se abstuviese	se abstuviesen	se hubiese abstenido	se hubiesen abstenido

imperativo	
—	**abstengámonos**
abstente; no te abstengas	**absteneos; no os abstengáis**
absténgase	**absténganse**

Words and expressions related to this verb

la abstención abstention, forbearance
abstenerse de to abstain from, to refrain from
la abstinencia abstinence, fasting
hacer abstinencia to fast

el, la abstencionista abstentionist
el abstencionismo abstentionism
el día de abstinencia day of fasting

to annoy, to bore, to vex

The Seven Simple Tenses		The Seven Compound Tenses	
Singular	Plural	Singular	Plural
1 presente de indicativo		8 perfecto de indicativo	
aburro	aburrimos	he aburrido	hemos aburrido
aburres	aburrís	has aburrido	habéis aburrido
aburre	aburren	ha aburrido	han aburrido
2 imperfecto de indicativo		9 pluscuamperfecto de indicativo	
aburría	aburríamos	había aburrido	habíamos aburrido
aburrías	aburríais	habías aburrido	habíais aburrido
aburría	aburrían	había aburrido	habían aburrido
3 pretérito		10 pretérito anterior	
aburrí	aburrimos	hube aburrido	hubimos aburrido
aburriste	aburristeis	hubiste aburrido	hubisteis aburrido
aburrió	aburrieron	hubo aburrido	hubieron aburrido
4 futuro		11 futuro perfecto	
aburriré	aburriremos	habré aburrido	habremos aburrido
aburrirás	aburriréis	habrás aburrido	habréis aburrido
aburrirá	aburrirán	habrá aburrido	habrán aburrido
5 potencial simple		12 potencial compuesto	
aburriría	aburriríamos	habría aburrido	habríamos aburrido
aburrirías	aburriríais	habrías aburrido	habríais aburrido
aburriría	aburrirían	habría aburrido	habrían aburrido
6 presente de subjuntivo		13 perfecto de subjuntivo	
aburra	aburramos	haya aburrido	hayamos aburrido
aburras	aburráis	hayas aburrido	hayáis aburrido
aburra	aburran	haya aburrido	hayan aburrido
7 imperfecto de subjuntivo		14 pluscuamperfecto de subjuntivo	
aburriera	aburriéramos	hubiera aburrido	hubiéramos aburrido
aburrieras	aburrierais	hubieras aburrido	hubierais aburrido
aburriera	aburrieran	hubiera aburrido	hubieran aburrido
OR		OR	
aburriese	aburriésemos	hubiese aburrido	hubiésemos aburrido
aburrieses	aburrieseis	hubieses aburrido	hubieseis aburrido
aburriese	aburriesen	hubiese aburrido	hubiesen aburrido

imperativo

—	aburramos
aburre; no aburras	aburrid; no aburráis
aburra	aburran

Sentences using this verb and words related to it
El profesor de español cree que Pedro está aburrido, que María está aburrida, que todos los alumnos en la clase están aburridos. Pero la verdad es que no se aburren.
Todos los alumnos se interesan en aprender español.

el aburrimiento   boredom, weariness
un aburridor, una aburridora   boring person
See also **aburrirse.**

una cara de aburrimiento   a bored look
la aburrición   annoyance, ennui

The subject pronouns are found on the page facing page 1.

7

to be bored, to grow tired, to grow weary

The Seven Simple Tenses		The Seven Compound Tenses	
Singular	Plural	Singular	Plural
1 presente de indicativo		8 perfecto de indicativo	
me aburro	nos aburrimos	me he aburrido	nos hemos aburrido
te aburres	os aburrís	te has aburrido	os habéis aburrido
se aburre	se aburren	se ha aburrido	se han aburrido
2 imperfecto de indicativo		9 pluscuamperfecto de indicativo	
me aburría	nos aburríamos	me había aburrido	nos habíamos aburrido
te aburrías	os aburríais	te habías aburrido	os habíais aburrido
se aburría	se aburrían	se había aburrido	se habían aburrido
3 pretérito		10 pretérito anterior	
me aburrí	nos aburrimos	me hube aburrido	nos hubimos aburrido
te aburriste	os aburristeis	te hubiste aburrido	os hubisteis aburrido
se aburrió	se aburrieron	se hubo aburrido	se hubieron aburrido
4 futuro		11 futuro perfecto	
me aburriré	nos aburriremos	me habré aburrido	nos habremos aburrido
te aburrirás	os aburriréis	te habrás aburrido	os habréis aburrido
se aburrirá	se aburrirán	se habrá aburrido	se habrán aburrido
5 potencial simple		12 potencial compuesto	
me aburriría	nos aburriríamos	me habría aburrido	nos habríamos aburrido
te aburrirías	os aburriríais	te habrías aburrido	os habríais aburrido
se aburriría	se aburrirían	se habría aburrido	se habrían aburrido
6 presente de subjuntivo		13 perfecto de subjuntivo	
me aburra	nos aburramos	me haya aburrido	nos hayamos aburrido
te aburras	os aburráis	te hayas aburrido	os hayáis aburrido
se aburra	se aburran	se haya aburrido	se hayan aburrido
7 imperfecto de subjuntivo		14 pluscuamperfecto de subjuntivo	
me aburriera	nos aburriéramos	me hubiera aburrido	nos hubiéramos aburrido
te aburrieras	os aburrierais	te hubieras aburrido	os hubierais aburrido
se aburriera	se aburrieran	se hubiera aburrido	se hubieran aburrido
OR		OR	
me aburriese	nos aburriésemos	me hubiese aburrido	nos hubiésemos aburrido
te aburrieses	os aburrieseis	te hubieses aburrido	os hubieseis aburrido
se aburriese	se aburriesen	se hubiese aburrido	se hubiesen aburrido

imperativo	
—	aburrámonos
abúrrete; no te aburras	aburríos; no os aburráis
abúrrase	abúrranse

Words and expressions related to this verb
**Hace treinta años que el profesor de español enseña la lengua en la misma escuela, pero
ne se aburre.**

el aburrimiento   boredom, weariness
aburridamente   tediously
See also **aburrir.**

aburrirse como una ostra   to be bored stiff
   (like an oyster)
¡Qué aburrimiento!   What a bore!

to finish, to end, to complete

The Seven Simple Tenses		The Seven Compound Tenses	
Singular	Plural	Singular	Plural
1 presente de indicativo		8 perfecto de indicativo	
acabo	acabamos	he acabado	hemos acabado
acabas	acabáis	has acabado	habéis acabado
acaba	acaban	ha acabado	han acabado
2 imperfecto de indicativo		9 pluscuamperfecto de indicativo	
acababa	acabábamos	había acabado	habíamos acabado
acababas	acababais	habías acabado	habíais acabado
acababa	acababan	había acabado	habían acabado
3 pretérito		10 pretérito anterior	
acabé	acabamos	hube acabado	hubimos acabado
acabaste	acabasteis	hubiste acabado	hubisteis acabado
acabó	acabaron	hubo acabado	hubieron acabado
4 futuro		11 futuro perfecto	
acabaré	acabaremos	habré acabado	habremos acabado
acabarás	acabaréis	habrás acabado	habréis acabado
acabará	acabarán	habrá acabado	habrán acabado
5 potencial simple		12 potencial compuesto	
acabaría	acabaríamos	habría acabado	habríamos acabado
acabarías	acabaríais	habrías acabado	habríais acabado
acabaría	acabarían	habría acabado	habrían acabado
6 presente de subjuntivo		13 perfecto de subjuntivo	
acabe	acabemos	haya acabado	hayamos acabado
acabes	acabéis	hayas acabado	hayáis acabado
acabe	acaben	haya acabado	hayan acabado
7 imperfecto de subjuntivo		14 pluscuamperfecto de subjuntivo	
acabara	acabáramos	hubiera acabado	hubiéramos acabado
acabaras	acabarais	hubieras acabado	hubierais acabado
acabara	acabaran	hubiera acabado	hubieran acabado
OR		OR	
acabase	acabásemos	hubiese acabado	hubiésemos acabado
acabases	acabaseis	hubieses acabado	hubieseis acabado
acabase	acabasen	hubiese acabado	hubiesen acabado

imperativo

—	acabemos
acaba; no acabes	acabad; no acabéis
acabe	acaben

Sentences using this verb and words related to it
Yo acabo de leer la lección de español, Miguel acaba de escribir una composición, y los otros alumnos acaban de hablar en español.

el acabamiento completion
acabar de + inf. to have just + past part.
acabar por to end by, to . . . finally
acabar con to put an end to

> Consult the back pages for the sections on verbs in idioms and with prepositions.

See also **acabar** on page 524.

The subject pronouns are found on the page facing page 1.

to accelerate, to speed, to hasten, to hurry

The Seven Simple Tenses		The Seven Compound Tenses	
Singular	Plural	Singular	Plural

1 presente de indicativo

acelero	aceleramos
aceleras	aceleráis
acelera	aceleran

8 perfecto de indicativo

he acelerado	hemos acelerado
has acelerado	habéis acelerado
ha acelerado	han acelerado

2 imperfecto de indicativo

aceleraba	acelerábamos
acelerabas	acelerabais
aceleraba	aceleraban

9 pluscuamperfecto de indicativo

había acelerado	habíamos acelerado
habías acelerado	habíais acelerado
había acelerado	habían acelerado

3 pretérito

aceleré	aceleramos
aceleraste	acelerasteis
aceleró	aceleraron

10 pretérito anterior

hube acelerado	hubimos acelerado
hubiste acelerado	hubisteis acelerado
hubo acelerado	hubieron acelerado

4 futuro

aceleraré	aceleraremos
acelerarás	aceleraréis
acelerará	acelerarán

11 futuro perfecto

habré acelerado	habremos acelerado
habrás acelerado	habréis acelerado
habrá acelerado	habrán acelerado

5 potencial simple

aceleraría	aceleraríamos
acelerarías	aceleraríais
aceleraría	acelerarían

12 potencial compuesto

habría acelerado	habríamos acelerado
habrías acelerado	habríais acelerado
habría acelerado	habrían acelerado

6 presente de subjuntivo

acelere	aceleremos
aceleres	acelereis
acelere	aceleren

13 perfecto de subjuntivo

haya acelerado	hayamos acelerado
hayas acelerado	hayáis acelerado
haya acelerado	hayan acelerado

7 imperfecto de subjuntivo

acelerara	aceleráramos
aceleraras	acelerarais
acelerara	aceleraran
OR	
acelerase	acelerásemos
acelerases	aceleraseis
acelerase	acelerasen

14 pluscuamperfecto de subjuntivo

hubiera acelerado	hubiéramos acelerado
hubieras acelerado	hubierais acelerado
hubiera acelerado	hubieran acelerado
OR	
hubiese acelerado	hubiésemos acelerado
hubieses acelerado	hubieseis acelerado
hubiese acelerado	hubiesen acelerado

imperativo

—	aceleremos
acelera; no aceleres	acelerad; no aceleréis
acelere	aceleren

Words related to this verb
aceleradamente   hastily, quickly, speedily
la aceleración   haste, acceleration

acelerante   accelerating
el aceleramiento   acceleration

Be sure to consult the sections on verbs used in idiomatic expressions, verbs with prepositions,
and the list of over 1,100 verbs conjugated like model verbs in the back pages.

The Seven Simple Tenses		The Seven Compound Tenses	
Singular	Plural	Singular	Plural
1 presente de indicativo		8 perfecto de indicativo	
acepto	aceptamos	he aceptado	hemos aceptado
aceptas	aceptáis	has aceptado	habéis aceptado
acepta	aceptan	ha aceptado	han aceptado
2 imperfecto de indicativo		9 pluscuamperfecto de indicativo	
aceptaba	aceptábamos	había aceptado	habíamos aceptado
aceptabas	aceptabais	habías aceptado	habíais aceptado
aceptaba	aceptaban	había aceptado	habían aceptado
3 pretérito		10 pretérito anterior	
acepté	aceptamos	hube aceptado	hubimos aceptado
aceptaste	aceptasteis	hubiste aceptado	hubisteis aceptado
aceptó	aceptaron	hubo aceptado	hubieron aceptado
4 futuro		11 futuro perfecto	
aceptaré	aceptaremos	habré aceptado	habremos aceptado
aceptarás	aceptaréis	habrás aceptado	habréis aceptado
aceptará	aceptarán	habrá aceptado	habrán aceptado
5 potencial simple		12 potencial compuesto	
aceptaría	aceptaríamos	habría aceptado	habríamos aceptado
aceptarías	aceptaríais	habrías aceptado	habríais aceptado
aceptaría	aceptarían	habría aceptado	habrían aceptado
6 presente de subjuntivo		13 perfecto de subjuntivo	
acepte	aceptemos	haya aceptado	hayamos aceptado
aceptes	aceptéis	hayas aceptado	hayáis aceptado
acepte	acepten	haya aceptado	hayan aceptado
7 imperfecto de subjuntivo		14 pluscuamperfecto de subjuntivo	
aceptara	aceptáramos	hubiera aceptado	hubiéramos aceptado
aceptaras	aceptarais	hubieras aceptado	hubierais aceptado
aceptara	aceptaran	hubiera aceptado	hubieran aceptado
OR		OR	
aceptase	aceptásemos	hubiese aceptado	hubiésemos aceptado
aceptases	aceptaseis	hubieses aceptado	hubieseis aceptado
aceptase	aceptasen	hubiese aceptado	hubiesen aceptado

imperativo

—	aceptemos
acepta; no aceptes	aceptad; no aceptéis
acepte	acepten

Words and expressions related to this verb
aceptable   acceptable
el aceptador, la aceptadora   acceptor
el aceptante, la aceptante   accepter
la aceptación   acceptance, acceptation

aceptar + inf.   to agree + inf.
aceptar empleo   to take a job
acepto, acepta   acceptable
aceptar o rechazar una oferta
    to accept or reject an offer

Enjoy verbs in Spanish proverbs on page 559.

The subject pronouns are found on the page facing page 1.

11

to bring near, to place near

The Seven Simple Tenses		The Seven Compound Tenses	
Singular	Plural	Singular	Plural
1 presente de indicativo		8 perfecto de indicativo	
acerco	acercamos	he acercado	hemos acercado
acercas	acercáis	has acercado	habéis acercado
acerca	acercan	ha acercado	han acercado
2 imperfecto de indicativo		9 pluscuamperfecto de indicativo	
acercaba	acercábamos	había acercado	habíamos acercado
acercabas	acercabais	habías acercado	habíais acercado
acercaba	acercaban	había acercado	habían acercado
3 pretérito		10 pretérito anterior	
acerqué	acercamos	hube acercado	hubimos acercado
acercaste	acercasteis	hubiste acercado	hubisteis acercado
acercó	acercaron	hubo acercado	hubieron acercado
4 futuro		11 futuro perfecto	
acercaré	acercaremos	habré acercado	habremos acercado
acercarás	acercaréis	habrás acercado	habréis acercado
acercará	acercarán	habrá acercado	habrán acercado
5 potencial simple		12 potencial compuesto	
acercaría	acercaríamos	habría acercado	habríamos acercado
acercarías	acercaríais	habrías acercado	habríais acercado
acercaría	acercarían	habría acercado	habrían acercado
6 presente de subjuntivo		13 perfecto de subjuntivo	
acerque	acerquemos	haya acercado	hayamos acercado
acerques	acerquéis	hayas acercado	hayáis acercado
acerque	acerquen	haya acercado	hayan acercado
7 imperfecto de subjuntivo		14 pluscuamperfecto de subjuntivo	
acercara	acercáramos	hubiera acercado	hubiéramos acercado
acercaras	acercarais	hubieras acercado	hubierais acercado
acercara	acercaran	hubiera acercado	hubieran acercado
OR		OR	
acercase	acercásemos	hubiese acercado	hubiésemos acercado
acercases	acercaseis	hubieses acercado	hubieseis acercado
acercase	acercasen	hubiese acercado	hubiesen acercado

imperativo	
—	acerquemos
acerca; no acerques	acercad; no acerquéis
acerque	acerquen

Words and expressions related to this verb
acerca de   about, regarding, with regard to
el acercamiento   approaching, approximation
cerca de   near
de cerca   close at hand, closely

acerca de esto   hereof
la cerca   fence, hedge
el cercado   fenced in area
mis parientes cercanos   my close relatives

See also **acercarse**.

The Seven Simple Tenses		The Seven Compound Tenses	
Singular	Plural	Singular	Plural
1 presente de indicativo		8 perfecto de indicativo	
me acerco	**nos acercamos**	**me he acercado**	**nos hemos acercado**
te acercas	**os acercáis**	**te has acercado**	**os habéis acercado**
se acerca	**se acercan**	**se ha acercado**	**se han acercado**
2 imperfecto de indicativo		9 pluscuamperfecto de indicativo	
me acercaba	**nos acercábamos**	**me había acercado**	**nos habíamos acercado**
te acercabas	**os acercabais**	**te habías acercado**	**os habíais acercado**
se acercaba	**se acercaban**	**se había acercado**	**se habían acercado**
3 pretérito		10 pretérito anterior	
me acerqué	**nos acercamos**	**me hube acercado**	**nos hubimos acercado**
te acercaste	**os acercasteis**	**te hubiste acercado**	**os hubisteis acercado**
se acercó	**se acercaron**	**se hubo acercado**	**se hubieron acercado**
4 futuro		11 futuro perfecto	
me acercaré	**nos acercaremos**	**me habré acercado**	**nos habremos acercado**
te acercarás	**os acercaréis**	**te habrás acercado**	**os habréis acercado**
se acercará	**se acercarán**	**se habrá acercado**	**se habrán acercado**
5 potencial simple		12 potencial compuesto	
me acercaría	**nos acercaríamos**	**me habría acercado**	**nos habríamos acercado**
te acercarías	**os acercaríais**	**te habrías acercado**	**os habríais acercado**
se acercaría	**se acercarían**	**se habría acercado**	**se habrían acercado**
6 presente de subjuntivo		13 perfecto de subjuntivo	
me acerque	**nos acerquemos**	**me haya acercado**	**nos hayamos acercado**
te acerques	**os acerquéis**	**te hayas acercado**	**os hayáis acercado**
se acerque	**se acerquen**	**se haya acercado**	**se hayan acercado**
7 imperfecto de subjuntivo		14 pluscuamperfecto de subjuntivo	
me acercara	**nos acercáramos**	**me hubiera acercado**	**nos hubiéramos acercado**
te acercaras	**os acercarais**	**te hubieras acercado**	**os hubierais acercado**
se acercara	**se acercaran**	**se hubiera acercado**	**se hubieran acercado**
OR		OR	
me acercase	**nos acercásemos**	**me hubiese acercado**	**nos hubiésemos acercado**
te acercases	**os acercaseis**	**te hubieses acercado**	**os hubieseis acercado**
se acercase	**se acercasen**	**se hubiese acercado**	**se hubiesen acercado**

imperativo

—	**acerquémonos**
acércate; no te acerques	**acercaos; no os acerquéis**
acérquese	**acérquense**

Words and expressions related to this verb
acerca de about, regarding, with regard to
el acercamiento approaching, approximation
cerca de near
de cerca close at hand, closely

cercanamente soon, shortly
cercano, cercana near, close
cercar to enclose, fence in
las cercanías neighborhood, suburbs

See also **acercar.**

to hit the mark, to hit upon, to do (something) right, to succeed in, to guess right

The Seven Simple Tenses		The Seven Compound Tenses	
Singular	Plural	Singular	Plural
1 presente de indicativo		8 perfecto de indicativo	
acierto	acertamos	he acertado	hemos acertado
aciertas	acertáis	has acertado	habéis acertado
acierta	aciertan	ha acertado	han acertado
2 imperfecto de indicativo		9 pluscuamperfecto de indicativo	
acertaba	acertábamos	había acertado	habíamos acertado
acertabas	acertabais	habías acertado	habíais acertado
acertaba	acertaban	había acertado	habían acertado
3 pretérito		10 pretérito anterior	
acerté	acertamos	hube acertado	hubimos acertado
acertaste	acertasteis	hubiste acertado	hubisteis acertado
acertó	acertaron	hubo acertado	hubieron acertado
4 futuro		11 futuro perfecto	
acertaré	acertaremos	habré acertado	habremos acertado
acertarás	acertaréis	habrás acertado	habréis acertado
acertará	acertarán	habrá acertado	habrán acertado
5 potencial simple		12 potencial compuesto	
acertaría	acertaríamos	habría acertado	habríamos acertado
acertarías	acertaríais	habrías acertado	habríais acertado
acertaría	acertarían	habría acertado	habrían acertado
6 presente de subjuntivo		13 perfecto de subjuntivo	
acierte	acertemos	haya acertado	hayamos acertado
aciertes	acertéis	hayas acertado	hayáis acertado
acierte	acierten	haya acertado	hayan acertado
7 imperfecto de subjuntivo		14 pluscuamperfecto de subjuntivo	
acertara	acertáramos	hubiera acertado	hubiéramos acertado
acertaras	acertarais	hubieras acertado	hubierais acertado
acertara	acertaran	hubiera acertado	hubieran acertado
OR		OR	
acertase	acertásemos	hubiese acertado	hubiésemos acertado
acertases	acertaseis	hubieses acertado	hubieseis acertado
acertase	acertasen	hubiese acertado	hubiesen acertado

imperativo

—	acertemos
acierta; no aciertes	acertad; no acertéis
acierte	acierten

Words and expressions related to this verb
acertado, acertada proper, fit, sensible
el acertador, la acertadora good guesser
acertar a to happen to + inf.
acertar con to come across, to find

Es cierto. It's certain/sure.

el acertamiento tact, ability
el acertijo riddle
acertadamente opportunely, correctly
ciertamente certainly

Get acquainted with what preposition goes with what verb on pages 541–549.

to acclaim, to applaud, to shout, to hail

The Seven Simple Tenses		The Seven Compound Tenses	
Singular	Plural	Singular	Plural
1 presente de indicativo		**8 perfecto de indicativo**	
aclamo	aclamamos	he aclamado	hemos aclamado
aclamas	aclamáis	has aclamado	habéis aclamado
aclama	aclaman	ha aclamado	han aclamado
2 imperfecto de indicativo		**9 pluscuamperfecto de indicativo**	
aclamaba	aclamábamos	había aclamado	habíamos aclamado
aclamabas	aclamabais	habías aclamado	habíais aclamado
aclamaba	aclamaban	había aclamado	habían aclamado
3 pretérito		**10 pretérito anterior**	
aclamé	aclamamos	hube aclamado	hubimos aclamado
aclamaste	aclamasteis	hubiste aclamado	hubisteis aclamado
aclamó	aclamaron	hubo aclamado	hubieron aclamado
4 futuro		**11 futuro perfecto**	
aclamaré	aclamaremos	habré aclamado	habremos aclamado
aclamarás	aclamaréis	habrás aclamado	habréis aclamado
aclamará	aclamarán	habrá aclamado	habrán aclamado
5 potencial simple		**12 potencial compuesto**	
aclamaría	aclamaríamos	habría aclamado	habríamos aclamado
aclamarías	aclamaríais	habrías aclamado	habríais aclamado
aclamaría	aclamarían	habría aclamado	habrían aclamado
6 presente de subjuntivo		**13 perfecto de subjuntivo**	
aclame	aclamemos	haya aclamado	hayamos aclamado
aclames	aclaméis	hayas aclamado	hayáis aclamado
aclame	aclamen	haya aclamado	hayan aclamado
7 imperfecto de subjuntivo		**14 pluscuamperfecto de subjuntivo**	
aclamara	aclamáramos	hubiera aclamado	hubiéramos aclamado
aclamaras	aclamarais	hubieras aclamado	hubierais aclamado
aclamara	aclamaran	hubiera aclamado	hubieran aclamado
OR		OR	
aclamase	aclamásemos	hubiese aclamado	hubiésemos aclamado
aclamases	aclamaseis	hubieses aclamado	hubieseis aclamado
aclamase	aclamasen	hubiese aclamado	hubiesen aclamado

imperativo	
—	aclamemos
aclama; no aclames	aclamad; no aclaméis
aclame	aclamen

Words and expressions related to this verb
aclamado, aclamada acclaimed
la aclamación acclaim, acclamation
la reclamación claim, demand
reclamar en juicio to sue

aclamable laudable
por aclamación unanimously
reclamar to claim, to demand, to reclaim
reclamar por daños to claim damages

The subject pronouns are found on the page facing page 1.   **15**

to explain, to clarify, to make clear, to rinse, to clear

The Seven Simple Tenses		The Seven Compound Tenses	
Singular	Plural	Singular	Plural
1 presente de indicativo		8 perfecto de indicativo	
aclaro	aclaramos	he aclarado	hemos aclarado
aclaras	aclaráis	has aclarado	habéis aclarado
aclara	aclaran	ha aclarado	han aclarado
2 imperfecto de indicativo		9 pluscuamperfecto de indicativo	
aclaraba	aclarábamos	había aclarado	habíamos aclarado
aclarabas	aclarabais	habías aclarado	habíais aclarado
aclaraba	aclaraban	había aclarado	habían aclarado
3 pretérito		10 pretérito anterior	
aclaré	aclaramos	hube aclarado	hubimos aclarado
aclaraste	aclarasteis	hubiste aclarado	hubisteis aclarado
aclaró	aclararon	hubo aclarado	hubieron aclarado
4 futuro		11 futuro perfecto	
aclararé	aclararemos	habré aclarado	habremos aclarado
aclararás	aclararéis	habrás aclarado	habréis aclarado
aclarará	aclararán	habrá aclarado	habrán aclarado
5 potencial simple		12 potencial compuesto	
aclararía	aclararíamos	habría aclarado	habríamos aclarado
aclararías	aclararíais	habrías aclarado	habríais aclarado
aclararía	aclararían	habría aclarado	habrían aclarado
6 presente de subjuntivo		13 perfecto de subjuntivo	
aclare	aclaremos	haya aclarado	hayamos aclarado
aclares	aclaréis	hayas aclarado	hayáis aclarado
aclare	aclaren	haya aclarado	hayan aclarado
7 imperfecto de subjuntivo		14 pluscuamperfecto de subjuntivo	
aclarara	aclaráramos	hubiera aclarado	hubiéramos aclarado
aclararas	aclararais	hubieras aclarado	hubierais aclarado
aclarara	aclararan	hubiera aclarado	hubieran aclarado
OR		OR	
aclarase	aclarásemos	hubiese aclarado	hubiésemos aclarado
aclarases	aclaraseis	hubieses aclarado	hubieseis aclarado
aclarase	aclarasen	hubiese aclarado	hubiesen aclarado

imperativo

—	aclaremos
aclara; no aclares	aclarad; no aclaréis
aclare	aclaren

Words and expressions related to this verb
una aclaración explanation
aclarado, aclarada cleared, made clear; rinsed
aclarar la voz to clear one's throat
poner en claro to clarify

aclarecer to make clear
¡Claro que sí! Of course!
¡Claro que no! Of course not!
¿Está claro? Is that clear?

Review the principal parts of important Spanish verbs on pages xvi–xvii.

to accompany, to escort, to go with, to keep company

The Seven Simple Tenses		The Seven Compound Tenses	
Singular	Plural	Singular	Plural
1 presente de indicativo		8 perfecto de indicativo	
acompaño	**acompañamos**	**he acompañado**	**hemos acompañado**
acompañas	**acompañáis**	**has acompañado**	**habéis acompañado**
acompaña	**acompañan**	**ha acompañado**	**han acompañado**
2 imperfecto de indicativo		9 pluscuamperfecto de indicativo	
acompañaba	**acompañábamos**	**había acompañado**	**habíamos acompañado**
acompañabas	**acompañabais**	**habías acompañado**	**habíais acompañado**
acompañaba	**acompañaban**	**había acompañado**	**habían acompañado**
3 pretérito		10 pretérito anterior	
acompañé	**acompañamos**	**hube acompañado**	**hubimos acompañado**
acompañaste	**acompañasteis**	**hubiste acompañado**	**hubisteis acompañado**
acompañó	**acompañaron**	**hubo acompañado**	**hubieron acompañado**
4 futuro		11 futuro perfecto	
acompañaré	**acompañaremos**	**habré acompañado**	**habremos acompañado**
acompañarás	**acompañaréis**	**habrás acompañado**	**habréis acompañado**
acompañará	**acompañarán**	**habrá acompañado**	**habrán acompañado**
5 potencial simple		12 potencial compuesto	
acompañaría	**acompañaríamos**	**habría acompañado**	**habríamos acompañado**
acompañarías	**acompañaríais**	**habrías acompañado**	**habríais acompañado**
acompañaría	**acompañarían**	**habría acompañado**	**habrían acompañado**
6 presente de subjuntivo		13 perfecto de subjuntivo	
acompañe	**acompañemos**	**haya acompañado**	**hayamos acompañado**
acompañes	**acompañéis**	**hayas acompañado**	**hayáis acompañado**
acompañe	**acompañen**	**haya acompañado**	**hayan acompañado**
7 imperfecto de subjuntivo		14 pluscuamperfecto de subjuntivo	
acompañara	**acompañáramos**	**hubiera acompañado**	**hubiéramos acompañado**
acompañaras	**acompañarais**	**hubieras acompañado**	**hubierais acompañado**
acompañara	**acompañaran**	**hubiera acompañado**	**hubieran acompañado**
OR		OR	
acompañase	**acompañásemos**	**hubiese acompañado**	**hubiésemos acompañado**
acompañases	**acompañaseis**	**hubieses acompañado**	**hubieseis acompañado**
acompañase	**acompañasen**	**hubiese acompañado**	**hubiesen acompañado**

imperativo

—	**acompañemos**
acompaña; no acompañes	**acompañad; no acompañéis**
acompañe	**acompañen**

Words and expressions related to this verb
el acompañador, la acompañadora   companion, chaperon, accompanist
el acompañamiento   accompaniment
el acompañado, la acompañada   assistant
un compañero, una compañera   friend, mate, companion;
        compañero de cuarto   roommate; **compañero de juego**   playmate

The subject pronouns are found on the page facing page 1.

to advise, to counsel

The Seven Simple Tenses		The Seven Compound Tenses	
Singular	Plural	Singular	Plural
1 presente de indicativo		8 perfecto de indicativo	
aconsejo	aconsejamos	he aconsejado	hemos aconsejado
aconsejas	aconsejáis	has aconsejado	habéis aconsejado
aconseja	aconsejan	ha aconsejado	han aconsejado
2 imperfecto de indicativo		9 pluscuamperfecto de indicativo	
aconsejaba	aconsejábamos	había aconsejado	habíamos aconsejado
aconsejabas	aconsejabais	habías aconsejado	habíais aconsejado
aconsejaba	aconsejaban	había aconsejado	habían aconsejado
3 pretérito		10 pretérito anterior	
aconsejé	aconsejamos	hube aconsejado	hubimos aconsejado
aconsejaste	aconsejasteis	hubiste aconsejado	hubisteis aconsejado
aconsejó	aconsejaron	hubo aconsejado	hubieron aconsejado
4 futuro		11 futuro perfecto	
aconsejaré	aconsejaremos	habré aconsejado	habremos aconsejado
aconsejarás	aconsejaréis	habrás aconsejado	habréis aconsejado
aconsejará	aconsejarán	habrá aconsejado	habrán aconsejado
5 potencial simple		12 potencial compuesto	
aconsejaría	aconsejaríamos	habría aconsejado	habríamos aconsejado
aconsejarías	aconsejaríais	habrías aconsejado	habríais aconsejado
aconsejaría	aconsejarían	habría aconsejado	habrían aconsejado
6 presente de subjuntivo		13 perfecto de subjuntivo	
aconseje	aconsejemos	haya aconsejado	hayamos aconsejado
aconsejes	aconsejéis	hayas aconsejado	hayáis aconsejado
aconseje	aconsejen	haya aconsejado	hayan aconsejado
7 imperfecto de subjuntivo		14 pluscuamperfecto de subjuntivo	
aconsejara	aconsejáramos	hubiera aconsejado	hubiéramos aconsejado
aconsejaras	aconsejarais	hubieras aconsejado	hubierais aconsejado
aconsejara	aconsejaran	hubiera aconsejado	hubieran aconsejado
OR		OR	
aconsejase	aconsejásemos	hubiese aconsejado	hubiésemos aconsejado
aconsejases	aconsejaseis	hubieses aconsejado	hubieseis aconsejado
aconsejase	aconsejasen	hubiese aconsejado	hubiesen aconsejado

imperativo	
—	aconsejemos
aconseja; no aconsejes	aconsejad; aconsejéis
aconseje	aconsejen

Words and expressions related to this verb

el aconsejador, la aconsejadora   adviser, counselor
aconsejar con   to consult
el consejo   advice, counsel
El tiempo da buen consejo.   Time will tell.

aconsejarse   to seek advice
aconsejarse de   to consult with
el aconsejamiento   counselling
desaconsejadamente   ill-advisedly

Enjoy verbs in Spanish proverbs on page 539.

to agree (upon)

The Seven Simple Tenses		The Seven Compound Tenses	
Singular	Plural	Singular	Plural
1　presente de indicativo		8　perfecto de indicativo	
acuerdo	**acordamos**	**he acordado**	**hemos acordado**
acuerdas	**acordáis**	**has acordado**	**habéis acordado**
acuerda	**acuerdan**	**ha acordado**	**han acordado**
2　imperfecto de indicativo		9　pluscuamperfecto de indicativo	
acordaba	**acordábamos**	**había acordado**	**habíamos acordado**
acordabas	**acordabais**	**habías acordado**	**habíais acordado**
acordaba	**acordaban**	**había acordado**	**habían acordado**
3　pretérito		10　pretérito anterior	
acordé	**acordamos**	**hube acordado**	**hubimos acordado**
acordaste	**acordasteis**	**hubiste acordado**	**hubisteis acordado**
acordó	**acordaron**	**hubo acordado**	**hubieron acordado**
4　futuro		11　futuro perfecto	
acordaré	**acordaremos**	**habré acordado**	**habremos acordado**
acordarás	**acordaréis**	**habrás acordado**	**habréis acordado**
acordará	**acordarán**	**habrá acordado**	**habrán acordado**
5　potencial simple		12　potencial compuesto	
acordaría	**acordaríamos**	**habría acordado**	**habríamos acordado**
acordarías	**acordaríais**	**habrías acordado**	**habríais acordado**
acordaría	**acordarían**	**habría acordado**	**habrían acordado**
6　presente de subjuntivo		13　perfecto de subjuntivo	
acuerde	**acordemos**	**haya acordado**	**hayamos acordado**
acuerdes	**acordéis**	**hayas acordado**	**hayáis acordado**
acuerde	**acuerden**	**haya acordado**	**hayan acordado**
7　imperfecto de subjuntivo		14　pluscuamperfecto de subjuntivo	
acordara	**acordáramos**	**hubiera acordado**	**hubiéramos acordado**
acordaras	**acordarais**	**hubieras acordado**	**hubierais acordado**
acordara	**acordaran**	**hubiera acordado**	**hubieran acordado**
OR		OR	
acordase	**acordásemos**	**hubiese acordado**	**hubiésemos acordado**
acordases	**acordaseis**	**hubieses acordado**	**hubieseis acordado**
acordase	**acordasen**	**hubiese acordado**	**hubiesen acordado**

imperativo

—	**acordemos**
acuerda; no acuerdes	**acordad; no acordéis**
acuerde	**acuerden**

Words and expressions related to this verb
la acordada　decision, resolution
acordadamente　jointly, by common consent
un acuerdo　agreement
de acuerdo　in agreement
de común acuerdo　unanimously,
　by mutual agreement

desacordar　to put out of tune
desacordante　discordant
desacordado, desacordada　out of tune (music)
estar de acuerdo con　to be in agreement with

See also **acordarse.**

The subject pronouns are found on the page facing page 1.

acordarse   Gerundio **acordándose**   Part. pas. **acordado**

to remember, to agree

The Seven Simple Tenses		The Seven Compound Tenses	
Singular	Plural	Singular	Plural
1 presente de indicativo		**8 perfecto de indicativo**	
me acuerdo	nos acordamos	me he acordado	nos hemos acordado
te acuerdas	os acordáis	te has acordado	os habéis acordado
se acuerda	se acuerdan	se ha acordado	se han acordado
2 imperfecto de indicativo		**9 pluscuamperfecto de indicativo**	
me acordaba	nos acordábamos	me había acordado	nos habíamos acordado
te acordabas	os acordabais	te habías acordado	os habíais acordado
se acordaba	se acordaban	se había acordado	se habían acordado
3 pretérito		**10 pretérito anterior**	
me acordé	nos acordamos	me hube acordado	nos hubimos acordado
te acordaste	os acordasteis	te hubiste acordado	os hubisteis acordado
se acordó	se acordaron	se hubo acordado	se hubieron acordado
4 futuro		**11 futuro perfecto**	
me acordaré	nos acordaremos	me habré acordado	nos habremos acordado
te acordarás	os acordaréis	te habrás acordado	os habréis acordado
se acordará	se acordarán	se habrá acordado	se habrán acordado
5 potencial simple		**12 potencial compuesto**	
me acordaría	nos acordaríamos	me habría acordado	nos habríamos acordado
te acordarías	os acordaríais	te habrías acordado	os habríais acordado
se acordaría	se acordarían	se habría acordado	se habrían acordado
6 presente de subjuntivo		**13 perfecto de subjuntivo**	
me acuerde	nos acordemos	me haya acordado	nos hayamos acordado
te acuerdes	os acordéis	te hayas acordado	os hayáis acordado
se acuerde	se acuerden	se haya acordado	se hayan acordado
7 imperfecto de subjuntivo		**14 pluscuamperfecto de subjuntivo**	
me acordara	nos acordáramos	me hubiera acordado	nos hubiéramos acordado
te acordaras	os acordarais	te hubieras acordado	os hubierais acordado
se acordara	se acordaran	se hubiera acordado	se hubieran acordado
OR		OR	
me acordase	nos acordásemos	me hubiese acordado	nos hubiésemos acordado
te acordases	os acordaseis	te hubieses acordado	os hubieseis acordado
se acordase	se acordasen	se hubiese acordado	se hubiesen acordado

imperativo	
—	**acordémenos**
acuérdate; no te acuerdes	**acordaos; no os acordéis**
acuérdese	**acuérdense**

Words and expressions related to this verb
si mal no me acuerdo   if I remember correctly, if my memory does not fail me
un acuerdo   agreement
de acuerdo   in agreement
de común acuerdo   unanimously, by mutual agreement
desacordarse   to become forgetful

See also **acordar**.

20

to go to bed, to lie down

The Seven Simple Tenses		The Seven Compound Tenses	
Singular	Plural	Singular	Plural
1 presente de indicativo		8 perfecto de indicativo	
me acuesto	nos acostamos	me he acostado	nos hemos acostado
te acuestas	os acostáis	te has acostado	os habéis acostado
se acuesta	se acuestan	se ha acostado	se han acostado
2 imperfecto de indicativo		9 pluscuamperfecto de indicativo	
me acostaba	nos acostábamos	me había acostado	nos habíamos acostado
te acostabas	os acostabais	te habías acostado	os habíais acostado
se acostaba	se acostaban	se había acostado	se habían acostado
3 pretérito		10 pretérito anterior	
me acosté	nos acostamos	me hube acostado	nos hubimos acostado
te acostaste	os acostasteis	te hubiste acostado	os hubisteis acostado
se acostó	se acostaron	se hubo acostado	se hubieron acostado
4 futuro		11 futuro perfecto	
me acostaré	nos acostaremos	me habré acostado	nos habremos acostado
te acostarás	os acostaréis	te habrás acostado	os habréis acostado
se acostará	se acostarán	se habrá acostado	se habrán acostado
5 potencial simple		12 potencial compuesto	
me acostaría	nos acostaríamos	me habría acostado	nos habríamos acostado
te acostarías	os acostaríais	te habrías acostado	os habríais acostado
se acostaría	se acostarían	se habría acostado	se habrían acostado
6 presente de subjuntivo		13 perfecto de subjuntivo	
me acueste	nos acostemos	me haya acostado	nos hayamos acostado
te acuestes	os acostéis	te hayas acostado	os hayáis acostado
se acueste	se acuesten	se haya acostado	se hayan acostado
7 imperfecto de subjuntivo		14 pluscuamperfecto de subjuntivo	
me acostara	nos acostáramos	me hubiera acostado	nos hubiéramos acostado
te acostaras	os acostarais	te hubieras acostado	os hubierais acostado
se acostara	se acostaran	se hubiera acostado	se hubieran acostado
OR		OR	
me acostase	nos acostásemos	me hubiese acostado	nos hubiésemos acostado
te acostases	os acostaseis	te hubieses acostado	os hubieseis acostado
se acostase	se acostasen	se hubiese acostado	se hubiesen acostado

imperativo

—	acostémonos; no nos acostemos
acuéstate; no te acuestes	acostaos; no os acostéis
acuéstese; no se acueste	acuéstense; no se acuesten

Sentences using this verb and words and expressions related to it
Todas las noches me acuesto a las diez, mi hermanito se acuesta a las ocho, y mis padres se acuestan a las once.

el acostamiento   lying down
acostado, acostada   in bed, lying down

acostar   to put to bed
acostarse con las gallinas   to go to bed very early (with the hens/chickens)

The subject pronouns are found on the page facing page 1

acostumbrar Gerundio **acostumbrando** Part. pas. **acostumbrado**

to be accustomed, to be in the habit of

The Seven Simple Tenses		The Seven Compound Tenses	
Singular	Plural	Singular	Plural
1 presente de indicativo		**8 perfecto de indicativo**	
acostumbro	acostumbramos	he acostumbrado	hemos acostumbrado
acostumbras	acostumbráis	has acostumbrado	habéis acostumbrado
acostumbra	acostumbran	ha acostumbrado	han acostumbrado
2 imperfecto de indicativo		**9 pluscuamperfecto de indicativo**	
acostumbraba	acostumbrábamos	había acostumbrado	habíamos acostumbrado
acostumbrabas	acostumbrabais	habías acostumbrado	habíais acostumbrado
acostumbraba	acostumbraban	había acostumbrado	habían acostumbrado
3 pretérito		**10 pretérito anterior**	
acostumbré	acostumbramos	hube acostumbrado	hubimos acostumbrado
acostumbraste	acostumbrasteis	hubiste acostumbrado	hubisteis acostumbrado
acostumbró	acostumbraron	hubo acostumbrado	hubieron acostumbrado
4 futuro		**11 futuro perfecto**	
acostumbraré	acostumbraremos	habré acostumbrado	habremos acostumbrado
acostumbrarás	acostumbraréis	habrás acostumbrado	habréis acostumbrado
acostumbrará	acostumbrarán	habrá acostumbrado	habrán acostumbrado
5 potencial simple		**12 potencial compuesto**	
acostumbraría	acostumbraríamos	habría acostumbrado	habríamos acostumbrado
acostumbrarías	acostumbraríais	habrías acostumbrado	habríais acostumbrado
acostumbraría	acostumbrarían	habría acostumbrado	habrían acostumbrado
6 presente de subjuntivo		**13 perfecto de subjuntivo**	
acostumbre	acostumbremos	haya acostumbrado	hayamos acostumbrado
acostumbres	acostumbréis	hayas acostumbrado	hayáis acostumbrado
acostumbre	acostumbren	haya acostumbrado	hayan acostumbrado
7 imperfecto de subjuntivo		**14 pluscuamperfecto de subjuntivo**	
acostumbrara	acostumbráramos	hubiera acostumbrado	hubiéramos acostumbrado
acostumbraras	acostumbrarais	hubieras acostumbrado	hubierais acostumbrado
acostumbrara	acostumbraran	hubiera acostumbrado	hubieran acostumbrado
OR		OR	
acostumbrase	acostumbrásemos	hubiese acostumbrado	hubiésemos acostumbrado
acostumbrases	acostumbraseis	hubieses acostumbrado	hubieseis acostumbrado
acostumbrase	acostumbrasen	hubiese acostumbrado	hubiesen acostumbrado

imperativo	
—	acostumbremos
acostumbra; no acostumbres	acostumbrad; no acostumbréis
acostumbre	acostumbren

Words and expressions related to this verb

acostumbradamente customarily
la costumbre custom, habit
de costumbre customary, usual
tener por costumbre to be in the habit of

acostumbrado, acostumbrada accustomed
acostumbrarse to become accustomed, to get used to
acostumbrarse a algo to become accustomed to something

> Increase your verb power with popular phrases, words, and expressions for tourists on pages 595–618.

to knife, to cut, to slash, to cut open

The Seven Simple Tenses	The Seven Compound Tenses

Singular	Plural	Singular	Plural
1 presente de indicativo		**8 perfecto de indicativo**	
acuchillo	**acuchillamos**	**he acuchillado**	**hemos acuchillado**
acuchillas	**acuchilláis**	**has acuchillado**	**habéis acuchillado**
acuchilla	**acuchillan**	**ha acuchillado**	**han acuchillado**
2 imperfecto de indicativo		**9 pluscuamperfecto de indicativo**	
acuchillaba	**acuchillábamos**	**había acuchillado**	**habíamos acuchillado**
acuchillabas	**acuchillabais**	**habías acuchillado**	**habíais acuchillado**
acuchillaba	**acuchillaban**	**había acuchillado**	**habían acuchillado**
3 pretérito		**10 pretérito anterior**	
acuchillé	**acuchillamos**	**hube acuchillado**	**hubimos acuchillado**
acuchillaste	**acuchillasteis**	**hubiste acuchillado**	**hubisteis acuchillado**
acuchilló	**acuchillaron**	**hubo acuchillado**	**hubieron acuchillado**
4 futuro		**11 futuro perfecto**	
acuchillaré	**acuchillaremos**	**habré acuchillado**	**habremos acuchillado**
acuchillarás	**acuchillaréis**	**habrás acuchillado**	**habréis acuchillado**
acuchillará	**acuchillarán**	**habrá acuchillado**	**habrán acuchillado**
5 potencial simple		**12 potencial compuesto**	
acuchillaría	**acuchillaríamos**	**habría acuchillado**	**habríamos acuchillado**
acuchillarías	**acuchillaríais**	**habrías acuchillado**	**habríais acuchillado**
acuchillaría	**acuchillarían**	**habría acuchillado**	**habrían acuchillado**
6 presente de subjuntivo		**13 perfecto de subjuntivo**	
acuchille	**acuchillemos**	**haya acuchillado**	**hayamos acuchillado**
acuchilles	**acuchilléis**	**hayas acuchillado**	**hayáis acuchillado**
acuchille	**acuchillen**	**haya acuchillado**	**hayan acuchillado**
7 imperfecto de subjuntivo		**14 pluscuamperfecto de subjuntivo**	
acuchillara	**acuchilláramos**	**hubiera acuchillado**	**hubiéramos acuchillado**
acuchillaras	**acuchillarais**	**hubieras acuchillado**	**hubierais acuchillado**
acuchillara	**acuchillaran**	**hubiera acuchillado**	**hubieran acuchillado**
OR		OR	
acuchillase	**acuchillásemos**	**hubiese acuchillado**	**hubiésemos acuchillado**
acuchillases	**acuchillaseis**	**hubieses acuchillado**	**hubieseis acuchillado**
acuchillase	**acuchillasen**	**hubiese acuchillado**	**hubiesen acuchillado**

imperativo

—	**acuchillemos**
acuchilla; no acuchilles	**acuchillad; no acuchilléis**
acuchille	**acuchillen**

Words and expressions related to this verb
un cuchillo   knife
un cuchillo de monte   hunting knife
un cuchillo de cocina   kitchen knife
ser cuchillo de otro   to be a thorn in someone's side
un acuchillador, una acuchilladora   quarrelsome person; bully

acuchillado, acuchillada   knifed, slashed
las mangas acuchilladas   slashed sleeves
(fashion, style)

The subject pronouns are found on the page facing page 1.

to attend, to be present frequently, to respond (to a call), to come to the rescue

The Seven Simple Tenses		The Seven Compound Tenses	
Singular	Plural	Singular	Plural
1 presente de indicativo		8 perfecto de indicativo	
acudo	acudimos	he acudido	hemos acudido
acudes	acudís	has acudido	habéis acudido
acude	acuden	ha acudido	han acudido
2 imperfecto de indicativo		9 pluscuamperfecto de indicativo	
acudía	acudíamos	había acudido	habíamos acudido
acudías	acudíais	habías acudido	habíais acudido
acudía	acudían	había acudido	habían acudido
3 pretérito		10 pretérito anterior	
acudí	acudimos	hube acudido	hubimos acudido
acudiste	acudisteis	hubiste acudido	hubisteis acudido
acudió	acudieron	hubo acudido	hubieron acudido
4 futuro		11 futuro perfecto	
acudiré	acudiremos	habré acudido	habremos acudido
acudirás	acudiréis	habrás acudido	habréis acudido
acudirá	acudirán	habrá acudido	habrán acudido
5 potencial simple		12 potencial compuesto	
acudiría	acudiríamos	habría acudido	habríamos acudido
acudirías	acudiríais	habrías acudido	habríais acudido
acudiría	acudirían	habría acudido	habrían acudido
6 presente de subjuntivo		13 perfecto de subjuntivo	
acuda	acudamos	haya acudido	hayamos acudido
acudas	acudáis	hayas acudido	hayáis acudido
acuda	acudan	haya acudido	hayan acudido
7 imperfecto de subjuntivo		14 pluscuamperfecto de subjuntivo	
acudiera	acudiéramos	hubiera acudido	hubiéramos acudido
acudieras	acudierais	hubieras acudido	hubierais acudido
acudiera	acudieran	hubiera acudido	hubieran acudido
OR		OR	
acudiese	acudiésemos	hubiese acudido	hubiésemos acudido
acudieses	acudieseis	hubieses acudido	hubieseis acudido
acudiese	acudiesen	hubiese acudido	hubiesen acudido

imperativo

—	acudamos
acude; no acudas	acudid; no acudáis
acuda	acudan

Words and expressions related to this verb

el acudimiento   aid
acudir en socorro de   to go to help
acudir con el remedio   to get there with the remedy
acudir a los tribunales   to go to court (law)

acudir a una cita   to keep an appointment
acudir a un examen   to take an exam
acudir a alguien   to give help to someone
acudir en ayuda de alguien   to come
to someone's rescue

The Seven Simple Tenses | The Seven Compound Tenses

Singular	Plural	Singular	Plural
1 presente de indicativo		8 perfecto de indicativo	
acuso	**acusamos**	**he acusado**	**hemos acusado**
acusas	**acusáis**	**has acusado**	**habéis acusado**
acusa	**acusan**	**ha acusado**	**han acusado**
2 imperfecto de indicativo		9 pluscuamperfecto de indicativo	
acusaba	**acusábamos**	**había acusado**	**habíamos acusado**
acusabas	**acusabais**	**habías acusado**	**habíais acusado**
acusaba	**acusaban**	**había acusado**	**habían acusado**
3 pretérito		10 pretérito anterior	
acusé	**acusamos**	**hube acusado**	**hubimos acusado**
acusaste	**acusasteis**	**hubiste acusado**	**hubisteis acusado**
acusó	**acusaron**	**hubo acusado**	**hubieron acusado**
4 futuro		11 futuro perfecto	
acusaré	**acusaremos**	**habré acusado**	**habremos acusado**
acusarás	**acusaréis**	**habrás acusado**	**habréis acusado**
acusará	**acusarán**	**habrá acusado**	**habrán acusado**
5 potencial simple		12 potencial compuesto	
acusaría	**acusaríamos**	**habría acusado**	**habríamos acusado**
acusarías	**acusaríais**	**habrías acusado**	**habríais acusado**
acusaría	**acusarían**	**habría acusado**	**habrían acusado**
6 presente de subjuntivo		13 perfecto de subjuntivo	
acuse	**acusemos**	**haya acusado**	**hayamos acusado**
acuses	**acuséis**	**hayas acusado**	**hayáis acusado**
acuse	**acusen**	**haya acusado**	**hayan acusado**
7 imperfecto de subjuntivo		14 pluscuamperfecto de subjuntivo	
acusara	**acusáramos**	**hubiera acusado**	**hubiéramos acusado**
acusaras	**acusarais**	**hubieras acusado**	**hubierais acusado**
acusara	**acusaran**	**hubiera acusado**	**hubieran acusado**
OR		OR	
acusase	**acusásemos**	**hubiese acusado**	**hubiésemos acusado**
acusases	**acusaseis**	**hubieses acusado**	**hubieseis acusado**
acusase	**acusasen**	**hubiese acusado**	**hubiesen acusado**

imperativo

—	**acusemos**
acusa; no acuses	**acusad; no acuséis**
acuse	**acusen**

Words and expressions related to this verb
el acusado, la acusada   defendant, accused
la acusación   accusation
el acusador, la acusadora   accuser

acusar de robo   to accuse of robbery
acusar recibo de una cosa   to acknowledge
   receipt of something
acusarse de un pecado   to confess a sin

The subject pronouns are found on the page facing page 1.

to advance, to keep on, to progress, to go ahead

The Seven Simple Tenses		The Seven Compound Tenses	
Singular	Plural	Singular	Plural
1 presente de indicativo		8 perfecto de indicativo	
adelanto	adlenatamos	he adelantado	hemos adelantado
adelantas	adelantáis	has adelantado	habéis adelantado
adelanta	adelantan	ha adelantado	han adelantado
2 imperfecto de indicativo		9 pluscuamperfecto de indicativo	
adelantaba	adelantábamos	había adelantado	habíamos adelantado
adelantabas	adelantabais	habías adelantado	habíais adelantado
adelantaba	adelantaban	había adelantado	habían adelantado
3 pretérito		10 pretérito anterior	
adelanté	adelantamos	hube adelantado	hubimos adelantado
adelantaste	adelantasteis	hubiste adelantado	hubisteis adelantado
adelantó	adelantaron	hubo adelantado	hubieron adelantado
4 futuro		11 futuro perfecto	
adelantaré	adelantaremos	habré adelantado	habremos adelantado
adelantarás	adelantaréis	habrás adelantado	habréis adelantado
adelantará	adelantarán	habrá adelantado	habrán adelantado
5 potencial simple		12 potencial compuesto	
adelantaría	adelantaríamos	habría adelantado	habríamos adelantado
adelantarías	adelantaríais	habrías adelantado	habríais adelantado
adelantaría	adelantarían	habría adelantado	habrían adelantado
6 presente de subjuntivo		13 perfecto de subjuntivo	
adelante	adelantemos	haya adelantado	hayamos adelantado
adelantes	adelantéis	hayas adelantado	hayáis adelantado
adelante	adelanten	haya adelantado	hayan adelantado
7 imperfecto de subjuntivo		14 pluscuamperfecto de subjuntivo	
adelantara	adelantáramos	hubiera adelantado	hubiéramos adelantado
adelantaras	adelantarais	hubieras adelantado	hubierais adelantado
adelantara	adelantaran	hubiera adelantado	hubieran adelantado
OR		OR	
adelantase	adelantasemos	hubiese adelantado	hubiésemos adelantado
adelantases	adelantaseis	hubieses adelantado	hubieseis adelantado
adelantase	adelantasen	hubiese adelantado	hubiesen adelantado

imperativo

—	adelantemos
adelanta; no adelantes	adelantad; no adelantéis
adelante	adelanten

Words and expressions related to this verb
el adelantamiento   advance, growth, increase, progress
adelante   ahead, forward; **¡Adelante!**   Come in! Go ahead!
adelantar dinero   to advance money; **un adelanto**   advance payment
en lo adelante   in the future; **los adelantos tecnológicos**   technological advances, progress
de aquí en adelante   henceforth; **de hoy en adelante**   from now on

For other words and expressions related to this verb, see **adelantarse.**

to go forward, to go ahead, to move ahead, to take the lead

The Seven Simple Tenses		The Seven Compound Tenses	
Singular	Plural	Singular	Plural
1 presente de indicativo		8 perfecto de indicativo	
me adelanto	**nos adelantamos**	**me he adelantado**	**nos hemos adelantado**
te adelantas	**os adelantáis**	**te has adelantado**	**os habéis adelantado**
se adelanta	**se adelantan**	**se ha adelantado**	**se han adelantado**
2 imperfecto de indicativo		9 pluscuamperfecto de indicativo	
me adelantaba	**nos adelantábamos**	**me había adelantado**	**nos habíamos adelantado**
te adelantabas	**os adelantabais**	**te habías adelantado**	**os habíais adelantado**
se adelantaba	**se adelantaban**	**se había adelantado**	**se habían adelantado**
3 pretérito		10 pretérito anterior	
me adelanté	**nos adelantamos**	**me hube adelantado**	**nos hubimos adelantado**
te adelantaste	**os adelantasteis**	**te hubiste adelantado**	**os hubisteis adelantado**
se adelantó	**se adelantaron**	**se hubo adelantado**	**se hubieron adelantado**
4 futuro		11 futuro perfecto	
me adelantaré	**nos adelantaremos**	**me habré adelantado**	**nos habremos adelantado**
te adelantarás	**os adelantaréis**	**te habrás adelantado**	**os habréis adelantado**
se adelantará	**se adelantarán**	**se habrá adelantado**	**se habrán adelantado**
5 potencial simple		12 potencial compuesto	
me adelantaría	**nos adelantaríamos**	**me habría adelantado**	**nos habríamos adelantado**
te adelantarías	**os adelantaríais**	**te habrías adelantado**	**os habríais adelantado**
se adelantaría	**se adelantarían**	**se habría adelantado**	**se habrían adelantado**
6 presente de subjuntivo		13 perfecto de subjuntivo	
me adelante	**nos adelantemos**	**me haya adelantado**	**nos hayamos adelantado**
te adelantes	**os adelantéis**	**te hayas adelantado**	**os hayáis adelantado**
se adelante	**se adelanten**	**se haya adelantado**	**se hayan adelantado**
7 imperfecto de subjuntivo		14 pluscuamperfecto de subjuntivo	
me adelantara	**nos adelantáramos**	**me hubiera adelantado**	**nos hubiéramos adelantado**
te adelantaras	**os adelantarais**	**te hubieras adelantado**	**os hubierais adelantado**
se adelantara	**se adelantaran**	**se hubiera adelantado**	**se hubieran adelantado**
OR		OR	
me adelantase	**nos adelantásemos**	**me hubiese adelantado**	**nos hubiésemos adelantado**
te adelantases	**os adelantaseis**	**te hubieses adelantado**	**os hubieseis adelantado**
se adelantase	**se adelantasen**	**se hubiese adelantado**	**se hubiesen adelantado**

imperativo

—	**adelantémonos**
adelántate; no te adelantes	**adelantaos; no os adelantéis**
adelántese	**adelántense**

Words and expressions related to this verb
adelantado, adelantada   bold; anticipated; fast (watch or clock)
adelantadamente   in anticipation, beforehand
más adelante   later on; farther on
llevar adelante   to carry on, to go ahead

For other words and expressions related to this verb, see **adelantar.**

The subject pronouns are found on the page facing page 1

to divine, to foretell, to guess, to solve

The Seven Simple Tenses		The Seven Compound Tenses	
Singular	Plural	Singular	Plural
1 presente de indicativo		**8 perfecto de indicativo**	
adivino	adivinamos	he adivinado	hemos adivinado
adivinas	adivináis	has adivinado	habéis adivinado
adivina	adivinan	ha adivinado	han adivinado
2 imperfecto de indicativo		**9 pluscuamperfecto de indicativo**	
adivinaba	adivinábamos	había adivinado	habíamos adivinado
adivinabas	adivinabais	habías adivinado	habíais adivinado
adivinaba	adivinaban	había adivinado	habían adivinado
3 pretérito		**10 pretérito anterior**	
adiviné	adivinamos	hube adivinado	hubimos adivinado
adivinaste	adivinasteis	hubiste adivinado	hubisteis adivinado
adivinó	adivinaron	hubo adivinado	hubieron adivinado
4 futuro		**11 futuro perfecto**	
adivinaré	adivinaremos	habré adivinado	habremos adivinado
adivinarás	adivinaréis	habrás adivinado	habréis adivinado
adivinará	adivinarán	habrá adivinado	habrán adivinado
5 potencial simple		**12 potencial compuesto**	
adivinaría	adivinaríamos	habría adivinado	habríamos adivinado
adivinarías	adivinaríais	habrías adivinado	habríais adivinado
adivinaría	adivinarían	habría adivinado	habrían adivinado
6 presente de subjuntivo		**13 perfecto de subjuntivo**	
adivine	adivinemos	haya adivinado	hayamos adivinado
adivines	adivinéis	hayas adivinado	hayáis adivinado
adivine	adivinen	haya adivinado	hayan adivinado
7 imperfecto de subjuntivo		**14 pluscuamperfecto de subjuntivo**	
adivinara	adivináramos	hubiera adivinado	hubiéramos adivinado
adivinaras	adivinarais	hubieras adivinado	hubierais adivinado
adivinara	adivinaran	hubiera adivinado	hubieran adivinado
OR		OR	
adivinase	adivinásemos	hubiese adivinado	hubiésemos adivinado
adivinases	adivinaseis	hubieses adivinado	hubieseis adivinado
adivinase	adivinasen	hubiese adivinado	hubiesen adivinado

imperativo

—	adivinemos
adivina; no adivines	adivinad; no adivinéis
adivine	adivinen

Words and expressions related to this verb

un adivino, una adivina prophet; fortune teller; guesser

la adivinación del pensamiento mind reading
¡Adivine quién soy! Guess who (I am)!

una adivinanza prophecy, prediction; enigma, riddle, puzzle
una adivinaja riddle, puzzle
adivinar el pensamiento de alguien to read a person's mind

Want to learn more idiomatic expressions that contain verbs? Check out pages 524–537.

The Seven Simple Tenses		The Seven Compound Tenses	
Singular	Plural	Singular	Plural
1 presente de indicativo		8 perfecto de indicativo	
admiro	**admiramos**	**he admirado**	**hemos admirado**
admiras	**admiráis**	**has admirado**	**habéis admirado**
admira	**admiran**	**ha admirado**	**han admirado**
2 imperfecto de indicativo		9 pluscuamperfecto de indicativo	
admiraba	**admirábamos**	**había admirado**	**habíamos admirado**
admirabas	**admirabais**	**habías admirado**	**habíais admirado**
admiraba	**admiraban**	**había admirado**	**habían admirado**
3 pretérito		10 pretérito anterior	
admiré	**admiramos**	**hube admirado**	**hubimos admirado**
admiraste	**admirasteis**	**hubiste admirado**	**hubisteis admirado**
admiró	**admiraron**	**hubo admirado**	**hubieron admirado**
4 futuro		11 futuro perfecto	
admiraré	**admiraremos**	**habré admirado**	**habremos admirado**
admirarás	**admiraréis**	**habrás admirado**	**habréis admirado**
admirará	**admirarán**	**habrá admirado**	**habrán admirado**
5 potencial simple		12 potencial compuesto	
admiraría	**admiraríamos**	**habría admirado**	**habríamos admirado**
admirarías	**admiraríais**	**habrías admirado**	**habríais admirado**
admiraría	**admirarían**	**habría admirado**	**habrían admirado**
6 presente de subjuntivo		13 perfecto de subjuntivo	
admire	**admiremos**	**haya admirado**	**hayamos admirado**
admires	**admiréis**	**hayas admirado**	**hayáis admirado**
admire	**admiren**	**haya admirado**	**hayan admirado**
7 imperfecto de subjuntivo		14 pluscuamperfecto de subjuntivo	
admirara	**admiráramos**	**hubiera admirado**	**hubiéramos admirado**
admiraras	**admirarais**	**hubieras admirado**	**hubierais admirado**
admirara	**admiraran**	**hubiera admirado**	**hubieran admirado**
OR		OR	
admirase	**admirásemos**	**hubiese admirado**	**hubiésemos admirado**
admirases	**admiraseis**	**hubieses admirado**	**hubieseis admirado**
admirase	**admirasen**	**hubiese admirado**	**hubiesen admirado**

imperativo

—	**admiremos**
admira; no admires	**admirad; no admiréis**
admire	**admiren**

Words and expressions related to this verb

el admirador, la admiradora   admirer
la admiración   admiration
admirable   admirable
admirablemente   admirably
admirativamente   admiringly, with admiration

sentir admiración por alguien   to feel admiration for someone
hablar en tono admirativo   to speak in an admiring tone
causar admiración   to inspire admiration

The subject pronouns are found on the page facing page 1.

admitir

Gerundio **admitiendo**   Part. pas. **admitido**

to admit, to grant, to permit

The Seven Simple Tenses		The Seven Compound Tenses	
Singular	Plural	Singular	Plural
1 presente de indicativo		8 perfecto de indicativo	
admito	admitimos	he admitido	hemos admitido
admites	admitís	has admitido	habéis admitido
admite	admiten	ha admitido	han admitido
2 imperfecto de indicativo		9 pluscuamperfecto de indicativo	
admitía	admitíamos	había admitido	habíamos admitido
admitías	admitíais	habías admitido	habíais admitido
admitía	admitían	había admitido	habían admitido
3 pretérito		10 pretérito anterior	
admití	admitimos	hube admitido	hubimos admitido
admitiste	admitisteis	hubiste admitido	hubisteis admitido
admitió	admitieron	hubo admitido	hubieron admitido
4 futuro		11 futuro perfecto	
admitiré	admitiremos	habré admitido	habremos admitido
admitirás	admitiréis	habrás admitido	habréis admitido
admitirá	admitirán	habrá admitido	habrán admitido
5 potencial simple		12 potencial compuesto	
admitiría	admitiríamos	habría admitido	habríamos admitido
admitirías	admitiríais	habrías admitido	habríais admitido
admitiría	admitirían	habría admitido	habrían admitido
6 presente de subjuntivo		13 perfecto de subjuntivo	
admita	admitamos	haya admitido	hayamos admitido
admitas	admitáis	hayas admitido	hayáis admitido
admita	admitan	haya admitido	hayan admitido
7 imperfecto de subjuntivo		14 pluscuamperfecto de subjuntivo	
admitiera	admitiéramos	hubiera admitido	hubiéramos admitido
admitieras	admitierais	hubieras admitido	hubierais admitido
admitiera	admitieran	hubiera admitido	hubieran admitido
OR		OR	
admitiese	admitiésemos	hubiese admitido	hubiésemos admitido
admitieses	admitieseis	hubieses admitido	hubieseis admitido
admitiese	admitiesen	hubiese admitido	hubiesen admitido

imperativo	
—	admitamos
admite; no admitas	admitid; no admitáis
admita	admitan

Words and expressions related to this verb

la admisión   acceptance, admission
admisible   admissible

admitir una aclamación   to accept a claim
el examen de admisión   entrance exam

> Consult the back pages for verbs used in idiomatic expressions, Spanish
> proverbs using verbs, weather expressions using verbs, verbs with prepositions,
> and over 1,100 verbs conjugated like model verbs.

The Seven Simple Tenses		The Seven Compound Tenses	
Singular	Plural	Singular	Plural
1 presente de indicativo		8 perfecto de indicativo	
adopto	adoptamos	he adoptado	hemos adoptado
adoptas	adoptáis	has adoptado	habéis adoptado
adopta	adoptan	ha adoptado	han adoptado
2 imperfecto de indicativo		9 pluscuamperfecto de indicativo	
adoptaba	adoptábamos	había adoptado	habíamos adoptado
adoptabas	adoptabais	habías adoptado	habíais adoptado
adaptaba	adoptaban	había adoptado	habían adoptado
3 pretérito		10 pretérito anterior	
adopté	adoptamos	hube adoptado	hubimos adoptado
adoptaste	adoptasteis	hubiste adoptado	hubisteis adoptado
adoptó	adoptaron	hubo adoptado	hubieron adoptado
4 futuro		11 futuro perfecto	
adoptaré	adoptaremos	habré adoptado	habremos adoptado
adoptarás	adoptaréis	habrás adoptado	habréis adoptado
adoptará	adoptarán	habrá adoptado	habrán adoptado
5 potencial simple		12 potencial compuesto	
adoptaría	adoptaríamos	habría adoptado	habríamos adoptado
adoptarías	adoptaríais	habrías adoptado	habríais adoptado
adoptaría	adoptarían	habría adoptado	habrían adoptado
6 presente de subjuntivo		13 perfecto de subjuntivo	
adopte	adoptemos	haya adoptado	hayamos adoptado
adoptes	adoptéis	hayas adoptado	hayáis adoptado
adopte	adopten	haya adoptado	hayan adoptado
7 imperfecto de subjuntivo		14 pluscuamperfecto de subjuntivo	
adoptara	adoptáramos	hubiera adoptado	hubiéramos adoptado
adoptaras	adoptarais	hubieras adoptado	hubierais adoptado
adoptara	adoptaran	hubiera adoptado	hubieran adoptado
OR		OR	
adoptase	adoptásemos	hubiese adoptado	hubiésemos adoptado
adoptases	adoptaseis	hubieses adoptado	hubieseis adoptado
adoptase	adoptasen	hubiese adoptado	hubiesen adoptado

imperativo

—	adoptemos
adopta; no adoptes	adoptad; no adoptéis
adopte	adopten

Words and expressions related to this verb

la adopción   adoption   **adoptable**   adoptable
el adopcionismo   adoptionism   **adoptado, adoptada**   adopted
el, la adopcionista   adoptionist   **adoptivamente**   adoptively

Enjoy verbs in Spanish proverbs on page 539.

The subject pronouns are found on the page facing page 1.   **31**

to adore, to worship

The Seven Simple Tenses		The Seven Compound Tenses	
Singular	Plural	Singular	Plural
1　presente de indicativo		8　perfecto de indicativo	
adoro	adoramos	he adorado	hemos adorado
adoras	adoráis	has adorado	habéis adorado
adora	adoran	ha adorado	han adorado
2　imperfecto de indicativo		9　pluscuamperfecto de indicativo	
adoraba	adorábamos	había adorado	habíamos adorado
adorabas	adorabais	habías adorado	habíais adorado
adoraba	adoraban	había adorado	habían adorado
3　pretérito		10　pretérito anterior	
adoré	adoramos	hube adorado	hubimos adorado
adoraste	adorasteis	hubiste adorado	hubisteis adorado
adoró	adoraron	hubo adorado	hubieron adorado
4　futuro		11　futuro perfecto	
adoraré	adoraremos	habré adorado	habremos adorado
adorarás	adoraréis	habrás adorado	habréis adorado
adorará	adorarán	habrá adorado	habrán adorado
5　potencial simple		12　potencial compuesto	
adoraría	adoraríamos	habría adorado	habríamos adorado
adorarías	adoraríais	habrías adorado	habríais adorado
adoraría	adorarían	habría adorado	habrían adorado
6　presente de subjuntivo		13　perfecto de subjuntivo	
adore	adoremos	haya adorado	hayamos adorado
adores	adoréis	hayas adorado	hayáis adorado
adore	adoren	haya adorado	hayan adorado
7　imperfecto de subjuntivo		14　pluscuamperfecto de subjuntivo	
adorara	adoráramos	hubiera adorado	hubiéramos adorado
adoraras	adorarais	hubieras adorado	hubierais adorado
adorara	adoraran	hubiera adorado	hubieran adorado
OR		OR	
adorase	adorásemos	hubiese adorado	hubiésemos adorado
adorases	adoraseis	hubieses adorado	hubieseis adorado
adorase	adorasen	hubiese adorado	hubiesen adorado

imperativo	
—	adoremos
adora; no adores	adorad; no adoréis
adore	adoren

Words and expressions related to this verb

el adorador, la adoradora　adorer, worshipper　　**adorablemente**　adorably, adoringly
adorable　adorable　　　　　　　　　　　　　　**adorado, adorada**　adored
la adoración　adoration, worship, veneration

Get your feet wet with verbs used in weather expressions on page 540.

to acquire, to get, to obtain

The Seven Simple Tenses		The Seven Compound Tenses	
Singular	Plural	Singular	Plural
1 presente de indicativo		8 perfecto de indicativo	
adquiero	**adquirimos**	**he adquirido**	**hemos adquirido**
adquieres	**adquirís**	**has adquirido**	**habéis adquirido**
adquiere	**adquieren**	**ha adquirido**	**han adquirido**
2 imperfecto de indicativo		9 pluscuamperfecto de indicativo	
adquiría	**adquiríamos**	**había adquirido**	**habíamos adquirido**
adquirías	**adquiríais**	**habías adquirido**	**habíais adquirido**
adquiría	**adquirían**	**había adquirido**	**habían adquirido**
3 pretérito		10 pretérito anterior	
adquirí	**adquirimos**	**hube adquirido**	**hubimos adquirido**
adquiriste	**adquiristeis**	**hubiste adquirido**	**hubisteis adquirido**
adquirió	**adquirieron**	**hubo adquirido**	**hubieron adquirido**
4 futuro		11 futuro perfecto	
adquiriré	**adquiriremos**	**habré adquirido**	**habremos adquirido**
adquirirás	**adquiriréis**	**habrás adquirido**	**habréis adquirido**
adquirirá	**adquirirán**	**habrá adquirido**	**habrán adquirido**
5 potencial simple		12 potencial compuesto	
adquiriría	**adquiriríamos**	**habría adquirido**	**habríamos adquirido**
adquirirías	**adquiriríais**	**habrías adquirido**	**habríais adquirido**
adquiriría	**adquirirían**	**habría adquirido**	**habrían adquirido**
6 presente de subjuntivo		13 perfecto de subjuntivo	
adquiera	**adquiramos**	**haya adquirido**	**hayamos adquirido**
adquieras	**adquiráis**	**hayas adquirido**	**hayáis adquirido**
adquiera	**adquieran**	**haya adquirido**	**hayan adquirido**
7 imperfecto de subjuntivo		14 pluscuamperfecto de subjuntivo	
adquiriera	**adquiriéramos**	**hubiera adquirido**	**hubiéramos adquirido**
adquirieras	**adquirierais**	**hubieras adquirido**	**hubierais adquirido**
adquiriera	**adquirieran**	**hubiera adquirido**	**hubieran adquirido**
OR		OR	
adquiriese	**adquiriésemos**	**hubiese adquirido**	**hubiésemos adquirido**
adquirieses	**adquirieseis**	**hubieses adquirido**	**hubieseis adquirido**
adquiriese	**adquiriesen**	**hubiese adquirido**	**hubiesen adquirido**

	imperativo	
—		**adquiramos**
adquiere; no adquieras		**adquirid; no adquiráis**
adquiera		**adquieran**

Words and expressions related to this verb
el adquiridor, la adquiridora   acquirer
el (la) adquirente, el (la) adquiriente
  acquirer
la adquisición   acquisition, attainment

adquirir los bienes dotales   to acquire a dowry
los bienes adquiridos   acquired wealth
adquirible   obtainable
adquirir un hábito   to acquire a habit

to advise, to give notice, to give warning, to take notice of, to warn

The Seven Simple Tenses		The Seven Compound Tenses	
Singular	Plural	Singular	Plural
1 presente de indicativo		**8 perfecto de indicativo**	
advierto	advertimos	he advertido	hemos advertido
adviertes	advertís	has advertido	habéis advertido
advierte	advierten	ha advertido	han advertido
2 imperfecto de indicativo		**9 pluscuamperfecto de indicativo**	
advertía	advertíamos	había advertido	habíamos advertido
advertías	advertíais	habías advertido	habíais advertido
advertía	advertían	había advertido	habían advertido
3 pretérito		**10 pretérito anterior**	
advertí	advertimos	hube advertido	hubimos advertido
advertiste	advertisteis	hubiste advertido	hubisteis advertido
advirtió	advirtieron	hubo advertido	hubieron advertido
4 futuro		**11 futuro perfecto**	
advertiré	advertiremos	habré advertido	habremos advertido
advertirás	advertiréis	habrás advertido	habréis advertido
advertirá	advertirán	habrá advertido	habrán advertido
5 potencial simple		**12 potencial compuesto**	
advertiría	advertiríamos	habría advertido	habríamos advertido
advertirías	advertiríais	habrías advertido	habríais advertido
advertiría	advertirían	habría advertido	habrían advertido
6 presente de subjuntivo		**13 perfecto de subjuntivo**	
advierta	advirtamos	haya advertido	hayamos advertido
adviertas	advirtáis	hayas advertido	hayáis advertido
advierta	adviertan	haya advertido	hayan advertido
7 imperfecto de subjuntivo		**14 pluscuamperfecto de subjuntivo**	
advirtiera	advirtiéramos	hubiera advertido	hubiéramos advertido
advirtieras	advirtierais	hubieras advertido	hubierais advertido
advirtiera	advirtieran	hubiera advertido	hubieran advertido
OR		OR	
advirtiese	advirtiésemos	hubiese advertido	hubiésemos advertido
advirtieses	advirtieseis	hubieses advertido	hubieseis advertido
advirtiese	advirtiesen	hubiese advertido	hubiesen advertido

	imperativo	
—		advirtamos
advierte; no adviertas		advertid; no advirtáis
advierta		adviertan

Words and expressions related to this verb

advertido, advertida   skillful, clever
la advertencia   warning, notice, foreword
advertidamente   advisedly
un advertimiento   notice, warning

después de repetidas advertencias
   after repeated warnings
hacer una advertencia a un niño
   to correct a child's inappropriate behavior

Want to learn more idiomatic expressions that contain verbs? Check out pages 524–537.

The Seven Simple Tenses		The Seven Compound Tenses	
Singular	Plural	Singular	Plural
1 presente de indicativo		8 perfecto de indicativo	
me afeito	nos afeitamos	me he afeitado	nos hemos afeitado
te afeitas	os afeitáis	te has afeitado	os habéis afeitado
se afeita	se afeitan	se ha afeitado	se han afeitado
2 imperfecto de indicativo		9 pluscuamperfecto de indicativo	
me afeitaba	nos afeitábamos	me había afeitado	nos habíamos afeitado
te afeitabas	os afeitabais	te habías afeitado	os habíais afeitado
se afeitaba	se afeitaban	se había afeitado	se habían afeitado
3 pretérito		10 pretérito anterior	
me afeité	nos afeitamos	me hube afeitado	nos hubimos afeitado
te afeitaste	os afeitasteis	te hubiste afeitado	os hubisteis afeitado
se afeitó	se afeitaron	se hubo afeitado	se hubieron afeitado
4 futuro		11 futuro perfecto	
me afeitaré	nos afeitaremos	me habré afeitado	nos habremos afeitado
te afeitarás	os afeitaréis	te habrás afeitado	os habréis afeitado
se afeitará	se afeitarán	se habrá afeitado	se habrán afeitado
5 potencial simple		12 potencial compuesto	
me afeitaría	nos afeitaríamos	me habría afeitado	nos habríamos afeitado
te afeitarías	os afeitaríais	te habrías afeitado	os habríais afeitado
se afeitaría	se afeitarían	se habría afeitado	se habrían afeitado
6 presente de subjuntivo		13 perfecto de subjuntivo	
me afeite	nos afeitemos	me haya afeitado	nos hayamos afeitado
te afeites	os afeitéis	te hayas afeitado	os hayáis afeitado
se afeite	se afeiten	se haya afeitado	se hayan afeitado
7 imperfecto de subjuntivo		14 pluscuamperfecto de subjuntivo	
me afeitara	nos afeitáramos	me hubiera afeitado	nos hubiéramos afeitado
te afeitaras	os afeitarais	te hubieras afeitado	os hubierais afeitado
se afeitara	se afeitaran	se hubiera afeitado	se hubieran afeitado
OR		OR	
me afeitase	nos afeitásemos	me hubiese afeitado	nos hubiésemos afeitado
te afeitases	os afeitaseis	te hubieses afeitado	os hubieseis afeitado
se afeitase	se afeitasen	se hubiese afeitado	se hubiesen afeitado

	imperativo	
—		**afeitémonos**
aféitate; no te afeites		**afeitaos; no os afeitéis**
aféitese		**aféitense**

Words related to this verb
afeitar   to shave
una afeitada   a shave
el afeite   cosmetic, makeup

afeitadamente   ornately
una afeitadora   shaving machine, shaver
la maquinilla (de afeitar) eléctrica
electric shaver, razor

Get acquainted with what preposition goes with what verb on pages 541–549.

The subject pronouns are found on the page facing page 1.

to grasp, to obtain, to seize, to catch, to clutch, to come upon

The Seven Simple Tenses		The Seven Compound Tenses	
Singular	Plural	Singular	Plural
1 presente de indicativo		**8 perfecto de indicativo**	
agarro	agarramos	he agarrado	hemos agarrado
agarras	agarráis	has agarrado	habéis agarrado
agarra	agarran	ha agarrado	han agarrado
2 imperfecto de indicativo		**9 pluscuamperfecto de indicativo**	
agarraba	agarrábamos	había agarrado	habíamos agarrado
agarrabas	agarrabais	habías agarrado	habíais agarrado
agarraba	agarraban	había agarrado	habían agarrado
3 pretérito		**10 pretérito anterior**	
agarré	agarramos	hube agarrado	hubimos agarrado
agarraste	agarrasteis	hubiste agarrado	hubisteis agarrado
agarró	agarraron	hubo agarrado	hubieron agarrado
4 futuro		**11 futuro perfecto**	
agarraré	agarraremos	habré agarrado	habremos agarrado
agarrarás	agarraréis	habrás agarrado	habréis agarrado
agarrará	agarrarán	habrá agarrado	habrán agarrado
5 potencial simple		**12 potencial compuesto**	
agarraría	agarraríamos	habría agarrado	habríamos agarrado
agarrarías	agarraríais	habrías agarrado	habríais agarrado
agarraría	agarrarían	habría agarrado	habrían agarrado
6 presente de subjuntivo		**13 perfecto de subjuntivo**	
agarre	agarremos	haya agarrado	hayamos agarrado
agarres	agarréis	hayas agarrado	hayáis agarrado
agarre	agarren	haya agarrado	hayan agarrado
7 imperfecto de subjuntivo		**14 pluscuamperfecto de subjuntivo**	
agarrara	agarráramos	hubiera agarrado	hubiéramos agarrado
agarraras	agarrarais	hubieras agarrado	hubierais agarrado
agarrara	agarraran	hubiera agarrado	hubieran agarrado
OR		OR	
agarrase	agarrásemos	hubiese agarrado	hubiésemos agarrado
agarrases	agarraseis	hubieses agarrado	hubieseis agarrado
agarrase	agarrasen	hubiese agarrado	hubiesen agarrado

imperativo	
—	agarremos
agarra; no agarres	agarrad; no agarréis
agarre	agarren

Words and expressions related to this verb

el agarro grasp
la agarrada quarrel, scrap
agarrarse a *or* **de** to seize

agarrarse una fiebre to catch a fever
agarrar de un pelo to provide an excuse
desgarrar to rend, rip, tear

Be sure to consult the back pages for sections on verbs used in idiomatic expressions, verbs with prepositions, and the list of over 1,100 verbs conjugated like model verbs.

to agitate, to wave, to shake up, to stir

The Seven Simple Tenses		The Seven Compound Tenses	
Singular	Plural	Singular	Plural
1 presente de indicativo		8 perfecto de indicativo	
agito	**agitamos**	**he agitado**	**hemos agitado**
agitas	**agitáis**	**has agitado**	**habéis agitado**
agita	**agitan**	**ha agitado**	**han agitado**
2 imperfecto de indicativo		9 pluscuamperfecto de indicativo	
agitaba	**agitábamos**	**había agitado**	**habíamos agitado**
agitabas	**agitabais**	**habías agitado**	**habíais agitado**
agitaba	**agitaban**	**había agitado**	**habían agitado**
3 pretérito		10 pretérito anterior	
agité	**agitamos**	**hube agitado**	**hubimos agitado**
agitaste	**agitasteis**	**hubiste agitado**	**hubisteis agitado**
agitó	**agitaron**	**hubo agitado**	**hubieron agitado**
4 futuro		11 futuro perfecto	
agitaré	**agitaremos**	**habré agitado**	**habremos agitado**
agitarás	**agitaréis**	**habrás agitado**	**habréis agitado**
agitará	**agitarán**	**habrá agitado**	**habrán agitado**
5 potencial simple		12 potencial compuesto	
agitaría	**agitaríamos**	**habría agitado**	**habríamos agitado**
agitarías	**agitaríais**	**habrías agitado**	**habríais agitado**
agitaría	**agitarían**	**habría agitado**	**habrían agitado**
6 presente de subjuntivo		13 perfecto de subjuntivo	
agite	**agitemos**	**haya agitado**	**hayamos agitado**
agites	**agitéis**	**hayas agitado**	**hayáis agitado**
agite	**agiten**	**haya agitado**	**hayan agitado**
7 imperfecto de subjuntivo		14 pluscuamperfecto de subjuntivo	
agitara	**agitáramos**	**hubiera agitado**	**hubiéramos agitado**
agitaras	**agitarais**	**hubieras agitado**	**hubierais agitado**
agitara	**agitaran**	**hubiera agitado**	**hubieran agitado**
OR		OR	
agitase	**agitásemos**	**hubiese agitado**	**hubiésemos agitado**
agitases	**agitaseis**	**hubieses agitado**	**hubieseis agitado**
agitase	**agitasen**	**hubiese agitado**	**hubiesen agitado**

imperativo

—	**agitemos**
agita; no agites	**agitad; no agitéis**
agite	**agiten**

Words related to this verb
la agitación   agitation, excitement
agitado, agitada   agitated, excited
agitarse   to fidget, to become agitated

agitable   agitable
un agitador, una agitadora   agitator, shaker

Don't miss the definitions of basic grammatical terms with examples
in English and Spanish on pages 666–677.

to exhaust, to use up

The Seven Simple Tenses		The Seven Compound Tenses	
Singular	Plural	Singular	Plural
1 presente de indicativo		8 perfecto de indicativo	
agoto	agotamos	he agotado	hemos agotado
agotas	agotáis	has agotado	habéis agotado
agota	agotan	ha agotado	han agotado
2 imperfecto de indicativo		9 pluscuamperfecto de indicativo	
agotaba	agotábamos	había agotado	habíamos agotado
agotabas	agotabais	habías agotado	habíais agotado
agotaba	agotaban	había agotado	habían agotado
3 pretérito		10 pretérito anterior	
agoté	agotamos	hube agotado	hubimos agotado
agotaste	agotasteis	hubiste agotado	hubisteis agotado
agotó	agotaron	hubo agotado	hubieron agotado
4 futuro		11 futuro perfecto	
agotaré	agotaremos	habré agotado	habremos agotado
agotarás	agotaréis	habrás agotado	habréis agotado
agotará	agotarán	habrá agotado	habrán agotado
5 potencial simple		12 potencial compuesto	
agotaría	agotaríamos	habría agotado	habríamos agotado
agotarías	agotaríais	habrías agotado	habríais agotado
agotaría	agotarían	habría agotado	habrían agotado
6 presente de subjuntivo		13 perfecto de subjuntivo	
agote	agotemos	haya agotado	hayamos agotado
agotes	agotéis	hayas agotado	hayáis agotado
agote	agoten	haya agotado	hayan agotado
7 imperfecto de subjuntivo		14 pluscuamperfecto de subjuntivo	
agotara	agotáramos	hubiera agotado	hubiéramos agotado
agotaras	agotarais	hubieras agotado	hubierais agotado
agotara	agotaran	hubiera agotado	hubieran agotado
OR		OR	
agotase	agotásemos	hubiese agotado	hubiésemos agotado
agotases	agotaseis	hubieses agotado	hubieseis agotado
agotase	agotasen	hubiese agotado	hubiesen agotado

imperativo	
—	agotemos
agota; no agotes	agotad; no agotéis
agote	agoten

Words related to this verb
agotador, agotadora exhausting
el agotamiento exhaustion

agotable exhaustible
agotado, agotada exhausted; out of print, out of stock, sold out

If you don't know the Spanish verb for the English verb you have in mind,
look it up in the index on pages 505–518.

to please, to be pleasing

The Seven Simple Tenses		The Seven Compound Tenses	
Singular	Plural	Singular	Plural

1 presente de indicativo

		8 perfecto de indicativo	
agrado	agradamos	he agradado	hemos agradado
agradas	agradáis	has agradado	habéis agradado
agrada	agradan	ha agradado	han agradado

2 imperfecto de indicativo / **9 pluscuamperfecto de indicativo**

agradaba	agradábamos	había agradado	habíamos agradado
agradabas	agradabais	habías agradado	habíais agradado
agradaba	agradaban	había agradado	habían agradado

3 pretérito / **10 pretérito anterior**

agradé	agradamos	hube agradado	hubimos agradado
agradaste	agradasteis	hubiste agradado	hubisteis agradado
agradó	agradaron	hubo agradado	hubieron agradado

4 futuro / **11 futuro perfecto**

agradaré	agradaremos	habré agradado	habremos agradado
agradarás	agradaréis	habrás agradado	habréis agradado
agradará	agradarán	habrá agradado	habrán agradado

5 potencial simple / **12 potencial compuesto**

agradaría	agradaríamos	habría agradado	habríamos agradado
agradarías	agradaríais	habrías agradado	habríais agradado
agradaría	agradarían	habría agradado	habrían agradado

6 presente de subjuntivo / **13 perfecto de subjuntivo**

agrade	agrademos	haya agradado	hayamos agradado
agrades	agradéis	hayas agradado	hayáis agradado
agrade	agraden	haya agradado	hayan agradado

7 imperfecto de subjuntivo / **14 pluscuamperfecto de subjuntivo**

agradara	agradáramos	hubiera agradado	hubiéramos agradado
agradaras	agradarais	hubieras agradado	hubierais agradado
agradara	agradaran	hubiera agradado	hubieran agradado
OR		OR	
agradase	agradásemos	hubiese agradado	hubiésemos agradado
agradases	agradaseis	hubieses agradado	hubieseis agradado
agradase	agradasen	hubiese agradado	hubiesen agradado

imperativo

—	agrademos
agrada; no agrades	agradad; no agradéis
agrade	agraden

Words and expressions related to this verb
agradable   pleasing, pleasant, agreeable
agradablemente   agreeably, pleasantly
el agrado   pleasure, liking
Es de mi agrado.   It's to my liking.
de su agrado   to one's liking
ser del agrado de uno   to be to one's taste (liking)

Pablo es un muchacho agradador.
   Paul is eager to please.
María es una muchacha agradadora.
   Mary is eager to please.
desagradable   unpleasant, disagreeable

The subject pronouns are found on the page facing page 1.

39

agradecer
Gerundio **agradeciendo** Part. pas. **agradecido**

to thank, to be thankful for

The Seven Simple Tenses		The Seven Compound Tenses	
Singular	Plural	Singular	Plural
1 presente de indicativo		8 perfecto de indicativo	
agradezco	agradecemos	he agradecido	hemos agradecido
agradeces	agradecéis	has agradecido	habéis agradecido
agradece	agradecen	ha agradecido	han agradecido
2 imperfecto de indicativo		9 pluscuamperfecto de indicativo	
agradecía	agradecíamos	había agradecido	habíamos agradecido
agradecías	agradecíais	habías agradecido	habíais agradecido
agradecía	agradecían	había agradecido	habían agradecido
3 pretérito		10 pretérito anterior	
agradecí	agradecimos	hube agradecido	hubimos agradecido
agradeciste	agradecisteis	hubiste agradecido	hubisteis agradecido
agradeció	agradecieron	hubo agradecido	hubieron agradecido
4 futuro		11 futuro perfecto	
agradeceré	agradeceremos	habré agradecido	habremos agradecido
agradecerás	agradeceréis	habrás agradecido	habréis agradecido
agradecerá	agradecerán	habrá agradecido	habrán agradecido
5 potencial simple		12 potencial compuesto	
agradecería	agradeceríamos	habría agradecido	habríamos agradecido
agradecerías	agradeceríais	habrías agradecido	habríais agradecido
agradecería	agradecerían	habría agradecido	habrían agradecido
6 presente de subjuntivo		13 perfecto de subjuntivo	
agradezca	agradezcamos	haya agradecido	hayamos agradecido
agradezcas	agradezcáis	hayas agradecido	hayáis agradecido
agradezca	agradezcan	haya agradecido	hayan agradecido
7 imperfecto de subjuntivo		14 pluscuamperfecto de subjuntivo	
agradeciera	agradeciéramos	hubiera agradecido	hubiéramos agradecido
agradecieras	agradecierais	hubieras agradecido	hubierais agradecido
agradeciera	agradecieran	hubiera agradecido	hubieran agradecido
OR		OR	
agradeciese	agradeciésemos	hubiese agradecido	hubiésemos agradecido
agradecieses	agradecieseis	hubieses agradecido	hubieseis agradecido
agradeciese	agradeciesen	hubiese agradecido	hubiesen agradecido

imperativo

—	agradezcamos
agradece; no agradezcas	agradeced; no agradezcáis
agradezca	agradezcan

Words and expressions related to this verb
agradecido, agradecida thankful, grateful
el agradecimiento gratitude, gratefulness
muy agradecido much obliged

desagradecer to be ungrateful
desagradecidamente ungratefully

Don't miss the definitions of basic grammatical terms with examples
in English and Spanish on pages 666–677.

40

to enlarge, to grow larger, to increase, to exaggerate

The Seven Simple Tenses		The Seven Compound Tenses	
Singular	Plural	Singular	Plural
1 presente de indicativo		8 perfecto de indicativo	
agrando	agrandamos	he agrandado	hemos agrandado
agrandas	agrandáis	has agrandado	habéis agrandado
agranda	agrandan	ha agrandado	han agrandado
2 imperfecto de indicativo		9 pluscuamperfecto de indicativo	
agrandaba	agrandábamos	había agrandado	habíamos agrandado
agrandabas	agrandabais	habías agrandado	habíais agrandado
agrandaba	agrandaban	había agrandado	habían agrandado
3 pretérito		10 pretérito anterior	
agrandé	agrandamos	hube agrandado	hubimos agrandado
agrandaste	agrandasteis	hubiste agrandado	hubisteis agrandado
agrandó	agrandaron	hubo agrandado	hubieron agrandado
4 futuro		11 futuro perfecto	
agrandaré	agrandaremos	habré agrandado	habremos agrandado
agrandarás	agrandaréis	habrás agrandado	habréis agrandado
agrandará	agrandarán	habrá agrandado	habrán agrandado
5 potencial simple		12 potencial compuesto	
agrandaría	agrandaríamos	habría agrandado	habríamos agrandado
agrandarías	agrandaríais	habrías agrandado	habríais agrandado
agrandaría	agrandarían	habría agrandado	habrían agrandado
6 presente de subjuntivo		13 perfecto de subjuntivo	
agrande	agrandemos	haya agrandado	hayamos agrandado
agrandes	agrandéis	hayas agrandado	hayáis agrandado
agrande	agranden	haya agrandado	hayan agrandado
7 imperfecto de subjuntivo		14 pluscuamperfecto de subjuntivo	
agrandara	agrandáramos	hubiera agrandado	hubiéramos agrandado
agrandaras	agrandarais	hubieras agrandado	hubierais agrandado
agrandara	agrandaran	hubiera agrandado	hubieran agrandado
OR		OR	
agrandase	agrandásemos	hubiese agrandado	hubiésemos agrandado
agrandases	agrandaseis	hubieses agrandado	hubieseis agrandado
agrandase	agrandasen	hubiese agrandado	hubiesen agrandado

imperativo

—	agrandemos
agranda; no agrandes	agrandad; no agrandéis
agrande	agranden

Words and expressions related to this verb
el agrandamiento   aggrandizement, increase
en grande   in a grand way
grandemente   greatly

grande   great, big, large, grand, huge
vivir a lo grande   to live high (live it up)
dárselas de grande   to swagger

Want to learn more idiomatic expressions that contain verbs? Check out pages 524–537.

The subject pronouns are found on the page facing page 1.

to aggravate, to make worse

The Seven Simple Tenses		The Seven Compound Tenses	
Singular	Plural	Singular	Plural
1 presente de indicativo		8 perfecto de indicativo	
agravo	**agravamos**	**he agravado**	**hemos agravado**
agravas	**agraváis**	**has agravado**	**habéis agravado**
agrava	**agravan**	**ha agravado**	**han agravado**
2 imperfecto de indicativo		9 pluscuamperfecto de indicativo	
agravaba	**agravábamos**	**había agravado**	**habíamos agravado**
agravabas	**agravabais**	**habías agravado**	**habíais agravado**
agravaba	**agravaban**	**había agravado**	**habían agravado**
3 pretérito		10 pretérito anterior	
agravé	**agravamos**	**hube agravado**	**hubimos agravado**
agravaste	**agravasteis**	**hubiste agravado**	**hubisteis agravado**
agravó	**agravaron**	**hubo agravado**	**hubieron agravado**
4 futuro		11 futuro perfecto	
agravaré	**agravaremos**	**habré agravado**	**habremos agravado**
agravarás	**agravaréis**	**habrás agravado**	**habréis agravado**
agravará	**agravarán**	**habrá agravado**	**habrán agravado**
5 potencial simple		12 potencial compuesto	
agravaría	**agravaríamos**	**habría agravado**	**habríamos agravado**
agravarías	**agravaríais**	**habrías agravado**	**habríais agravado**
agravaría	**agravarían**	**habría agravado**	**habrían agravado**
6 presente de subjuntivo		13 perfecto de subjuntivo	
agrave	**agravemos**	**haya agravado**	**hayamos agravado**
agraves	**agravéis**	**hayas agravado**	**hayáis agravado**
agrave	**agraven**	**haya agravado**	**hayan agravado**
7 imperfecto de subjuntivo		14 pluscuamperfecto de subjuntivo	
agravara	**agraváramos**	**hubiera agravado**	**hubiéramos agravado**
agravaras	**agravarais**	**hubieras agravado**	**hubierais agravado**
agravara	**agravaran**	**hubiera agravado**	**hubieran agravado**
OR		OR	
agravase	**agravásemos**	**hubiese agravado**	**hubiésemos agravado**
agravases	**agravaseis**	**hubieses agravado**	**hubieseis agravado**
agravase	**agravasen**	**hubiese agravado**	**hubiesen agravado**

	imperativo	
—		**agravemos**
agrava; no agraves		**agravad; no agravéis**
agrave		**agraven**

Words related to this verb
agraviadamente   offensively   **agravante**   aggravating
agraviado, agraviada   insulted   **una agravación, un agravamiento**   aggravation
el agraviamiento   offense, wrongful injury

Learn more verbs in 30 practical situations for tourists on pages 564–594.

to add, to collect, to gather, to aggregate, to collate

The Seven Simple Tenses		The Seven Compound Tenses	
Singular	Plural	Singular	Plural
1 presente de indicativo		8 perfecto de indicativo	
agrego	**agregamos**	**he agregado**	**hemos agregado**
agregas	**agregáis**	**has agregado**	**habéis agregado**
agrega	**agregan**	**ha agregado**	**han agregado**
2 imperfecto de indicativo		9 pluscuamperfecto de indicativo	
agregaba	**agregábamos**	**había agregado**	**habíamos agregado**
agregabas	**agregabais**	**habías agregado**	**habíais agregado**
agregaba	**agregaban**	**había agregado**	**habían agregado**
3 pretérito		10 pretérito anterior	
agregué	**agregamos**	**hube agregado**	**hubimos agregado**
agregaste	**agregasteis**	**hubiste agregado**	**hubisteis agregado**
agregó	**agregaron**	**hubo agregado**	**hubieron agregado**
4 futuro		11 futuro perfecto	
agregaré	**agregaremos**	**habré agregado**	**habremos agregado**
agregarás	**agregaréis**	**habrás agregado**	**habréis agregado**
agregará	**agregarán**	**habrá agregado**	**habrán agregado**
5 potencial simple		12 potencial compuesto	
agregaría	**agregaríamos**	**habría agregado**	**habríamos agregado**
agregarías	**agregaríais**	**habrías agregado**	**habríais agregado**
agregaría	**agregarían**	**habría agregado**	**habrían agregado**
6 presente de subjuntivo		13 perfecto de subjuntivo	
agregue	**agreguemos**	**haya agregado**	**hayamos agregado**
agregues	**agreguéis**	**hayas agregado**	**hayáis agregado**
agregue	**agreguen**	**haya agregado**	**hayan agregado**
7 imperfecto de subjuntivo		14 pluscuamperfecto de subjuntivo	
agregara	**agregáramos**	**hubiera agregado**	**hubiéramos agregado**
agregaras	**agregarais**	**hubieras agregado**	**hubierais agregado**
agregara	**agregaran**	**hubiera agregado**	**hubieran agregado**
OR		OR	
agregase	**agregásemos**	**hubiese agregado**	**hubiésemos agregado**
agregases	**agregaseis**	**hubieses agregado**	**hubieseis agregado**
agregase	**agregasen**	**hubiese agregado**	**hubiesen agregado**

	imperativo	
—		**agreguemos**
agrega; no agregues		**agregad; no agreguéis**
agregue		**agreguen**

Words and expressions related to this verb
agregarse a   to join   **agregar dos a cinco**   to add two to five
un agregado comercial   commercial attaché

If you want to see a sample English verb fully conjugated in
all the tenses, check out pages xviii–xix.

---

to group

The Seven Simple Tenses		The Seven Compound Tenses	
Singular	Plural	Singular	Plural
1 presente de indicativo		**8 perfecto de indicativo**	
agrupo	agrupamos	he agrupado	hemos agrupado
agrupas	agrupáis	has agrupado	habéis agrupado
agrupa	agrupan	ha agrupado	han agrupado
2 imperfecto de indicativo		**9 pluscuamperfecto de indicativo**	
agrupaba	agrupábamos	había agrupado	habíamos agrupado
agrupabas	agrupabais	habías agrupado	habíais agrupado
agrupaba	agrupaban	había agrupado	habían agrupado
3 pretérito		**10 pretérito anterior**	
agrupé	agrupamos	hube agrupado	hubimos agrupado
agrupaste	agrupasteis	hubiste agrupado	hubisteis agrupado
agrupó	agruparon	hubo agrupado	hubieron agrupado
4 futuro		**11 futuro perfecto**	
agruparé	agruparemos	habré agrupado	habremos agrupado
agruparás	agruparéis	habrás agrupado	habréis agrupado
agrupará	agruparán	habrá agrupado	habrán agrupado
5 potencial simple		**12 potencial compuesto**	
agruparía	agruparíamos	habría agrupado	habríamos agrupado
agruparías	agruparíais	habrías agrupado	habríais agrupado
agruparía	agruparían	habría agrupado	habrían agrupado
6 presente de subjuntivo		**13 perfecto de subjuntivo**	
agrupe	agrupemos	haya agrupado	hayamos agrupado
agrupes	agrupéis	hayas agrupado	hayáis agrupado
agrupe	agrupen	haya agrupado	hayan agrupado
7 imperfecto de subjuntivo		**14 pluscuamperfecto de subjuntivo**	
agrupara	agrupáramos	hubiera agrupado	hubiéramos agrupado
agruparas	agruparais	hubieras agrupado	hubierais agrupado
agrupara	agruparan	hubiera agrupado	hubieran agrupado
OR		OR	
agrupase	agrupásemos	hubiese agrupado	hubiésemos agrupado
agrupases	agrupaseis	hubieses agrupado	hubieseis agrupado
agrupase	agrupasen	hubiese agrupado	hubiesen agrupado

imperativo	
—	agrupemos
agrupa; no agrupes	agrupad; no agrupéis
agrupe	agrupen

Words related to this verb
una agrupación, un agrupamiento group   **un grupo** group
  (cluster)   **una agrupación coral** choral group
agrupado, agrupada grouped

Check out the verb drills and verb tests with answers explained on pages 619–665.

to expect, to wait for

The Seven Simple Tenses		The Seven Compound Tenses	
Singular	Plural	Singular	Plural
1 presente de indicativo		8 perfecto de indicativo	
aguardo	**aguardamos**	**he aguardado**	**hemos aguardado**
aguardas	**aguardáis**	**has aguardado**	**habéis aguardado**
aguarda	**aguardan**	**ha aguardado**	**han aguardado**
2 imperfecto de indicativo		9 pluscuamperfecto de indicativo	
aguardaba	**aguardábamos**	**había aguardado**	**habíamos aguardado**
aguardabas	**aguardabais**	**habías aguardado**	**habíais aguardado**
aguardaba	**aguardaban**	**había aguardado**	**habían aguardado**
3 pretérito		10 pretérito anterior	
aguardé	**aguardamos**	**hube aguardado**	**hubimos aguardado**
aguardaste	**aguardasteis**	**hubiste aguardado**	**hubisteis aguardado**
aguardó	**aguardaron**	**hubo aguardado**	**hubieron aguardado**
4 futuro		11 futuro perfecto	
aguardaré	**aguardaremos**	**habré aguardado**	**habremos aguardado**
aguardarás	**aguardaréis**	**habrás aguardado**	**habréis aguardado**
aguardará	**aguardarán**	**habrá aguardado**	**habrán aguardado**
5 potencial simple		12 potencial compuesto	
aguardaría	**aguardaríamos**	**habría aguardado**	**habríamos aguardado**
aguardarías	**aguardaríais**	**habrías aguardado**	**habríais aguardado**
aguardaría	**aguardarían**	**habría aguardado**	**habrían aguardado**
6 presente de subjuntivo		13 perfecto de subjuntivo	
aguarde	**aguardemos**	**haya aguardado**	**hayamos aguardado**
aguardes	**aguardéis**	**hayas aguardado**	**hayáis aguardado**
aguarde	**aguarden**	**haya aguardado**	**hayan aguardado**
7 imperfecto de subjuntivo		14 pluscuamperfecto de subjuntivo	
aguardara	**aguardáramos**	**hubiera aguardado**	**hubiéramos aguardado**
aguardaras	**aguardarais**	**hubieras aguardado**	**hubierais aguardado**
aguardara	**aguardaran**	**hubiera aguardado**	**hubieran aguardado**
OR		OR	
aguardase	**aguardásemos**	**hubiese aguardado**	**hubiésemos aguardado**
aguardases	**aguardaseis**	**hubieses aguardado**	**hubieseis aguardado**
aguardase	**aguardasen**	**hubiese aguardado**	**hubiesen aguardado**

imperativo

—	**aguardemos**
aguarda; no aguardes	**aguardad; no aguardéis**
aguarde	**aguarden**

Words and expressions related to this verb
la aguardada   expecting, waiting
guardar   to guard, to watch (over)

guardar silencio   to keep silent
¡Dios guarde al Rey!   God save the King!

Consult the sections on verbs used in idiomatic expressions, verbs with prepositions, and the list of over 1,100 verbs conjugated like model verbs in the back pages.

ahorrar

Gerundio **ahorrando**   Part. pas. **ahorrado**

to economize, to save

The Seven Simple Tenses		The Seven Compound Tenses	
Singular	Plural	Singular	Plural
1 presente de indicativo		8 perfecto de indicativo	
ahorro	ahorramos	he ahorrado	hemos ahorrado
ahorras	ahorráis	has ahorrado	habéis ahorrado
ahorra	ahorran	ha ahorrado	han ahorrado
2 imperfecto de indicativo		9 pluscuamperfecto de indicativo	
ahorraba	ahorrábamos	había ahorrado	habíamos ahorrado
ahorrabas	ahorrabais	habías ahorrado	habíais ahorrado
ahorraba	ahorraban	había ahorrado	habían ahorrado
3 pretérito		10 pretérito anterior	
ahorré	ahorramos	hube ahorrado	hubimos ahorrado
ahorraste	ahorrasteis	hubiste ahorrado	hubisteis ahorrado
ahorró	ahorraron	hubo ahorrado	hubieron ahorrado
4 futuro		11 futuro perfecto	
ahorraré	ahorraremos	habré ahorrado	habremos ahorrado
ahorrarás	ahorraréis	habrás ahorrado	habréis ahorrado
ahorrará	ahorrarán	habrá ahorrado	habrán ahorrado
5 potencial simple		12 potencial compuesto	
ahorraría	ahorraríamos	habría ahorrado	habríamos ahorrado
ahorrarías	ahorraríais	habrías ahorrado	habríais ahorrado
ahorraría	ahorrarían	habría ahorrado	habrían ahorrado
6 presente de subjuntivo		13 perfecto de subjuntivo	
ahorre	ahorremos	haya ahorrado	hayamos ahorrado
ahorres	ahorréis	hayas ahorrado	hayáis ahorrado
ahorre	ahorren	haya ahorrado	hayan ahorrado
7 imperfecto de subjuntivo		14 pluscuamperfecto de subjuntivo	
ahorrara	ahorráramos	hubiera ahorrado	hubiéramos ahorrado
ahorraras	ahorrarais	hubieras ahorrado	hubierais ahorrado
ahorrara	ahorraran	hubiera ahorrado	hubieran ahorrado
OR		OR	
ahorrase	ahorrásemos	hubiese ahorrado	hubiésemos ahorrado
ahorrases	ahorraseis	hubieses ahorrado	hubieseis ahorrado
ahorrase	ahorrasen	hubiese ahorrado	hubiesen ahorrado

imperativo

—	ahorremos
ahorra; no ahorres	**ahorrad; no ahorréis**
ahorre	**ahorren**

Words and expressions related to this verb

ahorrado, ahorrada   thrifty
un ahorrador de tiempo   time saver
ahorrador, ahorradora   thrifty person, thrifty

el ahorramiento   saving, economy
no ahorrarse con nadie   not to be afraid
  of anybody

If you don't know the Spanish verb for an English verb you have in mind,
try the index on pages 505–518.

to reach, to overtake

The Seven Simple Tenses		The Seven Compound Tenses	
Singular	Plural	Singular	Plural
1 presente de indicativo		8 perfecto de indicativo	
alcanzo	alcanzamos	he alcanzado	hemos alcanzado
alcanzas	alcanzáis	has alcanzado	habéis alcanzado
alcanza	alcanzan	ha alcanzado	han alcanzado
2 imperfecto de indicativo		9 pluscuamperfecto de indicativo	
alcanzaba	alcanzábamos	había alcanzado	habíamos alcanzado
alcanzabas	alcanzabais	habías alcanzado	habíais alcanzado
alcanzaba	alcanzaban	había alcanzado	habían alcanzado
3 pretérito		10 pretérito anterior	
alcancé	alcanzamos	hube alcanzado	hubimos alcanzado
alcanzaste	alcanzasteis	hubiste alcanzado	hubisteis alcanzado
alcanzó	alcanzaron	hubo alcanzado	hubieron alcanzado
4 futuro		11 futuro perfecto	
alcanzaré	alcanzaremos	habré alcanzado	habremos alcanzado
alcanzarás	alcanzaréis	habrás alcanzado	habréis alcanzado
alcanzará	alcanzarán	habrá alcanzado	habrán alcanzado
5 potencial simple		12 potencial compuesto	
alcanzaría	alcanzaríamos	habría alcanzado	habríamos alcanzado
alcanzarías	alcanzaríais	habrías alcanzado	habríais alcanzado
alcanzaría	alcanzarían	habría alcanzado	habrían alcanzado
6 presente de subjuntivo		13 perfecto de subjuntivo	
alcance	alcancemos	haya alcanzado	hayamos alcanzado
alcances	alcancéis	hayas alcanzado	hayáis alcanzado
alcance	alcancen	haya alcanzado	hayan alcanzado
7 imperfecto de subjuntivo		14 pluscuamperfecto de subjuntivo	
alcanzara	alcanzáramos	hubiera alcanzado	hubiéramos alcanzado
alcanzaras	alcanzarais	hubieras alcanzado	hubierais alcanzado
alcanzara	alcanzaran	hubiera alcanzado	hubieran alcanzado
OR		OR	
alcanzase	alcanzásemos	hubiese alcanzado	hubiésemos alcanzado
alcanzases	alcanzaseis	hubieses alcanzado	hubieseis alcanzado
alcanzase	alcanzasen	hubiese alcanzado	hubiesen alcanzado

imperativo

—	alcancemos
alcanza; no alcances	alcanzad; no alcancéis
alcance	alcancen

Words and expressions related to this verb

el alcance   overtaking, reach
al alcance de   within reach of
dar alcance a   to overtake

al alcance del oído   within earshot
alcanzable   attainable, reachable
el alcanzador, la alcanzadora   pursuer

If you want an explanation of meanings and uses of Spanish and
English verb tenses and moods, see pages xx–xxxix.

to be glad, to rejoice, to be happy

The Seven Simple Tenses		The Seven Compound Tenses	
Singular	Plural	Singular	Plural
1 presente de indicativo		8 perfecto de indicativo	
me alegro	**nos alegramos**	**me he alegrado**	**nos hemos alegrado**
te alegras	**os alegráis**	**te has alegrado**	**os habéis alegrado**
se alegra	**se alegran**	**se ha alegrado**	**se han alegrado**
2 imperfecto de indicativo		9 pluscuamperfecto de indicativo	
me alegraba	**nos alegrábamos**	**me había alegrado**	**nos habíamos alegrado**
te alegrabas	**os alegrabais**	**te habías alegrado**	**os habíais alegrado**
se alegraba	**se alegraban**	**se había alegrado**	**se habían alegrado**
3 pretérito		10 pretérito anterior	
me alegré	**nos alegramos**	**me hube alegrado**	**nos hubimos alegrado**
te alegraste	**os alegrasteis**	**te hubiste alegrado**	**os hubisteis alegrado**
se alegró	**se alegraron**	**se hubo alegrado**	**se hubieron alegrado**
4 futuro		11 futuro perfecto	
me alegraré	**nos alegraremos**	**me habré alegrado**	**nos habremos alegrado**
te alegrarás	**os alegraréis**	**te habrás alegrado**	**os habréis alegrado**
se alegrará	**se alegrarán**	**se habrá alegrado**	**se habrán alegrado**
5 potencial simple		12 potencial compuesto	
me alegraría	**nos alegraríamos**	**me habría alegrado**	**nos habríamos alegrado**
te alegrarías	**os alegraríais**	**te habrías alegrado**	**os habríais alegrado**
se alegraría	**se alegrarían**	**se habría alegrado**	**se habrían alegrado**
6 presente de subjuntivo		13 perfecto de subjuntivo	
me alegre	**nos alegremos**	**me haya alegrado**	**nos hayamos alegrado**
te alegres	**os alegréis**	**te hayas alegrado**	**os hayáis alegrado**
se alegre	**se alegren**	**se haya alegrado**	**se hayan alegrado**
7 imperfecto de subjuntivo		14 pluscuamperfecto de subjuntivo	
me alegrara	**nos alegráramos**	**me hubiera alegrado**	**nos hubiéramos alegrado**
te alegraras	**os alegrarais**	**te hubieras alegrado**	**os hubierais alegrado**
se alegrara	**se alegraran**	**se hubiera alegrado**	**se hubieran alegrado**
OR		OR	
me alegrase	**nos alegrásemos**	**me hubiese alegrado**	**nos hubiésemos alegrado**
te alegrases	**os alegraseis**	**te hubieses alegrado**	**os hubieseis alegrado**
se alegrase	**se alegrasen**	**se hubiese alegrado**	**se hubiesen alegrado**

imperativo

—	**alegrémonos**
alégrate; no te alegres	**alegraos; no os alegréis**
alégrese	**alégrense**

Words and expressions related to this verb
la alegría   joy, rejoicing, mirth
alegro   allegro
tener mucha alegría   to be very glad
¡Qué alegría!   What joy!

alegremente   gladly, cheerfully
alegre   happy, joyful, merry, bright (color)
alegrar la fiesta   to liven up the party
saltar de alegría   to jump for joy

Increase your verb power with popular phrases,
words, and expressions for tourists on pages 595–618.

to lunch, to have lunch

The Seven Simple Tenses		The Seven Compound Tenses	
Singular	Plural	Singular	Plural
1 presente de indicativo		8 perfecto de indicativo	
almuerzo	**almorzamos**	**he almorzado**	**hemos almorzado**
almuerzas	**almorzáis**	**has almorzado**	**habéis almorzado**
almuerza	**almuerzan**	**ha almorzado**	**han almorzado**
2 imperfecto de indicativo		9 pluscuamperfecto de indicativo	
almorzaba	**almorzábamos**	**había almorzado**	**habíamos almorzado**
almorzabas	**almorzabais**	**habías almorzado**	**habíais almorzado**
almorzaba	**almorzaban**	**había almorzado**	**habían almorzado**
3 pretérito		10 pretérito anterior	
almorcé	**almorzamos**	**hube almorzado**	**hubimos almorzado**
almorzaste	**almorzasteis**	**hubiste almorzado**	**hubisteis almorzado**
almorzó	**almorzaron**	**hubo almorzado**	**hubieron almorzado**
4 futuro		11 futuro perfecto	
almorzaré	**almorzaremos**	**habré almorzado**	**habremos almorzado**
almorzarás	**almorzaréis**	**habrás almorzado**	**habréis almorzado**
almorzará	**almorzarán**	**habrá almorzado**	**habrán almorzado**
5 potencial simple		12 potencial compuesto	
almorzaría	**almorzaríamos**	**habría almorzado**	**habríamos almorzado**
almorzarías	**almorzaríais**	**habrías almorzado**	**habríais almorzado**
almorzaría	**almorzarían**	**habría almorzado**	**habrían almorzado**
6 presente de subjuntivo		13 perfecto de subjuntivo	
almuerce	**almorcemos**	**haya almorzado**	**hayamos almorzado**
almuerces	**almorcéis**	**hayas almorzado**	**hayáis almorzado**
almuerce	**almuercen**	**haya almorzado**	**hayan almorzado**
7 imperfecto de subjuntivo		14 pluscuamperfecto de subjuntivo	
almorzara	**almorzáramos**	**hubiera almorzado**	**hubiéramos almorzado**
almorzaras	**almorzarais**	**hubieras almorzado**	**hubierais almorzado**
almorzara	**almorzaran**	**hubiera almorzado**	**hubieran almorzado**
OR		OR	
almorzase	**almorzásemos**	**hubiese almorzado**	**hubiésemos almorzado**
almorzases	**almorzaseis**	**hubieses almorzado**	**hubieseis almorzado**
almorzase	**almorzasen**	**hubiese almorzado**	**hubiesen almorzado**

imperativo	
—	**almorcemos**
almuerza; no almuerces	**almorzad; no almorcéis**
almuerce	**almuercen**

Sentences using this verb and words related to it
Todos los días tomo el desayuno en casa, tomo el almuerzo en la escuela con mis amigos, y ceno con mi familia a las ocho.

el desayuno breakfast
el almuerzo lunch
la cena dinner, supper

cenar to have dinner, supper
una almorzada handful

Use the EE-zee guide to Spanish pronunciation on pages 562–563.

alquilar

Gerundio **alquilando**   Part. pas. **alquilado**

to hire, to rent

The Seven Simple Tenses		The Seven Compound Tenses	
Singular	Plural	Singular	Plural
1 presente de indicativo		**8 perfecto de indicativo**	
alquilo	alquilamos	he alquilado	hemos alquilado
alquilas	alquiláis	has alquilado	habéis alquilado
alauila	alquilan	ha alquilado	han alquilado
2 imperfecto de indicativo		**9 pluscuamperfecto de indicativo**	
alquilaba	alquilábamos	había alquilado	habíamos alquilado
alquilabas	alquilabais	habías alquilado	habíais alquilado
alquilaba	alquilaban	había alquilado	habían alquilado
3 pretérito		**10 pretérito anterior**	
alquilé	alquilamos	hube alquilado	hubimos alquilado
alquilase	alquilasteis	hubiste alquilado	hubisteis alquilado
alquiló	alquilaron	hubo alquilado	hubieron alquilado
4 futuro		**11 futuro perfecto**	
alquilaré	alquilaremos	habré alquilado	habremos alquilado
alquilarás	alquilaréis	habrás alquilado	habréis alquilado
alquilará	alquilarán	habrá alquilado	habrán alquilado
5 potencial simple		**12 potencial compuesto**	
alquilaría	alquilaríamos	habría alquilado	habríamos alquilado
alquilarías	alquilaríais	habrías alquilado	habríais alquilado
alquilaría	alquilarían	habría alquilado	habrían alquilado
6 presente de subjuntivo		**13 perfecto de subjuntivo**	
alquile	alquilemos	haya alquilado	hayamos alquilado
alquiles	alquiléis	hayas alquilado	hayáis alquilado
alquile	alquilen	haya alquilado	hayan alquilado
7 imperfecto de subjuntivo		**14 pluscuamperfecto de subjuntivo**	
alquilara	alquiláramos	hubiera alquilado	hubiéramos alquilado
alquilaras	alquilarais	hubieras alquilado	hubierais alquilado
alquilara`	alquilaran	hubiera alquilado	hubieran alquilado
OR		OR	
alquilase	alquilásemos	hubiese alquilado	hubiésemos alquilado
alquilases	alquilaseis	hubieses alquilado	hubieseis alquilado
alquilase	alquilasen	hubiese alquilado	hubiesen alquilado

imperativo

—	alquilemos
alquila; no alquiles	alquilad; no alquiléis
alquile	alquilen

Words and expressions related to this verb

alquilable   rentable
SE ALQUILA   FOR RENT
ALQUILA   AVAILABLE

desalquilar   to vacate, stop renting
desalquilarse   to become vacant, unrented
desalquilado, desalquilada   unrented, unlet, vacant

If you want to see a sample English verb fully conjugated
in all the tenses, check out pages xviii and xix.

to illuminate, to light, to enlighten

The Seven Simple Tenses		The Seven Compound Tenses	
Singular	Plural	Singular	Plural
1 presente de indicativo		8 perfecto de indicativo	
alumbro	**alumbramos**	**he alumbrado**	**hemos alumbrado**
alumbras	**alumbráis**	**has alumbrado**	**habéis alumbrado**
alumbra	**alumbran**	**ha alumbrado**	**han alumbrado**
2 imperfecto de indicativo		9 pluscuamperfecto de indicativo	
alumbraba	**alumbrábamos**	**había alumbrado**	**habíamos alumbrado**
alumbrabas	**alumbrabais**	**habías alumbrado**	**habíais alumbrado**
alumbraba	**alumbraban**	**había alumbrado**	**habían alumbrado**
3 pretérito		10 pretérito anterior	
alumbré	**alumbramos**	**hube alumbrado**	**hubimos alumbrado**
alumbraste	**alumbrasteis**	**hubiste alumbrado**	**hubisteis alumbrado**
alumbró	**alumbraron**	**hubo alumbrado**	**hubieron alumbrado**
4 futuro		11 futuro perfecto	
alumbraré	**alumbraremos**	**habré alumbrado**	**habremos alumbrado**
alumbrarás	**alumbraréis**	**habrás alumbrado**	**habréis alumbrado**
alumbrará	**alumbrarán**	**habrá alumbrado**	**habrán alumbrado**
5 potencial simple		12 potencial compuesto	
alumbraría	**alumbraríamos**	**habría alumbrado**	**habríamos alumbrado**
alumbrarías	**alumbraríais**	**habrías alumbrado**	**habríais alumbrado**
alumbraría	**alumbrarían**	**habría alumbrado**	**habrían alumbrado**
6 presente de subjuntivo		13 perfecto de subjuntivo	
alumbre	**alumbremos**	**haya alumbrado**	**hayamos alumbrado**
alumbres	**alumbréis**	**hayas alumbrado**	**hayáis alumbrado**
alumbre	**alumbren**	**haya alumbrado**	**hayan alumbrado**
7 imperfecto de subjuntivo		14 pluscuamperfecto de subjuntivo	
alumbrara	**alumbráramos**	**hubiera alumbrado**	**hubiéramos alumbrado**
alumbraras	**alumbrarais**	**hubieras alumbrado**	**hubierais alumbrado**
alumbrara	**alumbraran**	**hubiera alumbrado**	**hubieran alumbrado**
OR		OR	
alumbrase	**alumbrásemos**	**hubiese alumbrado**	**hubiésemos alumbrado**
alumbrases	**alumbraseis**	**hubieses alumbrado**	**hubieseis alumbrado**
alumbrase	**alumbrasen**	**hubiese alumbrado**	**hubiesen alumbrado**

imperativo

—	**alumbremos**
alumbra; no alumbres	**alumbrad; no alumbréis**
alumbre	**alumbren**

Words and expressions related to this verb
alumbrante   illuminating, enlightening
el alumbramiento   lighting
el alumbrado fluorescente   fluorescent lighting
el alumbrado reflejado (indirecto)   indirect lighting
la lumbre   fire, light; **calentarse a la lumbre**   to warm oneself by the fire

The subject pronouns are found on the page facing page 1.

alumbrarse Gerundio **alumbrándose** Part. pas. **alumbrado**

to be (get) high, to get tipsy, to become lively (from liquor)

The Seven Simple Tenses		The Seven Compound Tenses	
Singular	Plural	Singular	Plural

1 presente de indicativo

me alumbro	nos alumbramos		
te alumbras	os alumbráis		
se alumbra	se alumbran		

8 perfecto de indicativo

me he alumbrado	nos hemos alumbrado		
te has alumbrado	os habéis alumbrado		
se ha alumbrado	se han alumbrado		

2 imperfecto de indicativo

me alumbraba	nos alumbrábamos
te alumbrabas	os alumbrabais
se alumbraba	se alumbraban

9 pluscuamperfecto de indicativo

me había alumbrado	nos habíamos alumbrado
te habías alumbrado	os habíais alumbrado
se había alumbrado	se habían alumbrado

3 pretérito

me alumbré	nos alumbramos
te alumbraste	os alumbrasteis
se alumbró	se alumbraron

10 pretérito anterior

me hube alumbrado	nos hubimos alumbrado
te hubiste alumbrado	os hubisteis alumbrado
se hubo alumbrado	se hubieron alumbrado

4 futuro

me alumbraré	nos alumbraremos
te alumbrarás	os alumbraréis
se alumbrará	se alumbrarán

11 futuro perfecto

me habré alumbrado	nos habremos alumbrado
te habrás alumbrado	os habréis alumbrado
se habrá alumbrado	se habrán alumbrado

5 potencial simple

me alumbraría	nos alumbraríamos
te alumbrarías	os alumbraríais
se alumbraría	se alumbrarían

12 potencial compuesto

me habría alumbrado	nos habríamos alumbrado
te habrías alumbrado	os habríais alumbrado
se habría alumbrado	se habrían alumbrado

6 presente de subjuntivo

me alumbre	nos alumbremos
te alumbres	os alumbréis
se alumbre	se alumbren

13 perfecto de subjuntivo

me haya alumbrado	nos hayamos alumbrado
te hayas alumbrado	os hayáis alumbrado
se haya alumbrado	se hayan alumbrado

7 imperfecto de subjuntivo

me alumbrara	nos alumbráramos
te alumbraras	os alumbrarais
se alumbrara	se alumbraran
OR	
me alumbrase	nos alumbrásemos
te alumbrases	os alumbraseis
se alumbrase	se alumbrasen

14 pluscuamperfecto de subjuntivo

me hubiera alumbrado	nos hubiéramos alumbrado
te hubieras alumbrado	os hubierais alumbrado
se hubiera alumbrado	se hubieran alumbrado
OR	
me hubiese alumbrado	nos hubiésemos alumbrado
te hubieses alumbrado	os hubieseis alumbrado
se hubiese alumbrado	se hubiesen alumbrado

imperativo

—	alumbrémonos
alúmbrate; no te alumbres	alumbraos, no os alumbréis
alúmbrese	alúmbrense

For words and expressions related to this verb, see **alumbrar.**

Be sure to consult the back pages for sections on verbs used in idiomatic expressions, verbs with prepositions, and the list of over 1,100 verbs conjugated like model verbs.

Learn more verbs in 30 practical situations for tourists on pages 564–594.

to heave, to lift, to pick up, to raise (prices)

The Seven Simple Tenses		The Seven Compound Tenses	
Singular	Plural	Singular	Plural
1 presente de indicativo		**8 perfecto de indicativo**	
alzo	alzamos	he alzado	hemos alzado
alzas	alzáis	has alzado	habéis alzado
alza	alzan	ha alzado	han alzado
2 imperfecto de indicativo		**9 pluscuamperfecto de indicativo**	
alzaba	alzábamos	había alzado	habíamos alzado
alzabas	alzabais	habías alzado	habíais alzado
alzaba	alzaban	había alzado	habían alzado
3 pretérito		**10 pretérito anterior**	
alcé	alzamos	hube alzado	hubimos alzado
alzaste	alzasteis	hubiste alzado	hubisteis alzado
alzó	alzaron	hubo alzado	hubieron alzado
4 futuro		**11 futuro perfecto**	
alzaré	alzaremos	habré alzado	habremos alzado
alzarás	alzaréis	habrás alzado	habréis alzado
alzará	alzarán	habrá alzado	habrán alzado
5 potencial simple		**12 potencial compuesto**	
alzaría	alzaríamos	habría alzado	habríamos alzado
alzarías	alzaríais	habrías alzado	habríais alzado
alzaría	alzarían	habría alzado	habrían alzado
6 presente de subjuntivo		**13 perfecto de subjuntivo**	
alce	alcemos	haya alzado	hayamos alzado
alces	alcéis	hayas alzado	hayáis alzado
alce	alcen	haya alzado	hayan alzado
7 imperfecto de subjuntivo		**14 pluscuamperfecto de subjuntivo**	
alzara	alzáramos	hubiera alzado	hubiéramos alzado
alzaras	alzarais	hubieras alzado	hubierais alzado
alzara	alzaran	hubiera alzado	hubieran alzado
OR		OR	
alzase	alzásemos	hubiese alzado	hubiésemos alzado
alzases	alzaseis	hubieses alzado	hubieseis alzado
alzase	alzasen	hubiese alzado	hubiesen alzado

imperativo	
—	**alcemos**
alza; no alces	**alzad; no alcéis**
alce	**alcen**

Words and expressions related to this verb

alzar velas   to set the sails, to hoist sail
alzar con   to run off with, to steal
la alzadura   elevation
el alzamiento   raising, lifting

el alzo   robbery, theft
alzar la mano   to threaten, to raise one's hand
alzar la voz   to raise one's voice
alzar el codo   to drink to excess (to raise one's elbow)

amar

Gerundio **amando**   Part. pas. **amado**

to love

The Seven Simple Tenses		The Seven Compound Tenses	
Singular	Plural	Singular	Plural
1 presente de indicativo		**8 perfecto de indicativo**	
amo	amamos	he amado	hemos amado
amas	amáis	has amado	habéis amado
ama	aman	ha amado	han amado
2 imperfecto de indicativo		**9 pluscuamperfecto de indicativo**	
amaba	amábamos	había amado	habíamos amado
amabas	amabais	habías amado	habíais amado
amaba	amaban	había amado	habían amado
3 pretérito		**10 pretérito anterior**	
amé	amamos	hube amado	hubimos amado
amaste	amasteis	hubiste amado	hubisteis amado
amó	amaron	hubo amado	hubieron amado
4 futuro		**11 futuro perfecto**	
amaré	amaremos	habré amado	habremos amado
amarás	amaréis	habrás amado	habréis amado
amará	amarán	habrá amado	habrán amado
5 potencial simple		**12 potencial compuesto**	
amaría	amaríamos	habría amado	habríamos amado
amarías	amaríais	habrías amado	habríais amado
amaría	amarían	habría amado	habrían amado
6 presente de subjuntivo		**13 perfecto de subjuntivo**	
ame	amemos	haya amado	hayamos amado
ames	améis	hayas amado	hayáis amado
ame	amen	haya amado	hayan amado
7 imperfecto de subjuntivo		**14 pluscuamperfecto de subjuntivo**	
amara	amáramos	hubiera amado	hubiéramos amado
amaras	amarais	hubieras amado	hubierais amado
amara	amaran	hubiera amado	hubieran amado
OR		OR	
amase	amásemos	hubiese amado	hubiésemos amado
amases	amaseis	hubieses amado	hubieseis amado
amase	amasen	hubiese amado	hubiesen amado

	imperativo	
—		amemos
ama; no ames		amad; no améis
ame		amen

Words related to this verb
la amabilidad   amiability, kindness
amable   amiable, kind, affable

amablemente   amiably, kindly; **una carta amatoria**   love letter
el amor   love; **amante** lover

Want to learn more idiomatic expressions that contain verbs? Check out pages 524–537.

The Seven Simple Tenses		The Seven Compound Tenses	
Singular	Plural	Singular	Plural
1 presente de indicativo		**8 perfecto de indicativo**	
añado	**añadimos**	**he añadido**	**hemos añadido**
añades	**añadís**	**has añadido**	**habéis añadido**
añade	**añaden**	**ha añadido**	**han añadido**
2 imperfecto de indicativo		**9 pluscuamperfecto de indicativo**	
añadía	**añadíamos**	**había añadido**	**habíamos añadido**
añadías	**añadíais**	**habías añadido**	**habíais añadido**
añadía	**añadían**	**había añadido**	**habían añadido**
3 pretérito		**10 pretérito anterior**	
añadí	**añadimos**	**hube añadido**	**hubimos añadido**
añadiste	**añadisteis**	**hubiste añadido**	**hubisteis añadido**
añadió	**añadieron**	**hubo añadido**	**hubieron añadido**
4 futuro		**11 futuro perfecto**	
añadiré	**añadiremos**	**habré añadido**	**habremos añadido**
añadirás	**añadiréis**	**habrás añadido**	**habréis añadido**
añadirá	**añadirán**	**habrá añadido**	**habrán añadido**
5 potencial simple		**12 potencial compuesto**	
añadiría	**añadiríamos**	**habría añadido**	**habríamos añadido**
añadirías	**añadiríais**	**habrías añadido**	**habríais añadido**
añadiría	**añadirían**	**habría añadido**	**habrían añadido**
6 presente de subjuntivo		**13 perfecto de subjuntivo**	
añada	**añadamos**	**haya añadido**	**hayamos añadido**
añadas	**añadáis**	**hayas añadido**	**hayáis añadido**
añada	**añadan**	**haya añadido**	**hayan añadido**
7 imperfecto de subjuntivo		**14 pluscuamperfecto de subjuntivo**	
añadiera	**añadiéramos**	**hubiera añadido**	**hubiéramos añadido**
añadieras	**añadierais**	**hubieras añadido**	**hubierais añadido**
añadiera	**añadieran**	**hubiera añadido**	**hubieran añadido**
OR		OR	
añadiese	**añadiésemos**	**hubiese añadido**	**hubiésemos añadido**
añadieses	**añadieseis**	**hubieses añadido**	**hubieseis añadido**
añadiese	**añadiesen**	**hubiese añadido**	**hubiesen añadido**

	imperativo	
—		**añadamos**
añade; no añadas		**añadid; no añadáis**
añada		**añadan**

Words and expressions related to this verb

la añadidura increase, addition
por añadidura in addition, besides

de añadidura extra, for good measure
añadido, añadida added, additional

Enjoy verbs in Spanish proverbs on page 539.

The subject pronouns are found on the page facing page 1.

55

andar

Gerundio andando   **Part. pas. andado**

to walk

The Seven Simple Tenses		The Seven Compound Tenses	
Singular	Plural	Singular	Plural
1 presente de indicativo		8 perfecto de indicativo	
ando	andamos	he andado	hemos andado
andas	andáis	has andado	habéis andado
anda	andan	ha andado	han andado
2 imperfecto de indicativo		9 pluscuamperfecto de indicativo	
andaba	andábamos	había andado	habíamos andado
andabas	andabais	habías andado	habíais andado
andaba	andaban	había andado	habían andado
3 pretérito		10 pretérito anterior	
anduve	anduvimos	hube andado	hubimos andado
anduviste	anduvisteis	hubiste andado	hubisteis andado
anduvo	anduvieron	hubo andado	hubieron andado
4 futuro		11 futuro perfecto	
andaré	andaremos	habré andado	habremos andado
andarás	andaréis	habrás andado	habréis andado
andará	andarán	habrá andado	habrán andado
5 potencial simple		12 potencial compuesto	
andaría	andaríamos	habría andado	habríamos andado
andarías	andaríais	habrías andado	habríais andado
andaría	andarían	habría andado	habrían andado
6 presente de subjuntivo		13 perfecto de subjuntivo	
ande	andemos	haya andado	hayamos andado
andes	andéis	hayas andado	hayáis andado
ande	anden	haya andado	hayan andado
7 imperfecto de subjuntivo		14 pluscuamperfecto de subjuntivo	
anduviera	anduviéramos	hubiera andado	hubiéramos andado
anduvieras	anduvierais	hubieras andado	hubierais andado
anduviera	anduvieran	hubiera andado	hubieran andado
OR		OR	
anduviese	anduviésemos	hubiese andado	hubiésemos andado
anduvieses	anduvieseis	hubieses andado	hubieseis andado
anduviese	anduviesen	hubiese andado	hubiesen andado

	imperativo	
—	andemos
anda; no andes	andad; no andéis
ande	anden

Words and expressions related to this verb

las andanzas   events

buena andanza   good fortune

mala andanza   bad fortune

a todo andar   at full speed

¿Cómo andan los negocios?   How's business?

desandar   to retrace one's steps

Anda despacio que tengo prisa.   Make haste slowly.

Dime con quién andas y te diré quién eres.   Tell me who your friends are and I will tell you who you are.

56

to announce, to foretell, to proclaim

The Seven Simple Tenses		The Seven Compound Tenses	
Singular	Plural	Singular	Plural
1 presente de indicativo		8 perfecto de indicativo	
anuncio	**anunciamos**	**he anunciado**	**hemos anunciado**
anuncias	**anunciáis**	**has anunciado**	**habéis anunciado**
anuncia	**anuncian**	**ha anunciado**	**han anunciado**
2 imperfecto de indicativo		9 pluscuamperfecto de indicativo	
anunciaba	**anunciábamos**	**había anunciado**	**habíamos anunciado**
anunciabas	**anunciabais**	**habías anunciado**	**habíais anunciado**
anunciaba	**anunciaban**	**había anunciado**	**habían anunciado**
3 pretérito		10 pretérito anterior	
anuncié	**anunciamos**	**hube anunciado**	**hubimos anunciado**
anunciaste	**anunciasteis**	**hubiste anunciado**	**hubisteis anunciado**
anunció	**anunciaron**	**hubo anunciado**	**hubieron anunciado**
4 futuro		11 futuro perfecto	
anunciaré	**anunciaremos**	**habré anunciado**	**habremos anunciado**
anunciarás	**anunciaréis**	**habrás anunciado**	**habréis anunciado**
anunciará	**anunciarán**	**habrá anunciado**	**habrán anunciado**
5 potencial simple		12 potencial compuesto	
anunciaría	**anunciaríamos**	**habría anunciado**	**habríamos anunciado**
anunciarías	**anunciaríais**	**habrías anunciado**	**habríais anunciado**
anunciaría	**anunciarían**	**habría anunciado**	**habrían anunciado**
6 presente de subjuntivo		13 perfecto de subjuntivo	
anuncie	**anunciemos**	**haya anunciado**	**hayamos anunciado**
anuncies	**anunciéis**	**hayas anunciado**	**hayáis anunciado**
anuncie	**anuncien**	**haya anunciado**	**hayan anunciado**
7 imperfecto de subjuntivo		14 pluscuamperfecto de subjuntivo	
anunciara	**anunciáramos**	**hubiera anunciado**	**hubiéramos anunciado**
anunciaras	**anunciarais**	**hubieras anunciado**	**hubierais anunciado**
anunciara	**anunciaran**	**hubiera anunciado**	**hubieran anunciado**
OR		OR	
anunciase	**anunciásemos**	**hubiese anunciado**	**hubiésemos anunciado**
anunciases	**anunciaseis**	**hubieses anunciado**	**hubieseis anunciado**
anunciase	**anunciasen**	**hubiese anunciado**	**hubiesen anunciado**

imperativo

—	**anunciemos**
anuncia; no anuncies	**anunciad; no anunciéis**
anuncie	**anuncien**

Words related to this verb
el, la anunciante advertiser
la Anunciación Annunciation
el anunciador, la anunciadora advertiser,
  announcer

el anuncio advertisement, announcement
el cartel anunciador billboard
los anuncios por palabras classified
  advertisements

Get your feet wet with verbs used in weather expressions on page 540.

The subject pronouns are found on the page facing page 1.

apagar

Gerundio **apagando**   Part. pas. **apagado**

to put out (flame, fire), to extinguish, to turn off (flame, fire, light)

The Seven Simple Tenses		The Seven Compound Tenses	
Singular	Plural	Singular	Plural
1 presente de indicativo		**8 perfecto de indicativo**	
apago	apagamos	he apagado	hemos apagado
apagas	apagáis	has apagado	habéis apagado
apaga	apagan	ha apagado	han apagado
2 imperfecto de indicativo		**9 pluscuamperfecto de indicativo**	
apagaba	apagábamos	había apagado	habíamos apagado
apagabas	apagabais	habías apagado	habíais apagado
apagaba	apagaban	había apagado	habían apagado
3 pretérito		**10 pretérito anterior**	
apagué	apagamos	hube apagado	hubimos apagado
apagaste	apagasteis	hubiste apagado	hubisteis apagado
apagó	apagaron	hubo apagado	hubieron apagado
4 futuro		**11 futuro perfecto**	
apagaré	apagaremos	habré apagado	habremos apagado
apagarás	apagaréis	habrás apagado	habréis apagado
apagará	apagarán	habrá apagado	habrán apagado
5 potencial simple		**12 potencial compuesto**	
apagaría	apagaríamos	habría apagado	habríamos apagado
apagarías	apagaríais	habrías apagado	habríais apagado
apagaría	apagarían	habría apagado	habrían apagado
6 presente de subjuntivo		**13 perfecto de subjuntivo**	
apague	apaguemos	haya apagado	hayamos apagado
apagues	apaguéis	hayas apagado	hayáis apagado
apague	apaguen	haya apagado	hayan apagado
7 imperfecto de subjuntivo		**14 pluscuamperfecto de subjuntivo**	
apagara	apagáramos	hubiera apagado	hubiéramos apagado
apagaras	apagarais	hubieras apagado	hubierais apagado
apagara	apagaran	hubiera apagado	hubieran apagado
OR		OR	
apagase	apagásemos	hubiese apagado	hubiésemos apagado
apagases	apagaseis	hubieses apagado	hubieseis apagado
apagase	apagasen	hubiese apagado	hubiesen apagado

imperativo	
—	apaguemos
apaga; no apagues	apagad; no apaguéis
apague	apaguen

Words and expressions related to this verb

el apagafuegos, el apagaincendios   fire extinguisher
apagadizo, apagadiza   fire resistant
¡Apaga y vámonos!   Let's end this and let's go! Let's put an end to all this!

el apagavelas   candle extinguisher
el apagón   blackout (no electricity)

Enjoy verbs in Spanish proverbs on page 539.

to appear, to show up

The Seven Simple Tenses | The Seven Compound Tenses

Singular	Plural	Singular	Plural
1 presente de indicativo		8 perfecto de indicativo	
aparezco	**aparecemos**	**he aparecido**	**hemos aparecido**
apareces	**aparecéis**	**has aparecido**	**habéis aparecido**
aparece	**aparecen**	**ha aparecido**	**han aparecido**
2 imperfecto de indicativo		9 pluscuamperfecto de indicativo	
aparecía	**aparecíamos**	**había aparecido**	**habíamos aparecido**
aparecías	**aparecíais**	**habías aparecido**	**habíais aparecido**
aparecía	**aparecían**	**había aparecido**	**habían aparecido**
3 pretérito		10 pretérito anterior	
aparecí	**aparecimos**	**hube aparecido**	**hubimos aparecido**
apareciste	**aparecisteis**	**hubiste aparecido**	**hubisteis aparecido**
apareció	**aparecieron**	**hubo aparecido**	**hubieron aparecido**
4 futuro		11 futuro perfecto	
apareceré	**apareceremos**	**habré aparecido**	**habremos aparecido**
aparecerás	**apareceréis**	**habrás aparecido**	**habréis aparecido**
aparecerá	**aparecerán**	**habrá aparecido**	**habrán aparecido**
5 potencial simple		12 potencial compuesto	
aparecería	**apareceríamos**	**habría aparecido**	**habríamos aparecido**
aparecerías	**apareceríais**	**habrías aparecido**	**habríais aparecido**
aparecería	**aparecerían**	**habría aparecido**	**habrían aparecido**
6 presente de subjuntivo		13 perfecto de subjuntivo	
aparezca	**aparezcamos**	**haya aparecido**	**hayamos aparecido**
aparezcas	**aparezcáis**	**hayas aparecido**	**hayáis aparecido**
aparezca	**aparezcan**	**haya aparecido**	**hayan aparecido**
7 imperfecto de subjuntivo		14 pluscuamperfecto de subjuntivo	
apareciera	**apareciéramos**	**hubiera aparecido**	**hubiéramos aparecido**
aparecieras	**aparecierais**	**hubieras aparecido**	**hubierais aparecido**
apareciera	**aparecieran**	**hubiera aparecido**	**hubieran aparecido**
OR		OR	
apareciese	**apareciésemos**	**hubiese aparecido**	**hubiésemos aparecido**
aparecieses	**aparecieseis**	**hubieses aparecido**	**hubieseis aparecido**
apareciese	**apareciesen**	**hubiese aparecido**	**hubiesen aparecido**

imperativo

—	**aparezcamos**
aparece; no aparezcas	**apareced; no aparezcáis**
aparezca	**aparezcan**

Words and expressions related to this verb
un aparecimiento   apparition
un aparecido   ghost
una aparición   apparition, appearance
parecer   to seem, to appear
parecerse a   to look like

aparecerse en casa   to arrive home unexpectedly
aparecerse a alguno   to see a ghost
aparecerse entre sueños   to see someone in a
   dream

The subject pronouns are found on the page facing page 1.

aplaudir

Gerundio **aplaudiendo**   Part. pas. **aplaudido**

to applaud

The Seven Simple Tenses		The Seven Compound Tenses	
Singular	Plural	Singular	Plural
1 presente de indicativo		**8 perfecto de indicativo**	
aplaudo	aplaudimos	he aplaudido	hemos aplaudido
aplaudes	aplaudís	has aplaudido	habéis aplaudido
aplaude	aplauden	ha aplaudido	han aplaudido
2 imperfecto de indicativo		**9 pluscuamperfecto de indicativo**	
aplaudía	aplaudíamos	había aplaudido	habíamos aplaudido
aplaudías	aplaudíais	habías aplaudido	habíais aplaudido
aplaudía	aplaudían	había aplaudido	habían aplaudido
3 pretérito		**10 pretérito anterior**	
aplaudí	aplaudimos	hube aplaudido	hubimos aplaudido
aplaudiste	aplaudisteis	hubiste aplaudido	hubisteis aplaudido
aplaudió	aplaudieron	hubo aplaudido	hubieron aplaudido
4 futuro		**11 futuro perfecto**	
aplaudiré	aplaudiremos	habré aplaudido	habremos aplaudido
aplaudirás	aplaudiréis	habrás aplaudido	habréis aplaudido
aplaudirá	aplaudirán	habrá aplaudido	habrán aplaudido
5 potencial simple		**12 potencial compuesto**	
aplaudiría	aplaudiríamos	habría aplaudido	habríamos aplaudido
aplaudirías	aplaudiríais	habrías aplaudido	habríais aplaudido
aplaudiría	aplaudirían	habría aplaudido	habrían aplaudido
6 presente de subjuntivo		**13 perfecto de subjuntivo**	
aplauda	aplaudamos	haya aplaudido	hayamos aplaudido
aplaudas	aplaudáis	hayas aplaudido	hayáis aplaudido
aplauda	aplaudan	haya aplaudido	hayan aplaudido
7 imperfecto de subjuntivo		**14 pluscuamperfecto de subjuntivo**	
aplaudiera	aplaudiéramos	hubiera aplaudido	hubiéramos aplaudido
aplaudieras	aplaudierais	hubieras aplaudido	hubierais aplaudido
aplaudiera	aplaudieran	hubiera aplaudido	hubieran aplaudido
OR		OR	
aplaudiese	aplaudiésemos	hubiese aplaudido	hubiésemos aplaudido
aplaudieses	aplaudieseis	hubieses aplaudido	hubieseis aplaudido
aplaudiese	aplaudiesen	hubiese aplaudido	hubiesen aplaudido

	imperativo	
—	aplaudamos
aplaude; no aplaudas	aplaudid; no aplaudáis
aplauda	aplaudan

Words and expressions related to this verb
el aplauso   applause
el aplaudidor, la aplaudidora   applauder

con el aplauso de   to the applause of
una salva de aplausos   thunderous applause

Get acquainted with what preposition goes with what verb on pages 541–549.

to take power, to take possession

The Seven Simple Tenses		The Seven Compound Tenses	
Singular	Plural	Singular	Plural
1 presente de indicativo		8 perfecto de indicativo	
me apodero	**nos apoderamos**	**me he apoderado**	**nos hemos apoderado**
te apoderas	**os apoderáis**	**te has apoderado**	**os habéis apoderado**
se apodera	**se apoderan**	**se ha apoderado**	**se han apoderado**
2 imperfecto de indicativo		9 pluscuamperfecto de indicativo	
me apoderaba	**nos apoderábamos**	**me había apoderado**	**nos habíamos apoderado**
te apoderabas	**os apoderabais**	**te habías apoderado**	**os habíais apoderado**
se apoderaba	**se apoderaban**	**se había apoderado**	**se habían apoderado**
3 pretérito		10 pretérito anterior	
me apoderé	**nos apoderamos**	**me hube apoderado**	**nos hubimos apoderado**
te apoderaste	**os apoderasteis**	**te hubiste apoderado**	**os hubisteis apoderado**
se apoderó	**se apoderaron**	**se hubo apoderado**	**se hubieron apoderado**
4 futuro		11 futuro perfecto	
me apoderaré	**nos apoderaremos**	**me habré apoderado**	**nos habremos apoderado**
te apoderarás	**os apoderaréis**	**te habrás apoderado**	**os habréis apoderado**
se apoderará	**se apoderarán**	**se habrá apoderado**	**se habrán apoderado**
5 potencial simple		12 potencial compuesto	
me apoderaría	**nos apoderaríamos**	**me habría apoderado**	**nos habríamos apoderado**
te apoderarías	**os apoderaríais**	**te habrías apoderado**	**os habríais apoderado**
se apoderaría	**se apoderarían**	**se habría apoderado**	**se habrían apoderado**
6 presente de subjuntivo		13 perfecto de subjuntivo	
me apodere	**nos apoderemos**	**me haya apoderado**	**nos hayamos apoderado**
te apoderes	**os apoderéis**	**te hayas apoderado**	**os hayáis apoderado**
se apodere	**se apoderen**	**se haya apoderado**	**se hayan apoderado**
7 imperfecto de subjuntivo		14 pluscuamperfecto de subjuntivo	
me apoderara	**nos apoderáramos**	**me hubiera apoderado**	**nos hubiéramos apoderado**
te apoderaras	**os apoderarais**	**te hubieras apoderado**	**os hubierais apoderado**
se apoderara	**se apoderaran**	**se hubiera apoderado**	**se hubieran apoderado**
OR		OR	
me apoderase	**nos apoderásemos**	**me hubiese apoderado**	**nos hubiésemos apoderado**
te apoderases	**os apoderaseis**	**te hubieses apoderado**	**os hubieseis apoderado**
se apoderase	**se apoderasen**	**se hubiese apoderado**	**se hubiesen apoderado**

imperativo	
—	**apoderémonos**
apodérate; no te apoderes	**apoderaos; no os apoderéis**
apodérese	**apodérense**

Words and expressions related to this verb

poder   to be able

el poder   power

el apoderado   proxy

apoderarse de algo   to take possession of something

apoderado, apoderada   empowered

apoderar   to empower, to authorize

Get acquainted with what preposition goes with what verb on pages 541–549.

The subject pronouns are found on the page facing page 1.

apreciar

Gerundio **apreciando**   Part. pas. **apreciado**

to appreciate, to appraise, to esteem

The Seven Simple Tenses		The Seven Compound Tenses	
Singular	Plural	Singular	Plural
1 presente de indicativo		**8 perfecto de indicativo**	
aprecio	apreciamos	he apreciado	hemos apreciado
aprecias	apreciáis	has apreciado	habéis apreciado
aprecia	aprecian	ha apreciado	han apreciado
2 imperfecto de indicativo		**9 pluscuamperfecto de indicativo**	
apreciaba	apreciábamos	había apreciado	habíamos apreciado
apreciabas	apreciabais	habías apreciado	habíais apreciado
apreciaba	apreciaban	había apreciado	habían apreciado
3 pretérito		**10 pretérito anterior**	
aprecié	apreciamos	hube apreciado	hubimos apreciado
apreciaste	apreciasteis	hubiste apreciado	hubisteis apreciado
apreció	apreciaron	hubo apreciado	hubieron apreciado
4 futuro		**11 futuro perfecto**	
apreciaré	apreciaremos	habré apreciado	habremos apreciado
apreciarás	apreciaréis	habrás apreciado	habréis apreciado
apreciará	apreciarán	habrá apreciado	habrán apreciado
5 potencial simple		**12 potencial compuesto**	
apreciaría	apreciaríamos	habría apreciado	habríamos apreciado
apreciarías	apreciaríais	habrías apreciado	habríais apreciado
apreciaría	apreciarían	habría apreciado	habrían apreciado
6 presente de subjuntivo		**13 perfecto de subjuntivo**	
aprecie	apreciemos	haya apreciado	hayamos apreciado
aprecies	apreciéis	hayas apreciado	hayáis apreciado
aprecie	aprecien	haya apreciado	hayan apreciado
7 imperfecto de subjuntivo		**14 pluscuamperfecto de subjuntivo**	
apreciara	apreciáramos	hubiera apreciado	hubiéramos apreciado
apreciaras	apreciarais	hubieras apreciado	hubierais apreciado
apeciara	apreciaran	hubiera apreciado	hubieran apreciado
OR		OR	
apreciase	apreciásemos	hubiese apreciado	hubiésemos apreciado
apreciases	apreciaseis	hubieses apreciado	hubieseis apreciado
apreciase	apreciasen	hubiese apreciado	hubiesen apreciado

	imperativo	
—		apreciemos
aprecia; no aprecies		apreciad; no apreciéis
aprecie		aprecien

Words and expressions related to this verb

el aprecio   appreciation, esteem
la apreciación   appreciation, estimation
apreciable   appreciable; worthy
la apreciabilidad   appreciability

preciar   to appraise, to estimate
el precio   price; **no tener precio** to be priceless
un precio fijo   set price

Enjoy verbs in Spanish proverbs on page 539.

The Seven Simple Tenses		The Seven Compound Tenses	
Singular	Plural	Singular	Plural
1 presente de indicativo		**8 perfecto de indicativo**	
aprendo	aprendemos	he aprendido	hemos aprendido
aprendes	aprendéis	has aprendido	habéis aprendido
aprende	aprenden	ha aprendido	han aprendido
2 imperfecto de indicativo		**9 pluscuamperfecto de indicativo**	
aprendía	aprendíamos	había aprendido	habíamos aprendido
aprendías	aprendíais	habías aprendido	habíais aprendido
aprendía	aprendían	había aprendido	habían aprendido
3 pretérito		**10 pretérito anterior**	
aprendí	aprendimos	hube aprendido	hubimos aprendido
aprendiste	aprendisteis	hubiste aprendido	hubisteis aprendido
aprendió	aprendieron	hubo aprendido	hubieron aprendido
4 futuro		**11 futuro perfecto**	
aprenderé	aprenderemos	habré aprendido	habremos aprendido
aprenderás	aprenderéis	habrás aprendido	habréis aprendido
aprenderá	aprenderán	habrá aprendido	habrán aprendido
5 potencial simple		**12 potencial compuesto**	
aprendería	aprenderíamos	habría aprendido	habríamos aprendido
aprenderías	aprenderíais	habrías aprendido	habríais aprendido
aprendería	aprenderían	habría aprendido	habrían aprendido
6 presente de subjuntivo		**13 perfecto de subjuntivo**	
aprenda	aprendamos	haya aprendido	hayamos aprendido
aprendas	aprendáis	hayas aprendido	hayáis aprendido
aprenda	aprendan	haya aprendido	hayan aprendido
7 imperfecto de subjuntivo		**14 pluscuamperfecto de subjuntivo**	
aprendiera	aprendiéramos	hubiera aprendido	hubiéramos aprendido
aprendieras	aprendierais	hubieras aprendido	hubierais aprendido
aprendiera	aprendieran	hubiera aprendido	hubieran aprendido
OR		OR	
aprendiese	aprendiésemos	hubiese aprendido	hubiésemos aprendido
aprendieses	aprendieseis	hubieses aprendido	hubieseis aprendido
aprendiese	aprendiesen	hubiese aprendido	hubiesen aprendido

imperativo	
—	**aprendamos**
aprende; no aprendas	**aprended; no aprendáis**
aprenda	**aprendan**

Sentences using this verb and words and expressions related to it
Aprendo mucho en la escuela. En la clase de español aprendemos a hablar, a leer, y a escribir en español.

el aprendedor, la aprendedora   learner
el aprendizaje   apprenticeship
el aprendiz, la aprendiza   apprentice

aprender a + inf.   to learn + inf.
aprender de memoria   to memorize
aprender con   to study with

The subject pronouns are found on the page facing page 1.

to hasten, to hurry, to rush

The Seven Simple Tenses		The Seven Compound Tenses	
Singular	Plural	Singular	Plural
1 presente de indicativo		8 perfecto de indicativo	
me apresuro	nos apresuramos	me he apresurado	nos hemos apresurado
te apresuras	os apresuráis	te has apresurado	os habéis apresurado
se apresura	se apresuran	se ha apresurado	se han apresurado
2 imperfecto de indicativo		9 pluscuamperfecto de indicativo	
me apresuraba	nos apresurábamos	me había apresurado	nos habíamos apresurado
te apresurabas	os apresurabais	te habías apresurado	os habíais apresurado
se apresuraba	se apresuraban	se había apresurado	se habían apresurado
3 pretérito		10 pretérito anterior	
me apresuré	nos apresuramos	me hube apresurado	nos hubimos apresurado
te apresuraste	os apresurasteis	te hubiste apresurado	os hubisteis apresurado
se apresuró	se apresuraron	se hubo apresurado	se hubieron apresurado
4 futuro		11 futuro perfecto	
me apresuraré	nos apresuraremos	me habré apresurado	nos habremos apresurado
te apresurarás	os apresuraréis	te habrás apresurado	os habréis apresurado
se apresurará	se apresurarán	se habrá apresurado	se habrán apresurado
5 potencial simple		12 potencial compuesto	
me apresuraría	nos apresuraríamos	me habría apresurado	nos habríamos apresurado
te apresurarías	os apresuraríais	te habrías apresurado	os habríais apresurado
se apresuraría	se apresurarían	se habría apresurado	se habrían apresurado
6 presente de subjuntivo		13 perfecto de subjuntivo	
me apresure	nos apresuremos	me haya apresurado	nos hayamos apresurado
te apresures	os apresuréis	te hayas apresurado	os hayáis apresurado
se apresure	se apresuren	se haya apresurado	se hayan apresurado
7 imperfecto de subjuntivo		14 pluscuamperfecto de subjuntivo	
me apresurara	nos apresuráramos	me hubiera apresurado	nos hubiéramos apresurado
te apresuraras	os apresurarais	te hubieras apresurado	os hubierais apresurado
se apresurara	se apresuraran	se hubiera apresurado	se hubieran apresurado
OR		OR	
me apresurase	nos apresurásemos	me hubiese apresurado	nos hubiésemos apresurado
te apresurases	os apresuraseis	te hubieses apresurado	os hubieseis apresurado
se apresurase	se apresurasen	se hubiese apresurado	se hubiesen apresurado

imperativo	
—	apresurémonos
apresúrate; no te apresures	apresuraos; no os apresuréis
apresúrese	apresúrense

Words and expressions related to this verb

la apresuración haste
apresurado, apresurada hasty, quick
apresuradamente hastily
la prisa haste

el apresuramiento hastiness
apresurar to accelerate
apresurarse a + inf. to hurry + inf.
tener prisa to be in a hurry

Get acquainted with what preposition goes with what verb on pages 541–549.

to approve, to pass a test

The Seven Simple Tenses		The Seven Compound Tenses	
Singular	Plural	Singular	Plural
1 presente de indicativo		8 perfecto de indicativo	
apruebo	**aprobamos**	**he aprobado**	**hemos aprobado**
apruebas	**aprobáis**	**has aprobado**	**habéis aprobado**
aprueba	**aprueban**	**ha aprobado**	**han aprobado**
2 imperfecto de indicativo		9 pluscuamperfecto de indicativo	
aprobaba	**aprobábamos**	**había aprobado**	**habíamos aprobado**
aprobabas	**aprobabais**	**habías aprobado**	**habíais aprobado**
aprobaba	**aprobaban**	**había aprobado**	**habían aprobado**
3 pretérito		10 pretérito anterior	
aprobé	**aprobamos**	**hube aprobado**	**hubimos aprobado**
aprobaste	**aprobasteis**	**hubiste aprobado**	**hubisteis aprobado**
aprobó	**aprobaron**	**hubo aprobado**	**hubieron aprobado**
4 futuro		11 futuro perfecto	
aprobaré	**aprobaremos**	**habré aprobado**	**habremos aprobado**
aprobarás	**aprobaréis**	**habrás aprobado**	**habréis aprobado**
aprobará	**aprobarán**	**habrá aprobado**	**habrán aprobado**
5 potencial simple		12 potencial compuesto	
aprobaría	**aprobaríamos**	**habría aprobado**	**habríamos aprobado**
aprobarías	**aprobaríais**	**habrías aprobado**	**habríais aprobado**
aprobaía	**aprobarían**	**habría aprobado**	**habrían aprobado**
6 presente de subjuntivo		13 perfecto de subjuntivo	
apruebe	**aprobemos**	**haya aprobado**	**hayamos aprobado**
apruebes	**aprobéis**	**hayas aprobado**	**hayáis aprobado**
apruebe	**aprueben**	**haya aprobado**	**hayan aprobado**
7 imperfecto de subjuntivo		14 pluscuamperfecto de subjuntivo	
aprobara	**aprobáramos**	**hubiera aprobado**	**hubiéramos aprobado**
aprobaras	**aprobarais**	**hubieras aprobado**	**hubierais aprobado**
aprobara	**aprobaran**	**hubiera aprobado**	**hubieran aprobado**
OR		OR	
aprobase	**aprobásemos**	**hubiese aprobado**	**hubiésemos aprobado**
aprobases	**aprobaseis**	**hubieses aprobado**	**hubieseis aprobado**
aprobase	**aprobasen**	**hubiese aprobado**	**hubiesen aprobado**

imperativo

—	**aprobemos**
aprueba; no apruebes	**aprobad; no aprobéis**
apruebe	**aprueben**

Words and expressions related to this verb
la aprobación   approbation, approval, consent
aprobatoriamente   approvingly
el aprobado   passing grade in an exam
aprobado, aprobada   accepted, admitted, approved, passed (in an exam)
aprobado por mayoría   accepted by a majority
comprobar   to verify, compare, check prove; **desaprobar**   to disapprove
la desaprobación   disapproval

The subject pronouns are found on the page facing page 1.

aprovecharse

Gerundio **aprovechándose**   Part. pas. **aprovechado**

to take advantage, to avail oneself

The Seven Simple Tenses		The Seven Compound Tenses	
Singular	Plural	Singular	Plural

1 presente de indicativo

me aprovecho	nos aprovechamos	
te aprovechas	os aprovecháis	
se aprovecha	se aprovechan	

8 perfecto de indicativo

me he aprovechado	nos hemos aprovechado
te has aprovechado	os habéis aprovechado
se ha aprovechado	se han aprovechado

2 imperfecto de indicativo

me aprovechaba	nos aprovechábamos
te aprovechabas	os aprovechabais
se aprovechaba	se aprovechaban

9 pluscuamperfecto de indicativo

me había aprovechado	nos habíamos aprovechado
te habías aprovechado	os habíais aprovechado
se había aprovechado	se habían aprovechado

3 pretérito

me aproveché	nos aprovechamos
te aprovechaste	os aprovechasteis
se aprovechó	se aprovecharon

10 pretérito anterior

me hube aprovechado	nos hubimos aprovechado
te hubiste aprovechado	os hubisteis aprovechado
se hubo aprovechado	se hubieron aprovechado

4 futuro

me aprovecharé	nos aprovecharemos
te aprovecharás	os aprovecharéis
se aprovechará	se aprovecharán

11 futuro perfecto

me habré aprovechado	nos habremos aprovechado
te habrás aprovechado	os habréis aprovechado
se habrá aprovechado	se habrán aprovechado

5 potencial simple

me aprovecharía	nos aprovecharíamos
te aprovecharías	os aprovecharíais
se aprovecharía	se aprovecharían

12 potencial compuesto

me habría aprovechado	nos habríamos aprovechado
te habrías aprovechado	os habríais aprovechado
se habría aprovechado	se habrían aprovechado

6 presente de subjuntivo

me aproveche	nos aprovechemos
te aproveches	os aprovechéis
se aproveche	se aprovechen

13 perfecto de subjuntivo

me haya aprovechado	nos hayamos aprovechado
te hayas aprovechado	os hayáis aprovechado
se haya aprovechado	se hayan aprovechado

7 imperfecto de subjuntivo

me aprovechara	nos aprovecháramos
te aprovecharas	os aprovecharais
se aprovechara	se aprovecharan
OR	
me aprovechase	nos aprovechásemos
te aprovechases	os aprovechaseis
se aprovechase	se aprovechasen

14 pluscuamperfecto de subjuntivo

me hubiera aprovechado	nos hubiéramos aprovechado
te hubieras aprovechado	os hubierais aprovechado
se hubiera aprovechado	se hubieran aprovechado
OR	
me hubiese aprovechado	nos hubiésemos aprovechado
te hubieses aprovechado	os hubieseis aprovechado
se hubiese aprovechado	se hubiesen aprovechado

imperativo

—	aprovechémonos
aprovéchate; no te aproveches	aprovechaos; no os aprovechéis
aprovéchese	aprovéchense

Words and expressions related to this verb

aprovechado, aprovechada economical
aprovechable available, profitable
aprovechamiento use, utilization
aprovecharse de to take advantage of

aprovechar to make use of
aprovechar la ocasión to take the opportunity
aprovechón, aprovechona opportunist

Want to learn more idiomatic expressions that contain verbs? Check out pages 524–537.

to fret, to grieve, to worry

The Seven Simple Tenses		The Seven Compound Tenses	
Singular	Plural	Singular	Plural
1 presente de indicativo		8 perfecto de indicativo	
me apuro	nos apuramos	me he apurado	nos hemos apurado
te apuras	os apuráis	te has apurado	os habéis apurado
se apura	se apuran	se ha apurado	se han apurado
2 imperfecto de indicativo		9 pluscuamperfecto de indicativo	
me apuraba	nos apurábamos	me había apurado	nos habíamos apurado
te apurabas	os apurabais	te habías apurado	os habíais apurado
se apuraba	se apuraban	se había apurado	se habían apurado
3 pretérito		10 pretérito anterior	
me apuré	nos apuramos	me hube apurado	nos hubimos apurado
te apuraste	os apurasteis	te hubiste apurado	os hubisteis apurado
se apuró	se apuraron	se hubo apurado	se hubieron apurado
4 futuro		11 futuro perfecto	
me apuraré	nos apuraremos	me habré apurado	nos habremos apurado
te apurarás	os apuraréis	te habrás apurado	os habréis apurado
se apurará	se apurarán	se habrá apurado	se habrán apurado
5 potencial simple		12 potencial compuesto	
me apuraría	nos apuraríamos	me habría apurado	nos habríamos apurado
te apurarías	os apuraríais	te habrías apurado	os habríais apurado
se apuraría	se apurarían	se habría apurado	se habrían apurado
6 presente de subjuntivo		13 perfecto de subjuntivo	
me apure	nos apuremos	me haya apurado	nos hayamos apurado
te apures	os apuréis	te hayas apurado	os hayáis apurado
se apure	se apuren	se haya apurado	se hayan apurado
7 imperfecto de subjuntivo		14 pluscuamperfecto de subjuntivo	
me apurara	nos apuráramos	me hubiera apurado	nos hubiéramos apurado
te apuraras	os apurarais	te hubieras apurado	os hubierais apurado
se apurara	se apuraran	se hubiera apurado	se hubieran apurado
OR		OR	
me apurase	nos apurásemos	me hubiese apurado	nos hubiésemos apurado
te apurases	os apuraseis	te hubieses apurado	os hubieseis apurado
se apurase	se apurasen	se hubiese apurado	se hubiesen apurado

imperativo

—	apurémonos
apúrate; no te apures	apuraos; no os apuréis
apúrese	apúrense

Words and expressions related to this verb
apurar   to purify; to exhaust, consume; to annoy, to tease
apurar todos los recursos   to exhaust every recourse, every means
apurar la paciencia de uno   to wear out one's patience
apurarse por poco   to worry over trivialities
el apuro   difficulty, trouble
estar en un apuro   to be in a fix

The subject pronouns are found on the page facing page 1.

to root up (out), to pull up (out), to tear off (away), to snatch,
to start (a motor), to boot up (a computer)

The Seven Simple Tenses		The Seven Compound Tenses	
Singular	Plural	Singular	Plural
1 presente de indicativo		8 perfecto de indicativo	
arranco	arrancamos	he arrancado	hemos arrancado
arrancas	arrancáis	has arrancado	habéis arrancado
arranca	arrancan	ha arrancado	han arrancado
2 imperfecto de indicativo		9 pluscuamperfecto de indicativo	
arrancaba	arrancábamos	había arrancado	habíamos arrancado
arrancabas	arrancabais	habías arrancado	habíais arrancado
arrancaba	arrancaban	había arrancado	habían arrancado
3 pretérito		10 pretérito anterior	
arranqué	arrancamos	hube arrancado	hubimos arrancado
arrancaste	arancasteis	hubiste arrancado	hubisteis arrancado
arrancó	arrancaron	hubo arrancado	hubieron arrancado
4 futuro		11 futuro perfecto	
arrancaré	arrancaremos	habré arrancado	habremos arrancado
arrancarás	arancaréis	habrás arrancado	habréis arrancado
arrancará	arrancarán	habrá arrancado	habrán arrancado
5 potencial simple		12 potencial compuesto	
arrancaría	arrancaríamos	habría arrancado	habríamos arrancado
arrancarías	arrancaríais	habrías arrancado	habríais arrancado
arrancaría	arancarían	habría arrancado	habrían arrancado
6 presente de subjuntivo		13 perfecto de subjuntivo	
arranque	arranquemos	haya arrancado	hayamos arrancado
arranques	arranquéis	hayas arrancado	hayáis arrancado
arranque	arranquen	haya arrancado	hayan arrancado
7 imperfecto de subjuntivo		14 pluscuamperfecto de subjuntivo	
arrancara	arrancáramos	hubiera arrancado	hubiéramos arrancado
arrancaras	arrancarais	hubieras arrancado	hubierais arrancado
arrancara	arancaran	hubiera arrancado	hubieran arrancado
OR		OR	
arrancase	arrancásemos	hubiese arrancado	hubiésemos arrancado
arrancases	arrancaseis	hubieses arrancado	hubieseis arrancado
arrancase	arrancasen	hubiese arrancado	hubiesen arrancado

imperativo

—	arranquemos
arranca; no arranques	arrancad; no arranquéis
arranque	arranquen

Words and expressions related to this verb
un arrancarraíces tool to pull out roots
arrancar a to snatch away from
arrancar de raíz to cut up, to pull out by the root

una arrancadora tool for pulling out
la arrancadura extraction
el arrancador starter (engine)

If you don't know the Spanish verb for the English verb you have
in mind, look it up in the index on pages 505–518.

to fix, to arrange, to adjust, to regulate, to settle, to repair

The Seven Simple Tenses		The Seven Compound Tenses	
Singular	Plural	Singular	Plural
1 presente de indicativo		8 perfecto de indicativo	
arreglo	arreglamos	he arreglado	hemos arreglado
arreglas	arregláis	has arreglado	habéis arreglado
arregla	arreglan	ha arreglado	han arreglado
2 imperfecto de indicativo		9 pluscuamperfecto de indicativo	
arreglaba	arreglábamos	había arreglado	habíamos arreglado
arreglabas	arreglabais	habías arreglado	habíais arreglado
arreglaba	arreglaban	había arreglado	habían arreglado
3 pretérito		10 pretérito anterior	
arreglé	arreglamos	hube arreglado	hubimos arreglado
arreglaste	arreglasteis	hubiste arreglado	hubisteis arreglado
arregló	arreglaron	hubo arreglado	hubieron arreglado
4 futuro		11 futuro perfecto	
arreglaré	arreglaremos	habré arreglado	habremos arreglado
arreglarás	arrelgaréis	habrás arreglado	habréis arreglado
arreglará	arreglarán	habrá arreglado	habrán arreglado
5 potencial simple		12 potencial compuesto	
arreglaría	arreglaríamos	habría arreglado	habríamos arreglado
arreglarías	arreglaríais	habrías arreglado	habríais arreglado
arreglaría	arreglarían	habría arreglado	habrían arreglado
6 presente de subjuntivo		13 perfecto de subjuntivo	
arregle	arreglemos	haya arreglado	hayamos arreglado
arregles	arregléis	hayas arreglado	hayáis arreglado
arregle	arreglen	haya arreglado	hayan arreglado
7 imperfecto de subjuntivo		14 pluscuamperfecto de subjuntivo	
arreglara	arregláramos	hubiera arreglado	hubiéramos arreglado
arreglaras	arreglarais	hubieras arreglado	hubierais arreglado
arreglara	arreglaran	hubiera arreglado	hubieran arreglado
OR		OR	
arreglase	arreglásemos	hubiese arreglado	hubiésemos arreglado
arreglases	arreglaseis	hubieses arreglado	hubieseis arreglado
arreglase	arreglasen	hubiese arreglado	hubiesen arreglado

imperativo

—	arreglemos
arregla; no arregles	arreglad; no arregléis
arregle	arreglen

Words and expressions related to this verb

arregladamente regularly
arreglarse con to settle with, to reach an agreement with
arreglarse por las buenas to settle a matter in a friendly way

arreglar una factura to pay a bill
con arreglo a according to
un reglamento rule, regulation
un arreglo agreement, solution
arreglado, arreglada neat, orderly
arreglar una cuenta to settle an account

to fling, to hurl, to throw

The Seven Simple Tenses		The Seven Compound Tenses	
Singular	Plural	Singular	Plural
1 presente de indicativo		8 perfecto de indicativo	
arrojo	arrojamos	he arrojado	hemos arrojado
arrojas	arrojáis	has arrojado	habéis arrojado
arroja	arrojan	ha arrojado	han arrojado
2 imperfecto de indicativo		9 pluscuamperfecto de indicativo	
arrojaba	arrojábamos	había arrojado	habíamos arrojado
arrojabas	arrojabais	habías arrojado	habíais arrojado
arrojaba	arrojaban	había arrojado	habían arrojado
3 pretérito		10 pretérito anterior	
arrojé	arrojamos	hube arrojado	hubimos arrojado
arrojaste	arrojasteis	hubiste arrojado	hubisteis arrojado
arrojó	arrojaron	hubo arrojado	hubieron arrojado
4 futuro		11 futuro perfecto	
arrojaré	arrojaremos	habré arrojado	habremos arrojado
arrojarás	arrojaréis	habrás arrojado	habréis arrojado
arrojará	arrojarán	habrá arrojado	habrán arrojado
5 potencial simple		12 potencial compuesto	
arrojaría	arrojaríamos	habría arrojado	habríamos arrojado
arrojarías	arrojaríais	habrías arrojado	habríais arrojado
arrojaría	arrojarían	habría arrojado	habrían arrojado
6 presente de subjuntivo		13 perfecto de subjuntivo	
arroje	arrojemos	haya arrojado	hayamos arrojado
arrojes	arrojéis	hayas arrojado	hayáis arrojado
arroje	arrojen	haya arrojado	hayan arrojado
7 imperfecto de subjuntivo		14 pluscuamperfecto de subjuntivo	
arrojara	arrojáramos	hubiera arrojado	hubiéramos arrojado
arrojaras	arrojarais	hubieras arrojado	hubierais arrojado
arrojara	arrojaran	hubiera arrojado	hubieran arrojado
OR		OR	
arrojase	arrojásemos	hubiese arrojado	hubiésemos arrojado
arrojases	arrojaseis	hubieses arrojado	hubieseis arrojado
arrojase	arrojasen	hubiese arrojado	hubiesen arrojado

	imperativo	
—		arrojemos
arroja; no arrojes		arrojad; no arrojéis
arroje		arrojen

Words and expressions related to this verb
el arrojador, la arrojadora thrower
arrojado, arrojada fearless
el arrojo fearlessness

arrojar la esponja to throw in the towel
 (sponge)
el arrojallamas flame thrower
 (also **el lanzallamas**)

See also **lanzar.**

> If you want an explanation of meanings and uses of Spanish and English verb tenses and moods, see pages xx–xl.

to articulate, to pronounce distinctly

The Seven Simple Tenses		The Seven Compound Tenses	
Singular	Plural	Singular	Plural
1 presente de indicativo		**8 perfecto de indicativo**	
articulo	articulamos	he articulado	hemos articulado
articulas	articuláis	has articulado	habéis articulado
articula	articulan	ha articulado	han articulado
2 imperfecto de indicativo		**9 pluscuamperfecto de indicativo**	
articulaba	articulábamos	había articulado	habíamos articulado
articulabas	articulabais	habías articulado	habíais articulado
articulaba	articulaban	había articulado	habían articulado
3 pretérito		**10 pretérito anterior**	
articulé	articulamos	hube articulado	hubimos articulado
articulaste	articulasteis	hubiste articulado	hubisteis articulado
articuló	articularon	hubo articulado	hubieron articulado
4 futuro		**11 futuro perfecto**	
articularé	articularemos	habré articulado	habremos articulado
articularás	articularéis	habrás articulado	habréis articulado
articulará	articularán	habrá articulado	habrán articulado
5 potencial simple		**12 potencial compuesto**	
articularía	artricularíamos	habría articulado	habríamos articulado
articularías	articularíais	habrías articulado	habríais articulado
articularía	articularían	habría articulado	habrían articulado
6 presente de subjuntivo		**13 perfecto de subjuntivo**	
articule	articulemos	haya articulado	hayamos articulado
articules	articuléis	hayas articulado	hayáis articulado
articule	articulen	haya articulado	hayan articulado
7 imperfecto de subjuntivo		**14 pluscuamperfecto de subjuntivo**	
articulara	articuláramos	hubiera articulado	hubiéramos articulado
articularas	articularais	hubieras articulado	hubierais articulado
articulara	articularan	hubiera articulado	hubieran articulado
OR		OR	
articulase	articulásemos	hubiese articulado	hubiésemos articulado
articulases	articulaseis	hubieses articulado	hubieseis articulado
articulase	articulasen	hubiese articulado	hubiesen articulado

imperativo

—	articulemos
articula; no articules	articulad; no articuléis
articule	articulen

Words related to this verb
articuladamente clearly, distinctly
la articulación articulation, pronunciation
el, la articulista someone who writes articles

articular claramente   to articulate clearly
articular (expresar) las emociones claramente
to express emotions clearly

Consult the back pages for over 1,100 verbs conjugated like model verbs among the 501 in this book.

The subject pronouns are found on the page facing page 1.   **71**

asegurar

Gerundio **asegurando**   Part. pas. **asegurado**

to assure, to affirm, to assert, to insure

The Seven Simple Tenses		The Seven Compound Tenses	
Singular	Plural	Singular	Plural
1 presente de indicativo		**8 perfecto de indicativo**	
aseguro	aseguramos	he asegurado	hemos asegurado
aseguras	aseguráis	has asegurado	habéis asegurado
asegura	aseguran	ha asegurado	han asegurado
2 imperfecto de indicativo		**9 pluscuamperfecto de indicativo**	
aseguraba	asegurábamos	había asegurado	habíamos asegurado
asegurabas	asegurabais	habías asegurado	habíais asegurado
aseguraba	aseguraban	había asegurado	habían asegurado
3 pretérito		**10 pretérito anterior**	
aseguré	aseguramos	hube asegurado	hubimos asegurado
aseguraste	asegurasteis	hubiste asegurado	hubisteis asegurado
aseguró	aseguraron	hubo asegurado	hubieron asegurado
4 futuro		**11 futuro perfecto**	
aseguraré	aseguraremos	habré asegurado	habremos asegurado
asegurarás	aseguraréis	habrás asegurado	habréis asegurado
asegurará	asegurarán	habrá asegurado	habrán asegurado
5 potencial simple		**12 potencial compuesto**	
aseguraría	aseguraríamos	habría asegurado	habríamos asegurado
asegurarías	aseguraríais	habrías asegurado	habríais asegurado
aseguraría	asegurarían	habría asegurado	habrían asegurado
6 presente de subjuntivo		**13 perfecto de subjuntivo**	
asegure	aseguremos	haya asegurado	hayamos asegurado
asegures	aseguréis	hayas asegurado	hayáis asegurado
asegure	aseguren	haya asegurado	hayan asegurado
7 imperfecto de subjuntivo		**14 pluscuamperfecto de subjuntivo**	
asegurara	aseguráramos	hubiera asegurado	hubiéramos asegurado
aseguraras	asegurarais	hubieras asegurado	hubierais asegurado
asegurara	aseguraran	hubiera asegurado	hubieran asegurado
OR		OR	
asegurase	asegurásemos	hubiese asegurado	hubiésemos asegurado
asegurases	aseguraseis	hubieses asegurado	hubieseis asegurado
asegurase	asegurasen	hubiese asegurado	hubiesen asegurado

imperativo		
—	aseguremos	
asegura; no asegures	asegurad; no aseguréis	
asegure	aseguren	

Words and expressions related to this verb

la aseguración   insurance
asegurable   insurable
el asegurado, la asegurada   insured person
la seguridad   security, surety
seguramente   surely, securely

¡Ya puede usted asegurarlo!   You can
   be sure of it!
tener por seguro   for sure
de seguro   surely
el asegurador contra incendios   fire insurance
   underwriter

to seize, to grasp

The Seven Simple Tenses		The Seven Compound Tenses	
Singular	Plural	Singular	Plural
1 presente de indicativo		8 perfecto de indicativo	
asgo	**asimos**	**he asido**	**hemos asido**
ases	**asís**	**has asido**	**habéis asido**
ase	**asen**	**ha asido**	**han asido**
2 imperfecto de indicativo		9 pluscuamperfecto de indicativo	
asía	**asíamos**	**había asido**	**habíamos asido**
asías	**asíais**	**habías asido**	**habíais asido**
asía	**asían**	**había asido**	**habían asido**
3 pretérito		10 pretérito anterior	
así	**asimos**	**hube asido**	**hubimos asido**
asiste	**asisteis**	**hubiste asido**	**hubisteis asido**
asió	**asieron**	**hubo asido**	**hubieron asido**
4 futuro		11 futuro perfecto	
asiré	**asiremos**	**habré asido**	**habremos asido**
asirás	**asiréis**	**habrás asido**	**habréis asido**
asirá	**asirán**	**habrá asido**	**habrán asido**
5 potencial simple		12 potencial compuesto	
asiría	**asiríamos**	**habría asido**	**habríamos asido**
asirías	**asiríais**	**habrías asido**	**habríais asido**
asiría	**asirían**	**habría asido**	**habrían asido**
6 presente de subjuntivo		13 perfecto de subjuntivo	
asga	**asgamos**	**haya asido**	**hayamos asido**
asgas	**asgáis**	**hayas asido**	**hayáis asido**
asga	**asgan**	**haya asido**	**hayan asido**
7 imperfecto de subjuntivo		14 pluscuamperfecto de subjuntivo	
asiera	**asiéramos**	**hubiera asido**	**hubiéramos asido**
asieras	**asierais**	**hubieras asido**	**hubierais asido**
asiera	**asieran**	**hubiera asido**	**hubieran asido**
OR		OR	
asiese	**asiésemos**	**hubiese asido**	**hubiésemos asido**
asieses	**asieseis**	**hubieses asido**	**hubieseis asido**
asiese	**asiesen**	**hubiese asido**	**hubiesen asido**

	imperativo	
—		**asgamos**
ase; no asgas		**asid; no asgáis**
asga		**asgan**

Words and expressions related to this verb
asir de los cabellos   to grab by the hair
asirse a (or **de**)   to take hold of, to seize, grab
asirse con   to grapple with

asirse   to quarrel with each other
asir del brazo   to get hold of by the arm
asidos del brazo   arm in arm

Consult the sections on verbs used in idiomatic expressions, verbs with prepositions, and the list of over 1,100 verbs conjugated like model verbs in the back pages.

to attend, to assist, to be present

The Seven Simple Tenses		The Seven Compound Tenses	
Singular	Plural	Singular	Plural
1 presente de indicativo		8 perfecto de indicativo	
asisto	**asistimos**	**he asistido**	**hemos asistido**
asistes	**asistís**	**has asistido**	**habéis asistido**
asiste	**asisten**	**ha asistido**	**han asistido**
2 imperfecto de indicativo		9 pluscuamperfecto de indicativo	
asistía	**asistíamos**	**había asistido**	**habíamos asistido**
asistías	**asistíais**	**habías asistido**	**habíais asistido**
asistía	**asistían**	**había asistido**	**habían asistido**
3 pretérito		10 pretérito anterior	
asistí	**asistimos**	**hube asistido**	**hubimos asistido**
asististe	**asististeis**	**hubiste asistido**	**hubisteis asistido**
asistió	**asistieron**	**hubo asistido**	**hubieron asistido**
4 futuro		11 futuro perfecto	
asistiré	**asistiremos**	**habré asistido**	**habremos asistido**
asistirás	**asistiréis**	**habrás asistido**	**habréis asistido**
asistirá	**asistirán**	**habrá asistido**	**habrán asistido**
5 potencial simple		12 potencial compuesto	
asistiría	**asistiríamos**	**habría asistido**	**habríamos asistido**
asistirías	**asistiríais**	**habrías asistido**	**habríais asistido**
asistiría	**asistirían**	**habría asistido**	**habrían asistido**
6 presente de subjuntivo		13 perfecto de subjuntivo	
asista	**asistamos**	**haya asistido**	**hayamos asistido**
asistas	**asistáis**	**hayas asistido**	**hayáis asistido**
asista	**asistan**	**haya asistido**	**hayan asistido**
7 imperfecto de subjuntivo		14 pluscuamperfecto de subjuntivo	
asistiera	**asistiéramos**	**hubiera asistido**	**hubiéramos asistido**
asistieras	**asistierais**	**hubieras asistido**	**hubierais asistido**
asistiera	**asistieran**	**hubiera asistido**	**hubieran asistido**
OR		OR	
asistiese	**asistiésemos**	**hubiese asistido**	**hubiésemos asistido**
asistieses	**asistieseis**	**hubieses asistido**	**hubieseis asistido**
asistiese	**asistiesen**	**hubiese asistido**	**hubiesen asistido**

imperativo

—	**asistamos**
asiste; no asistas	**asistid; no asistáis**
asista	**asistan**

Words and expressions related to this verb
asistir a to attend, to be present at
la asistencia attendance, presence

la asistencia social social welfare
la asistencia técnica technical assistance

Don't miss the definitions of basic grammatical terms with examples
in English and Spanish on pages 666–677.

to be frightened, to be scared

The Seven Simple Tenses		The Seven Compound Tenses	
Singular	Plural	Singular	Plural
1 presente de indicativo		8 perfecto de indicativo	
me asusto	nos asustamos	me he asustado	nos hemos asustado
te asustas	os asustáis	te has asustado	os habéis asustado
se asusta	se asustan	se ha asustado	se han asustado
2 imperfecto de indicativo		9 pluscuamperfecto de indicativo	
me asustaba	nos asustábamos	me había asustado	nos habíamos asustado
te asustabas	os asustabais	te habías asustado	os habíais asustado
se asustaba	se asustaban	se había asustado	se habían asustado
3 pretérito		10 pretérito anterior	
me asusté	nos asustamos	me hube asustado	nos hubimos asustado
te asustaste	os asustasteis	te hubiste asustado	os hubisteis asustado
se asustó	se asustaron	se hubo asustado	se hubieron asustado
4 futuro		11 futuro perfecto	
me asustaré	nos asustaremos	me habré asustado	nos habremos asustado
te asustarás	os asustaréis	te habrás asustado	os habréis asustado
se asustará	se asustarán	se habrá asustado	se habrán asustado
5 potencial simple		12 potencial compuesto	
me asustaría	nos asustaríamos	me habría asustado	nos habríamos asustado
te asustarías	os asustaríais	te habrías asustado	os habríais asustado
se asustaría	se asustarían	se habría asustado	se habrían asustado
6 presente de subjuntivo		13 perfecto de subjuntivo	
me asuste	nos asustemos	me haya asustado	nos hayamos asustado
te asustes	os asustéis	te hayas asustado	os hayáis asustado
se asuste	se asusten	se haya asustado	se hayan asustado
7 imperfecto de subjuntivo		14 pluscuamperfecto de subjuntivo	
me asustara	nos asustáramos	me hubiera asustado	nos hubiéramos asustado
te asustaras	os asustarais	te hubieras asustado	os hubierais asustado
se asustara	se asustaran	se hubiera asustado	se hubieran asustado
OR		OR	
me asustase	nos asustásemos	me hubiese asustado	nos hubiésemos asustado
te asustases	os asustaseis	te hubieses asustado	os hubieseis asustado
se asustase	se asustasen	se hubiese asustado	se hubiesen asustado

imperativo

—	asustémonos
asústate; no te asustes	asustaos; no os asustéis
asústese	asústense

Words and expressions related to this verb
asustado, asustada   frightened, scared
asustadizo, asustadiza   easily frightened
asustador, asustadora   frightening
asustar   to frighten, to scare
Me asusto de pensarlo.   It frightens me
to think about it.
un susto   a fright, scare

asustarse de + inf.   to be afraid + inf.
asustarse por nada   to be frightened by the
slightest thing

Get acquainted with what preposition goes
with what verb on pages 541–549.

The subject pronouns are found on the page facing page 1.

to attack

The Seven Simple Tenses		The Seven Compound Tenses	
Singular	Plural	Singular	Plural
1 presente de indicativo		8 perfecto de indicativo	
ataco	**atacamos**	**he atacado**	**hemos atacado**
atacas	**atacáis**	**has atacado**	**habéis atacado**
ataca	**atacan**	**ha atacado**	**han atacado**
2 imperfecto de indicativo		9 pluscuamperfecto de indicativo	
atacaba	**atacábamos**	**había atacado**	**habíamos atacado**
atacabas	**atacabais**	**habías atacado**	**habíais atacado**
atacaba	**atacaban**	**había atacado**	**habían atacado**
3 pretérito		10 pretérito anterior	
ataqué	**atacamos**	**hube atacado**	**hubimos atacado**
atacaste	**atacasteis**	**hubiste atacado**	**hubisteis atacado**
atacó	**atacaron**	**hubo atacado**	**hubieron atacado**
4 futuro		11 futuro perfecto	
atacaré	**atacaremos**	**habré atacado**	**habremos atacado**
atacarás	**atacaréis**	**habrás atacado**	**habréis atacado**
atacará	**atacarán**	**habrá atacado**	**habrán atacado**
5 potencial simple		12 potencial compuesto	
atacaría	**atacaríamos**	**habría atacado**	**habríamos atacado**
atacarías	**atacaríais**	**habrías atacado**	**habríais atacado**
atacaría	**atacarían**	**habría atacado**	**habrían atacado**
6 presente de subjuntivo		13 perfecto de subjuntivo	
ataque	**ataquemos**	**haya atacado**	**hayamos atacado**
ataques	**ataquéis**	**hayas atacado**	**hayáis atacado**
ataque	**ataquen**	**haya atacado**	**hayan atacado**
7 imperfecto de subjuntivo		14 pluscuamperfecto de subjuntivo	
atacara	**atacáramos**	**hubiera atacado**	**hubiéramos atacado**
atacaras	**atacarais**	**hubieras atacado**	**hubierais atacado**
atacara	**atacaran**	**hubiera atacado**	**hubieran atacado**
OR		OR	
atacase	**atacásemos**	**hubiese atacado**	**hubiésemos atacado**
atacases	**atacaseis**	**hubieses atacado**	**hubieseis atacado**
atacase	**atacasen**	**hubiese atacado**	**hubiesen atacado**

imperativo

—	**ataquemos**
ataca; no ataques	**atacad; no ataquéis**
ataque	**ataquen**

Words related to this verb
el ataque attack   **el, la atacante** attacker
atacado, atacada attacked   **el atacador, la atacadora** aggressor

Check out the verb drills and verb tests with answers explained on pages 619–665.

to rely on, to depend on

The Seven Simple Tenses		The Seven Compound Tenses	
Singular	Plural	Singular	Plural
1 presente de indicativo		8 perfecto de indicativo	
me atengo	**nos atenemos**	**me he atenido**	**nos hemos atenido**
te atienes	**os atenéis**	**te has atenido**	**os habéis atenido**
se atiene	**se atienen**	**se ha atenido**	**se han atenido**
2 imperfecto de indicativo		9 pluscuamperfecto de indicativo	
me atenía	**nos ateníamos**	**me había atenido**	**nos habíamos atenido**
te atenías	**os ateníais**	**te habías atenido**	**os habíais atenido**
se atenía	**se atenían**	**se había atenido**	**se habían atenido**
3 pretérito		10 pretérito anterior	
me atuve	**nos atuvimos**	**me hube atenido**	**nos hubimos atenido**
te atuviste	**os atuvisteis**	**te hubiste atenido**	**os hubisteis atenido**
se atuvo	**se atuvieron**	**se hubo atenido**	**se hubieron atenido**
4 futuro		11 futuro perfecto	
me atendré	**nos atendremos**	**me habré atenido**	**nos habremos atenido**
te atendrás	**os atendréis**	**te habrás atenido**	**os habréis atenido**
se atendrá	**se atendrán**	**se habrá atenido**	**se habrán atenido**
5 potencial simple		12 potencial compuesto	
me atendría	**nos atendríamos**	**me habría atenido**	**nos habríamos atenido**
te atendrías	**os atendríais**	**te habrías atenido**	**os habríais atenido**
se atendría	**se atendrían**	**se habría atenido**	**se habrían atenido**
6 presente de subjuntivo		13 perfecto de subjuntivo	
me atenga	**nos atengamos**	**me haya atenido**	**nos hayamos atenido**
te antengas	**os atengáis**	**te hayas atenido**	**os hayáis atenido**
se atenga	**se atengan**	**se haya atenido**	**se hayan atenido**
7 imperfecto de subjuntivo		14 pluscuamperfecto de subjuntivo	
me atuviera	**nos atuviéramos**	**me hubiera atenido**	**nos hubiéramos atenido**
te atuvieras	**os atuvierais**	**te hubieras atenido**	**os hubierais atenido**
se atuviera	**se atuvieran**	**se hubiera atenido**	**se hubieran atenido**
OR		OR	
me atuviese	**nos atuviésemos**	**me hubiese atenido**	**nos hubiésemos atenido**
te atuvieses	**os atuvieseis**	**te hubieses atenido**	**os hubieseis atenido**
se atuviese	**se atuviesen**	**se hubiese atenido**	**se hubiesen atenido**

imperativo	
—	**atengámonos**
atente; no te atengas	**ateneos; no os atengáis**
aténgase	**aténganse**

Words and expressions related to this verb

mantener	to maintain	**atenerse al convenio**	to abide by the agreement
atenerse a	to depend on, to rely on	**atenerse a las reglas**	to abide by the rules

---

Be sure to consult the back pages for sections on verbs used in idiomatic expressions, verbs with prepositions, and the list of over 1,100 verbs conjugated like model verbs.

The subject pronouns are found on the page facing page 1.

atraer

to attract, to allure, to charm

The Seven Simple Tenses		The Seven Compound Tenses	
Singular	Plural	Singular	Plural
1 presente de indicativo		**8 perfecto de indicativo**	
atraigo	atraemos	he atraído	hemos atraído
atraes	atraéis	has atraído	habéis atraído
atrae	atraen	ha atraído	han atraído
2 imperfecto de indicativo		**9 pluscuamperfecto de indicativo**	
atraía	atraíamos	había atraído	habíamos atraído
atraías	atraíais	habías atraído	habíais atraído
atraía	atraían	había atraído	habían atraído
3 pretérito		**10 pretérito anterior**	
atraje	atrajimos	hube atraído	hubimos atraído
atrajiste	atrajisteis	hubiste atraído	hubisteis atraído
atrajo	atrajeron	hubo atraído	hubieron atraído
4 futuro		**11 futuro perfecto**	
atraeré	atraeremos	habré atraído	habremos atraído
atraerás	atraeréis	habrás atraído	habréis atraído
atraerá	atraerán	habrá atraído	habrán atraído
5 potencial simple		**12 potencial compuesto**	
atraería	atraeríamos	habría atraído	habríamos atraído
atraerías	atraeríais	habrías atraído	habríais atraído
atraería	atraerían	habría atraído	habrían atraído
6 presente de subjuntivo		**13 perfecto de subjuntivo**	
atraiga	atraigamos	haya atraído	hayamos atraído
atraigas	atraigáis	hayas atraído	hayáis atraído
atraiga	atraigan	haya atraído	hayan atraído
7 imperfecto de subjuntivo		**14 pluscuamperfecto de subjuntivo**	
atrajera	atrajéramos	hubiera atraído	hubiéramos atraído
atrajeras	atrajerais	hubieras atraído	hubierais atraído
atrajera	atrajeran	hubiera atraído	hubieran atraído
OR		OR	
atrajese	atrajésemos	hubiese atraído	hubiésemos atraído
atrajeses	atrajeseis	hubieses atraído	hubieseis atraído
atrajese	atrajesen	hubiese atraído	hubiesen atraído

imperativo

—	**atraigamos**
atrae; no atraigas	**atraed; no atraigáis**
atraiga	**atraigan**

Words and expressions related to this verb

la atracción attraction; **atracción sexual**
  sex appeal; **las atracciones** entertainment
atractivamente attractively
atractivo, atractiva attractive

atrayentemente attractively
atrayente appealing, attractive
el parque de atracciones amusement park
atraer las miradas to attract attention

Learn more verbs in 30 practical situations for tourists on pages 564–594.

to cross, to go through, to run through

The Seven Simple Tenses		The Seven Compound Tenses	
Singular	Plural	Singular	Plural
1 presente de indicativo		8 perfecto de indicativo	
atravieso	atravesamos	he atravesado	hemos atravesado
atraviesas	atravesáis	has atravesado	habéis atravesado
atraviesa	atraviesan	ha atravesado	han atravesado
2 imperfecto de indicativo		9 pluscuamperfecto de indicativo	
atravesaba	atravesábamos	había atravesado	habíamos atravesado
atravesabas	atravesabais	habías atravesado	habíais atravesado
atravesaba	atravesaban	había atravesado	habían atravesado
3 pretérito		10 pretérito anterior	
atravesé	atravesamos	hube atravesado	hubimos atravesado
atravesaste	atravesasteis	hubiste atravesado	hubisteis atravesado
atravesó	atravesaron	hubo atravesado	hubieron atravesado
4 futuro		11 futuro perfecto	
atravesaré	atravesaremos	habré atravesado	habremos atravesado
atravesarás	atravesaréis	habrás atravesado	habréis atravesado
atravesará	atravesarán	habrá atravesado	habrán atravesado
5 potencial simple		12 potencial compuesto	
atravesaría	atravesaríamos	habría atravesado	habríamos atravesado
atravesarías	atravesaríais	habrías atravesado	habríais atravesado
atravesaría	atravesarían	habría atravesado	habrían atravesado
6 presente de subjuntivo		13 perfecto de subjuntivo	
atraviese	atravesemos	haya atravesado	hayamos atravesado
atravieses	atraveséis	hayas atravesado	hayáis atravesado
atraviese	atraviesen	haya atravesado	hayan atravesado
7 imperfecto de subjuntivo		14 pluscuamperfecto de subjuntivo	
atravesara	atravesáramos	hubiera atravesado	hubiéramos atravesado
atravesaras	atravesarais	hubieras atravesado	hubierais atravesado
atravesara	atravesaran	hubiera atravesado	hubieran atravesado
OR		OR	
atravesase	atravesásemos	hubiese atravesado	hubiésemos atravesado
atravesases	atravesaseis	hubieses atravesado	hubieseis atravesado
atravesase	atravesasen	hubiese atravesado	hubiesen atravesado

imperativo

—	atravesemos
atraviesa; no atravieses	**atravesad; no atraveséis**
atraviese	**atraviesen**

Words and expressions related to this verb

atravesar con   to meet
travesar   to cross
mirar de través   to look out of the corner
   of one's eye

la travesía   crossing (sea), voyage
atravesado, atravesada   cross-eyed
atravesable   traversable
a través de   across, through

Increase your verb power with popular phrases,
words, and expressions for tourists on pages 595–618.

79

to dare, to venture

The Seven Simple Tenses		The Seven Compound Tenses	
Singular	Plural	Singular	Plural
1 presente de indicativo		8 perfecto de indicativo	
me atrevo	**nos atrevemos**	**me he atrevido**	**nos hemos atrevido**
te atreves	**os atrevéis**	**te has atrevido**	**os habéis atrevido**
se atreve	**se atreven**	**se ha atrevido**	**se han atrevido**
2 imperfecto de indicativo		9 pluscuamperfecto de indicativo	
me atrevía	**nos atrevíamos**	**me había atrevido**	**nos habíamos atrevido**
te atrevías	**os atrevíais**	**te habías atrevido**	**os habíais atrevido**
se atrevía	**se atrevían**	**se había atrevido**	**se habían atrevido**
3 pretérito		10 pretérito anterior	
me atreví	**nos atrevimos**	**me hube atrevido**	**nos hubimos atrevido**
te atreviste	**os atrevisteis**	**te hubiste atrevido**	**os hubisteis atrevido**
se atrevió	**se atrevieron**	**se hubo atrevido**	**se hubieron atrevido**
4 futuro		11 futuro perfecto	
me atreveré	**nos atreveremos**	**me habré atrevido**	**nos habremos atrevido**
te atreverás	**os atreveréis**	**te habrás atrevido**	**os habréis atrevido**
se atreverá	**se atreverán**	**se habrá atrevido**	**se habrán atrevido**
5 potencial simple		12 potencial compuesto	
me atrevería	**nos atreveríamos**	**me habría atrevido**	**nos habríamos atrevido**
te atreverías	**os atreveríais**	**te habrías atrevido**	**os habríais atrevido**
se atrevería	**se atreverían**	**se habría atrevido**	**se habrían atrevido**
6 presente de subjuntivo		13 perfecto de subjuntivo	
me atreva	**nos atrevamos**	**me haya atrevido**	**nos hayamos atrevido**
te atrevas	**os atreváis**	**te hayas atrevido**	**os hayáis atrevido**
se atreva	**se atrevan**	**se haya atrevido**	**se hayan atrevido**
7 imperfecto de subjuntivo		14 pluscuamperfecto de subjuntivo	
me atreviera	**nos atreviéramos**	**me hubiera atrevido**	**nos hubiéramos atrevido**
te atrevieras	**os atrevierais**	**te hubieras atrevido**	**os hubierais atrevido**
se atreviera	**se atrevieran**	**se hubiera atrevido**	**se hubieran atrevido**
OR		OR	
me atreviese	**nos atreviésemos**	**me hubiese atrevido**	**nos hubiésemos atrevido**
te atrevieses	**os atrevieseis**	**te hubieses atrevido**	**os hubieseis atrevido**
se atreviese	**se atreviesen**	**se hubiese atrevido**	**se hubiesen atrevido**

imperativo	
—	**atrevámonos**
atrévete; no te atrevas	**atreveos; no os atreváis**
atrévase	**atrévanse**

Words and expressions related to this verb

atrevido, atrevida daring, bold
el atrevimiento audacity, boldness
atrevidamente boldly, daringly
atreverse con *or* **contra** to be insolent to,
  to be offensive toward

¡Atrévete! You just dare!
Hazlo si te atreves. Do it if you dare.
atreverse a decir mentiras to dare to tell lies

Use the EE-zee guide to Spanish
pronunciation on pages 562–563.

The Seven Simple Tenses		The Seven Compound Tenses	
Singular	Plural	Singular	Plural

1 presente de indicativo

		8 perfecto de indicativo	
avanzo	avanzamos	he avanzado	hemos avanzado
avanzas	avanzáis	has avanzado	habéis avanzado
avanza	avanzan	ha avanzado	han avanzado

2 imperfecto de indicativo

		9 pluscuamperfecto de indicativo	
avanzaba	avanzábamos	había avanzado	habíamos avanzado
avanzabas	avanzabais	habías avanzado	habíais avanzado
avanzaba	avanzaban	había avanzado	habían avanzado

3 pretérito

		10 pretérito anterior	
avancé	avanzamos	hube avanzado	hubimos avanzado
avanzaste	avanzasteis	hubiste avanzado	hubisteis avanzado
avanzó	avanzaron	hubo avanzado	hubieron avanzado

4 futuro

		11 futuro perfecto	
avanzaré	avanzaremos	habré avanzado	habremos avanzado
avanzarás	avanzaréis	habrás avanzado	habréis avanzado
avanzará	avanzarán	habrá avanzado	habrán avanzado

5 potencial simple

		12 potencial compuesto	
avanzaría	avanzaríamos	habría avanzado	habríamos avanzado
avanzarías	avanzaríais	habrías avanzado	habríais avanzado
avanzaría	avanzarían	habría avanzado	habrían avanzado

6 presente de subjuntivo

		13 perfecto de subjuntivo	
avance	avancemos	haya avanzado	hayamos avanzado
avances	avancéis	hayas avanzado	hayáis avanzado
avance	avancen	haya avanzado	hayan avanzado

7 imperfecto de subjuntivo

		14 pluscuamperfecto de subjuntivo	
avanzara	avanzáramos	hubiera avanzado	hubiéramos avanzado
avanzaras	avanzarais	hubieras avanzado	hubierais avanzado
avanzara	avanzaran	hubiera avanzado	hubieran avanzado
OR		OR	
avanzase	avanzásemos	hubiese avanzado	hubiésemos avanzado
avanzases	avanzaseis	hubieses avanzado	hubieseis avanzado
avanzase	avanzasen	hubiese avanzado	hubiesen avanzado

imperativo

—	avancemos
avanza; no avances	avanzad; no avancéis
avance	avancen

Words and expressions related to this verb

avanzado, avanzada   advanced; **de edad avanzada**   advanced in years

la avanzada   advance guard, **los avances tecnológicos**   technological advances

If you don't know the Spanish verb for the English verb you have in mind,
look it up in the index on pages 505–518.

The subject pronouns are found on the page facing page 1.

to find out, to inquire, to investigate

The Seven Simple Tenses		The Seven Compound Tenses	
Singular	Plural	Singular	Plural
1 presente de indicativo		**8 perfecto de indicativo**	
averiguo	averiguamos	he averiguado	hemos averiguado
averiguas	averiguáis	has averiguado	habéis averiguado
averigua	averiguan	ha averiguado	han averiguado
2 imperfecto de indicativo		**9 pluscuamperfecto de indicativo**	
averiguaba	averiguábamos	había averiguado	habíamos averiguado
averiguabas	averiguabais	habías averiguado	habíais averiguado
averiguaba	averiguaban	había averiguado	habían averiguado
3 pretérito		**10 pretérito anterior**	
averigüé	averiguamos	hube averiguado	hubimos averiguado
averiguaste	averiguasteis	hubiste averiguado	hubisteis averiguado
averiguó	averiguaron	hubo averiguado	hubieron averiguado
4 futuro		**11 futuro perfecto**	
averiguaré	averiguaremos	habré averiguado	habremos averiguado
averiguarás	averiguaréis	habrás averiguado	habréis averiguado
averiguará	averiguarán	habrá averiguado	habrán averiguado
5 potencial simple		**12 potencial compuesto**	
averiguaría	averiguaríamos	habría averiguado	habríamos averiguado
averiguarías	averiguaríais	habrías averiguado	habríais averiguado
averiguaría	averiguarían	habría averiguado	habrían averiguado
6 presente de subjuntivo		**13 perfecto de subjuntivo**	
averigüe	averigüemos	haya averiguado	hayamos averiguado
averigües	averigüéis	hayas averiguado	hayáis averiguado
averigüe	averigüen	haya averiguado	hayan averiguado
7 imperfecto de subjuntivo		**14 pluscuamperfecto de subjuntivo**	
averiguara	averiguáramos	hubiera averiguado	hubiéramos averiguado
averiguaras	averiguarais	hubieras averiguado	hubierais averiguado
averiguara	averiguaran	hubiera averiguado	hubieran averiguado
OR		OR	
averiguase	averiguásemos	hubiese averiguado	hubiésemos averiguado
averiguases	averiguaseis	hubieses averiguado	hubieseis averiguado
averiguase	averiguasen	hubiese averiguado	hubiesen averiguado

imperativo	
—	averigüemos
averigua; no averigües	averiguad; no averigüéis
averigüe	averigüen

Words related to this verb
el averiguador, la averiguadora   investigator   **averiguable**   investigable, verifiable
la averiguación   inquiry, investigation   **averiguadamente**   surely, certainly

> Don't miss the definitions of basic grammatical terms with examples
> in English and Spanish on pages 666–677.

to help, to aid, to assist

The Seven Simple Tenses		The Seven Compound Tenses	
Singular	Plural	Singular	Plural
1 presente de indicativo		8 perfecto de indicativo	
ayudo	**ayudamos**	**he ayudado**	**hemos ayudado**
ayudas	**ayudáis**	**has ayudado**	**habéis ayudado**
ayuda	**ayudan**	**ha ayudado**	**han ayudado**
2 imperfecto de indicativo		9 pluscuamperfecto de indicativo	
ayudaba	**ayudábamos**	**había ayudado**	**habíamos ayudado**
ayudabas	**ayudabais**	**habías ayudado**	**habíais ayudado**
ayudaba	**ayudaban**	**había ayudado**	**habían ayudado**
3 pretérito		10 pretérito anterior	
ayudé	**ayudamos**	**hube ayudado**	**hubimos ayudado**
ayudaste	**ayudasteis**	**hubiste ayudado**	**hubisteis ayudado**
ayudó	**ayudaron**	**hubo ayudado**	**hubieron ayudado**
4 futuro		11 futuro perfecto	
ayudaré	**ayudaremos**	**habré ayudado**	**habremos ayudado**
ayudarás	**ayudaréis**	**habrás ayudado**	**habréis ayudado**
ayudará	**ayudarán**	**habrá ayudado**	**habrán ayudado**
5 potencial simple		12 potencial compuesto	
ayudaría	**ayudaríamos**	**habría ayudado**	**habríamos ayudado**
ayudarías	**ayudaríais**	**habrías ayudado**	**habríais ayudado**
ayudaría	**ayudarían**	**habría ayudado**	**habrían ayudado**
6 presente de subjuntivo		13 perfecto de subjuntivo	
ayude	**ayudemos**	**haya ayudado**	**hayamos ayudado**
ayudes	**ayudéis**	**hayas ayudado**	**hayáis ayudado**
ayude	**ayuden**	**haya ayudado**	**hayan ayudado**
7 imperfecto de subjuntivo		14 pluscuamperfecto de subjuntivo	
ayudara	**ayudáramos**	**hubiera ayudado**	**hubiéramos ayudado**
ayudaras	**ayudarais**	**hubieras ayudado**	**hubierais ayudado**
ayudara	**ayudaran**	**hubiera ayudado**	**hubieran ayudado**
OR		OR	
ayudase	**ayudásemos**	**hubiese ayudado**	**hubiésemos ayudado**
ayudases	**ayudaseis**	**hubieses ayudado**	**hubieseis ayudado**
ayudase	**ayudasen**	**hubiese ayudado**	**hubiesen ayudado**

imperativo

—	**ayudemos**
ayuda; no ayudes	**ayudad; no ayudéis**
ayude	**ayuden**

Words and expressions related to this verb
la ayuda   aid, assistance, help
ayuda de cámara   valet
un ayudador, una ayudadora   helper
ayudante   assistant

la ayuda financiera   financial aid
A quien madruga, Dios le ayuda.
The early bird catches the worm.

Enjoy verbs in Spanish proverbs on page 539.

bailar

Gerundio **bailando**   Part. pas. **bailado**

to dance

The Seven Simple Tenses		The Seven Compound Tenses	
Singular	Plural	Singular	Plural
1 presente de indicativo		**8 perfecto de indicativo**	
bailo	bailamos	he bailado	hemos bailado
bailas	bailáis	has bailado	habéis bailado
baila	bailan	ha bailado	han bailado
2 imperfecto de indicativo		**9 pluscuamperfecto de indicativo**	
bailaba	bailábamos	había bailado	habíamos bailado
bailabas	bailabais	habías bailado	habíais bailado
bailaba	bailaban	había bailado	habían bailado
3 pretérito		**10 pretérito anterior**	
bailé	bailamos	hube bailado	hubimos bailado
bailaste	bailasteis	hubiste bailado	hubisteis bailado
bailó	bailaron	hubo bailado	hubieron bailado
4 futuro		**11 futuro perfecto**	
bailaré	bailaremos	habré bailado	habremos bailado
bailarás	bailaréis	habrás bailado	habréis bailado
bailará	bailarán	habrá bailado	habrán bailado
5 potencial simple		**12 potencial compuesto**	
bailaría	bailaríamos	habría bailado	habríamos bailado
bailarías	bailaríais	habrías bailado	habríais bailado
bailaría	bailarían	habría bailado	habrían bailado
6 presente de subjuntivo		**13 perfecto de subjuntivo**	
baile	bailemos	haya bailado	hayamos bailado
bailes	bailéis	hayas bailado	hayáis bailado
baile	bailen	haya bailado	hayan bailado
7 imperfecto de subjuntivo		**14 pluscuamperfecto de subjuntivo**	
bailara	bailáramos	hubiera bailado	hubiéramos bailado
bailaras	bailarais	hubieras bailado	hubierais bailado
bailara	bailaran	hubiera bailado	hubieran bailado
OR		OR	
bailase	bailásemos	hubiese bailado	hubiésemos bailado
bailases	bailaseis	hubieses bailado	hubieseis bailado
bailase	bailasen	hubiese bailado	hubiesen bailado

	imperativo	
—	**bailemos**
baila; no bailes	**bailad; no bailéis**
baile	**bailen**

Sentences using this verb and words related to it

Cuando el gato va a sus devociones, bailan los ratones.   When the cat is away, the mice will play.
un baile   dance; **un bailete**   ballet

un bailarín, una bailarina   dancer (professional)
un bailador, una bailadora   dancer
la música bailable   dance music

Enjoy verbs in Spanish proverbs on page 539.

to lower, to let down, to come down, to go down, to descend

The Seven Simple Tenses		The Seven Compound Tenses	
Singular	Plural	Singular	Plural
1 presente de indicativo		8 perfecto de indicativo	
bajo	bajamos	he bajado	hemos bajado
bajas	bajáis	has bajado	habéis bajado
baja	bajan	ha bajado	han bajado
2 imperfecto de indicativo		9 pluscuamperfecto de indicativo	
bajaba	bajábamos	había bajado	habíamos bajado
bajabas	bajabais	habías bajado	habíais bajado
bajaba	bajaban	había bajado	habían bajado
3 pretérito		10 pretérito anterior	
bajé	bajamos	hube bajado	hubimos bajado
bajaste	bajasteis	hubiste bajado	hubisteis bajado
bajó	bajaron	hubo bajado	hubieron bajado
4 futuro		11 futuro perfecto	
bajaré	bajaremos	habré bajado	habremos bajado
bajarás	bajaréis	habrás bajado	habréis bajado
bajará	bajarán	habrá bajado	habrán bajado
5 potencial simple		12 potencial compuesto	
bajaría	bajaríamos	habría bajado	habríamos bajado
bajarías	bajaríais	habrías bajado	habríais bajado
bajaría	bajarían	habría bajado	habrían bajado
6 presente de subjuntivo		13 perfecto de subjuntivo	
baje	bajemos	haya bajado	hayamos bajado
bajes	bajéis	hayas bajado	hayáis bajado
baje	bajen	haya bajado	hayan bajado
7 imperfecto de subjuntivo		14 pluscuamperfecto de subjuntivo	
bajara	bajáramos	hubiera bajado	hubiéramos bajado
bajaras	bajarais	hubieras bajado	hubierais bajado
bajara	bajaran	hubiera bajado	hubieran bajado
OR		OR	
bajase	bajásemos	hubiese bajado	hubiésemos bajado
bajases	bajaseis	hubieses bajado	hubieseis bajado
bajase	bajasen	hubiese bajado	hubiesen bajado

imperativo	
—	bajemos
baja; no bajes	bajad; no bajéis
baje	bajen

Words and expressions related to this verb
la baja reduction (fall) in prices
la bajada descent
bajamente basely
en voz baja in a low voice
bajo down, below

rebajar to reduce
bajar de to get off
bajar de valor to decline in value
el piso bajo ground floor
una rebaja rebate, discount

The subject pronouns are found on the page facing page 1.

balbucear

Gerundio **balbuceando**   Part. pas. **balbuceado**

to stammer, to hesitate (in speech)

The Seven Simple Tenses		The Seven Compound Tenses	
Singular	Plural	Singular	Plural
1 presente de indicativo		**8 perfecto de indicativo**	
balbuceo	balbuceamos	he balbuceado	hemos balbuceado
balbuceas	balbuceáis	has balbuceado	habéis balbuceado
balbucea	balbucean	ha balbuceado	han balbuceado
2 imperfecto de indicativo		**9 pluscuamperfecto de indicativo**	
balbuceaba	balbuceábamos	había balbuceado	habíamos balbuceado
balbuceabas	balbuceabais	habías balbuceado	habíais balbuceado
balbuceaba	balbuceaban	había balbuceado	habían balbuceado
3 pretérito		**10 pretérito anterior**	
balbuceé	balbuceamos	hube balbuceado	hubimos balbuceado
babluceaste	balbuceasteis	hubiste balbuceado	hubisteis balbuceado
balbuceó	balbucearon	hubo balbuceado	hubieron balbuceado
4 futuro		**11 futuro perfecto**	
balbucearé	balbucearemos	habré balbuceado	habremos balbuceado
balbucearás	balbucearéis	habrás balbuceado	habréis balbuceado
balbuceará	balbucerán	habrá balbuceado	habrán balbuceado
5 potencial simple		**12 potencial compuesto**	
balbucearía	balbucearíamos	habría balbuceado	habríamos balbuceado
balbucearías	balbucearíais	habrías balbuceado	habríais balbuceado
balbucearía	balbucearían	habría balbuceado	habrían balbuceado
6 presente de subjuntivo		**13 perfecto de subjuntivo**	
balbucee	balbuceemos	haya balbuceado	hayamos balbuceado
balbucees	balbuceéis	hayas balbuceado	hayáis balbuceado
balbucee	balbuceen	haya balbuceado	hayan balbuceado
7 imperfecto de subjuntivo		**14 pluscuamperfecto de subjuntivo**	
balbuceara	balbuceáramos	hubiera balbuceado	hubiéramos balbuceado
balbucearas	balbucearais	hubieras balbuceado	hubierais balbuceado
balbuceara	balbucearan	hubiera balbuceado	hubieran balbuceado
OR		OR	
balbucease	balbuceásemos	hubiese balbuceado	hubiésemos balbuceado
balbuceases	balbuceaseis	hubieses balbuceado	hubieseis balbuceado
balbucease	balbuceasen	hubiese balbuceado	hubiesen balbuceado

imperativo	
—	balbuceemos
balbucea; no balbucees	balbucead; no balbuceéis
balbucee	balbuceen

Words related to this verb
balbuciente lisping, stammering
el balbuceo, la balbucencia stuttering, stammering, lisp

Be sure to consult the back pages for sections on verbs used in idiomatic expressions, verbs with prepositions, and the list of over 1,100 verbs conjugated like model verbs.

to bathe oneself, to take a bath

The Seven Simple Tenses		The Seven Compound Tenses	
Singular	Plural	Singular	Plural
1 presente de indicativo		8 perfecto de indicativo	
me baño	**nos bañamos**	**me he bañado**	**nos hemos bañado**
te bañas	**os bañáis**	**te has bañado**	**os habéis bañado**
se baña	**se bañan**	**se ha bañado**	**se han bañado**
2 imperfecto de indicativo		9 pluscuamperfecto de indicativo	
me bañaba	**nos bañábamos**	**me había bañado**	**nos habíamos bañado**
te bañabas	**os bañabais**	**te habías bañado**	**os habíais bañado**
se bañaba	**se bañaban**	**se había bañado**	**se habían bañado**
3 pretérito		10 pretérito anterior	
me bañé	**nos bañamos**	**me hube bañado**	**nos hubimos bañado**
te bañaste	**os bañasteis**	**te hubiste bañado**	**os hubisteis bañado**
se bañó	**se bañaron**	**se hubo bañado**	**se hubieron bañado**
4 futuro		11 futuro perfecto	
me bañaré	**nos bañaremos**	**me habré bañado**	**nos habremos bañado**
te bañarás	**os bañaréis**	**te habrás bañado**	**os habréis bañado**
se bañará	**se bañarán**	**se habrá bañado**	**se habrán bañado**
5 potencial simple		12 potencial compuesto	
me bañaría	**nos bañaríamos**	**me habría bañado**	**nos habríamos bañado**
te bañarías	**os bañaríais**	**te habrías bañado**	**os habríais bañado**
se bañaría	**se bañarían**	**se habría bañado**	**se habrían bañado**
6 presente de subjuntivo		13 perfecto de subjuntivo	
me bañe	**nos bañemos**	**me haya bañado**	**nos hayamos bañado**
te bañes	**os bañéis**	**te hayas bañado**	**os hayáis bañado**
se bañe	**se bañen**	**se haya bañado**	**se hayan bañado**
7 imperfecto de subjuntivo		14 pluscuamperfecto de subjuntivo	
me bañara	**nos bañáramos**	**me hubiera bañado**	**nos hubiéramos bañado**
te bañaras	**os bañarais**	**te hubieras bañado**	**os hubierais bañado**
se bañara	**se bañaran**	**se hubiera bañado**	**se hubieran bañado**
OR		OR	
me bañase	**nos bañásemos**	**me hubiese bañado**	**nos hubiésemos bañado**
te bañases	**os bañaseis**	**te hubieses bañado**	**os hubieseis bañado**
se bañase	**se bañasen**	**se hubiese bañado**	**se hubiesen bañado**

imperativo

—	**bañémonos**
báñate; no te bañes	**bañaos; no os bañéis**
báñese	**báñense**

Words and expressions related to this verb

una bañera, una bañadera   bathtub
un bañador, una bañadora   bather
un baño   bath, bathing
un baño de vapor   steam bath

bañar un papel de lágrimas   to write a mournful letter
bañar a la luz   to light up, to illuminate
bañar   to bathe

barrer

Gerundio **barriendo**   Part. pas. **barrido**

to sweep, to whisk

The Seven Simple Tenses		The Seven Compound Tenses	
Singular	Plural	Singular	Plural
1 presente de indicativo		**8 perfecto de indicativo**	
barro	barremos	he barrido	hemos barrido
barres	barréis	has barrido	habéis barrido
barre	barren	ha barrido	han barrido
2 imperfecto de indicativo		**9 pluscuamperfecto de indicativo**	
barría	barríamos	había barrido	habíamos barrido
barrías	barríais	habías barrido	habíais barrido
barria	barrían	había barrido	habían barrido
3 pretérito		**10 pretérito anterior**	
barrí	barrimos	hube barrido	hubimos barrido
barriste	barristeis	hubiste barrido	hubisteis barrido
barrió	barrieron	hubo barrido	hubieron barrido
4 futuro		**11 futuro perfecto**	
barreré	barreremos	habré barrido	habremos barrido
barrerás	barreréis	habrás barrido	habréis barrido
barrerá	barrerán	habrá barrido	habrán barrido
5 potencial simple		**12 potencial compuesto**	
barrería	barreríamos	habría barrido	habríamos barrido
barrerías	barreríais	habrías barrido	habríais barrido
barrería	barrerían	habría barrido	habrían barrido
6 presente de subjuntivo		**13 perfecto de subjuntivo**	
barra	barramos	haya barrido	hayamos barrido
barras	barráis	hayas barrido	hayáis barrido
barra	barran	haya barrido	hayan barrido
7 imperfecto de subjuntivo		**14 pluscuamperfecto de subjuntivo**	
barriera	barriéramos	hubiera barrido	hubiéramos barrido
barrieras	barrierais	hubieras barrido	hubierais barrido
barriera	barrieran	hubiera barrido	hubieran barrido
OR		OR	
barriese	barriésemos	hubiese barrido	hubiésemos barrido
barrieses	barrieseis	hubieses barrido	hubieseis barrido
barriese	barriesen	hubiese barrido	hubiesen barrido

imperativo	
—	barramos
barre; no barras	barred; no barráis
barra	barran

Words and expressions related to this verb

la barredera   street sweeper machine

el barredero de alfombra   carpet sweeper

la barredura   sweeping

la barredora eléctrica (also **la aspiradora**) vacuum cleaner

---

Increase your verb power with popular phrases, words, and expressions for tourists on pages 595–618.

---

to be enough, to be sufficient, to suffice

The Seven Simple Tenses		The Seven Compound Tenses	
Singular	Plural	Singular	Plural
1 presente de indicativo		8 perfecto de indicativo	
basta	**bastan**	**ha bastado**	**han bastado**
2 imperfecto de indicativo		9 pluscuamperfecto de indicativo	
bastaba	**bastaban**	**había bastado**	**habían bastado**
3 pretérito		10 pretérito anterior	
bastó	**bastaron**	**hubo bastado**	**hubieron bastado**
4 futuro		11 futuro perfecto	
bastará	**bastarán**	**habré bastado**	**habrán bastado**
5 potencial simple		12 potencial compuesto	
bastaría	**bastarían**	**habría bastado**	**habrían bastado**
6 presente de subjuntivo		13 perfecto de subjuntivo	
que baste	**que basten**	**haya bastado**	**hayan bastado**
7 imperfecto de subjuntivo		14 pluscuamperfecto de subjuntivo	
que bastara	**que bastaran**	**hubiera bastado**	**hubieran bastado**
OR		OR	
que bastase	**que bastasen**	**hubiese bastado**	**hubiesen bastado**

imperativo

¡Que baste!   **¡Que basten!**

Common expression related to this verb
¡Basta!   Enough! That will do!
This is an impersonal verb and it is used mainly in the third person singular and plural.
It is a regular ar verb and can be conjugated in all the persons.

Consult the back pages for verbs used in idiomatic expressions,
verbs and prepositions, and Spanish proverbs using verbs.

to baptize, to christen

The Seven Simple Tenses		The Seven Compound Tenses	
Singular	Plural	Singular	Plural
1 presente de indicativo		8 perfecto de indicativo	
bautizo	**bautizamos**	**he bautizado**	**hemos bautizado**
bautizas	**bautizáis**	**has bautizado**	**habéis bautizado**
bautiza	**bautizan**	**ha bautizado**	**han bautizado**
2 imperfecto de indicativo		9 pluscuamperfecto de indicativo	
bautizaba	**bautizábamos**	**había bautizado**	**habíamos bautizado**
bautizabas	**bautizabais**	**habías bautizado**	**habíais bautizado**
bautizaba	**bautizaban**	**había bautizado**	**habían bautizado**
3 pretérito		10 pretérito anterior	
bauticé	**bautizamos**	**hube bautizado**	**hubimos bautizado**
bautizaste	**bautizasteis**	**hubiste bautizado**	**hubisteis bautizado**
bautizó	**bautizaron**	**hubo bautizado**	**hubieron bautizado**
4 futuro		11 futuro perfecto	
bautizaré	**bautizaremos**	**habré bautizado**	**habremos bautizado**
bautizarás	**bautizaréis**	**habrás bautizado**	**habréis bautizado**
bautizará	**bautizarán**	**habrá bautizado**	**habrán bautizado**
5 potencial simple		12 potencial compuesto	
bautizaría	**bautizaríamos**	**habría bautizado**	**habríamos bautizado**
bautizarías	**bautizaríais**	**habrías bautizado**	**habríais bautizado**
bautizaría	**bautizarían**	**habría bautizado**	**habrían bautizado**
6 presente de subjuntivo		13 perfecto de subjuntivo	
bautice	**bauticemos**	**haya bautizado**	**hayamos bautizado**
bautices	**bauticéis**	**hayas bautizado**	**hayáis bautizado**
bautice	**bauticen**	**haya bautizado**	**hayan bautizado**
7 imperfecto de subjuntivo		14 pluscuamperfecto de subjuntivo	
bautizara	**bautizáramos**	**hubiera bautizado**	**hubiéramos bautizado**
bautizaras	**bautizarais**	**hubieras bautizado**	**hubierais bautizado**
bautizara	**bautizaran**	**hubiera bautizado**	**hubieran bautizado**
OR		OR	
bautizase	**bautizásemos**	**hubiese bautizado**	**hubiésemos bautizado**
bautizases	**bautizaseis**	**hubieses bautizado**	**hubieseis bautizado**
bautizase	**bautizasen**	**hubiese bautizado**	**hubiesen bautizado**

imperativo

—	**bauticemos**
bautiza; no bautices	**bautizad; no bauticéis**
bautice	**bauticen**

Words and expressions related to this verb

el bautisterio bapistery
el bautismo baptism, christening
bautismal baptismal

el, la Bautista Baptist
bautizar una calle to name a street

Get your feet wet with verbs used in weather expressions on page 540.

The Seven Simple Tenses		The Seven Compound Tenses	
Singular	Plural	Singular	Plural
1 presente de indicativo		8 perfecto de indicativo	
bebo	**bebemos**	**he bebido**	**hemos bebido**
bebes	**bebéis**	**has bebido**	**habéis bebido**
bebe	**beben**	**ha bebido**	**han bebido**
2 imperfecto de indicativo		9 pluscuamperfecto de indicativo	
bebía	**bebíamos**	**había bebido**	**habíamos bebido**
bebías	**bebíais**	**habías bebido**	**habíais bebido**
bebía	**bebían**	**había bebido**	**habían bebido**
3 pretérito		10 pretérito anterior	
bebí	**bebimos**	**hube bebido**	**hubimos bebido**
bebiste	**bebisteis**	**hubiste bebido**	**hubisteis bebido**
bebió	**bebieron**	**hubo bebido**	**hubieron bebido**
4 futuro		11 futuro perfecto	
beberé	**beberemos**	**habré bebido**	**habremos bebido**
beberás	**beberéis**	**habrás bebido**	**habréis bebido**
beberá	**beberán**	**habrá bebido**	**habrán bebido**
5 potencial simple		12 potencial compuesto	
bebería	**beberíamos**	**habría bebido**	**habríamos bebido**
beberías	**beberíais**	**habrías bebido**	**habríais bebido**
bebería	**beberían**	**habría bebido**	**habrían bebido**
6 presente de subjuntivo		13 perfecto de subjuntivo	
beba	**bebamos**	**haya bebido**	**hayamos bebido**
bebas	**bebáis**	**hayas bebido**	**hayáis bebido**
beba	**beban**	**haya bebido**	**hayan bebido**
7 imperfecto de subjuntivo		14 pluscuamperfecto de subjuntivo	
bebiera	**bebiéramos**	**hubiera bebido**	**hubiéramos bebido**
bebieras	**bebierais**	**hubieras bebido**	**hubierais bebido**
bebiera	**bebieran**	**hubiera bebido**	**hubieran bebido**
OR		OR	
bebiese	**bebiésemos**	**hubiese bebido**	**hubiésemos bebido**
bebieses	**bebieseis**	**hubieses bebido**	**hubieseis bebido**
bebiese	**bebiesen**	**hubiese bebido**	**hubiesen bebido**

imperativo

—	**bebamos**
bebe; no bebas	**bebed; no bebáis**
beba	**beban**

Words and expressions related to this verb
una bebida   drink, beverage
beber de   to drink from
beber a la salud   to drink to health

beber como una cuba   to drink like a fish
querer beber la sangre a otro   to hate
   somebody bitterly

Want to learn more idiomatic expressions that contain verbs? Check out pages 524–537.

bendecir Gerundio **bendiciendo** Part. pas. **bendecido (bendito,**
when used as an adj. with **estar)**

to bless, to consecrate

The Seven Simple Tenses | The Seven Compound Tenses

Singular	Plural	Singular	Plural
1 presente de indicativo		8 perfecto de indicativo	
bendigo	bendecimos	he bendecido	hemos bendecido
bendices	bendecís	has bendecido	habéis bendecido
bendice	bendicen	ha bendecido	han bendecido
2 imperfecto de indicativo		9 pluscuamperfecto de indicativo	
bendecía	bendecíamos	había bendecido	habíamos bendecido
bendecías	bendecíais	habías bendecido	habíais bendecido
bendecía	bendecían	había bendecido	habían bendecido
3 pretérito		10 pretérito anterior	
bendije	bendijimos	hube bendecido	hubimos bendecido
bendijiste	bendijisteis	hubiste bendecido	hubisteis bendecido
bendijo	bendijeron	hubo bendecido	hubieron bendecido
4 futuro		11 futuro perfecto	
bendeciré	bendeciremos	habré bendecido	habremos bendecido
bendecirás	bendeciréis	habrás bendecido	habréis bendecido
bendecirá	bendecirán	habrá bendecido	habrán bendecido
5 potencial simple		12 potencial compuesto	
bendeciría	bendeciríamos	habría bendecido	habríamos bendecido
bendecirías	bendeciríais	habrías bendecido	habríais bendecido
bendeciría	bendecirían	habría bendecido	habrían bendecido
6 presente de subjuntivo		13 perfecto de subjuntivo	
bendiga	bendigamos	haya bendecido	hayamos bendecido
bendigas	bendigáis	hayas bendecido	hayáis bendecido
bendiga	bendigan	haya bendecido	hayan bendecido
7 imperfecto de subjuntivo		14 pluscuamperfecto de subjuntivo	
bendijera	bendijéramos	hubiera bendecido	hubiéramos bendecido
bendijeras	bendijerais	hubieras bendecido	hubierais bendecido
bendijera	bendijeran	hubiera bendecido	hubieran bendecido
OR		OR	
bendijese	bendijésemos	hubiese bendecido	hubiésemos bendecido
bendijeses	bendijeseis	hubieses bendecido	hubieseis bendecido
bendijese	bendijesen	hubiese bendecido	hubiesen bendecido

imperativo

—	bendigamos
bendice; no bendigas	bendecid; no bendigáis
bendiga	bendigan

Words and expressions related to this verb
la bendición   benediction, blessing
las bendiciones nupciales   marriage

un bendecidor, una bendecidora   blesser
el pan bendito   communion bread (blessed)

See also **maldecir.**
See also the note on the bottom of page 371.

Enjoy verbs in Spanish proverbs on page 539.

to erase, to cross out

The Seven Simple Tenses		The Seven Compound Tenses	
Singular	Plural	Singular	Plural
1 presente de indicativo		8 perfecto de indicativo	
borro	borramos	he borrado	hemos borrado
borras	borráis	has borrado	habéis borrado
borra	borran	ha borrado	han borrado
2 imperfecto de indicativo		9 pluscuamperfecto de indicativo	
borraba	borrábamos	había borrado	habíamos borrado
borrabas	borrabais	habías borrado	habíais borrado
borraba	borraban	había borrado	habían borrado
3 pretérito		10 pretérito anterior	
borré	borramos	hube borrado	hubimos borrado
borraste	borrasteis	hubiste borrado	hubisteis borrado
borró	borraron	hubo borrado	hubieron borrado
4 futuro		11 futuro perfecto	
borraré	borraremos	habré borrado	habremos borrado
borrarás	borraréis	habrás borrado	habréis borrado
borrará	borrarán	habrá borrado	habrán borrado
5 potencial simple		12 potencial compuesto	
borraría	borraríamos	habría borrado	habríamos borrado
borrarías	borraríais	habrías borrado	habríais borrado
borraría	borrarían	habría borrado	habrían borrado
6 presente de subjuntivo		13 perfecto de subjuntivo	
borre	borremos	haya borrado	hayamos borrado
borres	borréis	hayas borrado	hayáis borrado
borre	borren	haya borrado	hayan borrado
7 imperfecto de subjuntivo		14 pluscuamperfecto de subjuntivo	
borrara	borráramos	hubiera borrado	hubiéramos borrado
borraras	borrarais	hubieras borrado	hubierais borrado
borrara	borraran	hubiera borrado	hubieran borrado
OR		OR	
borrase	borrásemos	hubiese borrado	hubiésemos borrado
borrases	borraseis	hubieses borrado	hubieseis borrado
borrase	borrasen	hubiese borrado	hubiesen borrado

	imperativo	
—		borremos
borra; no borres		borrad; no borréis
borre		borren

Words and expressions related to this verb

la goma de borrar   rubber eraser
la borradura   erasure
el borrador   eraser (chalk), rough draft
la tecla de borrado   delete key (computer)

desborrar   to burl (to clean off the knots from cloth)
emborrar   to pad, to stuff, to wad; to gulp down food

bostezar

Gerundio **bostezando**   Part. pas. **bostezado**

to yawn, to gape

The Seven Simple Tenses		The Seven Compound Tenses	
Singular	Plural	Singular	Plural
1 presente de indicativo		8 perfecto de indicativo	
bostezo	**bostezamos**	**he bostezado**	**hemos bostezado**
bostezas	**bostezáis**	**has bostezado**	**habéis bostezado**
bosteza	**bostezan**	**ha bostezado**	**han bostezado**
2 imperfecto de indicativo		9 pluscuamperfecto de indicativo	
bostezaba	**bostezábamos**	**había bostezado**	**habíamos bostezado**
bostezabas	**bostezabais**	**habías bostezado**	**habíais bostezado**
bostezaba	**bostezeban**	**había bostezado**	**habían bostezado**
3 pretérito		10 pretérito anterior	
bostecé	**bostezamos**	**hube bostezado**	**hubimos bostezado**
bostezaste	**bostezasteis**	**hubiste bostezado**	**hubisteis bostezado**
bostezó	**bostezaron**	**hubo bostezado**	**hubieron bostezado**
4 futuro		11 futuro perfecto	
bostezaré	**bostezaremos**	**habré bostezado**	**habremos bostezado**
bostezarás	**bostezaréis**	**habrás bostezado**	**habréis bostezado**
bostezará	**bostezarán**	**habrá bostezado**	**habrán bostezado**
5 potencial simple		12 potencial compuesto	
bostezaría	**bostezaríamos**	**habría bostezado**	**habríamos bostezado**
bostezarías	**bostezaríais**	**habrías bostezado**	**habríais bostezado**
bostezaría	**bostezarían**	**habría bostezado**	**habrían bostezado**
6 presente de subjuntivo		13 perfecto de subjuntivo	
bostece	**bostecemos**	**haya bostezado**	**hayamos bostezado**
bosteces	**bostecéis**	**hayas bostezado**	**hayáis bostezado**
bostece	**bostecen**	**haya bostezado**	**hayan bostezado**
7 imperfecto de subjuntivo		14 pluscuamperfecto de subjuntivo	
bostezara	**bostezáramos**	**hubiera bostezado**	**hubiéramos bostezado**
bostezaras	**bostezarais**	**hubieras bostezado**	**hubierais bostezado**
bostezara	**bostezaran**	**hubiera bostezado**	**hubieran bostezado**
OR		OR	
bostezase	**bostezásemos**	**hubiese bostezado**	**hubiésemos bostezado**
bostezases	**bostezaseis**	**hubieses bostezado**	**hubieseis bostezado**
bostezase	**bostezasen**	**hubiese bostezado**	**hubiesen bostezado**

	imperativo	
—		**bostecemos**
bosteza; no bosteces		**bostezad; no bostecéis**
bostece		**bostecen**

Words related to this verb
un bostezo yawn
bostezante yawning, gaping

un bostezador, una bostezadora a person who yawns frequently

Be sure to consult the back pages for sections on verbs used in idiomatic expressions, verbs with prepositions, and the list of over 1,100 verbs conjugated like model verbs.

to fling, to cast (away), to throw (away), to launch

The Seven Simple Tenses		The Seven Compound Tenses	
Singular	Plural	Singular	Plural
1 presente de indicativo		8 perfecto de indicativo	
boto	botamos	he botado	hemos botado
botas	botáis	has botado	habéis botado
bota	botan	ha botado	han botado
2 imperfecto de indicativo		9 pluscuamperfecto de indicativo	
botaba	botábamos	había botado	habíamos botado
botabas	botabais	habías botado	habíais botado
botaba	botaban	había botado	habían botado
3 pretérito		10 pretérito anterior	
boté	botamos	hube botado	hubimos botado
botaste	botasteis	hubiste botado	hubisteis botado
botó	botaron	hubo botado	hubieron botado
4 futuro		11 futuro perfecto	
botaré	botaremos	habré botado	habremos botado
botarás	botaréis	habrás botado	habréis botado
botará	botarán	habrá botado	habrán botado
5 potencial simple		12 potencial compuesto	
botaría	botaríamos	habría botado	habríamos botado
botarías	botaríais	habrías botado	habríais botado
botaría	botarían	habría botado	habrían botado
6 presente de subjuntivo		13 perfecto de subjuntivo	
bote	botemos	haya botado	hayamos botado
botes	botéis	hayas botado	hayáis botado
bote	boten	haya botado	hayan botado
7 imperfecto de subjuntivo		14 pluscuamperfecto de subjuntivo	
botara	botáramos	hubiera botado	hubiéramos botado
botaras	botarais	hubieras botado	hubierais botado
botara	botaran	hubiera botado	hubieran botado
OR		OR	
botase	botásemos	hubiese botado	hubiésemos botado
botases	botaseis	hubieses botado	hubieseis botado
botase	botasen	hubiese botado	hubiesen botado

	imperativo
—	botemos
bota; no botes	botad; no botéis
bote	boten

Words and expressions related to this verb

un bote   thrust, blow; boat; **un bote de remos**   rowboat
rebotar   to bend back; to repel, to bounce back, rebound
un rebote   bounce, rebound; **de rebote**   indirectly

dar bote   to buck
el bote automóvil   powerboat
el bote de salvavidas   lifeboat

Use the EE-zee guide to Spanish pronunciation on pages 562–563.

The subject pronouns are found on the page facing page 1.   **95**

broncear

Gerundio **bronceando**   Part. pas. **bronceado**

to bronze, to tan

The Seven Simple Tenses		The Seven Compound Tenses	
Singular	Plural	Singular	Plural
1 presente de indicativo		**8 perfecto de indicativo**	
bronceo	bronceamos	he bronceado	hemos bronceado
bronceas	bronceáis	has bronceado	habéis bronceado
broncea	broncean	ha bronceado	han bronceado
2 imperfecto de indicativo		**9 pluscuamperfecto de indicativo**	
bronceaba	bronceábamos	había bronceado	habíamos bronceado
bronceabas	bronceabais	habías bronceado	habíais bronceado
bronceaba	bronceaban	había bronceado	habían bronceado
3 pretérito		**10 pretérito anterior**	
bronceé	bronceamos	hube bronceado	hubimos bronceado
bronceaste	bronceasteis	hubiste bronceado	hubisteis bronceado
bronceó	broncearon	hubo bronceado	hubieron bronceado
4 futuro		**11 futuro perfecto**	
broncearé	broncearemos	habré bronceado	habremos bronceado
broncearás	broncearéis	habrás bronceado	habréis bronceado
bronceará	broncearán	habrá bronceado	habrán bronceado
5 potencial simple		**12 potencial compuesto**	
broncearía	broncearíamos	habría bronceado	habríamos bronceado
broncearías	broncearíais	habrías bronceado	habríais bronceado
broncearía	broncearían	habría bronceado	habrían bronceado
6 presente de subjuntivo		**13 perfecto de subjuntivo**	
broncee	bronceemos	haya bronceado	hayamos bronceado
broncees	bronceéis	hayas bronceado	hayáis bronceado
broncee	bronceen	haya bronceado	hayan bronceado
7 imperfecto de subjuntivo		**14 pluscuamperfecto de subjuntivo**	
bronceara	bronceáramos	hubiera bronceado	hubiéramos bronceado
broncearas	broncearais	hubieras bronceado	hubierais bronceado
bronceara	broncearan	hubiera bronceado	hubieran bronceado
OR		OR	
broncease	bronceásemos	hubiese bronceado	hubiésemos bronceado
bronceases	bronceaseis	hubieses bronceado	hubieseis bronceado
broncease	bronceasen	hubiese bronceado	hubiesen bronceado

	imperativo	
—		bronceemos
broncea; no broncees		broncead; no bronceéis
broncee		bronceen

Words related to this verb
el bronce   bronze
bronceado, bronceada   bronze colored, sunburned, tanned
broncearse   to tan, bronze oneself (skin)

Be sure to consult the back pages for sections on verbs used in idiomatic expressions, verbs with prepositions, and the list of over 1,100 verbs conjugated like model verbs.

to boil, to bustle, to hustle, to stir

The Seven Simple Tenses		The Seven Compound Tenses	
Singular	Plural	Singular	Plural
1 presente de indicativo		8 perfecto de indicativo	
bullo	**bullimos**	**he bullido**	**hemos bullido**
bulles	**bullís**	**has bullido**	**habéis bullido**
bulle	**bullen**	**ha bullido**	**han bullido**
2 imperfecto de indicativo		9 pluscuamperfecto de indicativo	
bullía	**bullíamos**	**había bullido**	**habíamos bullido**
bullías	**bullíais**	**habías bullido**	**habíais bullido**
bullía	**bullían**	**había bullido**	**habían bullido**
3 pretérito		10 pretérito anterior	
bullí	**bullimos**	**hube bullido**	**hubimos bullido**
bulliste	**bullisteis**	**hubiste bullido**	**hubisteis bullido**
bulló	**bulleron**	**hubo bullido**	**hubieron bullido**
4 futuro		11 futuro perfecto	
bulliré	**bulliremos**	**habré bullido**	**habremos bullido**
bullirás	**bulliréis**	**habrás bullido**	**habréis bullido**
bullirá	**bullirán**	**habrá bullido**	**habrán bullido**
5 potencial simple		12 potencial compuesto	
bulliría	**bulliríamos**	**habría bullido**	**habríamos bullido**
bullirías	**bulliríais**	**habrías bullido**	**habríais bullido**
bulliría	**bullirían**	**habría bullido**	**habrían bullido**
6 presente de subjuntivo		13 perfecto de subjuntivo	
bulla	**bullamos**	**haya bullido**	**hayamos bullido**
bullas	**bulláis**	**hayas bullido**	**hayáis bullido**
bulla	**bullan**	**haya bullido**	**hayan bullido**
7 imperfecto de subjuntivo		14 pluscuamperfecto de subjuntivo	
bullera	**bulléramos**	**hubiera bullido**	**hubiéramos bullido**
bulleras	**bullerais**	**hubieras bullido**	**hubierais bullido**
bullera	**bulleran**	**hubiera bullido**	**hubieran bullido**
OR		OR	
bullese	**bullésemos**	**hubiese bullido**	**hubiésemos bullido**
bulleses	**bulleseis**	**hubieses bullido**	**hubieseis bullido**
bullese	**bullesen**	**hubiese bullido**	**hubiesen bullido**

imperativo

—	**bullamos**
bulle; no bullas	**bullid; no bulláis**
bulla	**bullan**

Words related to this verb
un, una bullebulle busybody
el bullicio noise, bustle
bulliciosamente noisily

bullente bubbling
la bulla bustle, noise; mob
un bullaje noisy crowd

Review the principal parts of important Spanish verbs on pages xvi and xvii.

to make fun of, to poke fun at, to ridicule

The Seven Simple Tenses		The Seven Compound Tenses	
Singular	Plural	Singular	Plural
1 presente de indicativo		8 perfecto de indicativo	
me burlo	nos burlamos	me he burlado	nos hemos burlado
te burlas	os burláis	te has burlado	os habéis burlado
se burla	se burlan	se ha burlado	se han burlado
2 imperfecto de indicativo		9 pluscuamperfecto de indicativo	
me burlaba	nos burlábamos	me había burlado	nos habíamos burlado
te burlabas	os burlabais	te habías burlado	os habíais burlado
se burlaba	se burlaban	se había burlado	se habían burlado
3 pretérito		10 pretérito anterior	
me burlé	nos burlamos	me hube burlado	nos hubimos burlado
te burlaste	os burlasteis	te hubiste burlado	os hubisteis burlado
se burló	se burlaron	se hubo burlado	se hubieron burlado
4 futuro		11 futuro perfecto	
me burlaré	nos burlaremos	me habré burlado	nos habremos burlado
te burlarás	os burlaréis	te habrás burlado	os habréis burlado
se burlará	se burlarán	se habrá burlado	se habrán burlado
5 potencial simple		12 potencial compuesto	
me burlaría	nos burlaríamos	me habría burlado	nos habríamos burlado
te burlarías	os burlaríais	te habrías burlado	os habríais burlado
se burlaría	se burlarían	se habría burlado	se habrían burlado
6 presente de subjuntivo		13 perfecto de subjuntivo	
me burle	nos burlemos	me haya burlado	nos hayamos burlado
te burles	os burléis	te hayas burlado	os hayáis burlado
se burle	se burlen	se haya burlado	se hayan burlado
7 imperfecto de subjuntivo		14 pluscuamperfecto de subjuntivo	
me burlara	nos burláramos	me hubiera burlado	nos hubiéramos burlado
te burlaras	os burlarais	te hubieras burlado	os hubierais burlado
se burlara	se burlaran	se hubiera burlado	se hubieran burlado
OR		OR	
me burlase	nos burlásemos	me hubiese burlado	nos hubiésemos burlado
te burlases	os burlaseis	te hubieses burlado	os hubieseis burlado
se burlase	se burlasen	se hubiese burlado	se hubiesen burlado

imperativo

—	burlémonos
búrlate; no te burles	burlaos; no os burléis
búrlese	búrlense

Words and expressions related to this verb

el burlador, la burladora practical joker, jester, wag
burlescamente comically
de burlas for fun
la burlería trick

burlesco, burlesca burlesque
burlarase de alguien to make fun of someone
burlar a alguien to deceive someone
hacer burla de to make fun of
una burla jeer

to look for, to seek

The Seven Simple Tenses		The Seven Compound Tenses	
Singular	Plural	Singular	Plural
1 presente de indicativo		8 perfecto de indicativo	
busco	buscamos	he buscado	hemos buscado
buscas	buscáis	has buscado	habéis buscado
busca	buscan	ha buscado	han buscado
2 imperfecto de indicativo		9 pluscuamperfecto de indicativo	
buscaba	buscábamos	había buscado	habíamos buscado
buscabas	buscabais	habías buscado	habíais buscado
buscaba	buscaban	había buscado	habían buscado
3 pretérito		10 pretérito anterior	
busqué	buscamos	hube buscado	hubimos buscado
buscaste	buscasteis	hubiste buscado	hubisteis buscado
buscó	buscaron	hubo buscado	hubieron buscado
4 futuro		11 futuro perfecto	
buscaré	buscaremos	habré buscado	habremos buscado
buscarás	buscaréis	habrás buscado	habréis buscado
buscará	buscarán	habrá buscado	habrán buscado
5 potencial simple		12 potencial compuesto	
buscaría	buscaríamos	habría buscado	habríamos buscado
buscarías	buscaríais	habrías buscado	habríais buscado
buscaría	buscarían	habría buscado	habrían buscado
6 presente de subjuntivo		13 perfecto de subjuntivo	
busque	busquemos	haya buscado	hayamos buscado
busques	busquéis	hayas buscado	hayáis buscado
busque	busquen	haya buscado	hayan buscado
7 imperfecto de subjuntivo		14 pluscuamperfecto de subjuntivo	
buscara	buscáramos	hubiera buscado	hubiéramos buscado
buscaras	buscarais	hubieras buscado	hubierais buscado
buscara	buscaran	hubiera buscado	hubieran buscado
OR		OR	
buscase	buscásemos	hubiese buscado	hubiésemos buscado
buscases	buscaseis	hubieses buscado	hubieseis buscado
buscase	buscasen	hubiese buscado	hubiesen buscado

imperativo

—	busquemos
busca; no busques	buscad; no busquéis
busque	busquen

Sentences using this verb and words related to it
¿**Qué busca Ud.?**   What are you looking for?
Busco mis libros.   I'm looking for my books.
la busca, la buscada   research, search

la búsqueda   search
rebuscar   to search into meticulously
el rebuscamiento   meticulous searching

Get acquainted with what preposition goes with what verb on pages 541–549.

to be contained, to fit into

The Seven Simple Tenses		The Seven Compound Tenses	
Singular	Plural	Singular	Plural
1 presente de indicativo		8 perfecto de indicativo	
quepo	cabemos	he cabido	hemos cabido
cabes	cabéis	has cabido	habéis cabido
cabe	caben	ha cabido	han cabido
2 imperfecto de indicativo		9 pluscuamperfecto de indicativo	
cabía	cabíamos	había cabido	habíamos cabido
cabías	cabíais	habías cabido	habíais cabido
cabía	cabían	había cabido	habían cabido
3 pretérito		10 pretérito anterior	
cupe	cupimos	hube cabido	hubimos cabido
cupiste	cupisteis	hubiste cabido	hubisteis cabido
cupo	cupieron	hubo cabido	hubieron cabido
4 futuro		11 futuro perfecto	
cabré	cabremos	habré cabido	habremos cabido
cabrás	cabréis	habrás cabido	habréis cabido
cabrá	cabrán	habrá cabido	habrán cabido
5 potencial simple		12 potencial compuesto	
cabría	cabríamos	habría cabido	habríamos cabido
cabrías	cabríais	habrías cabido	habríais cabido
cabría	cabrían	habría cabido	habrían cabido
6 presente de subjuntivo		13 perfecto de subjuntivo	
quepa	quepamos	haya cabido	hayamos cabido
quepas	quepáis	hayas cabido	hayáis cabido
quepa	quepan	haya cabido	hayan cabido
7 imperfecto de subjuntivo		14 pluscuamperfecto de subjuntivo	
cupiera	cupiéramos	hubiera cabido	hubiéramos cabido
cupieras	cupierais	hubieras cabido	hubierais cabido
cupiera	cupieran	hubiera cabido	hubieran cabido
OR		OR	
cupiese	cupiésemos	hubiese cabido	hubiésemos cabido
cupieses	cupieseis	hubieses cabido	hubieseis cabido
cupiese	cupiesen	hubiese cabido	hubiesen cabido

	imperativo	
—		quepamos
cabe; no quepas		cabed; no quepáis
quepa		quepan

Common idiomatic expressions using this verb
Pablo no cabe en sí. Paul has a swelled head.
No quepo aquí. I don't have enough room here.
No cabe duda de que . . . There is no doubt that . . .

No me cabe en la cabeza. I don't get (understand) it.
Todo cabe. All is possible. (It all fits.)

Can't recognize an irregular verb form? Check out pages 519–523.

The Seven Simple Tenses		The Seven Compound Tenses	
Singular	Plural	Singular	Plural
1 presente de indicativo		**8 perfecto de indicativo**	
caigo	caemos	he caído	hemos caído
caes	caéis	has caído	habéis caído
cae	caen	ha caído	han caído
2 imperfecto de indicativo		**9 pluscuamperfecto de indicativo**	
caía	caíamos	había caído	habíamos caído
caías	caíais	habías caído	habíais caído
caía	caían	había caído	habían caído
3 pretérito		**10 pretérito anterior**	
caí	caímos	hube caído	hubimos caído
caíste	caísteis	hubiste caído	hubisteis caído
cayó	cayeron	hubo caído	hubieron caído
4 futuro		**11 futuro perfecto**	
caeré	caeremos	habré caído	habremos caído
caerás	caeréis	habrás caído	habréis caído
caerá	caerán	habrá caído	habrán caído
5 potencial simple		**12 potencial compuesto**	
caería	caeríamos	habría caído	habríamos caído
caerías	caeríais	habrías caído	habríais caído
caería	caerían	habría caído	habrían caído
6 presente de subjuntivo		**13 perfecto de subjuntivo**	
caiga	caigamos	haya caído	hayamos caído
caigas	caigáis	hayas caído	hayáis caído
caiga	caigan	haya caído	hayan caído
7 imperfecto de subjuntivo		**14 pluscuamperfecto de subjuntivo**	
cayera	cayéramos	hubiera caído	hubiéramos caído
cayeras	cayerais	hubieras caído	hubierais caído
cayera	cayeran	hubiera caído	hubieran caído
OR		OR	
cayese	cayésemos	hubiese caído	hubiésemos caído
cayeses	cayeseis	hubieses caído	hubieseis caído
cayese	cayesen	hubiese caído	hubiesen caído

imperativo

—	caigamos
cae; no caigas	caed; no caigáis
caiga	caigan

Words and expressions related to this verb

la caída   the fall
a la caída del sol   at sunset
a la caída de la tarde   at the end of the afternoon
caer enfermo (enferma)   to fall sick
dejar caer   to drop

See also **caerse.**

caer de espaldas   to fall backwards
decaer   to decay, decline
recaer   to relapse, fall back
caer con   to come down with

Can't recognize an irregular verb form? Check out pages 519–523.

to fall, to fall down, to tumble

The Seven Simple Tenses		The Seven Compound Tenses	
Singular	Plural	Singular	Plural
1 presente de indicativo		8 perfecto de indicativo	
me caigo	nos caemos	me he caído	nos hemos caído
te caes	os caéis	te has caído	os habéis caído
se cae	se caen	se ha caído	se han caído
2 imperfecto de indicativo		9 pluscuamperfecto de indicativo	
me caía	nos caíamos	me había caído	nos habíamos caído
te caías	os caíais	te habías caído	os habíais caído
se caía	se caían	se había caído	se habían caído
3 pretérito		10 pretérito anterior	
me caí	nos caímos	me hube caído	nos hubimos caído
te caíste	os caísteis	te hubiste caído	os hubisteis caído
se cayó	se cayeron	se hubo caído	se hubieron caído
4 futuro		11 futuro perfecto	
me caeré	nos caeremos	me habré caído	nos habremos caído
te caerás	os caeréis	te habrás caído	os habréis caído
se caerá	se caerán	se habrá caído	se habrán caído
5 potencial simple		12 potencial compuesto	
me caería	nos caeríamos	me habría caído	nos habríamos caído
te caerías	os caeríais	te habrías caído	os habríais caído
se caería	se caerían	se habría caído	se habrían caído
6 presente de subjuntivo		13 perfecto de subjuntivo	
me caiga	nos caigamos	me haya caído	nos hayamos caído
te caigas	os caigáis	te hayas caído	os hayáis caído
se caiga	se caigan	se haya caído	se hayan caído
7 imperfecto de subjuntivo		14 pluscuamperfecto de subjuntivo	
me cayera	nos cayéramos	me hubiera caído	nos hubiéramos caído
te cayeras	os cayerais	te hubieras caído	os hubierais caído
se cayera	se cayeran	se hubiera caído	se hubieran caído
OR		OR	
me cayese	nos cayésemos	me hubiese caído	nos hubiésemos caído
te cayeses	os cayeseis	te hubieses caído	os hubieseis caído
se cayese	se cayesen	se hubiese caído	se hubiesen caído

	imperativo	
—		caigámonos
cáete; no te caigas		caeos; no os caigáis
cáigase		cáiganse

Words and expressions related to this verb
caer de lo alto   to fall from above
caer de plano   to fall flat
caer en la cuenta   to catch on, to realize,
  to get the point

caerse a pedazos   to fall to pieces
dejar caer la voz   to drop one's voice
caerse de risa   to roll on the floor with
  laughter

For other words and expressions related to this verb, see **caer.**

to heat (up), to warm (up)

The Seven Simple Tenses		The Seven Compound Tenses	
Singular	Plural	Singular	Plural
1 presente de indicativo		8 perfecto de indicativo	
caliento	**calentamos**	**he calentado**	**hemos calentado**
calientas	**calentáis**	**has calentado**	**habéis calentado**
calienta	**calientan**	**ha calentado**	**han calentado**
2 imperfecto de indicativo		9 pluscuamperfecto de indicativo	
calentaba	**calentábamos**	**había calentado**	**habíamos calentado**
calentabas	**calentabais**	**habías calentado**	**habíais calentado**
calentaba	**calentaban**	**había calentado**	**habían calentado**
3 pretérito		10 pretérito anterior	
calenté	**calentamos**	**hube calentado**	**hubimos calentado**
calentaste	**calentasteis**	**hubiste calentado**	**hubisteis calentado**
calentó	**calentaron**	**hubo calentado**	**hubieron calentado**
4 futuro		11 futuro perfecto	
calentaré	**calentaremos**	**habré calentado**	**habremos calentado**
calentarás	**calentaréis**	**habrás calentado**	**habréis calentado**
calentará	**calentarán**	**habrá calentado**	**habrán calentado**
5 potencial simple		12 potencial compuesto	
calentaría	**calentaríamos**	**habría calentado**	**habríamos calentado**
calentarías	**calentaríais**	**habrías calentado**	**habríais calentado**
calentaría	**calentarían**	**habría calentado**	**habrían calentado**
6 presente de subjuntivo		13 perfecto de subjuntivo	
caliente	**calentemos**	**haya calentado**	**hayamos calentado**
calientes	**calentéis**	**hayas calentado**	**hayáis calentado**
caliente	**calienten**	**haya calentado**	**hayan calentado**
7 imperfecto de subjuntivo		14 pluscuamperfecto de subjuntivo	
calentara	**calentáramos**	**hubiera calentado**	**hubiéramos calentado**
calentaras	**calentarais**	**hubieras calentado**	**hubierais calentado**
calentara	**calentaran**	**hubiera calentado**	**hubieran calentado**
OR		OR	
calentase	**calentásemos**	**hubiese calentado**	**hubiésemos calentado**
calentases	**calentaseis**	**hubieses calentado**	**hubieseis calentado**
calentase	**calentasen**	**hubiese calentado**	**hubiesen calentado**

imperativo	
—	**calentemos**
calienta; no calientes	**calentad; no calentéis**
caliente	**calienten**

Words and expressions related to this verb
calentar a uno las orejas   to reprimand (scold) a person
calentarse   to warm oneself
calentarse la cabeza   to rack one's brains
calentarse a la lumbre   to warm oneself by the fire
el calor   heat; **Hace calor esta noche.**   It is warm this evening.
recalentar   to warm over, reheat

The subject pronouns are found on the page facing page 1.

to be silent, to keep quiet

The Seven Simple Tenses		The Seven Compound Tenses	
Singular	Plural	Singular	Plural
1 presente de indicativo		**8 perfecto de indicativo**	
me callo	nos callamos	me he callado	nos hemos callado
te callas	os calláis	te has callado	os habéis callado
se calla	se callan	se ha callado	se han callado
2 imperfecto de indicativo		**9 pluscuamperfecto de indicativo**	
me callaba	nos callábamos	me había callado	nos habíamos callado
te callabas	os callabais	te habías callado	os habíais callado
se callaba	se callaban	se había callado	se habían callado
3 pretérito		**10 pretérito anterior**	
me callé	nos callamos	me hube callado	nos hubimos callado
te callaste	os callasteis	te hubiste callado	os hubisteis callado
se calló	se callaron	se hubo callado	se hubieron callado
4 futuro		**11 futuro perfecto**	
me callaré	nos callaremos	me habré callado	nos habremos callado
te callarás	os callaréis	te habrás callado	os habréis callado
se callará	se callarán	se habrá callado	se habrán callado
5 potencial simple		**12 potencial compuesto**	
me callaría	nos callaríamos	me habría callado	nos habríamos callado
te callarías	os callaríais	te habrías callado	os habríais callado
se callaría	se callarían	se habría callado	se habrían callado
6 presente de subjuntivo		**13 perfecto de subjuntivo**	
me calle	nos callemos	me haya callado	nos hayamos callado
te calles	os calléis	te hayas callado	os hayáis callado
se calle	se callen	se haya callado	se hayan callado
7 imperfecto de subjuntivo		**14 pluscuamperfecto de subjuntivo**	
me callara	nos calláramos	me hubiera callado	nos hubiéramos callado
te callaras	os callarais	te hubieras callado	os hubierais callado
se callara	se callaran	se hubiera callado	se hubieran callado
OR		OR	
me callase	nos callásemos	me hubiese callado	nos hubiésemos callado
te callases	os callaseis	te hubieses callado	os hubieseis callado
se callase	se callasen	se hubiese callado	se hubiesen callado

	imperativo	
—		callémonos
cállate; no te calles		callaos; no os calléis
cállese		cállense

Common idiomatic expressions related to this verb
Quien calla, otorga.   Silence means consent (**otorgar**/to grant, to consent)
¡Cállese Ud.!   Keep quiet!
¡Cállate la boca!   Shut your mouth!
callarse la boca   to shut one's mouth

Don't miss the definitions of basic grammatical terms with examples in English and Spanish on pages 666–677.

to shoe, to wear (shoes), to put on (shoes)

The Seven Simple Tenses		The Seven Compound Tenses	
Singular	Plural	Singular	Plural
1 presente de indicativo		**8 perfecto de indicativo**	
calzo	calzamos	he calzado	hemos calzado
calzas	calzáis	has calzado	habéis calzado
calza	calzan	ha calzado	han calzado
2 imperfecto de indicativo		**9 pluscuamperfecto de indicativo**	
calzaba	calzábamos	había calzado	habíamos calzado
calzabas	calzabais	habías calzado	habíais calzado
calzaba	calzaban	había calzado	habían calzado
3 pretérito		**10 pretérito anterior**	
calcé	calzamos	hube calzado	hubimos calzado
calzaste	calzasteis	hubiste calzado	hubisteis calzado
calzó	calzaron	hubo calzado	hubieron calzado
4 futuro		**11 futuro perfecto**	
calzaré	calzaremos	habré calzado	habremos calzado
calzarás	calzaréis	habrás calzado	habréis calzado
calzará	calzarán	habrá calzado	habrán calzado
5 potencial simple		**12 potencial compuesto**	
calzaría	calzaríamos	habría calzado	habríamos calzado
calzarías	calzaríais	habrías calzado	habríais calzado
calzaría	calzarían	habría calzado	habrían calzado
6 presente de subjuntivo		**13 perfecto de subjuntivo**	
calce	calcemos	haya calzado	hayamos calzado
calces	calcéis	hayas calzado	hayáis calzado
calce	calcen	haya calzado	hayan calzado
7 imperfecto de subjuntivo		**14 pluscuamperfecto de subjuntivo**	
calzara	calzáramos	hubiera calzado	hubiéramos calzado
calzaras	calzarais	hubieras calzado	hubierais calzado
calzara	calzaran	hubiera calzado	hubieran calzado
OR		OR	
calzase	calzásemos	hubiese calzado	hubiésemos calzado
calzases	calzaseis	hubieses calzado	hubieseis calzado
calzase	calzasen	hubiese calzado	hubiesen calzado

imperativo

—	**calcemos**
calza; no calces	**calzad; no calcéis**
calce	**calcen**

Words related to this verb
la calza stocking
un calzadillo small shoe
un calzador shoehorn
un calcetín sock
la calceta stocking

medias calzas knee high stockings
las calzonarias suspenders
calcetar to knit stockings, socks;
    hacer calceta to knit

Learn more verbs in 30 practical situations for tourists on pages 564–594.

cambiar

Gerundio **cambiando**   Part. pas. **cambiado**

to change, to exchange

The Seven Simple Tenses		The Seven Compound Tenses	
Singular	Plural	Singular	Plural
1 presente de indicativo		**8 perfecto de indicativo**	
cambio	cambiamos	he cambiado	hemos cambiado
cambias	cambiáis	has cambiado	habéis cambiado
cambia	cambian	ha cambiado	han cambiado
2 imperfecto de indicativo		**9 pluscuamperfecto de indicativo**	
cambiaba	cambiábamos	había cambiado	habíamos cambiado
cambiabas	cambiabais	habías cambiado	habíais cambiado
cambiaba	cambiaban	había cambiado	habían cambiado
3 pretérito		**10 pretérito anterior**	
cambié	cambiamos	hube cambiado	hubimos cambiado
cambiaste	cambiasteis	hubiste cambiado	hubisteis cambiado
cambió	cambiaron	hubo cambiado	hubieron cambiado
4 futuro		**11 futuro perfecto**	
cambiaré	cambiaremos	habré cambiado	habremos cambiado
cambiarás	cambiaréis	habrás cambiado	habréis cambiado
cambiará	cambiarán	habrá cambiado	habrán cambiado
5 potencial simple		**12 potencial compuesto**	
cambiaría	cambiaríamos	habría cambiado	habríamos cambiado
cambiarías	cambiaríais	habrías cambiado	habríais cambiado
cambiaría	cambiarían	habría cambiado	habrían cambiado
6 presente de subjuntivo		**13 perfecto de subjuntivo**	
cambie	cambiemos	haya cambiado	hayamos cambiado
cambies	cambiéis	hayas cambiado	hayáis cambiado
cambie	cambien	haya cambiado	hayan cambiado
7 imperfecto de subjuntivo		**14 pluscuamperfecto de subjuntivo**	
cambiara	cambiáramos	hubiera cambiado	hubiéramos cambiado
cambiaras	cambiarais	hubieras cambiado	hubierais cambiado
cambiara	cambiaran	hubiera cambiado	hubieran cambiado
OR		OR	
cambiase	cambiásemos	hubiese cambiado	hubiésemos cambiado
cambiases	cambiaseis	hubieses cambiado	hubieseis cambiado
cambiase	cambiasen	hubiese cambiado	hubiesen cambiado

	imperativo
—	cambiemos
cambia; no cambies	**cambiad; no cambiéis**
cambie	**cambien**

Common idiomatic expressions using this verb

cambiar de ropa   to change one's clothing
cambiar de opinión   to change one's mind
el cambio   exchange, change
el cambio de voz   change of voice

cambiar una rueda   to change a wheel
cambiar de costumbres   to change one's habits
cambiar de idea   to change one's mind
cambiar el horario   to change the timetable

Increase your verb power with popular phrases, words, and expressions for tourists on pages 595–618.

to walk, to move along

The Seven Simple Tenses		The Seven Compound Tenses	
Singular	Plural	Singular	Plural
1 presente de indicativo		8 perfecto de indicativo	
camino	caminamos	he caminado	hemos caminado
caminas	camináis	has caminado	habéis caminado
camina	caminan	ha caminado	han caminado
2 imperfecto de indicativo		9 pluscuamperfecto de indicativo	
caminaba	caminábamos	había caminado	habíamos caminado
caminabas	caminabais	habías caminado	habíais caminado
caminaba	caminaban	había caminado	habían caminado
3 pretérito		10 pretérito anterior	
caminé	caminamos	hube caminado	hubimos caminado
caminaste	caminasteis	hubiste caminado	hubisteis caminado
caminó	caminaron	hubo caminado	hubieron caminado
4 futuro		11 futuro perfecto	
caminaré	caminaremos	habré caminado	habremos caminado
caminarás	caminaréis	habrás caminado	habréis caminado
caminará	caminarán	habrá caminado	habrán caminado
5 potencial simple		12 potencial compuesto	
caminaría	caminaríamos	habría caminado	habríamos caminado
caminarías	caminaríais	habrías caminado	habríais caminado
caminaría	caminarían	habría caminado	habrían caminado
6 presente de subjuntivo		13 perfecto de subjuntivo	
camine	caminemos	haya caminado	hayamos caminado
camines	caminéis	hayas caminado	hayáis caminado
camine	caminen	haya caminado	hayan caminado
7 imperfecto de subjuntivo		14 pluscuamperfecto de subjuntivo	
caminara	camináramos	hubiera caminado	hubiéramos caminado
caminaras	caminarais	hubieras caminado	hubierais caminado
caminara	caminaran	hubiera caminado	hubieran caminado
OR		OR	
caminase	caminásemos	hubiese caminado	hubiésemos caminado
caminases	caminaseis	hubieses caminado	hubieseis caminado
caminase	caminasen	hubiese caminado	hubiesen caminado

	imperativo
—	caminemos
camina; no camines	caminad; no caminéis
camine	caminen

Words and expressions related to this verb
el camino   road, highway
el camino de hierro   railroad
en camino de   on the way to
una caminata   a long walk
hacer de un camino dos mandados   to kill
  two birds with one stone

el camino real   highway, highroad
estar en camino   to be on one's way
quedarse a medio camino   to stop halfway
por buen camino   on the right road
al buen camino   on the right track
un camión   truck

The subject pronouns are found on the page facing page 1.

cansarse   Gerundio **cansándose**   Part. pas. **cansado**

to become tired, to become weary, to get tired

The Seven Simple Tenses		The Seven Compound Tenses	
Singular	Plural	Singular	Plural
1 presente de indicativo		8 perfecto de indicativo	
me canso	**nos cansamos**	**me he cansado**	**nos hemos cansado**
te cansas	**os cansáis**	**te has cansado**	**os habéis cansado**
se cansa	**se cansan**	**se ha cansado**	**se han cansado**
2 imperfecto de indicativo		9 pluscuamperfecto de indicativo	
me cansaba	**nos cansábamos**	**me había cansado**	**nos habíamos cansado**
te cansabas	**os cansabais**	**te habías cansado**	**os habíais cansado**
se cansaba	**se cansaban**	**se había cansado**	**se habían cansado**
3 pretérito		10 pretérito anterior	
me cansé	**nos cansamos**	**me hube cansado**	**nos hubimos cansado**
te cansaste	**os cansasteis**	**te hubiste cansado**	**os hubisteis cansado**
se cansó	**se cansaron**	**se hubo cansado**	**se hubieron cansado**
4 futuro		11 futuro perfecto	
me cansaré	**nos cansaremos**	**me habré cansado**	**nos habremos cansado**
te cansarás	**os cansaréis**	**te habrás cansado**	**os habréis cansado**
se cansará	**se cansarán**	**se habrá cansado**	**se habrán cansado**
5 potencial simple		12 potencial compuesto	
me cansaría	**nos cansaríamos**	**me habría cansado**	**nos habríamos cansado**
te cansarías	**os cansaríais**	**te habrías cansado**	**os habríais cansado**
se cansaría	**se cansarían**	**se habría cansado**	**se habrían cansado**
6 presente de subjuntivo		13 perfecto de subjuntivo	
me canse	**nos cansemos**	**me haya cansado**	**nos hayamos cansado**
te canses	**os canséis**	**te hayas cansado**	**os hayáis cansado**
se canse	**se cansen**	**se haya cansado**	**se hayan cansado**
7 imperfecto de subjuntivo		14 pluscuamperfecto de subjuntivo	
me cansara	**nos cansáramos**	**me hubiera cansado**	**nos hubiéramos cansado**
te cansaras	**os cansarais**	**te hubieras cansado**	**os hubierais cansado**
se cansara	**se cansaran**	**se hubiera cansado**	**se hubieran cansado**
OR		OR	
me cansase	**nos cansásemos**	**me hubiese cansado**	**nos hubiésemos cansado**
te cansases	**os cansaseis**	**te hubieses cansado**	**os hubieseis cansado**
se cansase	**se cansasen**	**se hubiese cansado**	**se hubiesen cansado**

	imperativo	
—		**cansémonos**
cánsate; no te canses		**cansaos; no os canséis**
cánsese		**cánsense**

Sentences using this verb and words and expressions related to it
María se cansa, Pedro se cansa y yo me canso. Nosotros nos cansamos.

la cansera fatigue	cansarse de esperar to get tired of waiting
el cansancio fatigue, weariness	cansado, cansada tired, exhausted
cansar to fatigue, to tire, to weary	**María está cansada.** Mary is tired.
el descanso rest, relief; el descansadero resting place	cansarse fácilmente to get tired easily

108   Enjoy verbs in Spanish proverbs on page 539.

The Seven Simple Tenses		The Seven Compound Tenses	
Singular	Plural	Singular	Plural
1 presente de indicativo		8 perfecto de indicativo	
canto	cantamos	he cantado	hemos cantado
cantas	cantáis	has cantado	habéis cantado
canta	cantan	ha cantado	han cantado
2 imperfecto de indicativo		9 pluscuamperfecto de indicativo	
cantaba	cantábamos	había cantado	habíamos cantado
cantabas	cantabais	habías cantado	habíais cantado
cantaba	cantaban	había cantado	habían cantado
3 pretérito		10 pretérito anterior	
canté	cantamos	hube cantado	hubimos cantado
cantaste	cantasteis	hubiste cantado	hubisteis cantado
cantó	cantaron	hubo cantado	hubieron cantado
4 futuro		11 futuro perfecto	
cantaré	cantaremos	habré cantado	habremos cantado
cantarás	cantaréis	habrás cantado	habréis cantado
cantará	cantarán	habrá cantado	habrán cantado
5 potencial simple		12 potencial compuesto	
cantaría	cantaríamos	habría cantado	habríamos cantado
cantarías	cantaríais	habrías cantado	habríais cantado
cantaría	cantarían	habría cantado	habrían cantado
6 presente de subjuntivo		13 perfecto de subjuntivo	
cante	cantemos	haya cantado	hayamos cantado
cantes	cantéis	hayas cantado	hayáis cantado
cante	canten	haya cantado	hayan cantado
7 imperfecto de subjuntivo		14 pluscuamperfecto de subjuntivo	
cantara	cantáramos	hubiera cantado	hubiéramos cantado
cantaras	cantarais	hubieras cantado	hubierais cantado
cantara	cantaran	hubiera cantado	hubieran cantado
OR		OR	
cantase	cantásemos	hubiese cantado	hubiésemos cantado
cantases	cantaseis	hubieses cantado	hubieseis cantado
cantase	cantasen	hubiese cantado	hubiesen cantado

	imperativo	
—	cantemos
canta; no cantes	cantad; no cantéis
cante	canten

Sentences using this verb and words related to it
Quien canta su mal espanta. When you sing you drive away your grief.

una canción song
una cantata cantata (music)
encantar to enchant
cantador, cantadora singer

una cantatriz woman singer
cantor, cantora, cantante singer
encantado, encantada enchanted
un canto song

to characterize

The Seven Simple Tenses		The Seven Compound Tenses	
Singular	Plural	Singular	Plural
1 presente de indicativo		8 perfecto de indicativo	
caracterizo	caracterizamos	he caracterizado	hemos caracterizado
caracterizas	caracterizáis	has caracterizado	habéis caracterizado
caracteriza	caracterizan	ha caracterizado	han caracterizado
2 imperfecto de indicativo		9 pluscuamperfecto de indicativo	
caracterizaba	caracterizábamos	había caracterizado	habíamos caracterizado
caracterizabas	caracterizabais	habías caracterizado	habíais caracterizado
caracterizaba	caracterizaban	había caracterizado	habían caracterizado
3 pretérito		10 pretérito anterior	
caractericé	caracterizamos	hube caracterizado	hubimos caracterizado
caracterizaste	caracterizasteis	hubiste caracterizado	hubisteis caracterizado
caracterizó	caracterizaron	hubo caracterizado	hubieron caracterizado
4 futuro		11 futuro perfecto	
caracterizaré	caracterizaremos	habré caracterizado	habremos caracterizado
caracterizarás	caracterizaréis	habrás caracterizado	habréis caracterizado
caracterizará	caracterizarán	habrá caracterizado	habrán caracterizado
5 potencial simple		12 potencial compuesto	
caracterizaría	caracterizaríamos	habría caracterizado	habríamos caracterizado
caracterizarías	caracterizaríais	habrías caracterizado	habríais caracterizado
caracterizaría	caracterizarían	habría caracterizado	habrían caracterizado
6 presente de subjuntivo		13 perfecto de subjuntivo	
caracterice	caractericemos	haya caracterizado	hayamos caracterizado
caracterices	caractericéis	hayas caracterizado	hayáis caracterizado
caracterice	caractericen	haya caracterizado	hayan caracterizado
7 imperfecto de subjuntivo		14 pluscuamperfecto de subjuntivo	
caracterizara	caracterizáramos	hubiera caracterizado	hubiéramos caracterizado
caracterizaras	caracterizarais	hubieras caracterizado	hubierais caracterizado
caracterizara	caracterizaran	hubiera caracterizado	hubieran caracterizado
OR		OR	
caracterizase	caracterizásemos	hubiese caracterizado	hubiésemos caracterizado
caracterizases	caracterizaseis	hubieses caracterizado	hubieseis caracterizado
caracterizase	caracterizasen	hubiese caracterizado	hubiesen caracterizado

imperativo

—	**caractericemos**
caracteriza; no caracterices	**caracterizad; no caractericéis**
caracterice	**caractericen**

Words related to this verb

el carácter   character (of a person); do not confuse with **personaje**   character (in a play)
característico, característica   characteristic; **tener buen (mal) carácter**
    to be good- (bad-) natured
característicamente   characteristically
la caracterización   characterization

Check out the verb drills and verb tests with answers explained on pages 619–665.

to load, to burden, to charge (a battery)

The Seven Simple Tenses		The Seven Compound Tenses	
Singular	Plural	Singular	Plural
1 presente de indicativo		8 perfecto de indicativo	
cargo	cargamos	he cargado	hemos cargado
cargas	cargáis	has cargado	habéis cargado
carga	cargan	ha cargado	han cargado
2 imperfecto de indicativo		9 pluscuamperfecto de indicativo	
cargaba	cargábamos	había cargado	habíamos cargado
cargabas	cargabais	habías cargado	habíais cargado
cargaba	cargaban	había cargado	habían cargado
3 pretérito		10 pretérito anterior	
cargué	cargamos	hube cargado	hubimos cargado
cargaste	cargasteis	hubiste cargado	hubisteis cargado
cargó	cargaron	hubo cargado	hubieron cargado
4 futuro		11 futuro perfecto	
cargaré	cargaremos	habré cargado	habremos cargado
cargarás	cargaréis	habrás cargado	habréis cargado
cargará	cargarán	habrá cargado	habrán cargado
5 potencial simple		12 potencial compuesto	
cargaría	cargaríamos	habría cargado	habríamos cargado
cargarías	cargaríais	habrías cargado	habríais cargado
cargaría	cargarían	habría cargado	habrían cargado
6 presente de subjuntivo		13 perfecto de subjuntivo	
cargue	carguemos	haya cargado	hayamos cargado
cargues	carguéis	hayas cargado	hayáis cargado
cargue	carguen	haya cargado	hayan cargado
7 imperfecto de subjuntivo		14 pluscuamperfecto de subjuntivo	
cargara	cargáramos	hubiera cargado	hubiéramos cargado
cargaras	cargarais	hubieras cargado	hubierais cargado
cargara	cargaran	hubiera cargado	hubieran cargado
OR		OR	
cargase	cargásemos	hubiese cargado	hubiésemos cargado
cargases	cargaseis	hubieses cargado	hubieseis cargado
cargase	cargasen	hubiese cargado	hubiesen cargado

imperativo

—	carguemos
carga; no cargues	cargad; no carguéis
cargue	carguen

Words and expressions related to this verb

cargoso, cargosa burdensome   **una carga** load, responsibility
la cargazón cargo   **el telecarga** download, upload (computer)
una cargazón de cabeza heaviness of the head   **el cargador** shipper
el cargamento shipment

Review the principal parts of important Spanish verbs on pages xvi and xvii.

to get married, to marry

The Seven Simple Tenses		The Seven Compound Tenses	
Singular	Plural	Singular	Plural
1 presente de indicativo		**8 perfecto de indicativo**	
me caso	nos casamos	me he casado	nos hemos casado
te casas	os casáis	te has casado	os habéis casado
se casa	se casan	se ha casado	se han casado
2 imperfecto de indicativo		**9 pluscuamperfecto de indicativo**	
me casaba	nos casábamos	me había casado	nos habíamos casado
te casabas	os casabais	te habías casado	os habíais casado
se casaba	se casaban	se había casado	se habían casado
3 pretérito		**10 pretérito anterior**	
me casé	nos casamos	me hube casado	nos hubimos casado
te casaste	os casasteis	te hubiste casado	os hubisteis casado
se casó	se casaron	se hubo casado	se hubieron casado
4 futuro		**11 futuro perfecto**	
me casaré	nos casaremos	me habré casado	nos habremos casado
te casarás	os casaréis	te habrás casado	os habréis casado
se casará	se casarán	se habrá casado	se habrán casado
5 potencial simple		**12 potencial compuesto**	
me casaría	nos casaríamos	me habría casado	nos habríamos casado
te casarías	os casaríais	te habrías casado	os habríais casado
se casaría	se casarían	se habría casado	se habrían casado
6 presente de subjuntivo		**13 perfecto de subjuntivo**	
me case	nos casemos	me haya casado	nos hayamos casado
te cases	os caséis	te hayas casado	os hayáis casado
se case	se casen	se haya casado	se hayan casado
7 imperfecto de subjuntivo		**14 pluscuamperfecto de subjuntivo**	
me casara	nos casáramos	me hubiera casado	nos hubiéramos casado
te casaras	os casarais	te hubieras casado	os hubierais casado
se casara	se casaran	se hubiera casado	se hubieran casado
OR		OR	
me casase	nos casásemos	me hubiese casado	nos hubiésemos casado
te casases	os casaseis	te hubieses casado	os hubieseis casado
se casase	se casasen	se hubiese casado	se hubiesen casado

imperativo	
—	casémonos
cásate; no te cases	casaos; no os caséis
cásese	cásense

Words and expressions related to this verb

Antes que te cases, mira lo que haces.   Look before you leap. (Before you get married, look at what you're doing); **un casamiento por amor**   a love marriage

un casmiento ventajoso   a marriage of convenience

casarse con alguien   to marry someone

los recién casados   newlyweds

Enjoy more verbs in Spanish proverbs on page 539.

to celebrate, to praise

The Seven Simple Tenses		The Seven Compound Tenses	
Singular	Plural	Singular	Plural
1 presente de indicativo		**8 perfecto de indicativo**	
celebro	celebramos	he celebrado	hemos celebrado
celebras	celebráis	has celebrado	habéis celebrado
celebra	celebran	ha celebrado	han celebrado
2 imperfecto de indicativo		**9 pluscuamperfecto de indicativo**	
celebraba	celebrábamos	había celebrado	habíamos celebrado
celebrabas	celebrabais	habías celebrado	habíais celebrado
celebraba	celebraban	había celebrado	habían celebrado
3 pretérito		**10 pretérito anterior**	
celebré	celebramos	hube celebrado	hubimos celebrado
celebraste	celebrasteis	hubiste celebrado	hubisteis celebrado
celebró	celebraron	hubo celebrado	hubieron celebrado
4 futuro		**11 futuro perfecto**	
celebraré	celebraremos	habré celebrado	habremos celebrado
celebrarás	celebraréis	habrás celebrado	habréis celebrado
celebrará	celebrarán	habrá celebrado	habrán celebrado
5 potencial simple		**12 potencial compuesto**	
celebraría	celebraríamos	habría celebrado	habríamos celebrado
celebrarías	celebraríais	habrías celebrado	habríais celebrado
celebraría	celebrarían	habría celebrado	habrían celebrado
6 presente de subjuntivo		**13 perfecto de subjuntivo**	
celebre	celebremos	haya celebrado	hayamos celebrado
celebres	celebréis	hayas celebrado	hayáis celebrado
celebre	celebren	haya celebrado	hayan celebrado
7 imperfecto de subjuntivo		**14 pluscuamperfecto de subjuntivo**	
celebrara	celebráramos	hubiera celebrado	hubiéramos celebrado
celebraras	celebrarais	hubieras celebrado	hubierais celebrado
celebrara	celebraran	hubiera celebrado	hubieran celebrado
OR		OR	
celebrase	celebrásemos	hubiese celebrado	hubiésemos celebrado
celebrases	celebraseis	hubieses celebrado	hubieseis celebrado
celebrase	celebrasen	hubiese celebrado	hubiesen celebrado

imperativo	
—	celebremos
celebra; no celebres	celebrad; no celebréis
celebre	celebren

Words and expressions related to this verb
célebre famous, celebrated, renowned
la celebridad fame, celebrity
la celebración celebration

celebrado, celebrada popular, celebrated
ganar celebridad to win fame
una persona célebre a celebrity

Check out the verb drills and verb tests with answers explained on pages 619–665.

| cenar | Gerundio **cenando** | Part. pas. **cenado** |

to have supper, to eat supper, to dine, to have dinner

The Seven Simple Tenses		The Seven Compound Tenses	
Singular	Plural	Singular	Plural
1 presente de indicativo		8 perfecto de indicativo	
ceno	cenamos	he cenado	hemos cenado
cenas	cenáis	has cenado	habéis cenado
cena	cenan	ha cenado	han cenado
2 imperfecto de indicativo		9 pluscuamperfecto de indicativo	
cenaba	cenábamos	había cenado	habíamos cenado
cenabas	cenabais	habías cenado	habíais cenado
cenaba	cenaban	había cenado	habían cenado
3 pretérito		10 pretérito anterior	
cené	cenamos	hube cenado	hubimos cenado
cenaste	cenasteis	hubiste cenado	hubisteis cenado
cenó	cenaron	hubo cenado	hubieron cenado
4 futuro		11 futuro perfecto	
cenaré	cenaremos	habré cenado	habremos cenado
cenarás	cenaréis	habrás cenado	habréis cenado
cenará	cenarán	habrá cenado	habrán cenado
5 potencial simple		12 potencial compuesto	
cenaría	cenaríamos	habría cenado	habríamos cenado
cenarías	cenaríais	habrías cenado	habríais cenado
cenaría	cenarían	habría cenado	habrían cenado
6 presente de subjuntivo		13 perfecto de subjuntivo	
cene	cenemos	haya cenado	hayamos cenado
cenes	cenéis	hayas cenado	hayáis cenado
cene	cenen	haya cenado	hayan cenado
7 imperfecto de subjuntivo		14 pluscuamperfecto de subjuntivo	
cenara	cenáramos	hubiera cenado	hubiéramos cenado
cenaras	cenarais	hubieras cenado	hubierais cenado
cenara	cenaran	hubiera cenado	hubieran cenado
OR		OR	
cenase	cenásemos	hubiese cenado	hubiésemos cenado
cenases	cenaseis	hubieses cenado	hubieseis cenado
cenase	cenasen	hubiese cenado	hubiesen cenado

	imperativo	
—	cenemos
cena; no cenes	cenad; no cenéis
cene	cenen

Sentences using this verb and words related to it
—Carlos, ¿A qué hora cenas?
—Ceno a las ocho con mi familia en casa.

la cena   supper (dinner); **quedarse sin cenar**   to go (remain) without dinner
La última cena   (*The Last Supper,* fresco by Leonardo da Vinci)
la hora de cenar   dinnertime; suppertime; **una cena de despedida**   farewell dinner

Use the EE-zee guide to Spanish pronunciation on pages 562–563.

to brush

The Seven Simple Tenses		The Seven Compound Tenses	
Singular	Plural	Singular	Plural
1 presente de indicativo		**8 perfecto de indicativo**	
cepillo	cepillamos	he cepillado	hemos cepillado
capillas	cepilláis	has cepillado	habéis cepillado
capilla	cepillan	ha cepillado	han cepillado
2 imperfecto de indicativo		**9 pluscuamperfecto de indicativo**	
cepillaba	cepillábamos	había cepillado	habíamos cepillado
cepillabas	cepillabais	habías cepillado	habíais cepillado
cepillaba	cepillaban	había cepillado	habían cepillado
3 pretérito		**10 pretérito anterior**	
cepillé	cepillamos	hube cepillado	hubimos cepillado
cepillaste	cepillasteis	hubiste cepillado	hubisteis cepillado
cepilló	cepillaron	hubo cepillado	hubieron cepillado
4 futuro		**11 futuro perfecto**	
cepillaré	cepillaremos	habré cepillado	habremos cepillado
cepillarás	cepillaréis	habrás cepillado	habréis cepillado
cepillará	cepillarán	habrá cepillado	habrán cepillado
5 potencial simple		**12 potencial compuesto**	
cepillaría	cepillaríamos	habría cepillado	habríamos cepillado
cepillarías	cepillaríais	habrías cepillado	habríais cepillado
cepillaría	cepillarían	habría cepillado	habrían cepillado
6 presente de subjuntivo		**13 perfecto de subjuntivo**	
cepille	cepillemos	haya cepillado	hayamos cepillado
cepilles	cepilléis	hayas cepillado	hayáis cepillado
cepille	cepillen	haya cepillado	hayan cepillado
7 imperfecto de subjuntivo		**14 pluscuamperfecto de subjuntivo**	
cepillara	cepilláramos	hubiera cepillado	hubiéramos cepillado
cepillaras	cepillarais	hubieras cepillado	hubierais cepillado
cepillara	cepillaran	hubiera cepillado	hubieran cepillado
OR		OR	
cepillase	cepillásemos	hubiese cepillado	hubiésemos cepillado
cepillases	cepillaseis	hubieses cepillado	hubieseis cepillado
cepillase	cepillasen	hubiese cepillado	hubiesen cepillado

imperativo	
—	cepillemos
cepilla; no cepilles	cepillad; no cepilléis
cepille	cepillen

Words and expressions related to this verb
un cepillo brush
un cepillo para el cabello hairbursh;
  un cepillo de cabeza hairbrush
un buen cepillado a good brushing
cepillarse to brush oneself
Juanito, cepíllate los dientes. Johnny, brush your teeth.

un cepillo de dientes toothbrush
un cepillo para la ropa clothesbrush;
  un cepillo de ropa clothesbrush
Me cepillé el pelo/I brushed my hair

to close

The Seven Simple Tenses		The Seven Compound Tenses	
Singular	Plural	Singular	Plural
1 presente de indicativo		8 perfecto de indicativo	
cierro	cerramos	he cerrado	hemos cerrado
cierras	cerráis	has cerrado	habéis cerrado
cierra	cierran	ha cerrado	han cerrado
2 imperfecto de indicativo		9 pluscuamperfecto de indicativo	
cerraba	cerrábamos	había cerrado	habíamos cerrado
cerrabas	cerrabais	habías cerrado	habíais cerrado
cerraba	cerraban	había cerrado	habían cerrado
3 pretérito		10 pretérito anterior	
cerré	cerramos	hube cerrado	hubimos cerrado
cerraste	cerrasteis	hubiste cerrado	hubisteis cerrado
cerró	cerraron	hubo cerrado	hubieron cerrado
4 futuro		11 futuro perfecto	
cerraré	cerraremos	habré cerrado	habremos cerrado
cerrarás	cerraréis	habrás cerrado	habréis cerrado
cerrará	cerrarán	habrá cerrado	habrán cerrado
5 potencial simple		12 potencial compuesto	
cerraría	cerraríamos	habría cerrado	habríamos cerrado
cerrarías	cerraríais	habrías cerrado	habríais cerrado
cerraría	cerrarían	habría cerrado	habrían cerrado
6 presente de subjuntivo		13 perfecto de subjuntivo	
cierre	cerremos	haya cerrado	hayamos cerrado
cierres	cerréis	hayas cerrado	hayáis cerrado
cierre	cierren	haya cerrado	hayan cerrado
7 imperfecto de subjuntivo		14 pluscuamperfecto de subjuntivo	
cerrara	cerráramos	hubiera cerrado	hubiéramos cerrado
cerraras	cerrarais	hubieras cerrado	hubierais cerrado
cerrara	cerraran	hubiera cerrado	hubieran cerrado
OR		OR	
cerrase	cerrásemos	hubiese cerrado	hubiésemos cerrado
cerrases	cerraseis	hubieses cerrado	hubieseis cerrado
cerrase	cerrasen	hubiese cerrado	hubiesen cerrado

imperativo	
—	cerremos
cierra; no cierres	cerrad; no cerréis
cierre	cierren

Words and expressions related to this verb
cerrar los ojos   to close one's eyes
cerrar los oídos   to turn a deaf ear
cerrar la boca   to shut up, to keep silent
la cerradura   lock
La puerta está cerrada.   The door is closed.
Las ventanas están cerradas.   The windows are closed.

encerrar   to lock up, to confine
encerrarse   to live in seclusion, to retire
cerrar con llave   to lock up (to close with a key)
una cerradura de combinación   combination lock
cerrar una cuenta   to close an account

to certify, to register (a letter), to attest

The Seven Simple Tenses		The Seven Compound Tenses	
Singular	Plural	Singular	Plural

1 presente de indicativo

certifico	certificamos	
certificas	certificáis	
certifica	certifican	

8 perfecto de indicativo

he certificado	hemos certificado
has certificado	habéis certificado
ha certificado	han certificado

2 imperfecto de indicativo

certificaba	certificábamos
certificabas	certificabais
certificaba	certificaban

9 pluscuamperfecto de indicativo

había certificado	habíamos certificado
habías certificado	habíais certificado
había certificado	habían certificado

3 pretérito

certifiqué	certificamos
certificaste	certificasteis
certificó	certificaron

10 pretérito anterior

hube certificado	hubimos certificado
hubiste certificado	hubisteis certificado
hubo certificado	hubieron certificado

4 futuro

certificaré	certificaremos
certificarás	certificaréis
certificará	certificarán

11 futuro perfecto

habré certificado	habremos certificado
habrás certificado	habréis certificado
habrá certificado	habrán certificado

5 potencial simple

certificaría	certificaríamos
certificarías	certificaríais
certificaría	certificarían

12 potencial compuesto

habría certificado	habríamos certificado
habrías certificado	habríais certificado
habría certificado	habrían certificado

6 presente de subjuntivo

certifique	certifiquemos
certifiques	certifiquéis
certifique	certifiquen

13 perfecto de subjuntivo

haya certificado	hayamos certificado
hayas certificado	hayáis certificado
haya certificado	hayan certificado

7 imperfecto de subjuntivo

certificara	certificáramos
certificaras	certificarais
certificara	certificaran
OR	
certificase	certificásemos
certificases	certificaseis
certificase	certificasen

14 pluscuamperfecto de subjuntivo

hubiera certificado	hubiéramos certificado
hubieras certificado	hubierais certificado
hubiera certificado	hubieran certificado
OR	
hubiese certificado	hubiésemos certificado
hubieses certificado	hubieseis certificado
hubiese certificado	hubiesen certificado

imperativo

—	certifiquemos
certifica; no certifiques	certificad; no certifiquéis
certifique	certifiquen

Words related to this verb

la certificación   certificate, certification
certificador, certificadora   certifier
la certidumbre   certainty

la certeza   certainty
la certinidad   assurance, certainty
tener la certeza de que . . .   to be sure that . . .

Get acquainted with what preposition goes with what verb on pages 541–549.

The subject pronouns are found on the page facing page 1.

charlar

Gerundio **charlando**   Part. pas. **charlado**

to chat, to prattle

The Seven Simple Tenses		The Seven Compound Tenses	
Singular	Plural	Singular	Plural
1 presente de indicativo		8 perfecto de indicativo	
charlo	charlamos	he charlado	hemos charlado
charlas	charláis	has charlado	habéis charlado
charla	charlan	ha charlado	han charlado
2 imperfecto de indicativo		9 pluscuamperfecto de indicativo	
charlaba	charlábamos	había charlado	habíamos charlado
charlabas	charlabais	habías charlado	habíais charlado
charlaba	charlaban	había charlado	habían charlado
3 pretérito		10 pretérito anterior	
charlé	charlamos	hube charlado	hubimos charlado
charlaste	charlasteis	hubiste charlado	hubisteis charlado
charló	charlaron	hubo charlado	hubieron charlado
4 futuro		11 futuro perfecto	
charlaré	charlaremos	habré charlado	habremos charlado
charlarás	charlaréis	habrás charlado	habréis charlado
charlará	charlarán	habrá charlado	habrán charlado
5 potencial simple		12 potencial compuesto	
charlaría	charlaríamos	habría charlado	habríamos charlado
charlarías	charlaríais	habrías charlado	habríais charlado
charlaría	charlarían	habría charlado	habrían charlado
6 presente de subjuntivo		13 perfecto de subjuntivo	
charle	charlemos	haya charlado	hayamos charlado
charles	charléis	hayas charlado	hayáis charlado
charle	charlen	haya charlado	hayan charlado
7 imperfecto de subjuntivo		14 pluscuamperfecto de subjuntivo	
charlara	charláramos	hubiera charlado	hubiéramos charlado
charlaras	charlarais	hubieras charlado	hubierais charlado
charlara	charlaran	hubiera charlado	hubieran charlado
OR		OR	
charlase	charlásemos	hubiese charlado	hubiésemos charlado
charlases	charlaseis	hubieses charlado	hubieseis charlado
charlase	charlasen	hubiese charlado	hubiesen charlado

imperativo	
—	charlemos
charla; no charles	charlad; no charléis
charle	charlen

Words and expressions related to this verb
charlar por los codos   to talk one's head off; **una charla**   to talk, chat
la charladuría   chitchat, gossip, idle talk
un charlatán, una charlatana   chatterbox, charlatan, quack, talkative, gossip
charlatanear   to gossip; **charlador, charladora**   talkative, chatterbox

Get your feet wet with verbs used in weather expressions on page 540.

118

to mumble, to mutter

The Seven Simple Tenses		The Seven Compound Tenses	
Singular	Plural	Singular	Plural
1 presente de indicativo		8 perfecto de indicativo	
chisto	chistamos	he chistado	hemos chistado
chistas	chistáis	has chistado	habéis chistado
chista	chistan	ha chistado	han chistado
2 imperfecto de indicativo		9 pluscuamperfecto de indicativo	
chistaba	chistábamos	había chistado	habíamos chistado
chistabas	chistabais	habías chistado	habíais chistado
chistaba	chistaban	había chistado	habían chistado
3 pretérito		10 pretérito anterior	
chisté	chistamos	hube chistado	hubimos chistado
chistaste	chistasteis	hubiste chistado	hubisteis chistado
chistó	chistaron	hubo chistado	hubieron chistado
4 futuro		11 futuro perfecto	
chistaré	chistaremos	habré chistado	habremos chistado
chistarás	chistaréis	habrás chistado	habréis chistado
chistará	chistarán	habrá chistado	habrán chistado
5 potencial simple		12 potencial compuesto	
chistaría	chistaríamos	habría chistado	habríamos chistado
chistarías	chistaríais	habrías chistado	habríais chistado
chistaría	chistarían	habría chistado	habrían chistado
6 presente de subjuntivo		13 perfecto de subjuntivo	
chiste	chistemos	haya chistado	hayamos chistado
chistes	chistéis	hayas chistado	hayáis chistado
chiste	chisten	haya chistado	hayan chistado
7 imperfecto de subjuntivo		14 pluscuamperfecto de subjuntivo	
chistara	chistáramos	hubiera chistado	hubiéramos chistado
chistaras	chistarais	hubieras chistado	hubierais chistado
chistara	chistaran	hubiera chistado	hubieran chistado
OR		OR	
chistase	chistásemos	hubiese chistado	hubiésemos chistado
chistases	chistaseis	hubieses chistado	hubieseis chistado
chistase	chistasen	hubiese chistado	hubiesen chistado

	imperativo	
—	chistemos	
chista; no chistes	chistad; no chistéis	
chiste	chisten	

Words and expressions related to this verb

no chistar   to remain silent, not to say a word
un chiste   joke, witty saying
contar un chiste   to tell a joke
chistoso, chistosa   funny, witty

hacer chiste de una cosa   to make a joke of something
sin chistar ni mistar   without saying a word
caer en el chiste   to get the joke

Enjoy more verbs in Spanish proverbs on page 539.

The subject pronouns are found on the page facing page 1.

to suck

The Seven Simple Tenses		The Seven Compound Tenses	
Singular	Plural	Singular	Plural
1 presente de indicativo		8 perfecto de indicativo	
chupo	chupamos	he chupado	hemos chupado
chupas	chupáis	has chupado	habéis chupado
chupa	chupan	ha chupado	han chupado
2 imperfecto de indicativo		9 pluscuamperfecto de indicativo	
chupaba	chupábamos	había chupado	habíamos chupado
chupabas	chupabais	habías chupado	habíais chupado
chupaba	chupaban	había chupado	habían chupado
3 pretérito		10 pretérito anterior	
chupé	chupamos	hube chupado	hubimos chupado
chupaste	chupasteis	hubiste chupado	hubisteis chupado
chupó	chuparon	hubo chupado	hubieron chupado
4 futuro		11 futuro perfecto	
chuparé	chuparemos	habré chupado	habremos chupado
chuparás	chuparéis	habrás chupado	habréis chupado
chupará	chuparán	habrá chupado	habrán chupado
5 potencial simple		12 potencial compuesto	
chuparía	chuparíamos	habría chupado	habríamos chupado
chuparías	chuparíais	habrías chupado	habríais chupado
chuparía	chuparían	habría chupado	habrían chupado
6 presente de subjuntivo		13 perfecto de subjuntivo	
chupe	chupemos	haya chupado	hayamos chupado
chupes	chupéis	hayas chupado	hayáis chupado
chupe	chupen	haya chupado	hayan chupado
7 imperfecto de subjuntivo		14 pluscuamperfecto de subjuntivo	
chupara	chupáramos	hubiera chupado	hubiéramos chupado
chuparas	chuparais	hubieras chupado	hubierais chupado
chupara	chuparan	hubiera chupado	hubieran chupado
OR		OR	
chupase	chupásemos	hubiese chupado	hubiésemos chupado
chupases	chupaseis	hubieses chupado	hubieseis chupado
chupase	chupasen	hubiese chupado	hubiesen chupado

imperativo	
—	chupemos
chupa; no chupes	chupad; no chupéis
chupe	chupen

Words and expressions related to this verb
un chupadero, un chupaderito   teething ring
la chupada, la chupadura   suck, sucking
andarse en chupaderitos   to use ineffective
  means for a task
chuparse los dedos   to lick one's
  lips (fingers)

mejillas chupadas   hollow cheeks
está chupado   it's as easy as ABC
chupado, chupada   skinny
chupar un limón   to suck a lemon

If you don't know the Spanish verb for the English verb you have in mind, look it up in the index on pages 505–518.

The Seven Simple Tenses		The Seven Compound Tenses	
Singular	Plural	Singular	Plural
1 presente de indicativo		8 perfecto de indicativo	
cocino	**cocinamos**	**he cocinado**	**hemos cocinado**
cocinas	**cocináis**	**has cocinado**	**habéis cocinado**
cocina	**cocinan**	**ha cocinado**	**han cocinado**
2 imperfecto de indicativo		9 pluscuamperfecto de indicativo	
cocinaba	**cocinábamos**	**había cocinado**	**habíamos cocinado**
cocinabas	**cocinabais**	**habías cocinado**	**habíais cocinado**
cocinaba	**cocinaban**	**había cocinado**	**habían cocinado**
3 pretérito		10 pretérito anterior	
cociné	**cocinamos**	**hube cocinado**	**hubimos cocinado**
cocinaste	**cocinasteis**	**hubiste cocinado**	**hubisteis cocinado**
cocinó	**cocinaron**	**hubo cocinado**	**hubieron cocinado**
4 futuro		11 futuro perfecto	
cocinaré	**cocinaremos**	**habré cocinado**	**habremos cocinado**
cocinarás	**cocinaréis**	**habrás cocinado**	**habréis cocinado**
cocinará	**cocinarán**	**habrá cocinado**	**habrán cocinado**
5 potencial simple		12 potencial compuesto	
cocinaría	**cocinaríamos**	**habría cocinado**	**habríamos cocinado**
cocinarías	**cocinaríais**	**habrías cocinado**	**habríais cocinado**
cocinaría	**cocinarían**	**habría cocinado**	**habrían cocinado**
6 presente de subjuntivo		13 perfecto de subjuntivo	
cocine	**cocinemos**	**haya cocinado**	**hayamos cocinado**
cocines	**cocinéis**	**hayas cocinado**	**hayáis cocinado**
cocine	**cocinen**	**haya cocinado**	**hayan cocinado**
7 imperfecto de subjuntivo		14 pluscuamperfecto de subjuntivo	
cocinara	**cocináramos**	**hubiera cocinado**	**hubiéramos cocinado**
cocinaras	**cocinarais**	**hubieras cocinado**	**hubierais cocinado**
cocinara	**cocinaran**	**hubiera cocinado**	**hubieran cocinado**
OR		OR	
cocinase	**cocinásemos**	**hubiese cocinado**	**hubiésemos cocinado**
cocinases	**cocinaseis**	**hubieses cocinado**	**hubieseis cocinado**
cocinase	**cocinasen**	**hubiese cocinado**	**hubiesen cocinado**

imperativo

—	**cocinemos**
cocina; no cocines	**cocinad; no cocinéis**
cocine	**cocinen**

Words related to this verb
la cocina   kitchen; cooking, cuisine
cocer   to cook, to bake, to boil
el cocinero, la cocinera   cook, kitchen chef
la cocinilla   portable stove

el cocimiento   cooking
el cocido   plate of boiled meat and vegetables;
stew
hacer la cocina   to cook, do the cooking
un libro de cocina   a cookbook

The subject pronouns are found on the page facing page 1.

to seize, to take, to grasp, to grab, to catch, to get (understand)

The Seven Simple Tenses		The Seven Compound Tenses	
Singular	Plural	Singular	Plural
1 presente de indicativo		8 perfecto de indicativo	
cojo	cogemos	he cogido	hemos cogido
coges	cogéis	has cogido	habéis cogido
coge	cogen	ha cogido	han cogido
2 imperfecto de indicativo		9 pluscuamperfecto de indicativo	
cogía	cogíamos	había cogido	habíamos cogido
cogías	cogíais	habías cogido	habíais cogido
cogía	cogían	había cogido	habían cogido
3 pretérito		10 pretérito anterior	
cogí	cogimos	hube cogido	hubimos cogido
cogiste	cogisteis	hubiste cogido	hubisteis cogido
cogió	cogieron	hubo cogido	hubieron cogido
4 futuro		11 futuro perfecto	
cogeré	cogeremos	habré cogido	habremos cogido
cogerás	cogeréis	habrás cogido	habréis cogido
cogerá	cogerán	habrá cogido	habrán cogido
5 potencial simple		12 potencial compuesto	
cogería	cogeríamos	habría cogido	habríamos cogido
cogerías	cogeríais	habrías cogido	habríais cogido
cogería	cogerían	habría cogido	habrían cogido
6 presente de subjuntivo		13 perfecto de subjuntivo	
coja	cojamos	haya cogido	hayamos cogido
cojas	cojáis	hayas cogido	hayáis cogido
coja	cojan	haya cogido	hayan cogido
7 imperfecto de subjuntivo		14 pluscuamperfecto de subjuntivo	
cogiera	cogiéramos	hubiera cogido	hubiéramos cogido
cogieras	cogierais	hubieras cogido	hubierais cogido
cogiera	cogieran	hubiera cogido	hubieran cogido
OR		OR	
cogiese	cogiésemos	hubiese cogido	hubiésemos cogido
cogieses	cogieseis	hubieses cogido	hubieseis cogido
cogiese	cogiesen	hubiese cogido	hubiesen cogido

imperativo	
—	cojamos
coge; no cojas	coged; no cojáis
coja	cojan

Sentences using this verb and words related to it
Quien siembra vientos recoge tempestades.   If you sow the wind, you will reap the whirlwind.

la cogida gathering of fruits, a catch	**recoger** to pick (up), to gather, to reap
el cogedor collector, dustpan	**acoger** to greet, to receive, to welcome
escoger to choose, to select	**encoger** to shorten, to shrink
coger catarro (o resfriado) to catch cold	**descoger** to expand, to extend

The Seven Simple Tenses		The Seven Compound Tenses	
Singular	Plural	Singular	Plural
1 presente de indicativo		**8 perfecto de indicativo**	
colijo	colegimos	he colegido	hemos colegido
coliges	colegís	has colegido	habéis colegido
colige	coligen	ha colegido	han colegido
2 imperfecto de indicativo		**9 pluscuamperfecto de indicativo**	
colegía	colegíamos	había colegido	habíamos colegido
colegías	colegíais	habías colegido	habíais colegido
colegía	colegían	había colegido	habían colegido
3 pretérito		**10 pretérito anterior**	
colegí	colegimos	hube colegido	hubimos colegido
colegiste	colegisteis	hubiste colegido	hubisteis colegido
coligió	coligieron	hubo colegido	hubieron colegido
4 futuro		**11 futuro perfecto**	
colegiré	colegiremos	habré colegido	habremos colegido
colegirás	colegiréis	habrás colegido	habréis colegido
colegirá	colegirán	habrá colegido	habrán colegido
5 potencial simple		**12 potencial compuesto**	
colegiría	colegiríamos	habría colegido	habríamos colegido
colegirías	colegiríais	habrías colegido	habríais colegido
colegiría	colegirían	habría colegido	habrían colegido
6 presente de subjuntivo		**13 perfecto de subjuntivo**	
colija	colijamos	haya colegido	hayamos colegido
colijas	colijáis	hayas colegido	hayáis colegido
colija	colijan	haya colegido	hayan colegido
7 imperfecto de subjuntivo		**14 pluscuamperfecto de subjuntivo**	
coligiera	coligiéramos	hubiera colegido	hubiéramos colegido
coligieras	coligierais	hubieras colegido	hubierais colegido
coligiera	coligieran	hubiera colegido	hubieran colegido
OR		OR	
coligiese	coligiésemos	hubiese colegido	hubiésemos colegido
coligieses	coligieseis	hubieses colegido	hubieseis colegido
coligiese	coligiesen	hubiese colegido	hubiesen colegido

imperativo

—	colijamos
colige; no colijas	colegid; no colijáis
colija	colijan

Words related to this verb
el colegio college, school
la colección collection

colectivo, colectiva collective
el colegio electoral electoral college

Consult the sections on verbs used in idiomatic expressions, verbs with prepositions, and the list of over 1,100 verbs conjugated like model verbs in the back pages.

to hang (up)

The Seven Simple Tenses		The Seven Compound Tenses	
Singular	Plural	Singular	Plural
1 presente de indicativo		8 perfecto de indicativo	
cuelgo	**colgamos**	**he colgado**	**hemos colgado**
cuelgas	**colgáis**	**has colgado**	**habéis colgado**
cuelga	**cuelgan**	**ha colgado**	**han colgado**
2 imperfecto de indicativo		9 pluscuamperfecto de indicativo	
colgaba	**colgábamos**	**había colgado**	**habíamos colgado**
colgabas	**colgabais**	**habías colgado**	**habíais colgado**
colgaba	**colgaban**	**había colgado**	**habían colgado**
3 pretérito		10 pretérito anterior	
colgué	**colgamos**	**hube colgado**	**hubimos colgado**
colgaste	**colgasteis**	**hubiste colgado**	**hubisteis colgado**
colgó	**colgaron**	**hubo colgado**	**hubieron colgado**
4 futuro		11 futuro perfecto	
colgaré	**colgaremos**	**habré colgado**	**habremos colgado**
colgarás	**colgaréis**	**habrás colgado**	**habréis colgado**
colgará	**colgarán**	**habrá colgado**	**habrán colgado**
5 potencial simple		12 potencial compuesto	
colgaría	**colgaríamos**	**habría colgado**	**habríamos colgado**
colgarías	**colgaríais**	**habrías colgado**	**habríais colgado**
colgaría	**colgarían**	**habría colgado**	**habrían colgado**
6 presente de subjuntivo		13 perfecto de subjuntivo	
cuelgue	**colguemos**	**haya colgado**	**hayamos colgado**
cuelgues	**colguéis**	**hayas colgado**	**hayáis colgado**
cuelgue	**cuelguen**	**haya colgado**	**hayan colgado**
7 imperfecto de subjuntivo		14 pluscuamperfecto de subjuntivo	
colgara	**colgáramos**	**hubiera colgado**	**hubiéramos colgado**
colgaras	**colgarais**	**hubieras colgado**	**hubierais colgado**
colgara	**colgaran**	**hubiera colgado**	**hubieran colgado**
OR		OR	
colgase	**colgásemos**	**hubiese colgado**	**hubiésemos colgado**
colgases	**colgaseis**	**hubieses colgado**	**hubieseis colgado**
colgase	**colgasen**	**hubiese colgado**	**hubiesen colgado**

	imperativo	
—		**colguemos**
cuelga; no cuelgues		**colgad; no colguéis**
cuelgue		**cuelguen**

Words related to this verb

el colgadero   hanger, hook on which to hang things
dejar colgado (colgada)   to be left disappointed

la colgadura   drapery, tapestry
colgar la ropa   to hang up the clothes
colgar el teléfono   to hang up the telephone
el puente colgante   suspension bridge

If you want to see a sample English verb fully conjugated in all the tenses, check out pages xviii and xix.

to put, to place

The Seven Simple Tenses		The Seven Compound Tenses	
Singular	Plural	Singular	Plural
1 presente de indicativo		**8 perfecto de indicativo**	
coloco	colocamos	he colocado	hemos colocado
colocas	colocáis	has colocado	habéis colocado
coloca	colocan	ha colocado	han colocado
2 imperfecto de indicativo		**9 pluscuamperfecto de indicativo**	
colocaba	colocábamos	había colocado	habíamos colocado
colocabas	colocabais	habías colocado	habíais colocado
colocaba	colocaban	había colocado	habían colocado
3 pretérito		**10 pretérito anterior**	
coloqué	colocamos	hube colocado	hubimos colocado
colocaste	colocasteis	hubiste colocado	hubisteis colocado
colocó	colocaron	hubo colocado	hubieron colocado
4 futuro		**11 futuro perfecto**	
colocaré	colocaremos	habré colocado	habremos colocado
colocarás	colocaréis	habrás colocado	habréis colocado
colocará	colocarán	habrá colocado	habrán colocado
5 potencial simple		**12 potencial compuesto**	
colocaría	colocaríamos	habría colocado	habríamos colocado
colocarías	colocaríais	habrías colocado	habríais colocado
colocaría	colocarían	habría colocado	habrían colocado
6 presente de subjuntivo		**13 perfecto de subjuntivo**	
coloque	coloquemos	haya colocado	hayamos colocado
coloques	coloquéis	hayas colocado	hayáis colocado
coloque	coloquen	haya colocado	hayan colocado
7 imperfecto de subjuntivo		**14 pluscuamperfecto de subjuntivo**	
colocara	colocáramos	hubiera colocado	hubiéramos colocado
colocaras	colocarais	hubieras colocado	hubierais colocado
colocara	colocaran	hubiera colocado	hubieran colocado
OR		OR	
colocase	colocásemos	hubiese colocado	hubiésemos colocado
colocases	colocaseis	hubieses colocado	hubieseis colocado
colocase	colocasen	hubiese colocado	hubiesen colocado

	imperativo
—	coloquemos
coloca; no coloques	colocad; no coloquéis
coloque	coloquen

Words and expressions related to this verb
la colocación   job, employment, position
colocar dinero   to invest money

colocar un pedido   to place an order
la agencia de colocaciones   job placement agency

Can't recognize an irregular verb form? Check out pages 519–523.

The subject pronouns are found on the page facing page 1.

comenzar

Gerundio **comenzando**   Part. pas. **comenzado**

to begin, to start, to commence

The Seven Simple Tenses		The Seven Compound Tenses	
Singular	Plural	Singular	Plural
1 presente de indicativo		**8 perfecto de indicativo**	
comienzo	comenzamos	he comenzado	hemos comenzado
comienzas	comenzáis	has comenzado	habéis comenzado
comienza	comienzan	ha comenzado	han comenzado
2 imperfecto de indicativo		**9 pluscuamperfecto de indicativo**	
comenzaba	comenzábamos	había comenzado	habíamos comenzado
comenzabas	comenzabais	habías comenzado	habíais comenzado
comenzaba	comenzaban	había comenzado	habían comenzado
3 pretérito		**10 pretérito anterior**	
comencé	comenzamos	hube comenzado	hubimos comenzado
comenzaste	comenzasteis	hubiste comenzado	hubisteis comenzado
comenzó	comenzaron	hubo comenzado	hubieron comenzado
4 futuro		**11 futuro perfecto**	
comenzaré	comenzaremos	habré comenzado	habremos comenzado
comenzarás	comenzaréis	habrás comenzado	habréis comenzado
comenzará	comenzarán	habrá comenzado	habrán comenzado
5 potencial simple		**12 potencial compuesto**	
comenzaría	comenzaríamos	habría comenzado	habríamos comenzado
comenzarías	comenzaríais	habrías comenzado	habríais comenzado
comenzaría	comenzarían	habría comenzado	habrían comenzado
6 presente de subjuntivo		**13 perfecto de subjuntivo**	
comience	comencemos	haya comenzado	hayamos comenzado
comiences	comencéis	hayas comenzado	hayáis comenzado
comience	comiencen	haya comenzado	hayan comenzado
7 imperfecto de subjuntivo		**14 pluscuamperfecto de subjuntivo**	
comenzara	comenzáramos	hubiera comenzado	hubiéramos comenzado
comenzaras	comenzarais	hubieras comenzado	hubierais comenzado
comenzara	comenzaran	hubiera comenzado	hubieran comenzado
OR		OR	
comenzase	comenzásemos	hubiese comenzado	hubiésemos comenzado
comenzases	comenzaseis	hubieses comenzado	hubieseis comenzado
comenzase	comenzasen	hubiese comenzado	hubiesen comenzado

	imperativo
—	comencemos
comienza; no comiences	comenzad; no comencéis
comience	comiencen

Words and expressions related to this verb

—¿Qué tiempo hace?
—Comienza a llover.

el comienzo beginning
comenzante beginner

El comenzante comenzó al comienzo.
The beginner began at the beginning.

comenzar a + inf.   to begin + inf.
comenzar por + inf.   to begin by + pres. part.

Get acquainted with what preposition goes with what verb on pages 541–549.

The Seven Simple Tenses		The Seven Compound Tenses	
Singular	Plural	Singular	Plural
1 presente de indicativo		8 perfecto de indicativo	
como	comemos	he comido	hemos comido
comes	coméis	has comido	habéis comido
come	comen	ha comido	han comido
2 imperfecto de indicativo		9 pluscuamperfecto de indicativo	
comía	comíamos	había comido	habíamos comido
comías	comíais	habías comido	habíais comido
comía	comían	había comido	habían comido
3 pretérito		10 pretérito anterior	
comí	comimos	hube comido	hubimos comido
comiste	comisteis	hubiste comido	hubisteis comido
comió	comieron	hubo comido	hubieron comido
4 futuro		11 futuro perfecto	
comeré	comeremos	habré comido	habremos comido
comerás	comeréis	habrás comido	habréis comido
comerá	comerán	habrá comido	habrán comido
5 potencial simple		12 potencial compuesto	
comería	comeríamos	habría comido	habríamos comido
comerías	comeríais	habrías comido	habríais comido
comería	comerían	habría comido	habrían comido
6 presente de subjuntivo		13 perfecto de subjuntivo	
coma	comamos	haya comido	hayamos comido
comas	comáis	hayas comido	hayáis comido
coma	coman	haya comido	hayan comido
7 imperfecto de subjuntivo		14 pluscuamperfecto de subjuntivo	
comiera	comiéramos	hubiera comido	hubiéramos comido
comieras	comierais	hubieras comido	hubierais comido
comiera	comieran	hubiera comido	hubieran comido
OR		OR	
comiese	comiésemos	hubiese comido	hubiésemos comido
comieses	comieseis	hubieses comido	hubieseis comido
comiese	comiesen	hubiese comido	hubiesen comido

imperativo	
—	comamos
come; no comas	comed; no comáis
coma	coman

Words and expressions related to this verb

ganar de comer to earn a living
la comida meal
cama y comida bed and board
comer fuera de casa to eat out; dine out
dar de comer a los niños to feed the children
comer con muchas ganas to eat heartily

comerse to eat up
el comedor dining room
comer con gana to eat heartily
comer de todo to eat everything
comer para vivir to eat to live
comer como un pajarito to eat like a little bird

The subject pronouns are found on the page facing page 1.

componer

Gerundio **componiendo**　　Part. pas. **compuesto**

to compose

The Seven Simple Tenses		The Seven Compound Tenses	
Singular	Plural	Singular	Plural
1　presente de indicativo		**8　perfecto de indicativo**	
compongo	componemos	he compuesto	hemos compuesto
compones	componéis	has compuesto	habéis compuesto
compone	componen	ha compuesto	han compuesto
2　imperfecto de indicativo		**9　pluscuamperfecto de indicativo**	
componía	componíamos	había compuesto	habíamos compuesto
componías	componíais	habías compuesto	habíais compuesto
componía	componían	había compuesto	habían compuesto
3　pretérito		**10　pretérito anterior**	
compuse	compusimos	hube compuesto	hubimos compuesto
compusiste	compusisteis	hubiste compuesto	hubisteis compuesto
compuso	compusieron	hubo compuesto	hubieron compuesto
4　futuro		**11　futuro perfecto**	
compondré	compondremos	habré compuesto	habremos compuesto
compondrás	compondréis	habrás compuesto	habréis compuesto
compondrá	compondrán	habrá compuesto	habrán compuesto
5　potencial simple		**12　potencial compuesto**	
compondría	compondríamos	habría compuesto	habríamos compuesto
compondrías	compondríais	habrías compuesto	habríais compuesto
compondría	compondrían	habría compuesto	habrían compuesto
6　presente de subjuntivo		**13　perfecto de subjuntivo**	
compongo	compongamos	haya compuesto	hayamos compuesto
compongas	compongáis	hayas compuesto	hayáis compuesto
componga	compongan	haya compuesto	hayan compuesto
7　imperfecto de subjuntivo		**14　pluscuamperfecto de subjuntivo**	
compusiera	compusiéramos	hubiera compuesto	hubiéramos compuesto
compusieras	compusierais	hubieras compuesto	hubierais compuesto
compusiera	compusieran	hubiera compuesto	hubieran compuesto
OR		OR	
compusiese	compusiésemos	hubiese compuesto	hubiésemos compuesto
compusieses	compusieseis	hubieses compuesto	hubieseis compuesto
compusiese	compusiesen	hubiese compuesto	hubiesen compuesto

	imperativo	
—		**compongamos**
compón; no compongas		**componed; no compongáis**
componga		**compongan**

Words and expressions related to this verb

el compuesto　compound, mixture
compuestamente　neatly, orderly
deponer　to depose
imponer　to impose
la composición　composition

el compositor, la compositora　composer (music)
exponer　to expose, to exhibit
indisponer　to indispose

Don't miss the definitions of basic grammatical terms with examples in English and Spanish on pages 666–677.

to buy, to purchase

The Seven Simple Tenses		The Seven Compound Tenses	
Singular	Plural	Singular	Plural
1 presente de indicativo		8 perfecto de indicativo	
compro	compramos	he comprado	hemos comprado
compras	compráis	has comprado	habéis comprado
compra	compran	ha comprado	han comprado
2 imperfecto de indicativo		9 pluscuamperfecto de indicativo	
compraba	comprábamos	había comprado	habíamos comprado
comprabas	comprabais	habías comprado	habíais comprado
compraba	compraban	había comprado	habían comprado
3 pretérito		10 pretérito anterior	
compré	compramos	hube comprado	hubimos comprado
compraste	comprasteis	hubiste comprado	hubisteis comprado
compró	compraron	hubo comprado	hubieron comprado
4 futuro		11 futuro perfecto	
compraré	compraremos	habré comprado	habremos comprado
comprarás	compraréis	habrás comprado	habréis comprado
comprará	comprarán	habrá comprado	habrán comprado
5 potencial simple		12 potencial compuesto	
compraría	compraríamos	habría comprado	habríamos comprado
comprarías	compraríais	habrías comprado	habríais comprado
compraría	comprarían	habría comprado	habrían comprado
6 presente de subjuntivo		13 perfecto de subjuntivo	
compre	compremos	haya comprado	hayamos comprado
compres	compréis	hayas comprado	hayáis comprado
compre	compren	haya comprado	hayan comprado
7 imperfecto de subjuntivo		14 pluscuamperfecto de subjuntivo	
comprara	compráramos	hubiera comprado	hubiéramos comprado
compraras	comprarais	hubieras comprado	hubierais comprado
comprara	compraran	hubiera comprado	hubieran comprado
OR		OR	
comprase	comprásemos	hubiese comprado	hubiésemos comprado
comprases	compraseis	hubieses comprado	hubieseis comprado
comprase	comprasen	hubiese comprado	hubiesen comprado

imperativo

—	compremos
compra; no compres	comprad; no compréis
compre	compren

Words and expressions related to this verb
comprador, compradora   shopper, buyer
la compra   purchase
comprar al contado   to buy for cash
ir de compras   to go shopping

comprar al fiado, comprar a crédito
   to buy on credit
comprar con rebaja   to buy at a discount
hacer compras   to shop

Want to learn more idiomatic expressions that contain verbs? Check out pages 524–537.

The subject pronouns are found on the page facing page 1.

comprender

Gerundio **comprendiendo**   Part. pas. **comprendido**

to understand

The Seven Simple Tenses		The Seven Compound Tenses	
Singular	Plural	Singular	Plural

1   presente de indicativo

		8 perfecto de indicativo	
comprendo	comprendemos	he comprendido	hemos comprendido
comprendes	comprendéis	has comprendido	habéis comprendido
comprende	comprenden	ha comprendido	han comprendido

2   imperfecto de indicativo

		9 pluscuamperfecto de indicativo	
comprendía	comprendíamos	había comprendido	habíamos comprendido
comprendías	comprendíais	habías comprendido	habíais comprendido
comprendía	comprendían	había comprendido	habían comprendido

3   pretérito

		10 pretérito anterior	
comprendí	comprendimos	hube comprendido	hubimos comprendido
comprendiste	comprendisteis	hubiste comprendido	hubisteis comprendido
comprendió	comprendieron	hubo comprendido	hubieron comprendido

4   futuro

		11 futuro perfecto	
comprenderé	comprenderemos	habré comprendido	habremos comprendido
comprenderás	comprenderéis	habrás comprendido	habréis comprendido
comprenderá	comprenderán	habrá comprendido	habrán comprendido

5   potencial simple

		12 potencial compuesto	
comprendería	comprenderíamos	habría comprendido	habríamos comprendido
comprenderías	comprenderíais	habrías comprendido	habríais comprendido
comprendería	comprenderían	habría comprendido	habrían comprendido

6   presente de subjuntivo

		13 perfecto de subjuntivo	
comprenda	comprendamos	haya comprendido	hayamos comprendido
comprendas	comprendáis	hayas comprendido	hayáis comprendido
comprenda	comprendan	haya comprendido	hayan comprendido

7   imperfecto de subjuntivo

		14 pluscuamperfecto de subjuntivo	
comprendiera	comprendiéramos	hubiera comprendido	hubiéramos comprendido
comprendieras	comprendierais	hubieras comprendido	hubierais comprendido
comprendiera	comprendieran	hubiera comprendido	hubieran comprendido
OR		OR	
comprendiese	comprendiésemos	hubiese comprendido	hubiésemos comprendido
comprendieses	comprendieseis	hubieses comprendido	hubieseis comprendido
comprendiese	comprendiesen	hubiese comprendido	hubiesen comprendido

imperativo

—	comprendamos
comprende; no comprendas	comprended; no comprendáis
comprenda	comprendan

Words related to this verb

la comprensión   comprehension, understanding

la comprensibilidad   comprehensibility, intelligibility

comprensivo, comprensiva   comprehensive

comprensible   comprehensible, understandable

comprenderse   to understand one another

Increase your verb power with popular phrases, words, and expressions for tourists on pages 595–618.

to lead, to conduct, to drive

The Seven Simple Tenses		The Seven Compound Tenses	
Singular	Plural	Singular	Plural
1 presente de indicativo		8 perfecto de indicativo	
conduzco	**conducimos**	**he conducido**	**hemos conducido**
conduces	**conducís**	**has conducido**	**habéis conducido**
conduce	**conducen**	**ha conducido**	**han conducido**
2 imperfecto de indicativo		9 pluscuamperfecto de indicativo	
conducía	**conducíamos**	**había conducido**	**habíamos conducido**
conducías	**conducíais**	**habías conducido**	**habíais conducido**
conducía	**conducían**	**había conducido**	**habían conducido**
3 pretérito		10 pretérito anterior	
conduje	**condujimos**	**hube conducido**	**hubimos conducido**
condujiste	**condujisteis**	**hubiste conducido**	**hubisteis conducido**
condujo	**condujeron**	**hubo conducido**	**hubieron conducido**
4 futuro		11 futuro perfecto	
conduciré	**conduciremos**	**habré conducido**	**habremos conducido**
conducirás	**conduciréis**	**habrás conducido**	**habréis conducido**
conducirá	**conducirán**	**habrá conducido**	**habrán conducido**
5 potencial simple		12 potencial compuesto	
conduciría	**conduciríamos**	**habría conducido**	**habríamos conducido**
conducirías	**conduciríais**	**habrías conducido**	**habríais conducido**
conduciría	**conducirían**	**habría conducido**	**habrían conducido**
6 presente de subjuntivo		13 perfecto de subjuntivo	
conduzca	**conduzcamos**	**haya conducido**	**hayamos conducido**
conduzcas	**conduzcáis**	**hayas conducido**	**hayáis conducido**
conduzca	**conduzcan**	**haya conducido**	**hayan conducido**
7 imperfecto de subjuntivo		14 pluscuamperfecto de subjuntivo	
condujera	**condujéramos**	**hubiera conducido**	**hubiéramos conducido**
condujeras	**condujerais**	**hubieras conducido**	**hubierais conducido**
condujera	**condujeran**	**hubiera conducido**	**hubieran conducido**
OR		OR	
condujese	**condujésemos**	**hubiese conducido**	**hubiésemos conducido**
condujeses	**condujeseis**	**hubieses conducido**	**hubieseis conducido**
condujese	**condujesen**	**hubiese conducido**	**hubiesen conducido**

imperativo

—	**conduzcamos**
conduce; no conduzcas	**conducid; no conduzcáis**
conduzca	**conduzcan**

Words and expressions related to this verb
conductor, conductora   conductor, driver
el conducto   conduit, duct
la conducta   conduct, behavior
conducente   conducive

conducir de prisa   to drive fast
¿Sabe Ud. conducir?   Do you know how
   to drive?
un permiso de conducir   driver's license

Can't recognize an irregular verb form? Check out pages 519–523.

to confess

The Seven Simple Tenses		The Seven Compound Tenses	
Singular	Plural	Singular	Plural
1 presente de indicativo		**8 perfecto de indicativo**	
confieso	confesamos	he confesado	hemos confesado
confiesas	confesáis	has confesado	habéis confesado
confiesa	confiesan	ha confesado	han confesado
2 imperfecto de indicativo		**9 pluscuamperfecto de indicativo**	
confesaba	confesábamos	había confesado	habíamos confesado
confesabas	confesabais	habías confesado	habíais confesado
confesaba	confesaban	había confesado	habían confesado
3 pretérito		**10 pretérito anterior**	
confesé	confesamos	hube confesado	hubimos confesado
confesaste	confesasteis	hubiste confesado	hubisteis confesado
confesó	confesaron	hubo confesado	hubieron confesado
4 futuro		**11 futuro perfecto**	
confesaré	confesaremos	habré confesado	habremos confesado
confesarás	confesaréis	habrás confesado	habréis confesado
confesará	confesarán	habrá confesado	habrán confesado
5 potencial simple		**12 potencial compuesto**	
confesaría	confesaríamos	habría confesado	habríamos confesado
confesarías	confesaríais	habrías confesado	habríais confesado
confesaría	confesarían	habría confesado	habrían confesado
6 presente de subjuntivo		**13 perfecto de subjuntivo**	
confiese	confesemos	haya confesado	hayamos confesado
confieses	confeséis	hayas confesado	hayáis confesado
confiese	confiesen	haya confesado	hayan confesado
7 imperfecto de subjuntivo		**14 pluscuamperfecto de subjuntivo**	
confesara	confesáramos	hubiera confesado	hubiéramos confesado
confesaras	confesarais	hubieras confesado	hubierais confesado
confesara	confesaran	hubiera confesado	hubieran confesado
OR		OR	
confesase	confesásemos	hubiese confesado	hubiésemos confesado
confesases	confesaseis	hubieses confesado	hubieseis confesado
confesase	confesasen	hubiese confesado	hubiesen confesado

imperativo

—	confesemos
confiesa; no confieses	confesad; no confeséis
confiese	confiesen

Words and expressions related to this verb
la confesión confession
el confesionario confessional (box)
el confesor confessor

confesar de plano to confess openly
un, una confesante penitent
confesarse a Dios to confess to God

Learn more verbs in 30 practical situations for tourists on pages 564–594.

to know, to be acquainted with

The Seven Simple Tenses		The Seven Compound Tenses	
Singular	Plural	Singular	Plural
1 presente de indicativo		8 perfecto de indicativo	
conozco	**conocemos**	**he conocido**	**hemos conocido**
conoces	**conocéis**	**has conocido**	**habéis conocido**
conoce	**conocen**	**ha conocido**	**han conocido**
2 imperfecto de indicativo		9 pluscuamperfecto de indicativo	
conocía	**conocíamos**	**había conocido**	**habíamos conocido**
conocías	**conocíais**	**habías conocido**	**habíais conocido**
conocía	**conocían**	**había conocido**	**habían conocido**
3 pretérito		10 pretérito anterior	
conocí	**conocimos**	**hube conocido**	**hubimos conocido**
conociste	**conocisteis**	**hubiste conocido**	**hubisteis conocido**
conoció	**conocieron**	**hubo conocido**	**hubieron conocido**
4 futuro		11 futuro perfecto	
conoceré	**conoceremos**	**habré conocido**	**habremos conocido**
conocerás	**conoceréis**	**habrás conocido**	**habréis conocido**
conocerá	**conocerán**	**habrá conocido**	**habrán conocido**
5 potencial simple		12 potencial compuesto	
conocería	**conoceríamos**	**habría conocido**	**habríamos conocido**
conocerías	**conoceríais**	**habrías conocido**	**habríais conocido**
conocería	**conocerían**	**habría conocido**	**habrían conocido**
6 presente de subjuntivo		13 perfecto de subjuntivo	
conozco	**conozcamos**	**haya conocido**	**hayamos conocido**
conozcas	**conozcáis**	**hayas conocido**	**hayáis conocido**
conozca	**conozcan**	**haya conocido**	**hayan conocido**
7 imperfecto de subjuntivo		14 pluscuamperfecto de subjuntivo	
conociera	**conociéramos**	**hubiera conocido**	**hubiéramos conocido**
conocieras	**conocierais**	**hubieras conocido**	**hubierais conocido**
conociera	**conocieran**	**hubiera conocido**	**hubieran conocido**
OR		OR	
conociese	**conociésemos**	**hubiese conocido**	**hubiésemos conocido**
conocieses	**conocieseis**	**hubieses conocido**	**hubieseis conocido**
conociese	**conociesen**	**hubiese conocido**	**hubiesen conocido**

imperativo

—	**conozcamos**
conoce; no conozcas	**conoced; no conozcáis**
conozca	**conozcan**

Sentences using this verb and words related to it

—¿**Conoce Ud. a esa mujer?**
—**Sí, la conozco.**
un conocido, una conocida   an acquaintance
el conocimiento   knowledge

poner en conocimiento de   to inform (about)
reconocer   to recognize, to admit
desconocer   to be ignorant of
muy conocido   very well known

Get acquainted with what preposition goes with what verb on pages 541–549.

conseguir

Gerundio consiguiendo   Part. pas. **conseguido**

to attain, to get, to obtain

The Seven Simple Tenses		The Seven Compound Tenses	
Singular	Plural	Singular	Plural
1 presente de indicativo		**8 perfecto de indicativo**	
consigo	conseguimos	he conseguido	hemos conseguido
consigues	conseguís	has conseguido	habéis conseguido
consigue	consiguen	ha conseguido	han conseguido
2 imperfecto de indicativo		**9 pluscuamperfecto de indicativo**	
conseguía	conseguíamos	había conseguido	habíamos conseguido
conseguías	conseguíais	habías conseguido	habíais conseguido
conseguía	conseguían	había conseguido	habían conseguido
3 pretérito		**10 pretérito anterior**	
conseguí	conseguimos	hube conseguido	hubimos conseguido
conseguiste	conseguisteis	hubiste conseguido	hubisteis conseguido
consiguió	consiguieron	hubo conseguido	hubieron conseguido
4 futuro		**11 futuro perfecto**	
conseguiré	conseguiremos	habré conseguido	habremos conseguido
conseguirás	conseguiréis	habrás conseguido	habréis conseguido
conseguirá	conseguirán	habrá conseguido	habrán conseguido
5 potencial simple		**12 potencial compuesto**	
conseguiría	conseguiríamos	habría conseguido	habríamos conseguido
conseguirías	conseguiríais	habrías conseguido	habríais conseguido
conseguiría	conseguirían	habría conseguido	habrían conseguido
6 presente de subjuntivo		**13 perfecto de subjuntivo**	
consiga	consigamos	haya conseguido	hayamos conseguido
consigas	consigáis	hayas conseguido	hayáis conseguido
consiga	consigan	haya conseguido	hayan conseguido
7 imperfecto de subjuntivo		**14 pluscuamperfecto de subjuntivo**	
consiguiera	consiguiéramos	hubiera conseguido	hubiéramos conseguido
consiguieras	consiguierais	hubieras conseguido	hubierais conseguido
consiguiera	consiguieran	hubiera conseguido	hubieran conseguido
OR		OR	
consiguiese	consiguiésemos	hubiese conseguido	hubiésemos conseguido
consiguieses	consiguieseis	hubieses conseguido	hubieseis conseguido
consiguiese	consiguiesen	hubiese conseguido	hubiesen conseguido

	imperativo	
—		**consigamos**
	consigue; no consigas	**conseguid; no consigáis**
	consiga	**consigan**

Words and expressions related to this verb

el conseguimiento attainment
el consiguiente consequent (syllogism)
de consiguiente, por consiguiente consequently
consiguientemente consequently

See also **seguir**.

dar por conseguido to take for granted
conseguir un permiso to get a permit
conseguir billetes to get tickets
conseguir una buena colocación
    to get a good job

Enjoy verbs in Spanish proverbs on page 539.

to constitute, to make up

The Seven Simple Tenses		The Seven Compound Tenses	
Singular	Plural	Singular	Plural
1 presente de indicativo		8 perfecto de indicativo	
constituyo	constituimos	he constituido	hemos constituido
constituyes	constituís	has constituido	habéis constituido
constituye	constituyen	ha constituido	han constituido
2 imperfecto de indicativo		9 pluscuamperfecto de indicativo	
constituía	constituíamos	había constituido	habíamos constituido
constituías	constituíais	habías constituido	habíais constituido
constituía	constituían	había constituido	habían constituido
3 pretérito		10 pretérito anterior	
constituí	constituimos	hube constituido	hubimos constituido
constituiste	constituisteis	hubiste constituido	hubisteis constituido
constituyó	constituyeron	hubo constituido	hubieron constituido
4 futuro		11 futuro perfecto	
constituiré	constituiremos	habré constituido	habremos constituido
constituirás	constituiréis	habrás constituido	habréis constituido
constituirá	constituirán	habrá constituido	habrán constituido
5 potencial simple		12 potencial compuesto	
constituiría	constituiríamos	habría constituido	habríamos constituido
constituirías	constituiríais	habrías constituido	habríais constituido
constituiría	constituirían	habría constituido	habrían constituido
6 presente de subjuntivo		13 perfecto de subjuntivo	
constituya	constituyamos	haya constituido	hayamos constituido
constituyas	constituyáis	hayas constituido	hayáis constituido
constituya	constituyan	haya constituido	hayan constituido
7 imperfecto de subjuntivo		14 pluscuamperfecto de subjuntivo	
constituyera	constituyéramos	hubiera constituido	hubiéramos constituido
constituyeras	constituyerais	hubieras constituido	hubierais constituido
constituyera	constituyeran	hubiera constituido	hubieran constituido
OR		OR	
constituyese	constituyésemos	hubiese constituido	hubiésemos constituido
constituyeses	constituyeseis	hubieses constituido	hubieseis constituido
constituyese	constituyesen	hubiese constituido	hubiesen constituido

imperativo

	constituyamos
constituye; no constituyas	constituid; no constituyáis
constituya	constituyan

Words related to this verb

constitutivo, constitutiva constitutive, essential
la constitución constitution
el constitucionalismo constitutionalism

constituyente constituent
instituir to institute, to instruct, to teach
restituir to restore, to give back

If you don't know the Spanish verb for the English verb you have in mind, look it up
in the index on pages 505–518.

The subject pronouns are found on the page facing page 1.

to construct, to build

The Seven Simple Tenses		The Seven Compound Tenses	
Singular	Plural	Singular	Plural
1 presente de indicativo		8 perfecto de indicativo	
construyo	construimos	he construido	hemos construido
construyes	construís	has construido	habéis construido
construye	construyen	ha construido	han construido
2 imperfecto de indicativo		9 pluscuamperfecto de indicativo	
construía	construíamos	había construido	habíamos construido
construías	construíais	habías construido	habíais construido
construía	construían	había construido	habían construido
3 pretérito		10 pretérito anterior	
construí	construimos	hube construido	hubimos construido
construiste	construisteis	hubiste construido	hubisteis construido
construyó	construyeron	hubo construido	hubieron construido
4 futuro		11 futuro perfecto	
construiré	construiremos	habré construido	habremos construido
construirás	construiréis	habrás construido	habréis construido
construirá	construirán	habrá construido	habrán construido
5 potencial simple		12 potencial compuesto	
construiría	construiríamos	habría construido	habríamos construido
construirías	construiríais	habrías construido	habríais construido
construiría	construirían	habría construido	habrían construido
6 presente de subjuntivo		13 perfecto de subjuntivo	
construya	construyamos	haya construido	hayamos construido
construyas	construyáis	hayas construido	hayáis construido
construya	construyan	haya construido	hayan construido
7 imperfecto de subjuntivo		14 pluscuamperfecto de subjuntivo	
construyera	construyéramos	hubiera construido	hubiéramos construido
construyeras	construyerais	hubieras construido	hubierais construido
construyera	construyeran	hubiera construido	hubieran construido
OR		OR	
construyese	construyésemos	hubiese construido	hubiésemos construido
construyeses	construyeseis	hubieses construido	hubieseis construido
construyese	construyesen	hubiese construido	hubiesen construido

	imperativo	
—		construyamos
construye; no construyas		construid; no construyáis
construya		construyan

Words related to this verb
la construcción   construction
constructor, constructora   builder
la construcción naval   shipbuilding
reconstruir   to reconstruct

construible   constructible
el edificio en construcción   building under construction

Use the EE-zee guide to Spanish pronunciation on pages 562–563.

to count, to relate, to tell

The Seven Simple Tenses		The Seven Compound Tenses	
Singular	Plural	Singular	Plural

1 presente de indicativo

cuento	contamos		
cuentas	contáis		
cuenta	cuentan		

8 perfecto de indicativo

he contado	hemos contado
has contado	habéis contado
ha contado	han contado

2 imperfecto de indicativo

contaba	contábamos
contabas	contabais
contaba	contaban

9 pluscuamperfecto de indicativo

había contado	habíamos contado
habías contado	habíais contado
había contado	habían contado

3 pretérito

conté	contamos
contaste	contasteis
contó	contaron

10 pretérito anterior

hube contado	hubimos contado
hubiste contado	hubisteis contado
hubo contado	hubieron contado

4 futuro

contaré	contaremos
contarás	contaréis
contará	contarán

11 futuro perfecto

habré contado	habremos contado
habrás contado	habréis contado
habrá contado	habrán contado

5 potencial simple

contaría	contaríamos
contarías	contaríais
contaría	contarían

12 potencial compuesto

habría contado	habríamos contado
habrías contado	habríais contado
habría contado	habrían contado

6 presente de subjuntivo

cuente	contemos
cuentes	contéis
cuente	cuenten

13 perfecto de subjuntivo

haya contado	hayamos contado
hayas contado	hayáis contado
haya contado	hayan contado

7 imperfecto de subjuntivo

contara	contáramos
contaras	contarais
contara	contaran
OR	
contase	contásemos
contases	contaseis
contase	contasen

14 pluscuamperfecto de subjuntivo

hubiera contado	hubiéramos contado
hubieras contado	hubierais contado
hubiera contado	hubieran contado
OR	
hubiese contado	hubiésemos contado
hubieses contado	hubieseis contado
hubiese contado	hubiesen contado

imperativo

—	contemos
cuenta; no cuentes	contad; no contéis
cuente	cuenten

Words and expressions related to this verb
un cuento story, tale
estar en el cuento to be informed
contar con to depend on, to count on,
  to rely on

recontar to recount
descontar to discount, to deduct
la cuenta bill, check
una cuenta bancaria bank account

Enjoy verbs in Spanish proverbs on page 539.

The subject pronouns are found on the page facing page 1.

contener

Gerundio conteniendo   **Part. pas. contenido**

to contain, to hold, to restrain

The Seven Simple Tenses		The Seven Compound Tenses	
Singular	Plural	Singular	Plural
1 presente de indicativo		**8 perfecto de indicativo**	
contengo	contenemos	he contenido	hemos contenido
contienes	contenéis	has contenido	habéis contenido
contiene	contienen	ha contenido	han contenido
2 imperfecto de indicativo		**9 pluscuamperfecto de indicativo**	
contenía	conteníamos	había contenido	habíamos contenido
contenías	conteníais	habías contenido	habíais contenido
contenía	contenían	había contenido	habían contenido
3 pretérito		**10 pretérito anterior**	
contuve	contuvimos	hube contenido	hubimos contenido
contuviste	contuvisteis	hubiste contenido	hubisteis contenido
contuvo	contuvieron	hubo contenido	hubieron contenido
4 futuro		**11 futuro perfecto**	
contendré	contendremos	habré contenido	habremos contenido
contendrás	contendréis	habrás contenido	habréis contenido
contendrá	contendrán	habrá contenido	habrán contenido
5 potencial simple		**12 potencial compuesto**	
contendría	contendríamos	habría contenido	habríamos contenido
contendrías	contendríais	habrías contenido	habríais contenido
contendría	contendrían	habría contenido	habrían contenido
6 presente de subjuntivo		**13 perfecto de subjuntivo**	
contenga	contengamos	haya contenido	hayamos contenido
contengas	contegáis	hayas contenido	hayáis contenido
contenga	contengan	haya contenido	hayan contenido
7 imperfecto de subjuntivo		**14 pluscuamperfecto de subjuntivo**	
contuviera	contuviéramos	hubiera contenido	hubiéramos contenido
contuvieras	contuvierais	hubieras contenido	hubierais contenido
contuviera	contuvieran	hubiera contenido	hubieran contenido
OR		OR	
contuviese	contuviésemos	hubiese contenido	hubiésemos contenido
contuvieses	contuvieseis	hubieses contenido	hubieseis contenido
contuviese	contuviesen	hubiese contenido	hubiesen contenido

	imperativo	
—		contengamos
conten; no contengas		contened; no contegáis
contenga		contengan

Words related to this verb
el contenido content, contents
conteniente containing
contenido, contenida contained

contenerse to contain oneself
contenible containable
contener la risa to keep a straight face (to contain laughter)

See also **tener.**

Get your feet wet with verbs used in weather expressions on page 540.

to answer, to reply (to)

The Seven Simple Tenses		The Seven Compound Tenses	
Singular	Plural	Singular	Plural

1   presente de indicativo

contesto	contestamos		
contestas	contestáis		
contesta	contestan		

8   perfecto de indicativo

he contestado	hemos contestado
has contestado	habéis contestado
ha contestado	han contestado

2   imperfecto de indicativo

contestaba	contestábamos
contestabas	contestabais
contestaba	contestaban

9   pluscuamperfecto de indicativo

había contestado	habíamos contestado
habías contestado	habíais contestado
había contestado	habían contestado

3   pretérito

contesté	contestamos
contestaste	contestasteis
contestó	contestaron

10   pretérito anterior

hube contestado	hubimos contestado
hubiste contestado	hubisteis contestado
hubo contestado	hubieron contestado

4   futuro

contestaré	contestaremos
contestarás	contestaréis
contestará	contestarán

11   futuro perfecto

habré contestado	habremos contestado
habrás contestado	habréis contestado
habrá contestado	habrán contestado

5   potencial simple

contestaría	contestaríamos
contestarías	contestaríais
contestaría	contestarían

12   potencial compuesto

habría contestado	habríamos contestado
habrías contestado	habríais contestado
habría contestado	habrían contestado

6   presente de subjuntivo

conteste	contestemos
contestes	contestéis
conteste	contesten

13   perfecto de subjuntivo

haya contestado	hayamos contestado
hayas contestado	hayáis contestado
haya contestado	hayan contestado

7   imperfecto de subjuntivo

contestara	contestáramos
contestaras	contestarais
contestara	contestaran
OR	
contestase	contestásemos
contestases	contestaseis
contestase	contestasen

14   pluscuamperfecto de subjuntivo

hubiera contestado	hubiéramos contestado
hubieras contestado	hubierais contestado
hubiera contestado	hubieran contestado
OR	
hubiese contestado	hubiésemos contestado
hubieses contestado	hubieseis contestado
hubiese contestado	hubiesen contestado

imperativo

—	**contestemos**
contesta; no contestes	**contestad; no contestéis**
conteste	**contesten**

Words related to this verb
la contestación   answer, reply
contestable   contestable
protestar   to protest
contestar el teléfono   to answer the telephone

un contestador automático   an answering machine
contestar una pregunta   to answer a question

Check out the verb drills and verb tests with answers explained on pages 619–665.

The subject pronouns are found on the page facing page 1.

to continue

The Seven Simple Tenses		The Seven Compound Tenses	
Singular	Plural	Singular	Plural
1 presente de indicativo		8 perfecto de indicativo	
continúo	continuamos	he continuado	hemos continuado
continúas	continuáis	has continuado	habéis continuado
continúa	continúan	ha continuado	han continuado
2 imperfecto de indicativo		9 pluscuamperfecto de indicativo	
continuaba	continuábamos	había continuado	habíamos continuado
continuabas	continuabais	habías continuado	habíais continuado
continuaba	continuaban	había continuado	habían continuado
3 pretérito		10 pretérito anterior	
continué	continuamos	hube continuado	hubimos continuado
continuaste	continuasteis	hubiste continuado	hubisteis continuado
continuó	continuaron	hubo continuado	hubieron continuado
4 futuro		11 futuro perfecto	
continuaré	continuaremos	habré continuado	habremos continuado
continuarás	continuaréis	habrás continuado	habréis continuado
continuará	continuarán	habrá continuado	habrán continuado
5 potencial simple		12 potencial compuesto	
continuaría	continuaríamos	habría continuado	habríamos continuado
continuarías	continuaríais	habrías continuado	habríais continuado
continuaría	continuarían	habría continuado	habrían continuado
6 presente de subjuntivo		13 perfecto de subjuntivo	
continúe	continuemos	haya continuado	hayamos continuado
continúes	continuéis	hayas continuado	hayáis continuado
continúe	continúen	haya continuado	hayan continuado
7 imperfecto de subjuntivo		14 pluscuamperfecto de subjuntivo	
continuara	continuáramos	hubiera continuado	hubiéramos continuado
continuaras	continuarais	hubieras continuado	hubierais continuado
continuara	continuaran	hubiera continuado	hubieran continuado
OR		OR	
continuase	continuásemos	hubiese continuado	hubiésemos continuado
continusases	continuaseis	hubieses continuado	hubieseis continuado
continuase	continuasen	hubiese continuado	hubiesen continuado

	imperativo	
—	continuemos
continúa; no continúes	continuad; no continuéis
continúe	continúen

Words and expressions related to this verb
la **continuación**   continuation
continuamente   continually
a **continuación**   following, next
descontinuar   to discontinue

la **descontinuación**   discontinuation
continuo, continua   continuous
la **coninuidad**   continuity

Review the principal parts of important Spanish verbs on pages xvi and xvii.

to contribute, to pay taxes

The Seven Simple Tenses		The Seven Compound Tenses	
Singular	Plural	Singular	Plural
1 presente de indicativo		8 perfecto de indicativo	
contribuyo	**contribuimos**	**he contribuido**	**hemos contribuido**
contribuyes	**contribuís**	**has contribuido**	**habéis contribuido**
contribuye	**contribuyen**	**ha contribuido**	**han contribuido**
2 imperfecto de indicativo		9 pluscuamperfecto de indicativo	
contribuía	**contribuíamos**	**había contribuido**	**habíamos contribuido**
contribuías	**contribuíais**	**habías contribuido**	**habíais contribuido**
contribuía	**contribuían**	**había contribuido**	**habían contribuido**
3 pretérito		10 pretérito anterior	
contribuí	**contribuimos**	**hube contribuido**	**hubimos contribuido**
contribuiste	**contribuisteis**	**hubiste contribuido**	**hubisteis contribuido**
contribuyó	**contribuyeron**	**hubo contribuido**	**hubieron contribuido**
4 futuro		11 futuro perfecto	
contribuiré	**contribuiremos**	**habré contribuido**	**habremos contribuido**
contribuirás	**contribuiréis**	**habrás contribuido**	**habréis contribuido**
contribuirá	**contribuirán**	**habrá contribuido**	**habrán contribuido**
5 potencial simple		12 potencial compuesto	
contribuiría	**contribuiríamos**	**habría contribuido**	**habríamos contribuido**
contribuirías	**contribuiríais**	**habrías contribuido**	**habríais contribuido**
contribuiría	**contribuirían**	**habría contribuido**	**habrían contribuido**
6 presente de subjuntivo		13 perfecto de subjuntivo	
contribuya	**contribuyamos**	**haya contribuido**	**hayamos contribuido**
contribuyas	**contribuyáis**	**hayas contribuido**	**hayáis contribuido**
contribuya	**contribuyan**	**haya contribuido**	**hayan contribuido**
7 imperfecto de subjuntivo		14 pluscuamperfecto de subjuntivo	
contribuyera	**contribuyéramos**	**hubiera contribuido**	**hubiéramos contribuido**
contribuyeras	**contribuyerais**	**hubieras contribuido**	**hubierais contribuido**
contribuyera	**contribuyeran**	**hubiera contribuido**	**hubieran contribuido**
OR		OR	
contribuyese	**contribuyésemos**	**hubiese contribuido**	**hubiésemos contribuido**
contribuyeses	**contribuyeseis**	**hubieses contribuido**	**hubieseis contribuido**
contribuyese	**contribuyesen**	**hubiese contribuido**	**hubiesen contribuido**

imperativo

—	**contribuyamos**
contribuye; no contribuyas	**contribuid; no contribuyáis**
contribuya	**contribuyan**

Words related to this verb
contribuidor, contribuidora   contributor
la contribución   contribution tax
contributario, contribuyente   taxpayer

la contribución directa   direct tax
la contribución de guerra   war tax (levy)

If you want to see a sample English verb fully conjugated in all the tenses,
check out pages xviii and xix.

convencer   Gerundio **convenciendo**   Part. pas. **convencido**

to convince

The Seven Simple Tenses		The Seven Compound Tenses	
Singular	Plural	Singular	Plural
1 presente de indicativo		8 perfecto de indicativo	
convenzo	convencemos	he convencido	hemos convencido
convences	convencéis	has convencido	habéis convencido
convence	convencen	ha convencido	han convencido
2 imperfecto de indicativo		9 pluscuamperfecto de indicativo	
convencía	convencíamos	había convencido	habíamos convencido
convencías	convencíais	habías convencido	habíais convencido
convencía	convencían	había convencido	habían convencido
3 pretérito		10 pretérito anterior	
convencí	convencimos	hube convencido	hubimos convencido
convenciste	convencisteis	hubiste convencido	hubisteis convencido
convenció	convencieron	hubo convencido	hubieron convencido
4 futuro		11 futuro perfecto	
convenceré	convenceremos	habré convencido	habremos convencido
convencerás	convenceréis	habrás convencido	habréis convencido
convencerá	convencerán	habrá convencido	habrán convencido
5 potencial simple		12 potencial compuesto	
convencería	convenceríamos	habría convencido	habríamos convencido
convencerías	convenceríais	habrías convencido	habríais convencido
convencería	convencerían	habría convencido	habrían convencido
6 presente de subjuntivo		13 perfecto de subjuntivo	
convenza	convenzamos	haya convencido	hayamos convencido
convenzas	convenzáis	hayas convencido	hayáis convencido
convenza	convenzan	haya convencido	hayan convencido
7 imperfecto de subjuntivo		14 pluscuamperfecto de subjuntivo	
convenciera	convenciéramos	hubiera convencido	hubiéramos convencido
convencieras	convencierais	hubieras convencido	hubierais convencido
convenciera	convencieran	hubiera convencido	hubieran convencido
OR		OR	
convenciese	convenciésemos	hubiese convencido	hubiésemos convencido
convencieses	convencieseis	hubieses convencido	hubieseis convencido
convenciese	convenciesen	hubiese convencido	hubiesen convencido

	imperativo	
—		convenzamos
convence; no convenzas		convenced; no convenzáis
convenza		convenzan

Words related to this verb

el convencimiento conviction   **convencible** convincible
convencido, convencida convinced   **convencedor, convencedora** convincing

For other words and expressions related to this verb, see **vencer.**

If you want an explanation of meanings and uses of Spanish
and English verb tenses and moods, see pages xx–xl.

to agree, to convene, to be fitting

The Seven Simple Tenses		The Seven Compound Tenses	
Singular	Plural	Singular	Plural
1 presente de indicativo		8 perfecto de indicativo	
convengo	convenimos	he convenido	hemos convenido
convienes	convenís	has convenido	habéis convenido
conviene	convienen	ha convenido	han convenido
2 imperfecto de indicativo		9 pluscuamperfecto de indicativo	
convenía	conveníamos	había convenido	habíamos convenido
convenías	conveníais	habías convenido	habíais convenido
convenía	convenían	había convenido	habían convenido
3 pretérito		10 pretérito anterior	
convine	convinimos	hube convenido	hubimos convenido
conviniste	convinisteis	hubiste convenido	hubisteis convenido
convino	convinieron	hubo convenido	hubieron convenido
4 futuro		11 futuro perfecto	
convendré	convendremos	habré convenido	habremos convenido
convendrás	convendréis	habrás convenido	habréis convenido
convendrá	convendrán	habrá convenido	habrán convenido
5 potencial simple		12 potencial compuesto	
convendría	convendríamos	habría convenido	habríamos convenido
convendrías	convendríais	habrías convenido	habríais convenido
convendría	convendrían	habría convenido	habrían convenido
6 presente de subjuntivo		13 perfecto de subjuntivo	
convenga	convengamos	haya convenido	hayamos convenido
convengas	convengáis	hayas convenido	hayáis convenido
convenga	convengan	haya convenido	hayan convenido
7 imperfecto de subjuntivo		14 pluscuamperfecto de subjuntivo	
conviniera	conviniéramos	hubiera convenido	hubiéramos convenido
convinieras	convinierais	hubieras convenido	hubierais convenido
conviniera	convinieran	hubiera convenido	hubieran convenido
OR		OR	
conviniese	conviniésemos	hubiese convenido	hubiésemos convenido
convinieses	convinieseis	hubieses convenido	hubieseis convenido
conviniese	conviniesen	hubiese convenido	hubiesen convenido

imperativo	
—	convengamos
conven; no convengas	convenid; no convengáis
convenga	convengan

Words and expressions related to this verb
convenir + inf.   to be important + inf.
convenir en + inf.   to agree + inf.
convenido, convenida   agreed

el convenio   agreement
conveniente   convenient
la convención   convention

For other words and expressions related to this verb, see **venir.**

Can't recognize an irregular verb form? Check out pages 519–523.

convertir　　　　Gerundio **convirtiendo**　　　　Part. pas. **convertido**

to convert

The Seven Simple Tenses		The Seven Compound Tenses	
Singular	Plural	Singular	Plural
1　presente de indicativo		**8　perfecto de indicativo**	
convierto	convertimos	he convertido	hemos convertido
conviertes	convertís	has convertido	habéis convertido
convierte	convierten	ha convertido	han convertido
2　imperfecto de indicativo		**9　pluscuamperfecto de indicativo**	
convertía	convertíamos	había convertido	habíamos convertido
convertías	convertíais	habías convertido	habíais convertido
convertía	convertían	había convertido	habían convertido
3　pretérito		**10　pretérito anterior**	
convertí	convertimos	hube convertido	hubimos convertido
convertiste	convertisteis	hubiste convertido	hubisteis convertido
convirtió	convirtieron	hubo convertido	hubieron convertido
4　futuro		**11　futuro perfecto**	
convertiré	convertiremos	habré convertido	habremos convertido
convertirás	convertiréis	habrás convertido	habréis convertido
convertirá	convertirán	habrá convertido	habrán convertido
5　potencial simple		**12　potencial compuesto**	
convertiría	convertiríamos	habría convertido	habríamos convertido
convertirías	convertiríais	habrías convertido	habríais convertido
convertiría	convertirían	habría convertido	habrían convertido
6　presente de subjuntivo		**13　perfecto de subjuntivo**	
convierta	convirtamos	haya convertido	hayamos convertido
conviertas	convirtáis	hayas convertido	hayáis convertido
convierta	conviertan	haya convertido	hayan convertido
7　imperfecto de subjuntivo		**14　pluscuamperfecto de subjuntivo**	
convirtiera	convirtiéramos	hubiera convertido	hubiéramos convertido
convirtieras	convirtierais	hubieras convertido	hubierais convertido
convirtiera	convirtieran	hubiera convertido	hubieran convertido
OR		OR	
convirtiese	convirtiésemos	hubiese convertido	hubiésemos convertido
convirtieses	convirtieseis	hubieses convertido	hubieseis convertido
convirtiese	convirtiesen	hubiese convertido	hubiesen convertido

imperativo	
—	**convirtamos**
convierte; no conviertas	**convertid; no convirtáis**
convierta	**conviertan**

Words and expressions related to this verb

convertir en dinero　to convert into cash
convertido, convertida　converted, changed
convertir el agua en vino　to turn water
　into wine

la conversión　conversion
convertible　convertible
convertirse　to convert (oneself), to be
　converted, to change religion

Learn more verbs in 30 practical situations for tourists on pages 564–594.

to call together, to convene, to convoke, to summon

The Seven Simple Tenses		The Seven Compound Tenses	
Singular	Plural	Singular	Plural
1 presente de indicativo		8 perfecto de indicativo	
convoco	convocamos	he convocado	hemos convocado
convocas	convocáis	has convocado	habéis convocado
convoca	convocan	ha convocado	han convocado
2 imperfecto de indicativo		9 pluscuamperfecto de indicativo	
convocaba	convocábamos	había convocado	habíamos convocado
convocabas	convocabais	habías convocado	habíais convocado
convocaba	convocaban	había convocado	habían convocado
3 pretérito		10 pretérito anterior	
convoqué	convocamos	hube convocado	hubimos convocado
convocaste	convocasteis	hubiste convocado	hubisteis convocado
convocó	convocaron	hubo convocado	hubieron convocado
4 futuro		11 futuro perfecto	
convocaré	convocaremos	habré convocado	habremos convocado
convocarás	convocaréis	habrás convocado	habréis convocado
convocará	convocarán	habrá convocado	habrán convocado
5 potencial simple		12 potencial compuesto	
convocaría	convocaríamos	habría convocado	habríamos convocado
convcoarías	convocaríais	habrías convocado	habríais convocado
convocaría	convocarían	habría convocado	habrían convocado
6 presente de subjuntivo		13 perfecto de subjuntivo	
convoque	convoquemos	haya convocado	hayamos convocado
convoques	convoquéis	hayas convocado	hayáis convocado
convoque	convoquen	haya convocado	hayan convocado
7 imperfecto de subjuntivo		14 pluscuamperfecto de subjuntivo	
convocara	convocáramos	hubiera convocado	hubiéramos convocado
convocaras	convocarais	hubieras convocado	hubierais convocado
convocara	convocaran	hubiera convocado	hubieran convocado
OR		OR	
convocase	convocásemos	hubiese convocado	hubiésemos convocado
convocases	convocaseis	hubieses convocado	hubieseis convocado
convocase	convocasen	hubiese convocado	hubiesen convocado

imperativo

—	convoquemos
convoca; no convoques	convocad; no convoquéis
convoque	convoquen

Words and expressions related to this verb
la convocación convocation
la vocación vocation, calling
el vacabulario vocabulary

un vocablo word, expression, term
jugar del vocablo to pun, to make a pun
la convocatoria convocation, calling together

Use the EE-zee guide to Spanish pronunciation on pages 562–563.

The subject pronouns are found on the page facing page 1.

145

to correct

The Seven Simple Tenses		The Seven Compound Tenses	
Singular	Plural	Singular	Plural
1 presente de indicativo		8 perfecto de indicativo	
corrijo	corregimos	he corregido	hemos corregido
corriges	corregís	has corregido	habéis corregido
corrige	corrigen	ha corregido	han corregido
2 imperfecto de indicativo		9 pluscuamperfecto de indicativo	
corregía	corregíamos	había corregido	habíamos corregido
corregías	corregíais	habías corregido	habíais corregido
corregía	corregían	había corregido	habían corregido
3 pretérito		10 pretérito anterior	
corregí	corregimos	hube corregido	hubimos corregido
corregiste	corregisteis	hubiste corregido	hubisteis corregido
corrigió	corrigieron	hubo corregido	hubieron corregido
4 futuro		11 futuro perfecto	
corregiré	corregiremos	habré corregido	habremos corregido
corregirás	corregiréis	habrás corregido	habréis corregido
corregirá	corregirán	habrá corregido	habrán corregido
5 potencial simple		12 potencial compuesto	
corregiría	corregiríamos	habría corregido	habríamos corregido
corregirías	corregiríais	habrías corregido	habríais corregido
corregiría	corregirían	habría corregido	habrían corregido
6 presente de subjuntivo		13 perfecto de subjuntivo	
corrija	corrijamos	haya corregido	hayamos corregido
corrijas	corrijáis	hayas corregido	hayáis corregido
corrija	corrijan	haya corregido	hayan corregido
7 imperfecto de subjuntivo		14 pluscuamperfecto de subjuntivo	
corrigiera	corrigiéramos	hubiera corregido	hubiéramos corregido
corrigieras	corrigierais	hubieras corregido	hubierais corregido
corrigiera	corrigieran	hubiera corregido	hubieran corregido
OR		OR	
corrigiese	corrigiésemos	hubiese corregido	hubiésemos corregido
corrigieses	corrigieseis	hubieses corregido	hubieseis corregido
corrigiese	corrigiesen	hubiese corregido	hubiesen corregido

	imperativo
—	**corrijamos**
corrige; no corrijas	**corregid; no corrijáis**
corrija	**corrijan**

Words and expressions related to this verb
corregir pruebas   to read proofs
corregible   corrigible
incorregible   incorrigible
la corrección   correction

correcto, correcta   correct
correctamente   correctly
correccional   correctional
el correccional   reformatory

Can't recognize an irregular verb form? Check out pages 519–523.

to run, to race, to flow

The Seven Simple Tenses		The Seven Compound Tenses	
Singular	Plural	Singular	Plural

1   presente de indicativo

corro	corremos
corres	corréis
corre	corren

8   perfecto de indicativo

he corrido	hemos corrido
has corrido	habéis corrido
ha corrido	han corrido

2   imperfecto de indicativo

corría	corríamos
corrías	corríais
corría	corrían

9   pluscuamperfecto de indicativo

había corrido	habíamos corrido
habías corrido	habíais corrido
había corrido	habían corrido

3   pretérito

corrí	corrimos
corriste	corristeis
corrió	corrieron

10   pretérito anterior

hube corrido	hubimos corrido
hubiste corrido	hubisteis corrido
hubo corrido	hubieron corrido

4   futuro

correré	correremos
correrás	correréis
correrá	correrán

11   futuro perfecto

habré corrido	habremos corrido
habrás corrido	habréis corrido
habrá corrido	habrán corrido

5   potencial simple

correría	correríamos
correrías	correríais
correría	correrían

12   potencial compuesto

habría corrido	habríamos corrido
habrías corrido	habríais corrido
habría corrido	habrían corrido

6   presente de subjuntivo

corra	corramos
corras	corráis
corra	corran

13   perfecto de subjuntivo

haya corrido	hayamos corrido
hayas corrido	hayáis corrido
haya corrido	hayan corrido

7   imperfecto de subjuntivo

corriera	corriéramos
corrieras	corrierais
corriera	corrieran
OR	
corriese	corriésemos
corrieses	corrieseis
corriese	corriesen

14   pluscuamperfecto de subjuntivo

hubiera corrido	hubiéramos corrido
hubieras corrido	hubierais corrido
hubiera corrido	hubieran corrido
OR	
hubiese corrido	hubiésemos corrido
hubieses corrido	hubieseis corrido
hubiese corrido	hubiesen corrido

imperativo

—	corramos
corre; no corras	corred; no corráis
corra	corran

Words and expressions related to this verb

el correo   mail, post
correo aéreo   air mail
echar una carta al correo   to mail (post) a letter
la corrida   race
de corrida   at full speed

descorrer   to flow (liquids); to draw a curtain or drape
por correo aparte   under separate cover (mail)
recorrer   to travel on, to go over

The subject pronouns are found on the page facing page 1.

to cut, to cut off, to cut out

The Seven Simple Tenses		The Seven Compound Tenses	
Singular	Plural	Singular	Plural
1 presente de indicativo		8 perfecto de indicativo	
corto	cortamos	he cortado	hemos cortado
cortas	cortáis	has cortado	habéis cortado
corta	cortan	ha cortado	han cortado
2 imperfecto de indicativo		9 pluscuamperfecto de indicativo	
cortaba	cortábamos	había cortado	habíamos cortado
cortabas	cortabais	habías cortado	habíais cortado
cortaba	cortaban	había cortado	habían cortado
3 pretérito		10 pretérito anterior	
corté	cortamos	hube cortado	hubimos cortado
cortaste	cortasteis	hubiste cortado	hubisteis cortado
cortó	cortaron	hubo cortado	hubieron cortado
4 futuro		11 futuro perfecto	
cortaré	cortaremos	habré cortado	habremos cortado
cortarás	cortaréis	habrás cortado	habréis cortado
cortará	cortarán	habrá cortado	habrán cortado
5 potencial simple		12 potencial compuesto	
cortaría	cortaríamos	habría cortado	habríamos cortado
cortarías	cortaríais	habrías cortado	habríais cortado
cortaría	cortarían	habría cortado	habrían cortado
6 presente de subjuntivo		13 perfecto de subjuntivo	
corte	cortemos	haya cortado	hayamos cortado
cortes	cortéis	hayas cortado	hayáis cortado
corte	corten	haya cortado	hayan cortado
7 imperfecto de subjuntivo		14 pluscuamperfecto de subjuntivo	
cortara	cortáramos	hubiera cortado	hubiéramos cortado
cortaras	cortarais	hubieras cortado	hubierais cortado
cortara	cortaran	hubiera cortado	hubieran cortado
OR		OR	
cortase	cortásemos	hubiese cortado	hubiésemos cortado
cortases	cortaseis	hubieses cortado	hubieseis cortado
cortase	cortasen	hubiese cortado	hubiesen cortado

imperativo	
—	cortemos
corta; no cortes	cortad; no cortéis
corte	corten

Words and expressions related to this verb
cortar el agua   to cut off the water
cortar las alas a uno   to cut a person down, "to cut off one's wings"
cortar el vino con agua   to dilute wine
corto, corta   short; **corto de oído**   hard of hearing
recortar   to trim, cut off, cut away; **un recorte**   clipping from a newspaper
un corte del pelo   haircut

The Seven Simple Tenses		The Seven Compound Tenses	
Singular	Plural	Singular	Plural
1 presente de indicativo		8 perfecto de indicativo	
cuesta	**cuestan**	**ha costado**	**han costado**
2 imperfecto de indicativo		9 pluscuamperfecto de indicativo	
costaba	**costaban**	**había costado**	**habían costado**
3 pretérito		10 pretérito anterior	
costó	**costaron**	**hubo costado**	**hubieron costado**
4 futuro		11 futuro perfecto	
costará	**costarán**	**habrá costado**	**habrán costado**
5 potencial simple		12 potencial compuesto	
costaría	**costarían**	**habría costado**	**habrían costado**
6 presente de subjuntivo		13 perfecto de subjuntivo	
que cueste	**que cuesten**	**que haya costado**	**que hayan costado**
7 imperfecto de subjuntivo		14 pluscuamperfecto de subjuntivo	
que costara	**que costaran**	**que hubiera costado**	**que hubieran costado**
OR		OR	
que costase	**que costasen**	**que hubiese costado**	**que hubiesen costado**

imperativo

¡Que cueste! **¡Que cuesten!**

Sentences using this verb and words and expressions related to it

—**¿Cuánto cuesta este libro?** **Cuesta + inf.** It is difficult to . . .
—**Cuesta diez euros.** **Cuesta creerlo.** It's difficult to believe it.

costoso, costosa costly, expensive
el costo price, cost
el costo de la vida the cost of living
costear to finance

costar un ojo de la cara to be very expensive
  (to cost an arm and a leg)
cueste lo que cueste at any cost

The subject pronouns are found on the page facing page 1.

to grow

The Seven Simple Tenses		The Seven Compound Tenses	
Singular	Plural	Singular	Plural
1 presente de indicativo		**8 perfecto de indicativo**	
crezco	crecemos	he crecido	hemos crecido
creces	crecéis	has crecido	habéis crecido
crece	crecen	ha crecido	han crecido
2 imperfecto de indicativo		**9 pluscuamperfecto de indicativo**	
crecía	crecíamos	había crecido	habíamos crecido
crecías	crecíais	habías crecido	habíais crecido
crecía	crecían	había crecido	habían crecido
3 pretérito		**10 pretérito anterior**	
crecí	crecimos	hube crecido	hubimos crecido
creciste	crecisteis	hubiste crecido	hubisteis crecido
creció	crecieron	hubo crecido	hubieron crecido
4 futuro		**11 futuro perfecto**	
creceré	creceremos	habré crecido	habremos crecido
crecerás	creceréis	habrás crecido	habréis crecido
crecerá	crecerán	habrá crecido	habrán crecido
5 potencial simple		**12 potencial compuesto**	
crecería	creceríamos	habría crecido	habríamos crecido
crecerías	creceríais	habrías crecido	habríais crecido
crecería	crecerían	habría crecido	habrían crecido
6 presente de subjuntivo		**13 perfecto de subjuntivo**	
crezca	crezcamos	haya crecido	hayamos crecido
crezcas	crezcáis	hayas crecido	hayáis crecido
crezca	crezcan	haya crecido	hayan crecido
7 imperfecto de subjuntivo		**14 pluscuamperfecto de subjuntivo**	
creciera	creciéramos	hubiera crecido	hubiéramos crecido
crecieras	crecierais	hubieras crecido	hubierais crecido
creciera	crecieran	hubiera crecido	hubieran crecido
OR		OR	
creciese	creciésemos	hubiese crecido	hubiésemos crecido
crecieses	crecieseis	hubieses crecido	hubieseis crecido
creciese	creciesen	hubiese crecido	hubiesen crecido

imperativo	
—	crezcamos
crece; no crezcas	creced; no crezcáis
crezca	crezcan

Words and expressions related to this verb

crecer como la mala hierba to grow like a weed
crecidamente abundantly
el crescendo crescendo (music)

la luna creciente crescent moon
el crecimiento growth
la crecida swelling of a river
creciente growing, increasing

Don't miss the definitions of basic grammatical terms with
examples in English and Spanish on pages 666–677.

The Seven Simple Tenses		The Seven Compound Tenses	
Singular	Plural	Singular	Plural
1 presente de indicativo		8 perfecto de indicativo	
creo	**creemos**	**he creído**	**hemos creído**
crees	**creéis**	**has creído**	**habéis creído**
cree	**creen**	**ha creído**	**han creído**
2 imperfecto de indicativo		9 pluscuamperfecto de indicativo	
creía	**creíamos**	**había creído**	**habíamos creído**
creías	**creíais**	**habías creído**	**habíais creído**
creía	**creían**	**había creído**	**habían creído**
3 pretérito		10 pretérito anterior	
creí	**creímos**	**hube creído**	**hubimos creído**
creíste	**creísteis**	**hubiste creído**	**hubisteis creído**
creyó	**creyeron**	**hubo creído**	**hubieron creído**
4 futuro		11 futuro perfecto	
creeré	**creeremos**	**habré creído**	**habremos creído**
creerás	**creeréis**	**habrás creído**	**habréis creído**
creerá	**creerán**	**habrá creído**	**habrán creído**
5 potencial simple		12 potencial compuesto	
creería	**creeríamos**	**habría creído**	**habríamos creído**
creería	**creeríais**	**habrías creído**	**habríais creído**
creería	**creerían**	**habría creído**	**habrían creído**
6 presente de subjuntivo		13 perfecto de subjuntivo	
crea	**creamos**	**haya creído**	**hayamos creído**
creas	**creáis**	**hayas creído**	**hayáis creído**
crea	**crean**	**haya creído**	**hayan creído**
7 imperfecto de subjuntivo		14 pluscuamperfecto de subjuntivo	
creyera	**creyéramos**	**hubiera creído**	**hubiéramos creído**
creyeras	**creyerais**	**hubieras creído**	**hubierais creído**
creyera	**creyeran**	**hubiera creído**	**hubieran creído**
OR		OR	
creyese	**creyésemos**	**hubiese creído**	**hubiésemos creído**
creyeses	**creyeseis**	**hubieses creído**	**hubieseis creído**
creyese	**creyesen**	**hubiese creído**	**hubiesen creído**

imperativo	
—	**creamos**
cree; no creas	**creed; no creáis**
crea	**crean**

Words and expressions related to this verb
Ver es creer   Seeing is believing.
¡Ya lo creo!   Of course!
crédulo, crédula   credulous
descreer   to disbelieve
Creo que sí.   I think so.

la credulidad   credulity
el credo   creed
dar crédito   to believe
Creo que no.   I don't think so.
No me lo creo.   I can't believe it.

The subject pronouns are found on the page facing page 1.

to breed, to raise, to bring up (rear)

The Seven Simple Tenses		The Seven Compound Tenses	
Singular	Plural	Singular	Plural
1 presente de indicativo		8 perfecto de indicativo	
crío	**criamos**	**he criado**	**hemos criado**
crías	**criáis**	**has criado**	**habéis criado**
cría	**crían**	**ha criado**	**han criado**
2 imperfecto de indicativo		9 pluscuamperfecto de indicativo	
criaba	**criábamos**	**había criado**	**habíamos criado**
criabas	**criabais**	**habías criado**	**habíais criado**
criaba	**criaban**	**había criado**	**habían criado**
3 pretérito		10 pretérito anterior	
crié	**criamos**	**hube criado**	**hubimos criado**
criaste	**criasteis**	**hubiste criado**	**hubisteis criado**
crió	**criaron**	**hubo criado**	**hubieron criado**
4 futuro		11 futuro perfecto	
criaré	**criaremos**	**habré criado**	**habremos criado**
criarás	**criaréis**	**habrás criado**	**habréis criado**
criará	**criarán**	**habrá criado**	**habrán criado**
5 potencial simple		12 potencial compuesto	
criaría	**criaríamos**	**habría criado**	**habríamos criado**
criarías	**criaríais**	**habrías criado**	**habríais criado**
criaría	**criarían**	**habría criado**	**habrían criado**
6 presente de subjuntivo		13 perfecto de subjuntivo	
críe	**criemos**	**haya criado**	**hayamos criado**
críes	**criéis**	**hayas criado**	**hayáis criado**
críe	**críen**	**haya criado**	**hayan criado**
7 imperfecto de subjuntivo		14 pluscuamperfecto de subjuntivo	
criara	**criáramos**	**hubiera criado**	**hubiéramos criado**
criaras	**criarais**	**hubieras criado**	**hubierais criado**
criara	**criaran**	**hubiera criado**	**hubieran criado**
OR		OR	
criase	**criásemos**	**hubiese criado**	**hubiésemos criado**
criases	**criaseis**	**hubieses criado**	**hubieseis criado**
criase	**criasen**	**hubiese criado**	**hubiesen criado**

	imperativo	
—		**criemos**
cría; no críes		**criad; no criéis**
críe		**críen**

Words and expressions related to this verb

la criandera la criadora wet nurse
el criado, la criada servant
la crianza nursing
dar crianza to educate, to bring up

mal crianza bad manners, impoliteness
Dios los cría y ellos se juntan Birds of a feather flock together.

Enjoy more verbs in Spanish proverbs on page 539.

The Seven Simple Tenses		The Seven Compound Tenses	
Singular	Plural	Singular	Plural
1 presente de indicativo		**8 perfecto de indicativo**	
cruzo	cruzamos	he cruzado	hemos cruzado
cruzas	cruzáis	has cruzado	habéis cruzado
cruza	cruzan	ha cruzado	han cruzado
2 imperfecto de indicativo		**9 pluscuamperfecto de indicativo**	
cruzaba	cruzábamos	había cruzado	habíamos cruzado
cruzabas	cruzabais	habías cruzado	habíais cruzado
cruzaba	cruzaban	había cruzado	habían cruzado
3 pretérito		**10 pretérito anterior**	
crucé	cruzamos	hube cruzado	hubimos cruzado
cruzaste	cruzasteis	hubiste cruzado	hubisteis cruzado
cruzó	cruzaron	hubo cruzado	hubieron cruzado
4 futuro		**11 futuro perfecto**	
cruzaré	cruzaremos	habré cruzado	habremos cruzado
cruzarás	cruzaréis	habrás cruzado	habréis cruzado
cruzará	cruzarán	habrá cruzado	habrán cruzado
5 potencial simple		**12 potencial compuesto**	
cruzaría	cruzaríamos	habría cruzado	habríamos cruzado
cruzarías	cruzaríais	habrías cruzado	habríais cruzado
cruzaría	cruzarían	habría cruzado	habrían cruzado
6 presente de subjuntivo		**13 perfecto de subjuntivo**	
cruce	crucemos	haya cruzado	hayamos cruzado
cruces	crucéis	hayas cruzado	hayáis cruzado
cruce	crucen	haya cruzado	hayan cruzado
7 imperfecto de subjuntivo		**14 pluscuamperfecto de subjuntivo**	
cruzara	cruzáramos	hubiera cruzado	hubiéramos cruzado
cruzaras	cruzarais	hubieras cruzado	hubierais cruzado
cruzara	cruzaran	hubiera cruzado	hubieran cruzado
OR		OR	
cruzase	cruzásemos	hubiese cruzado	hubiésemos cruzado
cruzases	cruzaseis	hubieses cruzado	hubieseis cruzado
cruzase	cruzasen	hubiese cruzado	hubiesen cruzado

imperativo

—	crucemos
cruza; no cruces	cruzad; no crucéis
cruce	crucen

Sentences using this verb and words related to it
El que no se aventura no cruza el mar. Nothing ventured, nothing gained.

el cruzamiento crossing   **la cruz** cross
la cruzada crusade, crossroads   **la Cruz de Malta** Maltese Cross

Enjoy more verbs in Spanish proverbs on page 539.

to cover

The Seven Simple Tenses		The Seven Compound Tenses	
Singular	Plural	Singular	Plural
1 presente de indicativo		**8 perfecto de indicativo**	
cubro	cubrimos	he cubierto	hemos cubierto
cubres	cubrís	has cubierto	habéis cubierto
cubre	cubren	ha cubierto	han cubierto
2 imperfecto de indicativo		**9 pluscuamperfecto de indicativo**	
cubría	cubríamos	había cubierto	habíamos cubierto
cubrías	cubríais	habías cubierto	habíais cubierto
cubría	cubrían	había cubierto	habían cubierto
3 pretérito		**10 pretérito anterior**	
cubrí	cubrimos	hube cubierto	hubimos cubierto
cubriste	cubristeis	hubiste cubierto	hubisteis cubierto
cubrió	cubrieron	hubo cubierto	hubieron cubierto
4 futuro		**11 futuro perfecto**	
cubriré	cubriremos	habré cubierto	habremos cubierto
cubrirás	cubriréis	habrás cubierto	habréis cubierto
cubrirá	cubrirán	habrá cubierto	habrán cubierto
5 potencial simple		**12 potencial compuesto**	
cubriría	cubriríamos	habría cubierto	habríamos cubierto
cubrirías	cubriríais	habrías cubierto	habríais cubierto
cubriría	cubrirían	habría cubierto	habrían cubierto
6 presente de subjuntivo		**13 perfecto de subjuntivo**	
cubra	cubramos	haya cubierto	hayamos cubierto
cubras	cubráis	hayas cubierto	hayáis cubierto
cubra	cubran	haya cubierto	hayan cubierto
7 imperfecto de subjuntivo		**14 pluscuamperfecto de subjuntivo**	
cubriera	cubriéramos	hubiera cubierto	hubiéramos cubierto
cubrieras	cubrierais	hubieras cubierto	hubierais cubierto
cubriera	cubrieran	hubiera cubierto	hubieran cubierto
OR		OR	
cubriese	cubriésemos	hubiese cubierto	hubiésemos cubierto
cubrieses	cubrieseis	hubieses cubierto	hubieseis cubierto
cubriese	cubriesen	hubiese cubierto	hubiesen cubierto

imperativo	
—	cubramos
cubre; no cubras	cubrid; no cubráis
cubra	cubran

Words and expressions related to this verb

la cubierta cover, wrapping
la cubierta del motor hood of an automobile
el cubrimiento covering
el cubierto place setting (meal)
cubrir los gastos to cover expenses
cubiertamente covertly

encubrir to hide, to conceal, to mask
el encubrimiento hiding, concealment
descubrir to discover
bajo cubierto under cover
a cubierto de under cover of
el cielo está cubierto the sky is overcast

Get your feet wet with verbs used in weather expressions on page 540.

to take care of oneself

The Seven Simple Tenses		The Seven Compound Tenses	
Singular	Plural	Singular	Plural
1 presente de indicativo		8 perfecto de indicativo	
me cuido	**nos cuidamos**	**me he cuidado**	**nos hemos cuidado**
te cuidas	**os cuidáis**	**te has cuidado**	**os habéis cuidado**
se cuida	**se cuidan**	**se ha cuidado**	**se han cuidado**
2 imperfecto de indicativo		9 pluscuamperfecto de indicativo	
me cuidaba	**nos cuidábamos**	**me había cuidado**	**nos habíamos cuidado**
te cuidabas	**os cuidabais**	**te habías cuidado**	**os habíais cuidado**
se cuidaba	**se cuidaban**	**se había cuidado**	**se habían cuidado**
3 pretérito		10 pretérito anterior	
me cuidé	**nos cuidamos**	**me hube cuidado**	**nos hubimos cuidado**
te cuidaste	**os cuidasteis**	**te hubiste cuidado**	**os hubisteis cuidado**
se cuidó	**se cuidaron**	**se hubo cuidado**	**se hubieron cuidado**
4 futuro		11 futuro perfecto	
me cuidaré	**nos cuidaremos**	**me habré cuidado**	**nos habremos cuidado**
te cuidarás	**os cuidaréis**	**te habrás cuidado**	**os habréis cuidado**
se cuidará	**se cuidarán**	**se habrá cuidado**	**se habrán cuidado**
5 potencial simple		12 potencial compuesto	
me cuidaría	**nos cuidaríamos**	**me habría cuidado**	**nos habríamos cuidado**
te cuidarías	**os cuidaríais**	**te habrías cuidado**	**os habríais cuidado**
se cuidaría	**se cuidarían**	**se habría cuidado**	**se habrían cuidado**
6 presente de subjuntivo		13 perfecto de subjuntivo	
me cuide	**nos cuidemos**	**me haya cuidado**	**nos hayamos cuidado**
te cuides	**os cuidéis**	**te hayas cuidado**	**os hayáis cuidado**
se cuide	**se cuiden**	**se haya cuidado**	**se hayan cuidado**
7 imperfecto de subjuntivo		14 pluscuamperfecto de subjuntivo	
me cuidara	**nos cuidáramos**	**me hubiera cuidado**	**nos hubiéramos cuidado**
te cuidaras	**os cuidarais**	**te hubieras cuidado**	**os hubierais cuidado**
se cuidara	**se cuidaran**	**se hubiera cuidado**	**se hubieran cuidado**
OR		OR	
me cuidase	**nos cuidásemos**	**me hubiese cuidado**	**nos hubiésemos cuidado**
te cuidases	**os cuidaseis**	**te hubieses cuidado**	**os hubieseis cuidado**
se cuidase	**se cuidasen**	**se hubiese cuidado**	**se hubiesen cuidado**

	imperativo	
—		**cuidémonos**
cuídate; no te cuides		**cuidaos; no os cuidéis**
cuídese		**cuídense**

Words and expressions related to this verb

cuidar de to care for, to look after	**¡Cuidado!** Careful!
cuidarse de to care about, to be careful	**cuidadoso, cuidadosa** careful
el cuidado care, concern	**al cuidado de** under the care of
con cuidado with care	**tener cuidado** to be careful
descuidar to neglect, overlook	**descuidarse de** not to bother about
el descuido negligence, neglect	**descuidarse de + inf.** to neglect + inf.

The subject pronouns are found on the page facing page 1.   **155**

cumplir   Gerundio **cumpliendo**   Part. pas. **cumplido**

to fulfill, to keep (a promise), to reach one's birthday (use with **años**)

The Seven Simple Tenses		The Seven Compound Tenses	
Singular	Plural	Singular	Plural
1 presente de indicativo		8 perfecto de indicativo	
cumplo	**cumplimos**	**he cumplido**	**hemos cumplido**
cumples	**cumplís**	**has cumplido**	**habéis cumplido**
cumple	**cumplen**	**ha cumplido**	**han cumplido**
2 imperfecto de indicativo		9 pluscuamperfecto de indicativo	
cumplía	**cumplíamos**	**había cumplido**	**habíamos cumplido**
cumplías	**cumplíais**	**habías cumplido**	**habíais cumplido**
cumplía	**cumplían**	**había cumplido**	**habían cumplido**
3 pretérito		10 pretérito anterior	
cumplí	**cumplimos**	**hube cumplido**	**hubimos cumplido**
cumpliste	**cumplisteis**	**hubiste cumplido**	**hubisteis cumplido**
cumplió	**cumplieron**	**hubo cumplido**	**hubieron cumplido**
4 futuro		11 futuro perfecto	
cumpliré	**cumpliremos**	**habré cumplido**	**habremos cumplido**
cumplirás	**cumpliréis**	**habrás cumplido**	**habréis cumplido**
cumplirá	**cumplirán**	**habrá cumplido**	**habrán cumplido**
5 potencial simple		12 potencial compuesto	
cumpliría	**cumpliríamos**	**habría cumplido**	**habríamos cumplido**
cumplirías	**cumpliríais**	**habrías cumplido**	**habríais cumplido**
cumpliría	**cumplirían**	**habría cumplido**	**habrían cumplido**
6 presente de subjuntivo		13 perfecto de subjuntivo	
cumpla	**cumplamos**	**haya cumplido**	**hayamos cumplido**
cumplas	**cumpláis**	**hayas cumplido**	**hayáis cumplido**
cumpla	**cumplan**	**haya cumplido**	**hayan cumplido**
7 imperfecto de subjuntivo		14 pluscuamperfecto de subjuntivo	
cumpliera	**cumpliéramos**	**hubiera cumplido**	**hubiéramos cumplido**
cumplieras	**cumplierais**	**hubieras cumplido**	**hubierais cumplido**
cumpliera	**cumplieran**	**hubiera cumplido**	**hubieran cumplido**
OR		OR	
cumpliese	**cumpliésemos**	**hubiese cumplido**	**hubiésemos cumplido**
cumplieses	**cumplieseis**	**hubieses cumplido**	**hubieseis cumplido**
cumpliese	**cumpliesen**	**hubiese cumplido**	**hubiesen cumplido**

imperativo	
—	**cumplamos**
cumple; no cumplas	**cumplid; no cumpláis**
cumpla	**cumplan**

Words and expressions related to this verb
el cumpleaños birthday
cumplidamente completely
el cumplimiento completion
cumplir con to fulfill one's obligations

cumplir ... años to reach the age of . . .
Hoy cumplo diez y siete años. Today is my seventeenth birthday.
¡Feliz cumpleaños! Happy birthday!

Use the EE-zee guide to Spanish pronunciation on pages 562–563

The Seven Simple Tenses		The Seven Compound Tenses	
Singular	Plural	Singular	Plural
1　presente de indicativo		8　perfecto de indicativo	
doy	**damos**	**he dado**	**hemos dado**
das	**dais**	**has dado**	**habéis dado**
da	**dan**	**ha dado**	**han dado**
2　imperfecto de indicativo		9　pluscuamperfecto de indicativo	
daba	**dábamos**	**había dado**	**habíamos dado**
dabas	**dabais**	**habías dado**	**habíais dado**
daba	**daban**	**había dado**	**habían dado**
3　pretérito		10　pretérito anterior	
di	**dimos**	**hube dado**	**hubimos dado**
diste	**disteis**	**hubiste dado**	**hubisteis dado**
dio	**dieron**	**hubo dado**	**hubieron dado**
4　futuro		11　futuro perfecto	
daré	**daremos**	**habré dado**	**habremos dado**
darás	**daréis**	**habrás dado**	**habréis dado**
dará	**darán**	**habrá dado**	**habrán dado**
5　potencial simple		12　potencial compuesto	
daría	**daríamos**	**habría dado**	**habríamos dado**
darías	**daríais**	**habrías dado**	**habríais dado**
daría	**darían**	**habría dado**	**habrían dado**
6　presente de subjuntivo		13　perfecto de subjuntivo	
dé	**demos**	**haya dado**	**hayamos dado**
des	**deis**	**hayas dado**	**hayáis dado**
dé	**den**	**haya dado**	**hayan dado**
7　imperfecto de subjuntivo		14　pluscuamperfecto de subjuntivo	
diera	**diéramos**	**hubiera dado**	**hubiéramos dado**
dieras	**dierais**	**hubieras dado**	**hubierais dado**
diera	**dieran**	**hubiera dado**	**hubieran dado**
OR		OR	
diese	**diésemos**	**hubiese dado**	**hubiésemos dado**
dieses	**dieseis**	**hubieses dado**	**hubieseis dado**
diese	**diesen**	**hubiese dado**	**hubiesen dado**

imperativo

—	**demos**
da; no des	**dad; no deis**
dé	**den**

Common idiomatic expressions using this verb

A Dios rogando y con el mazo dando.　Put your faith in God and keep your powder dry.

El tiempo da buen consejo.　Time will tell.

dar la mano (las manos) a alguien　to shake hands with someone

dar de comer　to feed

darse　to give oneself up, to give in

For more idiomatic expressions using **dar,** see pages 525–526.

The subject pronouns are found on the page facing page 1.

deber

Gerundio **debiendo**   Part. pas. **debido**

to owe, must, ought

The Seven Simple Tenses		The Seven Compound Tenses	
Singular	Plural	Singular	Plural
1 presente de indicativo		**8 perfecto de indicativo**	
debo	debemos	he debido	hemos debido
debes	debéis	has debido	habéis debido
debe	deben	ha debido	han debido
2 imperfecto de indicativo		**9 pluscuamperfecto de indicativo**	
debía	debíamos	había debido	habíamos debido
debías	debíais	habías debido	habíais debido
debía	debían	había debido	habían debido
3 pretérito		**10 pretérito anterior**	
debí	debimos	hube debido	hubimos debido
debiste	debisteis	hubiste debido	hubisteis debido
debió	debieron	hubo debido	hubieron debido
4 futuro		**11 futuro perfecto**	
deberé	deberemos	habré debido	habremos debido
deberás	deberéis	habrás debido	habréis debido
deberá	deberán	habrá debido	habrán debido
5 potencial simple		**12 potencial compuesto**	
debería	deberíamos	habría debido	habríamos debido
deberías	deberíais	habrías debido	habríais debido
debería	deberían	habría debido	habrían debido
6 presente de subjuntivo		**13 perfecto de subjuntivo**	
deba	debamos	haya debido	hayamos debido
debas	debáis	hayas debido	hayáis debido
deba	deban	haya debido	hayan debido
7 imperfecto de subjuntivo		**14 pluscuamperfecto de subjuntivo**	
debiera	debiéramos	hubiera debido	hubiéramos debido
debieras	debierais	hubieras debido	hubierais debido
debiera	debieran	hubiera debido	hubieran debido
OR		OR	
debiese	debiésemos	hubiese debido	hubiésemos debido
debieses	debieseis	hubieses debido	hubieseis debido
debiese	debiesen	hubiese debido	hubiesen debido

	imperativo	
—		debamos
debe; no debas		debed; no debáis
deba		deban

Sentences using this verb and words related to it

el deber   duty, obligation; **los deberes** homework
debido, debida   due; **debido a**   due to
la deuda   debt

estar en deuda con   to be indebted to; **el deudor, la deudora**   debtor
José debe de haber llegado.   Joseph must have arrived.

See also **deber** on pages 526–534.

The Seven Simple Tenses		The Seven Compound Tenses	
Singular	Plural	Singular	Plural
1 presente de indicativo		8 perfecto de indicativo	
decido	decidimos	he decidido	hemos decidido
decides	decidís	has decidido	habéis decidido
decide	deciden	ha decidido	han decidido
2 imperfecto de indicativo		9 pluscuamperfecto de indicativo	
decidía	decidíamos	había decidido	habíamos decidido
decidías	decidíais	habías decidido	habíais decidido
decidía	decidían	había decidido	habían decidido
3 pretérito		10 pretérito anterior	
decidí	decidimos	hube decidido	hubimos decidido
decidiste	decidisteis	hubiste decidido	hubisteis decidido
decidió	decidieron	hubo decidido	hubieron decidido
4 futuro		11 futuro perfecto	
decidiré	decidiremos	habré decidido	habremos decidido
decidirás	decidiréis	habrás decidido	habréis decidido
decidirá	decidirán	habrá decidido	habrán decidido
5 potencial simple		12 potencial compuesto	
decidiría	decidiríamos	habría decidido	habríamos decidido
decidirías	decidiríais	habrías decidido	habríais decidido
decidiría	decidirían	habría decidido	habrían decidido
6 presente de subjuntivo		13 perfecto de subjuntivo	
decida	decidamos	haya decidido	hayamos decidido
decidas	decidáis	hayas decidido	hayáis decidido
decida	decidan	haya decidido	hayan decidido
7 imperfecto de subjuntivo		14 pluscuamperfecto de subjuntivo	
decidiera	decidiéramos	hubiera decidido	hubiéramos decidido
decidieras	decidierais	hubieras decidido	hubierais decidido
decidiera	decidieran	hubiera decidido	hubieran decidido
OR		OR	
decidiese	decidiésemos	hubiese decidido	hubiésemos decidido
decidieses	decidieseis	hubieses decidido	hubieseis decidido
decidiese	decidiesen	hubiese decidido	hubiesen decidido

imperativo

—	**decidamos**
decide; no decidas	**decidid; no decidáis**
decida	**decidan**

Words and expressions related to this verb

la decisión   decision
decididamente   decidedly
decisivamente   decisively
decisivo, decisiva   decisive

decidir a + inf.   to persuade + inf.; to decide + inf.
decidirse   to make up one's mind, to be determined
estar decidido (decidida) a + inf.
    to make up one's mind

Want to learn more idiomatic expressions that contain verbs? Check out pages 524–537.

decir

to say, to tell

The Seven Simple Tenses		The Seven Compound Tenses	
Singular	Plural	Singular	Plural
1 presente de indicativo		**8 perfecto de indicativo**	
digo	decimos	he dicho	hemos dicho
dices	decís	has dicho	habéis dicho
dice	dicen	ha dicho	han dicho
2 imperfecto de indicativo		**9 pluscuamperfecto de indicativo**	
decía	decíamos	había dicho	habíamos dicho
decías	decíais	habías dicho	habíais dicho
decía	decían	había dicho	habían dicho
3 pretérito		**10 pretérito anterior**	
dije	dijimos	hube dicho	hubimos dicho
dijiste	dijisteis	hubiste dicho	hubisteis dicho
dijo	dijeron	hubo dicho	hubieron dicho
4 futuro		**11 futuro perfecto**	
diré	diremos	habré dicho	habremos dicho
dirás	diréis	habrás dicho	habréis dicho
dirá	dirán	habrá dicho	habrán dicho
5 potencial simple		**12 potencial compuesto**	
diría	diríamos	habría dicho	habríamos dicho
dirías	diríais	habrías dicho	habríais dicho
diría	dirían	habría dicho	habrían dicho
6 presente de subjuntivo		**13 perfecto de subjuntivo**	
diga	digamos	haya dicho	hayamos dicho
digas	digáis	hayas dicho	hayáis dicho
diga	digan	haya dicho	hayan dicho
7 imperfecto de subjuntivo		**14 pluscuamperfecto de subjuntivo**	
dijera	dijéramos	hubiera dicho	hubiéramos dicho
dijeras	dijerais	hubieras dicho	hubierais dicho
dijera	dijeran	hubiera dicho	hubieran dicho
OR		OR	
dijese	dijésemos	hubiese dicho	hubiésemos dicho
dijeses	dijeseis	hubieses dicho	hubieseis dicho
dijese	dijesen	hubiese dicho	hubiesen dicho

imperativo	
—	digamos
di; no digas	decid; no digáis
diga	digan

Sentences using this verb and words related to it

Dicho y hecho.   No sooner said than done.

querer decir   to mean

Dime con quién andas y te diré quién eres.   Tell me who your friends are and I will tell you who you are.

Diga or **Dígame**   Hello (telephone)

un decir   a familiar saying

See also **decir** on page 526.

See also **decir** on page 526.

160   Can't recognize an irregular verb form? Check out pages 519–523.

The Seven Simple Tenses		The Seven Compound Tenses	
Singular	Plural	Singular	Plural
1 presente de indicativo		8 perfecto de indicativo	
declaro	declaramos	he declarado	hemos declarado
declaras	declaráis	has declarado	habéis declarado
declara	declaran	ha declarado	han declarado
2 imperfecto de indicativo		9 pluscuamperfecto de indicativo	
declaraba	declarábamos	había declarado	habíamos declarado
declarabas	declarabais	habías declarado	habíais declarado
declaraba	declaraban	había declarado	habían declarado
3 pretérito		10 pretérito anterior	
declaré	declaramos	hube declarado	hubimos declarado
declaraste	declarasteis	hubiste declarado	hubisteis declarado
declaró	declararon	hubo declarado	hubieron declarado
4 futuro		11 futuro perfecto	
declararé	declararemos	habré declarado	habremos declarado
declararás	declararéis	habrás declarado	habréis declarado
declarará	declararán	habrá declarado	habrán declarado
5 potencial simple		12 potencial compuesto	
declararía	declararíamos	habría declarado	habríamos declarado
declararías	declararíais	habrías declarado	habríais declarado
declararía	declararían	habría declarado	habrían declarado
6 presente de subjuntivo		13 perfecto de subjuntivo	
declare	declaremos	haya declarado	hayamos declarado
declares	declaréis	hayas declarado	hayáis declarado
declare	declaren	haya declarado	hayan declarado
7 imperfecto de subjuntivo		14 pluscuamperfecto de subjuntivo	
declarara	declaráramos	hubiera declarado	hubiéramos declarado
declararas	declararais	hubieras declarado	hubierais declarado
declarara	declararan	hubiera declarado	hubieran declarado
OR		OR	
declarase	declarásemos	hubiese declarado	hubiésemos declarado
declarases	declaraseis	hubieses declarado	hubieseis declarado
declarase	declarasen	hubiese declarado	hubiesen declarado

	imperativo
—	declaremos
declara; no declares	declarad; no declaréis
declare	declaren

Words related to this verb
una declaración declaration   **declarativo, declarativa** declarative
declarado, declarada declared   **una declamación** declamation, recitation

---

If you want an explanation of meanings and uses of Spanish and English
verb tenses and moods, see pages xx–xl.

The subject pronouns are found on the page facing page 1.

to devote oneself

The Seven Simple Tenses		The Seven Compound Tenses	
Singular	Plural	Singular	Plural
1 presente de indicativo		**8 perfecto de indicativo**	
me dedico	nos dedicamos	me he dedicado	nos hemos dedicado
te dedicas	os dedicáis	te has dedicado	os habéis dedicado
se dedica	se dedican	se ha dedicado	se han dedicado
2 imperfecto de indicativo		**9 pluscuamperfecto de indicativo**	
me dedicaba	nos dedicábamos	me había dedicado	nos habíamos dedicado
te dedicabas	os dedicabais	te habías dedicado	os habíais dedicado
se dedicaba	se dedicaban	se había dedicado	se habían dedicado
3 pretérito		**10 pretérito anterior**	
me dediqué	nos dedicamos	me hube dedicado	nos hubimos dedicado
te dedicaste	os dedicasteis	te hubiste dedicado	os hubisteis dedicado
se dedicó	se dedicaron	se hubo dedicado	se hubieron dedicado
4 futuro		**11 futuro perfecto**	
me dedicaré	nos dedicaremos	me habré dedicado	nos habremos dedicado
te dedicarás	os dedicaréis	te habrás dedicado	os habréis dedicado
se dedicará	se dedicarán	se habrá dedicado	se habrán dedicado
5 potencial simple		**12 potencial compuesto**	
me dedicaría	nos dedicaríamos	me habría dedicado	nos habríamos dedicado
te dedicarías	os dedicaríais	te habrías dedicado	os habríais dedicado
se dedicaría	se dedicarían	se habría dedicado	se habrían dedicado
6 presente de subjuntivo		**13 perfecto de subjuntivo**	
me dedique	nos dediquemos	me haya dedicado	nos hayamos dedicado
te dediques	os dediquéis	te hayas dedicado	os hayáis dedicado
se dedique	se dediquen	se haya dedicado	se hayan dedicado
7 imperfecto de subjuntivo		**14 pluscuamperfecto de subjuntivo**	
me dedicara	nos dedicáramos	me hubiera dedicado	nos hubiéramos dedicado
te dedicaras	os dedicarais	te hubieras dedicado	os hubierais dedicado
se dedicara	se dedicaran	se hubiera dedicado	se hubieran dedicado
OR		OR	
me dedicase	nos dedicásemos	me hubiese dedicado	nos hubiésemos dedicado
te dedicases	os dedicaseis	te hubieses dedicado	os hubieseis dedicado
se dedicase	se dedicasen	se hubiese dedicado	se hubiesen dedicado

imperativo

—	**dediquémonos**
dedícate; no te dediques	**dedicaos; no os dediquéis**
dedíquese	**dedíquense**

Words related to this verb
predicar   to preach, predicate
dedicarse a   to devote oneself to
dedicar   to dedicate, consecrate

dedicado, dedicada   dedicated
una dedicación   dedication
dedicar algo a   to dedicate something to

Get acquainted with what preposition goes with what verb on pages 541–549.

The Seven Simple Tenses | The Seven Compound Tenses

Singular	Plural	Singular	Plural
1 presente de indicativo		**8 perfecto de indicativo**	
defiendo	**defendemos**	**he defendido**	**hemos defendido**
defiendes	**defendéis**	**has defendido**	**habéis defendido**
defiende	**defienden**	**ha defendido**	**han defendido**
2 imperfecto de indicativo		**9 pluscuamperfecto de indicativo**	
defendía	**defendíamos**	**había defendido**	**habíamos defendido**
defendías	**defendíais**	**habías defendido**	**habíais defendido**
defendía	**defendían**	**había defendido**	**habían defendido**
3 pretérito		**10 pretérito anterior**	
defendí	**defendimos**	**hube defendido**	**hubimos defendido**
defendiste	**defendisteis**	**hubiste defendido**	**hubisteis defendido**
defendió	**defendieron**	**hubo defendido**	**hubieron defendido**
4 futuro		**11 futuro perfecto**	
defenderé	**defenderemos**	**habré defendido**	**habremos defendido**
defenderás	**defenderéis**	**habrás defendido**	**habréis defendido**
defenderá	**defenderán**	**habrá defendido**	**habrán defendido**
5 potencial simple		**12 potencial compuesto**	
defendería	**defenderíamos**	**habría defendido**	**habríamos defendido**
defenderías	**defenderíais**	**habrías defendido**	**habríais defendido**
defendería	**defenderían**	**habría defendido**	**habrían defendido**
6 presente de subjuntivo		**13 perfecto de subjuntivo**	
defienda	**defendamos**	**haya defendido**	**hayamos defendido**
defiendas	**defendáis**	**hayas defendido**	**hayáis defendido**
defienda	**defiendan**	**haya defendido**	**hayan defendido**
7 imperfecto de subjuntivo		**14 pluscuamperfecto de subjuntivo**	
defendiera	**defendiéramos**	**hubiera defendido**	**hubiéramos defendido**
defendieras	**defendierais**	**hubieras defendido**	**hubierais defendido**
defendiera	**defendieran**	**hubiera defendido**	**hubieran defendido**
OR		OR	
defendiese	**defendiésemos**	**hubiese defendido**	**hubiésemos defendido**
defendieses	**defendieseis**	**hubieses defendido**	**hubieseis defendido**
defendiese	**defendiesen**	**hubiese defendido**	**hubiesen defendido**

imperativo

—	**defendamos**
defiende; no defiendas	**defended; no defendáis**
defienda	**defiendan**

Words related to this verb

defendible defensible
la defensa defense
defensivo, defensiva defensive
defensor, defensora defender, supporter, protector

el defensorio defense, plea
estar a la defensiva to be on the defensive
en defensa propia in self-defense
defender la patria contra el enemigo to defend one's country against the enemy

The subject pronouns are found on the page facing page 1.

dejar
Gerundio **dejando**　　　Part. pas. **dejado**

to let, to permit, to allow, to leave

The Seven Simple Tenses		The Seven Compound Tenses	
Singular	Plural	Singular	Plural
1　presente de indicativo		**8　perfecto de indicativo**	
dejo	dejamos	he dejado	hemos dejado
dejas	dejáis	has dejado	habéis dejado
deja	dejan	ha dejado	han dejado
2　imperfecto de indicativo		**9　pluscuamperfecto de indicativo**	
dejaba	dejábamos	había dejado	habíamos dejado
dejabas	dejabais	habías dejado	habíais dejado
dejaba	dejaban	había dejado	habían dejado
3　pretérito		**10　pretérito anterior**	
dejé	dejamos	hube dejado	hubimos dejado
dejaste	dejasteis	hubiste dejado	hubisteis dejado
dejó	dejaron	hubo dejado	hubieron dejado
4　futuro		**11　futuro perfecto**	
dejaré	dejaremos	habré dejado	habremos dejado
dejarás	dejaréis	habrás dejado	habréis dejado
dejará	dejarán	habrá dejado	habrán dejado
5　potencial simple		**12　potencial compuesto**	
dejaría	dejaríamos	habría dejado	habríamos dejado
dejarías	dejaríais	habrías dejado	habríais dejado
dejaría	dejarían	habría dejado	habrían dejado
6　presente de subjuntivo		**13　perfecto de subjuntivo**	
deje	dejemos	haya dejado	hayamos dejado
dejes	dejéis	hayas dejado	hayáis dejado
deje	dejen	haya dejado	hayan dejado
7　imperfecto de subjuntivo		**14　pluscuamperfecto de subjuntivo**	
dejara	dejáramos	hubiera dejado	hubiéramos dejado
dejaras	dejarais	hubieras dejado	hubierais dejado
dejara	dejaran	hubiera dejado	hubieran dejado
OR		OR	
dejase	dejásemos	hubiese dejado	hubiésemos dejado
dejases	dejaseis	hubieses dejado	hubieseis dejado
dejase	dejasen	hubiese dejado	hubiesen dejado

	imperativo	
—		dejemos
deja; no dejes		dejad; no dejéis
deje		dejen

Words and expressions related to this verb

dejar caer　to drop (to let fall)
el dejo　abandonment
dejado, dejada　dejected

dejarse　to abandon (neglect) oneself
dejar atrás　to leave behind
dejar de + inf.　to stop + pres. part.

See also **dejar** on pages 526 and 527.

Want to learn more idiomatic expressions that contain verbs? Check out pages 524–537.

to be delinquent, to violate the law

The Seven Simple Tenses		The Seven Compound Tenses	
Singular	Plural	Singular	Plural
1 presente de indicativo		8 perfecto de indicativo	
delinco	**delinquimos**	**he delinquido**	**hemos delinquido**
delinques	**delinquís**	**has delinquido**	**habéis delinquido**
delinque	**delinquen**	**ha delinquido**	**han delinquido**
2 imperfecto de indicativo		9 pluscuamperfecto de indicativo	
delinquía	**delinquíamos**	**había delinquido**	**habíamos delinquido**
delinquías	**delinquíais**	**habías delinquido**	**habíais delinquido**
delinquía	**delinquían**	**había delinquido**	**habían delinquido**
3 pretérito		10 pretérito anterior	
delinquí	**delinquimos**	**hube delinquido**	**hubimos delinquido**
delinquiste	**delinquisteis**	**hubiste delinquido**	**hubisteis delinquido**
delinquió	**delinquieron**	**hubo delinquido**	**hubieron delinquido**
4 futuro		11 futuro perfecto	
delinquiré	**delinquiremos**	**habré delinquido**	**habremos delinquido**
delinquirás	**delinquiréis**	**habrás delinquido**	**habréis delinquido**
delinquirá	**delinquirán**	**habrá delinquido**	**habrán delinquido**
5 potencial simple		12 potencial compuesto	
delinquiría	**delinquiríamos**	**habría delinquido**	**habríamos delinquido**
delinquirías	**delinquiríais**	**habrías delinquido**	**habríais delinquido**
delinquiría	**delinquirían**	**habría delinquido**	**habrían delinquido**
6 presente de subjuntivo		13 perfecto de subjuntivo	
delinca	**delincamos**	**haya delinquido**	**hayamos delinquido**
delincas	**delincáis**	**hayas delinquido**	**hayáis delinquido**
delinca	**delincan**	**haya delinquido**	**hayan delinquido**
7 imperfecto de subjuntivo		14 pluscuamperfecto de subjuntivo	
delinquiera	**delinquiéramos**	**hubiera delinquido**	**hubiéramos delinquido**
delinquieras	**delinquierais**	**hubieras delinquido**	**hubierais delinquido**
delinquiera	**delinquieran**	**hubiera delinquido**	**hubieran delinquido**
OR		OR	
delinquiese	**delinquiésemos**	**hubiese delinquido**	**hubiésemos delinquido**
delinquieses	**delinquieseis**	**hubieses delinquido**	**hubieseis delinquido**
delinquiese	**delinquiesen**	**hubiese delinquido**	**hubiesen delinquido**

imperativo	
—	**delincamos**
delinque; no delincas	**delinquid; no delincáis**
delinca	**delincan**

Words related to this verb
el delinquimiento, la delincuencia
   delinquency
delincuente   delinquent

la delincuencia juvenil   juvenile delinquency
delincuente habitual   habitual offender

Review the principal parts of important Spanish verbs on pages xvi and xvii.

demostrar

Gerundio **demostrando**   Part. pas. **demostrado**

to demonstrate, to prove

The Seven Simple Tenses		The Seven Compound Tenses	
Singular	Plural	Singular	Plural
1 presente de indicativo		8 perfecto de indicativo	
demuestro	demostramos	he demostrado	hemos demostrado
demuestras	demostráis	has demostrado	habéis demostrado
demuestra	demuestran	ha demostrado	han demostrado
2 imperfecto de indicativo		9 pluscuamperfecto de indicativo	
demostraba	demostrábamos	había demostrado	habíamos demostrado
demostrabas	demostrabais	habías demostrado	habíais demostrado
demostraba	demostraban	había demostrado	habían demostrado
3 pretérito		10 pretérito anterior	
demostré	demostramos	hube demostrado	hubimos demostrado
demostraste	demostrasteis	hubiste demostrado	hubisteis demostrado
demostró	demostraron	hubo demostrado	hubieron demostrado
4 futuro		11 futuro perfecto	
demostraré	demostraremos	habré demostrado	habremos demostrado
demostrarás	demostraréis	habrás demostrado	habréis demostrado
demostrará	demostrarán	habrá demostrado	habrán demostrado
5 potencial simple		12 potencial compuesto	
demostraría	demostraríamos	habría demostrado	habríamos demostrado
demostrarías	demostraríais	habrías demostrado	habríais demostrado
demostraría	demostrarían	habría demostrado	habrían demostrado
6 presente de subjuntivo		13 perfecto de subjuntivo	
demuestre	demostremos	haya demostrado	hayamos demostrado
demuestres	demostréis	hayas demostrado	hayáis demostrado
demuestre	demuestren	haya demostrado	hayan demostrado
7 imperfecto de subjuntivo		14 pluscuamperfecto de subjuntivo	
demostrara	demostráramos	hubiera demostrado	hubiéramos demostrado
demostraras	demostrarais	hubieras demostrado	hubierais demostrado
demostrara	demostraran	hubiera demostrado	hubieran demostrado
OR		OR	
demostrase	demostrásemos	hubiese demostrado	hubiésemos demostrado
demostrases	demostraseis	hubieses demostrado	hubieseis demostrado
demostrase	demostrasen	hubiese demostrado	hubiesen demostrado

imperativo	
—	demostremos
demuestra; no demuestres	demostrad; no demostréis
demuestre	demuestren

Words related to this verb

demostrativo, demostrativa   demonstrative   **demostrable**   demonstrable
la demostración   demonstration, proof   **mostrar**   to show, to exhibit
demostrador, demostradora   demonstrator   **la demostración de cariño**   show of affection

If you want to see a sample English verb fully conjugated in all the tenses,
check out pages xviii and xix.

The Seven Simple Tenses		The Seven Compound Tenses	
Singular	Plural	Singular	Plural
1 presente de indicativo		8 perfecto de indicativo	
denuncio	denunciamos	he denunciado	hemos denunciado
denuncias	denunciáis	has denunciado	habéis denunciado
denuncia	denuncian	ha denunciado	han denunciado
2 imperfecto de indicativo		9 pluscuamperfecto de indicativo	
denunciaba	denunciábamos	había denunciado	habíamos denunciado
denunciabas	denunciabais	habías denunciado	habíais denunciado
denunciaba	denunciaban	había denunciado	habían denunciado
3 pretérito		10 pretérito anterior	
denuncié	denunciamos	hube denunciado	hubimos denunciado
denunciaste	denunciasteis	hubiste denunciado	hubisteis denunciado
denunció	denunciaron	hubo denunciado	hubieron denunciado
4 futuro		11 futuro perfecto	
denunciaré	denunciaremos	habré denunciado	habremos denunciado
denunciarás	denunciaréis	habrás denunciado	habréis denunciado
denunciará	denunciarán	habrá denunciado	habrán denunciado
5 potencial simple		12 potencial compuesto	
denunciaría	denunciaríamos	habría denunciado	habríamos denunciado
denunciarías	denunciaríais	habrías denunciado	habríais denunciado
denunciaría	denunciarían	habría denunciado	habrían denunciado
6 presente de subjuntivo		13 perfecto de subjuntivo	
denuncie	denunciemos	haya denunciado	hayamos denunciado
denuncies	denunciéis	hayas denunciado	hayáis denunciado
denuncie	denuncien	haya denunciado	hayan denunciado
7 imperfecto de subjuntivo		14 pluscuamperfecto de subjuntivo	
denunciara	denunciáramos	hubiera denunciado	hubiéramos denunciado
denunciaras	denunciarais	hubieras denunciado	hubierais denunciado
denunciara	denunciaran	hubiera denunciado	hubieran denunciado
OR		OR	
denunciase	denunciásemos	hubiese denunciado	hubiésemos denunciado
denunciases	denunciaseis	hubieses denunciado	hubieseis denunciado
denunciase	denunciasen	hubiese denunciado	hubiesen denunciado

imperativo

—	**denunciemos**
denuncia; no denuncies	**denunciad; no denunciéis**
denuncie	**denuncien**

Words and expressions related to this verb
una denuncia, una denunciación   denunciation   **denunciar un robo**   to report a theft
un denuncio   denouncement   **una denuncia falsa**   a false accusation

If you want an explanation of meanings and uses of Spanish and
English verb tenses and moods, see pages xx–xl.

The subject pronouns are found on the page facing page 1.

depender

Gerundio **dependiendo**   Part. pas. **dependido**

to depend

The Seven Simple Tenses		The Seven Compound Tenses	
Singular	Plural	Singular	Plural
1 presente de indicativo		**8 perfecto de indicativo**	
dependo	dependemos	he dependido	hemos dependido
dependes	dependéis	has dependido	habéis dependido
depende	dependen	ha dependido	han dependido
2 imperfecto de indicativo		**9 pluscuamperfecto de indicativo**	
dependía	dependíamos	había dependido	habíamos dependido
dependías	dependíais	habías dependido	habíais dependido
dependía	dependían	había dependido	habían dependido
3 pretérito		**10 pretérito anterior**	
dependí	dependimos	hube dependido	hubimos dependido
dependiste	dependisteis	hubiste dependido	hubisteis dependido
dependió	dependieron	hubo dependido	hubieron dependido
4 futuro		**11 futuro perfecto**	
dependeré	dependeremos	habré dependido	habremos dependido
dependerás	dependeréis	habrás dependido	habréis dependido
dependerá	dependerán	habrá dependido	habrán dependido
5 potencial simple		**12 potencial compuesto**	
dependería	dependeríamos	habría dependido	habríamos dependido
dependerías	dependeríais	habrías dependido	habríais dependido
dependería	dependerían	habría dependido	habrían dependido
6 presente de subjuntivo		**13 perfecto de subjuntivo**	
dependa	dependamos	haya dependido	hayamos dependido
dependas	dependáis	hayas dependido	hayáis dependido
dependa	dependan	haya dependido	hayan dependido
7 imperfecto de subjuntivo		**14 pluscuamperfecto de subjuntivo**	
dependiera	dependiéramos	hubiera dependido	hubiéramos dependido
dependieras	dependierais	hubieras dependido	hubierais dependido
dependiera	dependieran	hubiera dependido	hubieran dependido
OR		OR	
dependiese	dependiésemos	hubiese dependido	hubiésemos dependido
dependieses	dependieseis	hubieses dependido	hubieseis dependido
dependiese	dependiesen	hubiese dependido	hubiesen dependido

imperativo	
—	dependamos
depende; no dependas	depended; no dependáis
dependa	dependan

Words and expressions related to this verb

depender de   to depend on, to rely on
no depender de nadie   to stand on one's own two feet
un dependiente, una dependienta   dependent, employee, clerk
la dependencia   dependence, dependency
pender   to dangle, hang, to be pending
suspender   to suspend, hang, hang up; **suspender pagos**   to stop payment

to knock down, to overthrow, to tear down, to throw down

The Seven Simple Tenses		The Seven Compound Tenses	
Singular	Plural	Singular	Plural
1 presente de indicativo		8 perfecto de indicativo	
derribo	**derribamos**	**he derribado**	**hemos derribado**
derribas	**derribáis**	**has derribado**	**habéis derribado**
derriba	**derriban**	**ha derribado**	**han derribado**
2 imperfecto de indicativo		9 pluscuamperfecto de indicativo	
derribaba	**derribábamos**	**había derribado**	**habíamos derribado**
derribabas	**derribabais**	**habías derribado**	**habíais derribado**
derribaba	**derribaban**	**había derribado**	**habían derribado**
3 pretérito		10 pretérito anterior	
derribé	**derribamos**	**hube derribado**	**hubimos derribado**
derribaste	**derribasteis**	**hubiste derribado**	**hubisteis derribado**
derribó	**derribaron**	**hubo derribado**	**hubieron derribado**
4 futuro		11 futuro perfecto	
derribaré	**derribaremos**	**habré derribado**	**habremos derribado**
derribarás	**derribaréis**	**habrás derribado**	**habréis derribado**
derribará	**derribarán**	**habrá derribado**	**habrán derribado**
5 potencial simple		12 potencial compuesto	
derribaría	**derribaríamos**	**habría derribado**	**habríamos derribado**
derribarías	**derribaríais**	**habrías derribado**	**habríais derribado**
derribaría	**derribarían**	**habría derribado**	**habrían derribado**
6 presente de subjuntivo		13 perfecto de subjuntivo	
derribe	**derribemos**	**haya derribado**	**hayamos derribado**
derribes	**derribéis**	**hayas derribado**	**hayáis derribado**
derribe	**derriben**	**haya derribado**	**hayan derribado**
7 imperfecto de subjuntivo		14 pluscuamperfecto de subjuntivo	
derribara	**derribáramos**	**hubiera derribado**	**hubiéramos derribado**
derribaras	**derribarais**	**hubieras derribado**	**hubierais derribado**
derribara	**derribaran**	**hubiera derribado**	**hubieran derribado**
OR		OR	
derribase	**derribásemos**	**hubiese derribado**	**hubiésemos derribado**
derribases	**derribaseis**	**hubieses derribado**	**hubieseis derribado**
derribase	**derribasen**	**hubiese derribado**	**hubiesen derribado**

imperativo

—	**derribemos**
derriba; no derribes	**derribad; no derribéis**
derribe	**derriben**

Words and expressions related to this verb
derribar a tiros to shoot down
derribado, derribada demolished, humiliated
el derribador, la derribadora overthrower

los derribos rubble
derribar al criminal to bring the criminal
down

If you don't know the Spanish verb for an English verb you have in mind,
look it up in the index on pages 505–518.

The subject pronouns are found on the page facing page 1.

desayunarse

desayunarse   Gerundio **desayunándose**   Part. pas. **desayunado**

to breakfast, to have breakfast

The Seven Simple Tenses		The Seven Compound Tenses	
Singular	Plural	Singular	Plural
1 presente de indicativo		**8 perfecto de indicativo**	
me desayuno	nos desayunamos	me he desayunado	nos hemos desayunado
te desayunas	os desayunáis	te has desayunado	os habéis desayunado
se desayuna	se desayunan	se ha desayunado	se han desayunado
2 imperfecto de indicativo		**9 pluscuamperfecto de indicativo**	
me desayunaba	nos desayunábamos	me había desayunado	nos habíamos desayunado
te desayunabas	os desayunabais	te habías desayunado	os habíais desayunado
se desayunaba	se desayunaban	se había desayunado	se habían desayunado
3 pretérito		**10 pretérito anterior**	
me desayuné	nos desayunamos	me hube desayunado	nos hubimos desayunado
te desayunaste	os desayunasteis	te hubiste desayunado	os hubisteis desayunado
se desayunó	se desayunaron	se hubo desayunado	se hubieron desayunado
4 futuro		**11 futuro perfecto**	
me desayunaré	nos desayunaremos	me habré desayunado	nos habremos desayunado
te desayunarás	os desayunaréis	te habrás desayunado	os habréis desayunado
se desayunará	se desayunarán	se habrá desayunado	se habrán desayunado
5 potencial simple		**12 potencial compuesto**	
me desayunaría	nos desayunaríamos	me habría desayunado	nos habríamos desayunado
te desayunarías	os desayunaríais	te habrías desayunado	os habríais desayunado
se desayunaría	se desayunarían	se habría desayunado	se habrían desayunado
6 presente de subjuntivo		**13 perfecto de subjuntivo**	
me desayune	nos desayunemos	me haya desayunado	nos hayamos desayunado
te desayunes	os desayunéis	te hayas desayunado	os hayáis desayunado
se desayune	se desayunen	se haya desayunado	se hayan desayunado
7 imperfecto de subjuntivo		**14 pluscuamperfecto de subjuntivo**	
me desayunara	nos desayunáramos	me hubiera desayunado	nos hubiéramos desayunado
te desayunaras	os desayunarais	te hubieras desayunado	os hubierais desayunado
se desayunara	se desayunaran	se hubiera desayunado	se hubieran desayunado
OR		OR	
me desayunase	nos desayunásemos	me hubiese desayunado	nos hubiésemos desayunado
te desayunases	os desayunaseis	te hubieses desayunado	os hubieseis desayunado
se desayunase	se desayunasen	se hubiese desayunado	se hubiesen desayunado

imperativo

—	desayunémonos
desayúnate; no te desayunes	desayunaos; no os desayunéis
desayúnese	desayúnense

Sentences using this verb and words related to it
—¿Qué toma Ud. en el desayuno todas las mañanas?
—Tomo leche, café con crema, pan tostado y un huevo.

desayunar	to breakfast	**ayunar**	to fast (not to eat)
el desayuno	breakfast	**el ayuno**	fast, fasting

Get your feet wet with verbs used in weather expressions on page 540.

The Seven Simple Tenses		The Seven Compound Tenses	
Singular	Plural	Singular	Plural

1 presente de indicativo

descanso	descansamos
descansas	descansáis
descansa	descansan

8 perfecto de indicativo

he descansado	hemos descansado
has descansado	habéis descansado
ha descansado	han descansado

2 imperfecto de indicativo

descansaba	descansábamos
descansabas	descansabais
descansaba	descansaban

9 pluscuamperfecto de indicativo

había descansado	habíamos descansado
habías descansado	habíais descansado
había descansado	habían descansado

3 pretérito

descansé	descansamos
descansaste	descansasteis
descansó	descansaron

10 pretérito anterior

hube descansado	hubimos descansado
hubiste descansado	hubisteis descansado
hubo descansado	hubieron descansado

4 futuro

descansaré	descansaremos
descansarás	descansaréis
descansará	descansarán

11 futuro perfecto

habré descansado	habremos descansado
habrás descansado	habréis descansado
habrá descansado	habrán descansado

5 potencial simple

descansaría	descansaríamos
descansarías	descansaríais
descansaría	descansarían

12 potencial compuesto

habría descansado	habríamos descansado
habrías descansado	habríais descansado
habría descansado	habrían descansado

6 presente de subjuntivo

descanse	descansemos
descanses	descanséis
descanse	descansen

13 perfecto de subjuntivo

haya descansado	hayamos descansado
hayas descansado	hayáis descansado
haya descansado	hayan descansado

7 imperfecto de subjuntivo

descansara	descansáramos
descansaras	descansarais
descansara	descansaran
OR	
descansase	descansásemos
descansases	descansaseis
descansase	descansasen

14 pluscuamperfecto de subjuntivo

hubiera descansado	hubiéramos descansado
hubieras descansado	hubierais descansado
hubiera descansado	hubieran descansado
OR	
hubiese descansado	hubiésemos descansado
hubieses descansado	hubieseis descansado
hubiese descansado	hubiesen descansado

imperativo

—	descansemos
descansa; no descanses	descansad; no descanséis
descanse	descansen

Words and expressions related to this verb

el descanso rest, relief, break
el descansadero resting place
la cansera fatigue
cansar to fatigue, to tire, to weary

el descansillo landing on a staircase
el descanso a discreción at ease (military)
cansarse de esperar to be tired of waiting
el descanso por enfermedad sick leave

The subject pronouns are found on the page facing page 1.

describir

Gerundio **describiendo**   Part. pas. **descrito**

to describe, to delineate

The Seven Simple Tenses		The Seven Compound Tenses	
Singular	Plural	Singular	Plural
1 presente de indicativo		**8 perfecto de indicativo**	
describo	describimos	he descrito	hemos descrito
describes	describís	has descrito	habéis descrito
describe	describen	ha descrito	han descrito
2 imperfecto de indicativo		**9 pluscuamperfecto de indicativo**	
describía	describíamos	había descrito	habíamos descrito
describías	describíais	habías descrito	habíais descrito
describía	describían	había descrito	habían descrito
3 pretérito		**10 pretérito anterior**	
describí	describimos	hube descrito	hubimos descrito
describiste	describisteis	hubiste descrito	hubisteis descrito
describió	describieron	hubo descrito	hubieron descrito
4 futuro		**11 futuro perfecto**	
describiré	describiremos	habré descrito	habremos descrito
describirás	describiréis	habrás descrito	habréis descrito
describirá	describirán	habrá descrito	habrán descrito
5 potencial simple		**12 potencial compuesto**	
describiría	describiríamos	habría descrito	habríamos descrito
describirías	describiríais	habrías descrito	habríais descrito
describiría	describirían	habría descrito	habrían descrito
6 presente de subjuntivo		**13 perfecto de subjuntivo**	
describa	describamos	haya descrito	hayamos descrito
describas	describáis	hayas descrito	hayáis descrito
describa	describan	haya descrito	hayan descrito
7 imperfecto de subjuntivo		**14 pluscuamperfecto de subjuntivo**	
describiera	describiéramos	hubiera descrito	hubiéramos descrito
describieras	describierais	hubieras descrito	hubierais descrito
describiera	describieran	hubiera descrito	hubieran descrito
OR		OR	
describiese	describiésemos	hubiese descrito	hubiésemos descrito
describieses	describieseis	hubieses descrito	hubieseis descrito
describiese	describiesen	hubiese descrito	hubiesen descrito

	imperativo	
—		**describamos**
describe; no describas		**describid; no describáis**
describa		**describan**

Words and expressions related to this verb

la descripción description
descriptor, descriptora describer
descriptivo, descriptiva descriptive

escribir to write
escribir a mano to write by hand
escribir a máquina to typewrite

For other words and expressions related to this verb, see **escribir** and **subscribir**.

Don't miss the definitions of basic grammatical terms with examples in English and Spanish on pages 666–677.

to discover, to reveal, to uncover, to unveil

The Seven Simple Tenses		The Seven Compound Tenses	
Singular	Plural	Singular	Plural
1 presente de indicativo		8 perfecto de indicativo	
descubro	**descubrimos**	**he descubierto**	**hemos descubierto**
descubres	**descubrís**	**has descubierto**	**habéis descubierto**
descubre	**descubren**	**ha descubierto**	**han descubierto**
2 imperfecto de indicativo		9 pluscuamperfecto de indicativo	
descubría	**descubríamos**	**había descubierto**	**habíamos descubierto**
descubrías	**descubríais**	**habías descubierto**	**habíais descubierto**
descubría	**descubrían**	**había descubierto**	**habían descubierto**
3 pretérito		10 pretérito anterior	
descubrí	**descubrimos**	**hube descubierto**	**hubimos descubierto**
descubriste	**descubristeis**	**hubiste descubierto**	**hubisteis descubierto**
descubrió	**descubrieron**	**hubo descubierto**	**hubieron descubierto**
4 futuro		11 futuro perfecto	
descubriré	**descubriremos**	**habré descubierto**	**habremos descubierto**
descubrirás	**descubriréis**	**habrás descubierto**	**habréis descubierto**
descubrirá	**descubrirán**	**habrá descubierto**	**habrán descubierto**
5 potencial simple		12 potencial compuesto	
descubriría	**descubriríamos**	**habría descubierto**	**habríamos descubierto**
descubrirías	**descubriríais**	**habrías descubierto**	**habríais descubierto**
descubriría	**descubrirían**	**habría descubierto**	**habrían descubierto**
6 presente de subjuntivo		13 perfecto de subjuntivo	
descubra	**descubramos**	**haya descubierto**	**hayamos descubierto**
descubras	**descubráis**	**hayas descubierto**	**hayáis descubierto**
descubra	**descubran**	**haya descubierto**	**hayan descubierto**
7 imperfecto de subjuntivo		14 pluscuamperfecto de subjuntivo	
descubriera	**descubriéramos**	**hubiera descubierto**	**hubiéramos descubierto**
descubrieras	**descubrierais**	**hubieras descubierto**	**hubierais descubierto**
descubriera	**descubrieran**	**hubiera descubierto**	**hubieran descubierto**
OR		OR	
descubriese	**descubriésemos**	**hubiese descubierto**	**hubiésemos descubierto**
descubrieses	**descubrieseis**	**hubieses descubierto**	**hubieseis descubierto**
descubriese	**descubriesen**	**hubiese descubierto**	**hubiesen descubierto**

imperativo

—	**descubramos**
descubre; no descubras	**descubrid; no descubráis**
descubra	**descubran**

Words and expressions related to this verb

descubrirse to take off one's hat
el descubrimiento discovery
descubridor, descubridora discoverer
a la descubierta clearly, openly

cubrir to cover
cubrir el costo to cover the cost
cubrir la mesa to cover the table
descubrir un nuevo antibiótico to discover a new antibiotic

The subject pronouns are found on the page facing page 1.

173

to desire, to wish, to want

The Seven Simple Tenses		The Seven Compound Tenses	
Singular	Plural	Singular	Plural
1 presente de indicativo		8 perfecto de indicativo	
deseo	deseamos	he deseado	hemos deseado
deseas	deseáis	has deseado	habéis deseado
desea	desean	ha deseado	han deseado
2 imperfecto de indicativo		9 pluscuamperfecto de indicativo	
deseaba	deseábamos	había deseado	habíamos deseado
deseabas	deseabais	habías deseado	habíais deseado
deseaba	deseaban	había deseado	habían deseado
3 pretérito		10 pretérito anterior	
deseé	deseamos	hube deseado	hubimos deseado
deseaste	deseasteis	hubiste deseado	hubisteis deseado
deseó	desearon	hubo deseado	hubieron deseado
4 futuro		11 futuro perfecto	
desearé	desearemos	habré deseado	habremos deseado
desearás	desaréis	habrás deseado	habréis deseado
deseará	desearán	habrá deseado	habrán deseado
5 potencial simple		12 potencial compuesto	
desearía	desearíamos	habría deseado	habríamos deseado
desearías	desearíais	habrías deseado	habríais deseado
desearía	desearían	habría deseado	habrían deseado
6 presente de subjuntivo		13 perfecto de subjuntivo	
desee	deseemos	haya deseado	hayamos deseado
desees	deseéis	hayas deseado	hayáis deseado
desee	deseen	haya deseado	hayan deseado
7 imperfecto de subjuntivo		14 pluscuamperfecto de subjuntivo	
deseara	deseáramos	hubiera deseado	hubiéramos deseado
desearas	desearais	hubieras deseado	hubierais deseado
deseara	desearan	hubiera deseado	hubieran deseado
OR		OR	
desease	deseásemos	hubiese deseado	hubiésemos deseado
deseases	deseaseis	hubieses deseado	hubieseis deseado
desease	deseasen	hubiese deseado	hubiesen deseado

imperativo

—	deseemos
desea; no desees	**desead; no deseéis**
desee	**deseen**

Words and expressions related to this verb
el deseo   desire
deseoso, deseosa   desirous
tener deseo de + inf.   to be eager + inf.
deseable   desirable

el deseador, la deseadora   desirer, wisher
deseablemente   desirably
poco deseable   undesirable
desear hacer algo   to wish to do something

to play (a part), to act (a part), to discharge,
to perform (a duty), to take out of pawn

The Seven Simple Tenses		The Seven Compound Tenses	
Singular	Plural	Singular	Plural
1 presente de indicativo		8 perfecto de indicativo	
desempeño	desempeñamos	he desempeñado	hemos desempeñado
desempeñas	desempeñáis	has desempeñado	habéis desempeñado
desempeña	desempeñan	ha desempeñado	han desempeñado
2 imperfecto de indicativo		9 pluscuamperfecto de indicativo	
desempeñaba	desempeñábamos	había desempeñado	habíamos desempeñado
desempeñabas	desempeñabais	habías desempeñado	habíais desempeñado
desempeñaba	desempeñaban	había desempeñado	habían desempeñado
3 pretérito		10 pretérito anterior	
desempeñé	desempeñamos	hube desempeñado	hubimos desempeñado
desempeñaste	desempeñasteis	hubiste desempeñado	hubisteis desempeñado
desempeñó	desempeñaron	hubo desempeñado	hubieron desempeñado
4 futuro		11 futuro perfecto	
desempeñaré	desempeñaremos	habré desempeñado	habremos desempeñado
desempeñarás	desempeñaréis	habrás desempeñado	habréis desempeñado
desempeñará	desempeñarán	habrá desempeñado	habrán desempeñado
5 potencial simple		12 potencial compuesto	
desempeñaría	desempeñaríamos	habría desempeñado	habríamos desempeñado
desempeñarías	desempeñaríais	habrías desempeñado	habríais desempeñado
desempeñaría	desempeñarían	habría desempeñado	habrían desempeñado
6 presente de subjuntivo		13 perfecto de subjuntivo	
desempeñe	desempeñemos	haya desempeñado	hayamos desempeñado
desempeñes	desempeñéis	hayas desempeñado	hayáis desempeñado
desempeñe	desempeñen	haya desempeñado	hayan desempeñado
7 imperfecto de subjuntivo		14 pluscuamperfecto de subjuntivo	
desempeñara	desempeñáramos	hubiera desempeñado	hubiéramos desempeñado
desempeñaras	desempeñarais	hubieras desempeñado	hubierais desempeñado
desempeñara	desempeñaran	hubiera desempeñado	hubieran desempeñado
OR		OR	
desempeñase	desempeñásemos	hubiese desempeñado	hubiésemos desempeñado
desempeñases	desempeñaseis	hubieses desempeñado	hubieseis desempeñado
desempeñase	desempeñasen	hubiese desempeñado	hubiesen desempeñado

imperativo	
—	**desempeñemos**
desempeña; no desempeñes	**desempeñad; no desempeñéis**
desempeñe	**desempeñen**

Words and expressions related to this verb
desempeñado, desempeñada out of debt
el desempeño payment of a debt
desempeñar un cargo to take a job

empeñar to pawn, to pledge
una casa de empeños pawnshop
el empeño pawn, pledge, obligation

Check out the verb drills and verb tests with answers explained on pages 619–665.

to undo, to destroy, to take apart

The Seven Simple Tenses		The Seven Compound Tenses	
Singular	Plural	Singular	Plural
1 presente de indicativo		8 perfecto de indicativo	
deshago	deshacemos	he deshecho	hemos deshecho
deshaces	deshacéis	has deshecho	habéis deshecho
deshace	deshacen	ha deshecho	han deshecho
2 imperfecto de indicativo		9 pluscuamperfecto de indicativo	
deschacía	deshacíamos	había deshecho	habíamos deshecho
deshacías	deshacíais	habías deshecho	habíais deshecho
deshacía	deshacían	había deshecho	habían deshecho
3 pretérito		10 pretérito anterior	
deshice	deshicimos	hube deshecho	hubimos deshecho
deshiciste	deshicisteis	hubiste deshecho	hubisteis deshecho
deshizo	deshicieron	hubo deshecho	hubieron deshecho
4 futuro		11 futuro perfecto	
desharé	desharemos	habré deshecho	habremos deshecho
desharás	desharéis	habrás deshecho	habréis deshecho
deshará	desharán	habrá deshecho	habrán deshecho
5 potencial simple		12 potencial compuesto	
desharía	desharíamos	habría deshecho	habríamos deshecho
desharías	desharíais	habrías deshecho	habríais deshecho
desharía	desharían	habría deshecho	habrían deshecho
6 presente de subjuntivo		13 perfecto de subjuntivo	
deshaga	deshagamos	haya deshecho	hayamos deshecho
deshagas	deshagáis	hayas deshecho	hayáis deshecho
deshaga	deshagan	haya deshecho	hayan deshecho
7 imperfecto de subjuntivo		14 pluscuamperfecto de subjuntivo	
deshiciera	deschiciéramos	hubiera deshecho	hubiéramos deshecho
deshicieras	deshicierais	hubieras deshecho	hubierais deshecho
deshiciera	deshicieran	hubiera deshecho	hubieran deshecho
OR		OR	
deshiciese	deshiciésemos	hubiese deshecho	hubiésemos deshecho
deshicieses	deshicieseis	hubieses deshecho	hubieseis deshecho
deshiciese	deshiciesen	hubiese deshecho	hubiesen deshecho

imperativo

—	deshagamos
deshaz; no deshagas	deshaced; no deshagáis
deshaga	deshagan

Words and expressions related to this verb
deshecho, deshecha   destroyed, wasted, undone
el deshechizo   breaking off a magic spell
hacer la deshecha   to pretend, to feign

Use the EE-zee guide to Spanish pronunciation on pages 562 and 563.

to take leave of, to say good-bye to

The Seven Simple Tenses		The Seven Compound Tenses	
Singular	Plural	Singular	Plural
1 presente de indicativo		8 perfecto de indicativo	
me despido	**nos despedimos**	**me he despedido**	**nos hemos despedido**
te despides	**os despedís**	**te has despedido**	**os habéis despedido**
se despide	**se despiden**	**se ha despedido**	**se han despedido**
2 imperfecto de indicativo		9 pluscuamperfecto de indicativo	
me despedía	**nos despedíamos**	**me había despedido**	**nos habíamos despedido**
te despedías	**os despedíais**	**te habías despedido**	**os habíais despedido**
se despedía	**se despedían**	**se había despedido**	**se habían despedido**
3 pretérito		10 pretérito anterior	
me despedí	**nos despedimos**	**me hube despedido**	**nos hubimos despedido**
te despediste	**os despedisteis**	**te hubiste despedido**	**os hubisteis despedido**
se despidió	**se despidieron**	**se hubo despedido**	**se hubieron despedido**
4 futuro		11 futuro perfecto	
me despediré	**nos despediremos**	**me habré despedido**	**nos habremos despedido**
te despedirás	**os despediréis**	**te habrás despedido**	**os habréis despedido**
se despedirá	**se despedirán**	**se habrá despedido**	**se habrán despedido**
5 potencial simple		12 potencial compuesto	
me despediría	**nos despediríamos**	**me habría despedido**	**nos habríamos despedido**
te despedirías	**os despediríais**	**te habrías despedido**	**os habríais despedido**
se despediría	**se despedirían**	**se habría despedido**	**se habrían despedido**
6 presente de subjuntivo		13 perfecto de subjuntivo	
me despida	**nos despidamos**	**me haya despedido**	**nos hayamos despedido**
te despidas	**os despidáis**	**te hayas despedido**	**os hayáis despedido**
se despida	**se despidan**	**se haya despedido**	**se hayan despedido**
7 imperfecto de subjuntivo		14 pluscuamperfecto de subjuntivo	
me despidiera	**nos despidiéramos**	**me hubiera despedido**	**nos hubiéramos despedido**
te despidieras	**os despidierais**	**te hubieras despedido**	**os hubierais despedido**
se despidiera	**se despidieran**	**se hubiera despedido**	**se hubieran despedido**
OR		OR	
me despidiese	**nos despidiésemos**	**me hubiese despedido**	**nos hubiésemos despedido**
te despidieses	**os despidieseis**	**te hubieses despedido**	**os hubieseis despedido**
se despidiese	**se despidiesen**	**se hubiese despedido**	**se hubiesen despedido**

imperativo	
—	**despidámonos**
despídete; no te despidas	**despedíos; nos despidáis**
despídase	**despídanse**

Words and expressions related to this verb
despedirse a la francesa   to take French leave
despedir   to dismiss
un despedimiento, una despedida   dismissal, discharge, farewell
despedirse de   to take leave of, to say good-bye to

Get acquainted with what preposition goes with what verb on pages 541–549.

The subject pronouns are found on the page facing page 1.

despegar

Gerundio **despegando**   Part. pas. **despegado**

to detach, to unglue, to unstick, to take off (airplane)

The Seven Simple Tenses		The Seven Compound Tenses	
Singular	Plural	Singular	Plural
1 presente de indicativo		**8 perfecto de indicativo**	
despego	despegamos	he despegado	hemos despegado
despegas	despegáis	has despegado	habéis despegado
despega	despegan	ha despegado	han despegado
2 imperfecto de indicativo		**9 pluscuamperfecto de indicativo**	
despegaba	despegábamos	había despegado	habíamos despegado
despegabas	despegabais	habías despegado	habíais despegado
despegaba	despegaban	había despegado	habían despegado
3 pretérito		**10 pretérito anterior**	
despegué	despegamos	hube despegado	hubimos despegado
despegaste	despegasteis	hubiste despegado	hubisteis despegado
despegó	despegaron	hubo despegado	hubieron despegado
4 futuro		**11 futuro perfecto**	
despegaré	despegaremos	habré despegado	habremos despegado
despegarás	despergaréis	habrás despegado	habréis despegado
despegará	despegarán	habrá despegado	habrán despegado
5 potencial simple		**12 potencial compuesto**	
despegaría	despegaríamos	habría despegado	habríamos despegado
despegarías	despegaríais	habrías despegado	habríais despegado
despegaría	despegarían	habría despegado	habrían despegado
6 presente de subjuntivo		**13 perfecto de subjuntivo**	
despegue	despeguemos	haya despegado	hayamos despegado
despegues	despeguéis	hayas despegado	hayáis despegado
despegue	despeguen	haya despegado	hayan despegado
7 imperfecto de subjuntivo		**14 pluscuamperfecto de subjuntivo**	
despegara	despegáramos	hubiera despegado	hubiéramos despegado
despegaras	despegarais	hubieras despegado	hubierais despegado
despegara	despegaran	hubiera despegado	hubieran despegado
OR		OR	
despegase	despegásemos	hubiese despegado	hubiésemos despegado
despegases	despegaseis	hubieses despegado	hubieseis despegado
despegase	despegasen	hubiese despegado	hubiesen despegado

	imperativo
—	despeguemos
despega; no despegues	despegad; no despeguéis
despegue	despeguen

Words and expressions related to this verb
despegar los labios   to speak
el despegue   take-off (airplane)
despegadamente   without concern

despegarse   to become distant, indifferent; to grow displeased
el despego, el despegamiento   aversion, indifference

For other words and expressions related to this verb, see **pegar.**

Gerundio **desperezándose**   Part. pas. **desperezado**   **desperezarse**

to stretch oneself, to stretch one's arms and legs

The Seven Simple Tenses		The Seven Compound Tenses	
Singular	Plural	Singular	Plural
1 presente de indicativo		**8 perfecto de indicativo**	
me desperezo	nos desperezamos	me he desperezado	nos hemos desperezado
te desperezas	os desperezáis	te has desperezado	os habéis desperezado
se despereza	se desperezan	se ha desperezado	se han desperezado
2 imperfecto de indicativo		**9 pluscuamperfecto de indicativo**	
me desperezaba	nos desperezábamos	me había desperezado	nos habíamos desperezado
te desperezabas	os desperezabais	te habías desperezado	os habíais desperezado
se desperezaba	se desperezaban	se había desperezado	se habían desperezado
3 pretérito		**10 pretérito anterior**	
me desperecé	nos desperezamos	me hube desperezado	nos hubimos desperezado
te desperezaste	os desperezasteis	te hubiste desperezado	os hubisteis desperezado
se desperezó	se desperezaron	se hubo desperezado	se hubieron desperezado
4 futuro		**11 futuro perfecto**	
me desperezaré	nos desperezaremos	me habré desperezado	nos habremos desperezado
te desperezarás	os desperezaréis	te habrás desperezado	os habréis desperezado
se desperezará	se desperezarán	se habrá desperezado	se habrán desperezado
5 potencial simple		**12 potencial compuesto**	
me desperezaría	nos desperezaríamos	me habría desperezado	nos habríamos desperezado
te desperezarías	os desperezaríais	te habrías desperezado	os habríais desperezado
se desperezaría	se desperezarían	se habría desperezado	se habrían desperezado
6 presente de subjuntivo		**13 perfecto de subjuntivo**	
me desperece	nos desperecemos	me haya desperezado	nos hayamos desperezado
te despereces	os desperecéis	te hayas desperezado	os hayáis desperezado
se desperece	se desperecen	se haya desperezado	se hayan desperezado
7 imperfecto de subjuntivo		**14 pluscuamperfecto de subjuntivo**	
me desperezara	nos desperezáramos	me hubiera desperezado	nos hubiéramos desperezado
te desperezaras	os desperezarais	te hubieras desperezado	os hubierais desperezado
se desperezara	se desperezaran	se hubiera desperezado	se hubieran desperezado
OR		OR	
me desperezase	nos desperezásemos	me hubiese desperezado	nos hubiésemos desperezado
te desperezases	os desperezaseis	te hubieses desperezado	os hubieseis desperezado
se desperezase	se desperezasen	se hubiese desperezado	se hubiesen desperezado

imperativo

—	desperecémonos
desperézate; no te despereces	desperezaos; no os desperecéis
desperécese	desperécense

Words related to this verb
el desperezo stretching one's arms and legs
perezoso, perezosa lazy

perezosamente lazily
la pereza laziness

Learn more verbs in 30 practical situations for tourists on pages 564–594.

despertarse

Gerundio **despertándose**   Part. pas. **despertado**

to wake up oneself

The Seven Simple Tenses		The Seven Compound Tenses	
Singular	Plural	Singular	Plural
1 presente de indicativo		**8 perfecto de indicativo**	
me despierto	nos despertamos	me he despertado	nos hemos despertado
te despiertas	os despertáis	te has despertado	os habéis despertado
se despierta	se despiertan	se ha despertado	se han despertado
2 imperfecto de indicativo		**9 pluscuamperfecto de indicativo**	
me despertaba	nos despertábamos	me había despertado	nos habíamos despertado
te despertabas	os despertabais	te habías despertado	os habíais despertado
se despertaba	se despertaban	se había despertado	se habían despertado
3 pretérito		**10 pretérito anterior**	
me desperté	nos despertamos	me hube despertado	nos hubimos despertado
te despertaste	os despertasteis	te hubiste despertado	os hubisteis despertado
se despertó	se despertaron	se hubo despertado	se hubieron despertado
4 futuro		**11 futuro perfecto**	
me despertaré	nos despertaremos	me habré despertado	nos habremos despertado
te despertarás	os despertaréis	te habrás despertado	os habréis despertado
se despertará	se despertarán	se habrá despertado	se habrán despertado
5 potencial simple		**12 potencial compuesto**	
me despertaría	nos despertaríamos	me habría despertado	nos habríamos despertado
te despertarías	os despertaríais	te habrías despertado	os habríais despertado
se despertaría	se despertarían	se habría despertado	se habrían despertado
6 presente de subjuntivo		**13 perfecto de subjuntivo**	
me despierte	nos despertemos	me haya despertado	nos hayamos despertado
te despiertes	os despertéis	te hayas despertado	os hayáis despertado
se despierte	se despierten	se haya despertado	se hayan despertado
7 imperfecto de subjuntivo		**14 pluscuamperfecto de subjuntivo**	
me despertara	nos despertáramos	me hubiera despertado	nos hubiéramos despertado
te despertaras	os despertarais	te hubieras despertado	os hubierais despertado
se despertara	se despertaran	se hubiera despertado	se hubieran despertado
OR		OR	
me despertase	nos despertásemos	me hubiese despertado	nos hubiésemos despertado
te despertases	os despertaseis	te hubieses despertado	os hubieseis despertado
se despertase	se despertasen	se hubiese despertado	se hubiesen despertado

	imperativo	
—		despertémonos
despiértate; no te despiertes		despertaos; no os despertéis
despiértese		despiértense

Words and expressions related to this verb
despertar   to awaken (someone), to enliven
un despertador   alarm clock
el despertamiento   awakening, arousal

despierto, despierta   wide awake, alert
María sueña despierta.   Mary daydreams.
despertarse a las siete de la mañana   to wake up at seven in the morning

If you want an explanation of meanings and uses of Spanish and English verb tenses and moods, see pages xx–xxl.

The Seven Simple Tenses		The Seven Compound Tenses	
Singular	Plural	Singular	Plural
1 presente de indicativo		**8 perfecto de indicativo**	
destruyo	**destruimos**	**he destruido**	**hemos destruido**
destruyes	**destruís**	**has destruido**	**habéis destruido**
destruye	**destruyen**	**ha destruido**	**han destruido**
2 imperfecto de indicativo		**9 pluscuamperfecto de indicativo**	
destruía	**destruíamos**	**había destruido**	**habíamos destruido**
destruías	**destruíais**	**habías destruido**	**habíais destruido**
destruía	**destruían**	**había destruido**	**habían destruido**
3 pretérito		**10 pretérito anterior**	
destruí	**destruimos**	**hube destruido**	**hubimos destruido**
destruiste	**destruisteis**	**hubiste destruido**	**hubisteis destruido**
destruyó	**destruyeron**	**hubo destruido**	**hubieron destruido**
4 futuro		**11 futuro perfecto**	
destruiré	**destruiremos**	**habré destruido**	**habremos destruido**
destruirás	**destruiréis**	**habrás destruido**	**habréis destruido**
destruirá	**destruirán**	**habrá destruido**	**habrán destruido**
5 potencial simple		**12 potencial compuesto**	
destruiría	**destruiríamos**	**habría destruido**	**habríamos destruido**
destruirías	**destruiríais**	**habrías destruido**	**habríais destruido**
destruiría	**destruirían**	**habría destruido**	**habrían destruido**
6 presente de subjuntivo		**13 perfecto de subjuntivo**	
destruya	**destruyamos**	**haya destruido**	**hayamos destruido**
destruyas	**destruyáis**	**hayas destruido**	**hayáis destruido**
destruya	**destruyan**	**haya destruido**	**hayan destruido**
7 imperfecto de subjuntivo		**14 pluscuamperfecto de subjuntivo**	
destruyera	**destruyéramos**	**hubiera destruido**	**hubiéramos destruido**
destruyeras	**destruyerais**	**hubieras destruido**	**hubierais destruido**
destruyera	**destruyeran**	**hubiera destruido**	**hubieran destruido**
OR		OR	
destruyese	**destruyésemos**	**hubiese destruido**	**hubiésemos destruido**
destruyeses	**destruyeseis**	**hubieses destruido**	**hubieseis destruido**
destruyese	**destruyesen**	**hubiese destruido**	**hubiesen destruido**

imperativo

—	**destruyamos**
destruye; no destruyas	**destruid; no destruyáis**
destruya	**destruyan**

Words and expressions related to this verb

destructor, destructora destructor, destroyer
la destrucción destruction
destruíble destructible

destructivo, destructiva destructive
destruidor, destruidora destroyer
destructivamente destructively

Increase your verb power with popular phrases, words,
and expressions for tourists on pages 595–618.

The subject pronouns are found on the page facing page 1.

to undress oneself, to get undressed

The Seven Simple Tenses		The Seven Compound Tenses	
Singular	Plural	Singular	Plural
1 presente de indicativo		8 perfecto de indicativo	
me desvisto	nos desvestimos	me he desvestido	nos hemos desvestido
te desvistes	os desvestís	te has desvestido	os habéis desvestido
se desviste	se desvisten	se ha desvestido	se han desvestido
2 imperfecto de indicativo		9 pluscuamperfecto de indicativo	
me desvestía	nos desvestíamos	me había desvestido	nos habíamos desvestido
te desvestías	os desvestíais	te habías desvestido	os habíais desvestido
se desvestía	se desvestían	se había desvestido	se habían desvestido
3 pretérito		10 pretérito anterior	
me desvestí	nos desvestimos	me hube desvestido	nos hubimos desvestido
te desvestiste	os desvestisteis	te hubiste desvestido	os hubisteis desvestido
se desvistió	se desvistieron	se hubo desvestido	se hubieron desvestido
4 futuro		11 futuro perfecto	
me desvestiré	nos desvestiremos	me habré desvestido	nos habremos desvestido
te desvestirás	os desvestiréis	te habrás desvestido	os habréis desvestido
se desvestirá	se desvestirán	se habrá desvestido	se habrán desvestido
5 potencial simple		12 potencial compuesto	
me desvestiría	nos desvestiríamos	me habría desvestido	nos habríamos desvestido
te desvestirías	os desvestiríais	te habrías desvestido	os habríais desvestido
se desvestiría	se desvestirían	se habría desvestido	se habrían desvestido
6 presente de subjuntivo		13 perfecto de subjuntivo	
me desvista	nos desvistamos	me haya desvestido	nos hayamos desvestido
te desvistas	os desvistáis	te hayas desvestido	os hayáis desvestido
se desvista	se desvistan	se haya desvestido	se hayan desvestido
7 imperfecto de subjuntivo		14 pluscuamperfecto de subjuntivo	
me desvistiera	nos desvistiéramos	me hubiera desvestido	nos hubiéramos desvestido
te desvistieras	os desvistierais	te hubieras desvestido	os hubierais desvestido
se desvistiera	se desvistieran	se hubiera desvestido	se hubieran desvestido
OR		OR	
me desvistiese	nos desvistiésemos	me hubiese desvestido	nos hubiésemos desvestido
te desvistieses	os desvistieseis	te hubieses desvestido	os hubieseis desvestido
se desvistiese	se desvistiesen	se hubiese desvestido	se hubiesen desvestido

	imperativo	
—		desvistámonos
desvístete; no te desvistas		desvestíos; no os desvistáis
desvístase		desvístanse

Words and expressions related to this verb
vestir   to clothe, to dress
vestirse   to clothe oneself, to dress oneself
el vestido   clothing, clothes, dress
vestidos usados   secondhand clothing

bien vestido   well-dressed
vestir de blanco   to dress in white
vestir de uniforme   to dress in uniform
el vestido de etiqueta   evening clothes

Don't miss the definitions of basic grammatical terms with examples
in English and Spanish on pages 666–677.

to stop (someone or something), to detain

The Seven Simple Tenses		The Seven Compound Tenses	
Singular	Plural	Singular	Plural
1 presente de indicativo		8 perfecto de indicativo	
detengo	detenemos	he detenido	hemos detenido
detienes	detenéis	has detenido	habéis detenido
detiene	detienen	ha detenido	han detenido
2 imperfecto de indicativo		9 pluscuamperfecto de indicativo	
detenía	deteníamos	había detenido	habíamos detenido
detenías	deteníais	habías detenido	habíais detenido
detenía	detenían	había detenido	habían detenido
3 pretérito		10 pretérito anterior	
detuve	detuvimos	hube detenido	hubimos detenido
detuviste	detuvisteis	hubiste detenido	hubisteis detenido
detuvo	detuvieron	hubo detenido	hubieron detenido
4 futuro		11 futuro perfecto	
detendré	detendremos	habré detenido	habremos detenido
detendrás	detendréis	habrás detenido	habréis detenido
detendrá	detendrán	habrá detenido	habrán detenido
5 potencial simple		12 potencial compuesto	
detendría	detendríamos	habría detenido	habríamos detenido
detendrías	detendríais	habrías detenido	habríais detenido
detendría	detendrían	habría detenido	habrían detenido
6 presente de subjuntivo		13 perfecto de subjuntivo	
detenga	detengamos	haya detenido	hayamos detenido
detengas	detengáis	hayas detenido	hayáis detenido
detenga	detengan	haya detenido	hayan detenido
7 imperfecto de subjuntivo		14 pluscuamperfecto de subjuntivo	
detuviera	detuviéramos	hubiera detenido	hubiéramos detenido
detuvieras	detuvierais	hubieras detenido	hubierais detenido
detuviera	detuvieran	hubiera detenido	hubieran detenido
OR		OR	
detuviese	detuviésemos	hubiese detenido	hubiésemos detenido
detuvieses	detuvieseis	hubieses detenido	hubieseis detenido
detuviese	detuviesen	hubiese detenido	hubiesen detenido

	imperativo	
—		detengamos
detén; no detengas		detened; no detengáis
detenga		detengan

Words related to this verb

el detenimiento   delay
detenidamente   cautiously
sostener   to support, to sustain
la detención   detention, detainment

detenerse a + inf.   to stop + inf.
el sostenimiento   support, sustenance
el detenido, la detenida   person under arrest
sin detención   without delay

See also **tener.**

The subject pronouns are found on the page facing page 1.

183

to stop (oneself)

The Seven Simple Tenses		The Seven Compound Tenses	
Singular	Plural	Singular	Plural
1 presente de indicativo		8 perfecto de indicativo	
me detengo	**nos detenemos**	**me he detenido**	**nos hemos detenido**
te detienes	**os detenéis**	**te has detenido**	**os habéis detenido**
se detiene	**se detienen**	**se ha detenido**	**se han detenido**
2 imperfecto de indicativo		9 pluscuamperfecto de indicativo	
me detenía	**nos deteníamos**	**me había detenido**	**nos habíamos detenido**
te detenías	**os deteníais**	**te habías detenido**	**os habíais detenido**
se detenía	**se detenían**	**se había detenido**	**se habían detenido**
3 pretérito		10 pretérito anterior	
me detuve	**nos detuvimos**	**me hube detenido**	**nos hubimos detenido**
te detuviste	**os detuvisteis**	**te hubiste detenido**	**os hubisteis detenido**
se detuvo	**se detuvieron**	**se hubo detenido**	**se hubieron detenido**
4 futuro		11 futuro perfecto	
me detendré	**nos detendremos**	**me habré detenido**	**nos habremos detenido**
te detendrás	**os detendréis**	**te habrás detenido**	**os habréis detenido**
se detendrá	**se detendrán**	**se habrá detenido**	**se habrán detenido**
5 potencial simple		12 potencial compuesto	
me detendría	**nos detendríamos**	**me habría detenido**	**nos habríamos detenido**
te detendrías	**os detendríais**	**te habrías detenido**	**os habríais detenido**
se detendría	**se detendrían**	**se habría detenido**	**se habrían detenido**
6 presente de subjuntivo		13 perfecto de subjuntivo	
me detenga	**nos detengamos**	**me haya detenido**	**nos hayamos detenido**
te detengas	**os detangáis**	**te hayas detenido**	**os hayáis detenido**
se detenga	**se detengan**	**se haya detenido**	**se hayan detenido**
7 imperfecto de subjuntivo		14 pluscuamperfecto de subjuntivo	
me detuviera	**nos detuviéramos**	**me hubiera detenido**	**nos hubiéramos detenido**
te detuvieras	**os detuvierais**	**te hubieras detenido**	**os hubierais detenido**
se detuviera	**se detuvieran**	**se hubiera detenido**	**se hubieran detenido**
OR		OR	
me detuviese	**nos detuviésemos**	**me hubiese detenido**	**nos hubiésemos detenido**
te detuvieses	**os detuvieseis**	**te hubieses detenido**	**os hubieseis detenido**
se detuviese	**se detuviesen**	**se hubiese detenido**	**se hubiesen detenido**

	imperativo	
—		**detengámonos**
detente; no te detengas		**deteneos; no os detengáis**
deténgase		**deténganse**

Words and expressions related to this verb

detener to stop (someone or something), to detain

detenerse en una idea to dwell on an idea

detenedor, detenedora detainer

See also **detener.**

If you don't know the Spanish verb for an English verb you have in mind, try the index on pages 505–518.

to return (an object), to refund, to give back

The Seven Simple Tenses		The Seven Compound Tenses	
Singular	Plural	Singular	Plural
1 presente de indicativo		**8 perfecto de indicativo**	
devuelvo	devolvemos	he devuelto	hemos devuelto
devuelves	devolvéis	has devuelto	habéis devuelto
devuelve	devuelven	ha devuelto	han devuelto
2 imperfecto de indicativo		**9 pluscuamperfecto de indicativo**	
devolvía	devolvíamos	había devuelto	habíamos devuelto
devolvías	devolvíais	habías devuelto	habíais devuelto
devolvía	devolvían	había devuelto	habían devuelto
3 pretérito		**10 pretérito anterior**	
devolví	devolvimos	hube devuelto	hubimos devuelto
devolviste	devolvisteis	hubiste devuelto	hubisteis devuelto
devolvió	devolvieron	hubo devuelto	hubieron devuelto
4 futuro		**11 futuro perfecto**	
devolveré	devolveremos	habré devuelto	habremos devuelto
devolverás	devolveréis	habrás devuelto	habréis devuelto
devolverá	devolverán	habrá devuelto	habrán devuelto
5 potencial simple		**12 potencial compuesto**	
devolvería	devolveríamos	habría devuelto	habríamos devuelto
devolverías	devolveríais	habrías devuelto	habríais devuelto
devolvería	devolverían	habría devuelto	habrían devuelto
6 presente de subjuntivo		**13 perfecto de subjuntivo**	
devuelva	devolvamos	haya devuelto	hayamos devuelto
devuelvas	devolváis	hayas devuelto	hayáis devuelto
devuelva	devuelvan	haya devuelto	hayan devuelto
7 imperfecto de subjuntivo		**14 pluscuamperfecto de subjuntivo**	
devolviera	devolviéramos	hubiera devuelto	hubiéramos devuelto
devolvieras	devolvierais	hubieras devuelto	hubierais devuelto
devolviera	devolvieran	hubiera devuelto	hubieran devuelto
OR		OR	
devolviese	devolviésemos	hubiese devuelto	hubiésemos devuelto
devolvieses	devolvieseis	hubieses devuelto	hubieseis devuelto
devolviese	devolviesen	hubiese devuelto	hubiesen devuelto

	imperativo
—	devolvamos
devuelve; no devuelvas	devolved; no devolváis
devuelva	devuelvan

Words and expressions related to this verb
—¿**Ha devuelto Ud. los libros a la biblioteca?**   —Sí, señora, los devolví ayer.
devolutivo, devolutiva returnable   **devolver** to vomit
volver to return, to go back   **la devolución** return, giving back

For other words and expressions related to this verb, see **revolver** and **volver**.

See also **devolver** on page 537.

The subject pronouns are found on the page facing page 1.

dibujar

Gerundio **dibujando**   Part. pas. **dibujado**

to design, to draw, to sketch

The Seven Simple Tenses		The Seven Compound Tenses	
Singular	Plural	Singular	Plural
1 presente de indicativo		**8 perfecto de indicativo**	
dibujo	dibujamos	he dibujado	hemos dibujado
dibujas	dibujáis	has dibujado	habéis dibujado
dibuja	dibujan	ha dibujado	han dibujado
2 imperfecto de indicativo		**9 pluscuamperfecto de indicativo**	
dibujaba	dibujábamos	había dibujado	habíamos dibujado
dibujabas	dibujabais	habías dibujado	habíais dibujado
dibujaba	dibujaban	había dibujado	habían dibujado
3 pretérito		**10 pretérito anterior**	
dibujé	dibujamos	hube dibujado	hubimos dibujado
dibujaste	dibujasteis	hubiste dibujado	hubisteis dibujado
dibujó	dibujaron	hubo dibujado	hubieron dibujado
4 futuro		**11 futuro perfecto**	
dibujaré	dibujaremos	habré dibujado	habremos dibujado
dibujarás	dibujaréis	habrás dibujado	habréis dibujado
dibujará	dibujarán	habrá dibujado	habrán dibujado
5 potencial simple		**12 potencial compuesto**	
dibujaría	dibujaríamos	habría dibujado	habríamos dibujado
dibujarías	dibujaríais	habrías dibujado	habríais dibujado
dibujaría	dibujarían	habría dibujado	habrían dibujado
6 presente de subjuntivo		**13 perfecto de subjuntivo**	
dibuje	dibujemos	haya dibujado	hayamos dibujado
dibujes	dibujéis	hayas dibujado	hayáis dibujado
dibuje	dibujen	haya dibujado	hayan dibujado
7 imperfecto de subjuntivo		**14 pluscuamperfecto de subjuntivo**	
dibujara	dibujáramos	hubiera dibujado	hubiéramos dibujado
dibujaras	dibujarais	hubieras dibujado	hubierais dibujado
dibujara	dibujaran	hubiera dibujado	hubieran dibujado
OR		OR	
dibujase	dibujásemos	hubiese dibujado	hubiésemos dibujado
dibujases	dibujaseis	hubieses dibujado	hubieseis dibujado
dibujase	dibujasen	hubiese dibujado	hubiesen dibujado

imperativo	
—	dibujemos
dibuja; no dibujes	dibujad; no dibujéis
dibuje	dibujen

Words and expressions related to this verb

un dibujo   drawing, design, sketch
el, la dibujante   designer, illustrator, sketcher
dibujos humorísticos   comics
el dibujo asistido por ordenador   computer-assisted drawing

dibujo a la pluma   pen and ink drawing
dibujos animados   animated cartoons

The Seven Simple Tenses		The Seven Compound Tenses	
Singular	Plural	Singular	Plural
1 presente de indicativo		8 perfecto de indicativo	
dirijo	**dirigimos**	**he dirigido**	**hemos dirigido**
diriges	**dirigís**	**has dirigido**	**habéis dirigido**
dirige	**dirigen**	**ha dirigido**	**han dirigido**
2 imperfecto de indicativo		9 pluscuamperfecto de indicativo	
dirigía	**dirigíamos**	**había dirigido**	**habíamos dirigido**
dirigías	**dirigíais**	**habías dirigido**	**habíais dirigido**
dirigía	**dirigían**	**había dirigido**	**habían dirigido**
3 pretérito		10 pretérito anterior	
dirigí	**dirigimos**	**hube dirigido**	**hubimos dirigido**
dirigiste	**dirigisteis**	**hubiste dirigido**	**hubisteis dirigido**
dirigió	**dirigieron**	**hubo dirigido**	**hubieron dirigido**
4 futuro		11 futuro perfecto	
dirigiré	**dirigiremos**	**habré dirigido**	**habremos dirigido**
dirigirás	**dirigiréis**	**habrás dirigido**	**habréis dirigido**
dirigirá	**dirigirán**	**habrá dirigido**	**habrán dirigido**
5 potencial simple		12 potencial compuesto	
dirigiría	**dirigiríamos**	**habría dirigido**	**habríamos dirigido**
dirigirías	**dirigiríais**	**habrías dirigido**	**habríais dirigido**
dirigiría	**dirigirían**	**habría dirigido**	**habrían dirigido**
6 presente de subjuntivo		13 perfecto de subjuntivo	
dirija	**dirijamos**	**haya dirigido**	**hayamos dirigido**
dirijas	**dirijáis**	**hayas dirigido**	**hayáis dirigido**
dirija	**dirijan**	**haya dirigido**	**hayan dirigido**
7 imperfecto de subjuntivo		14 pluscuamperfecto de subjuntivo	
dirigiera	**dirigiéramos**	**hubiera dirigido**	**hubiéramos dirigido**
dirigieras	**dirigierais**	**hubieras dirigido**	**hubierais dirigido**
dirigiera	**dirigieran**	**hubiera dirigido**	**hubieran dirigido**
OR		OR	
dirigiese	**dirigiésemos**	**hubiese dirigido**	**hubiésemos dirigido**
dirigieses	**dirigieseis**	**hubieses dirigido**	**hubieseis dirigido**
dirigiese	**dirigiesen**	**hubiese dirigido**	**hubiesen dirigido**

imperativo

—	**dirijamos**
dirige; no dirijas	**dirigid; no dirijáis**
dirija	**dirijan**

Words and expressions related to this verb

el director, la directora   director

director de orquesta   orchestra conductor

el dirigente, la dirigente   leader

dirigir la palabra a   to address, to speak to

dirigible   manageable

el dirigible   dirigible, blimp (aviation)

dirigirse a   to make one's way to, to go to

dirigir el baile   to run the show

Can't recognize an irregular verb form? Check out pages 519–523.

to apologize, to excuse (oneself)

The Seven Simple Tenses		The Seven Compound Tenses	
Singular	Plural	Singular	Plural
1 presente de indicativo		8 perfecto de indicativo	
me disculpo	**nos disculpamos**	**me he disculpado**	**nos hemos disculpado**
te disculpas	**os disculpáis**	**te has disculpado**	**os habéis disculpado**
se disculpa	**se disculpan**	**se ha disculpado**	**se han disculpado**
2 imperfecto de indicativo		9 pluscuamperfecto de indicativo	
me disculpaba	**nos disculpábamos**	**me había disculpado**	**nos habíamos disculpado**
te disculpabas	**os disculpabais**	**te habías disculpado**	**os habíais disculpado**
se disculpaba	**se disculpaban**	**se había disculpado**	**se habían disculpado**
3 pretérito		10 pretérito anterior	
me disculpé	**nos disculpamos**	**me hube disculpado**	**nos hubimos disculpado**
te disculpaste	**os disculpasteis**	**te hubiste disculpado**	**os hubisteis disculpado**
se disculpó	**se disculparon**	**se hubo disculpado**	**se hubieron disculpado**
4 futuro		11 futuro perfecto	
me disculparé	**nos disculparemos**	**me habré disculpado**	**nos habremos disculpado**
te disculparás	**os disculparéis**	**te habrás disculpado**	**os habréis disculpado**
se disculpará	**se disculparán**	**se habrá disculpado**	**se habrán disculpado**
5 potencial simple		12 potencial compuesto	
me disculparía	**nos disculparíamos**	**me habría disculpado**	**nos habríamos disculpado**
te disculparías	**os disculparíais**	**te habrías disculpado**	**os habríais disculpado**
se disculparía	**se disculparían**	**se habría disculpado**	**se habrían disculpado**
6 presente de subjuntivo		13 perfecto de subjuntivo	
me disculpe	**nos disculpemos**	**me haya disculpado**	**nos hayamos disculpado**
te disculpes	**os disculpéis**	**te hayas disculpado**	**os hayáis disculpado**
se disculpe	**se disculpen**	**se haya disculpado**	**se hayan disculpado**
7 imperfecto de subjuntivo		14 pluscuamperfecto de subjuntivo	
me disculpara	**nos disculpáramos**	**me hubiera disculpado**	**nos hubiéramos disculpado**
te disculparas	**os disculparais**	**te hubieras disculpado**	**os hubierais disculpado**
se disculpara	**se disculparan**	**se hubiera disculpado**	**se hubieran disculpado**
OR		OR	
me disculpase	**nos disculpásemos**	**me hubiese disculpado**	**nos hubiésemos disculpado**
te disculpases	**os disculpaseis**	**te hubieses disculpado**	**os hubieseis disculpado**
se disculpase	**se disculpasen**	**se hubiese disculpado**	**se hubiesen disculpado**

imperativo

—	**disculpémonos**
discúlpate; no te disculpes	**disculpaos; no os disculpéis**
discúlpese	**discúlpense**

Words and expressions related to this verb

disculpar to excuse, to pardon (someone)
disculparse con to apologize to, to make
  excuses to
disculparse de to apologize for, to make
  excuses for

una disculpa excuse, apology
la culpa fault, blame, guilt
tener la culpa to be guilty
culpar to blame, to accuse
culparse to blame oneself
dar disculpas to make excuses

The Seven Simple Tenses		The Seven Compound Tenses	
Singular	Plural	Singular	Plural
1 presente de indicativo		**8 perfecto de indicativo**	
discuto	discutimos	he discutido	hemos discutido
discutes	discutís	has discutido	habéis discutido
discute	discuten	ha discutido	han discutido
2 imperfecto de indicativo		**9 pluscuamperfecto de indicativo**	
discutía	discutíamos	había discutido	habíamos discutido
discutías	discutíais	habías discutido	habíais discutido
discutía	discutían	había discutido	habían discutido
3 pretérito		**10 pretérito anterior**	
discutí	discutimos	hube discutido	hubimos discutido
discutiste	discutisteis	hubiste discutido	hubisteis discutido
discutió	discutieron	hubo discutido	hubieron discutido
4 futuro		**11 futuro perfecto**	
discutiré	discutiremos	habré discutido	habremos discutido
discutirás	discutiréis	habrás discutido	habréis discutido
discutirá	discutirán	habrá discutido	habrán discutido
5 potencial simple		**12 potencial compuesto**	
discutiría	discutiríamos	habría discutido	habríamos discutido
discutirías	discutiríais	habrías discutido	habríais discutido
discutiría	discutirían	habría discutido	habrían discutido
6 presente de subjuntivo		**13 perfecto de subjuntivo**	
discuta	discutamos	haya discutido	hayamos discutido
discutas	discutáis	hayas discutido	hayáis discutido
discuta	discutan	haya discutido	hayan discutido
7 imperfecto de subjuntivo		**14 pluscuamperfecto de subjuntivo**	
discutiera	discutiéramos	hubiera discutido	hubiéramos discutido
discutieras	discutierais	hubieras discutido	hubierais discutido
discutiera	discutieran	hubiera discutido	hubieran discutido
OR		OR	
discutiese	discutiésemos	hubiese discutido	hubiésemos discutido
discutieses	discutieseis	hubieses discutido	hubieseis discutido
discutiese	discutiesen	hubiese discutido	hubiesen discutido

imperativo	
—	**discutamos**
discute; no discutas	**discutid; no discutáis**
discuta	**discutan**

Words and expressions related to this verb

discutir sobre   to argue about
discutible   debatable, disputable
la discusión   discussion, argument

un discurso   discourse, speech
el discurso de la corona   King (Queen's) speech
discutir el precio   to argue over the price

Use the EE-zee guide to Spanish pronunciation on pages 562 and 563.

The subject pronouns are found on the page facing page 1.

dispensar

Gerundio **dispensando** Part. pas. **dispensado**

to excuse, to dispense, to distribute, to exempt

The Seven Simple Tenses		The Seven Compound Tenses	
Singular	Plural	Singular	Plural
1 presente de indicativo		**8 perfecto de indicativo**	
dispenso	dispensamos	he dispensado	hemos dispensado
dispensas	dispensáis	has dispensado	habéis dispensado
dispensa	dispensan	ha dispensado	han dispensado
2 imperfecto de indicativo		**9 pluscuamperfecto de indicativo**	
dispensaba	dispensábamos	había dispensado	habíamos dispensado
dispensabas	dispensabais	habías dispensado	habíais dispensado
dispensaba	dispensaban	había dispensado	habían dispensado
3 pretérito		**10 pretérito anterior**	
dispensé	dispensamos	hube dispensado	hubimos dispensado
dispensaste	dispensasteis	hubiste dispensado	hubisteis dispensado
dispensó	dispensaron	hubo dispensado	hubieron dispensado
4 futuro		**11 futuro perfecto**	
dispensaré	dispensaremos	habré dispensado	habremos dispensado
dispensarás	dispensaréis	habrás dispensado	habréis dispensado
dispensará	dispensarán	habrá dispensado	habrán dispensado
5 potencial simple		**12 potencial compuesto**	
dispensaría	dispensaríamos	habría dispensado	habríamos dispensado
dispensarías	dispensaríais	habrías dispensado	habríais dispensado
dispensaría	dispensarían	habría dispensado	habrían dispensado
6 presente de subjuntivo		**13 perfecto de subjuntivo**	
dispense	dispensemos	haya dispensado	hayamos dispensado
dispenses	dispenséis	hayas dispensado	hayáis dispensado
dispense	dispensen	haya dispensado	hayan dispensado
7 imperfecto de subjuntivo		**14 pluscuamperfecto de subjuntivo**	
dispensara	dispensáramos	hubiera dispensado	hubiéramos dispensado
dispensaras	dispensarais	hubieras dispensado	hubierais dispensado
dispensara	dispensaran	hubiera dispensado	hubieran dispensado
OR		OR	
dispensase	dispensásemos	hubiese dispensado	hubiésemos dispensado
dispensases	dispensaseis	hubieses dispensado	hubieseis dispensado
dispensase	dispensasen	hubiese dispensado	hubiesen dispensado

	imperativo
—	dispensemos
dispensa; no dispenses	dispensad; no dispenséis
dispense	dispensen

Words and expressions related to this verb

¡Dispénseme! Excuse me!
la dispensación dispensation
el dispensario dispensary, clinic

dispensar de + inf. to excuse from + pres. part.
la dispensa privilege, exemption

Increase your verb power with popular phrases, words, and expressions for tourists on pages 595–618.

The Seven Simple Tenses		The Seven Compound Tenses	
Singular	Plural	Singular	Plural
1 presente de indicativo		**8 perfecto de indicativo**	
distingo	distinguimos	he distinguido	hemos distinguido
distingues	distinguís	has distinguido	habéis distinguido
distingue	distinguen	ha distinguido	han distinguido
2 imperfecto de indicativo		**9 pluscuamperfecto de indicativo**	
distinguía	distinguíamos	había distinguido	habíamos distinguido
distinguías	distinguíais	habías distinguido	habíais distinguido
distinguía	distinguían	había distinguido	habían distinguido
3 pretérito		**10 pretérito anterior**	
distinguí	distinguimos	hube distinguido	hubimos distinguido
distinguiste	distinguisteis	hubiste distinguido	hubisteis distinguido
distinguió	distinguieron	hubo distinguido	hubieron distinguido
4 futuro		**11 futuro perfecto**	
distinguiré	distinguiremos	habré distinguido	habremos distinguido
distinguirás	distinguiréis	habrás distinguido	habréis distinguido
distinguirá	distinguirán	habrá distinguido	habrán distinguido
5 potencial simple		**12 potencial compuesto**	
distinguiría	distinguiríamos	habría distinguido	habríamos distinguido
distinguirías	distinguiríais	habrías distinguido	habríais distinguido
distinguiría	distinguirían	habría distinguido	habrían distinguido
6 presente de subjuntivo		**13 perfecto de subjuntivo**	
distinga	distingamos	haya distinguido	hayamos distinguido
distingas	distingáis	hayas distinguido	hayáis distinguido
distinga	distingan	haya distinguido	hayan distinguido
7 imperfecto de subjuntivo		**14 pluscuamperfecto de subjuntivo**	
distinguiera	distinguiéramos	hubiera distinguido	hubiéramos distinguido
distinguieras	distinguierais	hubieras distinguido	hubierais distinguido
distinguiera	distinguieran	hubiera distinguido	hubieran distinguido
OR		OR	
distinguiese	distinguiésemos	hubiese distinguido	hubiésemos distinguido
distinguieses	distinguieseis	hubieses distinguido	hubieseis distinguido
distinguiese	distinguiesen	hubiese distinguido	hubiesen distinguido

	imperativo	
—		distingamos
distingue; no distingas		distinguid; no distingáis
distinga		distingan

Words related to this verb
distinguirse to distinguish oneself
distintivo, distintiva distinctive
el distingo restriction

a distinción de as distinct from
distinto, distinta different, distinct, clear
la distinción distinction

If you want to see a sample English verb fully conjugated in
all the tenses, check out pages xviii and xix.

divertirse

Gerundio **divirtiéndose**   Part. pas. **divertido**

to have a good time, to enjoy oneself, to amuse oneself

The Seven Simple Tenses		The Seven Compound Tenses	
Singular	Plural	Singular	Plural
1 presente de indicativo		8 perfecto de indicativo	
me divierto	**nos divertimos**	**me he divertido**	**nos hemos divertido**
te diviertes	**os divertís**	**te has divertido**	**os habéis divertido**
se divierte	**se divierten**	**se ha divertido**	**se han divertido**
2 imperfecto de indicativo		9 pluscuamperfecto de indicativo	
me divertía	**nos divertíamos**	**me había divertido**	**nos habíamos divertido**
te divertías	**os divertíais**	**te habías divertido**	**os habíais divertido**
se divertía	**se divertían**	**se había divertido**	**se habían divertido**
3 pretérito		10 pretérito anterior	
me divertí	**nos divertimos**	**me hube divertido**	**nos hubimos divertido**
te divertiste	**os divertisteis**	**te hubiste divertido**	**os hubisteis divertido**
se divirtió	**se divirtieron**	**se hubo divertido**	**se hubieron divertido**
4 futuro		11 futuro perfecto	
me divertiré	**nos divertiremos**	**me habré divertido**	**nos habremos divertido**
te divertirás	**os divertiréis**	**te habrás divertido**	**os habréis divertido**
se divertirá	**se divertirán**	**se habrá divertido**	**se habrán divertido**
5 potencial simple		12 potencial compuesto	
me divertiría	**nos divertiríamos**	**me habría divertido**	**nos habríamos divertido**
te divertirías	**os divertiríais**	**te habrías divertido**	**os habríais divertido**
se divertiría	**se divertirían**	**se habría divertido**	**se habrían divertido**
6 presente de subjuntivo		13 perfecto de subjuntivo	
me divierta	**nos divirtamos**	**me haya divertido**	**nos hayamos divertido**
te diviertas	**os divirtáis**	**te hayas divertido**	**os hayáis divertido**
se divierta	**se diviertan**	**se haya divertido**	**se hayan divertido**
7 imperfecto de subjuntivo		14 pluscuamperfecto de subjuntivo	
me divirtiera	**nos divirtiéramos**	**me hubiera divertido**	**nos hubiéramos divertido**
te divirtieras	**os divirtierais**	**te hubieras divertido**	**os hubierais divertido**
se divirtiera	**se divirtieran**	**se hubiera divertido**	**se hubieran divertido**
OR		OR	
me divirtiese	**nos divirtiésemos**	**me hubiese divertido**	**nos hubiésemos divertido**
te divirtieses	**os divirtieseis**	**te hubieses divertido**	**os hubieseis divertido**
se divirtiese	**se divirtiesen**	**se hubiese divertido**	**se hubiesen divertido**

imperativo

—	**divirtámonos; no nos divirtamos**
diviértete; no te diviertas	**divertíos; no os divirtáis**
diviértase; no se divierta	**diviértanse; no se diviertan**

Words related to this verb

el divertimiento   amusement, diversion
diverso, diversa   diverse, different
la diversión   entertainment, pastime

divertir   to entertain
divertido, divertida   amusing, entertaining
una película divertida   an entertaining film

Learn more verbs in 30 practical situations for tourists on pages 564–594.

to be (get) divorced

The Seven Simple Tenses		The Seven Compound Tenses	
Singular	Plural	Singular	Plural
1 presente de indicativo		8 perfecto de indicativo	
me divorcio	**nos divorciamos**	**me he divorciado**	**nos hemos divorciado**
te divorcias	**os divorciáis**	**te has divorciado**	**os habéis divorciado**
se divorcia	**se divorcian**	**se ha divorciado**	**se han divorciado**
2 imperfecto de indicativo		9 pluscuamperfecto de indicativo	
me divorciaba	**nos divorciábamos**	**me había divorciado**	**nos habíamos divorciado**
te divorciabas	**os divorciabais**	**te habías divorciado**	**os habíais divorciado**
se divorciaba	**se divorciaban**	**se había divorciado**	**se habían divorciado**
3 pretérito		10 pretérito anterior	
me divorcié	**nos divorciamos**	**me hube divorciado**	**nos hubimos divorciado**
te divorciaste	**os divorciasteis**	**te hubiste divorciado**	**os hubisteis divorciado**
se divorció	**se divorciaron**	**se hubo divorciado**	**se hubieron divorciado**
4 futuro		11 futuro perfecto	
me divorciaré	**nso divorciaremos**	**me habré divorciado**	**nos habremos divorciado**
te divorciarás	**os divorciaréis**	**te habrás divorciado**	**os habréis divorciado**
se divoricará	**se divorciarán**	**se habrá divorciado**	**se habrán divorciado**
5 potencial simple		12 potencial compuesto	
me divorciaría	**nos divorciaríamos**	**me habría divorciado**	**nos habríamos divorciado**
te divorciarías	**os divorciaríais**	**te habrías divorciado**	**os habríais divorciado**
se divoricaría	**se divorciarían**	**se habría divorciado**	**se habrían divorciado**
6 presente de subjuntivo		13 perfecto de subjuntivo	
me divorcie	**nos divorciemos**	**me haya divorciado**	**nos hayamos divorciado**
te divorcies	**os divorciéis**	**te hayas divorciado**	**os hayáis divorciado**
se divorcie	**se divorcien**	**se haya divorciado**	**se hayan divorciado**
7 imperfecto de subjuntivo		14 pluscuamperfecto de subjuntivo	
me divorciara	**nos divorciáramos**	**me hubiera divorciado**	**nos hubiéramos divorciado**
te divorciaras	**os divorciarais**	**te hubieras divorciado**	**os hubierais divorciado**
se divorciara	**se divorciaran**	**se hubiera divorciado**	**se hubieran divorciado**
OR		OR	
me divorciase	**nos divorciásemos**	**me hubiese divorciado**	**nos hubiésemos divorciado**
te divorciases	**os divorciaseis**	**te hubieses divorciado**	**os hubieseis divorciado**
se divorciase	**se divorciasen**	**se hubiese divorciado**	**se hubiesen divorciado**

imperativo

—	**divorciémonos**
divórciate; no te divorcies	**divorciaos; no os divorciéis**
divórciese	**divórciense**

Words related to this verb
divorciarse de   to get a divorce from
el divorcio   divorce, separation
una mujer divorciada, un hombre divorciado   divorced woman, man

Check out the verb drills and verb tests with answers explained on pages 619–665.

The subject pronouns are found on the page facing page 1.

to ache, to pain, to hurt, to cause grief, to cause regret

The Seven Simple Tenses		The Seven Compound Tenses	
Singular	Plural	Singular	Plural
1 presente de indicativo		8 perfecto de indicativo	
duelo	**dolemos**	**he dolido**	**hemos dolido**
dueles	**doléis**	**has dolido**	**habéis dolido**
duele	**duelen**	**ha dolido**	**han dolido**
2 imperfecto de indicativo		9 pluscuamperfecto de indicativo	
dolía	**dolíamos**	**había dolido**	**habíamos dolido**
dolías	**dolíais**	**habías dolido**	**habíais dolido**
dolía	**dolían**	**había dolido**	**habían dolido**
3 pretérito		10 pretérito anterior	
dolí	**dolimos**	**hube dolido**	**hubimos dolido**
doliste	**dolisteis**	**hubiste dolido**	**hubisteis dolido**
dolió	**dolieron**	**hubo dolido**	**hubieron dolido**
4 futuro		11 futuro perfecto	
doleré	**doleremos**	**habré dolido**	**habremos dolido**
dolerás	**doleréis**	**habrás dolido**	**habréis dolido**
dolerá	**dolerán**	**habrá dolido**	**habrán dolido**
5 potencial simple		12 potencial compuesto	
dolería	**doleríamos**	**habría dolido**	**habríamos dolido**
dolerías	**doleríais**	**habrías dolido**	**habríais dolido**
dolería	**dolerían**	**habría dolido**	**habrían dolido**
6 presente de subjuntivo		13 perfecto de subjuntivo	
duela	**dolamos**	**haya dolido**	**hayamos dolido**
duelas	**doláis**	**hayas dolido**	**hayáis dolido**
duela	**duelan**	**haya dolido**	**hayan dolido**
7 imperfecto de subjuntivo		14 pluscuamperfecto de subjuntivo	
doliera	**doliéramos**	**hubiera dolido**	**hubiéramos dolido**
dolieras	**dolierais**	**hubieras dolido**	**hubierais dolido**
doliera	**dolieran**	**hubiera dolido**	**hubieran dolido**
OR		OR	
doliese	**doliésemos**	**hubiese dolido**	**hubiésemos dolido**
dolieses	**dolieseis**	**hubieses dolido**	**hubieseis dolido**
doliese	**doliesen**	**hubiese dolido**	**hubiesen dolido**

imperativo

—	**dolamos**
duele; no duelas	**doled; no doláis**
duela	**duelan**

Words and expressions related to this verb
dolerse de   to complain about, to regret
un dolor   ache, hurt, pain, regret
causar dolor   to pain
estar con dolores   to be in labor
Me duelo de haber dicho tales cosas.

   I regret having said such things.

tener dolor de cabeza   to have a headache
tener dolor de muelas   to have a toothache
tener dolor do oído   to have an earache
un dolor sordo   dull nagging pain
dolerse de sus pecados   to repent of one's sins
José se duele de sus pecados.

   José repents of his sins.

The Seven Simple Tenses		The Seven Compound Tenses	
Singular	Plural	Singular	Plural
1 presente de indicativo		8 perfecto de indicativo	
duermo	**dormimos**	**he dormido**	**hemos dormido**
duermes	**dormís**	**has dormido**	**habéis dormido**
duerme	**duermen**	**ha dormido**	**han dormido**
2 imperfecto de indicativo		9 pluscuamperfecto de indicativo	
dormía	**dormíamos**	**había dormido**	**habíamos dormido**
dormías	**dormíais**	**habías dormido**	**habíais dormido**
dormía	**dormían**	**había dormido**	**habían dormido**
3 pretérito		10 pretérito anterior	
dormí	**dormimos**	**hube dormido**	**hubimos dormido**
dormiste	**dormisteis**	**hubiste dormido**	**hubisteis dormido**
durmió	**durmieron**	**hubo dormido**	**hubieron dormido**
4 futuro		11 futuro perfecto	
dormiré	**dormiremos**	**habré dormido**	**habremos dormido**
dormirás	**dormiréis**	**habrás dormido**	**habréis dormido**
dormirá	**dormirán**	**habrá dormido**	**habrán dormido**
5 potencial simple		12 potencial compuesto	
dormiría	**dormiríamos**	**habría dormido**	**habríamos dormido**
dormirías	**dormiríais**	**habrías dormido**	**habríais dormido**
dormiría	**dormirían**	**habría dormido**	**habrían dormido**
6 presente de subjuntivo		13 perfecto de subjuntivo	
duerma	**durmamos**	**haya dormido**	**hayamos dormido**
duermas	**durmáis**	**hayas dormido**	**hayáis dormido**
duerma	**duerman**	**haya dormido**	**hayan dormido**
7 imperfecto de subjuntivo		14 pluscuamperfecto de subjuntivo	
durmiera	**durmiéramos**	**hubiera dormido**	**hubiéramos dormido**
durmieras	**durmierais**	**hubieras dormido**	**hubierais dormido**
durmiera	**durmieran**	**hubiera dormido**	**hubieran dormido**
OR		OR	
durmiese	**durmiésemos**	**hubiese dormido**	**hubiésemos dormido**
durmieses	**durmieseis**	**hubieses dormido**	**hubieseis dormido**
durmiese	**durmiesen**	**hubiese dormido**	**hubiesen dormido**

imperativo

—	**durmamos**
duerme; no duermas	**dormid; no durmáis**
duerma	**duerman**

Words and expressions related to this verb

dormirse   to fall asleep; (pres. part.:
  durmiéndose)
dormir a pierna suelta   to sleep soundly
dormitar   to doze
el dormitorio   bedroom, dormitory
dormilón, dormilona   sleepyhead

dormir como una piedra   to sleep like
  a log (**piedra**/stone)
dormir la siesta   to take an afternoon nap
dormir la mona   to sleep off a hangover
la dormición   dormition
tener la pierna dormida   to have one's leg
  fall asleep

The subject pronouns are found on the page facing page 1.

to take a shower, to shower oneself

The Seven Simple Tenses		The Seven Compound Tenses	
Singular	Plural	Singular	Plural
1 presente de indicativo		8 perfecto de indicativo	
me ducho	**nos duchamos**	**me he duchado**	**nos hemos duchado**
te duchas	**os ducháis**	**te has duchado**	**os habéis duchado**
se ducha	**se duchan**	**se ha duchado**	**se han duchado**
2 imperfecto de indicativo		9 pluscuamperfecto de indicativo	
me duchaba	**nos duchábamos**	**me había duchado**	**nos habíamos duchado**
te duchabas	**os duchabais**	**te habías duchado**	**os habíais duchado**
se duchaba	**se duchaban**	**se había duchado**	**se habían duchado**
3 pretérito		10 pretérito anterior	
me duché	**nos duchamos**	**me hube duchado**	**nos hubimos duchado**
te duchaste	**os duchasteis**	**te hubiste duchado**	**os hubisteis duchado**
se duchó	**se ducharon**	**se hubo duchado**	**se hubieron duchado**
4 futuro		11 futuro perfecto	
me ducharé	**nos ducharemos**	**me habré duchado**	**nos habremos duchado**
te ducharás	**os ducharéis**	**te habrás duchado**	**os habréis duchado**
se duchará	**se ducharán**	**se habrá duchado**	**se habrán duchado**
5 potencial simple		12 potencial compuesto	
me ducharía	**nos ducharíamos**	**me habría duchado**	**nos habríamos duchado**
te ducharías	**os ducharíais**	**te habrías duchado**	**os habríais duchado**
se ducharía	**se ducharían**	**se habría duchado**	**se habrían duchado**
6 presente de subjuntivo		13 perfecto de subjuntivo	
me duche	**nos duchemos**	**me haya duchado**	**nos hayamos duchado**
te duches	**os duchéis**	**te hayas duchado**	**os hayáis duchado**
se duche	**se duchen**	**se haya duchado**	**se hayan duchado**
7 imperfecto de subjuntivo		14 pluscuamperfecto de subjuntivo	
me duchara	**nos ducháramos**	**me hubiera duchado**	**nos hubiéramos duchado**
te ducharas	**os ducharais**	**te hubieras duchado**	**os hubierais duchado**
se duchara	**se ducharan**	**se hubiera duchado**	**se hubieran duchado**
OR		OR	
me duchase	**nos duchásemos**	**me hubiese duchado**	**nos hubiésemos duchado**
te duchases	**os duchaseis**	**te hubieses duchado**	**os hubieseis duchado**
se duchase	**se duchasen**	**se hubiese duchado**	**se hubiesen duchado**

	imperativo	
—		**duchémonos**
dúchate; no te duches		**duchaos; no os duchéis**
dúchese		**dúchense**

Sentences using this verb and words related to it
**Por lo general, me ducho todas las mañanas, pero esta mañana no me duché y mi padre me dijo:
—¡Dúchate!**

una ducha   shower, douche
tomar una ducha   to take a shower   **darse una ducha**   to have a shower

---

   Use the EE-zee guide to Spanish pronunciation on pages 562 and 563.

The Seven Simple Tenses		The Seven Compound Tenses	
Singular	Plural	Singular	Plural

1 presente de indicativo

Singular	Plural
dudo	dudamos
dudas	dudáis
duda	dudan

8 perfecto de indicativo

Singular	Plural
he dudado	hemos dudado
has dudado	habéis dudado
ha dudado	han dudado

2 imperfecto de indicativo

dudaba	dudábamos
dudabas	dudabais
dudaba	dudaban

9 pluscuamperfecto de indicativo

había dudado	habíamos dudado
habías dudado	habíais dudado
había dudado	habían dudado

3 pretérito

dudé	dudamos
dudaste	dudasteis
dudó	dudaron

10 pretérito anterior

hube dudado	hubimos dudado
hubiste dudado	hubisteis dudado
hubo dudado	hubieron dudado

4 futuro

dudaré	dudaremos
dudarás	dudaréis
dudará	dudarán

11 futuro perfecto

habré dudado	habremos dudado
habrás dudado	habréis dudado
habrá dudado	habrán dudado

5 potencial simple

dudaría	dudaríamos
dudarías	dudaríais
dudaría	dudarían

12 potencial compuesto

habría dudado	habríamos dudado
habrías dudado	habríais dudado
habría dudado	habrían dudado

6 presente de subjuntivo

dude	dudemos
dudes	dudéis
dude	duden

13 perfecto de subjuntivo

haya dudado	hayamos dudado
hayas dudado	hayáis dudado
haya dudado	hayan dudado

7 imperfecto de subjuntivo

dudara	dudáramos
dudaras	dudarais
dudara	dudaran
OR	
dudase	dudásemos
dudases	dudaseis
dudase	dudasen

14 pluscuamperfecto de subjuntivo

hubiera dudado	hubiéramos dudado
hubieras dudado	hubierais dudado
hubiera dudado	hubieran dudado
OR	
hubiese dudado	hubiésemos dudado
hubieses dudado	hubieseis dudado
hubiese dudado	hubiesen dudado

imperativo

—	dudemos
duda; no dudes	dudad; no dudéis
dude	duden

Words and expressions related to this verb

la duda doubt
sin duda undoubtedly, without a doubt
dudoso, dudosa doubtful
dudosamente doubtfully, hesitantly
dudar haber dicho eso to doubt having said that

poner en duda to doubt, to question
No cabe duda. There is no doubt.
No lo dudo. I don't doubt it.
dudar de algo to doubt something
dudar entre los dos to be unable to decide between the two

The subject pronouns are found on the page facing page 1.

echar

to cast, to fling, to hurl, to pitch, to throw

The Seven Simple Tenses		The Seven Compound Tenses	
Singular	Plural	Singular	Plural
1 presente de indicativo		**8 perfecto de indicativo**	
echo	echamos	he echado	hemos echado
echas	echáis	has echado	habéis echado
echa	echan	ha echado	han echado
2 imperfecto de indicativo		**9 pluscuamperfecto de indicativo**	
echaba	echábamos	había echado	habíamos echado
echabas	echabais	habías echado	habíais echado
echaba	echaban	había echado	habían echado
3 pretérito		**10 pretérito anterior**	
eché	echamos	hube echado	hubimos echado
echaste	echasteis	hubiste echado	hubisteis echado
echó	echaron	hubo echado	hubieron echado
4 futuro		**11 futuro perfecto**	
echaré	echaremos	habré echado	habremos echado
echarás	echaréis	habrás echado	habréis echado
echará	echarán	habrá echado	habrán echado
5 potencial simple		**12 potencial compuesto**	
echaría	echaríamos	habría echado	habríamos echado
echarías	echaríais	habrías echado	habríais echado
echaría	echarían	habría echado	habrían echado
6 presente de subjuntivo		**13 perfecto de subjuntivo**	
eche	echemos	haya echado	hayamos echado
eches	echéis	hayas echado	hayáis echado
eche	echen	haya echado	hayan echado
7 imperfecto de subjuntivo		**14 pluscuamperfecto de subjuntivo**	
echara	echáramos	hubiera echado	hubiéramos echado
echaras	echarais	hubieras echado	hubierais echado
echara	echaran	hubiera echado	hubieran echado
OR		OR	
echase	echásemos	hubiese echado	hubiésemos echado
echases	echaseis	hubieses echado	hubieseis echado
echase	echasen	hubiese echado	hubiesen echado

	imperativo	
—		echemos
echa; no eches		echad; no echéis
eche		echen

Words and expressions related to this verb
echar mano a   to grab; **echar de menos a una persona**   to miss a person
echar una carta al correo   to mail (post) a letter; **echar raíces**   to take root
una echada, un echamiento   cast, throw, casting, throwing
echarse   to lie down, rest, stretch out (oneself)
desechar   to reject

Enjoy verbs in Spanish proverbs on page 539.

to execute, to carry out, to perform

The Seven Simple Tenses		The Seven Compound Tenses	
Singular	Plural	Singular	Plural

1 presente de indicativo

		8 perfecto de indicativo	
ejecuto	ejecutamos	he ejecutado	hemos ejecutado
ejecutas	ejecutáis	has ejecutado	habéis ejecutado
ejecuta	ejecutan	ha ejecutado	han ejecutado

2 imperfecto de indicativo

		9 pluscuamperfecto de indicativo	
ejecutaba	ejecutábamos	había ejecutado	habíamos ejecutado
ejecutabas	ejecutabais	habías ejecutado	habíais ejecutado
ejecutaba	ejecutaban	había ejecutado	habían ejecutado

3 pretérito

		10 pretérito anterior	
ejecuté	ejecutamos	hube ejecutado	hubimos ejecutado
ejecutaste	ejecutasteis	hubiste ejecutado	hubisteis ejecutado
ejecutó	ejecutaron	hubo ejecutado	hubieron ejecutado

4 futuro

		11 futuro perfecto	
ejecutaré	ejecutaremos	habré ejecutado	habremos ejecutado
ejecutarás	ejecutaréis	habrás ejecutado	habréis ejecutado
ejecutará	ejecutarán	habrá ejecutado	habrán ejecutado

5 potencial simple

		12 potencial compuesto	
ejecutaría	ejecutaríamos	habría ejecutado	habríamos ejecutado
ejecutarías	ejecutaríais	habrías ejecutado	habríais ejecutado
ejecutaría	ejecutarían	habría ejecutado	habrían ejecutado

6 presente de subjuntivo

		13 perfecto de subjuntivo	
ejecute	ejecutemos	haya ejecutado	hayamos ejecutado
ejecutes	ejecutéis	hayas ejecutado	hayáis ejecutado
ejecute	ejecuten	haya ejecutado	hayan ejecutado

7 imperfecto de subjuntivo

		14 pluscuamperfecto de subjuntivo	
ejecutara	ejecutáramos	hubiera ejecutado	hubiéramos ejecutado
ejecutaras	ejecutarais	hubieras ejecutado	hubierais ejecutado
ejecutara	ejecutaran	hubiera ejecutado	hubieran ejecutado
OR		OR	
ejecutase	ejecutásemos	hubiese ejecutado	hubiésemos ejecutado
ejecutases	ejecutaseis	hubieses ejecutado	hubieseis ejecutado
ejecutase	ejecutasen	hubiese ejecutado	hubiesen ejecutado

imperativo

—	ejecutemos
ejecuta; no ejecutes	ejecutad; no ejecutéis
ejecute	ejecuten

Words and expressions related to this verb
un ejecutivo, una ejecutiva   executive
un ejecutor de la justicia   executioner
ejecutor, ejecutora   executor, executant

ejecutar un ajuste   to make an agreement
ejecutar un contrato   to carry out a contract
la ejecución   execution of a murderer, condemned person; execution of a plan, of a theatrical performance

The subject pronouns are found on the page facing page 1.

ejercer

Gerundio **ejerciendo**   Part. pas. **ejercido**

to exercise, to practice (a profession)

The Seven Simple Tenses		The Seven Compound Tenses	
Singular	Plural	Singular	Plural
1 presente de indicativo		**8 perfecto de indicativo**	
ejerzo	**ejercemos**	**he ejercido**	**hemos ejercido**
ejerces	**ejercéis**	**has ejercido**	**habéis ejercido**
ejerce	**ejercen**	**ha ejercido**	**han ejercido**
2 imperfecto de indicativo		**9 pluscuamperfecto de indicativo**	
ejercía	**ejercíamos**	**había ejercido**	**habíamos ejercido**
ejercías	**ejercíais**	**habías ejercido**	**habíais ejercido**
ejercía	**ejercían**	**había ejercido**	**habían ejercido**
3 pretérito		**10 pretérito anterior**	
ejercí	**ejercimos**	**hube ejercido**	**hubimos ejercido**
ejerciste	**ejercisteis**	**hubiste ejercido**	**hubisteis ejercido**
ejerció	**ejercieron**	**hubo ejercido**	**hubieron ejercido**
4 futuro		**11 futuro perfecto**	
ejerceré	**ejerceremos**	**habré ejercido**	**habremos ejercido**
ejercerás	**ejerceréis**	**habrás ejercido**	**habréis ejercido**
ejercerá	**ejercerán**	**habrá ejercido**	**habrán ejercido**
5 potencial simple		**12 potencial compuesto**	
ejercería	**ejerceríamos**	**habría ejercido**	**habríamos ejercido**
ejercerías	**ejerceríais**	**habrías ejercido**	**habríais ejercido**
ejercería	**ejercerían**	**habría ejercido**	**habrían ejercido**
6 presente de subjuntivo		**13 perfecto de subjuntivo**	
ejerza	**ejerzamos**	**haya ejercido**	**hayamos ejercido**
ejerzas	**ejerzáis**	**hayas ejercido**	**hayáis ejercido**
ejerza	**ejerzan**	**haya ejercido**	**hayan ejercido**
7 imperfecto de subjuntivo		**14 pluscuamperfecto de subjuntivo**	
ejerciera	**ejerciéramos**	**hubiera ejercido**	**hubiéramos ejercido**
ejercieras	**ejercierais**	**hubieras ejercido**	**hubierais ejercido**
ejerciera	**ejercieran**	**hubiera ejercido**	**hubieran ejercido**
OR		OR	
ejerciese	**ejerciésemos**	**hubiese ejercido**	**hubiésemos ejercido**
ejercieses	**ejercieseis**	**hubieses ejercido**	**hubieseis ejercido**
ejerciese	**ejerciesen**	**hubiese ejercido**	**hubiesen ejercido**

imperativo

—	**ejerzamos**
ejerce; no ejerzas	**ejerced; no ejerzáis**
ejerza	**ejerzan**

Words and expressions related to this verb
el ejercicio exercise
hacer ejercicios to drill, to exercise
el ejército army
ejercitar to drill, to exercise, to train
ejercer la medicina to practice medicine

los ejercicios escritos written exercises (tests)
ejercer el derecho de voto to exercise (use)
  one's right to vote
ejercitar a un estudiante en inglés to drill
  a student in English

to elect, to select, to choose

The Seven Simple Tenses		The Seven Compound Tenses	
Singular	Plural	Singular	Plural
1 presente de indicativo		8 perfecto de indicativo	
elijo	**elegimos**	**he elegido**	**hemos elegido**
eliges	**elegís**	**has elegido**	**habéis elegido**
elige	**eligen**	**ha elegido**	**han elegido**
2 imperfecto de indicativo		9 pluscuamperfecto de indicativo	
elegía	**elegíamos**	**había elegido**	**habíamos elegido**
elegías	**elegíais**	**habías elegido**	**habíais elegido**
elegía	**elegían**	**había elegido**	**habían elegido**
3 pretérito		10 pretérito anterior	
elegí	**elegimos**	**hube elegido**	**hubimos elegido**
elegiste	**elegisteis**	**hubiste elegido**	**hubisteis elegido**
eligió	**eligieron**	**hubo elegido**	**hubieron elegido**
4 futuro		11 futuro perfecto	
elegiré	**elegiremos**	**habré elegido**	**habremos elegido**
elegirás	**elegiréis**	**habrás elegido**	**habréis elegido**
elegirá	**elegirán**	**habrá elegido**	**habrán elegido**
5 potencial simple		12 potencial compuesto	
elegiría	**elegiríamos**	**habría elegido**	**habríamos elegido**
elegirías	**elegiríais**	**habrías elegido**	**habríais elegido**
elegiría	**elegirían**	**habría elegido**	**habrían elegido**
6 presente de subjuntivo		13 perfecto de subjuntivo	
elija	**elijamos**	**haya elegido**	**hayamos elegido**
elijas	**elijáis**	**hayas elegido**	**hayáis elegido**
elija	**elijan**	**haya elegido**	**hayan elegido**
7 imperfecto de subjuntivo		14 pluscuamperfecto de subjuntivo	
eligiera	**eligiéramos**	**hubiera elegido**	**hubiéramos elegido**
eligieras	**eligierais**	**hubieras elegido**	**hubierais elegido**
eligiera	**eligieran**	**hubiera elegido**	**hubieran elegido**
OR		OR	
eligiese	**eligiésemos**	**hubiese elegido**	**hubiésemos elegido**
eligieses	**eligieseis**	**hubieses elegido**	**hubieseis elegido**
eligiese	**eligiesen**	**hubiese elegido**	**hubiesen elegido**

imperativo

—	**elijamos**
elige; no elijas	**elegid; no elijáis**
elija	**elijan**

Words related to this verb

elegible   eligible
la elegibilidad   eligibility
la elección   election

elegir + inf.   to choose + inf.
reelegir   to reelect
el elector, la electora   elector, voter

Get acquainted with what preposition goes with what verb on pages 541–549.

embeber

Gerundio **embebiendo**   Part. pas. **embebido**

to soak in, to soak up, to suck in, to imbibe

The Seven Simple Tenses		The Seven Compound Tenses	
Singular	Plural	Singular	Plural
1 presente de indicativo		**8 perfecto de indicativo**	
embebo	embebemos	he embebido	hemos embebido
embebes	embebéis	has embebido	habéis embebido
embebe	embeben	ha embebido	han embebido
2 imperfecto de indicativo		**9 pluscuamperfecto de indicativo**	
embebía	embebíamos	había embebido	habíamos embebido
embebía	embebíais	habías embebido	habíais embebido
embebía	embebían	había embebido	habían embebido
3 pretérito		**10 pretérito anterior**	
embebí	embebimos	hube embebido	hubimos embebido
embebiste	embebisteis	hubiste embebido	hubisteis embebido
embebió	embebieron	hubo embebido	hubieron embebido
4 futuro		**11 futuro perfecto**	
embeberé	embeberemos	habré embebido	habremos embebido
embeberás	embeberéis	habrás embebido	habréis embebido
embeberá	embeberán	habrá embebido	habrán embebido
5 potencial simple		**12 potencial compuesto**	
embebería	embeberíamos	habría embebido	habríamos embebido
embeberías	embeberíais	habrías embebido	habríais embebido
embebería	embeberían	habría embebido	habrían embebido
6 presente de subjuntivo		**13 perfecto de subjuntivo**	
embeba	embebamos	haya embebido	hayamos embebido
embebas	embebáis	hayas embebido	hayáis embebido
embeba	embeban	haya embebido	hayan embebido
7 imperfecto de subjuntivo		**14 pluscuamperfecto de subjuntivo**	
embebiera	embebiéramos	hubiera embebido	hubiéramos embebido
embebieras	embebierais	hubieras embebido	hubierais embebido
embebiera	embebieran	hubiera embebido	hubieran embebido
OR		OR	
embebiese	embebiésemos	hubiese embebido	hubiésemos embebido
embebieses	embebieseis	hubieses embebido	hubieseis embebido
embebiese	embebiesen	hubiese embebido	hubiesen embebido

	imperativo	
—		embebamos
embebe; no embebas		embebed; no embebáis
embeba		embeban

Words related to this verb

una columna embebida   imbedded column
  (architecture)
embebedor, embebedora   absorbent, imbibing
beber   to drink
una bebida   drink, beverage
embeber algo en agua   to soak something in water

embeberse en   to absorb oneself, to
  immerse oneself in
embeberse en un libro   to absorb oneself
  in a book, to become absorbed in a book

to begin, to start

The Seven Simple Tenses		The Seven Compound Tenses	
Singular	Plural	Singular	Plural
1 presente de indicativo		8 perfecto de indicativo	
empiezo	empezamos	he empezado	hemos empezado
empiezas	empezáis	has empezado	habéis empezado
empieza	empiezan	ha empezado	han empezado
2 imperfecto de indicativo		9 pluscuamperfecto de indicativo	
empezaba	empezábamos	había empezado	habíamos empezado
empezabas	empezabais	habías empezado	habíais empezado
empezaba	empezaban	había empezado	habían empezado
3 pretérito		10 pretérito anterior	
empecé	empezamos	hube empezado	hubimos empezado
empezaste	empezasteis	hubiste empezado	hubisteis empezado
empezó	empezaron	hubo empezado	hubieron empezado
4 futuro		11 futuro perfecto	
empezaré	empezaremos	habré empezado	habremos empezado
empezarás	empezaréis	habrás empezado	habréis empezado
empezará	empezarán	habrá empezado	habrán empezado
5 potencial simple		12 potencial compuesto	
empezaría	empezaríamos	habría empezado	habríamos empezado
empezarías	empezaríais	habrías empezado	habríais empezado
empezaría	empezarían	habría empezado	habrían empezado
6 presente de subjuntivo		13 perfecto de subjuntivo	
empiece	empecemos	haya empezado	hayamos empezado
empieces	empecéis	hayas empezado	hayáis empezado
empiece	empiecen	haya empezado	hayan empezado
7 imperfecto de subjuntivo		14 pluscuamperfecto de subjuntivo	
empezara	empezáramos	hubiera empezado	hubiéramos empezado
empezaras	empezarais	hubieras empezado	hubierais empezado
empezara	empezaran	hubiera empezado	hubieran empezado
OR		OR	
empezase	empezásemos	hubiese empezado	hubiésemos empezado
empezases	empezaseis	hubieses empezado	hubieseis empezado
empezase	empezasen	hubiese empezado	hubiesen empezado

imperativo

—	**empecemos**
empieza; no empieces	**empezad; no empecéis**
empiece	**empiecen**

Common idiomatic expressions using this verb
empezar por + inf.   to begin by + pres. part.
empezar a + inf.   to begin + inf.; **Ricardo empieza a escribir en inglés.**
par empezar   to begin with

Get acquainted with what preposition goes with what verb on pages 541–549.

to employ, to use

The Seven Simple Tenses		The Seven Compound Tenses	
Singular	Plural	Singular	Plural
1 presente de indicativo		**8 perfecto de indicativo**	
empleo	empleamos	he empleado	hemos empleado
empleas	empleáis	has empleado	habéis empleado
emplea	emplean	ha empleado	han empleado
2 imperfecto de indicativo		**9 pluscuamperfecto de indicativo**	
empleaba	empleábamos	había empleado	habíamos empleado
empleabas	empleabais	habías empleado	habíais empleado
empleaba	empleaban	había empleado	habían empleado
3 pretérito		**10 pretérito anterior**	
empleé	empleamos	hube empleado	hubimos empleado
empleaste	empleasteis	hubiste empleado	hubisteis empleado
empleó	emplearon	hubo empleado	hubieron empleado
4 futuro		**11 futuro perfecto**	
emplearé	emplearemos	habré empleado	habremos empleado
emplearás	emplearéis	habrás empleado	habréis empleado
empleará	emplearán	habrá empleado	habrán empleado
5 potencial simple		**12 potencial compuesto**	
emplearía	emplearíamos	habría empleado	habríamos empleado
emplearías	emplearíais	habrías empleado	habríais empleado
emplearía	emplearían	habría empleado	habrían empleado
6 presente de subjuntivo		**13 perfecto de subjuntivo**	
emplee	empleemos	haya empleado	hayamos empleado
emplees	empleéis	hayas empleado	hayáis empleado
emplee	empleen	haya empleado	hayan empleado
7 imperfecto de subjuntivo		**14 pluscuamperfecto de subjuntivo**	
empleara	empleáramos	hubiera empleado	hubiéramos empleado
emplearas	emplearais	hubieras empleado	hubierais empleado
empleara	emplearan	hubiera empleado	hubieran empleado
OR		OR	
emplease	empleásemos	hubiese empleado	hubiésemos empleado
empleases	empleaseis	hubieses empleado	hubieseis empleado
emplease	empleasen	hubiese empleado	hubiesen empleado

imperativo		
—		empleemos
emplea; no emplees		emplead; no empleéis
emplee		empleen

Words and expressions related to this verb
un empleado, una empleada employee
el empleo job, employment, occupation, use
un empleador, una empleadora employer
EMPLEO SOLICITADO POSITION WANTED

Use the EE-zee guide to Spanish pronunciation on pages 562 and 563.

to incite, to inflame, to kindle, to light

The Seven Simple Tenses		The Seven Compound Tenses	
Singular	Plural	Singular	Plural
1 presente de indicativo		8 perfecto de indicativo	
enciendo	**encendemos**	**he encendido**	**hemos encendido**
enciendes	**encendéis**	**has encendido**	**habéis encendido**
enciende	**encienden**	**ha encendido**	**han encendido**
2 imperfecto de indicativo		9 pluscuamperfecto de indicativo	
encendía	**encendíamos**	**había encendido**	**habíamos encendido**
encendías	**encendíais**	**habías encendido**	**habíais encendido**
encendía	**encendían**	**había encendido**	**habían encendido**
3 pretérito		10 pretérito anterior	
encendí	**encendimos**	**hube encendido**	**hubimos encendido**
encendiste	**encendisteis**	**hubiste encendido**	**hubisteis encendido**
encendió	**encendieron**	**hubo encendido**	**hubieron encendido**
4 futuro		11 futuro perfecto	
encenderé	**encenderemos**	**habré encendido**	**habremos encendido**
encenderás	**encenderéis**	**habrás encendido**	**habréis encendido**
encenderá	**encenderán**	**habrá encendido**	**habrán encendido**
5 potencial simple		12 potencial compuesto	
encendería	**encenderíamos**	**habría encendido**	**habríamos encendido**
encenderías	**encenderíais**	**habrías encendido**	**habríais encendido**
encendería	**encenderían**	**habría encendido**	**habrían encendido**
6 presente de subjuntivo		13 perfecto de subjuntivo	
encienda	**encendamos**	**haya encendido**	**hayamos encendido**
enciendas	**encendáis**	**hayas encendido**	**hayáis encendido**
encienda	**enciendan**	**haya encendido**	**hayan encendido**
7 imperfecto de subjuntivo		14 pluscuamperfecto de subjuntivo	
encendiera	**encendiéramos**	**hubiera encendido**	**hubiéramos encendido**
encendieras	**encendierais**	**hubieras encendido**	**hubierais encendido**
encendiera	**encendieran**	**hubiera encendido**	**hubieran encendido**
OR		OR	
encendiese	**encendiésemos**	**hubiese encendido**	**hubiésemos encendido**
encendieses	**encendieseis**	**hubieses encendido**	**hubieseis encendido**
encendiese	**encendiesen**	**hubiese encendido**	**hubiesen encendido**

imperativo	
—	**encendamos**
enciende; no enciendas	**encended; no encendáis**
encienda	**enciendan**

Words and expressions related to this verb
encenderse en ira   to burn up with anger
encendido, encendida   inflamed; **encendido de color**   highly colored
incendiar   to set on fire; **incendiarse**   to catch fire
un incendio   fire; **un extintor de incendio**   fire extinguisher

The subject pronouns are found on the page facing page 1.

encerrar

to enclose, to lock up, to confine

The Seven Simple Tenses		The Seven Compound Tenses	
Singular	Plural	Singular	Plural
1 presente de indicativo		**8 perfecto de indicativo**	
encierro	encerramos	he encerrado	hemos encerrado
encierras	encerráis	has encerrado	habéis encerrado
encierra	encierran	ha encerrado	han encerrado
2 imperfecto de indicativo		**9 pluscuamperfecto de indicativo**	
encerraba	encerrábamos	había encerrado	habíamos encerrado
encerrabas	encerrabais	habías encerrado	habíais encerrado
encerraba	encerraban	había encerrado	habían encerrado
3 pretérito		**10 pretérito anterior**	
encerré	encerramos	hube encerrado	hubimos encerrado
encerraste	encerrasteis	hubiste encerrado	hubisteis encerrado
encerró	encerraron	hubo encerrado	hubieron encerrado
4 futuro		**11 futuro perfecto**	
encerraré	encerraremos	habré encerrado	habremos encerrado
encerrarás	encerraréis	habrás encerrado	habréis encerrado
encerrará	encerrarán	habrá encerrado	habrán encerrado
5 potencial simple		**12 potencial compuesto**	
encerraría	encerraríamos	habría encerrado	habríamos encerrado
encerrarías	encerraríais	habrías encerrado	habríais encerrado
encerraría	encerrarían	habría encerrado	habrían encerrado
6 presente de subjuntivo		**13 perfecto de subjuntivo**	
encierre	encerremos	haya encerrado	hayamos encerrado
encierres	encerréis	hayas encerrado	hayáis encerrado
encierre	encierren	haya encerrado	hayan encerrado
7 imperfecto de subjuntivo		**14 pluscuamperfecto de subjuntivo**	
encerrara	encerráramos	hubiera encerrado	hubiéramos encerrado
encerraras	encerrarais	hubieras encerrado	hubierais encerrado
encerrara	encerraran	hubiera encerrado	hubieran encerrado
OR		OR	
encerrase	encerrásemos	hubiese encerrado	hubiésemos encerrado
encerrases	encerraseis	hubieses encerrado	hubieseis encerrado
encerrase	encerrasen	hubiese encerrado	hubiesen encerrado

imperativo	
—	encerremos
encierra; no encierres	encerrad; no encerréis
encierre	encierren

Words related to this verb
encerrado, encerrada   closed, locked, shut
encerrarse   to live in seclusion; to be locked up, closeted, shut in

For other words and expressions related to this verb, see **cerrar.**

Learn more verbs in 30 practical situations for tourists on pages 564–594.

to meet, to encounter, to find

The Seven Simple Tenses		The Seven Compound Tenses	
Singular	Plural	Singular	Plural
1 presente de indicativo		8 perfecto de indicativo	
encuentro	encontramos	he encontrado	hemos encontrado
encuentras	encontráis	has encontrado	habéis encontrado
encuentra	encuentran	ha encontrado	han encontrado
2 imperfecto de indicativo		9 pluscuamperfecto de indicativo	
encontraba	encontrábamos	había encontrado	habíamos encontrado
encontrabas	encontrabais	habías encontrado	habíais encontrado
encontraba	encontraban	había encontrado	habían encontrado
3 pretérito		10 pretérito anterior	
encontré	encontramos	hube encontrado	hubimos encontrado
encontraste	encontrasteis	hubiste encontrado	hubisteis encontrado
encontró	encontraron	hubo encontrado	hubieron encontrado
4 futuro		11 futuro perfecto	
encontraré	encontraremos	habré encontrado	habremos encontrado
encontrarás	encontraréis	habrás encontrado	habréis encontrado
encontrará	encontrarán	habrá encontrado	habrán encontrado
5 potencial simple		12 potencial compuesto	
encontraría	encontraríamos	habría encontrado	habríamos encontrado
encontrarías	encontraríais	habrías encontrado	habríais encontrado
encontraría	encontrarían	habría encontrado	habrían encontrado
6 presente de subjuntivo		13 perfecto de subjuntivo	
encuentre	encontremos	haya encontrado	hayamos encontrado
encuentres	encontréis	hayas encontrado	hayáis encontrado
encuentre	encuentren	haya encontrado	hayan encontrado
7 imperfecto de subjuntivo		14 pluscuamperfecto de subjuntivo	
encontrara	encontráramos	hubiera encontrado	hubiéramos encontrado
encontraras	encontrarais	hubieras encontrado	hubierais encontrado
encontrara	encontraran	hubiera encontrado	hubieran encontrado
OR		OR	
encontrase	encontrásemos	hubiese encontrado	hubiésemos encontrado
encontrases	encontraseis	hubieses encontrado	hubieseis encontrado
encontrase	encontrasen	hubiese encontrado	hubiesen encontrado

imperativo	
—	encontremos
encuentra; no encuentres	encontrad; no encontréis
encuentre	encuentren

Words and expressions related to this verb
un encuentro   encounter, meeting
salir al encuentro de   to go to meet
encontrarse con alguien   to meet someone, to run across someone
   (pres. part.: **encontrándose**)

Can't recognize an irregular verb form? Check out pages 519–523.

The subject pronouns are found on the page facing page 1.

enfadarse

Gerundio enfadándose   Part. pas. **enfadado**

to become angry, annoyed, irritated

The Seven Simple Tenses		The Seven Compound Tenses	
Singular	Plural	Singular	Plural
1 presente de indicativo		**8 perfecto de indicativo**	
me enfado	nos enfadamos	me he enfadado	nos hemos enfadado
te enfadas	os enfadáis	te has enfadado	os habéis enfadado
se enfada	se enfadan	se ha enfadado	se han enfadado
2 imperfecto de indicativo		**9 pluscuamperfecto de indicativo**	
me enfadaba	nos enfadábamos	me había enfadado	nos habíamos enfadado
te enfadabas	os enfadabais	te habías enfadado	os habíais enfadado
se enfadaba	se enfadaban	se había enfadado	se habían enfadado
3 pretérito		**10 pretérito anterior**	
me enfadé	nos enfadamos	me hube enfadado	nos hubimos enfadado
te enfadaste	os enfadasteis	te hubiste enfadado	os hubisteis enfadado
se enfadó	se enfadaron	se hubo enfadado	se hubieron enfadado
4 futuro		**11 futuro perfecto**	
me enfadaré	nos enfadaremos	me habré enfadado	nos habremos enfadado
te enfadarás	os enfadaréis	te habrás enfadado	os habréis enfadado
se enfadará	se enfadarán	se habrá enfadado	se habrán enfadado
5 potencial simple		**12 potencial compuesto**	
me enfadaría	nos enfadaríamos	me habría enfadado	nos habríamos enfadado
te enfadarías	os enfadaríais	te habrías enfadado	os habríais enfadado
se enfadaría	se enfadarían	se habría enfadado	se habrían enfadado
6 presente de subjuntivo		**13 perfecto de subjuntivo**	
me enfade	nos enfademos	me haya enfadado	nos hayamos enfadado
te enfades	os enfadéis	te hayas enfadado	os hayáis enfadado
se enfade	se enfaden	se haya enfadado	se hayan enfadado
7 imperfecto de subjuntivo		**14 pluscuamperfecto de subjuntivo**	
me enfadara	nos enfadáramos	me hubiera enfadado	nos hubiéramos enfadado
te enfadaras	os enfadarais	te hubieras enfadado	os hubierais enfadado
se enfadara	se enfadaran	se hubiera enfadado	se hubieran enfadado
OR		OR	
me enfadase	nos enfadásemos	me hubiese enfadado	nos hubiésemos enfadado
te enfadases	os enfadaseis	te hubieses enfadado	os hubieseis enfadado
se enfadase	se enfadasen	se hubiese enfadado	se hubiesen enfadado

imperativo	
—	enfadémonos
enfádate; no te enfades	enfadaos; no os enfadéis
enfádese	enfádense

Words related to this verb

enfadoso, enfadosa   annoying
el enfado   anger, vexation
enfadadizo, enfadadiza   irritable

enfadosamente   annoyingly, angrily
enfadar   to anger, to annoy, to irritate
enfadarse por cualquier   to get angry about anything

If you don't know the Spanish verb for the English verb you have in mind, look it up in the index on pages 505–518.

to get sick, to fall sick, to become sick, to fall ill, to become ill

The Seven Simple Tenses		The Seven Compound Tenses	
Singular	Plural	Singular	Plural
1 presente de indicativo		8 perfecto de indicativo	
me enfermo	nos enfermamos	me he enfermado	nos hemos enfermado
te enfermas	os enfermáis	te has enfermado	os habéis enfermado
se enferma	se enferman	se ha enfermado	se han enfermado
2 imperfecto de indicativo		9 pluscuamperfecto de indicativo	
me enfermaba	nos enfermábamos	me había enfermado	nos habíamos enfermado
te enfermabas	os enfermabais	te habías enfermado	os habíais enfermado
se enfermaba	se enfermaban	se había enfermado	se habían enfermado
3 pretérito		10 pretérito anterior	
me enfermé	nos enfermamos	me hube enfermado	nos hubimos enfermado
te enfermaste	os enfermasteis	te hubiste enfermado	os hubisteis enfermado
se enfermó	se enfermaron	se hubo enfermado	se hubieron enfermado
4 futuro		11 futuro perfecto	
me enfermaré	nos enfermaremos	me habré enfermado	nos habremos enfermado
te enfermarás	os enfermaréis	te habrás enfermado	os habréis enfermado
se enfermará	se enfermarán	se habrá enfermado	se habrán enfermado
5 potencial simple		12 potencial compuesto	
me enfermaría	nos enfermaríamos	me habría enfermado	nos habríamos enfermado
te enfermarías	os enfermaríais	te habrías enfermado	os habríais enfermado
se enfermaría	se enfermarían	se habría enfermado	se habrían enfermado
6 presente de subjuntivo		13 perfecto de subjuntivo	
me enferme	nos enfermemos	me haya enfermado	nos hayamos enfermado
te enfermes	os enferméis	te hayas enfermado	os hayáis enfermado
se enferme	se enfermen	se haya enfermado	se hayan enfermado
7 imperfecto de subjuntivo		14 pluscuamperfecto de subjuntivo	
me enfermara	nos enfermáramos	me hubiera enfermado	nos hubiéramos enfermado
te enfermaras	os enfermarais	te hubieras enfermado	os hubierais enfermado
se enfermara	se enfermaran	se hubiera enfermado	se hubieran enfermado
OR		OR	
me enfermase	nos enfermásemos	me hubiese enfermado	nos hubiésemos enfermado
te enfermases	os enfermaseis	te hubieses enfermado	os hubieseis enfermado
se enfermase	se enfermasen	se hubiese enfermado	se hubiesen enfermado

imperativo	
—	enfermémonos
enférmate; no te enfermes	enfermaos; no os enferméis
enférmese	enférmense

Words and expressions related to this verb

la enfermedad illness, sickness
la enfermería infirmary
enfermo de amor lovesick
enfermar to fall sick, to make sick
un enfermo, una enferma patient
enfermoso, enfermosa sickly
un enfermero, una enfermera nurse

enfermero (enfermera) ambulante visiting nurse
caer enfermo (enferma) to get sick, to fall sick
enfermizo, enfermiza sickly, ailing, unhealthy
enfermo interno in-patient
estar enfermo (enferma) to be sick

The subject pronouns are found on the page facing page 1.

to become angry, to get angry, to get cross

The Seven Simple Tenses		The Seven Compound Tenses	
Singular	Plural	Singular	Plural
1 presente de indicativo		**8 perfecto de indicativo**	
me enojo	nos enojamos	me he enojado	nos hemos enojado
te enojas	os enojáis	te has enojado	os habéis enojado
se enoja	se enojan	se ha enojado	se han enojado
2 imperfecto de indicativo		**9 pluscuamperfecto de indicativo**	
me enojaba	nos enojábamos	me había enojado	nos habíamos enojado
te enojabas	os enojabais	te habías enojado	os habíais enojado
se enojaba	se enojaban	se había enojado	se habían enojado
3 pretérito		**10 pretérito anterior**	
me enojé	nos enojamos	me hube enojado	nos hubimos enojado
te enojaste	os enojasteis	te hubiste enojado	os hubisteis enojado
se enojó	se enojaron	se hubo enojado	se hubieron enojado
4 futuro		**11 futuro perfecto**	
me enojaré	nos enojaremos	me habré enojado	nos habremos enojado
te enojarás	os enojaréis	te habrás enojado	os habréis enojado
se enojará	se enojarán	se habrá enojado	se habrán enojado
5 potencial simple		**12 potencial compuesto**	
me enojaría	nos enojaríamos	me habría enojado	nos habríamos enojado
te enojarías	os enojaríais	te habrías enojado	os habríais enojado
se enojaría	se enojarían	se habría enojado	se habrían enojado
6 presente de subjuntivo		**13 perfecto de subjuntivo**	
me enoje	nos enojemos	me haya enojado	nos hayamos enojado
te enojes	os enojéis	te hayas enojado	os hayáis enojado
se enoje	se enojen	se haya enojado	se hayan enojado
7 imperfecto de subjuntivo		**14 pluscuamperfecto de subjuntivo**	
me enojara	nos enojáramos	me hubiera enojado	nos hubiéramos enojado
te enojaras	os enojarais	te hubieras enojado	os hubierais enojado
se enojara	se enojaran	se hubiera enojado	se hubieran enojado
OR		OR	
me enojase	nos enojásemos	me hubiese enojado	nos hubiésemos enojado
te enojases	os enojaseis	te hubieses enojado	os hubieseis enojado
se enojase	se enojasen	se hubiese enojado	se hubiesen enojado

imperativo	
—	enojémonos
enójate; no te enojes	enojaos; no os enojéis
enójese	enójense

Words and expressions related to this verb

enojar to annoy, to irritate, to make angry, to vex; **enojarse de** to become angry at someone
el enojo anger, annoyance; **enojadizo, enojadiza** ill-tempered, irritable
enojoso, enojosa irritating, troublesome
enojosamente angrily
enojado, enojada angry; **una enojada** fit of anger
enojarse con (contra) alguien to become angry with someone

to teach, to show, to point out

The Seven Simple Tenses		The Seven Compound Tenses	
Singular	Plural	Singular	Plural
1 presente de indicativo		8 perfecto de indicativo	
enseño	**enseñamos**	**he enseñado**	**hemos enseñado**
enseñas	**enseñáis**	**has enseñado**	**habéis enseñado**
enseña	**enseñan**	**ha enseñado**	**han enseñado**
2 imperfecto de indicativo		9 pluscuamperfecto de indicativo	
enseñaba	**enseñábamos**	**había enseñado**	**habíamos enseñado**
enseñabas	**enseñabais**	**habías enseñado**	**habíais enseñado**
enseñaba	**enseñaban**	**había enseñado**	**habían enseñado**
3 pretérito		10 pretérito anterior	
enseñé	**enseñamos**	**hube enseñado**	**hubimos enseñado**
enseñaste	**enseñasteis**	**hubiste enseñado**	**hubisteis enseñado**
enseñó	**enseñaron**	**hubo enseñado**	**hubieron enseñado**
4 futuro		11 futuro perfecto	
enseñaré	**enseñaremos**	**habré enseñado**	**habremos enseñado**
enseñarás	**enseñaréis**	**habrás enseñado**	**habréis enseñado**
enseñará	**enseñarán**	**habrá enseñado**	**habrán enseñado**
5 potencial simple		12 potencial compuesto	
enseñaría	**enseñaríamos**	**habría enseñado**	**habríamos enseñado**
enseñarías	**enseñaríais**	**habrías enseñado**	**habríais enseñado**
enseñaría	**enseñarían**	**habría enseñado**	**habrían enseñado**
6 presente de subjuntivo		13 perfecto de subjuntivo	
enseñe	**enseñemos**	**haya enseñado**	**hayamos enseñado**
enseñes	**enseñéis**	**hayas enseñado**	**hayáis enseñado**
enseñe	**enseñen**	**haya enseñado**	**hayan enseñado**
7 imperfecto de subjuntivo		14 pluscuamperfecto de subjuntivo	
enseñara	**enseñáramos**	**hubiera enseñado**	**hubiéramos enseñado**
enseñaras	**enseñarais**	**hubieras enseñado**	**hubierais enseñado**
enseñara	**enseñaran**	**hubiera enseñado**	**hubieran enseñado**
OR		OR	
enseñase	**enseñásemos**	**hubiese enseñado**	**hubiésemos enseñado**
enseñases	**enseñaseis**	**hubieses enseñado**	**hubieseis enseñado**
enseñase	**enseñasen**	**hubiese enseñado**	**hubiesen enseñado**

imperativo	
—	**enseñemos**
enseña; no enseñes	**enseñad; no enseñéis**
enseñe	**enseñen**

Words and expressions related to this verb

enseñarse   to teach oneself
enseñar a + inf.   to teach + inf.
el enseñamiento, la enseñanza   teaching, education
 la enseñanza primaria   primary education
 la enseñanza secundaria   secondary (high school)
  education
 la enseñanza superior   higher education

diseñar   to design
el diseño   design
la enseña   emblem, standard
bien enseñado   well-bred
mal enseñado   ill-bred
un perro bien enseñado   a house-trained
 dog

211

The subject pronouns are found on the page facing page 1.

entender

Gerundio **entendiendo** Part. pas. **entendido**

to understand

The Seven Simple Tenses		The Seven Compound Tenses	
Singular	Plural	Singular	Plural
1 presente de indicativo		8 perfecto de indicativo	
entiendo	**entendemos**	**he entendido**	**hemos entendido**
entiendes	**entendéis**	**has entendido**	**habéis entendido**
entiende	**entienden**	**ha entendido**	**han entendido**
2 imperfecto de indicativo		9 pluscuamperfecto de indicativo	
entendía	**entendíamos**	**había entendido**	**habíamos entendido**
entendías	**entendíais**	**habías entendido**	**habíais entendido**
entendía	**entendían**	**había entendido**	**habían entendido**
3 pretérito		10 pretérito anterior	
entendí	**entendimos**	**hube entendido**	**hubimos entendido**
entendiste	**entendisteis**	**hubiste entendido**	**hubisteis entendido**
entendió	**entendieron**	**hubo entendido**	**hubieron entendido**
4 futuro		11 futuro perfecto	
entenderé	**entenderemos**	**habré entendido**	**habremos entendido**
entenderás	**entenderéis**	**habrás entendido**	**habréis entendido**
entenderá	**entenderán**	**habrá entendido**	**habrán entendido**
5 potencial simple		12 potencial compuesto	
entendería	**entenderíamos**	**habría entendido**	**habríamos entendido**
entenderías	**entenderíais**	**habrías entendido**	**habríais entendido**
entendería	**entenderían**	**habría entendido**	**habrían entendido**
6 presente de subjuntivo		13 perfecto de subjuntivo	
entienda	**entendamos**	**haya entendido**	**hayamos entendido**
entiendas	**entendáis**	**hayas entendido**	**hayáis entendido**
entienda	**entiendan**	**haya entendido**	**hayan entendido**
7 imperfecto de subjuntivo		14 pluscuamperfecto de subjuntivo	
entendiera	**entendiéramos**	**hubiera entendido**	**hubiéramos entendido**
entendieras	**entendierais**	**hubieras entendido**	**hubierais entendido**
entendiera	**entendieran**	**hubiera entendido**	**hubieran entendido**
OR		OR	
entendiese	**entendiésemos**	**hubiese entendido**	**hubiésemos entendido**
entendieses	**entendieseis**	**hubieses entendido**	**hubieseis entendido**
entendiese	**entendiesen**	**hubiese entendido**	**hubiesen entendido**

	imperativo	
—		**entendamos**
entiende; no entiendas		**entended; no entendáis**
entienda		**entiendan**

Words and expressions related to this verb

dar a entender to insinuate, to hint
Yo me entiendo. I have my reasons.
según mi entender according to my opinion
el entendimiento comprehension, understanding

¿Qué entiende Ud. por eso? What do you mean by that?
entenderse bien to get along well with each other
desentenderse de to have nothing to do with

to enter, to go (in), to come (in)

The Seven Simple Tenses		The Seven Compound Tenses	
Singular	Plural	Singular	Plural
1 presente de indicativo		8 perfecto de indicativo	
entro	entramos	he entrado	hemos entrado
entras	entráis	has entrado	habéis entrado
entra	entran	ha entrado	han entrado
2 imperfecto de indicativo		9 pluscuamperfecto de indicativo	
entraba	entrábamos	había entrado	habíamos entrado
entrabas	entrabais	habías entrado	habíais entrado
entraba	entraban	había entrado	habían entrado
3 pretérito		10 pretérito anterior	
entré	entramos	hube entrado	hubimos entrado
entraste	entrasteis	hubiste entrado	hubisteis entrado
entró	entraron	hubo entrado	hubieron entrado
4 futuro		11 futuro perfecto	
entraré	entraremos	habré entrado	habremos entrado
entrarás	entraréis	habrás entrado	habréis entrado
entrará	entrarán	habrá entrado	habrán entrado
5 potencial simple		12 potencial compuesto	
entraría	entraríamos	habría entrado	habríamos entrado
entrarías	entraríais	habrías entrado	habríais entrado
entraría	entrarían	habría entrado	habrían entrado
6 presente de subjuntivo		13 perfecto de subjuntivo	
entre	entremos	haya entrado	hayamos entrado
entres	entréis	hayas entrado	hayáis entrado
entre	entren	haya entrado	hayan entrado
7 imperfecto de subjuntivo		14 pluscuamperfecto de subjuntivo	
entrara	entráramos	hubiera entrado	hubiéramos entrado
entraras	entrarais	hubieras entrado	hubierais entrado
entrara	entraran	hubiera entrado	hubieran entrado
OR		OR	
entrase	entrásemos	hubiese entrado	hubiésemos entrado
entrases	entraseis	hubieses entrado	hubieseis entrado
entrase	entrasen	hubiese entrado	hubiesen entrado

imperativo

—	entremos
entra; no entres	entrad; no entréis
entre	entren

Words and expressions related to this verb
la entrada   entrance
entrada general   standing room (theater, movies)
entrado (entrada) en años   advanced in years
entrar por la puerta   to enter through the door

entrar en órbita   to go into orbit
entrar en   to enter, to go in
entrar en un club   to join a club
entrar en una profesión   to enter into (take up) a profession

to deliver, to hand over, to give

The Seven Simple Tenses		The Seven Compound Tenses	
Singular	Plural	Singular	Plural
1 presente de indicativo		8 perfecto de indicativo	
entrego	entregamos	he entregado	hemos entregado
entregas	entregáis	has entregado	habéis entregado
entrega	entregan	ha entregado	han entregado
2 imperfecto de indicativo		9 pluscuamperfecto de indicativo	
entregaba	entregábamos	había entregado	habíamos entregado
entregabas	entregabais	habías entregado	habíais entregado
entregaba	entregaban	había entregado	habían entregado
3 pretérito		10 pretérito anterior	
entregué	entregamos	hube entregado	hubimos entregado
entregaste	entregasteis	hubiste entregado	hubisteis entregado
entregó	entregaron	hubo entregado	hubieron entregado
4 futuro		11 futuro perfecto	
entregaré	entregaremos	habré entregado	habremos entregado
entregarás	entregaréis	habrás entregado	habréis entregado
entregará	entregarán	habrá entregado	habrán entregado
5 potencial simple		12 potencial compuesto	
entregaría	entregaríamos	habría entregado	habríamos entregado
entregarías	entregaríais	habrías entregado	habríais entregado
entregaría	entregarían	habría entregado	habrían entregado
6 presente de subjuntivo		13 perfecto de subjuntivo	
entregue	entreguemos	haya entregado	hayamos entregado
entregues	entreguéis	hayas entregado	hayáis entregado
entregue	entreguen	haya entregado	hayan entregado
7 imperfecto de subjuntivo		14 pluscuamperfecto de subjuntivo	
entregara	entregáramos	hubiera entregado	hubiéramos entregado
entregaras	entregarais	hubieras entregado	hubierais entregado
entregara	entregaran	hubiera entregado	hubieran entregado
OR		OR	
entregase	entregásemos	hubiese entregado	hubiésemos entregado
entregases	entregaseis	hubieses entregado	hubieseis entregado
entregase	entregasen	hubiese entregado	hubiesen entregado

	imperativo	
—	entreguemos
entrega; no entregues	entregad; no entreguéis
entregue	entreguen

Words and expressions related to this verb
entregarse   to surrender, to give in
entragarse en brazos de uno   to trust someone completely
entregado, entregada   delivered
la entrega   delivery, installment, handing over

entregar al profesor los ejercicios   to hand in the exercises to the teacher
entregar a domicilio   to deliver to a residence (home delivery)

to enunciate, to state

The Seven Simple Tenses		The Seven Compound Tenses	
Singular	Plural	Singular	Plural
1 presente de indicativo		8 perfecto de indicativo	
enuncio	**enunciamos**	**he enunciado**	**hemos enunciado**
enuncias	**enunciáis**	**has enunciado**	**habéis enunciado**
enuncia	**enuncian**	**ha enunciado**	**han enunciado**
2 imperfecto de indicativo		9 pluscuamperfecto de indicativo	
enunciaba	**enunciábamos**	**había enunciado**	**habíamos enunciado**
enunciabas	**enunciabais**	**habías enunciado**	**habíais enunciado**
enunciaba	**enunciaban**	**había enunciado**	**habían enunciado**
3 pretérito		10 pretérito anterior	
enuncié	**enunciamos**	**hube enunciado**	**hubimos enunciado**
enunciaste	**enunciasteis**	**hubiste enunciado**	**hubisteis enunciado**
enunció	**enunciaron**	**hubo enunciado**	**hubieron enunciado**
4 futuro		11 futuro perfecto	
enunciaré	**enunciaremos**	**habré enunciado**	**habremos enunciado**
enunciarás	**enunciaréis**	**habrás enunciado**	**habréis enunciado**
enunciará	**enunciarán**	**habrá enunciado**	**habrán enunciado**
5 potencial simple		12 potencial compuesto	
enunciaría	**enunciaríamos**	**habría enunciado**	**habríamos enunciado**
enunciarías	**enunciaríais**	**habrías enunciado**	**habríais enunciado**
enunciaría	**enunciarían**	**habría enunciado**	**habrían enunciado**
6 presente de subjuntivo		13 perfecto de subjuntivo	
enuncie	**enunciemos**	**haya enunciado**	**hayamos enunciado**
enuncies	**enunciéis**	**hayas enunciado**	**hayáis enunciado**
enuncie	**enuncien**	**haya enunciado**	**hayan enunciado**
7 imperfecto de subjuntivo		14 pluscuamperfecto de subjuntivo	
enunciara	**enunciáramos**	**hubiera enunciado**	**hubiéramos enunciado**
enunciaras	**enunciarais**	**hubieras enunciado**	**hubierais enunciado**
enunciara	**enunciaran**	**hubiera enunciado**	**hubieran enunciado**
OR		OR	
enunciase	**enunciásemos**	**hubiese enunciado**	**hubiésemos enunciado**
enunciases	**enunciaseis**	**hubieses enunciado**	**hubieseis enunciado**
enunciase	**enunciasen**	**hubiese enunciado**	**hubiesen enunciado**

imperativo

—	**enunciemos**
enuncia; no enuncies	**enunciad; no enunciéis**
enuncie	**enuncien**

Words related to this verb
la enunciación   enunciation, statement, declaration
enunciativo, enunciativa   enunciative

Increase your verb power with popular phrases, words, and expressions for tourists on pages 595–618.

The subject pronouns are found on the page facing page 1.

to send

The Seven Simple Tenses		The Seven Compound Tenses	
Singular	Plural	Singular	Plural
1 presente de indicativo		8 perfecto de indicativo	
envío	enviamos	he enviado	hemos enviado
envías	enviáis	has enviado	habéis enviado
envía	envían	ha enviado	han enviado
2 imperfecto de indicativo		9 pluscuamperfecto de indicativo	
enviaba	enviábamos	había enviado	habíamos enviado
enviabas	enviabais	habías enviado	habíais enviado
enviaba	enviaban	había enviado	habían enviado
3 pretérito		10 pretérito anterior	
envié	enviamos	hube enviado	hubimos enviado
enviaste	enviasteis	hubiste enviado	hubisteis enviado
envió	enviaron	hubo enviado	hubieron enviado
4 futuro		11 futuro perfecto	
enviaré	enviaremos	habré enviado	habremos enviado
enviarás	enviaréis	habrás enviado	habréis enviado
enviará	enviarán	habrá enviado	habrán enviado
5 potencial simple		12 potencial compuesto	
enviaría	enviaríamos	habría enviado	habríamos enviado
enviarías	enviaríais	habrías enviado	habríais enviado
enviaría	enviarían	habría enviado	habrían enviado
6 presente de subjuntivo		13 perfecto de subjuntivo	
envíe	enviemos	haya enviado	hayamos enviado
envíes	enviéis	hayas enviado	hayáis enviado
envíe	envíen	haya enviado	hayan enviado
7 imperfecto de subjuntivo		14 pluscuamperfecto de subjuntivo	
enviara	enviáramos	hubiera enviado	hubiéramos enviado
enviaras	enviarais	hubieras enviado	hubierais enviado
enviara	enviaran	hubiera enviado	hubieran enviado
OR		OR	
enviase	enviásemos	hubiese enviado	hubiésemos enviado
enviases	enviaseis	hubieses enviado	hubieseis enviado
enviase	enviasen	hubiese enviado	hubiesen enviado

	imperativo	
—		enviemos
envía; no envíes		enviad; no enviéis
envíe		envíen

Words and expressions related to this verb

enviar a alguien a pasear   to send someone
   to take a walk
el envío   dispatch; **un enviado**   envoy
la enviada   shipment
reenviar   to send back; to forward

un enviado especial   special newspaper
   correspondent
enviar un fax   to send a fax
enviar por correo electrónico   to e-mail,
   send by e-mail

   Review the principal parts of important Spanish verbs on pages xvi and xvii.

The Seven Simple Tenses		The Seven Compound Tenses	
Singular	Plural	Singular	Plural
1 presente de indicativo		8 perfecto de indicativo	
envuelvo	**envolvemos**	**he envuelto**	**hemos envuelto**
envuelves	**envolvéis**	**has envuelto**	**habéis envuelto**
envuelve	**envuelven**	**ha envuelto**	**han envuelto**
2 imperfecto de indicativo		9 pluscuamperfecto de indicativo	
envolvía	**envolvíamos**	**había envuelto**	**habíamos envuelto**
envolvías	**envolvíais**	**habías envuelto**	**habíais envuelto**
envolvía	**envolvían**	**había envuelto**	**habían envuelto**
3 pretérito		10 pretérito anterior	
envolví	**envolvimos**	**hube envuelto**	**hubimos envuelto**
envolviste	**envolvisteis**	**hubiste envuelto**	**hubisteis envuelto**
envolvió	**envolvieron**	**hubo envuelto**	**hubieron envuelto**
4 futuro		11 futuro perfecto	
envolveré	**envolveremos**	**habré envuelto**	**habremos envuelto**
envolverás	**envolveréis**	**habrás envuelto**	**habréis envuelto**
envolverá	**envolverán**	**habrá envuelto**	**habrán envuelto**
5 potencial simple		12 potencial compuesto	
envolvería	**envolveríamos**	**habría envuelto**	**habríamos envuelto**
envolverías	**envolveríais**	**habrías envuelto**	**habríais envuelto**
envolvería	**envolverían**	**habría envuelto**	**habrían envuelto**
6 presente de subjuntivo		13 perfecto de subjuntivo	
envuelva	**envolvamos**	**haya envuelto**	**hayamos envuelto**
envuelvas	**envolváis**	**hayas envuelto**	**hayáis envuelto**
envuelva	**envuelvan**	**haya envuelto**	**hayan envuelto**
7 imperfecto de subjuntivo		14 pluscuamperfecto de subjuntivo	
envolviera	**envolviéramos**	**hubiera envuelto**	**hubiéramos envuelto**
envolvieras	**envolvierais**	**hubieras envuelto**	**hubierais envuelto**
envolviera	**envolvieran**	**hubiera envuelto**	**hubieran envuelto**
OR		OR	
envolviese	**envolviésemos**	**hubiese envuelto**	**hubiésemos envuelto**
envolvieses	**envolvieseis**	**hubieses envuelto**	**hubieseis envuelto**
envolviese	**envolviesen**	**hubiese envuelto**	**hubiesen envuelto**

imperativo

—	**envolvamos**
envuele; no envuelvas	**envolved; no envolváis**
envuelva	**envuelvan**

Words related to this verb

envolverse   to have an affair, to become involved
el envolvimiento   wrapping; involvement

envuelto, envuelta   wrapped
una envoltura   wrapping, wrapper, cover

Check out the verb drills and verb tests with answers explained on pages 619–665.

equivocarse   Gerundio **equivocándose**   Part. pas. **equivocado**

to be mistaken, to make a mistake

The Seven Simple Tenses		The Seven Compound Tenses	
Singular	Plural	Singular	Plural
1 presente de indicativo		8 perfecto de indicativo	
me equivoco	**nos equivocamos**	**me he equivocado**	**nos hemos equivocado**
te equivocas	**os equivocáis**	**te has equivocado**	**os habéis equivocado**
se equivoca	**se equivocan**	**se ha equivocado**	**se han equivocado**
2 imperfecto de indicativo		9 pluscuamperfecto de indicativo	
me equivocaba	**nos equivocábamos**	**me había equivocado**	**nos habíamos equivocado**
te equivocabas	**os equivocabais**	**te habías equivocado**	**os habíais equivocado**
se equivocaba	**se equivocaban**	**se había equivocado**	**se habían equivocado**
3 pretérito		10 pretérito anterior	
me equivoqué	**nos equivocamos**	**me hube equivocado**	**nos hubimos equivocado**
te equivocaste	**os equivocasteis**	**te hubiste equivocado**	**os hubisteis equivocado**
se equivocó	**se equivocaron**	**se hubo equivocado**	**se hubieron equivocado**
4 futuro		11 futuro perfecto	
me equivocaré	**nos equivocaremos**	**me habré equivocado**	**nos habremos equivocado**
te equivocarás	**os equivocaréis**	**te habrás equivocado**	**os habréis equivocado**
se equivocará	**se equivocarán**	**se habrá equivocado**	**se habrán equivocado**
5 potencial simple		12 potencial compuesto	
me equivocaría	**nos equivocaríamos**	**me habría equivocado**	**nos habríamos equivocado**
te equivocarías	**os equivocaríais**	**te habrías equivocado**	**os habríais equivocado**
se equivocaría	**se equivocarían**	**se habría equivocado**	**se habrían equivocado**
6 presente de subjuntivo		13 perfecto de subjuntivo	
me equivoque	**nos equivoquemos**	**me haya equivocado**	**nos hayamos equivocado**
te equivoques	**os equivoquéis**	**te hayas equivocado**	**os hayáis equivocado**
se equivoque	**se equivoquen**	**se haya equivocado**	**se hayan equivocado**
7 imperfecto de subjuntivo		14 pluscuamperfecto de subjuntivo	
me equivocara	**nos equivocáramos**	**me hubiera equivocado**	**nos hubiéramos equivocado**
te equivocaras	**os equivocarais**	**te hubieras equivocado**	**os hubierais equivocado**
se equivocara	**se equivocaran**	**se hubiera equivocado**	**se hubieran equivocado**
OR		OR	
me equivocase	**nos equivocásemos**	**me hubiese equivocado**	**nos hubiésemos equivocado**
te equivocases	**os equivocaseis**	**te hubieses equivocado**	**os hubieseis equivocado**
se equivocase	**se equivocasen**	**se hubiese equivocado**	**se hubiesen equivocado**

	imperativo
—	**equivoquémonos**
equivócate; no te equivoques	**equivocaos; no os equivoquéis**
equivóquese	**equivóquense**

Words and expressions related to this verb
equivoquista quibbler
equivocado, equivocada mistaken
una equivocación error, mistake, equivocation
equivocarse de fecha to be mistaken about the date

estar equivocado (equivocada) to be mistaken
cometer una equivocación to make a mistake

to raise, to stand up straight

The Seven Simple Tenses		The Seven Compound Tenses	
Singular	Plural	Singular	Plural
1 presente de indicativo		**8 perfecto de indicativo**	
irgo (yergo)	**erguimos**	**he erguido**	**hemos erguido**
irgues (yergues)	**erguís**	**has erguido**	**habéis erguido**
irgue (yergue)	**irguen (yerguen)**	**ha erguido**	**han erguido**
2 imperfecto de indicativo		**9 pluscuamperfecto de indicativo**	
erguía	**erguíamos**	**había erguido**	**habíamos erguido**
erguías	**erguíais**	**habías erguido**	**habíais erguido**
erguía	**erguían**	**había erguido**	**habían erguido**
3 pretérito		**10 pretérito anterior**	
erguí	**erguimos**	**hube erguido**	**hubimos erguido**
erguiste	**erguisteis**	**hubiste erguido**	**hubisteis erguido**
irguió	**irguieron**	**hubo erguido**	**hubieron erguido**
4 futuro		**11 futuro perfecto**	
erguiré	**erguiremos**	**habré erguido**	**habremos erguido**
erguirás	**erguiréis**	**habrás erguido**	**habréis erguido**
erguirá	**erguirán**	**habrá erguido**	**habrán erguido**
5 potencial simple		**12 potencial compuesto**	
erguiría	**erguiríamos**	**habría erguido**	**habríamos erguido**
erguirías	**erguiríais**	**habrías erguido**	**habríais erguido**
erguiría	**erguirían**	**habría erguido**	**habrían erguido**
6 presente de subjuntivo		**13 perfecto de subjuntivo**	
irga (yerga)	**irgamos (yergamos)**	**haya erguido**	**hayamos erguido**
irgas (yergas)	**irgáis (yergáis)**	**hayas erguido**	**hayáis erguido**
irga (yerga)	**irgan (yergan)**	**haya erguido**	**hayan erguido**
7 imperfecto de subjuntivo		**14 pluscuamperfecto de subjuntivo**	
irguiera	**irguiéramos**	**hubiera erguido**	**hubiéramos erguido**
irguieras	**irguierais**	**hubieras erguido**	**hubierais erguido**
irguiera	**irguieran**	**hubiera erguido**	**hubieran erguido**
OR		OR	
irguiese	**irguiésemos**	**hubiese erguido**	**hubiésemos erguido**
irguieses	**irguieseis**	**hubieses erguido**	**hubieseis erguido**
irguiese	**irguiesen**	**hubiese erguido**	**hubiesen erguido**

imperativo

—	**irgamos (yergamos)**
irgue (yergue); no irgas (yergas)	**erguid; no irgáis (yergáis)**
irga (yerga)	**irgan (yergan)**

Words and expressions related to this verb
enguirse   to swell up with pride, to stiffen
un erguimiento   straightening, raising,
   erection

erguido, erguida   erect, proud
erguir las orejas   to prick up one's ears
erguirse de repente   to stand up suddenly

Can't recognize an irregular verb form? Check out pages 519–523.

errar   Gerundio **errando**   Part. pas. **errado**

to err, to wander, to roam, to miss

The Seven Simple Tenses		The Seven Compound Tenses	
Singular	Plural	Singular	Plural
1 presente de indicativo		8 perfecto de indicativo	
yerro	**erramos**	**he errado**	**hemos errado**
yerras	**erráis**	**has errado**	**habéis errado**
yerra	**yerran**	**ha errado**	**han errado**
2 imperfecto de indicativo		9 pluscuamperfecto de indicativo	
erraba	**errábamos**	**había errado**	**habíamos errado**
errabas	**errabais**	**habías errado**	**habíais errado**
erraba	**erraban**	**había errado**	**habían errado**
3 pretérito		10 pretérito anterior	
erré	**erramos**	**hube errado**	**hubimos errado**
erraste	**errasteis**	**hubiste errado**	**hubisteis errado**
erró	**erraron**	**hubo errado**	**hubieron errado**
4 futuro		11 futuro perfecto	
erraré	**erraremos**	**habré errado**	**habremos errado**
errarás	**erraréis**	**habrás errado**	**habréis errado**
errará	**errarán**	**habrá errado**	**habrán errado**
5 potencial simple		12 potencial compuesto	
erraría	**erraríamos**	**habría errado**	**habríamos errado**
errarías	**erraríais**	**habrías errado**	**habríais errado**
erraría	**errarían**	**habría errado**	**habrían errado**
6 presente de subjuntivo		13 perfecto de subjuntivo	
yerre	**erremos**	**haya errado**	**hayamos errado**
yerres	**erréis**	**hayas errado**	**hayáis errado**
yerre	**yerren**	**haya errado**	**hayan errado**
7 imperfecto de subjuntivo		14 pluscuamperfecto de subjuntivo	
errara	**erráramos**	**hubiera errado**	**hubiéramos errado**
erraras	**errarais**	**hubieras errado**	**hubierais errado**
errara	**erraran**	**hubiera errado**	**hubieran errado**
OR		OR	
errase	**errásemos**	**hubiese errado**	**hubiésemos errado**
errases	**erraseis**	**hubieses errado**	**hubieseis errado**
errase	**errasen**	**hubiese errado**	**hubiesen errado**

	imperativo	
—		**erremos**
yerra; no yerres		**errad; no erréis**
yerre		**yerren**

Words and expressions related to this verb

una errata   erratum, typographical error
errante   errant, wandering
un error   error, mistake

deshacer un yerro   to amend an error
un error de imprenta   misprint
un yerro   error, fault, mistake

Can't recognize an irregular verb form? Check out pages 519–523.

220

to choose, to select, to pick

The Seven Simple Tenses		The Seven Compound Tenses	
Singular	Plural	Singular	Plural

1   presente de indicativo

Singular	Plural
escojo	escogemos
escoges	escogéis
escoge	escogen

8   perfecto de indicativo

Singular	Plural
he escogido	hemos escogido
has escogido	habéis escogido
ha escogido	han escogido

2   imperfecto de indicativo

escogía	escogíamos
escogías	escogíais
escogía	escogían

9   pluscuamperfecto de indicativo

había escogido	habíamos escogido
habías escogido	habíais escogido
había escogido	habían escogido

3   pretérito

escogí	escogimos
escogiste	escogisteis
escogió	escogieron

10   pretérito anterior

hube escogido	hubimos escogido
hubiste escogido	hubisteis escogido
hubo escogido	hubieron escogido

4   futuro

escogeré	escogeremos
escogerás	escogeréis
escogerá	escogerán

11   futuro perfecto

habré escogido	habremos escogido
habrás escogido	habréis escogido
habrá escogido	habrán escogido

5   potencial simple

escogería	escogeríamos
escogerías	escogeríais
escogería	escogerían

12   potencial compuesto

habría escogido	habríamos escogido
habrías escogido	habríais escogido
habría escogido	habrían escogido

6   presente de subjuntivo

escoja	escojamos
escojas	escojáis
escoja	escojan

13   perfecto de subjuntivo

haya escogido	hayamos escogido
hayas escogido	hayáis escogido
haya escogido	hayan escogido

7   imperfecto de subjuntivo

escogiera	escogiéramos
escogieras	escogierais
escogiera	escogieran
OR	
escogiese	escogiésemos
escogieses	escogieseis
escogiese	escogiesen

14   pluscuamperfecto de subjuntivo

hubiera escogido	hubiéramos escogido
hubieras escogido	hubierais escogido
hubiera escogido	hubieran escogido
OR	
hubiese escogido	hubiésemos escogido
hubieses escogido	hubieseis escogido
hubiese escogido	hubiesen escogido

imperativo

—	escojamos
escoge; no escojas	escoged; no escojáis
escoja	escojan

Words and expressions related to this verb

un escogimiento   choice, selection
escogedor, escogedora   chooser
escogido, escogida   chosen

escoger entre dos colores   to choose between
   two colors
las obras escogidas   the selected works

See also **coger.**

Can't recognize an irregular verb form? Check out pages 519–523.

to write

The Seven Simple Tenses		The Seven Compound Tenses	
Singular	Plural	Singular	Plural
1 presente de indicativo		8 perfecto de indicativo	
escribo	**escribimos**	**he escrito**	**hemos escrito**
escribes	**escribís**	**has escrito**	**habéis escrito**
escribe	**escriben**	**ha escrito**	**han escrito**
2 imperfecto de indicativo		9 pluscuamperfecto de indicativo	
escribía	**escribíamos**	**había escrito**	**habíamos escrito**
escribías	**escribíais**	**habías escrito**	**habíais escrito**
escribía	**escribían**	**había escrito**	**habían escrito**
3 pretérito		10 pretérito anterior	
escribí	**escribimos**	**hube escrito**	**hubimos escrito**
escribiste	**escribisteis**	**hubiste escrito**	**hubisteis escrito**
escribió	**escribieron**	**hubo escrito**	**hubieron escrito**
4 futuro		11 futuro perfecto	
escribiré	**escribiremos**	**habré escrito**	**habremos escrito**
escribirás	**escribiréis**	**habrás escrito**	**habréis escrito**
escribirá	**escribirán**	**habrá escrito**	**habrán escrito**
5 potencial simple		12 potencial compuesto	
escribiría	**escribiríamos**	**habría escrito**	**habríamos escrito**
escribirías	**escribiríais**	**habrías escrito**	**habríais escrito**
escribiría	**escribirían**	**habría escrito**	**habrían escrito**
6 presente de subjuntivo		13 perfecto de subjuntivo	
escriba	**escribamos**	**haya escrito**	**hayamos escrito**
escribas	**escribáis**	**hayas escrito**	**hayáis escrito**
escriba	**escriban**	**haya escrito**	**hayan escrito**
7 imperfecto de subjuntivo		14 pluscuamperfecto de subjuntivo	
escribiera	**escribiéramos**	**hubiera escrito**	**hubiéramos escrito**
escribieras	**escribierais**	**hubieras escrito**	**hubierais escrito**
escribiera	**escribieran**	**hubiera escrito**	**hubieran escrito**
OR		OR	
escribiese	**escribiésemos**	**hubiese escrito**	**hubiésemos escrito**
escribieses	**escribieseis**	**hubieses escrito**	**hubieseis escrito**
escribiese	**escribiesen**	**hubiese escrito**	**hubiesen escrito**

imperativo

—	**escribamos**
escribe; no escribas	**escribid; no escribáis**
escriba	**escriban**

Words and expressions related to this verb
una máquina de escribir typewriter
escribir a máquina to typewrite
un escritorio writing desk
escritor, escritora writer, author
por escrito in writing

escribir a mano to write by hand
describir to describe
la descripción description
descriptor, descriptora describer
el examen escrito written exam

Check out the verb drills and verb tests with answers explained on pages 619–665.

The Seven Simple Tenses		The Seven Compound Tenses	
Singular	Plural	Singular	Plural
1 presente de indicativo		8 perfecto de indicativo	
escucho	**escuchamos**	**he escuchado**	**hemos escuchado**
escuchas	**escucháis**	**has escuchado**	**habéis escuchado**
escucha	**escuchan**	**ha escuchado**	**han escuchado**
2 imperfecto de indicativo		9 pluscuamperfecto de indicativo	
escuchaba	**escuchábamos**	**había escuchado**	**habíamos escuchado**
escuchabas	**escuchabais**	**habías escuchado**	**habíais escuchado**
escuchaba	**escuchaban**	**había escuchado**	**habían escuchado**
3 pretérito		10 pretérito anterior	
escuché	**escuchamos**	**hube escuchado**	**hubimos escuchado**
escuchaste	**escuchasteis**	**hubiste escuchado**	**hubisteis escuchado**
escuchó	**escucharon**	**hubo escuchado**	**hubieron escuchado**
4 futuro		11 futuro perfecto	
escucharé	**escucharemos**	**habré escuchado**	**habremos escuchado**
escucharás	**escucharéis**	**habrás escuchado**	**habréis escuchado**
escuchará	**escucharán**	**habrá escuchado**	**habrán escuchado**
5 potencial simple		12 potencial compuesto	
escucharía	**escucharíamos**	**habría escuchado**	**habríamos escuchado**
escucharías	**escucharíais**	**habrías escuchado**	**habríais escuchado**
escucharía	**escucharían**	**habría escuchado**	**habrían escuchado**
6 presente de subjuntivo		13 perfecto de subjuntivo	
escuche	**escuchemos**	**haya escuchado**	**hayamos escuchado**
escuches	**escuchéis**	**hayas escuchado**	**hayáis escuchado**
escuche	**escuchen**	**haya escuchado**	**hayan escuchado**
7 imperfecto de subjuntivo		14 pluscuamperfecto de subjuntivo	
escuchara	**escucháramos**	**hubiera escuchado**	**hubiéramos escuchado**
escucharas	**escucharais**	**hubieras escuchado**	**hubierais escuchado**
escuchara	**escucharan**	**hubiera escuchado**	**hubieran escuchado**
OR		OR	
escuchase	**escuchásemos**	**hubiese escuchado**	**hubiésemos escuchado**
escuchases	**escuchaseis**	**hubieses escuchado**	**hubieseis escuchado**
escuchase	**escuchasen**	**hubiese escuchado**	**hubiesen escuchado**

imperativo

—	**escuchemos**
escucha; no escuches	**escuchad; no escuchéis**
escuche	**escuchen**

Words and expressions related to this verb
escuchar + noun   to listen to + noun
  Escucho un disco.   I'm listening to a record.
escuchador, escuchadora, escuchante   listener

escuchar música   to listen to music
escuchar detrás de las puertas   to listen
  behind doors

Get acquainted with what preposition goes with what verb on pages 541–549.

to scatter, to spread

The Seven Simple Tenses		The Seven Compound Tenses	
Singular	Plural	Singular	Plural
1 presente de indicativo		8 perfecto de indicativo	
esparzo	esparcimos	he esparcido	hemos esparcido
esparces	esparcís	has esparcido	habéis esparcido
esparce	esparcen	ha esparcido	han esparcido
2 imperfecto de indicativo		9 pluscuamperfecto de indicativo	
esparcía	esparcíamos	había esparcido	habíamos esparcido
esparcías	esparcíais	habías esparcido	habíais esparcido
esparcía	esparcían	había esparcido	habían esparcido
3 pretérito		10 pretérito anterior	
esparcí	esparcimos	hube esparcido	hubimos esparcido
esparciste	esparcisteis	hubiste esparcido	hubisteis esparcido
esparció	esparcieron	hubo esparcido	hubieron esparcido
4 futuro		11 futuro perfecto	
esparciré	esparciremos	habré esparcido	habremos esparcido
esparcirás	esparciréis	habrás esparcido	habréis esparcido
esparcirá	esparcirán	habrá esparcido	habrán esparcido
5 potencial simple		12 potencial compuesto	
esparciría	esparciríamos	habría esparcido	habríamos esparcido
esparcirías	esparciríais	habrías esparcido	habríais esparcido
esparciría	esparcirían	habría esparcido	habrían esparcido
6 presente de subjuntivo		13 perfecto de subjuntivo	
esparza	esparzamos	haya esparcido	hayamos esparcido
esparzas	esparzáis	hayas esparcido	hayáis esparcido
esparza	esparzan	haya esparcido	hayan esparcido
7 imperfecto de subjuntivo		14 pluscuamperfecto de subjuntivo	
esparciera	esparciéramos	hubiera esparcido	hubiéramos esparcido
esparcieras	esparcierais	hubieras esparcido	hubierais esparcido
esparciera	esparcieran	hubiera esparcido	hubieran esparcido
OR		OR	
esparciese	esparciésemos	hubiese esparcido	hubiésemos esparcido
esparcieses	esparcieseis	hubieses esparcido	hubieseis esparcido
esparciese	esparciesen	hubiese esparcido	hubiesen esparcido

	imperativo	
—		esparzamos
esparce; no esparzas		esparcid; no esparzáis
esparza		esparzan

Words and expressions related to this verb
el esparcimiento　scattering, spreading
esparcidamente　separately, sparsely
el esparcidor, la esparcidora　spreader, scatterer

flores esparcidas por las calles　flowers
　scattered over the streets

Get your feet wet with verbs used in weather expressions on page 540.

to expect, to hope, to wait (for)

The Seven Simple Tenses		The Seven Compound Tenses	
Singular	Plural	Singular	Plural
1 presente de indicativo		8 perfecto de indicativo	
espero	**esperamos**	**he esperado**	**hemos esperado**
esperas	**esperáis**	**has esperado**	**habéis esperado**
espera	**esperan**	**ha esperado**	**han esperado**
2 imperfecto de indicativo		9 pluscuamperfecto de indicativo	
esperaba	**esperábamos**	**había esperado**	**habíamos esperado**
esperabas	**esperabais**	**habías esperado**	**habíais esperado**
esperaba	**esperaban**	**había esperado**	**habían esperado**
3 pretérito		10 pretérito anterior	
esperé	**esperamos**	**hube esperado**	**hubimos esperado**
esperaste	**esperasteis**	**hubiste esperado**	**hubisteis esperado**
esperó	**esperaron**	**hubo esperado**	**hubieron esperado**
4 futuro		11 futuro perfecto	
esperaré	**esperaremos**	**habré esperado**	**habremos esperado**
esperarás	**esperaréis**	**habrás esperado**	**habréis esperado**
esperará	**esperarán**	**habrá esperado**	**habrán esperado**
5 potencial simple		12 potencial compuesto	
esperaría	**esperaríamos**	**habría esperado**	**habríamos esperado**
esperarías	**esperaríais**	**habrías esperado**	**habríais esperado**
esperaría	**esperarían**	**habría esperado**	**habrían esperado**
6 presente de subjuntivo		13 perfecto de subjuntivo	
espere	**esperemos**	**haya esperado**	**hayamos esperado**
esperes	**esperéis**	**hayas esperado**	**hayáis esperado**
espere	**esperen**	**haya esperado**	**hayan esperado**
7 imperfecto de subjuntivo		14 pluscuamperfecto de subjuntivo	
esperara	**esperáramos**	**hubiera esperado**	**hubiéramos esperado**
esperaras	**esperarais**	**hubieras esperado**	**hubierais esperado**
esperara	**esperaran**	**hubiera esperado**	**hubieran esperado**
OR		OR	
esperase	**esperásemos**	**hubiese esperado**	**hubiésemos esperado**
esperases	**esperaseis**	**hubieses esperado**	**hubieseis esperado**
esperase	**esperasen**	**hubiese esperado**	**hubiesen esperado**

	imperativo	
—	**esperemos**
espera; no esperes	**esperad; no esperéis**
espere	**esperen**

Words and expressions related to this verb
Mientras hay vida hay esperanza.
  When there is life there is hope.
la esperanza   hope
No hay esperanza.   There is no hope.

dar esperanzas   to give encouragement
desesperar   to despair

Enjoy more verbs in Spanish proverbs on page 539.

to ski

The Seven Simple Tenses		The Seven Compound Tenses	
Singular	Plural	Singular	Plural
1 presente de indicativo		8 perfecto de indicativo	
esquío	esquiamos	he esquiado	hemos esquiado
esquías	esquiáis	has esquiado	habéis esquiado
esquía	esquían	ha esquiado	han esquiado
2 imperfecto de indicativo		9 pluscuamperfecto de indicativo	
esquiaba	esquiábamos	había esquiado	habíamos esquiado
esquiabas	esquiabais	habías esquiado	habíais esquiado
esquiaba	esquiaban	había esquiado	habían esquiado
3 pretérito		10 pretérito anterior	
esquié	esquiamos	hube esquiado	hubimos esquiado
esquiaste	esquiasteis	hubiste esquiado	hubisteis esquiado
esquió	esquiaron	hubo esquiado	hubieron esquiado
4 futuro		11 futuro perfecto	
esquiaré	esquiaremos	habré esquiado	habremos esquiado
esquiarás	esquiaréis	habrás esquiado	habréis esquiado
esquiará	esquiarán	habrá esquiado	habrán esquiado
5 potencial simple		12 potencial compuesto	
esquiaría	esquiaríamos	habría esquiado	habríamos esquiado
esquiarías	esquiaríais	habrías esquiado	habríais esquiado
esquiaría	esquiarían	habría esquiado	habrían esquiado
6 presente de subjuntivo		13 perfecto de subjuntivo	
esquíe	esquiemos	haya esquiado	hayamos esquiado
esquíes	esquiéis	hayas esquiado	hayáis esquiado
esquíe	esquíen	haya esquiado	hayan esquiado
7 imperfecto de subjuntivo		14 pluscuamperfecto de subjuntivo	
esquiara	esquiáramos	hubiera esquiado	hubiéramos esquiado
esquiaras	esquiarais	hubieras esquiado	hubierais esquiado
esquiara	esquiaran	hubiera esquiado	hubieran esquiado
OR		OR	
esquiase	esquiásemos	hubiese esquiado	hubiésemos esquiado
esquiases	esquiaseis	hubieses esquiado	hubieseis esquiado
esquiase	esquiasen	hubiese esquiado	hubiesen esquiado

	imperativo
—	esquiemos
esquía; no esquíes	esquiad; no esquiéis
esquíe	esquíen

Sentences using this verb and words and expressions related to it

el esquí   ski, skiing
un esquiador, una esquiadora   skier
el esquí alpino   Alpine skiing
el esquí acuático   water-skiing

Me gusta el esquí.   I like skiing.
Me gusta esquiar.   I like to ski.
el esquí de fondo   cross-country skiing

Learn more verbs in 30 practical situations for tourists on pages 564–594.

to establish, to set up

The Seven Simple Tenses		The Seven Compound Tenses	
Singular	Plural	Singular	Plural
1 presente de indicativo		8 perfecto de indicativo	
establezco	establecemos	he establecido	hemos establecido
estableces	establecéis	has establecido	habéis establecido
establece	establecen	ha establecido	han establecido
2 imperfecto de indicativo		9 pluscuamperfecto de indicativo	
establecía	establecíamos	había establecido	habíamos establecido
establecías	establecíais	habías establecido	habíais establecido
establecía	establecían	había establecido	habían establecido
3 pretérito		10 pretérito anterior	
establecí	establecimos	hube establecido	hubimos establecido
estableciste	establecisteis	hubiste establecido	hubisteis establecido
estableció	establecieron	hubo establecido	hubieron establecido
4 futuro		11 futuro perfecto	
estableceré	estableceremos	habré establecido	habremos establecido
establecerás	estableceréis	habrás establecido	habréis establecido
establecerá	establecerán	habrá establecido	habrán establecido
5 potencial simple		12 potencial compuesto	
establecería	estableceríamos	habría establecido	habríamos establecido
establecerías	estableceríais	habrías establecido	habríais establecido
establecería	establecerían	habría establecido	habrían establecido
6 presente de subjuntivo		13 perfecto de subjuntivo	
establezca	establezcamos	haya establecido	hayamos establecido
establezcas	establezcáis	hayas establecido	hayáis establecido
establezca	establezcan	haya establecido	hayan establecido
7 imperfecto de subjuntivo		14 pluscuamperfecto de subjuntivo	
estableciera	estableciéramos	hubiera establecido	hubiéramos establecido
establecieras	establecierais	hubieras establecido	hubierais establecido
estableciera	establecieran	hubiera establecido	hubieran establecido
OR		OR	
estableciese	estableciésemos	hubiese establecido	hubiésemos establecido
establecieses	establecieseis	hubieses establecido	hubieseis establecido
estableciese	estableciesen	hubiese establecido	hubiesen establecido

imperativo		
—		establezcamos
establece; no establezcas		estableced; no establezcáis
establezca		establezcan

Words and expressions related to this verb
establecer normas   to set up standards
un establecedor, una establecedora   founder
un establecimiento   establishment
establemente   firmly, stably
establecerse   to set oneself up, as in business;
   to settle down

establecer un campamento   to set up camp
un establecimiento comercial   commercial
   establishment

The subject pronouns are found on the page facing page 1.

The Seven Simple Tenses		The Seven Compound Tenses	
Singular	Plural	Singular	Plural
1 presente de indicativo		8 perfecto de indicativo	
estoy	**estamos**	**he estado**	**hemos estado**
estás	**estáis**	**has estado**	**habéis estado**
está	**están**	**ha estado**	**han estado**
2 imperfecto de indicativo		9 pluscuamperfecto de indicativo	
estaba	**estábamos**	**había estado**	**habíamos estado**
estabas	**estabais**	**habías estado**	**habíais estado**
estaba	**estaban**	**había estado**	**habían estado**
3 pretérito		10 pretérito anterior	
estuve	**estuvimos**	**hube estado**	**hubimos estado**
estuviste	**estuvisteis**	**hubiste estado**	**hubisteis estado**
estuvo	**estuvieron**	**hubo estado**	**hubieron estado**
4 futuro		11 futuro perfecto	
estaré	**estaremos**	**habré estado**	**habremos estado**
estarás	**estaréis**	**habrás estado**	**habréis estado**
estará	**estarán**	**habrá estado**	**habrán estado**
5 potencial simple		12 potencial compuesto	
estaría	**estaríamos**	**habría estado**	**habríamos estado**
estarías	**estaríais**	**habrías estado**	**habríais estado**
estaría	**estarían**	**habría estado**	**habrían estado**
6 presente de subjuntivo		13 perfecto de subjuntivo	
esté	**estemos**	**haya estado**	**hayamos estado**
estés	**estéis**	**hayas estado**	**hayáis estado**
esté	**estén**	**haya estado**	**hayan estado**
7 imperfecto de subjuntivo		14 pluscuamperfecto de subjuntivo	
estuviera	**estuviéramos**	**hubiera estado**	**hubiéramos estado**
estuvieras	**estuvierais**	**hubieras estado**	**hubierais estado**
estuviera	**estuvieran**	**hubiera estado**	**hubieran estado**
OR		OR	
estuviese	**estuviésemos**	**hubiese estado**	**hubiésemos estado**
estuvieses	**estuvieseis**	**hubieses estado**	**hubieseis estado**
estuviese	**estuviesen**	**hubiese estado**	**hubiesen estado**

imperativo

—	**estemos**
está; no estés	**estad; no estéis**
esté	**estén**

Common idiomatic expressions using this verb
—**¿Cómo está Ud.?**
—**Estoy muy bien, gracias. ¿Y usted?**
—**Estoy enfermo hoy.**

estar para + inf.   to be about + inf.
  Estoy para salir.   I am about to go out.
estar por   to be in favor of

Consult the back pages for **estar** used in more idiomatic expressions on pages 527, 535, and 536.

to estimate, to esteem, to respect, to value

The Seven Simple Tenses		The Seven Compound Tenses	
Singular	Plural	Singular	Plural
1 presente de indicativo		8 perfecto de indicativo	
estimo	estimamos	he estimado	hemos estimado
estimas	estimáis	has estimado	habéis estimado
estima	estiman	ha estimado	han estimado
2 imperfecto de indicativo		9 pluscuamperfecto de indicativo	
estimaba	estimábamos	había estimado	habíamos estimado
estimabas	estmabais	habías estimado	habíais estimado
estimaba	estimaban	había estimado	habían estimado
3 pretérito		10 pretérito anterior	
estimé	estimamos	hube estimado	hubimos estimado
estimaste	estimasteis	hubiste estimado	hubisteis estimado
estimó	estimaron	hubo estimado	hubieron estimado
4 futuro		11 futuro perfecto	
estimaré	estimaremos	habré estimado	habremos estimado
estimarás	estimaréis	habrás estimado	habréis estimado
estimará	estimarán	habrá estimado	habrán estimado
5 potencial simple		12 potencial compuesto	
estimaría	estimaríamos	habría estimado	habríamos estimado
estimarías	estimaríais	habrías estimado	habríais estimado
estimaría	estimarían	habría estimado	habrían estimado
6 presente de subjuntivo		13 perfecto de subjuntivo	
estime	estimemos	haya estimado	hayamos estimado
estimes	estiméis	hayas estimado	hayáis estimado
estime	estimen	haya estimado	hayan estimado
7 imperfecto de subjuntivo		14 pluscuamperfecto de subjuntivo	
estimara	estimáramos	hubiera estimado	hubiéramos estimado
estimaras	estimarais	hubieras estimado	hubierais estimado
estimara	estimaran	hubiera estimado	hubieran estimado
OR		OR	
estimase	estimásemos	hubiese estimado	hubiésemos estimado
estimases	estimaseis	hubieses estimado	hubieseis estimado
estimase	estimasen	hubiese estimado	hubiesen estimado

	imperativo
—	estimemos
estima; no estimes	estimad; no estiméis
estime	estimen

Words and expressions related to this verb
la estima   esteem, respect
la estimabilidad   worthiness, worth
la estimación   estimation, esteem

estimar con exceso   to overestimate
estimar en menos   to underestimate
estimar oportuno   to deem (see) fit

Want to learn more idiomatic expressions that contain verbs? Check out pages 524–537.

The subject pronouns are found on the page facing page 1.

estudiar

Gerundio **estudiando**   Part. pas. **estudiado**

to study

The Seven Simple Tenses		The Seven Compound Tenses	
Singular	Plural	Singular	Plural
1 presente de indicativo		**8 perfecto de indicativo**	
estudio	estudiamos	he estudiado	hemos estudiado
estudias	estudiáis	has estudiado	habéis estudiado
estudia	estudian	ha estudiado	han estudiado
2 imperfecto de indicativo		**9 pluscuamperfecto de indicativo**	
estudiaba	estudiábamos	había estudiado	habíamos estudiado
estudiabas	estudiabais	habías estudiado	habíais estudiado
estudiaba	estudiaban	había estudiado	habían estudiado
3 pretérito		**10 pretérito anterior**	
estudié	estudiamos	hube estudiado	hubimos estudiado
estudiaste	estudiasteis	hubiste estudiado	hubisteis estudiado
estudió	estudiaron	hubo estudiado	hubieron estudiado
4 futuro		**11 futuro perfecto**	
estudiaré	estudiaremos	habré estudiado	habremos estudiado
estudiarás	estudiaréis	habrás estudiado	habréis estudiado
estudiará	estudiarán	habrá estudiado	habrán estudiado
5 potencial simple		**12 potencial compuesto**	
estudiaría	estudiaríamos	habría estudiado	habríamos estudiado
estudiarías	estudiaríais	habrías estudiado	habríais estudiado
estudiaría	estudiarían	habría estudiado	habrían estudiado
6 presente de subjuntivo		**13 perfecto de subjuntivo**	
estudie	estudiemos	haya estudiado	hayamos estudiado
estudies	estudiéis	hayas estudiado	hayáis estudiado
estudie	estudien	haya estudiado	hayan estudiado
7 imperfecto de subjuntivo		**14 pluscuamperfecto de subjuntivo**	
estudiara	estudiáramos	hubiera estudiado	hubiéramos estudiado
estudiaras	estudiarais	hubieras estudiado	hubierais estudiado
estudiara	estudiaran	hubiera estudiado	hubieran estudiado
OR		OR	
estudiase	estudiásemos	hubiese estudiado	hubiésemos estudiado
estudiases	estudiaseis	hubieses estudiado	hubieseis estudiado
estudiase	estudiasen	hubiese estudiado	hubiesen estudiado

	imperativo	
—		estudiemos
estudia; no estudies		estudiad; no estudiéis
estudie		estudien

Words and expressions related to this verb

un, una estudiante student
el estudio study, studio, study room
estudioso, estudiosa studious

altos estudios advanced studies
estudiosamente studiously
estudiante de intercambio exchange student

> Don't miss the definitions of basic grammatical terms with examples
> in English and Spanish on pages 666–677.

to demand, to urge, to require

The Seven Simple Tenses		The Seven Compound Tenses	
Singular	Plural	Singular	Plural
1 presente de indicativo		**8 perfecto de indicativo**	
exijo	exigimos	he exigido	hemos exigido
exiges	exigís	has exigido	habéis exigido
exige	exigen	ha exigido	han exigido
2 imperfecto de indicativo		**9 pluscuamperfecto de indicativo**	
exigía	exigíamos	había exigido	habíamos exigido
exigías	exigíais	habías exigido	habíais exigido
exigía	exigían	había exigido	habían exigido
3 pretérito		**10 pretérito anterior**	
exigí	exigimos	hube exigido	hubimos exigido
exigiste	exigisteis	hubiste exigido	hubisteis exigido
exigió	exigieron	hubo exigido	hubieron exigido
4 futuro		**11 futuro perfecto**	
exigiré	exigiremos	habré exigido	habremos exigido
exigirás	exigiréis	habrás exigido	habréis exigido
exigirá	exigirán	habrá exigido	habrán exigido
5 potencial simple		**12 potencial compuesto**	
exigiría	exigiríamos	habría exigido	habríamos exigido
exigirías	exigiríais	habrías exigido	habríais exigido
exigiría	exigirían	habría exigido	habrían exigido
6 presente de subjuntivo		**13 perfecto de subjuntivo**	
exija	exijamos	haya exigido	hayamos exigido
exijas	exijáis	hayas exigido	hayáis exigido
exija	exijan	haya exigido	hayan exigido
7 imperfecto de subjuntivo		**14 pluscuamperfecto de subjuntivo**	
exigiera	exigiéramos	hubiera exigido	hubiéramos exigido
exigieras	exigierais	hubieras exigido	hubierais exigido
exigiera	exigieran	hubiera exigido	hubieran exigido
OR		OR	
exigiese	exigiésemos	hubiese exigido	hubiésemos exigido
exigieses	exigieseis	hubieses exigido	hubieseis exigido
exigiese	exigiesen	hubiese exigido	hubiesen exigido

imperativo

—	exijamos
exige; no exijas	exigid; no exijáis
exija	exijan

Words and expressions related to this verb
exigente exacting, demanding
la exigencia exigency, requirement
exigible demanding, payable on demand
exigir el pago to demand payment

una persona muy exigente a very demanding person
exigir algo de buena calidad to insist upon something of good quality

Can't recognize an irregular verb form? Check out pages 519–523.

to explain

The Seven Simple Tenses		The Seven Compound Tenses	
Singular	Plural	Singular	Plural
1 presente de indicativo		**8 perfecto de indicativo**	
explico	explicamos	he explicado	hemos explicado
explicas	explicáis	has explicado	habéis explicado
explica	explican	ha explicado	han explicado
2 imperfecto de indicativo		**9 pluscuamperfecto de indicativo**	
explicaba	explicábamos	había explicado	habíamos explicado
explicabas	explicabais	habías explicado	habíais explicado
explicaba	explicaban	había explicado	habían explicado
3 pretérito		**10 pretérito anterior**	
expliqué	explicamos	hube explicado	hubimos explicado
explicaste	explicasteis	hubiste explicado	hubisteis explicado
explicó	explicaron	hubo explicado	hubieron explicado
4 futuro		**11 futuro perfecto**	
explicaré	explicaremos	habré explicado	habremos explicado
explicarás	explicaréis	habrás explicado	habréis explicado
explicará	explicarán	habrá explicado	habrán explicado
5 potencial simple		**12 potencial compuesto**	
explicaría	explicaríamos	habría explicado	habríamos explicado
explicarías	explicaríais	habrías explicado	habríais explicado
explicaría	explicarían	habría explicado	habrían explicado
6 presente de subjuntivo		**13 perfecto de subjuntivo**	
explique	expliquemos	haya explicado	hayamos explicado
expliques	expliquéis	hayas explicado	hayáis explicado
explique	expliquen	haya explicado	hayan explicado
7 imperfecto de subjuntivo		**14 pluscuamperfecto de subjuntivo**	
explicara	explicáramos	hubiera explicado	hubiéramos explicado
explicaras	explicarais	hubieras explicado	hubierais explicado
explicara	explicaran	hubiera explicado	hubieran explicado
OR		OR	
explicase	explicásemos	hubiese explicado	hubiésemos explicado
explicases	explicaseis	hubieses explicado	hubieseis explicado
explicase	explicasen	hubiese explicado	hubiesen explicado

	imperativo	
—		expliquemos
explica; no expliques		explicad; no expliquéis
explique		expliquen

Words and expressions related to this verb
una explicación explanation
explícito, explícita explicit
explícitamente explicitly

explicativo, explicativa explanatory
pedir explicaciones to ask for an explanation

Check out the verb drills and verb tests with answers explained on pages 619–665.

The Seven Simple Tenses		The Seven Compound Tenses	
Singular	Plural	Singular	Plural
1 presente de indicativo		8 perfecto de indicativo	
expreso	**expresamos**	**he expresado**	**hemos expresado**
expresas	**expresáis**	**has expresado**	**habéis expresado**
expresa	**expresan**	**ha expresado**	**han expresado**
2 imperfecto de indicativo		9 pluscuamperfecto de indicativo	
expresaba	**expresábamos**	**había expresado**	**habíamos expresado**
expresabas	**expresabais**	**habías expresado**	**habíais expresado**
expresaba	**expresaban**	**había expresado**	**habían expresado**
3 pretérito		10 pretérito anterior	
expresé	**expresamos**	**hube expresado**	**hubimos expresado**
expresaste	**expresasteis**	**hubiste expresado**	**hubisteis expresado**
expresó	**expresaron**	**hubo expresado**	**hubieron expresado**
4 futuro		11 futuro perfecto	
expresaré	**expresaremos**	**habré expresado**	**habremos expresado**
expresarás	**expresaréis**	**habrás expresado**	**habréis expresado**
expresará	**expresarán**	**habrá expresado**	**habrán expresado**
5 potencial simple		12 potencial compuesto	
expresaría	**expresaríamos**	**habría expresado**	**habríamos expresado**
expresarías	**expresaríais**	**habrías expresado**	**habríais expresado**
expresaría	**expresarían**	**habría expresado**	**habrían expresado**
6 presente de subjuntivo		13 perfecto de subjuntivo	
exprese	**expresemos**	**haya expresado**	**hayamos expresado**
expreses	**expreséis**	**hayas expresado**	**hayáis expresado**
exprese	**expresen**	**haya expresado**	**hayan expresado**
7 imperfecto de subjuntivo		14 pluscuamperfecto de subjuntivo	
expresara	**expresáramos**	**hubiera expresado**	**hubiéramos expresado**
expresaras	**expresarais**	**hubieras expresado**	**hubierais expresado**
expresara	**expresaran**	**hubiera expresado**	**hubieran expresado**
OR		OR	
expresase	**expresásemos**	**hubiese expresado**	**hubiésemos expresado**
expresases	**expresaseis**	**hubieses expresado**	**hubieseis expresado**
expresase	**expresasen**	**hubiese expresado**	**hubiesen expresado**

imperativo

—	**expresemos**
expresa; no expreses	**expresad; no expreséis**
exprese	**expresen**

Words and expressions related to this verb

expresarse   to express oneself
una expresión   expression, phrase
expresamente   expressly, on purpose
expresivamente   expressively

el expresionismo   expressionism (art)
expreso   express (train, etc.)
una expresión idiomática   idiomatic expression
expresiones de mi parte   regards from me, kindest regards

The subject pronouns are found on the page facing page 1.

to fabricate, to manufacture

The Seven Simple Tenses		The Seven Compound Tenses	
Singular	Plural	Singular	Plural
1 presente de indicativo		**8 perfecto de indicativo**	
fabrico	fabricamos	he fabricado	hemos fabricado
fabricas	fabricáis	has fabricado	habéis fabricado
fabrica	fabrican	ha fabricado	han fabricado
2 imperfecto de indicativo		**9 pluscuamperfecto de indicativo**	
fabricaba	fabricábamos	había fabricado	habíamos fabricado
fabricabas	fabricabais	habías fabricado	habíais fabricado
fabricaba	fabricaban	había fabricado	habían fabricado
3 pretérito		**10 pretérito anterior**	
fabriqué	fabricamos	hube fabricado	hubimos fabricado
fabricaste	fabricasteis	hubiste fabricado	hubisteis fabricado
fabricó	fabricaron	hubo fabricado	hubieron fabricado
4 futuro		**11 futuro perfecto**	
fabricaré	fabricaremos	habré fabricado	habremos fabricado
fabricarás	fabricaréis	habrás fabricado	habréis fabricado
fabricará	fabricarán	habrá fabricado	habrán fabricado
5 potencial simple		**12 potencial compuesto**	
fabricaría	fabricaríamos	habría fabricado	habríamos fabricado
fabricarías	fabricaríais	habrías fabricado	habríais fabricado
fabricaría	fabricarían	habría fabricado	habrían fabricado
6 presente de subjuntivo		**13 perfecto de subjuntivo**	
fabrique	fabriquemos	haya fabricado	hayamos fabricado
fabriques	fabriquéis	hayas fabricado	hayáis fabricado
fabrique	fabriquen	haya fabricado	hayan fabricado
7 imperfecto de subjuntivo		**14 pluscuamperfecto de subjuntivo**	
fabricara	fabricáramos	hubiera fabricado	hubiéramos fabricado
fabricaras	fabricarais	hubieras fabricado	hubierais fabricado
fabricara	fabricaran	hubiera fabricado	hubieran fabricado
OR		OR	
fabricase	fabricásemos	hubiese fabricado	hubiésemos fabricado
fabricases	fabricaseis	hubieses fabricado	hubieseis fabricado
fabricase	fabricasen	hubiese fabricado	hubiesen fabricado

imperativo	
—	fabriquemos
fabrica; no fabriques	fabricad; no fabriquéis
fabrique	fabriquen

Words and expressions related to this verb
la fábrica   factory
la fabricación   fabrication, manufacturing
de fabricación casera   homemade

el fabricante   manufacturer
fabricación en serie   mass production
prefabricar   to prefabricate

Get acquainted with what preposition goes with what verb on pages 541–549.

to be lacking, to be wanting, to lack, to miss, to need

The Seven Simple Tenses		The Seven Compound Tenses	
Singular	Plural	Singular	Plural
1 presente de indicativo		8 perfecto de indicativo	
falto	faltamos	he faltado	hemos faltado
faltas	faltáis	has faltado	habéis faltado
falta	faltan	ha faltado	han faltado
2 imperfecto de indicativo		9 pluscuamperfecto de indicativo	
faltaba	faltábamos	había faltado	habíamos faltado
faltabas	faltabais	habías faltado	habíais faltado
faltaba	faltaban	había faltado	habían faltado
3 pretérito		10 pretérito anterior	
falté	faltamos	hube faltado	hubimos faltado
faltaste	faltasteis	hubiste faltado	hubisteis faltado
faltó	faltaron	hubo faltado	hubieron faltado
4 futuro		11 futuro perfecto	
faltaré	faltaremos	habré faltado	habremos faltado
faltarás	faltaréis	habrás faltado	habréis faltado
faltará	faltarán	habrá faltado	habrán faltado
5 potencial simple		12 potencial compuesto	
faltaría	faltaríamos	habría faltado	habríamos faltado
faltarías	faltaríais	habrías faltado	habríais faltado
faltaría	faltarían	habría faltado	habrían faltado
6 presente de subjuntivo		13 perfecto de subjuntivo	
falte	faltemos	haya faltado	hayamos faltado
faltes	faltéis	hayas faltado	hayáis faltado
falte	falten	haya faltado	hayan faltado
7 imperfecto de subjuntivo		14 pluscuamperfecto de subjuntivo	
faltara	faltáramos	hubiera faltado	hubiéramos faltado
faltaras	faltarais	hubieras faltado	hubierais faltado
faltara	faltaran	hubiera faltado	hubieran faltado
OR		OR	
faltase	faltásemos	hubiese faltado	hubiésemos faltado
faltases	faltaseis	hubieses faltado	hubieseis faltado
faltase	faltasen	hubiese faltado	hubiesen faltado

	imperativo	
—		faltemos
falta; no faltes		faltad; no faltéis
falte		falten

Common idiomatic expressions using this verb
a falta de   for lack of
sin falta   without fail, without fault
la falta   lack, want
faltante   lacking, wanting

¡No faltaba más!   That's the limit!
faltar poco para + inf.   not to be long before
hacer falta   to be necessary
poner faltas a   to find fault with

Get your feet wet with verbs used in weather expressions on page 540.

The subject pronouns are found on the page facing page 1.

to congratulate, to felicitate

The Seven Simple Tenses		The Seven Compound Tenses	
Singular	Plural	Singular	Plural
1 presente de indicativo		8 perfecto de indicativo	
felicito	**felicitamos**	**he felicitado**	**hemos felicitado**
felicitas	**felicitáis**	**has felicitado**	**habéis felicitado**
felicita	**felicitan**	**ha felicitado**	**han felicitado**
2 imperfecto de indicativo		9 pluscuamperfecto de indicativo	
felicitaba	**felicitábamos**	**había felicitado**	**habíamos felicitado**
felicitabas	**felicitabais**	**habías felicitado**	**habíais felicitado**
felicitaba	**felicitaban**	**había felicitado**	**habían felicitado**
3 pretérito		10 pretérito anterior	
felicité	**felicitamos**	**hube felicitado**	**hubimos felicitado**
felicitaste	**felicitasteis**	**hubiste felicitado**	**hubisteis felicitado**
felicitó	**felicitaron**	**hubo felicitado**	**hubieron felicitado**
4 futuro		11 futuro perfecto	
felicitaré	**felicitaremos**	**habré felicitado**	**habremos felicitado**
felicitarás	**felicitaréis**	**habrás felicitado**	**habréis felicitado**
felicitará	**felicitarán**	**habrá felicitado**	**habrán felicitado**
5 potencial simple		12 potencial compuesto	
felicitaría	**felicitaríamos**	**habría felicitado**	**habríamos felicitado**
felicitarías	**felicitaríais**	**habrías felicitado**	**habríais felicitado**
felicitaría	**felicitarían**	**habría felicitado**	**habrían felicitado**
6 presente de subjuntivo		13 perfecto de subjuntivo	
felicite	**felicitemos**	**haya felicitado**	**hayamos felicitado**
felicites	**felicitéis**	**hayas felicitado**	**hayáis felicitado**
felicite	**feliciten**	**haya felicitado**	**hayan felicitado**
7 imperfecto de subjuntivo		14 pluscuamperfecto de subjuntivo	
felicitara	**felicitáramos**	**hubiera felicitado**	**hubiéramos felicitado**
felicitaras	**felicitarais**	**hubieras felicitado**	**hubierais felicitado**
felicitara	**felicitaran**	**hubiera felicitado**	**hubieran felicitado**
OR		OR	
felicitase	**felicitásemos**	**hubiese felicitado**	**hubiésemos felicitado**
felicitases	**felicitaseis**	**hubieses felicitado**	**hubieseis felicitado**
felicitase	**felicitasen**	**hubiese felicitado**	**hubiesen felicitado**

	imperativo	
—		**felicitemos**
felicita; no felicites		**felicitad; no felicitéis**
felicite		**feliciten**

Words and expressions related to this verb

la felicitación, las felicitaciones
   congratulations
la felicidad happiness, good fortune
felizmente happily, fortunately

feliz happy, fortunate, lucky (*pl.* **felices**)
felice happy (in poetry)
¡Feliz Año Nuevo! Happy New Year!
¡Feliz Cumpleaños! Happy Birthday!

If you want to see a sample English verb fully conjugated
in all the tenses, check out pages xviii and xix.

to feast, to entertain, to celebrate

The Seven Simple Tenses		The Seven Compound Tenses	
Singular	Plural	Singular	Plural
1 presente de indicativo		8 perfecto de indicativo	
festejo	**festejamos**	**he festejado**	**hemos festejado**
festejas	**festejáis**	**has festejado**	**habéis festejado**
festeja	**festejan**	**ha festejado**	**han festejado**
2 imperfecto de indicativo		9 pluscuamperfecto de indicativo	
festejaba	**festejábamos**	**había festejado**	**habíamos festejado**
festejabas	**festejabais**	**habías festejado**	**habíais festejado**
fetsejaba	**festejaban**	**había festejado**	**habían festejado**
3 pretérito		10 pretérito anterior	
festejé	**fetejamos**	**hube festejado**	**hubimos festejado**
festejaste	**festejasteis**	**hubiste festejado**	**hubisteis festejado**
festejó	**festejaron**	**hubo festejado**	**hubieron festejado**
4 futuro		11 futuro perfecto	
festejaré	**festejaremos**	**habré festejado**	**habremos festejado**
festejarás	**festejaréis**	**habrás festejado**	**habréis festejado**
festejará	**festejarán**	**habrá festejado**	**habrán festejado**
5 potencial simple		12 potencial compuesto	
festejaría	**festejaríamos**	**habría festejado**	**habríamos festejado**
festejarías	**festejaríais**	**habrías festejado**	**habríais festejado**
festejaría	**festejarían**	**habría festejado**	**habrían festejado**
6 presente de subjuntivo		13 perfecto de subjuntivo	
festeje	**festejemos**	**haya festejado**	**hayamos festejado**
festejes	**festejéis**	**hayas festejado**	**hayáis festejado**
festeje	**festejen**	**haya festejado**	**hayan festejado**
7 imperfecto de subjuntivo		14 pluscuamperfecto de subjuntivo	
festejara	**festejáramos**	**hubiera festejado**	**hubiéramos festejado**
festejaras	**festejarais**	**hubieras festejado**	**hubierais festejado**
festejara	**festejaran**	**hubiera festejado**	**hubieran festejado**
OR		OR	
festejase	**festejásemos**	**hubiese festejado**	**hubiésemos festejado**
festejases	**festejaseis**	**hubieses festejado**	**hubieseis festejado**
festejase	**festejasen**	**hubiese festejado**	**hubiesen festejado**

	imperativo	
—		**festejemos**
festeja; no festejes		**festejad; no festejéis**
festeje		**festejen**

Words and expressions related to this verb

un festejo   banquet, feast, celebration
una fiesta   feast, holy day, festivity
la Fiesta de la Raza   Columbus Day

la fiesta nacional   national holiday
la fiesta de todos los santos   All Saints' Day
la fiesta de cumpleaños   birthday party

> If you want an explanation of meanings and uses of Spanish and
> English verb tenses and moods, see pages xx–xl.

to confide, to trust

The Seven Simple Tenses		The Seven Compound Tenses	
Singular	Plural	Singular	Plural
1 presente de indicativo		**8 perfecto de indicativo**	
fío	fiamos	he fiado	hemos fiado
fías	fiáis	has fiado	habéis fiado
fía	fían	ha fiado	han fiado
2 imperfecto de indicativo		**9 pluscuamperfecto de indicativo**	
fiaba	fiábamos	había fiado	habíamos fiado
fiabas	fiabais	habías fiado	habíais fiado
fiaba	fiaban	había fiado	habían fiado
3 pretérito		**10 pretérito anterior**	
fié	fiamos	hube fiado	hubimos fiado
fiaste	fiasteis	hubiste fiado	hubisteis fiado
fió	fiaron	hubo fiado	hubieron fiado
4 futuro		**11 futuro perfecto**	
fiaré	fiaremos	habré fiado	habremos fiado
fiarás	fiaréis	habrás fiado	habréis fiado
fiará	fiarán	habrá fiado	habrán fiado
5 potencial simple		**12 potencial compuesto**	
fiaría	fiaríamos	habría fiado	habríamos fiado
fiarías	fiaríais	habrías fiado	habríais fiado
fiaría	fiarían	habría fiado	habrían fiado
6 presente de subjuntivo		**13 perfecto de subjuntivo**	
fíe	fiemos	haya fiado	hayamos fiado
fíes	fiéis	hayas fiado	hayáis fiado
fíe	fíen	haya fiado	hayan fiado
7 imperfecto de subjuntivo		**14 pluscuamperfecto de subjuntivo**	
fiara	fiáramos	hubiera fiado	hubiéramos fiado
fiaras	fiarais	hubieras fiado	hubierais fiado
fiara	fiaran	hubiera fiado	hubieran fiado
OR		OR	
fiase	fiásemos	hubiese fiado	hubiésemos fiado
fiases	fiaseis	hubieses fiado	hubieseis fiado
fiase	fiasen	hubiese fiado	hubiesen fiado

imperativo	
—	fiemos
fía; no fíes	fiad; no fiéis
fíe	fíen

Words and expressions related to this verb
fiarse de to have confidence in, to trust
la fianza security, surety, guarantee
al fiado on credit, on trust
fiable trustworthy

fiar en to trust in
comprar al fiado to buy on credit
en libertad bajo fianza free on bail
no se fía no credit

> If you don't know the Spanish verb for the English verb you have in mind, look it up in the index on pages 505–518.

to take notice, to pay attention, to settle

The Seven Simple Tenses		The Seven Compound Tenses	
Singular	Plural	Singular	Plural
1 presente de indicativo		8 perfecto de indicativo	
me fijo	nos fijamos	me he fijado	nos hemos fijado
te fijas	os fijáis	te has fijado	os habéis fijado
se fija	se fijan	se ha fijado	se han fijado
2 imperfecto de indicativo		9 pluscuamperfecto de indicativo	
me fijaba	nos fijábamos	me había fijado	nos habíamos fijado
te fijabas	os fijabais	te habías fijado	os habíais fijado
se fijaba	se fijaban	se había fijado	se habían fijado
3 pretérito		10 pretérito anterior	
me fijé	nos fijamos	me hube fijado	nos hubimos fijado
te fijaste	os fijasteis	te hubiste fijado	os hubisteis fijado
se fijó	se fijaron	se hubo fijado	se hubieron fijado
4 futuro		11 futuro perfecto	
me fijaré	nos fijaremos	me habré fijado	nos habremos fijado
te fijarás	os fijaréis	te habrás fijado	os habréis fijado
se fijará	se fijarán	se habrá fijado	se habrán fijado
5 potencial simple		12 potencial compuesto	
me fijaría	nos fijaríamos	me habría fijado	nos habríamos fijado
te fijarías	os fijaríais	te habrías fijado	os habríais fijado
se fijaría	se fijarían	se habría fijado	se habrían fijado
6 presente de subjuntivo		13 perfecto de subjuntivo	
me fije	nos fijemos	me haya fijado	nos hayamos fijado
te fijes	os fijéis	te hayas fijado	os hayáis fijado
se fije	se fijen	se haya fijado	se hayan fijado
7 imperfecto de subjuntivo		14 pluscuamperfecto de subjuntivo	
me fijara	nos fijáramos	me hubiera fijado	nos hubiéramos fijado
te fijaras	os fijarais	te hubieras fijado	os hubierais fijado
se fijara	se fijaran	se hubiera fijado	se hubieran fijado
OR		OR	
me fijase	nos fijásemos	me hubiese fijado	nos hubiésemos fijado
te fijases	os fijaseis	te hubieses fijado	os hubieseis fijado
se fijase	se fijasen	se hubiese fijado	se hubiesen fijado

imperativo	
—	fijémonos
fíjate; no te fijes	fijaos; no os fijéis
fíjese	fíjense

Words and expressions related to this verb
fijar   to clinch, to fasten, to fix; **fijo**   (when used as an adj.)
fijarse en   to take notice of, to pay attention to, to settle in
hora fija   set time, set hour, time agreed on; **de fijo**   surely
fijamente   fixedly, assuredly; **fijar el precio**   to fix the price
una fija   door hinge; **una fijación**   fixation   PROHIBIDO FIJAR CARTELES POST NO BILLS
la fijación de precios   price fixing

The subject pronouns are found on the page facing page 1.

fingir

Gerundio **fingiendo**   Part. pas. **fingido**

to feign, to pretend

The Seven Simple Tenses		The Seven Compound Tenses	
Singular	Plural	Singular	Plural
1 presente de indicativo		**8 perfecto de indicativo**	
finjo	fingimos	he fingido	hemos fingido
finges	fingís	has fingido	habéis fingido
finge	fingen	ha fingido	han fingido
2 imperfecto de indicativo		**9 pluscuamperfecto de indicativo**	
fingía	fingíamos	había fingido	habíamos fingido
fingías	fingíais	habías fingido	habíais fingido
fingía	fingían	había fingido	habían fingido
3 pretérito		**10 pretérito anterior**	
fingí	fingimos	hube fingido	hubimos fingido
fingiste	finisteis	hubiste fingido	hubisteis fingido
fingió	fingieron	hubo fingido	hubieron fingido
4 futuro		**11 futuro perfecto**	
fingiré	fingiremos	habré fingido	habremos fingido
fingirás	fingiréis	habrás fingido	habréis fingido
fingirá	fingirán	habrá fingido	habrán fingido
5 potencial simple		**12 potencial compuesto**	
fingiría	fingiríamos	habría fingido	habríamos fingido
fingirías	fingiríais	habrías fingido	habríais fingido
fingiría	fingirían	habría fingido	habrían fingido
6 presente de subjuntivo		**13 perfecto de subjuntivo**	
finja	finjamos	haya fingido	hayamos fingido
finjas	finjáis	hayas fingido	hayáis fingido
finja	finjan	haya fingido	hayan fingido
7 imperfecto de subjuntivo		**14 pluscuamperfecto de subjuntivo**	
fingiera	fingiéramos	hubiera fingido	hubiéramos fingido
fingieras	fingierais	hubieras fingido	hubierais fingido
fingiera	fingieran	hubiera fingido	hubieran fingido
OR		OR	
fingiese	fingiésemos	hubiese fingido	hubiésemos fingido
fingieses	fingieseis	hubieses fingido	hubieseis fingido
fingiese	fingiesen	hubiese fingido	hubiesen fingido

imperativo	
—	**finjamos**
finge; no finjas	**fingid; no finjáis**
finja	**finjan**

Words and expressions related to this verb
fingir + inf.   to pretend + inf.
el fingimiento   deceit, pretense, feigning
un fingidor, una fingidora   faker, feigner
fingidamente   fictitiously
fingir sorpresa   to fake surprise

fingirse amigos   to pretend to be friends
nombre fingido   assumed (fake) name
fingir alegría   to fake happiness

Can't recognize an irregular verb form? Check out pages 519–523.

The Seven Simple Tenses		The Seven Compound Tenses	
Singular	Plural	Singular	Plural
1 presente de indicativo		8 perfecto de indicativo	
firmo	firmamos	he firmado	hemos firmado
firmas	firmáis	has firmado	habéis firmado
firma	firman	ha firmado	han firmado
2 imperfecto de indicativo		9 pluscuamperfecto de indicativo	
firmaba	firmábamos	había firmado	habíamos firmado
firmabas	firmabais	habías firmado	habíais firmado
firmaba	firmaban	había firmado	habían firmado
3 pretérito		10 pretérito anterior	
firmé	firmamos	hube firmado	hubimos firmado
firmaste	firmasteis	hubiste firmado	hubisteis firmado
firmó	firmaron	hubo firmado	hubieron firmado
4 futuro		11 futuro perfecto	
firmaré	firmaremos	habré firmado	habremos firmado
firmarás	firmaréis	habrás firmado	habréis firmado
firmará	firmarán	habrá firmado	habrán firmado
5 potencial simple		12 potencial compuesto	
firmaría	firmaríamos	habría firmado	habríamos firmado
firmarías	firmaríais	habrías firmado	habríais firmado
firmaría	firmarían	habría firmado	habrían firmado
6 presente de subjuntivo		13 perfecto de subjuntivo	
firme	firmemos	haya firmado	hayamos firmado
firmes	firméis	hayas firmado	hayáis firmado
firme	firmen	haya firmado	hayan firmado
7 imperfecto de subjuntivo		14 pluscuamperfecto de subjuntivo	
firmara	firmáramos	hubiera firmado	hubiéramos firmado
firmaras	firmarais	hubieras firmado	hubierais firmado
firmara	firmaran	hubiera firmado	hubieran firmado
OR		OR	
firmase	firmásemos	hubiese firmado	hubiésemos firmado
firmases	firmaseis	hubieses firmado	hubieseis firmado
firmase	firmasen	hubiese firmado	hubiesen firmado

imperativo	
—	firmemos
firma; no firmes	firmad; no firméis
firme	firmen

Words and expressions related to this verb

firmar y sellar to sign and seal
el, la firmante signer
confirmar to confirm

de firme steadily
en lo firme in the right
color firme fast color

Check out the verb drills and verb tests with answers explained on pages 619–665.

formar

Gerundio **formando**   Part. pas. **formado**

to form, to shape

The Seven Simple Tenses		The Seven Compound Tenses	
Singular	Plural	Singular	Plural
1 presente de indicativo		**8 perfecto de indicativo**	
formo	formamos	he formado	hemos formado
formas	formáis	has formado	habéis formado
forma	forman	ha formado	han formado
2 imperfecto de indicativo		**9 pluscuamperfecto de indicativo**	
formaba	formábamos	había formado	habíamos formado
formabas	formabais	habías formado	habíais formado
formaba	formaban	había formado	habían formado
3 pretérito		**10 pretérito anterior**	
formé	formamos	hube formado	hubimos formado
formaste	formasteis	hubiste formado	hubisteis formado
formó	formaron	hubo formado	hubieron formado
4 futuro		**11 futuro perfecto**	
formaré	formaremos	habré formado	habremos formado
formarás	formaréis	habrás formado	habréis formado
formará	formarán	habrá formado	habrán formado
5 potencial simple		**12 potencial compuesto**	
formaría	formaríamos	habría formado	habríamos formado
formarías	formaríais	habrías formado	habríais formado
formaría	formarían	habría formado	habrían formado
6 presente de subjuntivo		**13 perfecto de subjuntivo**	
forme	formemos	haya formado	hayamos formado
formes	forméis	hayas formado	hayáis formado
forme	formen	haya formado	hayan formado
7 imperfecto de subjuntivo		**14 pluscuamperfecto de subjuntivo**	
formara	formáramos	hubiera formado	hubiéramos formado
formaras	formarais	hubieras formado	hubierais formado
formara	formaran	hubiera formado	hubieran formado
OR		OR	
formase	formásemos	hubiese formado	hubiésemos formado
formases	formaseis	hubieses formado	hubieseis formado
formase	formasen	hubiese formado	hubiesen formado

	imperativo	
—	formemos
forma; no formes	formad; no forméis
forme	formen

Words and expressions related to this verb

formativo, formativa formative
formante forming
transformar to transform
la forma form, shape
de esta forma in this way

la formación formation
formalmente formally
la formalidad formality
de forma que ... so that ...
de una forma o de otra somehow or other, one way or another

242

to wash dishes, to scrub

The Seven Simple Tenses		The Seven Compound Tenses	
Singular	Plural	Singular	Plural
1 presente de indicativo		8 perfecto de indicativo	
friego	**fregamos**	**he fregado**	**hemos fregado**
friegas	**fregáis**	**has fregado**	**habéis fregado**
friega	**friegan**	**ha fregado**	**han fregado**
2 imperfecto de indicativo		9 pluscuamperfecto de indicativo	
fregaba	**fregábamos**	**había fregado**	**habíamos fregado**
fregabas	**fregabais**	**habías fregado**	**habíais fregado**
fregaba	**fregaban**	**había fregado**	**habían fregado**
3 pretérito		10 pretérito anterior	
fregué	**fregamos**	**hube fregado**	**hubimos fregado**
fregaste	**fregasteis**	**hubiste fregado**	**hubisteis fregado**
fregó	**fregaron**	**hubo fregado**	**hubieron fregado**
4 futuro		11 futuro perfecto	
fregaré	**fregaremos**	**habré fregado**	**habremos fregado**
fregarás	**fregaréis**	**habrás fregado**	**habréis fregado**
fregará	**fregarán**	**habrá fregado**	**habrán fregado**
5 potencial simple		12 potencial compuesto	
fregaría	**fregaríamos**	**habría fregado**	**habríamos fregado**
fregarías	**fregaríais**	**habrías fregado**	**habríais fregado**
fregaría	**fregarían**	**habría fregado**	**habrían fregado**
6 presente de subjuntivo		13 perfecto de subjuntivo	
friegue	**freguemos**	**haya fregado**	**hayamos fregado**
friegues	**freguéis**	**hayas fregado**	**hayáis fregado**
friegue	**frieguen**	**haya fregado**	**hayan fregado**
7 imperfecto de subjuntivo		14 pluscuamperfecto de subjuntivo	
fregara	**fregáramos**	**hubiera fregado**	**hubiéramos fregado**
fregaras	**fregarais**	**hubieras fregado**	**hubierais fregado**
fregara	**fregaran**	**hubiera fregado**	**hubieran fregado**
OR		OR	
fregase	**fregásemos**	**hubiese fregado**	**hubiésemos fregado**
fregases	**fregaseis**	**hubieses fregado**	**hubieseis fregado**
fregase	**fregasen**	**hubiese fregado**	**hubiesen fregado**

imperativo	
—	**freguemos**
friega; no friegues	**fregad; no freguéis**
friegue	**frieguen**

Words and expressions related to this verb

el fregador   sink; dish mop, scrubbing brush
el fregadero   kitchen sink

la fregadura   scouring, mopping, scrubbing
refregar   to rub; **el refregamiento**   rubbing, scrubbing

Can't recognize an irregular verb form? Check out pages 519–523.

The subject pronouns are found on the page facing page 1.

The Seven Simple Tenses		The Seven Compound Tenses	
Singular	Plural	Singular	Plural
1 presente de indicativo		8 perfecto de indicativo	
frío	**freímos**	**he frito**	**hemos frito**
fríes	**freís**	**has frito**	**habéis frito**
fríe	**fríen**	**ha frito**	**han frito**
2 imperfecto de indicativo		9 pluscuamperfecto de indicativo	
freía	**freíamos**	**había frito**	**habíamos frito**
freías	**freíais**	**habías frito**	**habíais frito**
freía	**freían**	**había frito**	**habían frito**
3 pretérito		10 pretérito anterior	
freí	**freímos**	**hube frito**	**hubimos frito**
freíste	**freísteis**	**hubiste frito**	**hubisteis frito**
frió	**frieron**	**hubo frito**	**hubieron frito**
4 futuro		11 futuro perfecto	
freiré	**freiremos**	**habré frito**	**habremos frito**
freirás	**freiréis**	**habrás frito**	**habréis frito**
freirá	**freirán**	**habrá frito**	**habrán frito**
5 potencial simple		12 potencial compuesto	
freiría	**freiríamos**	**habría frito**	**habríamos frito**
freirías	**freiríais**	**habrías frito**	**habríais frito**
freiría	**freirían**	**habría frito**	**habrían frito**
6 presente de subjuntivo		13 perfecto de subjuntivo	
fría	**friamos**	**haya frito**	**hayamos frito**
frías	**friáis**	**hayas frito**	**hayáis frito**
fría	**frían**	**haya frito**	**hayan frito**
7 imperfecto de subjuntivo		14 pluscuamperfecto de subjuntivo	
friera	**friéramos**	**hubiera frito**	**hubiéramos frito**
frieras	**frierais**	**hubieras frito**	**hubierais frito**
friera	**frieran**	**hubiera frito**	**hubieran frito**
OR		OR	
friese	**friésemos**	**hubiese frito**	**hubiésemos frito**
frieses	**frieseis**	**hubieses frito**	**hubieseis frito**
friese	**friesen**	**hubiese frito**	**hubiesen frito**

	imperativo	
—		**friamos**
fríe; no frías		**freíd; no friáis**
fría		**frían**

Words and expressions related to this verb

patatas fritas   fried potatoes, French fries
patatas fritas a la inglesa   potato chips
las fritillas   fritters
frito, frita   fried

la fritada   fried food
la fritura   fry
el pescado frito   fried fish
los huevos fritos   fried eggs

Increase your verb power with popular phrases, words, and expressions for tourists on pages 595–618.

The Seven Simple Tenses		The Seven Compound Tenses	
Singular	Plural	Singular	Plural
1 presente de indicativo		8 perfecto de indicativo	
fumo	**fumamos**	he fumado	hemos fumado
fumas	**fumáis**	has fumado	habéis fumado
fuma	**fuman**	ha fumado	han fumado
2 imperfecto de indicativo		9 pluscuamperfecto de indicativo	
fumaba	**fumábamos**	había fumado	habíamos fumado
fumabas	**fumabais**	habías fumado	habíais fumado
fumaba	**fumaban**	había fumado	habían fumado
3 pretérito		10 pretérito anterior	
fumé	**fumamos**	hube fumado	hubimos fumado
fumaste	**fumasteis**	hubiste fumado	hubisteis fumado
fumó	**fumaron**	hubo fumado	hubieron fumado
4 futuro		11 futuro perfecto	
fumaré	**fumaremos**	habré fumado	habremos fumado
fumarás	**fumaréis**	habrás fumado	habréis fumado
fumará	**fumarán**	habrá fumado	habrán fumado
5 potencial simple		12 potencial compuesto	
fumaría	**fumaríamos**	habría fumado	habríamos fumado
fumarías	**fumaríais**	habrías fumado	habríais fumado
fumaría	**fumarían**	habría fumado	habrían fumado
6 presente de subjuntivo		13 perfecto de subjuntivo	
fume	**fumemos**	haya fumado	hayamos fumado
fumes	**fuméis**	hayas fumado	hayáis fumado
fume	**fumen**	haya fumado	hayan fumado
7 imperfecto de subjuntivo		14 pluscuamperfecto de subjuntivo	
fumara	**fumáramos**	hubiera fumado	hubiéramos fumado
fumaras	**fumarais**	hubieras fumado	hubierais fumado
fumara	**fumaran**	hubiera fumado	hubieran fumado
OR		OR	
fumase	**fumásemos**	hubiese fumado	hubiésemos fumado
fumases	**fumaseis**	hubieses fumado	hubieseis fumado
fumase	**fumasen**	hubiese fumado	hubiesen fumado

imperativo

—	**fumemos**
fuma; no fumes	**fumad; no fuméis**
fume	**fumen**

Words and expressions related to this verb

un fumador, una fumadora   smoker
una fumada, una fumarada   puff of smoke
fumar como una chimenea   to smoke like
  a chimney

un fumadero   smoking room
SE PROHIBE FUMAR   NO SMOKING
fumarse una clase   to cut (skip) a class

Fumar no es bueno para la salud/Smoking is not good for one's health.
  (see page 538, *Spanish infinitive and its principal uses*)

The subject pronouns are found on the page facing page 1.

funcionar Gerundio **funcionando** Part. pas. **funcionado**

to function, to run (machine)

The Seven Simple Tenses		The Seven Compound Tenses	
Singular	Plural	Singular	Plural
1 presente de indicativo		**8 perfecto de indicativo**	
funciono	funcionamos	he funcionado	hemos funcionado
funcionas	funcionáis	has funcionado	habéis funcionado
funciona	funcionan	ha funcionado	han funcionado
2 imperfecto de indicativo		**9 pluscuamperfecto de indicativo**	
funcionaba	funcionábamos	había funcionado	habíamos funcionado
funcionabas	funcionabais	habías funcionado	habíais funcionado
funcionaba	funcionaban	había funcionado	habían funcionado
3 pretérito		**10 pretérito anterior**	
funcioné	funcionamos	hube funcionado	hubimos funcionado
funcionaste	funcionasteis	hubiste funcionado	hubisteis funcionado
funcionó	funcionaron	hubo funcionado	hubieron funcionado
4 futuro		**11 futuro perfecto**	
funcionaré	funcionaremos	habré funcionado	habremos funcionado
funcionarás	funcionaréis	habrás funcionado	habréis funcionado
funcionará	funcionarán	habrá funcionado	habrán funcionado
5 potencial simple		**12 potencial compuesto**	
funcionaría	funcionaríamos	habría funcionado	habríamos funcionado
funcionarías	funcionaríais	habrías funcionado	habríais funcionado
funcionaría	funcionarían	habría funcionado	habrían funcionado
6 presente de subjuntivo		**13 perfecto de subjuntivo**	
funcione	funcionemos	haya funcionado	hayamos funcionado
funciones	funcionéis	hayas funcionado	hayáis funcionado
funcione	funcionen	haya funcionado	hayan funcionado
7 imperfecto de subjuntivo		**14 pluscuamperfecto de subjuntivo**	
funcionara	funcionáramos	hubiera funcionado	hubiéramos funcionado
funcionaras	funcionarais	hubieras funcionado	hubierais funcionado
funcionara	funcionaran	hubiera funcionado	hubieran funcionado
OR		OR	
funcionase	funcionásemos	hubiese funcionado	hubiésemos funcionado
funcionases	funionaseis	hubieses funcionado	hubieseis funcionado
funcionase	funcionasen	hubiese funcionado	hubiesen funcionado

	imperativo	
—		funcionemos
	funciona; no funciones	funcionad; no funcionéis
	funcione	funcionen

Words and expressions related to this verb

una función function
función de títeres puppet show
un funcionario de aduanas customs official
el funcionado, la funcionada civil servant
un funcionario público public official

> If you want to see a sample English verb fully conjugated in
> all the tenses, check out pages xviii and xix.

to earn, to gain, to win

The Seven Simple Tenses		The Seven Compound Tenses	
Singular	Plural	Singular	Plural
1 presente de indicativo		8 perfecto de indicativo	
gano	ganamos	he ganado	hemos ganado
ganas	ganáis	has ganado	habéis ganado
gana	ganan	ha ganado	han ganado
2 imperfecto de indicativo		9 pluscuamperfecto de indicativo	
ganaba	ganábamos	había ganado	habíamos ganado
ganabas	ganabais	habías ganado	habíais ganado
ganaba	ganaban	había ganado	habían ganado
3 pretérito		10 pretérito anterior	
gané	ganamos	hube ganado	hubimos ganado
ganaste	ganasteis	hubiste ganado	hubisteis ganado
ganó	ganaron	hubo ganado	hubieron ganado
4 futuro		11 futuro perfecto	
ganaré	ganaremos	habré ganado	habremos ganado
ganarás	ganaréis	habrás ganado	habréis ganado
ganará	ganarán	habrá ganado	habrán ganado
5 potencial simple		12 potencial compuesto	
ganaría	ganaríamos	habría ganado	habríamos ganado
ganarías	ganaríais	habrías ganado	habríais ganado
ganaría	ganarían	habría ganado	habrían ganado
6 presente de subjuntivo		13 perfecto de subjuntivo	
gane	ganemos	haya ganado	hayamos ganado
ganes	ganéis	hayas ganado	hayáis ganado
gane	ganen	haya ganado	hayan ganado
7 imperfecto de subjuntivo		14 pluscuamperfecto de subjuntivo	
ganara	ganáramos	hubiera ganado	hubiéramos ganado
ganaras	ganarais	hubieras ganado	hubierais ganado
ganara	ganaran	hubiera ganado	hubieran ganado
OR		OR	
ganase	ganásemos	hubiese ganado	hubiésemos ganado
ganases	ganaseis	hubieses ganado	hubieseis ganado
ganase	ganasen	hubiese ganado	hubiesen ganado

imperativo

—	ganemos
gana; no ganes	ganad; no ganéis
gane	ganen

Words and expressions related to this verb
ganar el pan, ganar la vida   to earn a living
la ganancia   profit, gain
ganador, ganadora   winner
ganar dinero   to earn (make) money
ganar a uno en inteligencia   to surpass
  someone in intelligence

desganar   to dissuade
desganarse   to lose one's appetite; to be bored
ganar el premio gordo   to win first prize
ir ganando   to be winning, to be in the lead

The subject pronouns are found on the page facing page 1.

247

to spend (money), to wear out, to waste

The Seven Simple Tenses		The Seven Compound Tenses	
Singular	Plural	Singular	Plural
1 presente de indicativo		8 perfecto de indicativo	
gasto	**gastamos**	**he gastado**	**hemos gastado**
gastas	**gastáis**	**has gastado**	**habéis gastado**
gasta	**gastan**	**ha gastado**	**han gastado**
2 imperfecto de indicativo		9 pluscuamperfecto de indicativo	
gastaba	**gastábamos**	**había gastado**	**habíamos gastado**
gastabas	**gastabais**	**habías gastado**	**habíais gastado**
gastaba	**gastaban**	**había gastado**	**habían gastado**
3 pretérito		10 pretérito anterior	
gasté	**gastamos**	**hube gastado**	**hubimos gastado**
gastaste	**gastasteis**	**hubiste gastado**	**hubisteis gastado**
gastó	**gastaron**	**hubo gastado**	**hubieron gastado**
4 futuro		11 futuro perfecto	
gastaré	**gastaremos**	**habré gastado**	**habremos gastado**
gastarás	**gastaréis**	**habrás gastado**	**habréis gastado**
gastará	**gastarán**	**habrá gastado**	**habrán gastado**
5 potencial simple		12 potencial compuesto	
gastaría	**gastaríamos**	**habría gastado**	**habríamos gastado**
gastarías	**gastaríais**	**habrías gastado**	**habríais gastado**
gastaría	**gastarían**	**habría gastado**	**habrían gastado**
6 presente de subjuntivo		13 perfecto de subjuntivo	
gaste	**gastemos**	**haya gastado**	**hayamos gastado**
gastes	**gastéis**	**hayas gastado**	**hayáis gastado**
gaste	**gasten**	**haya gastado**	**hayan gastado**
7 imperfecto de subjuntivo		14 pluscuamperfecto de subjuntivo	
gastara	**gastáramos**	**hubiera gastado**	**hubiéramos gastado**
gastaras	**gastarais**	**hubieras gastado**	**hubierais gastado**
gastara	**gastaran**	**hubiera gastado**	**hubieran gastado**
OR		OR	
gastase	**gastásemos**	**hubiese gastado**	**hubiésemos gastado**
gastases	**gastaseis**	**hubieses gastado**	**hubieseis gastado**
gastase	**gastasen**	**hubiese gastado**	**hubiesen gastado**

imperativo	
—	**gastemos**
gasta; no gastes	**gastad; no gastéis**
gaste	**gasten**

Words and expressions related to this verb
el gasto expense, expenditure
cubrir gastos to cover expenses
un gastador, una gastadora spendthrift, wasteful
pagar los gastos to foot the bill, to pay the tab
malgastar to squander, misspend, waste

gastar el tiempo to waste time
con poco gasto at little cost (expense)
el dinero para gastos menudos pocket money

See also **gastar** on page 527.

to grieve, to groan, to moan, to howl

The Seven Simple Tenses		The Seven Compound Tenses	
Singular	Plural	Singular	Plural
1 presente de indicativo		8 perfecto de indicativo	
gimo	**gemimos**	**he gemido**	**hemos gemido**
gimes	**gemís**	**has gemido**	**habéis gemido**
gime	**gimen**	**ha gemido**	**han gemido**
2 imperfecto de indicativo		9 pluscuamperfecto de indicativo	
gemía	**gemíamos**	**había gemido**	**habíamos gemido**
gemías	**gemíais**	**habías gemido**	**habíais gemido**
gemía	**gemían**	**había gemido**	**habían gemido**
3 pretérito		10 pretérito anterior	
gemí	**gemimos**	**hube gemido**	**hubimos gemido**
gemiste	**gemisteis**	**hubiste gemido**	**hubisteis gemido**
gimió	**gimieron**	**hubo gemido**	**hubieron gemido**
4 futuro		11 futuro perfecto	
gemiré	**gemiremos**	**habré gemido**	**habremos gemido**
gemirás	**gemiréis**	**habrás gemido**	**habréis gemido**
gemirá	**gemirán**	**habrá gemido**	**habrán gemido**
5 potencial simple		12 potencial compuesto	
gemiría	**gemiríamos**	**habría gemido**	**habríamos gemido**
gemirías	**gemiríais**	**habrías gemido**	**habríais gemido**
gemiría	**gemirían**	**habría gemido**	**habrían gemido**
6 presente de subjuntivo		13 perfecto de subjuntivo	
gima	**gimamos**	**haya gemido**	**hayamos gemido**
gimas	**gimáis**	**hayas gemido**	**hayáis gemido**
gima	**giman**	**haya gemido**	**hayan gemido**
7 imperfecto de subjuntivo		14 pluscuamperfecto de subjuntivo	
gimiera	**gimiéramos**	**hubiera gemido**	**hubiéramos gemido**
gimieras	**gimierais**	**hubieras gemido**	**hubierais gemido**
gimiera	**gimieran**	**hubiera gemido**	**hubieran gemido**
OR		OR	
gimiese	**gimiésemos**	**hubiese gemido**	**hubiésemos gemido**
gimieses	**gimieseis**	**hubieses gemido**	**hubieseis gemido**
gimiese	**gimiesen**	**hubiese gemido**	**hubiesen gemido**

imperativo

—	**gimamos**
gime; no gimas	**gemid; no gimáis**
gima	**giman**

Words related to this verb

gemidor, gemidora   lamenter, griever   **gemiquear**   to whine, to blubber
el gemido   lamentation, howl, groan, moan   **el gemiqueo**   whining, blubbering

Don't miss the definitions of basic grammatical terms with examples
in English and Spanish on pages 666–677.

The subject pronouns are found on the page facing page 1.   **249**

gobernar

Gerundio **gobernando**   Part. pas. **gobernado**

to govern, to rule

The Seven Simple Tenses		The Seven Compound Tenses	
Singular	Plural	Singular	Plural
1 presente de indicativo		**8 perfecto de indicativo**	
gobierno	gobernamos	he gobernado	hemos gobernado
gobiernas	gobernáis	has gobernado	habéis gobernado
gobierna	gobiernan	ha gobernado	han gobernado
2 imperfecto de indicativo		**9 pluscuamperfecto de indicativo**	
gobernaba	gobernábamos	había gobernado	habíamos gobernado
gobernabas	gobernabais	habías gobernado	habíais gobernado
gobernaba	gobernaban	había gobernado	habían gobernado
3 pretérito		**10 pretérito anterior**	
goberné	gobernamos	hube gobernado	hubimos gobernado
gobernaste	gobernasteis	hubiste gobernado	hubisteis gobernado
gobernó	gobernaron	hubo gobernado	hubieron gobernado
4 futuro		**11 futuro perfecto**	
gobernaré	gobernaremos	habré gobernado	habremos gobernado
gobernarás	gobernaréis	habrás gobernado	habréis gobernado
gobernará	gobernarán	habrá gobernado	habrán gobernado
5 potencial simple		**12 potencial compuesto**	
gobernaría	gobernaríamos	habría gobernado	habríamos gobernado
gobernarías	gobernaríais	habrías gobernado	habríais gobernado
gobernaría	gobernarían	habría gobernado	habrían gobernado
6 presente de subjuntivo		**13 perfecto de subjuntivo**	
gobierne	gobernemos	haya gobernado	hayamos gobernado
gobiernes	gobernéis	hayas gobernado	hayáis gobernado
gobierne	gobiernen	haya gobernado	hayan gobernado
7 imperfecto de subjuntivo		**14 pluscuamperfecto de subjuntivo**	
gobernara	gobernáramos	hubiera gobernado	hubiéramos gobernado
gobernaras	gobernarais	hubieras gobernado	hubierais gobernado
gobernara	gobernaran	hubiera gobernado	hubieran gobernado
OR		OR	
gobernase	gobernásemos	hubiese gobernado	hubiésemos gobernado
gobernases	gobernaseis	hubieses gobernado	hubieseis gobernado
gobernase	gobernasen	hubiese gobernado	hubiesen gobernado

imperativo	
—	gobernemos
gobierna; no gobiernes	gobernad; no gobernéis
gobierne	gobiernen

Words and expressions related to this verb

un gobernador, una gobernadora governor
el gobierno government
el gobierno central central government
el gobierno de la casa home management, housekeeping

un gobierno fantoche puppet government
la gobernación governing
el gobierno parlamentario parliamentary government
el gobierno militar military government

The Seven Simple Tenses		The Seven Compound Tenses	
Singular	Plural	Singular	Plural
1 presente de indicativo		8 perfecto de indicativo	
gozo	gozamos	he gozado	hemos gozado
gozas	gozáis	has gozado	habéis gozado
goza	gozan	ha gozado	han gozado
2 imperfecto de indicativo		9 pluscuamperfecto de indicativo	
gozaba	gozábamos	había gozado	habíamos gozado
gozabas	gozabais	habías gozado	habíais gozado
gozaba	gozaban	había gozado	habían gozado
3 pretérito		10 pretérito anterior	
gocé	gozamos	hube gozado	hubimos gozado
gozaste	gozasteis	hubiste gozado	hubisteis gozado
gozó	gozaron	hubo gozado	hubieron gozado
4 futuro		11 futuro perfecto	
gozaré	gozaremos	habré gozado	habremos gozado
gozarás	gozaréis	habrás gozado	habréis gozado
gozará	gozarán	habrá gozado	habrán gozado
5 potencial simple		12 potencial compuesto	
gozaría	gozaríamos	habría gozado	habríamos gozado
gozarías	gozaríais	habrías gozado	habríais gozado
gozaría	gozarían	habría gozado	habrían gozado
6 presente de subjuntivo		13 perfecto de subjuntivo	
goce	gocemos	haya gozado	hayamos gozado
goces	gocéis	hayas gozado	hayáis gozado
goce	gocen	haya gozado	hayan gozado
7 imperfecto de subjuntivo		14 pluscuamperfecto de subjuntivo	
gozara	gozáramos	hubiera gozado	hubiéramos gozado
gozaras	gozarais	hubieras gozado	hubierais gozado
gozara	gozaran	hubiera gozado	hubieran gozado
OR		OR	
gozase	gozásemos	hubiese gozado	hubiésemos gozado
gozases	gozaseis	hubieses gozado	hubieseis gozado
gozase	gozasen	hubiese gozado	hubiesen gozado

	imperativo	
—		gocemos
goza; no goces		gozad; no gocéis
goce		gocen

Words and expressions related to this verb

el goce   enjoyment
gozador, gozadora, gozante   enjoyer
el gozo   joy, pleasure
saltar de gozo   to jump with joy
gozosamente   joyfully

gozarla   to have a good time
gozar de buena salud   to enjoy good health
gozoso, gozosa   joyful

to shout, to scream, to shriek, to cry out

The Seven Simple Tenses		The Seven Compound Tenses	
Singular	Plural	Singular	Plural
1 presente de indicativo		8 perfecto de indicativo	
grito	gritamos	he gritado	hemos gritado
gritas	gritáis	has gritado	habéis gritado
grita	gritan	ha gritado	han gritado
2 imperfecto de indicativo		9 pluscuamperfecto de indicativo	
gritaba	gritábamos	había gritado	habíamos gritado
gritabas	gritabais	habías gritado	habíais gritado
gritaba	gritaban	había gritado	habían gritado
3 pretérito		10 pretérito anterior	
grité	gritamos	hube gritado	hubimos gritado
gritaste	gritasteis	hubiste gritado	hubisteis gritado
gritó	gritaron	hubo gritado	hubieron gritado
4 futuro		11 futuro perfecto	
gritaré	gritaremos	habré gritado	habremos gritado
gritarás	gritaréis	habrás gritado	habréis gritado
gritará	gritarán	habrá gritado	habrán gritado
5 potencial simple		12 potencial compuesto	
gritaría	gritaríamos	habría gritado	habríamos gritado
gritarías	gritaríais	habrías gritado	habríais gritado
gritaría	gritarían	habría gritado	habrían gritado
6 presente de subjuntivo		13 perfecto de subjuntivo	
grite	gritemos	haya gritado	hayamos gritado
grites	gritéis	hayas gritado	hayáis gritado
grite	griten	haya gritado	hayan gritado
7 imperfecto de subjuntivo		14 pluscuamperfecto de subjuntivo	
gritara	gritáramos	hubiera gritado	hubiéramos gritado
gritaras	gritarais	hubieras gritado	hubierais gritado
gritara	gritaran	hubiera gritado	hubieran gritado
OR		OR	
gritase	gritásemos	hubiese gritado	hubiésemos gritado
gritases	gritaseis	hubieses gritado	hubieseis gritado
gritase	gritasen	hubiese gritado	hubiesen gritado

	imperativo
—	gritemos
grita; no grites	gritad; no gritéis
grite	griten

Words and expressions related to this verb

el grito   cry, scream, shout

a gritos   at the top of one's voice, loudly

la grita, la gritería   outcry, shouting

un gritón, una gritona   screamer

dar grita a   to hoot at

gritar a un actor   to boo an actor

Increase your verb power with popular phrases, words,
and expressions for tourists on pages 595–618.

to grumble, to grunt, to growl, to creak

The Seven Simple Tenses		The Seven Compound Tenses	
Singular	Plural	Singular	Plural
1 presente de indicativo		8 perfecto de indicativo	
gruño	**gruñimos**	**he gruñido**	**hemos gruñido**
gruñes	**gruñís**	**has gruñido**	**habéis gruñido**
gruñe	**gruñen**	**ha gruñido**	**han gruñido**
2 imperfecto de indicativo		9 pluscuamperfecto de indicativo	
gruñía	**gruñíamos**	**había gruñido**	**habíamos gruñido**
gruñías	**gruñíais**	**habías gruñido**	**habíais gruñido**
gruñía	**gruñían**	**había gruñido**	**habían gruñido**
3 pretérito		10 pretérito anterior	
gruñí	**gruñimos**	**hube gruñido**	**hubimos gruñido**
gruñiste	**gruñisteis**	**hubiste gruñido**	**hubisteis gruñido**
gruñó	**gruñeron**	**hubo gruñido**	**hubieron gruñido**
4 futuro		11 futuro perfecto	
gruñiré	**gruñiremos**	**habré gruñido**	**habremos gruñido**
gruñirás	**gruñiréis**	**habrás gruñido**	**habréis gruñido**
gruñirá	**gruñirán**	**habrá gruñido**	**habrán gruñido**
5 potencial simple		12 potencial compuesto	
gruñiría	**gruñiríamos**	**habría gruñido**	**habríamos gruñido**
gruñirías	**gruñiríais**	**habrías gruñido**	**habríais gruñido**
gruñiría	**gruñirían**	**habría gruñido**	**habrían gruñido**
6 presente de subjuntivo		13 perfecto de subjuntivo	
gruña	**gruñamos**	**haya gruñido**	**hayamos gruñido**
gruñas	**gruñáis**	**hayas gruñido**	**hayáis gruñido**
gruña	**gruñan**	**haya gruñido**	**hayan gruñido**
7 imperfecto de subjuntivo		14 pluscuamperfecto de subjuntivo	
gruñera	**gruñéramos**	**hubiera gruñido**	**hubiéramos gruñido**
gruñeras	**gruñerais**	**hubieras gruñido**	**hubierais gruñido**
gruñera	**gruñeran**	**hubiera gruñido**	**hubieran gruñido**
OR		OR	
gruñese	**gruñésemos**	**hubiese gruñido**	**hubiésemos gruñido**
gruñeses	**gruñeseis**	**hubieses gruñido**	**hubieseis gruñido**
gruñese	**gruñesen**	**hubiese gruñido**	**hubiesen gruñido**

	imperativo	
—	**gruñamos**	
gruñe; no gruñas	**gruñid; no gruñáis**	
gruña	**gruñan**	

Words related to this verb
gruñón, gruñona   cranky, grumpy, grouchy
el gruñido, el gruñimiento   grunting, grunt, growling, growl
gruñidor, gruñidora   growler, grumbler

Use the EE-zee guide to Spanish pronunciation on pages 562 and 563.

The subject pronouns are found on the page facing page 1.

guiar

Gerundio **guiando**　　　Part. pas. **guiado**

to lead, to guide

The Seven Simple Tenses		The Seven Compound Tenses	
Singular	Plural	Singular	Plural
1　presente de indicativo		**8　perfecto de indicativo**	
guío	guiamos	he guiado	hemos guiado
guías	guiáis	has guiado	habéis guiado
guía	guían	ha guiado	han guiado
2　imperfecto de indicativo		**9　pluscuamperfecto de indicativo**	
guiaba	guiábamos	había guiado	habíamos guiado
guiabas	guiabais	habías guiado	habíais guiado
guiaba	guiaban	había guiado	habían guiado
3　pretérito		**10　pretérito anterior**	
guié	guiamos	hube guiado	hubimos guiado
guiaste	guiasteis	hubiste guiado	hubisteis guiado
guió	guiaron	hubo guiado	hubieron guiado
4　futuro		**11　futuro perfecto**	
guiaré	guiaremos	habré guiado	habremos guiado
guiarás	guiaréis	habrás guiado	habréis guiado
guiará	guiarán	habrá guiado	habrán guiado
5　potencial simple		**12　potencial compuesto**	
guiaría	guiaríamos	habría guiado	habríamos guiado
guiarías	guiaríais	habrías guiado	habríais guiado
guiaría	guiarían	habría guiado	habrían guiado
6　presente de subjuntivo		**13　perfecto de subjuntivo**	
guíe	guiemos	haya guiado	hayamos guiado
guíes	guiéis	hayas guiado	hayáis guiado
guíe	guíen	haya guiado	hayan guiado
7　imperfecto de subjuntivo		**14　pluscuamperfecto de subjuntivo**	
guiara	guiáramos	hubiera guiado	hubiéramos guiado
guiaras	guiarais	hubieras guiado	hubierais guiado
guiara	guiaran	hubiera guiado	hubieran guiado
OR		OR	
guiase	guiásemos	hubiese guiado	hubiésemos guiado
guiases	guiaseis	hubieses guiado	hubieseis guiado
guiase	guiasen	hubiese guiado	hubiesen guiado

imperativo	
—	guiemos
guía; no guíes	guiad; no guiéis
guíe	guíen

Words and expressions related to this verb

el guía　guide, leader
la guía　guidebook
guiarse por　to be guided by, to be governed by
guiar a alguien en los estudios　to guide
　(direct) someone in studies

la guía de teléfonos　telephone directory
la guía de bicicleta　handlebar of a bicycle
la guía turística　tourist guidebook

254

Use the EE-zee guide to Spanish pronunciation on pages 562 and 563.

The Seven Simple Tenses		The Seven Compound Tenses	
Singular	Plural	Singular	Plural
1 presente de indicativo		8 perfecto de indicativo	
gusta	**gustan**	**ha gustado**	**han gustado**
2 imperfecto de indicativo		9 pluscuamperfecto de indicativo	
gustaba	**gustaban**	**había gustado**	**habían gustado**
3 pretérito		10 pretérito anterior	
gustó	**gustaron**	**hubo gustado**	**hubieron gustado**
4 futuro		11 futuro perfecto	
gustará	**gustarán**	**habrá gustado**	**habrán gustado**
5 potencial simple		12 potencial compuesto	
gustaría	**gustarían**	**habría gustado**	**habrían gustado**
6 presente de subjuntivo		13 perfecto de subjuntivo	
que guste	**que gusten**	**que haya gustado**	**que hayan gustado**
7 imperfecto de subjuntivo		14 pluscuamperfecto de subjuntivo	
que gustara	**que gustaran**	**que hubiera gustado**	**que hubieran gustado**
OR		OR	
que gustase	**que gustasen**	**que hubiese gustado**	**que hubiesen gustado**

imperativo

¡Que guste!   **¡Que gusten!**

Sentences using this verb and words and expressions related to it

Me gusta el café.   I like coffee.
  Me gustan la leche y el café.   I like milk and coffee.
  A María le gustan los dulces.   Mary likes candy.
  A José y a Elena les gustan los deportes.   Joseph and Helen like sports.

el gusto   taste, pleasure, liking   **dar gusto**   to please
gustoso, gustosa   tasty, pleasing   **tener gusto en**   to be glad to

This verb is commonly used in the third person singular or plural, as in the above examples. See also **gustar** on page 528. Consult pages 524–537 for more verbs used in idiomatic expressions.

haber

Gerundio **habiendo**   Part. pas. **habido**

to have (as an auxiliary, helping verb to form the compound tenses)

The Seven Simple Tenses		The Seven Compound Tenses	
Singular	Plural	Singular	Plural
1 presente de indicativo		8 perfecto de indicativo	
he	hemos	he habido	hemos habido
has	habéis	has habido	habéis habido
ha	han	ha habido	han habido
2 imperfecto de indicativo		9 pluscuamperfecto de indicativo	
había	habíamos	había habido	habíamos habido
habías	habíais	habías habido	habíais habido
había	habían	había habido	habían habido
3 pretérito		10 pretérito anterior	
hube	hubimos	hube habido	hubimos habido
hubiste	hubisteis	hubiste habido	hubisteis habido
hubo	hubieron	hubo habido	hubieron habido
4 futuro		11 futuro perfecto	
habré	habremos	habré habido	habremos habido
habrás	habréis	habrás habido	habréis habido
habrá	habrán	habrá habido	habrán habido
5 potencial simple		12 potencial compuesto	
habría	habríamos	habría habido	habríamos habido
habrías	habríais	habrías habido	habríais habido
habría	habrían	habría habido	habrían habido
6 presente de subjuntivo		13 perfecto de subjuntivo	
haya	hayamos	haya habido	hayamos habido
hayas	hayáis	hayas habido	hayáis habido
haya	hayan	haya habido	hayan habido
7 imperfecto de subjuntivo		14 pluscuamperfecto de subjuntivo	
hubiera	hubiéramos	hubiera habido	hubiéramos habido
hubieras	hubierais	hubieras habido	hubierais habido
hubiera	hubieran	hubiera habido	hubieran habido
OR		OR	
hubiese	hubiésemos	hubiese habido	hubiésemos habido
hubieses	hubieseis	hubieses habido	hubieseis habido
hubiese	hubiesen	hubiese habido	hubiesen habido

imperativo

—	hayamos
hé; no hayas	habed; no hayáis
haya	hayan

Words and expressions related to this verb

el haber   credit (in bookkeeping); **hay . . .**   there is . . ., there are . . .

los haberes   assets, possessions, property; **He aquí la verdad.**   Here is the truth.

habérselas con alguien   to have a showdown with someone; **No hay de qué.**   You're welcome.

See also **haber** on pages 528 and 529.

Want to learn more idiomatic expressions that contain verbs? Check out pages 524–537.

to inhabit, to dwell, to live, to reside

The Seven Simple Tenses		The Seven Compound Tenses	
Singular	Plural	Singular	Plural
1　presente de indicativo		8　perfecto de indicativo	
habito	habitamos	he habitado	hemos habitado
habitas	habitáis	has habitado	habéis habitado
habita	habitan	ha habitado	han habitado
2　imperfecto de indicativo		9　pluscuamperfecto de indicativo	
habitaba	habitábamos	había habitado	habíamos habitado
habitabas	habitabais	habías habitado	habíais habitado
habitaba	habitaban	había habitado	habían habitado
3　pretérito		10　pretérito anterior	
habité	habitamos	hube habitado	hubimos habitado
habitaste	habitasteis	hubiste habitado	hubisteis habitado
habitó	habitaron	hubo habitado	hubieron habitado
4　futuro		11　futuro perfecto	
habitaré	habitaremos	habré habitado	habremos habitado
habitarás	habitaréis	habrás habitado	habréis habitado
habitará	habitarán	habrá habitado	habrán habitado
5　potencial simple		12　potencial compuesto	
habitaría	habitaríamos	habría habitado	habríamos habitado
habitarías	habitaríais	habrías habitado	habríais habitado
habitaría	habitarían	habría habitado	habrían habitado
6　presente de subjuntivo		13　perfecto de subjuntivo	
habite	habitemos	haya habitado	hayamos habitado
habites	habitéis	hayas habitado	hayáis habitado
habite	habiten	haya habitado	hayan habitado
7　imperfecto de subjuntivo		14　pluscuamperfecto de subjuntivo	
habitara	habitáramos	hubiera habitado	hubiéramos habitado
habitaras	habitarais	hubieras habitado	hubierais habitado
habitara	habitaran	hubiera habitado	hubieran habitado
OR		OR	
habitase	habitásemos	hubiese habitado	hubiésemos habitado
habitases	habitaseis	hubieses habitado	hubieseis habitado
habitase	habitasen	hubiese habitado	hubiesen habitado

imperativo	
—	habitemos
habita; no habites	habitad; no habitéis
habite	habiten

Words related to this verb
la habitación　habitation, residence, dwelling, abode
habitador, habitadora　inhabitant
la habitabilidad　habitability
el, la habitante　inhabitant

la habitación individual　single room
la habitación doble　double room
el piso con tres habitaciones　apartment
　with three rooms

Get your feet wet with verbs used in weather expressions on page 540.

The subject pronouns are found on the page facing page 1.

hablar

Gerundio **hablando**   Part. pas. **hablado**

to talk, to speak

The Seven Simple Tenses		The Seven Compound Tenses	
Singular	Plural	Singular	Plural
1 presente de indicativo		**8 perfecto de indicativo**	
hablo	hablamos	he hablado	hemos hablado
hablas	habláis	has hablado	habéis hablado
habla	hablan	ha hablado	han hablado
2 imperfecto de indicativo		**9 pluscuamperfecto de indicativo**	
hablaba	hablábamos	había hablado	habíamos hablado
hablabas	hablabais	habías hablado	habíais hablado
hablaba	hablaban	había hablado	habían hablado
3 pretérito		**10 pretérito anterior**	
hablé	hablamos	hube hablado	hubimos hablado
hablaste	hablasteis	hubiste hablado	hubisteis hablado
habló	hablaron	hubo hablado	hubieron hablado
4 futuro		**11 futuro perfecto**	
hablaré	hablaremos	habré hablado	habremos hablado
hablarás	hablaréis	habrás hablado	habréis hablado
hablará	hablarán	habrá hablado	habrán hablado
5 potencial simple		**12 potencial compuesto**	
hablaría	hablaríamos	habría hablado	habríamos hablado
hablarías	hablaríais	habrías hablado	habríais hablado
hablaría	hablarían	habría hablado	habrían hablado
6 presente de subjuntivo		**13 perfecto de subjuntivo**	
hable	hablemos	haya hablado	hayamos hablado
hables	habléis	hayas hablado	hayáis hablado
hable	hablen	haya hablado	hayan hablado
7 imperfecto de subjuntivo		**14 pluscuamperfecto de subjuntivo**	
hablara	habláramos	hubiera hablado	hubiéramos hablado
hablaras	hablarais	hubieras hablado	hubierais hablado
hablara	hablaran	hubiera hablado	hubieran hablado
OR		OR	
hablase	hablásemos	hubiese hablado	hubiésemos hablado
hablases	hablaseis	hubieses hablado	hubieseis hablado
hablase	hablasen	hubiese hablado	hubiesen hablado

	imperativo	
—		hablemos
habla; no hables		hablad; no habléis
hable		hablen

Words and expressions related to this verb

hablador, habladora   talkative, chatterbox
hablar a gritos   to shout
hablar entre dientes   to mumble
de habla inglesa   English-speaking
hablar al oído   to whisper in one's ear

la habladuría   gossip, idle rumor
de habla española   Spanish-speaking
hispanohablante   Spanish-speaking
Aquí se habla español.   Spanish is spoken here.

Enjoy verbs in Spanish proverbs on page 539.

The Seven Simple Tenses		The Seven Compound Tenses	
Singular	Plural	Singular	Plural
1 presente de indicativo		8 perfecto de indicativo	
hago	**hacemos**	**he hecho**	**hemos hecho**
haces	**hacéis**	**has hecho**	**habéis hecho**
hace	**hacen**	**ha hecho**	**han hecho**
2 imperfecto de indicativo		9 pluscuamperfecto de indicativo	
hacía	**hacíamos**	**había hecho**	**habíamos hecho**
hacías	**hacíais**	**habías hecho**	**habíais hecho**
hacía	**hacían**	**había hecho**	**habían hecho**
3 pretérito		10 pretérito anterior	
hice	**hicimos**	**hube hecho**	**hubimos hecho**
hiciste	**hicisteis**	**hubiste hecho**	**hubisteis hecho**
hizo	**hicieron**	**hubo hecho**	**hubieron hecho**
4 futuro		11 futuro perfecto	
haré	**haremos**	**habré hecho**	**habremos hecho**
harás	**haréis**	**habrás hecho**	**habréis hecho**
hará	**harán**	**habrá hecho**	**habrán hecho**
5 potencial simple		12 potencial compuesto	
haría	**haríamos**	**habría hecho**	**habríamos hecho**
harías	**haríais**	**habrías hecho**	**habríais hecho**
haría	**harían**	**habría hecho**	**habrían hecho**
6 presente de subjuntivo		13 perfecto de subjuntivo	
haga	**hagamos**	**haya hecho**	**hayamos hecho**
hagas	**hagáis**	**hayas hecho**	**hayáis hecho**
haga	**hagan**	**haya hecho**	**hayan hecho**
7 imperfecto de subjuntivo		14 pluscuamperfecto de subjuntivo	
hiciera	**hiciéramos**	**hubiera hecho**	**hubiéramos hecho**
hicieras	**hicierais**	**hubieras hecho**	**hubierais hecho**
hiciera	**hicieran**	**hubiera hecho**	**hubieran hecho**
OR		OR	
hiciese	**hiciésemos**	**hubiese hecho**	**hubiésemos hecho**
hicieses	**hicieseis**	**hubieses hecho**	**hubieseis hecho**
hiciese	**hiciesen**	**hubiese hecho**	**hubiesen hecho**

imperativo

—	**hagamos**
haz; no hagas	**haced; no hagáis**
haga	**hagan**

Common idiomatic expressions using this verb

Dicho y hecho.   No sooner said than done.

La práctica hace maestro al novicio.   Practice makes perfect.

Si a Roma fueres, haz como vieres.   When in Rome do as the Romans do. [Note that it is not uncommon to use the future subjunctive in proverbs, as in *fueres* (**ir** or **ser**) and *vieres* (**ver**); see page xxxvii.] See also **hacer** on pages 530, 531, and 533.

Consult pages 524–537 for verbs used in idiomatic expressions.

The subject pronouns are found on the page facing page 1.

hallar

Gerundio hallando   Part. pas. **hallado**

to find, to discover, to locate

The Seven Simple Tenses		The Seven Compound Tenses	
Singular	Plural	Singular	Plural
1 presente de indicativo		8 perfecto de indicativo	
hallo	hallamos	he hallado	hemos hallado
hallas	halláis	has hallado	habéis hallado
halla	hallan	ha hallado	han hallado
2 imperfecto de indicativo		9 pluscuamperfecto de indicativo	
hallaba	hallábamos	había hallado	habíamos hallado
hallabas	hallabais	habías hallado	habíais hallado
hallaba	hallaban	había hallado	habían hallado
3 pretérito		10 pretérito anterior	
hallé	hallamos	hube hallado	hubimos hallado
hallaste	hallasteis	hubiste hallado	hubisteis hallado
halló	hallaron	hubo hallado	hubieron hallado
4 futuro		11 futuro perfecto	
hallaré	hallaremos	habré hallado	habremos hallado
hallarás	hallaréis	habrás hallado	habréis hallado
hallará	hallarán	habrá hallado	habrán hallado
5 potencial simple		12 potencial compuesto	
hallaría	hallaríamos	habría hallado	habríamos hallado
hallarías	hallaríais	habrías hallado	habríais hallado
hallaría	hallarían	habría hallado	habrían hallado
6 presente de subjuntivo		13 perfecto de subjuntivo	
halle	hallemos	haya hallado	hayamos hallado
halles	halléis	hayas hallado	hayáis hallado
halle	hallen	haya hallado	hayan hallado
7 imperfecto de subjuntivo		14 pluscuamperfecto de subjuntivo	
hallara	halláramos	hubiera hallado	hubiéramos hallado
hallaras	hallarais	hubieras hallado	hubierais hallado
hallara	hallaran	hubiera hallado	hubieran hallado
OR		OR	
hallase	hallásemos	hubiese hallado	hubiésemos hallado
hallases	hallaseis	hubieses hallado	hubieseis hallado
hallase	hallasen	hubiese hallado	hubiesen hallado

	imperativo	
—	hallemos
halla; no halles	hallad; no halléis
halle	hallen

Words and expressions related to this verb

hallar bien con   to be well pleased with
un hallazgo   a find, something found
hallador, halladora   discoverer, finder

la hallada   discovery, find
bien hallado   at ease
mal hallado   uneasy, ill at ease

Learn more verbs in 30 practical situations for tourists on pages 564–594.

The Seven Simple Tenses	The Seven Compound Tenses
Singular Plural	Singular Plural
1 presente de indicativo	8 perfecto de indicativo
hiela	**ha helado**
OR	
está helando	
2 imperfecto de indicativo	9 pluscuamperfecto de indicativo
helaba	**había helado**
OR	
estaba helando	
3 pretérito	10 pretérito anterior
heló	**hubo helado**
4 futuro	11 futuro perfecto
helará	**habrá helado**
5 potencial simple	12 potencial compuesto
helaría	**habría helado**
6 presente de subjuntivo	13 perfecto de subjuntivo
hiele	**haya helado**
7 imperfecto de subjuntivo	14 pluscuamperfecto de subjuntivo
helara	**hubiera helado**
OR	OR
helase	**hubiese helado**

imperativo
¡Que hiele! (Let it freeze!)

Words and expressions related to this verb

la helada   frost (**helada blanca**/hoarfrost)
el hielo   ice
el helado   ice cream; sherbet (**el sorbete**)
la heladería   ice cream shop

la heladora   ice cream machine
el heladero   ice cream man (ice cream vendor)
romper el hielo   to break the ice

This verb is presented here in the third person singular referring to the weather. It can be used as a personal verb in the three persons of the singular and plural. The verb is then conjugated like a regular **-ar** type verb. Remember that when the vowel **e** in the stem is stressed, it changes to **ie**, as in the verb **pensar** among the 501 verbs in this book.

For other verbs used in weather expressions, see page 540.

heredar

Gerundio heredando   Part. pas. **heredado**

to inherit

The Seven Simple Tenses		The Seven Compound Tenses	
Singular	Plural	Singular	Plural
1 presente de indicativo		**8 perfecto de indicativo**	
heredo	heredamos	he heredado	hemos heredado
heredas	heredáis	has heredado	habéis heredado
hereda	heredan	ha heredado	han heredado
2 imperfecto de indicativo		**9 pluscuamperfecto de indicativo**	
heredaba	heredábamos	había heredado	habíamos heredado
heredabas	heredabais	habías heredado	habíais heredado
heredaba	heredaban	había heredado	habían heredado
3 pretérito		**10 pretérito anterior**	
heredé	heredamos	hube heredado	hubimos heredado
heredaste	heredasteis	hubiste heredado	hubisteis heredado
heredó	heredaron	hubo heredado	hubieron heredado
4 futuro		**11 futuro perfecto**	
heredaré	heredaremos	habré heredado	habremos heredado
heredarás	heredaréis	habrás heredado	habréis heredado
heredará	heredarán	habrá heredado	habrán heredado
5 potencial simple		**12 potencial compuesto**	
heredaría	heredaríamos	habría heredado	habríamos heredado
heredarías	heredaríais	habrías heredado	habríais heredado
heredaría	heredarían	habría heredado	habrían heredado
6 presente de subjuntivo		**13 perfecto de subjuntivo**	
herede	heredemos	haya heredado	hayamos heredado
heredes	heredéis	hayas heredado	hayáis heredado
herede	hereden	haya heredado	hayan heredado
7 imperfecto de subjuntivo		**14 pluscuamperfecto de subjuntivo**	
heredara	heredáramos	hubiera heredado	hubiéramos heredado
heredaras	heredarais	hubieras heredado	hubierais heredado
heredara	heredaran	hubiera heredado	hubieran heredado
OR		OR	
heredase	heredásemos	hubiese heredado	hubiésemos heredado
heredases	heredaseis	hubieses heredado	hubieseis heredado
heredase	heredasen	hubiese heredado	hubiesen heredado

	imperativo	
—		heredemos
hereda; no heredes		heredad; no heredéis
herede		hereden

Words and expressions related to this verb

el heredero heir; **la heredera** heiress
heredable inheritable
hereditario, hereditaria hereditary
la herencia inheritance

la enfermedad hereditaria hereditary disease
heredar una fortuna de sus padres to inherit
a fortune from one's parents

to harm, to hurt, to wound

The Seven Simple Tenses		The Seven Compound Tenses	
Singular	Plural	Singular	Plural
1 presente de indicativo		8 perfecto de indicativo	
hiero	**herimos**	**he herido**	**hemos herido**
hieres	**herís**	**has herido**	**habéis herido**
hiere	**hieren**	**ha herido**	**han herido**
2 imperfecto de indicativo		9 pluscuamperfecto de indicativo	
hería	**heríamos**	**había herido**	**habíamos herido**
herías	**heríais**	**habías herido**	**habíais herido**
hería	**herían**	**había herido**	**habían herido**
3 pretérito		10 pretérito anterior	
herí	**herimos**	**hube herido**	**hubimos herido**
heriste	**heristeis**	**hubiste herido**	**hubisteis herido**
hirió	**hirieron**	**hubo herido**	**hubieron herido**
4 futuro		11 futuro perfecto	
heriré	**heriremos**	**habré herido**	**habremos herido**
herirás	**heriréis**	**habrás herido**	**habréis herido**
herirá	**herirán**	**habrá herido**	**habrán herido**
5 potencial simple		12 potencial compuesto	
heriría	**heriríamos**	**habría herido**	**habríamos herido**
herirías	**heriríais**	**habrías herido**	**habríais herido**
heriría	**herirían**	**habría herido**	**habrían herido**
6 presente de subjuntivo		13 perfecto de subjuntivo	
hiera	**hiramos**	**haya herido**	**hayamos herido**
hieras	**hiráis**	**hayas herido**	**hayáis herido**
hiera	**hieran**	**haya herido**	**hayan herido**
7 imperfecto de subjuntivo		14 pluscuamperfecto de subjuntivo	
hiriera	**hiriéramos**	**hubiera herido**	**hubiéramos herido**
hirieras	**hirierais**	**hubieras herido**	**hubierais herido**
hiriera	**hirieran**	**hubiera herido**	**hubieran herido**
OR		OR	
hiriese	**hiriésemos**	**hubiese herido**	**hubiésemos herido**
hirieses	**hirieseis**	**hubieses herido**	**hubieseis herido**
hiriese	**hiriesen**	**hubiese herido**	**hubiesen herido**

imperativo

—	**hiramos**
hiere; no hieras	**herid; no hiráis**
hiera	**hieran**

Words and expressions related to this verb
la herida wound
mal herido, mal herida seriously wounded

una herida abierta open wound
a grito herido in loud cries

Can't recognize an irregular verb form? Check out pages 519–523.

The subject pronouns are found on the page facing page 1.

huir

Gerundio **huyendo**   Part. pas. **huido**

to escape, to flee, to run away, to slip away

The Seven Simple Tenses		The Seven Compound Tenses	
Singular	Plural	Singular	Plural
1 presente de indicativo		**8 perfecto de indicativo**	
huyo	huimos	he huido	hemos huido
huyes	huís	has huido	habéis huido
huye	huyen	ha huido	han huido
2 imperfecto de indicativo		**9 pluscuamperfecto de indicativo**	
huía	huíamos	había huido	habíamos huido
huías	huíais	habías huido	habíais huido
huía	huían	había huido	habían huido
3 pretérito		**10 pretérito anterior**	
huí	huimos	hube huido	hubimos huido
huiste	huisteis	hubiste huido	hubisteis huido
huyó	huyeron	hubo huido	hubieron huido
4 futuro		**11 futuro perfecto**	
huiré	huiremos	habré huido	habremos huido
huirás	huiréis	habrás huido	habréis huido
huirá	huirán	habrá huido	habrán huido
5 potencial simple		**12 potencial compuesto**	
huiría	huiríamos	habría huido	habríamos huido
huirías	huiríais	habrías huido	habríais huido
huiría	huirían	habría huido	habrían huido
6 presente de subjuntivo		**13 perfecto de subjuntivo**	
huya	huyamos	haya huido	hayamos huido
huyas	huyáis	hayas huido	hayáis huido
huya	huyan	haya huido	hayan huido
7 imperfecto de subjuntivo		**14 pluscuamperfecto de subjuntivo**	
huyera	huyéramos	hubiera huido	hubiéramos huido
huyeras	huyerais	hubieras huido	hubierais huido
huyera	huyeran	hubiera huido	hubieran huido
OR		OR	
huyese	huyésemos	hubiese huido	hubiésemos huido
huyeses	huyeseis	hubieses huido	hubieseis huido
huyese	huyesen	hubiese huido	hubiesen huido

	imperativo	
—		huyamos
huye; no huyas		huid; no huyáis
huya		huyan

Words and expressions related to this verb

huir de to keep away from
la huida escape, flight
huidizo, huidiza fugitive, evasive
huir del vicio to flee from vice

huidor, huidora fleeing, fugitive
rehuir to avoid, refuse, shun (**yo rehúyo**)
¡Huye! Run! Flee!
¡Cómo huyen las horas! How time flies!
(**las horas**/the hours)

to be ignorant of, not to know

The Seven Simple Tenses		The Seven Compound Tenses	
Singular	Plural	Singular	Plural
1 presente de indicativo		8 perfecto de indicativo	
ignoro	ignoramos	he ignorado	hemos ignorado
ignoras	ignoráis	has ignorado	habéis ignorado
ignora	ignoran	ha ignorado	han ignorado
2 imperfecto de indicativo		9 pluscuamperfecto de indicativo	
ignoraba	ignorábamos	había ignorado	habíamos ignorado
ignorabas	ignorabais	habías ignorado	habíais ignorado
ignoraba	ignoraban	había ignorado	habían ignorado
3 pretérito		10 pretérito anterior	
ignoré	ignoramos	hube ignorado	hubimos ignorado
ignoraste	ignorasteis	hubiste ignorado	hubisteis ignorado
ignoró	ignoraron	hubo ignorado	hubieron ignorado
4 futuro		11 futuro perfecto	
ignoraré	ignoraremos	habré ignorado	habremos ignorado
ignorarás	ignoraréis	habrás ignorado	habréis ignorado
ignorará	ignorarán	habrá ignorado	habrán ignorado
5 potencial simple		12 potencial compuesto	
ignoararía	ignoraríamos	habría ignorado	habríamos ignorado
ignoararías	ignoraríais	habrías ignorado	habríais ignorado
ignoraría	ignorarían	habría ignorado	habrían ignorado
6 presente de subjuntivo		13 perfecto de subjuntivo	
ignore	ignoremos	haya ignorado	hayamos ignorado
ignores	ignoréis	hayas ignorado	hayáis ignorado
ignore	ignoren	haya ignorado	hayan ignorado
7 imperfecto de subjuntivo		14 pluscuamperfecto de subjuntivo	
ignorara	ignoráramos	hubiera ignorado	hubiéramos ignorado
ignoraras	ignorarais	hubieras ignorado	hubierais ignorado
ignorara	ignoraran	hubiera ignorado	hubieran ignorado
OR		OR	
ignorase	ignorásemos	hubiese ignorado	hubiésemos ignorado
ignorases	ignoraseis	hubieses ignorado	hubieseis ignorado
ignorase	ignorasen	hubiese ignorado	hubiesen ignorado

imperativo	
—	ignoremos
ignora; no ignores	ignorad; no ignoréis
ignore	ignoren

Words and expressions related to this verb
la ignorancia ignorance
ignorante ignorant
ignoto, ignota unknown
no ignorar que . . . to be well aware that . . .

ignorantemente ignorantly
ignominioso, ignominiosa disgraceful, ignominious
la ignominia disgrace, infamy, ignominy
un ignorantón, una ignorantona an ignoramus

The subject pronouns are found on the page facing page 1.

265

impedir

Gerundio **impidiendo**   Part. pas. **impedido**

to hinder, to impede, to prevent

The Seven Simple Tenses		The Seven Compound Tenses	
Singular	Plural	Singular	Plural
1 presente de indicativo		8 perfecto de indicativo	
impido	**impedimos**	**he impedido**	**hemos impedido**
impides	**impedís**	**has impedido**	**habéis impedido**
impide	**impiden**	**ha impedido**	**han impedido**
2 imperfecto de indicativo		9 pluscuamperfecto de indicativo	
impedía	**impedíamos**	**había impedido**	**habíamos impedido**
impedías	**impedíais**	**habías impedido**	**habíais impedido**
impedía	**impedían**	**había impedido**	**habían impedido**
3 pretérito		10 pretérito anterior	
impedí	**impedimos**	**hube impedido**	**hubimos impedido**
impediste	**impedisteis**	**hubiste impedido**	**hubisteis impedido**
impidió	**impidieron**	**hubo impedido**	**hubieron impedido**
4 futuro		11 futuro perfecto	
impediré	**impediremos**	**habré impedido**	**habremos impedido**
impedirás	**impediréis**	**habrás impedido**	**habréis impedido**
impedirá	**impedirán**	**habrá impedido**	**habrán impedido**
5 potencial simple		12 potencial compuesto	
impediría	**impediríamos**	**habría impedido**	**habríamos impedido**
impedirías	**impediríais**	**habrías impedido**	**habríais impedido**
impediría	**impedirían**	**habría impedido**	**habrían impedido**
6 presente de subjuntivo		13 perfecto de subjuntivo	
impida	**impidamos**	**haya impedido**	**hayamos impedido**
impidas	**impidáis**	**hayas impedido**	**hayáis impedido**
impida	**impidan**	**haya impedido**	**hayan impedido**
7 imperfecto de subjuntivo		14 pluscuamperfecto de subjuntivo	
impidiera	**impidiéramos**	**hubiera impedido**	**hubiéramos impedido**
impidieras	**impidierais**	**hubieras impedido**	**hubierais impedido**
impidiera	**impidieran**	**hubiera impedido**	**hubieran impedido**
OR		OR	
impidiese	**impidiésemos**	**hubiese impedido**	**hubiésemos impedido**
impidieses	**impidieseis**	**hubieses impedido**	**hubieseis impedido**
impidiese	**impidiesen**	**hubiese impedido**	**hubiesen impedido**

imperativo	
—	**impidamos**
impide; no impidas	**impedid; no impidáis**
impida	**impidan**

Words and expressions related to this verb

impediente   impeding, hindering
un impedimento   impediment, hindrance
impedir algo a uno   to prevent somebody from doing something

impeditivo, impeditiva   hindering, preventive
un impedido, una impedida   disabled, handicapped person

See also **pedir.**

to matter, to be important

The Seven Simple Tenses		The Seven Compound Tenses	
Singular	Plural	Singular	Plural
1 presente de indicativo		8 perfecto de indicativo	
importa	**importan**	**ha importado**	**han importado**
2 imperfecto de indicativo		9 pluscuamperfecto de indicativo	
importaba	**importaban**	**había importado**	**habían importado**
3 pretérito		10 pretérito anterior	
importó	**importaron**	**hubo importado**	**hubieron importado**
4 futuro		11 futuro perfecto	
importará	**importarán**	**habrá importado**	**habrán importado**
5 potencial simple		12 potencial compuesto	
importaría	**importarían**	**habría importado**	**habrían importado**
6 presente de subjuntivo		13 perfecto de subjuntivo	
que importe	**que importen**	**que haya importado**	**que hayan importado**
7 imperfecto de subjuntivo		14 pluscuamperfecto de subjuntivo	
que importara	**que importaran**	**que hubiera importado**	**que hubieran importado**
OR		OR	
que importase	**que importasen**	**que hubiese importado**	**que hubiesen importado**

imperativo

¡Que importe!   **¡Que importen!**

Words and expressions related to this verb
No importa.   It does not matter.
Eso no importa.   That does not matter.
No me importaría.   It wouldn't matter to me.
la importancia   importance
importante   important

dar importancia a   to value
de gran importancia   of great importance
darse importancia   to be pretentious
¿Qué importa?   What difference does it make?

This verb can be conjugated regularly in all the persons but it is used most commonly as an impersonal verb in the third person.

The subject pronouns are found on the page facing page 1.

267

to imprint, to impress, to print, to fix in the mind

The Seven Simple Tenses		The Seven Compound Tenses	
Singular	Plural	Singular	Plural
1 presente de indicativo		**8 perfecto de indicativo**	
imprimo	imprimimos	he impreso	hemos impreso
imprimes	imprimís	has impreso	habéis impreso
imprime	imprimen	ha impreso	han impreso
2 imperfecto de indicativo		**9 pluscuamperfecto de indicativo**	
imprimía	imprimíamos	había impreso	habíamos impreso
imprimías	imprimíais	habías impreso	habíais impreso
imprimía	imprimían	había impreso	habían impreso
3 pretérito		**10 pretérito anterior**	
imprimí	imprimimos	hube impreso	hubimos impreso
imprimiste	imprimisteis	hubiste impreso	hubisteis impreso
imprimió	imprimieron	hubo impreso	hubieron impreso
4 futuro		**11 futuro perfecto**	
inprimiré	imprimiremos	habré impreso	habremos impreso
imprimirás	imprimiréis	habrás impreso	habréis impreso
imprimirá	imprimirán	habrá impreso	habrán impreso
5 potencial simple		**12 potencial compuesto**	
imprimiría	imprimiríamos	habría impreso	habríamos impreso
imprimirías	imprimiríais	habrías impreso	habríais impreso
imprimiría	imprimirían	habría impreso	habrían impreso
6 presente de subjuntivo		**13 perfecto de subjuntivo**	
imprima	imprimamos	haya impreso	hayamos impreso
imprimas	imprimáis	hayas impreso	hayáis impreso
imprima	impriman	haya impreso	hayan impreso
7 imperfecto de subjuntivo		**14 pluscuamperfecto de subjuntivo**	
imprimiera	imprimiéramos	hubiera impreso	hubiéramos impreso
imprimieras	imprimierais	hubieras impreso	hubierais impreso
imprimiera	imprimieran	hubiera impreso	hubieran impreso
OR		OR	
imprimiese	imprimiésemos	hubiese impreso	hubiésemos impreso
imprimieses	imprimieseis	hubieses impreso	hubieseis impreso
imprimiese	imprimiesen	hubiese impreso	hubiesen impreso

imperativo		
—		**imprimamos**
imprime; no imprimas		**imprimid; no imprimáis**
imprima		**impriman**

Words and expressions related to this verb
imprimible   printable
el imprimátur   imprimatur
impreso, impresa   printed, stamped

impresos   printed matter
el impresor, la impresora   printer, owner of a printing shop

Want to learn more idiomatic expressions that contain verbs? Check out pages 524–537.

Gerundio **incluyendo**   Part. pas. **incluido**   **incluir**
(**incluso,** when used as an *adj.*)

to include, to enclose

The Seven Simple Tenses | The Seven Compound Tenses

Singular	Plural	Singular	Plural
1 presente de indicativo		8 perfecto de indicativo	
incluyo	**incluimos**	**he incluido**	**hemos incluido**
incluyes	**incluís**	**has incluido**	**habéis incluido**
incluye	**incluyen**	**ha incluido**	**han incluido**
2 imperfecto de indicativo		9 pluscuamperfecto de indicativo	
incluía	**incluíamos**	**había incluido**	**habíamos incluido**
incluías	**incluíais**	**habías incluido**	**habíais incluido**
incluía	**incluían**	**había incluido**	**habían incluido**
3 pretérito		10 pretérito anterior	
incluí	**incluimos**	**hube incluido**	**hubimos incluido**
incluiste	**incluisteis**	**hubiste incluido**	**hubisteis incluido**
incluyó	**incluyeron**	**hubo incluido**	**hubieron incluido**
4 futuro		11 futuro perfecto	
incluiré	**incluiremos**	**habré incluido**	**habremos incluido**
incluirás	**incluiréis**	**habrás incluido**	**habréis incluido**
incluirá	**incluirán**	**habrá incluido**	**habrán incluido**
5 potencial simple		12 potencial compuesto	
incluiría	**incluiríamos**	**habría incluido**	**habríamos incluido**
incluirías	**incluiríais**	**habrías incluido**	**habríais incluido**
incluiría	**incluirían**	**habría incluido**	**habrían incluido**
6 presente de subjuntivo		13 perfecto de subjuntivo	
incluya	**incluyamos**	**haya incluido**	**hayamos incluido**
incluyas	**incluyáis**	**hayas incluido**	**hayáis incluido**
incluya	**incluyan**	**haya incluido**	**hayan incluido**
7 imperfecto de subjuntivo		14 pluscuamperfecto de subjuntivo	
incluyera	**incluyéramos**	**hubiera incluido**	**hubiéramos incluido**
incluyeras	**incluyerais**	**hubieras incluido**	**hubierais incluido**
incluyera	**incluyeran**	**hubiera incluido**	**hubieran incluido**
OR		OR	
incluyese	**incluyésemos**	**hubiese incluido**	**hubiésemos incluido**
incluyeses	**incluyeseis**	**hubieses incluido**	**hubieseis incluido**
incluyese	**incluyesen**	**hubiese incluido**	**hubiesen incluido**

imperativo

—	**incluyamos**
incluye; no incluyas	**incluid; no incluyáis**
incluya	**incluyan**

Words and expressions related to this verb
inclusivo, inclusiva inclusive, including
la inclusión inclusion
una inclusa foundling home
el dinero incluso the money enclosed,
  included

la carta inclusa the letter enclosed, included
inclusivamente inclusively
sin incluir not including
con inclusión de including
todo incluido everything included

to indicate, to point out

The Seven Simple Tenses		The Seven Compound Tenses	
Singular	Plural	Singular	Plural
1 presente de indicativo		**8 perfecto de indicativo**	
indico	indicamos	he indicado	hemos indicado
indicas	indicáis	has indicado	habéis indicado
indica	indican	ha indicado	han indicado
2 imperfecto de indicativo		**9 pluscuamperfecto de indicativo**	
indicaba	indicábamos	había indicado	habíamos indicado
indicabas	indicabais	habías indicado	habíais indicado
indicaba	indicaban	había indicado	habían indicado
3 pretérito		**10 pretérito anterior**	
indiqué	indicamos	hube indicado	hubimos indicado
indicaste	indicasteis	hubiste indicado	hubisteis indicado
indicó	indicaron	hubo indicado	hubieron indicado
4 futuro		**11 futuro perfecto**	
indicaré	indicaremos	habré indicado	habremos indicado
indicarás	indicaréis	habrás indicado	habréis indicado
indicará	indicarán	habrá indicado	habrán indicado
5 potencial simple		**12 potencial compuesto**	
indicaría	indicaríamos	habría indicado	habríamos indicado
indicarías	indicaríais	habrías indicado	habríais indicado
indicaría	indicarían	habría indicado	habrían indicado
6 presente de subjuntivo		**13 perfecto de subjuntivo**	
indique	indiquemos	haya indicado	hayamos indicado
indiques	indiquéis	hayas indicado	hayáis indicado
indique	indiquen	haya indicado	hayan indicado
7 imperfecto de subjuntivo		**14 pluscuamperfecto de subjuntivo**	
indicara	indicáramos	hubiera indicado	hubiéramos indicado
indicaras	indicarais	hubieras indicado	hubierais indicado
indicara	indicaran	hubiera indicado	hubieran indicado
OR		OR	
indicase	indicásemos	hubiese indicado	hubiésemos indicado
indicases	indicaseis	hubieses indicado	hubieseis indicado
indicase	indicasen	hubiese indicado	hubiesen indicado

imperativo

—	indiquemos
indica; no indiques	indicad; no indiquéis
indique	indiquen

Words and expressions related to this verb
indicativo, indicativa indicative
la indicación indication
el indicador indicator; **el indicador de humo** smoke detector

una falsa indicación a wrong direction
el indicador de horarios travel timetable (trains, *etc.*)
el indicador de velocidad speedometer

to induce, to influence, to persuade, to lead

The Seven Simple Tenses		The Seven Compound Tenses	
Singular	Plural	Singular	Plural
1 presente de indicativo		8 perfecto de indicativo	
induzco	**inducimos**	**he inducido**	**hemos inducido**
induces	**inducís**	**has inducido**	**habéis inducido**
induce	**inducen**	**ha inducido**	**han inducido**
2 imperfecto de indicativo		9 pluscuamperfecto de indicativo	
inducía	**inducíamos**	**había inducido**	**habíamos inducido**
inducías	**inducíais**	**habías inducido**	**habíais inducido**
inducía	**inducían**	**había inducido**	**habían inducido**
3 pretérito		10 pretérito anterior	
induje	**indujimos**	**hube inducido**	**hubimos inducido**
indujiste	**indujisteis**	**hubiste inducido**	**hubisteis inducido**
indujo	**indujeron**	**hubo inducido**	**hubieron inducido**
4 futuro		11 futuro perfecto	
induciré	**induciremos**	**habré inducido**	**habremos inducido**
inducirás	**induciréis**	**habrás inducido**	**habréis inducido**
inducirá	**inducirán**	**habrá inducido**	**habrán inducido**
5 potencial simple		12 potencial compuesto	
induciría	**induciríamos**	**habría inducido**	**habríamos inducido**
inducirías	**induciríais**	**habrías inducido**	**habríais inducido**
induciría	**inducirían**	**habría inducido**	**habrían inducido**
6 presente de subjuntivo		13 perfecto de subjuntivo	
induzca	**induzcamos**	**haya inducido**	**hayamos inducido**
induzcas	**induzcáis**	**hayas inducido**	**hayáis inducido**
induzca	**induzcan**	**haya inducido**	**hayan inducido**
7 imperfecto de subjuntivo		14 pluscuamperfecto de subjuntivo	
indujera	**indujéramos**	**hubiera inducido**	**hubiéramos inducido**
indujeras	**indujerais**	**hubieras inducido**	**hubierais inducido**
indujera	**indujeran**	**hubiera inducido**	**hubieran inducido**
OR		OR	
indujese	**indujésemos**	**hubiese inducido**	**hubiésemos inducido**
indujeses	**indujeseis**	**hubieses inducido**	**hubieseis inducido**
indujese	**indujesen**	**hubiese inducido**	**hubiesen inducido**

imperativo	
—	**induzcamos**
induce; no induzcas	**inducid; no induzcáis**
induzca	**induzcan**

Words and expressions related to this verb
inducidor, inducidora   inducer
el inducimiento   inducement

la inducción   induction
inducir a + inf.   to persuade to + inf.

Can't recognize an irregular verb form? Check out pages 519–523.

influir

Gerundio influyendo   **Part. pas. influido**

to influence, have influence on

The Seven Simple Tenses		The Seven Compound Tenses	
Singular	Plural	Singular	Plural
1 presente de indicativo		**8 perfecto de indicativo**	
influyo	influimos	he influido	hemos influido
influyes	influís	has influido	habéis influido
influye	influyen	ha influido	han influido
2 imperfecto de indicativo		**9 pluscuamperfecto de indicativo**	
influía	influíamos	había influido	habíamos influido
influías	influíais	habías influido	habíais influido
influía	influían	había influido	habían influido
3 pretérito		**10 pretérito anterior**	
influí	influimos	hube influido	hubimos influido
influiste	influisteis	hubiste influido	hubisteis influido
influyó	influyeron	hubo influido	hubieron influido
4 futuro		**11 futuro perfecto**	
influiré	influiremos	habré influido	habremos influido
influirás	influiréis	habrás influido	habréis influido
influirá	influirán	habrá influido	habrán influido
5 potencial simple		**12 potencial compuesto**	
influiría	influiríamos	habría influido	habríamos influido
influirías	influiríais	habrías influido	habríais influido
influiría	influirían	habría influido	habrían influido
6 presente de subjuntivo		**13 perfecto de subjuntivo**	
influya	influyamos	haya influido	hayamos influido
influyas	influyáis	hayas influido	hayáis influido
influya	influyan	haya influido	hayan influido
7 imperfecto de subjuntivo		**14 pluscuamperfecto de subjuntivo**	
influyera	influyéramos	hubiera influido	hubiéramos influido
influyeras	influyerais	hubieras influido	hubierais influido
influyera	influyeran	hubiera influido	hubieran influido
OR		OR	
influyese	influyésemos	hubiese influido	hubiésemos influido
influyeses	influyeseis	hubieses influido	hubieseis influido
influyese	influyesen	hubiese influido	hubiesen influido

imperativo	
—	influyamos
influye; no influyas	influid; no influyáis
influya	influyan

Words and expressions related to this verb

la influencia influence
influente influential, influencing
influir en to affect, to have an influence on, upon
influir sobre alguien para que + subjunctive to influence someone to + inf.
(Check out the subjunctive on pages xxvii to xxxi.)

If you want an explanation of meanings and uses of Spanish and English verb tenses and moods, see pages xx to xl.

272

to inform oneself, to find out

The Seven Simple Tenses		The Seven Compound Tenses	
Singular	Plural	Singular	Plural
1 presente de indicativo		8 perfecto de indicativo	
me informo	**nos informamos**	**me he informado**	**nos hemos informado**
te informas	**os informáis**	**te has informado**	**os habéis informado**
se informa	**se informan**	**se ha informado**	**se han informado**
2 imperfecto de indicativo		9 pluscuamperfecto de indicativo	
me informaba	**nos informábamos**	**me había informado**	**nos habíamos informado**
te informabas	**os informabais**	**te habías informado**	**os habíais informado**
se informaba	**se informaban**	**se había informado**	**se habían informado**
3 pretérito		10 pretérito anterior	
me informé	**nos informamos**	**me hube informado**	**nos hubimos informado**
te informaste	**os informasteis**	**te hubiste informado**	**os hubisteis informado**
se informó	**se informaron**	**se hubo informado**	**se hubieron informado**
4 futuro		11 futuro perfecto	
me informaré	**nos informaremos**	**me habré informado**	**nos habremos informado**
te informarás	**os informaréis**	**te habrás informado**	**os habréis informado**
se informará	**se informarán**	**se habrá informado**	**se habrán informado**
5 potencial simple		12 potencial compuesto	
me informaría	**nos informaríamos**	**me habría informado**	**nos habríamos informado**
te informarías	**os informaríais**	**te habrías informado**	**os habríais informado**
se informaría	**se informarían**	**se habría informado**	**se habrían informado**
6 presente de subjuntivo		13 perfecto de subjuntivo	
me informe	**nos informemos**	**me haya informado**	**nos hayamos informado**
te informes	**os informéis**	**te hayas informado**	**os hayáis informado**
se informe	**se informen**	**se haya informado**	**se hayan informado**
7 imperfecto de subjuntivo		14 pluscuamperfecto de subjuntivo	
me informara	**nos informáramos**	**me hubiera informado**	**nos hubiéramos informado**
te informaras	**os informarais**	**te hubieras informado**	**os hubierais informado**
se informara	**se informaran**	**se hubiera informado**	**se hubieran informado**
OR		OR	
me informase	**nos informásemos**	**me hubiese informado**	**nos hubiésemos informado**
te informases	**os informaseis**	**te hubieses informado**	**os hubieseis informado**
se informáse	**se informasen**	**se hubiese informado**	**se hubiesen informado**

	imperativo	
—	**informémonos**
infórmate; no te informes	**informaos; no os informéis**
infórmese	**infórmense**

Words and expressions related to this verb

el informe, los informes   information
un informe en confianza   confidential report
informativo, informativa   informative, informational
informarse de   to find out about

el, la informante   informant
informar   to inform, report
informar contra   to inform against
la información   information, report
información económica   financial news

The subject pronouns are found on the page facing page 1.

inscribir   Gerundio **inscribiendo**   Part. pas. **inscrito** (**inscripto,** *as an adj.*)
to inscribe, to record, to register

The Seven Simple Tenses		The Seven Compound Tenses	
Singular	Plural	Singular	Plural
1 presente de indicativo		**8 perfecto de indicativo**	
inscribo	inscribimos	he inscrito	hemos inscrito
inscribes	inscribís	has inscrito	habéis inscrito
inscribe	inscriben	ha inscrito	han inscrito
2 imperfecto de indicativo		**9 pluscuamperfecto de indicativo**	
inscribía	inscribíamos	había inscrito	habíamos inscrito
inscribías	inscribíais	habías inscrito	habíais inscrito
inscribía	inscribían	había inscrito	habían inscrito
3 pretérito		**10 pretérito anterior**	
inscribí	inscribimos	hube inscrito	hubimos inscrito
inscribiste	inscribisteis	hubiste inscrito	hubisteis inscrito
inscribió	inscribieron	hubo inscrito	hubieron inscrito
4 futuro		**11 futuro perfecto**	
inscribiré	inscribiremos	habré inscrito	habremos inscrito
inscribirás	inscribiréis	habrás inscrito	habréis inscrito
inscribirá	inscribirán	habrá inscrito	habrán inscrito
5 potencial simple		**12 potencial compuesto**	
inscribiría	inscribiríamos	habría inscrito	habríamos inscrito
inscribirías	inscribiríais	habrías inscrito	habríais inscrito
inscribiría	inscribirían	habría inscrito	habrían inscrito
6 presente de subjuntivo		**13 perfecto de subjuntivo**	
inscriba	inscribamos	haya inscrito	hayamos inscrito
inscribas	inscribáis	hayas inscrito	hayáis inscrito
inscriba	inscriban	haya inscrito	hayan inscrito
7 imperfecto de subjuntivo		**14 pluscuamperfecto de subjuntivo**	
inscribiera	inscribiéramos	hubiera inscrito	hubiéramos inscrito
inscribieras	inscribierais	hubieras inscrito	hubierais inscrito
inscribiera	inscribieran	hubiera inscrito	hubieran inscrito
OR		OR	
inscribiese	inscribiésemos	hubiese inscrito	hubiésemos inscrito
inscribieses	inscribieseis	hubieses inscrito	hubieseis inscrito
inscribiese	inscribiesen	hubiese inscrito	hubiesen inscrito

	imperativo	
—		**inscribamos**
inscribe; no inscribas		**inscribid; no inscribáis**
inscriba		**inscriban**

Words and expressions related to this verb
la inscripción   inscription, registration
inscripto, inscripta   inscribed, registered
escribir   to write

describir   to describe, to sketch
la descripción   description
inscribirse en un concurso   to register one's
   name (to sign up) in a competition

If you don't know the Spanish verb for the English verb you
have in mind, look it up in the index on pages 505–518.

The Seven Simple Tenses		The Seven Compound Tenses	
Singular	Plural	Singular	Plural

1   presente de indicativo

		8 perfecto de indicativo	
me inscribo	nos inscribimos	me he inscrito	nos hemos inscrito
te inscribes	os inscribís	te has inscrito	os habéis inscrito
se inscribe	se inscriben	se ha inscrito	se han inscrito

2   imperfecto de indicativo

		9 pluscuamperfecto de indicativo	
me inscribía	nos inscribíamos	me había inscrito	nos habíamos inscrito
te inscribías	os inscribíais	te habías inscrito	os habíais inscrito
se inscribía	se inscribían	se había inscrito	se habían inscrito

3   pretérito

		10 pretérito anterior	
me inscribí	nos inscribimos	me hube inscrito	nos hubimos inscrito
te inscribiste	os inscribisteis	te hubiste inscrito	os hubisteis inscrito
se inscribió	se inscribieron	se hubo inscrito	se hubieron inscrito

4   futuro

		11 futuro perfecto	
me inscribiré	nos inscribiremos	me habré inscrito	nos habremos inscrito
te inscribirás	os inscribiréis	te habrás inscrito	os habréis inscrito
se inscribirá	se inscribirán	se habrá inscrito	se habrán inscrito

5   potencial simple

		12 potencial compuesto	
me inscribiría	nos inscribiríamos	me habría inscrito	nos habríamos inscrito
te inscribirías	os inscribiríais	te habrías inscrito	os habríais inscrito
se inscribiría	se inscribirían	se habría inscrito	se habrían inscrito

6   presente de subjuntivo

		13 perfecto de subjuntivo	
me inscriba	nos inscribamos	me haya inscrito	nos hayamos inscrito
te inscribas	os inscribáis	te hayas inscrito	os hayáis inscrito
se inscriba	se inscriban	se haya inscrito	se hayan inscrito

7   imperfecto de subjuntivo

		14 pluscuamperfecto de subjuntivo	
me inscribiera	nos inscribiéramos	me hubiera inscrito	nos hubiéramos inscrito
te inscribieras	os inscribierais	te hubieras inscrito	os hubierais inscrito
se inscribiera	se inscribieran	se hubiera inscrito	se hubieran inscrito
OR		OR	
me inscribiese	nos inscribiésemos	me hubiese inscrito	nos hubiésemos inscrito
te inscribieses	os inscribieseis	te hubieses inscrito	os hubieseis inscrito
se inscribiese	se inscribiesen	se hubiese inscrito	se hubiesen inscrito

imperativo

—	inscribámonos
inscríbete; no te inscribas	inscribíos; no os inscribáis
inscríbase	inscríbanse

For words and expressions related to this verb, see **inscribir**.

Don't miss the definitions of basic grammatical terms with examples
in English and Spanish on pages 666–677.

insistir

Gerundio insistiendo   **Part. pas.** insistido

to insist, to persist, to stress

The Seven Simple Tenses		The Seven Compound Tenses	
Singular	Plural	Singular	Plural
1 presente de indicativo		**8 perfecto de indicativo**	
insisto	insistimos	he insistido	hemos insistido
insistes	insistís	has insistido	habéis insistido
insiste	insisten	ha insistido	han insistido
2 imperfecto de indicativo		**9 pluscuamperfecto de indicativo**	
insistía	insistíamos	había insistido	habíamos insistido
insistías	insistíais	habías insistido	habíais insistido
insistía	insistían	había insistido	habían insistido
3 pretérito		**10 pretérito anterior**	
insistí	insistimos	hube insistido	hubimos insistido
insististe	insististeis	hubiste insistido	hubisteis insistido
insistió	insistieron	hubo insistido	hubieron insistido
4 futuro		**11 futuro perfecto**	
insistiré	insistiremos	habré insistido	habremos insistido
insistirás	insistiréis	habrás insistido	habréis insistido
insistirá	insistirán	habrá insistido	habrán insistido
5 potencial simple		**12 potencial compuesto**	
insistiría	insistiríamos	habría insistido	habríamos insistido
insistirías	insistiríais	habrías insistido	habríais insistido
insistiría	insistirían	habría insistido	habrían insistido
6 presente de subjuntivo		**13 perfecto de subjuntivo**	
insista	insistamos	haya insistido	hayamos insistido
insistas	insistáis	hayas insistido	hayáis insistido
insista	insistan	haya insistido	hayan insistido
7 imperfecto de subjuntivo		**14 pluscuamperfecto de subjuntivo**	
insistiera	insistiéramos	hubiera insistido	hubiéramos insistido
insistieras	insistierais	hubieras insistido	hubierais insistido
insistiera	insistieran	hubiera insistido	hubieran insistido
OR		OR	
insistiese	insistiésemos	hubiese insistido	hubiésemos insistido
insistieses	insistieseis	hubieses insistido	hubieseis insistido
insistiese	insistiesen	hubiese insistido	hubiesen insistido

	imperativo	
—	insistamos	
insiste; no insistas	insistid; no insistáis	
insista	insistan	

Words related to this verb

insistir en   to insist on, to persist in
la insistencia   insistence, persistence

insistente   insistent
insistir en la importancia de   to stress the importance of

If you want to see a sample English verb fully conjugated in all the tenses, check out pages xviii and xix.

to be interested in

The Seven Simple Tenses		The Seven Compound Tenses	
Singular	Plural	Singular	Plural

1   presente de indicativo

me intereso	nos interesamos
te interesas	os interesáis
se interesa	se interesan

8   perfecto de indicativo

me he interesado	nos hemos interesado
te has interesado	os habéis interesado
se ha interesado	se han interesado

2   imperfecto de indicativo

me interesaba	nos interesábamos
te interesabas	os interesabais
se interesaba	se interesaban

9   pluscuamperfecto de indicativo

me había interesado	nos habíamos interesado
te habías interesado	os habíais interesado
se había interesado	se habían interesado

3   pretérito

me interesé	nos interesamos
te interesaste	os interesasteis
se interesó	se interesaron

10   pretérito anterior

me hube interesado	nos hubimos interesado
te hubiste interesado	os hubisteis interesado
se hubo interesado	se hubieron interesado

4   futuro

me interesaré	nos interesaremos
te interesarás	os interesaréis
se interesará	se interesarán

11   futuro perfecto

me habré interesado	nos habremos interesado
te habrás interesado	os habréis interesado
se habrá interesado	se habrán interesado

5   potencial simple

me interesaría	nos interesaríamos
te interesarías	os interesaríais
se interesaría	se interesarían

12   potencial compuesto

me habría interesado	nos habríamos interesado
te habrías interesado	os habríais interesado
se habría interesado	se habrían interesado

6   presente de subjuntivo

me interese	nos interesemos
te intereses	os intereséis
se interese	se interesen

13   perfecto de subjuntivo

me haya interesado	nos hayamos interesado
te hayas interesado	os hayáis interesado
se haya interesado	se hayan interesado

7   imperfecto de subjuntivo

me interesara	nos interesáramos
te interesaras	os interesarais
se interesara	se interesaran
OR	
me interesase	nos interesásemos
te interesases	os interesaseis
se interesase	se interesasen

14   pluscuamperfecto de subjuntivo

me hubiera interesado	nos hubiéramos interesado
te hubieras interesado	os hubierais interesado
se hubiera interesado	se hubieran interesado
OR	
me hubiese interesado	nos hubiésemos interesado
te hubieses interesado	os hubieseis interesado
se hubiese interesado	se hubiesen interesado

imperativo

—	interesémonos
interésate; no te intereses	interesaos; no os intereséis
interésese	interésense

Words and expressions related to this verb

interesarse en   to be interested in
interesar   to interest
el interés   interest
en interés de   on behalf of
desinteresarse   to become disinterested;
   to lose interest

interesante   interesting
interesado, interesada   interested
sin interés   uninteresting
desinteresar   to disinterest
desinteresado, desinteresada   disinterested
el desinterés   disinterest

The subject pronouns are found on the page facing page 1.

introducir

Gerundio introduciendo   Part. pas. **introducido**

to introduce

The Seven Simple Tenses		The Seven Compound Tenses	
Singular	Plural	Singular	Plural
1 presente de indicativo		**8 perfecto de indicativo**	
introduzco	**introducimos**	**he introducido**	**hemos introducido**
introduces	**introducís**	**has introducido**	**habéis introducido**
introduce	**introducen**	**ha introducido**	**han introducido**
2 imperfecto de indicativo		**9 pluscuamperfecto de indicativo**	
introducía	**introducíamos**	**había introducido**	**habíamos introducido**
introducías	**introducíais**	**habías introducido**	**habíais introducido**
introducía	**introducían**	**había introducido**	**habían introducido**
3 pretérito		**10 pretérito anterior**	
introduje	**introdujimos**	**hube introducido**	**hubimos introducido**
introdujiste	**introdujisteis**	**hubiste introducido**	**hubisteis introducido**
introdujo	**introdujeron**	**hubo introducido**	**hubieron introducido**
4 futuro		**11 futuro perfecto**	
introduciré	**introduciremos**	**habré introducido**	**habremos introducido**
introducirás	**introduciréis**	**habrás introducido**	**habréis introducido**
introducirá	**introducirán**	**habrá introducido**	**habrán introducido**
5 potencial simple		**12 potencial compuesto**	
introduciría	**introduciríamos**	**habría introducido**	**habríamos introducido**
introducirías	**introduciríais**	**habrías introducido**	**habríais introducido**
introduciría	**introducirían**	**habría introducido**	**habrían introducido**
6 presente de subjuntivo		**13 perfecto de subjuntivo**	
introduzca	**introduzcamos**	**haya introducido**	**hayamos introducido**
introduzcas	**introduzcáis**	**hayas introducido**	**hayáis introducido**
introduzca	**introduzcan**	**haya introducido**	**hayan introducido**
7 imperfecto de subjuntivo		**14 pluscuamperfecto de subjuntivo**	
introdujera	**introdujéramos**	**hubiera introducido**	**hubiéramos introducido**
introdujeras	**introdujerais**	**hubieras introducido**	**hubierais introducido**
introdujera	**introdujeran**	**hubiera introducido**	**hubieran introducido**
OR		OR	
introdujese	**introdujésemos**	**hubiese introducido**	**hubiésemos introducido**
introdujeses	**introdujeseis**	**hubieses introducido**	**hubieseis introducido**
introdujese	**introdujesen**	**hubiese introducido**	**hubiesen introducido**

	imperativo	
—		**introduzcamos**
introduce; no introduzcas		**introducid; no introduzcáis**
introduzca		**introduzcan**

Words related to this verb
la introducción introduction
introductor, introductora introducer
introducir a una persona en la oficina
  to show a person into the office

introductivo, introductiva introductive, introductory

Use the EE-zee guide to Spanish pronunciation on pages 562 and 563.

The Seven Simple Tenses		The Seven Compound Tenses	
Singular	Plural	Singular	Plural
1 presente de indicativo		8 perfecto de indicativo	
invito	**invitamos**	**he invitado**	**hemos invitado**
invitas	**invitáis**	**has invitado**	**habéis invitado**
invita	**invitan**	**ha invitado**	**han invitado**
2 imperfecto de indicativo		9 pluscuamperfecto de indicativo	
invitaba	**invitábamos**	**había invitado**	**habíamos invitado**
invitabas	**invitabais**	**habías invitado**	**habíais invitado**
invitaba	**invitaban**	**había invitado**	**habían invitado**
3 pretérito		10 pretérito anterior	
invité	**invitamos**	**hube invitado**	**hubimos invitado**
invitaste	**invitasteis**	**hubiste invitado**	**hubisteis invitado**
invitó	**invitaron**	**hubo invitado**	**hubieron invitado**
4 futuro		11 futuro perfecto	
invitaré	**invitaremos**	**habré invitado**	**habremos invitado**
invitarás	**invitaréis**	**habrás invitado**	**habréis invitado**
invitará	**invitarán**	**habrá invitado**	**habrán invitado**
5 potencial simple		12 potencial compuesto	
invitaría	**invitaríamos**	**habría invitado**	**habríamos invitado**
invitarías	**invitaríais**	**habrías invitado**	**habríais invitado**
invitaría	**invitarían**	**habría invitado**	**habrían invitado**
6 presente de subjuntivo		13 perfecto de subjuntivo	
invite	**invitemos**	**haya invitado**	**hayamos invitado**
invites	**invitéis**	**hayas invitado**	**hayáis invitado**
invite	**inviten**	**haya invitado**	**hayan invitado**
7 imperfecto de subjuntivo		14 pluscuamperfecto de subjuntivo	
invitara	**invitáramos**	**hubiera invitado**	**hubiéramos invitado**
invitaras	**invitarais**	**hubieras invitado**	**hubierais invitado**
invitara	**invitaran**	**hubiera invitado**	**hubieran invitado**
OR		OR	
invitase	**invitásemos**	**hubiese invitado**	**hubiésemos invitado**
invitases	**invitaseis**	**hubieses invitado**	**hubieseis invitado**
invitase	**invitasen**	**hubiese invitado**	**hubiesen invitado**

imperativo

—	**invitemos**
invita; no invites	**invitad; no invitéis**
invite	**inviten**

Words related to this verb

invitar a + inf. to invite + inf.
la invitación invitation
un invitado, una invitada guest

el invitador host
la invitadora hostess
evitar to avoid

Want to learn more idiomatic expressions that contain verbs? Check out pages 524–537.

The subject pronouns are found on the page facing page 1.

to go

The Seven Simple Tenses		The Seven Compound Tenses	
Singular	Plural	Singular	Plural
1 presente de indicativo		8 perfecto de indicativo	
voy	**vamos**	**he ido**	**hemos ido**
vas	**vais**	**has ido**	**habéis ido**
va	**van**	**ha ido**	**han ido**
2 imperfecto de indicativo		9 pluscuamperfecto de indicativo	
iba	**íbamos**	**había ido**	**habíamos ido**
ibas	**ibais**	**habías ido**	**habíais ido**
iba	**iban**	**había ido**	**habían ido**
3 pretérito		10 pretérito anterior	
fui	**fuimos**	**hube ido**	**hubimos ido**
fuiste	**fuisteis**	**hubiste ido**	**hubisteis ido**
fue	**fueron**	**hubo ido**	**hubieron ido**
4 futuro		11 futuro perfecto	
iré	**iremos**	**habré ido**	**habremos ido**
irás	**iréis**	**habrás ido**	**habréis ido**
irá	**irán**	**habrá ido**	**habrán ido**
5 potencial simple		12 potencial compuesto	
iría	**iríamos**	**habría ido**	**habríamos ido**
irías	**iríais**	**habrías ido**	**habríais ido**
iría	**irían**	**habría ido**	**habrían ido**
6 presente de subjuntivo		13 perfecto de subjuntivo	
vaya	**vayamos**	**haya ido**	**hayamos ido**
vayas	**vayáis**	**hayas ido**	**hayáis ido**
vaya	**vayan**	**haya ido**	**hayan ido**
7 imperfecto de subjuntivo		14 pluscuamperfecto de subjuntivo	
fuera	**fuéramos**	**hubiera ido**	**hubiéramos ido**
fueras	**fuerais**	**hubieras ido**	**hubierais ido**
fuera	**fueran**	**hubiera ido**	**hubieran ido**
OR		OR	
fuese	**fuésemos**	**hubiese ido**	**hubiésemos ido**
fueses	**fueseis**	**hubieses ido**	**hubieseis ido**
fuese	**fuesen**	**hubiese ido**	**hubiesen ido**

	imperativo	
—		**vamos (no vayamos)**
ve; no vayas		**id; no vayáis**
vaya		**vayan**

Common idiomatic expressions using this verb

ir de compras   to go shopping
ir de brazo   to walk arm in arm
¿Cómo le va?   How goes it? How are you?
Cuando el gato va a sus devociones, bailan los ratones.
     When the cat is away, the mice will play.

ir a caballo   to ride horseback
un billete de ida y vuelta   return ticket
¡Qué va!   Nonsense!

See also **ir, irse** on page 532.

Can't recognize an irregular verb form?
Check out pages 519–523.

The Seven Simple Tenses | The Seven Compound Tenses

Singular	Plural	Singular	Plural
1 presente de indicativo		8 perfecto de indicativo	
me voy	**nos vamos**	**me he ido**	**nos hemos ido**
te vas	**os vais**	**te has ido**	**os habéis ido**
se va	**se van**	**se ha ido**	**se han ido**
2 imperfecto de indicativo		9 pluscuamperfecto de indicativo	
me iba	**nos íbamos**	**me había ido**	**nos habíamos ido**
te ibas	**os ibais**	**te habías ido**	**os habíais ido**
se iba	**se iban**	**se había ido**	**se habían ido**
3 pretérito		10 pretérito anterior	
me fui	**nos fuimos**	**me hube ido**	**nos hubimos ido**
te fuiste	**os fuisteis**	**te hubiste ido**	**os hubisteis ido**
se fue	**se fueron**	**se hubo ido**	**se hubieron ido**
4 futuro		11 futuro perfecto	
me iré	**nos iremos**	**me habré ido**	**nos habremos ido**
te irás	**os iréis**	**te habrás ido**	**os habréis ido**
se irá	**se irán**	**se habrá ido**	**se habrán ido**
5 potencial simple		12 potencial compuesto	
me iría	**nos iríamos**	**me habría ido**	**nos habríamos ido**
te irías	**os iríais**	**te habrías ido**	**os habríais ido**
se iría	**se irían**	**se habría ido**	**se habrían ido**
6 presente de subjuntivo		13 perfecto de subjuntivo	
me vaya	**nos vayamos**	**me haya ido**	**nos hayamos ido**
te vayas	**os vayáis**	**te hayas ido**	**os hayáis ido**
se vaya	**se vayan**	**se haya ido**	**se hayan ido**
7 imperfecto de subjuntivo		14 pluscuamperfecto de subjuntivo	
me fuera	**nos fuéramos**	**me hubiera ido**	**nos hubiéramos ido**
te fueras	**os fuerais**	**te hubieras ido**	**os hubierais ido**
se fuera	**se fueran**	**se hubiera ido**	**se hubieran ido**
OR		OR	
me fuese	**nos fuésemos**	**me hubiese ido**	**nos hubiésemos ido**
te fueses	**os fueseis**	**te hubieses ido**	**os hubieseis ido**
se fuese	**se fuesen**	**se hubiese ido**	**se hubiesen ido**

imperativo

—	**vámonos; no nos vayamos**
vete; no te vayas	**idos; no os vayáis**
váyase; no se vaya	**váyanse; no se vayan**

Common idiomatic expressions using this verb

¡Vámonos! Let's go! Let's leave!   **¡Vete!** Go away! **¡Váyase!** Go away!

Si a Roma fueres, haz como vieres. When in Rome do as the Romans do. [Note that it is not uncommon to use the future subjunctive in proverbs, as in *fueres* (**ir** or **ser**) and *vieres* (**ver**); see page xxxvii.]

For additional common idiomatic expressions, see **ir**, which is related to **irse**. See also **ir, irse** on page 532.

to play (a game, sport)

The Seven Simple Tenses		The Seven Compound Tenses	
Singular	Plural	Singular	Plural
1 presente de indicativo		8 perfecto de indicativo	
juego	**jugamos**	**he jugado**	**hemos jugado**
juegas	**jugáis**	**has jugado**	**habéis jugado**
juega	**juegan**	**ha jugado**	**han jugado**
2 imperfecto de indicativo		9 pluscuamperfecto de indicativo	
jugaba	**jubábamos**	**había jugado**	**habíamos jugado**
jugabas	**jugabaís**	**habías jugado**	**habíais jugado**
jugaba	**jugaban**	**había jugado**	**habían jugado**
3 pretérito		10 pretérito anterior	
jugué	**jugamos**	**hube jugado**	**hubimos jugado**
jugaste	**jugasteis**	**hubiste jugado**	**hubisteis jugado**
jugó	**jugaron**	**hubo jugado**	**hubieron jugado**
4 futuro		11 futuro perfecto	
jugaré	**jugaremos**	**habré jugado**	**habremos jugado**
jugarás	**jugaréis**	**habrás jugado**	**habréis jugado**
jugará	**jugarán**	**habrá jugado**	**habrán jugado**
5 potencial simple		12 potencial compuesto	
jugaría	**jugaríamos**	**habría jugado**	**habríamos jugado**
jugarías	**jugaríais**	**habrías jugado**	**habríais jugado**
jugaría	**jugarían**	**habría jugado**	**habrían jugado**
6 presente de subjuntivo		13 perfecto de subjuntivo	
juegue	**juguemos**	**haya jugado**	**hayamos jugado**
juegues	**juguéis**	**hayas jugado**	**hayáis jugado**
juegue	**jueguen**	**haya jugado**	**hayan jugado**
7 imperfecto de subjuntivo		14 pluscuamperfecto de subjuntivo	
jugara	**jugáramos**	**hubiera jugado**	**hubiéramos jugado**
jugaras	**jugarais**	**hubieras jugado**	**hubierais jugado**
jugara	**jugaran**	**hubiera jugado**	**hubieran jugado**
OR		OR	
jugase	**jugásemos**	**hubiese jugado**	**hubiésemos jugado**
jugases	**jugaseis**	**hubieses jugado**	**hubieseis jugado**
jugase	**jugasen**	**hubiese jugado**	**hubiesen jugado**

	imperativo	
—	**juguemos**
juega; no juegues	**jugad; no juguéis**
juegue	**jueguen**

Words and expressions related to this verb

un juguete   toy, plaything
jugador, jugadora   player
un juego   game
la casa de juego   gambling house
el juego de té   tea set (service)
juego sucio   foul (dishonest) play

jugar a los naipes   to play cards
jugar al tenis   to play tennis
jugar al béisbol   to play baseball
hacer doble juego   to be two-faced
¡Hagan juego!   Place your bets!
el juego de palabras   play on words, pun

See also **jugar** on page 532.

to join, to unite, to connect

The Seven Simple Tenses		The Seven Compound Tenses	
Singular	Plural	Singular	Plural
1 presente de indicativo		8 perfecto de indicativo	
junto	**juntamos**	**he juntado**	**hemos juntado**
juntas	**juntáis**	**has juntado**	**habéis juntado**
junta	**juntan**	**ha juntado**	**han juntado**
2 imperfecto de indicativo		9 pluscuamperfecto de indicativo	
juntaba	**juntábamos**	**había juntado**	**habíamos juntado**
juntabas	**juntabais**	**habías juntado**	**habíais juntado**
juntaba	**juntaban**	**había juntado**	**habían juntado**
3 pretérito		10 pretérito anterior	
junté	**juntamos**	**hube juntado**	**hubimos juntado**
juntaste	**juntasteis**	**hubiste juntado**	**hubisteis juntado**
juntó	**juntaron**	**hubo juntado**	**hubieron juntado**
4 futuro		11 futuro perfecto	
juntaré	**juntaremos**	**habré juntado**	**habremos juntado**
juntarás	**juntaréis**	**habrás juntado**	**habréis juntado**
juntará	**juntarán**	**habrá juntado**	**habrán juntado**
5 potencial simple		12 potencial compuesto	
juntaría	**juntaríamos**	**habría juntado**	**habríamos juntado**
juntarías	**juntaríais**	**habrías juntado**	**habríais juntado**
juntaría	**juntarían**	**habría juntado**	**habrían juntado**
6 presente de subjuntivo		13 perfecto de subjuntivo	
junte	**juntemos**	**haya juntado**	**hayamos juntado**
juntes	**juntéis**	**hayas juntado**	**hayáis juntado**
junte	**junten**	**haya juntado**	**hayan juntado**
7 imperfecto de subjuntivo		14 pluscuamperfecto de subjuntivo	
juntara	**juntáramos**	**hubiera juntado**	**hubiéramos juntado**
juntaras	**juntarais**	**hubieras juntado**	**hubierais juntado**
juntara	**juntaran**	**hubiera juntado**	**hubieran juntado**
OR		OR	
juntase	**juntásemos**	**hubiese juntado**	**hubiésemos juntado**
juntases	**juntaseis**	**hubieses juntado**	**hubieseis juntado**
juntase	**juntasen**	**hubiese juntado**	**hubiesen juntado**

imperativo

—	**juntemos**
junta; no juntes	**juntad; no juntéis**
junte	**junten**

Words and expressions related to this verb
juntar con   to associate with
juntarse   to assemble, gather together
la junta   junta, conference, convention, meeting

juntar meriendas   to join forces
vivir juntos   to live together

Consult the back pages for sections on verbs used in idiomatic expressions, verbs with prepositions, and the list of over 1,100 verbs conjugated like model verbs.

The subject pronouns are found on the page facing page 1.

283

to swear, to take an oath

The Seven Simple Tenses		The Seven Compound Tenses	
Singular	Plural	Singular	Plural
1 presente de indicativo		8 perfecto de indicativo	
juro	juramos	he jurado	hemos jurado
juras	juráis	has jurado	habéis jurado
jura	juran	ha jurado	han jurado
2 imperfecto de indicativo		9 pluscuamperfecto de indicativo	
juraba	jurábamos	había jurado	habíamos jurado
jurabas	jurabais	habías jurado	habíais jurado
juraba	juraban	había jurado	habían jurado
3 pretérito		10 pretérito anterior	
juré	juramos	hube jurado	hubimos jurado
juraste	jurasteis	hubiste jurado	hubisteis jurado
juró	juraron	hubo jurado	hubieron jurado
4 futuro		11 futuro perfecto	
juraré	juraremos	habré jurado	habremos jurado
jurarás	juraréis	habrás jurado	habréis jurado
jurará	jurarán	habrá jurado	habrán jurado
5 potencial simple		12 potencial compuesto	
juraría	juraríamos	habría jurado	habríamos jurado
jurarías	juraríais	habrías jurado	habríais jurado
juraría	jurarían	habría jurado	habrían jurado
6 presente de subjuntivo		13 perfecto de subjuntivo	
jure	juremos	haya jurado	hayamos jurado
jures	juréis	hayas jurado	hayáis jurado
jure	juren	haya jurado	hayan jurado
7 imperfecto de subjuntivo		14 pluscuamperfecto de subjuntivo	
jurara	juráramos	hubiera jurado	hubiéramos jurado
juraras	jurarais	hubieras jurado	hubierais jurado
jurara	juraran	hubiera jurado	hubieran jurado
OR		OR	
jurase	jurásemos	hubiese jurado	hubiésemos jurado
jurases	juraseis	hubieses jurado	hubieseis jurado
jurase	jurasen	hubiese jurado	hubiesen jurado

imperativo	
—	juremos
jura; no jures	jurad; no juréis
jure	juren

Words and expressions related to this verb
jurar en falso   to commit perjury
jurar decir la verdad   to swear to tell the
  truth
un juramento   oath; **juramento falso**
  perjury

juramentarse   to take an oath, to be sworn in
jurar como un carretero   to swear like a
  trooper
bajo juramento   under oath

Gerundio **juzgando**   Part. pas. **juzgado**   **juzgar**

to judge

The Seven Simple Tenses		The Seven Compound Tenses	
Singular	Plural	Singular	Plural
1 presente de indicativo		**8 perfecto de indicativo**	
juzgo	juzgamos	he juzgado	hemos juzgado
juzgas	juzgáis	has juzgado	habéis juzgado
juzga	juzgan	ha juzgado	han juzgado
2 imperfecto de indicativo		**9 pluscuamperfecto de indicativo**	
juzgaba	juzgábamos	había juzgado	habíamos juzgado
juzgabas	juzgabais	habías juzgado	habíais juzgado
juzgaba	juzgaban	había juzgado	habían juzgado
3 pretérito		**10 pretérito anterior**	
juzgué	juzgamos	hube juzgado	hubimos juzgado
juzgaste	juzgasteis	hubiste juzgado	hubisteis juzgado
juzgó	juzgaron	hubo juzgado	hubieron juzgado
4 futuro		**11 futuro perfecto**	
juzgaré	juzgaremos	habré juzgado	habremos juzgado
juzgarás	juzgaréis	habrás juzgado	habréis juzgado
juzgará	juzgarán	habrá juzgado	habrán juzgado
5 potencial simple		**12 potencial compuesto**	
juzgaría	juzgaríamos	habría juzgado	habríamos juzgado
juzgarías	juzgaríais	habrías juzgado	habríais juzgado
juzgaría	juzgarían	habría juzgado	habrían juzgado
6 presente de subjuntivo		**13 perfecto de subjuntivo**	
juzgue	juzguemos	haya juzgado	hayamos juzgado
juzgues	juzguéis	hayas juzgado	hayáis juzgado
juzgue	juzguen	haya juzgado	hayan juzgado
7 imperfecto de subjuntivo		**14 pluscuamperfecto de subjuntivo**	
juzgara	juzgáramos	hubiera juzgado	hubiéramos juzgado
juzgaras	juzgarais	hubieras juzgado	hubierais juzgado
juzgara	juzgaran	hubiera juzgado	hubieran juzgado
OR		OR	
juzgase	juzgásemos	hubiese juzgado	hubiésemos juzgado
juzgases	juzgaseis	hubieses juzgado	hubieseis juzgado
juzgase	juzgasen	hubiese juzgado	hubiesen juzgado

imperativo

—	juzguemos
juzga; no juzgues	juzgad; no juzguéis
juzgue	juzguen

Words and expressions related to this verb

a juzgar por judging by
juzgar de to pass judgment on
el juzgado court of justice
el juez judge (**los jueces**)
juzgar mal to misjudge
juzgado, juzgada judged

juez de paz, juez municipal justice of the peace
prejuzgar to prejudge
juzgar a un asesino to judge a murderer
no poderse juzgar por las apariencias not to be able to judge by appearances

The subject pronouns are found on the page facing page 1.

285

lanzar   Gerundio **lanzando**   Part. pas. **lanzado**

to throw, to hurl, to fling, to launch

The Seven Simple Tenses		The Seven Compound Tenses	
Singular	Plural	Singular	Plural
1 presente de indicativo		8 perfecto de indicativo	
lanzo	lanzamos	he lanzado	hemos lanzado
lanzas	lanzáis	has lanzado	habéis lanzado
lanza	lanzan	ha lanzado	han lanzado
2 imperfecto de indicativo		9 pluscuamperfecto de indicativo	
lanzaba	lanzábamos	había lanzado	habíamos lanzado
lanzabas	lanzabais	habías lanzado	habíais lanzado
lanzaba	lanzaban	había lanzado	habían lanzado
3 pretérito		10 pretérito anterior	
lancé	lanzamos	hube lanzado	hubimos lanzado
lanzaste	lanzasteis	hubiste lanzado	hubisteis lanzado
lanzó	lanzaron	hubo lanzado	hubieron lanzado
4 futuro		11 futuro perfecto	
lanzaré	lanzaremos	habré lanzado	habremos lanzado
lanzarás	lanzaréis	habrás lanzado	habréis lanzado
lanzará	lanzarán	habrá lanzado	habrán lanzado
5 potencial simple		12 potencial compuesto	
lanzaría	lanzaríamos	habría lanzado	habríamos lanzado
lanzarías	lanzaríais	habrías lanzado	habríais lanzado
lanzaría	lanzarían	habría lanzado	habrían lanzado
6 presente de subjuntivo		13 perfecto de subjuntivo	
lance	lancemos	haya lanzado	hayamos lanzado
lances	lancéis	hayas lanzado	hayáis lanzado
lance	lancen	haya lanzado	hayan lanzado
7 imperfecto de subjuntivo		14 pluscuamperfecto de subjuntivo	
lanzara	lanzáramos	hubiera lanzado	hubiéramos lanzado
lanzaras	lanzarais	hubieras lanzado	hubierais lanzado
lanzara	lanzaran	hubiera lanzado	hubieran lanzado
OR		OR	
lanzase	lanzásemos	hubiese lanzado	hubiésemos lanzado
lanzases	lanzaseis	hubieses lanzado	hubieseis lanzado
lanzase	lanzasen	hubiese lanzado	hubiesen lanzado

	imperativo	
—		lancemos
lanza; no lances		lanzad; no lancéis
lance		lancen

Words and expressions related to this verb

la lanza   lance, spear
el lanzamiento   casting, throwing, launching
el lanzador, la lanzadora   thrower, pitcher
  (sports)
lanzarse   to throw oneself
See also **arrojar**.

quebrar lanzas   to quarrel
ser una lanza   to be an expert
la plataforma de lanzamiento   launching pad
lanzarse al agua   to jump into the water

to hurt oneself, to feel sorry for, to complain, to regret

The Seven Simple Tenses		The Seven Compound Tenses	
Singular	Plural	Singular	Plural
1 presente de indicativo		8 perfecto de indicativo	
me lastimo	nos lastimamos	me he lastimado	nos hemos lastimado
te lastimas	os lastimáis	te has lastimado	os habéis lastimado
se lastima	se lastiman	se ha lastimado	se han lastimado
2 imperfecto de indicativo		9 pluscuamperfecto de indicativo	
me lastimaba	nos lastimábamos	me había lastimado	nos habíamos lastimado
te lastimabas	os lastimabais	te habías lastimado	os habíais lastimado
se lastimaba	se lastimaban	se había lastimado	se habían lastimado
3 pretérito		10 pretérito anterior	
me lastimé	nos lastimamos	me hube lastimado	nos hubimos lastimado
te lastimaste	os lastimasteis	te hubiste lastimado	os hubisteis lastimado
se lastimó	se lastimaron	se hubo lastimado	se hubieron lastimado
4 futuro		11 futuro perfecto	
me lastimaré	nos lastimaremos	me habré lastimado	nos habremos lastimado
te lastimarás	os lastimaréis	te habrás lastimado	os habréis lastimado
se lastimará	se lastimarán	se habrá lastimado	se habrán lastimado
5 potencial simple		12 potencial compuesto	
me lastimaría	nos lastimaríamos	me habría lastimado	nos habríamos lastimado
te lastimarías	os lastimaríais	te habrías lastimado	os habríais lastimado
se lastimaría	se lastimarían	se habría lastimado	se habrían lastimado
6 presente de subjuntivo		13 perfecto de subjuntivo	
me lastime	nos lastimemos	me haya lastimado	nos hayamos lastimado
te lastimes	os lastiméis	te hayas lastimado	os hayáis lastimado
se lastime	se lastimen	se haya lastimado	se hayan lastimado
7 imperfecto de subjuntivo		14 pluscuamperfecto de subjuntivo	
me lastimara	nos lastimáramos	me hubiera lastimado	nos hubiéramos lastimado
te lastimaras	os lastimarais	te hubieras lastimado	os hubierais lastimado
se lastimara	se lastimaran	se hubiera lastimado	se hubieran lastimado
OR		OR	
me lastimase	nos lastimásemos	me hubiese lastimado	nos hubiésemos lastimado
te lastimases	os lastimaseis	te hubieses lastimado	os hubieseis lastimado
se lastimase	se lastimasen	se hubiese lastimado	se hubiesen lastimado

imperativo	
—	lastimémonos
lastímate; no te lastimes	lastimaos; no os lastiméis
lastímese	lastímense

Words and expressions related to this verb
lastimar   to hurt, damage, injure, offend
lastimarse de   to feel sorry for, to complain about
una lástima   pity; **¡Qué lástima!**   What a pity! What a shame!
tener lástima   to feel sorry

Consult pages 541–549 for the section on verbs with prepositions.

The subject pronouns are found on the page facing page 1.

lavar

Gerundio **lavando**   Part. pas. **lavado**

to wash

The Seven Simple Tenses		The Seven Compound Tenses	
Singular	Plural	Singular	Plural
1 presente de indicativo		8 perfecto de indicativo	
lavo	lavamos	he lavado	hemos lavado
lavas	laváis	has lavado	habéis lavado
lava	lavan	ha lavado	han lavado
2 imperfecto de indicativo		9 pluscuamperfecto de indicativo	
lavaba	lavábamos	había lavado	habíamos lavado
lavabas	lavabais	habías lavado	habíais lavado
lavaba	lavaban	había lavado	habían lavado
3 pretérito		10 pretérito anterior	
lavé	lavamos	hube lavado	hubimos lavado
lavaste	lavasteis	hubiste lavado	hubisteis lavado
lavó	lavaron	hubo lavado	hubieron lavado
4 futuro		11 futuro perfecto	
lavaré	lavaremos	habré lavado	habremos lavado
lavarás	lavaréis	habrás lavado	habréis lavado
lavará	lavarán	habrá lavado	habrán lavado
5 potencial simple		12 potencial compuesto	
lavaría	lavaríamos	habría lavado	habríamos lavado
lavarías	lavaríais	habrías lavado	habríais lavado
lavaría	lavarían	habría lavado	habrían lavado
6 presente de subjuntivo		13 perfecto de subjuntivo	
lave	lavemos	haya lavado	hayamos lavado
laves	lavéis	hayas lavado	hayáis lavado
lave	laven	haya lavado	hayan lavado
7 imperfecto de subjuntivo		14 pluscuamperfecto de subjuntivo	
lavara	laváramos	hubiera lavado	hubiéramos lavado
lavaras	lavarais	hubieras lavado	hubierais lavado
lavara	lavaran	hubiera lavado	hubieran lavado
OR		OR	
lavase	lavásemos	hubiese lavado	hubiésemos lavado
lavases	lavaseis	hubieses lavado	hubieseis lavado
lavase	lavasen	hubiese lavado	hubiesen lavado

imperativo

—	lavemos
lava; no laves	lavad; no lavéis
lave	laven

Words and expressions related to this verb

el lavatorio, el lavabo   lavatory, washroom, washstand
lavandero, lavandera   launderer
la lavandería   laundry shop

el lavamanos   washstand, washbowl
lavar en seco   to dry clean
la máquina de lavar ropa   clothes washing machine

See also **lavarse.**

The Seven Simple Tenses		The Seven Compound Tenses	
Singular	Plural	Singular	Plural

1 presente de indicativo

me lavo	nos lavamos		
te lavas	os laváis		
se lava	se lavan		

8 perfecto de indicativo

me he lavado	nos hemos lavado
te has lavado	os habéis lavado
se ha lavado	se han lavado

2 imperfecto de indicativo

me lavaba	nos lavábamos
te lavabas	os lavabais
se lavaba	se lavaban

9 pluscuamperfecto de indicativo

me había lavado	nos habíamos lavado
te habías lavado	os habíais lavado
se había lavado	se habían lavado

3 pretérito

me lavé	nos lavamos
te lavaste	os lavasteis
se lavó	se lavaron

10 pretérito anterior

me hube lavado	nos hubimos lavado
te hubiste lavado	os hubisteis lavado
se hubo lavado	se hubieron lavado

4 futuro

me lavaré	nos lavaremos
te lavarás	os lavaréis
se lavará	se lavarán

11 futuro perfecto

me habré lavado	nos habremos lavado
te habrás lavado	os habréis lavado
se habrá lavado	se habrán lavado

5 potencial simple

me lavaría	nos lavaríamos
te lavarías	os lavaríais
se lavaría	se lavarían

12 potencial compuesto

me habría lavado	nos habríamos lavado
te habrías lavado	os habríais lavado
se habría lavado	se habrían lavado

6 presente de subjuntivo

me lave	nos lavemos
te laves	os lavéis
se lave	se laven

13 perfecto de subjuntivo

me haya lavado	nos hayamos lavado
te hayas lavado	os hayáis lavado
se haya lavado	se hayan lavado

7 imperfecto de subjuntivo

me lavara	nos laváramos
te lavaras	os lavarais
se lavara	se lavaran
OR	
me lavase	nos lavásemos
te lavases	os lavaseis
se lavase	se lavasen

14 pluscuamperfecto de subjuntivo

me hubiera lavado	nos hubiéramos lavado
te hubieras lavado	os hubierais lavado
se hubiera lavado	se hubieran lavado
OR	
me hubiese lavado	nos hubiésemos lavado
te hubieses lavado	os hubieseis lavado
se hubiese lavado	se hubiesen lavado

imperativo

—	lavémonos; no nos lavemos
lávate; no te laves	lavaos; no os lavéis
lávese; no se lave	lávense; no se laven

Words and expressions related to this verb

el lavatorio, el lavabo   lavatory, washroom, washstand

lavandero, lavandera   launderer

la lavandería   laundry shop

la lavativa   enema

la lavadora de vajilla   dishwashing machine

For other words and expressions related to this verb, see **lavar.**

The subject pronouns are found on the page facing page 1.

to read

The Seven Simple Tenses		The Seven Compound Tenses	
Singular	Plural	Singular	Plural
1 presente de indicativo		8 perfecto de indicativo	
leo	**leemos**	**he leído**	**hemos leído**
lees	**leéis**	**has leído**	**habéis leído**
lee	**leen**	**ha leído**	**han leído**
2 imperfecto de indicativo		9 pluscuamperfecto de indicativo	
leía	**leíamos**	**había leído**	**habíamos leído**
leías	**leíais**	**habías leído**	**habíais leído**
leía	**leían**	**había leído**	**habían leído**
3 pretérito		10 pretérito anterior	
leí	**leímos**	**hube leído**	**hubimos leído**
leíste	**leísteis**	**hubiste leído**	**hubisteis leído**
leyó	**leyeron**	**hubo leído**	**hubieron leído**
4 futuro		11 futuro perfecto	
leeré	**leeremos**	**habré leído**	**habremos leído**
leerás	**leeréis**	**habrás leído**	**habréis leído**
leerá	**leerán**	**habrá leído**	**habrán leído**
5 potencial simple		12 potencial compuesto	
leería	**leeríamos**	**habría leído**	**habríamos leído**
leerías	**leeríais**	**habrías leído**	**habríais leído**
leería	**leerían**	**habría leído**	**habrían leído**
6 presente de subjuntivo		13 perfecto de subjuntivo	
lea	**leamos**	**haya leído**	**hayamos leído**
leas	**leáis**	**hayas leído**	**hayáis leído**
lea	**lean**	**haya leído**	**hayan leído**
7 imperfecto de subjuntivo		14 pluscuamperfecto de subjuntivo	
leyera	**leyéramos**	**hubiera leído**	**hubiéramos leído**
leyeras	**leyerais**	**hubieras leído**	**hubierais leído**
leyera	**leyeran**	**hubiera leído**	**hubieran leído**
OR		OR	
leyese	**leyésemos**	**hubiese leído**	**hubiésemos leído**
leyeses	**leyeseis**	**hubieses leído**	**hubieseis leído**
leyese	**leyesen**	**hubiese leído**	**hubiesen leído**

imperativo	
—	**leamos**
lee; no leas	**leed; no leáis**
lea	**lean**

Words and expressions related to this verb

la lectura reading
  Me gusta la lectura. I like reading.
la lección lesson
lector, lectora reader
leer mal to misread

releer to read again, to reread
leer entre líneas to read between the lines
un, una leccionista private tutor
leer para sí to read to oneself
leer pruebas de imprenta to proofread

The Seven Simple Tenses		The Seven Compound Tenses	
Singular	Plural	Singular	Plural
1 presente de indicativo		8 perfecto de indicativo	
levanto	**levantamos**	**he levantado**	**hemos levantado**
levantas	**levantáis**	**has levantado**	**habéis levantado**
levanta	**levantan**	**ha levantado**	**han levantado**
2 imperfecto de indicativo		9 pluscuamperfecto de indicativo	
levantaba	**levantábamos**	**había levantado**	**habíamos levantado**
levantabas	**levantabais**	**habías levantado**	**habíais levantado**
levantaba	**levantaban**	**había levantado**	**habían levantado**
3 pretérito		10 pretérito anterior	
levanté	**levantamos**	**hube levantado**	**hubimos levantado**
levantaste	**levantasteis**	**hubiste levantado**	**hubisteis levantado**
levantó	**levantaron**	**hubo levantado**	**hubieron levantado**
4 futuro		11 futuro perfecto	
levantaré	**levantaremos**	**habré levantado**	**habremos levantado**
levantarás	**levantaréis**	**habrás levantado**	**habréis levantado**
levantará	**levantarán**	**habrá levantado**	**habrán levantado**
5 potencial simple		12 potencial compuesto	
levantaría	**levantaríamos**	**habría levantado**	**habríamos levantado**
levantarías	**levantaríais**	**habrías levantado**	**habríais levantado**
levantaría	**levantarían**	**habría levantado**	**habrían levantado**
6 presente de subjuntivo		13 perfecto de subjuntivo	
levante	**levantemos**	**haya levantado**	**hayamos levantado**
levantes	**levantéis**	**hayas levantado**	**hayáis levantado**
levante	**levanten**	**haya levantado**	**hayan levantado**
7 imperfecto de subjuntivo		14 pluscuamperfecto de subjuntivo	
levantara	**levantáramos**	**hubiera levantado**	**hubiéramos levantado**
levantaras	**levantarais**	**hubieras levantado**	**hubierais levantado**
levantara	**levantaran**	**hubiera levantado**	**hubieran levantado**
OR		OR	
levantase	**levantásemos**	**hubiese levantado**	**hubiésemos levantado**
levantases	**levantaseis**	**hubieses levantado**	**hubieseis levantado**
levantase	**levantasen**	**hubiese levantado**	**hubiesen levantado**

imperativo

—	**levantemos**
levanta; no levantes	**levantad; no levantéis**
levante	**levanten**

Words and expressions related to this verb
levantar los manteles   to clear the table
levantar con algo   to get away with
   something
el Levante   Levant, East

el levantamiento   elevation, raising
levantar fuego   to make a disturbance
levantar la cabeza   to take heart (courage)
levantar la voz   to raise one's voice

See also **levantarse.**

The subject pronouns are found on the page facing page 1.

levantarse

Gerundio **levantándose**   Part. pas. **levantado**

to get up, to rise

The Seven Simple Tenses		The Seven Compound Tenses	
Singular	Plural	Singular	Plural
1 presente de indicativo		**8 perfecto de indicativo**	
me levanto	nos levantamos	me he levantado	nos hemos levantado
te levantas	os levantáis	te has levantado	os habéis levantado
se levanta	se levantan	se ha levantado	se han levantado
2 imperfecto de indicativo		**9 pluscuamperfecto de indicativo**	
me levantaba	nos levantábamos	me había levantado	nos habíamos levantado
te levantabas	os levantabais	te habías levantado	os habíais levantado
se levantaba	se levantaban	se había levantado	se habían levantado
3 pretérito		**10 pretérito anterior**	
me levanté	nos levantamos	me hube levantado	nos hubimos levantado
te levantaste	os levantasteis	te hubiste levantado	os hubisteis levantado
se levantó	se levantaron	se hubo levantado	se hubieron levantado
4 futuro		**11 futuro perfecto**	
me levantaré	nos levantaremos	me habré levantado	nos habremos levantado
te levantarás	os levantaréis	te habrás levantado	os habréis levantado
se levantará	se levantarán	se habrá levantado	se habrán levantado
5 potencial simple		**12 potencial compuesto**	
me levantaría	nos levantaríamos	me habría levantado	nos habríamos levantado
te levantarías	os levantaríais	te habrías levantado	os habríais levantado
se levantaría	se levantarían	se habría levantado	se habrían levantado
6 presente de subjuntivo		**13 perfecto de subjuntivo**	
me levante	nos levantemos	me haya levantado	nos hayamos levantado
te levantes	os levantéis	te hayas levantado	os hayáis levantado
se levante	se levanten	se haya levantado	se hayan levantado
7 imperfecto de subjuntivo		**14 pluscuamperfecto de subjuntivo**	
me levantara	nos levantáramos	me hubiera levantado	nos hubiéramos levantado
te levantaras	os levantarais	te hubieras levantado	os hubierais levantado
se levantara	se levantaran	se hubiera levantado	se hubieran levantado
OR		OR	
me levantase	nos levantásemos	me hubiese levantado	nos hubiésemos levantado
te levantases	os levantaseis	te hubieses levantado	os hubieseis levantado
se levantase	se levantasen	se hubiese levantado	se hubiesen levantado

imperativo	
—	levantémonos; no nos levantemos
levántate; no te levantes	levantaos; no os levantéis
levántese; no se levante	levántense; no se levanten

Words and expressions related to this verb

levantar los manteles   to clear the table
levantar con algo   to get away with something
el Levante   Levant, East
el levantamiento   elevation, raising

levantar la sesión   to adjourn
levantar la voz   to raise one's voice
levantarse de la cama   to get out of bed

See also **levantar.**

The Seven Simple Tenses		The Seven Compound Tenses	
Singular	Plural	Singular	Plural
1 presente de indicativo		**8 perfecto de indicativo**	
limpio	**limpiamos**	**he limpiado**	**hemos limpiado**
limpias	**limpiáis**	**has limpiado**	**habéis limpiado**
limpia	**limpian**	**ha limpiado**	**han limpiado**
2 imperfecto de indicativo		**9 pluscuamperfecto de indicativo**	
limpiaba	**limpiábamos**	**había limpiado**	**habíamos limpiado**
limpiabas	**limpiabais**	**habías limpiado**	**habíais limpiado**
limpiaba	**limpiaban**	**había limpiado**	**habían limpiado**
3 pretérito		**10 pretérito anterior**	
limpié	**limpiamos**	**hube limpiado**	**hubimos limpiado**
limpiaste	**limpiasteis**	**hubiste limpiado**	**hubisteis limpiado**
limpió	**limpiaron**	**hubo limpiado**	**hubieron limpiado**
4 futuro		**11 futuro perfecto**	
limpiaré	**limpiaremos**	**habré limpiado**	**habremos limpiado**
limpiarás	**limpiaréis**	**habrás limpiado**	**habréis limpiado**
llimpiará	**limpiarán**	**habrá limpiado**	**habrán limpiado**
5 potencial simple		**12 potencial compuesto**	
limpiaría	**limpiaríamos**	**habría limpiado**	**habríamos limpiado**
limpiarías	**limpiaríais**	**habrías limpiado**	**habríais limpiado**
limpiaría	**limpiarían**	**habría limpiado**	**habrían limpiado**
6 presente de subjuntivo		**13 perfecto de subjuntivo**	
limpie	**limpiemos**	**haya limpiado**	**hayamos limpiado**
limpies	**limpiéis**	**hayas limpiado**	**hayáis limpiado**
limpie	**limpien**	**haya limpiado**	**hayan limpiado**
7 imperfecto de subjuntivo		**14 pluscuamperfecto de subjuntivo**	
limpiara	**limiáramos**	**hubiera limpiado**	**hubiéramos limpiado**
limpiaras	**limpiarais**	**hubieras limpiado**	**hubierais limpiado**
limpiara	**limpiaran**	**hubiera limpiado**	**hubieran limpiado**
OR		OR	
limpiase	**limpiásemos**	**hubiese limpiado**	**hubiésemos limpiado**
limpiases	**limpiaseis**	**hubieses limpiado**	**hubieseis limpiado**
limpiase	**limpiasen**	**hubiese limpiado**	**hubiesen limpiado**

	imperativo	
—	**limpiemos**	
limpia; no limpies	**limpiad; no limpiéis**	
limpie	**limpien**	

Words and expressions related to this verb
limpiar en seco   to dry clean; **limpiar las faltriqueras a uno**   to pick someone's pocket
la limpieza   cleaning, cleanliness; **limpieza de manos**   integrity
jugar limpio   to play fair

For other words and expressions related to this verb, see **limpiarse.**

limpiarse

Gerundio **limpiándose**   Part. pas. **limpiado**

to clean oneself

The Seven Simple Tenses		The Seven Compound Tenses	
Singular	Plural	Singular	Plural
1 presente de indicativo		8 perfecto de indicativo	
me limpio	nos limpiamos	me he limpiado	nos hemos limpiado
te limpias	os limpiáis	te has limpiado	os habéis limpiado
se limpia	se limpian	se ha limpiado	se han limpiado
2 imperfecto de indicativo		9 pluscuamperfecto de indicativo	
me limpiaba	nos limpiábamos	me había limpiado	nos habíamos limpiado
te limpiabas	os limpiabais	te habías limpiado	os habíais limpiado
se limpiaba	se limpiaban	se había limpiado	se habían limpiado
3 pretérito		10 pretérito anterior	
me limpié	nos limpiamos	me hube limpiado	nos hubimos limpiado
te limpiaste	os limpiasteis	te hubiste limpiado	os hubisteis limpiado
se limpió	se limpiaron	se hubo limpiado	se hubieron limpiado
4 futuro		11 futuro perfecto	
me limpiaré	nos limpiaremos	me habré limpiado	nos habremos limpiado
te limpiarás	os limpiaréis	te habrás limpiado	os habréis limpiado
se limpiará	se limpiarán	se habrá limpiado	se habrán limpiado
5 potencial simple		12 potencial compuesto	
me limpiaría	nos limpiaríamos	me habría limpiado	nos habríamos limpiado
te limpiarías	os limpiaríais	te habrías limpiado	os habríais limpiado
se limpiaría	se limpiarían	se habría limpiado	se habrían limpiado
6 presente de subjuntivo		13 perfecto de subjuntivo	
me limpie	nos limpiemos	me haya limpiado	nos hayamos limpiado
te limpies	os limpiéis	te hayas limpiado	os hayáis limpiado
se limpie	se limpien	se haya limpiado	se hayan limpiado
7 imperfecto de subjuntivo		14 pluscuamperfecto de subjuntivo	
me limpiara	nos limpiáramos	me hubiera limpiado	nos hubiéramos limpiado
te limpiaras	os limpiarais	te hubieras limpiado	os hubierais limpiado
se limpiara	se limpiaran	se hubiera limpiado	se hubieran limpiado
OR		OR	
me limpiase	nos limpiásemos	me hubiese limpiado	nos hubiésemos limpiado
te limpiases	os limpiaseis	te hubieses limpiado	os hubieseis limpiado
se limpiase	se limpiasen	se hubiese limpiado	se hubiesen limpiado

	imperativo	
—		limpiémonos
límpiate; no te limpies		limpiaos; no os limpiéis
límpiese		límpiense

Words related to this verb
un limpiapipas pipe cleaner
un limpianieve snowplow

un limpiadientes toothpick
un limpiachimeneas chimney sweep

For other words and expressions related to this verb, see **limpiar.**

Want to learn more idiomatic expressions that contain verbs? Check out pages 524–537.

The Seven Simple Tenses		The Seven Compound Tenses	
Singular	Plural	Singular	Plural
1 presente de indicativo		**8 perfecto de indicativo**	
llamo	llamamos	he llamado	hemos llamado
llamas	llamáis	has llamado	habéis llamado
llama	llaman	ha llamado	han llamado
2 imperfecto de indicativo		**9 pluscuamperfecto de indicativo**	
llamaba	llamábamos	había llamado	habíamos llamado
llamabas	llamabais	habías llamado	habíais llamado
llamaba	llamaban	había llamado	habían llamado
3 pretérito		**10 pretérito anterior**	
llamé	llamamos	hube llamado	hubimos llamado
llamaste	llamasteis	hubiste llamado	hubisteis llamado
llamó	llamaron	hubo llamado	hubieron llamado
4 futuro		**11 futuro perfecto**	
llamaré	llamaremos	habré llamado	habremos llamado
llamarás	llamaréis	habrás llamado	habréis llamado
llamará	llamarán	habrá llamado	habrán llamado
5 potencial simple		**12 potencial compuesto**	
llamaría	llamaríamos	habría llamado	habríamos llamado
llamarías	llamaríais	habrías llamado	habríais llamado
llamaría	llamarían	habría llamado	habrían llamado
6 presente de subjuntivo		**13 perfecto de subjuntivo**	
llame	llamemos	haya llamado	hayamos llamado
llames	llaméis	hayas llamado	hayáis llamado
llame	llamen	haya llamado	hayan llamado
7 imperfecto de subjuntivo		**14 pluscuamperfecto de subjuntivo**	
llamara	llamáramos	hubiera llamado	hubiéramos llamado
llamaras	llamarais	hubieras llamado	hubierais llamado
llamara	llamaran	hubiera llamado	hubieran llamado
OR		OR	
llamase	llamásemos	hubiese llamado	hubiésemos llamado
llamases	llamaseis	hubieses llamado	hubieseis llamado
llamase	llamasen	hubiese llamado	hubiesen llamado

imperativo

—	llamemos
llama; no llames	llamad; no llaméis
llame	llamen

Words and expressions related to this verb
llamar al doctor   to call the doctor
llamar por teléfono   to telephone
llamar la atención sobre   to call attention to

llamar por los nombres   to call the roll
una allamada   call, knock, ring

See also **llamarse.**

to be called, to be named

The Seven Simple Tenses		The Seven Compound Tenses	
Singular	Plural	Singular	Plural
1 presente de indicativo		**8 perfecto de indicativo**	
me llamo	nos llamamos	me he llamado	nos hemos llamado
te llamas	os llamáis	te has llamado	os habéis llamado
se llama	se llaman	se ha llamado	se han llamado
2 imperfecto de indicativo		**9 pluscuamperfecto de indicativo**	
me llamaba	nos llamábamos	me había llamado	nos habíamos llamado
te llamabas	os llamabais	te habías llamado	os habíais llamado
se llamaba	se llamaban	se había llamado	se habían llamado
3 pretérito		**10 pretérito anterior**	
me llamé	nos llamamos	me hube llamado	nos hubimos llamado
te llamaste	os llamasteis	te hubiste llamado	os hubisteis llamado
se llamó	se llamaron	se hubo llamado	se hubieron llamado
4 futuro		**11 futuro perfecto**	
me llamaré	nos llamaremos	me habré llamado	nos habremos llamado
te llamarás	os llamaréis	te habrás llamado	os habréis llamado
se llamará	se llamarán	se habrá llamado	se habrán llamado
5 potencial simple		**12 potencial compuesto**	
me llamaría	nos llamaríamos	me habría llamado	nos habríamos llamado
te llamarías	os llamaríais	te habrías llamado	os habríais llamado
se llamaría	se llamarían	se habría llamado	se habrían llamado
6 presente de subjuntivo		**13 perfecto de subjuntivo**	
me llame	nos llamemos	me haya llamado	nos hayamos llamado
te llames	os llaméis	te hayas llamado	os hayáis llamado
se llame	se llamen	se haya llamado	se hayan llamado
7 imperfecto de subjuntivo		**14 pluscuamperfecto de subjuntivo**	
me llamara	nos llamáramos	me hubiera llamado	nos hubiéramos llamado
te llamaras	os llamarais	te hubieras llamado	os hubierais llamado
se llamara	se llamaran	se hubiera llamado	se hubieran llamado
OR		OR	
me llamase	nos llamásemos	me hubiese llamado	nos hubiésemos llamado
te llamases	os llamaseis	te hubieses llamado	os hubieseis llamado
se llamase	se llamasen	se hubiese llamado	se hubiesen llamado

imperativo	
—	llamémonos; no nos llamemos
llámate; no te llames	llamaos; no os llaméis
llámese; no se llame	llámense; no se llamen

Common idiomatic expressions using this verb
—¿Cómo se llama usted?   What is your name? (How do you call yourself?)
—Me llamo Juan Morales.   My name is Juan Morales.
—¿Y cómo se llaman sus hermanos?   And what are your brother's and sister's names?
—Se llaman Teresa y Pedro.   Their names are Teresa and Peter.

For other words and expressions related to this verb, see **llamar.**

The Seven Simple Tenses		The Seven Compound Tenses	
Singular	Plural	Singular	Plural
1 presente de indicativo		**8 perfecto de indicativo**	
llego	**llegamos**	**he llegado**	**hemos llegado**
llegas	**llegáis**	**has llegado**	**habéis llegado**
llega	**llegan**	**ha llegado**	**han llegado**
2 imperfecto de indicativo		**9 pluscuamperfecto de indicativo**	
llegaba	**llegábamos**	**había llegado**	**habíamos llegado**
llegabas	**llegabais**	**habías llegado**	**habíais llegado**
llegaba	**llegaban**	**había llegado**	**habían llegado**
3 pretérito		**10 pretérito anterior**	
llegué	**llegamos**	**hube llegado**	**hubimos llegado**
llegaste	**llegasteis**	**hubiste llegado**	**hubisteis llegado**
llegó	**llegaron**	**hubo llegado**	**hubieron llegado**
4 futuro		**11 futuro perfecto**	
llegaré	**llegaremos**	**habré llegado**	**habremos llegado**
llegarás	**llegaréis**	**habrás llegado**	**habréis llegado**
llegará	**llegarán**	**habrá llegado**	**habrán llegado**
5 potencial simple		**12 potencial compuesto**	
llegaría	**llegaríamos**	**habría llegado**	**habríamos llegado**
llegarías	**llegaríais**	**habrías llegado**	**habríais llegado**
llegaría	**llegarían**	**habría llegado**	**habrían llegado**
6 presente de subjuntivo		**13 perfecto de subjuntivo**	
llegue	**lleguemos**	**haya llegado**	**hayamos llegado**
llegues	**lleguéis**	**hayas llegado**	**hayáis llegado**
llegue	**lleguen**	**haya llegado**	**hayan llegado**
7 imperfecto de subjuntivo		**14 pluscuamperfecto de subjuntivo**	
llegara	**llegáramos**	**hubiera llegado**	**hubiéramos llegado**
llegaras	**llegarais**	**hubieras llegado**	**hubierais llegado**
llegara	**llegaran**	**hubiera llegado**	**hubieran llegado**
OR		OR	
llegase	**llegásemos**	**hubiese llegado**	**hubiésemos llegado**
llegases	**llegaseis**	**hubieses llegado**	**hubieseis llegado**
llegase	**llegasen**	**hubiese llegado**	**hubiesen llegado**

imperativo	
—	**lleguemos**
llega; no llegues	**llegad; no lleguéis**
llegue	**lleguen**

Words and expressions related to this verb
llegar a ser   to become
    Luis y Luisa quieren llegar a ser médicos.   Louis and Louise want to become doctors.
llegar a saber   to find out   **llegar a**   to reach
la llegada   arrival   **al llegar**   on arrival, upon arriving
llegar tarde   to arrive late   See also **llegar** on page 533.

Consult pages 524–537 for verbs used in idiomatic expressions.

The subject pronouns are found on the page facing page 1.

to fill

The Seven Simple Tenses		The Seven Compound Tenses	
Singular	Plural	Singular	Plural
1 presente de indicativo		8 perfecto de indicativo	
lleno	llenamos	he llenado	hemos llenado
llenas	llenáis	has llenado	habéis llenado
llena	llenan	ha llenado	han llenado
2 imperfecto de indicativo		9 pluscuamperfecto de indicativo	
llenaba	llenábamos	había llenado	habíamos llenado
llenabas	llenabais	habías llenado	habíais llenado
llenaba	llenaban	había llenado	habían llenado
3 pretérito		10 pretérito anterior	
llené	llenamos	hube llenado	hubimos llenado
llenaste	llenasteis	hubiste llenado	hubisteis llenado
llenó	llenaron	hubo llenado	hubieron llenado
4 futuro		11 futuro perfecto	
llenaré	llenaremos	habré llenado	habremos llenado
llenarás	llenaréis	habrás llenado	habréis llenado
llenará	llenarán	habrá llenado	habrán llenado
5 potencial simple		12 potencial compuesto	
llenaría	llenaríamos	habría llenado	habríamos llenado
llenarías	llenaríais	habrías llenado	habríais llenado
llenaría	llenarían	habría llenado	habrían llenado
6 presente de subjuntivo		13 perfecto de subjuntivo	
llene	llenemos	haya llenado	hayamos llenado
llenes	llenéis	hayas llenado	hayáis llenado
llene	llenen	haya llenado	hayan llenado
7 imperfecto de subjuntivo		14 pluscuamperfecto de subjuntivo	
llenara	llenáramos	hubiera llenado	hubiéramos llenado
llenaras	llenarais	hubieras llenado	hubierais llenado
llenara	llenaran	hubiera llenado	hubieran llenado
OR		OR	
llenase	llenásemos	hubiese llenado	hubiésemos llenado
llenases	llenaseis	hubieses llenado	hubieseis llenado
llenase	llenasen	hubiese llenado	hubiesen llenado

imperativo

—	llenemos
llena; no llenes	llenad; no llenéis
llene	llenen

Words and expressions related to this verb

lleno, llena full, filled
la llenura abundance, fullness
llenamente fully

lleno de bote a bote full to the brim
llenar un pedido to fill an order
llenar un formulario to fill out a form

Use the EE-zee guide to Spanish pronunciation on pages 562 and 563.

to carry (away), to take (away), to wear

The Seven Simple Tenses		The Seven Compound Tenses	
Singular	Plural	Singular	Plural
1 presente de indicativo		8 perfecto de indicativo	
llevo	**llevamos**	**he llevado**	**hemos llevado**
llevas	**lleváis**	**has llevado**	**habéis llevado**
lleva	**llevan**	**ha llevado**	**han llevado**
2 imperfecto de indicativo		9 pluscuamperfecto de indicativo	
llevaba	**llevábamos**	**había llevado**	**habíamos llevado**
llevabas	**llevabais**	**habías llevado**	**habíais llevado**
llevaba	**llevaban**	**había llevado**	**habían llevado**
3 pretérito		10 pretérito anterior	
llevé	**llevamos**	**hube llevado**	**hubimos llevado**
llevaste	**llevasteis**	**hubiste llevado**	**hubisteis llevado**
llevó	**llevaron**	**hubo llevado**	**hubieron llevado**
4 futuro		11 futuro perfecto	
llevaré	**llevaremos**	**habré llevado**	**habremos llevado**
llevarás	**llevaréis**	**habrás llevado**	**habréis llevado**
llevará	**llevarán**	**habrá llevado**	**habrán llevado**
5 potencial simple		12 potencial compuesto	
llevaría	**llevaríamos**	**habría llevado**	**habríamos llevado**
llevarías	**llevaríais**	**habrías llevado**	**habríais llevado**
llevaría	**llevarían**	**habría llevado**	**habrían llevado**
6 presente de subjuntivo		13 perfecto de subjuntivo	
lleve	**llevemos**	**haya llevado**	**hayamos llevado**
lleves	**llevéis**	**hayas llevado**	**hayáis llevado**
lleve	**lleven**	**haya llevado**	**hayan llevado**
7 imperfecto de subjuntivo		14 pluscuamperfecto de subjuntivo	
llevara	**lleváramos**	**hubiera llevado**	**hubiéramos llevado**
llevaras	**llevarais**	**hubieras llevado**	**hubierais llevado**
llevara	**llevaran**	**hubiera llevado**	**hubieran llevado**
OR		OR	
llevase	**llevásemos**	**hubiese llevado**	**hubiésemos llevado**
llevases	**llevaseis**	**hubieses llevado**	**hubieseis llevado**
llevase	**llevasen**	**hubiese llevado**	**hubiesen llevado**

imperativo	
—	**llevemos**
lleva; no lleves	**llevad; no llevéis**
lleve	**lleven**

Words and expressions related to this verb
llevar a cabo   to carry through, to accomplish
llevar una caída   to have a fall
llevador, llevadora   carrier
llevar puesto   to wear
llevarse algo de alguien   to take something from someone

llevar una vida de perros   to lead a dog's life
llevarse bien con alguien   to get along well with someone
llevar conmigo   to take with me

See also **llevar** on page 533.

The subject pronouns are found on the page facing page 1.

llorar
to weep, to cry, to whine

The Seven Simple Tenses		The Seven Compound Tenses	
Singular	Plural	Singular	Plural
1 presente de indicativo		**8 perfecto de indicativo**	
lloro	lloramos	he llorado	hemos llorado
lloras	lloráis	has llorado	habéis llorado
llora	lloran	ha llorado	han llorado
2 imperfecto de indicativo		**9 pluscuamperfecto de indicativo**	
lloraba	llorábamos	había llorado	habíamos llorado
llorabas	llorabais	habías llorado	habíais llorado
lloraba	lloraban	había llorado	habían llorado
3 pretérito		**10 pretérito anterior**	
lloré	lloramos	hube llorado	hubimos llorado
lloraste	llorasteis	hubiste llorado	hubisteis llorado
lloró	lloraron	hubo llorado	hubieron llorado
4 futuro		**11 futuro perfecto**	
lloraré	lloraremos	habré llorado	habremos llorado
llorarás	lloraréis	habrás llorado	habréis llorado
llorará	llorarán	habrá llorado	habrán llorado
5 potencial simple		**12 potencial compuesto**	
lloraría	lloraríamos	habría llorado	habríamos llorado
llorarías	lloraríais	habrías llorado	habríais llorado
lloraría	llorarían	habría llorado	habrían llorado
6 presente de subjuntivo		**13 perfecto de subjuntivo**	
llore	lloremos	haya llorado	hayamos llorado
llores	lloréis	hayas llorado	hayáis llorado
llore	lloren	haya llorado	hayan llorado
7 imperfecto de subjuntivo		**14 pluscuamperfecto de subjuntivo**	
llorara	lloráramos	hubiera llorado	hubiéramos llorado
lloraras	llorarais	hubieras llorado	hubierais llorado
llorara	lloraran	hubiera llorado	hubieran llorado
OR		OR	
llorase	llorásemos	hubiese llorado	hubiésemos llorado
llorases	lloraseis	hubieses llorado	hubieseis llorado
llorase	llorasen	hubiese llorado	hubiesen llorado

imperativo	
—	lloremos
llora; no llores	llorad; no lloréis
llore	lloren

Words and expressions related to this verb
lloroso, llorosa tearful, sorrowful
el lloro weeping, crying
llorador, lloradora weeper
lloriquear to whimper, to whine
llorar con un ojo to shed crocodile tears

llorar por to weep (cry) for
llorar por cualquier cosa to cry about anything
llorar a lágrima viva to cry one's eyes out
romper a llorar to burst into tears

300

The Seven Simple Tenses	The Seven Compound Tenses
Singular Plural	Singular Plural
1 presente de indicativo	8 perfecto de indicativo
llueve	**ha llovido**
OR	
está lloviendo	
2 imperfecto de indicativo	9 pluscuamperfecto de indicativo
llovía	**había llovido**
OR	
estaba lloviendo	
3 pretérito	10 pretérito anterior
llovió	**hubo llovido**
4 futuro	11 futuro perfecto
lloverá	**habrá llovido**
5 potencial simple	12 potencial compuesto
llovería	**habría llovido**
6 presente de subjuntivo	13 perfecto de subjuntivo
llueva	**haya llovido**
7 imperfecto de subjuntivo	14 pluscuamperfecto de subjuntivo
lloviera	**hubiera llovido**
OR	OR
lloviese	**hubiese llovido**

imperativo

¡Que llueva!   Let it rain!

Words and expressions related to this verb

la lluvia   rain
lluvioso, lluviosa   rainy
llover a cántaros   to rain in torrents
llueva o no   rain or shine

la llovizna   drizzle
llover chuzos   to rain canes (cats and dogs)
tiempo lluvioso   rainy weather
lloviznar   to drizzle

Get your feet wet with verbs used in weather expressions on page 540.

The subject pronouns are found on the page facing page 1.   **301**

luchar
Gerundio **luchando**   Part. pas. **luchado**

to fight, to strive, to struggle, to wrestle

The Seven Simple Tenses		The Seven Compound Tenses	
Singular	Plural	Singular	Plural
1 presente de indicativo		**8 perfecto de indicativo**	
lucho	luchamos	he luchado	hemos luchado
luchas	lucháis	has luchado	habéis luchado
lucha	luchan	ha luchado	han luchado
2 imperfecto de indicativo		**9 pluscuamperfecto de indicativo**	
luchaba	luchábamos	había luchado	habíamos luchado
luchabas	luchabais	habías luchado	habíais luchado
luchaba	luchaban	había luchado	habían luchado
3 pretérito		**10 pretérito anterior**	
luché	luchamos	hube luchado	hubimos luchado
luchaste	luchasteis	hubiste luchado	hubisteis luchado
luchó	lucharon	hubo luchado	hubieron luchado
4 futuro		**11 futuro perfecto**	
lucharé	lucharemos	habré luchado	habremos luchado
lucharás	lucharéis	habrás luchado	habréis luchado
luchará	lucharán	habrá luchado	habrán luchado
5 potencial simple		**12 potencial compuesto**	
lucharía	lucharíamos	habría luchado	habríamos luchado
lucharías	lucharíais	habrías luchado	habríais luchado
lucharía	lucharían	habría luchado	habrían luchado
6 presente de subjuntivo		**13 perfecto de subjuntivo**	
luche	luchemos	haya luchado	hayamos luchado
luches	luchéis	hayas luchado	hayáis luchado
luche	luchen	haya luchado	hayan luchado
7 imperfecto de subjuntivo		**14 pluscuamperfecto de subjuntivo**	
luchara	lucháramos	hubiera luchado	hubiéramos luchado
lucharas	lucharais	hubieras luchado	hubierais luchado
luchara	lucharan	hubiera luchado	hubieran luchado
OR		OR	
luchase	luchásemos	hubiese luchado	hubiésemos luchado
luchases	luchaseis	hubieses luchado	hubieseis luchado
luchase	luchasen	hubiese luchado	hubiesen luchado

	imperativo
—	luchemos
lucha; no luches	luchad; no luchéis
luche	luchen

Words and expressions related to this verb
luchar por + inf.   to struggle + inf.
un luchador, una luchadora   wrestler, fighter
la lucha   battle, combat, fight, struggle, quarrel

la lucha cuerpo a cuerpo   hand-to-hand fighting
luchar por la libertad   to struggle for freedom

Get acquainted with what preposition goes with what verb on pages 541–549.

to curse

The Seven Simple Tenses		The Seven Compound Tenses	
Singular	Plural	Singular	Plural
1 presente de indicativo		8 perfecto de indicativo	
maldigo	maldecimos	he maldecido	hemos maldecido
maldices	maldecís	has maldecido	habéis maldecido
maldice	maldicen	ha maldecido	han maldecido
2 imperfecto de indicativo		9 pluscuamperfecto de indicativo	
maldecía	maldecíamos	había maldecido	habíamos maldecido
maldecías	maldecíais	habías maldecido	habíais maldecido
maldecía	maldecían	había maldecido	habían maldecido
3 pretérito		10 pretérito anterior	
maldije	maldijimos	hube maldecido	hubimos maldecido
maldijiste	maldijisteis	hubiste maldecido	hubisteis maldecido
maldijo	maldijeron	hubo maldecido	hubieron maldecido
4 futuro		11 futuro perfecto	
maldeciré	maldeciremos	habré maldecido	habremos maldecido
maldecirás	maleciréis	habrás maldecido	habréis maldecido
maldecirá	maldecirán	habrá maldecido	habrán maldecido
5 potencial simple		12 potencial compuesto	
maldeciría	maldeciríamos	habría maldecido	habríamos maldecido
maldecirías	maldeciríais	habrías maldecido	habríais maldecido
maldeciría	maldecirían	habría maldecido	habrían maldecido
6 presente de subjuntivo		13 perfecto de subjuntivo	
maldiga	maldigamos	haya maldecido	hayamos maldecido
maldigas	maldigáis	hayas maldecido	hayáis maldecido
maldiga	maldigan	haya maldecido	hayan maldecido
7 imperfecto de subjuntivo		14 pluscuamperfecto de subjuntivo	
maldijera	maldijéramos	hubiera maldecido	hubiéramos maldecido
maldijeras	maldijerais	hubieras maldecido	hubierais maldecido
maldijera	maldijeran	hubiera maldecido	hubieran maldecido
OR		OR	
maldijese	maldijésemos	hubiese maldecido	hubiésemos maldecido
maldijeses	maldijeseis	hubieses maldecido	hubieseis maldecido
maldijese	maldijesen	hubiese maldecido	hubiesen maldecido

imperativo	
—	maldigamos
maldice; no maldigas	maldecid; no maldigáis
maldiga	maldigan

Words and expressions related to this verb
maldecir de to speak ill of
una maldición curse, malediction
maldiciente slanderous
maldito, maldita damned

un, una maldiciente slanderer
maldecido, maldecida wicked
maldispuesto, maldispuesta ill-disposed
los malditos the damned

See also **bendecir.** See also note on the bottom of page 371.

The subject pronouns are found on the page facing page 1.

303

manejar

Gerundio **manejando**   Part. pas. **manejado**

to manage, to handle, to drive, to operate (a vehicle)

The Seven Simple Tenses		The Seven Compound Tenses	
Singular	Plural	Singular	Plural
1 presente de indicativo		**8 perfecto de indicativo**	
manejo	manejamos	he manejado	hemos manejado
manejas	manejáis	has manejado	habéis manejado
maneja	manejan	ha manejado	han manejado
2 imperfecto de indicativo		**9 pluscuamperfecto de indicativo**	
manejaba	manejábamos	había manejado	habíamos manejado
manejabas	manejabais	habías manejado	habíais manejado
manejaba	manejaban	había manejado	habían manejado
3 pretérito		**10 pretérito anterior**	
manejé	manejamos	hube manejado	hubimos manejado
manejaste	manejasteis	hubiste manejado	hubisteis manejado
manejó	manejaron	hubo manejado	hubieron manejado
4 futuro		**11 futuro perfecto**	
manejaré	manejaremos	habré manejado	habremos manejado
manejarás	manejaréis	habrás manejado	habréis manejado
manejará	manejarán	habrá manejado	habrán manejado
5 potencial simple		**12 potencial compuesto**	
manejaría	manejaríamos	habría manejado	habríamos manejado
manejarías	manejaríais	habrías manejado	habríais manejado
manejaría	manejarían	habría manejado	habrían manejado
6 presente de subjuntivo		**13 perfecto de subjuntivo**	
maneje	manejemos	haya manejado	hayamos manejado
manejes	manejéis	hayas manejado	hayáis manejado
maneje	manejen	haya manejado	hayan manejado
7 imperfecto de subjuntivo		**14 pluscuamperfecto de subjuntivo**	
manejara	manejáramos	hubiera manejado	hubiéramos manejado
manejaras	manejarais	hubieras manejado	hubierais manejado
manejara	manejaran	hubiera manejado	hubieran manejado
OR		OR	
manejase	manejásemos	hubiese manejado	hubiésemos manejado
manejases	manejaseis	hubieses manejado	hubieseis manejado
manejase	manejasen	hubiese manejado	hubiesen manejado

imperativo	
—	manejemos
maneja; no manejes	manejad; no manejéis
maneje	manejen

Words and expressions related to this verb

el manejo management; driving
el manejo doméstico housekeeping
el manejo a distancia remote control

manejable manageable
la manejabilidad manageability
le mano hand

If you want an explanation of meanings and uses of Spanish
and English verb tenses and moods, see pages xx–xl.

to maintain, to keep up, to support, to provide for

The Seven Simple Tenses		The Seven Compound Tenses	
Singular	Plural	Singular	Plural
1 presente de indicativo		8 perfecto de indicativo	
mantengo	mantenemos	he mantenido	hemos mantenido
mantienes	mantenéis	has mantenido	habéis mantenido
mantiene	mantienen	ha mantenido	han mantenido
2 imperfecto de indicativo		9 pluscuamperfecto de indicativo	
mantenía	manteníamos	había mantenido	habíamos mantenido
mantenías	manteníais	habías mantenido	habíais mantenido
mantenía	mantenían	había mantenido	habían mantenido
3 pretérito		10 pretérito anterior	
mantuve	mantuvimos	hube mantenido	hubimos mantenido
mantuviste	mantuvisteis	hubiste mantenido	hubisteis mantenido
mantuvo	mantuvieron	hubo mantenido	hubieron mantenido
4 futuro		11 futuro perfecto	
mantendré	mantendremos	habré mantenido	habremos mantenido
mantendrás	mantendréis	habrás mantenido	habréis mantenido
mantendrá	mantendrán	habrá mantenido	habrán mantenido
5 potencial simple		12 potencial compuesto	
mantendría	mantendríamos	habría mantenido	habríamos mantenido
mantendrías	mantendríais	habrías mantenido	habríais mantenido
mantendría	mantendrían	habría mantenido	habrían mantenido
6 presente de subjuntivo		13 perfecto de subjuntivo	
mentenga	mantengamos	haya mantenido	hayamos mantenido
mantengas	mantengáis	hayas mantenido	hayáis mantenido
mantenga	mantengan	haya mantenido	hayan mantenido
7 imperfecto de subjuntivo		14 pluscuamperfecto de subjuntivo	
mantuviera	mantuviéramos	hubiera mantenido	hubiéramos mantenido
mantuvieras	mantuvierais	hubieras mantenido	hubierais mantenido
mantuviera	mantuvieran	hubiera mantenido	hubieran mantenido
OR		OR	
mantuviese	mantuviésemos	hubiese mantenido	hubiésemos mantenido
mantuvieses	mantuvieseis	hubieses mantenido	hubieseis mantenido
mantuviese	mantuviesen	hubiese mantenido	hubiesen mantenido

imperativo

—	mantengamos
manten; no mantengas	mantened; no mantengáis
mantenga	mantengan

Words and expressions related to this verb
mantener el orden   to keep (maintain) order
el mantenimiento, la mantenencia
   maintenance, support
mantener la palabra   to keep one's word
mantenerse   to support oneself

mantener su opinión   to maintain one's
   opinion
mantener a distancia   to keep at a distance

The subject pronouns are found on the page facing page 1.

to mark, to note, to observe

The Seven Simple Tenses		The Seven Compound Tenses	
Singular	Plural	Singular	Plural
1 presente de indicativo		8 perfecto de indicativo	
marco	marcamos	he marcado	hemos marcado
marcas	marcáis	has marcado	habéis marcado
marca	marcan	ha marcado	han marcado
2 imperfecto de indicativo		9 pluscuamperfecto de indicativo	
marcaba	marcábamos	había marcado	habíamos marcado
marcabas	marcabais	habías marcado	habíais marcado
marcaba	marcaban	había marcado	habían marcado
3 pretérito		10 pretérito anterior	
marqué	marcamos	hube marcado	hubimos marcado
marcaste	marcasteis	hubiste marcado	hubisteis marcado
marcó	marcaron	hubo marcado	hubieron marcado
4 futuro		11 futuro perfecto	
marcaré	marcaremos	habré marcado	habremos marcado
marcarás	marcaréis	habrás marcado	habréis marcado
marcará	marcarán	habrá marcado	habrán marcado
5 potencial simple		12 potencial compuesto	
marcaría	marcaríamos	habría marcado	habríamos marcado
marcarías	marcaríais	habrías marcado	habríais marcado
marcaría	marcarían	habría marcado	habrían marcado
6 presente de subjuntivo		13 perfecto de subjuntivo	
marque	marquemos	haya marcado	hayamos marcado
marques	marquéis	hayas marcado	hayáis marcado
marque	marquen	haya marcado	hayan marcado
7 imperfecto de subjuntivo		14 pluscuamperfecto de subjuntivo	
marcara	marcáramos	hubiera marcado	hubiéramos marcado
marcaras	marcarais	hubieras marcado	hubierais marcado
marcara	marcaran	hubiera marcado	hubieran marcado
OR		OR	
marcase	marcásemos	hubiese marcado	hubiésemos marcado
marcases	marcaseis	hubieses marcado	hubieseis marcado
marcase	marcasen	hubiese marcado	hubiesen marcado

	imperativo	
—		marquemos
marca; no marques		marcad; no marquéis
marque		marquen

Words and expressions related to this verb

marcar un número to dial a telephone number

marcado, marcada marked, remarkable

marcadamente markedly, notably

marcar una canasta to score a basket (basketball)

marcar las cartas to mark the cards

Review the principal parts of important Spanish verbs on pages xvi–xvii.

to walk, to march, to function (machine), to run (machine)

The Seven Simple Tenses		The Seven Compound Tenses	
Singular	Plural	Singular	Plural
1 presente de indicativo		8 perfecto de indicativo	
marcho	**marchamos**	**he marchado**	**hemos marchado**
marchas	**marcháis**	**has marchado**	**habéis marchado**
marcha	**marchan**	**ha marchado**	**han marchado**
2 imperfecto de indicativo		9 pluscuamperfecto de indicativo	
marchaba	**marchábamos**	**había marchado**	**habíamos marchado**
marchabas	**marchabais**	**habías marchado**	**habíais marchado**
marchaba	**marchaban**	**había marchado**	**habían marchado**
3 pretérito		10 pretérito anterior	
marché	**marchamos**	**hube marchado**	**hubimos marchado**
marchaste	**marchasteis**	**hubiste marchado**	**hubisteis marchado**
marchó	**marcharon**	**hubo marchado**	**hubieron marchado**
4 futuro		11 futuro perfecto	
marcharé	**marcharemos**	**habré marchado**	**habremos marchado**
marcharás	**marcharéis**	**habrás marchado**	**habréis marchado**
marchará	**marcharán**	**habrá marchado**	**habrán marchado**
5 potencial simple		12 potencial compuesto	
marcharía	**marcharíamos**	**habría marchado**	**habríamos marchado**
marcharías	**marcharíais**	**habrías marchado**	**habríais marchado**
marcharía	**marcharían**	**habría marchado**	**habrían marchado**
6 presente de subjuntivo		13 perfecto de subjuntivo	
marche	**marchemos**	**haya marchado**	**hayamos marchado**
marches	**marchéis**	**hayas marchado**	**hayáis marchado**
marche	**marchen**	**haya marchado**	**hayan marchado**
7 imperfecto de subjuntivo		14 pluscuamperfecto de subjuntivo	
marchara	**marcháramos**	**hubiera marchado**	**hubiéramos marchado**
marcharas	**marcharais**	**hubieras marchado**	**hubierais marchado**
marchara	**marcharan**	**hubiera marchado**	**hubieran marchado**
OR		OR	
marchase	**marchásemos**	**hubiese marchado**	**hubiésemos marchado**
marchases	**marchaseis**	**hubieses marchado**	**hubieseis marchado**
marchase	**marchasen**	**hubiese marchado**	**hubiesen marchado**

imperativo

—	**marchemos**
marcha; no marches	**marchad; no marchéis**
marche	**marchen**

Words and expressions related to this verb
la marcha   march
a largas marchas   speedily, with speed
¡En marcha! Forward march!
poner en marcha   to put in motion, to start
Esto no marcha   This won't work; This
   will not do.

Todo marcha bien.   Everything is going okay.
marcharse   to go away, to leave
marcharse por las buenas   to leave for good,
   never to return

to go away, to leave

The Seven Simple Tenses		The Seven Compound Tenses	
Singular	Plural	Singular	Plural
1 presente de indicativo		8 perfecto de indicativo	
me marcho	nos marchamos	me he marchado	nos hemos marchado
te marchas	os marcháis	te has marchado	os habéis marchado
se marcha	se marchan	se ha marchado	se han marchado
2 imperfecto de indicativo		9 pluscuamperfecto de indicativo	
me marchaba	nos marchábamos	me había marchado	nos habíamos marchado
te marchabas	os marchabais	te habías marchado	os habíais marchado
se marchaba	se marchaban	se había marchado	se habían marchado
3 pretérito		10 pretérito anterior	
me marché	nos marchamos	me hube marchado	nos hubimos marchado
te marchaste	os marchasteis	te hubiste marchado	os hubisteis marchado
se marchó	se marcharon	se hubo marchado	se hubieron marchado
4 futuro		11 futuro perfecto	
me marcharé	nos marcharemos	me habré marchado	nos habremos marchado
te marcharás	os marcharéis	te habrás marchado	os habréis marchado
se marchará	se marcharán	se habrá marchado	se habrán marchado
5 potencial simple		12 potencial compuesto	
me marcharía	nos marcharíamos	me habría marchado	nos habríamos marchado
te marcharías	os marcharíais	te habrías marchado	os habríais marchado
se marcharía	se marcharían	se habría marchado	se habrían marchado
6 presente de subjuntivo		13 perfecto de subjuntivo	
me marche	nos marchemos	me haya marchado	nos hayamos marchado
te marches	os marchéis	te hayas marchado	os hayáis marchado
se marche	se marchen	se haya marchado	se hayan marchado
7 imperfecto de subjuntivo		14 pluscuamperfecto de subjuntivo	
me marchara	nos marcháramos	me hubiera marchado	nos hubiéramos marchado
te marcharas	os marcharais	te hubieras marchado	os hubierais marchado
se marchara	se marcharan	se hubiera marchado	se hubieran marchado
OR		OR	
me marchase	nos marchásemos	me hubiese marchado	nos hubiésemos marchado
te marchases	os marchaseis	te hubieses marchado	os hubieseis marchado
se marchase	se marchasen	se hubiese marchado	se hubiesen marchado

	imperativo	
—		marchémonos
márchate; no te marches		marchaos; no os marchéis
márchese		márchense

For words and expressions related to this verb, see **marchar** which is related to it.

Also, be sure to consult the back pages for verbs used in idiomatic expressions, Spanish proverbs using verbs, weather expressions using verbs, verbs with prepositions, and over 1,100 Spanish verbs conjugated like model verbs among the 501 verbs in this book.

The Seven Simple Tenses		The Seven Compound Tenses	
Singular	Plural	Singular	Plural
1 presente de indicativo		8 perfecto de indicativo	
mato	**matamos**	**he matado**	**hemos matado**
matas	**matáis**	**has matado**	**habéis matado**
mata	**matan**	**ha matado**	**han matado**
2 imperfecto de indicativo		9 pluscuamperfecto de indicativo	
mataba	**matábamos**	**había matado**	**habíamos matado**
matabas	**matabais**	**habías matado**	**habíais matado**
mataba	**mataban**	**había matado**	**habían matado**
3 pretérito		10 pretérito anterior	
maté	**matamos**	**hube matado**	**hubimos matado**
mataste	**matasteis**	**hubiste matado**	**hubisteis matado**
mató	**mataron**	**hubo matado**	**hubieron matado**
4 futuro		11 futuro perfecto	
mataré	**mataremos**	**habré matado**	**habremos matado**
matarás	**mataréis**	**habrás matado**	**habréis matado**
matará	**matarán**	**habrá matado**	**habrán matado**
5 potencial simple		12 potencial compuesto	
mataría	**mataríamos**	**habría matado**	**habríamos matado**
matarías	**mataríais**	**habrías matado**	**habríais matado**
mataría	**matarían**	**habría matado**	**habrían matado**
6 presente de subjuntivo		13 perfecto de subjuntivo	
mate	**matemos**	**haya matado**	**hayamos matado**
mates	**matéis**	**hayas matado**	**hayáis matado**
mate	**maten**	**haya matado**	**hayan matado**
7 imperfecto de subjuntivo		14 pluscuamperfecto de subjuntivo	
matara	**matáramos**	**hubiera matado**	**hubiéramos matado**
mataras	**matarais**	**hubieras matado**	**hubierais matado**
matara	**mataran**	**hubiera matado**	**hubieran matado**
OR		OR	
matase	**matásemos**	**hubiese matado**	**hubiésemos matado**
matases	**mataseis**	**hubieses matado**	**hubieseis matado**
matase	**matasen**	**hubiese matado**	**hubiesen matado**

	imperativo	
—		**matemos**
mata; no mates		**matad; no matéis**
mate		**maten**

Words and expressions related to this verb
el mate   checkmate (chess)
dar jaque mate   to checkmate (chess)
dar mate a   to checkmate (chess)
matador, matadora   killer; **el matador**
  bullfighter (kills the bull)

matar el tiempo   to kill time
estar a matar con alguien   to be angry at
  someone
matar a preguntas   to bombard with
  questions

The subject pronouns are found on the page facing page 1.

to measure, to weigh, to scan (verses)

The Seven Simple Tenses		The Seven Compound Tenses	
Singular	Plural	Singular	Plural
1 presente de indicativo		8 perfecto de indicativo	
mido	medimos	he medido	hemos medido
mides	medís	has medido	habéis medido
mide	miden	ha medido	han medido
2 imperfecto de indicativo		9 pluscuamperfecto de indicativo	
medía	medíamos	había medido	habíamos medido
medías	medíais	habías medido	habíais medido
medía	medían	había medido	habían medido
3 pretérito		10 pretérito anterior	
medí	medimos	hube medido	hubimos medido
mediste	medisteis	hubiste medido	hubisteis medido
midió	midieron	hubo medido	hubieron medido
4 futuro		11 futuro perfecto	
mediré	mediremos	habré medido	habremos medido
medirás	mediréis	habrás medido	habréis medido
medirá	medirán	habrá medido	habrán medido
5 potencial simple		12 potencial compuesto	
mediría	mediríamos	habría medido	habríamos medido
medirías	mediríais	habrías medido	habríais medido
mediría	medirían	habría medido	habrían medido
6 presente de subjuntivo		13 perfecto de subjuntivo	
mida	midamos	haya medido	hayamos medido
midas	midáis	hayas medido	hayáis medido
mida	midan	haya medido	hayan medido
7 imperfecto de subjuntivo		14 pluscuamperfecto de subjuntivo	
midiera	midiéramos	hubiera medido	hubiéramos medido
midieras	midierais	hubieras medido	hubierais medido
midiera	midieran	hubiera medido	hubieran medido
OR		OR	
midiese	midiésemos	hubiese medido	hubiésemos medido
midieses	midieseis	hubieses medido	hubieseis medido
midiese	midiesen	hubiese medido	hubiesen medido

imperativo	
—	midamos
mide; no midas	medid; no midáis
mida	midan

Common idiomatic expressions using this verb

medir las calles   to walk the streets out of a job
medir el suelo   to fall flat on the ground
la medida   measurement
pesos y medidas   weights and measurements

medir sus pasos   to watch one's step
medir las palabras   to weigh one's words
medirse con alguien   to measure oneself
against someone

Consult the sections on verbs used in idiomatic expressions, verbs with prepositions, and the list of over 1,100 verbs conjugated like model verbs in the back pages.

The Seven Simple Tenses		The Seven Compound Tenses	
Singular	Plural	Singular	Plural
1 presente de indicativo		8 perfecto de indicativo	
mejoro	mejoramos	he mejorado	hemos mejorado
mejoras	mejoráis	has mejorado	habéis mejorado
mejora	mejoran	ha mejorado	han mejorado
2 imperfecto de indicativo		9 pluscuamperfecto de indicativo	
mejoraba	mejorábamos	había mejorado	habíamos mejorado
mejorabas	mejorabais	habías mejorado	habíais mejorado
mejoraba	mejoraban	había mejorado	habían mejorado
3 pretérito		10 pretérito anterior	
mejoré	mejoramos	hube mejorado	hubimos mejorado
mejoraste	mejorasteis	hubiste mejorado	hubisteis mejorado
mejoró	mejoraron	hubo mejorado	hubieron mejorado
4 futuro		11 futuro perfecto	
mejoraré	mejoraremos	habré mejorado	habremos mejorado
mejorarás	mejoraréis	habrás mejorado	habréis mejorado
mejorará	mejorarán	habrá mejorado	habrán mejorado
5 potencial simple		12 potencial compuesto	
mejoraría	mejoraríamos	habría mejorado	habríamos mejorado
mejorarías	mejoraríais	habrías mejorado	habríais mejorado
mejoraría	mejorarían	habría mejorado	habrían mejorado
6 presente de subjuntivo		13 perfecto de subjuntivo	
mejore	mejoremos	haya mejorado	hayamos mejorado
mejores	mejoréis	hayas mejorado	hayáis mejorado
mejore	mejoren	haya mejorado	hayan mejorado
7 imperfecto de subjuntivo		14 pluscuamperfecto de subjuntivo	
mejorara	mejoráramos	hubiera mejorado	hubiéramos mejorado
mejoraras	mejorarais	hubieras mejorado	hubierais mejorado
mejorara	mejoraran	hubiera mejorado	hubieran mejorado
OR		OR	
mejorase	mejorásemos	hubiese mejorado	hubiésemos mejorado
mejorases	mejoraseis	hubieses mejorado	hubieseis mejorado
mejorase	mejorasen	hubiese mejorado	hubiesen mejorado

	imperativo
—	mejoremos
mejora; no mejores	mejorad; no mejoréis
mejore	mejoren

Words and expressions related to this verb
la mejora, la mejoría   improvement, betterment
mejor   better, best
tanto mejor   so much the better
desmejorar   to spoil, make worse
mejorarse   to get well, recover, improve oneself

mejor dicho   rather
mejor que mejor   even better
lo mejor   the best
desmejorarse   to decay, decline, get worse; lose one's health

mencionar

Gerundio **mencionando**   Part. pas. **mencionado**

to mention

The Seven Simple Tenses		The Seven Compound Tenses	
Singular	Plural	Singular	Plural
1 presente de indicativo		**8 perfecto de indicativo**	
menciono	mencionamos	he mencionado	hemos mencionado
mencionas	mencionáis	has mencionado	habéis mencionado
menciona	mencionan	ha mencionado	han mencionado
2 imperfecto de indicativo		**9 pluscuamperfecto de indicativo**	
mencionaba	mencionábamos	había mencionado	habíamos mencionado
mencionabas	mencionabais	habías mencionado	habíais mencionado
mencionaba	mencionaban	había mencionado	habían mencionado
3 pretérito		**10 pretérito anterior**	
mencioné	mencionamos	hube mencionado	hubimos mencionado
mencionaste	mencionasteis	hubiste mencionado	hubisteis mencionado
mencionó	mencionaron	hubo mencionado	hubieron mencionado
4 futuro		**11 futuro perfecto**	
mencionaré	mencionaremos	habré mencionado	habremos mencionado
mencionarás	mencionaréis	habrás mencionado	habréis mencionado
mencionará	mencionarán	habrá mencionado	habrán mencionado
5 potencial simple		**12 potencial compuesto**	
mencionaría	mencionaríamos	habría mencionado	habríamos mencionado
mencionarías	mencionaríais	habrías mencionado	habríais mencionado
mencionaría	mencionarían	habría mencionado	habrían mencionado
6 presente de subjuntivo		**13 perfecto de subjuntivo**	
mencione	mencionemos	haya mencionado	hayamos mencionado
menciones	mencionéis	hayas mencionado	hayáis mencionado
mencione	mencionen	haya mencionado	hayan mencionado
7 imperfecto de subjuntivo		**14 pluscuamperfecto de subjuntivo**	
mencionara	mencionáramos	hubiera mencionado	hubiéramos mencionado
mencionaras	mencionarais	hubieras mencionado	hubierais mencionado
mencionara	mencionaran	hubiera mencionado	hubieran mencionado
OR		OR	
mencionase	mencionásemos	hubiese mencionado	hubiésemos mencionado
mencionases	mencionaseis	hubieses mencionado	hubieseis mencionado
mencionase	mencionasen	hubiese mencionado	hubiesen mencionado

	imperativo
—	mencionemos
menciona; no menciones	mencionad; no mencionéis
mencione	mencionen

Words and expressions related to this verb
la mención   mention
mención honorífica   honorable mention
digno de mención   worthy of mention

en mención   under discussion
hacer mención de   to make mention of
sin mencionar a   not to mention

Review the principal parts of important Spanish verbs on pages xvi–xvii.

to lie, to tell a lie

The Seven Simple Tenses		The Seven Compound Tenses	
Singular	Plural	Singular	Plural
1 presente de indicativo		8 perfecto de indicativo	
miento	**mentimos**	**he mentido**	**hemos mentido**
mientes	**mentís**	**has mentido**	**habéis mentido**
miente	**mienten**	**ha mentido**	**han mentido**
2 imperfecto de indicativo		9 pluscuamperfecto de indicativo	
mentía	**mentíamos**	**había mentido**	**habíamos mentido**
mentías	**mentíais**	**habías mentido**	**habíais mentido**
mentía	**mentían**	**había mentido**	**habían mentido**
3 pretérito		10 pretérito anterior	
mentí	**mentimos**	**hube mentido**	**hubimos mentido**
mentiste	**mentisteis**	**hubiste mentido**	**hubisteis mentido**
mintió	**mintieron**	**hubo mentido**	**hubieron mentido**
4 futuro		11 futuro perfecto	
mentiré	**mentiremos**	**habré mentido**	**habremos mentido**
mentirás	**mentiréis**	**habrás mentido**	**habréis mentido**
mentirá	**mentirán**	**habrá mentido**	**habrán mentido**
5 potencial simple		12 potencial compuesto	
mentiría	**mentiríamos**	**habría mentido**	**habríamos mentido**
mentirías	**mentiríais**	**habrías mentido**	**habríais mentido**
mentiría	**mentirían**	**habría mentido**	**habrían mentido**
6 presente de subjuntivo		13 perfecto de subjuntivo	
mienta	**mintamos**	**haya mentido**	**hayamos mentido**
mientas	**mintáis**	**hayas mentido**	**hayáis mentido**
mienta	**mientan**	**haya mentido**	**hayan mentido**
7 imperfecto de subjuntivo		14 pluscuamperfecto de subjuntivo	
mintiera	**mintiéramos**	**hubiera mentido**	**hubiéramos mentido**
mintieras	**mintierais**	**hubieras mentido**	**hubierais mentido**
mintiera	**mintieran**	**hubiera mentido**	**hubieran mentido**
OR		OR	
mintiese	**mintiésemos**	**hubiese mentido**	**hubiésemos mentido**
mintieses	**mintieseis**	**hubieses mentido**	**hubieseis mentido**
mintiese	**mintiesen**	**hubiese mentido**	**hubiesen mentido**

imperativo

—	**mintamos**
miente; no mientas	**mentid; no mintáis**
mienta	**mientan**

Words and expressions related to this verb

una mentira   a lie
un mentirón   a great lie
una mentirilla   a fib

mentido, mentida   deceptive, false
mentirosamente   falsely
¡Parece mentira!   I just don't believe it!

Can't recognize an irregular verb form? Check out pages 519–523.

to merit, to deserve

The Seven Simple Tenses		The Seven Compound Tenses	
Singular	Plural	Singular	Plural
1 presente de indicativo		8 perfecto de indicativo	
merezco	merecemos	he merecido	hemos merecido
mereces	merecéis	has merecido	habéis merecido
merece	merecen	ha merecido	han merecido
2 imperfecto de indicativo		9 pluscuamperfecto de indicativo	
merecía	merecíamos	había merecido	habíamos merecido
merecías	merecíais	habías merecido	habíais merecido
merecía	merecían	había merecido	habían merecido
3 pretérito		10 pretérito anterior	
merecí	merecimos	hube merecido	hubimos merecido
mereciste	merecisteis	hubiste merecido	hubisteis merecido
mereció	merecieron	hubo merecido	hubieron merecido
4 futuro		11 futuro perfecto	
mereceré	mereceremos	habré merecido	habremos merecido
merecerás	mereceréis	habrás merecido	habréis merecido
merecerá	merecerán	habrá merecido	habrán merecido
5 potencial simple		12 potencial compuesto	
merecería	mereceríamos	habría merecido	habríamos merecido
merecerías	mereceríais	habrías merecido	habríais merecido
merecería	merecerían	habría merecido	habrían merecido
6 presente de subjuntivo		13 perfecto de subjuntivo	
merezca	merezcamos	haya merecido	hayamos merecido
merezcas	merezcáis	hayas merecido	hayáis merecido
merezca	merezcan	haya merecido	hayan merecido
7 imperfecto de subjuntivo		14 pluscuamperfecto de subjuntivo	
mereciera	mereciéramos	hubiera merecido	hubiéramos merecido
merecieras	merecierais	hubieras merecido	hubierais merecido
mereciera	merecieran	hubiera merecido	hubieran merecido
OR		OR	
mereciese	mereciésemos	hubiese merecido	hubiésemos merecido
merecieses	merecieseis	hubieses merecido	hubieseis merecido
mereciese	mereciesen	hubiese merecido	hubiesen merecido

	imperativo	
—		merezcamos
merece; no merezcas		mereced; no merezcáis
merezca		merezcan

Words and expressions related to this verb
merecer la pena to be worth the trouble
el merecimiento, el mérito merit
meritísimo, meritísima most deserving
merced a . . . thanks to . . .
merecidamente deservedly

por sus propios méritos on one's own merits
hacer mérito de to make mention of
vuestra merced your honor, your grace; sir
merecer una bofetada to deserve a slap
  (in the face)

to look, to look at, to watch

The Seven Simple Tenses		The Seven Compound Tenses	
Singular	Plural	Singular	Plural
1 presente de indicativo		8 perfecto de indicativo	
miro	miramos	he mirado	hemos mirado
miras	miráis	has mirado	habéis mirado
mira	miran	ha mirado	han mirado
2 imperfecto de indicativo		9 pluscuamperfecto de indicativo	
miraba	mirábamos	había mirado	habíamos mirado
mirabas	mirabais	habías mirado	habíais mirado
miraba	miraban	había mirado	habían mirado
3 pretérito		10 pretérito anterior	
miré	miramos	hube mirado	hubimos mirado
miraste	mirasteis	hubiste mirado	hubisteis mirado
miró	miraron	hubo mirado	hubieron mirado
4 futuro		11 futuro perfecto	
miraré	miraremos	habré mirado	habremos mirado
mirarás	miraréis	habrás mirado	habréis mirado
mirará	mirarán	habrá mirado	habrán mirado
5 potencial simple		12 potencial compuesto	
miraría	miraríamos	habría mirado	habríamos mirado
mirarías	miraríais	habrías mirado	habríais mirado
miraría	mirarían	habría mirado	habrían mirado
6 presente de subjuntivo		13 perfecto de subjuntivo	
mire	miremos	haya mirado	hayamos mirado
mires	miréis	hayas mirado	hayáis mirado
mire	miren	haya mirado	hayan mirado
7 imperfecto de subjuntivo		14 pluscuamperfecto de subjuntivo	
mirara	miráramos	hubiera mirado	hubiéramos mirado
miraras	mirarais	hubieras mirado	hubierais mirado
mirara	miraran	hubiera mirado	hubieran mirado
OR		OR	
mirase	mirásemos	hubiese mirado	hubiésemos mirado
mirases	miraseis	hubieses mirado	hubieseis mirado
mirase	mirasen	hubiese mirado	hubiesen mirado

imperativo

—	miremos
mira; no mires	mirad; no miréis
mire	miren

Words and expressions related to this verb
mirar la televisión to watch television
¡Mira! Look! Look out! See here! Listen!
¡Antes que te cases, mira lo que haces!
Look before you leap! (Before you get married, look at what you are doing!)

mirar por to look after
mirar a to face, to look out on
mirar por encima del hombro to look down one's nose at

Enjoy verbs in Spanish proverbs on page 539.

The subject pronouns are found on the page facing page 1.

315

to look at oneself, to look at each other (**uno a otro; unos a otros**)

The Seven Simple Tenses		The Seven Compound Tenses	
Singular	Plural	Singular	Plural
1 presente de indicativo		8 perfecto de indicativo	
me miro	nos miramos	me he mirado	nos hemos mirado
te miras	os miráis	te has mirado	os habéis mirado
se mira	se miran	se ha mirado	se han mirado
2 imperfecto de indicativo		9 pluscuamperfecto de indicativo	
me miraba	nos mirábamos	me había mirado	nos habíamos mirado
te mirabas	os mirabais	te habías mirado	os habíais mirado
se miraba	se miraban	se había mirado	se habían mirado
3 pretérito		10 pretérito anterior	
me miré	nos miramos	me hube mirado	nos hubimos mirado
te miraste	os mirasteis	te hubiste mirado	os hubisteis mirado
se miró	se miraron	se hubo mirado	se hubieron mirado
4 futuro		11 futuro perfecto	
me miraré	nos miraremos	me habré mirado	nos habremos mirado
te mirarás	os miraréis	te habrás mirado	os habréis mirado
se mirará	se mirarán	se habrá mirado	se habrán mirado
5 potencial simple		12 potencial compuesto	
me miraría	nos miraríamos	me habría mirado	nos habríamos mirado
te mirarías	os miraríais	te habrías mirado	os habríais mirado
se miraría	se mirarían	se habría mirado	se habrían mirado
6 presente de subjuntivo		13 perfecto de subjuntivo	
me mire	nos miremos	me haya mirado	nos hayamos mirado
te mires	os miréis	te hayas mirado	os hayáis mirado
se mire	se miren	se haya mirado	se hayan mirado
7 imperfecto de subjuntivo		14 pluscuamperfecto de subjuntivo	
me mirara	nos miráramos	me hubiera mirado	nos hubiéramos mirado
te miraras	os mirarais	te hubieras mirado	os hubierais mirado
se mirara	se miraran	se hubiera mirado	se hubieran mirado
OR		OR	
me mirase	nos mirásemos	me hubiese mirado	nos hubiésemos mirado
te mirases	os miraseis	te hubieses mirado	os hubieseis mirado
se mirase	se mirasen	se hubiese mirado	se hubiesen mirado

	imperativo	
—	mirémonos	
mírate; no te mires	miraos; no os miréis	
mírese	mírense	

Words and expressions related to this verb
mirar to look (at), to watch
mirar la televisión to watch television
mirarse las uñas to twiddle one's tumbs
(to be idle)
mirarse unos a otros to look at each other
in awe

mirarse al espejo to look at oneself in
the mirror
¡Mira! Look! Look out!
echar una mirada a to take a look at
mirar alrededor to look around

to get wet, to wet oneself

The Seven Simple Tenses		The Seven Compound Tenses	
Singular	Plural	Singular	Plural
1 presente de indicativo		8 perfecto de indicativo	
me mojo	**nos mojamos**	**me he mojado**	**nos hemos mojado**
te mojas	**os mojáis**	**te has mojado**	**os habéis mojado**
se moja	**se mojan**	**se ha mojado**	**se han mojado**
2 imperfecto de indicativo		9 pluscuamperfecto de indicativo	
me mojaba	**nos mojábamos**	**me había mojado**	**nos habíamos mojado**
te mojabas	**os mojabais**	**te habías mojado**	**os habíais mojado**
se mojaba	**se mojaban**	**se había mojado**	**se habían mojado**
3 pretérito		10 pretérito anterior	
me mojé	**nos mojamos**	**me hube mojado**	**nos hubimos mojado**
te mojaste	**os mojasteis**	**te hubiste mojado**	**os hubisteis mojado**
se mojó	**se mojaron**	**se hubo mojado**	**se hubieron mojado**
4 futuro		11 futuro perfecto	
me mojaré	**nos mojaremos**	**me habré mojado**	**nos habremos mojado**
te mojarás	**os mojaréis**	**te habrás mojado**	**os habréis mojado**
se mojará	**se mojarán**	**se habrá mojado**	**se habrán mojado**
5 potencial simple		12 potencial compuesto	
me mojaría	**nos mojaríamos**	**me habría mojado**	**nos habríamos mojado**
te mojarías	**os mojaríais**	**te habrías mojado**	**os habríais mojado**
se mojaría	**se mojarían**	**se habría mojado**	**se habrían mojado**
6 presente de subjuntivo		13 perfecto de subjuntivo	
me moje	**nos mojemos**	**me haya mojado**	**nos hayamos mojado**
te mojes	**os mojéis**	**te hayas mojado**	**os hayáis mojado**
se moje	**se mojen**	**se haya mojado**	**se hayan mojado**
7 imperfecto de subjuntivo		14 pluscuamperfecto de subjuntivo	
me mojara	**nos mojáramos**	**me hubiera mojado**	**nos hubiéramos mojado**
te mojaras	**os mojarais**	**te hubieras mojado**	**os hubierais mojado**
se mojara	**se mojaran**	**se hubiera mojado**	**se hubieran mojado**
OR		OR	
me mojase	**nos mojásemos**	**me hubiese mojado**	**nos hubiésemos mojado**
te mojases	**os mojaseis**	**te hubieses mojado**	**os hubieseis mojado**
se mojase	**se mojasen**	**se hubiese mojado**	**se hubiesen mojado**

	imperativo	
—		**mojémonos**
mójate; no te mojes		**mojaos; no os mojéis**
mójese		**mójense**

Words and expressions related to this verb

mojado, mojada   wet, drenched, soaked
mojar   to wet, to moisten; to interfere, to meddle
mojar en   to get mixed up in
remojar   to soak; **remojar el gaznate**   to wet one's whistle (to drink something)

mojarse por la lluvia   to get wet from the rain
¡Cuidado! Piso mojado.   Caution! Wet floor.

montar

Gerundio **montando**   Part. pas. **montado**

to mount, to go up, to climb, to get on, to wind (a watch)

The Seven Simple Tenses		The Seven Compound Tenses	
Singular	Plural	Singular	Plural
1 presente de indicativo		8 perfecto de indicativo	
monto	montamos	he montado	hemos montado
montas	montáis	has montado	habéis montado
monta	montan	ha montado	han montado
2 imperfecto de indicativo		9 pluscuamperfecto de indicativo	
montaba	montábamos	había montado	habíamos montado
montabas	montabais	habías montado	habíais montado
montaba	montaban	había montado	habían montado
3 pretérito		10 pretérito anterior	
monté	montamos	hube montado	hubimos montado
montaste	montasteis	hubiste montado	hubisteis montado
montó	montaron	hubo montado	hubieron montado
4 futuro		11 futuro perfecto	
montaré	montaremos	habré montado	habremos montado
montarás	montaréis	habrás montado	habréis montado
montará	montarán	habrá montado	habrán montado
5 potencial simple		12 potencial compuesto	
montaría	montaríamos	habría montado	habríamos montado
montarías	montaríais	habrías montado	habríais montado
montaría	montarían	habría montado	habrían montado
6 presente de subjuntivo		13 perfecto de subjuntivo	
monte	montemos	haya montado	hayamos montado
montes	montéis	hayas montado	hayáis montado
monte	monten	haya montado	hayan montado
7 imperfecto de subjuntivo		14 pluscuamperfecto de subjuntivo	
montara	montáramos	hubiera montado	hubiéramos montado
montaras	montarais	hubieras montado	hubierais montado
montara	montaran	hubiera montado	hubieran montado
OR		OR	
montase	montásemos	hubiese montado	hubiésemos montado
montases	montaseis	hubieses montado	hubieseis montado
montase	montasen	hubiese montado	hubiesen montado

	imperativo	
—		montemos
monta; no montes		montad; no montéis
monte		monten

Words and expressions related to this verb

montar a caballo   to ride horseback
montar en pelo   to ride bareback
montar a horcajadas   to straddle
el monte   mount, mountain
la montaña   mountain

montarse   to mount, to get on top
remontar   to frighten away, to scare away, to
    go back up, to get back on; to go back (in time)
trasmontar   to go over mountains
montar a   to amount to

The Seven Simple Tenses		The Seven Compound Tenses	
Singular	Plural	Singular	Plural
1 presente de indicativo		8 perfecto de indicativo	
muerdo	**mordemos**	**he mordido**	**hemos mordido**
muerdes	**mordéis**	**has mordido**	**habéis mordido**
muerde	**muerden**	**ha mordido**	**han mordido**
2 imperfecto de indicativo		9 pluscuamperfecto de indicativo	
mordía	**mordíamos**	**había mordido**	**habíamos mordido**
mordías	**mordíais**	**habías mordido**	**habíais mordido**
mordía	**mordían**	**había mordido**	**habían mordido**
3 pretérito		10 pretérito anterior	
mordí	**mordimos**	**hube mordido**	**hubimos mordido**
mordiste	**mordisteis**	**hubiste mordido**	**hubisteis mordido**
mordió	**mordieron**	**hubo mordido**	**hubieron mordido**
4 futuro		11 futuro perfecto	
morderé	**morderemos**	**habré mordido**	**habremos mordido**
morderás	**morderéis**	**habrás mordido**	**habréis mordido**
morderá	**morderán**	**habrá mordido**	**habrán mordido**
5 potencial simple		12 potencial compuesto	
mordería	**morderíamos**	**habría mordido**	**habríamos mordido**
morderías	**morderíais**	**habrías mordido**	**habríais mordido**
mordería	**morderían**	**habría mordido**	**habrían mordido**
6 presente de subjuntivo		13 perfecto de subjuntivo	
muerda	**mordamos**	**haya mordido**	**hayamos mordido**
muerdas	**mordáis**	**hayas mordido**	**hayáis mordido**
muerda	**muerdan**	**haya mordido**	**hayan mordido**
7 imperfecto de subjuntivo		14 pluscuamperfecto de subjuntivo	
mordiera	**mordiéramos**	**hubiera mordido**	**hubiéramos mordido**
mordieras	**mordierais**	**hubieras mordido**	**hubierais mordido**
mordiera	**mordieran**	**hubiera mordido**	**hubieran mordido**
OR		OR	
mordiese	**mordiésemos**	**hubiese mordido**	**hubiésemos mordido**
mordieses	**mordieseis**	**hubieses mordido**	**hubieseis mordido**
mordiese	**mordiesen**	**hubiese mordido**	**hubiesen mordido**

imperativo

—	**mordamos**
muerde; no muerdas	**morded; no mordáis**
muerda	**muerdan**

Words and expressions related to this verb

Perro que ladra no muerde.   A barking dog
   does not bite.
una mordaza   gag
la mordacidad   mordancy

mordazmente   bitingly
una mordedura   a bite
morderse   to bite oneself
Me mordí el labio.   I bit my lip.

Enjoy more verbs in Spanish proverbs on page 539.

The subject pronouns are found on the page facing page 1.

to die

The Seven Simple Tenses		The Seven Compound Tenses	
Singular	Plural	Singular	Plural
1 presente de indicativo		8 perfecto de indicativo	
muero	morimos	he muerto	hemos muerto
mueres	morís	has muerto	habéis muerto
muere	mueren	ha muerto	han muerto
2 imperfecto de indicativo		9 pluscuamperfecto de indicativo	
moría	moríamos	había muerto	habíamos muerto
morías	moríais	habías muerto	habíais muerto
moría	morían	había muerto	habían muerto
3 pretérito		10 pretérito anterior	
morí	morimos	hube muerto	hubimos muerto
moriste	moristeis	hubiste muerto	hubisteis muerto
murió	murieron	hubo muerto	hubieron muerto
4 futuro		11 futuro perfecto	
moriré	moriremos	habré muerto	habremos muerto
morirás	moriréis	habrás muerto	habréis muerto
morirá	morirán	habrá muerto	habrán muerto
5 potencial simple		12 potencial compuesto	
moriría	moriríamos	habría muerto	habríamos muerto
morirías	moriríais	habrías muerto	habríais muerto
moriría	morirían	habría muerto	habrían muerto
6 presente de subjuntivo		13 perfecto de subjuntivo	
muera	muramos	haya muerto	hayamos muerto
mueras	muráis	hayas muerto	hayáis muerto
muera	mueran	haya muerto	hayan muerto
7 imperfecto de subjuntivo		14 pluscuamperfecto de subjuntivo	
muriera	muriéramos	hubiera muerto	hubiéramos muerto
murieras	murierais	hubieras muerto	hubierais muerto
muriera	murieran	hubiera muerto	hubieran muerto
OR		OR	
muriese	muriésemos	hubiese muerto	hubiésemos muerto
murieses	murieseis	hubieses muerto	hubieseis muerto
muriese	muriesen	hubiese muerto	hubiesen muerto

	imperativo	
—		muramos
muere; no mueras		morid; no muráis
muera		mueran

Words and expressions related to this verb
la muerte death
mortal fatal, mortal
la mortalidad mortality
morir de risa to die laughing
morirse de hambre to starve to death (to die of hunger)

entremorir to burn out, to flicker
morir de repente to drop dead
hasta morir until death
morirse de miedo to be scared to death
morirse de frío to freeze to death (to die of freezing cold)

to show, to point out, to display

The Seven Simple Tenses		The Seven Compound Tenses	
Singular	Plural	Singular	Plural
1 presente de indicativo		8 perfecto de indicativo	
muestro	**mostramos**	**he mostrado**	**hemos mostrado**
muestras	**mostráis**	**has mostrado**	**habéis mostrado**
muestra	**muestran**	**ha mostrado**	**han mostrado**
2 imperfecto de indicativo		9 pluscuamperfecto de indicativo	
mostraba	**mostrábamos**	**había mostrado**	**habíamos mostrado**
mostrabas	**mostrabais**	**habías mostrado**	**habíais mostrado**
mostraba	**mostraban**	**había mostrado**	**habían mostrado**
3 pretérito		10 pretérito anterior	
mostré	**mostramos**	**hube mostrado**	**hubimos mostrado**
mostraste	**mostrasteis**	**hubiste mostrado**	**hubisteis mostrado**
mostró	**mostraron**	**hubo mostrado**	**hubieron mostrado**
4 futuro		11 futuro perfecto	
mostraré	**mostraremos**	**habré mostrado**	**habremos mostrado**
mostrarás	**mostraréis**	**habrás mostrado**	**habréis mostrado**
mostrará	**mostrarán**	**habrá mostrado**	**habrán mostrado**
5 potencial simple		12 potencial compuesto	
mostraría	**mostraríamos**	**habría mostrado**	**habríamos mostrado**
mostrarías	**mostraríais**	**habrías mostrado**	**habríais mostrado**
mostraría	**mostrarían**	**habría mostrado**	**habrían mostrado**
6 presente de subjuntivo		13 perfecto de subjuntivo	
muestre	**mostremos**	**haya mostrado**	**hayamos mostrado**
muestres	**mostréis**	**hayas mostrado**	**hayáis mostrado**
muestre	**muestren**	**haya mostrado**	**hayan mostrado**
7 imperfecto de subjuntivo		14 pluscuamperfecto de subjuntivo	
mostrara	**mostráramos**	**hubiera mostrado**	**hubiéramos mostrado**
mostraras	**mostrarais**	**hubieras mostrado**	**hubierais mostrado**
mostrara	**mostraran**	**hubiera mostrado**	**hubieran mostrado**
OR		OR	
mostrase	**mostrásemos**	**hubiese mostrado**	**hubiésemos mostrado**
mostrases	**mostraseis**	**hubieses mostrado**	**hubieseis mostrado**
mostrase	**mostrasen**	**hubiese mostrado**	**hubiesen mostrado**

imperativo

—	**mostremos**
muestra; no muestres	**mostrad; no mostréis**
muestre	**muestren**

Words and expressions related to this verb
mostrador   counter (in a store where merchandise is displayed under a glass case)
mostrarse   to show oneself, to appear

See also **demostrar.**

Check out the verb drills and verb tests with answers explained on pages 619–665.

mover

to move, to persuade, to excite

The Seven Simple Tenses		The Seven Compound Tenses	
Singular	Plural	Singular	Plural
1 presente de indicativo		8 perfecto de indicativo	
muevo	**movemos**	**he movido**	**hemos movido**
mueves	**movéis**	**has movido**	**habéis movido**
mueve	**mueven**	**ha movido**	**han movido**
2 imperfecto de indicativo		9 pluscuamperfecto de indicativo	
movía	**movíamos**	**había movido**	**habíamos movido**
movías	**movíais**	**habías movido**	**habíais movido**
movía	**movían**	**había movido**	**habían movido**
3 pretérito		10 pretérito anterior	
moví	**movimos**	**hube movido**	**hubimos movido**
moviste	**movisteis**	**hubiste movido**	**hubisteis movido**
movió	**movieron**	**hubo movido**	**hubieron movido**
4 futuro		11 futuro perfecto	
moveré	**moveremos**	**habré movido**	**habremos movido**
moverás	**moveréis**	**habrás movido**	**habréis movido**
moverá	**moverán**	**habrá movido**	**habrán movido**
5 potencial simple		12 potencial compuesto	
movería	**moveríamos**	**habría movido**	**habríamos movido**
moverías	**moveríais**	**habrías movido**	**habríais movido**
movería	**moverían**	**habría movido**	**habrían movido**
6 presente de subjuntivo		13 perfecto de subjuntivo	
mueva	**movamos**	**haya movido**	**hayamos movido**
muevas	**mováis**	**hayas movido**	**hayáis movido**
mueva	**muevan**	**haya movido**	**hayan movido**
7 imperfecto de subjuntivo		14 pluscuamperfecto de subjuntivo	
moviera	**moviéramos**	**hubiera movido**	**hubiéramos movido**
movieras	**movierais**	**hubieras movido**	**hubierais movido**
moviera	**movieran**	**hubiera movido**	**hubieran movido**
OR		OR	
moviese	**moviésemos**	**hubiese movido**	**hubiésemos movido**
movieses	**movieseis**	**hubieses movido**	**hubieseis movido**
moviese	**moviesen**	**hubiese movido**	**hubiesen movido**

	imperativo	
—	**movamos**
mueve; no muevas	**moved; no mováis**
mueva	**muevan**

Words and expressions related to this verb
mover a alguien a + inf.   to move someone + inf.
la movilidad   mobility
el movimiento   movement, motion
mover cielo y tierra   to move heaven and earth
remover   to move, transfer, remove; **removerse**
   to move away

conmover   to move (one's emotions),
   to touch, stir, upset, shake
conmoverse   to be moved, touched
promover   to promote, to further

to change one's clothes, to change one's place of residence, to move

The Seven Simple Tenses		The Seven Compound Tenses	
Singular	Plural	Singular	Plural
1 presente de indicativo		8 perfecto de indicativo	
me mudo	nos mudamos	me he mudado	nos hemos mudado
te mudas	os mudáis	te has mudado	os habéis mudado
se muda	se mudan	se ha mudado	se han mudado
2 imperfecto de indicativo		9 pluscuamperfecto de indicativo	
me mudaba	nos mudábamos	me había mudado	nos habíamos mudado
te mudabas	os mudabais	te habías mudado	os habíais mudado
se mudaba	se mudaban	se había mudado	se habían mudado
3 pretérito		10 pretérito anterior	
me mudé	nos mudamos	me hube mudado	nos hubimos mudado
te mudaste	os mudasteis	te hubiste mudado	os hubisteis mudado
se mudó	se mudaron	se hubo mudado	se hubieron mudado
4 futuro		11 futuro perfecto	
me mudaré	nos mudaremos	me habré mudado	nos habremos mudado
te mudarás	os mudaréis	te habrás mudado	os habréis mudado
se mudará	se mudarán	se habrá mudado	se habrán mudado
5 potencial simple		12 potencial compuesto	
me mudaría	nos mudaríamos	me habría mudado	nos habríamos mudado
te mudarías	os mudaríais	te habrías mudado	os habríais mudado
se mudaría	se mudarían	se habría mudado	se habrían mudado
6 presente de subjuntivo		13 perfecto de subjuntivo	
me mude	nos mudemos	me haya mudado	nos hayamos mudado
te mudes	os mudéis	te hayas mudado	os hayáis mudado
se mude	se muden	se haya mudado	se hayan mudado
7 imperfecto de subjuntivo		14 pluscuamperfecto de subjuntivo	
me mudara	nos mudáramos	me hubiera mudado	nos hubiéramos mudado
te mudaras	os mudarais	te hubieras mudado	os hubierais mudado
se mudara	se mudaran	se hubiera mudado	se hubieran mudado
OR		OR	
me mudasen	nos mudásemos	me hubiese mudado	nos hubiésemos mudado
te mudases	os mudaseis	te hubieses mudado	os hubieseis mudado
se mudase	se mudasen	se hubiese mudado	se hubiesen mudado

imperativo

—	mudémonos
múdate; no te mudes	**mudaos; no os mudéis**
múdese	**múdense**

Words and expressions related to this verb

transmudar, trasmudar   to transmute
la mudanza   moving (change)
un carro de mudanzas   moving van
demudar   to change facial expression
mudar   to change

mudarse de casa   to move from one house to another
mudarse de ropa   to change clothes
demudarse   to be changed (face)

> Be sure to consult the back pages for sections on verbs used in idiomatic expressions, verbs with prepositions, and the list of over 1,100 verbs conjugated like model verbs.

323

nacer

Gerundio **naciendo**   Part. pas. **nacido**

to be born

The Seven Simple Tenses		The Seven Compound Tenses	
Singular	Plural	Singular	Plural
1 presente de indicativo		**8 perfecto de indicativo**	
nazco	nacemos	he nacido	hemos nacido
naces	nacéis	has nacido	habéis nacido
nace	nacen	ha nacido	han nacido
2 imperfecto de indicativo		**9 pluscuamperfecto de indicativo**	
nacía	nacíamos	había nacido	habíamos nacido
nacías	nacíais	habías nacido	habíais nacido
nacía	nacían	había nacido	habían nacido
3 pretérito		**10 pretérito anterior**	
nací	nacimos	hube nacido	hubimos nacido
naciste	nacisteis	hubiste nacido	hubisteis nacido
nació	nacieron	hubo nacido	hubieron nacido
4 futuro		**11 futuro perfecto**	
naceré	naceremos	habré nacido	habremos nacido
nacerás	naceréis	habrás nacido	habréis nacido
nacerá	nacerán	habrá nacido	habrán nacido
5 potencial simple		**12 potencial compuesto**	
nacería	naceríamos	habría nacido	habríamos nacido
nacerías	naceríais	habrías nacido	habríais nacido
nacería	nacerían	habría nacido	habrían nacido
6 presente de subjuntivo		**13 perfecto de subjuntivo**	
nazca	nazcamos	haya nacido	hayamos nacido
nazcas	nazcáis	hayas nacido	hayáis nacido
nazca	nazcan	haya nacido	hayan nacido
7 imperfecto de subjuntivo		**14 pluscuamperfecto de subjuntivo**	
naciera	naciéramos	hubiera nacido	hubiéramos nacido
nacieras	nacierais	hubieras nacido	hubierais nacido
naciera	nacieran	hubiera nacido	hubieran nacido
OR		OR	
naciese	naciésemos	hubiese nacido	hubiésemos nacido
nacieses	nacieseis	hubieses nacido	hubieseis nacido
naciese	naciesen	hubiese nacido	hubiesen nacido

imperativo	
—	nazcamos
nace; no nazcas	naced; no nazcáis
nazca	nazcan

Words and expressions related to this verb

bien nacido (nacida) well-bred; **mal nacido (nacida)** ill-bred
el nacimiento birth
renacer to be born again, to be reborn

nacer tarde to be born yesterday (not much intelligence)
nacer de pies to be born with a silver spoon in one's mouth

Learn more verbs in 30 practical situations for tourists on pages 564–594.

The Seven Simple Tenses		The Seven Compound Tenses	
Singular	Plural	Singular	Plural
1 presente de indicativo		8 perfecto de indicativo	
nado	**nadamos**	**he nadado**	**hemos nadado**
nadas	**nadáis**	**has nadado**	**habéis nadado**
nada	**nadan**	**ha nadado**	**han nadado**
2 imperfecto de indicativo		9 pluscuamperfecto de indicativo	
nadaba	**nadábamos**	**había nadado**	**habíamos nadado**
nadabas	**nadabais**	**habías nadado**	**habíais nadado**
nadaba	**nadaban**	**había nadado**	**habían nadado**
3 pretérito		10 pretérito anterior	
nadé	**nadamos**	**hube nadado**	**hubimos nadado**
nadaste	**nadasteis**	**hubiste nadado**	**hubisteis nadado**
nadó	**nadaron**	**hubo nadado**	**hubieron nadado**
4 futuro		11 futuro perfecto	
nadaré	**nadaremos**	**habré nadado**	**habremos nadado**
nadarás	**nadaréis**	**habrás nadado**	**habréis nadado**
nadará	**nadarán**	**habrá nadado**	**habrán nadado**
5 potencial simple		12 potencial compuesto	
nadaría	**nadaríamos**	**habría nadado**	**habríamos nadado**
nadarías	**nadaríais**	**habrías nadado**	**habríais nadado**
nadaría	**nadarían**	**habría nadado**	**habrían nadado**
6 presente de subjuntivo		13 perfecto de subjuntivo	
nade	**nademos**	**haya nadado**	**hayamos nadado**
nades	**nadéis**	**hayas nadado**	**hayáis nadado**
nade	**naden**	**haya nadado**	**hayan nadado**
7 imperfecto de subjuntivo		14 pluscuamperfecto de subjuntivo	
nadara	**nadáramos**	**hubiera nadado**	**hubiéramos nadado**
nadaras	**nadarais**	**hubieras nadado**	**hubierais nadado**
nadara	**nadaran**	**hubiera nadado**	**hubieran nadado**
OR		OR	
nadase	**nadásemos**	**hubiese nadado**	**hubiésemos nadado**
nadases	**nadaseis**	**hubieses nadado**	**hubieseis nadado**
nadase	**nadasen**	**hubiese nadado**	**hubiesen nadado**

imperativo

—	**nademos**
nada; no nades	**nadad; no nadéis**
nade	**naden**

Words and expressions related to this verb

nadador, nadadora   swimmer
la natación   swimming

nadar entre dos aguas   to be undecided
nadar en   to revel in, to delight in, to take
great pleasure in

Consult page 540 for weather expressions using verbs.

The subject pronouns are found on the page facing page 1.

navegar
Gerundio **navegando**   Part. pas. **navegado**

to navigate, to sail

The Seven Simple Tenses		The Seven Compound Tenses	
Singular	Plural	Singular	Plural
1 presente de indicativo		**8 perfecto de indicativo**	
navego	navegamos	he navegado	hemos navegado
navegas	navegáis	has navegado	habéis navegado
navega	navegan	ha navegado	han navegado
2 imperfecto de indicativo		**9 pluscuamperfecto de indicativo**	
navegaba	navegábamos	había navegado	habíamos navegado
navegabas	navegabais	habías navegado	habíais navegado
navegaba	navegaban	había navegado	habían navegado
3 pretérito		**10 pretérito anterior**	
navegué	navegamos	hube navegado	hubimos navegado
navegaste	navegasteis	hubiste navegado	hubisteis navegado
navegó	navegaron	hubo navegado	hubieron navegado
4 futuro		**11 futuro perfecto**	
navegaré	navegaremos	habré navegado	habremos navegado
navegarás	navegaréis	habrás navegado	habréis navegado
navegará	navegarán	habrá navegado	habrán navegado
5 potencial simple		**12 potencial compuesto**	
navegaría	navegaríamos	habría navegado	habríamos navegado
navegarías	navegaríais	habrías navegado	habríais navegado
navegaría	navegarían	habría navegado	habrían navegado
6 presente de subjuntivo		**13 perfecto de subjuntivo**	
navegue	naveguemos	haya navegado	hayamos navegado
navegues	naveguéis	hayas navegado	hayáis navegado
navegue	naveguen	haya navegado	hayan navegado
7 imperfecto de subjuntivo		**14 pluscuamperfecto de subjuntivo**	
navegara	navegáramos	hubiera navegado	hubiéramos navegado
navegaras	navegarais	hubieras navegado	hubierais navegado
navegara	navegaran	hubiera navegado	hubieran navegado
OR		OR	
navegase	navegásemos	hubiese navegado	hubiésemos navegado
navegases	navegaseis	hubieses navegado	hubieseis navegado
navegase	navegasen	hubiese navegado	hubiesen navegado

imperativo	
—	naveguemos
navega; no navegues	navegad; no naveguéis
navegue	naveguen

Words and expressions related to this verb

la navegación navigation
navegación de ultramar overseas shipping
navegar a distancia de to steer clear away
la nave ship
saber navegar to know how to navigate
navegar a la vela to sail

naval naval, nautical
navegable navigable
una naveta, una navecilla small ship
una nave cósmica spaceship
navegar los mares to sail the seas
la navegación fluvial river navigation

The Seven Simple Tenses | The Seven Compound Tenses

Singular	Plural	Singular	Plural
1 presente de indicativo		8 perfecto de indicativo	
necesito	**necesitamos**	**he necesitado**	**hemos necesitado**
necesitas	**necesitáis**	**has necesitado**	**habéis necesitado**
necesita	**necesitan**	**ha necesitado**	**han necesitado**
2 imperfecto de indicativo		9 pluscuamperfecto de indicativo	
necesitaba	**necesitábamos**	**había necesitado**	**habíamos necesitado**
necesitabas	**necesitabais**	**habías necesitado**	**habíais necesitado**
necesitaba	**necesitaban**	**había necesitado**	**habían necesitado**
3 pretérito		10 pretérito anterior	
necesité	**necesitamos**	**hube necesitado**	**hubimos necesitado**
necesitaste	**necesitasteis**	**hubiste necesitado**	**hubisteis necesitado**
necesitó	**necesitaron**	**hubo necesitado**	**hubieron necesitado**
4 futuro		11 futuro perfecto	
necesitaré	**necesitaremos**	**habré necesitado**	**habremos necesitado**
necesitarás	**necesitaréis**	**habrás necesitado**	**habréis necesitado**
necesitará	**necesitarán**	**habrá necesitado**	**habrán necesitado**
5 potencial simple		12 potencial compuesto	
necesitaría	**necesitaríamos**	**habría necesitado**	**habríamos necesitado**
necesitarías	**necesitaríais**	**habrías necesitado**	**habríais necesitado**
necesitaría	**necesitarían**	**habría necesitado**	**habrían necesitado**
6 presente de subjuntivo		13 perfecto de subjuntivo	
necesite	**necesitemos**	**haya necesitado**	**hayamos necesitado**
necesites	**necesitéis**	**hayas necesitado**	**hayáis necesitado**
necesite	**necesiten**	**haya necesitado**	**hayan necesitado**
7 imperfecto de subjuntivo		14 pluscuamperfecto de subjuntivo	
necesitara	**necesitáramos**	**hubiera necesitado**	**hubiéramos necesitado**
necesitaras	**necesitarais**	**hubieras necesitado**	**hubierais necesitado**
necesitara	**necesitaran**	**hubiera necesitado**	**hubieran necesitado**
OR		OR	
necesitase	**necesitásemos**	**hubiese necesitado**	**hubiésemos necesitado**
necesitases	**necesitaseis**	**hubieses necesitado**	**hubieseis necesitado**
necesitase	**necesitasen**	**hubiese necesitado**	**hubiesen necesitado**

imperativo

	necesitemos
necesita; no necesites	**necesitad; no necesitéis**
necesite	**necesiten**

Words and expressions related to this verb
la necesidad   necessity
por necesidad   from necessity
necesario, necesaria   necessary

necesitar + inf.   to have + inf., to need + inf.
un necesitado, una necesitada   needy person
necesariamente   necessarily

Increase your verb power with popular phrases, words,
and expressions for tourists on pages 595–618.

The subject pronouns are found on the page facing page 1.

to deny

The Seven Simple Tenses		The Seven Compound Tenses	
Singular	Plural	Singular	Plural
1 presente de indicativo		**8 perfecto de indicativo**	
niego	**negamos**	**he negado**	**hemos negado**
niegas	**negáis**	**has negado**	**habéis negado**
niega	**niegan**	**ha negado**	**han negado**
2 imperfecto de indicativo		**9 pluscuamperfecto de indicativo**	
negaba	**negábamos**	**había negado**	**habíamos negado**
negabas	**negabais**	**habías negado**	**habíais negado**
negaba	**negaban**	**había negado**	**habían negado**
3 pretérito		**10 pretérito anterior**	
negué	**negamos**	**hube negado**	**hubimos negado**
negaste	**negasteis**	**hubiste negado**	**hubisteis negado**
negó	**negaron**	**hubo negado**	**hubieron negado**
4 futuro		**11 futuro perfecto**	
negaré	**negaremos**	**habré negado**	**habremos negado**
negarás	**negaréis**	**habrás negado**	**habréis negado**
negará	**negarán**	**habrá negado**	**habrán negado**
5 potencial simple		**12 potencial compuesto**	
negaría	**negaríamos**	**habría negado**	**habríamos negado**
negarías	**negaríais**	**habrías negado**	**habríais negado**
negaría	**negarían**	**habría negado**	**habrían negado**
6 presente de subjuntivo		**13 perfecto de subjuntivo**	
niegue	**neguemos**	**haya negado**	**hayamos negado**
niegues	**neguéis**	**hayas negado**	**hayáis negado**
niegue	**nieguen**	**haya negado**	**hayan negado**
7 imperfecto de subjuntivo		**14 pluscuamperfecto de subjuntivo**	
negara	**negáramos**	**hubiera negado**	**hubiéramos negado**
negaras	**negarais**	**hubieras negado**	**hubierais negado**
negara	**negaran**	**hubiera negado**	**hubieran negado**
OR		OR	
negase	**negásemos**	**hubiese negado**	**hubiésemos negado**
negases	**negaseis**	**hubieses negado**	**hubieseis negado**
negase	**negasen**	**hubiese negado**	**hubiesen negado**

imperativo

—	**neguemos**
niega; no niegues	**negad; no neguéis**
niegue	**nieguen**

Words and expressions related to this verb

negador, negadora   denier
negativo, negativa   negative
la negación   denial, negation
negable   deniable

negar haber + past part.   to deny having + past part.
negarse a   to refuse
renegar   to abhor, to deny vehemently

Can't recognize an irregular verb form? Check out pages 519–523.

The Seven Simple Tenses	The Seven Compound Tenses
Singular Plural	Singular Plural
1 presente de indicativo **nieva** OR **está nevando**	8 perfecto de indicativo **ha nevado**
2 imperfecto de indicativo **nevaba** OR **estaba nevando**	9 pluscuamperfecto de indicativo **había nevado**
3 pretérito **nevó**	10 pretérito anterior **hubo nevado**
4 futuro **nevará**	11 futuro perfecto **habrá nevado**
5 potencial simple **nevaría**	12 potencial compuesto **habría nevado**
6 presente de subjuntivo **nieve**	13 perfecto de subjuntivo **haya nevado**
7 imperfecto de subjuntivo **nevara** OR **nevase**	14 pluscuamperfecto de subjuntivo **hubiera nevado** OR **hubiese nevado**

imperativo
¡Que nieve!   Let it snow!

Words and expressions related to this verb
la nieve   snow
    Me gusta la nieve.   I like snow.
nevado, nevada   snowy, snow covered
la nevada   snowfall; the state of Nevada, U.S.A.

la nevera   refrigerator
un copo de nieve   snowflake
una bola de nieve   snowball

Get your feet wet with verbs used in weather expressions on page 540.

The subject pronouns are found on the page facing page 1.

obedecer
Gerundio **obedeciendo** Part. pas. **obedecido**

to obey

The Seven Simple Tenses		The Seven Compound Tenses	
Singular	Plural	Singular	Plural
1 presente de indicativo		8 perfecto de indicativo	
obedezco	**obedecemos**	**he obedecido**	**hemos obedecido**
obedeces	**obedecéis**	**has obedecido**	**habéis obedecido**
obedece	**obedecen**	**ha obedecido**	**han obedecido**
2 imperfecto de indicativo		9 pluscuamperfecto de indicativo	
obedecía	**obedecíamos**	**había obedecido**	**habíamos obedecido**
obedecías	**obedecíais**	**habías obedecido**	**habíais obedecido**
obedecía	**obedecían**	**había obedecido**	**habían obedecido**
3 pretérito		10 pretérito anterior	
obedecí	**obedecimos**	**hube obedecido**	**hubimos obedecido**
obedeciste	**obedecisteis**	**hubiste obedecido**	**hubisteis obedecido**
obedeció	**obedecieron**	**hubo obedecido**	**hubieron obedecido**
4 futuro		11 futuro perfecto	
obedeceré	**obedeceremos**	**habré obedecido**	**habremos obedecido**
obedecerás	**obedeceréis**	**habrás obedecido**	**habréis obedecido**
obedecerá	**obedecerán**	**habrá obedecido**	**habrán obedecido**
5 potencial simple		12 potencial compuesto	
obedecería	**obedeceríamos**	**habría obedecido**	**habríamos obedecido**
obedecerías	**obedeceríais**	**habrías obedecido**	**habríais obedecido**
obedecería	**obedecerían**	**habría obedecido**	**habrían obedecido**
6 presente de subjuntivo		13 perfecto de subjuntivo	
obedezca	**obedezcamos**	**haya obedecido**	**hayamos obedecido**
obedezcas	**obedezcáis**	**hayas obedecido**	**hayáis obedecido**
obedezca	**obedezcan**	**haya obedecido**	**hayan obedecido**
7 imperfecto de subjuntivo		14 pluscuamperfecto de subjuntivo	
obedeciera	**obedeciéramos**	**hubiera obedecido**	**hubiéramos obedecido**
obedecieras	**obedecierais**	**hubieras obedecido**	**hubierais obedecido**
obedeciera	**obedecieran**	**hubiera obedecido**	**hubieran obedecido**
OR		OR	
obedeciese	**obedeciésemos**	**hubiese obedecido**	**hubiésemos obedecido**
obedecieses	**obedecieseis**	**hubieses obedecido**	**hubieseis obedecido**
obedeciese	**obedeciesen**	**hubiese obedecido**	**hubiesen obedecido**

imperativo

—	**obedezcamos**
obedece; no obedezcas	**obedeced; no obedezcáis**
obedezca	**obedezcan**

Words related to this verb

el obedecimiento, la obediencia obedience
obediente obedient
obedecer las leyes to obey the law
desobediente disobedient

obedientemente obediently
desobedecer to disobey
obedecer a sus padres to obey one's parents
la desobediencia disobedience

to observe, to notice

The Seven Simple Tenses		The Seven Compound Tenses	
Singular	Plural	Singular	Plural
1 presente de indicativo		**8 perfecto de indicativo**	
observo	observamos	he observado	hemos observado
observas	observáis	has observado	habéis observado
observa	observan	ha observado	han observado
2 imperfecto de indicativo		**9 pluscuamperfecto de indicativo**	
observaba	observábamos	había observado	habíamos observado
observabas	observabais	habías observado	habíais observado
osbervaba	observaban	había observado	habían observado
3 pretérito		**10 pretérito anterior**	
observé	observamos	hube observado	hubimos observado
observaste	observasteis	hubiste observado	hubisteis observado
observó	observaron	hubo observado	hubieron observado
4 futuro		**11 futuro perfecto**	
observaré	observaremos	habré observado	habremos observado
observarás	observaréis	habrás observado	habréis observado
observará	observarán	habrá observado	habrán observado
5 potencial simple		**12 potencial compuesto**	
observaría	observaríamos	habría observado	habríamos observado
observarías	observaríais	habrías observado	habríais observado
observaría	observarían	habría observado	habrían observado
6 presente de subjuntivo		**13 perfecto de subjuntivo**	
observe	observemos	haya observado	hayamos observado
observes	observéis	hayas observado	hayáis observado
observe	observen	haya observado	hayan observado
7 imperfecto de subjuntivo		**14 pluscuamperfecto de subjuntivo**	
observara	observáramos	hubiera observado	hubiéramos observado
observaras	observarais	hubieras observado	hubierais observado
observara	observaran	hubiera observado	hubieran observado
OR		OR	
observase	observásemos	hubiese observado	hubiésemos observado
observases	observaseis	hubieses observado	hubieseis observado
observase	observasen	hubiese observado	hubiesen observado

imperativo

—	observemos
observa; no observes	observad; no observéis
observe	observen

Words and expressions related to this verb
el observatorio   observatory
la observación   observation

la observancia   observance
observante   observant

Be sure to consult the back pages for sections on verbs used in idiomatic expressions,
verbs with prepositions, and the list of over 1,100 verbs conjugated like model verbs.

The subject pronouns are found on the page facing page 1.

to obtain, to get

The Seven Simple Tenses		The Seven Compound Tenses	
Singular	Plural	Singular	Plural
1 presente de indicativo		8 perfecto de indicativo	
obtengo	**obtenemos**	**he obtenido**	**hemos obtenido**
obtienes	**obtenéis**	**has obtenido**	**habéis obtenido**
obtiene	**obtienen**	**ha obtenido**	**han obtenido**
2 imperfecto de indicativo		9 pluscuamperfecto de indicativo	
obtenía	**obteníamos**	**había obtenido**	**habíamos obtenido**
obtenías	**obteníais**	**habías obtenido**	**habíais obtenido**
obtenía	**obtenían**	**había obtenido**	**habían obtenido**
3 pretérito		10 pretérito anterior	
obtuve	**obtuvimos**	**hube obtenido**	**hubimos obtenido**
obtuviste	**obtuvisteis**	**hubiste obtenido**	**hubisteis obtenido**
obtuvo	**obtuvieron**	**hubo obtenido**	**hubieron obtenido**
4 futuro		11 futuro perfecto	
obtendré	**obtendremos**	**habré obtenido**	**habremos obtenido**
obtendrás	**obtendréis**	**habrás obtenido**	**habréis obtenido**
obtendrá	**obtendrán**	**habrá obtenido**	**habrán obtenido**
5 potencial simple		12 potencial compuesto	
obtendría	**obtendríamos**	**habría obtenido**	**habríamos obtenido**
obtendrías	**obtendríais**	**habrías obtenido**	**habríais obtenido**
obtendría	**obtendrían**	**habría obtenido**	**habrían obtenido**
6 presente de subjuntivo		13 perfecto de subjuntivo	
obtenga	**obtengamos**	**haya obtenido**	**hayamos obtenido**
obtengas	**obtengáis**	**hayas obtenido**	**hayáis obtenido**
obtenga	**obtengan**	**haya obtenido**	**hayan obtenido**
7 imperfecto de subjuntivo		14 pluscuamperfecto de subjuntivo	
obtuviera	**obtuviéramos**	**hubiera obtenido**	**hubiéramos obtenido**
obtuvieras	**obtuvierais**	**hubieras obtenido**	**hubierais obtenido**
obtuviera	**obtuvieran**	**hubiera obtenido**	**hubieran obtenido**
OR		OR	
obtuviese	**obtuviésemos**	**hubiese obtenido**	**hubiésemos obtenido**
obtuvieses	**obtuvieseis**	**hubieses obtenido**	**hubieseis obtenido**
obtuviese	**obtuviesen**	**hubiese obtenido**	**hubiesen obtenido**

	imperativo	
—		**obtengamos**
obtén; no obtengas		**obtened; obtengáis**
obtenga		**obtengan**

Words related to this verb
obtenible   obtainable, available
obtener una colocación   to get a job
la obtención   obtainment

obtener buenos resultados   to get good results
obtener malos resultados   to get bad results

See also the verb **tener.**

The Seven Simple Tenses		The Seven Compound Tenses	
Singular	Plural	Singular	Plural
1 presente de indicativo		**8 perfecto de indicativo**	
me oculto	**nos ocultamos**	**me he ocultado**	**nos hemos ocultado**
te ocultas	**os ocultáis**	**te has ocultado**	**os habéis ocultado**
se oculta	**se ocultan**	**se ha ocultado**	**se han ocultado**
2 imperfecto de indicativo		**9 pluscuamperfecto de indicativo**	
me ocultaba	**nos ocultábamos**	**me había ocultado**	**nos habíamos ocultado**
te ocultabas	**os ocultabais**	**te habías ocultado**	**os habíais ocultado**
se ocultaba	**se ocultaban**	**se había ocultado**	**se habían ocultado**
3 pretérito		**10 pretérito anterior**	
me oculté	**nos ocultamos**	**me hube ocultado**	**nos hubimos ocultado**
te ocultaste	**os ocultasteis**	**te hubiste ocultado**	**os hubisteis ocultado**
se ocultó	**se ocultaron**	**se hubo ocultado**	**se hubieron ocultado**
4 futuro		**11 futuro perfecto**	
me ocultaré	**nos ocultaremos**	**me habré ocultado**	**nos habremos ocultado**
te ocultarás	**os ocultaréis**	**te habrás ocultado**	**os habréis ocultado**
se ocultará	**se ocultarán**	**se habrá ocultado**	**se habrán ocultado**
5 potencial simple		**12 potencial compuesto**	
me ocultaría	**nos ocultaríamos**	**me habría ocultado**	**nos habríamos ocultado**
te ocultarías	**os ocultaríais**	**te habrías ocultado**	**os habríais ocultado**
se ocultaría	**se ocultarían**	**se habría ocultado**	**se habrían ocultado**
6 presente de subjuntivo		**13 perfecto de subjuntivo**	
me oculte	**nos ocultemos**	**me haya ocultado**	**nos hayamos ocultado**
te ocultes	**os ocultéis**	**te hayas ocultado**	**os hayáis ocultado**
se oculte	**se oculten**	**se haya ocultado**	**se hayan ocultado**
7 imperfecto de subjuntivo		**14 pluscuamperfecto de subjuntivo**	
me ocultara	**nos ocultáramos**	**me hubiera ocultado**	**nos hubiéramos ocultado**
te ocultaras	**os ocultarais**	**te hubieras ocultado**	**os hubierais ocultado**
se ocultara	**se ocultaran**	**se hubiera ocultado**	**se hubieran ocultado**
OR		OR	
me ocultase	**nos ocultásemos**	**me hubiese ocultado**	**nos hubiésemos ocultado**
te ocultases	**os ocultaseis**	**te hubieses ocultado**	**os hubieseis ocultado**
se ocultase	**se ocultasen**	**se hubiese ocultado**	**se hubiesen ocultado**

imperativo

—	**ocultémonos**
ocúltate; no te ocultes	**ocultaos; no os ocultéis**
ocúltese	**ocúltense**

Words and expressions related to this verb
ocultar   to hide, conceal
ocultar una cosa de una persona   to hide something from someone
ocultarsele a uno   to hide oneself from someone
oculto, oculta   occult; hidden, concealed; **en oculto**   secretly
las Ciencias ocultas   the Occult Sciences

The subject pronouns are found on the page facing page 1.

ocupar

Gerundio **ocupando**   Part. pas. **ocupado**

to occupy

The Seven Simple Tenses		The Seven Compound Tenses	
Singular	Plural	Singular	Plural
1 presente de indicativo		**8 perfecto de indicativo**	
ocupo	ocupamos	he ocupado	hemos ocupado
ocupas	ocupáis	has ocupado	habéis ocupado
ocupa	ocupan	ha ocupado	han ocupado
2 imperfecto de indicativo		**9 pluscuamperfecto de indicativo**	
ocupaba	ocupábamos	había ocupado	habíamos ocupado
ocupabas	ocupabais	habías ocupado	habíais ocupado
ocupaba	ocupaban	había ocupado	habían ocupado
3 pretérito		**10 pretérito anterior**	
ocupé	ocupamos	hube ocupado	hubimos ocupado
ocupaste	ocupasteis	hubiste ocupado	hubisteis ocupado
ocupó	ocuparon	hubo ocupado	hubieron ocupado
4 futuro		**11 futuro perfecto**	
ocuparé	ocuparemos	habré ocupado	habremos ocupado
ocuparás	ocuparéis	habrás ocupado	habréis ocupado
ocupará	ocuparán	habrá ocupado	habrán ocupado
5 potencial simple		**12 potencial compuesto**	
ocuparía	ocuparíamos	habría ocupado	habríamos ocupado
ocuparías	ocuparíais	habrías ocupado	habríais ocupado
ocuparía	ocuparían	habría ocupado	habrían ocupado
6 presente de subjuntivo		**13 perfecto de subjuntivo**	
ocupe	ocupemos	haya ocupado	hayamos ocupado
ocupes	ocupéis	hayas ocupado	hayáis ocupado
ocupe	ocupen	haya ocupado	hayan ocupado
7 imperfecto de subjuntivo		**14 pluscuamperfecto de subjuntivo**	
ocupara	ocupáramos	hubiera ocupado	hubiéramos ocupado
ocuparas	ocuparais	hubieras ocupado	hubierais ocupado
ocupara	ocuparan	hubiera ocupado	hubieran ocupado
OR		OR	
ocupase	ocupasemos	hubiese ocupado	hubiésemos ocupado
ocupases	ocupaseis	hubieses ocupado	hubieseis ocupado
ocupase	ocupasen	hubiese ocupado	hubiesen ocupado

	imperativo	
—		ocupemos
ocupa; no ocupes		ocupad; no ocupéis
ocupe		ocupen

Words and expressions related to this verb

ocupado, ocupada   busy, occupied
la ocupación   occupation
ocuparse de (en)   to be busy with, in, to
  be engaged in
un, una ocupante   occupant

See also **preocuparse.**

desocupar   to vacate
ocuparse con algo   to be busy with something

to occur, to happen

The Seven Simple Tenses		The Seven Compound Tenses	
Singular	Plural	Singular	Plural
1 presente de indicativo		8 perfecto de indicativo	
ocurre	**ocurren**	**ha ocurrido**	**han ocurrido**
2 imperfecto de indicativo		9 pluscuamperfecto de indicativo	
ocurría	**ocurrían**	**había ocurrido**	**habían ocurrido**
3 pretérito		10 pretérito anterior	
ocurrió	**ocurrieron**	**hubo ocurrido**	**hubieron ocurrido**
4 futuro		11 futuro perfecto	
ocurrirá	**ocurrirán**	**habrá ocurrido**	**habrán ocurrido**
5 potencial simple		12 potencial compuesto	
ocurriría	**ocurrirían**	**habría ocurrido**	**habrían ocurrido**
6 presente de subjuntivo		13 perfecto de subjuntivo	
ocurra	**ocurran**	**haya ocurrido**	**hayan ocurrido**
7 imperfecto de subjuntivo		14 pluscuamperfecto de subjuntivo	
ocurriera	**ocurrieran**	**hubiera ocurrido**	**hubieran ocurrido**
OR		OR	
ocurriese	**ocurriesen**	**hubiese ocurrido**	**hubiesen ocurrido**

imperativo

¡Que ocurra!   **¡Que ocurran!**
Let it occur!   Let them occur!

Words related to this verb
ocurrente   occurring; funny, witty, humorous
la ocurrencia   occurrence, happening, event; witticism
This verb is generally used in the third person singular and plural.

Consult the sections on verbs used in idiomatic expressions, verbs with prepositions, and the list of over 1,100 verbs conjugated like model verbs in the back pages.

to offer

The Seven Simple Tenses		The Seven Compound Tenses	
Singular	Plural	Singular	Plural
1 presente de indicativo		8 perfecto de indicativo	
ofrezco	**ofrecemos**	**he ofrecido**	**hemos ofrecido**
ofreces	**ofrecéis**	**has ofrecido**	**habéis ofrecido**
ofrece	**ofrecen**	**ha ofrecido**	**han ofrecido**
2 imperfecto de indicativo		9 pluscuamperfecto de indicativo	
ofrecía	**ofrecíamos**	**había ofrecido**	**habíamos ofrecido**
ofrecías	**ofrecíais**	**habías ofrecido**	**habíais ofrecido**
ofrecía	**ofrecían**	**había ofrecido**	**habían ofrecido**
3 pretérito		10 pretérito anterior	
ofrecí	**ofrecimos**	**hube ofrecido**	**hubimos ofrecido**
ofreciste	**ofrecisteis**	**hubiste ofrecido**	**hubisteis ofrecido**
ofreció	**ofrecieron**	**hubo ofrecido**	**hubieron ofrecido**
4 futuro		11 futuro perfecto	
ofreceré	**ofreceremos**	**habré ofrecido**	**habremos ofrecido**
ofrecerás	**ofreceréis**	**habrás ofrecido**	**habréis ofrecido**
ofrecerá	**ofrecerán**	**habrá ofrecido**	**habrán ofrecido**
5 potencial simple		12 potencial compuesto	
ofrecería	**ofreceríamos**	**habría ofrecido**	**habríamos ofrecido**
ofrecerías	**ofreceríais**	**habrías ofrecido**	**habríais ofrecido**
ofrecería	**ofrecerían**	**habría ofrecido**	**habrían ofrecido**
6 presente de subjuntivo		13 perfecto de subjuntivo	
ofrezca	**ofrezcamos**	**haya ofrecido**	**hayamos ofrecido**
ofrezcas	**ofrezcáis**	**hayas ofrecido**	**hayáis ofrecido**
ofrezca	**ofrezcan**	**haya ofrecido**	**hayan ofrecido**
7 imperfecto de subjuntivo		14 pluscuamperfecto de subjuntivo	
ofreciera	**ofreciéramos**	**hubiera ofrecido**	**hubiéramos ofrecido**
ofrecieras	**ofrecierais**	**hubieras ofrecido**	**hubierais ofrecido**
ofreciera	**ofrecieran**	**hubiera ofrecido**	**hubieran ofrecido**
OR		OR	
ofreciese	**ofreciésemos**	**hubiese ofrecido**	**hubiésemos ofrecido**
ofrecieses	**ofrecieseis**	**hubieses ofrecido**	**hubieseis ofrecido**
ofreciese	**ofreciesen**	**hubiese ofrecido**	**hubiesen ofrecido**

	imperativo	
—		**ofrezcamos**
ofrece; no ofrezcas		**ofreced; no ofrezcáis**
ofrezca		**ofrezcan**

Words related to this verb

ofreciente offering
el ofrecimiento offer, offering
la ofrenda gift
ofrecer + inf. to offer + inf.
el ofrecedor, la ofrecedora offerer

ofrecer el brazo to offer one's arm
ofrecerse to offer oneself
ofrecerse para hacer un trabajo to offer oneself to do a job
ofrecer su ayuda to offer your help
ofrecer ventajas to offer advantages

The Seven Simple Tenses		The Seven Compound Tenses	
Singular	Plural	Singular	Plural
1 presente de indicativo		8 perfecto de indicativo	
oigo	**oímos**	**he oído**	**hemos oído**
oyes	**oís**	**has oído**	**habéis oído**
oye	**oyen**	**ha oído**	**han oído**
2 imperfecto de indicativo		9 pluscuamperfecto de indicativo	
oía	**oíamos**	**había oído**	**habíamos oído**
oías	**oíais**	**habías oído**	**habíais oído**
oía	**oían**	**había oído**	**habían oído**
3 pretérito		10 pretérito anterior	
oí	**oímos**	**hube oído**	**hubimos oído**
oíste	**oísteis**	**hubiste oído**	**hubisteis oído**
oyó	**oyeron**	**hubo oído**	**hubieron oído**
4 futuro		11 futuro perfecto	
oiré	**oiremos**	**habré oído**	**habremos oído**
oirás	**oiréis**	**habrás oído**	**habréis oído**
oirá	**oirán**	**habrá oído**	**habrán oído**
5 potencial simple		12 potencial compuesto	
oiría	**oiríamos**	**habría oído**	**habríamos oído**
oirías	**oiríais**	**habrías oído**	**habríais oído**
oiría	**oirían**	**habría oído**	**habrían oído**
6 presente de subjuntivo		13 perfecto de subjuntivo	
oiga	**oigamos**	**haya oído**	**hayamos oído**
oigas	**oigáis**	**hayas oído**	**hayáis oído**
oiga	**oigan**	**haya oído**	**hayan oído**
7 imperfecto de subjuntivo		14 pluscuamperfecto de subjuntivo	
oyera	**oyéramos**	**hubiera oído**	**hubiéramos oído**
oyeras	**oyerais**	**hubieras oído**	**hubierais oído**
oyera	**oyeran**	**hubiera oído**	**hubieran oído**
OR		OR	
oyese	**oyésemos**	**hubiese oído**	**hubiésemos oído**
oyeses	**oyeseis**	**hubieses oído**	**hubieseis oído**
oyese	**oyesen**	**hubiese oído**	**hubiesen oído**

imperativo

—	**oigamos**
oye; no oigas	**oíd; no oigáis**
oiga	**oigan**

Words and expressions related to this verb
la oída   hearing; **de oídas**   by hearsay
dar oídos   to lend an ear
oír decir   to hear tell, to hear say
oír hablar de   to hear of, to hear talk of

por oídos, de oídos   by hearing
al oído   confidentially
el oído   hearing (sense)
desoír   to ignore, to be deaf to

Can't recognize an irregular verb form? Check out pages 519–523.

oler

Gerundio **oliendo**

Part. pas. **olido**

to smell, to scent

The Seven Simple Tenses		The Seven Compound Tenses	
Singular	Plural	Singular	Plural
1 presente de indicativo		8 perfecto de indicativo	
huelo	**olemos**	**he olido**	**hemos olido**
hueles	**oléis**	**has olido**	**habéis olido**
huele	**huelen**	**ha olido**	**han olido**
2 imperfecto de indicativo		9 pluscuamperfecto de indicativo	
olía	**olíamos**	**había olido**	**habíamos olido**
olías	**olíais**	**habías olido**	**habíais olido**
olía	**olían**	**había olido**	**habían olido**
3 pretérito		10 pretérito anterior	
olí	**olimos**	**hube olido**	**hubimos olido**
oliste	**olisteis**	**hubiste olido**	**hubisteis olido**
olió	**olieron**	**hubo olido**	**hubieron olido**
4 futuro		11 futuro perfecto	
oleré	**oleremos**	**habré olido**	**habremos olido**
olerás	**oleréis**	**habrás olido**	**habréis olido**
olerá	**olerán**	**habrá olido**	**habrán olido**
5 potencial simple		12 potencial compuesto	
olería	**oleríamos**	**habría olido**	**habríamos olido**
olerías	**oleríais**	**habrías olido**	**habríais olido**
olería	**olerían**	**habría olido**	**habrían olido**
6 presente de subjuntivo		13 perfecto de subjuntivo	
huela	**olamos**	**haya olido**	**hayamos olido**
huelas	**oláis**	**hayas olido**	**hayáis olido**
huela	**huelan**	**haya olido**	**hayan olido**
7 imperfecto de subjuntivo		14 pluscuamperfecto de subjuntivo	
oliera	**oliéramos**	**hubiera olido**	**hubiéramos olido**
olieras	**olierais**	**hubieras olido**	**hubierais olido**
oliera	**olieran**	**hubiera olido**	**hubieran olido**
OR		OR	
oliese	**oliésemos**	**hubiese olido**	**hubiésemos olido**
olieses	**olieseis**	**hubieses olido**	**hubieseis olido**
oliese	**oliesen**	**hubiese olido**	**hubiesen olido**

	imperativo	
—		**olamos**
huele; no huelas		**oled; no oláis**
huela		**huelan**

Words and expressions related to this verb

el olfato, la olfacción   olfaction (the sense of smelling, act of smelling)
olfatear   to sniff
oler a   to smell of; **oler a rosa**   to smell like a rose
No huele bien   It looks fishy (It doesn't smell good.)

Can't recognize an irregular verb form? Check out pages 519–523.

The Seven Simple Tenses		The Seven Compound Tenses	
Singular	Plural	Singular	Plural
1 presente de indicativo		**8 perfecto de indicativo**	
olvido	olvidamos	he olvidado	hemos olvidado
olvidas	olvidáis	has olvidado	habéis olvidado
olvida	olvidan	ha olvidado	han olvidado
2 imperfecto de indicativo		**9 pluscuamperfecto de indicativo**	
olvidaba	olvidábamos	había olvidado	habíamos olvidado
olvidabas	olvidabais	habías olvidado	habíais olvidado
olvidaba	olvidaban	había olvidado	habían olvidado
3 pretérito		**10 pretérito anterior**	
olvidé	olvidamos	hube olvidado	hubimos olvidado
olvidaste	olvidasteis	hubiste olvidado	hubisteis olvidado
olvidó	olvidaron	hubo olvidado	hubieron olvidado
4 futuro		**11 futuro perfecto**	
olvidaré	olvidaremos	habré olvidado	habremos olvidado
olvidarás	olvidaréis	habrás olvidado	habréis olvidado
olvidará	olvidarán	habrá olvidado	habrán olvidado
5 potencial simple		**12 potencial compuesto**	
olvidaría	olvidaríamos	habría olvidado	habríamos olvidado
olvidarías	olvidaríais	habrías olvidado	habríais olvidado
olvidaría	olvidarían	habría olvidado	habrían olvidado
6 presente de subjuntivo		**13 perfecto de subjuntivo**	
olvide	olvidemos	haya olvidado	hayamos olvidado
olvides	olvidéis	hayas olvidado	hayáis olvidado
olvide	olviden	haya olvidado	hayan olvidado
7 imperfecto de subjuntivo		**14 pluscuamperfecto de subjuntivo**	
olvidara	olvidáramos	hubiera olvidado	hubiéramos olvidado
olvidaras	olvidarais	hubieras olvidado	hubierais olvidado
olvidara	olvidaran	hubiera olvidado	hubieran olvidado
OR		OR	
olvidase	olvidásemos	hubiese olvidado	hubiésemos olvidado
olvidases	olvidaseis	hubieses olvidado	hubieseis olvidado
olvidase	olvidasen	hubiese olvidado	hubiesen olvidado

imperativo	
—	olvidemos
olvida; no olvides	olvidad; no olvidéis
olvide	olviden

Words and expressions related to this verb

olvidado, olvidada   forgotten
olvidadizo, olvidadiza   forgetful
el ovido   forgetfulness, oblivion
Se me olvidó   It slipped my mind.

olvidar + inf.   to forget + inf.
olvidarse de   to forget
olvidarse de + inf.   to forget + inf.
olvidar la hora   to forget the time

The subject pronouns are found on the page facing page 1.

oponer

to oppose

The Seven Simple Tenses		The Seven Compound Tenses	
Singular	Plural	Singular	Plural
1 presente de indicativo		8 perfecto de indicativo	
opongo	oponemos	he opuesto	hemos opuesto
opones	oponéis	has opuesto	habéis opuesto
opone	oponen	ha opuesto	han opuesto
2 imperfecto de indicativo		9 pluscuamperfecto de indicativo	
oponía	oponíamos	había opuesto	habíamos opuesto
oponías	oponíais	habías opuesto	habíais opuesto
oponía	oponían	había opuesto	habían opuesto
3 pretérito		10 pretérito anterior	
opuse	opusimos	hube opuesto	hubimos opuesto
opusiste	opusisteis	hubiste opuesto	hubisteis opuesto
opuso	opusieron	hubo opuesto	hubieron opuesto
4 futuro		11 futuro perfecto	
opondré	opondremos	habré opuesto	habremos opuesto
opondrás	opondréis	habrás opuesto	habréis opuesto
opondrá	opondrán	habrá opuesto	habrán opuesto
5 potencial simple		12 potencial compuesto	
opondría	opondríamos	habría opuesto	habríamos opuesto
opondrías	opondríais	habrías opuesto	habríais opuesto
opondría	opondrían	habría opuesto	habrían opuesto
6 presente de subjuntivo		13 perfecto de subjuntivo	
oponga	opongamos	haya opuesto	hayamos opuesto
opongas	opongáis	hayas opuesto	hayáis opuesto
oponga	opongan	haya opuesto	hayan opuesto
7 imperfecto de subjuntivo		14 pluscuamperfecto de subjuntivo	
opusiera	opusiéramos	hubiera opuesto	hubiéramos opuesto
opusieras	opusierais	hubieras opuesto	hubierais opuesto
opusiera	opusieran	hubiera opuesto	hubieran opuesto
OR		OR	
opusiese	opusiésemos	hubiese opuesto	hubiésemos opuesto
opusieses	opusieseis	hubieses opuesto	hubieseis opuesto
opusiese	opusiesen	hubiese opuesto	hubiesen opuesto

	imperativo	
—		opongamos
opón; no opongas		oponed; no opongáis
oponga		opongan

Words related to this verb

oponerse a to be against
oponible opposable
oponerse to oppose each other
el, la oponente opponent

la oposición opposition
el, la oposicionista oppositionist
oponerse a una moción to oppose a motion

to order, to command, to put in order, to arrange

The Seven Simple Tenses		The Seven Compound Tenses	
Singular	Plural	Singular	Plural
1 presente de indicativo		8 perfecto de indicativo	
ordeno	ordenamos	he ordenado	hemos ordenado
ordenas	ordenáis	has ordenado	habéis ordenado
ordena	ordenan	ha ordenado	han ordenado
2 imperfecto de indicativo		9 pluscuamperfecto de indicativo	
ordenaba	ordenábamos	había ordenado	habíamos ordenado
ordenabas	ordenabais	habías ordenado	habíais ordenado
ordenaba	ordenaban	había ordenado	habían ordenado
3 pretérito		10 pretérito anterior	
ordené	ordenamos	hube ordenado	hubimos ordenado
ordenaste	ordenasteis	hubiste ordenado	hubisteis ordenado
ordenó	ordenaron	hubo ordenado	hubieron ordenado
4 futuro		11 futuro perfecto	
ordenaré	ordenaremos	habré ordenado	habremos ordenado
ordenarás	ordenaréis	habrás ordenado	habréis ordenado
ordenará	ordenarán	habrá ordenado	habrán ordenado
5 potencial simple		12 potencial compuesto	
ordenaría	ordenaríamos	habría ordenado	habríamos ordenado
ordenarías	ordenaríais	habrías ordenado	habríais ordenado
ordenaría	ordenarían	habría ordenado	habrían ordenado
6 presente de subjuntivo		13 perfecto de subjuntivo	
ordene	ordenemos	haya ordenado	hayamos ordenado
ordenes	ordenéis	hayas ordenado	hayáis ordenado
ordene	ordenen	haya ordenado	hayan ordenado
7 imperfecto de subjuntivo		14 pluscuamperfecto de subjuntivo	
ordenara	ordenáramos	hubiera ordenado	hubiéramos ordenado
ordenaras	ordenarais	hubieras ordenado	hubierais ordenado
ordenara	ordenaran	hubiera ordenado	hubieran ordenado
OR		OR	
ordenase	ordenásemos	hubiese ordenado	hubiésemos ordenado
ordenases	ordenaseis	hubieses ordenado	hubieseis ordenado
ordenase	ordenasen	hubiese ordenado	hubiesen ordenado

	imperativo	
—		ordenemos
ordena; no ordenes		ordenad; no ordenéis
ordene		ordenen

Words and expressions related to this verb
el orden, los órdenes   order, orders
el orden del día   order of the day
ordenadamente   in order, orderly,
    methodically

ordenarse   to become ordained, to take
    holy orders
llamar al orden   to call to order

Enjoy verbs in Spanish proverbs beginning on page 539.

organizar

to organize, to arrange, to set up

The Seven Simple Tenses		The Seven Compound Tenses	
Singular	Plural	Singular	Plural
1 presente de indicativo		**8 perfecto de indicativo**	
organizo	organizamos	he organizado	hemos organizado
organizas	organizáis	has organizado	habéis organizado
organiza	organizan	ha organizado	han organizado
2 imperfecto de indicativo		**9 pluscuamperfecto de indicativo**	
organizaba	organizábamos	había organizado	habíamos organizado
organizabas	organizabais	habías organizado	habíais organizado
organizaba	organizaban	había organizado	habían organizado
3 pretérito		**10 pretérito anterior**	
organicé	organizamos	hube organizado	hubimos organizado
organizaste	organizasteis	hubiste organizado	hubisteis organizado
organizó	organizaron	hubo organizado	hubieron organizado
4 futuro		**11 futuro perfecto**	
organizaré	organizaremos	habré organizado	habremos organizado
organizarás	organizaréis	habrás organizado	habréis organizado
organizará	organizarán	habrá organizado	habrán organizado
5 potencial simple		**12 potencial compuesto**	
organizaría	organizaríamos	habría organizado	habríamos organizado
organizarías	organizaríais	habrías organizado	habríais organizado
organizaría	organizarían	habría organizado	habrían organizado
6 presente de subjuntivo		**13 perfecto de subjuntivo**	
organice	organicemos	haya organizado	hayamos organizado
organices	organicéis	hayas organizado	hayáis organizado
organice	organicen	haya organizado	hayan organizado
7 imperfecto de subjuntivo		**14 pluscuamperfecto de subjuntivo**	
organizara	organizáramos	hubiera organizado	hubiéramos organizado
organizaras	organizarais	hubieras organizado	hubierais organizado
organizara	organizaran	hubiera organizado	hubieran organizado
OR		OR	
organizase	organizásemos	hubiese organizado	hubiésemos organizado
organizases	organizaseis	hubieses organizado	hubieseis organizado
organizase	organizasen	hubiese organizado	hubiesen organizado

	imperativo	
—		organicemos
organiza; no organices		organizad; no organicéis
organice		organicen

Words and expressions related to this verb

organizado, organizada organized
la organización organization
organizar una fiesta to organize a party

el organizador, la organizadora organizer
organizable organizable
la Organización de las Naciones Unidas
(**ONU**) the United Nations Organization
(UNO, UN)

to dare, to venture

The Seven Simple Tenses		The Seven Compound Tenses	
Singular	Plural	Singular	Plural
1 presente de indicativo		8 perfecto de indicativo	
oso	osamos	he osado	hemos osado
osas	osáis	has osado	habéis osado
osa	osan	ha osado	han osado
2 imperfecto de indicativo		9 pluscuamperfecto de indicativo	
osaba	osábamos	había osado	habíamos osado
osabas	osabais	habías osado	habíais osado
osaba	osaban	había osado	habían osado
3 pretérito		10 pretérito anterior	
osé	osamos	hube osado	hubimos osado
osaste	osasteis	hubiste osado	hubisteis osado
osó	osaron	hubo osado	hubieron osado
4 futuro		11 futuro perfecto	
osaré	osaremos	habré osado	habremos osado
osarás	osaréis	habrás osado	habréis osado
osará	osarán	habrá osado	habrán osado
5 potencial simple		12 potencial compuesto	
osaría	osaríamos	habría osado	habríamos osado
osarías	osaríais	habrías osado	habríais osado
osaría	osarían	habría osado	habrían osado
6 presente de subjuntivo		13 perfecto de subjuntivo	
ose	osemos	haya osado	hayamos osado
oses	oséis	hayas osado	hayáis osado
ose	osen	haya osado	hayan osado
7 imperfecto de subjuntivo		14 pluscuamperfecto de subjuntivo	
osara	osáramos	hubiera osado	hubiéramos osado
osaras	osarais	hubieras osado	hubierais osado
osara	osaran	hubiera osado	hubieran osado
OR		OR	
osase	osásemos	hubiese osado	hubiésemos osado
osases	osaseis	hubieses osado	hubieseis osado
osase	osasen	hubiese osado	hubiesen osado

imperativo

—	osemos
osa; no oses	osad; no oséis
ose	osen

Words and expressions related to this verb
osado, osada   audacious, bold, daring   **la osadía**   audacity, boldness
osadamente   boldly, daringly

Check out the verb drills and verb tests with answers explained on pages 619–665.

The subject pronouns are found on the page facing page 1.

to pay (for)

The Seven Simple Tenses		The Seven Compound Tenses	
Singular	Plural	Singular	Plural
1 presente de indicativo		8 perfecto de indicativo	
pago	**pagamos**	**he pagado**	**hemos pagado**
pagas	**pagáis**	**has pagado**	**habéis pagado**
paga	**pagan**	**ha pagado**	**han pagado**
2 imperfecto de indicativo		9 pluscuamperfecto de indicativo	
pagaba	**pagábamos**	**había pagado**	**habíamos pagado**
pagabas	**pagabais**	**habías pagado**	**habíais pagado**
pagaba	**pagaban**	**había pagado**	**habían pagado**
3 pretérito		10 pretérito anterior	
pagué	**pagamos**	**hube pagado**	**hubimos pagado**
pagaste	**pagasteis**	**hubiste pagado**	**hubisteis pagado**
pagó	**pagaron**	**hubo pagado**	**hubieron pagado**
4 futuro		11 futuro perfecto	
pagaré	**pagaremos**	**habré pagado**	**habremos pagado**
pagarás	**pagaréis**	**habrás pagado**	**habréis pagado**
pagará	**pagarán**	**habrá pagado**	**habrán pagado**
5 potencial simple		12 potencial compuesto	
pagaría	**pagaríamos**	**habría pagado**	**habríamos pagado**
pagarías	**pagaríais**	**habrías pagado**	**habríais pagado**
pagaría	**pagarían**	**habría pagado**	**habrían pagado**
6 presente de subjuntivo		13 perfecto de subjuntivo	
pague	**paguemos**	**haya pagado**	**hayamos pagado**
pagues	**paguéis**	**hayas pagado**	**hayáis pagado**
pague	**paguen**	**haya pagado**	**hayan pagado**
7 imperfecto de subjuntivo		14 pluscuamperfecto de subjuntivo	
pagara	**pagáramos**	**hubiera pagado**	**hubiéramos pagado**
pagaras	**pagarais**	**hubieras pagado**	**hubierais pagado**
pagara	**pagaran**	**hubiera pagado**	**hubieran pagado**
OR		OR	
pagase	**pagásemos**	**hubiese pagado**	**hubiésemos pagado**
pagases	**pagaseis**	**hubieses pagado**	**hubieseis pagado**
pagase	**pagasen**	**hubiese pagado**	**hubiesen pagado**

imperativo	
—	**paguemos**
paga; no pagues	**pagad; no paguéis**
pague	**paguen**

Words and expressions related to this verb

la paga payment
pagable payable
pagador, pagadora payer
el pagaré promissory note, I.O.U.
pagar un crimen to pay for a crime
pagar las culpas to pay for one's sins

pagar al contado to pay in cash
pagar contra entrega C.O.D. (Collect on delivery)
pagar la cuenta to pay the bill
pagar un ojo de la cara to pay an arm and a leg; to pay through your nose

to stop (someone or something)

The Seven Simple Tenses		The Seven Compound Tenses	
Singular	Plural	Singular	Plural
1 presente de indicativo		8 perfecto de indicativo	
paro	paramos	he parado	hemos parado
paras	paráis	has parado	habéis parado
para	paran	ha parado	han parado
2 imperfecto de indicativo		9 pluscuamperfecto de indicativo	
paraba	parábamos	había parado	habíamos parado
parabas	parabais	habías parado	habíais parado
paraba	paraban	había parado	habían parado
3 pretérito		10 pretérito anterior	
paré	paramos	hube parado	hubimos parado
paraste	parasteis	hubiste parado	hubisteis parado
paró	pararon	hubo parado	hubieron parado
4 futuro		11 futuro perfecto	
pararé	pararemos	habré parado	habremos parado
pararás	pararéis	habrás parado	habréis parado
parará	pararán	habrá parado	habrán parado
5 potencial simple		12 potencial compuesto	
pararía	pararíamos	habría parado	habríamos parado
pararías	pararíais	habrías parado	habríais parado
pararía	pararían	habría parado	habrían parado
6 presente de subjuntivo		13 perfecto de subjuntivo	
pare	paremos	haya parado	hayamos parado
pares	paréis	hayas parado	hayáis parado
pare	paren	haya parado	hayan parado
7 imperfecto de subjuntivo		14 pluscuamperfecto de subjuntivo	
parara	paráramos	hubiera parado	hubiéramos parado
pararas	pararais	hubieras parado	hubierais parado
parara	pararan	hubiera parado	hubieran parado
OR		OR	
parase	parásemos	hubiese parado	hubiésemos parado
parases	paraseis	hubieses parado	hubieseis parado
parase	parasen	hubiese parado	hubiesen parado

imperativo	
—	paremos
para; no pares	parad; no paréis
pare	paren

Words and expressions related to this verb
parar en mal   to end badly
PARADA   STOP
la parada de coches   taxi stand
pararse en   to pay attention to

la parada del autobús   bus stop
parar en seco   dead stop
una paradeta   short stop
sin parar   right away (without stopping)

For other words and expressions related to this verb, see **pararse.**

The subject pronouns are found on the page facing page 1.

pararse

Gerundio **parándose**

Part. pas. **parado**

to stop (oneself)

The Seven Simple Tenses		The Seven Compound Tenses	
Singular	Plural	Singular	Plural
1 presente de indicativo		**8 perfecto de indicativo**	
me paro	nos paramos	me he parado	nos hemos parado
te paras	os paráis	te has parado	os habéis parado
se para	se paran	se ha parado	se han parado
2 imperfecto de indicativo		**9 pluscuamperfecto de indicativo**	
me paraba	nos parábamos	me había parado	nos habíamos parado
te parabas	os parabais	te habías parado	os habíais parado
se paraba	se paraban	se había parado	se habían parado
3 pretérito		**10 pretérito anterior**	
me paré	nos paramos	me hube parado	nos hubimos parado
te paraste	os parasteis	te hubiste parado	os hubisteis parado
se paró	se pararon	se hubo parado	se hubieron parado
4 futuro		**11 futuro perfecto**	
me pararé	nos pararemos	me habré parado	nos habremos parado
te pararás	os pararéis	te habrás parado	os habréis parado
se parará	se pararán	se habrá parado	se habrán parado
5 potencial simple		**12 potencial compuesto**	
me pararía	nos pararíamos	me habría parado	nos habríamos parado
te pararías	os pararíais	te habrías parado	os habríais parado
se pararía	se pararían	se habría parado	se habrían parado
6 presente de subjuntivo		**13 perfecto de subjuntivo**	
me pare	nos paremos	me haya parado	nos hayamos parado
te pares	os paréis	te hayas parado	os hayáis parado
se pare	se paren	se haya parado	se hayan parado
7 imperfecto de subjuntivo		**14 pluscuamperfecto de subjuntivo**	
me parara	nos paráramos	me hubiera parado	nos hubiéramos parado
te pararas	os pararais	te hubieras parado	os hubierais parado
se parara	se pararan	se hubiera parado	se hubieran parado
OR		OR	
me parase	nos parásemos	me hubiese parado	nos hubiésemos parado
te parases	os paraseis	te hubieses parado	os hubieseis parado
se parase	se parasen	se hubiese parado	se hubiesen parado

imperativo	
—	**parémonos**
párate; no te pares	**paraos; no os paréis**
párese	**párense**

Words and expressions related to this verb
la parada stop
una paradeta, una paradilla pause
una parada en seco dead stop

parar to stop (someone or something)
no poder parar to be restless
parar en mal to end badly

For other words and expressions related to this verb, see **parar**.

Get acquainted with what preposition goes with what verb on pages 541–549.

to seem, to appear

The Seven Simple Tenses		The Seven Compound Tenses	
Singular	Plural	Singular	Plural
1 presente de indicativo		**8 perfecto de indicativo**	
parezco	parecemos	he parecido	hemos parecido
pareces	parecéis	has parecido	habéis parecido
parece	parecen	ha parecido	han parecido
2 imperfecto de indicativo		**9 pluscuamperfecto de indicativo**	
parecía	parecíamos	había parecido	habíamos parecido
parecías	parecíais	habías parecido	habíais parecido
parecía	parecían	había parecido	habían parecido
3 pretérito		**10 pretérito anterior**	
parecí	parecimos	hube parecido	hubimos parecido
pareciste	parecisteis	hubiste parecido	hubisteis parecido
pareció	parecieron	hubo parecido	hubieron parecido
4 futuro		**11 futuro perfecto**	
pareceré	pareceremos	habré parecido	habremos parecido
parecerás	pareceréis	habrás parecido	habréis parecido
parecerá	parecerán	habrá parecido	habrán parecido
5 potencial simple		**12 potencial compuesto**	
parecería	pareceríamos	habría parecido	habríamos parecido
parecerías	pareceríais	habrías parecido	habríais parecido
parecería	parecerían	habría parecido	habrían parecido
6 presente de subjuntivo		**13 perfecto de subjuntivo**	
parezca	parezcamos	haya parecido	hayamos parecido
parezcas	parezcáis	hayas parecido	hayáis parecido
parezca	parezcan	haya parecido	hayan parecido
7 imperfecto de subjuntivo		**14 pluscuamperfecto de subjuntivo**	
pareciera	pareciéramos	hubiera parecido	hubiéramos parecido
parecieras	parecierais	hubieras parecido	hubierais parecido
pareciera	parecieran	hubiera parecido	hubieran parecido
OR		OR	
pareciese	pareciésemos	hubiese parecido	hubiésemos parecido
parecieses	parecieseis	hubieses parecido	hubieseis parecido
pareciese	pareciesen	hubiese parecido	hubiesen parecido

imperativo	
—	parezcamos
parece; no parezcas	pareced; no parezcáis
parezca	parezcan

Words and expressions related to this verb
a lo que parece   according to what it seems
al parecer   seemingly, apparently
pareciente   similar
parecerse a   to resemble each other, to look alike

Me parece . . .   It seems to me . . .
por el bien parecer   for the sake of
appearances
parecer cansado (cansada)   to look (seem) tired

See also **parecerse.**

The subject pronouns are found on the page facing page 1.

to resemble each other, to look alike

The Seven Simple Tenses		The Seven Compound Tenses	
Singular	Plural	Singular	Plural
1 presente de indicativo		8 perfecto de indicativo	
me parezco	**nos parecemos**	**me he parecido**	**nos hemos parecido**
te pareces	**os parecéis**	**te has parecido**	**os habéis parecido**
se parece	**se parecen**	**se ha parecido**	**se han parecido**
2 imperfecto de indicativo		9 pluscuamperfecto de indicativo	
me parecía	**nos parecíamos**	**me había parecido**	**nos habíamos parecido**
te parecías	**os parecíais**	**te habías parecido**	**os habíais parecido**
se parecía	**se parecían**	**se había parecido**	**se habían parecido**
3 pretérito		10 pretérito anterior	
me parecí	**nos parecimos**	**me hube parecido**	**nos hubimos parecido**
te pareciste	**os parecisteis**	**te hubiste parecido**	**os hubisteis parecido**
se pareció	**se parecieron**	**se hubo parecido**	**se hubieron parecido**
4 futuro		11 futuro perfecto	
me pareceré	**nos pareceremos**	**me habré parecido**	**nos habremos parecido**
te parecerás	**os pareceréis**	**te habrás parecido**	**os habréis parecido**
se parecerá	**se parecerán**	**se habrá parecido**	**se habrán parecido**
5 potencial simple		12 potencial compuesto	
me parecería	**nos pareceríamos**	**me habría parecido**	**nos habríamos parecido**
te parecerías	**os pareceríais**	**te habrías parecido**	**os habríais parecido**
se parecería	**se parecerían**	**se habría parecido**	**se habrían parecido**
6 presente de subjuntivo		13 perfecto de subjuntivo	
me parezca	**nos parezcamos**	**me haya parecido**	**nos hayamos parecido**
te parezcas	**os parezcáis**	**te hayas parecido**	**os hayáis parecido**
se parezca	**se parezcan**	**se haya parecido**	**se hayan parecido**
7 imperfecto de subjuntivo		14 pluscuamperfecto de subjuntivo	
me pareciera	**nos pareciéramos**	**me hubiera parecido**	**nos hubiéramos parecido**
te parecieras	**os parecierais**	**te hubieras parecido**	**os hubierais parecido**
se pareciera	**se parecieran**	**se hubiera parecido**	**se hubieran parecido**
OR		OR	
me pareciese	**nos pareciésemos**	**me hubiese parecido**	**nos hubiésemos parecido**
te parecieses	**os parecieseis**	**te hubieses parecido**	**os hubieseis parecido**
se pareciese	**se pareciesen**	**se hubiese parecido**	**se hubiesen parecido**

imperativo	
—	**parezcámonos**
parécete; no te parezcas	**pareceos; no os parezcáis**
parézcase	**parézcanse**

Words and expressions related to this verb
parecer   to seem, to appear
a lo que parece   according to what it seems

al parecer   seemingly, apparently
pareciente   similar

See also **parecer.**

Learn more verbs in 30 practical situations for tourists on pages 564–594.

to leave, to depart, to divide, to split

The Seven Simple Tenses		The Seven Compound Tenses	
Singular	Plural	Singular	Plural
1 presente de indicativo		8 perfecto de indicativo	
parto	partimos	he partido	hemos partido
partes	partís	has partido	habéis partido
parte	parten	ha partido	han partido
2 imperfecto de indicativo		9 pluscuamperfecto de indicativo	
partía	partíamos	había partido	habíamos partido
partías	partíais	habías partido	habíais partido
partía	partían	había partido	habían partido
3 pretérito		10 pretérito anterior	
partí	partimos	hube partido	hubimos partido
partiste	partisteis	hubiste partido	hubisteis partido
partió	partieron	hubo partido	hubieron partido
4 futuro		11 futuro perfecto	
partiré	partiremos	habré partido	habremos partido
partirás	partiréis	habrás partido	habréis partido
partirá	partirán	habrá partido	habrán partido
5 potencial simple		12 potencial compuesto	
partiría	partiríamos	habría partido	habríamos partido
partirías	partiríais	habrías partido	habríais partido
partiría	partirían	habría partido	habrían partido
6 presente de subjuntivo		13 perfecto de subjuntivo	
parta	partamos	haya partido	hayamos partido
partas	partáis	hayas partido	hayáis partido
parta	partan	haya partido	hayan partido
7 imperfecto de subjuntivo		14 pluscuamperfecto de subjuntivo	
partiera	partiéramos	hubiera partido	hubiéramos partido
partieras	partierais	hubieras partido	hubierais partido
partiera	partieran	hubiera partido	hubieran partido
OR		OR	
partiese	partiésemos	hubiese partido	hubiésemos partido
partieses	partieseis	hubieses partido	hubieseis partido
partiese	partiesen	hubiese partido	hubiesen partido

imperativo

—	partamos
parte; no partas	partid; no partáis
parta	partan

Words and expressions related to this verb
a partir de   beginning with, starting from
tomar partido   to take sides, to make up
   one's mind
la partida   departure

partirse   to become divided
repartir   to distribute
partir algo en dos   to divide something
   in two

See also **repartir.**

pasar   Gerundio **pasando**   Part. pas. **pasado**

to pass (by), to happen, to spend (time)

The Seven Simple Tenses		The Seven Compound Tenses	
Singular	Plural	Singular	Plural
1 presente de indicativo		**8 perfecto de indicativo**	
paso	pasamos	he pasado	hemos pasado
pasas	pasáis	has pasado	habéis pasado
pasa	pasan	ha pasado	han pasado
2 imperfecto de indicativo		**9 pluscuamperfecto de indicativo**	
pasaba	pasábamos	había pasado	habíamos pasado
pasabas	pasabais	habías pasado	habíais pasado
pasaba	pasaban	había pasado	habían pasado
3 pretérito		**10 pretérito anterior**	
pasé	pasamos	hube pasado	hubimos pasado
pasaste	pasasteis	hubiste pasado	hubisteis pasado
pasó	pasaron	hubo pasado	hubieron pasado
4 futuro		**11 futuro perfecto**	
pasaré	pasaremos	habré pasado	habremos pasado
pasarás	pasaréis	habrás pasado	habréis pasado
pasará	pasarán	habrá pasado	habrán pasado
5 potencial simple		**12 potencial compuesto**	
pasaría	pasaríamos	habría pasado	habríamos pasado
pasarías	pasaríais	habrías pasado	habríais pasado
pasaría	pasarían	habría pasado	habrían pasado
6 presente de subjuntivo		**13 perfecto de subjuntivo**	
pase	pasemos	haya pasado	hayamos pasado
pases	paséis	hayas pasado	hayáis pasado
pase	pasen	haya pasado	hayan pasado
7 imperfecto de subjuntivo		**14 pluscuamperfecto de subjuntivo**	
pasara	pasáramos	hubiera pasado	hubiéramos pasado
pasaras	pasarais	hubieras pasado	hubierais pasado
pasara	pasaran	hubiera pasado	hubieran pasado
OR		OR	
pasase	pasásemos	hubiese pasado	hubiésemos pasado
pasases	pasaseis	hubieses pasado	hubieseis pasado
pasase	pasasen	hubiese pasado	hubiesen pasado

imperativo	
—	pasemos
pasa; no pases	pasad; no paséis
pase	pasen

Words and expressions related to this verb

pasajero, pasajera   passenger, traveler
¡Que lo pase Ud. bien!   Good luck, good bye!
¿Qué pasa?   What's happening? What's
  going on?

el pasatiempo   amusement, pastime
¿Qué te pasa?   What's the matter with you?
¡Pase un buen día!   Have a nice day!
pasar un examen   to take an exam

Consult pages 524–537 for the section on verbs used in
idiomatic expressions. See also **pasar** on page 527.

to take a walk, to parade

The Seven Simple Tenses		The Seven Compound Tenses	
Singular	Plural	Singular	Plural
1 presente de indicativo		8 perfecto de indicativo	
me paseo	nos paseamos	me he paseado	nos hemos paseado
te paseas	os paseáis	te has paseado	os habéis paseado
se pasea	se pasean	se ha paseado	se han paseado
2 imperfecto de indicativo		9 pluscuamperfecto de indicativo	
me paseaba	nos paseábamos	me había paseado	nos habíamos paseado
te paseabas	os paseabais	te habías paseado	os habíais paseado
se paseaba	se paseaban	se había paseado	se habían paseado
3 pretérito		10 pretérito anterior	
me paseé	nos paseamos	me hube paseado	nos hubimos paseado
te paseaste	os paseasteis	te hubiste paseado	os hubisteis paseado
se paseó	se pasearon	se hubo paseado	se hubieron paseado
4 futuro		11 futuro perfecto	
me pasearé	nos pasearemos	me habré paseado	nos habremos paseado
te pasearás	os pasearéis	te habrás paseado	os habréis paseado
se paseará	se pasearán	se habrá paseado	se habrán paseado
5 potencial simple		12 potencial compuesto	
me pasearía	nos pasearíamos	me habría paseado	nos habríamos paseado
te pasearías	os pasearíais	te habrías paseado	os habríais paseado
se pasearía	se pasearían	se habría paseado	se habrían paseado
6 presente de subjuntivo		13 perfecto de subjuntivo	
me pasee	nos paseemos	me haya paseado	nos hayamos paseado
te pasees	os paseéis	te hayas paseado	os hayáis paseado
se pasee	se paseen	se haya paseado	se hayan paseado
7 imperfecto de subjuntivo		14 pluscuamperfecto de subjuntivo	
me paseara	nos paseáramos	me hubiera paseado	nos hubiéramos paseado
te pasearas	os pasearais	te hubieras paseado	os hubierais paseado
se paseara	se pasearan	se hubiera paseado	se hubieran paseado
OR		OR	
me pasease	nos paseásemos	me hubiese paseado	nos hubiésemos paseado
te paseases	os paseaseis	te hubieses paseado	os hubieseis paseado
se pasease	se paseasen	se hubiese paseado	se hubiesen paseado

imperativo

—	paseémonos
paséate; no te pasees	paseaos; no os paseéis
paséese	paséense

Words and expressions related to this verb
un pase   pass, permit
un, una paseante   stroller
un paseo   a walk, a promenade
dar un paseo   to take a walk
ir de paseo   to go out for a walk

un paseo campestre   picnic
sacar a paseo   to take out for a walk
pasear   to walk (a child, a dog, etc.)
pasear en bicicleta   to go bicycling
el paseíllo   opening parade at bullfight

The subject pronouns are found on the page facing page 1.

pedir

Gerundio **pidiendo** Part. pas. **pedido**

to ask for, to request

The Seven Simple Tenses		The Seven Compound Tenses	
Singular	Plural	Singular	Plural
1 presente de indicativo		**8 perfecto de indicativo**	
pido	pedimos	he pedido	hemos pedido
pides	pedís	has pedido	habéis pedido
pide	piden	ha pedido	han pedido
2 imperfecto de indicativo		**9 pluscuamperfecto de indicativo**	
pedía	pedíamos	había pedido	habíamos pedido
pedías	pedíais	habías pedido	habíais pedido
pedía	pedían	había pedido	habían pedido
3 pretérito		**10 pretérito anterior**	
pedí	pedimos	hube pedido	hubimos pedido
pediste	pedisteis	hubiste pedido	hubisteis pedido
pidió	pidieron	hubo pedido	hubieron pedido
4 futuro		**11 futuro perfecto**	
pediré	pediremos	habré pedido	habremos pedido
pedirás	pediréis	habrás pedido	habréis pedido
pedirá	pedirán	habrá pedido	habrán pedido
5 potencial simple		**12 potencial compuesto**	
pediría	pediríamos	habría pedido	habríamos pedido
pedirías	pediríais	habrías pedido	habríais pedido
pediría	pedirían	habría pedido	habrían pedido
6 presente de subjuntivo		**13 perfecto de subjuntivo**	
pida	pidamos	haya pedido	hayamos pedido
pidas	pidáis	hayas pedido	hayáis pedido
pida	pidan	haya pedido	hayan pedido
7 imperfecto de subjuntivo		**14 pluscuamperfecto de subjuntivo**	
pidiera	pidiéramos	hubiera pedido	hubiéramos pedido
pidieras	pidierais	hubieras pedido	hubierais pedido
pidiera	pidieran	hubiera pedido	hubieran pedido
OR		OR	
pidiese	pidiésemos	hubiese pedido	hubiésemos pedido
pidieses	pidieseis	hubieses pedido	hubieseis pedido
pidiese	pidiesen	hubiese pedido	hubiesen pedido

	imperativo	
—		pidamos
pide; no pidas		pedid; no pidáis
pida		pidan

Words and expressions related to this verb
un pedimento   petition
hacer un pedido   to place an order

See also **despedirse.**
See also **pedir** on page 533.

un pedido   request, order
colocar un pedido   to place an order
pedir prestado   to borrow
una petición   petition, request
un pedidor, una pedidora   client, petitioner
pedir socorro   to ask for help

to beat, to hit, to slap, to stick, to glue, to paste

The Seven Simple Tenses		The Seven Compound Tenses	
Singular	Plural	Singular	Plural
1 presente de indicativo		8 perfecto de indicativo	
pego	**pegamos**	**he pegado**	**hemos pegado**
pegas	**pegáis**	**has pegado**	**habéis pegado**
pega	**pegan**	**ha pegado**	**han pegado**
2 imperfecto de indicativo		9 pluscuamperfecto de indicativo	
pegaba	**pebábamos**	**había pegado**	**habíamos pegado**
pegabas	**pegabais**	**habías pegado**	**habíais pegado**
pegaba	**pegaban**	**había pegado**	**habían pegado**
3 pretérito		10 pretérito anterior	
pegué	**pegamos**	**hube pegado**	**hubimos pegado**
pegaste	**pesgasteis**	**hubiste pegado**	**hubisteis pegado**
pegó	**pegaron**	**hubo pegado**	**hubieron pegado**
4 futuro		11 futuro perfecto	
pegaré	**pegaremos**	**habré pegado**	**habremos pegado**
pegarás	**pegaréis**	**habrás pegado**	**habréis pegado**
pegará	**pegarán**	**habrá pegado**	**habrán pegado**
5 potencial simple		12 potencial compuesto	
pegaría	**pegaríamos**	**habría pegado**	**habríamos pegado**
pegarías	**pegaríais**	**habrías pegado**	**habríais pegado**
pegaría	**pegarían**	**habría pegado**	**habrían pegado**
6 presente de subjuntivo		13 perfecto de subjuntivo	
pegue	**peguemos**	**haya pegado**	**hayamos pegado**
pegues	**peguéis**	**hayas pegado**	**hayáis pegado**
pegue	**peguen**	**haya pegado**	**hayan pegado**
7 imperfecto de subjuntivo		14 pluscuamperfecto de subjuntivo	
pegara	**pegáramos**	**hubiera pegado**	**hubiéramos pegado**
pegaras	**pegarais**	**hubieras pegado**	**hubierais pegado**
pegara	**pegaran**	**hubiera pegado**	**hubieran pegado**
OR		OR	
pegase	**pegásemos**	**hubiese pegado**	**hubiésemos pegado**
pegases	**pegaseis**	**hubieses pegado**	**hubieseis pegado**
pegase	**pegasen**	**hubiese pegado**	**hubiesen pegado**

	imperativo	
—	**peguemos**
pega; no pegues	**pegad; no peguéis**
pegue	**peguen**

Words and expressions related to this verb

pegar fuego to set fire to		**pegarse las sábanas** to sleep late in the morning
pegar saltos to jump		**pegársele a uno** to deceive someone
pegar voces to shout		**no pegar los ojos** to spend a sleepless night
el pegamento glue		**una pegatina** sticker

For other words and expressions related to this verb, see **despegar.**

The subject pronouns are found on the page facing page 1.

peinarse

Gerundio **peinándose**   Part. pas. **peinado**

to comb one's hair

The Seven Simple Tenses		The Seven Compound Tenses	
Singular	Plural	Singular	Plural
1 presente de indicativo		8 perfecto de indicativo	
me peino	nos peinamos	me he peinado	nos hemos peinado
te peinas	os peináis	te has peinado	os habéis peinado
se peina	se peinan	se ha peinado	se han peinado
2 imperfecto de indicativo		9 pluscuamperfecto de indicativo	
me peinaba	nos peinábamos	me había peinado	nos habíamos peinado
te peinabas	os peinabais	te habías peinado	os habíais peinado
se peinaba	se peinaban	se había peinado	se habían peinado
3 pretérito		10 pretérito anterior	
me peiné	nos peinamos	me hube peinado	nos hubimos peinado
te peinaste	os peinasteis	te hubiste peinado	os hubisteis peinado
se peinó	se peinaron	se hubo peinado	se hubieron peinado
4 futuro		11 futuro perfecto	
me peinaré	nos peinaremos	me habré peinado	nos habremos peinado
te peinarás	os peinaréis	te habrás peinado	os habréis peinado
se peinará	se peinarán	se habrá peinado	se habrán peinado
5 potencial simple		12 potencial compuesto	
me peinaría	nos peinaríamos	me habría peinado	nos habríamos peinado
te peinarías	os peinaríais	te habrías peinado	os habríais peinado
se peinaría	se peinarían	se habría peinado	se habrían peinado
6 presente de subjuntivo		13 perfecto de subjuntivo	
me peine	nos peinemos	me haya peinado	nos hayamos peinado
te peines	os peinéis	te hayas peinado	os hayáis peinado
se peine	se peinen	se haya peinado	se hayan peinado
7 imperfecto de subjuntivo		14 pluscuamperfecto de subjuntivo	
me peinara	nos peináramos	me hubiera peinado	nos hubiéramos peinado
te peinaras	os peinarais	te hubieras peinado	os hubierais peinado
se peinara	se peinaran	se hubiera peinado	se hubieran peinado
OR		OR	
me peinase	nos peinásemos	me hubiese peinado	nos hubiésemos peinado
te peinases	os peinaseis	te hubieses peinado	os hubieseis peinado
se peinase	se peinasen	se hubiese peinado	se hubiesen peinado

	imperativo
—	peinémonos
péinate; no te peines	peinaos; no os peinéis
péinese	péinense

Words and expressions related to this verb

un peine a comb
una peineta shell comb (used by women as an ornament in the hair)
un peinado hairdo, hair style

un peinador dressing gown
peinar to comb; **peinarse** to comb one's hair
despeinarse to dishevel, to take down one's hair

Learn more verbs in 30 practical situations for tourists on pages 564–594.

The Seven Simple Tenses		The Seven Compound Tenses	
Singular	Plural	Singular	Plural
1 presente de indicativo		8 perfecto de indicativo	
pienso	**pensamos**	**he pensado**	**hemos pensado**
piensas	**pensáis**	**has pensado**	**habéis pensado**
piensa	**piensan**	**ha pensado**	**han pensado**
2 imperfecto de indicativo		9 pluscuamperfecto de indicativo	
pensaba	**pensábamos**	**había pensado**	**habíamos pensado**
pensabas	**pensabais**	**habías pensado**	**habíais pensado**
pensaba	**pensaban**	**había pensado**	**habían pensado**
3 pretérito		10 pretérito anterior	
pensé	**pensamos**	**hube pensado**	**hubimos pensado**
pensaste	**pensasteis**	**hubiste pensado**	**hubisteis pensado**
pensó	**pensaron**	**hubo pensado**	**hubieron pensado**
4 futuro		11 futuro perfecto	
pensaré	**pensaremos**	**habré pensado**	**habremos pensado**
pensarás	**pensaréis**	**habrás pensado**	**habréis pensado**
pensará	**pensarán**	**habrá pensado**	**habrán pensado**
5 potencial simple		12 potencial compuesto	
pensaría	**pensaríamos**	**habría pensado**	**habríamos pensado**
pensarías	**pensaríais**	**habrías pensado**	**habríais pensado**
pensaría	**pensarían**	**habría pensado**	**habrían pensado**
6 presente de subjuntivo		13 perfecto de subjuntivo	
piense	**pensemos**	**haya pensado**	**hayamos pensado**
pienses	**penséis**	**hayas pensado**	**hayáis pensado**
piense	**piensen**	**haya pensado**	**hayan pensado**
7 imperfecto de subjuntivo		14 pluscuamperfecto de subjuntivo	
pensara	**pensáramos**	**hubiera pensado**	**hubiéramos pensado**
pensaras	**pensarais**	**hubieras pensado**	**hubierais pensado**
pensara	**pensaran**	**hubiera pensado**	**hubieran pensado**
OR		OR	
pensase	**pensásemos**	**hubiese pensado**	**hubiésemos pensado**
pensases	**pensaseis**	**hubieses pensado**	**hubieseis pensado**
pensase	**pensasen**	**hubiese pensado**	**hubiesen pensado**

imperativo	
—	**pensemos**
piensa; no pienses	**pensad; no penséis**
piense	**piensen**

Words and expressions related to this verb

¿Qué piensa Ud. de eso?   What do you think of that?
¿En qué piensa Ud.?   What are you thinking of?
pensativo, pensativa   thoughtful, pensive
un pensador, una pensadora   thinker

pensar + inf.   to intend + inf.
pensar en   to think of, about
sin pensar   thoughtlessly
repensar   to think over (again)

See also **pensar** on pages 533 and 534.

See also **pensar** on pages 533 and 534.

The subject pronouns are found on the page facing page 1.

percibir

Gerundio **percibiendo** Part. pas. **percibido**

to perceive

The Seven Simple Tenses		The Seven Compound Tenses	
Singular	Plural	Singular	Plural
1 presente de indicativo		**8 perfecto de indicativo**	
percibo	percibimos	he percibido	hemos percibido
percibes	percibís	has percibido	habéis percibido
percibe	perciben	ha percibido	han percibido
2 imperfecto de indicativo		**9 pluscuamperfecto de indicativo**	
percibía	percibíamos	había percibido	habíamos percibido
percibías	percibíais	habías percibido	habíais percibido
percibía	percibían	había percibido	habían percibido
3 pretérito		**10 pretérito anterior**	
percibí	percibimos	hube percibido	hubimos percibido
percibiste	percibisteis	hubiste percibido	hubisteis percibido
percibió	percibieron	hubo percibido	hubieron percibido
4 futuro		**11 futuro perfecto**	
percibiré	percibiremos	habré percibido	habremos percibido
percibirás	percibiréis	habrás percibido	habréis percibido
percibirá	percibirán	habrá percibido	habrán percibido
5 potencial simple		**12 potencial compuesto**	
percibiría	percibiríamos	habría percibido	habríamos percibido
percibirías	percibiríais	habrías percibido	habríais percibido
percibiría	percibirían	habría percibido	habrían percibido
6 presente de subjuntivo		**13 perfecto de subjuntivo**	
perciba	percibamos	haya percibido	hayamos percibido
percibas	percibáis	hayas percibido	hayáis percibido
perciba	perciban	haya percibido	hayan percibido
7 imperfecto de subjuntivo		**14 pluscuamperfecto de subjuntivo**	
percibiera	percibiéramos	hubiera percibido	hubiéramos percibido
percibieras	percibierais	hubieras percibido	hubierais percibido
percibiera	percibieran	hubiera percibido	hubieran percibido
OR		OR	
percibiese	percibiésemos	hubiese percibido	hubiésemos percibido
percibieses	percibieseis	hubieses percibido	hubieseis percibido
percibiese	percibiesen	hubiese percibido	hubiesen percibido

	imperativo
—	**percibamos**
percibe; no percibas	**percibid; no percibáis**
perciba	**perciban**

Words and expressions related to this verb

la percepción   perception
la perceptibilidad   perceptibility
perceptible   perceptible, perceivable

perceptiblemente   perceptibly
perceptivo, perceptiva   perceptive
imperceptible   imperceptible

Check out the verb drills and verb tests with answers explained on pages 619–665.

The Seven Simple Tenses		The Seven Compound Tenses	
Singular	Plural	Singular	Plural
1 presente de indicativo		8 perfecto de indicativo	
pierdo	**perdemos**	**he perdido**	**hemos perdido**
pierdes	**perdéis**	**has perdido**	**habéis perdido**
pierde	**pierden**	**ha perdido**	**han perdido**
2 imperfecto de indicativo		9 pluscuamperfecto de indicativo	
perdía	**perdíamos**	**había perdido**	**habíamos perdido**
perdías	**perdíais**	**habías perdido**	**habíais perdido**
perdía	**perdían**	**había perdido**	**habían perdido**
3 pretérito		10 pretérito anterior	
perdí	**perdimos**	**hube perdido**	**hubimos perdido**
perdiste	**perdisteis**	**hubiste perdido**	**hubisteis perdido**
perdió	**perdieron**	**hubo perdido**	**hubieron perdido**
4 futuro		11 futuro perfecto	
perderé	**perderemos**	**habré perdido**	**habremos perdido**
perderás	**perderéis**	**habrás perdido**	**habréis perdido**
perderá	**perderán**	**habrá perdido**	**habrán perdido**
5 potencial simple		12 potencial compuesto	
perdería	**perderíamos**	**habría perdido**	**habríamos perdido**
perderías	**perderíais**	**habrías perdido**	**habríais perdido**
perdería	**perderían**	**habría perdido**	**habrían perdido**
6 presente de subjuntivo		13 perfecto de subjuntivo	
pierda	**perdamos**	**haya perdido**	**hayamos perdido**
pierdas	**perdáis**	**hayas perdido**	**hayáis perdido**
pierda	**pierdan**	**haya perdido**	**hayan perdido**
7 imperfecto de subjuntivo		14 pluscuamperfecto de subjuntivo	
perdiera	**perdiéramos**	**hubiera perdido**	**hubiéramos perdido**
perdieras	**perdierais**	**hubieras perdido**	**hubierais perdido**
perdiera	**perdieran**	**hubiera perdido**	**hubieran perdido**
OR		OR	
perdiese	**perdiésemos**	**hubiese perdido**	**hubiésemos perdido**
perdieses	**perdieseis**	**hubieses perdido**	**hubieseis perdido**
perdiese	**perdiesen**	**hubiese perdido**	**hubiesen perdido**

imperativo

—	**perdamos**
pierde; no pierdas	**perded; no perdáis**
pierda	**pierdan**

Words and expressions related to this verb
un perdedor, una perdedora   loser
la pérdida   loss
¡Pierda Ud. cuidado!   Don't worry!
perdidamente enamorado (enamorada)
    passionately in love
perder de vista a (alguien)   to lose sight of (someone)

estar perdido (perdida)   to be lost
perder el juicio   to go mad (crazy)
perder los estribos   to lose self-control
perderse   to lose one's way, to get lost
la perdición   loss, ruin, perdition

The subject pronouns are found on the page facing page 1.

perdonar

Gerundio **perdonando**   Part. pas. **perdonado**

to pardon, to forgive, to excuse

The Seven Simple Tenses		The Seven Compound Tenses	
Singular	Plural	Singular	Plural
1 presente de indicativo		8 perfecto de indicativo	
perdono	perdonamos	he perdonado	hemos perdonado
perdonas	perdonáis	has perdonado	habéis perdonado
perdona	perdonan	ha perdonado	han perdonado
2 imperfecto de indicativo		9 pluscuamperfecto de indicativo	
perdonaba	perdonábamos	había perdonado	habíamos perdonado
perdonabas	perdonabais	habías perdonado	habíais perdonado
perdonaba	perdonaban	había perdonado	habían perdonado
3 pretérito		10 pretérito anterior	
perdoné	perdonamos	hube perdonado	hubimos perdonado
perdonaste	perdonasteis	hubiste perdonado	hubisteis perdonado
perdonó	perdonaron	hubo perdonado	hubieron perdonado
4 futuro		11 futuro perfecto	
perdonaré	perdonaremos	habré perdonado	habremos perdonado
perdonarás	perdonaréis	habrás perdonado	habréis perdonado
perdonará	perdonarán	habrá perdonado	habrán perdonado
5 potencial simple		12 potencial compuesto	
perdonaría	perdonaríamos	habría perdonado	habríamos perdonado
perdonarías	perdonaríais	habrías perdonado	habríais perdonado
perdonaría	perdonarían	habría perdonado	habrían perdonado
6 presente de subjuntivo		13 perfecto de subjuntivo	
perdone	perdonemos	haya perdonado	hayamos perdonado
perdones	perdonéis	hayas perdonado	hayáis perdonado
perdone	perdonen	haya perdonado	hayan perdonado
7 imperfecto de subjuntivo		14 pluscuamperfecto de subjuntivo	
perdonara	perdonáramos	hubiera perdonado	hubiéramos perdonado
perdonaras	perdonarais	hubieras perdonado	hubierais perdonado
perdonara	perdonaran	hubiera perdonado	hubieran perdonado
OR		OR	
perdonase	perdonásemos	hubiese perdonado	hubiésemos perdonado
perdonases	perdonaseis	hubieses perdonado	hubieseis perdonado
perdonase	perdonasen	hubiese perdonado	hubiesen perdonado

	imperativo	
—		perdonemos
	perdona; no perdones	perdonad; no perdonéis
	perdone	perdonen

Words and expressions related to this verb

el perdón   pardon, forgiveness
perdonable   pardonable, forgivable
imperdonable   unpardonable

Perdóneme   Pardon me.
donar   to donate; **el don**   gift
¡Perdón!   I'm sorry!

If you want to see a sample English verb fully conjugated
in all the tenses, check out pages xviii and xix.

to permit, to admit, to allow, to grant

The Seven Simple Tenses		The Seven Compound Tenses	
Singular	Plural	Singular	Plural
1 presente de indicativo		**8 perfecto de indicativo**	
permito	permitimos	he permitido	hemos permitido
permites	permitís	has permitido	habéis permitido
permite	permiten	ha permitido	han permitido
2 imperfecto de indicativo		**9 pluscuamperfecto de indicativo**	
permitía	permitíamos	había permitido	habíamos permitido
permitías	permitíais	habías permitido	habíais permitido
permitía	permitían	había permitido	habían permitido
3 pretérito		**10 pretérito anterior**	
permití	permitimos	hube permitido	hubimos permitido
permitiste	permitisteis	hubiste permitido	hubisteis permitido
permitió	permitieron	hubo permitido	hubieron permitido
4 futuro		**11 futuro perfecto**	
permitiré	permitiremos	habré permitido	habremos permitido
permitirás	permitiréis	habrás permitido	habréis permitido
permitirá	permitirán	habrá permitido	habrán permitido
5 potencial simple		**12 potencial compuesto**	
permitiría	permitiríamos	habría permitido	habríamos permitido
permitirías	permitiríais	habrías permitido	habríais permitido
permitiría	permitirían	habría permitido	habrían permitido
6 presente de subjuntivo		**13 perfecto de subjuntivo**	
permita	permitamos	haya permitido	hayamos permitido
permitas	permitáis	hayas permitido	hayáis permitido
permita	permitan	haya permitido	hayan permitido
7 imperfecto de subjuntivo		**14 pluscuamperfecto de subjuntivo**	
permitiera	permitiéramos	hubiera permitido	hubiéramos permitido
permitieras	permitierais	hubieras permitido	hubierais permitido
permitiera	permitieran	hubiera permitido	hubieran permitido
OR		OR	
permitiese	permitiésemos	hubiese permitido	hubiésemos permitido
permitieses	permitieseis	hubieses permitido	hubieseis permitido
permitiese	permitiesen	hubiese permitido	hubiesen permitido

imperativo	
—	permitamos
permite; no permitas	permitid; no permitáis
permita	permitan

Words and expressions related to this verb
el permiso permit, permission
¡Con permiso! Excuse me!
la permisión permission
emitir to emit
No se permite + inf. It is not permitted to + inf.

admitir to admit
permitirse + inf. to take the liberty + inf.
el permiso de conducir driver's license
transmitir to transmit

to pertain, to appertain, to belong

The Seven Simple Tenses		The Seven Compound Tenses	
Singular	Plural	Singular	Plural
1 presente de indicativo		8 perfecto de indicativo	
pertenezco	pertenecemos	he pertenecido	hemos pertenecido
perteneces	pertenecéis	has pertenecido	habéis pertenecido
pertenece	pertenecen	ha pertenecido	han pertenecido
2 imperfecto de indicativo		9 pluscuamperfecto de indicativo	
pertenecía	pertenecíamos	había pertenecido	habíamos pertenecido
pertenecías	pertenecíais	habías pertenecido	habíais pertenecido
pertenecía	pertenecían	había pertenecido	habían pertenecido
3 pretérito		10 pretérito anterior	
pertenecí	pertenecimos	hube pertenecido	hubimos pertenecido
perteneciste	pertenecisteis	hubiste pertenecido	hubisteis pertenecido
perteneció	pertenecieron	hubo pertenecido	hubieron pertenecido
4 futuro		11 futuro perfecto	
perteneceré	perteneceremos	habré pertenecido	habremos pertenecido
pertenecerás	pertenecéréis	habrás pertenecido	habréis pertenecido
pertenecerá	pertenecerán	habrá pertenecido	habrán pertenecido
5 potencial simple		12 potencial compuesto	
pertenecería	perteneceríamos	habría pertenecido	habríamos pertenecido
pertenecerías	perteneceríais	habrías pertenecido	habríais pertenecido
pertenecería	pertenecerían	habría pertenecido	habrían pertenecido
6 presente de subjuntivo		13 perfecto de subjuntivo	
pertenezca	pertenezcamos	haya pertenecido	hayamos pertenecido
pertenezcas	pertenezcáis	hayas pertenecido	hayáis pertenecido
pertenezca	pertenezcan	haya pertenecido	hayan pertenecido
7 imperfecto de subjuntivo		14 pluscuamperfecto de subjuntivo	
perteneciera	perteneciéramos	hubiera pertenecido	hubiéramos pertenecido
pertenecieras	pertenecierais	hubieras pertenecido	hubierais pertenecido
perteneciera	pertenecieran	hubiera pertenecido	hubieran pertenecido
OR		OR	
perteneciese	perteneciésemos	hubiese pertenecido	hubiésemos pertenecido
pertenecieses	pertenecieseis	hubieses pertenecido	hubieseis pertenecido
perteneciese	perteneciesen	hubiese pertenecido	hubiesen pertenecido

	imperativo	
—	pertenezcamos
pertenece; no pertenezcas	perteneced; no pertenezcáis
pertenezca	pertenezcan

Words and expressions related to this verb

el pertenecido   ownership, proprietorship
perteneciente   belonging, pertaining
la pertinencia   pertinence, relevance
pertinente   pertinent, relevant

la pertenencia   right of possession, ownership
ser de la pertenencia de   to be in the domain of
la tenencia ilícita   illegal possession

If you want an explanation of meanings and uses of Spanish
and English verb tenses and moods, see pages xx–xl.

The Seven Simple Tenses		The Seven Compound Tenses	
Singular	Plural	Singular	Plural
1　presente de indicativo		8　perfecto de indicativo	
pinto	**pintamos**	**he pintado**	**hemos pintado**
pintas	**pintáis**	**has pintado**	**habéis pintado**
pinta	**pintan**	**ha pintado**	**han pintado**
2　imperfecto de indicativo		9　pluscuamperfecto de indicativo	
pintaba	**pintábamos**	**había pintado**	**habíamos pintado**
pintabas	**pintabais**	**habías pintado**	**habíais pintado**
pintaba	**pintaban**	**había pintado**	**habían pintado**
3　pretérito		10　pretérito anterior	
pinté	**pintamos**	**hube pintado**	**hubimos pintado**
pintaste	**pintasteis**	**hubiste pintado**	**hubisteis pintado**
pintó	**pintaron**	**hubo pintado**	**hubieron pintado**
4　futuro		11　futuro perfecto	
pintaré	**pintaremos**	**habré pintado**	**habremos pintado**
pintarás	**pintaréis**	**habrás pintado**	**habréis pintado**
pintará	**pintarán**	**habrá pintado**	**habrán pintado**
5　potencial simple		12　potencial compuesto	
pintaría	**pintaríamos**	**habría pintado**	**habríamos pintado**
pintarías	**pintaríais**	**habrías pintado**	**habríais pintado**
pintaría	**pintarían**	**habría pintado**	**habrían pintado**
6　presente de subjuntivo		13　perfecto de subjuntivo	
pinte	**pintemos**	**haya pintado**	**hayamos pintado**
pintes	**pintéis**	**hayas pintado**	**hayáis pintado**
pinte	**pinten**	**haya pintado**	**hayan pintado**
7　imperfecto de subjuntivo		14　pluscuamperfecto de subjuntivo	
pintara	**pintáramos**	**hubiera pintado**	**hubiéramos pintado**
pintaras	**pintarais**	**hubieras pintado**	**hubierais pintado**
pintara	**pintaran**	**hubiera pintado**	**hubieran pintado**
OR		OR	
pintase	**pintásemos**	**hubiese pintado**	**hubiésemos pintado**
pintases	**pintaseis**	**hubieses pintado**	**hubieseis pintado**
pintase	**pintasen**	**hubiese pintado**	**hubiesen pintado**

imperativo

—	**pintemos**
pinta; no pintes	**pintad; no pintéis**
pinte	**pinten**

Words and expressions related to this verb

un pintor, una pintora　painter (artist)
una pintura　painting (picture)
un pintor de brocha gorda　house (sign) painter
una pintura al fresco　fresco painting

una pintura al óleo　oil painting
una pintura al pastel　pastel painting
pinturero, pinturera　conceited person
pintoresco, pintoresca　picturesque

The subject pronouns are found on the page facing page 1.

to make up (one's face), to tint, to color (one's hair, lips, etc.)

The Seven Simple Tenses		The Seven Compound Tenses	
Singular	Plural	Singular	Plural
1 presente de indicativo		8 perfecto de indicativo	
me pinto	nos pintamos	me he pintado	nos hemos pintado
te pintas	os pintáis	te has pintado	os habéis pintado
se pinta	se pintan	se ha pintado	se han pintado
2 imperfecto de indicativo		9 pluscuamperfecto de indicativo	
me pintaba	nos pintábamos	me había pintado	nos habíamos pintado
te pintabas	os pintabais	te habías pintado	os habíais pintado
se pintaba	se pintaban	se había pintado	se habían pintado
3 pretérito		10 pretérito anterior	
me pinté	nos pintamos	me hube pintado	nos hubimos pintado
te pintaste	os pintasteis	te hubiste pintado	os hubisteis pintado
se pintó	se pintaron	se hubo pintado	se hubieron pintado
4 futuro		11 futuro perfecto	
me pintaré	nos pintaremos	me habré pintado	nos habremos pintado
te pintarás	os pintaréis	te habrás pintado	os habréis pintado
se pintará	se pintarán	se habrá pintado	se habrán pintado
5 potencial simple		12 potencial compuesto	
me pintaría	nos pintaríamos	me habría pintado	nos habríamos pintado
te pintarías	os pintaríais	te habrías pintado	os habríais pintado
se pintaría	se pintarían	se habría pintado	se habrían pintado
6 presente de subjuntivo		13 perfecto de subjuntivo	
me pinte	nos pintemos	me haya pintado	nos hayamos pintado
te pintes	os pintéis	te hayas pintado	os hayáis pintado
se pinte	se pinten	se haya pintado	se hayan pintado
7 imperfecto de subjuntivo		14 pluscuamperfecto de subjuntivo	
me pintara	nos pintáramos	me hubiera pintado	nos hubiéramos pintado
te pintaras	os pintarais	te hubieras pintado	os hubierais pintado
se pintara	se pintaran	se hubiera pintado	se hubieran pintado
OR		OR	
me pintase	nos pintásemos	me hubiese pintado	nos hubiésemos pintado
te pintases	os pintaseis	te hubieses pintado	os hubieseis pintado
se pintase	se pintasen	se hubiese pintado	se hubiesen pintado

	imperativo	
—	pintémonos	
píntate; no te pintes	pintaos; no os pintéis	
píntese	píntense	

When using this verb to mean to color one's hair, lips, etc., you must mention **el pelo, los labios,** etc.

For words related to this verb see the verb **pintar.**

Get acquainted with what preposition goes with what verb on pages 541–549.

to tread (on), to step on, to trample

The Seven Simple Tenses		The Seven Compound Tenses	
Singular	Plural	Singular	Plural
1 presente de indicativo		8 perfecto de indicativo	
piso	pisamos	he pisado	hemos pisado
pisas	pisáis	has pisado	habéis pisado
pisa	pisan	ha pisado	han pisado
2 imperfecto de indicativo		9 pluscuamperfecto de indicativo	
pisaba	pisábamos	había pisado	habíamos pisado
pisabas	pisabais	habías pisado	habíais pisado
pisaba	pisaban	había pisado	habían pisado
3 pretérito		10 pretérito anterior	
pisé	pisamos	hube pisado	hubimos pisado
pisaste	pisasteis	hubiste pisado	hubisteis pisado
pisó	pisaron	hubo pisado	hubieron pisado
4 futuro		11 futuro perfecto	
pisaré	pisaremos	habré pisado	habremos pisado
pisarás	pisaréis	habrás pisado	habréis pisado
pisará	pisarán	habrá pisado	habrán pisado
5 potencial simple		12 potencial compuesto	
pisaría	pisaríamos	habría pisado	habríamos pisado
pisarías	pisaríais	habrías pisado	habríais pisado
pisaría	pisarían	habría pisado	habrían pisado
6 presente de subjuntivo		13 perfecto de subjuntivo	
pise	pisemos	haya pisado	hayamos pisado
pises	piséis	hayas pisado	hayáis pisado
pise	pisen	haya pisado	hayan pisado
7 imperfecto de subjuntivo		14 pluscuamperfecto de subjuntivo	
pisara	pisáramos	hubiera pisado	hubiéramos pisado
pisaras	pisarais	hubieras pisado	hubierais pisado
pisara	pisaran	hubiera pisado	hubieran pisado
OR		OR	
pisase	pisásemos	hubiese pisado	hubiésemos pisado
pisases	pisaseis	hubieses pisado	hubieseis pisado
pisase	pisasen	hubiese pisado	hubiesen pisado

imperativo	
—	pisemos
pisa; no pises	pisad; no piséis
pise	pisen

Words and expressions related to this verb
la pisa   kicking
el piso   floor, story (of a building)
el piso alto   top floor
repisar   to pack down
pisotear   to trample

el piso principal   main floor
el piso bajo   ground floor
el pisoteo   abuse, trampling
la repisa   shelf; **repisa de ventana**   windowsill
¡Piso mojado!   Wet floor!

to gratify, to humor, to please

The Seven Simple Tenses		The Seven Compound Tenses	
Singular	Plural	Singular	Plural
1 presente de indicativo		8 perfecto de indicativo	
plazco	**placemos**	**he placido**	**hemos placido**
places	**placéis**	**has placido**	**habéis placido**
place	**placen**	**ha placido**	**han placido**
2 imperfecto de indicativo		9 pluscuamperfecto de indicativo	
placía	**placíamos**	**había placido**	**habíamos placido**
placías	**placíais**	**habías placido**	**habíais placido**
placía	**placían**	**había placido**	**habían placido**
3 pretérito		10 pretérito anterior	
plací	**placimos**	**hube placido**	**hubimos placido**
placiste	**placisteis**	**hubiste placido**	**hubisteis placido**
plació	**placieron**	**hubo placido**	**hubieron placido**
4 futuro		11 futuro perfecto	
placeré	**placeremos**	**habré placido**	**habremos placido**
placerás	**placeréis**	**habrás placido**	**habréis placido**
placerá	**placerán**	**habrá placido**	**habrán placido**
5 potencial simple		12 potencial compuesto	
placería	**placeríamos**	**habría placido**	**habríamos placido**
placerías	**placeríais**	**habrías placido**	**habríais placido**
placería	**placerían**	**habría placido**	**habrían placido**
6 presente de subjuntivo		13 perfecto de subjuntivo	
plazca	**plazcamos**	**haya placido**	**hayamos placido**
plazcas	**plazcáis**	**hayas placido**	**hayáis placido**
plazca	**plazcan**	**haya placido**	**hayan placido**
7 imperfecto de subjuntivo		14 pluscuamperfecto de subjuntivo	
placiera	**placiéramos**	**hubiera placido**	**hubiéramos placido**
placieras	**placierais**	**hubieras placido**	**hubierais placido**
placiera	**placieran**	**hubiera placido**	**hubieran placido**
OR		OR	
placiese	**placiésemos**	**hubiese placido**	**hubiésemos placido**
placieses	**placieseis**	**hubieses placido**	**hubieseis placido**
placiese	**placiesen**	**hubiese placido**	**hubiesen placido**

imperativo

—	**plazcamos**
place; no plazcas	**placed; no plazcáis**
plazca	**plazcan**

Words related to this verb

el placer pleasure
la placidez contentment
placenteramente joyfully
el placero, la placera market merchant

placentero, placentera agreeable, pleasant
placible agreeable, placid; **plácido** placid, pleasant
implacable implacable, inexorable

In poetry, **plugo** is sometimes used instead of **plació**, **pluguieron** instead of **placieron**, **plegue** instead of **plazca**, **pluguiera** instead of **placiera**, and **pluguiese** instead of **placiese**.

to chat, to talk over, to discuss

The Seven Simple Tenses		The Seven Compound Tenses	
Singular	Plural	Singular	Plural

1   presente de indicativo

platico	platicamos	
platicas	platicáis	
platica	platican	

8   perfecto de indicativo

he platicado	hemos platicado
has platicado	habéis platicado
ha platicado	han platicado

2   imperfecto de indicativo

platicaba	platicábamos
platicabas	platicabais
platicaba	platicaban

9   pluscuamperfecto de indicativo

había platicado	habíamos platicado
habías platicado	habíais platicado
había platicado	habían platicado

3   pretérito

platiqué	platicamos
platicaste	platicasteis
platicó	platicaron

10   pretérito anterior

hube platicado	hubimos platicado
hubiste platicado	hubisteis platicado
hubo platicado	hubieron platicado

4   futuro

platicaré	platicaremos
platicarás	platicaréis
platicará	platicarán

11   futuro perfecto

habré platicado	habremos platicado
habrás platicado	habréis platicado
habrá platicado	habrán platicado

5   potencial simple

platicaría	platicaríamos
platicarías	platicaríais
platicaría	platicarían

12   potencial compuesto

habría platicado	habríamos platicado
habrías platicado	habríais platicado
habría platicado	habrían platicado

6   presente de subjuntivo

platique	platiquemos
platiques	platiquéis
platique	platiquen

13   perfecto de subjuntivo

haya platicado	hayamos platicado
hayas platicado	hayáis platicado
haya platicado	hayan platicado

7   imperfecto de subjuntivo

platicara	platicáramos
platicaras	platicarais
platicara	platicaran
OR	
platicase	platicásemos
platicases	platicaseis
platicase	platicasen

14   pluscuamperfecto de subjuntivo

hubiera platicado	hubiéramos platicado
hubieras platicado	hubierais platicado
hubiera platicado	hubieran platicado
OR	
hubiese platicado	hubiésemos platicado
hubieses platicado	hubieseis platicado
hubiese platicado	hubiesen platicado

imperativo

—	**platiquemos**
platica; no platiques	**platicad; no platiquéis**
platique	**platiquen**

Words related to this verb
una plática   chat, talk, conversation
un platicador, una platicadora   talker; *as an adj.,* talkative

Consult the back pages for the sections on verbs used in idiomatic expressions,
Spanish proverbs using verbs, weather expressions using verbs, verbs with prepositions,
and over 1,100 Spanish verbs conjugated like the 501 model verbs.

The subject pronouns are found on the page facing page 1.

to be able, can

The Seven Simple Tenses		The Seven Compound Tenses	
Singular	Plural	Singular	Plural
1 presente de indicativo		8 perfecto de indicativo	
puedo	podemos	he podido	hemos podido
puedes	podéis	has podido	habéis podido
puede	pueden	ha podido	han podido
2 imperfecto de indicativo		9 pluscuamperfecto de indicativo	
podía	podíamos	había podido	habíamos podido
podías	podíais	habías podido	habíais podido
podía	podían	había podido	habían podido
3 pretérito		10 pretérito anterior	
pude	pudimos	hube podido	hubimos podido
pudiste	pudisteis	hubiste podido	hubisteis podido
pudo	pudieron	hubo podido	hubieron podido
4 futuro		11 futuro perfecto	
podré	podremos	habré podido	habremos podido
podrás	podréis	habrás podido	habréis podido
podrá	podrán	habrá podido	habrán podido
5 potencial simple		12 potencial compuesto	
podría	podríamos	habría podido	habríamos podido
podrías	podríais	habrías podido	habríais podido
podría	podrían	habría podido	habrían podido
6 presente de subjuntivo		13 perfecto de subjuntivo	
pueda	podamos	haya podido	hayamos podido
puedas	podáis	hayas podido	hayáis podido
pueda	puedan	haya podido	hayan podido
7 imperfecto de subjuntivo		14 pluscuamperfecto de subjuntivo	
pudiera	pudiéramos	hubiera podido	hubiéramos podido
pudieras	pudierais	hubieras podido	hubierais podido
pudiera	pudieran	hubiera podido	hubieran podido
OR		OR	
pudiese	pudiésemos	hubiese podido	hubiésemos podido
pudieses	pudieseis	hubieses podido	hubieseis podido
pudiese	pudiesen	hubiese podido	hubiesen podido

imperativo

—	podamos
puede; no puedas	poded; no podáis
pueda	puedan

Words and expressions related to this verb
el poder power
apoderar to empower
apoderarse de to take possession, to take over
poderoso, poderosa powerful
No se puede. It can't be done.

poderosamente powerfully
el poderío power, strength
estar en el poder to be in power
Querer es poder Where there's a will
  there's a way.

See also **poder** on page 534.

Enjoy more verbs in Spanish proverbs on page 539.

to put, to place, to turn on (TV, radio)

The Seven Simple Tenses		The Seven Compound Tenses	
Singular	Plural	Singular	Plural
1 presente de indicativo		8 perfecto de indicativo	
pongo	**ponemos**	**he puesto**	**hemos puesto**
pones	**ponéis**	**has puesto**	**habéis puesto**
pone	**ponen**	**ha puesto**	**han puesto**
2 imperfecto de indicativo		9 pluscuamperfecto de indicativo	
ponía	**poníamos**	**había puesto**	**habíamos puesto**
ponías	**poníais**	**habías puesto**	**habíais puesto**
ponía	**ponían**	**había puesto**	**habían puesto**
3 pretérito		10 pretérito anterior	
puse	**pusimos**	**hube puesto**	**hubimos puesto**
pusiste	**pusisteis**	**hubiste puesto**	**hubisteis puesto**
puso	**pusieron**	**hubo puesto**	**hubieron puesto**
4 futuro		11 futuro perfecto	
pondré	**pondremos**	**habré puesto**	**habremos puesto**
pondrás	**pondréis**	**habrás puesto**	**habréis puesto**
pondrá	**pondrán**	**habrá puesto**	**habrán puesto**
5 potencial simple		12 potencial compuesto	
pondría	**pondríamos**	**habría puesto**	**habríamos puesto**
pondrías	**pondríais**	**habrías puesto**	**habríais puesto**
pondría	**pondrían**	**habría puesto**	**habrían puesto**
6 presente de subjuntivo		13 perfecto de subjuntivo	
ponga	**pongamos**	**haya puesto**	**hayamos puesto**
pongas	**pongáis**	**hayas puesto**	**hayáis puesto**
ponga	**pongan**	**haya puesto**	**hayan puesto**
7 imperfecto de subjuntivo		14 pluscuamperfecto de subjuntivo	
pusiera	**pusiéramos**	**hubiera puesto**	**hubiéramos puesto**
pusieras	**pusierais**	**hubieras puesto**	**hubierais puesto**
pusiera	**pusieran**	**hubiera puesto**	**hubieran puesto**
OR		OR	
pusiese	**pusiésemos**	**hubiese puesto**	**hubiésemos puesto**
pusieses	**pusieseis**	**hubieses puesto**	**hubieseis puesto**
pusiese	**pusiesen**	**hubiese puesto**	**hubiesen puesto**

imperativo

—	**pongamos**
pon; no pongas	**poned; no pongáis**
ponga	**pongan**

Common idiomatic expressions using this verb
poner fin a   to put a stop to
poner la mesa   to set the table
poner de acuerdo   to reach an agreement
posponer   to postpone

la puesta de sol   sunset
bien puesto, bien puesta   well placed
reponer   to replace, to put back
poner una duda en claro   to clear up a doubt

For additional words and expressions related to this verb, see **ponerse** and **componer.**
See also **poner, ponerse** on pages 533 and 534.

The subject pronouns are found on the page facing page 1.

to put on (clothing), to become, to set (of sun)

The Seven Simple Tenses		The Seven Compound Tenses	
Singular	Plural	Singular	Plural
1 presente de indicativo		**8 perfecto de indicativo**	
me pongo	nos ponemos	me he puesto	nos hemos puesto
te pones	os ponéis	te has puesto	os habéis puesto
se pone	se ponen	se ha puesto	se han puesto
2 imperfecto de indicativo		**9 pluscuamperfecto de indicativo**	
me ponía	nos poníamos	me había puesto	nos habíamos puesto
te ponías	os poníais	te habías puesto	os habíais puesto
se ponía	se ponían	se había puesto	se habían puesto
3 pretérito		**10 pretérito anterior**	
me puse	nos pusimos	me hube puesto	nos hubimos puesto
te pusiste	os pusisteis	te hubiste puesto	os hubisteis puesto
se puso	se pusieron	se hubo puesto	se hubieron puesto
4 futuro		**11 futuro perfecto**	
me pondré	nos pondremos	me habré puesto	nos habremos puesto
te pondrás	os pondréis	te habrás puesto	os habréis puesto
se pondrá	se pondrán	se habrá puesto	se habrán puesto
5 potencial simple		**12 potencial compuesto**	
me pondría	nos pondríamos	me habría puesto	nos habríamos puesto
te pondrías	os pondríais	te habrías puesto	os habríais puesto
se pondría	se pondrían	se habría puesto	se habrían puesto
6 presente de subjuntivo		**13 perfecto de subjuntivo**	
me ponga	nos pongamos	me haya puesto	nos hayamos puesto
te pongas	os pongáis	te hayas puesto	os hayáis puesto
se ponga	se pongan	se haya puesto	se hayan puesto
7 imperfecto de subjuntivo		**14 pluscuamperfecto de subjuntivo**	
me pusiera	nos pusiéramos	me hubiera puesto	nos hubiéramos puesto
te pusieras	os pusierais	te hubieras puesto	os hubierais puesto
se pusiera	se pusieran	se hubiera puesto	se hubieran puesto
OR		OR	
me pusiese	nos pusiésemos	me hubiese puesto	nos hubiésemos puesto
te pusieses	os pusieseis	te hubieses puesto	os hubieseis puesto
se pusiese	se pusiesen	se hubiese puesto	se hubiesen puesto

imperativo	
—	pongámonos
ponte; no te pongas	poneos; no os pongáis
póngase	pónganse

Common idiomatic expressions using this verb
ponerse el abrigo   to put on one's overcoat
ponerse a + inf.   to begin, to start + inf.
María se puso pálida.   Mary became pale.

reponerse   to calm down, to recover (one's health)
indisponerse   to become ill

For additional words and expressions related to this verb, see **componer, poner,** and **suponer.**
See also the back pages for verbs used in idiomatic expressions.

to possess, to own

The Seven Simple Tenses		The Seven Compound Tenses	
Singular	Plural	Singular	Plural
1 presente de indicativo		8 perfecto de indicativo	
poseo	poseemos	he poseído	hemos poseído
posees	poseéis	has poseído	habéis poseído
posee	poseen	ha poseído	han poseído
2 imperfecto de indicativo		9 pluscuamperfecto de indicativo	
poseía	poseíamos	había poseído	habíamos poseído
poseías	poseíais	habías poseído	habíais poseído
poseía	poseían	había poseído	habían poseído
3 pretérito		10 pretérito anterior	
poseí	poseímos	hube poseído	hubimos poseído
poseiste	poseísteis	hubiste poseído	hubisteis poseído
poseyó	poseyeron	hubo poseído	hubieron poseído
4 futuro		11 futuro perfecto	
poseeré	poseeremos	habré poseído	habremos poseído
poseerás	poseeréis	habrás poseído	habréis poseído
poseerá	poseerán	habrá poseído	habrán poseído
5 potencial simple		12 potencial compuesto	
poseería	poseeríamos	habría poseído	habríamos poseído
poseerías	poseeríais	habrías poseído	habríais poseído
poseería	poseerían	habría poseído	habrían poseído
6 presente de subjuntivo		13 perfecto de subjuntivo	
posea	poseamos	haya poseído	hayamos poseído
poseas	poseáis	hayas poseído	hayáis poseído
posea	posean	haya poseído	hayan poseído
7 imperfecto de subjuntivo		14 pluscuamperfecto de subjuntivo	
poseyera	poseyéramos	hubiera poseído	hubiéramos poseído
poseyeras	poseyerais	hubieras poseído	hubierais poseído
poseyera	poseyeran	hubiera poseído	hubieran poseído
OR		OR	
poseyese	poseyésemos	hubiese poseído	hubiésemos poseído
poseyeses	poseyeseis	hubieses poseído	hubieseis poseído
poseyese	poseyesen	hubiese poseído	hubiesen poseído

imperativo

—	poseamos
posee; no poseas	poseed; no poseáis
posea	posean

Words related to this verb
el poseedor, la poseedora   owner, possessor
la posesión   possession
poseerse   to control oneself

dar posesión de   to give possession of
el posesor, la posesora   owner, possessor
desposeer   to dispossess

Review the principal parts of important Spanish verbs on pages xvi–xvii.

The subject pronouns are found on the page facing page 1.

practicar
Gerundio **practicando**   Part. pas. **practicado**

to practice

The Seven Simple Tenses		The Seven Compound Tenses	
Singular	Plural	Singular	Plural
1 presente de indicativo		**8 perfecto de indicativo**	
practico	practicamos	he practicado	hemos practicado
practicas	practicáis	has practicado	habéis practicado
practica	practican	ha practicado	han practicado
2 imperfecto de indicativo		**9 pluscuamperfecto de indicativo**	
practicaba	practicábamos	había practicado	habíamos practicado
practicabas	practicabais	habías practicado	habíais practicado
practicaba	practicaban	había practicado	habían practicado
3 pretérito		**10 pretérito anterior**	
practiqué	practicamos	hube practicado	hubimos practicado
practicaste	practicasteis	hubiste practicado	hubisteis practicado
practicó	practicaron	hubo practicado	hubieron practicado
4 futuro		**11 futuro perfecto**	
practicaré	practicaremos	habré practicado	habremos practicado
practicarás	practicaréis	habrás practicado	habréis practicado
practicará	practicarán	habrá practicado	habrán practicado
5 potencial simple		**12 potencial compuesto**	
practicaría	practicaríamos	habría practicado	habríamos practicado
practicarías	practicaríais	habrías practicado	habríais practicado
practicaría	practicarían	habría practicado	habrían practicado
6 presente de subjuntivo		**13 perfecto de subjuntivo**	
practique	practiquemos	haya practicado	hayamos practicado
practiques	practiquéis	hayas practicado	hayáis practicado
practique	practiquen	haya practicado	hayan practicado
7 imperfecto de subjuntivo		**14 pluscuamperfecto de subjuntivo**	
practicara	practicáramos	hubiera practicado	hubiéramos practicado
practicaras	practicarais	hubieras practicado	hubierais practicado
practicara	practicaran	hubiera practicado	hubieran practicado
OR		OR	
practicase	practicásemos	hubiese practicado	hubiésemos practicado
practicases	practicaseis	hubieses practicado	hubieseis practicado
practicase	practicasen	hubiese practicado	hubiesen practicado

imperativo	
—	practiquemos
practica; no practiques	practicad; no practiquéis
practique	practiquen

Words and expressions related to this verb
práctico, práctica practical
la práctica practice, habit
en la práctica in practice
practicar investigaciones to look into, to investigate

practicar un informe to make a report
practicar una buena acción to do a good deed
practicar el fútbol to play soccer
practicar las artes marciales to practice martial arts

to predict, to forecast, to foretell

The Seven Simple Tenses		The Seven Compound Tenses	
Singular	Plural	Singular	Plural
1 presente de indicativo		8 perfecto de indicativo	
predigo	**predecimos**	**he predicho**	**hemos predicho**
predices	**predecís**	**has predicho**	**habéis predicho**
predice	**predicen**	**ha predicho**	**han predicho**
2 imperfecto de indicativo		9 pluscuamperfecto de indicativo	
predecía	**predecíamos**	**había predicho**	**habíamos predicho**
predecías	**predecíais**	**habías predicho**	**habíais predicho**
predecía	**predecían**	**había predicho**	**habían predicho**
3 pretérito		10 pretérito anterior	
predije	**predijimos**	**hube predicho**	**hubimos predicho**
predijiste	**predijisteis**	**hubiste predicho**	**hubisteis predicho**
predijo	**predijeron**	**hubo predicho**	**hubieron predicho**
4 futuro		11 futuro perfecto	
prediciré	**prediciremos**	**habré predicho**	**habremos predicho**
predicirás	**predeciréis**	**habrás predicho**	**habréis predicho**
predicirá	**predicirán**	**habrá predicho**	**habrán predicho**
5 potencial simple		12 potencial compuesto	
prediciría	**prediciríamos**	**habría predicho**	**habríamos predicho**
predicirías	**prediciríais**	**habrías predicho**	**habríais predicho**
prediciría	**predicirían**	**habría predicho**	**habrían predicho**
6 presente de subjuntivo		13 perfecto de subjuntivo	
prediga	**predigamos**	**haya predicho**	**hayamos predicho**
predigas	**predigáis**	**hayas predicho**	**hayáis predicho**
prediga	**predigan**	**haya predicho**	**hayan predicho**
7 imperfecto de subjuntivo		14 pluscuamperfecto de subjuntivo	
predijera	**predijéramos**	**hubiera predicho**	**hubiéramos predicho**
perdijeras	**predijerais**	**hubieras predicho**	**hubierais predicho**
predijera	**predijeran**	**hubiera predicho**	**hubieran predicho**
OR		OR	
predijese	**predijésemos**	**hubiese predicho**	**hubiésemos predicho**
predijeses	**predijeseis**	**hubieses predicho**	**hubieseis predicho**
predijese	**predijesen**	**hubiese predicho**	**hubiesen predicho**

	imperativo	
—	**predigamos**	
predice; no predigas	**predecid; no predigáis**	
prediga	**predigan**	

Words and expressions related to this verb
decir   to say, to tell
una predicción   prediction
la predicción del tiempo   weather forecasting
la dicción   diction

This verb is conjugated like the irregular verb **decir,** except in the future and conditional (Tense Nos. 4 and 5), and in the 2d person., sing. (**tú**) of the imperative, which are regular.

predicar

predicar   Gerundio **predicando**   Part. pas. **predicado**

to preach

The Seven Simple Tenses		The Seven Compound Tenses	
Singular	Plural	Singular	Plural
1 presente de indicativo		**8 perfecto de indicativo**	
predico	predicamos	he predicado	hemos predicado
predicas	predicáis	has predicado	habéis predicado
predica	predican	ha predicado	han predicado
2 imperfecto de indicativo		**9 pluscuamperfecto de indicativo**	
predicaba	predicábamos	había predicado	habíamos predicado
predicabas	predicabais	habías predicado	habíais predicado
predicaba	predicaban	había predicado	habían predicado
3 pretérito		**10 pretérito anterior**	
prediqué	predicamos	hube predicado	hubimos predicado
predicaste	predicasteis	hubiste predicado	hubisteis predicado
predicó	predicaron	hubo predicado	hubieron predicado
4 futuro		**11 futuro perfecto**	
predicaré	predicaremos	habré predicado	habremos predicado
predicarás	predicaréis	habrás predicado	habréis predicado
predicará	predicarán	habrá predicado	habrán predicado
5 potencial simple		**12 potencial compuesto**	
predicaría	predicaríamos	habría predicado	habríamos predicado
predicarías	predicaríais	habrías predicado	habríais predicado
predicaría	predicarían	habría predicado	habrían predicado
6 presente de subjuntivo		**13 perfecto de subjuntivo**	
predique	prediquemos	haya predicado	hayamos predicado
prediques	prediquéis	hayas predicado	hayáis predicado
predique	prediquen	haya predicado	hayan predicado
7 imperfecto de subjuntivo		**14 pluscuamperfecto de subjuntivo**	
predicara	predicáramos	hubiera predicado	hubiéramos predicado
predicaras	predicarais	hubieras predicado	hubierais predicado
predicara	predicaran	hubiera predicado	hubieran predicado
OR		OR	
predicase	predicásemos	hubiese predicado	hubiésemos predicado
predicases	predicaseis	hubieses predicado	hubieseis predicado
predicase	predicasen	hubiese predicado	hubiesen predicado

imperativo	
—	prediquemos
predica; no prediques	predicad; no prediquéis
predique	prediquen

Words related to this verb

la predicación   preaching   **una prédica**   sermon
un predicador   preacher   **predicativo, predicativa**   predicative

If you don't know the Spanish verb for the English verb you have
in mind, look it up in the index on pages 505–518.

The Seven Simple Tenses		The Seven Compound Tenses	
Singular	Plural	Singular	Plural
1 presente de indicativo		8 perfecto de indicativo	
prefiero	**preferimos**	**he preferido**	**hemos preferido**
prefieres	**preferís**	**has preferido**	**habéis preferido**
prefiere	**prefieren**	**ha preferido**	**han preferido**
2 imperfecto de indicativo		9 pluscuamperfecto de indicativo	
prefería	**preferíamos**	**había preferido**	**habíamos preferido**
preferías	**preferíais**	**habías preferido**	**habíais preferido**
prefería	**preferían**	**había preferido**	**habían preferido**
3 pretérito		10 pretérito anterior	
preferí	**preferimos**	**hube preferido**	**hubimos preferido**
preferiste	**preferisteis**	**hubiste preferido**	**hubisteis preferido**
prefirió	**prefirieron**	**hubo preferido**	**hubieron preferido**
4 futuro		11 futuro perfecto	
preferiré	**preferiremos**	**habré preferido**	**habremos preferido**
preferirás	**preferiréis**	**habrás preferido**	**habréis preferido**
preferirá	**preferirán**	**habrá preferido**	**habrán preferido**
5 potencial simple		12 potencial compuesto	
preferiría	**preferiríamos**	**habría preferido**	**habríamos preferido**
preferirías	**preferiríais**	**habrías preferido**	**habríais preferido**
preferiría	**preferirían**	**habría preferido**	**habrían preferido**
6 presente de subjuntivo		13 perfecto de subjuntivo	
prefiera	**prefiramos**	**haya preferido**	**hayamos preferido**
prefieras	**prefiráis**	**hayas preferido**	**hayáis preferido**
prefiera	**prefieran**	**haya preferido**	**hayan preferido**
7 imperfecto de subjuntivo		14 pluscuamperfecto de subjuntivo	
prefiriera	**prefiriéramos**	**hubiera preferido**	**hubiéramos preferido**
prefirieras	**prefirierais**	**hubieras preferido**	**hubierais preferido**
prefiriera	**prefirieran**	**hubiera preferido**	**hubieran preferido**
OR		OR	
prefiriese	**prefiriésemos**	**hubiese preferido**	**hubiésemos preferido**
prefirieses	**prefirieseis**	**hubieses preferido**	**hubieseis preferido**
prefiriese	**prefiriesen**	**hubiese preferido**	**hubiesen preferido**

	imperativo	
—		**prefiramos**
prefiere; no prefieras		**preferid; no prefiráis**
prefiera		**prefieran**

Words related to this verb

preferiblemente   preferably
preferible   preferable
la preferencia   preference
preferido, preferida   preferred, favorite

de preferencia   preferably
preferentemente   preferably
referir   to refer, to relate

Enjoy verbs in Spanish proverbs on page 539.

The subject pronouns are found on the page facing page 1.

to ask, to inquire, to question

The Seven Simple Tenses		The Seven Compound Tenses	
Singular	Plural	Singular	Plural
1 presente de indicativo		8 perfecto de indicativo	
pregunto	**preguntamos**	**he preguntado**	**hemos preguntado**
preguntas	**preguntáis**	**has preguntado**	**habéis preguntado**
pregunta	**preguntan**	**ha preguntado**	**han preguntado**
2 imperfecto de indicativo		9 pluscuamperfecto de indicativo	
preguntaba	**preguntábamos**	**había preguntado**	**habíamos preguntado**
preguntabas	**preguntabais**	**habías preguntado**	**habíais preguntado**
preguntaba	**preguntaban**	**había preguntado**	**habían preguntado**
3 pretérito		10 pretérito anterior	
pregunté	**preguntamos**	**hube preguntado**	**hubimos preguntado**
preguntaste	**preguntasteis**	**hubiste preguntado**	**hubisteis preguntado**
preguntó	**preguntaron**	**hubo preguntado**	**hubieron preguntado**
4 futuro		11 futuro perfecto	
preguntaré	**preguntaremos**	**habré preguntado**	**habremos preguntado**
preguntarás	**preguntaréis**	**habrás preguntado**	**habréis preguntado**
preguntará	**preguntarán**	**habrá preguntado**	**habrán preguntado**
5 potencial simple		12 potencial compuesto	
preguntaría	**preguntaríamos**	**habría preguntado**	**habríamos preguntado**
preguntarías	**preguntaríais**	**habrías preguntado**	**habríais preguntado**
preguntaría	**preguntarían**	**habría preguntado**	**habrían preguntado**
6 presente de subjuntivo		13 perfecto de subjuntivo	
pregunte	**preguntemos**	**haya preguntado**	**hayamos preguntado**
preguntes	**preguntéis**	**hayas preguntado**	**hayáis preguntado**
pregunte	**pregunten**	**haya preguntado**	**hayan preguntado**
7 imperfecto de subjuntivo		14 pluscuamperfecto de subjuntivo	
preguntara	**preguntáramos**	**hubiera preguntado**	**hubiéramos preguntado**
preguntaras	**preguntarais**	**hubieras preguntado**	**hubierais preguntado**
preguntara	**preguntaran**	**hubiera preguntado**	**hubieran preguntado**
OR		OR	
preguntase	**preguntásemos**	**hubiese preguntado**	**hubiésemos preguntado**
preguntases	**preguntaseis**	**hubieses preguntado**	**hubieseis preguntado**
preguntase	**preguntasen**	**hubiese preguntado**	**hubiesen preguntado**

imperativo

—	**preguntemos**
pregunta; no preguntes	**preguntad; no preguntéis**
pregunte	**pregunten**

Words and expressions related to this verb
una pregunta question
hacer una pregunta to ask a question
un preguntón, una preguntona
  inquisitive individual

preguntarse to wonder, to ask oneself
preguntante inquiring
preguntador, preguntadora inquisitive

See also **preguntar** on page 533.

to be concerned, to worry, to be worried

The Seven Simple Tenses		The Seven Compound Tenses	
Singular	Plural	Singular	Plural
1 presente de indicativo		**8 perfecto de indicativo**	
me preocupo	nos preocupamos	me he preocupado	nos hemos preocupado
te preocupas	os preocupáis	te has preocupado	os habéis preocupado
se preocupa	se preocupan	se ha preocupado	se han preocupado
2 imperfecto de indicativo		**9 pluscuamperfecto de indicativo**	
me preocupaba	nos preocupábamos	me había preocupado	nos habíamos preocupado
te preocupabas	os preocupabais	te habías preocupado	os habíais preocupado
se preocupaba	se preocupaban	se había preocupado	se habían preocupado
3 pretérito		**10 pretérito anterior**	
me preocupé	nos preocupamos	me hube preocupado	nos hubimos preocupado
te preocupaste	os preocupasteis	te hubiste preocupado	os hubisteis preocupado
se preocupó	se preocuparon	se hubo preocupado	se hubieron preocupado
4 futuro		**11 futuro perfecto**	
me preocuparé	nos preocuparemos	me habré preocupado	nos habremos preocupado
te preocuparás	os preocuparéis	te habrás preocupado	os habréis preocupado
se preocupará	se preocuparán	se habrá preocupado	se habrán preocupado
5 potencial simple		**12 potencial compuesto**	
me preocuparía	nos preocuparíamos	me habría preocupado	nos habríamos preocupado
te preocuparías	os preocuparíais	te habrías preocupado	os habríais preocupado
se preocuparía	se preocuparían	se habría preocupado	se habrían preocupado
6 presente de subjuntivo		**13 perfecto de subjuntivo**	
me preocupe	nos preocupemos	me haya preocupado	nos hayamos preocupado
te preocupes	os preocupéis	te hayas preocupado	os hayáis preocupado
se preocupe	se preocupen	se haya preocupado	se hayan preocupado
7 imperfecto de subjuntivo		**14 pluscuamperfecto de subjuntivo**	
me preocupara	nos preocupáramos	me hubiera preocupado	nos hubiéramos preocupado
te preocuparas	os preocuparais	te hubieras preocupado	os hubierais preocupado
se preocupara	se preocuparan	se hubiera preocupado	se hubieran preocupado
OR		OR	
me preocupase	nos preocupásemos	me hubiese preocupado	nos hubiésemos preocupado
te preocupases	os preocupaseis	te hubieses preocupado	os hubieseis preocupado
se preocupase	se preocupasen	se hubiese preocupado	se hubiesen preocupado

	imperativo	
—		preocupémonos
preocúpate; no te preocupes		preocupaos; no os preocupéis
preocúpese		preocúpense

Words related to this verb
preocupar   to preoccupy, to worry
la preocupación   preoccupation, worry
¡no se preocupe!   don't worry

preocuparse de   to take care of, to worry
   about; **estar preocupado**   to be worried
ocupar   to occupy

For other words and expressions related to this verb, see **ocupar.**

preparar

Gerundio **preparando**   Part. pas. **preparado**

to prepare

The Seven Simple Tenses		The Seven Compound Tenses	
Singular	Plural	Singular	Plural
1 presente de indicativo		**8 perfecto de indicativo**	
preparo	preparamos	he preparado	hemos preparado
preparas	preparáis	has preparado	habéis preparado
prepara	preparan	ha preparado	han preparado
2 imperfecto de indicativo		**9 pluscuamperfecto de indicativo**	
preparaba	preparábamos	había preparado	habíamos preparado
preparabas	preparabais	habías preparado	habíais preparado
preparaba	preparaban	había preparado	habían preparado
3 pretérito		**10 pretérito anterior**	
preparé	preparamos	hube preparado	hubimos preparado
preparaste	preparasteis	hubiste preparado	hubisteis preparado
preparó	prepararon	hubo preparado	hubieron preparado
4 futuro		**11 futuro perfecto**	
prepararé	prepararemos	habré preparado	habremos preparado
prepararás	prepararéis	habrás preparado	habréis preparado
preparará	prepararán	habrá preparado	habrán preparado
5 potencial simple		**12 potencial compuesto**	
prepararía	prepararíamos	habría preparado	habríamos preparado
prepararías	prepararíais	habrías preparado	habríais preparado
prepararía	prepararían	habría preparado	habrían preparado
6 presente de subjuntivo		**13 perfecto de subjuntivo**	
prepare	preparemos	haya preparado	hayamos preparado
prepares	preparéis	hayas preparado	hayáis preparado
prepare	preparen	haya preparado	hayan preparado
7 imperfecto de subjuntivo		**14 pluscuamperfecto de subjuntivo**	
preparara	preparáramos	hubiera preparado	hubiéramos preparado
prepararas	prepararais	hubieras preparado	hubierais preparado
preparara	prepararan	hubiera preparado	hubieran preparado
OR		OR	
preparase	preparásemos	hubiese preparado	hubiésemos preparado
preparases	preparaseis	hubieses preparado	hubieseis preparado
preparase	preparasen	hubiese preparado	hubiesen preparado

imperativo	
—	preparemos
prepara; no prepares	preparad; no preparéis
prepare	preparen

Words related to this verb

preparatorio, preparatoria   preparatory   **la preparación**   preparation
el preparativo   preparation, preparative   **prepararse**   to prepeare oneself

---

Get your feet wet with verbs used in weather expressions on page 540.

to be prepared, to get ready, to prepare oneself

The Seven Simple Tenses		The Seven Compound Tenses	
Singular	Plural	Singular	Plural
1 presente de indicativo		**8 perfecto de indicativo**	
me preparo	nos preparamos	me he preparado	nos hemos preparado
te preparas	os preparáis	te has preparado	os habéis preparado
se prepara	se preparan	se ha preparado	se han preparado
2 imperfecto de indicativo		**9 pluscuamperfecto de indicativo**	
me preparaba	nos preparábamos	me había preparado	nos habíamos preparado
te preparabas	os preparabais	te habías preparado	os habíais preparado
se preparaba	se preparaban	se había preparado	se habían preparado
3 pretérito		**10 pretérito anterior**	
me preparé	nos preparamos	me hube preparado	nos hubimos preparado
te preparaste	os preparasteis	te hubiste preparado	os hubisteis preparado
se preparó	se prepararon	se hubo preparado	se hubieron preparado
4 futuro		**11 futuro perfecto**	
me prepararé	nos prepararemos	me habré preparado	nos habremos preparado
te prepararás	os prepararéis	te habrás preparado	os habréis preparado
se preparará	se prepararán	se habrá preparado	se habrán preparado
5 potencial simple		**12 potencial compuesto**	
me prepararía	nos prepararíamos	me habría preparado	nos habríamos preparado
te prepararías	os prepararíais	te habrías preparado	os habríais preparado
se prepararía	se prepararían	se habría preparado	se habrían preparado
6 presente de subjuntivo		**13 perfecto de subjuntivo**	
me prepare	nos preparemos	me haya preparado	nos hayamos preparado
te prepares	os preparéis	te hayas preparado	os hayáis preparado
se prepare	se preparen	se haya preparado	se hayan preparado
7 imperfecto de subjuntivo		**14 pluscuamperfecto de subjuntivo**	
me preparara	nos preparáramos	me hubiera preparado	nos hubiéramos preparado
te prepararas	os prepararais	te hubieras preparado	os hubierais preparado
se preparara	se prepararan	se hubiera preparado	se hubieran preparado
OR		OR	
me preparase	nos preparásemos	me hubiese preparado	nos hubiésemos preparado
te preparases	os preparaseis	te hubieses preparado	os hubieseis preparado
se preparase	se preparasen	se hubiese preparado	se hubiesen preparado

	imperativo
—	preparémonos
prepárate; no te prepares	preparaos; no os preparéis
prepárese	preparense

Words related to this verb
preparar to prepare   **el preparamiento, la preparación** preparation

---

Learn more verbs in 30 practical situations for tourists on pages 564–594.

---

presentar   Gerundio **presentando**   Part. pas. **presentado**

to present, to display, to show, to introduce

The Seven Simple Tenses		The Seven Compound Tenses	
Singular	Plural	Singular	Plural
1 presente de indicativo		8 perfecto de indicativo	
presento	**presentamos**	**he presentado**	**hemos presentado**
presentas	**presentáis**	**has presentado**	**habéis presentado**
presenta	**presentan**	**ha presentado**	**han presentado**
2 imperfecto de indicativo		9 pluscuamperfecto de indicativo	
presentaba	**presentábamos**	**había presentado**	**habíamos presentado**
presentabas	**presentabais**	**habías presentado**	**habíais presentado**
presentaba	**presentaban**	**había presentado**	**habían presentado**
3 pretérito		10 pretérito anterior	
presenté	**presentamos**	**hube presentado**	**hubimos presentado**
presentaste	**presentasteis**	**hubiste presentado**	**hubisteis presentado**
presentó	**presentaron**	**hubo presentado**	**hubieron presentado**
4 futuro		11 futuro perfecto	
presentaré	**presentaremos**	**habré presentado**	**habremos presentado**
presentarás	**presentaréis**	**habrás presentado**	**habréis presentado**
presentará	**presentarán**	**habrá presentado**	**habrán presentado**
5 potencial simple		12 potencial compuesto	
presentaría	**presentaríamos**	**habría presentado**	**habríamos presentado**
presentarías	**presentaríais**	**habrías presentado**	**habríais presentado**
presentaría	**presentarían**	**habría presentado**	**habrían presentado**
6 presente de subjuntivo		13 perfecto de subjuntivo	
presente	**presentemos**	**haya presentado**	**hayamos presentado**
presentes	**presentéis**	**hayas presentado**	**hayáis presentado**
presente	**presenten**	**haya presentado**	**hayan presentado**
7 imperfecto de subjuntivo		14 pluscuamperfecto de subjuntivo	
presentara	**presentáramos**	**hubiera presentado**	**hubiéramos presentado**
presentaras	**presentarais**	**hubieras presentado**	**hubierais presentado**
presentara	**presentaran**	**hubiera presentado**	**hubieran presentado**
OR		OR	
presentase	**presentásemos**	**hubiese presentado**	**hubiésemos presentado**
presentases	**presentaseis**	**hubieses presentado**	**hubieseis presentado**
presentase	**presentasen**	**hubiese presentado**	**hubiesen presentado**

imperativo

—	**presentemos**
presenta; no presentes	**presentad; no presentéis**
presente	**presenten**

Words and expressions related to this verb

representar   to represent
presentarse   to introduce oneself
el presente   present; present tense
por lo presente   for the present

al presente, de presente   at present
presentar armas   to present arms
la presentación   presentation
presentable   presentable

Enjoy verbs in Spanish proverbs on page 539.

378

The Seven Simple Tenses		The Seven Compound Tenses	
Singular	Plural	Singular	Plural
1 presente de indicativo		8 perfecto de indicativo	
presto	**prestamos**	**he prestado**	**hemos prestado**
prestas	**prestáis**	**has prestado**	**habéis prestado**
presta	**prestan**	**ha prestado**	**han prestado**
2 imperfecto de indicativo		9 pluscuamperfecto de indicativo	
prestaba	**prestábamos**	**había prestado**	**habíamos prestado**
prestabas	**prestabais**	**habías prestado**	**habíais prestado**
prestaba	**prestaban**	**había prestado**	**habían prestado**
3 pretérito		10 pretérito anterior	
presté	**prestamos**	**hube prestado**	**hubimos prestado**
prestaste	**prestasteis**	**hubiste prestado**	**hubisteis prestado**
prestó	**prestaron**	**hubo prestado**	**hubieron prestado**
4 futuro		11 futuro perfecto	
prestaré	**prestaremos**	**habré prestado**	**habremos prestado**
prestarás	**prestaréis**	**habrás prestado**	**habréis prestado**
prestará	**prestarán**	**habrá prestado**	**habrán prestado**
5 potencial simple		12 potencial compuesto	
prestaría	**prestaríamos**	**habría prestado**	**habríamos prestado**
prestarías	**prestaríais**	**habrías prestado**	**habríais prestado**
prestaría	**prestarían**	**habría prestado**	**habrían prestado**
6 presente de subjuntivo		13 perfecto de subjuntivo	
preste	**prestemos**	**haya prestado**	**hayamos prestado**
prestes	**prestéis**	**hayas prestado**	**hayáis prestado**
preste	**presten**	**haya prestado**	**hayan prestado**
7 imperfecto de subjuntivo		14 pluscuamperfecto de subjuntivo	
prestara	**prestáramos**	**hubiera prestado**	**hubiéramos prestado**
prestaras	**prestarais**	**hubieras prestado**	**hubierais prestado**
prestara	**prestaran**	**hubiera prestado**	**hubieran prestado**
OR		OR	
prestase	**prestásemos**	**hubiese prestado**	**hubiésemos prestado**
prestases	**prestaseis**	**hubieses prestado**	**hubieseis prestado**
prestase	**prestasen**	**hubiese prestado**	**hubiesen prestado**

imperativo

—	**prestemos**
presta; no prestes	**prestad; no prestéis**
preste	**presten**

Words and expressions related to this verb

pedir prestado to borrow
tomar prestado to borrow
prestador, prestadora lender
un préstamo loan

prestar atención to pay attention
una casa de préstamos pawn shop
un, una prestamista money lender
la prestación benefit, contribution

principiar

Gerundio principiando   **Part. pas. principiado**

to begin

The Seven Simple Tenses		The Seven Compound Tenses	
Singular	Plural	Singular	Plural
1 presente de indicativo		**8 perfecto de indicativo**	
principio	principiamos	he principiado	hemos principiado
principias	principiáis	has principiado	habéis principiado
principia	principian	ha principiado	han principiado
2 imperfecto de indicativo		**9 pluscuamperfecto de indicativo**	
principiaba	principiábamos	había principiado	habíamos principiado
principiabas	principiabais	habías principiado	habíais principiado
principiaba	principiaban	había principiado	habían principiado
3 pretérito		**10 pretérito anterior**	
principié	principiamos	hube principiado	hubimos principiado
principiaste	principiasteis	hubiste principiado	hubisteis principiado
principió	principiaron	hubo principiado	hubieron principiado
4 futuro		**11 futuro perfecto**	
principiaré	principiaremos	habré principiado	habremos principiado
principiarás	principiaréis	habrás principiado	habréis principiado
principiará	principiarán	habrá principiado	habrán principiado
5 potencial simple		**12 potencial compuesto**	
principiaría	principiaríamos	habría principiado	habríamos principiado
principiarías	principiaríais	habrías principiado	habríais principiado
principiaría	principiarían	habría principiado	habrían principiado
6 presente de subjuntivo		**13 perfecto de subjuntivo**	
principie	principiemos	haya principiado	hayamos principiado
principies	principiéis	hayas principiado	hayáis principiado
principie	principien	haya principiado	hayan principiado
7 imperfecto de subjuntivo		**14 pluscuamperfecto de subjuntivo**	
principiara	principiáramos	hubiera principiado	hubiéramos principiado
principiaras	principiarais	hubieras principiado	hubierais principiado
principiara	principiaran	hubiera principiado	hubieran principiado
OR		OR	
principiase	principiásemos	hubiese principiado	hubiésemos principiado
principiases	principiaseis	hubieses principiado	hubieseis principiado
principiase	principiasen	hubiese principiado	hubiesen principiado

	imperativo	
—		**principiemos**
principia; no principies		**principiad; no principiéis**
principie		**principien**

Words and expressions related to this verb

el principio   beginning, start; principle
a principios de   at the beginning of
desde el principio   from the beginning
principio de admiración   inverted
   exclamation point (¡)

en principio   in principle
el, la principiante   beginner
principio de interrogación   inverted question
   mark (¿)
al principio (a los principios)   at first, in
   the beginning
la edición principe   first edition (*editio princeps*)

380

to test, to prove, to try, to try on

The Seven Simple Tenses		The Seven Compound Tenses	
Singular	Plural	Singular	Plural
1 presente de indicativo		8 perfecto de indicativo	
pruebo	**probamos**	**he probado**	**hemos probado**
pruebas	**probáis**	**has probado**	**habéis probado**
prueba	**prueban**	**ha probado**	**han probado**
2 imperfecto de indicativo		9 pluscuamperfecto de indicativo	
probaba	**probábamos**	**había probado**	**habíamos probado**
probabas	**probabais**	**habías probado**	**habíais probado**
probaba	**probaban**	**había probado**	**habían probado**
3 pretérito		10 pretérito anterior	
probé	**probamos**	**hube probado**	**hubimos probado**
probaste	**probasteis**	**hubiste probado**	**hubisteis probado**
probó	**probaron**	**hubo probado**	**hubieron probado**
4 futuro		11 futuro perfecto	
probaré	**probaremos**	**habré probado**	**habremos probado**
probarás	**probaréis**	**habrás probado**	**habréis probado**
probará	**probarán**	**habrá probado**	**habrán probado**
5 potencial simple		12 potencial compuesto	
probaría	**probaríamos**	**habría probado**	**habríamos probado**
probarías	**probaríais**	**habrías probado**	**habríais probado**
probaría	**probarían**	**habría probado**	**habrían probado**
6 presente de subjuntivo		13 perfecto de subjuntivo	
pruebe	**probemos**	**haya probado**	**hayamos probado**
pruebes	**probéis**	**hayas probado**	**hayáis probado**
pruebe	**prueben**	**haya probado**	**hayan probado**
7 imperfecto de subjuntivo		14 pluscuamperfecto de subjuntivo	
probara	**probáramos**	**hubiera probado**	**hubiéramos probado**
probaras	**probarais**	**hubieras probado**	**hubierais probado**
probara	**probaran**	**hubiera probado**	**hubieran probado**
OR		OR	
probase	**probásemos**	**hubiese probado**	**hubiésemos probado**
probases	**probaseis**	**hubieses probado**	**hubieseis probado**
probase	**probasen**	**hubiese probado**	**hubiesen probado**

imperativo

—	**probemos**
prueba; no pruebes	**probad; no probéis**
pruebe	**prueben**

Words and expressions related to this verb
la prueba   proof, evidence, test
poner a prueba   to put to the test, to try out
probable   probable
probablemente   probably
el probador   fitting room, dressing room

probar de   to taste, to take a taste of
la probatura   test, experiment
la probación   proof, probation
la probabilidad   probability
probatorio, probatoria   probative

The subject pronouns are found on the page facing page 1.

381

probarse

Gerundio **probándose** Part. pas. **probado**

to try on (clothes)

The Seven Simple Tenses		The Seven Compound Tenses	
Singular	Plural	Singular	Plural
1 presente de indicativo		8 perfecto de indicativo	
me pruebo	nos probamos	me he probado	nos hemos probado
te pruebas	os probáis	te has probado	os habéis probado
se prueba	se prueban	se ha probado	se han probado
2 imperfecto de indicativo		9 pluscuamperfecto de indicativo	
me probaba	nos probábamos	me había probado	nos habíamos probado
te probabas	os probabais	te habías probado	os habíais probado
se probaba	se probaban	se había probado	se habían probado
3 pretérito		10 pretérito anterior	
me probé	nos probamos	me hube probado	nos hubimos probado
te probaste	os probasteis	te hubiste probado	os hubisteis probado
se probó	se probaron	se hubo probado	se hubieron probado
4 futuro		11 futuro perfecto	
me probaré	nos probaremos	me habré probado	nos habremos probado
te probarás	os probaréis	te habrás probado	os habréis probado
se probará	se probarán	se habrá probado	se habrán probado
5 potencial simple		12 potencial compuesto	
me probaría	nos probaríamos	me habría probado	nos habríamos probado
te probarías	os probaríais	te habrías probado	os habríais probado
se probaría	se probarían	se habría probado	se habrían probado
6 presente de subjuntivo		13 perfecto de subjuntivo	
me pruebe	nos probemos	me haya probado	nos hayamos probado
te pruebes	os probéis	te hayas probado	os hayáis probado
se pruebe	se prueben	se haya probado	se hayan probado
7 imperfecto de subjuntivo		14 pluscuamperfecto de subjuntivo	
me probara	nos probáramos	me hubiera probado	nos hubiéramos probado
te probaras	os probarais	te hubieras probado	os hubierais probado
se probara	se probaran	se hubiera probado	se hubieran probado
OR		OR	
me probase	nos probásemos	me hubiese probado	nos hubiésemos probado
te probases	os probaseis	te hubieses probado	os hubieseis probado
se probase	se probasen	se hubiese probado	se hubiesen probado

	imperativo	
—	probémonos
pruébate; no te pruebes	probaos; no os probéis
pruébese	pruébense

For words and expressions related to this verb, see **probar.**

Can't recognize an irregular verb form? Check out pages 519–523.

to proclaim, to promulgate

The Seven Simple Tenses		The Seven Compound Tenses	
Singular	Plural	Singular	Plural
1 presente de indicativo		8 perfecto de indicativo	
proclamo	proclamamos	he proclamado	hemos proclamado
proclamas	proclamáis	has proclamado	habéis proclamado
proclama	proclaman	ha proclamado	han proclamado
2 imperfecto de indicativo		9 pluscuamperfecto de indicativo	
proclamaba	proclamábamos	había proclamado	habíamos proclamado
proclamabas	proclamabais	habías proclamado	habíais proclamado
proclamaba	proclamaban	había proclamado	habían proclamado
3 pretérito		10 pretérito anterior	
proclamé	proclamamos	hube proclamado	hubimos proclamado
proclamaste	proclamasteis	hubiste proclamado	hubisteis proclamado
proclamó	proclamaron	hubo proclamado	hubieron proclamado
4 futuro		11 futuro perfecto	
proclamaré	proclamaremos	habré proclamado	habremos proclamado
proclamarás	proclamaréis	habrás proclamado	habréis proclamado
proclamará	proclamarán	habrá proclamado	habrán proclamado
5 potencial simple		12 potencial compuesto	
proclamaría	proclamaríamos	habría proclamado	habríamos proclamado
proclamarías	proclamaríais	habrías proclamado	habríais proclamado
proclamaría	proclamarían	habría proclamado	habrían proclamado
6 presente de subjuntivo		13 perfecto de subjuntivo	
proclame	proclamemos	haya proclamado	hayamos proclamado
proclames	proclaméis	hayas proclamado	hayáis proclamado
proclame	proclamen	haya proclamado	hayan proclamado
7 imperfecto de subjuntivo		14 pluscuamperfecto de subjuntivo	
proclamara	proclamáramos	hubiera proclamado	hubiéramos proclamado
proclamaras	proclamaras	hubieras proclamado	hubierais proclamado
proclamara	proclamaran	hubiera proclamado	hubieran proclamado
OR		OR	
proclamase	proclamásemos	hubiese proclamado	hubiésemos proclamado
proclamases	proclamaseis	hubieses proclamado	hubieseis proclamado
proclamase	proclamasen	hubiese proclamado	hubiesen proclamado

imperativo	
—	proclamemos
proclama; no proclames	proclamad; no proclaméis
proclame	proclamen

Words related to this verb
la proclamación, la proclama   proclamation   **clamar**   to cry out, to beseech
clamoroso, clamorosa   loud, resounding   **el clamor**   shout

---

Use the EE-zee guide to Spanish pronunciation on pages 562 and 563.

The subject pronouns are found on the page facing page 1.

producir

Gerundio **produciendo** Part. pas. **producido**

to produce, to cause

The Seven Simple Tenses		The Seven Compound Tenses	
Singular	Plural	Singular	Plural
1 presente de indicativo		8 perfecto de indicativo	
produzco	**producimos**	**he producido**	**hemos producido**
produces	**producís**	**has producido**	**habéis producido**
produce	**producen**	**ha producido**	**han producido**
2 imperfecto de indicativo		9 pluscuamperfecto de indicativo	
producía	**producíamos**	**había producido**	**habíamos producido**
producías	**producíais**	**habías producido**	**habíais producido**
producía	**producían**	**había producido**	**habían producido**
3 pretérito		10 pretérito anterior	
produje	**produjimos**	**hube producido**	**hubimos producido**
produjiste	**produjisteis**	**hubiste producido**	**hubisteis producido**
produjo	**produjeron**	**hubo producido**	**hubieron producido**
4 futuro		11 futuro perfecto	
produciré	**produciremos**	**habré producido**	**habremos producido**
producirás	**produciréis**	**habrás producido**	**habréis producido**
producirá	**producirán**	**habrá producido**	**habrán producido**
5 potencial simple		12 potencial compuesto	
produciría	**produciríamos**	**habría producido**	**habríamos producido**
producirías	**produciríais**	**habrías producido**	**habríais producido**
produciría	**producirían**	**habría producido**	**habrían producido**
6 presente de subjuntivo		13 perfecto de subjuntivo	
produzca	**produzcamos**	**haya producido**	**hayamos producido**
produzcas	**produzcáis**	**hayas producido**	**hayáis producido**
produzca	**produzcan**	**haya producido**	**hayan producido**
7 imperfecto de subjuntivo		14 pluscuamperfecto de subjuntivo	
produjera	**produjéramos**	**hubiera producido**	**hubiéramos producido**
produjeras	**produjerais**	**hubieras producido**	**hubierais producido**
produjera	**produjeran**	**hubiera producido**	**hubieran producido**
OR		OR	
produjese	**produjésemos**	**hubiese producido**	**hubiésemos producido**
produjeses	**produjeseis**	**hubieses producido**	**hubieseis producido**
produjese	**produjesen**	**hubiese producido**	**hubiesen producido**

	imperativo	
—		**produzcamos**
produce; no produzcas		**producid; no produzcáis**
produzca		**produzcan**

Words and expressions related to this verb
la productividad   productivity
productivo, productiva   productive
el producto   product, produce; proceeds
productos de belleza   cosmetics
reproducir   to reproduce
la producción   production

productos de aguja   needlework
productos de consumo   consumer goods
productos de tocador   toilet articles
un productor, una productora   producer
reproducir asexualmente   to clone

to prohibit, to forbid

The Seven Simple Tenses		The Seven Compound Tenses	
Singular	Plural	Singular	Plural
1 presente de indicativo		8 perfecto de indicativo	
prohibo	prohibimos	he prohibido	hemos prohibido
prohibes	prohibís	has prohibido	habéis prohibido
prohibe	prohiben	ha prohibido	han prohibido
2 imperfecto de indicativo		9 pluscuamperfecto de indicativo	
prohibía	prohibíamos	había prohibido	habíamos prohibido
prohibías	prohibíais	habías prohibido	habíais prohibido
prohibía	prohibían	había prohibido	habían prohibido
3 pretérito		10 pretérito anterior	
prohibí	prohibimos	hube prohibido	hubimos prohibido
prohibiste	prohibisteis	hubiste prohibido	hubisteis prohibido
prohibió	prohibieron	hubo prohibido	hubieron prohibido
4 futuro		11 futuro perfecto	
prohibiré	prohibiremos	habré prohibido	habremos prohibido
prohibirás	prohibiréis	habrás prohibido	habréis prohibido
prohibirá	prohibirán	habrá prohibido	habrán prohibido
5 potencial simple		12 potencial compuesto	
prohibirá	prohibiríamos	habría prohibido	habríamos prohibido
prohibirías	prohibiríais	habrías prohibido	habríais prohibido
prohibiría	prohibirían	habría prohibido	habrían prohibido
6 presente de subjuntivo		13 perfecto de subjuntivo	
prohiba	prohibamos	haya prohibido	hayamos prohibido
prohibas	prohibáis	hayas prohibido	hayáis prohibido
prohiba	prohiban	haya prohibido	hayan prohibido
7 imperfecto de subjuntivo		14 pluscuamperfecto de subjuntivo	
prohibiera	prohibiéramos	hubiera prohibido	hubiéramos prohibido
prohibieras	prohibierais	hubieras prohibido	hubierais prohibido
prohibiera	prohibieran	hubiera prohibido	hubieran prohibido
OR		OR	
prohibiese	prohibiésemos	hubiese prohibido	hubiésemos prohibido
prohibieses	prohibieseis	hubieses prohibido	hubieseis prohibido
prohibiese	prohibiesen	hubiese prohibido	hubiesen prohibido

	imperativo	
—	prohibamos	
prohibe; no prohibas	prohibid; no prohibáis	
prohiba	prohiban	

Words and expressions related to this verb
la prohibición prohibition
el, la prohibicionista prohibitionist
SE PROHIBE EL ESTACIONAMIENTO
   NO PARKING
SE PROHIBE FUMAR NO SMOKING
SE PROHIBE FIJAR CARTELES
   POST NO BILLS

prohibitivo, prohibitiva prohibitive
prohibitorio, prohibitoria prohibitory
SE PROHIBE LA ENTRADA KEEP OUT
SE PROHIBE ESCUPIR NO SPITTING

385

to pronounce

The Seven Simple Tenses		The Seven Compound Tenses	
Singular	Plural	Singular	Plural

1 presente de indicativo

		8 perfecto de indicativo	
pronuncio	pronunciamos	he pronunciado	hemos pronunciado
pronuncias	pronunciáis	has pronunciado	habéis pronunciado
pronuncia	pronuncian	ha pronunciado	han pronunciado

2 imperfecto de indicativo

		9 pluscuamperfecto de indicativo	
pronunciaba	pronunciábamos	había pronunciado	habíamos pronunciado
pronunciabas	pronunciabais	habías pronunciado	habíais pronunciado
pronunciaba	pronunciaban	había pronunciado	habían pronunciado

3 pretérito

		10 pretérito anterior	
pronuncié	pronunciamos	hube pronunciado	hubimos pronunciado
pronunciaste	pronunciasteis	hubiste pronunciado	hubisteis pronunciado
pronunció	pronunciaron	hubo pronunciado	hubieron pronunciado

4 futuro

		11 futuro perfecto	
pronunciaré	pronunciaremos	habré pronunciado	habremos pronunciado
pronunciarás	pronunciaréis	habrás pronunciado	habréis pronunciado
pronunciará	pronunciarán	habrá pronunciado	habrán pronunciado

5 potencial simple

		12 potencial compuesto	
pronunciaría	pronunciaríamos	habría pronunciado	habríamos pronunciado
pronunciarías	pronunciaríais	habrías pronunciado	habríais pronunciado
pronunciaría	pronunciarían	habría pronunciado	habrían pronunciado

6 presente de subjuntivo

		13 perfecto de subjuntivo	
pronuncie	pronunciemos	haya pronunciado	hayamos pronunciado
pronuncies	pronunciéis	hayas pronunciado	hayáis pronunciado
pronuncie	pronuncien	haya pronunciado	hayan pronunciado

7 imperfecto de subjuntivo

		14 pluscuamperfecto de subjuntivo	
pronunciara	pronunciáramos	hubiera pronunciado	hubiéramos pronunciado
pronunciaras	pronunciarais	hubieras pronunciado	hubierais pronunciado
pronunciara	pronunciaran	hubiera pronunciado	hubieran pronunciado
OR		OR	
pronunciase	pronunciásemos	hubiese pronunciado	hubiésemos pronunciado
pronunciases	pronunciaseis	hubieses pronunciado	hubieseis pronunciado
pronunciase	pronunciasen	hubiese pronunciado	hubiesen pronunciado

imperativo

—	**pronunciemos**
pronuncia; no pronuncies	**pronunciad; no pronunciéis**
pronuncie	**pronuncien**

Words and expressions related to this verb
la pronunciación pronunciation
pronunciado, pronunciada pronounced
pronunciar un discurso to make
 a speech
enunciar to enunciate

pronunciar una conferencia to deliver a lecture
anunciar to announce
denunciar to denounce
renunciar to renounce
el nuncio omen
impronunciable unpronounceable

The Seven Simple Tenses | The Seven Compound Tenses

Singular	Plural	Singular	Plural
1 presente de indicativo		8 perfecto de indicativo	
protejo	**protegemos**	**he protegido**	**hemos protegido**
proteges	**protegéis**	**has protegido**	**habéis protegido**
protege	**protegen**	**ha protegido**	**han protegido**
2 imperfecto de indicativo		9 pluscuamperfecto de indicativo	
protegía	**protegíamos**	**había protegido**	**habíamos protegido**
protegías	**protegíais**	**habías protegido**	**habíais protegido**
protegía	**protegían**	**había protegido**	**habían protegido**
3 pretérito		10 pretérito anterior	
protegí	**protegimos**	**hube protegido**	**hubimos protegido**
protegiste	**protegisteis**	**hubiste protegido**	**hubisteis protegido**
protegió	**protegieron**	**hubo protegido**	**hubieron protegido**
4 futuro		11 futuro perfecto	
protegeré	**protegeremos**	**habré protegido**	**habremos protegido**
protegerás	**protegeréis**	**habrás protegido**	**habréis protegido**
protegerá	**protegerán**	**habrá protegido**	**habrán protegido**
5 potencial simple		12 potencial compuesto	
protegería	**protegeríamos**	**habría protegido**	**habríamos protegido**
protegerías	**protegeríais**	**habrías protegido**	**habríais protegido**
protegería	**protegerían**	**habría protegido**	**habrían protegido**
6 presente de subjuntivo		13 perfecto de subjuntivo	
proteja	**protejamos**	**haya protegido**	**hayamos protegido**
protejas	**protejáis**	**hayas protegido**	**hayáis protegido**
proteja	**protejan**	**haya protegido**	**hayan protegido**
7 imperfecto de subjuntivo		14 pluscuamperfecto de subjuntivo	
protegiera	**protegiéramos**	**hubiera protegido**	**hubiéramos protegido**
protegieras	**protegierais**	**hubieras protegido**	**hubierais protegido**
protegiera	**protegieran**	**hubiera protegido**	**hubieran protegido**
OR		OR	
protegiese	**protegiésemos**	**hubiese protegido**	**hubiésemos protegido**
protegieses	**protegieseis**	**hubieses protegido**	**hubieseis protegido**
protegiese	**protegiesen**	**hubiese protegido**	**hubiesen protegido**

imperativo

—	**protejamos**
protege; no protejas	**proteged; no protejáis**
proteja	**protejan**

Words related to this verb

la protección   protection
protegido, protegida   protected, favorite,
   protégé
el protector, la protectriz   protector, protectress
protectorio, protectoria   protective

proteger contra   to protect against
proteger de   to protect from
sin protección   unprotected
excesivamente protector, protectora
   overprotective

pulir

to polish

The Seven Simple Tenses		The Seven Compound Tenses	
Singular	Plural	Singular	Plural
1 presente de indicativo		8 perfecto de indicativo	
pulo	**pulimos**	**he pulido**	**hemos pulido**
pules	**pulís**	**has pulido**	**habéis pulido**
pule	**pulen**	**ha pulido**	**han pulido**
2 imperfecto de indicativo		9 pluscuamperfecto de indicativo	
pulía	**pulíamos**	**había pulido**	**habíamos pulido**
pulías	**pulíais**	**habías pulido**	**habíais pulido**
pulía	**pulían**	**había pulido**	**habían pulido**
3 pretérito		10 pretérito anterior	
pulí	**pulimos**	**hube pulido**	**hubimos pulido**
puliste	**pulisteis**	**hubiste pulido**	**hubisteis pulido**
pulió	**pulieron**	**hubo pulido**	**hubieron pulido**
4 futuro		11 futuro perfecto	
puliré	**puliremos**	**habré pulido**	**habremos pulido**
pulirás	**puliréis**	**habrás pulido**	**habréis pulido**
pulirá	**pulirán**	**habrá pulido**	**habrán pulido**
5 potencial simple		12 potencial compuesto	
puliría	**puliríamos**	**habría pulido**	**habríamos pulido**
pulirías	**puliríais**	**habrías pulido**	**habríais pulido**
puliría	**pulirían**	**habría pulido**	**habrían pulido**
6 presente de subjuntivo		13 perfecto de subjuntivo	
pula	**pulamos**	**haya pulido**	**hayamos pulido**
pulas	**puláis**	**hayas pulido**	**hayáis pulido**
pula	**pulan**	**haya pulido**	**hayan pulido**
7 imperfecto de subjuntivo		14 pluscuamperfecto de subjuntivo	
puliera	**puliéramos**	**hubiera pulido**	**hubiéramos pulido**
pulieras	**pulierais**	**hubieras pulido**	**hubierais pulido**
puliera	**pulieran**	**hubiera pulido**	**hubieran pulido**
OR		OR	
puliese	**puliésemos**	**hubiese pulido**	**hubiésemos pulido**
pulieses	**pulieseis**	**hubieses pulido**	**hubieseis pulido**
puliese	**puliesen**	**hubiese pulido**	**hubiesen pulido**

imperativo

—	**pulamos**
pule; no pulas	**pulid; no puláis**
pula	**pulan**

Words related to this verb

el pulimento polish, gloss   **pulimentar** to polish; **la pulidez** polish, elegance, shine
una pulidora polishing machine   **pulidamente** neatly

Increase your verb power with popular phrases, words,
and expressions for tourists on pages 595–618.

The Seven Simple Tenses		The Seven Compound Tenses	
Singular	Plural	Singular	Plural
1 presente de indicativo		8 perfecto de indicativo	
me quedo	**nos quedamos**	**me he quedado**	**nos hemos quedado**
te quedas	**os quedáis**	**te has quedado**	**os habéis quedado**
se queda	**se quedan**	**se ha quedado**	**se han quedado**
2 imperfecto de indicativo		9 pluscuamperfecto de indicativo	
me quedaba	**nos quedábamos**	**me había quedado**	**nos habíamos quedado**
te quedabas	**os quedabais**	**te habías quedado**	**os habíais quedado**
se quedaba	**se quedaban**	**se había quedado**	**se habían quedado**
3 pretérito		10 pretérito anterior	
me quedé	**nos quedamos**	**me hube quedado**	**nos hubimos quedado**
te quedaste	**os quedasteis**	**te hubiste quedado**	**os hubisteis quedado**
se quedó	**se quedaron**	**se hubo quedado**	**se hubieron quedado**
4 futuro		11 futuro perfecto	
me quedaré	**nos quedaremos**	**me habré quedado**	**nos habremos quedado**
te quedarás	**os quedaréis**	**te habrás quedado**	**os habréis quedado**
se quedará	**se quedarán**	**se habrá quedado**	**se habrán quedado**
5 potencial simple		12 potencial compuesto	
me quedaría	**nos quedaríamos**	**me habría quedado**	**nos habríamos quedado**
te quedarías	**os quedaríais**	**te habrías quedado**	**os habríais quedado**
se quedaría	**se quedarían**	**se habría quedado**	**se habrían quedado**
6 presente de subjuntivo		13 perfecto de subjuntivo	
me quede	**nos quedemos**	**me haya quedado**	**nos hayamos quedado**
te quedes	**os quedéis**	**te hayas quedado**	**os hayáis quedado**
se quede	**se queden**	**se haya quedado**	**se hayan quedado**
7 imperfecto de subjuntivo		14 pluscuamperfecto de subjuntivo	
me quedara	**nos quedáramos**	**me hubiera quedado**	**nos hubiéramos quedado**
te quedaras	**os quedarais**	**te hubieras quedado**	**os hubierais quedado**
se quedara	**se quedaran**	**se hubiera quedado**	**se hubieran quedado**
OR		OR	
me quedase	**nos quedásemos**	**me hubiese quedado**	**nos hubiésemos quedado**
te quedases	**os quedaseis**	**te hubieses quedado**	**os hubieseis quedado**
se quedase	**se quedasen**	**se hubiese quedado**	**se hubiesen quedado**

imperativo	
—	**quedémonos**
quédate; no te quedes	**quedaos; no os quedéis**
quédese	**quédense**

Words and expressions related to this verb
la quedada   residence, stay
quedar   to remain, to be left; **¿Cuánto dinero queda?**   How much money is left?
    Me quedan dos dólares.   I have two dollars left (remaining).
quedar limpio   to be clean out (of money); to be broke
quedar bien   to turn out well
quedarse muerto (muerta)   to be speechless, dumbfounded

to complain, to grumble

The Seven Simple Tenses		The Seven Compound Tenses	
Singular	Plural	Singular	Plural
1 presente de indicativo		8 perfecto de indicativo	
me quejo	**nos quejamos**	**me he quejado**	**nos hemos quejado**
te quejas	**os quejáis**	**te has quejado**	**os habéis quejado**
se queja	**se quejan**	**se ha quejado**	**se han quejado**
2 imperfecto de indicativo		9 pluscuamperfecto de indicativo	
me quejaba	**nos quejábamos**	**me había quejado**	**nos habíamos quejado**
te quejabas	**os quejabais**	**te habías quejado**	**os habíais quejado**
se quejaba	**se quejaban**	**se había quejado**	**se habían quejado**
3 pretérito		10 pretérito anterior	
me quejé	**nos quejamos**	**me hube quejado**	**nos hubimos quejado**
te quejaste	**os quejasteis**	**te hubiste quejado**	**os hubisteis quejado**
se quejó	**se quejaron**	**se hubo quejado**	**se hubieron quejado**
4 futuro		11 futuro perfecto	
me quejaré	**nos quejaremos**	**me habré quejado**	**nos habremos quejado**
te quejarás	**os quejaréis**	**te habrás quejado**	**os habréis quejado**
se quejará	**se quejarán**	**se habrá quejado**	**se habrán quejado**
5 potencial simple		12 potencial compuesto	
me quejaría	**nos quejaríamos**	**me habría quejado**	**nos habríamos quejado**
te quejarías	**os quejaríais**	**te habrías quejado**	**os habríais quejado**
se quejaría	**se quejarían**	**se habría quejado**	**se habrían quejado**
6 presente de subjuntivo		13 perfecto de subjuntivo	
me queje	**nos quejemos**	**me haya quejado**	**nos hayamos quejado**
te quejes	**os quejéis**	**te hayas quejado**	**os hayáis quejado**
se queje	**se quejen**	**se haya quejado**	**se hayan quejado**
7 imperfecto de subjuntivo		14 pluscuamperfecto de subjuntivo	
me quejara	**nos quejáramos**	**me hubiera quejado**	**nos hubiéramos quejado**
te quejaras	**os quejarais**	**te hubieras quejado**	**os hubierais quejado**
se quejara	**se quejaran**	**se hubiera quejado**	**se hubieran quejado**
OR		OR	
me quejase	**nos quejásemos**	**me hubiese quejado**	**nos hubiésemos quejado**
te quejases	**os quejaseis**	**te hubieses quejado**	**os hubieseis quejado**
se quejase	**se quejasen**	**se hubiese quejado**	**se hubiesen quejado**

imperativo

—	**quejémonos**
quéjate; no te quejes	**quejaos; no os quejéis**
quéjese	**quéjense**

Words and expressions related to this verb
quejarse de   to complain about   **quejoso, quejosa**   annoyed
la queja   complaint   **un quejumbrón, una quejumbrona**   whiner
el quejido   groan, moan   **dar quejidos**   to moan, groan

Get acquainted with what preposition goes with what verb on pages 541–549.

to burn, to fire

The Seven Simple Tenses		The Seven Compound Tenses	
Singular	Plural	Singular	Plural
1 presente de indicativo		**8 perfecto de indicativo**	
quemo	quemamos	he quemado	hemos quemado
quemas	quemáis	has quemado	habéis quemado
quema	queman	ha quemado	han quemado
2 imperfecto de indicativo		**9 pluscuamperfecto de indicativo**	
quemaba	quemábamos	había quemado	habíamos quemado
quemabas	quemabais	habías quemado	habíais quemado
quemaba	quemaban	había quemado	habían quemado
3 pretérito		**10 pretérito anterior**	
quemé	quemamos	hube quemado	hubimos quemado
quemaste	quemasteis	hubiste quemado	hubisteis quemado
quemó	quemaron	hubo quemado	hubieron quemado
4 futuro		**11 futuro perfecto**	
quemaré	quemaremos	habré quemado	habremos quemado
quemarás	quemaréis	habrás quemado	habréis quemado
quemará	quemarán	habrá quemado	habrán quemado
5 potencial simple		**12 potencial compuesto**	
quemaría	quemaríamos	habría quemado	habríamos quemado
quemarías	quemaríais	habrías quemado	habríais quemado
quemaría	quemarían	habría quemado	habrían quemado
6 presente de subjuntivo		**13 perfecto de subjuntivo**	
queme	quememos	haya quemado	hayamos quemado
quemes	queméis	hayas quemado	hayáis quemado
queme	quemen	haya quemado	hayan quemado
7 imperfecto de subjuntivo		**14 pluscuamperfecto de subjuntivo**	
quemara	quemáramos	hubiera quemado	hubiéramos quemado
quemaras	quemarais	hubieras quemado	hubierais quemado
quemara	quemaran	hubiera quemado	hubieran quemado
OR		OR	
quemase	quemásemos	hubiese quemado	hubiésemos quemado
quemases	quemaseis	hubieses quemado	hubieseis quemado
quemase	quemasen	hubiese quemado	hubiesen quemado

imperativo	
—	quememos
quema; no quemes	quemad; no queméis
queme	quemen

Words and expressions related to this verb
la quemadura   burn, scald, sunburn
el quemador de gas   gas burner
la quema   fire

quemarse las cejas   to burn the midnight oil
huir de la quema   to run away from trouble
quemado   burned, burned out (emotionally, physically)

to want, to wish

The Seven Simple Tenses		The Seven Compound Tenses	
Singular	Plural	Singular	Plural
1 presente de indicativo		**8 perfecto de indicativo**	
quiero	queremos	he querido	hemos querido
quieres	queréis	has querido	habéis querido
quiere	quieren	ha querido	han querido
2 imperfecto de indicativo		**9 pluscuamperfecto de indicativo**	
quería	queríamos	había querido	habíamos querido
querías	queríais	habías querido	habíais querido
quería	querían	había querido	habían querido
3 pretérito		**10 pretérito anterior**	
quise	quisimos	hube querido	hubimos querido
quisiste	quisisteis	hubiste querido	hubisteis querido
quiso	quisieron	hubo querido	hubieron querido
4 futuro		**11 futuro perfecto**	
querré	querremos	habré querido	habremos querido
querrás	querréis	habrás querido	habréis querido
querrá	querrán	habrá querido	habrán querido
5 potencial simple		**12 potencial compuesto**	
querría	querríamos	habría querido	habríamos querido
querrías	querríais	habrías querido	habríais querido
querría	querrían	habría querido	habrían querido
6 presente de subjuntivo		**13 perfecto de subjuntivo**	
quiera	queramos	haya querido	hayamos querido
quieras	queráis	hayas querido	hayáis querido
quiera	quieran	haya querido	hayan querido
7 imperfecto de subjuntivo		**14 pluscuamperfecto de subjuntivo**	
quisiera	quisiéramos	hubiera querido	hubiéramos querido
quisieras	quisierais	hubieras querido	hubierais querido
quisiera	quisieran	hubiera querido	hubieran querido
OR		OR	
quisiese	quisiésemos	hubiese querido	hubiésemos querido
quisieses	quisieseis	hubieses querido	hubieseis querido
quisiese	quisiesen	hubiese querido	hubiesen querido

imperativo	
—	queramos
quiere; no quieras	quered; no queráis
quiera	quieran

Words and expressions related to this verb

querer decir to mean; **¿Qué quiere Ud. decir?** What do you mean?
   ¿Qué quiere decir esto? What does this mean?
querido, querida dear; **querido amigo, querida amiga** dear friend
querido mío, querida mía my dear
querer bien a to love
Querer es poder Where there's a will there's a way.

Enjoy verbs in more Spanish proverbs on page 539.

to take off (clothing), to remove oneself, to withdraw

The Seven Simple Tenses		The Seven Compound Tenses	
Singular	Plural	Singular	Plural
1 presente de indicativo		8 perfecto de indicativo	
me quito	nos quitamos	me he quitado	nos hemos quitado
te quitas	os quitáis	te has quitado	os habéis quitado
se quita	se quitan	se ha quitado	se han quitado
2 imperfecto de indicativo		9 pluscuamperfecto de indicativo	
me quitaba	nos quitábamos	me había quitado	nos habíamos quitado
te quitabas	os quitabais	te habías quitado	os habíais quitado
se quitaba	se quitaban	se había quitado	se habían quitado
3 pretérito		10 pretérito anterior	
me quité	nos quitamos	me hube quitado	nos hubimos quitado
te quitaste	os quitasteis	te hubiste quitado	os hubisteis quitado
se quitó	se quitaron	se hubo quitado	se hubieron quitado
4 futuro		11 futuro perfecto	
me quitaré	nos quitaremos	me habré quitado	nos habremos quitado
te quitarás	os quitaréis	te habrás quitado	os habréis quitado
se quitará	se quitarán	se habrá quitado	se habrán quitado
5 potencial simple		12 potencial compuesto	
me quitaría	nos quitaríamos	me habría quitado	nos habríamos quitado
te quitarías	os quitaríais	te habrías quitado	os habríais quitado
se quitaría	se quitarían	se habría quitado	se habrían quitado
6 presente de subjuntivo		13 perfecto de subjuntivo	
me quite	nos quitemos	me haya quitado	nos hayamos quitado
te quites	os quitéis	te hayas quitado	os hayáis quitado
se quite	se quiten	se haya quitado	se hayan quitado
7 imperfecto de subjuntivo		14 pluscuamperfecto de subjuntivo	
me quitara	nos quitáramos	me hubiera quitado	nos hubiéramos quitado
te quitaras	os quitarais	te hubieras quitado	os hubierais quitado
se quitara	se quitaran	se hubiera quitado	se hubieran quitado
OR		OR	
me quitase	nos quitásemos	me hubiese quitado	nos hubiésemos quitado
te quitases	os quitaseis	te hubieses quitado	os hubieseis quitado
se quitase	se quitasen	se hubiese quitado	se hubiesen quitado

	imperativo	
—		quitémonos
quítate; no te quites		quitaos; no os quitéis
quítese		quítense

Words and expressions related to this verb
la quita   release (from owing money), acquittance
¡Quita de ahí!   Get away from here!
quitar   to remove, to take away; to rob, to strip

una quitanieves   snowplow
la quitación   salary
el quitasol   parasol (sunshade)

Check out the verb drills and verb tests with answers explained on pages 619–665.

to scrape, to rub off, to erase, to wipe out, to fray

The Seven Simple Tenses		The Seven Compound Tenses	
Singular	Plural	Singular	Plural
1　presente de indicativo		8　perfecto de indicativo	
raigo	**raemos**	**he raído**	**hemos raído**
raes	**raéis**	**has raído**	**habéis raído**
rae	**raen**	**ha raído**	**han raído**
2　imperfecto de indicativo		9　pluscuamperfecto de indicativo	
raía	**raíamos**	**había raído**	**habíamos raído**
raías	**raíais**	**habías raído**	**habíais raído**
raía	**raían**	**había raído**	**habían raído**
3　pretérito		10　pretérito anterior	
raí	**raímos**	**hube raído**	**hubimos raído**
raíste	**raísteis**	**hubiste raído**	**hubisteis raído**
rayó	**rayeron**	**hubo raído**	**hubieron raído**
4　futuro		11　futuro perfecto	
raeré	**raeremos**	**habré raído**	**habremos raído**
raerás	**raeréis**	**habrás raído**	**habréis raído**
raerá	**raerán**	**habrá raído**	**habrán raído**
5　potencial simple		12　potencial compuesto	
raería	**raeríamos**	**habría raído**	**habríamos raído**
raerías	**raeríais**	**habrías raído**	**habríais raído**
rearía	**raerían**	**habría raído**	**habrían raído**
6　presente de subjuntivo		13　perfecto de subjuntivo	
raiga	**raigamos**	**haya raído**	**hayamos raído**
raigas	**raigáis**	**hayas raído**	**hayáis raído**
raiga	**raigan**	**haya raído**	**hayan raído**
7　imperfecto de subjuntivo		14　pluscuamperfecto de subjuntivo	
rayera	**rayéramos**	**hubiera raído**	**hubiéramos raído**
rayeras	**rayerais**	**hubieras raído**	**hubierais raído**
rayera	**rayeran**	**hubiera raído**	**hubieran raído**
OR		OR	
rayese	**rayésemos**	**hubiese raído**	**hubiésemos raído**
rayeses	**rayeseis**	**hubieses raído**	**hubieseis raído**
rayese	**rayesen**	**hubiese raído**	**hubiesen raído**

imperativo	
—	**raigamos**
rae; no raigas	**raed; no raigáis**
raiga	**raigan**

Words related to this verb
la raedura　scraping
el raedor, la raedora　scraper

raerse　to wear away, become threadbare
raedizo, raediza　easily scraped or scratched
raído, raída　worn, frayed

Increase your verb power with popular phrases, words, and expressions for tourists on pages 595–618.

to realize, to carry out, to fulfill

The Seven Simple Tenses		The Seven Compound Tenses	
Singular	Plural	Singular	Plural
1 presente de indicativo		8 perfecto de indicativo	
realizo	realizamos	he realizado	hemos realizado
realizas	realizáis	has realizado	habéis realizado
realiza	realizan	ha realizado	han realizado
2 imperfecto de indicativo		9 pluscuamperfecto de indicativo	
realizaba	realizábamos	había realizado	habíamos realizado
realizabas	realizabais	habías realizado	habíais realizado
realizaba	realizaban	había realizado	habían realizado
3 pretérito		10 pretérito anterior	
realicé	realizamos	hube realizado	hubimos realizado
realizaste	realizasteis	hubiste realizado	hubisteis realizado
realizó	realizaron	hubo realizado	hubieron realizado
4 futuro		11 futuro perfecto	
realizaré	realizaremos	habré realizado	habremos realizado
realizarás	realizaréis	habrás realizado	habréis realizado
realizará	realizarán	habrá realizado	habrán realizado
5 potencial simple		12 potencial compuesto	
realizaría	realizaríamos	habría realizado	habríamos realizado
realizarías	realizaríais	habrías realizado	habríais realizado
realizaría	realizarían	habría realizado	habrían realizado
6 presente de subjuntivo		13 perfecto de subjuntivo	
realice	realicemos	haya realizado	hayamos realizado
realices	realicéis	hayas realizado	hayáis realizado
realice	realicen	haya realizado	hayan realizado
7 imperfecto de subjuntivo		14 pluscuamperfecto de subjuntivo	
realizara	realizáramos	hubiera realizado	hubiéramos realizado
realizaras	realizarais	hubieras realizado	hubierais realizado
realizara	realizaran	hubiera realizado	hubieran realizado
OR		OR	
realizase	realizásemos	hubiese realizado	hubiésemos realizado
realizases	realizaseis	hubieses realizado	hubieseis realizado
realizase	realizasen	hubiese realizado	hubiesen realizado

imperativo	
—	realicemos
realiza; no realices	realizad; no realicéis
realice	realicen

Words and expressions related to this verb
realizar su deseo   to have one's wish
la realización   fulfillment, realization, production
realizarse   to become fulfilled, to be carried out
realizable   practical

el, la realista   realist
la realidad   reality
el realismo   realism
realmente   really

recibir

Gerundio **recibiendo**

Part. pas. **recibido**

to receive, to get

The Seven Simple Tenses		The Seven Compound Tenses	
Singular	Plural	Singular	Plural
1 presente de indicativo		**8 perfecto de indicativo**	
recibo	recibimos	he recibido	hemos recibido
recibes	recibís	has recibido	habéis recibido
recibe	reciben	ha recibido	han recibido
2 imperfecto de indicativo		**9 pluscuamperfecto de indicativo**	
recibía	recibíamos	había recibido	habíamos recibido
recibías	recibíais	habías recibido	habíais recibido
recibía	recibían	había recibido	habían recibido
3 pretérito		**10 pretérito anterior**	
recibí	recibimos	hube recibido	hubimos recibido
recibiste	recibisteis	hubiste recibido	hubisteis recibido
recibió	recibieron	hubo recibido	hubieron recibido
4 futuro		**11 futuro perfecto**	
recibiré	recibiremos	habré recibido	habremos recibido
recibirás	recibiréis	habrás recibido	habréis recibido
recibirá	recibirán	habrá recibido	habrán recibido
5 potencial simple		**12 potencial compuesto**	
recibiría	recibiríamos	habría recibido	habríamos recibido
recibirías	recibiríais	habrías recibido	habríais recibido
recibiría	recibirían	habría recibido	habrían recibido
6 presente de subjuntivo		**13 perfecto de subjuntivo**	
reciba	recibamos	haya recibido	hayamos recibido
recibas	recibáis	hayas recibido	hayáis recibido
reciba	reciban	haya recibido	hayan recibido
7 imperfecto de subjuntivo		**14 pluscuamperfecto de subjuntivo**	
recibiera	recibiéramos	hubiera recibido	hubiéramos recibido
recibieras	recibierais	hubieras recibido	hubierais recibido
recibiera	recibieran	hubiera recibido	hubieran recibido
OR		OR	
recibiese	recibiésemos	hubiese recibido	hubiésemos recibido
recibieses	recibieseis	hubieses recibido	hubieseis recibido
recibiese	recibiesen	hubiese recibido	hubiesen recibido

	imperativo	
—		recibamos
recibe; no recibas		recibid; no recibáis
reciba		reciban

Words and expressions related to this verb
un recibo receipt
acusar recibo to acknowledge receipt
la recepción reception
recibir a cuenta to receive on account

de recibo acceptable; **ser de recibo** to be acceptable
recibirse to be admitted, to be received, to graduate

> Don't miss the definitions of basic grammatical terms with examples in English and Spanish on pages 666–677.

to pick (up), to gather, to harvest, to collect

The Seven Simple Tenses		The Seven Compound Tenses	
Singular	Plural	Singular	Plural
1 presente de indicativo		8 perfecto de indicativo	
recojo	**recogemos**	**he recogido**	**hemos recogido**
recoges	**recogéis**	**has recogido**	**habéis recogido**
recoge	**recogen**	**ha recogido**	**han recogido**
2 imperfecto de indicativo		9 pluscuamperfecto de indicativo	
recogía	**recogíamos**	**había recogido**	**habíamos recogido**
recogías	**recogíais**	**habías recogido**	**habíais recogido**
recogía	**recogían**	**había recogido**	**habían recogido**
3 pretérito		10 pretérito anterior	
recogí	**recogimos**	**hube recogido**	**hubimos recogido**
recogiste	**recogisteis**	**hubiste recogido**	**hubisteis recogido**
recogió	**recogieron**	**hubo recogido**	**hubieron recogido**
4 futuro		11 futuro perfecto	
recogeré	**recogeremos**	**habré recogido**	**habremos recogido**
recogerás	**recogeréis**	**habrás recogido**	**habréis recogido**
recogerá	**recogerán**	**habrá recogido**	**habrán recogido**
5 potencial simple		12 potencial compuesto	
recogería	**recogeríamos**	**habría recogido**	**habríamos recogido**
recogerías	**recogeríais**	**habrías recogido**	**habríais recogido**
recogería	**recogerían**	**habría recogido**	**habrían recogido**
6 presente de subjuntivo		13 perfecto de subjuntivo	
recoja	**recojamos**	**haya recogido**	**hayamos recogido**
recojas	**recojáis**	**hayas recogido**	**hayáis recogido**
recoja	**recojan**	**haya recogido**	**hayan recogido**
7 imperfecto de subjuntivo		14 pluscuamperfecto de subjuntivo	
recogiera	**recogiéramos**	**hubiera recogido**	**hubiéramos recogido**
recogieras	**recogierais**	**hubieras recogido**	**hubierais recogido**
recogiera	**recogieran**	**hubiera recogido**	**hubieran recogido**
OR		OR	
recogiese	**recogiésemos**	**hubiese recogido**	**hubiésemos recogido**
recogieses	**recogieseis**	**hubieses recogido**	**hubieseis recogido**
recogiese	**recogiesen**	**hubiese recogido**	**hubiesen recogido**

imperativo

—	**recojamos**
recoge; no recojas	**recoged; no recojáis**
recoja	**recojan**

Words and expressions related to this verb
la recogida harvest; **la recogida de
 basuras** garbage collection
un recogegotas drip pan

un recogedor dustpan
recogerse to be withdrawn, isolated
recoger datos to gather information, data

For other words related to this verb, see **coger.**

The subject pronouns are found on the page facing page 1.

recomendar

recomendar   Gerundio **recomendando**   Part. pas. **recomendado**

to recommend, to commend, to advise

The Seven Simple Tenses		The Seven Compound Tenses	
Singular	Plural	Singular	Plural
1 presente de indicativo		8 perfecto de indicativo	
recomiendo	**recomendamos**	**he recomendado**	**hemos recomendado**
recomiendas	**recomendáis**	**has recomendado**	**habéis recomendado**
recomienda	**recomiendan**	**ha recomendado**	**han recomendado**
2 imperfecto de indicativo		9 pluscuamperfecto de indicativo	
recomendaba	**recomendábamos**	**había recomendado**	**habíamos recomendado**
recomendabas	**recomendabais**	**habías recomendado**	**habíais recomendado**
recomendaba	**recomendaban**	**había recomendado**	**habían recomendado**
3 pretérito		10 pretérito anterior	
recomendé	**recomendamos**	**hube recomendado**	**hubimos recomendado**
recomendaste	**recomendasteis**	**hubiste recomendado**	**hubisteis recomendado**
recomendó	**recomendaron**	**hubo recomendado**	**hubieron recomendado**
4 futuro		11 futuro perfecto	
recomendaré	**recomendaremos**	**habré recomendado**	**habremos recomendado**
recomendarás	**recomendaréis**	**habrás recomendado**	**habréis recomendado**
recomendará	**recomendarán**	**habrá recomendado**	**habrán recomendado**
5 potencial simple		12 potencial compuesto	
recomendaría	**recomendaríamos**	**habría recomendado**	**habríamos recomendado**
recomendarías	**recomendaríais**	**habrías recomendado**	**habríais recomendado**
recomendará	**recomendarían**	**habría recomendado**	**habrían recomendado**
6 presente de subjuntivo		13 perfecto de subjuntivo	
recomiende	**recomendemos**	**haya recomendado**	**hayamos recomendado**
recomiendes	**recomendéis**	**hayas recomendado**	**hayáis recomendado**
recomiende	**recomienden**	**haya recomendado**	**hayan recomendado**
7 imperfecto de subjuntivo		14 pluscuamperfecto de subjuntivo	
recomendara	**recomendáramos**	**hubiera recomendado**	**hubiéramos recomendado**
recomendaras	**recomendarais**	**hubieras recomendado**	**hubierais recomendado**
recomendara	**recomendaran**	**hubiera recomendado**	**hubieran recomendado**
OR		OR	
recomendase	**recomendásemos**	**hubiese recomendado**	**hubiésemos recomendado**
recomendases	**recomendaseis**	**hubieses recomendado**	**hubieseis recomendado**
recomendase	**recomendasen**	**hubiese recomendado**	**hubiesen recomendado**

imperativo	
—	**recomendemos**
recomienda; no recomiendes	**recomendad; no recomendéis**
recomiende	**recomienden**

Words related to this verb
la recomendación recommendation   **recomendable** commendable, praiseworthy
recomendablemente commendably   **recomendar + inf.** to urge + inf.

> If you want an explanation of meanings and uses of Spanish
> and English verb tenses and moods, see pages xx–xl.

to recognize, to acknowledge, to be grateful for

The Seven Simple Tenses		The Seven Compound Tenses	
Singular	Plural	Singular	Plural
1 presente de indicativo		8 perfecto de indicativo	
reconozco	reconocemos	he reconocido	hemos reconocido
reconoces	reconocéis	has reconocido	habéis reconocido
reconoce	reconocen	ha reconocido	han reconocido
2 imperfecto de indicativo		9 pluscuamperfecto de indicativo	
reconocía	reconocíamos	había reconocido	habíamos reconocido
reconocías	reconocíais	habías reconocido	habíais reconocido
reconocía	reconocían	había reconocido	habían reconocido
3 pretérito		10 pretérito anterior	
reconocí	reconocimos	hube reconocido	hubimos reconocido
reconociste	reconocisteis	hubiste reconocido	hubisteis reconocido
reconoció	reconocieron	hubo reconocido	hubieron reconocido
4 futuro		11 futuro perfecto	
reconoceré	reconoceremos	habré reconocido	habremos reconocido
reconocerás	reconoceréis	habrás reconocido	habréis reconocido
reconocerá	reconocerán	habrá reconocido	habrán reconocido
5 potencial simple		12 potencial compuesto	
reconocería	reconoceríamos	habría reconocido	habríamos reconocido
reconocerías	reconoceríais	habrías reconocido	habríais reconocido
reconocería	reconocerían	habría reconocido	habrían reconocido
6 presente de subjuntivo		13 perfecto de subjuntivo	
reconozca	reconozcamos	haya reconocido	hayamos reconocido
reconozcas	reconozcáis	hayas reconocido	hayáis reconocido
reconozca	reconozcan	haya reconocido	hayan reconocido
7 imperfecto de subjuntivo		14 pluscuamperfecto de subjuntivo	
reconociera	reconociéramos	hubiera reconocido	hubiéramos reconocido
reconocieras	reconocierais	hubieras reconocido	hubierais reconocido
reconociera	reconocieran	hubiera reconocido	hubieran reconocido
OR		OR	
reconociese	reconociésemos	hubiese reconocido	hubiésemos reconocido
reconocieses	reconocieseis	hubieses reconocido	hubieseis reconocido
reconociese	reconociesen	hubiese reconocido	hubiesen reconocido

imperativo	
—	reconozcamos
reconoce; no reconozcas	reconoced; no reconozcáis
reconozca	reconozcan

Words related to this verb
reconocible recognizable
el reconocimiento recognition, gratitude
el reconocimiento de la voz voice recognition

reconocimiento médico medical examination
reconocidamente gratefully

For other words and expressions related to this verb, see **conocer.**

The subject pronouns are found on the page facing page 1.

recordar
Gerundio **recordando**   Part. pas. **recordado**

to remember, to recall, to remind

The Seven Simple Tenses		The Seven Compound Tenses	
Singular	Plural	Singular	Plural
1 presente de indicativo		**8 perfecto de indicativo**	
recuerdo	recordamos	he recordado	hemos recordado
recuerdas	recordáis	has recordado	habéis recordado
recuerda	recuerdan	ha recordado	han recordado
2 imperfecto de indicativo		**9 pluscuamperfecto de indicativo**	
recordaba	recordábamos	había recordado	habíamos recordado
recordabas	recordabais	habías recordado	habíais recordado
recordaba	recordaban	había recordado	habían recordado
3 pretérito		**10 pretérito anterior**	
recordé	recordamos	hube recordado	hubimos recordado
recordaste	recordasteis	hubiste recordado	hubisteis recordado
recordó	recordaron	hubo recordado	hubieron recordado
4 futuro		**11 futuro perfecto**	
recordaré	recordaremos	habré recordado	habremos recordado
recordarás	recordaréis	habrás recordado	habréis recordado
recordará	recordarán	habrá recordado	habrán recordado
5 potencial simple		**12 potencial compuesto**	
recordaría	recordaríamos	habría recordado	habríamos recordado
recordarías	recordaríais	habrías recordado	habríais recordado
recordaría	recordarían	habría recordado	habrían recordado
6 presente de subjuntivo		**13 perfecto de subjuntivo**	
recuerde	recordemos	haya recordado	hayamos recordado
recuerdes	recordéis	hayas recordado	hayáis recordado
recuerde	recuerden	haya recordado	hayan recordado
7 imperfecto de subjuntivo		**14 pluscuamperfecto de subjuntivo**	
recordara	recordáramos	hubiera recordado	hubiéramos recordado
recordaras	recordarais	hubieras recordado	hubierais recordado
recordara	recordaran	hubiera recordado	hubieran recordado
OR		OR	
recordase	recordásemos	hubiese recordado	hubiésemos recordado
recordases	recordaseis	hubieses recordado	hubieseis recordado
recordase	recordasen	hubiese recordado	hubiesen recordado

imperativo

	recordemos
recuerda; no recuerdes	**recordad; no recordéis**
recuerde	**recuerden**

Words and expressions related to this verb
el recuerdo memory, recollection
los recuerdos regards, compliments
recordable memorable
el récord record
una tienda de recuerdos souvenir shop

recordar algo a uno to remind someone of something
un recordatorio memento, reminder
cuerdo rational, sensible
cuerdamente sensibly

to refer, to relate

The Seven Simple Tenses		The Seven Compound Tenses	
Singular	Plural	Singular	Plural
1 presente de indicativo		**8 perfecto de indicativo**	
refiero	**referimos**	**he referido**	**hemos referido**
refieres	**referís**	**has referido**	**habéis referido**
refiere	**refieren**	**ha referido**	**han referido**
2 imperfecto de indicativo		**9 pluscuamperfecto de indicativo**	
refería	**referíamos**	**había referido**	**habíamos referido**
referías	**referíais**	**habías referido**	**habíais referido**
refería	**referían**	**había referido**	**habían referido**
3 pretérito		**10 pretérito anterior**	
referí	**referimos**	**hube referido**	**hubimos referido**
referiste	**referisteis**	**hubiste referido**	**hubisteis referido**
refirió	**refirieron**	**hubo referido**	**hubieron referido**
4 futuro		**11 futuro perfecto**	
referiré	**referiremos**	**habré referido**	**habremos referido**
referirás	**referiréis**	**habrás referido**	**habréis referido**
referirá	**referirán**	**habrá referido**	**habrán referido**
5 potencial simple		**12 potencial compuesto**	
referiría	**referiríamos**	**habría referido**	**habríamos referido**
referirías	**referiríais**	**habrías referido**	**habríais referido**
referiría	**referirían**	**habría referido**	**habrían referido**
6 presente de subjuntivo		**13 perfecto de subjuntivo**	
refiera	**refiramos**	**haya referido**	**hayamos referido**
refieras	**refiráis**	**hayas referido**	**hayáis referido**
refiera	**refieran**	**haya referido**	**hayan referido**
7 imperfecto de subjuntivo		**14 pluscuamperfecto de subjuntivo**	
refiriera	**refiriéramos**	**hubiera referido**	**hubiéramos referido**
refirieras	**refirieras**	**hubieras referido**	**hubierais referido**
refiriera	**refirieran**	**hubiera referido**	**hubieran referido**
OR		OR	
refiriese	**refiriésemos**	**hubiese referido**	**hubiésemos referido**
refirieses	**refirieseis**	**hubieses referido**	**hubieseis referido**
refiriese	**refiriesen**	**hubiese referido**	**hubiesen referido**

imperativo

—	**refiramos**
refiere; no refieras	**referid; no refiráis**
refiera	**refieran**

Words related to this verb

la referencia reference, account (narration)
referente concerning, referring, relating (to)
el referéndum referendum
transferir to transfer

preferir to prefer
el referido; la referida the person referred to
conferir to confer, to grant

The subject pronouns are found on the page facing page 1.

to give as a present, to make a present of, to give as a gift

The Seven Simple Tenses		The Seven Compound Tenses	
Singular	Plural	Singular	Plural
1　presente de indicativo		8　perfecto de indicativo	
regalo	**regalamos**	**he regalado**	**hemos regalado**
regalas	**regaláis**	**has regalado**	**habéis regalado**
regala	**regalan**	**ha regalado**	**han regalado**
2　imperfecto de indicativo		9　pluscuamperfecto de indicativo	
regalaba	**regalábamos**	**había regalado**	**habíamos regalado**
regalabas	**regalabais**	**habías regalado**	**habíais regalado**
regalaba	**regalaban**	**había regalado**	**habían regalado**
3　pretérito		10　pretérito anterior	
regalé	**regalamos**	**hube regalado**	**hubimos regalado**
regalaste	**regalasteis**	**hubiste regalado**	**hubisteis regalado**
regaló	**regalaron**	**hubo regalado**	**hubieron regalado**
4　futuro		11　futuro perfecto	
regalaré	**regalaremos**	**habré regalado**	**habremos regalado**
regalarás	**regalaréis**	**habrás regalado**	**habréis regalado**
regalará	**regalarán**	**habrá regalado**	**habrán regalado**
5　potencial simple		12　potencial compuesto	
regalaría	**regalaríamos**	**habría regalado**	**habríamos regalado**
regalarías	**regalaríais**	**habrías regalado**	**habríais regalado**
regalaría	**regalarían**	**habría regalado**	**habrían regalado**
6　presente de subjuntivo		13　perfecto de subjuntivo	
regale	**regalemos**	**haya regalado**	**hayamos regalado**
regales	**regaléis**	**hayas regalado**	**hayáis regalado**
regale	**regalen**	**haya regalado**	**hayan regalado**
7　imperfecto de subjuntivo		14　pluscuamperfecto de subjuntivo	
regalara	**regaláramos**	**hubiera regalado**	**hubiéramos regalado**
regalaras	**regalarais**	**hubieras regalado**	**hubierais regalado**
regalara	**regalaran**	**hubiera regalado**	**hubieran regalado**
OR		OR	
regalase	**regalásemos**	**hubiese regalado**	**hubiésemos regalado**
regalases	**regalaseis**	**hubieses regalado**	**hubieseis regalado**
regalase	**regalasen**	**hubiese regalado**	**hubiesen regalado**

	imperativo	
—		**regalemos**
regala; no regales		**regalad; no regaléis**
regale		**regalen**

Words and expressions related to this verb
regalar el oído　to flatter
un regalo　gift, present
regaladamente　comfortably

un regalejo　small gift
de regalo　free, gratis, complimentary

Get acquainted with what preposition goes with what verb on pages 541–549.

to water, to irrigate, to sprinkle

The Seven Simple Tenses		The Seven Compound Tenses	
Singular	Plural	Singular	Plural

1   presente de indicativo

		8 perfecto de indicativo	
riego	regamos	he regado	hemos regado
riegas	regáis	has regado	habéis regado
riega	riegan	ha regado	han regado

2   imperfecto de indicativo

		9 pluscuamperfecto de indicativo	
regaba	regábamos	había regado	habíamos regado
regabas	regabais	habías regado	habíais regado
regaba	regaban	había regado	habían regado

3   pretérito

		10 pretérito anterior	
regué	regamos	hube regado	hubimos regado
regaste	regasteis	hubiste regado	hubisteis regado
regó	regaron	hubo regado	hubieron regado

4   futuro

		11 futuro perfecto	
regaré	regaremos	habré regado	habremos regado
regarás	regaréis	habrás regado	habréis regado
regará	regarán	habrá regado	habrán regado

5   potencial simple

		12 potencial compuesto	
regaría	regaríamos	habría regado	habríamos regado
regarías	regaríais	habrías regado	habríais regado
regaría	regarían	habría regado	habrían regado

6   presente de subjuntivo

		13 perfecto de subjuntivo	
riegue	reguemos	haya regado	hayamos regado
riegues	reguéis	hayas regado	hayáis regado
riegue	rieguen	haya regado	hayan regado

7   imperfecto de subjuntivo

		14 pluscuamperfecto de subjuntivo	
regara	regáramos	hubiera regado	hubiéramos regado
regaras	regarais	hubieras regado	hubierais regado
regara	regaran	hubiera regado	hubieran regado
OR		OR	
regase	regásemos	hubiese regado	hubiésemos regado
regases	regaseis	hubieses regado	hubieseis regado
regase	regasen	hubiese regado	hubiesen regado

	imperativo	
—	reguemos	
riega; no riegues	regad; no reguéis	
riegue	rieguen	

Words and expressions related to this verb

una regata   regatta, boat race; irrigation ditch
el riego   irrigation, sprinkling, watering
irrigar   to irrigate
la irrigación   irrigation

boca de riego   hydrant
una regadora   water sprinkler
una regadura   sprinkling, watering

The subject pronouns are found on the page facing page 1.

to return, to go back, to regress

The Seven Simple Tenses		The Seven Compound Tenses	
Singular	Plural	Singular	Plural

1 presente de indicativo

		8 perfecto de indicativo	
regreso	regresamos	he regresado	hemos regresado
regresas	regresáis	has regresado	habéis regresado
regresa	regresan	ha regresado	han regresado

2 imperfecto de indicativo

		9 pluscuamperfecto de indicativo	
regresaba	regresábamos	había regresado	habíamos regresado
regresabas	regresabais	habías regresado	habíais regresado
regresaba	regresaban	había regresado	habían regresado

3 pretérito

		10 pretérito anterior	
regresé	regresamos	hube regresado	hubimos regresado
regresaste	regresasteis	hubiste regresado	hubisteis regresado
regresó	regresaron	hubo regresado	hubieron regresado

4 futuro

		11 futuro perfecto	
regresaré	regesaremos	habré regresado	habremos regresado
regresarás	regresaréis	habrás regresado	habréis regresado
regresará	regresarán	habrá regresado	habrán regresado

5 potencial simple

		12 potencial compuesto	
regresaría	regresaríamos	habría regresado	habríamos regresado
regresarías	regresaríais	habrías regresado	habríais regresado
regresaría	regresarían	habría regresado	habrían regresado

6 presente de subjuntivo

		13 perfecto de subjuntivo	
regrese	regresemos	haya regresado	hayamos regresado
regreses	regreséis	hayas regresado	hayáis regresado
regrese	regresen	haya regresado	hayan regresado

7 imperfecto de subjuntivo

		14 pluscuamperfecto de subjuntivo	
regresara	regresáramos	hubiera regresado	hubiéramos regresado
regresaras	regresarais	hubieras regresado	hubierais regresado
regresara	regresaran	hubiera regresado	hubieran regresado
OR		OR	
regresase	regresásemos	hubiese regresado	hubiésemos regresado
regreases	regresaseis	hubieses regresado	hubieseis regresado
regresase	regresasen	hubiese regresado	hubiesen regresado

imperativo	
—	regresemos
regresa; no regreses	regresad; no regreséis
regrese	regresen

Words and expressions related to this verb

progresar to progress
la regresión regression
regresivo, regresiva regressive
progresar to advance, to progress

el regreso return
estar de regreso to be back (from a trip)
egresado, egresada graduate
egresar to graduate

The Seven Simple Tenses | | The Seven Compound Tenses

Singular	Plural	Singular	Plural
1 presente de indicativo		**8 perfecto de indicativo**	
río	**reímos**	**he reído**	**hemos reído**
ríes	**reís**	**has reído**	**habéis reído**
ríe	**ríen**	**ha reído**	**han reído**
2 imperfecto de indicativo		**9 pluscuamperfecto de indicativo**	
reía	**reíamos**	**había reído**	**habíamos reído**
reías	**reíais**	**habías reído**	**habíais reído**
reía	**reían**	**había reído**	**habían reído**
3 pretérito		**10 pretérito anterior**	
reí	**reímos**	**hube reído**	**hubimos reído**
reíste	**reísteis**	**hubiste reído**	**hubisteis reído**
rió	**rieron**	**hubo reído**	**hubieron reído**
4 futuro		**11 futuro perfecto**	
reiré	**reiremos**	**habré reído**	**habremos reído**
reirás	**reiréis**	**habrás reído**	**habréis reído**
reirá	**reirán**	**habrá reído**	**habrán reído**
5 potencial simple		**12 potencial compuesto**	
reiría	**reiríamos**	**habría reído**	**habríamos reído**
reirías	**reiríais**	**habrías reído**	**habríais reído**
reiría	**reirían**	**habría reído**	**habrían reído**
6 presente de subjuntivo		**13 perfecto de subjuntivo**	
ría	**riamos**	**haya reído**	**hayamos reído**
rías	**riáis**	**hayas reído**	**hayáis reído**
ría	**rían**	**haya reído**	**hayan reído**
7 imperfecto de subjuntivo		**14 pluscuamperfecto de subjuntivo**	
riera	**riéramos**	**hubiera reído**	**hubiéramos reído**
rieras	**rierais**	**hubieras reído**	**hubierais reído**
riera	**rieran**	**hubiera reído**	**hubieran reído**
OR		OR	
riese	**riésemos**	**hubiese reído**	**hubiésemos reído**
rieses	**rieseis**	**hubieses reído**	**hubieseis reído**
riese	**riesen**	**hubiese reído**	**hubiesen reído**

imperativo

—	**riamos**
ríe; no rías	**reíd; no riáis**
ría	**rían**

Common idiomatic expressions using this verb

reír a carcajadas   to laugh loudly
reír de   to laught at, to make fun of
la risa   laugh, laughter

risible   laughable
risueño, risueña   smiling
soltar la risa   to burst out in laughter

For additional words and expressions related to this verb, see **sonreír** and **reírse.**

to laugh

The Seven Simple Tenses		The Seven Compound Tenses	
Singular	Plural	Singular	Plural
1 presente de indicativo		8 perfecto de indicativo	
me río	**nos reímos**	**me he reído**	**nos hemos reído**
te ríes	**os reís**	**te has reído**	**os habéis reído**
se ríe	**se ríen**	**se ha reído**	**se han reído**
2 imperfecto de indicativo		9 pluscuamperfecto de indicativo	
me reía	**nos reíamos**	**me había reído**	**nos habíamos reído**
te reías	**os reíais**	**te habías reído**	**os habíais reído**
se reía	**se reían**	**se había reído**	**se habían reído**
3 pretérito		10 pretérito anterior	
me reí	**nos reímos**	**me hube reído**	**nos hubimos reído**
te reíste	**os reísteis**	**te hubiste reído**	**os hubisteis reído**
se rió	**se rieron**	**se hubo reído**	**se hubieron reído**
4 futuro		11 futuro perfecto	
me reiré	**nos reiremos**	**me habré reído**	**nos habremos reído**
te reirás	**os reiréis**	**te habrás reído**	**os habréis reído**
se reirá	**se reirán**	**se habrá reído**	**se habrán reído**
5 potencial simple		12 potencial compuesto	
me reiría	**nos reiríamos**	**me habría reído**	**nos habríamos reído**
te reirías	**os reiríais**	**te habrías reído**	**os habríais reído**
se reiría	**se reirían**	**se habría reído**	**se habrían reído**
6 presente de subjuntivo		13 perfecto de subjuntivo	
me ría	**nos riamos**	**me haya reído**	**nos hayamos reído**
te rías	**os riáis**	**te hayas reído**	**os hayáis reído**
se ría	**se rían**	**se haya reído**	**se hayan reído**
7 imperfecto de subjuntivo		14 pluscuamperfecto de subjuntivo	
me riera	**nos riéramos**	**me hubiera reído**	**nos hubiéramos reído**
te rieras	**os rierais**	**te hubieras reído**	**os hubierais reído**
se riera	**se rieran**	**se hubiera reído**	**se hubieran reído**
OR		OR	
me riese	**nos riésemos**	**me hubiese reído**	**nos hubiésemos reído**
te rieses	**os rieseis**	**te hubieses reído**	**os hubieseis reído**
se riese	**se riesen**	**se hubiese reído**	**se hubiesen reído**

imperativo	
—	**riámonos**
ríete; no te rías	**reíos; no os riáis**
ríase	**ríanse**

Words and expressions related to this verb
reírse de to laugh at, to make fun of
reírse de uno en sus propias barbas
  to laugh up one's sleeve
una cosa de risa a laughing matter

reír a carcajadas to laugh loudly
la risa laughter; **¡Qué risa!** What a laugh!
reírse en las barbas de alguien to laugh in
  someone's face

For other words related to this verb, see **sonreír** and **reír.**

to refill, to fill again, to stuff

The Seven Simple Tenses		The Seven Compound Tenses	
Singular	Plural	Singular	Plural

1   presente de indicativo

		8 perfecto de indicativo	
relleno	**rellenamos**	he rellenado	hemos rellenado
rellenas	**rellenáis**	has rellenado	habéis rellenado
rellena	**rellenan**	ha rellenado	han rellenado

2   imperfecto de indicativo

		9 pluscuamperfecto de indicativo	
rellenaba	**rellenábamos**	había rellenado	habíamos rellenado
rellenabas	**rellenabais**	habías rellenado	habíais rellenado
rellenaba	**rellenaban**	había rellenado	habían rellenado

3   pretérito

		10 pretérito anterior	
rellené	**rellenamos**	hube rellenado	hubimos rellenado
rellenaste	**rellenasteis**	hubiste rellenado	hubisteis rellenado
rellenó	**rellenaron**	hubo rellenado	hubieron rellenado

4   futuro

		11 futuro perfecto	
rellenaré	**rellenaremos**	habré rellenado	habremos rellenado
rellenarás	**rellenaréis**	habrás rellenado	habréis rellenado
rellenará	**rellenarán**	habrá rellenado	habrán rellenado

5   potencial simple

		12 potencial compuesto	
rellenaría	**rellenaríamos**	habría rellenado	habríamos rellenado
rellenarías	**rellenaríais**	habrías rellenado	habríais rellenado
rellenaría	**rellenarían**	habría rellenado	habrían rellenado

6   presente de subjuntivo

		13 perfecto de subjuntivo	
rellene	**rellenemos**	haya rellenado	hayamos rellenado
rellenes	**rellenéis**	hayas rellenado	hayáis rellenado
rellene	**rellenen**	haya rellenado	hayan rellenado

7   imperfecto de subjuntivo

		14 pluscuamperfecto de subjuntivo	
rellenara	**rellenáramos**	hubiera rellenado	hubiéramos rellenado
rellenaras	**rellenarais**	hubieras rellenado	hubierais rellenado
rellenara	**rellenaran**	hubiera rellenado	hubieran rellenado
OR		OR	
rellenase	**rellenásemos**	hubiese rellenado	hubiésemos rellenado
rellenases	**rellenaseis**	hubieses rellenado	hubieseis rellenado
rellenase	**rellenasen**	hubiese rellenado	hubiesen rellenado

imperativo

—	**rellenemos**
rellena; no rellenes	**rellenad; no rellenéis**
rellene	**rellenen**

Words and expressions related to this verb
el relleno   filling, stuffing   **rellenable**   refillable
relleno, rellena   stuffed, filled   **rellenarse**   to stuff oneself with food

For other words and expressions related to this verb, see **llenar.**

Don't miss the definitions of basic grammatical terms with examples
in English and Spanish on pages 666–677.

to remit, to forward, to transmit

The Seven Simple Tenses		The Seven Compound Tenses	
Singular	Plural	Singular	Plural
1 presente de indicativo		8 perfecto de indicativo	
remito	remitimos	he remitido	hemos remitido
remites	remitís	has remitido	habéis remitido
remite	remiten	ha remitido	han remitido
2 imperfecto de indicativo		9 pluscuamperfecto de indicativo	
remitía	remitíamos	había remitido	habíamos remitido
remitías	remitíais	habías remitido	habíais remitido
remitía	remitían	había remitido	habían remitido
3 pretérito		10 pretérito anterior	
remití	remitimos	hube remitido	hubimos remitido
remitise	remitisteis	hubiste remitido	hubisteis remitido
remitió	remitieron	hubo remitido	hubieron remitido
4 futuro		11 futuro perfecto	
remitiré	remitiremos	habré remitido	habremos remitido
remitirás	remitiréis	habrás remitido	habréis remitido
remitirá	remitirán	habrá remitido	habrán remitido
5 potencial simple		12 potencial compuesto	
remitiría	remitiríamos	habría remitido	habríamos remitido
remitirías	remitiríais	habrías remitido	habríais remitido
remitiría	remitirían	habría remitido	habrían remitido
6 presente de subjuntivo		13 perfecto de subjuntivo	
remita	remitamos	haya remitido	hayamos remitido
remitas	remitáis	hayas remitido	hayáis remitido
remita	remitan	haya remitido	hayan remitido
7 imperfecto de subjuntivo		14 pluscuamperfecto de subjuntivo	
remitiera	remitiéramos	hubiera remitido	hubiéramos remitido
remitieras	remitierais	hubieras remitido	hubierais remitido
remitiera	remitieran	hubiera remitido	hubieran remitido
OR		OR	
remitiese	remitiésemos	hubiese remitido	hubiésemos remitido
remitieses	remitieseis	hubieses remitido	hubieseis remitido
remitiese	remitiesen	hubiese remitido	hubiesen remitido

imperativo	
—	**remitamos**
remite; no remitas	**remitid; no remitáis**
remita	**remitan**

Words and expressions related to this verb

remitirse a   to refer oneself to

el, la remitente   sender, shipper

la remisión   remission

la remisión de los pecados   remission of sins

For an explanation of meanings and uses of Spanish and English
verb tenses and moods, see pages xx to xl.

to scold, to quarrel

The Seven Simple Tenses | The Seven Compound Tenses

Singular	Plural	Singular	Plural
1 presente de indicativo		8 perfecto de indicativo	
riño	**reñimos**	**he reñido**	**hemos reñido**
riñes	**reñís**	**has reñido**	**habéis reñido**
riñe	**riñen**	**ha reñido**	**han reñido**
2 imperfecto de indicativo		9 pluscuamperfecto de indicativo	
reñía	**reñíamos**	**había reñido**	**habíamos reñido**
reñías	**reñíais**	**habías reñido**	**habíais reñido**
reñía	**reñían**	**había reñido**	**habían reñido**
3 pretérito		10 pretérito anterior	
reñí	**reñimos**	**hube reñido**	**hubimos reñido**
reñiste	**reñisteis**	**hubiste reñido**	**hubisteis reñido**
riñó	**riñeron**	**hubo reñido**	**hubieron reñido**
4 futuro		11 futuro perfecto	
reñiré	**reñiremos**	**habré reñido**	**habremos reñido**
reñirás	**reñiréis**	**habrás reñido**	**habréis reñido**
reñirá	**reñirán**	**habrá reñido**	**habrán reñido**
5 potencial simple		12 potencial compuesto	
reñiría	**reñiríamos**	**habría reñido**	**habríamos reñido**
reñirías	**reñiríais**	**habrías reñido**	**habríais reñido**
reñiría	**reñirían**	**habría reñido**	**habrían reñido**
6 presente de subjuntivo		13 perfecto de subjuntivo	
riña	**riñamos**	**haya reñido**	**hayamos reñido**
riñas	**riñáis**	**hayas reñido**	**hayáis reñido**
riña	**riñan**	**haya reñido**	**hayan reñido**
7 imperfecto de subjuntivo		14 pluscuamperfecto de subjuntivo	
riñera	**riñéramos**	**hubiera reñido**	**hubiéramos reñido**
riñeras	**riñerais**	**hubieras reñido**	**hubierais reñido**
riñera	**riñeran**	**hubiera reñido**	**hubieran reñido**
OR		OR	
riñese	**riñésemos**	**hubiese reñido**	**hubiésemos reñido**
riñeses	**riñeseis**	**hubieses reñido**	**hubieseis reñido**
riñese	**riñesen**	**hubiese reñido**	**hubiesen reñido**

imperativo

—	**riñamos**
riñe; no riñas	**reñid; no riñáis**
riña	**riñan**

Words and expressions related to this verb

reñidor, reñidora quarreller	**la riña** quarrel, fight
reñidamente stubbornly	**reñir a alguien** to tell someone off
reñir por to fight over	**una reñidura** scolding

If you don't know the Spanish verb for the English verb you
have in mind, look it up in the index on pages 505–518.

The subject pronouns are found on the page facing page 1.

to mend, to repair, to notice, to observe

The Seven Simple Tenses		The Seven Compound Tenses	
Singular	Plural	Singular	Plural
1 presente de indicativo		8 perfecto de indicativo	
reparo	reparamos	he reparado	hemos reparado
reparas	reparáis	has reparado	habéis reparado
repara	reparan	ha reparado	han reparado
2 imperfecto de indicativo		9 pluscuamperfecto de indicativo	
reparaba	reparábamos	había reparado	habíamos reparado
reparabas	reparabais	habías reparado	habíais reparado
reparaba	reparaban	había reparado	habían reparado
3 pretérito		10 pretérito anterior	
reparé	reparamos	hube reparado	hubimos reparado
reparaste	reparasteis	hubiste reparado	hubisteis reparado
reparó	repararon	hubo reparado	hubieron reparado
4 futuro		11 futuro perfecto	
repararé	repararemos	habré reparado	habremos reparado
repararás	repararéis	habrás reparado	habréis reparado
reparará	repararán	habrá reparado	habrán reparado
5 potencial simple		12 potencial compuesto	
repararía	repararíamos	habría reparado	habríamos reparado
repararías	repararíais	habrías reparado	habríais reparado
repararía	repararían	habría reparado	habrían reparado
6 presente de subjuntivo		13 perfecto de subjuntivo	
repare	reparemos	haya reparado	hayamos reparado
repares	reparéis	hayas reparado	hayáis reparado
repare	reparen	haya reparado	hayan reparado
7 imperfecto de subjuntivo		14 pluscuamperfecto de subjuntivo	
reparara	reparáramos	hubiera reparado	hubiéramos reparado
repararas	repararais	hubieras reparado	hubierais reparado
reparara	repararan	hubiera reparado	hubieran reparado
OR		OR	
reparase	reparásemos	hubiese reparado	hubiésemos reparado
reparases	reparaseis	hubieses reparado	hubieseis reparado
reparase	reparasen	hubiese reparado	hubiesen reparado

	imperativo
—	reparemos
repara; no repares	reparad; no reparéis
repare	reparen

Words and expressions related to this verb
reparar en to notice, to pay attention to
un reparo repairs, repairing; notice
una reparación repairing, reparation

reparaciones provisionales temporary repairs
reparable reparable; noteworthy
un reparador, una reparadora repairer

Increase your verb power with popular phrases, words,
and expressions for tourists on pages 595–618.

to distribute, to deal cards

The Seven Simple Tenses		The Seven Compound Tenses	
Singular	Plural	Singular	Plural
1 presente de indicativo		**8 perfecto de indicativo**	
reparto	repartimos	he repartido	hemos repartido
repartes	repartís	has repartido	habéis repartido
reparte	reparten	ha repartido	han repartido
2 imperfecto de indicativo		**9 pluscuamperfecto de indicativo**	
repartía	repartíamos	había repartido	habíamos repartido
repartías	repartíais	habías repartido	habíais repartido
repartía	repartían	había repartido	habían repartido
3 pretérito		**10 pretérito anterior**	
repartí	repartimos	hube repartido	hubimos repartido
repartiste	repartisteis	hubiste repartido	hubisteis repartido
repartió	repartieron	hubo repartido	hubieron repartido
4 futuro		**11 futuro perfecto**	
repartiré	repartiremos	habré repartido	habremos repartido
repartirás	repartiréis	habrás repartido	habréis repartido
repartirá	repartirán	habrá repartido	habrán repartido
5 potencial simple		**12 potencial compuesto**	
repartiría	repartiríamos	habría repartido	habríamos repartido
repartirías	repartiríais	habrías repartido	habríais repartido
repartiría	repartirían	habría repartido	habrían repartido
6 presente de subjuntivo		**13 perfecto de subjuntivo**	
reparta	repartamos	haya repartido	hayamos repartido
repartas	repartáis	hayas repartido	hayáis repartido
reparta	repartan	haya repartido	hayan repartido
7 imperfecto de subjuntivo		**14 pluscuamperfecto de subjuntivo**	
repartiera	repartiéramos	hubiera repartido	hubiéramos repartido
repartieras	repartierais	hubieras repartido	hubierais repartido
repartiera	repartieran	hubiera repartido	hubieran repartido
OR		OR	
repartiese	repartiésemos	hubiese repartido	hubiésemos repartido
repartieses	repartieseis	hubieses repartido	hubieseis repartido
repartiese	repartiesen	hubiese repartido	hubiesen repartido

imperativo

—	**repartamos**
reparte; no repartas	**repartid; no repartáis**
reparta	**repartan**

Words and expressions related to this verb
repartir un dividendo   to declare a dividend
la repartición, el repartimiento   distribution
el reparto   distribution, cast (of actors)
repartible   distributable

See also **partir.**

Consult the back pages for the section on verbs used in idiomatic expressions.

to repeat

The Seven Simple Tenses		The Seven Compound Tenses	
Singular	Plural	Singular	Plural
1 presente de indicativo		8 perfecto de indicativo	
repito	**repetimos**	**he repetido**	**hemos repetido**
repites	**repetís**	**has repetido**	**habéis repetido**
repite	**repiten**	**ha repetido**	**han repetido**
2 imperfecto de indicativo		9 pluscuamperfecto de indicativo	
repetía	**repetíamos**	**había repetido**	**habíamos repetido**
repetías	**repetíais**	**habías repetido**	**habíais repetido**
repetía	**repetían**	**había repetido**	**habían repetido**
3 pretérito		10 pretérito anterior	
repetí	**repetimos**	**hube repetido**	**hubimos repetido**
repetiste	**repetisteis**	**hubiste repetido**	**hubisteis repetido**
repitió	**repitieron**	**hubo repetido**	**hubieron repetido**
4 futuro		11 futuro perfecto	
repetiré	**repetiremos**	**habré repetido**	**habremos repetido**
repetirás	**repetiréis**	**habrás repetido**	**habréis repetido**
repetirá	**repetirán**	**habrá repetido**	**habrán repetido**
5 potencial simple		12 potencial compuesto	
repetiría	**repetiríamos**	**habría repetido**	**habríamos repetido**
repetirías	**repetiríais**	**habrías repetido**	**habríais repetido**
repetiría	**repetirían**	**habría repetido**	**habrían repetido**
6 presente de subjuntivo		13 perfecto de subjuntivo	
repita	**repitamos**	**haya repetido**	**hayamos repetido**
repitas	**repitáis**	**hayas repetido**	**hayáis repetido**
repita	**repitan**	**haya repetido**	**hayan repetido**
7 imperfecto de subjuntivo		14 pluscuamperfecto de subjuntivo	
repitiera	**repitiéramos**	**hubiera repetido**	**hubiéramos repetido**
repitieras	**repitierais**	**hubieras repetido**	**hubierais repetido**
repitiera	**repitieran**	**hubiera repetido**	**hubieran repetido**
OR		OR	
repitiese	**repitiésemos**	**hubiese repetido**	**hubiésemos repetido**
repitieses	**repitieseis**	**hubieses repetido**	**hubieseis repetido**
repitiese	**repitiesen**	**hubiese repetido**	**hubiesen repetido**

	imperativo	
—		**repitamos**
repite; no repitas		**repetid; no repitáis**
repita		**repitan**

Words related to this verb
la repetición repetition
repetidamente repeatedly
repetidor, repetidora repeating

repetidas veces over and over again
repetido, repetida repeated
¡Que se repita! Encore!

Review the principal parts of important Spanish verbs on pages xvi–xvii.

to resolve, to solve (a problem)

The Seven Simple Tenses		The Seven Compound Tenses	
Singular	Plural	Singular	Plural
1 presente de indicativo		8 perfecto de indicativo	
resuelvo	**resolvemos**	**he resuelto**	**hemos resuelto**
resuelves	**resolvéis**	**has resuelto**	**habéis resuelto**
resuelve	**resuelven**	**ha resuelto**	**han resuelto**
2 imperfecto de indicativo		9 pluscuamperfecto de indicativo	
resolvía	**resolvíamos**	**había resuelto**	**habíamos resuelto**
resolvías	**resolvíais**	**habías resuelto**	**habíais resuelto**
resolvía	**resolvían**	**había resuelto**	**habían resuelto**
3 pretérito		10 pretérito anterior	
resolví	**resolvimos**	**hube resuelto**	**hubimos resuelto**
resolviste	**resolvisteis**	**hubiste resuelto**	**hubisteis resuelto**
resolvió	**resolvieron**	**hubo resuelto**	**hubieron resuelto**
4 futuro		11 futuro perfecto	
resolveré	**resolveremos**	**habré resuelto**	**habremos resuelto**
resolverás	**resolveréis**	**habrás resuelto**	**habréis resuelto**
resolverá	**resolverán**	**habrá resuelto**	**habrán resuelto**
5 potencial simple		12 potencial compuesto	
resolvería	**resolveríamos**	**habría resuelto**	**habríamos resuelto**
resolverías	**resolveríais**	**habrías resuelto**	**habríais resuelto**
resolvería	**resolverían**	**habría resuelto**	**habrían resuelto**
6 presente de subjuntivo		13 perfecto de subjuntivo	
resuelva	**resolvamos**	**haya resuelto**	**hayamos resuelto**
resuelvas	**resolváis**	**hayas resuelto**	**hayáis resuelto**
resuelva	**resuelvan**	**haya resuelto**	**hayan resuelto**
7 imperfecto de subjuntivo		14 pluscuamperfecto de subjuntivo	
resolviera	**resolviéramos**	**hubiera resuelto**	**hubiéramos resuelto**
resolvieras	**resolvierais**	**hubieras resuelto**	**hubierais resuelto**
resolviera	**resolvieran**	**hubiera resuelto**	**hubieran resuelto**
OR		OR	
resolviese	**resolviésemos**	**hubiese resuelto**	**hubiésemos resuelto**
resolvieses	**resolvieseis**	**hubieses resuelto**	**hubieseis resuelto**
resolviese	**resolviesen**	**hubiese resuelto**	**hubiesen resuelto**

imperativo	
—	**resolvamos**
resuelve; no resuelvas	**resolved; no resolváis**
resuelva	**resuelvan**

Words and expressions related to this verb
resolver un conflicto   to settle a dispute
resolverse   to resolve (oneself)
resolverse a + inf.   to resolve – inf.
una resolución   resolution

una resolución definitiva   final decision
resolutivamente   resolutely
resoluto, resoluta   resolute
resuelto, resuelta   firm, resolute

responder
Gerundio **respondiendo** Part. pas. **respondido**

to answer, to reply, to respond

The Seven Simple Tenses		The Seven Compound Tenses	
Singular	Plural	Singular	Plural
1 presente de indicativo		**8 perfecto de indicativo**	
respondo	respondemos	he respondido	hemos respondido
respondes	respondéis	has respondido	habéis respondido
responde	responden	ha respondido	han respondido
2 imperfecto de indicativo		**9 pluscuamperfecto de indicativo**	
respondía	respondíamos	había respondido	habíamos respondido
respondías	respondíais	habías respondido	habíais respondido
respondía	respondían	había respondido	habían respondido
3 pretérito		**10 pretérito anterior**	
respondí	respondimos	hube respondido	hubimos respondido
respondiste	respondisteis	hubiste respondido	hubisteis respondido
respondió	respondieron	hubo respondido	hubieron respondido
4 futuro		**11 futuro perfecto**	
responderé	responderemos	habré respondido	habremos respondido
responderás	responderéis	habrás respondido	habréis respondido
responderá	responderán	habrá respondido	habrán respondido
5 potencial simple		**12 potencial compuesto**	
respondería	responderíamos	habría respondido	habríamos respondido
responderías	responderíais	habrías respondido	habríais respondido
respondería	responderían	habría respondido	habrían respondido
6 presente de subjuntivo		**13 perfecto de subjuntivo**	
responda	respondamos	haya respondido	hayamos respondido
respondas	respondáis	hayas respondido	hayáis respondido
responda	respondan	haya respondido	hayan respondido
7 imperfecto de subjuntivo		**14 pluscuamperfecto de subjuntivo**	
respondiera	respondiéramos	hubiera respondido	hubiéramos respondido
respondieras	respondierais	hubieras respondido	hubierais respondido
respondiera	respondieran	hubiera respondido	hubieran respondido
OR		OR	
respondiese	respondiésemos	hubiese respondido	hubiésemos respondido
respondieses	respondieseis	hubieses respondido	hubieseis respondido
respondiese	respondiesen	hubiese respondido	hubiesen respondido

imperativo

—	respondamos
responde; no respondas	responded; no respondáis
responda	respondan

Words and expressions related to this verb
una respuesta answer, reply, response
respondiente respondent
la correspondencia correspondence
correspondientemente correspondingly
responsivo, responsiva responsive

corresponder to correspond
corresponder a to reciprocate
responder a la pregunta to answer the
  question, to respond to the question

Enjoy verbs in Spanish proverbs on page 539.

to retire, to withdraw

The Seven Simple Tenses		The Seven Compound Tenses	
Singular	Plural	Singular	Plural
1 presente de indicativo		8 perfecto de indicativo	
retiro	**retiramos**	**he retirado**	**hemos retirado**
retiras	**retiráis**	**has retirado**	**habéis retirado**
retira	**retiran**	**ha retirado**	**han retirado**
2 imperfecto de indicativo		9 pluscuamperfecto de indicativo	
retiraba	**retirábamos**	**había retirado**	**habíamos retirado**
retirabas	**retirabais**	**habías retirado**	**habíais retirado**
retiraba	**retiraban**	**había retirado**	**habían retirado**
3 pretérito		10 pretérito anterior	
retiré	**retiramos**	**hube retirado**	**hubimos retirado**
retiraste	**retirasteis**	**hubiste retirado**	**hubisteis retirado**
retiró	**retiraron**	**hubo retirado**	**hubieron retirado**
4 futuro		11 futuro perfecto	
retiraré	**retiraremos**	**habré retirado**	**habremos retirado**
retirarás	**retiraréis**	**habrás retirado**	**habréis retirado**
retirará	**retirarán**	**habrá retirado**	**habrán retirado**
5 potencial simple		12 potencial compuesto	
retiraría	**retiraríamos**	**habría retirado**	**habríamos retirado**
retirarías	**retiraríais**	**habrías retirado**	**habríais retirado**
retiraría	**retirarían**	**habría retirado**	**habrían retirado**
6 presente de subjuntivo		13 perfecto de subjuntivo	
retire	**retiremos**	**haya retirado**	**hayamos retirado**
retires	**retiréis**	**hayas retirado**	**hayáis retirado**
retire	**retiren**	**haya retirado**	**hayan retirado**
7 imperfecto de subjuntivo		14 pluscuamperfecto de subjuntivo	
retirara	**retiráramos**	**hubiera retirado**	**hubiéramos retirado**
retiraras	**retirarais**	**hubieras retirado**	**hubierais retirado**
retirara	**retiraran**	**hubiera retirado**	**hubieran retirado**
OR		OR	
retirase	**retirásemos**	**hubiese retirado**	**hubiésemos retirado**
retirases	**retiraseis**	**hubieses retirado**	**hubieseis retirado**
retirase	**retirasen**	**hubiese retirado**	**hubiesen retirado**

imperativo

—	**retiremos**
retira; no retires	**retirad; no retiréis**
retire	**retiren**

Words and expressions related to this verb

retirarse   to retire
retirarse a dormir   to turn in (go to bed)
el retiro   retirement, withdrawal
El Retiro (El Buen Retiro)   name of a
   famous beautiful park in Madrid

la retirada   retirement, retreat
el retiramiento   retirement
pasar al retiro   to go into retirement
retirar dinero (del banco)   to make a
   withdrawal (from the bank)

The subject pronouns are found on the page facing page 1.

415

to delay, to retard

The Seven Simple Tenses		The Seven Compound Tenses	
Singular	Plural	Singular	Plural
1 presente de indicativo		8 perfecto de indicativo	
retraso	retrasamos	he retrasado	hemos retrasado
retrasas	retrasáis	has retrasado	habéis retrasado
retrasa	retrasan	ha retrasado	han retrasado
2 imperfecto de indicativo		9 pluscuamperfecto de indicativo	
retrasaba	retrasábamos	había retrasado	habíamos retrasado
retrasabas	retrasabais	habías retrasado	habíais retrasado
retrasaba	retrasaban	había retrasado	habían retrasado
3 pretérito		10 pretérito anterior	
retrasé	retrasamos	hube retrasado	hubimos retrasado
retrasaste	retrasasteis	hubiste retrasado	hubisteis retrasado
retrasó	retrasaron	hubo retrasado	hubieron retrasado
4 futuro		11 futuro perfecto	
retrasaré	retrasaremos	habré retrasado	habremos retrasado
retrasarás	retrasaréis	habrás retrasado	habréis retrasado
retrasará	retrasarán	habrá retrasado	habrán retrasado
5 potencial simple		12 potencial compuesto	
retrasaría	retrasaríamos	habría retrasado	habríamos retrasado
retrasarías	retrasaríais	habrías retrasado	habríais retrasado
retrasaría	retrasarían	habría retrasado	habrían retrasado
6 presente de subjuntivo		13 perfecto de subjuntivo	
retrase	retrasemos	haya retrasado	hayamos retrasado
retrases	retraséis	hayas retrasado	hayáis retrasado
retrase	retrasen	haya retrasado	hayan retrasado
7 imperfecto de subjuntivo		14 pluscuamperfecto de subjuntivo	
retrasara	retrasáramos	hubiera retrasado	hubiéramos retrasado
retrasaras	retrasarais	hubieras retrasado	hubierais retrasado
retrasara	retrasaran	hubiera retrasado	hubieran retrasado
OR		OR	
retrasase	retrasásemos	hubiese retrasado	hubiésemos retrasado
retrasases	retrasaseis	hubieses retrasado	hubieseis retrasado
retrasase	retrasasen	hubiese retrasado	hubiesen retrasado

imperativo	
—	retrasemos
retrasa; no retrases	retrasad; no retraséis
retrase	retrasen

Words and expressions related to this verb
retrasarse en + inf.   to be slow in, to be late + pres. part.
el retraso   delay, lag, slowness
con retraso   late (behind time)
atrasar   to be slow, slow down (watch, clock); **el atraso**   delay, tardiness; **en atraso**   in arrears
atrás   backward, back; **atrás de**   behind, back of; **días atrás**   days ago; **hacia atrás** backwards; **quedarse atrás**   to lag behind

to assemble, to get together, to meet, to gather

The Seven Simple Tenses		The Seven Compound Tenses	
Singular	Plural	Singular	Plural
1 presente de indicativo		8 perfecto de indicativo	
me reúno	**nos reunimos**	**me he reunido**	**nos hemos reunido**
te reúnes	**os reunís**	**te has reunido**	**os habéis reunido**
se reúne	**se reúnen**	**se ha reunido**	**se han reunido**
2 imperfecto de indicativo		9 pluscuamperfecto de indicativo	
me reunía	**nos reuníamos**	**me había reunido**	**nos habíamos reunido**
te reunías	**os reuníais**	**te habías reunido**	**os habíais reunido**
se reunía	**se reunían**	**se había reunido**	**se habían reunido**
3 pretérito		10 pretérito anterior	
me reuní	**nos reunimos**	**me hube reunido**	**nos hubimos reunido**
te reuniste	**os reunisteis**	**te hubiste reunido**	**os hubisteis reunido**
se reunió	**se reunieron**	**se hubo reunido**	**se hubieron reunido**
4 futuro		11 futuro perfecto	
me reuniré	**nos reuniremos**	**me habré reunido**	**nos habremos reunido**
te reunirás	**os reuniréis**	**te habrás reunido**	**os habréis reunido**
se reunirá	**se reunirán**	**se habrá reunido**	**se habrán reunido**
5 potencial simple		12 potencial compuesto	
me reuniría	**nos reuniríamos**	**me habría reunido**	**nos habríamos reunido**
te reunirías	**os reuniríais**	**te habrías reunido**	**os habríais reunido**
se reuniría	**se reunirían**	**se habría reunido**	**se habrían reunido**
6 presente de subjuntivo		13 perfecto de subjuntivo	
me reúna	**nos reunamos**	**me haya reunido**	**nos hayamos reunido**
te reúnas	**os reunáis**	**te hayas reunido**	**os hayáis reunido**
se reúna	**se reúnan**	**se haya reunido**	**se hayan reunido**
7 imperfecto de subjuntivo		14 pluscuamperfecto de subjuntivo	
me reuniera	**nos reuniéramos**	**me hubiera reunido**	**nos hubiéramos reunido**
te reunieras	**os reunierais**	**te hubieras reunido**	**os hubierais reunido**
se reuniera	**se reunieran**	**se hubiera reunido**	**se hubieran reunido**
OR		OR	
me reuniese	**nos reuniésemos**	**me hubiese reunido**	**nos hubiésemos reunido**
te reunieses	**os reunieseis**	**te hubieses reunido**	**os hubieseis reunido**
se reuniese	**se reuniesen**	**se hubiese reunido**	**se hubiesen reunido**

	imperativo
—	**reunámonos**
reúnete; no te reúnas	**reuníos; no os reunáis**
reúnase	**reúnanse**

Words and expressions related to this verb
reunirse con   to meet with
la reunión   reunion, meeting, gathering
una reunión en masa   mass meeting

una reunión plenaria   full meeting
la libertad de reunión   free assemblage
una reunión extraordinaria   special meeting

For other words related to this verb, see **unir.**

revocar   Gerundio **revocando**   Part. pas. **revocado**

to revoke, to repeal

The Seven Simple Tenses		The Seven Compound Tenses	
Singular	Plural	Singular	Plural
1 presente de indicativo		**8 perfecto de indicativo**	
revoco	revocamos	he revocado	hemos revocado
revocas	revocáis	has revocado	habéis revocado
revoca	revocan	ha revocado	han revocado
2 imperfecto de indicativo		**9 pluscuamperfecto de indicativo**	
revocaba	revocábamos	había revocado	habíamos revocado
revocabas	revocabais	habías revocado	habíais revocado
revocaba	revocaban	había revocado	habían revocado
3 pretérito		**10 pretérito anterior**	
revoqué	revocamos	hube revocado	hubimos revocado
revocaste	revocasteis	hubiste revocado	hubisteis revocado
revocó	revocaron	hubo revocado	hubieron revocado
4 futuro		**11 futuro perfecto**	
revocaré	revocaremos	habré revocado	habremos revocado
revocarás	revocaréis	habrás revocado	habréis revocado
revocará	revocarán	habrá revocado	habrán revocado
5 potencial simple		**12 potencial compuesto**	
revocaría	revocaríamos	habría revocado	habríamos revocado
revocarías	revocaríais	habrías revocado	habríais revocado
revocaría	revocarían	habría revocado	habrían revocado
6 presente de subjuntivo		**13 perfecto de subjuntivo**	
revoque	revoquemos	haya revocado	hayamos revocado
revoques	revoquéis	hayas revocado	hayáis revocado
revoque	revoquen	haya revocado	hayan revocado
7 imperfecto de subjuntivo		**14 pluscuamperfecto de subjuntivo**	
revocara	revocáramos	hubiera revocado	hubiéramos revocado
revocaras	revocarais	hubieras revocado	hubierais revocado
revocara	revocaran	hubiera revocado	hubieran revocado
OR		OR	
revocase	revocásemos	hubiese revocado	hubiésemos revocado
revocases	revocaseis	hubieses revocado	hubieseis revocado
revocase	revocasen	hubiese revocado	hubiesen revocado

	imperativo
—	revoquemos
revoca; no revoques	revocad; no revoquéis
revoque	revoquen

Words and expressions related to this verb

la revocación revocation
revocable revocable, reversible
revocablemente revocably

irrevocabilidad irrevocability
irrevocable irrevocable, irreversible
irrevocablemente irrevocably

If you want to see a sample English verb fully conjugated in all the tenses, check out pages xviii and xix.

to revolve, to turn around, to turn over, to turn upside down

The Seven Simple Tenses		The Seven Compound Tenses	
Singular	Plural	Singular	Plural
1 presente de indicativo		8 perfecto de indicativo	
revuelvo	**revolvemos**	**he revuelto**	**hemos revuelto**
revuelves	**revolvéis**	**has revuelto**	**habéis revuelto**
revuelve	**revuelven**	**ha revuelto**	**han revuelto**
2 imperfecto de indicativo		9 pluscuamperfecto de indicativo	
revolvía	**revolvíamos**	**había revuelto**	**habíamos revuelto**
revolvías	**revolvíais**	**habías revuelto**	**habíais revuelto**
revolvía	**revolvían**	**había revuelto**	**habían revuelto**
3 pretérito		10 pretérito anterior	
revolví	**revolvimos**	**hube revuelto**	**hubimos revuelto**
revolviste	**revolvisteis**	**hubiste revuelto**	**hubisteis revuelto**
revolvió	**revolvieron**	**hubo revuelto**	**hubieron revuelto**
4 futuro		11 futuro perfecto	
revolveré	**revolveremos**	**habré revuelto**	**habremos revuelto**
revolverás	**revolveréis**	**habrás revuelto**	**habréis revuelto**
revolverá	**revolverán**	**habrá revuelto**	**habrán revuelto**
5 potencial simple		12 potencial compuesto	
revolvería	**revolveríamos**	**habría revuelto**	**habríamos revuelto**
revolverías	**revolveríais**	**habrías revuelto**	**habríais revuelto**
revolvería	**revolverían**	**habría revuelto**	**habrían revuelto**
6 presente de subjuntivo		13 perfecto de subjuntivo	
revuelva	**revolvamos**	**haya revuelto**	**hayamos revuelto**
revuelvas	**revolváis**	**hayas revuelto**	**hayáis revuelto**
revuelva	**revuelvan**	**haya revuelto**	**hayan revuelto**
7 imperfecto de subjuntivo		14 pluscuamperfecto de subjuntivo	
revolviera	**revolviéramos**	**hubiera revuelto**	**hubiéramos revuelto**
revolvieras	**revolvierais**	**hubieras revuelto**	**hubierais revuelto**
revolviera	**revolvieran**	**hubiera revuelto**	**hubieran revuelto**
OR		OR	
revolviese	**revolviésemos**	**hubiese revuelto**	**hubiésemos revuelto**
revolvieses	**revolvieseis**	**hubieses revuelto**	**hubieseis revuelto**
revolviese	**revolviesen**	**hubiese revuelto**	**hubiesen revuelto**

imperativo

—	**revolvamos**
revuelve; no revuelvas	**revolved; no revolváis**
revuelva	**revuelvan**

Words and expressions related to this verb
huevos revueltos   scrambled eggs
la revolución   revolution

el revolvimiento   revolving, revolution
revueltamente   confusedly

For other words and expressions related to this verb, see **devolver** and **volver.**

Try a few of the verb tests on pages 619–665 with answers explained.

robar Gerundio **robando** Part. pas. **robado**

to rob, to steal

The Seven Simple Tenses		The Seven Compound Tenses	
Singular	Plural	Singular	Plural
1 presente de indicativo		8 perfecto de indicativo	
robo	robamos	he robado	hemos robado
robas	robáis	has robado	habéis robado
roba	roban	ha robado	han robado
2 imperfecto de indicativo		9 pluscuamperfecto de indicativo	
robaba	robábamos	había robado	habíamos robado
robabas	robabais	habías robado	habíais robado
robaba	robaban	había robado	habían robado
3 pretérito		10 pretérito anterior	
robé	robamos	hube robado	hubimos robado
robaste	robasteis	hubiste robado	hubisteis robado
robó	robaron	hubo robado	hubieron robado
4 futuro		11 futuro perfecto	
robaré	robaremos	habré robado	habremos robado
robarás	robaréis	habrás robado	habréis robado
robará	robarán	habrá robado	habrán robado
5 potencial simple		12 potencial compuesto	
robaría	robaríamos	habría robado	habríamos robado
robarías	robaríais	habrías robado	habríais robado
robaría	robarían	habría robado	habrían robado
6 presente de subjuntivo		13 perfecto de subjuntivo	
robe	robemos	haya robado	hayamos robado
robes	robéis	hayas robado	hayáis robado
robe	roben	haya robado	hayan robado
7 imperfecto de subjuntivo		14 pluscuamperfecto de subjuntivo	
robara	robáramos	hubiera robado	hubiéramos robado
robaras	robarais	hubieras robado	hubierais robado
robara	robaran	hubiera robado	hubieran robado
OR		OR	
robase	robásemos	hubiese robado	hubiésemos robado
robases	robaseis	hubieses robado	hubieseis robado
robase	robasen	hubiese robado	hubiesen robado

imperativo

—	robemos
roba; no robes	robad; no robéis
robe	roben

Words and expressions related to this verb

robarle algo a alguien   to rob somebody of something   **un antirrobo**   theft protection device,
robado, robada   stolen   burglar alarm
un robador, una robadora   robber, thief   **el robo**   robbery, theft

> If you want to see a sample English verb fully conjugated in all the tenses,
> check out pages xviii and xix.

to supplicate, to ask, to ask for, to request, to beg, to pray

The Seven Simple Tenses		The Seven Compound Tenses	
Singular	Plural	Singular	Plural
1 presente de indicativo		8 perfecto de indicativo	
ruego	**rogamos**	**he rogado**	**hemos rogado**
ruegas	**rogáis**	**has rogado**	**habéis rogado**
ruega	**ruegan**	**ha rogado**	**han rogado**
2 imperfecto de indicativo		9 pluscuamperfecto de indicativo	
rogaba	**rogábamos**	**había rogado**	**habíamos rogado**
rogabas	**rogabais**	**habías rogado**	**habíais rogado**
rogaba	**rogaban**	**había rogado**	**habían rogado**
3 pretérito		10 pretérito anterior	
rogué	**rogamos**	**hube rogado**	**hubimos rogado**
rogaste	**rogasteis**	**hubiste rogado**	**hubisteis rogado**
rogó	**rogaron**	**hubo rogado**	**hubieron rogado**
4 futuro		11 futuro perfecto	
rogaré	**rogaremos**	**habré rogado**	**habremos rogado**
rogarás	**rogaréis**	**habrás rogado**	**habréis rogado**
rogará	**rogarán**	**habrá rogado**	**habrán rogado**
5 potencial simple		12 potencial compuesto	
rogaría	**rogaríamos**	**habría rogado**	**habríamos rogado**
rogarías	**rogaríais**	**habrías rogado**	**habríais rogado**
rogaría	**rogarían**	**habría rogado**	**habrían rogado**
6 presente de subjuntivo		13 perfecto de subjuntivo	
ruegue	**roguemos**	**haya rogado**	**hayamos rogado**
ruegues	**roguéis**	**hayas rogado**	**hayáis rogado**
ruegue	**rueguen**	**haya rogado**	**hayan rogado**
7 imperfecto de subjuntivo		14 pluscuamperfecto de subjuntivo	
rogara	**rogáramos**	**hubiera rogado**	**hubiéramos rogado**
rogaras	**rogarais**	**hubieras rogado**	**hubierais rogado**
rogara	**rogaran**	**hubiera rogado**	**hubieran rogado**
OR		OR	
rogase	**rogásemos**	**hubiese rogado**	**hubiésemos rogado**
rogases	**rogaseis**	**hubieses rogado**	**hubieseis rogado**
rogase	**rogasen**	**hubiese rogado**	**hubiesen rogado**

imperativo

—	**roguemos**
ruega; no ruegues	**rogad; no roguéis**
ruegue	**rueguen**

Sentences using this verb and words related to it
A Dios rogando y con el mazo dando.   Put your faith in God and keep your powder dry.
rogador, rogadora   suppliant, requester
rogativo, rogativa   supplicatory
rogar por   to plead for

derogar   to abolish, to repeal
una prerrogativa   prerogative

The subject pronouns are found on the page facing page 1.

romper   Gerundio **rompiendo**   Part. pas. **roto**

to break, to shatter, to tear

The Seven Simple Tenses		The Seven Compound Tenses	
Singular	Plural	Singular	Plural
1 presente de indicativo		8 perfecto de indicativo	
rompo	**rompemos**	**he roto**	**hemos roto**
rompes	**rompéis**	**has roto**	**habéis roto**
rompe	**rompen**	**ha roto**	**han roto**
2 imperfecto de indicativo		9 pluscuamperfecto de indicativo	
rompía	**rompíamos**	**había roto**	**habíamos roto**
rompías	**rompíais**	**habías roto**	**habíais roto**
rompía	**rompían**	**había roto**	**habían roto**
3 pretérito		10 pretérito anterior	
rompí	**rompimos**	**hube roto**	**hubimos roto**
rompiste	**rompisteis**	**hubiste roto**	**hubisteis roto**
rompió	**rompieron**	**hubo roto**	**hubieron roto**
4 futuro		11 futuro perfecto	
romperé	**romperemos**	**habré roto**	**habremos roto**
romperás	**romperéis**	**habrás roto**	**habréis roto**
romperá	**romperán**	**habrá roto**	**habrán roto**
5 potencial simple		12 potencial compuesto	
rompería	**romperíamos**	**habría roto**	**habríamos roto**
romperías	**romperíais**	**habrías roto**	**habríais roto**
rompería	**romperían**	**habría roto**	**habrían roto**
6 presente de subjuntivo		13 perfecto de subjuntivo	
rompa	**rompamos**	**haya roto**	**hayamos roto**
rompas	**rompáis**	**hayas roto**	**hayáis roto**
rompa	**rompan**	**haya roto**	**hayan roto**
7 imperfecto de subjuntivo		14 pluscuamperfecto de subjuntivo	
rompiera	**rompiéramos**	**hubiera roto**	**hubiéramos roto**
rompieras	**rompierais**	**hubieras roto**	**hubierais roto**
rompiera	**rompieran**	**hubiera roto**	**hubieran roto**
OR		OR	
rompiese	**rompiésemos**	**hubiese roto**	**hubiésemos roto**
rompieses	**rompieseis**	**hubieses roto**	**hubieseis roto**
rompiese	**rompiesen**	**hubiese roto**	**hubiesen roto**

imperativo

—	**rompamos**
rompe; no rompas	**romped; no rompáis**
rompa	**rompan**

Words and expressions related to this verb
un rompenueces nutcracker
una rompedura breakage, rupture
romperse la cabeza to rack one's brains
romper con to break relations with
romper a + inf. to start suddenly + inf.

romper a llorar to break into tears
romper las relaciones to break off relations,
  an engagement
romper el hielo to break the ice
romperse la pierna (el brazo) to break a leg
  (an arm) [on oneself]
roto, rota broken

to know, to know how

The Seven Simple Tenses		The Seven Compound Tenses	
Singular	Plural	Singular	Plural
1 presente de indicativo		8 perfecto de indicativo	
sé	sabemos	he sabido	hemos sabido
sabes	sabéis	has sabido	habéis sabido
sabe	saben	ha sabido	han sabido
2 imperfecto de indicativo		9 pluscuamperfecto de indicativo	
sabía	sabíamos	había sabido	habíamos sabido
sabías	sabíais	habías sabido	habíais sabido
sabía	sabían	había sabido	habían sabido
3 pretérito		10 pretérito anterior	
supe	supimos	hube sabido	hubimos sabido
supiste	supisteis	hubiste sabido	hubisteis sabido
supo	supieron	hubo sabido	hubieron sabido
4 futuro		11 futuro perfecto	
sabré	sabremos	habré sabido	habremos sabido
sabrás	sabréis	habrás sabido	habréis sabido
sabrá	sabrán	habrá sabido	habrán sabido
5 potencial simple		12 potencial compuesto	
sabría	sabríamos	habría sabido	habríamos sabido
sabrías	sabríais	habrías sabido	habríais sabido
sabría	sabrían	habría sabido	habrían sabido
6 presente de subjuntivo		13 perfecto de subjuntivo	
sepa	sepamos	haya sabido	hayamos sabido
sepas	sepáis	hayas sabido	hayáis sabido
sepa	sepan	haya sabido	hayan sabido
7 imperfecto de subjuntivo		14 pluscuamperfecto de subjuntivo	
supiera	supiéramos	hubiera sabido	hubiéramos sabido
supieras	supierais	hubieras sabido	hubierais sabido
supiera	supieran	hubiera sabido	hubieran sabido
OR		OR	
supiese	supiésemos	hubiese sabido	hubiésemos sabido
supieses	supieseis	hubieses sabido	hubieseis sabido
supiese	supiesen	hubiese sabido	hubiesen sabido

imperativo

—	sepamos
sabe; no sepas	sabed; no sepáis
sepa	sepan

Words and expressions related to this verb
sabio, sabia wise, learned
un sabidillo, una sabidilla a know-it-all
  individual
la sabiduría knowledge, learning, wisdom
¿Sabe Ud. nadar? Do you know how to swim?

Sí, yo sé nadar. Yes, I know how to swim.
Que yo sepa . . . As far as I know . . .
¡Quién sabe! Who knows! Perhaps! Maybe!
la señorita Sabelotodo Miss Know-It-All
el señor Sabelotodo Mr. Know-It-All

See also **saber** on page 534.

The subject pronouns are found on the page facing page 1.

423

to take out, to get

The Seven Simple Tenses		The Seven Compound Tenses	
Singular	Plural	Singular	Plural
1 presente de indicativo		8 perfecto de indicativo	
saco	sacamos	he sacado	hemos sacado
sacas	sacáis	has sacado	habéis sacado
saca	sacan	ha sacado	han sacado
2 imperfecto de indicativo		9 pluscuamperfecto de indicativo	
sacaba	sacábamos	había sacado	habíamos sacado
sacabas	sacabais	habías sacado	habíais sacado
sacaba	sacaban	había sacado	habían sacado
3 pretérito		10 pretérito anterior	
saqué	sacamos	hube sacado	hubimos sacado
sacaste	sacasteis	hubiste sacado	hubisteis sacado
sacó	sacaron	hubo sacado	hubieron sacado
4 futuro		11 futuro perfecto	
sacaré	sacaremos	habré sacado	habremos sacado
sacarás	sacaréis	habrás sacado	habréis sacado
sacará	sacarán	habrá sacado	habrán sacado
5 potencial simple		12 potencial compuesto	
sacaría	sacaríamos	habría sacado	habríamos sacado
sacarías	sacaríais	habrías sacado	habríais sacado
sacaría	sacarían	habría sacado	habrían sacado
6 presente de subjuntivo		13 perfecto de subjuntivo	
saque	saquemos	haya sacado	hayamos sacado
saques	saquéis	hayas sacado	hayáis sacado
saque	saquen	haya sacado	hayan sacado
7 imperfecto de subjuntivo		14 pluscuamperfecto de subjuntivo	
sacara	sacáramos	hubiera sacado	hubiéramos sacado
sacaras	sacarais	hubieras sacado	hubierais sacado
sacara	sacaran	hubiera sacado	hubieran sacado
OR		OR	
sacase	sacásemos	hubiese sacado	hubiésemos sacado
sacases	sacaseis	hubieses sacado	hubieseis sacado
sacase	sacasen	hubiese sacado	hubiesen sacado

imperativo

—	saquemos
saca; no saques	sacad; no saquéis
saque	saquen

Words and expressions related to this verb
sacar agua   to draw water
sacar a paseo   to take out for a walk; ensacar   to put in a bag, to bag
un saco   bag, sack; saco de noche   overnight bag; un saco de dormir   sleeping bag
un sacapuntas   pencil sharpener
una saca   withdrawal; un sacacorchos   corkscrew

to shake, to jerk, to jolt

The Seven Simple Tenses		The Seven Compound Tenses	
Singular	Plural	Singular	Plural
1 presente de indicativo		8 perfecto de indicativo	
sacudo	**sacudimos**	**he sacudido**	**hemos sacudido**
sacudes	**sacudís**	**has sacudido**	**habéis sacudido**
sacude	**sacuden**	**ha sacudido**	**han sacudido**
2 imperfecto de indicativo		9 pluscuamperfecto de indicativo	
sacudía	**sacudíamos**	**había sacudido**	**habíamos sacudido**
sacudías	**sacudíais**	**habías sacudido**	**habíais sacudido**
sacudía	**sacudían**	**había sacudido**	**habían sacudido**
3 pretérito		10 pretérito anterior	
sacudí	**sacudimos**	**hube sacudido**	**hubimos sacudido**
sacudiste	**sacudisteis**	**hubiste sacudido**	**hubisteis sacudido**
sacudió	**sacudieron**	**hubo sacudido**	**hubieron sacudido**
4 futuro		11 futuro perfecto	
sacudiré	**sacudiremos**	**habré sacudido**	**habremos sacudido**
sacudirás	**sacudiréis**	**habrás sacudido**	**habréis sacudido**
sacudirá	**sacudirán**	**habrá sacudido**	**habrán sacudido**
5 potencial simple		12 potencial compuesto	
sacudiría	**sacudiríamos**	**habría sacudido**	**habríamos sacudido**
sacudirías	**sacudiríais**	**habrías sacudido**	**habríais sacudido**
sacudiría	**sacudirían**	**habría sacudido**	**habrían sacudido**
6 presente de subjuntivo		13 perfecto de subjuntivo	
sacuda	**sacudamos**	**haya sacudido**	**hayamos sacudido**
sacudas	**sacudáis**	**hayas sacudido**	**hayáis sacudido**
sacuda	**sacudan**	**haya sacudido**	**hayan sacudido**
7 imperfecto de subjuntivo		14 pluscuamperfecto de subjuntivo	
sacudiera	**sacudiéramos**	**hubiera sacudido**	**hubiéramos sacudido**
sacudieras	**sacudierais**	**hubieras sacudido**	**hubierais sacudido**
sacudiera	**sacudieran**	**hubiera sacudido**	**hubieran sacudido**
OR		OR	
sacudiese	**sacudiésemos**	**hubiese sacudido**	**hubiésemos sacudido**
sacudieses	**sacudieseis**	**hubieses sacudido**	**hubieseis sacudido**
sacudiese	**sacudiesen**	**hubiese sacudido**	**hubiesen sacudido**

imperativo

—	**sacudamos**
sacude; no sacudas	**sacudid; no sacudáis**
sacuda	**sacudan**

Words and expressions related to this verb
un sacudimiento   shaking, jolt, jerk
un sacudión   violent jolt
una sacudida   jerk, jolt, shake

sacudir el yugo   to shake off the yoke (to become independent)
a sacudidas   in jerks

Learn more verbs in 30 practical situations for tourists on pages 564–594.

to go out, to leave

The Seven Simple Tenses		The Seven Compound Tenses	
Singular	Plural	Singular	Plural
1 presente de indicativo		**8 perfecto de indicativo**	
salgo	salimos	he salido	hemos salido
sales	salís	has salido	habéis salido
sale	salen	ha salido	han salido
2 imperfecto de indicativo		**9 pluscuamperfecto de indicativo**	
salía	salíamos	había salido	habíamos salido
salías	salíais	habías salido	habíais salido
salía	salían	había salido	habían salido
3 pretérito		**10 pretérito anterior**	
salí	salimos	hube salido	hubimos salido
saliste	salisteis	hubiste salido	hubisteis salido
salió	salieron	hubo salido	hubieron salido
4 futuro		**11 futuro perfecto**	
saldré	saldremos	habré salido	habremos salido
saldrás	saldréis	habrás salido	habréis salido
saldrá	saldrán	habrá salido	habrán salido
5 potencial simple		**12 potencial compuesto**	
saldría	saldríamos	habría salido	habríamos salido
saldrías	saldríais	habrías salido	habríais salido
saldría	saldrían	habría salido	habrían salido
6 presente de subjuntivo		**13 perfecto de subjuntivo**	
salga	salgamos	haya salido	hayamos salido
salgas	salgáis	hayas salido	hayáis salido
salga	salgan	haya salido	hayan salido
7 imperfecto de subjuntivo		**14 pluscuamperfecto de subjuntivo**	
saliera	saliéramos	hubiera salido	hubiéramos salido
salieras	salierais	hubieras salido	hubierais salido
saliera	salieran	hubiera salido	hubieran salido
OR		OR	
saliese	saliésemos	hubiese salido	hubiésemos salido
salieses	salieseis	hubieses salido	hubieseis salido
saliese	saliesen	hubiese salido	hubiesen salido

imperativo	
—	salgamos
sal; no salgas	salid; no salgáis
salga	salgan

Words and expressions related to this verb
la salida   exit
sin salida   no exit, dead-end street
salir de compras   to go out shopping
salir mal   to go wrong, to do badly

saliente   salient, prominent
salir al encuentro de   to go to meet
salir de   to leave from, to get out of
salga lo que salga   come what may

See also **salir** on pages 526 and 527.

If you want an explanation of meanings and
uses of Spanish and English verb tenses
and moods, see pages xx–xxxix.

to jump, to leap, to hop, to spring

The Seven Simple Tenses		The Seven Compound Tenses	
Singular	Plural	Singular	Plural
1 presente de indicativo		8 perfecto de indicativo	
salto	saltamos	he saltado	hemos saltado
saltas	saltáis	has saltado	habéis saltado
salta	saltan	ha saltado	han saltado
2 imperfecto de indicativo		9 pluscuamperfecto de indicativo	
saltaba	saltábamos	había saltado	habíamos saltado
saltabas	saltabais	habías saltado	habíais saltado
saltaba	saltaban	había saltado	habían saltado
3 pretérito		10 pretérito anterior	
salté	saltamos	hube saltado	hubimos saltado
saltaste	saltasteis	hubiste saltado	hubisteis saltado
saltó	saltaron	hubo saltado	hubieron saltado
4 futuro		11 futuro perfecto	
saltaré	saltaremos	habré saltado	habremos saltado
saltarás	saltaréis	habrás saltado	habréis saltado
saltará	saltarán	habrá saltado	habrán saltado
5 potencial simple		12 potencial compuesto	
saltaría	saltaríamos	habría saltado	habríamos saltado
saltarías	saltaríais	habrías saltado	habríais saltado
saltaría	saltarían	habría saltado	habrían saltado
6 presente de subjuntivo		13 perfecto de subjuntivo	
salte	saltemos	haya saltado	hayamos saltado
saltes	saltéis	hayas saltado	hayáis saltado
salte	salten	haya saltado	hayan saltado
7 imperfecto de subjuntivo		14 pluscuamperfecto de subjuntivo	
saltara	saltáramos	hubiera saltado	hubiéramos saltado
saltaras	saltarais	hubieras saltado	hubierais saltado
saltara	saltaran	hubiera saltado	hubieran saltado
OR		OR	
saltase	saltásemos	hubiese saltado	hubiésemos saltado
saltases	saltaseis	hubieses saltado	hubieseis saltado
saltase	saltasen	hubiese saltado	hubiesen saltado

imperativo	
—	saltemos
salta; no saltes	saltad; no saltéis
salte	salten

Words and expressions related to this verb

hacer saltar la banca   to break the bank
  (in gambling)
saltar de gozo   to jump with joy
saltar por   to jump over
el saltimbanqui   acrobat

un salto   jump, leap
un salto de esquí   ski jump
un salto de cisne   swan dive
un salto mortal   somersault
saltear   to sauté

The subject pronouns are found on the page facing page 1.

427

saludar

to greet, to salute

The Seven Simple Tenses		The Seven Compound Tenses	
Singular	Plural	Singular	Plural
1 presente de indicativo		**8 perfecto de indicativo**	
saludo	saludamos	he saludado	hemos saludado
saludas	saludáis	has saludado	habéis saludado
saluda	saludan	ha saludado	han saludado
2 imperfecto de indicativo		**9 pluscuamperfecto de indicativo**	
saludaba	saludábamos	había saludado	habíamos saludado
saludabas	saludabais	habías saludado	habíais saludado
saludaba	saludaban	había saludado	habían saludado
3 pretérito		**10 pretérito anterior**	
saludé	saludamos	hube saludado	hubimos saludado
saludaste	saludasteis	hubiste saludado	hubisteis saludado
saludó	saludaron	hubo saludado	hubieron saludado
4 futuro		**11 futuro perfecto**	
saludaré	saludaremos	habré saludado	habremos saludado
saludarás	saludaréis	habrás saludado	habréis saludado
saludará	saludarán	habrá saludado	habrán saludado
5 potencial simple		**12 potencial compuesto**	
saludaría	saludaríamos	habría saludado	habríamos saludado
saludarías	saludaríais	habrías saludado	habríais saludado
saludaría	saludarían	habría saludado	habrían saludado
6 presente de subjuntivo		**13 perfecto de subjuntivo**	
salude	saludemos	haya saludado	hayamos saludado
saludes	saludéis	hayas saludado	hayáis saludado
salude	saluden	haya saludado	hayan saludado
7 imperfecto de subjuntivo		**14 pluscuamperfecto de subjuntivo**	
saludara	saludáramos	hubiera saludado	hubiéramos saludado
saludaras	saludarais	hubieras saludado	hubierais saludado
saludara	saludaran	hubiera saludado	hubieran saludado
OR		OR	
saludase	saludásemos	hubiese saludado	hubiésemos saludado
saludases	saludaseis	hubieses saludado	hubieseis saludado
saludase	saludasen	hubiese saludado	hubiesen saludado

imperativo

—	saludemos
saluda; no saludes	saludad; no saludéis
salude	saluden

Words and expressions related to this verb
la salutación greeting, salutation
el saludo salutation, greeting, salute
el saludo final closing (of a letter)
saludarse uno a otro to greet each other

la salud health; **¡A su salud!** To your health!
estar bien de salud to be in good health
estar mal de salud to be in bad health
¡Salud! Bless you! (to someone who sneezes)

Consult the back pages for the section on verbs with prepositions.

The Seven Simple Tenses		The Seven Compound Tenses	
Singular	Plural	Singular	Plural
1 presente de indicativo		**8 perfecto de indicativo**	
satisfago	satisfacemos	he satisfecho	hemos satisfecho
satisfaces	satisfacéis	has satisfecho	habéis satisfecho
satisface	satisfacen	ha satisfecho	han satisfecho
2 imperfecto de indicativo		**9 pluscuamperfecto de indicativo**	
satisfacía	satisfacíamos	había satisfecho	habíamos satisfecho
satisfacías	satisfacíais	habías satisfecho	habíais satisfecho
satisfacía	satisfacían	había satisfecho	habían satisfecho
3 pretérito		**10 pretérito anterior**	
satisfice	satisficimos	hube satisfecho	hubimos satisfecho
satisficiste	satisficisteis	hubiste satisfecho	hubisteis satisfecho
satisfizo	satisficieron	hubo satisfecho	hubieron satisfecho
4 futuro		**11 futuro perfecto**	
satisfaré	satisfaremos	habré satisfecho	habremos satisfecho
satisfarás	satisfaréis	habrás satisfecho	habréis satisfecho
satisfará	satisfarán	habrá satisfecho	habrán satisfecho
5 potencial simple		**12 potencial compuesto**	
satisfaría	satisfaríamos	habría satisfecho	habríamos satisfecho
satisfarías	satisfaríais	habrías satisfecho	habríais satisfecho
satisfaría	satisfarían	habría satisfecho	habrían satisfecho
6 presente de subjuntivo		**13 perfecto de subjuntivo**	
satisfaga	satisfagamos	haya satisfecho	hayamos satisfecho
satisfagas	satisfagáis	hayas satisfecho	hayáis satisfecho
satisfaga	satisfagan	haya satisfecho	hayan satisfecho
7 imperfecto de subjuntivo		**14 pluscuamperfecto de subjuntivo**	
satisficiera	satisficiéramos	hubiera satisfecho	hubiéramos satisfecho
satisficieras	satisficierais	hubieras satisfecho	hubierais satisfecho
satisficiera	satisficieran	hubiera satisfecho	hubieran satisfecho
OR		OR	
satisficiese	satisficiésemos	hubiese satisfecho	hubiésemos satisfecho
satisficieses	satisficieseis	hubieses satisfecho	hubieseis satisfecho
satisficiese	satisficiesen	hubiese satisfecho	hubiesen satisfecho

imperativo

—	satisfagamos
satisfaz (satisface); no satisfagas	satisfaced; no satisfagáis
satisfaga	satisfagan

Words and expressions related to this verb

la satisfacción   satisfaction
a satisfacción   satisfactorily
a satisfacción de   to the satisfaction of
insatisfecho, insatisfecha   dissatisfied
insaciable   insatiable

satisfecho, satisfecha   satisfied
satisfactorio, satisfactoria   satisfactory
satisfaciente   satisfying
saciar   to satisfy, to satiate
la saciedad   satiety, satiation

The subject pronouns are found on the page facing page 1.

to dry, to wipe dry

The Seven Simple Tenses		The Seven Compound Tenses	
Singular	Plural	Singular	Plural
1 presente de indicativo		8 perfecto de indicativo	
seco	**secamos**	**he secado**	**hemos secado**
secas	**secáis**	**has secado**	**habéis secado**
seca	**secan**	**ha secado**	**han secado**
2 imperfecto de indicativo		9 pluscuamperfecto de indicativo	
secaba	**secábamos**	**había secado**	**habíamos secado**
secabas	**secabais**	**habías secado**	**habíais secado**
secaba	**secaban**	**había secado**	**habían secado**
3 pretérito		10 pretérito anterior	
sequé	**secamos**	**hube secado**	**hubimos secado**
secaste	**secasteis**	**hubiste secado**	**hubisteis secado**
secó	**secaron**	**hubo secado**	**hubieron secado**
4 futuro		11 futuro perfecto	
secaré	**secaremos**	**habré secado**	**habremos secado**
secarás	**secaréis**	**habrás secado**	**habréis secado**
secará	**secarán**	**habrá secado**	**habrán secado**
5 potencial simple		12 potencial compuesto	
secaría	**secaríamos**	**habría secado**	**habríamos secado**
secarías	**secaríais**	**habrías secado**	**habríais secado**
secaría	**secarían**	**habría secado**	**habrían secado**
6 presente de subjuntivo		13 perfecto de subjuntivo	
seque	**sequemos**	**haya secado**	**hayamos secado**
seques	**sequéis**	**hayas secado**	**hayáis secado**
seque	**sequen**	**haya secado**	**hayan secado**
7 imperfecto de subjuntivo		14 pluscuamperfecto de subjuntivo	
secara	**secáramos**	**hubiera secado**	**hubiéramos secado**
secaras	**secarais**	**hubieras secado**	**hubierais secado**
secara	**secaran**	**hubiera secado**	**hubieran secado**
OR		OR	
secase	**secásemos**	**hubiese secado**	**hubiésemos secado**
secases	**secaseis**	**hubieses secado**	**hubieseis secado**
secase	**secasen**	**hubiese secado**	**hubiesen secado**

imperativo	
—	**sequemos**
seca; no seques	**secad; no sequéis**
seque	**sequen**

Words and expressions related to this verb

seco, seca dry, dried up   **limpiar en seco** to dry-clean
la seca drought   **en seco** high and dry
secado al sol sun dried   **¡Seco y volteado!** Bottoms up!

For other words and expressions related to this verb, see **secarse.**

Use the EE-zee guide to Spanish pronunciation on pages 562 and 563.

The Seven Simple Tenses		The Seven Compound Tenses	
Singular	Plural	Singular	Plural

1   presente de indicativo

me seco	nos secamos
te secas	os secáis
se seca	se secan

8   perfecto de indicativo

me he secado	nos hemos secado
te has secado	os habéis secado
se ha secado	se han secado

2   imperfecto de indicativo

me secaba	nos secábamos
te secabas	os secabais
se secaba	se secaban

9   pluscuamperfecto de indicativo

me había secado	nos habíamos secado
te habías secado	os habíais secado
se había secado	se habían secado

3   pretérito

me sequé	nos secamos
te secaste	os secasteis
se secó	se secaron

10   pretérito anterior

me hube secado	nos hubimos secado
te hubiste secado	os hubisteis secado
se hubo secado	se hubieron secado

4   futuro

me secaré	nos secaremos
te secarás	os secaréis
se secará	se secarán

11   futuro perfecto

me habré secado	nos habremos secado
te habrás secado	os habréis secado
se habrá secado	se habrán secado

5   potencial simple

me secaría	nos secaríamos
te secarías	os secaríais
se secaría	se secarían

12   potencial compuesto

me habría secado	nos habríamos secado
te habrías secado	os habríais secado
se habría secado	se habrían secado

6   presente de subjuntivo

me seque	nos sequemos
te seques	os sequéis
se seque	se sequen

13   perfecto de subjuntivo

me haya secado	nos hayamos secado
te hayas secado	os hayáis secado
se haya secado	se hayan secado

7   imperfecto de subjuntivo

me secara	nos secáramos
te secaras	os secarais
se secara	se secaran
OR	
me secase	nos secásemos
te secases	os secaseis
se secase	se secasen

14   pluscuamperfecto de subjuntivo

me hubiera secado	nos hubiéramos secado
te hubieras secado	os hubierais secado
se hubiera secado	se hubieran secado
OR	
me hubiese secado	nos hubiésemos secado
te hubieses secado	os hubieseis secado
se hubiese secado	se hubiesen secado

imperativo

—	sequémonos
sécate; no te seques	secaos; no os sequéis
séquese	séquense

Words and expressions related to this verb
la secadora   dryer
secado, secada   dried

a secas   plainly, simply
el vino seco   dry wine

For other words and expressions related to this verb, see **secar.**

Enjoy verbs in Spanish proverbs on page 539.

to follow, to pursue, to continue

The Seven Simple Tenses		The Seven Compound Tenses	
Singular	Plural	Singular	Plural
1 presente de indicativo		8 perfecto de indicativo	
sigo	**seguimos**	**he seguido**	**hemos seguido**
sigues	**seguís**	**has seguido**	**habéis seguido**
sigue	**siguen**	**ha seguido**	**han seguido**
2 imperfecto de indicativo		9 pluscuamperfecto de indicativo	
seguía	**seguíamos**	**había seguido**	**habíamos seguido**
seguías	**seguíais**	**habías seguido**	**habíais seguido**
seguía	**seguían**	**había seguido**	**habían seguido**
3 pretérito		10 pretérito anterior	
seguí	**seguimos**	**hube seguido**	**hubimos seguido**
seguiste	**seguisteis**	**hubiste seguido**	**hubisteis seguido**
siguió	**siguieron**	**hubo seguido**	**hubieron seguido**
4 futuro		11 futuro perfecto	
seguiré	**seguiremos**	**habré seguido**	**habremos seguido**
seguirás	**seguiréis**	**habrás seguido**	**habréis seguido**
seguirá	**seguirán**	**habrá seguido**	**habrán seguido**
5 potencial simple		12 potencial compuesto	
seguiría	**seguiríamos**	**habría seguido**	**habríamos seguido**
seguirías	**seguiríais**	**habrías seguido**	**habríais seguido**
seguiría	**seguirían**	**habría seguido**	**habrían seguido**
6 presente de subjuntivo		13 perfecto de subjuntivo	
siga	**sigamos**	**haya seguido**	**hayamos seguido**
sigas	**sigáis**	**hayas seguido**	**hayáis seguido**
siga	**sigan**	**haya seguido**	**hayan seguido**
7 imperfecto de subjuntivo		14 pluscuamperfecto de subjuntivo	
siguiera	**siguiéramos**	**hubiera seguido**	**hubiéramos seguido**
siguieras	**siguierais**	**hubieras seguido**	**hubierais seguido**
siguiera	**siguieran**	**hubiera seguido**	**hubieran seguido**
OR		OR	
siguiese	**siguiésemos**	**hubiese seguido**	**hubiésemos seguido**
siguieses	**siguieseis**	**hubieses seguido**	**hubieseis seguido**
siguiese	**siguiesen**	**hubiese seguido**	**hubiesen seguido**

imperativo	
—	**sigamos**
sigue; no sigas	**seguid; no sigáis**
siga	**sigan**

Words and expressions related to this verb

según   according to
al día siguiente   on the following day
las frases siguientes   the following sentences
seguir + pres. part.   to keep on + pres. part.;
   Siga leyendo   Keep on reading.
seguido, seguida   continuous

conseguir   to attain, to get, to obtain
proseguir   to continue, proceed
perseguir   to pursue
seguirle los pasos a uno   to keep one's eye
   on someone
un seguidor, una seguidora   follower

to signal, to indicate, to point out, to show

The Seven Simple Tenses		The Seven Compound Tenses	
Singular	Plural	Singular	Plural
1 presente de indicativo		8 perfecto de indicativo	
señalo	señalamos	he señalado	hemos señalado
señalas	señaláis	has señalado	habéis señalado
señala	señalan	ha señalado	han señalado
2 imperfecto de indicativo		9 pluscuamperfecto de indicativo	
señalaba	señalábamos	había señalado	habíamos señalado
señalabas	señalabais	habías señalado	habíais señalado
señalaba	señalaban	había señalado	habían señalado
3 pretérito		10 pretérito anterior	
señalé	señalamos	hube señalado	hubimos señalado
señalaste	señalasteis	hubiste señalado	hubisteis señalado
señaló	señalaron	hubo señalado	hubieron señalado
4 futuro		11 futuro perfecto	
señalaré	señalaremos	habré señalado	habremos señalado
señalarás	señalaréis	habrás señalado	habréis señalado
señalará	señalarán	habrá señalado	habrán señalado
5 potencial simple		12 potencial compuesto	
señalaría	señalaríamos	habría señalado	habríamos señalado
señalarías	señalaríais	habrías señalado	habríais señalado
señalaría	señalarían	habría señalado	habrían señalado
6 presente de subjuntivo		13 perfecto de subjuntivo	
señale	señalemos	haya señalado	hayamos señalado
señales	señaléis	hayas señalado	hayáis señalado
señale	señalen	haya señalado	hayan señalado
7 imperfecto de subjuntivo		14 pluscuamperfecto de subjuntivo	
señalara	señaláramos	hubiera señalado	hubiéramos señalado
señalaras	señalarais	hubieras señalado	hubierais señalado
señalara	señalaran	hubiera señalado	hubieran señalado
OR		OR	
señalase	señalásemos	hubiese señalado	hubiésemos señalado
señalases	señalaseis	hubieses señalado	hubieseis señalado
señalase	señalasen	hubiese señalado	hubiesen señalado

imperativo	
—	señalemos
señala; no señales	señalad; no señaléis
señale	señalen

Words and expressions related to this verb
señalar un día   to set a day
señalar una fecha   to set a date
señalar con el dedo   to point out, to
   indicate (with your finger)

una seña   mark, sign, signal
por señas   by signs
dar señas de   to show signs of
una señal   sign, mark; señal de parada   stop sign

Want to learn more idiomatic expressions that contain verbs? Check out pages 524–537.

to sit down

The Seven Simple Tenses		The Seven Compound Tenses	
Singular	Plural	Singular	Plural
1 presente de indicativo		8 perfecto de indicativo	
me siento	**nos sentamos**	**me he sentado**	**nos hemos sentado**
te sientas	**os sentáis**	**te has sentado**	**os habéis sentado**
se sienta	**se sientan**	**se ha sentado**	**se han sentado**
2 imperfecto de indicativo		9 pluscuamperfecto de indicativo	
me sentaba	**nos sentábamos**	**me había sentado**	**nos habíamos sentado**
te sentabas	**os sentabais**	**te habías sentado**	**os habíais sentado**
se sentaba	**se sentaban**	**se había sentado**	**se habían sentado**
3 pretérito		10 pretérito anterior	
me senté	**nos sentamos**	**me hube sentado**	**nos hubimos sentado**
te sentaste	**os sentasteis**	**te hubiste sentado**	**os hubisteis sentado**
se sentó	**se sentaron**	**se hubo sentado**	**se hubieron sentado**
4 futuro		11 futuro perfecto	
me sentaré	**nos sentaremos**	**me habré sentado**	**nos habremos sentado**
te sentarás	**os sentaréis**	**te habrás sentado**	**os habréis sentado**
se sentará	**se sentarán**	**se habrá sentado**	**se habrán sentado**
5 potencial simple		12 potencial compuesto	
me sentaría	**nos sentaríamos**	**me habría sentado**	**nos habríamos sentado**
te sentarías	**os sentaríais**	**te habrías sentado**	**os habríais sentado**
se sentaría	**se sentarían**	**se habría sentado**	**se habrían sentado**
6 presente de subjuntivo		13 perfecto de subjuntivo	
me siente	**nos sentemos**	**me haya sentado**	**nos hayamos sentado**
te sientes	**os sentéis**	**te hayas sentado**	**os hayáis sentado**
se siente	**se sienten**	**se haya sentado**	**se hayan sentado**
7 imperfecto de subjuntivo		14 pluscuamperfecto de subjuntivo	
me sentara	**nos sentáramos**	**me hubiera sentado**	**nos hubiéramos sentado**
te sentaras	**os sentarais**	**te hubieras sentado**	**os hubierais sentado**
se sentara	**se sentaran**	**se hubiera sentado**	**se hubieran sentado**
OR		OR	
me sentase	**nos sentásemos**	**me hubiese sentado**	**nos hubiésemos sentado**
te sentases	**os sentaseis**	**te hubieses sentado**	**os hubieseis sentado**
se sentase	**se sentasen**	**se hubiese sentado**	**se hubiesen sentado**

imperativo	
—	**sentémonos; no nos sentemos**
siéntate; no te sientes	**sentaos; no os sentéis**
siéntese; no se siente	**siéntense; no se sienten**

Words and expressions related to this verb
un asiento   a seat
sentado, sentada   seated
¡Siéntese Ud.!   Sit down!

sentar, asentar   to seat
una sentada   a sitting; **de una sentada**
  in one sitting
¡Vamos a sentarnos!   Let's sit down!

Can't recognize an irregular verb form? Check out pages 519–523.

Gerundio **sintiendo**   Part. pas. **sentido**   **sentir**

to feel sorry, to regret, to feel

The Seven Simple Tenses | The Seven Compound Tenses

Singular	Plural
1 presente de indicativo	
siento	sentimos
sientes	sentís
siente	sienten
2 imperfecto de indicativo	
sentía	sentíamos
sentías	sentíais
sentía	sentían
3 pretérito	
sentí	sentimos
sentiste	sentisteis
sintió	sintieron
4 futuro	
sentiré	sentiremos
sentirás	sentiréis
sentirá	sentirán
5 potencial simple	
sentiría	sentiríamos
sentirías	sentiríais
sentiría	sentirían
6 presente de subjuntivo	
sienta	sintamos
sientas	sintáis
sienta	sientan
7 imperfecto de subjuntivo	
sintiera	sintiéramos
sintieras	sintierais
sintiera	sintieran
OR	
sintiese	sintiésemos
sintieses	sintieseis
sintiese	sintiesen

Singular	Plural
8 perfecto de indicativo	
he sentido	hemos sentido
has sentido	habéis sentido
ha sentido	han sentido
9 pluscuamperfecto de indicativo	
había sentido	habíamos sentido
habías sentido	habíais sentido
había sentido	habían sentido
10 pretérito anterior	
hube sentido	hubimos sentido
hubiste sentido	hubisteis sentido
hubo sentido	hubieron sentido
11 futuro perfecto	
habré sentido	habremos sentido
habrás sentido	habréis sentido
habrá sentido	habrán sentido
12 potencial compuesto	
habría sentido	habríamos sentido
habrías sentido	habríais sentido
habría sentido	habrían sentido
13 perfecto de subjuntivo	
haya sentido	hayamos sentido
hayas sentido	hayáis sentido
haya sentido	hayan sentido
14 pluscuamperfecto de subjuntivo	
hubiera sentido	hubiéramos sentido
hubieras sentido	hubierais sentido
hubiera sentido	hubieran sentido
OR	
hubiese sentido	hubiésemos sentido
hubieses sentido	hubieseis sentido
hubiese sentido	hubiesen sentido

imperativo

—	sintamos
siente; no sientas	sentid; no sintáis
sienta	sientan

Words and expressions related to this verb
Lo siento. I regret it; I'm sorry.
el sentimiento feeling, sentiment
sentimentalmente sentimentally
sentir admiración por alguien to feel
admiration for someone

el sentir feeling; judgment
una persona sentimental sentimentalist
el sentimentalismo sentimentalism

For additional words and expressions related to this verb, see **sentirse.**

The subject pronouns are found on the page facing page 1.

to feel (well, ill)

The Seven Simple Tenses		The Seven Compound Tenses	
Singular	Plural	Singular	Plural
1 presente de indicativo		8 perfecto de indicativo	
me siento	nos sentimos	me he sentido	nos hemos sentido
te sientes	os sentís	te has sentido	os habéis sentido
se siente	se sienten	se ha sentido	se han sentido
2 imperfecto de indicativo		9 pluscuamperfecto de indicativo	
me sentía	nos sentíamos	me había sentido	nos habíamos sentido
te sentías	os sentíais	te habías sentido	os habíais sentido
se sentía	se sentían	se había sentido	se habían sentido
3 pretérito		10 pretérito anterior	
me sentí	nos sentimos	me hube sentido	nos hubimos sentido
te sentiste	os sentisteis	te hubiste sentido	os hubisteis sentido
se sintió	se sintieron	se hubo sentido	se hubieron sentido
4 futuro		11 futuro perfecto	
me sentiré	nos sentiremos	me habré sentido	nos habremos sentido
te sentirás	os sentiréis	te habrás sentido	os habréis sentido
se sentirá	se sentirán	se habrá sentido	se habrán sentido
5 potencial simple		12 potencial compuesto	
me sentiría	nos sentiríamos	me habría sentido	nos habríamos sentido
te sentirías	os sentiríais	te habrías sentido	os habríais sentido
se sentiría	se sentirían	se habría sentido	se habrían sentido
6 presente de subjuntivo		13 perfecto de subjuntivo	
me sienta	nos sintamos	me haya sentido	nos hayamos sentido
te sientas	os sintáis	te hayas sentido	os hayáis sentido
se sienta	se sientan	se haya sentido	se hayan sentido
7 imperfecto de subjuntivo		14 pluscuamperfecto de subjuntivo	
me sintiera	nos sintiéramos	me hubiera sentido	nos hubiéramos sentido
te sintieras	os sintierais	te hubieras sentido	os hubierais sentido
se sintiera	se sintieran	se hubiera sentido	se hubieran sentido
OR		OR	
me sintiese	nos sintiésemos	me hubiese sentido	nos hubiésemos sentido
te sintieses	os sintieseis	te hubieses sentido	os hubieseis sentido
se sintiese	se sintiesen	se hubiese sentido	se hubiesen sentido

imperativo	
—	sintámonos
siéntete; no te sientas	sentíos; no os sintáis
siéntase	siéntanse

Words and expressions related to this verb

¿**Cómo se siente Ud.?**   How do you feel?   **Me siento mal.**   I feel sick.

el sentido   sense; **los sentidos**   the senses

For additional words and expressions related to this verb, see **sentir.**

Don't miss the definitions of basic grammatical terms with examples
in English and Spanish on pages 666–677.

---

to separate, to detach, to sort, to set apart

The Seven Simple Tenses		The Seven Compound Tenses	
Singular	Plural	Singular	Plural
1 presente de indicativo		8 perfecto de indicativo	
separo	**separamos**	**he separado**	**hemos separado**
separas	**separáis**	**has separado**	**habéis separado**
separa	**separan**	**ha separado**	**han separado**
2 imperfecto de indicativo		9 pluscuamperfecto de indicativo	
separaba	**separábamos**	**había separado**	**habíamos separado**
separabas	**separabais**	**habías separado**	**habíais separado**
separaba	**separaban**	**había separado**	**habían separado**
3 pretérito		10 pretérito anterior	
separé	**separamos**	**hube separado**	**hubimos separado**
separaste	**separasteis**	**hubiste separado**	**hubisteis separado**
separó	**separaron**	**hubo separado**	**hubieron separado**
4 futuro		11 futuro perfecto	
separaré	**separaremos**	**habré separado**	**habremos separado**
separarás	**separaréis**	**habrás separado**	**habréis separado**
separará	**separarán**	**habrá separado**	**habrán separado**
5 potencial simple		12 potencial compuesto	
separaría	**separaríamos**	**habría separado**	**habríamos separado**
separarías	**separaríais**	**habrías separado**	**habríais separado**
separaría	**separarían**	**habría separado**	**habrían separado**
6 presente de subjuntivo		13 perfecto de subjuntivo	
separe	**separemos**	**haya separado**	**hayamos separado**
separes	**separéis**	**hayas separado**	**hayáis separado**
separe	**separen**	**haya separado**	**hayan separado**
7 imperfecto de subjuntivo		14 pluscuamperfecto de subjuntivo	
separara	**separáramos**	**hubiera separado**	**hubiéramos separado**
separaras	**separarais**	**hubieras separado**	**hubierais separado**
separara	**separaran**	**hubiera separado**	**hubieran separado**
OR		OR	
separase	**separásemos**	**hubiese separado**	**hubiésemos separado**
separases	**separaseis**	**hubieses separado**	**hubieseis separado**
separase	**separasen**	**hubiese separado**	**hubiesen separado**

imperativo

—	**separemos**
separa; no separes	**separad; no separéis**
separe	**separen**

Words and expressions related to this verb
la separación separation
separante separating
separar un asiento to reserve a seat
por separado separately

una separata reprint
separativo, separativa separative
separado, separada separate, separated
separadamente separately

Use the EE-zee guide to Spanish pronunciation on pages 562 and 563.

The subject pronouns are found on the page facing page 1.

The Seven Simple Tenses		The Seven Compound Tenses	
Singular	Plural	Singular	Plural
1 presente de indicativo		8 perfecto de indicativo	
soy	somos	he sido	hemos sido
eres	sois	has sido	habéis sido
es	son	ha sido	han sido
2 imperfecto de indicativo		9 pluscuamperfecto de indicativo	
era	éramos	había sido	habíamos sido
eras	erais	habías sido	habíais sido
era	eran	había sido	habían sido
3 pretérito		10 pretérito anterior	
fui	fuimos	hube sido	hubimos sido
fuiste	fuisteis	hubiste sido	hubisteis sido
fue	fueron	hubo sido	hubieron sido
4 futuro		11 futuro perfecto	
seré	seremos	habré sido	habremos sido
serás	seréis	habrás sido	habréis sido
será	serán	habrá sido	habrán sido
5 potencial simple		12 potencial compuesto	
sería	seríamos	habría sido	habríamos sido
serías	seríais	habrías sido	habríais sido
sería	serían	habría sido	habrían sido
6 presente de subjuntivo		13 perfecto de subjuntivo	
sea	seamos	haya sido	hayamos sido
seas	seáis	hayas sido	hayáis sido
sea	sean	haya sido	hayan sido
7 imperfecto de subjuntivo		14 pluscuamperfecto de subjuntivo	
fuera	fuéramos	hubiera sido	hubiéramos sido
fueras	fuerais	hubieras sido	hubierais sido
fuera	fueran	hubiera sido	hubieran sido
OR		OR	
fuese	fuésemos	hubiese sido	hubiésemos sido
fueses	fueseis	hubieses sido	hubieseis sido
fuese	fuesen	hubiese sido	hubiesen sido

imperativo	
—	seamos
sé; no seas	sed; no seáis
sea	sean

Common idiomatic expressions using this verb

Dime con quién andas y te diré quién eres.   Tell me who your friends are and I will tell you
who you are.

es decir   that is, that is to say; **Si yo fuera usted . . .**   If I were you . . .

¿Qué hora es?   What time is it? **Es la una.**   It's one o'clock. **Son las dos.**   It's two o'clock.

See also **ser** on pages 534, 535, and 536.

Can't recognize an irregular verb form? Check out pages 519–523.

The Seven Simple Tenses		The Seven Compound Tenses	
Singular	Plural	Singular	Plural
1 presente de indicativo		8 perfecto de indicativo	
sirvo	servimos	he servido	hemos servido
sirves	servís	has servido	habéis servido
sirve	sirven	ha servido	han servido
2 imperfecto de indicativo		9 pluscuamperfecto de indicativo	
servía	servíamos	había servido	habíamos servido
servías	servíais	habías servido	habíais servido
servía	servían	había servido	habían servido
3 pretérito		10 pretérito anterior	
serví	servimos	hube servido	hubimos servido
serviste	servisteis	hubiste servido	hubisteis servido
sirvió	sirvieron	hubo servido	hubieron servido
4 futuro		11 futuro perfecto	
serviré	serviremos	habré servido	habremos servido
servirás	serviréis	habrás servido	habréis servido
servirá	servirán	habrá servido	habrán servido
5 potencial simple		12 potencial compuesto	
serviría	serviríamos	habría servido	habríamos servido
servirías	serviríais	habrías servido	habríais servido
serviría	servirían	habría servido	habrían servido
6 presente de subjuntivo		13 perfecto de subjuntivo	
sirva	sirvamos	haya servido	hayamos servido
sirvas	sirváis	hayas servido	hayáis servido
sirva	sirvan	haya servido	hayan servido
7 imperfecto de subjuntivo		14 pluscuamperfecto de subjuntivo	
sirviera	sirviéramos	hubiera servido	hubiéramos servido
sirvieras	sirvierais	hubieras servido	hubierais servido
sirviera	sirvieran	hubiera servido	hubieran servido
OR		OR	
sirviese	sirviésemos	hubiese servido	hubiésemos servido
sirvieses	sirvieseis	hubieses servido	hubieseis servido
sirviese	sirviesen	hubiese servido	hubiesen servido

imperativo	
—	sirvamos
sirve; no sirvas	servid; no sirváis
sirva	sirvan

Words and expressions related to this verb

servidor, servidora   servant, waiter, waitress
el servicio   service
una servilleta   table napkin
servirse   to serve oneself
¡Sírvase usted!   Help yourself!
el servicio de soporte técnico   technical support service

Esto no sirve para nada   This serves no purpose; This is good for nothing.
servir para   to be good for, to be used for

socorrer
Gerundio **socorriendo**   Part. pas. **socorrido**

to help, to aid, to assist, to succor

The Seven Simple Tenses		The Seven Compound Tenses	
Singular	Plural	Singular	Plural
1 presente de indicativo		**8 perfecto de indicativo**	
socorro	socorremos	he socorrido	hemos socorrido
socorres	socorréis	has socorrido	habéis socorrido
socorre	socorren	ha socorrido	han socorrido
2 imperfecto de indicativo		**9 pluscuamperfecto de indicativo**	
socorría	socorríamos	había socorrido	habíamos socorrido
soccorrías	socorríais	habías socorrido	habíais socorrido
socorría	socorrían	había socorrido	habían socorrido
3 pretérito		**10 pretérito anterior**	
socorrí	socorrimos	hube socorrido	hubimos socorrido
socorriste	socorristeis	hubiste socorrido	hubisteis socorrido
socorrió	socorrieron	hubo socorrido	hubieron socorrido
4 futuro		**11 futuro perfecto**	
socorreré	socorreremos	habré socorrido	habremos socorrido
socorrerás	socorreréis	habrás socorrido	habréis socorrido
socorrerá	socorrerán	habrá socorrido	habrán socorrido
5 potencial simple		**12 potencial compuesto**	
socorrería	socorreríamos	habría socorrido	habríamos socorrido
socorrerías	socorreríais	habrías socorrido	habríais socorrido
socorrería	socorrerían	habría socorrido	habrían socorrido
6 presente de subjuntivo		**13 perfecto de subjuntivo**	
socorra	socorramos	haya socorrido	hayamos socorrido
socorras	socorráis	hayas socorrido	hayáis socorrido
socorra	socorran	haya socorrido	hayan socorrido
7 imperfecto de subjuntivo		**14 pluscuamperfecto de subjuntivo**	
socorriera	socorriéramos	hubiera socorrido	hubiéramos socorrido
socorrieras	socorrierais	hubieras socorrido	hubierais socorrido
socorriera	socorrieran	hubiera socorrido	hubieran socorrido
OR		OR	
socorriese	socorriésemos	hubiese socorrido	hubiésemos socorrido
socorrieses	socorrieseis	hubieses socorrido	hubieseis socorrido
socorriese	socorriesen	hubiese socorrido	hubiesen socorrido

	imperativo
—	socorramos
socorre; no socorras	socorred; no socorráis
socorra	socorran

Words and expressions related to this verb
el socorro   help; **¡Socorro! ¡Socorro!**   Help! Help!   **socorrido, socorrida**   helpful
un puesto de socorro   first-aid station   **socorrista**   first-aid provider

Check out the verb drills and verb tests with answers explained on pages 619–665.

to choke, to smother, to suffocate, to stifle

The Seven Simple Tenses		The Seven Compound Tenses	
Singular	Plural	Singular	Plural
1 presente de indicativo		8 perfecto de indicativo	
sofoco	**sofocamos**	**he sofocado**	**hemos sofocado**
sofocas	**sofocáis**	**has sofocado**	**habéis sofocado**
sofoca	**sofocan**	**ha sofocado**	**han sofocado**
2 imperfecto de indicativo		9 pluscuamperfecto de indicativo	
sofocaba	**sofocábamos**	**había sofocado**	**habíamos sofocado**
sofocabas	**sofocabais**	**habías sofocado**	**habíais sofocado**
sofocaba	**sofocaban**	**había sofocado**	**habían sofocado**
3 pretérito		10 pretérito anterior	
sofoqué	**sofocamos**	**hube sofocado**	**hubimos sofocado**
sofocaste	**sofocasteis**	**hubiste sofocado**	**hubisteis sofocado**
sofocó	**sofocaron**	**hubo sofocado**	**hubieron sofocado**
4 futuro		11 futuro perfecto	
sofocaré	**sofocaremos**	**habré sofocado**	**habremos sofocado**
sofocarás	**sofocaréis**	**habrás sofocado**	**habréis sofocado**
sofocará	**sofocarán**	**habrá sofocado**	**habrán sofocado**
5 potencial simple		12 potencial compuesto	
sofocaría	**sofocaríamos**	**habría sofocado**	**habríamos sofocado**
sofocarías	**sofocaríais**	**habrías sofocado**	**habríais sofocado**
sofocaría	**sofocarían**	**habría sofocado**	**habrían sofocado**
6 presente de subjuntivo		13 perfecto de subjuntivo	
sofoque	**sofoquemos**	**haya sofocado**	**hayamos sofocado**
sofoques	**sofoquéis**	**hayas sofocado**	**hayáis sofocado**
sofoque	**sofoquen**	**haya sofocado**	**hayan sofocado**
7 imperfecto de subjuntivo		14 pluscuamperfecto de subjuntivo	
sofocara	**sofocáramos**	**hubiera sofocado**	**hubiéramos sofocado**
sofocaras	**sofocarais**	**hubieras sofocado**	**hubierais sofocado**
sofocara	**sofocaran**	**hubiera sofocado**	**hubieran sofocado**
OR		OR	
sofocase	**sofocásemos**	**hubiese sofocado**	**hubiésemos sofocado**
sofocases	**sofocaseis**	**hubieses sofocado**	**hubieseis sofocado**
sofocase	**sofocasen**	**hubiese sofocado**	**hubiesen sofocado**

imperativo

—	**sofoquemos**
sofoca; no sofoques	**sofocad; no sofoquéis**
sofoque	**sofoquen**

Words and expressions related to this verb
sofocarse   to get out of breath
sofocarse por   to get excited over
sofocador, sofocadora   stifling, stuffy

la sofocación   suffocation, choking
sofocante   suffocating, stifling
el sofoco   suffocation

Review the principal parts of important Spanish verbs on pages xvi–xvii.

soler Gerundio **soliendo** Part. pas. **solido**

to be accustomed to, to be in the habit of, to have the custom of

The Seven Simple Tenses		The Seven Compound Tenses	
Singular	Plural	Singular	Plural
1 presente de indicativo		8 perfecto de indicativo	
suelo	solemos	he solido	hemos solido
sueles	soléis	has solido	habéis solido
suele	suelen	ha solido	han solido
2 imperfecto de indicativo		9 pluscuamperfecto de indicativo	
solía	solíamos	había solido	habíamos solido
solías	solíais	habías solido	habíais solido
solía	solían	había solido	habían solido
3 pretérito		10 pretérito anterior	
solí	solimos	hube solido	hubimos solido
soliste	solisteis	hubiste solido	hubisteis solido
solió	solieron	hubo solido	hubieron solido
4 futuro		11 futuro perfecto	
[not in use]		[not in use]	
5 potencial simple		12 potencial compuesto	
[not in use]		[not in use]	
6 presente de subjuntivo		13 perfecto de subjuntivo	
suela	solamos	haya solido	hayamos solido
suelas	soláis	hayas solido	hayáis solido
suela	suelan	haya solido	hayan solido
7 imperfecto de subjuntivo		14 pluscuamperfecto de subjuntivo	
soliera	soliéramos	hubiera solido	hubiéramos solido
solieras	solierais	hubieras solido	hubierais solido
soliera	solieran	hubiera solido	hubieran solido
OR		OR	
soliese	soliésemos	hubiese solido	hubiésemos solido
solieses	solieseis	hubieses solido	hubieseis solido
soliese	soliesen	hubiese solido	hubiesen solido

imperativo
[not in use]

This verb is defective and it is used primarily in the five simple tenses given above. When used, it is followed by an infinitive.

Suelo acostarme a las diez. Mi hermanito suele acostarse a las ocho y mis padres suelen acostarse a las once. Durante las vacaciones del verano pasado, solía levantarme tarde.

Get acquainted with what preposition goes with what verb on pages 541–549.

442

to sob, to whimper

The Seven Simple Tenses		The Seven Compound Tenses	
Singular	Plural	Singular	Plural
1 presente de indicativo		8 perfecto de indicativo	
sollozo	**sollozamos**	**he sollozado**	**hemos sollozado**
sollozas	**sollozáis**	**has sollozado**	**habéis sollozado**
solloza	**sollozan**	**ha sollozado**	**han sollozado**
2 imperfecto de indicativo		9 pluscuamperfecto de indicativo	
sollozaba	**sollozábamos**	**había sollozado**	**habíamos sollozado**
sollozabas	**sollozabais**	**habías sollozado**	**habíais sollozado**
sollozaba	**sollozaban**	**había sollozado**	**habían sollozado**
3 pretérito		10 pretérito anterior	
sollocé	**sollozamos**	**hube sollozado**	**hubimos sollozado**
sollozaste	**sollozasteis**	**hubiste sollozado**	**hubisteis sollozado**
sollozó	**sollozaron**	**hubo sollozado**	**hubieron sollozado**
4 futuro		11 futuro perfecto	
sollozaré	**sollozaremos**	**habré sollozado**	**habremos sollozado**
sollozarás	**sollozaréis**	**habrás sollozado**	**habréis sollozado**
sollozará	**sollozarán**	**habrá sollozado**	**habrán sollozado**
5 potencial simple		12 potencial compuesto	
sollozaría	**sollozaríamos**	**habría sollozado**	**habríamos sollozado**
sollozarías	**sollozaríais**	**habrías sollozado**	**habríais sollozado**
sollozaría	**sollozarían**	**habría sollozado**	**habrían sollozado**
6 presente de subjuntivo		13 perfecto de subjuntivo	
solloce	**sollocemos**	**haya sollozado**	**hayamos sollozado**
solloces	**sollocéis**	**hayas sollozado**	**hayáis sollozado**
solloce	**sollocen**	**haya sollozado**	**hayan sollozado**
7 imperfecto de subjuntivo		14 pluscuamperfecto de subjuntivo	
sollozara	**sollozáramos**	**hubiera sollozado**	**hubiéramos sollozado**
sollozaras	**sollozarais**	**hubieras sollozado**	**hubierais sollozado**
sollozara	**sollozaran**	**hubiera sollozado**	**hubieran sollozado**
OR		OR	
sollozase	**sollozásemos**	**hubiese sollozado**	**hubiésemos sollozado**
sollozases	**sollozaseis**	**hubieses sollozado**	**hubieseis sollozado**
sollozase	**sollozasen**	**hubiese sollozado**	**hubiesen sollozado**

	imperativo	
—		**sollocemos**
solloza; no solloces		**sollozad; no sollocéis**
solloce		**sollocen**

Words related to this verb
un sollozo   sob
estallar en sollozos   to burst into sobs   **sollozante**   sobbing

---

Be sure to consult the back pages for sections on verbs used in idiomatic expressions,
verbs with prepositions, and the list of over 1,100 verbs conjugated like model verbs.

to subdue, to subject, to surrender, to submit

The Seven Simple Tenses		The Seven Compound Tenses	
Singular	Plural	Singular	Plural
1 presente de indicativo		8 perfecto de indicativo	
someto	sometemos	he sometido	hemos sometido
sometes	sometéis	has sometido	habéis sometido
somete	someten	ha sometido	han sometido
2 imperfecto de indicativo		9 pluscuamperfecto de indicativo	
sometía	sometíamos	había sometido	habíamos sometido
sometías	sometíais	habías sometido	habíais sometido
sometía	sometían	había sometido	habían sometido
3 pretérito		10 pretérito anterior	
sometí	sometimos	hube sometido	hubimos sometido
sometiste	sometisteis	hubiste sometido	hubisteis sometido
sometió	sometieron	hubo sometido	hubieron sometido
4 futuro		11 futuro perfecto	
someteré	someteremos	habré sometido	habremos sometido
someterás	someteréis	habrás sometido	habréis sometido
someterá	someterán	habrá sometido	habrán sometido
5 potencial simple		12 potencial compuesto	
sometería	someteríamos	habría sometido	habríamos sometido
someterías	someteríais	habrías sometido	habríais sometido
sometería	someterían	habría sometido	habrían sometido
6 presente de subjuntivo		13 perfecto de subjuntivo	
someta	sometamos	haya sometido	hayamos sometido
sometas	sometáis	hayas sometido	hayáis sometido
someta	sometan	haya sometido	hayan sometido
7 imperfecto de subjuntivo		14 pluscuamperfecto de subjuntivo	
sometiera	sometiéramos	hubiera sometido	hubiéramos sometido
sometieras	sometierais	hubieras sometido	hubierais sometido
sometiera	sometieran	hubiera sometido	hubieran sometido
OR		OR	
sometiese	sometiésemos	hubiese sometido	hubiésemos sometido
sometieses	sometieseis	hubieses sometido	hubieseis sometido
sometiese	sometiesen	hubiese sometido	hubiesen sometido

imperativo	
—	sometamos
somete; no sometas	someted; no sometáis
someta	sometan

Words and expressions related to this verb

someterse to surrender, to humble oneself
sometido, sometida submissive, docile
la sumisión submission

el sometimiento submission
someter la renuncia to resign
someter a prueba to put to the test

Increase your verb power with popular phrases, words,
and expressions for tourists on pages 595–618.

444

to ring, to echo, to resound, to sound

The Seven Simple Tenses		The Seven Compound Tenses	
Singular	Plural	Singular	Plural
1 presente de indicativo		8 perfecto de indicativo	
sueno	sonamos	he sonado	hemos sonado
suenas	sonáis	has sonado	habéis sonado
suena	suenan	ha sonado	han sonado
2 imperfecto de indicativo		9 pluscuamperfecto de indicativo	
sonaba	sonábamos	había sonado	habíamos sonado
sonabas	sonabais	habías sonado	habíais sonado
sonaba	sonaban	había sonado	habían sonado
3 pretérito		10 pretérito anterior	
soné	sonamos	hube sonado	hubimos sonado
sonaste	sonasteis	hubiste sonado	hubisteis sonado
sonó	sonaron	hubo sonado	hubieron sonado
4 futuro		11 futuro perfecto	
sonaré	sonaremos	habré sonado	habremos sonado
sonarás	sonaréis	habrás sonado	habréis sonado
sonará	sonarán	habrá sonado	habrán sonado
5 potencial simple		12 potencial compuesto	
sonaría	sonaríamos	habría sonado	habríamos sonado
sonarías	sonaríais	habrías sonado	habríais sonado
sonaría	sonarían	habría sonado	habrían sonado
6 presente de subjuntivo		13 perfecto de subjuntivo	
suene	sonemos	haya sonado	hayamos sonado
suenes	sonéis	hayas sonado	hayáis sonado
suene	suenen	haya sonado	hayan sonado
7 imperfecto de subjuntivo		14 pluscuamperfecto de subjuntivo	
sonara	sonáramos	hubiera sonado	hubiéramos sonado
sonaras	sonarais	hubieras sonado	hubierais sonado
sonara	sonaran	hubiera sonado	hubieran sonado
OR		OR	
sonase	sonásemos	hubiese sonado	hubiésemos sonado
sonases	sonaseis	hubieses sonado	hubieseis sonado
sonase	sonasen	hubiese sonado	hubiesen sonado

imperativo	
—	sonemos
suena; no suenes	sonad; no sonéis
suene	suenen

Words and expressions related to this verb
sonar a   to seem like
sonarse (las narices)   to blow one's nose
sonante   sonant, sonorous, sounding
el sonar   sonar

una sonata   sonata
una sonatina   sonatina
sonar la alarma   to ring the alarm
el sonido   sound

Check out the verb drills and verb tests with answers explained on pages 619–665.

The subject pronouns are found on the page facing page 1.

soñar — Gerundio soñando — Part. pas. soñado

to dream

The Seven Simple Tenses		The Seven Compound Tenses	
Singular	Plural	Singular	Plural
1 presente de indicativo		**8 perfecto de indicativo**	
sueño	soñamos	he soñado	hemos soñado
sueñas	soñáis	has soñado	habéis soñado
sueña	sueñan	ha soñado	han soñado
2 imperfecto de indicativo		**9 pluscuamperfecto de indicativo**	
soñaba	soñábamos	había soñado	habíamos soñado
soñabas	soñabais	habías soñado	habíais soñado
soñaba	soñaban	había soñado	habían soñado
3 pretérito		**10 pretérito anterior**	
soñé	soñamos	hube soñado	hubimos soñado
soñaste	soñasteis	hubiste soñado	hubisteis soñado
soñó	soñaron	hubo soñado	hubieron soñado
4 futuro		**11 futuro perfecto**	
soñaré	soñaremos	habré soñado	habremos soñado
soñarás	soñaréis	habrás soñado	habréis soñado
soñará	soñarán	habrá soñado	habrán soñado
5 potencial simple		**12 potencial compuesto**	
soñaría	soñaríamos	habría soñado	habríamos soñado
soñarías	soñaríais	habrías soñado	habríais soñado
soñaría	soñarían	habría soñado	habrían soñado
6 presente de subjuntivo		**13 perfecto de subjuntivo**	
sueñe	soñemos	haya soñado	hayamos soñado
sueñes	soñéis	hayas soñado	hayáis soñado
sueñe	sueñen	haya soñado	hayan soñado
7 imperfecto de subjuntivo		**14 pluscuamperfecto de subjuntivo**	
soñara	soñáramos	hubiera soñado	hubiéramos soñado
soñaras	soñarais	hubieras soñado	hubierais soñado
soñara	soñaran	hubiera soñado	hubieran soñado
OR		OR	
soñase	soñásemos	hubiese soñado	hubiésemos soñado
soñases	soñaseis	hubieses soñado	hubieseis soñado
soñase	soñasen	hubiese soñado	hubiesen soñado

imperativo	
—	soñemos
sueña; no sueñes	soñad; no soñéis
sueñe	sueñen

Words and expressions related to this verb

soñar con to dream of
soñar despierto to daydream
soñador, soñadora dreamer
el sueño sleep, dream
el insomnio insomnia

tener sueño to be sleepy
un sueño hecho realidad a dream come true
sueño pesado sound sleep
echar un sueño to take a nap
el sonámbulo (somnámbulo) sleepwalker

Get acquainted with what preposition goes with what verb on pages 541–549.

The Seven Simple Tenses		The Seven Compound Tenses	
Singular	Plural	Singular	Plural

1 presente de indicativo

sonrío	sonreímos	
sonríes	sonreís	
sonríe	sonríen	

8 perfecto de indicativo

he sonreído	hemos sonreído
has sonreído	habéis sonreído
ha sonreído	han sonreído

2 imperfecto de indicativo

sonreía	sonreíamos
sonreías	sonreíais
sonreía	sonreían

9 pluscuamperfecto de indicativo

había sonreído	habíamos sonreído
habías sonreído	habíais sonreído
había sonreído	habían sonreído

3 pretérito

sonreí	sonreímos
sonreíste	sonreísteis
sonrió	sonrieron

10 pretérito anterior

hube sonreído	hubimos sonreído
hubiste sonreído	hubisteis sonreído
hubo sonreído	hubieron sonreído

4 futuro

sonreiré	sonreiremos
sonreirás	sonreiréis
sonreirá	sonreirán

11 futuro perfecto

habré sonreído	habremos sonreído
habrás sonreído	habréis sonreído
habrá sonreído	habrán sonreído

5 potencial simple

sonreiría	sonreiríamos
sonreirías	sonreiríais
sonreiría	sonreirían

12 potencial compuesto

habría sonreído	habríamos sonreído
habrías sonreído	habríais sonreído
habría sonreído	habrían sonreído

6 presente de subjuntivo

sonría	sonriamos
sonrías	sonriáis
sonría	sonrían

13 perfecto de subjuntivo

haya sonreído	hayamos sonreído
hayas sonreído	hayáis sonreído
haya sonreído	hayan sonreído

7 imperfecto de subjuntivo

sonriera	sonriéramos
sonrieras	sonrierais
sonriera	sonrieran
OR	
sonriese	sonriésemos
sonrieses	sonrieseis
sonriese	sonriesen

14 pluscuamperfecto de subjuntivo

hubiera sonreído	hubiéramos sonreído
hubieras sonreído	hubierais sonreído
hubiera sonreído	hubieran sonreído
OR	
hubiese sonreído	hubiésemos sonreído
hubieses sonreído	hubieseis sonreído
hubiese sonreído	hubiesen sonreído

imperativo

—	sonriamos
sonríe; no sonrías	sonreíd; no sonriáis
sonría	sonrían

Words and expressions related to this verb
sonriente smiling; **La Gioconda tiene una sonrisa bonita** The Mona Lisa has a pretty smile.
la sonrisa smile   **no perder la sonrisa** not to lose a smile; keep smiling

For additional words and expressions related to this verb, see **reír** and **reírse.**

soplar

Gerundio soplando   **Part. pas. soplado**

to blow, to blow out

The Seven Simple Tenses		The Seven Compound Tenses	
Singular	Plural	Singular	Plural
1 presente de indicativo		8 perfecto de indicativo	
soplo	soplamos	he soplado	hemos soplado
soplas	sopláis	has soplado	habéis soplado
sopla	soplan	ha soplado	han soplado
2 imperfecto de indicativo		9 pluscuamperfecto de indicativo	
soplaba	soplábamos	había soplado	habíamos soplado
soplabas	soplabais	habías soplado	habíais soplado
soplaba	soplaban	había soplado	habían soplado
3 pretérito		10 pretérito anterior	
soplé	soplamos	hube soplado	hubimos soplado
soplaste	soplasteis	hubiste soplado	hubisteis soplado
sopló	soplaron	hubo soplado	hubieron soplado
4 futuro		11 futuro perfecto	
soplaré	soplaremos	habré soplado	habremos soplado
soplarás	soplaréis	habrás soplado	habréis soplado
soplará	soplarán	habrá soplado	habrán soplado
5 potencial simple		12 potencial compuesto	
soplaría	soplaríamos	habría soplado	habríamos soplado
soplarías	soplaríais	habrías soplado	habríais soplado
soplaría	soplarían	habría soplado	habrían soplado
6 presente de subjuntivo		13 perfecto de subjuntivo	
sople	soplemos	haya soplado	hayamos soplado
soples	sopléis	hayas soplado	hayáis soplado
sople	soplen	haya soplado	hayan soplado
7 imperfecto de subjuntivo		14 pluscuamperfecto de subjuntivo	
soplara	sopláramos	hubiera soplado	hubiéramos soplado
soplaras	soplarais	hubieras soplado	hubierais soplado
soplara	soplaran	hubiera soplado	hubieran soplado
OR		OR	
soplase	soplásemos	hubiese soplado	hubiésemos soplado
soplases	soplaseis	hubieses soplado	hubieseis soplado
soplase	soplasen	hubiese soplado	hubiesen soplado

imperativo	
—	soplemos
sopla; no soples	soplad; no sopléis
sople	soplen

Words and expressions related to this verb
un soplamocos a punch in the nose
una sopladura air hole
un soplón, una soplona tattletale
saber de qué lado sopla el viento
   to know which way the wind blows

un soplete atomizador paint sprayer
un soplo puff; **en un soplo** in a jiffy
soplar a la policía to tip off the police
soplar la vela to blow out the candle
soplar con la boca to blow with the mouth
el viento sopla the wind blows

to surprise, to astonish

The Seven Simple Tenses	The Seven Compound Tenses

Singular	Plural	Singular	Plural
1 presente de indicativo		8 perfecto de indicativo	
sorprendo	**sorprendemos**	**he sorprendido**	**hemos sorprendido**
sorprendes	**sorprendéis**	**has sorprendido**	**habéis sorprendido**
sorprende	**sorprenden**	**ha sorprendido**	**han sorprendido**
2 imperfecto de indicativo		9 pluscuamperfecto de indicativo	
sorprendía	**sorprendíamos**	**había sorprendido**	**habíamos sorprendido**
sorprendías	**sorprendíais**	**habías sorprendido**	**habíais sorprendido**
sorprendía	**sorprendían**	**había sorprendido**	**habían sorprendido**
3 pretérito		10 pretérito anterior	
sorprendí	**sorprendimos**	**hube sorprendido**	**hubimos sorprendido**
sorprendiste	**sorprendisteis**	**hubiste sorprendido**	**hubisteis sorprendido**
sorprendió	**sorprendieron**	**hubo sorprendido**	**hubieron sorprendido**
4 futuro		11 futuro perfecto	
sorprenderé	**sorprenderemos**	**habré sorprendido**	**habremos sorprendido**
sorprenderás	**sorprenderéis**	**habrás sorprendido**	**habréis sorprendido**
sorprenderá	**sorprenderán**	**habrá sorprendido**	**habrán sorprendido**
5 potencial simple		12 potencial compuesto	
sorprendería	**sorprenderíamos**	**habría sorprendido**	**habríamos sorprendido**
sorprenderías	**sorprenderíais**	**habrías sorprendido**	**habríais sorprendido**
sorprendería	**sorprenderían**	**habría sorprendido**	**habrían sorprendido**
6 presente de subjuntivo		13 perfecto de subjuntivo	
sorprenda	**sorprendamos**	**haya sorprendido**	**hayamos sorprendido**
sorprendas	**sorprendáis**	**hayas sorprendido**	**hayáis sorprendido**
sorprenda	**sorprendan**	**haya sorprendido**	**hayan sorprendido**
7 imperfecto de subjuntivo		14 pluscuamperfecto de subjuntivo	
sorprendiera	**sorprendiéramos**	**hubiera sorprendido**	**hubiéramos sorprendido**
sorprendieras	**sorprendierais**	**hubieras sorprendido**	**hubierais sorprendido**
sorprendiera	**sorprendieran**	**hubiera sorprendido**	**hubieran sorprendido**
OR		OR	
sorprendiese	**sorprendiésemos**	**hubiese sorprendido**	**hubiésemos sorprendido**
sorprendieses	**sorprendieseis**	**hubieses sorprendido**	**hubieseis sorprendido**
sorprendiese	**sorprendiesen**	**hubiese sorprendido**	**hubiesen sorprendido**

imperativo

—	**sorprendamos**
sorprende; no sorprendas	**sorprended; no sorprendáis**
sorprenda	**sorprendan**

Words and expressions related to this verb

sorprender en el hecho   to catch in the act
una sorpresa   surprise
tomar por sorpresa   to take by surprise

coger de sorpresa   to take by surprise
sorprendente   surprising
sorprenderse   to be surprised, astonished

Get your feet wet with verbs used in weather expressions on page 540.

The subject pronouns are found on the page facing page 1.

to suspect

The Seven Simple Tenses		The Seven Compound Tenses	
Singular	Plural	Singular	Plural
1 presente de indicativo		8 perfecto de indicativo	
sospecho	sospechamos	he sospechado	hemos sospechado
sospechas	sospecháis	has sospechado	habéis sospechado
sospecha	sospechan	ha sospechado	han sospechado
2 imperfecto de indicativo		9 pluscuamperfecto de indicativo	
sospechaba	sospechábamos	había sospechado	habíamos sospechado
sospechabas	sospechabais	habías sospechado	habíais sospechado
sospechaba	sospechaban	había sospechado	habían sospechado
3 pretérito		10 pretérito anterior	
sospeché	sospechamos	hube sospechado	hubimos sospechado
sospechaste	sospechasteis	hubiste sospechado	hubisteis sospechado
sospechó	sospecharon	hubo sospechado	hubieron sospechado
4 futuro		11 futuro perfecto	
sospecharé	sospecharemos	habré sospechado	habremos sospechado
sospecharás	sospecharéis	habrás sospechado	habréis sospechado
sospechará	sospecharán	habrá sospechado	habrán sospechado
5 potencial simple		12 potencial compuesto	
sospecharía	sospecharíamos	habría sospechado	habríamos sospechado
sospecharías	sospecharíais	habrías sospechado	habríais sospechado
sospecharía	sospecharían	habría sospechado	habrían sospechado
6 presente de subjuntivo		13 perfecto de subjuntivo	
sospeche	sospechemos	haya sospechado	hayamos sospechado
sospeches	sospechéis	hayas sospechado	hayáis sospechado
sospeche	sospechen	haya sospechado	hayan sospechado
7 imperfecto de subjuntivo		14 pluscuamperfecto de subjuntivo	
sospechara	sospecháramos	hubiera sospechado	hubiéramos sospechado
sospecharas	sospecharais	hubieras sospechado	hubierais sospechado
sospechara	sospecharan	hubiera sospechado	hubieran sospechado
OR		OR	
sospechase	sospechásemos	hubiese sospechado	hubiésemos sospechado
sospechases	sospechaseis	hubieses sospechado	hubieseis sospechado
sospechase	sospechasen	hubiese sospechado	hubiesen sospechado

	imperativo	
—		sospechemos
sospecha; no sospeches		sospechad; no sospechéis
sospeche		sospechen

Words related to this verb
sospechar de to suspect **la sospecha** suspicion, doubt
sospechable suspicious **sospechoso, sospechosa** suspect

Want to learn more idiomatic expressions that contain verbs? Check out pages 524–537.

to sustain, to support, to maintain, to uphold

The Seven Simple Tenses		The Seven Compound Tenses	
Singular	Plural	Singular	Plural
1 presente de indicativo		8 perfecto de indicativo	
sostengo	**sostenemos**	**he sostenido**	**hemos sostenido**
sostienes	**sostenéis**	**has sostenido**	**habéis sostenido**
sostiene	**sostienen**	**ha sostenido**	**han sostenido**
2 imperfecto de indicativo		9 pluscuamperfecto de indicativo	
sostenía	**sosteníamos**	**había sostenido**	**habíamos sostenido**
sostenías	**sosteníais**	**habías sostenido**	**habíais sostenido**
sostenía	**sostenían**	**había sostenido**	**habían sostenido**
3 pretérito		10 pretérito anterior	
sostuve	**sostuvimos**	**hube sostenido**	**hubimos sostenido**
sostuviste	**sostuvisteis**	**hubiste sostenido**	**hubisteis sostenido**
sostuvo	**sostuvieron**	**hubo sostenido**	**hubieron sostenido**
4 futuro		11 futuro perfecto	
sostendré	**sostendremos**	**habré sostenido**	**habremos sostenido**
sostendrás	**sostendréis**	**habrás sostenido**	**habréis sostenido**
sostendrá	**sostendrán**	**habrá sostenido**	**habrán sostenido**
5 potencial simple		12 potencial compuesto	
sostendría	**sostendríamos**	**habría sostenido**	**habríamos sostenido**
sostendrías	**sostendríais**	**habrías sostenido**	**habríais sostenido**
sostendría	**sostendrían**	**habría sostenido**	**habrían sostenido**
6 presente de subjuntivo		13 perfecto de subjuntivo	
sostenga	**sostengamos**	**haya sostenido**	**hayamos sostenido**
sostengas	**sostengáis**	**hayas sostenido**	**hayáis sostenido**
sostenga	**sostengan**	**haya sostenido**	**hayan sostenido**
7 imperfecto de subjuntivo		14 pluscuamperfecto de subjuntivo	
sostuviera	**sostuviéramos**	**hubiera sostenido**	**hubiéramos sostenido**
sostuvieras	**sostuvierais**	**hubieras sostenido**	**hubierais sostenido**
sostuviera	**sostuvieran**	**hubiera sostenido**	**hubieran sostenido**
OR		OR	
sostuviese	**sostuviésemos**	**hubiese sostenido**	**hubiésemos sostenido**
sostuvieses	**sostuvieseis**	**hubieses sostenido**	**hubieseis sostenido**
sostuviese	**sostuviesen**	**hubiese sostenido**	**hubiesen sostenido**

imperativo	
—	**sostengamos**
sosten; no sostengas	**sostened; no sostengáis**
sostenga	**sostengan**

Words related to this verb
el sostén, el sostenimiento   support,
   sustenance
sosteniente   supporting, sustaining

sostenido, sostenida   supported, sustained
el sostenedor, la sostenedora   supporter
sostenerse   to support or maintain oneself

For other words and expressions related to this verb, see **tener.**

| subir | Gerundio **subiendo** | Part. pas. **subido** |

to go up, to come up, to climb, to rise, to mount, to get on (a train, bus, etc.)

The Seven Simple Tenses		The Seven Compound Tenses	
Singular	Plural	Singular	Plural
1 presente de indicativo		8 perfecto de indicativo	
subo	**subimos**	**he subido**	**hemos subido**
subes	**subís**	**has subido**	**habéis subido**
sube	**suben**	**ha subido**	**han subido**
2 imperfecto de indicativo		9 pluscuamperfecto de indicativo	
subía	**subíamos**	**había subido**	**habíamos subido**
subías	**subíais**	**habías subido**	**habíais subido**
subía	**subían**	**había subido**	**habían subido**
3 pretérito		10 pretérito anterior	
subí	**subimos**	**hube subido**	**hubimos subido**
subiste	**subisteis**	**hubiste subido**	**hubisteis subido**
subió	**subieron**	**hubo subido**	**hubieron subido**
4 futuro		11 futuro perfecto	
subiré	**subiremos**	**habré subido**	**habremos subido**
subirás	**subiréis**	**habrás subido**	**habréis subido**
subirá	**subirán**	**habrá subido**	**habrán subido**
5 potencial simple		12 potencial compuesto	
subiría	**subiríamos**	**habría subido**	**habríamos subido**
subirías	**subiríais**	**habrías subido**	**habríais subido**
subiría	**subirían**	**habría subido**	**habrían subido**
6 presente de subjuntivo		13 perfecto de subjuntivo	
suba	**subamos**	**haya subido**	**hayamos subido**
subas	**subáis**	**hayas subido**	**hayáis subido**
suba	**suban**	**haya subido**	**hayan subido**
7 imperfecto de subjuntivo		14 pluscuamperfecto de subjuntivo	
subiera	**subiéramos**	**hubiera subido**	**hubiéramos subido**
subieras	**subierais**	**hubieras subido**	**hubierais subido**
subiera	**subieran**	**hubiera subido**	**hubieran subido**
OR		OR	
subiese	**subiésemos**	**hubiese subido**	**hubiésemos subido**
subieses	**subieseis**	**hubieses subido**	**hubieseis subido**
subiese	**subiesen**	**hubiese subido**	**hubiesen subido**

imperativo

—	**subamos**
sube; no subas	**subid; no subáis**
suba	**suban**

Words related to this verb
subir a   to get on (a train, etc.)
subir pasajeros   to take on passengers
súbitamente, subitáneamente   all of a
   sudden, suddenly
la subida   ascent, increase

súbito, súbita   sudden
subirse a una escalera   to climb a ladder
Han subido los precios.   Prices have gone up.
subir la voz   to raise one's voice

to underline, to underscore, to emphasize

The Seven Simple Tenses		The Seven Compound Tenses	
Singular	Plural	Singular	Plural
1 presente de indicativo		8 perfecto de indicativo	
subrayo	subrayamos	he subrayado	hemos subrayado
subrayas	subrayáis	has subrayado	habéis subrayado
subraya	subrayan	ha subrayado	han subrayado
2 imperfecto de indicativo		9 pluscuamperfecto de indicativo	
subrayaba	subrayábamos	había subrayado	habíamos subrayado
subrayabas	subrayabais	habías subrayado	habíais subrayado
subrayaba	subrayaban	había subrayado	habían subrayado
3 pretérito		10 pretérito anterior	
subrayé	subrayamos	hube subrayado	hubimos subrayado
subrayaste	subrayasteis	hubiste subrayado	hubisteis subrayado
subrayó	subrayaron	hubo subrayado	hubieron subrayado
4 futuro		11 futuro perfecto	
subrayaré	subrayaremos	habré subrayado	habremos subrayado
subrayarás	subrayaréis	habrás subrayado	habréis subrayado
subrayará	subrayarán	habrá subrayado	habrán subrayado
5 potencial simple		12 potencial compuesto	
subrayaría	subrayaríamos	habría subrayado	habríamos subrayado
subrayarías	subrayaríais	habrías subrayado	habríais subrayado
subrayaría	subrayarían	habría subrayado	habrían subrayado
6 presente de subjuntivo		13 perfecto de subjuntivo	
subraye	subrayemos	haya subrayado	hayamos subrayado
subrayes	subrayéis	hayas subrayado	hayáis subrayado
subraye	subrayen	haya subrayado	hayan subrayado
7 imperfecto de subjuntivo		14 pluscuamperfecto de subjuntivo	
subrayara	subrayáramos	hubiera subrayado	hubiéramos subrayado
subrayaras	subrayarais	hubieras subrayado	hubierais subrayado
subrayara	subrayaran	hubiera subrayado	hubieran subrayado
OR		OR	
subrayase	subrayásemos	hubiese subrayado	hubiésemos subrayado
subrayases	subrayaseis	hubieses subrayado	hubieseis subrayado
subrayase	subrayasen	hubiese subrayado	hubiesen subrayado

imperativo

—	subrayemos
subraya; no subrayes	subrayad; no subrayéis
subraye	subrayen

Words and expressions related to this verb
subrayado, subrayada underlined, underlining   **el papel rayado** lined paper
rayar to draw lines, to rule or line paper, to cross out   **rayos X** X-rays
un rayo de sol sunbeam; **un rayo lunar** moonbeam

Learn more verbs in 30 practical situations for tourists on pages 564–594.

subscribir
Gerundio **subscribiendo**   Part. pas. **subscrito**

to subscribe, to agree to, to sign

The Seven Simple Tenses		The Seven Compound Tenses	
Singular	Plural	Singular	Plural
1 presente de indicativo		**8 perfecto de indicativo**	
subscribo	subscribimos	he subscrito	hemos subscrito
subscribes	subscribís	has subscrito	habéis subscrito
subscribe	subscriben	ha subscrito	han subscrito
2 imperfecto de indicativo		**9 pluscuamperfecto de indicativo**	
subscribía	subscribíamos	había subscrito	habíamos subscrito
subscribías	subscribíais	habías subscrito	habíais subscrito
subscribía	subscribían	había subscrito	habían subscrito
3 pretérito		**10 pretérito anterior**	
subscribí	subscribimos	hube subscrito	hubimos subscrito
subscribiste	subscribisteis	hubiste subscrito	hubisteis subscrito
subscribió	subscribieron	hubo subscrito	hubieron subscrito
4 futuro		**11 futuro perfecto**	
subscribiré	subscribiremos	habré subscrito	habremos subscrito
subscribirás	subscribiréis	habrás subscrito	habréis subscrito
subscribirá	subscribirán	habrá subscrito	habrán subscrito
5 potencial simple		**12 potencial compuesto**	
subscribiría	subscribiríamos	habría subscrito	habríamos subscrito
subscribirías	subscribiríais	habrías subscrito	habríais subscrito
subscribiría	subscribirían	habría subscrito	habrían subscrito
6 presente de subjuntivo		**13 perfecto de subjuntivo**	
subscriba	subscribamos	haya subscrito	hayamos subscrito
subscribas	subscribáis	hayas subscrito	hayáis subscrito
subscriba	subscriban	haya subscrito	hayan subscrito
7 imperfecto de subjuntivo		**14 pluscuamperfecto de subjuntivo**	
subscribiera	subscribiéramos	hubiera subscrito	hubiéramos subscrito
subscribieras	subscribierais	hubieras subscrito	hubierais subscrito
subscribiera	subscribieran	hubiera subscrito	hubieran subscrito
OR		OR	
subscribiese	subscribiésemos	hubiese subscrito	hubiésemos subscrito
subscribieses	subscribieseis	hubieses subscrito	hubieseis subscrito
subscribiese	subscribiesen	hubiese subscrito	hubiesen subscrito

imperativo	
—	**subscribamos**
subscribe; no subscribas	**subscribid; no subscribáis**
subscriba	**subscriban**

Words and expressions related to this verb
subscribirse a   to subscribe to (a magazine, etc.)
la subscripción   subscription
subscrito, subscrita   subscribed, signed

subscriptor, subscriptora   subscriber
suscribir (variant of **subscribir**)
   to subscribe

For other words and expressions related to this verb, see **describir** and **escribir.**

The Seven Simple Tenses		The Seven Compound Tenses	
Singular	Plural	Singular	Plural
1 presente de indicativo		8 perfecto de indicativo	
sucede	**suceden**	**ha sucedido**	**han sucedido**
2 imperfecto de indicativo		9 pluscuamperfecto de indicativo	
sucedía	**sucedían**	**había sucedido**	**habían sucedido**
3 pretérito		10 pretérito anterior	
sucedió	**sucedieron**	**hubo sucedido**	**hubieron sucedido**
4 futuro		11 futuro perfecto	
sucederá	**sucederán**	**habrá sucedido**	**habrán sucedido**
5 potencial simple		12 potencial compuesto	
sucedería	**sucederían**	**habría sucedido**	**habrían sucedido**
6 presente de subjuntivo		13 perfecto de subjuntivo	
suceda	**sucedan**	**haya sucedido**	**hayan sucedido**
7 imperfecto de subjuntivo		14 pluscuamperfecto de subjuntivo	
sucediera	**sucedieran**	**hubiera sucedido**	**hubieran sucedido**
OR		OR	
sucediese	**sucediesen**	**hubiese sucedido**	**hubiesen sucedido**

imperativo

¡Que suceda!   **¡Que sucedan!**
Let it happen!   Let them happen!

Words and expressions related to this verb
suceder a   to succeed to (a high position, etc.)
suceder con   to happen to

un sucedido   event, happening
sucediente   succeeding, following

Suceda lo que sucediere.   Come what may.
The verb form **sucediere** is the future subjunctive. For the formation and use of the future subjunctive, see page xxxvii.

The verb **suceder** is usually used impersonally. However, if you wish to use it to mean *to succeed,* conjugate it like **deber.** To express *to succeed (to be successful in something),* many people use **tener éxito.** See **tener** and pages 536–537.

to suffer, to endure, to bear up, to undergo

The Seven Simple Tenses		The Seven Compound Tenses	
Singular	Plural	Singular	Plural
1 presente de indicativo		8 perfecto de indicativo	
sufro	**sufrimos**	**he sufrido**	**hemos sufrido**
sufres	**sufrís**	**has sufrido**	**habéis sufrido**
sufre	**sufren**	**ha sufrido**	**han sufrido**
2 imperfecto de indicativo		9 pluscuamperfecto de indicativo	
sufría	**sufríamos**	**había sufrido**	**habíamos sufrido**
sufrías	**sufríais**	**habías sufrido**	**habíais sufrido**
sufría	**sufrían**	**había sufrido**	**habían sufrido**
3 pretérito		10 pretérito anterior	
sufrí	**sufrimos**	**hube sufrido**	**hubimos sufrido**
sufriste	**sufristeis**	**hubiste sufrido**	**hubisteis sufrido**
sufrió	**sufrieron**	**hubo sufrido**	**hubieron sufrido**
4 futuro		11 futuro perfecto	
sufriré	**sufriremos**	**habré sufrido**	**habremos sufrido**
sufrirás	**sufriréis**	**habrás sufrido**	**habréis sufrido**
sufrirá	**sufrirán**	**habrá sufrido**	**habrán sufrido**
5 potencial simple		12 potencial compuesto	
sufriría	**sufriríamos**	**habría sufrido**	**habríamos sufrido**
sufrirías	**sufriríais**	**habrías sufrido**	**habríais sufrido**
sufriría	**sufrirían**	**habría sufrido**	**habrían sufrido**
6 presente de subjuntivo		13 perfecto de subjuntivo	
sufra	**suframos**	**haya sufrido**	**hayamos sufrido**
sufras	**sufráis**	**hayas sufrido**	**hayáis sufrido**
sufra	**sufran**	**haya sufrido**	**hayan sufrido**
7 imperfecto de subjuntivo		14 pluscuamperfecto de subjuntivo	
sufriera	**sufriéramos**	**hubiera sufrido**	**hubiéramos sufrido**
sufrieras	**sufrierais**	**hubieras sufrido**	**hubierais sufrido**
sufriera	**sufrieran**	**hubiera sufrido**	**hubieran sufrido**
OR		OR	
sufriese	**sufriésemos**	**hubiese sufrido**	**hubiésemos sufrido**
sufrieses	**sufrieseis**	**hubieses sufrido**	**hubieseis sufrido**
sufriese	**sufriesen**	**hubiese sufrido**	**hubiesen sufrido**

	imperativo	
—		**suframos**
sufre; no sufras		**sufrid; no sufráis**
sufra		**sufran**

Words and expressions related to this verb
el sufrimiento   suffering
sufrible   sufferable
insufrible   insufferable
sufridor, sufridora   suffering

sufrir una multa   to be given a fine
sufrir un accidente   to have an accident
sufrir una pérdida   to suffer a loss

If you don't know the Spanish verb for the English verb you have in mind, look it up in the index on pages 505–518.

to hint, to insinuate, to suggest

The Seven Simple Tenses		The Seven Compound Tenses	
Singular	Plural	Singular	Plural
1 presente de indicativo		8 perfecto de indicativo	
sugiero	**sugerimos**	**he sugerido**	**hemos sugerido**
sugieres	**sugerís**	**has sugerido**	**habéis sugerido**
sugiere	**sugieren**	**ha sugerido**	**han sugerido**
2 imperfecto de indicativo		9 pluscuamperfecto de indicativo	
sugería	**sugeríamos**	**había sugerido**	**habíamos sugerido**
sugerías	**sugeríais**	**habías sugerido**	**habíais sugerido**
sugería	**sugerían**	**había sugerido**	**habían sugerido**
3 pretérito		10 pretérito anterior	
sugerí	**sugerimos**	**hube sugerido**	**hubimos sugerido**
sugeriste	**sugeristeis**	**hubiste sugerido**	**hubisteis sugerido**
sugirió	**sugirieron**	**hubo sugerido**	**hubieron sugerido**
4 futuro		11 futuro perfecto	
sugeriré	**sugeriremos**	**habré sugerido**	**habremos sugerido**
sugerirás	**sugeriréis**	**habrás sugerido**	**habréis sugerido**
sugerirá	**sugerirán**	**habrá sugerido**	**habrán sugerido**
5 potencial simple		12 potencial compuesto	
sugeriría	**sugeriríamos**	**habría sugerido**	**habríamos sugerido**
sugerirías	**sugeriríais**	**habrías sugerido**	**habríais sugerido**
sugeriría	**sugerirían**	**habría sugerido**	**habrían sugerido**
6 presente de subjuntivo		13 perfecto de subjuntivo	
sugiera	**sugiramos**	**haya sugerido**	**hayamos sugerido**
sugieras	**sugiráis**	**hayas sugerido**	**hayáis sugerido**
sugiera	**sugieran**	**haya sugerido**	**hayan sugerido**
7 imperfecto de subjuntivo		14 pluscuamperfecto de subjuntivo	
sugiriera	**sugiriéramos**	**hubiera sugerido**	**hubiéramos sugerido**
sugirieras	**sugirierais**	**hubieras sugerido**	**hubierais sugerido**
sugiriera	**sugirieran**	**hubiera sugerido**	**hubieran sugerido**
OR		OR	
sugiriese	**sugiriésemos**	**hubiese sugerido**	**hubiésemos sugerido**
sugirieses	**sugirieseis**	**hubieses sugerido**	**hubieseis sugerido**
sugiriese	**sugiriesen**	**hubiese sugerido**	**hubiesen sugerido**

imperativo

—	**sugiramos**
sugiere; no sugieras	**sugerid; no sugiráis**
sugiera	**sugieran**

Words and expressions related to this verb
una sugestión, una sugerencia   suggestion
sugestionable   easily influenced
sugestivo, sugestiva   suggestive
sugerente   suggestive

Increase your verb power with popular phrases, words,
and expressions for tourists on pages 595–618.

---

to submerge, to plunge, to immerse, to sink

The Seven Simple Tenses		The Seven Compound Tenses	
Singular	Plural	Singular	Plural
1 presente de indicativo		8 perfecto de indicativo	
sumerjo	**sumergimos**	**he sumergido**	**hemos sumergido**
sumerges	**sumergís**	**has sumergido**	**habéis sumergido**
sumerge	**sumergen**	**ha sumergido**	**han sumergido**
2 imperfecto de indicativo		9 pluscuamperfecto de indicativo	
sumergía	**sumergíamos**	**había sumergido**	**habíamos sumergido**
sumergías	**sumergíais**	**habías sumergido**	**habíais sumergido**
sumergía	**sumergían**	**había sumergido**	**habían sumergido**
3 pretérito		10 pretérito anterior	
sumergí	**sumergimos**	**hube sumergido**	**hubimos sumergido**
sumergiste	**sumergisteis**	**hubiste sumergido**	**hubisteis sumergido**
sumergió	**sumergieron**	**hubo sumergido**	**hubieron sumergido**
4 futuro		11 futuro perfecto	
sumergiré	**sumergiremos**	**habré sumergido**	**habremos sumergido**
sumergirás	**sumergiréis**	**habrás sumergido**	**habréis sumergido**
sumergirá	**sumergirán**	**habrá sumergido**	**habrán sumergido**
5 potencial simple		12 potencial compuesto	
sumergiría	**sumergiríamos**	**habría sumergido**	**habríamos sumergido**
sumergirías	**sumergiríais**	**habrías sumergido**	**habríais sumergido**
sumergiría	**sumergirían**	**habría sumergido**	**habrían sumergido**
6 presente de subjuntivo		13 perfecto de subjuntivo	
sumerja	**sumerjamos**	**haya sumergido**	**hayamos sumergido**
sumerjas	**sumerjáis**	**hayas sumergido**	**hayáis sumergido**
sumerja	**sumerjan**	**haya sumergido**	**hayan sumergido**
7 imperfecto de subjuntivo		14 pluscuamperfecto de subjuntivo	
sumergiera	**sumergiéramos**	**hubiera sumergido**	**hubiéramos sumergido**
sumergieras	**sumergierais**	**hubieras sumergido**	**hubierais sumergido**
sumergiera	**sumergieran**	**hubiera sumergido**	**hubieran sumergido**
OR		OR	
sumergiese	**sumergiésemos**	**hubiese sumergido**	**hubiésemos sumergido**
sumergieses	**sumergieseis**	**hubieses sumergido**	**hubieseis sumergido**
sumergiese	**sumergiesen**	**hubiese sumergido**	**hubiesen sumergido**

imperativo

—	**sumerjamos**
sumerge; no sumerjas	**sumergid; no sumerjáis**
sumerja	**sumerjan**

Words related to this verb
el sumergimiento submersion, sinking
el sumergible submarine

la sumersión submersion
emerger to emerge

If you want to see a sample English verb fully conjugated in all
the tenses, check out pages xviii and xix.

to suppose, to assume

The Seven Simple Tenses		The Seven Compound Tenses	
Singular	Plural	Singular	Plural
1 presente de indicativo		8 perfecto de indicativo	
supongo	**suponemos**	**he supuesto**	**hemos supuesto**
supones	**suponéis**	**has supuesto**	**habéis supuesto**
supone	**suponen**	**ha supuesto**	**han supuesto**
2 imperfecto de indicativo		9 pluscuamperfecto de indicativo	
suponía	**suponíamos**	**había supuesto**	**habíamos supuesto**
suponías	**suponíais**	**habías supuesto**	**habíais supuesto**
suponía	**suponían**	**había supuesto**	**habían supuesto**
3 pretérito		10 pretérito anterior	
supuse	**supusimos**	**hube supuesto**	**hubimos supuesto**
supusiste	**supusisteis**	**hubiste supuesto**	**hubisteis supuesto**
supuso	**supusieron**	**hubo supuesto**	**hubieron supuesto**
4 futuro		11 futuro perfecto	
supondré	**supondremos**	**habré supuesto**	**habremos supuesto**
supondrás	**supondréis**	**habrás supuesto**	**habréis supuesto**
supondrá	**supondrán**	**habrá supuesto**	**habrán supuesto**
5 potencial simple		12 potencial compuesto	
supondría	**supondríamos**	**habría supuesto**	**habríamos supuesto**
supondrías	**supondríais**	**habrías supuesto**	**habríais supuesto**
supondría	**supondrían**	**habría supuesto**	**habrían supuesto**
6 presente de subjuntivo		13 perfecto de subjuntivo	
suponga	**supongamos**	**haya supuesto**	**hayamos supuesto**
supongas	**supongáis**	**hayas supuesto**	**hayáis supuesto**
suponga	**supongan**	**haya supuesto**	**hayan supuesto**
7 imperfecto de subjuntivo		14 pluscuamperfecto de subjuntivo	
supusiera	**supusiéramos**	**hubiera supuesto**	**hubiéramos supuesto**
supusieras	**supusierais**	**hubieras supuesto**	**hubierais supuesto**
supusiera	**supusieran**	**hubiera supuesto**	**hubieran supuesto**
OR		OR	
supusiese	**supusiésemos**	**hubiese supuesto**	**hubiésemos supuesto**
supusieses	**supusieseis**	**hubieses supuesto**	**hubieseis supuesto**
supusiese	**supusiesen**	**hubiese supuesto**	**hubiesen supuesto**

imperativo

—	**supongamos**
supón; no supongas	**suponed; no supongáis**
suponga	**supongan**

Words related to this verb
un suponer, una suposición   supposition
poner   to put

proponer   to propose
por supuesto   of course

For additional words and expressions related to this verb, see **poner, ponerse,** and **componer.**

suprimir Gerundio **suprimiendo** Part. pas. **suprimido** (**supreso**, *as an adj.*)

to suppress, to abolish, to cancel (in mathematics),
to eliminate, to delete (for a computer)

The Seven Simple Tenses		The Seven Compound Tenses	
Singular	Plural	Singular	Plural
1 presente de indicativo		8 perfecto de indicativo	
suprimo	**suprimios**	**he suprimido**	**hemos suprimido**
suprimes	**suprimís**	**has suprimido**	**habéis suprimido**
suprime	**suprimen**	**ha suprimido**	**han suprimido**
2 imperfecto de indicativo		9 pluscuamperfecto de indicativo	
suprimía	**suprimíamos**	**había suprimido**	**habíamos suprimido**
suprimías	**suprimíais**	**habías suprimido**	**habíais suprimido**
suprimía	**suprimían**	**había suprimido**	**habían suprimido**
3 pretérito		10 pretérito anterior	
suprimí	**suprimimos**	**hube suprimido**	**hubimos suprimido**
suprimiste	**suprimisteis**	**hubiste suprimido**	**hubisteis suprimido**
suprimió	**suprimieron**	**hubo suprimido**	**hubieron suprimido**
4 futuro		11 futuro perfecto	
suprimiré	**suprimiremos**	**habré suprimido**	**habremos suprimido**
suprimirás	**suprimiréis**	**habrás suprimido**	**habréis suprimido**
suprimirá	**suprimirán**	**habrá suprimido**	**habrán suprimido**
5 potencial simple		12 potencial compuesto	
suprimiría	**suprimiríamos**	**habría suprimido**	**habríamos suprimido**
suprimirías	**suprimiríais**	**habrías suprimido**	**habríais suprimido**
suprimiría	**suprimirían**	**habría suprimido**	**habrían suprimido**
6 presente de subjuntivo		13 perfecto de subjuntivo	
suprima	**suprimamos**	**haya suprimido**	**hayamos suprimido**
suprimas	**suprimáis**	**hayas suprimido**	**hayáis suprimido**
suprima	**supriman**	**haya suprimido**	**hayan suprimido**
7 imperfecto de subjuntivo		14 pluscuamperfecto de subjuntivo	
suprimiera	**suprimiéramos**	**hubiera suprimido**	**hubiéramos suprimido**
suprimieras	**suprimierais**	**hubieras suprimido**	**hubierais suprimido**
suprimiera	**suprimieran**	**hubiera suprimido**	**hubieran suprimido**
OR		OR	
suprimiese	**suprimiésemos**	**hubiese suprimido**	**hubiésemos suprimido**
suprimieses	**suprimieseis**	**hubieses suprimido**	**hubieseis suprimido**
suprimiese	**suprimiesen**	**hubiese suprimido**	**hubiesen suprimido**

imperativo

—	**suprimamos**
suprime; no suprimas	**suprimid; no suprimáis**
suprima	**supriman**

Words related to this verb
la supresión suppression
suprimido, suprimida suppressed

suprimible suppressible
supreso, supresa suppressed

Want to learn more idiomatic expressions that contain verbs? Check out pages 524–537.

to surge, to spout up, to spurt up, to spring up,
to arise, to appear, to emerge, to loom up

The Seven Simple Tenses		The Seven Compound Tenses	
Singular	Plural	Singular	Plural
1 presente de indicativo		8 perfecto de indicativo	
surjo	surgimos	he surgido	hemos surgido
surges	surgís	has surgido	habéis surgido
surge	surgen	ha surgido	han surgido
2 imperfecto de indicativo		9 pluscuamperfecto de indicativo	
surgía	surgíamos	había surgido	habíamos surgido
surgías	surgíais	habías surgido	habíais surgido
surgía	surgían	había surgido	habían surgido
3 pretérito		10 pretérito anterior	
surgí	surgimos	hube surgido	hubimos surgido
surgiste	surgisteis	hubiste surgido	hubisteis surgido
surgió	surgieron	hubo surgido	hubieron surgido
4 futuro		11 futuro perfecto	
surgiré	surgiremos	habré surgido	habremos surgido
surgirás	surgiréis	habrás surgido	habréis surgido
surgirá	surgirán	habrá surgido	habrán surgido
5 potencial simple		12 potencial compuesto	
surgiría	surgiríamos	habría surgido	habríamos surgido
surgirías	surgiríais	habrías surgido	habríais surgido
surgiría	surgirían	habría surgido	habrían surgido
6 presente de subjuntivo		13 perfecto de subjuntivo	
surja	surjamos	haya surgido	hayamos surgido
surjas	surjáis	hayas surgido	hayáis surgido
surja	surjan	haya surgido	hayan surgido
7 imperfecto de subjuntivo		14 pluscuamperfecto de subjuntivo	
surgiera	surgiéramos	hubiera surgido	hubiéramos surgido
surgieras	surgierais	hubieras surgido	hubierais surgido
surgiera	surgieran	hubiera surgido	hubieran surgido
OR		OR	
surgiese	surgiésemos	hubiese surgido	hubiésemos surgido
surgieses	surgieseis	hubieses surgido	hubieseis surgido
surgiese	surgiesen	hubiese surgido	hubiesen surgido

	imperativo	
—		**surjamos**
surge; no surjas		**surgid; no surjáis**
surja		**surjan**

Words related to this verb
surgente surging, salient   **el resurgimiento** reappearance, recovery
resurgir to reappear

Este muchacho es muy grande; surge entre los otros muchachos.
This boy is very big; he towers over the other boys.

surgir also has the meaning of *to anchor* (nautical)
el surgidor, la surgidora person who anchors

The subject pronouns are found on the page facing page 1.

to sigh

The Seven Simple Tenses		The Seven Compound Tenses	
Singular	Plural	Singular	Plural
1 presente de indicativo		8 perfecto de indicativo	
suspiro	**suspiramos**	**he suspirado**	**hemos suspirado**
suspiras	**suspiráis**	**has suspirado**	**habéis suspirado**
suspira	**suspiran**	**ha suspirado**	**han suspirado**
2 imperfecto de indicativo		9 pluscuamperfecto de indicativo	
suspiraba	**suspirábamos**	**había suspirado**	**habíamos suspirado**
suspirabas	**suspirabais**	**habías suspirado**	**habíais suspirado**
suspiraba	**suspiraban**	**había suspirado**	**habían suspirado**
3 pretérito		10 pretérito anterior	
suspiré	**suspiramos**	**hube suspirado**	**hubimos suspirado**
suspiraste	**suspirasteis**	**hubiste suspirado**	**hubisteis suspirado**
suspiró	**suspiraron**	**hubo suspirado**	**hubieron suspirado**
4 futuro		11 futuro perfecto	
suspiraré	**suspiraremos**	**habré suspirado**	**habremos suspirado**
suspirarás	**suspiraréis**	**habrás suspirado**	**habréis suspirado**
suspirará	**suspirarán**	**habrá suspirado**	**habrán suspirado**
5 potencial simple		12 potencial compuesto	
suspiraría	**suspiraríamos**	**habría suspirado**	**habríamos suspirado**
suspirarías	**suspiraríais**	**habrías suspirado**	**habríais suspirado**
suspiraría	**suspirarían**	**habría suspirado**	**habrían suspirado**
6 presente de subjuntivo		13 perfecto de subjuntivo	
suspire	**suspiremos**	**haya suspirado**	**hayamos suspirado**
suspires	**suspiréis**	**hayas suspirado**	**hayáis suspirado**
suspire	**suspiren**	**haya suspirado**	**hayan suspirado**
7 imperfecto de subjuntivo		14 pluscuamperfecto de subjuntivo	
suspirara	**suspiráramos**	**hubiera suspirado**	**hubiéramos suspirado**
suspiraras	**suspirarais**	**hubieras suspirado**	**hubierais suspirado**
suspirara	**suspiraran**	**hubiera suspirado**	**hubieran suspirado**
OR		OR	
suspirase	**suspirásemos**	**hubiese suspirado**	**hubiésemos suspirado**
suspirases	**suspiraseis**	**hubieses suspirado**	**hubieseis suspirado**
suspirase	**suspirasen**	**hubiese suspirado**	**hubiesen suspirado**

imperativo	
—	**suspiremos**
suspira; no suspires	**suspirad; no suspiréis**
suspire	**suspiren**

Words and expressions related to this verb

suspirar por to long for
el suspiro sigh, breath; **exhalar el último suspiro** to breathe one's last breath

el espíritu spirit
exasperar to exasperate
inspirar to inspire, to inhale
la inspiración inspiration

Don't miss the definitions of basic grammatical terms with examples in English and Spanish on pages 666–677.

to pluck, to play (a stringed musical instrument)

The Seven Simple Tenses		The Seven Compound Tenses	
Singular	Plural	Singular	Plural
1 presente de indicativo		8 perfecto de indicativo	
taño	**tañemos**	**he tañido**	**hemos tañido**
tañes	**tañéis**	**has tañido**	**habéis tañido**
tañe	**tañen**	**ha tañido**	**han tañido**
2 imperfecto de indicativo		9 pluscuamperfecto de indicativo	
tañía	**tañíamos**	**había tañido**	**habíamos tañido**
tañías	**tañíais**	**habías tañido**	**habíais tañido**
tañía	**tañían**	**había tañido**	**habían tañido**
3 pretérito		10 pretérito anterior	
tañí	**tañimos**	**hube tañido**	**hubimos tañido**
tañiste	**tañisteis**	**hubiste tañido**	**hubisteis tañido**
tañó	**tañeron**	**hubo tañido**	**hubieron tañido**
4 futuro		11 futuro perfecto	
tañeré	**tañeremos**	**habré tañido**	**habremos tañido**
tañerás	**tañeréis**	**habrás tañido**	**habréis tañido**
tañerá	**tañerán**	**habrá tañido**	**habrán tañido**
5 potencial simple		12 potencial compuesto	
tañería	**tañeríamos**	**habría tañido**	**habríamos tañido**
tañerías	**tañeríais**	**habrías tañido**	**habríais tañido**
tañería	**tañerían**	**habría tañido**	**habrían tañido**
6 presente de subjuntivo		13 perfecto de subjuntivo	
taña	**tañamos**	**haya tañido**	**hayamos tañido**
tañas	**tañáis**	**hayas tañido**	**hayáis tañido**
taña	**tañan**	**haya tañido**	**hayan tañido**
7 imperfecto de subjuntivo		14 pluscuamperfecto de subjuntivo	
tañera	**tañéramos**	**hubiera tañido**	**hubiéramos tañido**
tañeras	**tañerais**	**hubieras tañido**	**hubierais tañido**
tañera	**tañeran**	**hubiera tañido**	**hubieran tañido**
OR		OR	
tañese	**tañésemos**	**hubiese tañido**	**hubiésemos tañido**
tañeses	**tañeseis**	**hubieses tañido**	**hubieseis tañido**
tañese	**tañesen**	**hubiese tañido**	**hubiesen tañido**

imperativo

—	**tañamos**
tañe; no tañas	**tañed; no tañáis**
taña	**tañan**

Words related to this verb

el tañido   sound, tone; twang of a stringed musical instrument;
  el tañimiento   plucking, strumming of a stringed musical instrument

---

Review the principal parts of important Spanish verbs on pages xvi–xvii.

---

to telephone

The Seven Simple Tenses		The Seven Compound Tenses	
Singular	Plural	Singular	Plural
1 presente de indicativo		8 perfecto de indicativo	
telefoneo	**telefoneamos**	**he telefoneado**	**hemos telefoneado**
telefoneas	**telefoneáis**	**has telefoneado**	**habéis telefoneado**
telefonea	**telefonean**	**ha telefoneado**	**han telefoneado**
2 imperfecto de indicativo		9 pluscuamperfecto de indicativo	
telefoneaba	**telefoneábamos**	**había telefoneado**	**habíamos telefoneado**
telefoneabas	**telefoneabais**	**habías telefoneado**	**habíais telefoneado**
telefoneaba	**telefoneaban**	**había telefoneado**	**habían telefoneado**
3 pretérito		10 pretérito anterior	
telefoneé	**telefoneamos**	**hube telefoneado**	**hubimos telefoneado**
telefoneaste	**telefoneasteis**	**hubiste telefoneado**	**hubisteis telefoneado**
telefoneó	**telefonearon**	**hubo telefoneado**	**hubieron telefoneado**
4 futuro		11 futuro perfecto	
telefonearé	**telefonearemos**	**habré telefoneado**	**habremos telefoneado**
telefonearás	**telefonearéis**	**habrás telefoneado**	**habréis telefoneado**
telefoneará	**telefonearán**	**habrá telefoneado**	**habrán telefoneado**
5 potencial simple		12 potencial compuesto	
telefonearía	**telefonearíamos**	**habría telefoneado**	**habríamos telefoneado**
telefonearías	**telefonearíais**	**habrías telefoneado**	**habríais telefoneado**
telefonearía	**telefonearían**	**habría telefoneado**	**habrían telefoneado**
6 presente de subjuntivo		13 perfecto de subjuntivo	
telefonee	**telefoneemos**	**haya telefoneado**	**hayamos telefoneado**
telefonees	**telefoneéis**	**hayas telefoneado**	**hayáis telefoneado**
telefonee	**telefoneen**	**haya telefoneado**	**hayan telefoneado**
7 imperfecto de subjuntivo		14 pluscuamperfecto de subjuntivo	
telefoneara	**telefoneáramos**	**hubiera telefoneado**	**hubiéramos telefoneado**
telefonearas	**telefonearais**	**hubieras telefoneado**	**hubierais telefoneado**
telefoneara	**telefonearan**	**hubiera telefoneado**	**hubieran telefoneado**
OR		OR	
telefonease	**telefoneásemos**	**hubiese telefoneado**	**hubiésemos telefoneado**
telefoneases	**telefoneaseis**	**hubieses telefoneado**	**hubieseis telefoneado**
telefonease	**telefoneasen**	**hubiese telefoneado**	**hubiesen telefoneado**

imperativo

—	**telefoneemos**
telefonea; no telefonees	**telefonead; no telefoneéis**
telefonee	**telefoneen**

Words and expressions related to this verb

el teléfono telephone
telefonista telephone operator
telefónico, telefónica telephonic
marcar el número de teléfono to dial
  a telephone number

la guía telefónica telephone book
la cabina telefónica telephone booth
el número de teléfono telephone number
por teléfono by telephone
una buscapersonas pager
un teléfono celular cell phone

For additional related vocabulary, see also making a telephone call on page 569.

to telegraph, to cable

The Seven Simple Tenses		The Seven Compound Tenses	
Singular	Plural	Singular	Plural
1 presente de indicativo		8 perfecto de indicativo	
telegrafío	telegrafiamos	he telegrafiado	hemos telegrafiado
telegrafías	telegrafiáis	has telegrafiado	habéis telegrafiado
telegrafía	telegrafían	ha telegrafiado	han telegrafiado
2 imperfecto de indicativo		9 pluscuamperfecto de indicativo	
telegrafiaba	telegrafiábamos	había telegrafiado	habíamos telegrafiado
telegrafiabas	telegrafiabais	habías telegrafiado	habíais telegrafiado
telegrafiaba	telegrafiaban	había telegrafiado	habían telegrafiado
3 pretérito		10 pretérito anterior	
telegrafié	telegrafiamos	hube telegrafiado	hubimos telegrafiado
telegrafiaste	telegrafiasteis	hubiste telegrafiado	hubisteis telegrafiado
telegrafió	telegrafiaron	hubo telegrafiado	hubieron telegrafiado
4 futuro		11 futuro perfecto	
telegrafiaré	telegrafiaremos	habré telegrafiado	habremos telegrafiado
telegrafiarás	telegrafiaréis	habrás telegrafiado	habréis telegrafiado
telegrafiará	telegrafiarán	habrá telegrafiado	habrán telegrafiado
5 potencial simple		12 potencial compuesto	
telegrafiaría	telegrafiaríamos	habría telegrafiado	habríamos telegrafiado
telegrafiarías	telegrafiaríais	habrías telegrafiado	habríais telegrafiado
telegrafiaría	telegrafiarían	habría telegrafiado	habrían telegrafiado
6 presente de subjuntivo		13 perfecto de subjuntivo	
telegrafíe	telegrafiemos	haya telegrafiado	hayamos telegrafiado
telegrafíes	telegrafiéis	hayas telegrafiado	hayáis telegrafiado
telegrafíe	telegrafíen	haya telegrafiado	hayan telegrafiado
7 imperfecto de subjuntivo		14 pluscuamperfecto de subjuntivo	
telegrafiara	telegrafiáramos	hubiera telegrafiado	hubiéramos telegrafiado
telegrafiaras	telegrafiarais	hubieras telegrafiado	hubierais telegrafiado
telegrafiara	telegrafiaran	hubiera telegrafiado	hubieran telegrafiado
OR		OR	
telegrafiase	telegrafiásemos	hubiese telegrafiado	hubiésemos telegrafiado
telegrafiases	telegrafiaseis	hubieses telegrafiado	hubieseis telegrafiado
telegrafiase	telegrafiasen	hubiese telegrafiado	hubiesen telegrafiado

imperativo

—	telegrafiemos
telegrafía; no telegrafíes	telegrafiad; no telegrafiéis
telegrafíe	telegrafíen

Words and expressions related to this verb

el telégrafo telegraph
el telegrama telegram, cablegram
telegrafista telegraph operator

la telegrafía telegraphy
el telégrafo sin hilos wireless telegraph
telegrafiar la intención to telegraph (one's) intentions

Learn more verbs in 30 practical situations for tourists on pages 564–594.

temblar

Gerundio **temblando**　　　Part. pas. **temblado**

to tremble, to quake, to quiver, to shake, to shiver

The Seven Simple Tenses		The Seven Compound Tenses	
Singular	Plural	Singular	Plural
1　presente de indicativo		8　perfecto de indicativo	
tiemblo	temblamos	he temblado	hemos temblado
tiemblas	tembláis	has temblado	habéis temblado
tiembla	tiemblan	ha temblado	han temblado
2　imperfecto de indicativo		9　pluscuamperfecto de indicativo	
temblaba	temblábamos	había temblado	habíamos temblado
temblabas	temblabais	habías temblado	habíais temblado
temblaba	temblaban	había temblado	habían temblado
3　pretérito		10　pretérito anterior	
temblé	temblamos	hube temblado	hubimos temblado
temblaste	temblasteis	hubiste temblado	hubisteis temblado
tembló	temblaron	hubo temblado	hubieron temblado
4　futuro		11　futuro perfecto	
temblaré	temblaremos	habré temblado	habremos temblado
temblarás	temblaréis	habrás temblado	habréis temblado
temblará	temblarán	habrá temblado	habrán temblado
5　potencial simple		12　potencial compuesto	
temblaría	temblaríamos	habría temblado	habríamos temblado
temblarías	temblaríais	habrías temblado	habríais temblado
temblaría	temblarían	habría temblado	habrían temblado
6　presente de subjuntivo		13　perfecto de subjuntivo	
tiemble	temblemos	haya temblado	hayamos temblado
tiembles	tembléis	hayas temblado	hayáis temblado
tiemble	tiemblen	haya temblado	hayan temblado
7　imperfecto de subjuntivo		14　pluscuamperfecto de subjuntivo	
temblara	tembláramos	hubiera temblado	hubiéramos temblado
temblaras	temblarais	hubieras temblado	hubierais temblado
temblara	temblaran	hubiera temblado	hubieran temblado
OR		OR	
temblase	temblásemos	hubiese temblado	hubiésemos temblado
temblases	temblaseis	hubieses temblado	hubieseis temblado
temblase	temblasen	hubiese temblado	hubiesen temblado

imperativo	
—	temblemos
tiembla; no tiembles	temblad; no tembléis
tiemble	tiemblen

Words and expressions related to this verb

temblante　trembling, shaking; **el temblante**　bracelet
el temblor　tremor, shaking; **temblón, temblona**　trembling
un temblor de tierra　earthquake; **un temblor de voz**　quivering of one's voice

---

If you want an explanation of meanings and uses of Spanish
and English verb tenses and moods, see pages xx–xl.

to fear, to dread

The Seven Simple Tenses		The Seven Compound Tenses	
Singular	Plural	Singular	Plural

1   presente de indicativo

		8 perfecto de indicativo	
temo	tememos	he temido	hemos temido
temes	teméis	has temido	habéis temido
teme	temen	ha temido	han temido

2   imperfecto de indicativo

		9 pluscuamperfecto de indicativo	
temía	temíamos	había temido	habíamos temido
temías	temíais	habías temido	habíais temido
temía	temían	había temido	habían temido

3   pretérito

		10 pretérito anterior	
temí	temimos	hube temido	hubimos temido
temiste	temisteis	hubiste temido	hubisteis temido
temió	temieron	hubo temido	hubieron temido

4   futuro

		11 futuro perfecto	
temeré	temeremos	habré temido	habremos temido
temerás	temeréis	habrás temido	habréis temido
temerá	temerán	habrá temido	habrán temido

5   potencial simple

		12 potencial compuesto	
temería	temeríamos	habría temido	habríamos temido
temerías	temeríais	habrías temido	habríais temido
temería	temerían	habría temido	habrían temido

6   presente de subjuntivo

		13 perfecto de subjuntivo	
tema	temamos	haya temido	hayamos temido
temas	temáis	hayas temido	hayáis temido
tema	teman	haya temido	hayan temido

7   imperfecto de subjuntivo

		14 pluscuamperfecto de subjuntivo	
temiera	temiéramos	hubiera temido	hubiéramos temido
temieras	temierais	hubieras temido	hubierais temido
temiera	temieran	hubiera temido	hubieran temido
OR		OR	
temiese	temiésemos	hubiese temido	hubiésemos temido
temieses	temieseis	hubieses temido	hubieseis temido
temiese	temiesen	hubiese temido	hubiesen temido

imperativo

—	**temamos**
teme; no temas	**temed; no temáis**
tema	**teman**

Words and expressions related to this verb

temer + inf.   to fear + inf.
temer por   to fear for
temedor, temedora   afraid, fearing
temedero, temedera   dreadful, fearful
intimidar   to intimidate

el temor   fear
la temeridad   temerity, daring
temeroso, temerosa   fearful
sin temor a nada   without fearing anything
tímido, tímida   shy

Consult pages 524-537 for the section on verbs used in idiomatic expressions.

to extend, to offer, to stretch, to spread out, to hang out (washing)

The Seven Simple Tenses		The Seven Compound Tenses	
Singular	Plural	Singular	Plural

1 presente de indicativo		8 perfecto de indicativo	
tiendo	tendemos	he tendido	hemos tendido
tiendes	tendéis	has tendido	habéis tendido
tiende	tienden	ha tendido	han tendido

2 imperfecto de indicativo		9 pluscuamperfecto de indicativo	
tendía	tendíamos	había tendido	habíamos tendido
tendías	tendíais	habías tendido	habíais tendido
tendía	tendían	había tendido	habían tendido

3 pretérito		10 pretérito anterior	
tendí	tendimos	hube tendido	hubimos tendido
tendiste	tendisteis	hubiste tendido	hubisteis tendido
tendió	tendieron	hubo tendido	hubieron tendido

4 futuro		11 futuro perfecto	
tenderé	tenderemos	habré tendido	habremos tendido
tenderás	tenderéis	habrás tendido	habréis tendido
tenderá	tenderán	habrá tendido	habrán tendido

5 potencial simple		12 potencial compuesto	
tendería	tenderíamos	habría tendido	habríamos tendido
tenderías	tenderíais	habrías tendido	habríais tendido
tendería	tenderían	habría tendido	habrían tendido

6 presente de subjuntivo		13 perfecto de subjuntivo	
tienda	tendamos	haya tendido	hayamos tendido
tiendas	tendáis	hayas tendido	hayáis tendido
tienda	tiendan	haya tendido	hayan tendido

7 imperfecto de subjuntivo		14 pluscuamperfecto de subjuntivo	
tendiera	tendiéramos	hubiera tendido	hubiéramos tendido
tendieras	tendierais	hubieras tendido	hubierais tendido
tendiera	tendieran	hubiera tendido	hubieran tendido
OR		OR	
tendiese	tendiésemos	hubiese tendido	hubiésemos tendido
tendieses	tendieseis	hubieses tendido	hubieseis tendido
tendiese	tendiesen	hubiese tendido	hubiesen tendido

imperativo	
—	tendamos
tiende; no tiendas	tended; no tendáis
tienda	tiendan

Words and expressions related to this verb

tender a + inf.   to tend + inf.
un tendero, una tendera   shopkeeper
un tenderete   booth, stand (for selling merchandise)

una tienda   shop, store; **tienda de pacotilla** junk store; **tienda de campaña**   tent
una tienda de ultramarinos   grocery store
una tendencia   trend

Use the EE-zee guide to Spanish pronunciation on pages 562 and 563.

The Seven Simple Tenses		The Seven Compound Tenses	
Singular	Plural	Singular	Plural
1 presente de indicativo		**8 perfecto de indicativo**	
tengo	tenemos	he tenido	hemos tenido
tienes	tenéis	has tenido	habéis tenido
tiene	tienen	ha tenido	han tenido
2 imperfecto de indicativo		**9 pluscuamperfecto de indicativo**	
tenía	teníamos	había tenido	habíamos tenido
tenías	teníais	habías tenido	habíais tenido
tenía	tenían	había tenido	habían tenido
3 pretérito		**10 pretérito anterior**	
tuve	tuvimos	hube tenido	hubimos tenido
tuviste	tuvisteis	hubiste tenido	hubisteis tenido
tuvo	tuvieron	hubo tenido	hubieron tenido
4 futuro		**11 futuro perfecto**	
tendré	tendremos	habré tenido	habremos tenido
tendrás	tendréis	habrás tenido	habréis tenido
tendrá	tendrán	habrá tenido	habrán tenido
5 potencial simple		**12 potencial compuesto**	
tendría	tendríamos	habría tenido	habríamos tenido
tendrías	tendríais	habrías tenido	habríais tenido
tendría	tendrían	habría tenido	habrían tenido
6 presente de subjuntivo		**13 perfecto de subjuntivo**	
tenga	tengamos	haya tenido	hayamos tenido
tengas	tengáis	hayas tenido	hayáis tenido
tenga	tengan	haya tenido	hayan tenido
7 imperfecto de subjuntivo		**14 pluscuamperfecto de subjuntivo**	
tuviera	tuviéramos	hubiera tenido	hubiéramos tenido
tuvieras	tuvierais	hubieras tenido	hubierais tenido
tuviera	tuvieran	hubiera tenido	hubieran tenido
OR		OR	
tuviese	tuviésemos	hubiese tenido	hubiésemos tenido
tuvieses	tuvieseis	hubieses tenido	hubieseis tenido
tuviese	tuviesen	hubiese tenido	hubiesen tenido

	imperativo
—	tengamos
ten; no tengas	tened; no tengáis
tenga	tengan

Common idiomatic expressions using this verb
Anda despacio que tengo prisa.   Make haste slowly.
tener prisa   to be in a hurry
tener hambre   to be hungry
tener sed   to be thirsty

tener frío   to be (feel) cold (persons)
tener calor   to be (feel) warm (persons)
retener   to retain

See also **tener** on pages 526, 536, and 537.

Enjoy verbs in Spanish proverbs on page 539.

tentar

Gerundio **tentando**   Part. pas. **tentado**

to examine by touch, to feel with the fingers, to attempt, to try

The Seven Simple Tenses		The Seven Compound Tenses	
Singular	Plural	Singular	Plural
1 presente de indicativo		**8 perfecto de indicativo**	
tiento	tentamos	he tentado	hemos tentado
tientas	tentáis	has tentado	habéis tentado
tienta	tientan	ha tentado	han tentado
2 imperfecto de indicativo		**9 pluscuamperfecto de indicativo**	
tentaba	tentábamos	había tentado	habíamos tentado
tentabas	tentabais	habías tentado	habíais tentado
tentaba	tentaban	había tentado	habían tentado
3 pretérito		**10 pretérito anterior**	
tenté	tenamos	hube tentado	hubimos tentado
tentaste	tentasteis	hubiste tentado	hubisteis tentado
tentó	tentaron	hubo tentado	hubieron tentado
4 futuro		**11 futuro perfecto**	
tentaré	tentaremos	habré tentado	habremos tentado
tentarás	tentaréis	habrás tentado	habréis tentado
tentará	tentarán	habrá tentado	habrán tentado
5 potencial simple		**12 potencial compuesto**	
tentaría	tentaríamos	habría tentado	habríamos tentado
tentarías	tentaríais	habrías tentado	habríais tentado
tentaría	tentarían	habría tentado	habrían tentado
6 presente de subjuntivo		**13 perfecto de subjuntivo**	
tiente	tentemos	haya tentado	hayamos tentado
tientes	tentéis	hayas tentado	hayáis tentado
tiente	tienten	haya tentado	hayan tentado
7 imperfecto de subjuntivo		**14 pluscuamperfecto de subjuntivo**	
tentara	tentáramos	hubiera tentado	hubiéramos tentado
tentaras	tentarais	hubieras tentado	hubierais tentado
tentara	tentaran	hubiera tentado	hubieran tentado
OR		OR	
tentase	tentásemos	hubiese tentado	hubiésemos tentado
tentases	tentaseis	hubieses tentado	hubieseis tentado
tentase	tentasen	hubiese tentado	hubiesen tentado

imperativo	
—	tentemos
tienta; no tientes	tentad; no tentéis
tiente	tienten

Words and expressions related to this verb
tentar a uno a + inf.   to tempt somebody + inf.
tentar al diablo   to tempt the devil (to look for trouble)
el tentador   the devil; **un tentador**   tempter; **una tentadora**   temptress
la tentación   temptation; **una tentativa**   attempt

If you want to see a sample English verb fully conjugated
in all the tenses, check out pages xviii and xix.

to end, to terminate, to finish

The Seven Simple Tenses		The Seven Compound Tenses	
Singular	Plural	Singular	Plural
1 presente de indicativo		**8 perfecto de indicativo**	
termino	terminamos	he terminado	hemos terminado
terminas	termináis	has terminado	habéis terminado
termina	terminan	ha terminado	han terminado
2 imperfecto de indicativo		**9 pluscuamperfecto de indicativo**	
terminaba	terminábamos	había terminado	habíamos terminado
terminabas	terminabais	habías terminado	habíais terminado
terminaba	terminaban	había terminado	habían terminado
3 pretérito		**10 pretérito anterior**	
terminé	terminamos	hube terminado	hubimos terminado
terminaste	terminasteis	hubiste terminado	hubisteis terminado
terminó	terminaron	hubo terminado	hubieron terminado
4 futuro		**11 futuro perfecto**	
terminaré	terminaremos	habré terminado	habremos terminado
terminarás	terminaréis	habrás terminado	habréis terminado
terminará	terminarán	habrá terminado	habrán terminado
5 potencial simple		**12 potencial compuesto**	
terminaría	terminaríamos	habría terminado	habríamos terminado
terminarías	terminaríais	habrías terminado	habríais terminado
terminaría	terminarían	habría terminado	habrían terminado
6 presente de subjuntivo		**13 perfecto de subjuntivo**	
termine	terminemos	haya terminado	hayamos terminado
termines	terminéis	hayas terminado	hayáis terminado
termine	terminen	haya terminado	hayan terminado
7 imperfecto de subjuntivo		**14 pluscuamperfecto de subjuntivo**	
terminara	termináramos	hubiera terminado	hubiéramos terminado
terminaras	terminarais	hubieras terminado	hubierais terminado
terminara	terminaran	hubiera terminado	hubieran terminado
OR		OR	
terminase	terminásemos	hubiese terminado	hubiésemos terminado
terminases	terminaseis	hubieses terminado	hubieseis terminado
terminase	terminasen	hubiese terminado	hubiesen terminado

imperativo	
—	terminemos
termina; no termines	terminad; no terminéis
termine	terminen

Words and expressions related to this verb

la terminación   termination, ending, completion
el término   end, ending; term
en otros términos   in other terms, in other words
determinar   to determine

llevar a término   to complete
estar en buenos términos con   to be on good terms with
la terminal aérea   air terminal
el terminal   terminal (electrical or computer)

tirar
Gerundio tirando **Part. pas. tirado**

to pull, to draw, to pitch (a ball), to shoot (a gun), to throw, to fling

The Seven Simple Tenses		The Seven Compound Tenses	
Singular	Plural	Singular	Plural
1 presente de indicativo		**8 perfecto de indicativo**	
tiro	tiramos	he tirado	hemos tirado
tiras	tiráis	has tirado	habéis tirado
tira	tiran	ha tirado	han tirado
2 imperfecto de indicativo		**9 pluscuamperfecto de indicativo**	
tiraba	tirábamos	había tirado	habíamos tirado
tirabas	tirabais	habías tirado	habíais tirado
tiraba	tiraban	había tirado	habían tirado
3 pretérito		**10 pretérito anterior**	
tiré	tiramos	hube tirado	hubimos tirado
tiraste	tirasteis	hubiste tirado	hubisteis tirado
tiró	tiraron	hubo tirado	hubieron tirado
4 futuro		**11 futuro perfecto**	
tiraré	tiraremos	habré tirado	habremos tirado
tirarás	tiraréis	habrás tirado	habréis tirado
tirará	tirarán	habrá tirado	habrán tirado
5 potencial simple		**12 potencial compuesto**	
tiraría	tiraríamos	habría tirado	habríamos tirado
tirarías	tiraríais	habrías tirado	habríais tirado
tiraría	tirarían	habría tirado	habrían tirado
6 presente de subjuntivo		**13 perfecto de subjuntivo**	
tire	tiremos	haya tirado	hayamos tirado
tires	tiréis	hayas tirado	hayáis tirado
tire	tiren	haya tirado	hayan tirado
7 imperfecto de subjuntivo		**14 pluscuamperfecto de subjuntivo**	
tirara	tiráramos	hubiera tirado	hubiéramos tirado
tiraras	tirarais	hubieras tirado	hubierais tirado
tirara	tiraran	hubiera tirado	hubieran tirado
OR		OR	
tirase	tirásemos	hubiese tirado	hubiésemos tirado
tirases	tiraseis	hubieses tirado	hubieseis tirado
tirase	tirasen	hubiese tirado	hubiesen tirado

imperativo	
—	tiremos
tira; no tires	tirad; no tiréis
tire	tiren

Words and expressions related to this verb

tirar a   to shoot at

tirar una línea   to draw a line

a tiro   within reach; **a tiro de piedra**   within a stone's throw; **ni a tiros**   not for love nor money; **al tiro**   right away

tirar la toalla   to throw in the towel; **tirarse al agua**   to jump in the water

If you don't know the Spanish verb for the English verb you have in mind, try the index on pages 505–518.

The Seven Simple Tenses		The Seven Compound Tenses	
Singular	Plural	Singular	Plural
1 presente de indicativo		8 perfecto de indicativo	
toco	**tocamos**	**he tocado**	**hemos tocado**
tocas	**tocáis**	**has tocado**	**habéis tocado**
toca	**tocan**	**ha tocado**	**han tocado**
2 imperfecto de indicativo		9 pluscuamperfecto de indicativo	
tocaba	**tocábamos**	**había tocado**	**habíamos tocado**
tocabas	**tocabais**	**habías tocado**	**habíais tocado**
tocaba	**tocaban**	**había tocado**	**habían tocado**
3 pretérito		10 pretérito anterior	
toqué	**tocamos**	**hube tocado**	**hubimos tocado**
tocaste	**tocasteis**	**hubiste tocado**	**hubisteis tocado**
tocó	**tocaron**	**hubo tocado**	**hubieron tocado**
4 futuro		11 futuro perfecto	
tocaré	**tocaremos**	**habré tocado**	**habremos tocado**
tocarás	**tocaréis**	**habrás tocado**	**habréis tocado**
tocará	**tocarán**	**habrá tocado**	**habrán tocado**
5 potencial simple		12 potencial compuesto	
tocaría	**tocaríamos**	**habría tocado**	**habríamos tocado**
tocarías	**tocaríais**	**habrías tocado**	**habríais tocado**
tocaría	**tocarían**	**habría tocado**	**habrían tocado**
6 presente de subjuntivo		13 perfecto de subjuntivo	
toque	**toquemos**	**haya tocado**	**hayamos tocado**
toques	**toquéis**	**hayas tocado**	**hayáis tocado**
toque	**toquen**	**haya tocado**	**hayan tocado**
7 imperfecto de subjuntivo		14 pluscuamperfecto de subjuntivo	
tocara	**tocáramos**	**hubiera tocado**	**hubiéramos tocado**
tocaras	**tocarais**	**hubieras tocado**	**hubierais tocado**
tocara	**tocaran**	**hubiera tocado**	**hubieran tocado**
OR		OR	
tocase	**tocásemos**	**hubiese tocado**	**hubiésemos tocado**
tocases	**tocaseis**	**hubieses tocado**	**hubieseis tocado**
tocase	**tocasen**	**hubiese tocado**	**hubiesen tocado**

imperativo

—	**toquemos**
toca; no toques	**tocad; no toquéis**
toque	**toquen**

Common idiomatic expressions using this verb

¿Sabe Ud. tocar el piano?   Do you know how to play the piano?

Sí, yo sé tocar el piano.   Yes, I know how to play the piano.

tocar a la puerta   to knock on the door

See also **tocar** on page 532.

el tocadiscos   record player

Aquel hombre está tocado.   That man is crazy.

tocar a uno   to be someone's turn; **Le toca a Juan.**   It's John's turn.

The subject pronouns are found on the page facing page 1.

tomar

Gerundio **tomando**   Part. pas. **tomado**

to take, to have (something to eat or drink)

The Seven Simple Tenses		The Seven Compound Tenses	
Singular	Plural	Singular	Plural
1 presente de indicativo		**8 perfecto de indicativo**	
tomo	tomamos	he tomado	hemos tomado
tomas	tomáis	has tomado	habéis tomado
toma	toman	ha tomado	han tomado
2 imperfecto de indicativo		**9 pluscuamperfecto de indicativo**	
tomaba	tomábamos	había tomado	habíamos tomado
tomabas	tomabais	habías tomado	habíais tomado
tomaba	tomaban	había tomado	habían tomado
3 pretérito		**10 pretérito anterior**	
tomé	tomamos	hube tomado	hubimos tomado
tomaste	tomasteis	hubiste tomado	hubisteis tomado
tomó	tomaron	hubo tomado	hubieron tomado
4 futuro		**11 futuro perfecto**	
tomaré	tomaremos	habré tomado	habremos tomado
tomarás	tomaréis	habrás tomado	habréis tomado
tomará	tomarán	habrá tomado	habrán tomado
5 potencial simple		**12 potencial compuesto**	
tomaría	tomaríamos	habría tomado	habríamos tomado
tomarías	tomaríais	habrías tomado	habríais tomado
tomaría	tomarían	habría tomado	habrían tomado
6 presente de subjuntivo		**13 perfecto de subjuntivo**	
tome	tomemos	haya tomado	hayamos tomado
tomes	toméis	hayas tomado	hayáis tomado
tome	tomen	haya tomado	hayan tomado
7 imperfecto de subjuntivo		**14 pluscuamperfecto de subjuntivo**	
tomara	tomáramos	hubiera tomado	hubiéramos tomado
tomaras	tomarais	hubieras tomado	hubierais tomado
tomara	tomaran	hubiera tomado	hubieran tomado
OR		OR	
tomase	tomásemos	hubiese tomado	hubiésemos tomado
tomases	tomaseis	hubieses tomado	hubieseis tomado
tomase	tomasen	hubiese tomado	hubiesen tomado

	imperativo	
—		tomemos
toma; no tomes		tomad; no toméis
tome		tomen

Sentences and expressions using this verb and words related to it

¿A qué hora toma Ud. el desayuno?   At what time do you have breakfast?
Tomo el desayuno a las siete y media.   I have breakfast at seven thirty.
¿Qué toma Ud. en el desayuno?   What do you have for breakfast?

tomar el tren   to catch the train
tomar el sol   to take a sunbath

tomar en cuenta   to consider
tomar parte en   to take part in

tomar el pelo *(hair)* **a uno** to pull someone's leg. See also **tomar** on page 533.

474

to toast, to tan, to roast (coffee)

The Seven Simple Tenses		The Seven Compound Tenses	
Singular	Plural	Singular	Plural
1 presente de indicativo		8 perfecto de indicativo	
tuesto	tostamos	he tostado	hemos tostado
tuestas	tostáis	has tostado	habéis tostado
tuesta	tuestan	ha tostado	han tostado
2 imperfecto de indicativo		9 pluscuamperfecto de indicativo	
tostaba	tostábamos	había tostado	habíamos tostado
tostabas	tostabais	habías tostado	habíais tostado
tostaba	tostaban	había tostado	habían tostado
3 pretérito		10 pretérito anterior	
tosté	tostamos	hube tostado	hubimos tostado
tostaste	tostasteis	hubiste tostado	hubisteis tostado
tostó	tostaron	hubo tostado	hubieron tostado
4 futuro		11 futuro perfecto	
tostaré	tostaremos	habré tostado	habremos tostado
tostarás	tostaréis	habrás tostado	habréis tostado
tostará	tostarán	habrá tostado	habrán tostado
5 potencial simple		12 potencial compuesto	
tostaría	tostaríamos	habría tostado	habríamos tostado
tostarías	tostaríais	habrías tostado	habríais tostado
tostaría	tostarían	habría tostado	habrían tostado
6 presente de subjuntivo		13 perfecto de subjuntivo	
tueste	tostemos	haya tostado	hayamos tostado
tuestes	tostéis	hayas tostado	hayáis tostado
tueste	tuesten	haya tostado	hayan tostado
7 imperfecto de subjuntivo		14 pluscuamperfecto de subjuntivo	
tostara	tostáramos	hubiera tostado	hubiéramos tostado
tostaras	tostarais	hubieras tostado	hubierais tostado
tostara	tostaran	hubiera tostado	hubieran tostado
OR		OR	
tostase	tostásemos	hubiese tostado	hubiésemos tostado
tostases	tostaseis	hubieses tostado	hubieseis tostado
tostase	tostasen	hubiese tostado	hubiesen tostado

imperativo

—	tostemos
tuesta; no tuestes	tostad; no tostéis
tueste	tuesten

Words and expressions related to this verb
un tostador toaster, toasting machine
pan tostado toast, toasted bread; **una tostada** piece of toast
el tostón crouton; **dar el tostón a uno** to get on someone's nerves
el tostadero de café coffee roaster
dar la tostada a uno to cheat someone

The subject pronouns are found on the page facing page 1.

trabajar

Gerundio **trabajando**   Part. pas. **trabajado**

to work, to labor

The Seven Simple Tenses		The Seven Compound Tenses	
Singular	Plural	Singular	Plural
1 presente de indicativo		**8 perfecto de indicativo**	
trabajo	trabajamos	he trabajado	hemos trabajado
trabajas	trabajáis	has trabajado	habéis trabajado
trabaja	trabajan	ha trabajado	han trabajado
2 imperfecto de indicativo		**9 pluscuamperfecto de indicativo**	
trabajaba	trabajábamos	había trabajado	habíamos trabajado
trabajabas	trabajabais	habías trabajado	habíais trabajado
trabajaba	trabajaban	había trabajado	habían trabajado
3 pretérito		**10 pretérito anterior**	
trabajé	trabajamos	hube trabajado	hubimos trabajado
trabajaste	trabajasteis	hubiste trabajado	hubisteis trabajado
trabajó	trabajaron	hubo trabajado	hubieron trabajado
4 futuro		**11 futuro perfecto**	
trabajaré	trabajaremos	habré trabajado	habremos trabajado
trabajarás	trabajaréis	habrás trabajado	habréis trabajado
trabajará	trabajarán	habrá trabajado	habrán trabajado
5 potencial simple		**12 potencial compuesto**	
trabajaría	trabajaríamos	habría trabajado	habríamos trabajado
trabajarías	trabajaríais	habrías trabajado	habríais trabajado
trabajaría	trabajarían	habría trabajado	habrían trabajado
6 presente de subjuntivo		**13 perfecto de subjuntivo**	
trabaje	trabajemos	haya trabajado	hayamos trabajado
trabajes	trabajéis	hayas trabajado	hayáis trabajado
trabaje	trabajen	haya trabajado	hayan trabajado
7 imperfecto de subjuntivo		**14 pluscuamperfecto de subjuntivo**	
trabajara	trabajáramos	hubiera trabajado	hubiéramos trabajado
trabajaras	trabajarais	hubieras trabajado	hubierais trabajado
trabajara	trabajaran	hubiera trabajado	hubieran trabajado
OR		OR	
trabajase	trabajásemos	hubiese trabajado	hubiésemos trabajado
trabajases	trabajaseis	hubieses trabajado	hubieseis trabajado
trabajase	trabajasen	hubiese trabajado	hubiesen trabajado

	imperativo
—	**trabajemos**
trabaja; no trabajes	**trabajad; no trabajéis**
trabaje	**trabajen**

Words and expressions related to this verb

el trabajo work
trabajador, trabajadora worker
trabajar de manos to do manual work
el trabajo de media jornada part-time employment

trabajar en + inf. to strive + inf.
tener trabajo que hacer to have work to do
trabajar a tiempo parcial to work part-time
los trabajos forzados hard labor

476

The Seven Simple Tenses		The Seven Compound Tenses	
Singular	Plural	Singular	Plural
1 presente de indicativo		8 perfecto de indicativo	
traduzco	**traducimos**	**he traducido**	**hemos traducido**
traduces	**traducís**	**has traducido**	**habéis traducido**
traduce	**traducen**	**ha traducido**	**han traducido**
2 imperfecto de indicativo		9 pluscuamperfecto de indicativo	
traducía	**traducíamos**	**había traducido**	**habíamos traducido**
traducías	**traducíais**	**habías traducido**	**habíais traducido**
traducía	**traducían**	**había traducido**	**habían traducido**
3 pretérito		10 pretérito anterior	
traduje	**tradujimos**	**hube traducido**	**hubimos traducido**
tradujiste	**tradujisteis**	**hubiste traducido**	**hubisteis traducido**
tradujo	**tradujeron**	**hubo traducido**	**hubieron traducido**
4 futuro		11 futuro perfecto	
traduciré	**traduciremos**	**habré traducido**	**habremos traducido**
traducirás	**traduciréis**	**habrás traducido**	**habréis traducido**
traducirá	**traducirán**	**habrá traducido**	**habrán traducido**
5 potencial simple		12 potencial compuesto	
traduciría	**traduciríamos**	**habría traducido**	**habríamos traducido**
traducirías	**traduciríais**	**habrías traducido**	**habríais traducido**
traduciría	**traducirían**	**habría traducido**	**habrían traducido**
6 presente de subjuntivo		13 perfecto de subjuntivo	
traduzca	**traduzcamos**	**haya traducido**	**hayamos traducido**
traduzcas	**traduzcáis**	**hayas traducido**	**hayáis traducido**
traduzca	**traduzcan**	**haya traducido**	**hayan traducido**
7 imperfecto de subjuntivo		14 pluscuamperfecto de subjuntivo	
tradujera	**tradujéramos**	**hubiera traducido**	**hubiéramos traducido**
tradujeras	**tradujerais**	**hubieras traducido**	**hubierais traducido**
tradujera	**tradujeran**	**hubiera traducido**	**hubieran traducido**
OR		OR	
tradujese	**tradujésemos**	**hubiese traducido**	**hubiésemos traducido**
tradujeses	**tradujeseis**	**hubieses traducido**	**hubieseis traducido**
tradujese	**tradujesen**	**hubiese traducido**	**hubiesen traducido**

	imperativo	
—	**traduzcamos**
traduce; no traduzcas	**traducid; no traduzcáis**
traduzca	**traduzcan**

Words related to this verb
la traducción   translation
traducible   translatable
traductor, traductora   translator
traducir del inglés al español   to translate
   from English to Spanish

traducir del español al inglés   to translate
   from Spanish to English
una traducción fiel   a faithful translation
intraducible   untranslatable

to bring

The Seven Simple Tenses | The Seven Compound Tenses

Singular	Plural	Singular	Plural
1 presente de indicativo		8 perfecto de indicativo	
traigo	traemos	he traído	hemos traído
traes	traéis	has traído	habéis traído
trae	traen	ha traído	han traído
2 imperfecto de indicativo		9 pluscuamperfecto de indicativo	
traía	traíamos	había traído	habíamos traído
traías	traíais	habías traído	habíais traído
traía	traían	había traído	habían traído
3 pretérito		10 pretérito anterior	
traje	trajimos	hube traído	hubimos traído
trajiste	trajisteis	hubiste traído	hubisteis traído
trajo	trajeron	hubo traído	hubieron traído
4 futuro		11 futuro perfecto	
traeré	traeremos	habré traído	habremos traído
traerás	traeréis	habrás traído	habréis traído
traerá	traerán	habrá traído	habrán traído
5 potencial simple		12 potencial compuesto	
traería	traeríamos	habría traído	habríamos traído
traerías	traeríais	habrías traído	habríais traído
traería	traerían	habría traído	habrían traído
6 presente de subjuntivo		13 perfecto de subjuntivo	
traiga	traigamos	haya traído	hayamos traído
traigas	traigáis	hayas traído	hayáis traído
traiga	traigan	haya traído	hayan traído
7 imperfecto de subjuntivo		14 pluscuamperfecto de subjuntivo	
trajera	trajéramos	hubiera traído	hubiéramos traído
trajeras	trajerais	hubieras traído	hubierais traído
trajera	trajeran	hubiera traído	hubieran traído
OR		OR	
trajese	trajésemos	hubiese traído	hubiésemos traído
trajeses	trajeseis	hubieses traído	hubieseis traído
trajese	trajesen	hubiese traído	hubiesen traído

imperativo

—	traigamos
trae; no traigas	traed; no traigáis
traiga	traigan

Words and expressions related to this verb
el traje   costume, dress, suit
el traje de baño   bathing suit
el traje hecho   ready-made suit
¡trae! ¡traiga!   Give it here!

traer y llevar   to spread rumors
contraer   to contract
traer entre manos   to have in mind
traer a la mente   to bring to mind

Review the principal parts of important Spanish verbs on pages xvi–xvii.

to try, to treat a subject

The Seven Simple Tenses		The Seven Compound Tenses	
Singular	Plural	Singular	Plural
1 presente de indicativo		8 perfecto de indicativo	
trato	**tratamos**	**he tratado**	**hemos tratado**
tratas	**tratáis**	**has tratado**	**habéis tratado**
trata	**tratan**	**ha tratado**	**han tratado**
2 imperfecto de indicativo		9 pluscuamperfecto de indicativo	
trataba	**tratábamos**	**había tratado**	**habíamos tratado**
tratabas	**tratabais**	**habías tratado**	**habíais tratado**
trataba	**trataban**	**había tratado**	**habían tratado**
3 pretérito		10 pretérito anterior	
traté	**tratamos**	**hube tratado**	**hubimos tratado**
trataste	**tratasteis**	**hubiste tratado**	**hubisteis tratado**
trató	**trataron**	**hubo tratado**	**hubieron tratado**
4 futuro		11 futuro perfecto	
trataré	**trataremos**	**habré tratado**	**habremos tratado**
tratarás	**trataréis**	**habrás tratado**	**habréis tratado**
tratará	**tratarán**	**habrá tratado**	**habrán tratado**
5 potencial simple		12 potencial compuesto	
trataría	**trataríamos**	**habría tratado**	**habríamos tratado**
tratarías	**trataríais**	**habrías tratado**	**habríais tratado**
trataría	**tratarían**	**habría tratado**	**habrían tratado**
6 presente de subjuntivo		13 perfecto de subjuntivo	
trate	**tratemos**	**haya tratado**	**hayamos tratado**
trates	**tratéis**	**hayas tratado**	**hayáis tratado**
trate	**traten**	**haya tratado**	**hayan tratado**
7 imperfecto de subjuntivo		14 pluscuamperfecto de subjuntivo	
tratara	**tratáramos**	**hubiera tratado**	**hubiéramos tratado**
trataras	**tratarais**	**hubieras tratado**	**hubierais tratado**
tratara	**trataran**	**hubiera tratado**	**hubieran tratado**
OR		OR	
tratase	**tratásemos**	**hubiese tratado**	**hubiésemos tratado**
tratases	**trataseis**	**hubieses tratado**	**hubieseis tratado**
tratase	**tratasen**	**hubiese tratado**	**hubiesen tratado**

imperativo

—	**tratemos**
trata; no trates	**tratad; no tratéis**
trate	**traten**

Words and expressions related to this verb

tratar de + inf.   to try + inf.

tratar con   to deal with

el trato   agreement; treatment

tratable   amiable, friendly

tratarse con   to have to do with

un tratado   treatise; treaty

¡Trato hecho!   It's a deal!

el tratamiento de textos   word processing

The subject pronouns are found on the page facing page 1.

tropezar　Gerundio **tropezando**　Part. pas. **tropezado**

to stumble, to blunder

The Seven Simple Tenses			The Seven Compound Tenses	
Singular	Plural		Singular	Plural
1 presente de indicativo			**8 perfecto de indicativo**	
tropiezo	tropezamos		he tropezado	hemos tropezado
tropiezas	tropezáis		has tropezado	habéis tropezado
tropieza	tropiezan		ha tropezado	han tropezado
2 imperfecto de indicativo			**9 pluscuamperfecto de indicativo**	
tropezaba	tropezábamos		había tropezado	habíamos tropezado
tropezabas	tropezabais		habías tropezado	habíais tropezado
tropezaba	tropezaban		había tropezado	habían tropezado
3 pretérito			**10 pretérito anterior**	
tropecé	tropezamos		hube tropezado	hubimos tropezado
tropezaste	tropezasteis		hubiste tropezado	hubisteis tropezado
tropezó	tropezaron		hubo tropezado	hubieron tropezado
4 futuro			**11 futuro perfecto**	
tropezaré	tropezaremos		habré tropezado	habremos tropezado
tropezarás	tropezaréis		habrás tropezado	habréis tropezado
tropezará	tropezarán		habrá tropezado	habrán tropezado
5 potencial simple			**12 potencial compuesto**	
tropezaría	tropezaríamos		habría tropezado	habríamos tropezado
tropezarías	tropezaríais		habrías tropezado	habríais tropezado
tropezaría	tropezarían		habría tropezado	habrían tropezado
6 presente de subjuntivo			**13 perfecto de subjuntivo**	
tropiece	tropecemos		haya tropezado	hayamos tropezado
tropieces	tropecéis		hayas tropezado	hayáis tropezado
tropiece	tropiecen		haya tropezado	hayan tropezado
7 imperfecto de subjuntivo			**14 pluscuamperfecto de subjuntivo**	
tropezara	tropezáramos		hubiera tropezado	hubiéramos tropezado
tropezaras	tropezarais		hubieras tropezado	hubierais tropezado
tropezara	tropezaran		hubiera tropezado	hubieran tropezado
OR			OR	
tropezase	tropezásemos		hubiese tropezado	hubiésemos tropezado
tropezases	tropezaseis		hubieses tropezado	hubieseis tropezado
tropezase	tropezasen		hubiese tropezado	hubiesen tropezado

imperativo	
—	tropecemos
tropieza; no tropieces	tropezad; no tropecéis
tropiece	tropiecen

Words and expressions related to this verb

tropezar con alguien　to run across someone, to meet someone unexpectedly
la tropezadura　stumbling
tropezador, tropezadora　tripper, stumbler
dar un tropezón　to trip, to stumble

Don't miss the definitions of basic grammatical terms with
examples in English and Spanish on pages 666–677.

480

to connect, to unite, to join, to bind, to attach

The Seven Simple Tenses		The Seven Compound Tenses	
Singular	Plural	Singular	Plural
1 presente de indicativo		8 perfecto de indicativo	
uno	**unimos**	**he unido**	**hemos unido**
unes	**unís**	**has unido**	**habéis unido**
une	**unen**	**ha unido**	**han unido**
2 imperfecto de indicativo		9 pluscuamperfecto de indicativo	
unía	**uníamos**	**había unido**	**habíamos unido**
unías	**uníais**	**habías unido**	**habíais unido**
unía	**unían**	**había unido**	**habían unido**
3 pretérito		10 pretérito anterior	
uní	**unimos**	**hube unido**	**hubimos unido**
uniste	**unisteis**	**hubiste unido**	**hubisteis unido**
unió	**unieron**	**hubo unido**	**hubieron unido**
4 futuro		11 futuro perfecto	
uniré	**uniremos**	**habré unido**	**habremos unido**
unirás	**uniréis**	**habrás unido**	**habréis unido**
unirá	**unirán**	**habrá unido**	**habrán unido**
5 potencial simple		12 potencial compuesto	
uniría	**uniríamos**	**habría unido**	**habríamos unido**
unirías	**uniríais**	**habrías unido**	**habríais unido**
uniría	**unirían**	**habría unido**	**habrían unido**
6 presente de subjuntivo		13 perfecto de subjuntivo	
una	**unamos**	**haya unido**	**hayamos unido**
unas	**unáis**	**hayas unido**	**hayáis unido**
una	**unan**	**haya unido**	**hayan unido**
7 imperfecto de subjuntivo		14 pluscuamperfecto de subjuntivo	
uniera	**uniéramos**	**hubiera unido**	**hubiéramos unido**
unieras	**unierais**	**hubieras unido**	**hubierais unido**
uniera	**unieran**	**hubiera unido**	**hubieran unido**
OR		OR	
uniese	**uniésemos**	**hubiese unido**	**hubiésemos unido**
unieses	**unieseis**	**hubieses unido**	**hubieseis unido**
uniese	**uniesen**	**hubiese unido**	**hubiesen unido**

	imperativo	
—		**unamos**
une; no unas		**unid; no unáis**
una		**unan**

Words and expressions related to this verb
unido, unida   united
los Estados Unidos   the United States
la unión   union, agreement, harmony

unirse   to be united; to get married
La unión hace la fuerza   There is strength in unity.
las Naciones Unidas (ONU)   the United Nations (UN)

For other words and expressions related to this verb, see **reunirse.**

Check out the verb drills and verb tests with answers explained on pages 619–665.

The subject pronouns are found on the page facing page 1.

to use, to employ, to wear

The Seven Simple Tenses		The Seven Compound Tenses	
Singular	Plural	Singular	Plural
1　presente de indicativo		8　perfecto de indicativo	
uso	usamos	he usado	hemos usado
usas	usáis	has usado	habéis usado
usa	usan	ha usado	han usado
2　imperfecto de indicativo		9　pluscuamperfecto de indicativo	
usaba	usábamos	había usado	habíamos usado
usabas	usabais	habías usado	habíais usado
usaba	usaban	había usado	habían usado
3　pretérito		10　pretérito anterior	
usé	usamos	hube usado	hubimos usado
usaste	usasteis	hubiste usado	hubisteis usado
usó	usaron	hubo usado	hubieron usado
4　futuro		11　futuro perfecto	
usaré	usaremos	habré usado	habremos usado
usarás	usaréis	habrás usado	habréis usado
usará	usarán	habrá usado	habrán usado
5　potencial simple		12　potencial compuesto	
usaría	usaríamos	habría usado	habríamos usado
usarías	usaríais	habrías usado	habríais usado
usaría	usarían	habría usado	habrían usado
6　presente de subjuntivo		13　perfecto de subjuntivo	
use	usemos	haya usado	hayamos usado
uses	uséis	hayas usado	hayáis usado
use	usen	haya usado	hayan usado
7　imperfecto de subjuntivo		14　pluscuamperfecto de subjuntivo	
usara	usáramos	hubiera usado	hubiéramos usado
usaras	usarais	hubieras usado	hubierais usado
usara	usaran	hubiera usado	hubieran usado
OR		OR	
usase	usásemos	hubiese usado	hubiésemos usado
usases	usaseis	hubieses usado	hubieseis usado
usase	usasen	hubiese usado	hubiesen usado

imperativo	
—	usemos
usa; no uses	usad; no uséis
use	usen

Words and expressions related to this verb

¿**Usa usted guantes?**　Do you wear gloves?
el uso　use, usage
usado, usada　used
desusar　to disuse

en buen uso　in good condition
en uso　in use, in service
usar + inf.　to be used + inf.
desusarse　to be no longer in use

If you want an explanation of meanings and uses of Spanish
and English verb tenses and moods, see pages xx–xxxix.

The Seven Simple Tenses		The Seven Compound Tenses	
Singular	Plural	Singular	Plural
1 presente de indicativo		8 perfecto de indicativo	
utilizo	utilizamos	he utilizado	hemos utilizado
utilizas	utilizáis	has utilizado	habéis utilizado
utiliza	utilizan	ha utilizado	han utilizado
2 imperfecto de indicativo		9 pluscuamperfecto de indicativo	
utilizaba	utilizábamos	había utilizado	habíamos utilizado
utilizabas	utilizabais	habías utilizado	habíais utilizado
utilizaba	utilizaban	había utilizado	habían utilizado
3 pretérito		10 pretérito anterior	
utilicé	utilizamos	hube utilizado	hubimos utilizado
utilizaste	utilizasteis	hubiste utilizado	hubisteis utilizado
utilizó	utilizaron	hubo utilizado	hubieron utilizado
4 futuro		11 futuro perfecto	
utilizaré	utilizaremos	habré utilizado	habremos utilizado
utilizarás	utilizaréis	habrás utilizado	habréis utilizado
utilizará	utilizarán	habrá utilizado	habrán utilizado
5 potencial simple		12 potencial compuesto	
utilizaría	utilizaríamos	habría utilizado	habríamos utilizado
utilizarías	utilizaríais	habrías utilizado	habríais utilizado
utilizaría	utilizarían	habría utilizado	habrían utilizado
6 presente de subjuntivo		13 perfecto de subjuntivo	
utilice	utilicemos	haya utilizado	hayamos utilizado
utilices	utilicéis	hayas utilizado	hayáis utilizado
utilice	utilicen	haya utilizado	hayan utilizado
7 imperfecto de subjuntivo		14 pluscuamperfecto de subjuntivo	
utilizara	utilizáramos	hubiera utilizado	hubiéramos utilizado
utilizaras	utilizarais	hubieras utilizado	hubierais utilizado
utilizara	utilizaran	hubiera utilizado	hubieran utilizado
OR		OR	
utilizase	utilizásemos	hubiese utilizado	hubiésemos utilizado
utilizases	utilizaseis	hubieses utilizado	hubieseis utilizado
utilizase	utilizasen	hubiese utilizado	hubiesen utilizado

	imperativo	
—	utilicemos	
utiliza; no utilices	utilizad; no utilicéis	
utilice	utilicen	

Words and expressions related to this verb
la utilización   utilization
utilizable   usable, available
útil   useful
el útil   tool

la utilidad   utility, usefulness
la utilidad pública   public utility
ser útil   to serve, to be useful
el programa de utilidad   utility program

The subject pronouns are found on the page facing page 1.

to empty

The Seven Simple Tenses		The Seven Compound Tenses	
Singular	Plural	Singular	Plural
1 presente de indicativo		8 perfecto de indicativo	
vacío	vaciamos	he vaciado	hemos vaciado
vacías	vaciáis	has vaciado	habéis vaciado
vacía	vacían	ha vaciado	han vaciado
2 imperfecto de indicativo		9 pluscuamperfecto de indicativo	
vaciaba	vaciábamos	había vaciado	habíamos vaciado
vaciabas	vaciabais	habías vaciado	habíais vaciado
vaciaba	vaciaban	había vaciado	habían vaciado
3 pretérito		10 pretérito anterior	
vacié	vaciamos	hube vaciado	hubimos vaciado
vaciaste	vaciasteis	hubiste vaciado	hubisteis vaciado
vació	vaciaron	hubo vaciado	hubieron vaciado
4 futuro		11 futuro perfecto	
vaciaré	vaciaremos	habré vaciado	habremos vaciado
vaciarás	vaciaréis	habrás vaciado	habréis vaciado
vaciará	vaciarán	habrá vaciado	habrán vaciado
5 potencial simple		12 potencial compuesto	
vaciaría	vaciaríamos	habría vaciado	habríamos vaciado
vaciarías	vaciaríais	habrías vaciado	habríais vaciado
vaciaría	vaciarían	habría vaciado	habrían vaciado
6 presente de subjuntivo		13 perfecto de subjuntivo	
vacíe	vaciemos	haya vaciado	hayamos vaciado
vacíes	vaciéis	hayas vaciado	hayáis vaciado
vacíe	vacíen	haya vaciado	hayan vaciado
7 imperfecto de subjuntivo		14 pluscuamperfecto de subjuntivo	
vaciara	vaciáramos	hubiera vaciado	hubiéramos vaciado
vaciaras	vaciarais	hubieras vaciado	hubierais vaciado
vaciara	vaciaran	hubiera vaciado	hubieran vaciado
OR		OR	
vaciase	vaciásemos	hubiese vaciado	hubiésemos vaciado
vaciases	vaciaseis	hubieses vaciado	hubieseis vaciado
vaciase	vaciasen	hubiese vaciado	hubiesen vaciado

	imperativo	
—		vaciemos
vacía; no vacíes		vaciad; no vaciéis
vacíe		vacíen

Words and expressions related to this verb
el vacío void; vacancy; **un vacío de aire** air pocket (aviation)
vacío, vacía empty; **evacuar** to evacuate
vacuo, vacua empty

Don't miss the definitions of basic grammatical terms with
examples in English and Spanish on pages 666–677.

The Seven Simple Tenses		The Seven Compound Tenses	
Singular	Plural	Singular	Plural
1 presente de indicativo		**8 perfecto de indicativo**	
valgo	valemos	he valido	hemos valido
vales	valéis	has valido	habéis valido
vale	valen	ha valido	han valido
2 imperfecto de indicativo		**9 pluscuamperfecto de indicativo**	
valía	valíamos	había valido	habíamos valido
valías	valíais	habías valido	habíais valido
valía	valían	había valido	habían valido
3 pretérito		**10 pretérito anterior**	
valí	valimos	hube valido	hubimos valido
valiste	valisteis	hubiste valido	hubisteis valido
valió	valieron	hubo valido	hubieron valido
4 futuro		**11 futuro perfecto**	
valdré	valdremos	habré valido	habremos valido
valdrás	valdréis	habrás valido	habréis valido
valdrá	valdrán	habrá valido	habrán valido
5 potencial simple		**12 potencial compuesto**	
valdría	valdríamos	habría valido	habríamos valido
valdrías	valdríais	habrías valido	habríais valido
valdría	valdrían	habría valido	habrían valido
6 presente de subjuntivo		**13 perfecto de subjuntivo**	
valga	valgamos	haya valido	hayamos valido
valgas	valgáis	hayas valido	hayáis valido
valga	valgan	haya valido	hayan valido
7 imperfecto de subjuntivo		**14 pluscuamperfecto de subjuntivo**	
valiera	valiéramos	hubiera valido	hubiéramos valido
valieras	valierais	hubieras valido	hubierais valido
valiera	valieran	hubiera valido	hubieran valido
OR		OR	
valiese	valiésemos	hubiese valido	hubiésemos valido
valieses	valieseis	hubieses valido	hubieseis valido
valiese	valiesen	hubiese valido	hubiesen valido

	imperativo	
—	valgamos
val *or* vale; no valgas	valed; no valgáis
valga	valgan

Sentences using this verb and words related to it
Más vale pájaro en mano que ciento volando.   A bird in the hand is worth two in the bush.
Más vale tarde que nunca.   Better late than never.
el valor   value, price, valor
valor facial   face value
la valía   value, worth

valorar   to appraise, to increase the value
No vale la pena   It's not worth the trouble.
valeroso   courageous

to stay awake, to guard, to watch over

The Seven Simple Tenses		The Seven Compound Tenses	
Singular	Plural	Singular	Plural
1 presente de indicativo		8 perfecto de indicativo	
velo	velamos	he velado	hemos velado
velas	veláis	has velado	habéis velado
vela	velan	ha velado	han velado
2 imperfecto de indicativo		9 pluscuamperfecto de indicativo	
velaba	velábamos	había velado	habíamos velado
velabas	velabais	habías velado	habíais velado
velaba	velaban	había velado	habían velado
3 pretérito		10 pretérito anterior	
velé	velamos	hube velado	hubimos velado
velaste	velasteis	hubiste velado	hubisteis velado
veló	velaron	hubo velado	hubieron velado
4 futuro		11 futuro perfecto	
velaré	velaremos	habré velado	habremos velado
velarás	velaréis	habrás velado	habréis velado
velará	velarán	habrá velado	habrán velado
5 potencial simple		12 potencial compuesto	
velaría	velaríamos	habría velado	habríamos velado
velarías	velaríais	habrías velado	habríais velado
velaría	velarían	habría velado	habrían velado
6 presente de subjuntivo		13 perfecto de subjuntivo	
vele	velemos	haya velado	hayamos velado
veles	veléis	hayas velado	hayáis velado
vele	velen	haya velado	hayan velado
7 imperfecto de subjuntivo		14 pluscuamperfecto de subjuntivo	
velara	veláramos	hubiera velado	hubiéramos velado
velaras	velarais	hubieras velado	hubierais velado
velara	velaran	hubiera velado	hubieran velado
OR		OR	
velase	velásemos	hubiese velado	hubiésemos velado
velases	velaseis	hubieses velado	hubieseis velado
velase	velasen	hubiese velado	hubiesen velado

imperativo	
—	velemos
vela; no veles	velad; no veléis
vele	velen

Words and expressions related to this verb
un velador   watchman, night guard; wooden candlestick
la vela   vigil; candle; **en vela**   without sleeping; **quedarse en velas**   to stay up (during the night)
velar a   to watch over (someone); **un velatorio**   wake
pasar la noche en vela   to toss and turn all night [or] to spend a sleepless night

to conquer, to overcome, to defeat

The Seven Simple Tenses		The Seven Compound Tenses	
Singular	Plural	Singular	Plural
1 presente de indicativo		8 perfecto de indicativo	
venzo	vencemos	he vencido	hemos vencido
vences	vencéis	has vencido	habéis vencido
vence	vencen	ha vencido	han vencido
2 imperfecto de indicativo		9 pluscuamperfecto de indicativo	
vencía	vencíamos	había vencido	habíamos vencido
vencías	vencíais	habías vencido	habíais vencido
vencía	vencían	había vencido	habían vencido
3 pretérito		10 pretérito anterior	
vencí	vencimos	hube vencido	hubimos vencido
venciste	vencisteis	hubiste vencido	hubisteis vencido
venció	vencieron	hubo vencido	hubieron vencido
4 futuro		11 futuro perfecto	
venceré	venceremos	habré vencido	habremos vencido
vencerás	venceréis	habrás vencido	habréis vencido
vencerá	vencerán	habrá vencido	habrán vencido
5 potencial simple		12 potencial compuesto	
vencería	venceríamos	habría vencido	habríamos vencido
vencerías	venceríais	habrías vencido	habríais vencido
vencería	vencerían	habría vencido	habrían vencido
6 presente de subjuntivo		13 perfecto de subjuntivo	
venza	venzamos	haya vencido	hayamos vencido
venzas	venzáis	hayas vencido	hayáis vencido
venza	venzan	haya vencido	hayan vencido
7 imperfecto de subjuntivo		14 pluscuamperfecto de subjuntivo	
venciera	venciéramos	hubiera vencido	hubiéramos vencido
vencieras	vencierais	hubieras vencido	hubierais vencido
venciera	vencieran	hubiera vencido	hubieran vencido
OR		OR	
venciese	venciésemos	hubiese vencido	hubiésemos vencido
vencieses	vencieseis	hubieses vencido	hubieseis vencido
venciese	venciesen	hubiese vencido	hubiesen vencido

imperativo	
—	venzamos
vence; no venzas	venced; no venzáis
venza	venzan

Words and expressions related to this verb
vencedor, vencedora victor
vencible conquerable
invencible invincible

darse por vencido to give in
vencerse to control oneself
la invencibilidad invincibility

See also **convencer.**

vender

Gerundio **vendiendo**   Part. pas. **vendido**

to sell

The Seven Simple Tenses		The Seven Compound Tenses	
Singular	Plural	Singular	Plural
1 presente de indicativo		**8 perfecto de indicativo**	
vendo	vendemos	he vendido	hemos vendido
vendes	vendéis	has vendido	habéis vendido
vende	venden	ha vendido	han vendido
2 imperfecto de indicativo		**9 pluscuamperfecto de indicativo**	
vendía	vendíamos	había vendido	habíamos vendido
vendías	vendíais	habías vendido	habíais vendido
vendía	vendían	había vendido	habían vendido
3 pretérito		**10 pretérito anterior**	
vendí	vendimos	hube vendido	hubimos vendido
vendiste	vendisteis	hubiste vendido	hubisteis vendido
vendió	vendieron	hubo vendido	hubieron vendido
4 futuro		**11 futuro perfecto**	
venderé	venderemos	habré vendido	habremos vendido
venderás	venderéis	habrás vendido	habréis vendido
venderá	venderán	habrá vendido	habrán vendido
5 potencial simple		**12 potencial compuesto**	
vendería	venderíamos	habría vendido	habríamos vendido
venderías	venderíais	habrías vendido	habríais vendido
vendería	venderían	habría vendido	habrían vendido
6 presente de subjuntivo		**13 perfecto de subjuntivo**	
venda	vendamos	haya vendido	hayamos vendido
vendas	vendáis	hayas vendido	hayáis vendido
venda	vendan	haya vendido	hayan vendido
7 imperfecto de subjuntivo		**14 pluscuamperfecto de subjuntivo**	
vendiera	vendiéramos	hubiera vendido	hubiéramos vendido
vendieras	vendierais	hubieras vendido	hubierais vendido
vendiera	vendieran	hubiera vendido	hubieran vendido
OR		OR	
vendiese	vendiésemos	hubiese vendido	hubiésemos vendido
vendieses	vendieseis	hubieses vendido	hubieseis vendido
vendiese	vendiesen	hubiese vendido	hubiesen vendido

imperativo

—	vendamos
vende; no vendas	vended; no vendáis
venda	vendan

Words and expressions related to this verb

vendedor, vendedora   seller, sales person
la venta   sale
el precio de venta   selling price
Aquí se venden libros.   Books are sold here.

vender a comisión   to sell on commission
vender al contado   to sell for cash
revender   to resell
estar en venta   to be on sale

Can't recognize an irregular verb form? Check out pages 519–523.

The Seven Simple Tenses | The Seven Compound Tenses

Singular	Plural	Singular	Plural
1 presente de indicativo		8 perfecto de indicativo	
vengo	**venimos**	**he venido**	**hemos venido**
vienes	**venís**	**has venido**	**habéis venido**
viene	**vienen**	**ha venido**	**han venido**
2 imperfecto de indicativo		9 pluscuamperfecto de indicativo	
venía	**veníamos**	**había venido**	**habíamos venido**
venías	**veníais**	**habías venido**	**habíais venido**
venía	**venían**	**había venido**	**habían venido**
3 pretérito		10 pretérito anterior	
vine	**vinimos**	**hube venido**	**hubimos venido**
viniste	**vinisteis**	**hubiste venido**	**hubisteis venido**
vino	**vinieron**	**hubo venido**	**hubieron venido**
4 futuro		11 futuro perfecto	
vendré	**vendremos**	**habré venido**	**habremos venido**
vendrás	**vendréis**	**habrás venido**	**habréis venido**
vendrá	**vendrán**	**habrá venido**	**habrán venido**
5 potencial simple		12 potencial compuesto	
vendría	**vendríamos**	**habría venido**	**habríamos venido**
vendrías	**vendríais**	**habrías venido**	**habríais venido**
vendría	**vendrían**	**habría venido**	**habrían venido**
6 presente de subjuntivo		13 perfecto de subjuntivo	
venga	**vengamos**	**haya venido**	**hayamos venido**
vengas	**vengáis**	**hayas venido**	**hayáis venido**
venga	**vengan**	**haya venido**	**hayan venido**
7 imperfecto de subjuntivo		14 pluscuamperfecto de subjuntivo	
viniera	**viniéramos**	**hubiera venido**	**hubiéramos venido**
vinieras	**vinierais**	**hubieras venido**	**hubierais venido**
viniera	**vinieran**	**hubiera venido**	**hubieran venido**
OR		OR	
viniese	**viniésemos**	**hubiese venido**	**hubiésemos venido**
vinieses	**vinieseis**	**hubieses venido**	**hubieseis venido**
viniese	**viniesen**	**hubiese venido**	**hubiesen venido**

imperativo

—	**vengamos**
ven; no vengas	**venid; no vengáis**
venga	**vengan**

Common idiomatic expressions using this verb
la semana que viene   next week
el mes que viene   next month
el porvenir   the future
Venga lo que venga.   Come what may.

See also **convenir.**

venir a las manos   to come to blows
venir a buscar   to come for, to get
Viene a ser lo mismo.   It amounts to the same thing.
venir a la mente   to come to mind
¡Bienvenido! ¡Bienvenida!   Welcome!

The subject pronouns are found on the page facing page 1.

to see

The Seven Simple Tenses		The Seven Compound Tenses	
Singular	Plural	Singular	Plural
1 presente de indicativo		**8 perfecto de indicativo**	
veo	vemos	he visto	hemos visto
ves	veis	has visto	habéis visto
ve	ven	ha visto	han visto
2 imperfecto de indicativo		**9 pluscuamperfecto de indicativo**	
veía	veíamos	había visto	habíamos visto
veías	veíais	habías visto	habíais visto
veía	veían	había visto	habían visto
3 pretérito		**10 pretérito anterior**	
vi	vimos	hube visto	hubimos visto
viste	visteis	hubiste visto	hubisteis visto
vio	vieron	hubo visto	hubieron visto
4 futuro		**11 futuro perfecto**	
veré	veremos	habré visto	habremos visto
verás	veréis	habrás visto	habréis visto
verá	verán	habrá visto	habrán visto
5 potencial simple		**12 potencial compuesto**	
vería	veríamos	habría visto	habríamos visto
verías	veríais	habrías visto	habríais visto
vería	verían	habría visto	habrían visto
6 presente de subjuntivo		**13 perfecto de subjuntivo**	
vea	veamos	haya visto	hayamos visto
veas	veáis	hayas visto	hayáis visto
vea	vean	haya visto	hayan visto
7 imperfecto de subjuntivo		**14 pluscuamperfecto de subjuntivo**	
viera	viéramos	hubiera visto	hubiéramos visto
vieras	vierais	hubieras visto	hubierais visto
viera	vieran	hubiera visto	hubieran visto
OR		OR	
viese	viésemos	hubiese visto	hubiésemos visto
vieses	vieseis	hubieses visto	hubieseis visto
viese	viesen	hubiese visto	hubiesen visto

	imperativo	
—	veamos
ve; no veas	ved; no veáis
vea	vean

Words and expressions related to this verb

¡**Vamos a ver!** Let's see!
¡**A ver!** Let's see!
Ver es creer. Seeing is believing.
la vista sight, seeing, view, vision
vivir para ver to live and learn
Está por ver. It remains to be seen.

a mi ver in my opinion
la veracidad veracity
¡**Ya se ve!** Of course! Certainly!
no tener nada que ver con to have nothing to do with
Hay que verlo para creerlo You have to see it to believe it.

to dress oneself, to get dressed

The Seven Simple Tenses		The Seven Compound Tenses	
Singular	Plural	Singular	Plural
1 presente de indicativo		8 perfecto de indicativo	
me visto	nos vestimos	me he vestido	nos hemos vestido
te vistes	os vestís	te has vestido	os habéis vestido
se viste	se visten	se ha vestido	se han vestido
2 imperfecto de indicativo		9 pluscuamperfecto de indicativo	
me vestía	nos vestíamos	me había vestido	nos habíamos vestido
te vestías	os vestíais	te habías vestido	os habíais vestido
se vestía	se vestían	se había vestido	se habían vestido
3 pretérito		10 pretérito anterior	
me vestí	nos vestimos	me hube vestido	nos hubimos vestido
te vestiste	os vestisteis	te hubiste vestido	os hubisteis vestido
se vistió	se vistieron	se hubo vestido	se hubieron vestido
4 futuro		11 futuro perfecto	
me vestiré	nos vestiremos	me habré vestido	nos habremos vestido
te vestirás	os vestiréis	te habrás vestido	os habréis vestido
se vestirá	se vestirán	se habrá vestido	se habrán vestido
5 potencial simple		12 potencial compuesto	
me vestiría	nos vestiríamos	me habría vestido	nos habríamos vestido
te vestirías	os vestiríais	te habrías vestido	os habríais vestido
se vestiría	se vestirían	se habría vestido	se habrían vestido
6 presente de subjuntivo		13 perfecto de subjuntivo	
me vista	nos vistamos	me haya vestido	nos hayamos vestido
te vistas	os vistáis	te hayas vestido	os hayáis vestido
se vista	se vistan	se haya vestido	se hayan vestido
7 imperfecto de subjuntivo		14 pluscuamperfecto de subjuntivo	
me vistiera	nos vistiéramos	me hubiera vestido	nos hubiéramos vestido
te vistieras	os vistierais	te hubieras vestido	os hubierais vestido
se vistiera	se vistieran	se hubiera vestido	se hubieran vestido
OR		OR	
me vistiese	nos vistiésemos	me hubiese vestido	nos hubiésemos vestido
te vistieses	os vistieseis	te hubieses vestido	os hubieseis vestido
se vistiese	se vistiesen	se hubiese vestido	se hubiesen vestido

imperativo

—	vistámonos; no nos vistamos
vístete; no te vistas	vestíos; no os vistáis
vístase; no se vista	vístanse; no se vistan

Words and expressions related to this verb

vestir   to clothe, to dress
desvestirse   to undress oneself, to get undressed
el vestido   clothing, clothes, dress
vestidos usados   secondhand clothing

bien vestido   well-dressed
vestir de uniforme   to dress in uniform
vestir de blanco   to dress in white
el vestuario   wardrobe; cloakroom
la vestimenta   clothes, garments

The subject pronouns are found on the page facing page 1.

The Seven Simple Tenses		The Seven Compound Tenses	
Singular	Plural	Singular	Plural
1 presente de indicativo		8 perfecto de indicativo	
viajo	**viajamos**	**he viajado**	**hemos viajado**
viajas	**viajáis**	**has viajado**	**habéis viajado**
viaja	**viajan**	**ha viajado**	**han viajado**
2 imperfecto de indicativo		9 pluscuamperfecto de indicativo	
viajaba	**viajábamos**	**había viajado**	**habíamos viajado**
viajabas	**viajabais**	**habías viajado**	**habíais viajado**
viajaba	**viajaban**	**había viajado**	**habían viajado**
3 pretérito		10 pretérito anterior	
viajé	**viajamos**	**hube viajado**	**hubimos viajado**
viajaste	**viajasteis**	**hubiste viajado**	**hubisteis viajado**
viajó	**viajaron**	**hubo viajado**	**hubieron viajado**
4 futuro		11 futuro perfecto	
viajaré	**viajaremos**	**habré viajado**	**habremos viajado**
viajarás	**viajaréis**	**habrás viajado**	**habréis viajado**
viajará	**viajarán**	**habrá viajado**	**habrán viajado**
5 potencial simple		12 potencial compuesto	
viajaría	**viajaríamos**	**habría viajado**	**habríamos viajado**
viajarías	**viajaríais**	**habrías viajado**	**habríais viajado**
viajaría	**viajarían**	**habría viajado**	**habrían viajado**
6 presente de subjuntivo		13 perfecto de subjuntivo	
viaje	**viajemos**	**haya viajado**	**hayamos viajado**
viajes	**viajéis**	**hayas viajado**	**hayáis viajado**
viaje	**viajen**	**haya viajado**	**hayan viajado**
7 imperfecto de subjuntivo		14 pluscuamperfecto de subjuntivo	
viajara	**viajáramos**	**hubiera viajado**	**hubiéramos viajado**
viajaras	**viajarais**	**hubieras viajado**	**hubierais viajado**
viajara	**viajaran**	**hubiera viajado**	**hubieran viajado**
OR		OR	
viajase	**viajásemos**	**hubiese viajado**	**hubiésemos viajado**
viajases	**viajaseis**	**hubieses viajado**	**hubieseis viajado**
viajase	**viajasen**	**hubiese viajado**	**hubiesen viajado**

imperativo

—	**viajemos**
viaja; no viajes	**viajad; no viajéis**
viaje	**viajen**

Words and expressions related to this verb

el viaje trip
hacer un viaje to take a trip
un viaje de ida y vuelta round trip
viajero, viajera traveler
el viaje de novios honeymoon

¡Buen viaje! Have a good trip!
un viaje de negocios business trip
un viaje redondo round trip
viajes espaciales space travel
el viaje de recreo pleasure trip

> *For more verbs useful when traveling in a Spanish-speaking country,*
> *see 30 practical situations for tourists beginning on page 564.*

to watch (over), to keep guard, to look out for

The Seven Simple Tenses		The Seven Compound Tenses	
Singular	Plural	Singular	Plural
1 presente de indicativo		**8 perfecto de indicativo**	
vigilo	vigilamos	he vigilado	hemos vigilado
vigilas	vigiláis	has vigilado	habéis vigilado
vigila	vigilan	ha vigilado	han vigilado
2 imperfecto de indicativo		**9 pluscuamperfecto de indicativo**	
vigilaba	vigilábamos	había vigilado	habíamos vigilado
vigilabas	vigilabais	habías vigilado	habíais vigilado
vigilaba	vigilaban	había vigilado	habían vigilado
3 pretérito		**10 pretérito anterior**	
vigilé	vigilamos	hube vigilado	hubimos vigilado
vigilaste	vigilasteis	hubiste vigilado	hubisteis vigilado
vigiló	vigilaron	hubo vigilado	hubieron vigilado
4 futuro		**11 futuro perfecto**	
vigilaré	vigilaremos	habré vigilado	habremos vigilado
vigilarás	vigilaréis	habrás vigilado	habréis vigilado
vigilará	vigilarán	habrá vigilado	habrán vigilado
5 potencial simple		**12 potencial compuesto**	
vigilaría	vigilaríamos	habría vigilado	habríamos vigilado
vigilarías	vigilaríais	habrías vigilado	habríais vigilado
vigilaría	vigilarían	habría vigilado	habrían vigilado
6 presente de subjuntivo		**13 perfecto de subjuntivo**	
vigile	vigilemos	haya vigilado	hayamos vigilado
vigiles	vigiléis	hayas vigilado	hayáis vigilado
vigile	vigilen	haya vigilado	hayan vigilado
7 imperfecto de subjuntivo		**14 pluscuamperfecto de subjuntivo**	
vigilara	vigiláramos	hubiera vigilado	hubiéramos vigilado
vigilaras	vigilarais	hubieras vigilado	hubierais vigilado
vigilara	vigilaran	hubiera vigilado	hubieran vigilado
OR		OR	
vigilase	vigilásemos	hubiese vigilado	hubiésemos vigilado
vigilases	vigilaseis	hubieses vigilado	hubieseis vigilado
vigilase	vigilasen	hubiese vigilado	hubiesen vigilado

	imperativo	
—	**vigilemos**	
vigila; no vigiles	**vigilad; no vigiléis**	
vigile	**vigilen**	

Words and expressions related to this verb
vigilar de cerca   to keep a close watch on
el, la vigilante   vigilante; vigilant, wakeful
la vigilancia   vigilance, watchfulness,
    surveillance

vigilantemente   vigilantly
vigilar sobre *or* **por**   to watch over
comer de vigilia   to abstain from meat
vigilante de noche   night watchman

The Seven Simple Tenses		The Seven Compound Tenses	
Singular	Plural	Singular	Plural
1 presente de indicativo		**8 perfecto de indicativo**	
visito	visitamos	he visitado	hemos visitado
visitas	visitáis	has visitado	habéis visitado
visita	visitan	ha visitado	han visitado
2 imperfecto de indicativo		**9 pluscuamperfecto de indicativo**	
visitaba	visitábamos	había visitado	habíamos visitado
visitabas	visitabais	habías visitado	habíais visitado
visitaba	visitaban	había visitado	habían visitado
3 pretérito		**10 pretérito anterior**	
visité	visitamos	hube visitado	hubimos visitado
visitaste	visitasteis	hubiste visitado	hubisteis visitado
visitó	visitaron	hubo visitado	hubieron visitado
4 futuro		**11 futuro perfecto**	
visitaré	visitaremos	habré visitado	habremos visitado
visitarás	visitaréis	habrás visitado	habréis visitado
visitará	visitarán	habrá visitado	habrán visitado
5 potencial simple		**12 potencial compuesto**	
visitaría	visitaríamos	habría visitado	habríamos visitado
visitarías	visitaríais	habrías visitado	habríais visitado
visitaría	visitarían	habría visitado	habrían visitado
6 presente de subjuntivo		**13 perfecto de subjuntivo**	
visite	visitemos	haya visitado	hayamos visitado
visites	visitéis	hayas visitado	hayáis visitado
visite	visiten	haya visitado	hayan visitado
7 imperfecto de subjuntivo		**14 pluscuamperfecto de subjuntivo**	
visitara	visitáramos	hubiera visitado	hubiéramos visitado
visitaras	visitarais	hubieras visitado	hubierais visitado
visitara	visitaran	hubiera visitado	hubieran visitado
OR		OR	
visitase	visitásemos	hubiese visitado	hubiésemos visitado
visitases	visitaseis	hubieses visitado	hubieseis visitado
visitase	visitasen	hubiese visitado	hubiesen visitado

	imperativo	
—		visitemos
visita; no visites		visitad; no visitéis
visite		visiten

Words and expressions related to this verb

una visita visit	**una visitación** visitation
visitante visitor	**pagar la visita** to return a visit
visitarse to visit one another	**tener visita** to have company
hacer una visita to pay a call, a visit	**una visita acompañada** guided tour

Can't recognize an irregular verb form? Check out pages 519–523.

The Seven Simple Tenses		The Seven Compound Tenses	
Singular	Plural	Singular	Plural
1 presente de indicativo		**8 perfecto de indicativo**	
vivo	vivimos	he vivido	hemos vivido
vives	vivís	has vivido	habéis vivido
vive	viven	ha vivido	han vivido
2 imperfecto de indicativo		**9 pluscuamperfecto de indicativo**	
vivía	vivíamos	había vivido	habíamos vivido
vivías	vivíais	habías vivido	habíais vivido
vivía	vivían	había vivido	habían vivido
3 pretérito		**10 pretérito anterior**	
viví	vivimos	hube vivido	hubimos vivido
viviste	vivisteis	hubiste vivido	hubisteis vivido
vivió	vivieron	hubo vivido	hubieron vivido
4 futuro		**11 futuro perfecto**	
viviré	viviremos	habré vivido	habremos vivido
vivirás	viviréis	habrás vivido	habréis vivido
vivirá	vivirán	habrá vivido	habrán vivido
5 potencial simple		**12 potencial compuesto**	
viviría	viviríamos	habría vivido	habríamos vivido
vivirías	viviríais	habrías vivido	habríais vivido
viviría	vivirían	habría vivido	habrían vivido
6 presente de subjuntivo		**13 perfecto de subjuntivo**	
viva	vivamos	haya vivido	hayamos vivido
vivas	viváis	hayas vivido	hayáis vivido
viva	vivan	haya vivido	hayan vivido
7 imperfecto de subjuntivo		**14 pluscuamperfecto de subjuntivo**	
viviera	viviéramos	hubiera vivido	hubiéramos vivido
vivieras	vivierais	hubieras vivido	hubierais vivido
viviera	vivieran	hubiera vivido	hubieran vivido
OR		OR	
viviese	viviésemos	hubiese vivido	hubiésemos vivido
vivieses	vivieseis	hubieses vivido	hubieseis vivido
viviese	viviesen	hubiese vivido	hubiesen vivido

imperativo	
—	vivamos
vive; no vivas	vivid; no viváis
viva	vivan

Words and expressions related to this verb

vivir de   to live on
la vida   life
en vida   while living, while alive
ganarse la vida   to earn one's living
una lengua viva   living language
¡Viva la reina!   Long live the queen!

vivir del aire   to live on thin air
vivir para ver   to live and learn (live and see)
vivir a oscuras   to live in ignorance
revivir   to revive
una mujer de mal vivir   prostitute
¡Viva el rey!   Long live the king!
¡La vida es así!   That's life!

The subject pronouns are found on the page facing page 1.

volar

Gerundio **volando**   Part. pas. **volado**

to fly

The Seven Simple Tenses		The Seven Compound Tenses	
Singular	Plural	Singular	Plural
1 presente de indicativo		**8 perfecto de indicativo**	
vuelo	volamos	he volado	hemos volado
vuelas	voláis	has volado	habéis volado
vuela	vuelan	ha volado	han volado
2 imperfecto de indicativo		**9 pluscuamperfecto de indicativo**	
volaba	volábamos	había volado	habíamos volado
volabas	volabais	habías volado	habíais volado
volaba	volaban	había volado	habían volado
3 pretérito		**10 pretérito anterior**	
volé	volamos	hube volado	hubimos volado
volaste	volasteis	hubiste volado	hubisteis volado
voló	volaron	hubo volado	hubieron volado
4 futuro		**11 futuro perfecto**	
volaré	volaremos	habré volado	habremos volado
volarás	volaréis	habrás volado	habréis volado
volará	volarán	habrá volado	habrán volado
5 potencial simple		**12 potencial compuesto**	
volaría	volaríamos	habría volado	habríamos volado
volarías	volaríais	habrías volado	habríais volado
volaría	volarían	habría volado	habrían volado
6 presente de subjuntivo		**13 perfecto de subjuntivo**	
vuele	volemos	haya volado	hayamos volado
vueles	voléis	hayas volado	hayáis volado
vuele	vuelen	haya volado	hayan volado
7 imperfecto de subjuntivo		**14 pluscuamperfecto de subjuntivo**	
volara	voláramos	hubiera volado	hubiéramos volado
volaras	volarais	hubieras volado	hubierais volado
volara	volaran	hubiera volado	hubieran volado
OR		OR	
volase	volásemos	hubiese volado	hubiésemos volado
volases	volaseis	hubieses volado	hubieseis volado
volase	volasen	hubiese volado	hubiesen volado

	imperativo
—	volemos
vuela; no vueles	**volad; no voléis**
vuele	**vuelen**

Words and expressions related to this verb
el vuelo   flight
Más vale pájaro en mano que ciento volando   A bird in the hand is worth two in the bush.
Las horas vuelan   The hours go flying by.   **¡Como vuela el tiempo!**   How time flies!
volear   to volley (a ball); **el voleo**   volley
el volante   steering wheel

Enjoy verbs in more Spanish proverbs on page 539.

The Seven Simple Tenses		The Seven Compound Tenses	
Singular	Plural	Singular	Plural
1 presente de indicativo		8 perfecto de indicativo	
vuelvo	**volvemos**	**he vuelto**	**hemos vuelto**
vuelves	**volvéis**	**has vuelto**	**habéis vuelto**
vuelve	**vuelven**	**ha vuelto**	**han vuelto**
2 imperfecto de indicativo		9 pluscuamperfecto de indicativo	
volvía	**volvíamos**	**había vuelto**	**habíamos vuelto**
volvías	**volvíais**	**habías vuelto**	**habíais vuelto**
volvía	**volvían**	**había vuelto**	**habían vuelto**
3 pretérito		10 pretérito anterior	
volví	**volvimos**	**hube vuelto**	**hubimos vuelto**
volviste	**volvisteis**	**hubiste vuelto**	**hubisteis vuelto**
volvió	**volvieron**	**hubo vuelto**	**hubieron vuelto**
4 futuro		11 futuro perfecto	
volveré	**volveremos**	**habré vuelto**	**habremos vuelto**
volverás	**volveréis**	**habrás vuelto**	**habréis vuelto**
volverá	**volverán**	**habrá vuelto**	**habrán vuelto**
5 potencial simple		12 potencial compuesto	
volvería	**volveríamos**	**habría vuelto**	**habríamos vuelto**
volverías	**volveríais**	**habrías vuelto**	**habríais vuelto**
volvería	**volverían**	**habría vuelto**	**habrían vuelto**
6 presente de subjuntivo		13 perfecto de subjuntivo	
vuelva	**volvamos**	**haya vuelto**	**hayamos vuelto**
vuelvas	**volváis**	**hayas vuelto**	**hayáis vuelto**
vuelva	**vuelvan**	**haya vuelto**	**hayan vuelto**
7 imperfecto de subjuntivo		14 pluscuamperfecto de subjuntivo	
volviera	**volviéramos**	**hubiera vuelto**	**hubiéramos vuelto**
volvieras	**volvierais**	**hubieras vuelto**	**hubierais vuelto**
volviera	**volvieran**	**hubiera vuelto**	**hubieran vuelto**
OR		OR	
volviese	**volviésemos**	**hubiese vuelto**	**hubiésemos vuelto**
volvieses	**volvieseis**	**hubieses vuelto**	**hubieseis vuelto**
volviese	**volviesen**	**hubiese vuelto**	**hubiesen vuelto**

imperativo

—	**volvamos**
vuelve; no vuelvas	**volved; no volváis**
vuelva	**vuelvan**

Common idiomatic expressions using this verb

volver en sí   to regain consciousness, to come to
volver sobre sus pasos   to retrace one's steps
una vuelta   turn, revolution, turning
dar una vuelta   to take a stroll
volverse triste   to become sad

un revólver   revolver, pistol
revolver   to revolve, to shake (up), to turn around
volverse   to turn around (oneself)
volverse loco   to go mad

See also **devolver** and **revolver**. See also **volver** on page 537.

The subject pronouns are found on the page facing page 1.

to vote, to vow

The Seven Simple Tenses		The Seven Compound Tenses	
Singular	Plural	Singular	Plural
1 presente de indicativo		8 perfecto de indicativo	
voto	votamos	he votado	hemos votado
votas	votáis	has votado	habéis votado
vota	votan	ha votado	han votado
2 imperfecto de indicativo		9 pluscuamperfecto de indicativo	
votaba	votábamos	había votado	habíamos votado
votabas	votabais	habías votado	habíais votado
votaba	votaban	había votado	habían votado
3 pretérito		10 pretérito anterior	
voté	votamos	hube votado	hubimos votado
votaste	votasteis	hubiste votado	hubisteis votado
votó	votaron	hubo votado	hubieron votado
4 futuro		11 futuro perfecto	
votaré	votaremos	habré votado	habremos votado
votarás	votaréis	habrás votado	habréis votado
votará	votarán	habrá votado	habrán votado
5 potencial simple		12 potencial compuesto	
votaría	votaríamos	habría votado	habríamos votado
votarías	votaríais	habrías votado	habríais votado
votaría	votarían	habría votado	habrían votado
6 presente de subjuntivo		13 perfecto de subjuntivo	
vote	votemos	haya votado	hayamos votado
votes	votéis	hayas votado	hayáis votado
vote	voten	haya votado	hayan votado
7 imperfecto de subjuntivo		14 pluscuamperfecto de subjuntivo	
votara	votáramos	hubiera votado	hubiéramos votado
votaras	votarais	hubieras votado	hubierais votado
votara	votaran	hubiera votado	hubieran votado
OR		OR	
votase	votásemos	hubiese votado	hubiésemos votado
votases	votaseis	hubieses votado	hubieseis votado
votase	votasen	hubiese votado	hubiesen votado

	imperativo	
—	votemos	
vota; no votes	votad; no votéis	
vote	voten	

Words and expressions related to this verb
votar en pro to vote for; **votar en contra** to vote against
el votador, la votadora voter
el voto vote, vow; **voto de gracias** vote of thanks; **voto activo** right to vote;
   voto de confianza vote of confidence; **echar votos** to curse, to swear
la votación voting; **la votación a mano alzada** voting by show of hands
la votación secreta secret ballot

   Get acquainted with what preposition goes with what verb on pages 541–549.

Gerundio **yaciendo**   Part. pas. **yacido**   **yacer**

to lie down, to be lying down, to lie in a grave

The Seven Simple Tenses | The Seven Compound Tenses

Singular	Plural	Singular	Plural
1 presente de indicativo		**8 perfecto de indicativo**	
yazco	yacemos	he yacido	hemos yacido
yaces	yacéis	has yacido	habéis yacido
yace	yacen	ha yacido	han yacido
2 imperfecto de indicativo		**9 pluscuamperfecto de indicativo**	
yacía	yacíamos	había yacido	habíamos yacido
yacías	yacíais	habías yacido	habíais yacido
yacía	yacían	había yacido	habían yacido
3 pretérito		**10 pretérito anterior**	
yací	yacimos	hube yacido	hubimos yacido
yaciste	yacisteis	hubiste yacido	hubisteis yacido
yació	yacieron	hubo yacido	hubieron yacido
4 futuro		**11 futuro perfecto**	
yaceré	yaceremos	habré yacido	habremos yacido
yacerás	yaceréis	habrás yacido	habréis yacido
yacerá	yacerán	habrá yacido	habrán yacido
5 potencial simple		**12 potencial compuesto**	
yacería	yaceríamos	habría yacido	habríamos yacido
yacerías	yaceríais	habrías yacido	habríais yacido
yacería	yacerían	habría yacido	habrían yacido
6 presente de subjuntivo		**13 perfecto de subjuntivo**	
yazca	yazcamos	haya yacido	hayamos yacido
yazcas	yazcáis	hayas yacido	hayáis yacido
yazca	yazcan	haya yacido	hayan yacido
7 imperfecto de subjuntivo		**14 pluscuamperfecto de subjuntivo**	
yaciera	yaciéramos	hubiera yacido	hubiéramos yacido
yacieras	yacierais	hubieras yacido	hubierais yacido
yaciera	yacieran	hubiera yacido	hubieran yacido
OR		OR	
yaciese	yaciésemos	hubiese yacido	hubiésemos yacido
yacieses	yacieseis	hubieses yacido	hubieseis yacido
yaciese	yaciesen	hubiese yacido	hubiesen yacido

imperativo

—	yazcamos
yaz *or* yace; no yazcas	yaced; no yazcáis
yazca	yazcan

Words and expressions related to this verb
la yacija bed, couch; grave, tomb
el yacimiento mineral deposit

Aquí yace don Juan Here lies Don Juan.
una estatua yacente statue lying in state (usually on a catafalque)

Be sure to consult the back pages for verbs used in idiomatic expressions, Spanish proverbs using verbs, weather expressions using verbs, verbs with prepositions, and over 1,100 Spanish verbs conjugated like model verbs among the 501 verbs in this book.

zumbar

Gerundio **zumbando**   Part. pas. **zumbado**

to buzz, to hum, to flutter around

The Seven Simple Tenses		The Seven Compound Tenses	
Singular	Plural	Singular	Plural
1 presente de indicativo		**8 perfecto de indicativo**	
zumbo	zumbamos	he zumbado	hemos zumbado
zumbas	zumbáis	has zumbado	habéis zumbado
zumba	zumban	ha zumbado	han zumbado
2 imperfecto de indicativo		**9 pluscuamperfecto de indicativo**	
zumbaba	zumbábamos	había zumbado	habíamos zumbado
zumbabas	zumbabais	habías zumbado	habíais zumbado
zumbaba	zumbaban	había zumbado	habían zumbado
3 pretérito		**10 pretérito anterior**	
zumbé	zumbamos	hube zumbado	hubimos zumbado
zumbaste	zumbasteis	hubiste zumbado	hubisteis zumbado
zumbó	zumbaron	hubo zumbado	hubieron zumbado
4 futuro		**11 futuro perfecto**	
zumbaré	zumbaremos	habré zumbado	habremos zumbado
zumbarás	zumbaréis	habrás zumbado	habréis zumbado
zumbará	zumbarán	habrá zumbado	habrán zumbado
5 potencial simple		**12 potencial compuesto**	
zumbaría	zumbaríamos	habría zumbado	habríamos zumbado
zumbarías	zumbaríais	habrías zumbado	habríais zumbado
zumbaría	zumbarían	habría zumbado	habrían zumbado
6 presente de subjuntivo		**13 perfecto de subjuntivo**	
zumbe	zumbemos	haya zumbado	hayamos zumbado
zumbes	zumbéis	hayas zumbado	hayáis zumbado
zumbe	zumben	haya zumbado	hayan zumbado
7 imperfecto de subjuntivo		**14 pluscuamperfecto de subjuntivo**	
zumbara	zumbáramos	hubiera zumbado	hubiéramos zumbado
zumbaras	zumbarais	hubieras zumbado	hubierais zumbado
zumbara	zumbaran	hubiera zumbado	hubieran zumbado
OR		OR	
zumbase	zumbásemos	hubiese zumbado	hubiésemos zumbado
zumbases	zumbaseis	hubieses zumbado	hubieseis zumbado
zumbase	zumbasen	hubiese zumbado	hubiesen zumbado

	imperativo
—	zumbemos
zumba; no zumbes	zumbad; no zumbéis
zumbe	zumben

Words and expressions related to this verb
Me zumban los cincuenta años.   I am close to fifty years old.
zumbarse de   to make fun of
zumbar una bofetada   to give a hard slap

un zumbo, un zumbido   buzz, hum; **un zumbido de ocupado**   busy signal of a telephone
un zumbador   buzzer

Want to learn more idiomatic expressions that contain verbs? Check out pages 524–537.

The Seven Simple Tenses		The Seven Compound Tenses	
Singular	Plural	Singular	Plural
1 presente de indicativo		8 perfecto de indicativo	
zurzo	**zurcimos**	**he zurcido**	**hemos zurcido**
zurces	**zurcís**	**has zurcido**	**habéis zurcido**
zurce	**zurcen**	**ha zurcido**	**han zurcido**
2 imperfecto de indicativo		9 pluscuamperfecto de indicativo	
zurcía	**zurcíamos**	**había zurcido**	**habíamos zurcido**
zurcías	**zurcíais**	**habías zurcido**	**habíais zurcido**
zurcía	**zurcían**	**había zurcido**	**habían zurcido**
3 pretérito		10 pretérito anterior	
zurcí	**zurcimos**	**hube zurcido**	**hubimos zurcido**
zurciste	**zurcisteis**	**hubiste zurcido**	**hubisteis zurcido**
zurció	**zurcieron**	**hubo zurcido**	**hubieron zurcido**
4 futuro		11 futuro perfecto	
zurciré	**zurciremos**	**habré zurcido**	**habremos zurcido**
zurcirás	**zurciréis**	**habrás zurcido**	**habréis zurcido**
zurcirá	**zurcirán**	**habrá zurcido**	**habrán zurcido**
5 potencial simple		12 potencial compuesto	
zurciría	**zurciríamos**	**habría zurcido**	**habríamos zurcido**
zurcirías	**zurciríais**	**habrías zurcido**	**habríais zurcido**
zurciría	**zurcirían**	**habría zurcido**	**habrían zurcido**
6 presente de subjuntivo		13 perfecto de subjuntivo	
zurza	**zurzamos**	**haya zurcido**	**hayamos zurcido**
zurzas	**zurzáis**	**hayas zurcido**	**hayáis zurcido**
zurza	**zurzan**	**haya zurcido**	**hayan zurcido**
7 imperfecto de subjuntivo		14 pluscuamperfecto de subjuntivo	
zurciera	**zurciéramos**	**hubiera zurcido**	**hubiéramos zurcido**
zurcieras	**zurcierais**	**hubieras zurcido**	**hubierais zurcido**
zurciera	**zurcieran**	**hubiera zurcido**	**hubieran zurcido**
OR		OR	
zurciese	**zurciésemos**	**hubiese zurcido**	**hubiésemos zurcido**
zurcieses	**zurcieseis**	**hubieses zurcido**	**hubieseis zurcido**
zurciese	**zurciesen**	**hubiese zurcido**	**hubiesen zurcido**

	imperativo	
—		**zurzamos**
zurce; no zurzas		**zurcid; no zurzáis**
zurza		**zurzan**

Words related to this verb
la zurcidura   darning, mending
zurcido, zurcida   darned, mended

un huevo de zurcir   darning ball (egg)
la aguja de zurcir   darning needle

Increase your verb power with popular phrases, words,
and expressions for tourists on pages 595–618.

The subject pronouns are found on the page facing page 1.

501

Appendix

The purpose of this index is to give you instantly the Spanish verb for the English verb you have in mind to use. This saves you time if you do not have a standard English-Spanish word dictionary at your fingertips.

When you find the Spanish verb you need through the English verb, look up its verb forms in this book where all verbs are listed alphabetically at the top of each page. If it is not listed among the 501 verbs in this book, consult the list of Over 1,100 Spanish Verbs Conjugated Like Model Verbs Among the 501, which begins on page 550.

The preposition *to* has been omitted in front of the English verb.

A

abandon   abandonar
able, to be   poder
abolish   abolir, suprimir
absolve   absolver
absorb   absorber
abstain   abstenerse
accede   acceder
accelerate   acelerar
accept   aceptar
acclaim   aclamar
accommodate   acomodar
accompany   acompañar
accuse   acusar
ache   doler
acknowledge   reconocer
acquainted with, to be   conocer
acquire   adquirir
acquit   absolver
act (a part)   desempeñar
activate   activar
add   agregar, añadir, sumar
adjust   arreglar
admire   admirar
admit   admitir, permitir
adopt   adoptar
adore   adorar
advance   adelantar, avanzar
advantage, to take   aprovecharse
advise   aconsejar, advertir,
    recomendar, avisar
affirm   asegurar
aggravate   agravar
aggregate   agregar

agitate   agitar
agree   convenir, acceder, acordarse
agree to   subscribir
agree upon   acordar
aid   ayudar, socorrer
allow   dejar, permitir
allure   atraer
amaze   asombrar
amuse oneself   divertirse
angry, to become   enfadarse
announce   anunciar
annoy   aburrir, enojar
annul   anular
anoint   untar
answer   contestar, responder
apologize   disculparse
appear   aparecer, surgir
appear (seem)   parecer
appertain   pertenecer
applaud   aclamar, aplaudir
appraise   apreciar
appreciate   apreciar
approach   acercarse
approve   aprobar
arrange   arreglar, ordenar,
    organizar, acomodar
arrive   llegar
articulate   articular
ask   preguntar, rogar
ask for   pedir, rogar
assail   asaltar
assault   asaltar
assemble   reunirse
assert   asegurar

assist　ayudar, socorrer
assume　suponer
assure　asegurar
astonish　asombrar, sorprender
attach　unir
attack　atacar
attain　conseguir, lograr
attempt　tentar
attend　acudir, asistir
attest　certificar
attract　atraer
augment　aumentar
avail oneself　aprovecharse
awaken　despertar

B

bake　cocer
baptize　bautizar
bath, to take a　bañarse
bathe oneself　bañarse
battle　batallar
be　estar, ser
be able　poder
be accustomed　acostumbrar, soler
be acquainted with　conocer
be bored　aburrirse
be born　nacer
be called　llamarse
be concerned　preocuparse
be contained in　caber
be divorced　divorciarse
be enough　bastar
be fitting　convenir
be frightened　asustarse
be (get) high (tipsy)　alumbrarse
be glad　alegrarse
be grateful for　reconocer
be guilty　delinquir
be happy　alegrarse
be ignorant of　ignorar
be important　importar
be in the habit of　acostumbrar, soler
be interested in　interesarse
be lacking　faltar
be lying down　yacer

be mistaken　equivocarse
be named　llamarse
be pleasing　agradar
be pleasing to　gustar
be prepared　prepararse
be present at　asistir
be present frequently　acudir
be scared　asustarse
be silent　callarse
be sorry for　lastimarse
be sufficient　bastar
be thankful for　agradecer
be wanting　faltar
be worth　valer
bear up (endure)　sufrir
beat　pegar
become　ponerse
become angry　calentarse, enfadarse, enojarse
become annoyed　enfadarse
become excited　calentarse
become ill　enfermarse
become irritated　enfadarse
become lively (from liquor)　alumbrarse
become sick　enfermarse
become tired　cansarse
become weary　cansarse
beg　implorar, rogar
begin　comenzar, empezar, iniciar, principiar
believe　creer
belong　pertenecer
bind　atar, unir
bite　morder
bless　bendecir
blow　soplar
blow out　soplar
blunder　tropezar
boil　bullir, cocer
boot up (a computer)　arrancar
bore　aburrir
bored, to be　aburrirse
born, to be　nacer
bow　inclinar
break　romper; — the law delinquir

breakfast, to (have) desayunar(se)
breed criar
bring traer
bring near acercar
bring up (breed, rear) criar
bronze broncear
brush cepillar
burden cargar
build construir
burn abrasar, quemar
bustle bullir
buy comprar
buzz zumbar

C

cable telegrafiar
calculate computar
call llamar
call together convocar
called, to be llamarse
calm tranquilizar
calm down tranquilizar
can poder
cancel (in mathematics) suprimir
carry (away) llevar
carry out ejecutar, realizar
cast echar
cast away botar
catch coger, agarrar
cause producir
cause grief doler
cause regret doler
celebrate celebrar, festejar
certify certificar
change cambiar
change one's clothing mudarse
change one's place of residence
    mudarse
characterize caracterizar
charge (a battery) cargar
charm atraer
chat charlar, platicar
choke sofocar
choose escoger, elegir
christen bautizar
clamp abrazar

clarify aclarar
clean limpiar
clean oneself limpiarse
clear aclarar
climb subir, montar
clinch fijar
clone reproducir asexualmente
    (see producir, page 384)
close cerrar
clothe vestir
clothe oneself vestirse
clutch agarrar
collate agregar
collect agregar, colegir, recoger
color (one's hair, *etc.*) pintarse
comb one's hair peinarse
come venir
come across or upon encontrarse,
    hallar
come down bajar
come (in) entrar
come to an agreement arreglarse
come to the rescue acudir
come up subir
come upon agarrar
command ordenar
commence comenzar
commend recomendar
compare comparar
complain lastimarse, quejarse
complete acabar, completar
compose componer
compromise arreglarse
compute computar
conduct conducir
confess confesar
confide fiar
confine encerrar
confirm confirmar
conform arreglarse
congratulate felicitar
conjugate conjugar
connect juntar, unir
conquer vencer
consecrate bendecir
consider considerar
constitute constituir

construct   construir
contain   contener
contained, to be   caber
continue   continuar, seguir
contradict   contradecir
contribute   contribuir
convene   convocar, convenir
convert   convertir
convince   convencer
convoke   convocar
cook   cocer, cocinar
copy   copiar
correct   corregir
cost   costar
counsel   aconsejar
count   contar
cover   cubrir, tapar
cover up   tapar
creak (as doors, hinges, *etc.*)   gruñir
crease   chafar
cross   atravesar, cruzar
cross out   borrar
crumple   chafar
cry out   gritar
cry (weep)   llorar
curse   maldecir
custom, to have the   soler
cut   acuchillar, cortar
cut off   cortar
cut open   acuchillar
cut out (eliminate)   suprimir,
   cortar

D
dance   bailar
dare   atreverse, osar
darn   zurcir
deal cards   repartir
debate   debatir
decide   decidir
declare   declarar
dedicate   dedicar
defeat   vencer
defend   defender
delay   retrasar
delete (for a computer)   suprimir

delineate   describir
deliver   entregar
demand   exigir, demandar
demonstrate   demostrar
denounce   denunciar
deny   negar
depart   partir
depend on   atenerse, depender
depreciate   desvalorizar
descend   bajar
describe   describir
deserve   merecer
design   dibujar
desire   desear
destroy   destruir, deshacer
detach   despegar, separar
detain   detener
devalue   desvalorizar
devote   dedicar
devote oneself   dedicarse
dial (phone)   marcar
die   morir
dine   cenar
direct   dirigir
discharge   desempeñar
discover   descubrir
discuss   discutir, platicar
disinfect   desinfectar
dismiss   despedir
dispense   dispensar
display   presentar, mostrar
distinguish   distinguir
distribute   dispensar, repartir
divide   partir
divine   adivinar
divorced, to be (get)   divorciarse
do   hacer
do (something) right   acertar
doubt   dudar
draw   dibujar
draw near   acercarse
draw (pull)   tirar
dread   temer
dream   soñar
drench   calar
dress   vestir
dress oneself   vestirse

drink   beber
drive (a car)   conducir, manejar
dry   secar
dry oneself   secarse
dwell   habitar

E

earn   ganar
ease   suavizar
eat   comer
eat breakfast   desayunar(se)
eat lunch   almorzar
eat supper   cenar
echo   sonar
economize   ahorrar
elect   elegir
eliminate   suprimir
embrace   abrazar
emphasize   subrayar
employ   emplear, usar
empty   vaciar
enclose   encerrar, incluir
encounter   encontrar
end   acabar, terminar
endure   sufrir
enjoy   gozar
enjoy oneself   divertirse
enlarge   agrandar
enliven   despertar
enroll   inscribirse
enter   entrar
entertain   festejar
entreat   implorar
enunciate   enunciar
erase   borrar, raer
erect   erguir
err   errar
escape   huir
escort   acompañar
establish   establecer
esteem   estimar, apreciar
estimate   estimar
exaggerate   agrandar
examine   considerar
examine by touch   tentar
exchange   cambiar

excite   mover
excuse   dispensar, perdonar
excuse oneself   disculparse
execute   ejecutar
exempt   dispensar
exercise   ejercer
exert   ejercer
exhaust   agotar
expect   aguardar, esperar
explain   aclarar, explicar
express   expresar
extend   tender
extinguish   apagar

F

fabricate   fabricar
fall   caer
fall asleep   dormirse
fall down   caerse
fall ill   enfermarse
fall sick   enfermarse
fasten   fijar
fatigue   cansar
fear   temer
feast   festejar
feel   sentir(se)
feel sorry   sentir
feel (touch)   tentar
feign   fingir, simular
felicitate   felicitar
fight   batallar, luchar
fill   llenar
fill again   rellenar
find   encontrar(se), hallar
find out   averiguar, informarse
finish   acabar, terminar
fire (burn)   abrasar, quemar
fit (into)   caber
fitting, to be   convenir
fix   arreglar
fix (fasten)   fijar
fix (in the mind)   imprimir
flatten   chafar
flee   huir
fling   arrojar, botar, echar, lanzar,
    tirar

flow   correr
fluctuate   vacilar
fly   volar
fly away   volarse
follow   seguir
forbid   prohibir
forecast   predecir
foretell   adivinar, predecir
forget   olvidar
forgive   perdonar
form   formar
forsake   abandonar
forward (remit)   remitir
fray   raer
freeze   helar
fret   apurarse
frighten   asombrar, asustar
fry   freír
fulfill   cumplir, realizar
fun of, to make   burlarse
function (machine)   marchar,
    funcionar

G
gain   ganar
gape   bostezar
gather   agregar, recoger
gather (unite, meet)   reunir(se)
get   adquirir, coger, conseguir,
    lograr, obtener, recibir,
    sacar
get angry   calentarse, enojarse
get cross   enojarse
get divorced   divorciarse
get dressed   vestirse
get excited   calentarse
get ill   enfermarse
get married   casarse
get on   montar, subir
get ready   prepararse
get sick   enfermarse
get tipsy   alumbrarse
get tired   cansarse
get together   reunirse
get undressed   desvestirse
get up   levantarse

get weary   cansarse
get wet   mojarse
give   dar
give as a gift   regalar
give as a present   regalar
give back (an object)   devolver
give (hand over)   entregar
give notice   advertir
give up   abandonar
give warning   advertir
glitter   brillar
glue   pegar
go   ir
go ahead   adelantar, adelantarse
go around, turn around   versar
go away   irse, marcharse
go back   regresar, volver
go down   bajar
go forward   adelantarse
go in   entrar
go out   salir
go through   atravesar
go to bed   acostarse
go up   subir, montar
go with   acompañar
good-by, to say   despedirse
good time, to have a   divertirse
govern   gobernar
grab   coger
grant   admitir, permitir
grasp   agarrar, asir, coger
gratify   placer
grease   untar
greet   saludar
grieve   apurarse, gemir
groan   gemir
group   agrupar
grow   crecer
grow larger   agrandar
grow tired   aburrirse
grow weary   aburrirse
growl   gruñir
grumble   gruñir, quejarse
grunt   gruñir
guard   velar
guess   adivinar
guide   guiar

H

habit, to be in the   soler
hail   aclamar
hand over   entregar
handle   manejar
hang out (washing)   tender
hang up   colgar
happen   pasar, suceder, ocurrir
harm   herir
harvest   recoger
hasten   apresurarse, acelerar
have (as an auxiliary verb)   haber
have (hold)   tener
have a good time   divertirse
have breakfast   desayunarse
have dinner   cenar
have influence on   influir
have lunch   almorzar
have something to eat or drink   tomar
have supper   cenar
have the custom of   soler
have to   deber, tener (que)
hear   oír
heat   calentar
heave   alzar
help   ayudar, socorrer
hesitate   vacilar
hesitate (in speech)   balbucear
hide (cover up)   tapar
hide oneself   ocultarse
hinder   impedir
hint   sugerir
hire (rent)   alquilar
hit   pegar
hit the mark   acertar
hit upon   acertar
hold   contener, tener
hold fast (overcome)   sujetar
hop   saltar
hope   esperar
hug   abrazar
hum   zumbar
humor   placer
hurl   arrojar, echar, lanzar
hurry   apresurarse, acelerar
hurt   doler, herir
hurt oneself   lastimarse

I

ill(to get, fall)   enfermarse
illuminate   alumbrar
illustrate   illustrar
imbibe   embeber
immerse   sumergir
immigrate   inmigrar
impede   impedir
implore   implorar
important, to be   importar
impress   impresionar
impress (imprint)   imprimir
imprint   imprimir
improve   mejorar
incite   encender
incline   inclinar
include   incluir
increase   agrandar, aumentar
indicate   indicar, señalar
induce   inducir
inflame   encender
influence   inducir, influir
inform   avisar
inform oneself   informarse
inhabit   habitar
inherit   heredar
initiate   iniciar
inquire   averiguar, preguntar
inscribe   inscribir
insinuate   sugerir
insist   insistir
insure   asegurar
intimidate   intimidar
introduce   introducir, presentar
intrust   fiar
investigate   averiguar
invite   invitar
irrigate   regar
irritate   enojar

J

jerk   sacudir
join   juntar, reunir, unir
jolt   sacudir
judge   juzgar
jump   saltar

K

keep (a promise)   **cumplir**
keep company   **acompañar**
keep guard   **vigilar**
keep quiet   **callarse**
keep still   **callarse**
keep up (maintain)   **mantener**
kill   **matar**
kindle   **encender**
knife   **acuchillar**
knock down   **abatir, derribar**
know   **conocer, saber**
know how   **saber**
know not, be unaware of   **ignorar**

L

labor   **trabajar**
lack   **faltar**
lacking, to be   **faltar**
land   **aterrizar**
laugh   **reír(se)**
launch   **lanzar, botar**
lead   **conducir, guiar, inducir**
leap   **saltar**
learn   **aprender**
leave   **dejar, marcharse, partir**
    salir
leave (go out)   **salir**
lend   **prestar**
let   **dejar**
let down   **bajar**
let go   **dejar, soltar**
let loose   **soltar**
lie down   **acostarse, yacer**
lie in a grave   **yacer**
lie (tell a lie)   **mentir**
lift   **alzar, levantar**
light   **alumbrar**
light (a flame)   **encender**
like (be pleasing to)   **gustar**
listen (to)   **escuchar**
live   **vivir**
live in (reside)   **habitar**
load   **cargar**
lock up   **encerrar**
look   **mirar**

look alike   **parecerse**
look at   **mirar**
look at oneself   **mirarse**
look for   **buscar**
look out (for)   **vigilar**
loosen   **soltar**
lose   **perder**
love   **amar**
lower   **bajar**
lunch   **almorzar**

M

maintain   **mantener, sostener**
make   **hacer**
make a mistake   **equivocarse**
make an impression   **impresionar**
make angry   **enojar**
make clear   **aclarar**
make fun of   **burlarse**
make presents   **regalar**
make up (constitute)   **constituir**
make up one's face   **maquillarse,**
    pintarse
make void (annul)   **anular**
make worse   **agravar**
manage   **manejar**
manufacture   **fabricar**
march   **marchar**
mark   **marcar, notar**
marry   **casarse**
matter   **importar**
measure   **medir**
meet   **encontrar(se), reuinir(se)**
mend   **zurcir, reparar**
mention   **mencionar**
merit   **merecer**
miss   **errar, faltar**
mistaken, to be   **equivocarse**
moan   **gemir**
moisten   **untar**
mount   **subir, montar**
move   **mover**
move ahead   **adelantarse**
move along   **caminar**
move (change residence)   **mudarse**
mumble   **chistar**

must   deber
mutter   chistar

N

name   llamar
named, to be   llamarse
navigate   navegar
need   faltar, necesitar
not to know   ignorar
note   marcar, notar
notice   notar, reparar
notify   avisar

O

obey   obedecer
observe   marcar, notar, observar,
    reparar
obtain   adquirir, agarrar, con-
    seguir, lograr, obtener, recibir
occupy   ocupar
occur   ocurrir
offend   ofender
offer   ofrecer
oil   untar
open   abrir
operate (a vehicle)   manejar
oppose   oponer
order   ordenar
organize   organizar
ought   deber
overcome   sujetar, vencer
overtake   alcanzar
overthrow   abatir, derribar, vencer
overturn   voltear
owe   deber
own   poseer

P

pain   doler
paint   pintar
parade   pasearse
pardon   perdonar
park (a vehicle)   estacionar
pass a test   aprobar

pass (by)   pasar
paste   pegar
pay   pagar
pay attention   fijarse
pay taxes   contribuir
perceive   percibir
perform   ejecutar
perform (a duty)   desempeñar
permit   admitir, dejar, permitir
persist   insistir
persuade   inducir, mover
pertain   pertenecer
petition   demandar
pick   recoger, (select) escoger
pick up   alzar, recoger
pitch   echar
pitch (a ball)   tirar
place   colocar, poner
place near   acercar
play (a game)   jugar
play (a string instrument)   tañer
play (music or a musical instrument)
    tocar
play (a part in)   desempeñar
play (a sport)   jugar
please   agradar, placer
pluck   tañer
plug up   tapar
plunge   sumergir
point out   enseñar, indicar, mostrar,
    señalar
poke fun at   burlarse
polish   pulir
possess   poseer
possession, to take   apoderarse
pour   verter
power, to take   apoderarse
practice   practicar
praise   celebrar
prattle   charlar
pray   rogar
preach   predicar
predict   predecir
prefer   preferir
prepare   preparar
prepare oneself   prepararse
present   presentar

pretend   fingir, simular
prevent   impedir
print   imprimir
proclaim   anunciar, proclamar
procure   lograr
produce   producir
progress   adelantar
prohibit   prohibir
promulgate   proclamar
pronounce   pronunciar
pronounce distinctly   articular
protect   proteger
prove   demostrar, probar
provide for   mantener
publish   publicar
pull   tirar
pull up (out)   arrancar
purchase   comprar
pursue   seguir
put   colocar, poner
put cosmetics on   maquillarse
put in, put into   meter
put in order   ordenar
put makeup on   maquillarse
put on clothing   ponerse
put on (shoes)   calzar
put out (flame, fire)   apagar

Q

quake   temblar
quarrel   reñir
question   preguntar
quiet down   tranquilizar
quiet, to keep   callarse
quiver   temblar

R

race   correr
rain   llover
raise (breed)   criar
raise (lift)   levantar
raise (prices)   alzar
reach   alcanzar
reach one's birthday   cumplir
read   leer

realize (fulfill)   realizar
rear (bring up, breed)   criar
recall   recordar
receive   recibir
recognize   reconocer
recommend   recomendar
record (inscribe)   inscribir
recycle   reciclar
refer   referir
refill   rellenar
refund   devolver
register   inscribirse
register (a letter)   certificar
regress   regresar
regret   lastimarse, sentir
regulate   arreglar
rejoice   alegrarse
relate   contar, referir
rely on   atenerse
remain   quedarse
remark   notar
remember   acordarse, recordar
remind   recordar
remit   remitir
remove (oneself)   quitarse
rent   alquilar
repair   arreglar, reparar
repeal   abolir, revocar
repeat   repetir
reply   contestar, responder
request   pedir, rogar
require   exigir
resemble each other   parecerse
reside   habitar
resolve   resolver
resound   sonar
respect   estimar
respond   responder
respond (to a call)   acudir
rest   descansar
restrain   contener
result   resultar
retard   retrasar
retire   retirar
return (an object)   devolver
return (go back)   regresar, volver
revoke   revocar

revolve   revolver, voltear
ridicule   burlarse
ring   sonar
rinse   aclarar
rise (get up)   levantarse
rise (go up)   subir
roam   errar
roast (coffee)   tostar
rob   robar
root up (out)   arrancar
rub off   raer
rule   gobernar
run   correr
run away   huir
run (machine)   marchar, funcionar
run through   atravesar
rush   apresurarse

S

sail   navegar
salute   saludar
satisfy   satisfacer
save (money)   ahorrar
say   decir
say good-by to   despedirse
scan (verses)   medir
scare   asustar
scatter   esparcir
scent   oler
scold   reñir
score (a goal)   marcar
scramble (eggs)   revolver
scrape   raer
scream   gritar
scrub   fregar
see   ver
seek   buscar
seem   parecer
seize   agarrar, asir, coger
select   escoger, elegir
sell   vender
send   enviar
separate   separar
serve   servir
set apart   separar
set (of sun)   ponerse

set on fire   incendiar
set up (organize)   organizar
set up straight   erguir
settle   arreglar, arreglarse
settle in   fijarse
shake   sacudir
shake (tremble)   temblar
shake up   agitar
sham   simular
shape   formar
shatter   romper
shave oneself   afeitarse
shine   brillar
shiver   temblar
shoe   calzar
shoot (a gun)   tirar
shout   aclamar, gritar
show   enseñar, mostrar, presentar, señalar
show up   aparecer
shower oneself   ducharse
shriek   gritar
sick (to get, fall)   enfermarse
sigh   suspirar
sign   subscribir, firmar
sign up   inscribirse
signal   señalar
simulate   simular
sing   cantar
sink   sumergir
sit down   sentarse
sit erect   erguirse
sketch   dibujar
ski   esquiar
slap   pegar
slash   acuchillar
sleep   dormir
slip away   huir
smell   oler
smile   sonreír
smoke   fumar
smooth   suavizar
smother   sofocar
snatch   arrancar
snow   nevar
soak   calar
soak in   embeber

soak up   embeber
sob   sollozar
soften   suavizar
solve (a problem)   resolver, adivinar
sort   separar
sound   sonar
sparkle   brillar
speak   hablar
speed   acelerar
spend (money)   gastar
spend (time)   pasar
spill   derramar
split   partir
spout   surgir
spread out   tender
spread (scatter)   esparcir
spring   saltar
sprinkle   regar
spurt   surgir
spy on   acechar
stagger   vacilar
stammer   balbucear
stand erect   erguirse
start   comenzar, empezar, iniciar
start (a motor)   arrancar
state   enunciar
station (park a vehicle)   estacionar
stay   quedarse
stay awake   velar
steal   robar
step on   pisar
stick   pegar
stifle   sofocar
still, to keep   callarse
stir   agitar
stop (oneself)   detenerse, pararse
stop (someone or something)
   detener, parar
stop up   tapar
store   almacenar
straighten up (oneself)   erguirse
stress   insistir
stretch   tender
stretch (oneself)   desperezarse
strive   luchar
struggle   batallar, luchar
study   estudiar

stuff   rellenar
stumble   tropezar
subdue   someter, sujetar
subject   someter, sujetar
submerge   sumergir
submit   someter
subscribe   subscribir, suscribir
succeed   lograr, suceder
succeed (in)   acertar
succor   socorrer
suck   chupar
suck in   embeber
sue   demandar
suffer   sufrir
suffice   bastar
suffocate   sofocar
suggest   sugerir
sum up   sumar
summon   convocar
supplicate   rogar
support   mantener, sostener
suppose   suponer
suppress   suprimir
surge   surgir
surprise   sorprender
surrender   someter
suspect   sospechar
sustain   sostener
swear   jurar
sweep   barrer
swim   nadar

T
take   coger, tomar
take a bath   bañarse
take a shower   ducharse
take a walk   pasearse
take advantage   aprovecharse
take apart   deshacer
take care of oneself   cuidarse
take an oath   jurar
take away   llevar
take leave of   despedirse
take notice (of)   advertir, fijarse
take off (airplane)   despegar
take off (clothing)   quitarse

take out of pawn   desempeñar
take out (something)   sacar
take possession   apoderarse
take power   apoderarse
take the lead   adelantarse
talk   hablar
talk over   platicar
tan   broncear, tostar
teach   enseñar
tear (break)   romper
tear down   derribar
tear off (away)   arrancar
telegraph   telegrafiar
telephone   telefonear
tell   contar, decir
tell a lie   mentir
temper   suavizar
tempt   tentar
terminate   terminar
test   probar
thank   agradecer
think   pensar
think over   considerar
throw   arrojar, echar, lanzar, tirar
throw away   botar
throw down   abatir, derribar
tie   atar
tilt   inclinar
tint (one's hair, *etc.*)   teñir
tire   cansar
toast   tostar
touch   tocar
trample   pisar
tranquilize   tranquilizar
translate   traducir
transmit   transmitir
travel   viajar
tread on   pisar
treat (a subject)   tratar
tremble   temblar
trot   trotar
try   probar, tentar, tratar
try on   probar(se)
tumble   caerse
turn   versar, voltear
turn around   versar, voltear
turn around (revolve)   revolver

turn off (flame, fire, light)   apagar
turn on (TV, radio)   poner
turn over   revolver
turn upside down   revolver

U

undergo   sufrir
underline   subrayar
underscore   subrayar
understand   comprender, entender
undo   deshacer
undress (oneself)   desvestirse
unfasten   soltar
unglue   despegar
unite   juntar, reunir, unir
unstick   despegar
untie   soltar
uphold   sostener
urge   exigir
use   usar, emplear
use up   agotar
utilize   utilizar

V

vacillate   vacilar
value   estimar
venture   osar, atreverse
verify   confirmar
vex   aburrir, enojar
vibrate   vibrar
visit   visitar
vote   votar
vow   votar

W

wait for   aguardar, esperar
wake up (oneself)   despertarse
walk   andar, caminar, marchar
walk, to take a   pasearse
wander   errar
want   desear, querer
wanting, to be   faltar
warm up   calentar
warn   advertir, avisar

wash   lavar
wash dishes   fregar
wash oneself   lavarse
waste   gastar
watch   mirar, acechar
watch over   velar, vigilar
water   regar
wave   agitar
waver   vacilar
wear   llevar, usar
wear out   gastar
wear (shoes)   calzar
weary   cansar
weep   llorar
weigh   medir
wet oneself   mojarse
whimper   sollozar
whine   llorar
whisk   barrer

win   ganar
wind (a watch)   montar
wipe dry   secar
wipe out   raer
wish   desear, querer
withdraw   quitarse, retirar
work   trabajar
worried, to be   preocuparse
worry   apurarse, preocuparse
worship   adorar
worth, to be   valer
wound   herir
wrap up   envolver
wrestle   luchar
write   escribir

Y

yawn   bostezar

The purpose of this index is to help you identify those verb forms that cannot be readily identified because they are irregular in some way. For example, if you come across the verb form *fui* (which is very common) in your Spanish readings, this index will tell you that *fui* is a form of *ir* or *ser*. Then you look up *ir* and *ser* in this book and you will find that verb form on the page where all the forms of *ir* and *ser* are given.

Verb forms whose first three or four letters are the same as the infinitive have not been included because they can easily be identified by referring to the alphabetical listing of the 501 verbs in this book.

After you find the verb of an irregular verb form, if it is not given among the 501 verbs, consult the list of Over 1,100 Spanish Verbs Conjugated Like Model Verbs, which begins on page 550.

A

abierto   abrir
acierto, *etc.*   acertar
acuerdo, *etc.*   acordar
acuesto, *etc.*   acostarse
alce, *etc.*   alzar
andes   andar
anduve, *etc.*   andar
apruebo, *etc.*   aprobar
ase, *etc.*   asir
asgo, *etc.*   asir
ataque, *etc.*   atacar
ate, *etc.*   atar

C

cabré, *etc.*   caber
caí, *etc.*   caer
caía, *etc.*   caer
caigo, *etc.*   caer
calce, *etc.*   calzar
caliento, *etc.*   calentar
cayera, *etc.*   caer
cierro, *etc.*   cerrar
cojo, *etc.*   coger
colija, *etc.*   colegir
consigo, *etc.*   conseguir
cuece, *etc.*   cocer
cuelgo, *etc.*   colgar
cuento, *etc.*   contar

cuesta, *etc.*   costar
cuezo, *etc.*   cocer
cupe, *etc.*   caber
cupiera, *etc.*   caber

D

da, *etc.*   dar
dad   dar
das   dar
dé   dar
demos   dar
den   dar
des   dar
di, *etc.*   dar, decir
dice, *etc.*   decir
diciendo   decir
dicho   decir
diera, *etc.*   dar
diese, *etc.*   dar
digo, *etc.*   decir
dije, *etc.*   decir
dimos, *etc.*   dar
dio   dar
diré, *etc.*   decir
diría, *etc.*   decir
diste   dar
doy   dar
duelo, *etc.*   doler
duermo, *etc.*   dormir

durmamos   dormir
durmiendo   dormir

E

eliges, *etc.*   elegir
eligiendo   elegir
eligiera, *etc.*   elegir
elijo, *etc.*   elegir
era, *etc.*   ser
eres   ser
es   ser
estoy   estar
estuve, *etc.*   estar
exija, *etc.*   exigir

F

fíe, *etc.*   fiar
finja, *etc.*   fingir
fío, *etc.*   fiar
friego, *etc.*   fregar
friendo   freír
friera, *etc.*   freír
frío, *etc.*   freír
frito   freír
fue, *etc.*   ir, ser
fuera, *etc.*   ir, ser
fuese, *etc.*   ir, ser
fui, *etc.*   ir, ser

G

gima, *etc.*   gemir
gimiendo   gemir
gimiera, *etc.*   gemir
gimiese, *etc.*   gemir
gimo, *etc.*   gemir
goce, *etc.*   gozar
gocé   gozar

H

ha   haber
había, *etc.*   haber
habré, *etc.*   haber
haga, *etc.*   hacer

hago, *etc.*   hacer
han   haber
haría, *etc.*   hacer
has   haber
haya, *etc.*   haber
haz   hacer
he   haber
hecho   hacer
hemos   haber
hice, *etc.*   hacer
hiciera, *etc.*   hacer
hiciese, *etc.*   hacer
hiela   helar
hiele   helar
hiera, *etc.*   herir
hiero, *etc.*   herir
hiramos   herir
hiriendo   herir
hiriera, *etc.*   herir
hiriese, *etc.*   herir
hizo   hacer
hube, *etc.*   haber
hubiera, *etc.*   haber
hubiese, *etc.*   haber
huela, *etc.*   oler
huelo, *etc.*   oler
huya, *etc.*   huir
huyendo   huir
huyera, *etc.*   huir
huyese, *etc.*   huir
huyo, *etc.*   huir

I

iba, *etc.*   ir
id   ir
ido   ir
idos   irse
irgo, *etc.*   erguir
irguiendo   erguir
irguiera, *etc.*   erguir
irguiese, *etc.*   erguir

J

juego, *etc.*   jugar
juegue, *etc.*   jugar

L

lea, *etc.*   leer
leído   leer
leo, *etc.*   leer
leyendo   leer
leyera, *etc.*   leer
leyese, *etc.*   leer
llueva   llover
llueve   llover

M

mida, *etc.*   medir
midiendo   medir
midiera, *etc.*   medir
midiese, *etc.*   medir
mido, *etc.*   medir
mienta, *etc.*   mentir
miento, *etc.*   mentir
mintiendo   mentir
mintiera, *etc.*   mentir
mintiese, *etc.*   mentir
muerda, *etc.*   morder
muerdo, *etc.*   morder
muero, *etc.*   morir
muerto   morir
muestre, *etc.*   mostrar
muestro, *etc.*   mostrar
mueva, *etc.*   mover
muevo, *etc.*   mover
muramos   morir
muriendo   morir
muriera, *etc.*   morir
muriese, *etc.*   morir

N

nazca, *etc.*   nacer
nazco   nacer
niego, *etc.*   negar
niegue, *etc.*   negar
nieva   nevar
nieve   nevar

O

oíd   oír
oiga, *etc.*   oír
oigo, *etc.*   oír
oliendo   oler
oliera, *etc.*   oler
oliese, *etc.*   oler
oye, *etc.*   oír
oyendo   oír
oyera, *etc.*   oír
oyese, *etc.*   oír

P

pida, *etc.*   pedir
pidamos   pedir
pidiendo   pedir
pidiera, *etc.*   pedir
pidiese, *etc.*   pedir
pido, *etc.*   pedir
pienso, *etc.*   pensar
pierda, *etc.*   perder
pierdo, *etc.*   perder
plegue   placer
plugo   placer
pluguiera   placer
pluguieron   placer
pluguiese   placer
ponga, *etc.*   poner
pongámonos   ponerse
ponte   ponerse
pruebe, *etc.*   probar
pruebo, *etc.*   probar
pude, *etc.*   poder
pudiendo   poder
pudiera, *etc.*   poder
pudiese, *etc.*   poder
puedo, *etc.*   poder
puesto   poner
puse, *etc.*   poner
pusiera, *etc.*   poner
pusiese, *etc.*   poner

Q

quepo, *etc.*   caber
quiebro   quebrar

quiero, *etc.*   querer
quise, *etc.*   querer
quisiera, *etc.*   querer
quisiese, *etc.*   querer

R

raí, *etc.*   raer
raía, *etc.*   raer
raiga, *etc.*   raer
raigo, *etc.*   raer
rayendo   raer
rayera, *etc.*   raer
rayese, *etc.*   raer
ría, *etc.*   reír
riamos   reír
riego, *etc.*   regar
riendo   reír
riera, *etc.*   reír
riese, *etc.*   reír
riña, *etc.*   reñir
riñendo   reñir
riñera, *etc.*   reñir
riñese, *etc.*   reñir
riño, *etc.*   reñir
río, *etc.*   reír
roto   romper
ruego, *etc.*   rogar
ruegue, *etc.*   rogar

S

sal, salgo, *etc.*   salir
saque, *etc.*   sacar
sé   saber, ser
sea, *etc.*   ser
sed   ser
sepa, *etc.*   saber
seque, *etc.*   secar
sido   ser
siendo   ser
siento, *etc.*   sentar, sentir
sigo, *etc.*   seguir
siguiendo   seguir
siguiera, *etc.*   seguir
siguiese, *etc.*   seguir
sintiendo   sentir

sintiera, *etc.*   sentir
sintiese, *etc.*   sentir
sintió   sentir
sirviendo   servir
sirvo, *etc.*   servir
sois   ser
somos   ser
son   ser
soy   ser
suela, *etc.*   soler
suelo, *etc.*   soler
suelto, *etc.*   soltar
sueno, *etc.*   sonar
sueño, *etc.*   soñar
supe, *etc.*   saber
supiera, *etc.*   saber
supiese, *etc.*   saber
surja, *etc.*   surgir

T

ten, tengo   tener
tiemblo, *etc.*   temblar
tiendo, *etc.*   tender
tienes, *etc.*   tener
tiento, *etc.*   tentar
toque, *etc.*   tocar
traigo, *etc.*   traer
traje, *etc.*   traer
tuesto, *etc.*   tostar
tuve, *etc.*   tener

U

uno, *etc.*   unir

V

va   ir
vais   ir
val, valgo, *etc.*   valer
vámonos   irse
vamos   ir
van   ir
vas   ir
vaya, *etc.*   ir
ve   ir, ver

vea, *etc.*   ver
ved   ver
ven   **venir, ver**
vendré, *etc.*   **venir**
venga, vengo   **venir**
veo, *etc.*   ver
ves   ver
vete   **irse**
vi   ver
viendo   ver
viene, *etc.*   **venir**
viera, *etc.*   ver
viese, *etc.*   ver
vimos, *etc.*   ver
vine, *etc.*   **venir**
vio   ver
viste   **ver, vestir**

vistiendo   **vestir**
vistiéndose   **vestirse**
vistiese   **vestirse**
visto   **ver, vestir**
voy   **ir**
vuelo, *etc.*   **volar**
vuelto   **volver**
vuelvo, *etc.*   **volver**

Y

yaz   **yacer**
yazco, *etc.*   **yacer**
yendo   **ir**
yergo, *etc.*   **erguir**
yerro, *etc.*   **errar**

On the pages containing 501 verbs given in this book, we offer simple sentences, idiomatic expressions, or words and expressions related to verbs. They can help build your Spanish vocabulary and knowledge of Spanish idioms.

When you look up the verb forms of a particular verb in this book, consult the following list so that you may learn some common idiomatic expressions. Consulting this list will save you time because you will not have to use a standard Spanish-English word dictionary to find out what the verbal idiom means. Also, if you do this, you will learn two things at the same time: the verb forms for a particular verb and verbal idioms.

Remember that not all verbs in the Spanish language are used in idioms. Those given below are used very frequently in Spanish readings and in conversation. Some of the following entries contain words, usually nouns, that are related to the verb entry. This, too, will help build your vocabulary. We also include a few proverbs containing verbs because they are interesting, colorful, useful, and they help build your knowledge of Spanish words and idiomatic expressions.

acabar de + inf.

The Spanish idiomatic expression **acabar de + inf.** is expressed in English as *to have just* + past participle.

In the present indicative:
María acaba de llegar.   Mary has just arrived.
Acabo de comer.   I have just eaten.
Acabamos de terminar la lección.   We have just finished the lesson.

In the imperfect indicative:
María acababa de llegar.   Mary had just arrived.
Acababa de comer.   I had just eaten.
Acabábamos de terminar la lección.   We had just finished the lesson.

Note:
(a) When you use **acabar** in the present tense, it indicates that the action of the main verb (+ inf.) has just occurred now in the present. In English, we express this by using *have just* + the past participle of the main verb: *Acabo de llegar/*I have just arrived. (See the other examples above under present indicative.)

(b) When you use **acabar** in the imperfect indicative, it indicates that the action of the main verb (+ inf.) had occurred at some time in the past when another action occurred in the past. In English, we express this by using *had just* + the past participle of the main verb: *Acabábamos de entrar en la casa cuando el teléfono sonó/*We had just entered the house when the telephone rang. (See the other examples above under imperfect indicative.)

Note also that when **acabar** is used in the imperfect indicative + the inf. of the main verb being expressed, the verb in the other clause is usually in the preterit.

conocer and **saber** (See also **poder** and **saber**)

These two verbs mean *to know* but they are each used in a distinct sense:

(a) Generally speaking, **conocer** means to know in the sense of *being acquainted* with a person, a place, or a thing: *¿Conoce Ud. a María?*/ Do you know Mary? *¿Conoce Ud. bien los Estados Unidos?*/Do you know the United States well? *¿Conoce Ud. este libro?*/Do you know (Are you acquainted with) this book?

In the preterit tense, **conocer** means *met* in the sense of *first met, first became acquainted with someone*: *¿Conoce Ud. a Elena?*/Do you know Helen? *Sí, (yo) la conocí anoche en casa de un amigo mío*/Yes, I met her (for the first time) last night at the home of one of my friends.

(b) Generally speaking, **saber** means to know a fact, to know something thoroughly: *¿Sabe Ud. qué hora es?*/Do you know what time it is? *¿Sabe Ud. la lección?*/Do you know the lesson?

When you use **saber + inf.**, it means *to know how*: *¿Sabe Ud. nadar?*/ Do you know how to swim? *Sí, (yo) sé nadar*/Yes, I know how to swim.

In the preterit tense, **saber** means *found out*: *¿Lo sabe Ud.?*/Do you know it? *Sí, lo supe ayer*/Yes, I found it out yesterday.

dar and darse

dar a to face (*El comedor da al jardín*/The dining room faces the garden.)
dar con algo to find something, to come upon something (*Esta mañana di con dinero en la calle*/This morning I found money in the street.)
dar con alguien to meet someone, to run into someone, to come across someone, to find someone (*Anoche, di con mi amiga Elena en el cine*/ Last night I met my friend Helen at the movies.)
dar cuerda al reloj to wind a watch
dar de beber a to give something to drink to
dar de comer a to feed, to give something to eat to (*Me gusta dar de comer a los pájaros en el parque*/I like to feed the birds in the park.)
dar en to hit against, to strike against
dar en el blanco to hit the target, to hit it right
dar gritos to shout
dar la bienvenida to welcome
dar la hora to strike the hour
dar la mano a alguien to shake hands with someone
dar las buenas noches a agluien to say good evening (good night) to someone
dar las gracias a alguien to thank someone
dar los buenos días a alguien to say good morning (hello) to someone
dar por + past part. to consider (*Lo doy por perdido*/I consider it lost.)
dar recuerdos a to give one's regards (best wishes) to

dar un abrazo   to embrace
dar un paseo   to take a walk
dar un paseo a caballo   to go horseback riding
dar un paseo en automóvil   to go for a drive
dar una vuelta   to go for a short walk, to go for a stroll
dar unas palmadas   to clap one's hands
dar voces   to shout
darse cuenta de   to realize, to be aware of, to take into account
darse la mano   to shake hands with each other
darse por + past part.   to consider onself (*Me doy por insultado*/I consider myself insulted.)
darse prisa   to hurry

deber, deber de and tener que

Generally speaking, use **deber** when you want to express a moral obligation, something you ought to do but that you may or may not actually do: *Debo estudiar esta noche pero estoy cansado y no me siento bien*/I ought to study tonight but I am tired and I do not feel well.

Generally speaking, **deber de + inf.** is used to express a supposition, something that is probable: *La señora Gómez debe de estar enferma porque sale de casa raramente*/Mrs. Gómez must be sick (is probably sick) because she goes out of the house rarely.

Generally speaking, use **tener que** when you want to say that you *have to* do something: *No puedo salir esta noche porque tengo que estudiar*/I cannot go out tonight because I have to study.

decir

decirle al oído   to whisper in one's ear
dicho y hecho   no sooner said than done
Es decir   That is to say . . .
querer decir   to mean (*¿Qué quiere decir este muchacho?*/What does this boy mean?)

dejar, salir, and salir de

These verbs mean *to leave,* but notice the difference in use:

Use **dejar** when you leave someone or when you leave something behind you: *El alumno dejó sus libros en la sala de clase*/The pupil left his books in the classroom.

Dejar also means *to let* or *to allow* or *to let go: ¡Déjelo!*/Let it! (Leave it!)

Use **salir de** when you mean *to leave* in the sense of *to go out of* (a place): *El alumno salió de la sala de clase*/The pupil left the classroom; *¿Dónde está su madre? Mi madre salió*/Where is your mother? My mother went out.

dejar de + inf. and dejar caer

Use **dejar de + inf.** when you mean *to stop* or *to fail to*: *Los alumnos dejaron de hablar cuando la profesora entró en la sala de clase*/The students stopped talking when the teacher came into the classroom; *¡No deje Ud. de llamarme!*/Don't fail to call me!

Dejar caer means *to drop*: *Luis dejó caer sus libros*/Louis dropped his books.

estar (See also ser and estar beginning on page 534)

está bien   all right, okay
estar a punto de + inf.   to be about + inf. (*Estoy a punto de salir*/I am about to go out.)
estar a sus anchas   to be comfortable
estar aburrido (aburrida)   to be bored
estar al día   to be up to date
estar bien   to be well
estar conforme con   to be in agreement with
estar de acuerdo   to agree
estar de acuerdo con   to be in agreement with
estar de boga   to be in fashion, to be fashionable
estar de buenas   to be in a good mood
estar de más   to be unnecessary
estar de pie   to be standing
estar de vuelta   to be back
estar en boga   to be in fashion, to be fashionable
estar listo (lista)   to be ready
estar mal   to be ill
estar para + inf.   to be about to (*Estoy para salir*/I am about to go out.)
estar por   to be in favor of
no estar para bromas   not to be in the mood for jokes

gastar and pasar

These two verbs mean *to spend*, but notice the difference in use:

Use **gastar** when you spend money: *No me gusta gastar mucho dinero*/I do not like to spend much money.

Use **pasar** when you spend time: *Me gustaría pasar un año en España*/I would like to spend a year in Spain.

gustar

    (a) Essentially, the verb gustar means *to be pleasing to* . . .

    (b) In English, we say, for example, *I like ice cream.* In Spanish, we say *Me gusta el helado;* that is to say, "Ice cream is pleasing to me (To me ice cream is pleasing)."

    (c) In English, the thing that you like is the direct object. In Spanish, the thing that you like is the subject. Also, in Spanish, the person who likes the thing is the indirect object: to me, to you, etc.: *A Roberto le gusta el helado*/Robert likes ice cream; in other words, "To Robert, ice cream is pleasing to him."

    (d) In Spanish, therefore, the verb gustar is used in the third person, either in the singular or plural, when you talk aobut something that you like—something that is pleasing to you. Therefore, the verb form must agree with the subject; if the thing liked is singular, the verb is third person singular; if the thing liked is plural, the verb gustar is third person plural: *Me gusta el café*/I like coffee; *Me gustan el café y la leche*/I like coffee and milk (Coffee and milk are pleasing to me).

    (e) When you mention the person or the persons who like something, you must use the preposition a in front of the person; you must also use the indirect object pronoun of the noun which is the person: *A los muchachos y a las muchachas les gusta jugar*/Boys and girls like to play; that is to say, "To play is pleasing to them, to boys and girls."

    (f) Other examples:

    Me gusta leer.   I like to read.

    Te gusta leer.   You (*familiar*) like to read.

    A Felipe le gusta el helado.   Philip likes ice cream.

    Al chico le gusta la leche.   The boy likes milk.

    A Carlota le gusta bailar.   Charlotte likes to dance.

    A las chicas les gustó el libro.   The girls liked the book.

    Nos gustó el cuento.   We liked the story.

    ¿Le gusta a Ud. el español?   Do you like Spanish?

    A Pedro y a Ana les gustó la película.   Peter and Anna liked the film.

    A mi amigo le gustaron los chocolates.   My friend liked the chocolates; that is to say, "The chocolates were pleasing (pleased) to him (to my friend)."

haber

    ha habido . . .   there has been . . ., there have been . . .

    había . . .   there was . . ., there were . . .

    habrá . . .   there will be . . .

    habría . . .   there would be . . .

    hubo . . .   there was . . ., there were . . .

haber, haber de + inf., and tener

The verb **haber** (to have) is used as an auxiliary verb (or helping verb) in order to form the seven compound tenses, which are as follows:

Compound Tenses	Example (in the 1st person sing.)
Present Perfect (or Perfect) Indicative	**he hablado** (I have spoken)
Pluperfect (or Past Perfect) Indicative	**había hablado** (I had spoken)
Preterit Perfect (or Past Anterior)	**hube hablado** (I had spoken)
Future Perfect (or Future Anterior)	**habré hablado** (I will have spoken)
Conditional Perfect	**habría hablado** (I would have spoken)
Present Perfect (or Past) Subjunctive	**haya hablado** (I may have spoken)
Pluperfect (or Past Perfect) Subjunctive	**hubiera hablado** *or* **hubiese hablado** (I might have spoken)

For an explanation of the formation of these tenses, see pages xxxviii–xl.

The verb **haber** is also used to form the perfect (or past) infinitive: *haber hablado* (to have spoken). As you can see, this is formed by using the infinitive form of haber + the past participle of the main verb.

The verb **haber** is also used to form the perfect participle: *habiendo hablado* (having spoken). As you can see, this is formed by using the present participle of haber + the past participle of the main verb.

The verb **haber + de + inf.** is equivalent to the English use of "to be supposed to . . ." or "to be to . . .": *María ha de traer un pastel, yo he de traer el helado, y mis amigos han de traer sus discos*/Mary is supposed to bring a pie, I am supposed to bring the ice cream, and my friends are to bring their records.

The verb **tener** is used to mean *to have* in the sense of *to possess* or *to hold*: *Tengo un perro y un gato*/I have a dog and a cat; *Tengo un lápiz en la mano*/ I have (am holding) a pencil in my hand.

In the preterit tense, **tener** can mean *received*: *Ayer mi padre tuvo un cheque*/ Yesterday my father received a check.

hay and hay que + inf.

The word **hay** is not a verb. You might regard it as an impersonal irregular from of **haber**. Actually, the word is composed of **ha** + the archaic **y**, meaning *there*. It is generally regarded as an adverbial expression because it points out that something or someone "is there." Its English equivalent is *There is . . .* or *There are . . .*, for example: *Hay muchos libros en la mesa*/ There are many books on the table; *Hay una mosca en la sopa*/There is a fly in the soup; *Hay veinte alumnos en esta clase*/There are twenty students in this class.

Hay que + inf. is an impersonal expression that denotes an obligation and it is commonly translated into English as: *One must . . .* or *It is necessary to . . . .* Examples: *Hay que estudiar para aprender*/It is necessary to study in order to learn; *Hay que comer para vivir*/One must eat in order to live.

hacer and **hacerse** (See also **Weather Expressions Using Verbs** on page 540)

hace poco   a little while ago

hace un año   a year ago

Hace un mes que partió el señor Molina.   Mr. Molina left one month ago.

hace una hora   an hour ago

hacer caso de   to pay attention to

hacer daño a algo   to harm something

hacer daño a alguien   to harm someone

hacer de   to act as (*El señor González siempre hace de jefe*/Mr. González always acts as a boss.)

hacer el baúl   to pack one's trunk

hacer el favor de + inf.   please (*Haga Ud. el favor de entrar*/Please come in.)

hacer el papel de   to play the role of

hacer la maleta   to pack one's suitcase

hacer pedazos   to smash, to break, to tear into pieces

hacer un viaje   to take a trip

hacer una broma   to play a joke

hacer una pregunta   to ask a question

hacer una visita   to pay a visit

hacerle falta   to need (*A Juan le hace falta un lápiz*/John needs a pencil.)

hacerse   to become (*Elena se hizo dentista*/Helen became a dentist.)

hacerse daño   to hurt oneself, to harm oneself

hacerse tarde   to be getting late (*Vámonos; se hace tarde*/Let's leave; it's getting late.)

¿Cuánto tiempo hace que + present tense . . . ?

(a) Use this formula when you want to ask *How long + the present perfect tense* in English:

¿Cuánto tiempo hace que Ud. estudia español?/How long have you been studying Spanish?

¿Cuánto tiempo hace que Ud. espera el autobús?/How long have you been waiting for the bus?

(b) When this formula is used, you generally expect the person to tell you how long a time it has been, e.g., one year, two months, a few minutes.

(c) This is used when the action began at some time in the past and continues up to the present moment. That is why you must use the present tense of the verb—the action of studying, waiting, etc., is still going on at the present.

Hace + length of time + que + present tense

(a) This formula is the usual answer to the question ¿Cuánto tiempo hace que + present tense . . . ?

(b) Since the question is asked in terms of *how long,* the usual answer is in terms of time: a year, two years, a few days, months, minutes, etc.:

Hace tres años que estudio español/I have been studying Spanish for three years.

Hace veinte minutos que espero el autobús/I have been waiting for the bus for twenty minutes.

(c) The same formula is used if you want to ask *how many weeks, how many months, how many minutes,* etc.:

¿Cuántos años hace que Ud. estudia español?/How many years have you been studying Spanish?

¿Cuántas horas hace que Ud. mira la televisión?/How many hours have you been watching television?

¿Desde cuándo + present tense . . . ?

¿Desde cuándo estudia Ud. español?/How long have you been studying Spanish?

Present tense + desde hace + length of time

Estudio español desde hace tres años/I have been studying Spanish for three years.

¿Cuánto tiempo hacía que + imperfect tense

(a) If the action of the verb began in the past and ended in the past, use the imperfect tense.

(b) This formula is equivalent to the English: *How long + past perfect tense:*
¿Cuánto tiempo hacía que Ud. hablaba cuando entré en la sala de clase?/ How long had you been talking when I entered the classroom?

(c) Note that the action of talking in this example began in the past and ended in the past when I entered the classroom.

Hacía + length of time + que + imperfect tense

The imperfect tense of the verb is used here because the action began in the past and ended in the past; it is not going on at the present moment.

Hacía una hora que yo hablaba cuando Ud. entró en la sala de clase/I had been talking for one hour when you entered the classroom.

¿Desde cuándo + imperfect tense . . . ?

¿Desde cuándo hablaba Ud. cuando yo entré en la sala de clase?/How long had you been talking when I entered the classroom?

Imperfect tense + desde hacía + length of time

(Yo) hablaba desde hacía una hora cuando Ud. entró en la sala de clase/I had been talking for one hour when you entered the classroom.

ir, irse

Use **ir** when you simply mean *to go: Voy al cine*/I am going to the movies.

Use **irse** when you mean *to leave* in the sense of *to go away: Mis padres se fueron al campo para visitar a mis abuelos*/My parents left for (went away to) the country to visit my grandparents.

ir a caballo   to ride horseback

ir a medias   to go halves

ir a pie   to walk (to go on foot)

ir bien   to get along well

ir con tiento   to go quietly, softly

ir delante   to go ahead

ir por   to go for, to go ahead

irse de prisa   to rush away

¡Qué va!   Nonsense! Rubbish!

¡Vaya!   You don't say!

Vaya con Dios.   God be with you.

jugar and tocar

Both these verbs mean *to play* but they have different uses. **Jugar a** means to play a sport, a game: *¿Juega Ud. al tenis?*/Do you play tennis?   *Me gusta jugar a la pelota*/I like to play ball.

The verb **tocar** means to play a musical instrument: *Carmen toca muy bien el piano*/Carmen plays the piano very well.

The verb **tocar** has other meanings, too. It is commonly used as follows: *to be one's turn,* in which case it takes an indirect object: *¿A quién le toca?*/Whose turn is it?   *Le toca a Juan*/It is John's turn.
to knock on a door (tocar a la puerta): *Alguien toca a la puerta*/Someone is knocking on (at) the door.

Essentially, **tocar** means *to touch.*

llegar a ser, hacerse and ponerse

These three verbs mean *to become*. Note the difference in use:

Use **llegar a ser** + a noun, e.g., *to become a doctor, to become a teacher;* in other words, the noun indicates the goal that you are striving for: *Quiero llegar a ser doctor*/I want to become a doctor. **Hacerse** is used similarly: *Juan se hizo abogado*/John became a lawyer.

Use **ponerse** + an adj., e.g., *to become pale, to become sick;* in other words, the adj. indicates the state or condition (physical or mental) that you have become: *Cuando vi el accidente, me puse pálido*/When I saw the accident, I became pale: *Mi madre se puso triste al oír la noticia desgraciada*/ My mother became sad upon hearing the unfortunate news.

llevar and tomar

These two verbs mean *to take* but note the difference in use:

Llevar means *to take* in the sense of carry or transport from place to place: *José llevó la silla de la cocina al comedor*/Joseph took the chair from the kitchen to the dining room.

The verb **llevar** is also used when you *take someone somewhere: Pedro llevó a María al baile anoche*/Peter took Mary to the dance last night.

As you probably know, **llevar** also means *to wear: María, ¿por qué llevas la falda nueva?*/Mary, why are you wearing your new skirt?

Tomar means *to take* in the sense of grab or catch: *La profesora tomó el libro y comenzó a leer a la clase*/The teacher took the book and began to read to the class; *Mi amigo tomó el tren esta mañana a las siete*/My friend took the train this morning at seven o'clock.

pedir and preguntar

Both these verbs mean *to ask* but note the difference:

Pedir means *to ask for something* or *to request: El alumno pidió un lápiz al profesor*/The pupil asked the teacher for a pencil.

Preguntar means *to inquire, to ask a question: La alumna preguntó a la profesora cómo estaba*/The pupil asked the teacher how she was.

pensar de and pensar en

Both these verbs mean *to think of* but note the difference:

Pensar is used with the prep. **de** when you ask someone what he/she thinks of someone or something, when you ask for someone's opinion: *¿Qué piensa Ud. de este libro?*/What do you think of this book? *Pienso que es bueno*/I think that it is good.

Pensar is used with the prep. **en** when you ask someone what or whom he/she is thinking about: *Miguel, no hablas mucho; ¿en qué piensas?*/ Michael, you are not talking much; of what are you thinking? (what are you thinking of?); *Pienso en las vacaciones de verano*/I'm thinking of summer vacation.

poder and **saber** (See also **conocer** and **saber**)

Both these verbs mean *can* but the difference in use is as follows:

Poder means *can* in the sense of *ability: No puedo ayudarle; lo siento*/ I cannot (am unable to) help you; I'm sorry.

Saber means *can* in the sense of *to know how: Este niño no sabe contar*/ This child can't (does not know how to) count.

In the preterit tense **poder** has the special meaning of *succeeded: Después de algunos minutos, Juan pudo abrir la puerta*/After a few minutes, John succeeded in opening the door.

In the preterit tense, **saber** has the special meaning of *found out: Lo supe ayer*/I found it out yesterday.

no poder más   to be exhausted, to be all in
No puede ser.   It's impossible. (It can't be.)

poner and **ponerse**

al poner del sol   at sunset
poner coto a   to put a stop to
poner el dedo en la llaga   to hit the nail right on the head
poner en claro   to explain simply and clearly
poner en duda   to doubt, to question
poner en marcha   to set in motion
poner en ridículo   to ridicule
poner los puntos sobre las íes   to mind one's p's and q's; to mind one's own business; to dot the i's
poner por escrito   to put in writing
ponerse de acuerdo   to reach an agreement
ponerse cómodo   to make oneself at home
ponerse en marcha   to start (out)
ponerse mal   to get sick

ser

Debe de ser . . .   It is probably . . .
Debe ser . . .   It ought to be . . .

Es de lamentar.   It's too bad.

Es de mi agrado.   It's to my liking.

Es hora de . . .   It is time to . . .

Es lástima or **Es una lástima.**   It's a pity; It's too bad.

Es que . . .   The fact is . . .

para ser   in spite of being (*Para ser tan viejo, él es muy ágil*/In spite of being so old, he is very nimble.)

sea lo que sea   whatever it may be

ser aficionado a   to be a fan of (*Soy aficionado al béisbol*/I'm a baseball fan.)

ser amable con   to be kind to (*Mi profesora de español es amable conmigo*/My Spanish teacher is kind to me.)

ser todo oídos   to be all ears (*Te escucho; soy todo oídos*/I'm listening to you; I'm all ears.)

si no fuera por . . .   if it were not for . . .

ser and **estar** (See also **estar** on page 527)

These two verbs mean *to be* but note the differences in use:

Generally speaking, use **ser** when you want to express *to be*.

Use **estar** when *to be* is used in the following ways:

(a) Health:
   (1) *¿Cómo está Ud.?*   How are you?
   (2) *Estoy bien.*   I am well.
   (3) *Estoy enfermo (enferma).*   I am sick.

(b) Location: persons, places, things
   (1) *Estoy en la sala de clase.*   I am in the classroom.
   (2) *La escuela está lejos.*   The school is far.
   (3) *Barcelona está en España.*   Barcelona is (located) in Spain.
   (4) *Los libros están en la mesa.*   The books are on the table.

(c) State or condition: persons
   (1) *Estoy contento (contenta).*   I am happy.
   (2) *Los alumnos están consados. (Las alumnas están cansadas.)* The students are tired.
   (3) *María está triste hoy.*   Mary is sad today.
   (4) *Estoy listo (lista).*   I am ready.
   (5) *Estoy pálido (pálida).*   I am pale.
   (6) *Estoy ocupado (ocupada).*   I am busy.
   (7) *Estoy seguro (segura).*   I am sure.
   (8) *Este hombre está vivo.*   This man is alive.
   (9) *Ese hombre está muerto.*   That man is dead
   (10) *Este hombre está borracho.*   This man is drunk.

(d) State or condition: things and places
   (1) *La ventana está abierta.*   The window is open.
   (2) *La taza está llena.* The cup is full.
   (3) *El té está caliente.*   The tea is hot.
   (4) *La limonada está fría.*   The lemonade is cold.
   (5) *La biblioteca está cerrada los domingos.*   The library is closed on Sundays.

(e) To form the progressive present of a verb, use the present tense of **estar** + the present part. of the main verb:
   Estoy estudiando en mi cuarto y no puedo salir esta noche.
   I am studying in my room and I cannot go out tonight.

(f) To form the progressive past of a verb, use the imperfect tense of **estar** + the present part. of the main verb:
   Mi hermano estaba leyendo cuando (yo) entré en el cuarto.
   My brother was reading when I entered (came into) the room.

ser aburrido   to be boring
ser de   to belong to; *Este libro es de María*/The book is Mary's.
ser de rigor   to be indispensable
ser de ver   to be worth seeing
se listo (lista)   to be clever

estar aburrido (aburrida)   to be bored
estar de buenas   to be lucky
estar de buen humor   to be in good spirits, a good mood
estar listo (lista)   to be ready

See also the verbs **ser** and **estar** among the 501 in this book.

tener and tenerse

¿Cuántos años tienes?   ¿Cuántos años tiene Ud.?   How old are you?
   Tengo diez y seis años.   I am sixteen years old.
¿Qué tienes?   ¿Qué tiene Ud.?   What's the matter?   What's the matter with you?   **No tengo nada.**   There's nothing wrong; There's nothing the matter (with me).
tener algo que hacer   to have something to do
tener apetito   to have an appetite
tener calor   to feel (to be) warm (persons)
tener cuidado   to be careful
tener dolor de cabeza   to have a headache
tener dolor de estómago   to have a stomachache
tener en cuenta   to take into account
tener éxito   to be successful
tener frío   to feel (to be) cold (persons)

tener ganas de + inf. to feel like + pres. part. (*Tengo ganas de tomar un helado*/I feel like having an ice cream.)

tener gusto en + inf. to be glad + inf. (*Tengo mucho gusto en conocerle*/I am very glad to meet you.)

tener hambre to feel (to be) hungry

tener la bondad de please, please be good enough to . . . (*Tenga la bondad de cerrar la puerta*/Please close the door.)

tener la culpa de algo to take the blame for something, to be to blame for something (*Tengo la culpa de eso*/I am to blame for that.)

tener lugar to take place (*El accidente tuvo lugar anoche*/The accident took place last night.)

tener miedo de to be afraid of

tener mucha sed to feel (to be) very thirsty (persons)

tener mucho calor to feel (to be) very warm (persons)

tener mucho frío to feel (to be) very cold (persons)

tener mucho que hacer to have a lot to do

tener poco que hacer to have little to do

tener por to consider as

tener prisa to be in a hurry

tener que + inf. to have + inf. (*Tengo que estudiar*/I have to study.)

tener que ver con to have to do with (*No tengo nada que ver con él*/I have nothing to do with him.)

tener razón to be right (*Usted tiene razón*/You are right.) **no tener razón** to be wrong (*Usted no tiene razón*/You are wrong.)

tener sed to feel (to be) thirsty (persons)

tener sueño to feel (to be) sleepy

tener suerte to be lucky

tener vergüenza de to be ashamed of

tenerse en pie to stand

volver and devolver

These two verbs mean *to return* but note the difference:

Volver means *to return* in the sense of *to come back: Voy a volver a casa*/I am going to return home. A synonym of **volver** is **regresar:** *Los muchachos regresaron a las ocho de la noche*/The boys came back (returned) at eight o'clock.

Devolver means *to return* in the sense of *to give back: Voy a devolver el libro a la biblioteca*/I am going to return the book to the library.

The Spanish Infinitive and Its Principal Uses: A Note

An infinitive is a verb that is not inflected; in other words, it does not change in form by inflection. In grammar, inflection takes place when a verb changes in form according to whether the subject of the sentence is singular in the 1st **(yo),** 2nd **(tú),** or 3rd **(Ud., él, ella)** person, or plural **(nosotros,** etc.), and according to the conjugated form of the verb in a particular tense, such as the present, preterit, imperfect, future, etc. An infinitive is generally considered to be a mood and it does not refer to a particular person, number, or tense. It is indeterminate and general. It is not conjugated in the tenses. The verb, however, is inflected because it is conjugated in the various tenses and changes in form. An infinitive remains in the same form: **hablar, comer, vivir.** In English, an infinitive is recognized by the preposition *to* in front of it, as in *to speak, to eat, to live.* When conjugated, *to speak* changes to *he, she speaks, I spoke, we have spoken,* etc. The change in the verb form is called inflection. The form of an infinitive is always the same because it is not conjugated and it is not inflected.

Here are three principal uses of the Spanish infinitive. For more examples in Spanish and English, please turn to page 541 where you will find an outline of what preposition (if any) goes with what verb plus an infinitive.

1. An infinitive can be used as a noun and it is masculine in gender. In English we use the present participle of a verb to function as a noun, in which case, we call it a *gerund.* In Spanish, however, the infinitive form of a verb is used. Examples:
    Leer es bueno/El leer es bueno/Reading is good.
    Fumar no es bueno para la salud/Smoking is not good for one's health.

2. An infinitive is used with some finite verbs (those that are conjugated in the various tenses) when affirmation or belief is conveyed. Examples:
    María siempre cree tener razón/Mary always believes she is right.
    Nosotros podemos venir a tu casa esta noche/We can come to your house tonight (this evening).

3. An infinitive can be used with idiomatic expressions that contain **que** or **de.** Examples:
    Tengo mucho que hacer esta mañana/I have a lot to do this morning.
    Mis amigos acaban de llegar/My friends have just arrived.

A Dios rogando y con el mazo dando. Put your faith in God and keep your powder dry. Praise the Lord and pass the ammunition.

Anda despacio que tengo prisa. Make haste slowly.

Antes que te cases, mira lo que haces. Look before you leap. Before you get married, look at what you're doing. [**casarse**/to get married; **mirar**/to look (at); **hacer**/to do, to make]

A quien madruga, Dios le ayuda. The early bird catches the worm. [**madrugar**/to get up early, at dawn; **ayudar**/to help]

Cuando el gato va a sus devociones, bailan los ratones. When the cat is away, the mice will play.

Dicho y hecho. No sooner said than done.

Dime con quién andas y te diré quién eres. Tell me who your friends are and I will tell you who you are.

Dios los cría y ellos se juntan. Birds of a feather flock together. [**criar**/to breed, to nurse; **juntarse**/to join together]

La práctica hace maestro al novicio. Practice makes perfect.

Las moscas no entran en una boca cerrada. Flies don't go into a closed mouth. [**entrar**/to enter; **cerrar**/to close]

El que mucho abarca poco aprieta. Do not bite off more than you can chew.

El que no se aventura no cruza la mar: Quien no se arriesga no pasa la mar. Nothing ventured, nothing gained.

El tiempo da buen consejo. Time will tell.

Más vale pájaro en mano que ciento volando. A bird in the hand is worth two in the bush.

Más vale tarde que nunca. Better late than never.

Mientras hay vida hay esperanza. Where there is life there is hope.

Perro que ladra no muerde. A barking dog does not bite.

Piedra movediza, el moho no la cobija. A rolling stone gathers no moss.

Querer es poder. Where there's a will there's a way.

Quien canta su mal espanta. When you sing you drive away your grief.

Quien siembra vientos recoge tempestades. If you sow the wind, you will reap the whirlwind.

Si a Roma fueres, haz como vieres. When in Rome do as the Romans do. [Note that it is not uncommon to use the future subjunctive in proverbs, as in *fueres* (**ir** or **ser**) and *vieres* (**ver**); see page xxxvii.]

Ver es creer. Seeing is believing.

Weather Expressions Using Verbs

Weather expressions using hacer and hay

¿Qué tiempo hace?   What is the weather like?
Hace buen tiempo.   The weather is good.
Hace calor.   It is warm (hot).
Hace fresco hoy.   It is cool today.
Hace frío.   It is cold.
Hace mal tiempo.   The weather is bad.
Hace sol.   It is sunny.
Hace viento.   It is windy.
¿Qué tiempo hacía cuando usted salió esta mañana?   What was the
   weather like when you went out this morning?
Hacía mucho frío ayer por la noche.   It was very cold yesterday evening.
Hacía mucho viento.   It was very windy.
¿Qué tiempo hará mañana?   What will the weather be like tomorrow?
Se dice que hará mucho calor.   They say it will be very hot.
Hay lodo.   It is muddy.   **Había lodo.**   It was muddy.
Hay luna.   The moon is shining *or* There is moonlight.   **Había luna ayer
   por la noche.**   There was moonlight yesterday evening.
¿Hay mucha nieve aquí en el invierno?   Is there much snow here in winter?
Hay neblina.   It is foggy.   **Había mucha neblina.**   It was very foggy.
Hay polvo.   It is dusty.   **Había mucho polvo.**   It was very dusty.

Other weather expressions using other verbs

Está lloviendo ahora.   It is raining now.
Está nevando.   It is snowing.
Esta mañana llovía cuando tomé el autobús.   This morning it was raining
   when I took the bus.
Estaba lloviendo cuando tomé el autobús.   It was raining when I took the
   bus.
Estaba nevando cuando me desperté.   It was snowing when I woke up.
¿Nieva mucho aquí en el invierno?   Does it snow much here in winter?
Las estrellas brillan.   The stars are shining.
¿Le gusta a usted la lluvia?   Do you like rain?
¿Le gusta a usted la nieve?   Do you like snow?
Sí. Me gusta la lluvia y me gusta la nieve.   Yes, I like rain and I like snow.
Pero no me gustan los días ventosos.   But I don't like windy days.
El viento sopla.   The wind blows.
El cielo está cubierto hoy.   The sky is overcast today.

Verbs with Prepositions

Spanish verbs are used with certain prepositions or no preposition at all. At times, the preposition used with a particular verb changes the meaning entirely, e.g., **contar** means *to count, to relate,* or *to tell;* **contar con** means *to rely on, to count on.*

When you look up a verb among the 501 to find its verb forms (or in the section of Over 1,100 Spanish Verbs Conjugated Like Model Verbs Among the 501), also consult all the categories given below so that you will learn what preposition that verb requires, if any.

The following are used frequently in Spanish readings and in conversation.

A. *Verbs of motion take the prep. a + inf.*

apresurarse a   to hasten to, to hurry to
dirigirse a   to go to, to go toward
ir a   to go to
regresar a   to return to
salir a   to go out to
venir a   to come to
volver a   to return to

> Examples:
> *Me apresuré a tomar el tren.*   I hurried to take the train.
> *El profesor se dirigió a abrir la puerta.*   The teacher went to open the door.
> *María fue a comer.*   Mary went to eat.

B. *The following verbs take the prep. a + inf.*

acertar a   to happen to
acostumbrarse a   to become used to, to become accustomed to
aficionarse a hacer algo   to become fond of doing something
alcanzar a   to succeed in (doing something)
aprender a   to learn to, to learn how to
aspirar a   to aspire to
atreverse a   to dare to
ayudar a (hacer algo)   to help to
comenzar a   to begin to
condenar a   to condemn to
convidar a   to invite to
decidirse a   to decide to
dedicarse a   to devote oneself to
detenerse a   to pause to, to stop to
disponerse a   to get ready to
echarse a   to begin to, to start to

empezar a   to begin to, to start to
enseñar a   to teach to
exponerse a   to run the risk of
invitar a   to invite to
negarse a   to refuse to
obligar a   to oblige to, to obligate to
ponerse a   to begin to, to start to
prepararse a   to prepare (oneself) to
principiar a   to begin to, to start to
resignarse a   to resign oneself to
resolverse a   to make up one's mind to
someter a   to submit to, to subdue to
venir a   to end up by
volver a   to (do something) again

Examples:
Me acostumbré a estudiar mis lecciones todas las noches.   I became used
   to studying my lessons every evening.
No me atreví a responder.   I did not dare to answer.
El hombre comenzó a llorar.   The man began to cry.
Me dispuse a salir.   I got ready to go out.
Me eché a llorar.   I began to cry.
El señor Gómez se negó a ir.   Mr. Gómez refused to go.
Juana se puso a correr.   Jane began to run.
El muchacho volvió a jugar.   The boy played again.

C. *The following verbs take the prep. a + noun (or pronoun if that is the required dependent element)*

acercarse a   to approach
acostumbrarse a   to become accustomed to, to become used to
aficionarse a   to become fond of
asemejarse a   to resemble, to look like
asistir a   to attend, to be present at
asomarse a   to appear at
cuidar a alguien   to take care of someone
dar a   to face, to overlook, to look out upon, to look out over
dedicarse a   to devote oneself to
echar una carta al correo   to mail, to post a letter
echar la culpa a alguien   to blame someone, to put the blame on someone
jugar a   to play (a game, sport, cards)
llegar a ser   to become
llevar a cabo   to carry out, to accomplish
oler a   to smell of, to smell like
parecerse a   to resemble, to look like
querer a   to love

saber a   to taste of, to taste like, to have the flavor of
ser aficionado a   to be fond of, to be a fan of
sonar a   to sound like
subir a   to get on, to get into (a bus, a train, a vehicle)
tocarle a una persona   to be a person's turn

Examples:
Nos acercamos a la ciudad.   We are approaching the city.
Una muchacha bonita se asomó a la puerta.   A pretty girl appeared at the door.
Mi cuarto da al jardín.   My room faces the garden.
Me dedico a mis estudios.   I devote myself to my studies.
Enrique llegó a ser profesor de matemáticas.   Henry became a mathematics teacher.
Jorge llevó a cabo sus responsabilidades.   George carried out his responsibilities.
Mi hermano se parece a mi padre y yo me parezco a mi madre.   My brother resembles my father and I resemble my mother.
Quiero a mi patria.   I love my country.
Soy aficionado a los deportes.   I am fond of sports.
Subí al tren.   I got on the train.
Le toca a Juan.   It is John's turn.

D. *The following verbs take the prep. con + inf.*

amenazar con   to threaten to
contar con   to count on, to rely on
contentarse con   to be satisfied with
soñar con   to dream of, to dream about

Examples:
Cuento con tener éxito.   I am counting on being successful.
Me contento con quedarme en casa.   I am satisfied with staying at home.
Sueño con ir a Chile.   I dream of going to Chile.

E. *The following verbs take the prep. con + noun (or pronoun if that is the required dependent element)*

acabar con   to finish, to put an end to, to make an end of, to finish off
casarse con   to marry, to get married to
conformarse con   to put up with
contar con   to count on, to rely on
contentarse con   to be satisfied with
cumplir con   to fulfill
dar con   to meet, to find, to come upon
encontrarse con   to run into, to meet by chance
entenderse con   to come to an understanding with
meterse con   to pick a quarrel with

quedarse con to keep, to hold on to
soñar con to dream of, to dream about
tropezar con to come upon, to run across unexpectedly, to run into

Examples:
José se casó con Ana. Joseph married Anna.
Me conformo con tus ideas. I put up with your ideas.
Contamos con nuestros padres. We count on our parents.
Me contento con poco dinero. I am satisfied with little money.
Siempre cumplo con mi promesa. I always fulfill my promise.
Anoche di con mis amigos en el cine. Last night I met my friends at
   the movies.
Ayer por la tarde me encontré con un amigo mío. Yesterday afternoon
   I ran into a friend of mine.
Me quedo con el dinero. I am keeping the money; I am holding on to
   the money.
Sueño con un verano agradable. I am dreaming of a pleasant summer.

F. The following verbs take the prep. de + inf.

acabar de to have just
acordarse de to remember to
alegrarse de to be glad to
arrepentirse de to repent
cansarse de to become tired of
cesar de to cease, to stop
dejar de to stop, to fail to
encargarse de to take charge of
haber de *see* the section Verbs Used in Idiomatic Expressions on page 524.
ocuparse de to be busy with, to attend to
olvidarse de to forget to
tratar de to try to
tratarse de to be a question of

Examples:
Guillermo acaba de llegar. William has just arrived.
Felipe acababa de partir. Philip had just left.
Me alegro de hablarle. I am glad to talk to you.
Me canso de esperar el autobús. I'm getting tired of waiting for the bus.
Cesó de llover. It stopped raining.
Jaime dejó de escribir la redacción. James failed to write the composition.
Mi padre se ocupa de preparar la comida. My father is busy preparing
   the meal.
Andrés se olvidó de estudiar. Andrew forgot to study.
Siempre trato de hacer un buen trabajo. I always try to do a good job.
Se trata de abstenerse. It is a question of abstaining.

G. *The following verbs take the prep. de + noun (or pronoun if that is the required dependent element)*

abusar de   to abuse, to overindulge in
acordarse de   to remember
alejarse de   to go away from
apartarse de   to keep away from
apoderarse de   to take possession of
aprovecharse de   to take advantage of
bajar de   to get out of, to descend from, to get off
burlarse de   to make fun of
cambiar de   to change (trains, buses, clothes, etc.)
cansarse de   to become tired of
carecer de   to lack
compadecerse de   to feel sorry for, to pity, to sympathize with
constar de   to consist of
cuidar de algo   to take care of something
depender de   to depend on
despedirse de   to say good-bye to, to take leave of
despojarse de   to take off (clothing)
disfrutar de   to enjoy
enamorarse de   to fall in love with
encogerse de hombros   to shrug one's shoulders
enterarse de   to find out about
fiarse de alguien   to trust someone
gozar de algo   to enjoy something
ocuparse de   to be busy with, to attend to
oír hablar de   to hear of, to hear about
olvidarse de   to forget
pensar de   to think of (**pensar de** is used when asking for an opinion)
perder de vista   to lose sight of
ponerse de acuerdo   to come to an agreement
preocuparse de   to worry about, to be concerned about
quejarse de   to complain about
reírse de   to laugh at
saber de memoria   to know by heart, to memorize
salir de   to go out of, to leave from
servir de   to serve as
servirse de   to make use of, to use
tratarse de   to be a question of, to deal with

Examples:
Me acuerdo de aquel hombre.   I remember that man.
Vamos a aprovecharnos de esta oportunidad.   Let's take advantage of this opportunity.

Después de bajar del tren, fui a comer.   After getting off the trian, I went to eat.
Todos los días cambio de ropa.   Every day I change my clothes.
Me canso de este trabajo.   I am getting tired of this work.
Esta composición carece de calidad.   This composition lacks quality.
Me compadezco de ese pobre hombre.   I pity that poor man.
Ahora tengo que despedirme de usted.   Now I have to say good-bye.
Eduardo se enamoró de Carmen.   Edward fell in love with Carmen.
Mi madre se ocupa de mi padre que está enfermo.   My mother is busy with my father who is sick.
Oí hablar de la boda de Anita.   I heard about Anita's wedding.
Carlos se olvidó del aniversario de sus padres.   Charles forgot about his parents' anniversary.
¿Qué piensa Ud. de nuestro profesor de español?   What do you think of our Spanish teacher?
¡Mira! ¡El mono se ríe de nosotros!   Look! The monkey is laughing at us.
Siempre salgo de casa a las ocho de la mañana.   I always leave (from, go out of) the house at eight in the morning.
En nuestro club, Cristóbal sirve de presidente.   In our club, Christopher serves as president.

H. *The following verbs generally take the prep. en + inf.*

acabar en   to end in
complacerse en   to be pleased to, to delight in
consentir en   to consent to
convenir en   to agree to, to agree on
empeñarse en   to persist in, to insist on
esforzarse en   to strive for, to force onself to, to try hard to
insistir en   to insist on
quedar en   to agree to, to agree on
tardar en   to be late (to delay) in

> Examples:
> *La señora Pardo consintió en asistir a la conferencia.*   Mrs. Pardo consented to attending the meeting.
> *El muchacho se empeñó en salir.*   The boy insisted on going out.
> *Mis amigos insistieron en venir a verme.*   My friends insisted on coming to see me.
> *El avión tardó en llegar.*   The plane was late in arriving.

I. *The following verbs generally take the prep. en + noun (or pronoun if that is the required dependent element)*

apoyarse en   to lean against, to lean on
confiar en   to rely on, to trust in
consistir en   to consist of
convertirse en   to become, to convert to
entrar en   to enter (into), to go into

fijarse en   to stare at, to notice, to take notice, to observe
meterse en   to get involved in, to plunge into
pensar en   to think of, to think about [**pensar en** is used when asking or when stating what or whom a person is thinking of]
ponerse en camino   to set out, to start out
reparar en   to notice, to observe
volver en sí   to regain consciousness, to be oneself again

Examples:
Me apoyé en la puerta.   I leaned against the door.
Entré en el restaurante.   I entered (I went into) the restaurant.
¿En qué piensa Ud.?   What are you thinking of?
Pienso en mi trabajo.   I am thinking of my work.
¿En quién piensa Ud.?   Whom are you thinking of?
Pienso en mi madre.   I am thinking of my mother.
¿En quiénes piensa Ud.?   Whom are you thinking of?
Pienso en mis padres.   I am thinking of my parents.

J. The following verbs generally take the prep. por + inf., noun, pronoun, adj., if that is the required dependent element

acabar por   to end up by
dar por   to consider, to regard as
darse por   to pretend (to be something), to think oneself (to be something)
estar por   to be in favor of
interesarse por   to take an interest in
pasar por   to be considered as
preguntar por   to ask for, to inquire about
tener por   to consider something, to have an opinion on something
tomar por   to take someone for

Examples:
Domingo acabó por casarse con Elena.   Dominic finally ended up by marrying Helen.
¿Mi libro de español? Lo doy por perdido.   My Spanish book? I consider it lost.
La señorita López se da por actriz.   Miss López pretends to be an actress.
Estamos por quedarnos en casa esta noche.   We are in favor of staying at home this evening.
El señor Pizarro pasa por experto.   Mr. Pizarro is considered an expert.
Pregunto por el señor Pardo. ¿Está en casa?   I am asking for Mr. Pardo. Is he at home?

K. Verb + NO PREPOSITION + inf. The following verbs do not ordinarily take a preposition when followed by an infinitive

deber + inf.   must, ought to
Debo hacer mis lecciones.   I must (ought to) do my lessons.

dejar + inf.   to allow to, to let
Mi madre me dejó salir.   My mother allowed me to go out.
Dejé caer mi libro.   I dropped my book (I let my book fall).

desear + inf.   to desire to, to wish to
Deseo tomar un café.   I wish to have a cup of coffee.

esperar + inf.   to expect to, to hope to
Espero ir a la América del Sur este invierno.   I expect to go to South America
  this winter.

hacer + inf.   to do, to make, to have something made or done
Tú me haces llorar.   You make me cry.
Mi padre hace construir una casita.   My father is having a small house built
  [by someone].

Note that the use of *hacer + inf.* can be described as the "causative (causal)"
use of *hacer* when there is an inf. directly after. it. The construction *hacer + inf.*
indicates that something is being made or being done by someone. Further
examples: *hacer firmar*/to have (something) signed (by someone); *hacer
confesar*/to have (someone) confess or to make (someone) confess. This
causative use of *hacer* is used in a verb tense that is needed + inf. form of
the verb which tells what action is being done or being made: *Mi padre hizo
construir una casita*/My father had a little house built; *Le haré confesar*/I shall
make him confess; *El señor López lo hizo firmar la carta*/Mr. López made him
sign the letter.

necesitar + inf.   to need
Necesito pasar una hora en la biblioteca.   I need to spend an hour in the library.

oír + inf.   to hear
Le oí entrar por la ventana.   I heard him enter through the window.
He oído hablar de su buena fortuna.   I have heard (talk) about your good fortune.
He oído decir que la señora Sierra está enferma.   I have heard (tell) that Mrs.
  Sierra is sick.

pensar + inf.   to intend to, to plan to
Pienso hacer un viaje a México.   I plan to take a trip to Mexico.

poder + inf.   to be able to, can
Puedo venir a verle a la una.   I can come to see you at one o'clock.

preferir + inf.   to prefer
Prefiero quedarme en casa esta noche.   I prefer to stay at home this evening.

prometer + inf.   to promise
Prometo venir a verle a las ocho.   I promise to come to see you at eight o'clock.

querer + inf.   to want to, to wish to
Quiero comer ahora.   I want to eat now.
¿Qué quiere decir este muchacho?   What does this boy mean?

saber + inf.   to know how to
¿Sabe Ud. nadar?   Do you know how to swim?
Sí, yo sé nadar.   Yes, I know how to swim.

ver + inf.   to see
Veo venir el tren.   I see the train coming.

L. *The following verbs do not ordinarily require a preposition, whereas in English a preposition is used*

agradecer   to thank for, to be thankful (to someone) for (something)
Le agradecí su paciencia.   I thanked him for his patience.

aprovechar   to take advantage of
¿No quiere Ud. aprovechar la oportunidad?   Don't you want to take advantage of the opportunity?

buscar   to look for, to search for
Busco mi libro.   I am looking for my book.

esuchar   to listen to
Escucho la música.   I am listening to the music.

esperar   to wait for
Espero el autobús.   I am waiting for the bus.

guardar cama   to stay in bed
La semana pasada guardé cama.   Last week I stayed in bed.

lograr   to succeed in
El alumno logró hacerlo.   The pupil succeeded in doing it.

mirar   to look at
Miro el cielo.   I am looking at the sky.

pagar   to pay for
Pagué los billetes.   I paid for the tickets.

pedir   to ask for
Pido un libro.   I am asking for a book.

soler + inf.   to be accustomed to, to be in the habit of
(Yo) suelo acompañar a mis amigos en el autobús.   I am in the habit of accompanying my friends on the bus.

Over 1,100 Spanish Verbs Conjugated Like Model Verbs Among the 501

The number after each verb is the page number in this book where a model verb is shown fully conjugated. At times there are two page references; for example, **sonarse** (to blow one's nose) is conjugated like **sonar** on page 445 because the **o** in the stem changes to **ue** and it is like **lavarse** on page 289, which is a reflexive **ar** type verb, as is **sonarse**. Don't forget to use the reflexive pronouns with reflexive verbs. Consult the entry **reflexive pronoun and reflexive verb** in the section on definitions of basic grammatical terms with examples in the back pages.

A

abajar, bajar to go down   85

abalanzar to balance   81

abalanzarse to hurl oneself   81

abalar to move, shake   54

abalear to shoot at, to wound or kill by gunshot   204

abalizar to mark with buoys   342

abanar to cool with a fan   247

abandonar to abandon   474

abanicar to fan   117

abaratar to make cheaper, reduce prices   309

abdicar to abdicate   99

abducir to abduct   131

aberrar to err, be mistaken   54

abjurar to abjure, renounce   284

ablandecer to soften   347

abnegar to abnegate, forego   328

abnegarse to go without, deny oneself   289, 328

abofetear to slap in the face   54

abominar to abominate   107

abonar to buy a subscription   54

abonarse to subscribe oneself   54, 289

abordar to board   54

aborrecer to abhor, detest   347

abrigar to shelter, protect   297

abrochar to button up, fasten   258

abrogar to abrogate, revoke, annul   421

abrumar, brumar to crush, oppress, overwhelm   245

absorber to absorb   127

abstraer to abstract   478

abusar to abuse   25

acachetear to slap in the face   54

acamar to flatten   54

acaparar to buy up, hoard   345

acceder to accede, agree   127

acechar to watch, spy on   198

acentuar to accentuate, mark with an accent   140

acertar to guess right   355

acoger to receive hospitably, welcome   122

acomodar to accommodate, arrange, hire   258

acompasar to measure   350

acopiar to classify, collect, gather   106

acorrer to run to someone's aid, help, assist   147

acostar to put to bed   21

acrecentar to increase   355

acrecer to augment, increase   150

activar to activate   288

actuar to act, behave   140

acumular to accumulate   84

adaptar to adapt   11

adestrar to train, instruct, direct   355

adicionar to add   54

administrar to administrate   213

adornar to adorn   54

adscribir to ascribe, assign, attribute   222

adular to adulate, flatter   258

advenir to arrive, come   489

afamar to make famous   54

afamarse to become famous   112

afanar to hurry; rob, steal   54

afear to deform, make ugly   54

afectar to affect   11

afeitar to shave   35

afianzar to fasten   286

aficionar to induce a liking for   341

aficionarse a to become fond of   341

afirmar to affirm, assert   241

afligir to afflict, distress   187

afluir to flow   264

afrontar to confront, face, defy   109

agraviar to wrong, injure, offend   54

agriar to make sour   54

agrietar to crack, split   54

aguachar to flood, fill with water   198

aguantar to bear, endure   54

aguar to dilute   82

ahogarse   to drown   289, 421

ahumar to cure in smoke, fill with smoke   54

adjustar to adjust   258

alambrar to fence with wire   51

alanzar to lance   286

alardear to boast, brag, show off   54

alargar to lengthen   421

alarmar to alarm   54

alentar to breathe; encourage, inspire   355

alienar to alienate   247

aligar to bind, tie   421

alimentar to feed, nourish   291

almacenar to store   114

alocar to make someone crazy   473

alojar to lodge, give accommodation to   85

amplificar to amplify, enlarge   117

analizar to analyze   90

animar to animate   54

anotar to annotate, write notes about   54

antepagar to pay in advance   344

anteponer to place before, to prefer   367

anular to annul, cancel   258

apaciguar to pacify, calm, soothe   82

aparar to prepare   345

apetecer to crave for, long for   59

aplicar to apply   99

apocar to lessen, reduce   99

apoderar to empower   61

apostar to bet, wager   475

aprehender to apprehend   63

aprestar to make ready, prepare   379

apresurar to accelerate, hurry   64

apretar to grip, press   355

apropiar to appropriate money, adapt   106

aprovechar to make use of   66

apurar to purify, exhaust, consume   67

arar to plow   54

argüir to argue, reason   264

armar to arm   54

arrendar to lease, let, rent, hire   355

arrepentirse de to repent for, regret   436

arrestar to arrest, detain   54

asaltar to assault, attack   427

asentar to seat, set down   355

asentir to assent, agree   373

asignar to assign, apportion, give   114

asomar to appear slowly (as through an opening)   474

asomarse to lean out, look out (as out of a window)   112

asombrar to amaze, astonish   113

aspirar to breathe in, inhale   29

asurarse to get burned   112

atar to bind, tie   309

atender to look after, attend to, pay attention   163

aterrizar to land   47

atravesar, travesar to cross, cross over, go through   355

atribuir to attribute   264

aumentar to augment, increase   318

autorizar to authorize   90

avenir to reconcile   489

aventurarse to venture, risk   48

avisar to advise, inform, warn, notify   343

ayunar to fast, go without food   170

B

bañar to bathe   87

batallar to fight, battle, struggle   260

batir to beat, whip   1

besar to kiss   233

blasfemar to blaspheme, curse   245

bogar to row   421

bonificar to increase production   117

boxear to box   204

bregar to fight, brawl   344

brillar to shine   258

brincar to bounce, jump, skip   430

brindar to offer, invite, drink a toast   54

bromear to joke   204

brumar, abrumar to crush, oppress, overwhelm   245

bufonearse to jest, joke   351

burbujear to bubble   54

C

cabecear to nod one's head when sleepy   54

cachar to break into pieces   198

calar to drench, soak   258

calcar to trace, copy   424

calcular to calculate   258

calificar to assess, rate, classify   117

calmar to calm   54

camorrear to quarrel   54

cancelar to cancel, strike out 54

candar to lock 109

cantalear to hum, sing softly 54

cantonear to idle, loaf, wander about 54

capar to castrate, cut off 334

captar to capture, win trust 54

carcajear to burst out laughing 54

carecer de to be in need of, to lack 336

cargarse de to be overloaded with 111, 112

castigar to chastise, punish 344

castrar to castrate; to dry a wound 54

catar to sample, taste 309

causar to cause 482

cautivar to capture; captivate, charm 288

cazar to hunt, chase 81

ceder to cede, yield 414

cegar to blind, block up, to grow blind 328

censurar to censure 72

cercar to fence in, enclose 12

cesar to cease, stop 233

chafar to crease, crumple (clothes) 258

chafarse to become flattened 289

chamar to barter, exchange 54

chamuscar to singe, scorch 99

chapar to cover, plate with silver or gold 334

charlar to chatter, prattle 258

chascar to crunch 99

chiflar to whistle, blow a whistle 258

chillar to scream, shriek 258

chinchar to annoy, irritate 258

chismear to gossip 258

chocar to collide, crash 424

chuchear to whisper 258

chufar to mock 258

circular to circulate, move 71

citar to make an appointment, cite, quote 494

civilizar to civilize, become civilized 90

clamar to cry out, wail 15

clarar to make clear, explain 16

clarificar to clarify 117

clasificar to classify 117

clavar to nail 54

cobijar to cover, shelter 54

cocer to cook 322, 487

codear to elbow, nudge 54

colar to filter, strain 475

colear to wag, move 54

colorar to color, give color to 32

colorear to color, tint 174

comandar to command 109

combatir to combat, fight 1

comentar to comment 109

cometer to commit, entrust 91

comparar to compare 345

compartir to divide, share 349

competir to compete, contest 412

compilar to compile 258

complacer to please 364

completar to complete 309

complicar to complicate 76

comprobar to check, verify, confirm 381

computar to compute, calculate 279

comunicar to communicate 232

concebir to conceive; imagine 352

conceder to concede 414

concentrar to concentrate 213

concertar to arrange, agree 355

concluir to conclude 269

condenar to condemn 114

confiar to trust, entrust 238

confirmar to confirm 241

confiscar to confiscate 99

conformar to conform 242

congelar to congeal, freeze 258

conjugar to conjugate 297

consentir to consent, allow 435

considerar to consider 225

consolar to console 137

conspirar to conspire, plot 315

constar to be clear, consistent 109

constatar to prove, verify 309

consultar to consult 309

contemplar to contemplate, meditate 258

contentar to gratify, please 109

contradecir (past part. **contradicho**) to contradict 303

contraponer to compare, contrast 367

contratar to contract, engage, hire 479

controlar to control 258

convalecer to convalesce 336

conversar to converse 343

copiar to copy 106

corresponder to correspond 414

corromper to corrupt 422

crear to create 174

criticar to criticize 117

cuestionar to debate, discuss 474

culpar to blame, accuse 334

culparse to blame oneself 188

cultivar to cultivate, grow 288

cumular to accumulate 258

curar to cure 72

D

dañar to damage, injure 109

dañarse to become damaged, injured 87

danzar to dance 81

datar to date (a letter, an account) 309

debatir to debate 408

decantar to exaggerate; pour off 109

decentar to cut into, begin cutting 355

declamar to declaim, recite 54

declinar to decline, get weak 107

decorar to decorate 32

dedicar to dedicate 424

deferir to defer; delegate 373

definir to define 349

deformar to deform 242

delatar to denounce, accuse 309

delegar to delegate 344

demandar to demand, petition, sue 197

demarcar to demarcate, delimit 424

demoler to demolish, pull down 322

denegar to deny, refuse 328

denotar to denote 11

dentar to teethe, provide with teeth; indent 355

deparar to provide, supply 345

departir to converse 349

depilar to depilate, remove hair 258

deplorar to deplore 32

depositar to deposit, place, put 258

depreciar to depreciate 386

derogar to derogate, abolish 421

derramar to spill 258

derretir to melt, dissolve 352

desacordar to be in discord 19

desacordarse to become forgetful 20

desalentar to make breathless, put out of breath 103

desalojar to move out, vacate 164

desamparar to abandon, forsake 345

desanimar to discourage 54

desaparecer to disappear 59

desapreciar to underestimate 62

desaprender to unlearn 63

desarrollar to develop 260

desarticular to disarticulate 71

desayudar to hinder, impede 83

desbaratar to ruin, wreck 109

descalificar to disqualify 117

descambiar to cancel an exchange 106

descaminar to mislead, lead astray 107

descargar to unload 111

descender to descend, go down 357

descolgar to unhook, take down from a hanging position 124

descollar to protrude, stand out 137

descomponer to disarrange, disrupt, disturb 367

desconcertar to disconcert, upset 355

desconectar to disconnect, switch off 258

descontar to discount, deduct; disregard 137

descuidarse to be negligent, careless 152

desdeñarse to be disdainful 87

desechar to reject 198

desencantar to disenchant 109

desenvolver to unwrap 497

desfijar to pull out, unfix 239

desgajar to rip off, tear off 54

desganarse to lose one's appetite 289

designar to designate 114

desinfectar to disinfect 258

desmentir to disprove, prove false 313

desnudar to undress 325

desnudarse to undress oneself 289

desobedecer to disobey 330

desocupar to vacate 334

desordenar to disarrange 341

desorganizar to disorganize 342

despedir to dismiss, fire, discharge 352, 177

despertar to wake up (someone) 355, 180

desplegar to unfold, unfurl, spread out 328

desterrar to banish, exile 355

desvalorizar to depreciate, devalue 47

desviar to divert 216

determinar to determine 471

dictar to dictate   11

diferir to differ; defer, postpone, delay   373

digerir to digest   373

discursar to discourse, make a speech   25

diseminar to disseminate, spread   107

disfrutar to enjoy   309

disimular to dissemble, pretend, cover up   71

disolver to dissolve   322

disponer to dispose   367

distraer to distract   478

distribuir to distribute   264

disturbar to disturb   9

disuadir to dissuade   349

divertir to amuse, distract, entertain   373, 192

dividir to divide   349

divulgar to divulge, make known   344

dorar to gild, cover with gold   32

dotar to endow, bequeath, give a dowry   11

driblar to dribble (sports)   258

E

editar to publish   252

educar to educate, instruct, rear, bring up   424

elaborar to elaborate; manufacture   93

embalar to pack, create   258

embarcar to embark, go on board   99

embargar to impede, hamper   344

embocar to cram down food, gulp down   424

emborronar to scribble   54

emitir to emit, send forth   349

empapar to drench, soak   345

enamorar to enamor, inspire love   54

enamorarse de to fall in love with   289

enchufar to connect, plug in   54

encomendar to commend, entrust   355

enfadar to anger, irritate   208

enfriar to cool, chill   216

engañarse to deceive oneself, be mistaken   87

engordar to fatten, grow fat, put on weight   54

enjuagar to rinse   298

enmendar to amend, revise, correct   355

enojar to annoy, irritate   210

enrollar to wind, roll up   260

ensayar to test, try, rehearse   54

ensillar to saddle   260

ensolver to include; reduce, condense   497

ensuciar to dirty, soil, stain   386

entenderse to understand each other, be understood   212

enterar to inform   213

enterarse de to find out about   289

enterrar to bury, inter; forget   116

entregarse to surrender, give in   214, 289

entretener to entertain, amuse   469

entretenerse to amuse oneself   77

entrever to catch a glimpse   490

entrevistar to interview   494

envestir to clothe   491

envolverse to become involved   217, 80

equipar to equip   334

equiparar to compare, match, make equal   345

equivaler to equal   485

equivocar to mistake   218

eructar to belch, burp   54

escalar to climb   258

escapar to escape   334

escarnecer to ridicule, mock   347

esconder to conceal, hide   414

esconderse to hide oneself   414, 80

escupir to spit   349

esforzar to strengthen, encourage   49

esforzarse to make an effort   49, 289

espantar to frighten, scare   109

esposar to handcuff   343

estacionar to station, park (a vehicle)   258

estrechar to narrow, tighten   198

evacuar to evacuate   140

evitar to avoid   252

evocar to evoke, recall   424

exagerar to exaggerate   258

examinar to examine   107

exasperar to exasperate   225

excitar to excite, stimulate   252

exclamar to exclaim   54

excluir to exclude   269

excusar to excuse   25

exhalar to exhale   260

existir to exist   276

expedir to expedite   352

explorar to explore   32

exponer to expose   367

exportar to export   109

extender to extend   357

extinguir to extinguish   191

extraer to extract, draw out   478

extrañar to surprise   211

F

facilitar to facilitate   236

fallar to trump, fail   260

falsear to falsify, misrepresent   204

falsificar to falsify, forge   424

familiarizar to familiarize   342

fantasear to daydream   204

farolear to boast, brag, show off   54

fascinar to fascinate   107

fastidiar to annoy, pester   230

fatigar to fatigue, tire   421

figurar to depict, draw, represent   72

figurarse to imagine   72, 289

fijar to fix, fasten   239

fluir to flow   272

formular to formulate   71

forzar to force   49

fotocopiar to photocopy   106

fotografiar to photograph   465

frotar to rub   498

fruncir to knit (eyebrows); to purse (lips)   501

frustrar to frustrate   213

fusilar to shoot   258

fusionar to combine, merge   107

fustigar to whip   344

G

galantear to woo, make eyes at   174

galopar to gallop   54

gandulear to idle, loaf   204

gansear to say, do stupid things   174

garabatear to scribble   464

garbear to show off   174

garlar to chatter, prattle   258

gatear to crawl   174

generar to generate, produce   213

girar to turn around, spin   213

golpear to crush, hit, strike   174

golpetear to pound, hammer   174

gorjear to warble, gurgle   204

gormar to vomit, spew   242

gotear to drip   204

grabar to engrave   247

gratar to brush, rub   247

gravar to burden   247

gravitar to gravitate   252

guardar to keep, guard, save   258

guipar to notice, see   54

guisar to cook   25

H

hacinar to pile up, stack   107

hadar to foretell   325

halagar to flatter   344

hambrear to starve   204

haraganear to idle, loaf   204

heder to stink   357

hervir to boil   373

holgar to rest, be idle   124

honrar to honor   32

hurtar to rob, steal   11

I

identificar to identify   117

iluminar to illuminate   107

ilusionar to fascinate   246

ilusionarse to have illusions   289

ilustrar to illustrate; enlighten, explain   213

imaginar to imagine   107

imbuir to imbue   264

imitar to imitate   252

implicar to implicate   424

implorar to implore   300

imponer to impose   367

impresionar to impress 107

incendiar to set on fire   106

incitar to incite   279

inclinar to incline, tilt   107

inferir to infer   401

influenciar to influence   386

informar to inform   242

iniciar to initiate, begin   386

inmigrar to immigrate   258

inocular to inoculate   71

inspirar to inspire   29

instituir to institute, found   264

instruir to instruct, teach   264

iterponer to interpose   367

interpretar to interpret   379

interrogar to interrogate, question   297

intimidar to intimidate   197

inventar to invent   279

invertir to invert, turn upside down   373

investigar to investigate   421

investir to invest, endow   352

invocar to appeal, call upon   424

irritar to irritate   279

J

jabonar to soap, lather   474

jacarear to annoy; to roam the streets at night making merry   204

jactarse to boast, brag   48

jadear to pant   204

jalar to pull   258

jamar to eat   54

jarapotear to stuff with drugs, medicines   204

jetar to dilute, dissolve   309

justar to joust, tilt   11

justificar to justify   117

L

ladrar to bark   54

ladronear to shoplift   204

lagrimar to cry, weep, shed tears 229

lamentar to lament 11

lamer to lick 91

laminar to laminate 107

limar to file, polish, smooth 229

llagar to injure, hurt, wound 298

llamear to blaze, flame 204

lloriquear to whimper, whine 204

lloviznar to drizzle 288

localizar to localize, locate, find 81

lograr to achieve, attain, get 29

lubricar to lubricate 470

lustrar to polish, cleanse 213

M

machar to beat, crush 307

magullar to batter, bruise 260

majar to crush, mash 85

malear to ruin, spoil 204

maleficiar to damage, harm, injure 386

malgastar to squander, waste 248

maliciar to fear, suspect 386

maltratar to maltreat, abuse 479

manchar to spot, stain, blot 307

mandar to command, order 258

manipular to manipulate 71

maquillarse to put on makeup 289

marcar to dial (phone), mark, score (a goal) 99

mascar, masticar to chew, masticate 99

meditar to meditate 252

mendigar to beg 344

merendar to have a snack, refreshment 355

meter to put in/into 444

mimar to pamper, spoil, indulge 315

mitigar to mitigate, allay, alleviate 344

modular to modulate 71

moler to grind, crush, mill 322

molestar to bother, annoy 248

monear to clown (monkey) around 204

murmurar to murmur, mutter 72

mutilar to mutilate 71

N

nacionalizar to nationalize, naturalize 90

narrar to narrate 213

naturalizar to naturalize, nationalize 90

nausear to feel nauseated, sick 204

necear to talk nonsense 204

negociar to negotiate 386

niñear to behave childishly 204

nombrar to name, appoint 113

notar to note 309

noticiar to inform, notify 386

notificar to notify, inform 117

numerar to number 225

nutrir to feed, nourish 349

O

obcecar to blind 99

objetar to object 309

obligar to oblige, compel 344

obliterar to obliterate, erase 225

obrar to build, work 113

obscurecer to darken 336

obsequiar to entertain, compliment 226

obstar to obstruct, impede, hinder 213

obstinarse to be obstinate, stubborn 289

obstruir to obstruct, to block 264

oficiar to officiate 386

ofuscar to dazzle 99

olfatear to smell, sniff 204

ominar to predict, foretell, forecast 107

omitir to omit 30

ondular to undulate, wind 71

operar to operate 225

opinar to opine, think, have an opinion 107

optar to opt, choose 11

orar to pray 32

ornar to adorn, decorate 247

oscilar to oscillate, swing 71

otorgar to grant, concede 421

P

padecer to suffer, endure 336

paginar to paginate 107

paladear to savor, taste, relish 204

palmear to clap hands 204

palpar to feel, touch 334

palpitar to palpitate, beat, throb 252

papar to swallow soft food without chewing 334

parpadear to blink, wink 204

participar to participate 334

patear, patalear to kick 204

patinar to skate, skid, slide 107

pausar to pause 25

pecar to sin 424

pelear to fight 204

penetrar to penetrate 213

perdurar to last a long time 213

perfumar to perfume   245

perjurar to commit perjury   284

permanecer to remain, stay   324

perseguir to pursue   432

persistir to persist   74

persuadir to persuade   349

pesar to weigh   25

pescar to fish   99

pestañear to wink, blink   204

picar to prick, puncture, pierce   424

pilotar, pilotear to pilot   54

plagar to infest, plague   344

planchar to iron   223

planear to plan, design, glide   204

plantar to plant   109

plegar to fold, pleat   328, 344

poblar to populate   475

posar to pose, put, lay down   482

posponer to postpone   367

preciar to appraise, value   62

preciarse to brag about oneself   289

precipitar to precipitate   252

predisponer to predispose   367

predominar to predominate   107

preponer to put before   367

prescribir to prescribe   222

preservar to preserve   288

presuponer to presuppose   367

prevaler to prevail   485

prevenir to warn   489

prever to foresee   490

privar to deprive   288

proceder to proceed   414

procesar to prosecute   404

procurar to endeavor, try, strive for   72

proferir to utter, say   373

profesar to profess   404

programar to program   54

progresar to progress   233

prolongar to prolong   344

prometer to promise   444

promulgar to promulgate, announce   344

propagar to propagate, spread   344

proponer to propose   367

proporcionar to furnish, supply, provide   107

proscribir to proscribe, banish   222

proseguir to continue, follow up, proceed   432

prosperar to prosper   225

protestar to protest   309

provenir to originate, come from   489

provocar to provoke   99

publicar to publish, issue   99

pugnar to fight   54

pujar to struggle   54

pulsar to pulse, throb   25

punchar to pierce, puncture   307

puntar to dot   494

Q

quebrar to break, smash   355

querellarse to file a legal complaint, bring suit against   297

quesear to make cheese   174

quietar to quiet, calm   309

quietarse to calm oneself   289

quillotrar to incite, excite   258

quimerizar to have fanciful ideas   81

R

rabiar to rage   106

racionar to ration   107

rascar to scratch, itch   99

rasgar to rip, tear   344

raspar to scrape   334

rasurarse to shave one's beard   292

reanimar to reanimate, revive   107

reaparecer to reappear   59

rearmar to rearm   54

reasegurar to reassure, reinsure   72

reasumir to resume, reassume   495

reatar to tie again, retie   309

rebajar to lower, reduce, bring down   85

rebatir to knock down again, beat again   1

rebuscar to search carefully, search into   99

recalentar to reheat, warm up, warm over   103

recapitular to recapitulate   71

recargar to reload, overload   111

rechazar to reject, repel   81

reciclar to recycle   258

recitar to recite   252

reclamar to reclaim, claim, demand, protest   15

reclinar to recline, lean   107

reclinarse en/sobre to lean on/upon   289

reconstruir to rebuild, reconstruct   264

reconvenir to reprimand, rebuke   489

recopilar to compile   258

recrear to amuse, entertain   174

recrearse to amuse, entertain oneself   289

recular to recoil, go backwards   71

recuperar to recuperate, recover   225

redactar to edit   213

reeditar to reprint, publish again   252

reelegir to reelect, elect again 201

refinar to refine 107

reflexionar to reflect 107

reformar to reform, alter, revise 242

reforzar to reinforce, strengthen 49

regalarse to indulge oneself 402, 289

registrar to register, record, examine 213

rehacer to do over, redo 259

rehuir to avoid, shun 264

rehusar to refuse 482

reiterar to reiterate, repeat 72

relanzar to throw back, repel 286

relatar to relate, narrate 309

relavar to wash again 288

relavarse to wash oneself again 289

releer to reread, read again 290

relumbrar to dazzle, sparkle 51

remandar to send over and over again 258

remarcar to mark again 306

rematar to kill off, terminate, finish off 309

remediar to remedy 230

remedir to remeasure 310

rememorar to remember 32

remendar to mend 355

remeter to put back 444

remirar to look at over again 315

remojar to soak 237

remontar to elevate, raise; frighten away 318

remorder to bite again 319

remover to remove, take away 322

renacer to be born again, be reborn 324

renegar to renege, deny; abhor 328

renunciar to renounce 386

reorganizar to reorganize 342

repararse to restrain oneself 410, 289

repasar to review, go over again 350

repensar to rethink, reconsider 355

repesar to weigh again 25

repintar to repaint 361

replantar to replant 109

replicar to retort, reply 99

reponer to put back 367

represar to repress, hold back 379

representar to represent 378

reprobar to reprove, fail in an exam 381

reprochar to reproach 198

reproducir to reproduce 384

repudiar to repudiate 230

repulir to polish again 388

repulsar to repulse, reject 2

requemar to burn again, over-cook 391

requerir to require 373

resaltar to bounce, rebound 427

resaludar to return someone's greeting 428

rescatar to ransom, rescue 309

reservar to reserve 288

resistir to resist 74

respetar to respect 54

respirar to breathe, respire 225

restaurar to restore 258

restituir to refund, give back 264

resucitar to resuscitate, bring back to life 252

resultar to result 427

resumir to summarize, sum up 481

resurgir to resurge, spring up again 461

retacar to hit twice (a ball) 76

retajar to cut around 85

retar to challenge 252

retardar to retard, slow down 197

retemblar to shake, tremble 355

retener to retain 469

retocar to touch up, retouch 473

retostar to toast again 475

retraducir to translate over again 477

retraer to bring again, bring back 478

retransmitir to retransmit, rebroadcast 30

retratar to paint a portrait 479

retribuir to repay, reward 264

retrotraer to antedate, date back 478

revender to resell 488

reventar to burst, explode 355

rever to review, revise 490

reverter to overflow 357

revertir to revert 34

revivir to revive 495

revolar to fly again 496

revolcar to knock down 424, 496

revolcarse to wallow, roll about 21, 424

revolotear to whirl up in the air 204

rezar to pray 53

ridiculizar to ridicule 342

rimar to rhyme 54

rizar to curl 342

rociar to spray, sprinkle 62

rodar to roll 475

rodear to surround 204

rodearse de to surround oneself with 204, 289

roncar to snore 424
ronchar to crunch, chew 223
rondar to patrol, prowl 213
rotar to rotate 309
rotular to label 71
rozar to scrape, scratch, rub 81
rubricar to initial, sign and seal 424
rular to roll 71
rumbar a to go in the direction of 54
rumiar to ruminate, meditate 62

S

saborear to savor, taste, relish 204
sacrificar to sacrifice 117
salar to salt, season with salt 71
saldar to settle, pay a debt 54
salivar to salivate 288
salpicar to splash 424
saltear to hold up, rob 204
salvar to save, rescue 288
sanar to cure, heal 54
sancionar to sanction, authorize; punish 107
sangrar to bleed 213
sangrarse to be bled 213, 289
saquear to pillage, loot, sack 204
satirizar to satirize 342
sedar to soothe, quiet 54
seducir to seduce 384
segar to cut, mow 328
segregar to segregate 421
sellar to seal, stamp 260
sembrar to sow 355
semejar to resemble 85
separarse to separate, come apart 289, 437
sepultar to bury 427
serrar to saw 116
signar to sign 114
signarse to cross oneself 289

significar to signify, mean 117
silbar to whistle 9
simbolizar to symbolize 342
simpatizar con to get along well with 342
simplificar to simplify 117
simular to simulate, feign, pretend 71
sintonizar to tune 342
sisar to snitch 9
sitiar to besiege 230
situar to situate, place, locate 140
sobar to knead, massage, rub, slap 54
sobregirar to overdraw 107
sobreponer to superimpose 367
sobresalir to stand out, excel 426
sobresaltar to attack, startle 427
sobrevenir to supervene, occur later 489
solicitar to solicit, request 252
solidificar to solidify 117
soltar to loosen, untie, let go 475
solucionar to solve 107
solventar to settle, pay a debt 109
sombrar to shade 54
sonarse to blow one's nose 289, 445
sonorizar to voice (phonetics) 342
sopapear to slap 204
soplarse to gobble up, wolf down 289, 448
soportar to support, endure, put up with 427
sorber to sip 91
sorregar to irrigate 328
sortear to raffle; avoid, dodge 204

sosegar to quiet, calm down 328
soterrar to bury; hide 355
suavizar to smooth, soften 342
subarrendar to sublet, sublease 355
subastar to auction 54
sublimar to exalt 54
subordinar to subordinate 341
subsistir to subsist 74
substituir to substitute 264
substraer to subtract, take away, remove 478
subvencionar to subsidize 312
subvenir to provide for needs 489
subvertir to subvert, disturb 263
sudar to sweat, perspire 54
sujetar to secure, fasten; subdue, subject 309
sumar to add, add up 54
suministrar to furnish, provide, supply 213
sumir to sink, submerge 460
superar to surpass, exceed 54
superponer to superpose 367
supervenir to happen, take place 489
suplantar to supplant, take the place of 109
suplicar to supplicate, entreat, implore 117
surcar to plow 424
surtir to supply, stock, provide 349
suscribir to subscribe 454
suspender to suspend, hang 91
sustraer to subtract, take away 478
susurrar to murmur, whisper 54
sutilizar to file, refine, polish, taper 342

T

tacar to mark, stain 473

tachar to cross out, strike out, eliminate 198

tajar to slice, carve, chop 85

talar to fell, cut down 54

tambalear to stagger 204

tamizar to sift 342

tapar to cover 334

tapiar to wall up, wall in 230

tapizar to upholster, hang tapestry 342

tardar to take a long time 197

tarjar to tally 85

tartamudear to stammer, stutter 204

tascar to gnaw, nibble 99

teclear to run one's fingers over piano or typewriter keys 204

tejar to tile 85

tejer to weave 91

teleguiar to guide by remote control 254

temblar to tremble, shudder, shake 355

teorizar to theorize 342

testar to make a will, testament 54

testificar to testify, bear witness 117

timar to cheat, swindle 229

timarse con to flirt with 289

timbrar to put a seal or stamp on 22

tintar to tint, dye 252

titular to title, entitle 71

tolerar to tolerate 225

tontear to act foolishly 204

torcer to twist 322, 487

tornar to turn 288

tornear to go round 204

torturar to torture 72

torturarse to worry excessively 289

tostarse to become sunburned 289, 475

trabar to bind, join, lock 54

trabarse de palabras to insult each other 289

tragar to swallow 421

traicionar to betray 107

trajinar to rush about 107

tramitar to negotiate, transact 252

trancar to stride along 424

tranquilizar to tranquilize 342

transcribir to transcribe 222

transferir, trasferir to transfer 373

transformar to transform 242

transfregar to rub together 328

transigir con to agree to 187

transitar to journey, travel 252

translimitar to go beyond the limits 252

transmitir to transmit 30

transpirar to perspire, sweat 315

transponer to transfer 367

transportar to transport 427

tranzar to break off, cut off; braid 81

trascender to transcend 357

trascolar to strain 475

trascolarse to percolate 289, 475

trascordarse to remember incorrectly, forget 20

trasegar to decant 328

trasferir, transferir to transfer 373

trasladar to transfer, move 213

trasladarse to move, change residence 289

traspasar to pierce 350

trasquilar to shear, clip, crop (hair) 258

trastornar to turn upside down, upset, disturb 54

trasvolar to fly over, fly across 496

tratarse de to be a question of 289, 479

travesar, atravesar to cross, cross over, go through 355

trazar to trace, draw, sketch 81

trenzar to braid, plait 81

trepar to climb, mount 334

tributar to pay tribute 213

tricotar to knit 252

trillar to make frequent use of 258

trinar to trill, warble 107

trinchar to slice (meat) 54

triplicar to triplicate, triple 424

triscar to mix up 99

triturar to crush, grind 72

triunfar to triumph 54

trizar to tear to shreds 81

trocar to exchange 19, 424

trocear to cut into pieces 204

trompicar to trip, stumble 424

tronar to thunder 475

tronchar to crack, split 54

tronzar to slice 81

trotar to trot 479

trucar to pocket a ball in billiards 424

truhanear to cheat, trick 204

trujamanear to interpret 204

tullecer to cripple, disable 336

tullir to cripple, disable 97

tumbar to knock down, knock over, overthrow 9

tundir to clip, shear; beat, thrash 349

turbar to disturb, upset, worry 9

tutear to use the tú form with someone 204

tutearse to use the tú form with each other 204, 289

U

ubicar to locate, situate   424
ufanarse de to boast of   87
ultimar to finish off   107
ultrajar to outrage   85
ulular to ululate, howl, screech, hoot   258
uncir to yoke   501
ungir to anoint   187
unificar to unify   117
uniformar to make uniform, standardize   242
untar to apply ointment, spread butter on   374
urdir to scheme, plot   349
urgir to urge, be urgent   187
usurpar to usurp, encroach   334
utilizarse to use, make use of   289, 483

V

vacar to become vacant   424
vaciarse to become empty   484, 289
vacilar to vacillate   115
vacunar to vaccinate   114
vacunarse to be vaccinated   114, 289
vagabundear to roam, idle, loaf   464
vagar to roam, wander   344
vaguear to idle, loaf   204
validar to validate   39

vallar to fence in, barricade   260
valorar, valorear to value, increase in value   54, 204
valorizar to value   342
valsar to waltz   25
variar to vary   484
vaticinar to vaticinate, prophesy, predict, foretell   471
vedar to prohibit, forbid   54
vendar to bandage   54
vengar to avenge   421
ventar to sniff, scent; blow (wind)   355
ventilar to ventilate   71
veranear to spend the summer   464
verificar to verify   117
versar to go round, turn   25
versificar to versify, write verses   117
verter to pour   357
vestir to clothe   491
vibrar to vibrate   258
vincular to relate, connect   71
vindicar to vindicate   424
violar to violate, rape   258
visar to visa, examine and endorse   25
vocalizar to vocalize   81
vocear to shout, cry out   204
vociferar to vociferate, shout   225
volcar to overturn, turn over, tilt   424, 496

voltear to turn over, roll over   204
vomitar to vomit   252

Y

yapar to give a little more, add a tip   334
yermar to strip, lay waste   54
yuxtaponer to juxtapose   367

Z

zafar to loosen, untie   54
zafarse de to escape from, get out of   54, 289
zaherir to wound with words, reproach, reprimand   263
zahondar to dig   339
zambullir to dive, plunge   97
zampar to stuff, cram food down one's throat, gobble down   334
zanjar to dig a ditch   85
zapatear to tap one's feet   464
zapear to chase away, scare away   204
zapuzar to plunge into water   81
zarandar, zarandear to shake about   54, 204
zunchar to fasten with a band   307
zurrar to spank, wallop   54

EE-zee Guide to Spanish Pronunciation

The purpose of this guide is to help you pronounce Spanish words as correctly as possible so you can communicate effectively. It is not intended to perfect your pronunciation of Spanish; that is accomplished by imitating correct spoken Spanish, which you must hear from persons who pronounce Spanish accurately.

The system of transcription of Spanish sound used here is English letters in italics. As soon as you catch on to this system, you will find it EE-zee. At first, you will have to refer to the list repeatedly until it is fixed in your mind. The sounds are arranged alphabetically in transcription form. This is the easiest way for you to find the transcription as you read the English letters next to the Spanish words.

Latin American pronunciation is used in the sound transcriptions. The same sounds are used in many regions of Spain but there are some areas where Castilian pronunciation is dominant; for example, the letter **c** before **e** or **i** and the letter **z** are pronounced *th*, as in the English word *thin,* and the double **ll** is similar to the sound in the English word *million.* This is something you should be aware of in case you are visiting those areas in Spain where you will hear those sounds. Examples:

ENGLISH WORD	SPANISH WORD	LATIN AMERICAN PRONUNCIATION	CASTILIAN PRONUNCIATION
basket	**cesta**	*SEHS-tah*	*th-EHS-tah*
thank you	**gracias**	*GRAH-syahs*	*GRAH-thee-ahs*
pencil	**lápiz**	*LAH-pees*	*LAH-peeth*
I call	**llamo**	*YAH-mo*	*LYAH-mo*

Transcription sounds that are printed in capital letters indicate that you must raise your voice on those sounds for correct stress. The simple rule of stressed vowel sounds in Spanish is as follows:

1. When a word ends in a vowel, **n,** or **s,** you must stress the vowel that *precedes* the last vowel or final syllable. Examples:

   casa *KAH-sah*　　**comen** *KOH-mehn*　　**comemos** *ko-MEH-mos*

2. When a word ends in a consonant other than **n** or **s,** you must stress the last vowel in the word. Examples:

   calor *kah-LOHR*　　**abril** *ah-BREEL*　　**arroz** *ahr-ROHS*　　**salud** *sah-LOODH*

3. When the pronunciation of a word does not follow the above two rules, you must write an accent mark over the vowel that is stressed. The only way to know this is to hear the word pronounced accurately so you will know whether or not an accent mark is needed. Examples:

   jabón *hah-BOHN*　　**árbol** *AHR-bohl*　　**lápiz** *LAH-pees*　　**sábado** *SAH-bah-dho*

4. An accent mark is written over a vowel at times to distinguish the meaning between two words spelled identically. Examples:

   yes **sí** *see*　　he **él** *ehl*　　that one **ése** *EH-seh*
   if **si** *see*　　the **el** *ehl*　　the book **ese libro** *EH-seh LEE-bro*

In some Spanish-speaking countries, the simple vowel **e** is at times pronounced open or closed and it can sound like *ay* in the English word *say* or *eh* as in the English word *egg*. In other countries, the final **s** in a word is not pronounced. This does not mean that one pronunciation is wrong and the other is correct. These are simply regional differences that have come about over decades and centuries of change. In fact, the meaning of a particular word may sometimes vary from place to place. For your purposes, while traveling in a Spanish-speaking country or region, you will be able to get along because the Spanish words and sound transcriptions in these two sections are of a standard level so you can communicate and be understood.

Now, become familiar with the EE-zee pronunciation guide. Remember, the transcriptions in italics serve only as a guide to pronouncing the Spanish. Practice pronouncing each sound first and then try it out by reading aloud some of the words and expressions on the pages that follow.

EE-zee GUIDE TO SPANISH PRONUNCIATION

Approximate pronunciation

TRANSCRIPTION LETTERS	ENGLISH WORD	SPANISH WORD	TRANSCRIPTION SOUNDS
ah	**ah!**	la	*lah*
ay	say	de	*dhay*
b	but	boca, vaso	*BOH-kah, BAH-so*
ch	church	mucho	*MOO-cho*
dh	they	de	*dhay*
eh	egg	el	*ehl*
ee	see	si	*see*
g	go	agua	*AH-gwah*
h	hello	gente, ojo	*HEHN-teh, OH-ho*
k	kit	como, **que**	*KOH-mo, kay*
ny	canyon	año	*AH-ny-o*
o	also	lomo	*LOH-mo*
oh	**oh!**	lo	*loh*
oo	too	tu	*too*
oy	toy	estoy	*ehs-TOY*
r	row	pero	*PEH-ro*
rr	burr	perro	*PEHR-ro*
s	see	si, brazo	*see, BRAH-so*
wah	watch	cuando	*KWAHN-dho*
weh	went	cuento	*KWEHN-toh*
y	yes	yo, llamo	*yoh, YAH-mo*

The purpose of this feature is to give you useful basic verbs, expressions, and words for thirty practical situations you may find yourself in while visiting Spain or any Spanish-speaking country or region of the world.

On each page where a situation is given, for example, in a restaurant or hotel, a few basic statements and questions are also included to help you communicate your thoughts effectively in the spoken language.

For the convenience of the traveler who cannot read or speak Spanish, next to the Spanish words there is a transcription of Spanish sounds in italicized English letters. They are not words either in Spanish or English and the hyphens, therefore, do not represent a division of words into syllables. They are merely sound transcriptions, and the hyphens indicate very short pauses or breath groups for about one second between sounds. In this way, the hyphens set apart the different transcriptions of sounds as listed in the EE-zee Pronunciation Guide on the preceding page. Study that page to become familiar with the simple system of transcription of sounds that we devised. Also, consult the Guide to Thirty Practical Situations where you can find quickly the page number of the situation that is of interest to you.

If there are other verbs you need to use, besides the ones given in this section, consult those in the main part of this book between pages 1 and 501.

¡Buen viaje!   *BWEHN BYAH-heh*   Have a good trip!

GUIDE TO THIRTY PRACTICAL SITUATIONS

Basic verbs, expressions, and words useful in this situation:

decir   *dhay-SEER*   to say, to tell

esperar   *ehs-peh-RAHR*   to wait (for)

llegar   *yeh-GAHR*   to arrive

ir   *eer*   to go

¿a qué hora?   *ah kay OH-rah*   at what time?

¿cuándo . . . ?   *KWAHN-dho*   when . . .?

dígame   *DHEE-gah-meh*   tell me

gracias   *GRAH-syahs*   thank you

el equipaje   *ehl eh-kee-PAH-heh*   baggage, luggage

poder   *po-DHER*   to be able, can

querer   *kay-REHR*   to want, to like

saber   *sah-BEHR*   to know

salir   *sah-LEER*   to leave

quisiera   *kee-SYEHR-ah*   I would like

el avión   *ehl ah-bee-OHN*   airplane

por favor   *pohr fah-BOHR*   please

el vuelo   *ehl BWEH-lo*   flight

el cambio   *ehl KAHM-bee-o*   money exchange

para   *PAH-rah*   for

Basic statements and questions useful in this situation:

1. **Yo quisiera saber a qué hora el avión sale para . . .**
   yoh kee-SYEHR-ah sah-BEHR an kay OH-rah ehl ah-bee-OHN SAH-leh PAH-rah
   I would like to know at what time the plane leaves for . . .

2. **¿A qué hora llega el avión a . . . ?**
   ah kay OH-rah YEH-gah ehl ah-bee-OHN ah
   At what time does the plane arrive at . . . ?

3. **Yo quisiera un asiento de primera clase, por favor.**
   yoh kee-SYEHR-ah oon ah-SYEHN-toh dhay pree-MEH-rah KLAH-seh, pohr fah-BOHR
   I would like a first class seat, please.

4. **Dígame, por favor, dónde está la sala de espera.**
   DHEE-gah-meh, pohr fah-BOHR, DHOHN-dhay ehs-TAH lah SAH-lah dhay ehs-PEH-rah
   Tell me, please, where the waiting room is located.

For more verbs, expressions, and popular words commonly used, consult page 595.

Basic verbs, expressions, and words useful in this situation:

tener   *tehn-EHR*   to have
costar   *kohs-TAHR*   to cost
preferir   *preh-feh-REER*   to prefer
bajar   *ba-HAHR*   to go down
la habitación   *lah ah-bee-tah-SYOHN*   room
dos camas   *dhos KAH-mahs*   two beds
no hay toallas   *noh AH-ee toh-AH-yahs*   there are no towels
privado   *pree-BAH-dho*   private
me gusta   *meh GOOS-tah*   I like

valer   *bah-LEHR*   to be worth
subir   *soo-BEER*   to go up
pagar   *pah-GAHR*   to pay
una cama   *OO-nah KAH-mah*   bed
una gran cama   *OO-nah gr-AHN KAH-mah*   a large bed
una ducha   *OO-nah DHOO-chah*   shower
un baño   *oon BAH-ny-o*   bathtub
¿hay . . . ?   *AH-ee*   is there . . . ?   are there . . . ?

Basic statements and questions useful in this situation:

1. **Buenos días. Quisiera una habitación para mí y mi esposa.**
   BWEH-nos DHEE-ahs. kee-SYEHR-ah OO-nah ah-bee-tah-SYOHN PAH-rah mee ee mee ehs-POH-sah
   Hello (Good day). I would like a room for me and my wife.

2. **Para una semana. Preferimos una habitación tranquila con un cuarto de baño privado, por favor.**
   PAH-rah OO-nah seh-MAH-nah. preh-feh-REE-mos OO-nah ah-bee-tah-SYOHN trahn-KEE-lah kohn oon KWAHR-toh dhay BAH-ny-o pree-BAH-dho, pohr fah-BOHR
   For one week. We prefer a quiet room with a private bathroom, please.

3. **¿Acepta usted tarjetas de crédito? Aquí tiene usted nuestros pasaportes.**
   ah-SEHP-tah oos-TEH-dh tahr-HEH-tahs dhay KREH-dhee-toh. ah-KEE tee-EHN-eh oos-TEH-dh NWEH-stros pah-sah-POHR-tehs
   Do you accept credit cards? Here are our passports.

4. **¿Cuál es el número de la habitación?**
   kwahl ehs ehl NOO-meh-ro dhay lah ah-bee-tah-SYOHN
   What is the room number?

For more verbs, expressions, and popular words commonly used, consult page 595.

Basic verbs, expressions, and words useful in this situation:

comprar   *kohm-PRAHR*   to buy

pagar al contado   *pah-GAHR ahl kohn-TAH-dho*   to pay in cash

un vendedor   *oon behn-dhay-DOHR*   salesman

un almacén   *oon ahl-mah-SEHN*   department store

¿en qué piso?   *ehn kay PEE-so*   on what floor?

la escalera mecánica   *lah ehs-kah-LEH-rah meh-KAH-nee-kah*   escalator

el precio   *ehl PREH-see-o*   price

buscar   *boos-KAHR*   to look for

¿puede usted . . . ?   *PWEH-dhay oos-TEH-dh*   can you . . . ?

una vendedora   *OO-nah behn-dhay-DOHR-ah*   saleslady

una tienda   *OO-nah-TYEHN-dha*   store, shop

un supermercado   *oon soo-pehr-mehr-KAH-dho*   supermarket

el ascensor   *ehl ah-sehn-SOHR*   elevator (lift)

¿cuánto cuesta?   *KWAHN-toh KWEH-stah*   how much does it cost?

Basic statements and questions useful in this situation:

1. **¿Puede indicarme dónde están los almacenes, por favor?**
   PWEH-dhay een-dhee-KAHR-meh DHOHN-dhay ehs-TAHN lohs ahl-mah-SEHN-ehs, pohr fah-BOHR
   Can you indicate to me where the department stores are located, please?

2. **Perdóneme. ¿Puede ayudarme? Busco una buena pastelería.**
   pehr-DHOH-neh-meh. PWEH-dhay ah-yoo-DHAHR-meh. BOOS-ko OO-nah BWEH-nah pahs-teh-leh-REE-ah
   Pardon me. Can you help me? I'm looking for a good pastry shop.

3. **Quisiera comprar juguetes. ¿Dónde se venden juguetes?**
   kee-SYEHR-ah kohm-PRAHR hoo-GAY-tehs. DHOHN-dhay seh BEHN-dhen hoo-GAY-tehs
   I would like to buy some toys. Where do they sell toys?

4. **Enséñeme algo más barato, por favor.**
   ehn-SEH-ny-eh-meh AHL-go mahs bah-RAH-toh, pohr fah-BOHR
   Show me something cheaper, please.

For more verbs, expressions, and popular words commonly used, consult page 595.

En una librería-papelería   *ehn OO-nah lee-brehr-EE-ah pah-pehl-eh-REE-ah*
In a bookstore—stationery shop

Basic verbs, expressions, and words useful in this situation:

leer   *leh-EHR*   to read
escribir   *ehs-kree-BEER*   to write
un libro   *oon LEE-bro*   book
a buen precio   *ah BWEHN PREH-see-o*
inexpensive
el arte   *ehl AHR-teh*   art
historia (f.)   *ees-TOHR-ee-ah*   history
un lápiz   *oon LAH-pees*   pencil
un sobre   *oon SOH-breh*   envelope
un plano de la ciudad   *oon PLAH-no*
dhay lah see-oo-DHAHD   city map

papel sin rayas (m.)   *pah-PEHL seen*
RAH-yahs   paper with no lines
muy costoso   *mwee kohs-TOH-so*
very expensive
libros de lance (m.)   *LEE-bros dhay*
LAHN-seh   used books
goma de borrar (f.)   *GOH-mah dhay*
bohr-RAHR   eraser
una novela   *OO-nah noh-BEH-lah*   novel
una guía turística   *OO-nah GEE-ah*
too-REE-stee-kah   tourist guide book

Basic statements and questions useful in this situation:

1. **Buenos días. Quisiera un libro de arte, por favor. Será un regalo.**
   BWEH-nos DHEE-ahs. kee-SYEHR-ah oon LEE-bro dhay AHR-teh, pohr fah-BOHR.
   seh-RAH oon reh-GAH-lo
   Hello. I would like an art book, please. It will be a gift.

2. **Prefiero el arte clásico. ¿Cuánto cuesta éste? ¡Oh! ¡Es muy caro!**
   preh-FYEH-ro ehl AHR-teh KLAH-see-ko. KWAHN-toh KWEH-stah EHS-teh. oh. ehs
   mwee KAH-ro
   I prefer classic art. How much does this one cost? Oh! It's very expensive.

3. **¿Tiene algo más barato? Necesito, también, revistas ilustradas y un cuaderno.**
   TYEH-neh AHL-go mahs bah-RAH-toh. neh-seh-SEE-toh, tahm-bee-EHN, reh-BEES-
   tahs ee-loo-STRAH-dhahs ee oon kwah-DHEHR-no
   Do you have something cheaper? I also need magazines and a notebook.

For more verbs, expressions, and popular words commonly used, consult page 595.

Basic verbs, expressions, and words useful in this situation:

llamar por teléfono   *yah-MAHR pohr teh-LEH-fo-no*   to telephone
marcar el número de teléfono   *mahr-KAHR ehl NOO-meh-ro dhay teh-LEH-fo-no*   to dial the telephone number
mi número es . . .   *mee NOO-meh-ro ehs*   my number is . . .
consultar   *kohn-sool-TAHR*   to consult
escucho   *ehs-KOO-cho*   I'm listening
¡cuelgue!   *KWEHL-geh*   hang up!
hablar   *ah-BLAHR*   to talk, to speak
¡descuelgue!   *dhehs-KWEHL-geh*   pick up (receiver of telephone)!

las cabinas telefónicas   *lahs kah-BEE-nahs teh-leh-FOH-nee-kahs*   telephone booths
las guías de teléfonos   *lahs GEE-ahs dhay teh-LEH-fo-nos*   telephone books
la (el) telefonista   *lah (ehl) teh-leh-fo-NEES-tah*   telephone operator
el número equivocado   *ehl NOO-meh-ro eh-kee-boh-KAH-dho*   the wrong number
¡diga!   *DHEE-gah*   hello! (answering a telephone call)

Basic statements and questions useful in this situation:

1. **Perdóneme. Quisiera consultar las guías de teléfonos. ¿Dónde están?**
   pehr-DHO-neh-meh. kee-SYEHR-ah kohn-sool-TAHR lahs GEE-ahs dhay teh-LEH-fo-nos. DHOHN-dhay ehs-TAHN
   Pardon me. I would like to consult the telephone books. Where are they?

2. **Quisiera telefonear a Nueva York. Quisiera poner una conferencia cuyo importe se carga al abonado solicitado.**
   kee-SYEHR-ah tehl-leh-fo-neh-AHR ah noo-EH-bha yohrk. kee-SYEHR-ah po-NEHR OO-nah kohn-feh-REHN-syah KOO-yo eem-POHR-teh seh KAHR-gah ahl ah-bo-NAH-dho so-lee-see-TAH-dho
   I would like to telephone New York. I would like to place a collect call.

3. **Perdóneme. ¿Puede ayudarme a hacer una llamada?**
   pehr-DHO-neh-meh. PWEH-dheh ah-yoo-DAHR-meh ah ah-SEHR OO-nah yah-MAH-dhah
   Pardon me. Can you help me make a telephone call?

More verbs and new words for this conversational situation:

una buscapersonas   pager
una cabina   booth
el cambio   change (in coins)
¿Dónde puedo enviar (recibir) un fax?   Where can I send (receive, get) a fax?
un fax   fax
una llamada   a call
pagar   to pay;   **por favor**   please
por teléfono   by phone
el teléfono celular   cell phone
quisiera   I would like

For more verbs, expressions, and popular words commonly used, consult page 595.

Basic verbs, expressions, and words useful in this situation:

lavar   *lah-BAHR*   to wash

secar   *seh-KAHR*   to dry

lejía (f.)   *leh-HEE-ah*   bleach

una ficha   *OO-nah FEE-chah*   token

el secador   *ehl seh-kah-DHOR*   dryer

almidón (m.)   *ahl-mee-DHOHN*   starch

la moneda   *lah mo-NEH-dhah*   change (coins)

necesito   *neh-seh-SEE-toh*   I need

¿cuántos minutos?   *KWAHN-tohs mee-NOO-tohs*   how many minutes?

sin lejía   *seen leh-HEE-ah*   without bleach

mucho   *MOO-cho*   much, a lot

un poquito   *oon po-KEE-toh*   very little

los copos de jabón   *lohs KOH-pos dhay hah-BOHN*   soap flakes

en necesario esperar   *ehs neh-seh-SAH-ree-o ehs-peh-RAHR*   it is necessary to wait

ayúdeme, por favor   *ah-YOO-dheh-meh pohr fah-BOHR*   help me, please

Basic statements and questions useful in this situation:

1. **Dispénseme, por favor. ¿Puede ayudarme? No sé nada de estas máquinas.**
   dhees-PEHN-seh-meh, pohr fah-BOHR. PWEH-dheh ah-yoo-DHAR-meh. noh seh NAH-dha dhay EHS-tahs MAH-kee-nahs
   Excuse me, please. Can you help me? I don't know anything about these machines.

2. **¿Cómo marchan estas máquinas?**
   KOH-mo MAHR-chahn EHS-tahs MAH-kee-nahs
   How do these machines work?

3. **¿Necesito fichas? ¿Dónde puedo conseguirlas?**
   neh-seh-SEE-toh FEE-chahs. DHOHN-dhay PWEH-dho kohn-seh-GEER-lahs
   Do I need tokens? Where can I get them?

4. **Usted es muy amable. Muchas gracias.**
   oos-TEH-dh ehs mwee ah-MAH-bleh. MOO-chahs GRAH-syahs
   You are very kind. Thank you very much.

For more verbs, expressions, and popular words commonly used, consult page 595.

Basic verbs, expressions, and words useful in this situation:

preparar   *preh-pah-RAHR*   to prepare

necesito aspirinas   *neh-seh-SEE-toh ahs-pee-REE-nahs*   I need aspirins

algo contra la tos   *AHL-go KOHN-trah lah tohs*   something for a cough

un resfriado   *oon rehs-free-AH-dho*   common cold

tengo un dolor de muelas   *TEHN-go oon dho-LOHR dhay MWEH-lahs*   I have a toothache

un cepillo de dientes   *oon seh-PEE-yo dhay dhee-YEHN-tehs*   toothbrush

polvo dentífrico (m.)   *POHL-bo dhen-TEE-free-ko*   tooth powder

una quemadura   *OO-nah kay-mah-DHOO-rah*   burn

crema (f.) **de afeitar**   *KREH-mah dhay ah-feh-ee-TAHR*   shaving cream

esta receta   *EHS-tah reh-SEH-tah*   this prescription

¿puedo . . .?   *PWEH-dho*   may I . . . ?

un dolor de garganta   *oon dho-LOHR dhay gahr-GAHN-tah*   sore throat

volver   *bohl-BEHR*   to return (come back)

yodo (m.)   *YOH-dho*   iodine

un jabón   *oon hah-BOHN*   soap

pastillas contra la tos   *pahs-TEE-yahs KOHN-trah lah tohs*   cough drops

pasta dentífrica (f.)   *PAHS-tah dhen-TEE-free-kah*   toothpaste; **con fluor**   *kohn floo-OHR*   with fluoride

un laxante   *oon lahk-SAHN-teh*   laxative

algo contra la diarrea   *AHL-go KOHN-trah lah dhee-AHR-reh-ah*   something for diarrhea

Basic statements and questions useful in this situation:

1. **Buenos días. Necesito algo para un dolor de garganta y una enjuagadura.**
   BWEH-nos DHEE-ahs. neh-seh-SEE-toh AHL-go PAH-RAH oon dho-LOHR dhay gahr-GAHN-tah ee OO-nah ehn-hoo-ah-gah-DOO-rah
   Hello. I need something for a sore throat and a mouthwash solution.

2. **¿Puede usted preparar esta receta? ¿Cuándo podré volver?**
   PWEH-dhay oos-TEH-dh preh-pah-RAHR EHS-tah reh-SEH-tah. KWAHN-dho po-dh-RAY bohl-BEHR
   Can you prepare this prescription? When may I come back?

3. **¿Y la posolagía? ¿Cuántos comprimidos por día?**
   ee lah po-so-lo-HEE-ah. KWAHN-tohs kohn-pree-MEE-dhos pohr DHEE-ah
   And the dosage? How many tablets a day?

For more verbs, expressions, and popular words commonly used, consult page 595.

Basic verbs, expressions, and words useful in this situation:

estar enfermo (enferma)   *ehs-TAHR ehn-FEHR-mo (ehn-FEHR-mah)*   to be sick

la angina   *lah ahn-HEE-nah*   angina

un constipado   *oon kohn-stee-PAH-dho*   head cold

estoy preñada   *ehs-TOY preh-ny-AH-dhah*   I'm pregnant

¿es grave?   *ehs GRAH-beh*   is it serious?

algunos días   *ahl-GOO-nos DHEE-ahs*   a few days

el vómito   *ehl BOH-mee-toh*   vomiting

el desmayo   *ehl dh-ehs-MAH-yo*   fainting spell

el estreñimiento   *ehl ehs-treh-ny-ee-mee-EHN-toh*   constipation

algunas semanas   *ahl-GOO-nahs seh-MAH-nahs*   a few weeks

la presión sanguínea   *lah preh-SYOHN sahn-GEE-neh-ah*   blood pressure

el insomnio   *ehl een-SOHM-nee-o*   insomnia

la fiebre   *lah fee-EH-breh*   fever

Basic statements and questions useful in this situation:

1. **¿Puede llamar a un médico, por favor? No me siento bien.**
   PWEH-dhay yah-MAHR ah oon MEH-dhee-ko, pohr fah-BOHR. noh meh see-EHN-toh bee-EHN
   Can you call a doctor, please? I don't feel well.

2. **Buenos días, doctor. Tengo un poco de fiebre y duermo mal.**
   BWEH-nos DHEE-ahs, dhok-TOR. TEHN-go oon POH-ko dhay fee-EH-breh ee dh-WEHR-mo mahl
   Hello, doctor. I have a little fever and I don't sleep well.

3. **Vomito cada mañana. ¿Estoy preñada?**
   boh-MEE-toh KAH-dhah mah-ny-AH-nah. ehs-TOY preh-ny-AH-dhah
   I vomit every morning. Am I pregnant?

4. **¿Cuánto le debo?**
   KWAHN-toh leh dh-EH-bo
   How much do I owe you?

For more verbs, expressions, and popular words commonly used, consult page 595.

Basic verbs, expressions, and words useful in this situation:

déme *dh-EH-meh* give me

quisiera *kee-SYEHR-ah* I would like

necesito *neh-seh-SEE-toh* I need

perfumes franceses *pehr-FOO-mehs frahn-SEH-sehs* French perfumes

un desodorante *oon dheh-so-dho-RAHN-teh* deodorant

¿cuánto vale? *KWAHN-toh BAH-leh* how much does it cost?

para un hombre *PAH-rah oon OHM-breh* for a man

¿tiene Ud . . . ? *TYEH-neh oos-TEH-dh* do you have . . . ?

estoy buscando . . . *ehs-TOY boos-KAHN-dho* I'm looking for . . .

un perfume español *oon pehr-FOO-meh ehs-pah-ny-OHL* Spanish perfume

un frasquito *oon frah-SKEE-toh* vial, small bottle

para mí *PAH-rah mee* for me

para una dama *PAH-rah OO-nah dh-AH-mah* for a lady

Basic statements and questions useful in this situation:

1. **Necesito un lápiz de labios y una pastilla de jabón.**
   neh-seh-SEE-toh OO-nLAH-pees dhay LAH-bee-os ee OO-nah pah-STEE-yah dhay hah-BOHN
   I need a lipstick and a small bar of soap.

2. **Mi marido necesita una maquinilla de afeitar.**
   mee mah-REE-dho neh-seh-SEE-tah OO-nah mah-kee-NEE-yah dhay ah-feh-ee-TAHR
   My husband needs a safety razor.

3. **Necesito, también, una esponja, un peine, y un perfume de mejor calidad.**
   neh-seh-SEE-toh, tahm-BYEHN, OO-nah ehs-POHN-hah, oon PEH-een-eh, ee oon pehr-FOO-meh dhay meh-HOHR kah-lee-dh-AHDH
   I need, also, a sponge, a comb, and a perfume of the best quality.

4. **¿Acepta Ud. tarjetas de crédito?**
   ah-SEHP-tah oos-TEH-dh tahr-HEH-tahs dhay KREH-dhee-toh
   Do you accept credit cards?

For more verbs, expressions, and popular words commonly used, consult page 595.

Basic verbs, expressions, and words useful in this situation:

recomendar   *reh-ko-mehn-DHAHR*   to recommend

somos cuatro   *SOH-mos KWAH-tro*   we are·four (four of us)

tomaré   *toh-mah-RAY*   I will have

tomaremos   *toh-mah-RAY-mos*   we will have

la propina   *lah pro-PEE-nah*   tip (gratuity)

cerca de la ventana   *SEHR-kah dhay lah behn-TAH-nah*   near the window

servir   *sehr-BEER*   to serve

comer   *ko-MEHR*   to eat

tráigame   *TRAH-ee-gah-meh*   bring me

déme   *DHAY-meh*   give me

dénos   *DHAY-nos*   give us

quisiera   *kee-SYEHR-ah*   I would like

la cuenta   *lah KWEHN-tah*   check (bill)

el servicio   *ehl sehr-VEE-see-o*   service

incluido   *een-kloo-EE-dho*   included

en la terraza   *ehn lah tehr-RAH-sah*   on the terrace

Basic statements and questions useful in this situation:

1. **¿Puede usted recomendarme un restaurante o una cafetería?**
   PWEH-dhay oos-TEH-dh reh-ko-mehn-DHAHR-meh oon rehs-tah-oo-RAHN-teh oh OO-nah kah-feh-tehr-EE-ah
   Can you recommend to me a restaurant or a cafeteria?

2. **Quisiera un bistec poco cocinado, patatas fritas, y una ensalada de tomates.**
   kee-SYEHR-ah oon bee-STEK POH-ko ko-see-NAH-doh, pah-TAH-tahs FREE-tahs, ee OO-nah ehn-sah-LAH-dha dhay toh-MAH-tehs
   I would like a steak, rare, fried potatoes, and a tomato salad.

3. **Necesito un tenedor, un cuchillo, y mucho pan, por favor.**
   neh-seh-SEE-toh oon teh-neh-dh-OHR, oon koo-CHEE-yo, ee MOO-cho pahn, pohr fah-BOHR
   I need a fork, a knife, and a lot of bread, please.

4. **Todo es satisfactorio. La cuenta, por favor. Muchas gracias.**
   TOH-dho ehs sah-tees-fahk-TOH-ree-o. lah KWEHN-tah, pohr fah-BOHR. MOO-chahs GRAH-syahs
   Everything is satisfactory. The check, please. Thank you very much.

For more verbs, expressions, and popular words commonly used, consult page 595.

En un taller de lavado y planchado · *ehn oon tah-YEHR dhay lah-BAH-dho ee plahn-CHAH-dho* · In a laundry service shop

Basic verbs, expressions, and words useful in this situation:

estar listo *ehs-TAHR LEE-sto* to be ready

necesito *neh-seh-SEE-toh* I need

me gustaría *meh goos-tah-REE-ah* I would like

la falda *lah FAHL-dha* skirt

la blusa *lah BLOO-sah* blouse

los pañuelos *lohs pah-ny-WEH-los* handkerchiefs

¿cuándo puedo volver? *KWAHN-dho PWEH-dho bohl-BEHR* when can I return?

¿cuánto le debo? *KWAHN-toh leh dh-EH-bo* how much do I owe you?

los calcetines *lohs kahl-seh-TEE-nehs* socks

la camisa *lah kah-MEE-sah* shirt

el sostén *ehl so-STEHN* bra (brassiere)

almidón (m.) *ahl-mee-DHOHN* starch

con un poquito de lejía *kohn oon po-KEE-toh dhay leh-HEE-ah* with very little bleach

sin almidón *seen ahl-mee-DHOHN* without starch

Basic statements and questions useful in this situation:

1. **Buenos días. Aquí tengo mucha ropa. ¿Cuándo estará todo listo?**
   BWEH-nos DHEE-ahs. ah-KEE tehn-go MOO-chah ROH-pah. KWAHN-dho ehs-tah-RAH TOH-dho LEE-sto
   Good day. Here I have a lot of clothes. When will it all be ready?

2. **Necesito esta ropa para mañana si es posible.**
   neh-seh-SEE-toh EHS-tah ROH-pah PAH-rah mah-ny-AH-nah see ehs po-SEE-bleh
   I need these clothes for tomorrow if it is possible.

3. **¿Puede usted plancharme los pañuelos?**
   PWEH-dhay oos-TEH-dh plahn-CHAHR-meh lohs pah-ny-WEH-los
   Can you iron the handkerchiefs for me?

4. **Está bien. Vuelvo mañana a las cuatro de la tarde. Muchas gracias. Adiós.**
   ehs-TAH bee-EHN. BWEHL-bo mah-ny-AH-nah ah lahs KWAH-tro dhay lah TAHR-dhay. MOO-chahs GRAH-syahs. ah-dhee-OHS
   Fine. I'll be back tomorrow at four in the afternoon. Thank you very much. Good-bye.

For more verbs, expressions, and popular words commonly used, consult page 595.

Basic verbs, expressions, and words useful in this situation:

¿qué película?   *kay peh-LEE-koo-lah*
what film (move)?

¿qué sesión?   *kay sehs-YOHN*   what
showing?

¿dónde están los retretes?   *DHOHN-dhay ehs-TAHN lohs reh-TREH-tehs*
where are the rest rooms?

en español   *ehn ehs-pah-ny-OHL*   in
Spanish

una butaca   *OO-nah boo-TAH-kah*
orchestra seat

déme   *DHAY-meh*   give me

¿qué espectáculo?   *kay ehs-pehk-TAH-koo-lo*   what show?

comenzar   *ko-mehn-SAHR*   to begin

¿cuántas horas?   *KWAHN-tahs OH-rahs*
how many hours?

las localidades   *lahs lo-kah-lee-DHA-dh-ehs*   the seats

en inglés   *ehn een-GLEHS*   in English

empezar   *ehm-peh-SAHR*   to begin

¿a qué hora?   *ah kay OH-rah*   at what
time?

Basic statements and questions useful in this situation:

1. **Dos billetes, por favor, para la película a las dos de esta tarde.**
   dhos bee-y-EH-tehs, pohr fah-BOHR, PAH-rah lah peh-LEE-koo-lah ah lahs dhos dhay EHS-tah TAHR-dhay
   Two tickets, please, for the movie at two o'clock this afternoon.

2. **Preferimos dos butacas pero no muy cerca de la pantalla.**
   preh-feh-REE-mos dhos boo-TAH-kahs PEH-ro noh mwee SEHR-kah dhay lah pahn-TAH-yah
   We prefer two orchestra seats but not very close to the screen.

3. **¿Cuánto valen los billetes?**
   KWAHN-toh BAH-lehn lohs bee-YEH-tehs
   How much do the tickets cost?

4. **Nos gustan mucho las películas policíacas.**
   nohn GOOs-tahn MOO-cho lahs peh-LEE-koo-lahs po-lee-SEE-ah-kahs
   We like detective movies very much.

For more verbs, expressions, and popular words commonly used, consult page 595.

En la estación de ferrocarril *ehn lah ehs-tah-SYOHN dhay fehr-roh-kahr-REEL*
At the railroad station

Basic verbs, expressions, and words useful in this situation:

un billete *oon bee-YEH-teh* ticket

el tren *ehl trehn* train

el andén *ehl ahn-DHEHN* platform

la vía *lah BEE-ah* track

la cantina *lah kahn-TEE-nah* snack bar

el equipaje *ehl eh-kee-PAH-heh*
baggage, luggage

el coche restaurante *ehl KOH-cheh
rehs-tah-oo-RAHN-teh* dining car

un carrito *oon kahr-REE-toh* luggage
cart

tengo *TEHN-go* I have

hacer cola *ah-SEHR KOH-lah* to stand
in line (queue up)

la entrada *la ehn-TRAH-dha* entrance

la salida *lah sah-LEE-dha* exit

informaciones *een-fohrm-ah-see-OH-
nehs* information

el coche cama *ehl KOH-cheh KAH-mah*
sleeping car

la maleta *lah mah-LEH-tah* valise,
suitcase

Basic statements and questions useful in this situation:

1. **Un billete de primera, por favor, para ir a . . .**
   oon bee-YEH-teh dhay pree-MEHR-ah, pohr fah-BOHR, PAH-rah eer ah
   One first class ticket, please, to go to . . .

2. **¿Cuánto cuesta un billete de ida? ¿Y de ida y vuelta?**
   *KWAHN-toh KWEHS-tah oon bee-YEH-teh dhay EE-dha. ee dhay EE-dha ee
   BWEHL-tah*
   How much does a one-way ticket cost? And a round-trip?

3. **¿A qué hora sale el tren para . . . ?**
   ah kay OH-rah SAH-leh ehl trehn PAH-rah
   At what time does the train leave for . . .?

4. **¿Es el tren rápido o local? ¿Tengo que trasbordar?**
   ehs ehl trehn RAH-pee-dho oh lo-KAHL. TEHN-go kay trahs-bohrdh-AHR
   Is the train an express or a local? Do I have to transfer?

For more verbs, expressions, and popular words commonly used, consult page 595.

Basic verbs, expressions, and words useful in this situation:

¿qué recomienda usted?   *kay reh-kohm-YEHN-dhah oos-TEH-dh*   what do you recommend?

comerlo aquí   *kohm-EHR-loh ah-KEE*   to eat it here

pastas danesas   *PAHS-tahs dahn-EH-sahs*   Danish pastries

el pastel de chocolate   *ehl pahs-TEHL dhay cho-ko-LAH-teh*   chocolate cake

un una tarta   *OO-nah TAHR-tah*   tart

aquélla   *ah-KEY-yah*   that one

cerca de mí   *SEHR-kah dhay mee*   near me

galletas (f.)   *gah-YEH-tahs*   cookies

quisiera   *kee-SYEHR-ah*   I would like

comprar   *kohm-PRAHR*   to buy

¿puedo . . .?   *PWEH-dho*   may I . . .?

déme   *DHAY-meh*   give me

bollos blancos   *BOH-yohs BLAN-kos*   small white rolls; **morenos**   *moh-REH-nos*   brown

el merengue   *ehl mehr-EHN-gay*   meringue

con miel   *kohn mee-EHL*   with honey

éste   *EHS-teh*   this one

aquéllas   *ah-KEH-yahs*   those

cerca de usted   *SEHR-kah dhay oos-TEH-dh*   near you

Basic statements and questions useful in this situation:

1. **Me gustaría un pastel que tuviera almendras.**
   meh goos-tah-REE-yah oon pahs-TEHL kay toov-YEH-ra ahl-MEHN-drahs
   I would like a pastry that contains almonds.

2. **¿Hay pasteles conteniendo nueces, castañas o avellanas?**
   AH-ee pahs-TEHL-ehs kohn-teh-ny-EHN-dho NWEH-sehs, kahs-TAH-ny-ahs oh ah-bay-YAHN-ahs
   Are there any pastries containing walnuts, chestnuts, or hazelnuts?

3. **Déme, también, este gran pastel de chocolate. ¡Tengo mucha hambre!**
   DHAY-meh, tahm-bee-EHN, EHS-teh grahn pahs-TEHL dhay cho-ko-LAH-teh. TEHN-go MOO-chah AHM-breh
   Give me, also, this big chocolate cake. I'm very hungry!

For more verbs, expressions, and popular words commonly used, consult page 595.

En un kiosco de periódicos   *ehn oon kee-YOHS-ko dhay peh-ree-OH-dhee-kos*
At a newsstand

Basic verbs, expressions, and words useful in this situation:

un periódico   *oon peh-ree-OH-dhee-ko*
newspaper
una revista   *OO-nah reh-BEES-tah*
magazine
un mapa de esta ciudad   *oon MAH-pah
dhay EHS-tah syoo-DHA-dh*   a map of
this city
déme, por favor   *DHAY-meh, pohr fah-
BOHR*   give me, please
en inglés   *ehn een-GLEHS*   in English
en alemán   *ehn ah-leh-MAHN*   in
German

una tarjeta postal ilustrada   *OO-nah
tahr-HEH-tah pohs-TAHL ee-loos-
TRAH-dhah*   picture post card
una guía turística   *OO-nah GEE-ah too-
REE-stee-kah*   tourist guidebook
¿cuánto por esta edición?   *KWAHN-toh
pohr EHS-tah eh-dhee-SYOHN*   how
much for this issue?
tomo   *TOH-mo*   I'll have; I'll take
en italiano   *ehn ee-tah-LYAH-no*   in
Italian

Basic statements and questions useful in this situation:

1. **¿Tiene periódicos de los Estados Unidos de América?**
   *TYEH-neh peh-ree-OH-dhee-kos dhay lohs ehs-TAH-dhos oo-NEE-dhos dhay ah-
   MEH-ree-kah*
   Do you have newspapers from the United States of America?

2. **Tomo este periódico, esta guía, esta revista, y este mapa.**
   *TOH-mo EHS-teh peh-ree-OH-dhee-ko, EHS-tah GEE-ah, EHS-tah reh-BEES-tah, ee
   EHS-teh MAH-pah*
   I'll take this newspaper, this guide, this magazine, and this map.

3. **Aquí tiene usted el dinero. Muchas gracias, señor (señora, señorita).**
   *ah-KEE TYEH-neh oos-TEH-dh el dhee-NEH-ro. MOO-chahs GRAH-syahs, sehn
   YOHR (sehn-YOH-rah, sehn-yoh-REE-tah)*
   Here is the money. Thank you very much, sir (madam, miss).

For more verbs, expressions, and popular words commonly used, consult page 595.

En una tienda de limpieza en seco
ehn OO-nah TYEHN-dhah dhay leem-PYEH-sah ehn SEH-ko In a dry cleaning store

Basic verbs, expressions, and words useful in this situation:

limpiar en seco *leem-pee-AHR ehn SEH-ko* to dry clean

planchar *plahn-CHAHR* to press

le traigo *leh TRAH-ee-go* I'm bringing to you

hay que . . . *AH-ee kay* it is necessary . . .

un sastre *oon SAHS-treh* tailor

un pantalón *oon pahn-tah-LOHN* pants, trousers, slacks

arreglar *ah-reh-GLAHR* to mend

estos botones *EHS-tos boh-TOH-nehs* these buttons

¿cuándo estará listo? *KWAHN-dho ehs-tah-RAH LEE-sto* when will it be ready?

la tintura *lah teen-TOO-rah* dyeing

una falda *OO-nah FAHL-dha* skirt

esta mancha *EHS-tah MAHN-chah* this stain

Basic statements and questions useful in this situation:

1. **¿Puede ayudarme? Busco una tienda de limpieza en seco.**
   PWEH-dhe ah-yoo-dh-AHR-meh. BOOS-ko OO-nah TYEHN-dha dhay leem-PYEH-sah ehn SEH-ko
   Can you help me? I'm looking for a dry cleaning store.

2. **¿Hay una tienda aquí en esta vecindad?**
   AH-ee OO-nah TYEHN-dha ah-KEE ehn EHS-tah beh-seen-dh-AH-dh
   Is there a store here in this neighborhood?

3. **¿Hace usted tinturas?**
   AH-seh oos-TEH-dh teen-TOO-rahs
   Do you do dyeing?

4. **Quíteme estas manchas, por favor.**
   KEE-teh-meh EHS-tahs MAHN-chahs, pohr fah-BOHR
   Remove these stains for me, please.

5. **Las manchas en esta corbata son de sopa.**
   lahs MAHN-chahs ehn EHS-tah kohr-BAH-tah sohn dhay SOH-pah
   The stains on this necktie are from soup.

For more verbs, expressions, and popular words commonly used, consult page 595.

En una peluquería para señoras y señores
ehn OO-nah peh-loo-kay-REE-ah PAH-rah sehn-YOH-rahs ee sehn-YOHR-ehs
In a hair stylist shop for men and women

Basic verbs, expressions, and words useful in this situation:

tener cita *teh-NEHR SEE-tah* to have an appointment

me gustaría tener un corte de pelo *meh goos-tah-REE-ah tehn-EHR oon KOHR-teh dhay PEH-lo* I would like to have a haircut

un nuevo corte *oon NWEH-bo KOHR-teh* a new cut

seco o mojado *SEH-ko oh mo-HAH-dho* dry or moist

un corte revuelto *oon KOHR-teh reh-BWEHL-toh* a wild, crazy hair style

me voy a la peluquería *meh boy ah lah peh-loo-kay-REE-ah* I'm going to the hair stylist shop

la peluquera *lah peh-loo-KAY-rah* hair stylist (woman)

el peluquero *ehl peh-loo-KAY-ro* hair stylist (man)

como este modelo *KOH-mo EHS-teh mo-dh-EH-lo* like this style

elegante *eh-leh-GAHN-teh* elegant

me gusta este modelo *meh GOOS-tah EHS-teh mo-dh-EH-lo* I like this style

un champú *oon chahm-POO* shampoo

eso es *EH-so ehs* that's right

Basic statements and questions useful in this situation:

1. **Buenos días, señorita (señora, señor). Mi nombre es . . . Quisiera una cita.**
   BWEH-nos DHEE-ahs, sehn-yoh-REE-tah (sehn-YOH-rah, sehn-YOHR). mee NOHM-breh ehs . . . kee-SYEHR-ah OO-nah SEE-tah
   Hello, miss (madam, sir). My name is . . . I would like an appointment.

2. **Para hoy. ¿Para esta mañana? ¿Esta tarde? ¿Mañana? ¿Ahora mismo?**
   PAH-rah oy. PAH-rah EHS-tah mah-ny-AH-nah. EHS-tah TAHR-dhay. mah-ny-AH-nah. ah-OH-rah MEES-mo
   For today. For this morning? This afternoon? Tomorrow? Right now?

3. **Me gustaría un corte revuelto. Primero, un champú, por favor.**
   meh goos-tah-REE-ah oon KOHR-teh reh-BWEHL-toh. pree-MEH-ro, oon chahm-POO, pohr fah-BOHR
   I would like a wild, crazy hair style. First, a shampoo, please.

For more verbs, expressions, and popular words commonly used, consult page 595.

Basic verbs, expressions, and words useful in this situation:

desear *dhay-seh-AHR* to desire, to want, to wish

cobrar un cheque *ko-BRAHR oon CHEH-keh* to cash a check

cambiar *kahm-BYAHR* to change (exchange money)

dólares americanos (m.) *dh-OH-lahr-ehs ah-meh-ree-KAHN-os* American dollars

libras esterlinas *LEE-brahs ehs-tehr-LEE-nahs* pounds sterling

cheques de viaje *CHEH-kehs dhay BYAH-heh* traveler's checks

pagar *pah-GAHR* to pay

recibir *reh-see-BEER* to receive, to get

necesitar *neh-seh-see-TAHR* to need

deber *dhay-BEHR* have to, must

dólares norteamericanos *dh-OH-lahr-ehs nor-teh-ah-meh-ree-KAHN-os* American dollars; **dólares canadienses** *dh-OH-lahr-ehs kah-nah-DYEHN-sehs* Canadian dollars

mi pasaporte *mee pah-sah-POHR-teh* passport

el banco más cercano *ehl BAHN-ko mahs sehr-KAH-no* the nearest bank

Basic statements and questions useful in this situation:

1. **Dígame, por favor, ¿dónde está el banco más cercano?**
   DHEE-gah-meh, pohr fah-BOHR, DHOHN-dhay ehs-TAH ehl BAHN-ko mahs sehr-KAH-no
   Tell me, please, where is the nearest bank?

2. **¿Puede usted darme mil euros en billetes de cien euros? Es más conveniente.**
   PWEH-dhay oos-TEH-dh DAHR-me meel EH-oo-ros ehn bee-YEH-tehs dhay see-EHN EH-oo-ros? ehs mahs kohn-behn-YEHN-teh
   Can you give me one thousand euros in bills of one hundred euros? It is more convenient.

3. **Deseo cambiar mil dólares americanos.**
   dhay-SEH-o kahm-BYAHR meel dh-OH-lah-rehs ah-meh-ree-KAHN-os
   I wish to change one thousand American dollars.

4. **Espero recibir dinero de los Estados Unidos (de Inglaterra, del Canadá, de Australia, de Italia)**
   ehs-PEH-ro reh-see-BEER dhee-NEH-ro dhay los ehs-TAH-dhos oo-NEE-dhos (dhay een-glah-TEHR-rah, dhehl kah-nah-DHAH, dhay ah-oo-STRAH-layh, dhay ee-TAH-lyah)
   I expect to receive money from the United States (from England, from Canada, from Australia, from Italy).

More verbs and new words for this conversational situation:

buscar to look for; **busco** I am looking for
el cajero automático automatic cash dispenser; ATM
Dígame Tell me; **Deme** Give me; **por favor** please
enviar to send; **quisiera enviar** I would like to send
el eurodólar Eurodollar, euro
extender un cheque to write a check; **firmar** to sign
necesitar to need; **necesito** I need
la tarjeta de débito (crédito) debit (credit) card

For more verbs, expressions, and popular words commonly used, consult page 595.

Basic verbs, expressions, and words useful in this situation:

alquilar   *ahl-kee-LAHR*   to rent, to hire
ir   *eer*   to go
tengo que . . .   *TEHN-go kay*   I have to . . .
mi permiso de conducir   *mee pehr-MEE-so dhay kohn-dhoo-SEER*   my driver's license
un coche   *oon KOH-cheh*   car, automobile
el tren   *ehl trehn*   train
el autocar   *ehl ah-oo-toh-KARH*   interurban (long distance) bus
la bicicleta   *lah bee-see-KLEH-tah*   bicycle

conducir   *kohn-dhoo-SEER*   to drive (a motor vehicle)
quisiera . . .   *kee-SYEHR-ah*   I would like . . .
al día   *ahl DHEE-ah*   by the day
a la semana   *ah lah seh-MAH-nah*   by the week
un camión   *oon kah-MYOHN*   truck
el autobús   *ehl ah-oo-toh-BOOS*   city bus
el metro   *ehl MEH-tro*   subway (tube)
el taxi   *ehl TAHK-see*   taxi
el estacionamiento   *ehl ehs-tah-syohn-ah-MYEHN-toh*   parking

Basic statements and questions useful in this situation:

1. **Quisiera alquilar un coche, por favor, por una semana.**
   kee-SYEHR-ah ahl-kee-LAHR oon KOH-cheh, pohr fah-BOHR, POHR OO-nah seh-MAH-nah
   I would like to rent a car, please, for one week.

2. **¿Es necesario dejar una fianza? ¿La gasolina está incluida?**
   ehs neh-seh-SAHR-yo dhay-HAHR OO-nah fee-AHN-sah. lah gah-so-LEE-nah ehs-TAH een-kloo-EE-dhah
   Is it necessary to leave a deposit? Is the gasoline included?

3. **¿Cuál es la dirección para ir a . . . ?**
   kwahl ehs lah dhee-rehk-SYOHN PAH-rah eer ah . . . .
   What is the direction to go to . . . ?

4. **¿Puede decirme si está lejos de aquí?**
   PWEH-dhay dhay-SEER-meh see ehs-TAH LEH-hos dhay ah-KEE
   Can you tell me if it is far from here?

For more verbs, expressions, and popular words commonly used, consult page 595.

Basic verbs, expressions, and words useful in this situation:

ir *eer* to go
bajar *bah-HAHR* to get off
un billete *oon bee-YEH-teh* ticket
cambiar *kahm-BYAHR* to change
la salida *lah sah-LEE-dha* exit
llegar *yeh-GAHR* to arrive
¿por dónde? *pohr DHOHN-dhay*
which way?
¿qué línea? *kay LEE-neh-ah* what line?
la escalera mecánica *lah ehs-kah-LEH-rah meh-KAH-nee-kah* escalator

trasbordar *trahs-bohr-DHAR* to transfer, change trains
la ventanilla *lah behn-tah-NEE-yah* ticket window
bajo *BAH-ho* I'm getting off
la entrada *lah ehn-TRAH-dhah* entrance
perdóneme *pehr-DHO-ne-meh* pardon me
ayúdeme, por favor *ah-YOO-dheh-meh, pohr fah-BOHR* help me, please

Basic statements and questions useful in this situation:

1. **Perdóneme. ¿Puede indicarme en dónde está situado el metro más cercano?**
   pehr-DHOH-neh-meh. PWEH-dhay een-dhee-KAHR-meh ehn DHOHN-dhay ehs-TAH see-too-AH-dho ehl MEH-tro mahs sehr-KAH-no
   Pardon me. Can you point out to me where the nearest subway is located?

2. **Quisiera ir a . . . ?Qué línea necesito tomar? ¿En qué estación debo bajar?**
   kee-SYEHR-ah eer ah . . . kay LEE-neh-ah neh-seh-SEE-toh toh-MAHR. ehn kay ehs-tah-SYOHN dh-EH-bo bah-HAHR
   I would like to go to . . . What line do I have to take? At what station do I get off?

3. **Dígame, por favor, como abrir esta puerta. Muéstreme.**
   DHEE-gah-meh, pohr fah-BOHR, KOH-mo ahb-REER EHS-tah PWEHR-tah. MWEHS-treh-meh
   Tell me, please, how to open this door. Show me.

4. **Déme, por favor, un fajo de billetes. ¿Cuánto le debo? Muchas gracias.**
   DHAY-meh, pohr fah-BOHR, oon FAH-ho dhay bee-YEH-tehs. KWAHN-toh leh DHEH-bo. MOO-chahs GRAH-syahs
   Give me, please, a booklet of tickets. How much do I owe you? Thank you very much.

For more verbs, expressions, and popular words commonly used, consult page 595.

En la oficina de correos   *ehn lah o-fee-SEE-nah dhay kohr-REH-os*
In the post office

Basic verbs, expressions, and words useful in this situation:

enviar *ehn-bee-AHR* to send

mandar un telegrama *mahn-dh-AHR oon tehl-leh-GRAH-mah* to send a telegram

el acuse de recibo *ehl ah-KOO-seh dhay reh-SEE-bo* return receipt

un sobre *oon SOH-breh* envelope

correo certificado *kohr-REH-o sehr-tee-fee-KAH-dho* registered mail

una estampilla *OO-nah ehs-tahm-PEE-yah* postage stamp

ningún valor *nee-GOON bah-LOHR* no value

¿dónde está? *DHOHN-dhay ehs-TAH* where is it located?

¿cuánto cuesta por palabra? *KWAHN-toh KWEHS-tah pohr pah-LAH-brah* How much does it cost for each word?

la dirección *lah dhee-rehk-SYOHN* the address

diez sellos aéreos *dhee-EHS SEH-yos ah-EHR-eh-os* ten air mail stamps

impresos *eem-PREH-sos* printed matter

lista de correos *LEE-stah dhay kohr-REH-os* general delivery

la aduana *lah ad-dh-WAH-nah* customs

Basic statements and questions useful in this situation:

1. **Quisiera enviar estas cartas y tarjetas a los Estados Unidos. Por correo aéreo.**
   kee-SYEHR-ah ehn-bee-AHR EHS-tahs KAHR-tahs ee tahr-HEH-tahs ah lohs ehs-TAH-dhos oo-NEE-dhos. pohr kohr-REH-o ah-EHR-eho-o
   I would like to send these letters and post cards to the United States. Air mail.

2. **Este paquete contiene libros. Son regalos.**
   EHS-teh pah-KEH-teh kohn-TYEHN-eh LEE-bros. sohn reh-GAH-los
   This package contains books. They are gifts.

3. **¿Hay correo para mí en la lista de correos? Mi nombre es . . .**
   AH-ee kohr-REH-o PAH-rah mee ehn lah LEE-stah dhay kohr-REH-os. mee NOHM-breh ehs . . .
   Is there any mail for me in general delivery? My name is . . .

For more verbs, expressions, and popular words commonly used, consult page 595.

En una tienda de fotos   *ehn OO-nah TYEHN-dhah dhay FOH-tos*
In a photo shop

Basic verbs, expressions, and words useful in this situation:

sacar fotos *sah-KAHR FOH-tos* to
  take photos

una foto *OO-nah FOH-toh* photo,
  snapshot

una cámara *OO-nah KAH-mah-rah*
  camera

¿qué número? *kay NOO-mehr-o* what
  number?

en colores *ehn koh-LOH-rehs* in color

una copia *OO-nah KOH-pee-ah* one
  copy

revelar un carrete *reh-behl-AHR oon
  kahr-REH-teh* to develop a roll (of film)

una foto de identidad *OO-nah FOH-toh
  dhay ee-dhen-tee-dh-AH-dh*
  identification photo

pronto *PROHN-toh* fast, quickly

en blanco y negro *ehn BLAHN-ko ee
  NEH-gro* in white and black

en acabado brillante *ehn ah-kah-BAH-
  dho bree-YAHN-teh* in a glossy finish

en acabado mate *ehn ah-kah-BAH-dho
  MAH-teh* in a matte finish

Basic statements and questions useful in this situation:

1. **Perdóneme. ¿Sabe usted si hay una tienda de fotos por aquí?**
   *pehr-DHOH-neh-meh. SAH-beh oos-TEH-dh see AH-ee OO-nah TYEHN-dhah dhay
   FOH-tos pohr ah-KEE*
   Pardon me. Do you know if there is a photo shop around here?

2. **Hágame el favor de revelar este carrete ¿Cuánto cuesta?**
   *AH-gah-meh ehl fah-BOHR dhay reh-behl-AHR EHS-teh kahr-REH-teh. KWAHN-toh
   KWEHS-tah*
   Please be good enough to develop this roll (of film). How much does it cost?

3. **En colores con acabado brillante.**
   ehn koh-LOHR-ehs kohn ah-kah-BAH-dho bree-YAHN-teh
   In color on a glossy finish.

4. **¿Cuándo puedo volver para recogerlas?**
   KWAHN-dho PWEH-dho bohl-BEHR PAH-rah reh-ko-HEHR-lahs
   When can I come back to pick them up?

More verbs and new words for this conversational situation:

una máquina fotográfica camera
una cámara digital digital camera
una videocámara camcorder
una pila battery
un carrete (de película) roll (of film)
un rollo de película roll of film
sacar instantáneas to take snapshots

el scanner scanner
la cámara fotográfica camera
el objetivo normal standard lens
la fotografía photography
el disparador shutter release
el contacto de cuboflash flash cube
  contact

For more verbs, expressions, and popular words commonly used, consult page 595.

Basic verbs, expressions, and words useful in this situation:

¿me puedo probar . . .?   *meh PWEH-dho proh-BAHR*   may I try on . . . ?
comprar   *kohm-PRAHR*   to buy
pagar al contado   *pah-GAHR-ahl kohn-TAH-dho*   to pay in cash
una blusa   *OO-nah BLOO-sah*   blouse
un sostén   *oon soh-STEHN*   bra (brassiere)
más corto   *mahs KOHR-toh*   shorter
medias (f.)   *MEH-dhee-ahs*   stockings
en seda (f.)   *ehn SEH-dhah*   in silk
un cinturón   *oon seen-toor-OHN*   belt
mangas cortas   *MAHN-gahs KOHR-tahs*   short sleeves
con rayas   *kohn RAH-yahs*   with stripes
un traje   *oon TRAH-heh*   suit

devolver un artículo   *deh-bohl-BEHR oon ahr-TEE-koo-lo*   to return an article
tomar   *toh-MAHR*   to take
un vestido   *oon behs-TEE-dho*   a dress
una falda   *OO-nah FAHL-dhah*   a skirt
zapatos   *sah-PAH-tohs*   shoes
un traje de noche   *oon TRAH-heh dhay NOH-cheh*   evening gown
más largo   *mahs LAHR-go*   longer
algo más elegante   *AHL-go mahs eh-leh-GAHN-teh*   something more elegant
un pantalón   *oon pahn-tah-LOHN*   pants, trousers, slacks
en cuero   *ehn KWEH-ro*   in leather
mangas largas   *MAHN-gahs LAHR-gahs*   long sleeves

Basic statements and questions useful in this situation:

1. **Quisiera comprar algunos artículos. ¿Puede ayudarme, por favor?**
   kee-SYEHR-ah kohm-PRAHR ahl-GOO-nos ahr-TEE-koo-los. PWEH-dhay ah-yoo-dh-AHR-meh, pohr fah-BOHR
   I would like to buy a few things. Can you help me, please?

2. **¿Me puedo probar este vestido? Es bonito.**
   meh PWEH-dho proh-BAHR EHS-teh behs-TEE-dho. ehs bo-NEE-toh
   May I try on this dress? It's pretty.

3. **No me gusta esta blusa. Es fea. ¿Tiene otras?**
   noh meh GOOS-tah EHS-tah BLOO-sah. ehs FEH-ah. TYEHN-eh OH-trahs
   I don't like this blouse. It's ugly. Do you have any others?

4. **Prefiero los colores rosado, rojo, amarillo, gris, verde, y azul.**
   preh-FYEH-ro lohs ko-LOH-rehs roh-SAH-dho, ROH-ho, ah-mah-REE-yo, greess, BEHR-dhay, ee ah-SOOL
   I prefer the colors pink, red, yellow, gray, green, and blue.

5. **¿Me puedo probar este traje? Me gusta mucho.**
   meh PWEH-dho proh-BAHR EHS-teh TRAH-heh. meh GOOS-tagh MOO-cho
   May I try on this suit? I like it very much.

6. **No me gusta esta camisa. Es fea. ¿Tiene otras?**
   noh meh GOOS-tah EHS-tah kah-MEE-sah. ehs FEH-ah. TYEHN-eh OH-trahs
   I don't like this shirt. It's ugly. Do you have any others?

For more verbs, expressions, and popular words commonly used, consult page 595.

En una tienda de ordenadores o en un cybercafé
ehn OO-nah TYEHN-da day or-day-na-DOR-ays oh en oon see-behr-kaFAY
In a computer store or in an Internet café

Basic verbs, expressions, and words useful in this situation:

un ordenador   *oon or-day-na-DOR*   or
una computadora   *OOna kom-poo-ta-DOR-ah*   computer

el programador or **la programadora de ordenadores** or **de computadoras**
computer programmer

¿dónde puedo . . .?   *DHOHN-dhay PWEH-dho*   where can I . . .?

arrancar (iniciar)   *ah-rahn-KAR (ee-nee-see-AR)*   to boot

bajar   *bah-HAR*   to download

el buscador   *el boos-ka-DOR*   search engine

el correo electrónico   *el koRAY-oh ay-lek-TRO-nee-ko*   e-mail

crashear   *krash-ay-AR*   to crash

una impresora   *OO-nah eem-pres-OR-a*   printer

el Internet, la Red   *ehl een-ter-NET, la RED*   (Net) Internet

un modem   *oon mo-dem*   modem

navegar (surfear)   *na-vay-GAR (soor-fay-AR)*   to navigate (to surf)

un ordenador portátil   *oon or-day-na-DOR por-TA-teel*   laptop computer

una página   *OO-nah PA-heen-a*   (web) page

el programa   *el pro-GRAM-a*   program

un programa antivirus   *oon pro-GRAM-a an-tee-VEE-roos*   antivirus

el servidor   *el ser-vee-DOR*   server

el teclado   *el tek-LA-doh*   keyboard

la traducción asistida por ordenador   *la tra-dooks-ee-OHN a-see-stee-da por or-day-na-DOR*   computer-assisted translation

el tratamiento de textos   *el tra-ta-mee-EN-toh day TEKS-tohs*   word processing

un virus   *oon VEE-roos*   virus

Basic statements and questions useful in this situation:

1. **¿Dónde puedo enviar el correo electrónico?**
   DHOHN-dhay PWEH-dho envee-AR el korAY-o el-ek-TRO-nee-ko
   Where can I send e-mail?

2. **Necesito enviar un mensaje instantáneo.**
   nay-say-SEE-toh envee-AR oon men-SAY-hay instan-TAN-ay-o
   I need to send an instant message.

3. **Quisiera charlar (conversar, hablar) con mi esposa (esposo).**
   kee-see-EHR-a char-LAR (kon-ver-SAR, ab-LAR) kon mee es-PO-sa (es-PO-so)
   I would like to chat (converse, talk) with my wife (husband).

4. **Quisiera instalar este programa. ¿Puede ayudarme?**
   kee-see-EHR-a een-sta-LAR ES-tay pro-GRAM-a. PWEH-day a-yoo-DAR-may
   I would like to install this program. Can you help me?

For more verbs, expressions, and popular words commonly used, consult page 595.

Basic verbs, expressions, and words useful in this situation:

probar   *pro-BAHR*   to take a taste
comer   *koh-MEHR*   to eat
con azúcar   *kohn ah-SOO-kahr*   with sugar
con leche   *kohn LEH-cheh*   with milk
con frutas   *kohn FROO-tahs*   with fruits
la especialidad de hoy   *lah ehs-peh-see-ah-lee-dh-AH-dh dhay oy*   today's special
mantequilla (f.)   *mahn-teh-KEE-yah*   butter
una gaseosa   *OO-nah gah-seh-OH-sah*   carbonated drink
tomar   *toh-MAHR*   to take, to have
más   *mahs*   more

poco   *POH-ko*   little (not much)
con limón   *kohn lee-MOHN*   with lemon
caliente   *kah-LYEHN-tay*   hot
un pastel con fresas   *oon pahs-TEHL kohn FREH-sahs*   a pastry with strawberries
con nata batida   *kohn NAH-tah bah-TEE-dha*   with whipped cream
algo crespo   *AHL-go KREHS-po*   something crispy
tostada (f.)   *tohs-TAH-dha*   toast
confitura (f.)   *kohn-fee-TOO-rah*   preserves (jam)
un bollo de crema   *oon BOH-yo dhay kr-EH-mah*   cream puff

Basic statements and questions useful in this situation:

1. **Buenos días. Una mesa para mí (para dos personas), por favor.**
   BWEH-nos DHEE-ahs. OO-nah MEH-sah PAH-rah mee (PAH-rah dhos pehr-SOH-nahs), pohr fah-BOHR
   Hello. A table for me (for two persons), please.

2. **Quisiera un té y un pastel con fresas y nata batida.**
   kee-SYEHR-ah oon tay ee oon pahs-TEHL kohn FREH-sahs ee NAH-tah bah-TEE-dha
   I would like some tea and a pastry with strawberries and whipped cream.

3. **Prefiero limón con el té. Para mi amigo (amiga), leche con el té.**
   preh-FYEH-ro lee-MOHN kohn ehl tay. PAH-rah mee ah-MEE-go (ah-MEE-gah), LEH-cheh kohn ehl tay
   I prefer lemon with the tea. For my friend, milk with the tea.

For more verbs, expressions, and popular words commonly used, consult page 595.

Basic verbs, expressions, and words useful in this situation:

hace sol   *AH-seh sohl*   it's sunny

hace buen tiempo   *AH-seh bwehn TYEHM-po*   the weather is good

está nevando   *ehs-TAH neh-BAHN-dho* it's snowing

hace viento   *AH-seh bee-YEHN-toh*   it's windy

un impermeable   *oon eem-pehr-meh-AH-bleh*   raincoat

dar un paseo   *dh-AHR oon pah-SEH-o* to take a walk

en el parque   *ehn ehl PAHR-kay*   in the park

hace calor   *AH-seh kah-LOHR*   it's warm (hot)

está lloviendo ahora   *ehs-TAH yo-bee-EHN-dho ah-OH-rah*   it's raining now

la lluvia   *lah YOO-bee-ah*   the rain

hace mal tiempo   *AH-seh mahl TYEHM-po*   the weather is bad

un paraguas   *oon pah-RAH-gwahs* umbrella

hace fresco hoy   *AH-seh FREHS-ko oy* it's cool today

hace frío   *AH-seh FREE-o*   it's cold

Basic statements and questions useful in this situation:

1. **¿Qué tiempo hace hoy? Tengo que salir.**
   kay TYEHM-po AH-seh oy. TEHN-go kay sah-LEER
   What's the weather like today? I have to go out.

2. **Me gustaría dar un paseo en el parque pero está lloviendo.**
   meh goos-tah-REE-ah dh-AHR oon pah-SEH-o ehn ehl PAHR-kay PEH-ro ehs-TAH yo-bee-EHN-dho
   I would like to take a walk in the park but it's raining.

3. **Necesito comprar un paraguas y un impermeable.**
   neh-seh-SEE-toh kohm-PRAHR oon pah-RAH-gwahs ee oon eem-pehr-meh-AH-bleh
   I need to buy an umbrella and a raincoat (mackintosh).

4. **¿Hay mucha nieve aquí en el invierno?**
   AH-ee MOO-chah ny-EH-beh ah-KEE ehn ehl een-bee-EHR-no
   Is there much snow here in winter?

For more verbs, expressions, and popular words commonly used, consult page 595.

Basic verbs, expressions, and words useful in this situation:

mirar   *meer-AHR*   to look (at)

desear   *dhay-seh-AHR*   to desire, to want, to wish

una flor   *OO-nah flohr*   flower

ofrecer   *oh-freh-SEHR*   to offer

escoger   *ehs-koh-HEHR*   to choose

es para ofrecer   *ehs PAH-rah oh-freh-SEHR*   it's to give as a gift

estoque (m.)   *ehs-TOH-keh*   gladiolus

claveles (m.)   *klah-BEH-lehs*   carnations

violetas (f.)   *bee-oh-LEH-tahs*   violets

una cinta   *OO-nah SEEN-tah*   ribbon

ver   *behr*   to see

un ramillete de flores   *oon rah-mee-YAY-teh dhay FLOHR-ehs*   bunch of flowers

encontrar   *ehn-kohn-TRAHR*   to find, meet

valer   *bah-LEHR*   to be worth

preferir   *preh-feh-REER*   to prefer

una planta bonita   *OO-nah PLAHN-tah bo-NEE-tah*   a pretty plant

rosas (f.)   *ROH-sahs*   roses

Basic statements and questions useful in this situation:

1. **Quisiera comprar algunas flores para ofrecer.**
   kee-SYEHR-ah kohm-PRAHR ahl-GOO-nahs FLOHR-ehs PAH-rah oh-freh-SEHR.
   I would like to buy some flowers as a gift.

2. **Me gusta mucho este ramillete de flores.**
   meh GOOS-tah MOO-cho EHS-teh rah-mee-YAY-teh dhay FLOHR-ehs.
   I like this bunch of flowers very much.

3. **Lo llevo conmigo. Me gustaría, también, rosas y violetas.**
   loh YAY-bo kohn-MEE-go. meh goos-tah-REE-ah, tahm-BYEHN, ROH-sahs ee bee-oh-LEH-tahs.
   I'll take it with me. I would like, also, roses and violets.

4. **¿Cuánto le debo? Voy a pagar al contado.**
   KWAHN-toh leh dh-EH-bo. boy ah pah-GAHR ahl kohn-TAH-dho.
   How much do I owe you? I'm going to pay in cash.

For more verbs, expressions, and popular words commonly used, consult page 595.

Basic verbs, expressions, and words useful in this situation:

nadar   *nad-dh-AHR*   to swim

una piscina   *OO-nah pee-SEE-nah*
swimming pool

flotar   *flo-TAHR*   to float

¿dónde puedo cambiarme?   *DHOHN-
day PWEH-dho kahm-bee-AHR-meh*
where can I change (my clothes)?

una limonada   *OO-nah lee-mo-NAH-dh-
ah*   lemonade

un balón   *oon bah-LOHN*   beach ball

una ducha   *OO-nah DHOO-chah*
shower

PROHIBIDO BANARSE   *proh-ee-BEE-dho
bah-ny-AHR-seh*   NO BATHING

el mar   *ehl mahr*   the sea

¿un helado de qué sabor?   *oon ehl-AH-
dho dhay kay sah-BOHR*   what flavor
ice cream?

bucear   *boo-seh-AHR*   to dive

un traje de baño   *oon TRAH-heh dhay
BAH-ny-o*   swim suit

quiero alquilar . . .   *KYEH-ro ahl-kee-
LAHR*   I would like to rent . . .

páseme una toalla   *PAH-seh-meh OO-
nah toh-AH-yah*   hand me a towel

el esquí náutico   *ehl ehs-KEE NAH-oo-
tee-ko*   water skiing

el agua   *ehl AH-gwah*   the water

en la arena   *ehn lah ah-REH-nah*   on
the sand

para niños   *PAH-rah NEE-ny-os*   for
children

una sombrilla   *OO-nah sohm-BREE-yah*
beach umbrella

Basic statements and questions useful in this situation:

1. **Quisiera pasar algunos días en la playa a . . .**
   kee-SYEHR-ah pah-SAHR al-GOO-nos DHEE-ahs ehn lah PLAH-yah ah
   I would like to spend a few days at the beach at . . .

2. **Quisiera alquilar una sombrilla. ¿Cuánto cuesta?**
   kee-SYEHR-ah ahl-kee-LAHR OO-nah sohn-BREE-yah. KWAHN-toh KWEHS-tah
   I would like to rent (hire) a beach umbrella. How much does it cost?

3. **No podemos nadar aquí. Es peligroso y es prohibido.**
   noh po-dh-EH-mos nah-dh-AHR ah-KEE. ehs peh-lee-GRO-so ee ehs proh-ee-BEE-dho.
   We can't swim here. It's dangerous and it is forbidden.

For more verbs, expressions, and popular words commonly used, consult page 595.

La partida   *lah pahr-TEE-dha*   The departure

Basic verbs, expressions, and words useful in this situation:

partir *pahr-TEER* to leave
arreglar mi cuenta *ahr-reh-GLAHR mee*
  KWEHN-tah to settle my account
¿cuánto le debo? *KWAHN-toh leh dh-*
  EH-bo how much do I owe you?
magnífico *mahg-NEE-fee-ko*
  magnificent
mi equipaje *mee eh-kee-PAH-heh* my
  baggage, luggage

mañana por la mañana *mah-ny-AH-nah*
  pohr lah mah-ny-AH-nah tomorrow
  morning
voy a salir *boy ah sah-LEER* I'm going
  to leave (check out)
temprano *tehm-PRAH-no* early
mi estancia *mee ehs-TAHN-see-ah* my
  stay
agradable *ah-grah-DHAH-bleh*
  pleasant
un recibo *oon reh-SEE-bo* receipt
llame un taxi *YAH-meh oon TAHK-see*
  call a taxi

Basic statements and questions useful in this situation:

1. **Voy (Vamos) a partir temprano mañana por la mañana.**
   boy (BAH-mos) ah pahr-TEER tehm-PRAH-no mah-ny-AH-nah pohr lah mah-ny-AH-nah
   I'm going (we're going) to leave early tomorrow morning.

2. **¿Antes de qué hora hay que desocupar la habitación?**
   AHN-tehs dhay kay OH-rah AH-ee kay dhay-so-koo-PAHR lah ah-bee-tah-SYOHN
   Before what time is it required to vacate the room?

3. **Me estancia en su hotel y en su país ha sido agradable.**
   mee ehs-TAHN-see-ah ehn soo o-TEHL ee ehn soo pah-EES ah SEE-dho ah-grah-
   DHAH-bleh
   My stay in your hotel and in your country has been pleasant.

4. **Quisiera arreglar mi cuenta ahora, por favor.**
   kee-SYEHR-ah ahr-reh-GLAHR mee KWEHN-tah ah-OH-rah, pohr fah-BOHR
   I would like to settle my account now, please.

For more verbs, expressions, and popular words commonly used, consult page 595.

Basic verbs, expressions, and words useful in this situation:

NADA QUE DECLARAR   *NAH-dha kay dhay-*
klah-RAHR   NOTHING TO DECLARE

yo no sé   *yoh noh seh*   I don't know

hable más despacio, por favor   *AH-bleh*
mahs dh-ehs-PAH-see-o, pohr fah-BOHR
speak more slowly, please

nada   *NAH-dha*   nothing

lo siento   *loh SYEHN-toh*   I'm sorry

ARTICULOS PARA DECLARAR   *ahr-TEE-*
koo-los PAH-rah dhay-klah-RAHR
ARTICLES TO DECLARE

presentar   *preh-sehn-TAHR*   to present

arrancar el ordenador portátil   *ah-rahn-*
KAHR ehl or-day-nah-DOR por-TA-teel
to turn on (boot up) the laptop computer

no comprendo   *noh kohm-PREHN-dho*
I don't understand

vuelvo a mi país   *BWEHL-bo ah mee*
pah-EES   I'm returning to my country

sí, comprendo   *see kohm-PREHN-dho*
yes, I understand

he aquí mi pasaporte   *ay ah-KEE mee*
pah-sah-POHR-teh   here is my passport

¿puedo marcharme?   *PWEH-dho mahr-*
CHAHR-meh   may I leave?

el control de seguridad   security check

cerrar el ordenador portátil   *say-RAHR*
ehl or-day-nah-DOR por-TA-teel   to turn
off the laptop computer

Basic statements and questions useful in this situation:

1. **Tengo una botella de vino y un frasco de perfume. Son regalos.**
   TEHN-go OO-nah boh-TEH-yah dhay BEE-no ee oon FRAHS-ko dhay pehr-FOO-meh.
   sohn reh-GAH-los
   I have one bottle of wine and one small bottle of perfume. They are gifts.

2. **Busco mis llaves para abrir las maletas. Un momento, por favor.**
   BOOS-ko mees YAH-behs PAH-rah ah-BREER lahs mah-LEH-tahs. oon mo-MEHN-
   toh, por fah-BOHR
   I'm looking for my keys to open the suitcases. Just a minute, please.

3. **Son artículos para mi uso personal.**
   sohn ahr-TEE-koo-los PAH-rah mee OO-so pehr-so-NAHL
   They are articles for my own personal use.

4. **Mi estancia en su país ha sido agradable. Muchas gracias. ¡Adiós!**
   Mee ehs-TAHN-see-ah ehn soo pah-EES ah SEE-dho ah-grah-DHAH-bleh. MOO-chahs
   GRAH-syahs. ah-dhee-OHS
   My stay in your country has been pleasant. Thank you very much. Good-bye!

For more verbs, expressions, and popular words commonly used, consult page 595.

Popular Phrases, Words, and Expressions for Tourists

This feature provides you with many popular phrases, words, expressions, abbreviations, signs, and notices that you will most likely need to understand when you hear them or when you see them posted in many public places in a Spanish-speaking country or region. There are also many you will need to use yourself when speaking Spanish.

All the entries in English and Spanish are given in one alphabetical listing because it is more convenient to look in one place instead of two for an entry. One listing also prevents you from looking inadvertently in a Spanish listing for an English word or in an English listing for a Spanish word. Also, cognates and near-cognates in both languages are reduced to a single entry. Spanish words are printed in boldface letters. After the Spanish phrase or word, you are given an approximate sound so you may pronounce the Spanish as well as possible to communicate effectively. Consult the EE-zee guide to Spanish pronunciation on page 562.

If you do not find the word or phrase you have in mind, perhaps it is given in the thirty situations that precede this section. Be sure to consult the Guide to Thirty Practical Situations on page 564. Also, if there is a Spanish verb you wish to use that is not given in this section, consult the 501 verbs in this book and the index of English-Spanish verbs that begins on page 505.

A

a, an **un** *oon;* **una** *OO-nah;* **un lápiz** *oon LAH-pees* a pencil; **una naranja** *OO-nah nah-RAHN-hah* an orange

ABORDO *ah BOHR-dho* ON BOARD

a little **un poco** *oon POH-ko*

a lot **mucho** *MOO-cho*

ABIERTO DE . . . HASTA . . . *ah-bee-EHR-toh dhay AH-stah* OPEN FROM . . . UNTIL . . .

ABIERTO TODOS LOS DIAS *ah-bee-EHR-toh TOH-dhos lohs DHEE-ahs* OPEN EVERY DAY

abortion **el aborto** *ehl ah-BOHR-toh*

about (approximately) **a eso de** *ah EH-so-dhay;* (concerning) **de** *dhay*

above **arriba** *ahr-REE-bah;* **sobre** *SOH-breh;* above all **sobre todo** *SOH-breh TOH-dho*

accelerate **acelerar** *ah-seh-leh-RAHR;* accelerator **el acelerador** *ehl ah-seh-leh-rae-DHOR*

accident **el accidente** *ehl ahk-see-dh-EHN-teh*

ache **tener dolor** *teh-NEHR dho-LOHR;* ache (pain) **un dolor** *oon dho-LOHR*

address **la dirección** *lah dhee-REHK-see-OHN*

adorable **adorable** *ad-dhor-AH-bleh*

ADUANA (f.) *ah-dh-WAH-nah* CUSTOMS

adventure **la aventura** *lah ah-behn-TOO-rah*

advertisement **un anuncio** *oon ah-NOON-see-oh*

advice **el consejo** *ehl kohn-SEH-ho*

AEROPUERTO (m.) *ah-eh-ro-PWEHR-toh* AIRPORT

affection **el cariño** *ehl kah-REE-ny-o;* affectionately **con cariño** *kohn kah-REE-ny-o*

after **después** *dh-ehs-PWEHS*

afternoon **la tarde** *lah TAHR-dhe*

afterwards **luego** *LWEH-go*

again **otra vez** *OH-trah behs;* **de nuevo** *dhay NWEH-bo*

ago **hace** *AH-seh*

agua mineral *AH-gwah mee-neh-RAHL* mineral water

aid **el socorro** *ehl so-KOHR-ro;* **la ayuda** *lah ah-YOO-dh-ah*

AIDS SIDA *SEE-dh-ah* (sexually transmitted infectious fatal disease)

air **el aire** *ehl AH-ee-reh*

air conditioned **aire acondicionado** *AH-ee-reh ah-kohn-dhee-see-oh-NAH-dho*

air mail **por correo aéreo** *pohr kohr-REH-o ah-EH-reh-o*

airline **la línea aérea** *lah LEE-neh-ah ah-EH-reh-ah*

airplane **un avión** *oon ah-bee-OHN*

all **todo** *TOH-dho;* all day **todo el día** *TOH-dho ehl DHEE-ah*

almost **casi** *KAH-see*

almuerzo *ahl-MWEHR-so* lunch

alone **solo** (man); **sola** (woman); I am alone **estoy solo** *ehs-TOY-SOH-lo;* **estoy sola** *ehs-TOY SOH-lah*

already **ya** *yah*

also **también** *tahm-BYEHN*

ALTO *AHL-toh* STOP

always **siempre** *SYEHM-preh*

ambulance **una ambulancia** *OO-nah ahm-boo-LAHN-syah*

American, I am **soy norteamericano** (man) *soy nohr-teh-ah-meh-ree-KAH-no;* **soy norteamericana** (woman) *soy nohr-teh-ah-meh-ree-KAH-nah*

amusing **divertido** *dhee-behr-TEE-dho*

and **y** *ee* (when **y** is followed by a Spanish word beginning with **i** or **hi,** the word for "and" is **e** *eh*); sons and daughters **hijos e hijas** *EE-hos eh EE-hahs*

and you? **¿y usted?** *ee oos-TEH-dh*

ANDENES (m.) *ahn-dh-EH-nehs* PLATFORMS (TRAINS)

annoy **molestar** *mo-lehs-TAHR*

another **otro** *OH-tro;* **otra** *OH-trah*

anybody **alguien** *AHL-gee-ehn*

anything **algo** *AHL-go*

aperitif **el aperitivo** *ehl ah-peh-ree-TEE-bo*

apple **una manzana** *OO-nah mahn-SAH-nah*

April **abril** *ah-BREEL*

árbol *AHR-bohl* tree

are there . . . ? is there . . . ? **¿hay . . . ?** *AH-ee*

arrested **arrestado** *ahr-rehs-TAH-dho*

arrival **la llegada** *lah yeh-GAH-dh-ah*

arroz *ahr-ROHS* rice

as little as **tan poco como** *tahn POH-ko KOH-mo*
as soon as possible **lo más pronto posible** *loh mahs PROHN-to po-SEE-bleh*
asados *ah-SAH-dhos* roasts
ASCENSOR (m.) *ah-sehn-SOHR* ELEVATOR (LIFT)
ashtray **un cenicero** *oon seh-nee-SEH-ro*
ask for someone **preguntar por alguien** *preh-goon-TAHR pohr AHL-gee-ehn*
ask (request) **preguntar** *preh-goon-TAHR*
asparagus **el aspárrago** *ehl ehs-PAHR-rah-go*
aspirin **la aspirina** *lah ahs-pee-REE-nah*
at **a** *ah;* **en** *ehn;* at the beach **a la playa** *ah lah PLAH-yah;* at home
  en casa *ehn KAH-sah;* at all costs **a todo costa** *ah TOH-dha KOHS-
  tah;* at full speed **a toda prisa** *ah TOH-dha PREE-sah;* at least **por lo
  menos** *pohr loh MEH-nos*
ATENCION (f.) *ah-tehn-see-OHN* CAUTION
audio-visual **audiovisual** *AH-oo-dhee-o-bee-soo-AHL*
August **agosto** *ah-GOH-sto*
Australia **Australia** *ah-oo-STRAH-lee-ah*
Australian, I am **soy australiano** (man) *soy ah-oo-strah-lee-AH-no;* **soy
  australiana** (woman) *soy ah-oo-strah-lee-AH-nah*
auto **el auto** *ehl AH-oo-toh*
automatic **automático** *ah-oo-toh-MAH-tee-ko*
automobile **un coche** *oon KOH-cheh;* **un automóvil** *oon ah-oo-toh-MOH-
  beel*
AVISO (m.) *ah-BEE-so* NOTICE
awful **terrible** *tehr-REE-bleh*

B

baby **el bebé** *ehl bay-BAY*
baby bottle **un biberón** *oon bee-beh-ROHN*
bad **malo** *MAH-lo;* too bad! **¡es lástima!** *ehs LAHS-teem-ah*
baggage **el equipaje** *ehl eh-kee-PAH-heh;* **el bagaje** *ehl bah-GAH-heh*
baggage cart **un carrito** *oon kahr-REE-toh*
baggage room **la sala de equipajes** *lah SAH-lah dhay eh-kee-PAH-hehs*
baggage room checking **la consigna** *lah kohn-SEEG-nah*
BAJADA (f.) *bah-HAH-dha* DOWNHILL
bakery **la panadería** *lah pah-nah-dh-eh-REE-ah*
bank **el banco** *ehl BAHN-ko*
bargains **gangas** (f.) *GAHN-gahs*
bath, to take a **tomar un baño** *toh-MAHR-oon BAH-ny-o*
bathroom **el cuarto de baño** *ehl KWAHR-toh dhay BAH-ny-o*
be quick! **¡dése prisa!** *dh-EH-seh PREE-sah*
beat it! (go away!) **¡váyase!** *BAH-yah-seh*
because **porque** *POHR-keh*
bed **la cama** *lah KAH-mah;* bed and board **pensión completa** *pehn-see-
  OHN kohn-PLEH-tah*
bed bug **una chinche** *OO-nah CHEEN-cheh*
bed cover, bedspread **una cubrecama** *OO-nah koo-breh-KAH-mah*

bed pan **un silleta de cama** *OO-nah see-YEH-tah dhay KAH-mah*; **una chata de cama** *OO-nah CHAH-tah dhay KAH-mah;* **un cómodo de cama** *oon KOH-mo-dho dhay KAH-mah*

beef **carne de vaca** *KAHR-neh dhay BAH-kah*

beefsteak **bistec** *bee-STEHK;* **biftec** *beef-TEHK;* **bisté** *bee-STEH*

beer **la cerveza** *lah sehr-BEH-sah*

behind **detrás** *dhay-TRAHS;* behind me **detrás de mí** *dhay-TRAHS dhay mee*

believe me! **¡créame!** *KREH-ah-meh*

between **entre** *EHN-treh*

bicycle **una bicicleta** *OO-nah bee-see-KLEH-tah*

BIENVENIDO *bee-yehn-beh-NEE-dho* WELCOME

bill (paid for services) **la cuenta** *lah KWEHN-tah*

black **negro** *NEH-gro*

black coffee **café solo** *kah-FEH SOH-lo*

bless my soul! **¡válgame Dios!** *BAHL-gah-meh dhee-OHS*

blood **la sangre** *lah SAHN-greh*

blue **azul** *ah-SOOL*

boat **un barco** *oon BAHR-ko;* **un bote** *oon BOH-teh;* **un buque** *oon BOO-keh*

book **un libro** *oon LEE-bro*

boss **el amo** *ehl AH-mo;* **ama** (woman) *AH-mah*

bottle **una botella** *OO-nah boh-TEH-yah*

bottle opener **un abridor para botella** *oon ah-bree-DOHR PAH-rah boh-TEH-yah*

bottled water **una botella de agua** *OO-nah boh-TEH-yah dhay AH-gwah*

boy **un muchacho** *oon moo-CHAH-cho;* **un chico** *oon CHEE-ko*

bread **el pan** *ehl pahn*

breakdown (vehicle) **la avería** *lah ah-beh-REE-ah*

breakfast **el desayuno** *ehl dhay-sah-YOO-no*

bring it, please **tráigalo, por favor** *TRAH-ee-gah-lo, pohr fah-BOHR*

bring me . . . , please **tráigame . . . , por favor** *TRAH-ee-gah-meh, pohr fah-BOHR*

British **británico** *bree-TAHN-ee-ko*

brown **marrón** *mahr-ROHN;* **pardo** *PAHR-dho*

bulb, electric light **una bombilla** *OO-nah bohm-BEE-yah*

bull **el toro** *ehl TOH-ro;* bull ring **la plaza de toros** *lah PLAH-sah dhay TOH-ros;* bullfight **la corrida de toros** *lah kohr-REE-dha dhay TOH-ros*

bus **un autobús** *oon ah-oo-toh-BOOS*

but **pero** *PEH-ro*

butter **la mantequilla** *lah mahn-teh-KEE-yah*

button **un botón** *oon boh-TOHN*

by the way (incidentally) **a propósito** *ah proh-POH-see-toh*

C

CABALLEROS (m.) *kah-bah-YEH-ros* GENTLEMEN

café *kah-FEH* coffee

CAIDA DE PIEDRAS (f.) *kah-EE-dhah dhay pee-EH-dh-rahs* FALLEN ROCK ZONE

CAJA (f.) *KAH-hah* CASHIER'S DESK

CALIENTE *kah-lee-EHN-teh* HOT

call now! **¡llame ahora!** *YAH-meh ah-OH-rah*

call the police! **¡llame a la policía!** *YAH-meh ah lah poh-lee-SEE-ah*

CAMBIO (m.) *KAHM-bee-o* CHANGE (MONEY EXCHANGE OFFICE)

can I . . . ? **¿puedo . . . ?** *PWEH-dho;* **con permiso** *kohn pehr-MEE-so*

can opener **un abrelatas** *oon ah-breh-LAH-tahs*

Canadian, I am **soy canadiense** (man or woman) *soy kah-nah-dh-ee-EHN-seh*

CANTINA (f.) *kahn-TEE-nah* SNACK BAR

car **un coche** *oon KOH-cheh*

careful **cuidado** *kwee-DAH-dho*

carne **KAHR-neh** meat

carne de cordero *KAHR-neh dhay kohr-dh-EH-ro* lamb

carne de vaca *KAHR-neh dhay BAH-kah* beef

CARRETERA PARTICULAR (f.) *kahr-reh-TEH-rah pahr-tee-koo-LAHR* PRIVATE ROAD

cart **un carrito** *oon kahr-REE-toh*

CEDA EL PASO *SEH-dhah ehl PAH-so* YIELD

cena *SEH-nah* dinner

centavos *sehn-TAH-bohs* cents

cereza *seh-REH-sah* cherry

CERRADO *sehr-RAH-dho* CLOSED

cerveza *sehr-BEH-sah* beer

change to, **cambiar** *kahm-bee-AHR*

cheaper **más barato** *mahs bah-RAH-toh*

check (paid for services) **la cuenta** *lah KWEHN-tah*

check baggage **facturar** *fahk-too-RAHR*

cheese **el questo** *ehl KEH-so*

cherry **la cereza** *lah seh-REH-sah*

chest (human body) **el pecho** *ehl PEH-cho*

child **un niño** (boy) *oon NEEN-yo;* **una niña** (girl) *OO-nah NEEN-yah*

chocolate **chocolate** *cho-ko-LAH-teh*

church **la iglesia** *lah eeg-LEH-syah*

cigarette lighter **un mechero** *oon meh-CHEH-ro*

clean **limpio** *LEEM-pee-o*

clock **el reloj** *ehl reh-LOH*

close the door, please **cierre la puerta, por favor** *see-EHR-eh lah PWEHR-tah, pohr fah-BOHR*

closed **cerrado** *sehr-RAH-dho*

clothes, clothing **la ropa** *lah ROH-pah*

coat hangers **los colgadores** *lohs kohl-gah-DOHR-ehs*

coat (overcoat) **el abrigo** *ehl ah-BREE-go*

COCHE RESTAURANTE (m.) *KOH-cheh rehs-tah-oo-RAHN-teh* DINING CAR

cockroach **la cucaracha** *lah koo-kah-RAH-chah*

coffee **el café** *ehl kah-FEH;* coffee black **un café solo** *oon kah-FEH SOH-lo;* with lots of milk **con mucha leche** *kohn MOO-chah LEH-cheh* cold **frío** *FREE-o*

cold, I feel **tengo frío** *TEHN-go FREE-o;* it's cold in my room **hace frío en mi habitación** *AH-seh FREE-o ehn mee ah-bee-tah-SYOHN*

cold water **agua fría** *AH-gwah FREE-ah*

come here! **¡venga acá!** *BEHN-gah ah-KAH*

come in! **¡entre!** *EHN-treh;* **¡adelante!** *ah-dh-eh-LAHN-teh*

come on! **¡vamos!** *BAH-mos*

COMPLETO *kohm-PLEH-toh* FULL

computer **la computadora** *lah kohm-poo-tah-dh-OH-rah*

concert **un concierto** *oon kohn-see-EHR-toh*

confession **la confesión** *lah kohn-feh-SYOHN*

CONSIGNA (f.) *kohn-SEEG-nah* BAGGAGE CHECKING

contrary, on the **al contrario** *ahl kohn-TRAH-ree-o*

CONTROL DE SEGURIDAD (m.) *kohn-TROL dhay seh-goo-ree-dh-AH-dh* SECURITY CONTROL

corkscrew **un sacacorchos** *oon sah-kah-KOHR-chos*

corner (inside) **el rincón** *ehl reen-KOHN;* outside corner (as on a street) **la esquina** *lah ehs-KEE-nah*

CORREO AEREO (m.) *kohr-REH-o ah-EHR-eh-o* AIR MAIL

could you tell me . . . ? **¿podría decirme . . . ?** *po-dh-REE-ah dh-eh-SEER-meh*

cream **la crema** *lah KREH-mah*

creamed **puré** *poor-REH*

credit card **una tarjeta de crédito** *OO-nah tahr-HEH-tah dhay KREH-dhee-toh*

CRUCE PELIGROSO (m.) *KROO-seh peh-lee-GROH-so* DANGEROUS CROSSROADS

cts. (centavos) *sehn-TAH-bos* cents

CUIDADO *kwee-dh-AH-dho* CAREFUL, CAUTION

CUIDADO CON EL TREN *kwee-dh-AH-dho kohn ehl trehn* RAILROAD CROSSING

cup **una taza** *OO-nah TAH-sah*

CURVA PELIGROSA (f.) *KOOR-bah pehl-ee-GROH-sah* DANGEROUS CURVE

customs **la aduana** *lah ah-dh-WAH-nah*

D

daily **al día** *ahl DHEE-ah;* **por día** *pohr DHEE-ah*

DAMAS (f.) *dh-AH-mahs* LADIES

dance **un baile** *oon BAH-ee-leh*

danger **peligro** *peh-LEE-gro*

dark **obscuro** *ohb-SKOO-ro*

day **el día** *ehl DHEE-ah*

dead **muerto** *MWEHR-toh;* **muerta** *MWEHR-tah*

dear me! **¡Dios mío!** *dhee-OHS MEE-o*

decaffeinated **descafeinado** *dh-ehs-kah-feh-ee-NAH-dho*

December **diciembre** *dhee-see-EHM-breh*

dentist **el (la) dentista** *ehl (lah) dhen-TEES-tah*

department store **el almacén** *ehl ahl-mah-SEHN*

DERECHA (f.) *dh-eh-REH-chah* RIGHT

DESCUENTOS (m.) *dh-ehs-KWEHN-tohs* DISCOUNTS

DESPACIO *dh-ehs-PAH-see-oh* SLOW

dessert **postre** *POH-streh*

DESVIACION (f.) *dh-ehs-bee-ah-see-OHN* DETOUR

diapers **los pañales** *lohs pah-ny-AH-lehs*

dictionary **el diccionario** *ehl dh-eek-see-o-NAH-ree-o*

dining room **el comedor** *ehl koh-meh-DHOR*

dinner **la cena** *lah SEH-nah*

DIRECCION PROHIBIDA (f.) *dh-ee-rehk-see-OHN pro-ee-BEE-dh-ah* NO ENTRY

DIRECCION UNICA (f.) *dh-ee-rehk-see-OHN OO-nee-kah* ONE-WAY STREET

dirty **sucio** *SOO-see-o;* dirty water **agua sucia** *AH-gwah SOO-see-ah*

dizzy, I feel **estoy aturdido** (man); **aturdida** (woman); *ehs-TOY ah-toor-DHEE-dho (ah-toor-DHEE-dha)*

do you speak English? **¿habla usted inglés?** *AH-blah oos-TEH-dh een-GLEHS;* French **francés** *frahn-SEHS;* German **alemán** *ah-leh-MAHN;* Greek **griego** *gree-EH-go;* Italian **italiano** *ee-tah-lee-AH-no*

dollar **el dólar** *ehl dh-OH-lahr*

don't mention it (you're welcome) **de nada** *dhay NAH-dha;* **por nada** *pohr NAH-dha;* **no hay de qué** *noh AH-ee dhay kay*

don't tell me! **¡no me diga!** *noh meh dh-EE-gah*

down **abajo** *ah-BAH-ho;* **debajo** *dhay-BAH-ho*

dozen **una docena** *OO-nah dho-SEH-nah*

dress **un vestido** *oon behs-TEE-dho*

drip (leak) **el escape** *ehl ehs-KAH-peh*

drugstore **la farmacia** *lah fahr-MAH-syah*

Dutch, I am **soy holandés** (man) *soy o-lahn-dh-EHS;* **holandesa** (woman) *o-lahn-dh-EHS-ah*

E

each **cada** *KAH-dha*

early **temprano** *tehm-PRAH-no*

EE.UU. (Estados Unidos) *ehs-TAH-dhos oo-NEE-dhos* United States (U.S.)

eggs **huevos** *WEH-bos;* scrambled eggs **huevos revueltos** *WEH-bos reh-BWEHL-tos;* omelet **tortilla** *tor-TEE-yah*

electricity **la electricidad** *lah eh-lehk-tree-see-dh-AH-dh*

eleven **once** *OHN-seh*

embassy **la embajada** *lah ehm-bah-HAH-dha*

emergency **una emergencia** *OO-nah ehm-ehr-HEHN-see-ah*

empty **vacío** *bah-SEE-o*

EMPUJE *ehm-POO-heh* PUSH

EN VENTA *ehn BEHN-tah* ON SALE

England **la Inglaterra** *lah een-glah-TEHR-rah*

English, I am **soy inglés** (man) *soy een-GLEHS;* **inglesa** (woman) *een-GLEHS-ah*

ENTRADA (f.) *ehn-TRAH-dha* ENTRANCE

ENTRADA PROHIBIDA (f.) *ehn-TRAH-dha pro-ee-BE-dha* KEEP OUT

ENTRE SIN GOLPEAR *EHN-treh seen gohl-peh-AHR* ENTER WITHOUT KNOCKING

envelope **un sobre** *oon SOH-breh*

EQUIPAJE (m.) *eh-kee-PAH-heh* BAGGAGE

error **un error** *oon ehr-ROHR*

ESCUELA (f.) *ehs-KWEH-lah* SCHOOL

ESTACION (f.) *ehs-tah-SYOHN* STATION

ESTACIONAMIENTO PROHIBIDO (m.) *ehs-tah-syohn-ah-mee-EHN-toh pro-ee-BEE-dho* NO PARKING

ESTANCO (m.) *ehs-TAHN-ko* TOBACCO SHOP

ESTIMADOS GRATIS (m.) *ehs-tee-MAH-dhos GRAH-tees* FREE ESTIMATES

evening **la noche** *lah NOH-cheh*

every **cada** *KAH-dha*

everybody **todo el mundo** *TOH-dho ehl MOON-dho*

exchange **el cambio** *ehl KAHM-bee-o*

excursion **la excursión** *lah ehs-koor-SYOHN*

excuse me **perdóneme** *pehr-DHOH-neh-meh;* **con permiso** *kohn pehr-MEE-so*

exit **la salida** *lah sah-LEE-dha*

expensive **caro** *KAH-ro;* less expensive **menos caro** *MEH-nos KAH-ro*

express train **el expreso** *ehl ehs-PREH-so*

eye **el ojo** *ehl OH-ho*

eye glasses **las gafas** *lahs GAH-fahs*

F

facing the courtyard **dando al patio** *DAHN-dho ahl PAH-tee-o;* —the garden —**al jardín** *ahl hahr-DHEEN;* —the street **a la calle** *ah lah KAH-yeh*

family **la familia** *lah fah-MEEL-yah*

far **lejos** *LEH-hos;* far from **lejos de** *LEH-hos dhay*

fare **la tarifa** *lah tah-REE-fah*

fast **rápido** *RAH-pee-dho*

father **el padre** *ehl PAH-dh-reh*

faucet **el grifo** *ehl GREE-fo*

fault **la culpa** *lah KOOL-pah*

February **febrero** *feh-BREH-ro*

FERIA (f.) *FEH-ree-ah* FAIR (country fair)

fever **la fiebre** *lah fee-EH-breh*

film **la película** *lah peh-LEE-koo-lah*

fine **bueno** *BWEH-no;* **bien** *bee-YEHN;* it's fine! **¡está bien!** *ehs-TAH-bee-YEHN*

fire **el fuego** *ehl FWEH-go*

first **primero** *pree-MEH-ro;* **primera** *pree-MEH-rah*

fish **el pescado** *ehl pehs-KAH-dho*

flag **la bandera** *lah bahn-dh-EH-rah*

flashlight **una linterna eléctrica** *OO-nah leen-TEHR-nah eh-LEHK-tree-kah*

flight (plane) **el vuelo** *ehl BWEH-lo;* to fly **volar** *bo-LAHR*

fly (insect) **una mosca** *OO-nah MOH-skah;* there is a fly in my soup! **¡hay una mosca en mi sopa!** *AH-ee OO-nah MOH-skah ehn mee SOH-pah*

food **la comida** *lah ko-MEE-dhah;* **el alimento** *ehl ah-lee-MEHN-toh*

foot **el pie** *ehl pee-EH*

for **para** *PAH-rah*

fork **un tenedor** *oon teh-neh-dh-OHR*

forty **cuarenta** *kwah-REHN-tah*
four **cuatro** *KWAH-tro*
fourteen **catorce** *kah-TOHR-seh*
fourth **cuarto** *KWAHR-toh*
free **gratis** *GRAH-tees*
fresh water **agua fresca** *AH-gwah FREHS-kah*
Friday **viernes** *bee-EHR-nehs*
fried **frito** *FREE-toh*
friend **el amigo** *ehl ah-MEE-go* (man); **la amiga** *lah ah-MEE-gah*
(woman)
friendly **amable** *ah-MAH-bleh*
FRIO (m.) *FREE-o* COLD
from **de** *dhay*
fruit **la fruta** *lah FROO-tah*
FUMADOR (m.) *foo-mah-dh-OHR* SMOKING CAR (ROOM)
funny **cómico** *KOH-mee-ko*

G
games **juegos** (m.) *HWEH-gos*
GANGAS (f.) *GAHN-gahs* BARGAINS
garlic **el ajo** *ehl AH-ho*
gas **gas** (m.) *gahss*
gasoline (petrol) **gasolina** (f.) *gah-so-LEE-nah*
generally **por lo general** *pohr loh hehn-eh-RAHL*
gentleman **el señor** *ehl seh-ny-OHR;* **el caballero** *ehl kah-bah-YEH-ro*
German, I am **soy alemán** (man) *soy ah-leh-MAHN;* **alemana** (woman)
ah-leh-MAHN-ah
get a doctor **llame a un doctor** *YAH-meh ah oon dh-ohk-TOHR*
get help right away **busque ayuda rápido** *BOOS-keh ah-YOO-dhah RAH-*
pee-dho
gift **un regalo** *oon reh-GAH-lo*
girl **la muchacha** *lah moo-CHAH-chah;* **la chica** *lah CHEE-kah*
GIROS POSTALES (m.) *HEE-ros pos-STAHL-ehs* MONEY ORDERS
give me **déme** *DHAY-meh;* give us **dénos** *DHAY-nos*
glass (drinking) **un vaso** *oon BAH-so*
gloves **guantes** *GWAHN-tehs*
go away! **¡váyase!** *BAH-yah-seh*
go down **bajar** *bah-HAHR*
go in **entrar** *ehn-TRAHR*
go out **salir** *sah-LEER*
go shopping **ir de compras** *eer dhay KOHM-prahs*
go to bed **acostarse** *ah-kos-TAHR-seh*
go up **subir** *soo-BEER*
God **Dios** *dhee-OHS*
GOLPEE, POR FAVOR *GOHl-peh-eh, pohr fah-BOHR* KNOCK, PLEASE
good **bueno** *BWEH-no;* **buena** *BWEH-nah*
good afternoon **buenas tardes** *BWEH-nahs TAHR-dh-ehs*

good-bye **adiós** *ah-dhee-OHS*
good day **buenos días** *BWEH-nos DHEE-ahs*
good evening **buenas noches** *BWEH-nahs NOH-chehs*
good idea **buena idea** *BWEH-nah ee-dh-EH-ah*
good morning **buenos días** *BWEH-nos DHEE-ahs*
good night **buenas noches** *BWEH-nahs NOH-chehs*
GRATIS *GRAH-tees* FREE
gray **gris** *greess*
Great Britain **la Gran Bretaña** *lah grahn breh-TAH-ny-ah*
Greek, I am **soy griego** (man) *soy gree-YAY-go;* **griega** (woman) *gree-YAY-gah*
green **verde** *BEHR-dhe*
greetings **saludos** *sah-LOO-dhos*
guide **guía** *GEE-ah*
guisantes *gee-SAHN-tehs* green peas
gum (chewing) **el chicle** *ehl CHEE-kleh*

H

h. (hora) *OH-rah* hour
half **medio** *MEHDH-yo;* **la mitad** *lah mee-TAHDH*
ham **el jamón** *ehl hah-MOHN*
handbag **la bolsa** *lah BOHL-sah*
hang up! (on telephone) **¡cuelgue!** *KWEHL-geh*
happy **feliz** *feh-LEESS*
hard-boiled egg **un huevo duro** *oon WEH-bo DHOO-ro*
have a nice day! **¡pase un buen día!** *PAH-seh oon bwehn DHEE-ah*
he **él** *ehl*
headache **un dolor de cabeza** *oon dh-oh-LOHR dhay kah-BEH-sah*
heart **el corazón** *ehl koh-rah-SOHN*
heat **el calor** *ehl kah-LOHR*
heavy (in weight) **pesado** *peh-SAH-dho*
HECHO EN . . . *EH-cho ehn* MADE IN . . .
helado *eh-LAH-dho* ice cream
hello! **¡hola!** *OH-lah;* (on phone) **¡diga!** *DHEE-gah*
help! **¡socorro!** *soh-KOHR-ro*
help me, please **ayúdeme, por favor** *ah-YOO-dh-eh-meh, pohr fah-BOHR*
here **aquí** *ah-KEE*
here it is! **¡aquí lo tiene usted!** *ah-KEE loh TYHEN-eh oos-TEH-dh*
hold the line (on phone) **no cuelgue** *noh KWEHL-geh*
HOMBRES (m.) *OHM-brehs* MEN
HORAS DE SERVICIO (f.) *OH-rahs dhay sehr-VEES-yo* SERVING HOURS
hospital **el hospital** *ehl os-pee-TAHL*
hot **caliente** *kah-LYEHN-teh;* it's very hot in my room **hace mucho calor en mi habitación** *AH-seh MOO-cho kah-LOHR ehn mee ah-bee-tah-SYOHN*
hot chocolate **chocolate caliente** *cho-ko-LAH-teh kah-LYEHN-teh*
hour **la hora** *lah OH-rah*
how **como** *KOH-mo*

how are things? **¿qué tal?** *kay tahl*
how are you? **¿cómo está usted?** *KOH-mo ehs-TAH oos-TEH-dh*
how do you say . . . in spanish? **¿cómo se dice . . . en español?** *KOH-mo seh*
  DHEE-seh . . . ehn ehs-pah-ny-OHL
how far? **¿a qué distancia?** *ah kay dhees-TAHN-syah*
how long? **¿cuánto tiempo?** *KWAHN-toh TYEHM-po*
how many? **¿cuántos?** *KWAHN-tohs*
how much? **¿cuánto?** *KWAHN-toh*
huevos (m.) *WEH-bos* eggs
hundred **ciento** *SYEHN-toh*
hurry up! **¡dése prisa!** *DHAY-seh PREE-sah*
husband **el marido** *ehl mah-REE-dho*

I

I **yo** *yoh*
I beg your pardon **perdóneme** *pehr-DHOH-neh-meh*
I certainly hope so! **¡ojalá!** *o-hah-LAH*
I certainly think so! **¡ya lo creo!** *yah loh KREH-o*
I don't like . . . **no me gusta . . .** *noh meh GOOS-tah*
I don't understand **no comprendo** *noh kohm-PREHN-dho;* **no entiendo**
  noh ehn-TYEHN-dho
I don't want **no quiero** *noh-KEYH-ro*
I hate **detesto** *dh-eh-TEHS-toh*
I have a family **tengo una familia** *TEHN-go OO-nah fah-MEEL-yah*
I have a husband **tengo un marido** *TEHN-go oon mah-REE-dho*
I have a problem **tengo un problema** *TEHN-go oon pro-BLEH-mah*
I have a wife **tengo una esposa** *TEHN-go OO-nah ehs-POH-sah*
I have no money **no tengo dinero** *noh TEHN-go dhee-NEH-ro*
I like . . . **me gusta . . .** *meh GOOS-tah*
I lost my . . . **perdí mi . . .** *pehr-DHEE mee*
I said . . . **dije . . .** *DHEE-heh*
I speak a little Spanish **hablo español un poco** *AH-blo ehs-pah-ny-OHL oon*
  POH-ko
I understand **comprendo** *kohm-PREHN-dho;* **entiendo** *ehn-TYEHN-dho*
I visited . . . **visité . . .** *bee-see-TEH*
I went . . . **fui . . .** *fwee*
I would like . . . **quisiera . . .** *kee-SYEH-rah*
ice cream **el helado** *ehl eh-LAH-dho*
ice cubes **hielo en cubitos** *YEH-lo ehn koo-BEE-tos*
if **si** *see*
I'll scream! **¡grito!** *GREE-toh*
I'm afraid **tengo miedo** *TEHN-go MYEH-dho*
I'm bleeding **me desangro** *meh dh-eh-SAHN-gro*
I'm going . . . **me voy . . .** *meh boy*
I'm going to have . . . **voy a tomar . . .** *boy ah toh-MAHR*
I'm hungry **tengo hambre** *TEHN-go AHM-breh*
I'm lost **me he perdido** *meh eh pehr-DHEE-dho*

I'm resting   **yo descanso**   *yoh dhay-SKAHN-so*
I'm right   **tengo razón**   *TEN-go rah-SOHN*
I'm sad   **estoy triste**   *eh-TOY TREE-steh*
I'm sick   **estoy enfermo** (man)   *ehs-TOY ehn-FEHR-mo;*   **enferma**   (woman)
   ehn-FEHR-mah
I'm sleepy   **tengo sueño**   *TEHN-go SWEH-ny-o*
I'm sorry   **lo siento**   *loh see-EHN-toh*
I'm thirsty   **tengo sed**   *TEHN-go SEH-dh*
I'm tired   **estoy cansado** (man)   *ehs-TOY kahn-SAH-dho;*   **cansada** (woman)
   kahn-SAH-dha
I'm wounded   **estoy herido**   *ehs-TOY ehr-EE-dho*
I'm wrong   **no tengo razón**   *noh TEHN-go rah-SOHN*
immediately   **en seguida**   *ehn seh-GEE-dha;*   **pronto**   *PROHN-toh*
in   **en**   *ehn;*   in a minute   **en un momento**   *ehn oon mo-MEHN-toh*
in front of me   **delante de mí**   *dh-eh-LAHN-teh dhay mee*
in the afternoon   **por la tarde**   *pohr lah TAHR-dh-eh*
in the distance   **a lo lejos**   *ah loh LEH-hos*
included   **incluido**   *een-kloo-EE-dho*
infant   **el bebé**   *ehl bay-BAY*
INFORMACIONES (f.)   *een-for-mah-see-OH-nehs*   INFORMATION
insects   **insectos**   *een-SEHK-tos*
inside   **dentro**   *dh-EHN-tro*
introduce   **presentar**   *preh-sehn-TAHR;*   this is my wife   **yo le presento a mi
   esposa**   *yoh leh preh-SEHN-toh-ah-mee ehs-POH-sah;*   my husband   **mi
   marido**   *mee mah-REE-dho*
iodine   **yodo**   *YOH-dho*
Irish, I'm   **soy irlandés** (man)   *soy eer-lahn-dh-EHS;*   **irlandesa** (woman)
   eer-lahn-dh-EH-sah
iron (press), to   **planchar**   *plahn-CHAHR*
is . . . ?   **¿es . . . ?**   *ehs;*   **¿está . . . ?**   *ehs-TAH*
is it closed?   **¿está cerrado?**   *ehs-TAH sehr-RAH-dho*
is it correct?   **¿es correcto?**   *ehs kor-REHK-toh*
is it necessary?   **¿es necesario?**   *ehs neh-seh-SAH-ree-o*
is it open?   **¿está abierto?**   *ehs-TAH ah-bee-EHR-toh*
is there?   **¿hay?**   *AH-ee*
is there any mail for me?   **¿hay correo para mí?**   *AH-ee kohr-REH-o PAH-rah mee*
it doesn't matter   **no importa**   *noh eem-POHR-tah*
Italian, I am   **soy italiano** (man)   *soy ee-tah-lee-AH-no;*   **italiana** (woman)
   ee-tah-lee-AH-nah
Italy   **Italia**   *ee-TAH-lee-ah*
it's a pleasure   **es un placer**   *ehs oon plah-SEHR*
it's dangerous   **es peligroso**   *ehs peh-lee-GROH-so*
it's early   **es temprano**   *ehs tehm-PRAH-no*
it's for me   **es para mí**   *ehs PAH-rah mee;*   it's for us   **es para nosotros**
   ehs PAH-rah no-SOH-tros;   it's for you   **es para usted**   *ehs PAH-rah oos-
   TEH-dh*
it's funny   **es cómico**   *ehs KOH-mee-ko*

it's late **es tarde** *ehs TAHR-dh-eh*
it's my fault **es culpa mía** *ehs KOOL-pah MEE-ah*
it's not possible **no es posible** *noh ehs po-SEE-bleh*
it's possible **es posible** *ehs po-SEE-bleh*
it's your fault **es culpa suya** *ehs KOOL-pah SOO-yah*
IZQUIERDA (f.) *ees-kee-EHR-dhah* LEFT

J

jabón (m.) *hah-BOHN* soap
jam (preserves) **la mermelada** *lah mehr-meh-LAH-dh-ah*
jamón (m.) *hah-MOHN* ham
January **enero** *eh-NEH-ro*
JOYAS (f.) *HOH-yahs* JEWELRY
juice **el jugo** *ehl HOO-go*
July **julio** *HOOL-ee-o*
June **junio** *HOON-ee-o*
just a minute **un momento** *oon mo-MEHN-toh*

K

keep it **guárdelo** *GWAHR-dhe-lo*
keep your hands to yourself **quite sus manos** *KEE-teh soos MAH-nos*
key **la llave** *lah YAH-beh*
kind (friendly) **amable** *ah-MAH-bleh*
kitchen **la cocina** *lah ko-SEE-nah*
knife **un cuchillo** *oon koo-CHEE-yo*

L

lady **la dama** *lah dh-AH-mah*
lamp **la lámpara** *lah-LAHM-pah-rah*
large **grande** *GRAHN-dh-eh;* larger **más grande** *mahs GRAHN-dh-eh*
last week **la semana pasada** *lah seh-MAH-nah pah-SAH-dha*
late **tarde** *TAHR-dh-eh*
lavatory **el lavabo** *ehl lah-BAH-bo*
laxative **el laxante** *ehl lahk-SAHN-teh*
leather **el cuero** *ehl KWEH-ro*
leave me alone! **¡váyase!** *BAH-yah-seh*
lechuga (f.) *leh-CHOO-gah* lettuce
left (opposite of right) **izquierda** *ees-kee-EHR-dhah*
legal services **servicios legales** *sehr-BEE-see-os leh-GAH-lehs*
legumbres (f.) *leh-GOOM-brehs* vegetables
lemon **el limón** *ehl lee-MOHN*
lemonade **la limonada** *lah lee-mo-NAH-dh-ah*
less **menos** *MEH-nos*
let me get by, please **con permiso, déjeme pasar, por favor** *kohn pehr-MEE-so, dhay-heh-meh pah-SAHR, pohr fah-BOHR*
let's go! **¡vamos!** *BAH-mos*
let's leave, let's go away! **¡vámonos!** *BAH-mo-nos*

letter   **una carta**   *OO-nah KAHR-tah*
LIBRE   *LEE-breh*   VACANT, UNOCCUPIED
light (color)   **claro**   *KLAH-ro;*   (in weight)   **ligero**   *lee-HEH-ro*
LISTA DE CORREOS   *LEE-stah dhay kohr-REH-os*   GENERAL DELIVERY (POST OFFICE)
listen to me   **escúcheme**   *ehs-KOO-cheh-meh*
little (in size)   **pequeño**   *peh-KEHN-yo;*   (in quantity)   **poco**   *POH-ko*
look   **¡mire!**   *MEE-reh*
look out!   **¡cuidado!**   *kwee-dh-AH-dho*
lost and found office   **la oficina de objetos perdidos**   *lah o-fee-SEE-nah dhay ob-HEH-tos pehr-dh-EE-dhos*
low   **bajo**   *BAH-ho*
lunch   **el almuerzo**   *ehl ahl-MWEHR-so*

M

machine does not work   **la máquina no funciona**   *lah MAH-kee-nah noh foon-see-OH-nah*
madam   **señora**   *seh-ny-OHR-ah* (abbreviation is **Sra.**)
magazine   **una revista**   *OO-nah reh-BEES-tah*
mail   **el correo**   *ehl kohr-REH-o*
mailbox   **el buzón**   *ehl boo-SOHN*
man   **un hombre**   *oon OHM-breh*
manager   **el gerente**   *ehl heh-REHN-teh*
many   **muchos**   *MOO-chos;*   many things   **muchas cosas**   *MOO-chahs KOH-sahs*
map   **un mapa**   *oon MAH-pah*
March   **marzo**   *MAHR-so*
mashed potatoes   **puré** (m.) **de patatas**   *poo-REH dhay pah-TAH-tahs*
matches   **cerillas** (f.)   *sehre-EE-yahs*
May   **mayo**   *MAH-yo*
may I . . . ?   **¿permite usted . . . ?**   *pehr-MEE-teh oos-TEH-dh*
maybe   **quizá**   *kee-SAH*
MAYOR VENTA (f.)   *mah-YOHR BEHN-tah*   MAJOR SALE
meal   **la comida**   *lah ko-MEE-dhah*
meat   **la carne**   *lah KAHR-neh*
menu   **el menú**   *ehl meh-NOO*
message   **el mensaje**   *ehl mehn-SAH-heh*
middle of July   **a mediados de julio**   *ah meh-dhee-AH-dhos dhay HOOL-ee-o*
midnight   **la medianoche**   *lah meh-dhee-ah-NOH-cheh*
milk   **la leche**   *lah LEH-cheh*
minute   **un minuto**   *oon mee-NOO-toh*
miss   **la señorita**   *lah seh-ny-o-REE-tah* (abbreviation is **Srta.**)
miss the train   **perder el tren**   *pehr-dh-EHR ehl trehn*
mistake   **un error**   *oon ehr-ROHR*
mister   **el señor**   *ehl seh-ny-OHR*
Monday   **el lunes**   *ehl LOO-nehs*
money   **el dinero**   *ehl dhee-NEH-ro*

money exchange **cambio de moneda** *KAHM-bee-o dhay mo-NEH-dha*
month **el mes** *ehl mehs*
more **más** *mahs*
mother **la madre** *lah MAh-dh-reh*
motorcycle **una motocicleta** *OO-nah mo-toh-see-KLEH-tah*
movies, at the **al cine** *ah! SEE-neh*
Mr. **señor** *seh-ny-OHR* (abbreviation is **Sr.**)
Mrs. **señora** *seh-ny-OH-rah* (abbreviation is **Sra.**)
much **mucho** *MOO-cho*
MUJERES (f.) *moo-HEH-rehs* WOMEN
museum **el museo** *ehl moo-SEH-o*
my daughter **mi hija** *mee EE-hah*
my family **mi familia** *mee fah-MEEL-yah*
my God! **¡Dios mío** *dhee-OHS MEE-o*
my husband **mi marido** *mee mah-REE-dho*
my money **mi dinero** *mee dhee-NEH-ro*
my purse **mi bolsa** *mee BOHL-sah*
my son **mi hijo** *mee EE-hoh*
my wallet **mi cartera** *mee kahr-TEH-rah*
my wife **mi esposa** *mee ehs-POH-sah*
my wristwatch **mi reloj de pulsera** *mee reh-LOH dhay pool-SEH-rah*

N
name **el nombre** *ehl NOHM-breh*
napkin **la servilleta** *lah sehr-bee-YEH-tah*
nationality **la nacionalidad** *lah nah-see-nah-lee-dh-AH-dh*
naturally **naturalmente** *nah-toor-ahl-MEHN-teh*
near **cerca de** *SEHR-kah dhay;* **cercano** *sehr-KAH-no*
never **nunca** *NOON-kah*
next to **al lado de** *ahl LAH-dho dhay*
next week **la semana próxima** *lah seh-MAHN-ah PROHK-see-mah*
night **la noche** *lah NOH-cheh*
nightclub **el cabaret** *ehl kah-bah-REHT*
nine **nueve** *NWEH-beh*
nineteen **diez y nueve** *dhee-EHS ee NWEH-beh*
ninety **noventa** *no-BEHN-tah*
ninth **noveno** *no-BEH-no*
no **no** *noh*
NO FUMADORES *noh foo-mah-dh-OHR-ehs* NO SMOKERS
NO OBSTRUYA LA ENTRADA *noh ob-STROO-yah lah ehn-TRAH-dha* DO NOT
    BLOCK ENTRANCE
no problem! **¡no hay problema!** *noh AH-ee proh-BLEHM-ah*
NO TOCAR *noh toh-KAHR* DO NOT TOUCH
no way! **¡de ninguna manera!** *dhay neen-GOO-nah mah-NEH-rah*
noise **el ruido** *ehl RWEE-dho*
none **ninguno** *neen-GOO-no*
not **no** *noh*

nothing **nada** *NAH-dh-ah;* nothing more **nada más** *NAH-dh-ah mahs*
November **noviembre** *no-be-EHM-breh*
now **ahora** *ah-OHR-ah*
number **el número** *ehl NOO-meh-ro*

O

OBRAS *OH-brahs* ROAD WORK
October **octubre** *ok-TOO-breh*
OCUPADO *o-koo-PAH-dho* OCCUPIED, IN USE
of course **claro que sí** *KLAH-ro kay see;* **por supuesto** *pohr soo-PWEH-sto*
office **la oficina** *lah o-fee-SEE-nah*
often **a menudo** *ah meh-NOO-dho*
okay, O.K. **está bien** *ehs-TAH bee-YEHN*
omelet **la tortilla** *lah tor-TEE-yah*
on **en** *ehn;* **sobre** *SOH-breh*
on the contrary **al contrario** *ahl kohn-TRAH-ree-o*
on vacation **de vacaciones** *dhay bah-kah-see-OHN-ehs*
once **una vez** *OO-nah behs*
one **un** *oon;* **una** *OO-nah*
only **solamente** *so-lah-MEHN-teh*
open **abierto** *ah-bee-EHR-toh*
orange **una naranja** *OO-nah nah-RAHN-hah*
outside **fuera** *FWEH-rah*
over here **acá** *ah-KAH*
over there **allá** *ah-YAH*
overcoat **el abrigo** *ehl ah-BREE-go*

P

paella (f.) *pah-EH-yah* rice with meat, green vegetables and shellfish
pain (ache) **un dolor** *oon dho-LOHR*
pan (m.) *pahn* bread
PARADA *pah-RAH-dhah* STOP
parade **un desfile** *oon dh-ehs-FEE-leh*
pardon me **perdóneme** *pehr-DHOH-neh-meh*
park **el parque** *ehl PAHR-kay;* to take a stroll in the park **dar un paseo en el parque** *dh-AHR oon pah-SEH-o ehn ehl PAHR-kay*
park, to (a vehicle) **estacionar** *ehs-tah-see-ohn-AHR;* **aparcar** *ah-pahr-KAHR*
party **una fiesta** *OO-nah fee-EHS-tah*
PASAJEROS (m.) *pah-sah-HEH-ros* PASSENGERS
PASO PROHIBIDO *PAH-so pro-ee-BEE-dho* NO ENTRY
passage **el pasaje** *ehl pah-SAH-heh*
passport lost **pasaporte perdido** *pah-sah-POHR-teh pehr-DHEE-dho*
pastry shop **una pastelería** *OO-nah pah-steh-leh-REE-yah*
patatas asadas (f.) *pah-TAH-tahs ah-SAH-dhas* roast potatoes; fried **fritas** *FREE-tahs*
payment **un pago** *oon PAH-go*
PEATONES (m.) *peh-ah-TOH-nehs* PEDESTRIANS

PELIGRO (m.) *peh-LEE-gro* DANGER; **DE MUERTE** *dhay moo-EHR-teh* OF DEATH

people **la gente** *lah HEHN-teh*

percent **por ciento** *pohr see-EHN-toh*

perhaps **quizá** *kee-SAH*

PERMITIDO FUMAR *pehr-mee-TEE-dho foo-MAHR* SMOKING PERMITTED

person **una persona** *OO-nah pehr-SOH-nah;* this person **esta persona** *EHS-tah pehr-SOH-nah*

pescado (m.) *pehs-KAH-dho* fish

pesetas (pts.) (f.) *peh-SEH-tahs* pesetas

pesos (m.) *PEH-sos* pesos

petrol (gasoline) **la gasolina** *lah gah-so-LEE-nah*

phone me **llámeme por teléfono** *YAH-meh-meh pohr teh-LEH-fo-no*

pick up (receiver of telephone) **descuelgue** *dh-ehs-KWEHL-geh*

pickpocket **un ratero** *oon rah-TEH-ro;* **una ratera** *OO-nah rah-TEH-rah*

pill **una píldora** *OO-nah PEEL-dho-rah*

pink **rosa** *ROH-sah*

pleasant **agradable** *ah-grah-DHAH-blay*

please **por favor** *pohr fah-BOHR*

pleased to meet you **el gusto es mío** *ehl GOOS-toh ehs MEE-o*

pleasure **el gusto** *ehl GOOS-toh;* **el placer** *ehl plah-SEHR*

pocket **el bolsillo** *ehl bohl-SEE-yo*

poison **el veneno** *ehl beh-NEH-no*

police **la policía** *lah po-lee-SEE-ah*

pollo (m.) *POH-yo* chicken

POR FAVOR *pohr fah-BOHR* PLEASE

porter **portero de equipajes** *pohr-TEH-ro dhay eh-kee-PAH-hehs*

postage stamp **un sello** *oon SEH-yo*

postres (m.) *POHS-trehs* desserts

potatoes **patatas** (f.) *pah-TAH-tahs;* **papas** (f.) *PAH-pahs*

PRECIO (m.) *PREH-see-o* PRICE

present (gift) **un regalo** *oon reh-GAH-lo*

preserves (jam) **la mermelada** *lah mehr-meh-LAH-dh-ah*

press (iron) **planchar** *plahn-CHAHR*

priest **el cura** *ehl KOO-rrah*

PRIVADO *pree-BAH-dho* PRIVATE

private bathroom **un cuarto de baño privado** *oon KWAHR-toh dhay BAH-ny-o pree-BAH-dho*

PROHIBIDO *pro-ee-BEE-dho* PROHIBITED

PROHIBIDO ADELANTAR *pro-ee-BEE-dho ah-dhay-lahn-TAHR* NO PASSING

PROHIBIDO APARCAR *pro-ee-BEE-dho ah-pahr-KAHR* NO PARKING

PROHIBIDO ENTRAR *pro-ee-BEE-dho ehn-TRAHR* KEEP OUT

PROHIBIDO FUMAR *pro-ee-BEE-dho foo-MAHR* NO SMOKING

pts. (pesetas) *peh-SEH-tahs* pesetas

PUESTO DE SOCORRO *PWEHS-toh dhay so-KOHR-ro* FIRST-AID STATION

purse **la bolsa** *lah BOHL-sah*

put this thing here **ponga esta cosa aquí** *POHN-gah EHS-tah KOH-sah ah-KEE;* put this thing there **ponga esta cosa allá** *POHN-gah EHS-tah KOH-sah ah-YAH*

Q

quality   **la calidad**   *lah kah-lee-dh-AH-dh*
question   **una pregunta**   *OO-nah preh-GOON-tah*
quick, quickly   **rápido**   *RAH-pee-dho;*   **pronto**   *PROHN-toh*
quiet   **quieto**   *kee-EH-toh*
quite enough, thank you   **bastante, gracias**   *bahs-TAHN-teh, GRAH-syahs*

R

radiator   **el radiador**   *ehl rah-dee-ah-dh-OHR*
railroad   **el ferrocarril**   *ehl fehr-roh-kahr-REEL*
rain   **la lluvia**   *lah YOO-bee-ah;*   is it raining?   **¿está lloviendo?**   *ehs-TAH yo-bee-EHN-dho*
raincoat   **un impermeable**   *oon eem-pehr-meh-AH-bleh*
razor blade   **una hojita de afeitar**   *OO-nah o-HEE-tah dhay ah-feh-ee-TAHR*
ready   **listo**   *LEE-sto*
REBAJAS (f.)   *reh-BAH-hahs*   SALE, BARGAINS
receipt   **un recibo**   *oon-reh-SEE-bo*
RECIEN PINTADO   *reh-see-EHN peen-TAH-dho*   WET PAINT
record (phonograph)   **un disco**   *oon DHEES-ko*
red   **rojo**   *ROH-ho*
repeat, please   **repita, por favor**   *reh-PEE-tah, pohr fah-BOHR*
RESERVADO   *reh-sehr-BAH-dho*   RESERVED
rest rooms   **los lavabos**   *lohs lah-BAH-bos*
RETRETES (m.)   *reh-TREH-tehs*   TOILETS, REST ROOMS
rice   **el arroz**   *ehl ahr-ROHS*
right (opposite of left)   **derecho**   *dh-eh-REH-cho*
right away   **pronto**   *PROHN-toh*
right now   **ahora mismo**   *ah-OH-rah MEES-mo*
ring me up (telephone)   **llámeme por teléfono**   *YAH-meh-meh pohr teh-LEH-fo-no*
roast beef   **el rosbif**   *ehl ros-BEEF*
round trip   **ida y vuelta**   *EE-dha ee BWEHL-tah*
running water   **el agua corriente**   *ehl AH-gwah kor-ree-EHN-teh*

S

SALA DE ESPERA (f.)   *SAH-lah dhay ehs-PEH-rah*   WAITING ROOM
salad   **la ensalada**   *lah ens-sah-LAH-dha*
SALDOS (m.)   *SAHL-dhos*   LIQUIDATION SALE
SALIDA (f.)   *sah-LEE-dha*   EXIT
SALIDA DE EMERGENCIA (f.)   *sah-LEE-dha dhay ehm-ehr-HEHN-see-ah*   EMERGENCY EXIT
salty   **salado**   *sah-LAH-dho*
Saturday   **el sábado**   *ehl SAH-bah-dho*
SE ALQUILA   *seh ahl-KEE-lah*   FOR RENT (FOR HIRE, TO LET)
SE HABLA INGLES   *seh AH-bleh een-GLEHS*   ENGLISH IS SPOKEN
SE PROHIBE ADELANTAR   *seh pro-EE-beh ah-dhay-lahn-TAHR*   NO PASSING
SE PROHIBE LA ENTRADA   *seh pro-EE-beh lah ehn-TRAH-dha*   KEEP OUT

SE VENDE *seh BEHN-dh-eh* FOR SALE

seat **un asiento** *oon ah-see-EHN-toh*

second **segundo** *seh-GOON-dho*

see you later **hasta luego** *AH-stah LWEH-go*

see you next week **hasta la semana próxima** *AH-stah lah seh-MAH-nah PROHK-see-mah*

see you soon **hasta pronto** *AH-stah PROHN-toh*

see you tomorrow **hasta mañana** *AH-stah mah-ny-AH-nah*

SELLOS (m.) *SEH-yos* POSTAGE STAMPS

SEMAFORO (m.) *seh-MAH-fo-ro* TRAFFIC LIGHTS

SENDERO (m.) PARA BICICLETAS *sehn-dh-EH-ro PAH-rah bee-see-KLEH-tahs* BICYCLE ROUTE

SENORES *seh-ny-OHR-ehs* GENTLEMEN

September **septiembre** *sehp-tee-EHM-breh*

service **el servicio** *ehl shr-BEE-see-o;* included **incluido** *een-kloo-EE-dho*

seven **siete** *see-EH-teh*

seventeen **diez y siete** *dhee-EHS ee see-EH-teh*

seventh **séptimo** *SEHP-tee-mo*

seventy **setenta** *seh-TEHN-tah*

several **varios** *BAH-ree-os*

she **ella** *EH-yah*

sherbet **sorbete** *sor-BEH-teh*

ship **el barco** *ehl BAHR-ko;* **buque** *BOO-keh;* **vapor** *bah-POHR*

shopping **ir de compras** *eer dhay KOHM-prahs*

show me **muéstreme** *MWEHS-treh-meh*

shower **la ducha** *lah dh-OO-chah*

shrimp **el camarón** *ehl kah-mah-ROHN*

shut your mouth **cierre la boca** *see-EHR-reh lah BOH-kah*

sick **enfermo** *ehn-FEHR-mo;* **enferma** *ehn-FEHR-mah*

sir **señor** *seh-ny-OHR*

six **seis** *SEH-ees*

sixteen **diez y seis** *dhee-EHS ee SEH-ees*

sixth **sexto** *SEHS-toh*

sixty **sesenta** *seh-SEHN-tah*

slowly **despacio** *dh-ehs-PAH-see-o*

small **pequeño** *peh-KEH-ny-o*

snack **un bocadillo** *oon bo-kah-dh-EE-yo*

soap **el jabón** *ehl hah-BOHN*

somebody, someone **alguien** *AHL-gee-ehn*

sopa *SOH-pah* soup

sorbete (m.) *sor-BEH-teh* sherbet

Spain **España** (f.) *ehs-PAH-ny-ah*

speak! **¡hable!** *AH-bleh*

special menu **el menú especial** *ehl mehn-OO ehs-peh-see-AHL*

spoon **la cuchara** *lah koo-CHAH-rah*

sports **los deportes** *lohs dhay-POHR-tehs*

Sr. (señor) *seh-ny-OHR* Mr., sir

Sra. (señora) *seh-ny-OH-rah*   Mrs., madam
Srta. (señorita) *seh-ny-oh-REE-tah*   Miss
stewardess (plane) **la azafata** *lah ah-sah-FAH-tah*
sticker (label) **la etiqueta** *lah eh-tee-KEH-tah*
stop! **¡deténgase!** *dhay-TEHN-gah-seh*
stop her! **¡deténgala!** *dhay-TEHN-gah-lah*
stop that man! **¡detenga a ese hombre!** *dahy-TEHN-gah ah EH-seh OHM-breh*
stop that person! **¡detenga a esa persona!** *dhay-TEHN-gah ah EH-sah pehr-SOH-nah*
stop that woman! **¡detenga a esa mujer!** *dhay-TEHN-gah ah EH-sah moo-HEHR*
stop thief! **¡al ladrón!** *ahl lah-dh-ROHN*
store **la tienda** *lah tee-EHN-dha*
straight away **pronto** *PROHN-toh*
strawberry **la fresa** *lah FREH-sah*
street **la calle** *lah KAH-yeh*
subway (tube) **el metro** *ehl MEH-tro*
sugar **el azúcar** *ehl ah-SOO-kahr*
suitcase **la maleta** *lah mah-LEH-tah*
summer excursion **excursión de verano** *ehs-koor-see-OHN dhay behr-AH-no*
Sunday **el domingo** *ehl dho-MEEN-go*
sure **seguro** *seh-GOO-ro*
syphilis **la sífilis** *lah SEE-fee-lees*

T

table **una mesa** *OO-nah MEH-sah*
tablet (pill) **un comprimido** *oon kohm-pree-MEE-dho*
tailor **el sastre** *ehl SAHS-treh*
take a trip **hacer un viaje** *ah-SEHR oon bee-AH-heh*
tap (faucet) **el grifo** *ehl GREE-fo*
tea **el té** *ehl teh*
teaspoon **la cucharita** *lah koo-chah-REE-tah*
telegram **el telegrama** *ehl teh-leh-GRAH-mah*
telephone **el teléfono** *ehl teh-LEH-fo-no*
telephone booth **la cabina telefónica** *lah kah-BEE-nah teh-leh-FOH-nee-kah*
television **la televisión** *lah teh-leh-bee-see-OHN*
tell me **dígame** *DHEE-gah-meh*
ten **diez** *dhee-EHS*
ternera (f.) *tehr-NEH-rah*   veal
thank you **gracias** *GRAH-syahs*
that's a good idea **es una buena idea** *ehs OO-nah BWEH-nah ee-dh-EH-ah*
that's all right **está bien** *ehs-TAH bee-YEHN*
that's funny **es cómico** *ehs KOH-mee-ko*
that's how it is! **¡es así!** *ehs ah-SEE*
that's right **eso es** *EH-so ehs*
theft **un robo** *oon ROH-bo*

there! **¡allá!** *ah-YAH*

there are . . . ; there is . . . **hay . . .** *AH-ee;* there aren't . . . ; there isn't . . . **no hay . . .** *noh AH-ee*

thermometer **el termómetro** *ehl tehr-MOH-meh-tro*

they **ellos** *EH-yos;* **ellas** *EH-yahs*

thief **un ladrón** *oon lah-dh-ROHN*

thing **la cosa** *lah KOH-sah*

third **tercero** *tehr-SEH-ro*

thirteen **trece** *TREH-seh*

thirty **treinta** *TREH-een-tah*

this evening **esta noche** *EHS-tah NOH-cheh*

thousand **mil** *meel*

three **tres** *trehs*

through **a través** *ah trah-BEHS*

Thursday **el jueves** *HWEH-behs*

ticket **un billete** *oon-bee-YEH-teh*

ticket window **la ventanilla** *lah behn-tah-NEE-yah*

time (hour) **la hora** *lah OH-rah;* what time is it? **¿qué hora es?** *kay OH-rah es*

timetable **el horario** *ehl o-RAH-ree-o*

tip (gratuity) **la propina** *lah pro-PEE-nah*

TIRAR *tee-RAHR* PULL

to **a** *ah*

toast (bread) **el pan tostado** *ehl pahn tos-TAH-dho;* **una tostada** *OO-nah tos-TAH-dhah*

tobacco **el tabaco** *ehl tah-BAH-ko*

today **hoy** *oy*

toilet paper (tissue) **el papel higiénico** *ehl pah-PEHL ee-hee-EHN-ee-ko*

toilets **los lavabos** *lohs lah-BAH-bos;* **los retretes** *lohs reh-TREH-tehs*

tomorrow **mañana** *mah-ny-AH-nah*

tonight **esta noche** *EHS-tah NOH-cheh*

too (also) **también** *tahm-bee-EHN*

too bad! **¡es lástima!** *ehs LAHS-tee-mah*

too much **demasiado** *dhay-mah-see-AH-dho*

TOQUE EL TIMBRE *TOH-kay ehl TEEM-breh* RING THE BELL

tourism **el turismo** *ehl too-REES-mo*

tourist **el (la) turista** *ehl (lah) too-REES-tah*

tourist office **la oficina de turismo** *lah-o-fee-SEE-nah dhay too-REES-mo*

towel **la toalla** *lah toh-AH-yah*

traffic **el tráfico** *ehl TRAH-fee-ko*

traffic light **el semáforo** *ehl seh-MAH-fo-ro*

train **el tren** *el trehn*

travel agency **una agencia de viajes** *OO-nah ah-HEHN-see-yah dhay bee-AH-hehs*

traveler's check **el cheque de viajeros** *ehl CHEH-kay dhay bee-ah-HEH-ros*

tube (subway) **el metro** *ehl MEH-tro*

Tuesday **el martes** *ehl MAHR-tehs*

TV set **el televisor** *ehl teh-leh-bee-SOHR*

twelve **doce** *DHOH-seh*

twenty **veinte** *BEH-een-teh*

twice **dos veces** *dhos BEH-sehs*

two **dos** *dhos*

two hundred **doscientos** *dhos-see-EHN-tos*

typewriter **una máquina de escribir** *OO-nah MAH-kee-nah dhay ehs-kree-BEER*

U

Ud., Vd. (usted) *oos-TEH-dh* you (singular, polite form)

Uds., Vds. (ustedes) *oos-TEH-dh-ehs* you (plural, polite form)

umbrella **el paraguas** *ehl pah-RAH-gwahs*

under **debajo** *dheh-BAH-ho*

understood **entendido** *ehn-tehn-DHEE-dho;* **comprendido** *kohm-prehn-DHEE-dho*

United States **los Estados Unidos** *lohs ehs-TAH-dhos oo-NEE-dhos*

until **hasta** *AH-stah*

up **arriba** *ahr-REE-bah*

urgent **urgente** *oor-HEHN-teh*

U.S.A. **EE.UU.**

usted *oos-TEH-dh* you

V

vacant room **una habitación libre** *OO-nah ah-bee-tah-see-OHN LEE-breh*

valise **la maleta** *lah mah-LEH-tah*

valuables **objetos de valor** *ob-HEH-tohs dhay bah-LOHR*

vanilla **la vainilla** *lah bah-ee-NEE-yah*

veal **la ternera** *lah tehr-NEH-rah*

vegetables **legumbres** *leh-GOOM-brehs*

VELOCIDAD LIMITADA (f.) *beh-lo-see-dh-AH-dh lee-mee-TAH-dh-ah* SPEED LIMIT

VENTA (f.) *BEHN-tah* SALE

very **muy** *mwee;* very much **muchísimo** *moo-CHEE-see-mo*

VIA (f.) *BEE-ah* TRACK

vinegar **el vinagre** *ehl bee-NAH-greh*

vino (m.) *BEE-no* wine

vomit **vomitar** *bo-mee-TAHR*

W

wait! **¡espere!** *ehs-PEH-reh*

waiter **el mesero** *ehl meh-SEH-ro;* **el camarero** *ehl kah-mah-REH-ro*

waiting room **la sala de espera** *lah SAH-lah dhay ehs-PEH-rah*

waitress **la mesera** *lah meh-SEH-rah;* **la camarera** *lah kah-mah-REH-rah*

wake me up **despiérteme** *dh-ehs-pee-EHR-teh-me*

wallet **la cartera de bolsillo** *lah kahr-TEH-rah dhay bohl-SEE-yo*
warm **caliente** *kah-lee-EHN-teh*
watch out! **¡cuidado!** *kwee-dh-AH-dho*
water **el agua** *ehl AH-gwah*
watermelon **la sandía** *lah sahn-dh-EE-ah*
W.C. (Water Closet) toilet
we **nosotros** *no-SOH-tros;* **nosotras** *no-SOH-trahs*
Wednesday **el miércoles** *ehl mee-EHR-ko-lehs*
week **la semana** *lah seh-MAH-nah*
weekend **el fin de semana** *ehl feen dhay seh-MAH-nah*
weekly **a la semana** *ah lah seh-MAH-nah*
well **bien** *bee-EHN*
what? **¿cómo?** *KOH-mo*
what did you say? **¿qué dijo?** *kay DHEE-ho*
what does this mean? **¿qué quiere decir esto?** *kay kee-EH-reh dhay-SEER EH-sto*
what time? **¿qué hora?** *kay OH-rah*
what time is it? **¿qué hora es?** *kay OH-rah ehs*
whatever **cualquier** *kwahl-kee-EHR*
what's that **¿qué es eso?** *kay ehs EH-so*
what's this? **¿qué es esto?** *kay ehs EH-sto*
what's your name? **¿cuál es su nombre?** *kwahl ehs soo NOHM-breh*
when? **¿cuándo?** *KWAHN-dho*
where? **¿dónde?** *DHOHN-dh-eh*
where are . . . ? **¿dónde están . . . ?** *DHOHN-dh-eh ehs-TAHN*
where are the children? **¿dónde están los niños?** *DHOHN-dh-eh ehs-TAHN lohs NEE-ny-os*
where are the women? **¿dónde están las mujeres?** *DHOHN-dh-eh ehs-TAHN lahs moo-HEH-rehs*
where can I find . . . ? **¿dónde puedo encontrar . . . ?** *DHOHN-dh-eh PWEH-dho ehn-kohn-TRAHR*
where is . . . ? **¿dónde está?** *DHOHN-dh-eh ehs-TAH*
which way . . . ? **¿por dónde?** *pohr DHOHN-dh-eh*
whipped potatoes **puré de patatas (de papas)** *poo-REH dhay pah-TAH-tahs (dhay PAH-pahs)*
white **blanco** *BLAHN-ko*
who **quien** *kee-EHN;* who are you? **¿quién es usted?** *kee-EHN ehs oos-TEH-dh;* who is it? **¿quién es?** *kee-EHN ehs;* who is talking? **¿quién habla?** *kee-EHN AH-blah*
why? **¿por qué?** *pohr kay*
wide **ancho** *AHN-cho*
wife **la esposa** *lah ehs-POH-sah*
willingly **de buena gana** *dhay BWEH-nah GAH-nah*
window **la ventana** *lah behn-TAH-nah*
wine **el vino** *ehl BEE-no*
with **con** *kohn;* without **sin** *seen*
woman **la mujer** *lah moo-HEHR*

women's rest room   **el lavabo para mujeres (damas)**   *ehl lah-BAH-bo PAH-rah moo-HEH-rehs (dh-AH-mahs)*
word   **la palabra**   *lah pah-LAH-brah*
wristwatch   **el reloj de pulsera**   *ehl reh-LOH dhay pool-SEH-rah*
write to me   **escríbame**   *ehs-KREE-bah-meh*

Y

year   **el año**   *ehl AH-ny-o*
yellow   **amarillo**   *ah-mah-REE-yo*
yes   **sí**   *see*
yesterday   **ayer**   *ah-YEHR*
yet   **todavía**   *toh-dha-BEE-ah;*   not yet   **todavía no**   *toh-dha-BEE-ah noh*
you   **usted**   *oos-TEH-dh* (polite, singular form);   **tú**   *too* (familiar, singular
   form when you know the person very well)
you are right   **usted tiene razón**   *oos-TEH-dh TYEHN-eh rah-SOHN*
you are wrong   **usted no tiene razón**   *oos-TEH-dh noh TYEHN-eh rah-SOHN*
you don't say!   **¡no me diga!**   *noh meh DHEE-gah*
you said   **usted dijo**   *oos-TEH-dh DHEE-ho*
your   **su**   *soo;*   **sus**   *soos*
you're welcome   **de nada**   *dhay NAH-dha;*   **por nada**   *pohr NAH-dha;*   **no
   hay de qué**   *noh AH-ee dhay kay*
youth hostel   **albergue juvenil** (m.)   *ahl-BEHR-geh hoo-behn-EEL*

Z

zipper   **un cierre relámpago**   *oon SYEHR-reh reh-LAHM-pah-go*
ZONA AZUL   *SOH-nah ah-SOOL*   LIMITED PARKING

Verb Drills and Tests with Answers Explained

The hundreds of verb forms in this part of the book will immerse you in the practice and improvement of your knowledge of Spanish verb forms, tenses, and uses. You will find a variety of types of questions to make your experience interesting, challenging, and rewarding. All verb forms used in the drills and tests are found in the preliminary pages, among the 501 verbs, and in the back pages of this book.

The answers and explanations begin on page 652. The explanations are brief and to the point, including references to pages in this book for study and review.

Tips: To figure out the correct verb form of the required tense, examine each sentence carefully. Take a good look at the subject of the verb. Is it 1st, 2d, or 3d person? Is it singular or plural? Is it masculine or feminine? Look for key elements that precede or follow the verb to determine the verb form and tense, for example, such words as yesterday, last week, today, at this moment, tomorrow, next year, a preposition, a certain conjunction, and other key words that indicate the need for an infinitive, present participle (**gerundio**), past participle, or the indicative or subjunctive moods in the required tense. The correct verb form depends on the sense and grammatical structure of the sentence.

The best way to learn irregular forms in the seven simple tenses is from study, practice, and experience. For the information of present and past participles, including irregulars, consult pages xi to xiii. As for the formation of regular verb forms, consult pages xxi to xxxix. For an easy way to form the seven compound tenses in Spanish, consult page xl from time to time.

Verb Test 1

SENTENCE COMPLETION

Directions: *Each of the following sentences contains a missing verb form. From the choices given, select the verb form of the tense that is required, according to the sense of the sentence, and write the letter of your choice on the line. At times, only the infinitive form is needed or a present or past participle. Answers and answer explanations begin on page 652.*

1. Margarita acaba de _____ un falda.
   A. compró   B. compré   C. comprar   D. compraste

2. Aquel hombre no _____ nadar.
   A. supe   B. sepa   C. sé   D. sabe

3. Hace mal tiempo. Está _____ .
   A. llover   B. lloviendo   C. llorando   D. llovido

4. Te _____ mañana, José. ¡Adiós!
   A. verá   B. veré   C. ver   D. vi

5. Me parece que María _____ pálida hoy.
    A. está   B. es   C. estuve   D. fue

6. Ricardo y Dora _____ cansados.
    A. son   B. están   C. fueron   D. fuimos

7. Voy a _____ temprano porque tomo el tren a las seis de la mañana.
    A. acostarse   B. me acuesto   C. acostarme   D. se acuesta

8. No _____ ganas de comer porque no me gusta esta sopa.
    A. tengo   B. quiero   C. tuvo   D. pago

9. Tengo que _____ la cocina y necesito una escoba.
    A. limpiar   B. limpio   C. limpiara   D. limpie

10. La madre ha _____ el cabello de la niña.
    A. lavado   B. lavando   C. lavar   D. lava

11. Mi abuelito _____ anoche.
    A. muere   B. murió   C. morí   D. morir

12. Aquí tiene usted el dinero que le _____ .
    A. quiero   B. necesito   C. debo   D. conozco

13. No se olviden ustedes que mañana la tienda _____ cerrada.
    A. será   B. estará   C. es   D. estuve

14. La maestra dijo a los alumnos: "_____ los libros en la página diez, por favor."
    A. Abren   B. Abrid   C. Abrieron   d. Abrían

15. En la ciudad de Madrid _____ divertirme porque hay muchos teatros y cines.
    A. puedes   B. puede   C. puedo   D. podemos

16. Los Reyes Magos han _____ muchos regalos a los niños.
    A. traemos   B. traen   C. traído   D. trajeran

17. Miguel _____ de escribir una carta.
    A. acaba   B. acabé   C. acabaré   D. acabar

18. Hace tres horas que (yo) _____ la televisión.
    A. miré   B. miró   C. miro   D. miraré

19. Cuando yo entré en la sala de estar, mi madre _____ y mi padre escribía.
    A. leía   B. leí   C. leyó   D. lee

20. Esta mañana mi hermana _____ en el cuarto de baño cuando me desperté.
    A. canté   B. cantará   C. cantaría   D. cantaba

DIALOGUE

Directions: *In the following dialogue thre are blank spaces indicating missing verb forms. Select the appropriate verb form according to the sense of what the speakers are saying and write the letter of your choice on the line. The situation is given below. First, read the entire selection once. During the second reading, make your choices.*

Situation: You are on the telephone talking to a clerk at the Teatro Colón. You are asking about a ticket for a show.

La señorita: ¡Teatro Colón! ¡Información y reservas!
Usted: ¿ _____ entradas para el sábado?

1. A. Había   B. Haber   C. Hubo   D. Hay

La señorita: Sí. Hay entradas de varios precios
Usted: _____ una por cien pesos, por favor.

2. A. Quise   B. Quiso   C. Quiera   D. Quisiera

La señorita: ¡Qué suerte tiene usted! Es la última entrada a este precio.
Usted: ¡Qué bueno! ¿Cómo _____ ?

3. A. pago   B. pagué   C. pagó   D. pagaba

La señorita: Si usted nos envía un cheque hoy, llegará mañana y le enviaremos la entrada.
Usted: ¿A qué hora _____ la función?

4. A. empecé   B. empezó   C. empieza   D. empiece

La señorita: A las dos y media de la tarde.
Usted: Muchas gracias. Usted _____ muy amable.

5. A. es   B. está   C. sea   D. fuera

PATTERN RESPONSES

Directions: *Answer the following questions in Spanish in complete sentences in the affirmative, using a pronoun for the subject. Add* **también** *(also). See page 519 for irregular verb forms that you cannot identify.*

Model: **Francisco comprende bien. ¿Y sus hermanos?**
                 (Francis understands well. And his brothers?)

You write: **Ellos comprenden bien, también.** (They understand well, also.)

1. Pedro estudia bien. ¿Y los otros alumnos?

   _____

2. Roberto escribe bien. ¿Y sus hermanas?

   _____

3. Sofía está leyendo un libro en la cama. ¿Y tú?

   _____

4. Isabel va de compras. ¿Y tus amigos?

   _____

5. Ricardo fue al cine. ¿Y tú?

   _____

6. Juan ha comido bien. ¿Y nosotros?

   _____

7. Ana está bien. ¿Y sus padres?

   _____

8. Juana se sentó. ¿Y las otras muchachas?

   _____

9. Mariana se lavó la cara. ¿Y tú?

   _____

10. Carlos sabe nadar. ¿Y tú?

    _____

11. Tú has cantado bien. ¿Y Luis?

    _____

12. El sénor Fuentes escogió un carro costoso. ¿Y usted?

    _____

13. Tú has terminado la lección. ¿Y los otros alumnos?

    _____

14. Yo escribí una carta. ¿Y Felipe?

    _____

15. Roberto tiene que estudiar. ¿Y tú?

_____

16. Yo he devuelto los libros a la biblioteca. ¿Y María?

_____

17. Manuel ha dicho la verdad. ¿Y nosotros?

_____

18. Tú te acuestas a las diez. ¿Y tus amigos?

_____

19. José ha leído un libro. ¿Y usted?

_____

20. Adolfo quiere hacerlo. ¿Y nosotros?

_____

Verb Test 4

SENTENCE COMPLETION

**Directions:** Each of the following sentences contains a missing verb form. From the choices given, select the verb form of the tense that is required, according to the sense of the sentence, and write the letter of your choice on the line. At times, only the infinitive form is needed or a present or past participle.

1. Cuando estábamos en Barcelona, _____ al cine todos los sábados.
  A. vamos   B. iremos   C. vayamos   D. íbamos

2. Cuando _____ en Málaga, íbamos a la playa todos los días.
  A. vivíamos   B. viviremos   C. vivamos   D. viviéramos

3. Mi madre era hermosa cuando _____ pequeña.
  A. es   B. fui   C. fue   D. era

4. ¿Qué hora _____ cuando usted telefoneó?
  A. era   B. fue   C. fuí   D. es

5. Cuando yo telefoneé, _____ las tres.
  A. fue   B. fueron   C. eran   D. son

6. Hacía dos horas que yo _____ la televisión cuando mi hermano entró.
  A. miraba   B. miró   C. miraré   D. miraría

7. Roberto dice que quiere _____ a mi casa.
  A. venir   B. viene   C. vendrá   D. vendría

8. ¿Has _____ mis guantes?
   A. ve   B. ver   C. visto   D. veía

9. Casandra dijo que _____ venir a mi casa.
   A. quería   B. quise   C. querrá   D. quiera

10. Ayer mi amigo _____ de Madrid.
    A. llegué   B. llegaste   C. llegó   D. llegará

11. Anoche María _____ a la iglesia.
    A. fui   B. fue   C. irá   D. iría

12. ¿Qué _____ en la calle ayer por la tarde?
    A. pasa   B. pasó   C. pasé   D. pasará

13. Antes de salir de casa esta mañana, yo _____ un buen desayuno.
    A. tomó   B. tomé   C. tome   D. tomara

14. Esta mañana salí de casa, tomé el autobús, y _____ a la escuela a las ocho.
    A. llego   B. llegó   C. llegué   D. llegaré

15. Yo _____ a Elena la semana pasada en el baile.
    A. conozco   B. conocí   C. conoció   D. conocería

16. ¿Cuándo _____ la verdad, José?
    A. sepa   B. supe   C. supiste   D. supiera

17. ¿El trabajo? Yo lo _____ la semana que viene.
    A. haré   B. hará   C. hice   D. hizo

18. El verano que viene nosotros _____ al campo.
    A. iremos   B. fuimos   C. vayamos   D. íbamos

19. María dice que _____ mañana.
    A. vine   B. vino   C. vendrá   D. venga

20. Si Miguel tuviera dinero, _____ a España.
    A. irá   B. iría   C. iré   D. va

DIALOGUE

Directions: In the following dialogue there are blank spaces indicating missing verb forms. Select the appropriate verb form according to the sense of what the speakers are saying and write the letter of your choice on the line. The situation is given below. First, read the entire selection once. During the second reading, make your choices.

Situation: Dolores, an exchange student from Barcelona, is visiting your school. The school principal has asked you to accompany her as a guide.

Dolores: ¡Qué escuela tan moderna! Me _____ mucho.
  1. A. gusto   B. gusta   C. gustaría   D. guste
Tú: Sí, es muy moderna.

Dolores: ¿Cuántos años hace que _____ (tú) a esta escuela?
  2. A. asistes   B. asiste   C. asistí   D. asistió

Tú: Ya _____ tres años.
  3. A. hace   B. hacen   C. haría   D. harían

Dolores: ¿A qué hora empieza y termina el día escolar?
Tú: _____ a las ocho y termina a las dos y media.
  4. A. Empieza   B. Empecé   C. Empezó   D. Empezará

Dolores: Me gustaría mucho asistir a unas clases.
Tú: Puedes _____ a mi clase de biología.
  5. A. viene   B. vine   C. venir   D. vino

Dolores: Me interesan más las lenguas extranjeras.
Tú: Entonces, _____ a mi clase de español.
  6. A. voy   B. vas   C. vamos   D. iríamos

CHANGING FROM ONE VERB TO ANOTHER

Directions: *The verb forms in the following statements are all in the imperative. Change each sentence by replacing the verb with the proper form of the verb in parentheses, keeping the imperative form. The verb form you write must be in the same person as the one you are replacing. In other words, you must recognize if the given verb form is 2d person singular (tú), 3d person singular (usted) or plural (ustedes), or 1st person plural (nosotros). See page 519 for irregular verb forms that you cannot identify.*

Model:	**Lea la oración. (escribir)** (Read the sentence.)
You write:	**Escriba la oración.** (Write the sentence.)

1. Lea la palabra. (decir)

   _____

2. Toma la leche. (beber)

   _____

3. Venga inmediatamente. (partir)

   _____

4. Abre la ventana. (cerrar)

   _____

5. Ponga la maleta sobre la cama. (tomar)

   _____

6. Pronuncie la palabra. (escribir)

   _____

7. Leamos la carta. (enviar)

   _____

8. Aprendan el poema. (leer)

   _____

9. Partamos ahora. (salir)

   _____

10. Siéntese, por favor. (levantarse)

    _____

11. Venda la casa. (comprar)

    _____

12. Salgan ahora. (venir)

    _____

13. Lávate. (secarse)

    _____

14. Compre estos guantes. (escoger)

_____

15. Cómalo. (beber)

_____

Verb Test 7

CHANGING FROM ONE TENSE TO ANOTHER

**Directions:** The following verb forms are all in the **future tense.** Change them to the **conditional,** keeping the same subject. See page 519 for irregular verb forms that you cannot identify.

Model: Yo iré.   You write: Yo iría.

1. Yo saldré.

_____

3. Nosotros seremos.

_____

5. María querrá.

_____

7. Ellos harán.

9. José bailará.

_____

11. Él será.

_____

13. Alberto se sentará.

_____

15. Nosotros nos sentaremos.

_____

17. Tú beberás.

_____

19. Miguel leerá.

_____

21. Vosotros iréis.

_____

23. Ellos vendrán.

_____

2. Ud. tendrá.

_____

4. Uds. estarán.

_____

6. Tú ganarás.

_____

8. Ella cantará.

10. Tú escribirás.

_____

12. Yo me lavaré.

_____

14. Nosotros nos sentiremos.

_____

16. Yo aprenderé.

_____

18. Ud. sabrá.

_____

20. Nosotros iremos.

_____

22. Uds. dirán.

_____

24. Ellas venderán.

_____

25. José y Dora serán.

_____

26. Los chicos comerán.

_____

27. María y yo haremos.

_____

28. Elena y Ana pondrán.

_____

29. Vosotros veréis.

_____

30. Yo estudiaré.

_____

Verb Test 8

PATTERN RESPONSES

Directions: *Answer the following questions in the negative in complete Spanish sentences. In answer (a), use* **No.** *In answer (b), use* **tampoco** *(either). Study models (a) and (b) carefully. Use a pronoun as subject in your answers. Place* **tampoco** *at the end of the sentence. See page 519 for irregular verb forms that you cannot identify.*

Model: (a) **¿Trabaja Ud.?**   You write: (a) **No. Yo no trabajo.**
                  (Do you work?)   (No. I don't work.)
            (b) **¿Y Carlos?**   (b) **Él no trabaja tampoco.**
                  (And Charles?)   (He does not work either.)

1. (a) ¿Saldrá Ud. de casa esta noche?

_____

   (b) ¿Y sus amigos?

_____

2. (a) ¿Quieres venir a mi casa esta tarde?

_____

   (b) ¿Y vosotros?

_____

3. (a) ¿Cantaste esta mañana?

_____

   (b) ¿Y María y José?

_____

4. (a) ¿Dices mentiras?

_____

   (b) ¿Y Francisca?

_____

5. (a) ¿Fue Ud. al cine ayer?

_____

   (b) ¿Y sus padres?

_____

CHANGING FROM ONE TENSE TO ANOTHER

*Directions: The following verb forms are all in the **imperfect indicative tense**. Change them to the **preterit tense**, keeping the same subject. See page 519 for irregular verb forms that you cannot identify.*

Model: **Yo trabajaba.** (I was working *or* I used to work.)

You write: **Yo trabajé.** (I worked.)

1. Yo iba al parque.

   _____

2. Elisa miraba la televisión.

   _____

3. El niño bebía la leche.

   _____

4. Margarita hacía la lección.

   _____

5. José hablaba mucho.

   _____

6. Mi amigo pagaba la cuenta.

   _____

7. Nosotros tomábamos el desayuno a las ocho.

   _____

8. Luis escribía cartas.

   _____

9. Marta aprendía la lección.

   _____

10. Los Señores López vivían en esta casa.

    _____

11. Yo hacía el trabajo.

    _____

12. La señorita traía el plato.

    _____

13. Pablo leía el poema.

    _____

14. Carlota decía la verdad.

    _____

15. La profesora abría el libro.

    _____

SENTENCE COMPLETION

Directions: *Each of the following sentences contains a missing verb form. From the choices given, select the verb form of the tense that is required, according to the sense of the sentence, and write the letter of your choice on the line. At times, only the infinitive form is needed or a present or past participle.*

1. Me _____ tomar una limonada ahora.
    A. gustaría   B. gusto   C. gusté   D. guste

2. Si mis padres tuvieran dinero, _____ a Barcelona.
    A. irían   B. irán   C. fueron   D. iban

3. María había _____ que vendría mañana.
    A. dijo   B. dice   C. dicho   D. decir

4. Claudia decía que _____ a mi casa esta tarde.
    A. vendría   B. viene   C. vine   D. venir

5. No se _____ aquí, Señor Robles, por favor.
    A. siente   B. sientes   C. sienta   D. sentó

6. Quiero que Jorge lo _____.
    A. hace   B. hacía   C. haga   D. hizo

7. Yo voy a _____ un café.
    A. tomo   B. tomar   C. tomando   D. tomado

8. En este momento, estoy _____ mis lecciones.
    A. estudiar   B. estudio   C. estudié   D. estudiando

9. El niño entró _____ en la casa.
    A. llorando   B. llorar   C. lloré   D. lloró

10. Prefiero que Juan lo _____ .
    A. hace   B. hizo   C. hice   D. haga

11. Dudo que Julia _____ a verme.
    A. viene   B. venga   C. vino   D. vendrá

12. Es necesario que Inés _____ bien.
    A. come   B. coma   C. comer   D. comiera

13. Le hablaré a Juan cuando _____ .
    A. llega   B. llegará   C. llegó   D. llegue

14. Me quedo aquí hasta que el Señor Hildago _____ .
    A. vuelve   B. volverá   C. vuelva   D. volvería

15. Démelo con tal que _____ bueno.
    A. sea   B. es   C. era   D. fue

16. Aunque Pablo _____ esta noche, no me quedo.
    A. viene   B. viniera   C. vendrá   D. venga

17. Busco un libro que _____ interesante.
    A. es   B. sea   C. será   D. sería

18. ¿Hay alguien aquí que _____ francés?
    A. hable   B. habla   C. hablara   D. hablaría

19. No hay nadie que _____ hacerlo.
    A. poder   B. puede   C. pueda   D. podrá

20. Yo insistí en que María lo _____ .
    A. hace   B. haga   C. hiciera   D. hará

Verb Test 11

CHANGING FROM ONE TENSE TO ANOTHER

Directions: *The following verb forms are all in the present indicative tense. Change them to the **pretérito**. Keep the same subject, of course. Consult page 519 for irregular verb forms that you cannot identify.*

Model: **Ella estudia.**

You write: **Ella estudió.**

1. Yo hablo.

_____

2. Tú aprendes.

_____

3. Ud. vive aquí.

_____

4. Él trabaja.

_____

5. Ella dice algo.

_____

6. Uds. van al cine.

_____

7. Vosotros pedís algo.

_____

8. Ellos son.

_____

9. Ellas beben café.

_____

10. Juana juega.

_____

11. Tú tocas.

_____

12. El perro muerde.

_____

13. Ellos oyen algo.

_____

14. Uds. escuchan.

_____

15. Yo estoy en casa.

_____

16. Gabriela viene.

_____

17. El niño duerme.

_____

18. Los alumnos leen.

_____

19. Nosotros comemos.

_____

20. Vosotros hacéis la lección.

_____

21. Nosotros vamos al teatro.

_____

22. Ellos piensan.

_____

23. Ellas tienen dinero.

_____

24. Alberto escribe.

_____

25. Ella muere.

_____

26. María y José comen.

_____

27. Yo oigo la música.

_____

28. Yo quiero comer.

_____

29. Ella está en la escuela.

_____

30. Yo voy a casa.

_____

Verb Test 12

COMPLETION OF VERB FORMS
(in the Seven Simple Tenses)

**Directions:** Complete each verb form in the tenses indicated by writing the correct letter or letters on the blank lines.

Presente de indicativo (Tense No. 1)

1. (hablar) Yo habl ____
2. (beber) Tú beb ____
3. (recibir) Ud. recib ____
4. (abrir) Uds. abr ____
5. (hacer) Ellos hac ____
6. (aprender) Nostros aprend ____
7. (leer) María le ____
8. (aceptar) Ellos acept ____
9. (amar) Yo am ____
10. (escribir) Tú escrib ____

Imperfecto de indicativo (Tense No. 2)

1. (cantar) Yo cant ____
2. (dar) Uds. d ____
3. (bañarse) Tú te bañ ____
4. (hacer) Nosotros hac ____
5. (hablar) Ud. habl ____
6. (hallar) Nosotros hall ____
7. (comprender) Yo comprend ____
8. (comer) Uds. com ____
9. (levantarse) Yo me levant ____
10. (vivir) Ella viv ____

Pretérito (Tense No. 3)

1. (hablar) Yo habl ___
2. (comprar) Tú compr ___
3. (aprender) Ud. aprend ___
4. (correr) Nosotros corr ___
5. (recibir) Uds. recib ___
6. (cantar) Él cant ___
7. (apresurarse) Ellos se apresur ___
8. (traer) Uds. traj ___
9. (vivir) Ella viv ___
10. (lavarse) Ellas se lav ___

Futuro (Tense No. 4)

1. (bailar) Yo bailar ___
2. (aprender) Tú aprender ___
3. (ir) Ud. ir ___
4. (venir) Uds. vendr ___
5. (irse) Nosotros nos ir ___
6. (recibir) Ud. recibir ___
7. (dar) Yo dar ___
8. (cantar) Ellos cantar ___
9. (comprender) Ella comprender ___
10. (vivir) Uds. vivir ___

Potencial simple (Tense No. 5)

1. (comprender) Ella comprender ___
2. (vivir) Uds. vivir ___
3. (comprar) Ellos comprar ___
4. (dar) Yo dar ___
5. (recibir) Ud. recibir ___
6. (saltar) Nosotros saltar ___
7. (dormir) Ella dormir ___
8. (entender) Ellos entender ___
9. (estar) Yo estar ___
10. (ser) Yo ser ___

Presente de subjuntivo (Tense No. 6)

1. (hablar) que yo habl ___
2. (aprender) que tú aprend ___
3. (recibir) que Ud. recib ___
4. (tener) que él teng ___
5. (estar) que ella est ___
6. (ser) que Ud. se ___
7. (cantar) que Uds. cant ___
8. (casarse) que nosotros nos cas ___
9. (venir) que ella veng ___
10. (comprender) que yo comprend ___

Imperfecto de subjuntivo (Tense No. 7)

1. (hablar) que yo habla ___
2. (aprender) que él aprendie ___
3. (vivir) que Ud. vivie ___
4. (bailar) que nosotros bailá ___
5. (bajar) que ella baja ___
6. (comprender) que ellos comprendie ___

PAST PARTICIPLES

Directions: *In this acrostic (**un acróstico**) complete each word in Spanish by writing the past participle of the infinitive given for each row. When you write the past participles for the infinitives given below, write them across next to the numbers. The first letter of each past participle is given. If you read the printed letters down from 1 to 9, you will read the Spanish word **enamorado**, which means* in love.

1.	E									
2.	N									
3.	A									
4.	M									
5.	O									
6.	R									
7.	A									
8.	D									
9.	O									

1.	escribir	**4.**	morir	**7.**	aprender
2.	nacer	**5.**	oír	**8.**	decir
3.	abrir	**6.**	reír	**9.**	obtener

DRILLING THE VERB HABER
(in the Seven Simple Tenses)

Note: You must know the verb **haber** (to have) in the seven simple tenses because they are needed to form the seven compound tenses, for example, the **perfecto de indicativo** (Tense No. 8), as in **yo he comido** (I have eaten). Practice these by writing them every day until you know them thoroughly. If you don't know them, see page 256. Also, review pages xxxviii and xxxix.

Directions: *Write the verb forms of **haber** in the seven simple tenses indicated.*

1. Presente de indicativo (Tense No. 1)

Singular	*Plural*
yo _____	nosotros (nosotras)_____
tú _____	vosotros (vosotras) _____
Ud./él/ella/*(or a noun)* _____	Uds./ellos/ellas/*(or a noun)*_____

Verb Drills and Tests with Answers Explained   635

2. Imperfecto de indicativo (Tense No. 2)

yo _____   nosotros (nosotras)_____

tú _____   vosotros (vosotras) _____

Ud./él/ella/(or a noun) _____   Uds./ellos/ellas/(or a noun)_____

3. Pretérito (Tense No. 3)

yo _____   nosotros (nosotras)_____

tú _____   vosotros (vosotras) _____

Ud./él/ella/(or a noun) _____   Uds./ellos/ellas/(or a noun)_____

4. Futuro (Tense No. 4)

yo _____   nosotros (nosotras)_____

tú _____   vosotros (vosotras) _____

Ud./él/ella/(or a noun) _____   Uds./ellos/ellas/(or a noun)_____

5. Potencial simple (Tense No. 5)

yo _____   nosotros (nosotras)_____

tú _____   vosotros (vosotras) _____

Ud./él/ella/(or a noun) _____   Uds./ellos/ellas/(or a noun)_____

6. Presente de subjuntivo (Tense No. 6)

que yo_____   que nosotros (nosotras)_____

que tú _____   que vosotros (vosotras) _____

que Ud./él/ella/(or a noun)_____   que Uds./ellos/ellas/(or a noun)_____

7. Imperfecto de subjuntivo (Tense No. 7)

que yo_____   que nosotros (nosotras)_____

que tú _____   que vosotros (vosotras) _____

que Ud./él/ella/(or a noun)_____   que Uds./ellos/ellas/(or a noun)_____

DRILLING THE VERB ESTAR
(in the Seven Simple Tenses)

Note: You must know the verb **estar** (to be) in the seven simple tenses because it is a commonly used verb. Besides, the present indicative tense of **estar** is needed to form the progressive present, as in **estoy estudiando** (I am studying). The imperfect indicative tense of **estar** is needed to form the progressive past, as in **estaba estudiando** (I was studying). Review no. 1 at the top of page xii. Also, review the bottom of page xxxvi to the top of page xxxvii. Review the formation of the present participles on page xi so that you may be able to form the progressive present and progressive past.

Directions: Write the verb forms of estar in the seven simple tenses indicated.

1. Presente de indicativo (Tense No. 1)

	Singular		*Plural*
yo	_____	nosotros (nosotras)	_____
tú	_____	vosotros (vosotras)	_____
Ud./él/ella/*(or a noun)*	_____	Uds./ellos/ellas/*(or a noun)*	_____

2. Imperfecto de indicativo (Tense No. 2)

yo	_____	nosotros (nosotras)	_____
tú	_____	vosotros (vosotras)	_____
Ud./él/ella/*(or a noun)*	_____	Uds./ellos/ellas/*(or a noun)*	_____

3. Pretérito (Tense No. 3)

yo	_____	nosotros (nosotras)	_____
tú	_____	vosotros (vosotras)	_____
Ud./él/ella/*(or a noun)*	_____	Uds./ellos/ellas/*(or a noun)*	_____

4. Futuro (Tense No. 4)

yo	_____	nosotros (nosotras)	_____
tú	_____	vosotros (vosotras)	_____
Ud./él/ella/*(or a noun)*	_____	Uds./ellos/ellas/*(or a noun)*	_____

Verb Drills and Tests with Answers Explained 637

5. Potencial simple (Tense No. 5)

yo _____   nosotros (nosotras)_____

tú _____   vosotros (vosotras) _____

Ud./él/ella/*(or a noun)* _____   Uds./ellos/ellas/*(or a noun)*_____

6. Presente de subjuntivo (Tense No. 6)

que yo_____   que nosotros (nosotras)_____

que tú _____   que vosotros (vosotras) _____

que Ud./él/ella/*(or a noun)*_____   que Uds./ellos/ellas/*(or a noun)*_____

7. Imperfecto de subjuntivo (Tense No. 7)

que yo_____   que nosotros (nosotras)_____

que tú _____   que vosotros (vosotras) _____

que Ud./él/ella/*(or a noun)*_____   que Uds./ellos/ellas/*(or a noun)*_____

Verb Test 16

CHANGING FROM ONE TENSE TO ANOTHER

Directions: *The following verb forms are all in the **perfecto de indicativo** (Tense No. 8). Change them to the **pluscuamperfecto de indicativo** (Tense No. 9), keeping the same subject. Keep in mind that to form the **pluscuamperfecto de indicativo** you need to use the imperfect indicative tense of **haber** plus the past participle of the verb you are working with. Review the formation of the past participles on pages xii and xiii. Also, review Verb Test 14.*

	Perfecto de indicativo		*Pluscuamperfecto de indicativo*
Model:	**María ha comido.**	You write:	**María había comido.**
	(Mary has eaten.)		(Mary had eaten.)

1. Yo he hablado.

_____

2. Tú has aprendido.

_____

3. Ud. ha salido.

_____

4. Él ha comprendido.

_____

5. Ella ha comprado.

_____

6. El chico ha comido.

_____

7. Nosotros hemos ido.

_____

8. Yo he abierto.

_____

9. Uds. han hecho.

_____

10. Ellas han caído.

_____

11. Yo he llegado.

_____

12. Tú has escrito.

_____

13. Ud. ha creído.

_____

14. Él ha dicho.

_____

15. Ella ha dado.

_____

16. La chica ha bebido.

_____

17. Nosotros hemos oído.

_____

18. Uds. han tenido.

_____

19. Ellos han puesto.

_____

20. Ellas han cubierto.

_____

Verb Test 17

SENTENCE COMPLETION

**Directions:** Each of the following sentences contains a missing verb form. From the choices given, select the verb form of the tense that is required, according to the sense of the sentence, and write the letter of your choice on the line. At times only the infinitive form is needed or a present or past participle.

1. ¡Ojalá que _____ los niños mañana!
   A. vienen   B. vendrán   C. vengan   D. vendrían

2. Yo se lo explicaba a Roberto para que lo _____ .
   A. comprender   B. comprende   C. comprenderá   D. comprendiera

3. Sí, sí. Yo he _____ con ella.
   A. hablando   B. hablado   C. hablo   D. hablé

4. Este profesor me habla como si _____ un niño.
   A. soy   B. fuera   C. fui   D. fue

5. ¿Quién ha _____ el premio?
   A. ganado   B. ganando   C. gana   D. ganó

6. No quiero _____ porque está lloviendo.
   A. salgo   B. salir   C. saliendo   D. sale

7. Juanito, ¿cuándo vas a _____ el ruido?
   A. terminar   B. terminando   C. terminas   D. terminado

8. ¿Qué quiere _____ este muchacho?
   A. dice   B. decir   C. diciendo   D. dicho

9. ¡Qué tiempo espléndido! ¡Está _____ !
   A. nevar   B. nevando   C. nevado   D. nevó

10. Cuando llegué a casa, mi hermano había _____ .
   A. salir   B. salido   C. saliendo   D. salía

PRESENT PARTICIPLES

Directions: In this word puzzle, find the present participle of each of the verbs listed below and draw a line around each one. To get you started, the first verb on the list **(comer)**, whose present participle is **comiendo,** is already done. The present participles are written horizontally or vertically. If you need to, review page xi before you start.

```
H  A  B  L  A  N  D  O  D
C  V  S  E  C  O  M  I  I
O  I  I  Y  E  N  D  O  C
M  V  E  E  V  I  V  R  I
I  I  N  N  B  L  A  I  E
E  E  D  D  A  N  D  E  N
N  N  O  O  E  S  T  N  D
D  D  E  S  T  A  N  D  O
O  O  Y  E  S  A  D  O  H
```

comer	hablar	reír
decir	ir	ser
estar	leer	vivir

DIALOGUE

Directions: In the following dialogue thre are blank spaces indicating missing verb forms. Select the appropriate verb form according to the sense of what the speakers are saying and write the letter of your choice on the line. The situation is given below.

Situation: You and your sister Julia are in a veterinarian's waiting room because your dog, Rojo, needs a rabies shot.

Julia :   ¡Diós mío! ¡Qué rido! ¿Por qué ladran todos los perros a la vez?
Tú: Me parece que _____ miedo.

  1. A. tiene   B. tienes   C. tienen   D. teniendo

Julia :   Ese gatito precioso allí parece dormido.
Tú: Verdad. Debe _____ enfermo.

2. A. ser   B. estar   C. tener   D. estando

Julia :   Mira a aquel chico tan pequeño con el perro enorme.
Tú: Sí. ¡ _____ muy cómico!

3. A. Es   B. Está   C. Son   D. Están

Julia :   ¡Qué quieto está Rojo! En casa siempre salta por todas partes.
Tú: _____ en un lugar extraño.

4. A. Es   B. Está   C. Son   D. Están

Julia :   Ya nos llaman. Y ahora Rojo quiere correr como siempre.
          ¿Qué haremos?
Tú: Yo lo _____ adentro.

5. A. llevo   B. llevaba   C. llevé   D. llevó

Verb Test 20

CHANGING FROM ONE VERB TO ANOTHER

*Directions: The verb forms in the following statements are all in the **pretérito**. Change each sentence by replacing the verb in the sentence with the proper form of the verb in parentheses, keeping the **pretérito**. Rewrite the statement in Spanish.*

Model: **Claudia habló. (cantar)** (Claudia spoke.)
You write: **Claudia cantó.** (Claudia sang.)

1. Roberto *aprendió* la lección. (escribir)

_____

2. La Señora Fuentes *se sentó.* (levantarse)

_____

3. Yo *recibí* un regalo. (ofrecer)

_____

4. María *pensó.* (trabajar)

_____

5. El alumno *escribió* una carta. (leer)

_____

6. El Señor Robles *llegó.* (morir)

_____

7. Margarita *entró.* (salir)

_____

8. Ricardo *cantó.* (hablar)

_____

9. Yo *vi* a María. (saludar)

_____

10. Mi padre *vio* un accidente. (tener)

_____

11. Mi hermana *comió* la comida. (hacer)

_____

12. ¿*Viajó* usted a España? (ir)

_____

13. ¿*Se levantaron* los chicos? (vestirse)

_____

14. Esta mañana yo *me apresuré.* (lavarse)

_____

15. Yo no *pude* hacerlo. (querer)

_____

MATCHING SPANISH VERB FORMS WITH ENGLISH VERB FORMS

Directions: *Match the following Spanish verb forms with the English equivalent verb forms by writing the number in column one on the blank line in column two.*

Column One	Column Two
1. Yo he comido	____ I came
2. Ud. puso	____ I have eaten
3. Ella quiere	____ You said
4. Ellos hicieron	____ You put
5. Tú ganas	____ She wants
6. Yo me afeito	____ You will buy
7. Nosotros dimos	____ We give
8. Uds. dieron	____ They made (did)
9. Está lloviendo	____ He became frightened
10. Ellos murieron	____ You win
11. Él se asustó	____ We gave
12. Nosotros damos	____ I am shaving myself
13. Uds. comprarán	____ You gave
14. Tú dijiste	____ It is raining
15. Yo vine	____ They died

CHANGING FROM ONE TENSE TO ANOTHER

Directions: *The verb forms are all in the **presente de indicativo** (Tense No. 1). Change them to the **pretérito** (Tense No. 3), keeping the same subject.*

	Presente de indicativo		Pretérito
Model:	**Yo como bien.**	**You write:**	**Yo comí bien.**
	(I eat well.)		(I ate well.)

1. Yo cojo la pelota.

_____

2. Ud. duerme demasiado.

_____

3. Tú vas al cine.

_____

4. Él habla mucho.

_____

5. Ella escribe una tarjeta.

_____

6. Nosotros comemos en este restaurante.

_____

7. Vosotros aceptáis el dinero.

_____

8. Uds. dan de comer a los pájaros.

_____

9. Yo voy al teatro.

_____

10. Ellas van a casa.

_____

11. Ellos están en la piscina.

_____

12. Yo me siento cerca de la ventana.

_____

13. Ud. se levanta.

_____

14. Nosotros nos apresuramos.

_____

15. Los muchahcos vienen a verme.

_____

16. Berta está enferma.

_____

17. Mi madre hace un bizcocho.

_____

18. Yo busco mis libros.

_____

19. La profesora abre la puerta.

_____

20. Me gusta el helado.

_____

Verb Test 23

PRETERIT PERFECT

Directions: *In this word puzzle, find the **pretérito perfecto** (also known as the **pretérito anterior**), which is Tense No. 10, of the three verbs given below. When you find those three verb forms, draw a line around each one. One is printed horizontally, another one is printed vertically, and another is printed backwards. To refresh your memory of what the **pretérito perfecto** is, review page xxxii.*

```
B  U  H  O  H  B  U  T  O
H  B  U  A  G  I  R  O  T
H  U  B  E  V  I  S  T  O
R  I  O  E  S  C  I  R  T
H  U  E  B  I  M  O  E  S
O  R  S  E  I  B  U  I  H
E  S  C  R  I  O  T  B  U
V  I  R  T  O  A  B  A  E
H  A  I  B  A  B  I  E  R
I  S  T  O  V  H  U  B  E
R  O  O  T  R  O  T  U  I
R  C  S  E  E  B  U  H  O
```

abrir   escribir   ver

DRILLING AGAIN THE VERB HABER
(in the Seven Simple Tenses)

Note: In Test 14 you drilled the verb **haber** in the seven simple tenses. Now, do it again here because you must know those verb forms in order to form the seven compound tenses (Tense Nos. 8 to 14). Practice these by writing them every day until you know them thoroughly. If you don't know them yet, see page 256. Also, review pages xxxi to xxxiv and pages xxxviii and xxxix.

*Directions: Write the verb forms of **haber** in the seven simple tenses indicated.*

1. Presente de indicativo (Tense No. 1)

Singular	*Plural*
yo _____	nosotros (nosotras)_____
tú _____	vosotros (vosotras) _____
Ud./él/ella/*(or a noun)* _____	Uds./ellos/ellas/*(or a noun)*_____

2. Imperfecto de indicativo (Tense No. 2)

yo _____	nosotros (nosotras)_____
tú _____	vosotros (vosotras) _____
Ud./él/ella/*(or a noun)* _____	Uds./ellos/ellas/*(or a noun)*_____

3. Pretérito (Tense No. 3)

yo _____	nosotros (nosotras)_____
tú _____	vosotros (vosotras) _____
Ud./él/ella/*(or a noun)* _____	Uds./ellos/ellas/*(or a noun)*_____

4. Futuro (Tense No. 4)

yo _____	nosotros (nosotras)_____
tú _____	vosotros (vosotras) _____
Ud./él/ella/*(or a noun)* _____	Uds./ellos/ellas/*(or a noun)*_____

5. Potencial simple (Tense No. 5)

yo _____	nosotros (nosotras)_____
tú _____	vosotros (vosotras) _____
Ud./él/ella/*(or a noun)* _____	Uds./ellos/ellas/*(or a noun)*_____

6. Presente de subjuntivo (Tense No. 6)

que yo_____   que nosotros (nosotras)_____

que tú _____   que vosotros (vosotras) _____

que Ud./él/ella/(*or a noun*)_____   que Uds./ellos/ellas/(*or a noun*)_____

7. Imperfecto de subjuntivo (Tense No. 7)

que yo_____   que nosotros (nosotras)_____

que tú _____   que vosotros (vosotras) _____

que Ud./él/ella/(*or a noun*)_____   que Uds./ellos/ellas/(*or a noun*)_____

Verb Test 25

PATTERN RESPONSES

*Directions: Answer the following questions in Spanish in complete sentences in the affirmative, using a pronoun for the subject. Add **también** (also). See page 519 for irregular verb forms that you cannot identify.*

Model: **Pedro escribe bien. ¿Y los otros alumnos?**
(Peter writes well. And the other students?)

You write: Ellos escriben bien, también.
(They write well, also.)

1. María sabe nadar. ¿Y tú?

   _____

2. Tú sales de la escuela a las tres. ¿Y los profesores?

   _____

3. Yo estoy sentado. ¿Y Juanita?

   _____

4. Tú eres inteligente. ¿Y tus hermanos?

   _____

5. Ud. sonríe de vez en cuando. ¿Y Pedro y Juana?

   _____

6. Isabel leyó el libro. ¿Y María y José?

_____

7. Ester recibió muchos regalos. ¿Y nosotros?

_____

8. Yo bebí café con leche. ¿Y Andrés?

_____

9. Los alumnos oyeron la música. ¿Y Ud.?

_____

10. Susana durmió mucho. ¿Y los niños?

_____

11. Pablo fue al cine. ¿Y tus amigos?

_____

12. Tú te acuestas a las diez. ¿Y tus padres?

_____

13. José ha dicho la verdad. ¿Y Gabriela y Margarita?

_____

14. Yo hice la lección. ¿Y los otros alumnos?

_____

15. Tú has cantado bien. ¿Y Luis?

_____

IDENTIFYING VERB FORMS IN A PASSAGE
FROM SPANISH LITERATURE

Directions: *Read the following literary passage twice. Then, identify the verb forms with their subjects printed in* **bold face** *by giving (a) the infinitive of the verb form, (b) the name of the tense in Spanish, and (c) the person and number of the verb form.*

Example: son

You write: (a) **ser**
(b) **presente de indicativo**
(c) **3d person plural**

Al ruido, **salió Sancho, diciendo:**

—**Señor don Quixote,** bien **puede** entrar, que al punto que **yo llegué se direon todos** por vencidos. **Baje, baje,** que **todos son** amigos y **hemos echado** pelillos a la mar, y nos **están aguardando** con una muy gentil olla de vaca, tocino, carnero, nabos y berzas, que **está diciendo:** "**¡Cóme**me, **cóme**me!"

Selection from *Don Quixote de la Mancha,*
by Miguel de Cervantes

1. salió

(a) _____

(b) _____

(c) _____

2. diciendo

(a) _____

(b) _____

(c) _____

3. puede

(a) _____

(b) _____

(c) _____

4. llegué

(a) _____

(b) _____

(c) _____

5. se dieron

(a) _____

(b) _____

(c) _____

6. baje

(a) _____

(b) _____

(c) _____

7. son

(a) _____

(b) _____

(c) _____

8. hemos echado

(a) _____

(b) _____

(c) _____

9. están aguardando

(a) _____

(b) _____

(c) _____

10. está diciendo

(a) _____

(b) _____

(c) _____

11. come

(a) _____

(b) _____

(c) _____

Answers to Verb Tests with Explanations

Test 1

1. **C** You need the infinitive form of the verb in C because of the preceding preposition **de.** Review section F on page 544. The forms of **comprar** in A, B, and D are in the preterit. Review them on page 129.

2. **D** You need the 3d person singular, pres. ind. of the verb in D because the subject **hombre** is 3d person singular. Review the other forms of **saber** in A, B, and C on page 423.

3. **B** You need to complete the progressive present with the present participle **lloviendo** in B. Review the bottom of page xxxvi and the top of page xxxvii. Review **llorar** on page 300 and **llover** on page 301.

4. **B** The 1st person singular, future, of **ver** is needed because future time is implied in the word **mañana.** You are telling José, "I will see you tomorrow." Choice A is 3d person singular, future. Review the forms of **ver** on page 490.

5. **A** A form of **estar** is needed because a temporary state or condition is indicated in the sentence: Mary is pale. Review the uses of **estar** on page 535. As for the other choices, review the forms of **estar** on page 228 and **ser** on page 438.

6. **B** Here, too, a form of **estar** is needed because a temporary state or condition is indicated in the sentence: Ricardo and Dora are tired. Review the uses of **estar** on page 535, specifically in (c) (1). Review the forms of **estar** on page 228. As for the forms of **ser** in A, C, and D, review those forms on page 438.

7. **C** You are dealing with the verb **acostarse.** You need the infinitive form **acostarme** in C because of the preceding preposition **a.** The **me** in **acostarme** is needed because **voy** (I am going) is stated. Review the examples in section A on page 541 where **ir,** a verb of motion, requires the preposition **a** + inf. Review the forms of **acostarse** in choices B and D on page 21.

8. **A** You must know the idiomatic expression **tener ganas de** + inf. Study the section on verbs used in idiomatic expressions beginning on page 524, in particular, idioms using **tener** on pages 536 and 537, where **tener ganas de** is listed. As for **tuvo** in C, it is preterit, 3d person singular. Study the forms of **tener** on page 469. As for **quiero** in B, study **querer** on page 392. Regarding choice D, **pago** is a form of **pagar** on page 344.

9. **A** You need the infinitive form **limpiar** because of the idiomatic expression **tener que** + inf., listed on page 537 with an example. Review the other forms of **limpiar** in B, C, and D on page 293.

10. **A** You need to complete the **perfecto de indicativo** (Tense No. 8) because **ha** is given as the helping verb. On page 288 review this tense and the other forms of **lavar** in choices B, C, and D. Also, review the formation of the **perfecto de indicativo** on page xxxi.

11. **B** The subject is 3d person singular. You need the 3d person singular of **morir** in the preterit, which is in choice B, because **anoche** (last night) is stated. Review the other forms of **morir** in choices A, C, and D on page 320.

12. **C** According to the meaning of the sentence, you are dealing with the verb **deber.** Study the forms on page 158. The other verbs in A, B, and D would make no sense in this sentence. Review them on pages 133, 327, and 392.

13. **B** A form of **estar** is needed because a temporary state or condition is indicated in the sentence: the store will be closed. The future tense is needed because

mañana (tomorrow) is stated. The subject **la tienda** is 3d person singular and so is the verb **estará.** Review the uses of **estar** on page 536, in particular, the example in (d) (5). Review the preterit of **estar** in choice D on page 228 and the forms of **ser** in choices A and C on page 438.

14. B   You need the imperative of **abrir** because the teacher told the pupils, "Open" the books. The 2d person plural familiar form of **vosotros** is needed because the teacher talked to her pupils in the familiar form. Review **abrid** in the imperative as well as the other choices of verb forms on page 4 where **abrir** is given in all its forms.

15. C   The form **puedo** (1st person singular, pres. ind.) is the correct choice because right after it is **divertirme** and they must agree in person; in other words, the statement is saying, "I can enjoy myself." Review **poder** on page 366 for the forms in choices A, B, C, and D.

16. C   You need to complete the **perfecto de indicativo** (Tense No. 8) by selecting the past participle **traído** because **han** is given as the helping verb. The sentence is saying that The Three Wise Men *have brought* many presents to the children. Review the forms of **traer** on page 478.

17. A   You are dealing with the idiomatic expression **acabar de + inf.** Review it on page 524. Also, review the forms of **acabar** on page 9.

18. C   The sentence states **"hace tres horas"** and it requires the pres. ind. of **mirar.** Review the explanation in (f) on page xxi. Review the other choices in A, B, and D on page 315 where all the forms of **mirar** are given.

19. A   The sentence states that when I entered the living room, my mother *was reading* and my father *was writing.* Review the uses of the **imperfecto de indicativo** in such a sentence structure and the explanation in (b) on page xxii. Review the other choices in B, C, and D on page 290 where all the forms of **leer** are given.

20. D   The sentence states that this morning my sister *was singing* in the bathroom when I woke up. The explanation here is the same as in no. 19 above. Review the other choices in A, B, and C on page 109 where all the forms of **cantar** are given.

Test 2

1. D   You are asking the clerk if *there are* tickets for Saturday. **Hay** is the word for *there are* or *there is.* Review the explanation at the bottom of page 529. Also, on page 256 review the forms of **haber** in choices A, B, and C.

2. D   The polite form of saying *I would like* or *I should like* is **quisiera,** which is the **imperfecto de subjuntivo** of **querer.** Review it at the top of page xxxi. Also, study the other forms of **querer** in choices A, B, and C on page 392.

3. A   You are asking the clerk, *How do I pay?* That means you need the 1st person singular of the **presente de indicativo** in A. Review the other forms of **pagar** in choices B, C, and D on page 344.

4. C   You need the 3d pers. sing. **empieza** in C because the subject, **la función** (the performance) is 3d pers. sing. Study the other forms of **empezar** in choices A, B, and D on page 203.

5. A   Review the explanation of the uses of **ser** and **estar** on pages 535 and 536. There is nothing in the sentence that requires a form of **estar** in B, or the **presente de subjuntivo** in C, and nothing that requires the **imperfecto de subjuntivo** in D. Review the forms of **estar** on page 228 and **ser** on page 438.

Test 3

1. **Ellos estudian bien, también.** Study the **presente de indicativo** of **estudiar** on page 230.
2. **Ellas escriben bien, también.** Study the **presente de indicativo** of **escribir** on page 222.
3. **Yo estoy leyendo un libro en la cama, también.** Study the formation of the progressive present beginning at the bottom of page xxxvi. Note the irregular present participle (**gerundio**) of **leer (leyendo)** on pages xi and 290.
4. **Ellos van de compras, también.** Study the **presente de indicativo** of **ir** on page 280 and the idiomatic expression **ir de compras** on the bottom of that page.
5. **Yo fui al cine, también.** Study the **pretérito** of **ir** on page 280.
6. **Nosotros hemos comido bien, también.** Study the **perfecto de indicativo** (Tense No. 8) of **comer** on page 127.
7. **Ellos están bien, también.** Study the **presente de indicativo** of **estar** on page 228.
8. **Ellas se sentaron, también.** Study the **pretérito** of **sentarse** on page 434.
9. **Yo me lavé la cara, también.** Study the **pretérito** of **lavarse** on page 289.
10. **Yo sé nadar, también.** Study the **presente de indicativo** of **saber** on page 423.
11. **Él ha cantado bien, también.** Study the **perfecto de indicativo** of **cantar** on page 109.
12. **Yo escogí un carro costoso, también.** Study the **pretérito** of **escoger** on page 221.
13. **Ellos han terminado la lección, también.** Study the **perfecto de indicativo** of **terminar** on page 471.
14. **Él escribió una carta, también.** Study the **pretérito** of **escribir** on page 222.
15. **Yo tengo que estudiar, también.** Study the **presente de indicativo** of **tener** on page 469 and the idiomatic expression **tener que + inf.** on page 537.
16. **Ella ha devuelto los libros a la biblioteca, también.** Study the **perfecto de indicativo** of **devolver** on page 185 and the difference between **volver** and **devolver** on pages 536 and 537. Note on page xiii that the past participle is irregular.
17. **Nosotros hemos dicho la verdad, también.** Study the **perfecto de indicativo** of **decir** on page 160 and the irregular past participle **dicho** on page xiii.
18. **Ellos se acuestan a las diez, también.** Study the **presente de indicativo** of **acostarse** on page 21 and note the change in spelling in the stem for **o** to **ue** when **o** in **acostarse** is stressed.
19. **Yo he leído un libro, también.** Study the **perfecto de indicativo** of **leer** on page 290. Note the irregular past participle **leído** on page xiii.
20. **Nosotros queremos hacerlo, también.** Study the **presente de indicativo** of **querer** on page 392 and note the change in spelling in the stem of this verb when it is stressed.

Test 4

1. D   You need the **imperfecto de indicativo** of **ir** because, according to the sense of the statement, the action was performed habitually in the past. Study the explanation and examples in (c) on page xxii. Also, review the forms of **ir** in choices A, B, and C on page 280.

2. A   You need the **imperfecto de indicativo** of **vivir** for the same reason and explanation given in the preceding statment no. 1 above. Review the forms of **vivir** in choices B, C, and D on page 495.

3. D   You need the **imperfecto de indicativo** of **ser** because, according to the sense of the statement, there is a description of a physical condition in the past. Study the explanation and examples in (d) on page xxii. Also, review the forms of **ser** in choices A, B, and C on page 438.

4. A   You need the **imperfecto de indicativo** of **ser** because you are asking what time it was in the past. Study the explanation and examples in (e) at the top of page xxiii. Also, review the forms of **ser** again on page 438.

5. **C** You need the **imperfecto de indicativo** of **ser** in the 3d person plural because the time stated is plural (**tres**). Study again the explanation and examples in (e) at the top of page xxiii. Review the **pretérito** of **telefonear** on page 464.

6. **A** And here, too, you need the **imperfecto de indicativo** of **mirar**. Study the explanation and examples in (f) on page xxiii. Also, review the forms of **mirar** in choices B, C, and D on page 315.

7. **A** You need the infinitive form of **venir** because in front of it there is a verb form (**quiere**). Robert says that *he wants to come* to my house. Review verbs that take no preposition + infinitive in section K, beginning on page 547. On page 548 **querer + inf.** is listed. Also, review the other forms of **venir** in choices B, C, and D on page 489.

8. **C** You must complete the **perfecto de indicativo** tense by using the past participle **visto** because the helping verb **ha** is stated in front of the missing verb form. Review this tense of **ver** and the choices in A, B, and D on page 490. Also study the irregular past participles on page xiii.

9. **A** You need the **imperfecto de indicativo** of **querer** because you are dealing with an indirect quotation in the past. Casandra said that *she wanted* to come to my house. Compare this sentence with the one in number 7 above. Study the explanation and example in (g) on page xxiii. Also, review the other forms of **querer** in choices B, C, and D on page 392.

10. **C** The adverb **ayer** (yesterday) tells us that the verb is in the past. The subject is **amigo** (friend), 3d person singular; therefore, the verb must be 3d person singular also. Choice C is 3d person singular in the **pretérito** of **llegar**. Review the other forms of **llegar** in choices A, B, and D on page 297.

11. **B** The adverb **anoche** (last night) tells us that the verb is in the past. The subject is **María,** which is 3d person singular; therefore, the verb must also be 3d person singular. Choice B is 3d person singular in the **pretérito** or **ir**. Review the other forms of **ir** in choices A, C, and D on page 280.

12. **B** **Ayer por la tarde** (yesterday afternoon) tells us that the verb is in the past. The statement asks *what happened* in the street. Review the forms of **pasar** on page 350 in the **presente de indicativo** (choice A), the **pretérito** (choices B and C), and in the **futuro** (choice D). Also, check out example 3 at the top of page xxiv.

13. **B** According to the sense of the sentence, the verb must be in the past. The subject is **yo,** 1st person singular; therefore, the verb must also be 1st person singular. Review the **pretérito** of **tomar** in choices A and B, as well as the choices in C and D on page 474.

14. **C** The two verbs in the sentence (**salí** and **tomé**) are in the **pretérito.** The missing verb form must also be in the same tense and person because of the sense indicated in the statement. Review the forms of **llegar** on page 297, **salir** on page 426, and **tomar** on page 474. Also, check out example 5 at the top of page xxiv.

15. **B** Because of the subject **yo,** you need the 1st person singular of **conocer** in the **pretérito.** According to the sense of the statement, **la semana pasada** (last week) indicates a past tense. Review the other choices of verb forms of **conocer** on page 133. Also, examine example number 1 in the middle of page xxiv.

16. **C** You are talking to José and are using the familiar **tú** form of the verb in the 2d person singular. You are asking him when he found out the truth. The only **tú** form in the **pretérito** among the choices is in C. Review the other forms of **saber** in the other choices on page 423. Also, note the special use of **saber** in the **pretérito** in example number 6 on page xxiv.

17. A The subject is **yo.** You need the **futuro,** 1st person singular, of **hacer** because **la semana que viene** (next week) is stated. Review the **futuro** and **pretérito** of **hacer** on page 259. Also, review the uses and formation of the future tense, with many examples, on pages xxv and xxvi.

18. A The subject is **nosotros.** You need the **futuro,** 1st person plural, of **ir** because **el verano que viene** (next summer) is stated. Review the other forms of **ir** in choices B, C, and D on page 280.

19. C Mary say that she *will come* tomorrow. The **futuro** of **venir** is needed in the 3d person singular because **María** is 3d person singular. Review the forms of **venir** among the other choices on page 489. It would make no sense to use the **pretérito** of **venir** in A and B because **mañana** (tomorrow) implies future time. Also, review the uses of the future tense on page xxv, in particular example (c), and the formation of that tense at the top of page xxvi.

20. B If Miguel had money, he *would go* to Spain. The only conditional form of **ir** is in B. A and C are future tense. D is the present tense. Review the forms of **ir** on page 280. Also, review the uses of the **potencial simple** (conditional) with examples on page xxvi, in particular example (a).

    Let's look at the dependent clause in this sentence: **Si Miguel** *tuviera* **dinero . . .** (If Miguel *had* money . . .). The form *tuviera* is the **imperfecto de subjuntivo** (Tense No. 7) of **tener** on page 469. That form is used because **si** (if) introduces the clause. Typical examples in English of this sort of thing are the following: If *I were* king, if *I were* you, he talks to me as if *I were* a child. These are contrary to fact conditions. Review the uses and formation of the **imperfecto de subjuntivo,** with examples, on page xxx, in particular, the example at the top of page xxxi.

Test 5

1. B Review the explanation and examples of the use of **gustar** on page 528 and the usual forms of the verb on page 255, as well as the examples on the bottom of that page.

2. A The subject **tú** agrees with the verb **asistes** because they are both 2d person singular, present indicative. Review the other tenses of **asistir** on page 74.

3. A Review the explanation and use of **hace** + length of time in example (f) on page xxi, at the bottom of page 530, and at the top of page 531. Also, review **hacer** on page 259.

4. A The use of **empieza** is in the question as well as in the answer. On page 203 study the forms of **empezar** in choices A, B, C, and D. Note that the second **e** in this verb changes to **ie** when it is stressed. Also, **z** changes to **c** when the vowel **e** follows it.

5. C You need the infinitive form **venir** because a verb form **(puedes)** precedes it. Review verbs that take no preposition + infinitive in section K, beginning on page 547. On page 548 **poder + inf.** is listed. What you are saying to Dolores is "You can come" (You *are able to come*). Review the forms of **venir** in choices A, B, C, and D on page 489.

6. C You are telling Dolores, "Then, *let's go* to my Spanish class." On page 280 review the forms of **ir** in the four choices, giving special attention to **vamos** *(let's go)* in the imperative near the bottom of that page. When you are not sure of the translation into English of a Spanish verb tense, review pages xviii and xix where there is a sample English verb conjugated in all the tenses.

Test 6

Note: In this test, the verb form given in each sentence is in the imperative (command) mood. You are also given a verb in parentheses to use in place of the one in the sentence. Review the **imperativo** on pages xxxiv to xxxvi. If you had any difficulty with the imperative forms of the verbs used in this test, you must turn to the page in this book among the 501 verbs and review the forms that are given near the bottom of each page under **imperativo.**

1. Diga la palabra.
2. Bebe la leche.
3. Parta inmediatamente.
4. Cierra la ventana.
5. Tome la maleta sobre la cama.
6. Escriba la palabra.
7. Enviemos la carta.
8. Lean el poema.
9. Salgamos ahora.
10. Levántese, por favor.
11. Compre la casa.
12. Vengan ahora.
13. Sécate.
14. Escoja estos guantes
15. Bébalo.

Test 7

Note: Review the formation of regular verbs in the future (futuro) (Tense No. 4) at the top of page xxvi and the conditional **(potencial simple)** (Tense No. 5) at the bottom of page xxvi.

1. Yo saldría.
2. Ud. tendría.
3. Nosotros seríamos.
4. Uds. estarían.
5. María querría.
6. Tú ganarías.
7. Ellos harían.
8. Ella cantaría.
9. José bailaría.
10. Tú escribirías.
11. Él sería.
12. Yo me lavaría.
13. Alberto se sentaría.
14. Nosotros nos sentiríamos.
15. Nosotros nos sentaríamos.
16. Yo aprendería.
17. Tú beberías.
18. Ud. sabría.
19. Miguel leería.
20. Nosotros iríamos.
21. Vosotros iríais.
22. Uds. dirían.
23. Ellos vendrían.
24. Ellas venderían.
25. José y Dora serían.
26. Los chicos comerían.
27. María y yo haríamos.
28. Elena y Ana pondrían.
29. Vosotros veríais.
30. Yo estudiaría.

Test 8

1. (a) No. Yo no saldré de casa esta noche.
   (b) Ellos no saldrán de casa esta noche tampoco.
   Review the **futuro** of **salir** among the 501 verbs in this book.
2. (a) No. Yo no quiero venir a tu casa esta tarde.
   (b) Nosotros no queremos venir a tu casa esta tarde tampoco.
   Review the **presente de indicativo** of **querer** among the 501 verbs.
3. (a) No. Yo no canté esta mañana.
   (b) Ellos no cantaron esta mañana tampoco.
   Review the **pretérito** of **cantar** among the 501 verbs.
4. (a) No. Yo no digo mentiras.
   (b) Ella no dice mentiras tampoco.
   Review the **presente de indicativo** of **decir** among the 501 verbs.
5. (a) No. Yo no fui al cine ayer.
   (b) Ellos no fueron al cine ayer tampoco.
   Review the **pretérito** of **ir** among the 501 verbs.

Test 9

1. Yo fui al parque.
2. Elisa miró la televisión.
3. El niño bebió la leche.
4. Margarita hizo la lección.
5. José habló mucho.
6. Mi amigo pagó la cuenta.
7. Nosotros tomamos el desayuno a las ocho.
8. Luis escribió cartas.
9. Marta aprendió la lección.
10. Los Señores López vivieron en esta casa.
11. Yo hice el trabajo.
12. La señorita trajo el plato.
13. Pablo leyó el poema.
14. Carlota dijo la verdad.
15. La profesora abrió el libro.

Test 10

1. A Review the explanations and examples of the **potencial simple** (Tense No. 5), in particular, example (b) on page xxvi. Review the other forms of **gustar** on page 255 and the examples at the bottom of that page. Also, review the explanations and examples of **gustar** on page 528.

2. A Review the explanation and examples in question number 20 in **Test 4.** The idea is the same here.

3. C You need to complete the **pluscuamperfecto de indicativo** (Tense No. 9) because **había** is given as the helping verb. On page 160 review this tense and the other forms of **decir** in choices A, B, and D. Also, review the formation of the **pluscuamperfecto de indicativo** on pages xxxi and xxxii. From time to time refer to the regular formation of past participles and the list of irregular past participles on pages xii and xiii where you will find **dicho.** Study example (c) 3 on page xxvi.

4. A Review the **potencial simple** (Tense No. 5) on page xxvi, in particular, example (c) 2. Review the other forms of **venir** among the 501 verbs.

5. A Review the **imperativo** on pages xxxiv to xxxvi and at the bottom of the page where **sentarse** is among the 501 verbs.

6. C Study the explanations and examples of the uses of the **presente de subjuntivo** (Tense No. 6) on pages xxvii to xxx. See example (e) on page xxvii. Review the other forms of **hacer** among the 501 verbs.

7. B Review the verbs of motion that take the preposition **a** + infinitive in section A on page 541. Study the other forms of **tomar** among the 501 verbs.

8. D Review the formation of the progressive present beginning at the bottom of page xxxvi. Study the regular formation of present participles and irregular present participles on pages xi and xii. Study the other forms of **estudiar** among the 501 verbs.

9. A Review example 2 on page xii. Also, review the other forms of **llorar** among the 501 verbs.

10. D Study the explanations and examples of the uses of the **presente de subjuntivo** (Tense No. 6) on pages xxvii to xxx. See statement (e) on page xxvii and example 3 at the top of page xxviii.

11. B See explanation (f), example 1 on page xxviii. Review the other forms of **venir** among the 501 verbs.

12. B See explanation (g), example 1 on page xxviii. Review the other forms of **comer** among the 501 verbs.

13. D See explanation (h) on page xxviii and example 1 at the top of page xxix. Review the other forms of **llegar** among the 501 verbs.

14. C See explanation (h) on page xxviii and example 4 at the top of page xxix. Review the other forms of **volver** among the 501 verbs.

15. A   See explanation (i), example 1 on page xxix. Review the other forms of **ser** among the 501 verbs.
16. D   See explanation (k) and the example on page xxix. Review the other forms of **venir** among the 501 verbs.
17. B   See explanation (l), example 1 on page xxix. Review the other forms of **ser** among the 501 verbs.
18. A   See explanation (l), example 2 on page xxix. Review the other forms of **hablar** among the 501 verbs.
19. C   See explanation (l), example 3 on page xxix. Review the other forms of **poder** among the 501 verbs.
20. C   Review the explanation, formation, and uses of the **imperfecto de subjuntivo** (Tense No. 7) on pages xxx and xxxi. See example 1 at the bottom of page xxx. Review the other forms of **hacer** among the 501 verbs.

Test 11

Note: The infinitive form of the verb is given in parentheses in front of the following answers in case you had difficulty identifying any of the irregular verb forms. They are given so you may verify the forms in the **presente de indicativo** and the **pretérito** by turning to the page where the verbs are arranged alphabetically among the 501 verbs in this book.

1. (hablar) Yo hablé.
2. (aprender) Tú aprendiste.
3. (vivir) Ud. vivió aquí.
4. (trabajar) Él trabajó.
5. (decir) Ella dijo algo.
6. (ir) Uds. fueron al cine.
7. (pedir) Vosotros pedisteis algo.
8. (ser) Ellos fueron.
9. (beber) Ellas bebieron café.
10. (jugar) Juana jugó.
11. (tocar) Tú tocaste.
12. (morder) El perro mordió.
13. (oír) Ellos oyeron algo.
14. (escuchar) Uds. escucharon.
15. (estar) Yo estuve en casa.
16. (venir) Gabriela vino.
17. (dormir) El niño durmió.
18. (leer) Los alumnos leyeron.
19. (comer) Nosotros comimos.
20. (hacer) Vosotros hicisteis la lección.
21. (ir) Nosotros fuimos al teatro.
22. (pensar) Ellos pensaron.
23. (tener) Ellos tuvieron dinero.
24. (escribir) Alberto escribió.
25. (morir) Ella murió.
26. (comer) María y José comieron.
27. (oír) Yo oí la música.
28. (querer) Yo quise comer.
29. (estar) Ella estuvo en la escuela.
30. (ir) Yo fui a casa.

Test 12

Presente de indicativo

1. Yo hablo.
2. Tú bebes.
3. Ud. recibe.
4. Uds. abren.
5. Ellos hacen.
6. Nosotros aprendemos.
7. María lee.
8. Ellos aceptan.
9. Yo amo.
10. Tú escribes.

Imperfecto de indicativo

1. Yo cantaba.
2. Uds. daban.
3. Tú te bañabas.
4. Nosotros hacíamos.
5. Ud. hablaba.
6. Nosotros hallábamos.
7. Yo comprendía.
8. Uds. comían.
9. Yo me levantaba.
10. Ella vivía.

Pretérito

1. Yo hablé.
2. Tú compraste.
3. Ud. aprendió.
4. Nosotros corrimos.
5. Uds. recibieron.
6. Él cantó.
7. Ellos se apresuraron.
8. Uds. trajeron.
9. Ella vivió.
10. Ellas se lavaron.

Futuro

1. Yo bailaré.
2. Tú aprenderás.
3. Ud. irá.
4. Uds. vendrán.
5. Nosotros nos iremos.
6. Ud. recibirá.
7. Yo daré.
8. Ellos cantarán.
9. Ella comprenderá.
10. Uds. vivirán.

Potencial simple

1. Ella comprendería.
2. Uds. vivirían.
3. Ellos comprarían.
4. Yo daría.
5. Ud. recibiría.
6. Nosotros saltaríamos.
7. Ella dormiría.
8. Ellos entenderían.
9. Yo estaría.
10. Yo sería.

Presente de subjuntivo

1. que yo hable
2. que tú aprendas
3. que Ud. reciba
4. que él tanga
5. que ella esté
6. que Ud. sea
7. que Uds. canten
8. que nosotros nos casemos
9. que ella venga
10. que yo comprenda

Imperfecto de subjuntivo

1. que yo hablara *or* hablase
2. que él aprendiera *or* aprendiese
3. que Ud. viviera *or* viviese
4. que nosotros bailáramos *or* bailásemos
5. que ella bajara *or* bajase
6. que ellos comprendieran *or* comprendiesen

Test 13

1. E S C R I T O
2. N A C I D O
3. A B I E R T O
4. M U E R T O
5. O Í D O
6. R E Í D O
7. A P R E N D I D O
8. D I C H O
9. O B T E N I D O

Test 14

Note: All the forms of **haber** in the seven simple tenses are given on page 256. Verify your work by consulting that page. Remember that these verb forms are needed to form the seven compound tenses that are also on that page.

Test 15

Note: All the forms of **estar** in the seven simple tenses are given on page 228. Verify your work by consulting that page. Remember that the verb forms in the **presente de indicativo** (Tense No. 1) of **estar** are needed to form the progressive present, as in **estoy trabajando** (I am working). The verb forms in the **imperfecto de indicativo** (Tense No. 2) of **estar** are needed to form the progressive past, as in **estaba trabajando** (I was working). Review the bottom of page xxxvi to the top of page xxxvii. Review the formation of the present participles on pages xi and xii so that you may be able to form the progressive present and progressive past.

Test 16

Note: Keep in mind that to form the **pluscuamperfecto de indicativo** (Tense No. 9) you need to use the **imperfecto de indicativo** (Tense No. 2) of **haber** plus the past participle of the verb you are working with. Review the formation of the past participles on pages xii and xiii. Also, review Test 14.

1. Yo había hablado.
2. Tú habías aprendido.
3. Ud. había salido.
4. Él había comprendido.
5. Ella había comprado.
6. El chico había comido.
7. Nosotros habíamos ido.
8. Yo había abierto.
9. Uds. habían hecho.
10. Ellas habían caído.
11. Yo había llegado.
12. Tú habías escrito.
13. Ud. había creído.
14. Él había dicho.
15. Ella había dado.
16. La chica había bebido.
17. Nosotros habíamos oído.
18. Uds. habían tenido.
19. Ellos habían puesto.
20. Ellas habían cubierto.

Test 17

1. C   See explanation (n) and the example on page xxx. Review the other forms of **venir** among the 501 verbs.
2. D   See the explanation, examples, and regular formation of the **imperfecto de subjuntivo** (Tense No. 7) on pages xxx and xxxi. Review the other forms of **comprender** among the 501 verbs.
3. B   You need to complete the **perfecto de indicativo** (Tense No. 8) by selecting the past participle **hablado** because **he** is given in front of the missing verb form. Review the other verb forms of **hablar** among the 501 verbs.
4. B   See the explanation, examples, and regular formation of the **imperfecto de subjuntivo** (Tense No. 7) on pages xxx and xxxi, in particular, the example at the top of page xxxi. Review the other forms of **ser** among the 501 verbs.
5. A   You need to complete the **perfecto de indicativo** (Tense No. 8) by selecting the past participle **ganado** because **ha** is given in front of the missing verb form. See the explanation, examples, and regular formation of the **perfecto de**

indicativo on page xxxi, in particular, example 3. Review the other forms of **ganar** among the 501 verbs.

6. **B** The infinitive form **salir** is needed because a verb form (**quiero**) precedes it. Review section K on pages 547 and 548 where you will find **querer** + infinitive. Review the other forms of **salir** among the 501 verbs.

7. **A** You need the infinitive form **terminar** because the preposition **a** precedes the missing verb form. Review section A on page 541 where you will find **ir** and other verbs of motion that take the preposition **a** + infinitive. Also, review the other forms of **terminar** among the 501 verbs.

8. **B** The infinitive form **decir** is needed because a verb form (**quiere**) precedes the missing verb form. Review section K on pages 547 and 548 where you will find **querer** + infinitive. See also the two examples given there. Review verbs used in idiomatic expressions beginning on page 524, in particular, under **decir** on page 526. Review the other forms of **decir** among the 501 verbs.

9. **B** You need to complete the progressive present by selecting the present participle **nevando** because **está** is given in front of the missing verb form. Review the formation of the progressive forms on pages xxxvi and xxxvii. Also, review the present participles on pages xi and xii. As for the other forms of **nevar** in the choices, turn to the page where **nevar** is given among the 501 verbs.

10. **B** The sentence means *When I arrived home, my brother had gone out.* You need to complete the **pluscuamperfecto de indicativo** (Tense No. 9) by selecting the past participle **salido** because the helping verb **había** is given in front of the missing verb form. Review the explanation, formation, and examples of this tense on pages xxxi and xxxii, in particular, example 1. As for the other forms of **salir** in the choices, turn to the page where **salir** is given among the 501 verbs.

Test 18

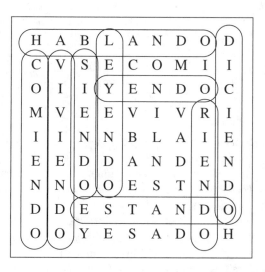

Test 19

1. **C** You need the 3d person plural, **presente de indicativo** of **tener** because you are telling Julia it seems to you that *they* (the dogs/**los perros**) *are* afraid. Note the idiomatic expression **tener miedo** (to be afraid), which is listed on page 537 in the section on verbs used in idiomatic expressions, beginning on page 524. Review the other forms of **tener** among the 501 verbs.

2. **B** You need **estar** because you are saying that the little cat must *be* sick. Review the uses of **estar** on pages 535 and 536. Also, the infinitive form **estar** is needed because **debe** is a verb that precedes the missing verb form. Generally speaking, the infinitive form of a verb is used when it is preceded by a conjugated verb form. Review the forms of the verbs in the choices among the 501 verbs: **estar, ser, tener.**

3. **A** Review again the difference in the uses of **ser** and **estar** on pages 535 and 536. Also, review the forms of these two verbs among the 501 verbs.

4. **B** You are telling Julia that Rojo, the dog, is quiet because he *is* in a strange place. Review the reason for **estar** in (b) and the examples on page 535.

5. **A** You need the **presente de indicativo** of **llevar** because the situation is taking place at the present time. Review the other choices of forms and tenses of **llevar** where the verb appears among the 501 verbs.

Test 20

Note: If you are still not sure of verb forms in the **pretérito,** you must review all the verbs used in this test by turning to the page where they appear among the 501 verbs.

1. Roberto escribió la lección.	9. Yo saludé a María.
2. La Señora Fuentes se levantó.	10. Mi padre tuvo un accidente.
3. Yo ofrecí un regalo.	11. Mi hermana hizo la comida.
4. María trabajó.	12. ¿Fue usted a España?
5. El alumno leyó una carta.	13. ¿Se vistieron los chicos?
6. El Señor Robles murió.	14. Esta mañana yo me lavé.
7. Margarita salió.	15. Yo no quise hacerlo.
8. Ricardo habló.	

Test 21

15, 1, 14, 2, 3, 13, 12, 4, 11, 5, 7, 6, 8, 9, 10

Test 22

Note: Review all the verbs used in the sentences in this test in the **presente de indicativo** (Tense No. 1) and in the **pretérito** (Tense No. 3) by turning to the page where they appear among the 501 verbs in this book. If you were not able to identify some of the irregular verb forms in the sentences, consult the index of common irregular Spanish verb forms identified by infinitive beginning on page 519. For example, in the first sentence, **cojo** is given as an irregular form of **coger.** Then, look up **coger** among the 501 verbs.

1. Yo cogí la pelota.	11. Ellos estuvieron en la piscina.
2. Ud. durmió demasiado.	12. Yo me senté cerca de la ventana.
3. Tú fuiste al cine.	13. Ud. se levantó.
4. Él habló mucho.	14. Nosotros nos apresuramos.
5. Ella escribió una tarjeta.	15. Los muchachos vinieron a verme.
6. Nosotros comimos en este restaurante.	16. Berta estuvo enferma.
7. Vosotros aceptasteis el dinero.	17. Mi madre hizo un bizcocho.
8. Uds. dieron de comer a los pájaros.	18. Yo busqué mis libros.
9. Yo fui al teatro.	19. La profesora brió la puerta.
10. Ellas fueron a casa.	20. Me gustó el helado. *[The subject in this sentence is **el helado.** See page 528.]*

Test 23

```
B  U  H  O  H  B  U  T  O
H  B  U  A  G  I  R  O  T
H  U  B  E  V  I  S  T  O
R  I  O  E  S  C  I  R  T
H  U  E  B  I  M  O  E  S
O  R  S  E  I  B  U  I  H
E  S  C  R  I  O  T  B  U
V  I  R  T  O  A  B  A  E
H  A  I  B  A  B  I  E  R
I  S  T  O  V  H  U  B  E
R  O  O  T  R  O  T  U  I
R  C  S  E  E  B  U  H  O
```

Test 24

Note: All the forms of **haber** in the seven simple tenses are given on page 256. Verify your work by consulting that page. Remember that these verb forms are needed to form the seven compound tenses (Tenses Nos. 8 to 14). Review again page xxxix.

Test 25

1. Yo sé nadar, también.
2. Ellos salen de la escuela a las tres, trambién.
3. Ella está sentada, también.
4. Ellos son inteligentes, también.
5. Ellos sonríen, también.
6. Ellos leyeron el libro, también.
7. Nosotros recibimos muchos regalos, también.
8. Él bebió café con leche, también.
9. Yo oí la música, también.
10. Ellos durmieron mucho, también.
11. Ellos fueron al cine, también.
12. Ellos se acuestan a las diez, también.
13. Ellas han dicho la verdad, también.
14. Ellos hicieron la lección, también.
15. Él ha cantado bien, también.

Test 26

Note: Turn to the page among the 501 verbs and verify the form of the verb given in (a) in the following answers. Also, consult the page references that are given here.

1. (a) **salir**
   (b) **pretérito**
   (c) 3d pers., sing. (The subject is Sancho.)
2. (a) **decir**
   (b) **gerundio** (pres. part.)
   (c) Review present participles on page xi.

3. (a) **poder**
    (b) **presente de indicativo**
    (c) 3d pers., sing. (**Ud.** understood. Sancho is talking to **Don Quixote.**)
4. (a) **llegar**
    (b) **pretérito**
    (c) 1st pers., sing.
5. (a) **darse**
    (b) **pretérito**
    (c) 3d pers., pl. See **darse** at the bottom of page 157.
6. (a) **bajar**
    (b) **imperativo**
    (c) 3d pers., sing. (**Ud.**) (**baje, baje**/come down, come down)
7. (a) **ser**
    (b) **presente de indicativo**
    (c) 3d pers., pl.
8. (a) **echar**
    (b) **perfecto de indicativo**
    (c) 1st pers., pl. (we have thrown)
9. (a) **aguardar**
    (b) progressive present
    (c) See pages xii, example 1, and xxxvi, (1) and (2), at the bottom of that page.
    (**nos están aguardando**/they are waiting for us)
10. (a) **decir**
    (b) progressive present
    (c) See pages xii, example 1, and xxxvi, (1) and (2), at the bottom of that page.
    (**la olla que está diciendo**/the pot that is saying)
11. (a) **comer**
    (b) **imperativo**
    (c) 2d pers., sing. (**tú**)
    (**come, come**/eat, eat; **¡cómeme, cómeme!**/eat me! eat me!)

Definitions of Basic Grammatical Terms with Examples

active voice When we speak or write in the active voice, the subject of the verb performs the action. The action falls on the direct object.

> *The robber opened the window/El ladrón abrió la ventana.*

The subject is *the robber.* The verb is *opened.* The direct object is *the window.* See also *passive voice* in this list. Compare the above sentence with the example in the passive voice. Review the section on passive voice and active voice on pages xiv and xv. See also page xiii, example 6.

adjective An adjective is a word that modifies a noun or a pronoun. In grammar, to modify a word means to describe, limit, expand, or make the meaning particular.

> *a beautiful garden/un jardín hermoso; she is pretty/ella es bonita*

The adjective *beautiful/hermoso* modifies the noun *garden/jardín.* The adjective *pretty/bonita* modifies the pronoun *she/ella.* In Spanish there are different kinds of adjectives. *See also* comparative adjective, demonstrative adjective, descriptive adjective, interrogative adjective, limiting adjective, possessive adjective, superlative adjective.

adverb An adverb is a word that modifies a verb, an adjective, or another adverb. An adverb says something about how, when, where, to what extent, or in what way.

> *Mary runs swiftly/María corre rápidamente.*

The adverb *swiftly/rápidamente* modifies the verb *runs/corre.* The adverb shows *how* she runs.

> *John is very handsome/Juan es muy guapo.*

The adverb *very/muy* modifies the adjective *handsome/guapo.* The adverb shows *how* handsome he is.

> *The boy is talking very fast now/El muchacho habla muy rápidamente ahora.*

The adverb *very/muy* modifies the adverb *fast/rápidamente.* The adverb shows *to what extent* he is talking *fast.* The adverb *now/ahora* tells us *when.*

> *The post office is there/La oficina de correos está allá.*

The adverb *there/allá* modifies the verb *is/está.* It tells us *where* the post office is.

> *Mary writes meticulously/María escribe meticulosamente.*

The adverb *meticulously/meticulosamente* modifies the verb *writes/escribe.* It tells us *in what way* she writes.

affirmative statement, negative statement A statement in the affirmative is the opposite of a statement in the negative. To negate an affirmative statement is to make it negative.

> Affirmative: *I like ice cream/Me gusta el helado.*
>
> Negative: *I do not like ice cream/No me gusta el helado.*

Review page 528.

agreement of adjective with noun Agreement is made on the adjective with the noun it modifies in gender (masculine or feminine) and number (singular or plural).

> *a white house/una casa blanca.*

The adjective **blanca** is feminine singular because the noun **una casa** is feminine singular

> *many white houses/muchas casas blancas.*

The adjective **blancas** is feminine plural because the noun **casas** is feminine plural.

agreement of verb with its subject A verb agrees in person (1st, 2d, or 3d) and in number (singular or plural) with its subject.

> *Paul tells the truth/Pablo dice la verdad.*

The verb **dice** (of **decir**) is 3d person singular because the subject *Pablo/Paul* is 3d person singular.

Where are the tourists going?/¿Adónde van los turistas?

The verb **van** (of **ir**) is 3d person plural because the subject *los turistas/the tourists* is 3d person plural. For subject pronouns in the singular and plural, review page xl.

antecedent   An antecedent is a word to which a relative pronoun refers. It comes *before* the pronoun.

The girl who is laughing loudly is my sister/
La muchacha que está riendo a carcajadas es mi hermana.

The antecedent is *girl/la muchacha.* The relative pronoun *who/que* refers to the girl.

The car that I bought is very expensive/
El carro que yo compré es muy costoso.

The antecedent is *car/el carro.* The relative pronoun *that/que* refers to the car. Review **comprar** and **reír** among the 501 verbs in this book. Note that **está riendo** is the progressive present. Review example 1 on page xii and examples (1) and (2) on page xxxvi. *See also* relative pronoun.

auxiliary verb   An auxiliary verb is a helping verb. In English grammar it is *to have.* In Spanish grammar it is *haber/to have.* An auxiliary verb is used to help form the compound tenses.

I have eaten/(Yo) he comido.

Review the forms of **haber** in the seven simple tenses on page 256. You need to know them to form the seven compound tenses. Also, review **comer** among the 501 verbs in this book.

cardinal number   A cardinal number is a number that expresses an amount, such as *one, two, three,* and so on. See also ordinal number.

clause   A clause is a group of words that contains a subject and a predicate. A predicate may contain more than one word. A conjugated verb form is revealed in the predicate.

Mrs. Gómez lives in a large apartment/
La señora Gómez vive en un gran apartamento.

The subject is *Mrs. Gómez/la señora Gómez.* The predicate is *lives in a large apartment/vive en un gran apartamento.* The verb is *lives/vive.* Review **vivir** among the 501 verbs in this book. *See also* dependent clause, independent clause, predicate.

comparative adjective   When making a comparison between two persons or things, an adjective is used to express the degree of comparison in the following ways.

Same degree of comparison:

Helen is as tall as Mary/Elena es tan alta como María.

Lesser degree of comparison

Jane is less intelligent than Eva/Juana es menos inteligente que Eva.

Higher degree of comparison:

This apple is more delicious than that one/Esta manzana es más deliciosa que ésa.

See also superlative adjective.

comparative adverb   An adverb is compared in the same way as an adjective is compared. *See* comparative adjective above.

Same degree of comparison:

Mr. Robles speaks as well as Mr. Vega/
El señor Robles habla tan bien como el señor Vega.

Definitions of Basic Grammatical Terms with Examples   667

Lesser degree of comparison:

Alice studies less diligently than her sister/
Alicia estudia menos diligentemente que su hermana.

Higher degree of comparison:

Albert works more slowly than his brother/
Alberto trabaja más lentamente que su hermano.

See also superlative adverb.

complex sentence   A complex sentence contains one independent clause and one or more dependent clauses.

One independent clause and one dependent clause:

Joseph works but his brother doesn't/
José trabaja pero su hermano no trabaja.

The independent clause is *Joseph works.* It makes sense when it stands alone because it expresses a complete thought. The dependent clause is *but his brother doesn't.* The dependent clause, which is introduced by the conjunction *but/pero,* does not make complete sense when it stands alone because it *depends* on the thought expressed in the independent clause.

One independent clause and two dependent clauses:

Anna is a good student because she studies but her sister never studies/
Ana es una buena alumna porque estudia pero su hermana nunca estudia.

The independent clause is *Anna is a good student.* It makes sense when it stands alone because it expresses a complete thought. The first dependent clause is *because she studies.* The dependent clause, which is introduced by the conjunction *because/porque,* does not make complete sense when it stands alone because it *depends* on the thought expressed in the independent clause. The second dependent clause is *but her sister never studies.* That dependent clause, which is introduced by the conjunction *but/pero,* does not make complete sense either when it stands alone because it *depends* on the thought expressed in the independent clause. *See also* dependent clause, independent clause.

compound sentence   A compound sentence contains two or more independent clauses.

*Mrs. Fuentes went to the supermarket, she bought a few
things, and then she went home/*
**La señora Fuentes fue al supermercado, compró
algunas cosas, y entonces fue a casa.**

This compound sentence contains three independent clauses. They are independent because they make sense when they stand alone. Review the explanation, uses, and examples of the **pretérito** (Tense No. 3) on page xxiv. Review **comprar** and **ir** among the 501 verbs in this book. *See also* independent clause.

conditional perfect tense   In Spanish grammar, the conditional (**el potencial**) is considered a mood. This tense is defined with examples on page xxxiii.

conditional present tense   In Spanish grammar, the conditional (**el potencial**) is considered a mood. This tense is defined with examples on pages xxvi and xxvii.

conjugation   The conjugation of a verb is the fixed order of all its forms showing their inflections (changes) in the three persons of the singular and plural in a particular tense. *See also* number and person (1st, 2d, 3d).

conjunction   A conjunction is a word that connects words or groups of words.

and/y, or/o, but/pero, because/porque
Charles and Charlotte/Carlos y Carlota

You can stay home or you can come with me/
(Tú) peudes quedarte en casa o venir conmigo.

contrary to fact This term refers to an "if" clause. *See* if (**si**) clause.

declarative sentence A declarative sentence makes a statement.

Review the **perfecto de indicativo** (Tense No. 8) on page xxxi and **terminar** among the 501 verbs in this book.

definite article The definite article in Spanish has four forms and they all mean *the*. They are **el, la, los, las.**

el libro/the book, la casa/the house,
los libros/the books, las casas/the houses.

The definite articles **la, los, las** are also used as direct object pronouns. *See* direct object pronoun.

demonstrative adjective A demonstrative adjective is an adjective that points out. It is placed in front of a noun.

this book/este libro; these books/estos libros;
this cup/esta taza; these flowers/estas flores

demonstrative pronoun .A demonstrative pronoun is a pronoun that points out. It takes the place of a noun. It agrees in gender and number with the noun it replaces.

I have two oranges; do you prefer this one or that one?/
Tengo dos naranjas; ¿prefiere usted ésta o ésa?
I prefer those [over there]/Prefiero aquéllas.

For demonstrative pronouns that are neuter, *see* neuter.

dependent clause A dependent clause is a group of words that contains a subject and a predicate. It does not express a complete thought when it stands alone. It is called *dependent* because it depends on the independent clause for a complete meaning. Subordinate clause is another term for dependent clause.

Edward is absent today because he is sick/
Eduardo está ausente hoy porque está enfermo.

The independent clause is *Edward is absent today.* The dependent clause is *because he is sick. See also* clause, independent clause.

descriptive adjective A descriptive adjective is an adjective that describes a person, place, or thing.

a pretty girl/una muchacha bonita; a big house/una casa grande;
an expensive car/un carro costoso.

See also adjective.

direct object noun A direct object noun receives the action of the verb *directly*. That is why it is called a direct object, as opposed to an indirect object. A direct object noun is normally placed *after* the verb.

I am writing a letter/Escribo una carta.

The direct object is the noun *letter/una carta. See also* direct object pronoun.

direct object pronoun A direct object pronoun receives the action of the verb *directly*. It takes the place of a direct object noun. In Spanish a pronoun that is a direct object of a verb is ordinarily placed *in front of* the verb.

I am writing it [the letter]/La escribo.

In the *affirmative imperative,* a direct object pronoun is placed *after* the verb and is joined to it, resulting in one word.

Write it [the letter] now!/¡Escríbala [Ud.] ahora!

An accent mark is added on the vowel **i** [**í**] in order to keep the emphasis on that vowel as it was in **escriba** before the direct object pronoun **la** was added to the verb form. Review the simple rule about stressed vowel sounds in Spanish and when accent marks are needed in examples 1, 2, 3, and 4 on page 562. *See also* imperative.

disjunctive pronoun   A disjunctive pronoun is a pronoun that is stressed; in other words, emphasis is placed on it. It is usually an object of a preposition. In Spanish usage, prepositional pronoun is another term for disjunctive pronoun.

for me/para mí; for you (fam.)/para ti;
con usted/with you; con él/with him; con ella/with her

Note the following exceptions with **con:**

conmigo/with me; contigo/with you (fam.);
consigo/with yourself (yourselves, himself, herself, themselves)

ending of a verb   In Spanish grammar the ending of a verb form changes according to the person and number of the subject and the tense of the verb.

To form the present indicative tense of a regular **-ar** type verb like **hablar,** drop **ar** of the infinitive and add the following endings; **-o, -as, -a** for the 1st, 2d, and 3d persons of the singular; **-amos, -áis, -an** for the 1st, 2d, and 3d persons of the plural. You then get: **hablo, hablas, habla; hablamos, habláis, hablan.** Review at the top of page xxii. *See also* stem of a verb.

feminine   In Spanish grammar the gender of a noun, pronoun, or adjective is feminine or masculine, not male or female.

Masculine			Feminine		
noun	*pronoun*	*adjective*	*noun*	*pronoun*	*adjective*
el hombre	**él**	**guapo**	**la mujer**	**ella**	**hermosa**
the man	he	handsome	the woman	she	beautiful

See also gender.

future perfect tense   This tense is defined with examples on pages xxxii and xxxiii. It is also called the future anterior.

future tense   This tense is defined with examples on pages xxv and xxvi.

gender   Gender means masculine or feminine.

Masculine: *the boy/el muchacho; the book/el libro*
Feminine: *the girl/la muchacha; the house/la casa*

gerund   In English grammar, a gerund is a word formed from a verb. It ends in *ing.* Actually, it is the present participle of a verb. However, it is not used as a verb. It is used as a noun.

Seeing is believing/Ver es creer/[to see is to believe].

However, in Spanish grammar, the infinitive form of the verb is used, as in the above example, when the verb is used as a noun.

The Spanish gerund is also a word formed from a verb. It is the present participle of a verb. The Spanish gerund [**el gerundio**] regularly ends in **ando** for **ar** type verbs (of the 1st conjugation), in **iendo** for **er** type verbs (of the 2d conjugation), and **iendo** for **ir** type verbs (of the 3d conjugation). There are also irregular present participles that end in **yendo.**

hablando/talking   comiendo/eating   viviendo/living

See also present participle.

if (si) clause   An "if" clause is defined with an example at the top of page xxxi where **como si** (as if) is used. Another term for an "if" clause is contrary to fact, as in English, if I were king . . ., if I were rich . . .

Si yo tuviera bastante dinreo, iría a España/
If I had enough money, I would go to Spain.

Review the **imperfecto de subjuntivo** (Tense No. 7) of **tener** on page 469 and the **potencial simple** (Tense No. 5) of **ir** on page 280. *See also* clause.

imperative   The imperative is a mood, not a tense. It is used to express a command. In Spanish it is used in the 2d person of the singular (**tú**), the 3d person of the singular (**usted**), the 1st person of the plural (**nosotros, nosotras**), the 2d person of the plural (**vosotros, vosotras**), and in the 3d person of the plural (**ustedes**). As an example, review the **imperativo** of **comer** among the 501 verbs in this book. Review the explanation of the **imperativo** with examples on pages xxxiv to xxxvi. *See also* person (1st, 2d, 3d).

imperfect indicativo tense   This tense is defined with examples on pages xxii and xxiii.

imperfect subjunctive tense   This tense is defined with examples on pages xxx and xxxi.

indefinite article   In English the indefinite articles are *a, an,* as in *a book, an apple*. They are indefinite because they do not refer to any definite or particular noun.

In Spanish there are two indefinite articles in the singular: one in the masculine form (**un**) and one in the feminine form (**una**).

Masculine singular: *un libro/a book*
Feminine singular: *una manzana/an apple*

In the plural they change to **unos** and **unas**.

unos libros/some books; **unas** *manzanas/some apples*

See also definite article.

indefinite pronoun   An indefinite pronoun is a pronoun that does not refer to any definite or particular noun.

something/algo; someone, somebody/alguien

independent clause   An independent clause is a group of words that contains a subject and a predicate. It expresses a complete thought when it stands alone.

The cat is sleeping on the bed/El gato está durmiendo sobre la cama.

See also clause, dependent clause, predicate.

indicative mood   The indicative mood is used in sentences that make a statement or ask a question. The indicative mood is used most of the time when we speak or write in English or Spanish.

I am going to the movies now/Voy al cine ahora.
When are you going?/¿Adónde vas?

indirect object noun   An indirect object noun receives the action of the verb *indirectly.*

I am writing a letter to Christine or *I am writing Christine a letter/*
Estoy escribiendo una carta a Cristina.

The verb is *am writing/estoy escribiendo.* The direct object noun is *a letter/una carta.* The indirect object noun is *Cristina/Christine. See also* indirect object pronoun.

indirect object pronoun   An indirect object pronoun takes the place of an indirect object noun. It receives the action of the verb *indirectly.*

I am writing a letter to her or *I am writing her a letter/*
Le escribo una carta (a ella).

The indirect object pronoun is *(to) her/le. See also* indirect object noun.

infinitive   An infinitive is a verb form. In English, it is normally stated with the preposition to, as in *to talk, to drink, to receive.* In Spanish, the infinitive form of a verb consists of three major types: those of the 1st conjugation that end in **-ar,** the 2d conjugation that end in **-er,** and the 3d conjugation that end in **-ir.** In Spanish grammar, the infinitive (**el infinitivo**) is considered a mood.

hablar/to talk, to speak; beber/to drink; recibir/to receive

All the verbs in this book on pages 1 to 501 are given in the infinitive form at the top of each page where they are arranged alphabetically.

interjection   An interjection is a word that expresses emotion, a feeling of joy, of sadness, an exclamation of surprise, and other exclamations consisting of one or two words.

Ah!/¡Ah! Ouch!/¡Ay! Darn it!/¡Caramba!/ My God!/¡Dios mío!

interrogative adjective   In Spanish, an interrogative adjective is an adjective that is used in a question. As an adjective, it is placed in front of a noun.

What book do you want?/¿Qué libro desea usted?

What time is it?/¿Qué hora es?

interrogative adverb   In Spanish, an interrogative adverb is an adverb that introduces a question. As an adverb, it modifies the verb.

How are you?/¿Cómo está usted?

How much does this book cost?/¿Cuándo cuesta este libro?

When will you arrive?/¿Cuándo llegará usted?

interrogative pronoun   An interrogative pronoun is a pronoun that asks a question. There are interrogative pronouns that refer to persons and those that refer to things.

Who is it?/¿Quién es?

What are you saying?/¿Qué dice usted?

interrogative sentence   An interrogative sentence asks a question.

What are you doing?/¿Qué hace usted?

intransitive verb   An intransitive verb is a verb that does not take a direct object.

The professor is talking/El profesor habla

An intransitive verb takes an indirect object.

The professor is talking to us/El profesor nos habla.

See also direct object pronoun, indirect object pronoun, transitive verb.

irregular verb   An irregular verb is a verb that does not follow a fixed pattern in its conjugation in the various verb tenses. Basic irregular verbs in Spanish:

estar/to be   hacer/to do, to make   ir/to go   ser/to be

See also conjugation, regular verb.

limiting adjective   A limiting adjective is an adjective that limits a quantity.

three lemons/tres limones; a few candies/ algunos dulces

main clause   Main clause is another term for independent clause. *See* independent clause.

masculine   In Spanish grammar the gender of a noun, pronoun, or adjective is masculine or feminine, not male or female. *See also* feminine, gender.

mood of verbs   Some grammarians use the term *the mode* instead of *the mood* of a verb. Either term means *the manner or way* a verb is expressed. In English and Spanish grammar a verb expresses an action or state of being in a particular mood. In Spanish grammar, there are five moods (**modos**); the infinitive (**el infinitivo**), the indicative (**el indicativo**), the imperative (**el imperativo**), the conditional (**el potencial**), and the subjunctive (**el subjuntivo**). In English grammar, there are three moods: the indicative mood, the imperative mood, and the subjunctive mood. Most of the time, in English and Spanish, we speak and write in the indicative mood.

negative statement, affirmative statement
    See affirmative statement, negative statement

neuter   A word that is neuter is neither masculine nor feminine. Common neuter demonstrative pronouns in Spanish are *esto/this, eso/that, aquello/that* [farther away].
    What's this?/¿Qué es esto? What's that?/¿Qué es eso?
For demonstrative pronouns that are not neuter, *see* demonstrative pronoun. There is also the neuter pronoun **lo.** It usually refers to an idea or statement. It is not normally translated into English but often the translation is *so.*
    ¿Estás enferma, María?/Are you sick, Mary? Sí, lo estoy/Yes, I am.
    No lo creo/I don't think so.
    Lo parece/It seems so.

noun   A noun is a word that names a person, animal, place, thing, condition or state, or quality.
    the man/el hombre, the woman/la mujer, the horse/el caballo,
    the house/la casa, the pencil/el lápiz,
    happiness/la felicidad, excellence/la excelencia
In Spanish the noun **el nombre** is the word for name and noun. Another word for noun in Spanish is *el sustantivo/substantive.*

number   In English and Spanish grammar, number means singular or plural.
    Masc. sing.:
        the boy/el muchacho; the pencil/el lápiz; the eye/el ojo
    Masc. pl.:
        the boys/los muchachos; the pencils/los lápices; the eyes/los ojos
    Fem. sing.:
        the girl/la muchacha; the house/la casa; the cow/la vaca
    Fem. pl.:
        the girls/las muchachas; the houses/las casas; the cows/las vacas

ordinal number   An ordinal number is a number that expresses position in a series, such as *first, second, third,* and so on. In English and Spanish grammar we talk about 1st person, 2d person, 3d person singular or plural regarding subjects and verbs.
    See also cardinal number and person (1st, 2d, 3d).

orthographical changes in verb forms   An orthographical change in a verb form is a change in spelling.
    The verb *conocer/to know, to be acquainted with* changes in spelling in the 1st person singular of the present indicative. The letter **z** is inserted in front of the second **c.** When formed regularly, the ending **er** of the infinitive drops and **o** is added for the 1st person singular form of the present indicative. That would result in **conoco,** a peculiar sound to the Spanish ear for a verb form of **conocer.** The letter **z** is added to keep the sound of **s** as it is in the infinitive **conocer.** Therefore, the spelling changes and the form is **yo conozco.** In other forms of **conocer** in the present indicative **z** is not inserted because they retain the sound of **s.**
    There are many verb forms in Spanish that contain orthographical changes. Review the verb **conocer** in the present indicative tense among the 501 verbs.

passive voice   When we speak or write in the active voice and change to the passive voice, the direct object becomes the subject, the subject becomes the object of a preposition, and the verb becomes *to be* plus the past participle of the active verb. The past participle functions as an adjective.

The window was opened by the robber/La ventana fue abierta por el ladrón.
The subject is *la ventana.* The verb is *fue.* The word *abierta* is a feminine adjective agreeing with *la ventana.* Actually, it is the past participle of *abrir/to open* but here it serves as an adjective. The object of the preposition *by/por* is the *robber/el ladrón. See also* active voice in this list. Compare the above sentence with the examples in the active voice. Review the section on passive voice and active voice on pages xiv and xv. *See also* page xiii, example 6.

past anterior tense   This tense is defined with examples on page xxxii. It is also called the *preterit perfect.*

past participle   A past participle is derived from a verb. It is used to form the compound tenses. Its auxiliary verb in English is *to have.* In Spanish, the auxiliary verb is *haber/to have.* It is part of the verb tense.

hablar/to speak, to talk	*I have spoken/he hablado*
comer/to eat	*I have eaten/he comido*
recibir/to receive	*I have received/he recibido*

Review pages xii and xiii for the regular formation of a past participle and a list of common irregular past participles. *See also* auxiliary verb.

past perfect tense   This tense is defined with examples on pages xxxi and xxxii. It is also called the pluperfect indicative tense.

past subjunctive tense   This tense is defined with examples on pages xxxiii and xxxiv. It is also called the present perfect subjunctive.

person (1st, 2d, 3d)   Verb forms in a particular tense are learned systematically according to person (1st, 2d, 3d) and number (singular, plural).

Example, showing the present indicative tense of the verb *ir/to go:*

Singular	Plural
1st person: *(yo) voy*	1st person: *(nosotros, nosotras) vamos*
2d person: *(tú) vas*	2d person: *(vosotros, vosotras) vais*
3d person: *(Ud., él, ella) va*	3d person: *(Uds., ellos, ellas) van*

personal pronoun   A personal pronoun is a pronoun that refers to a person. Review the subject pronouns on page xl. For examples of other types of pronouns, *see also* demonstrative pronoun, direct object pronoun, disjunctive pronoun, indefinite pronoun, indirect object pronoun, interrogative pronoun, possessive pronoun, reflexive pronoun, relative pronoun.

pluperfect indicative tense   This tense is defined with examples on pages xxxi and xxxii. It is also called the past perfect indicative tense.

pluperfect subjunctive tense   This tense is defined with examples on page xxxiv. It is also called the past perfect subjunctive tense.

plural   Plural means more than one. *See also* person (1st, 2d, 3d) and singular.

possessive adjective   A possessive adjective is an adjective that is placed in front of a noun to show possession.

my book/mi libro   my friend/mis amigos   our school/nuestra escuela

possessive pronoun   A possessive pronoun is a pronoun that shows possession. It takes the place of a possessive adjective with the noun. Its form agrees in gender (masculine or feminine) and number (singular or plural) with what it is replacing.
English:

mine, yours, his, hers, its, ours, theirs

Spanish:

Possessive Adjective	Possessive Pronoun
my book/mi libro	*mine/el mío*
my house/mi casa	*mine/la mía*
my shoes/mis zapatos	*mine/los míos*

predicate   The predicate is that part of the sentence that tells us something about the subject. The main word of the predicate is the verb.

Today the tourists are going to the Prado Museum/
Hoy los turistas van al Museo del Prado.

The subject is the *tourists/los turistas.* The predicate is *are going to the Prado Museum/* *van al Museo del Prado.* The verb is *are going/van.*

preposition   A preposition is a word that establishes a rapport between words.

with, without, to, at, between

with her/con ella without money/sin dinero to Spain/a España
at six o'clock/a las seis between you and me/entre tú y yo

Review verbs with prepositions beginning on page 541.

prepositional pronoun   A prepositional pronoun is a pronoun that is an object of a preposition. The term disjunctive pronoun is also used. For examples, *see* disjunctive pronoun.

present indicative tense   This tense is defined with examples on pages xxi and xxii.

present participle   A present participle is derived from a verb form. In English a present participle ends in *ing.* In Spanish a present participle is called **un gerundio.**

cantando/singing comiendo/eating yendo/going

Review pages xi and xii for regular and irregular present participles and their uses. *See also* gerund.

present perfect indicative tense   This tense is defined with examples on page xxxi.

present subjunctive tense   This tense is defined with examples on pages xxvii to xxx.

preterit tense   This tense is defined with examples on pages xxiv and xxv.

preterit perfect tense   This tense is defined with examples on page xxxii. It is also called the past anterior.

pronoun   A pronoun is a word that takes the place of a noun.

el hombre/él   la mujer/ella
the man/he   the woman/she

reflexive pronoun and reflexive verb   In English a reflexive pronoun is a personal pronoun that contains *self* or *selves.* In Spanish and English a reflexive pronoun is used with a verb that is called reflexive because the action of the verb falls on the reflexive pronoun. In Spanish there is a required set of reflexive pronouns for a reflexive verb.

lavarse	*(Yo) me lavo.*	*afeitarse*	*Pablo se ha afeitado.*
to wash oneself	*I wash myself.*	*to shave oneself*	*Paul has shaved himself.*

Review, for example, the reflexive verbs **afeitarse, lavarse, levantarse, llamarse** among the 501 verbs in this book to become familiar with the reflexive pronouns that go with reflexive verbs in the three persons of the singular and plural.

regular verb   A regular verb is a verb that is conjugated in the various tenses according to a fixed pattern. For examples, review page xxii at the top and page xxiii at the bottom. *See also* conjugation, irregular verb.

relative pronoun   A relative pronoun is a pronoun that refers to its antecedent.

The girl who is talking with John is my sister/
La muchacha que está hablando con Juan es mi hermana.

The antecedent is *girl/la muchacha.* The relative pronoun *who/que* refers to the girl.
See also antecedent.

sentence   A sentence is a group of words that contains a subject and a predicate. The verb
is contained in the predicate. A sentence expresses a complete thought.

The train leaves at two o'clock in the afternoon/
El tren sale a las dos de la tarde.

The subject is *train/el tren.* The predicate is *leaves at two o'clock in the afternoon/sale
a las dos de la tarde.* The verb is *leaves/sale. See also* complex sentence, compound
sentence, simple sentence.

simple sentence   A simple sentence is a sentence that contains one subject and one predicate. The verb is the core of the predicate. The verb is the most important word in a sentence because it tells us what the subject is doing.

Mary is eating an apple from her garden/
María está comiendo una manzana de su jardín.

The subject is *Mary/María.* The predicate is *is eating an apple from her garden/está
comiendo una manzana de su jardín.* The verb is *is eating/está comiendo.* The direct
object is *an apple/una manzana. From her garden/de su jardín* is an adverbial phrase.
It tells you from where the apple came. *See also* complex sentence, compound sentence.

singular   Singular means one. *See also* plural.

stem of a verb   The stem of a verb is what is left after we drop the ending of its infinitive
form. It is needed to add to it the required endings of a regular verb in a particular verb
tense.

Infinitive	Stem	Ending of infinitive
hablar/to talk	*habl*	*ar*
comer/to eat	*com*	*er*
escribir/to write	*escrib*	*ir*

See also ending of a verb.

stem-changing verb   In Spanish there are many verb forms that change in the stem. The
verb *dormir/to sleep* changes the vowel **o** in the stem to **ue** when the stress (emphasis,
accent) falls on that **o**; for example, **(yo) duermo.** When the stress does not fall on that
o, it does not change; for example, **(nosotros) dormimos.** Here, the stress is on the
vowel **i.**

Review the present indicative tense of **dormir** among the 501 verbs.

subject   A subject is that part of a sentence that is related to its verb. The verb says something about the subject.

Clara and Isabel are beautiful/Clara e Isabel son hermosas.

subjunctive mood   The subjunctive mood is the mood of a verb that is used in specific
cases, e.g., after certain verbs expressing a wish, doubt, emotion, fear, joy, uncertainty,
an indefinite expression, an indefinite antecedent, certain conjunctions, and others. The
subjunctive mood is used more frequently in Spanish than in English. Review the uses
of the subjunctive mood with examples on pages xxvii to xxxi and pages xxxiii to
xxxviii. *See also* mood of verbs.

subordinate clause   Subordinate clause is another term for dependent clause. *See*
dependent clause.

superlative adjective A superlative adjective is an adjective that expresses the highest degree when making a comparison of more than two persons or things.

Adjective	Comparative	Superlative
bueno/good	*mejor/better*	*el mejor/best*
alto/tall	*más alto/taller*	*el más alto/tallest*

See also comparative adjective.

superlative adverb A superlative adverb is an adverb that expresses the highest degree when making a comparison of more than two persons or things.

Adjective	Comparative	Superlative
lentamente	*más lentamente*	*lo más lentamente*
slowly	*more slowly*	*most slowly*

See also comparative adverb.

tense of verb In English and Spanish grammar, tense means time. The tense of the verb indicates the time of the action or state of being. The three major segments of time are past, present, and future. In Spanish there are fourteen major verb tenses, of which seven are simple tenses and seven are compound. Review pages xxxviii and xl for the names of the fourteen tenses in Spanish and English.

transitive verb A transitive verb is a verb that takes a direct object.

*I am closing the window/**Cierro la ventana.***

The subject is *I/(**Yo**)*. The verb is *am closing/**cierro***. The direct object is *the window/**la ventana**. See also* intransitive verb.

verb A verb is a word that expresses action or a state of being.

Action:

Los pájaros están volando/The birds are flying.

The verb is *están volando/are flying*.

State of being:

La señora López está contenta/Mrs. López is happy.

The verb is *está/is*.

NOTES